COLLINS
GEM
ENGLISH
DICTIONARY

Collins
London and Glasgow

First published 1902
New Editions 1936, 1954, 1963, 1981, 1985, 1987
Reprinted 1988

© Wm. Collins Sons & Co. Ltd.
1902, 1936, 1954, 1963, 1981, 1985, 1987

ISBN 0 00 458329 9

Printed in Great Britain
Collins Clear-Type Press

CONTENTS

EDITORIAL STAFF

Managing Editor
William T. McLeod

Editors
(for this edition)
Diana Adams, Danielle McGrath
(for previous editions)
Marian Makins, Margaret Martin,
Pamela Breckenridge, Michael Munro

Canadian Adviser
Patrick Drysdale
Editor, *A Dictionary of Canadianisms
on Historical Principles*

South African Adviser
M. V. Aldridge
Professor of Phonetics and
General Linguistics
University of the Witwatersrand

Australian Adviser
W. A. Krebs
Australian National University

PREFACE

COLLINS ENGLISH GEM DICTIONARY has for some eighty years been one of the most popular reference books in the world and certainly the most widely bought and widely used small English Dictionary. It has sold in huge quantities on every continent and been used by people of many countries and every walk of life and every age group.

There are many reasons for its success. One is the choice of vocabulary - a selection which prefers the words that are central to the contemporary living language and leaves to larger works those that are only rarely met with in normal speech and writing. Another is the truly remarkable amount of information that it contains. It has served many millions of people faithfully and well, whether as an indispensable writing-desk companion in home, office, or school, or a pocket help when travelling at home or abroad. To these many friends it is known simply and affectionately as "the Gem".

But language changes and dictionaries must change with it. During its lifetime this work has been completely revised and reset several times, apart from more frequent lesser revisions. This latest entirely new edition preserves those Gem features which have stood the test of daily use, but of course adds many new words and meanings that have established themselves in recent years. The latest computer typesetting techniques have permitted an overall increase in vocabulary without a corresponding increase in bulk.

We believe that the present Gem remains what previous editions have long been - the finest dictionary of its kind in the world - and that this latest edition will prove its worth to many old and new users.

WTM

ARRANGEMENT OF ENTRIES

All main entries are arranged in a single alphabetical listing, including abbreviations, foreign words, and combining forms or prefixes. Each such entry consists of a paragraph, with a main, or core, word at the head of it in large bold type. Derived or related words, in smaller bold type, appear later in the paragraph in alphabetical order, with phrases included at the end. Thus, **'labourer'** and **'laborious'** will be found under **'labour'**, **'lends itself to'** under **'lend'**, and so on. Alternative spellings are shown by bracketing optional letters, eg **'judg(e)'ment'** or by placing the variants side by side (**accurs'ed, accurst'**); but if the divergence in spelling is very great there is a separate entry.

The part of speech is shown by an abbreviation placed after the word (or its pronunciation), eg **'dog** *n.*,' for noun. Words which are used as more than one part of speech are only written out once, the change being indicated by a new part of speech label, eg **'ravage** *vt.* lay waste, plunder — *n.* destruction.' In the case of very short, simple entries, parts of speech may be combined, eg **'jest** *n./vi.* joke.' Spelling of verb parts is indicated in brackets after the verbal definitions, eg **'jab** ... stab abruptly (**-bb-**)'.

When a derived word is included within an entry, its meaning may be understood from the meaning of the headword or another derived word from within the paragraph.

Field labels and usage notes are added in italic type and abbreviated where there will be no confusion.

Although only '-ize' and '-ization' spellings are shown, the reader should understand that spellings in '-ise' and '-isation' are equally acceptable.

PRONUNCIATION

The pronunciation of many words is adequately shown simply by placing an accent (ʹ) immediately after the syllable that carries the main stress. All headwords are stressed except those that have only one syllable.

Where the stress mark alone is insufficient to clarify some peculiarity of pronunciation or misleading spelling, a simple phonetic respelling of the whole or part of the word is given in square brackets immediately after the headword. Typical examples are:

cache [kash]; **cachʹet** [kashʹā]; **caecum** [sēʹkəm]; **caissonʹ** [kə-soonʹ]; **capercaiʹlzie** [kap-ər-kāʹlyi]; **cappucciʹno** [-chēʹ-].

The special letters used in the phonetic respelling are listed below. All letters *not* listed have their normal pronunciation.

ā	mate	o͞o	food	ch	church
ah	calm	yoo	sinuous	ng	ring
aw	law	yo͞o	few	th	thin
ē	freeze	oi	boil	TH	this
ī	bite	ow	how	y	yes
ō	rope	ə	ago	H	loch
oo	book				

NOTES

1. The position of the stress mark in a headword generally indicates the length of the stressed vowel: if it comes immediately after the vowel, the vowel is usually long (**saʹvour**); if it comes after a

Pronunciation

consonant, the vowel is usually short (**sav'age**). But there are some exceptions (like **recite'**, **voli'tion**, **colli'sion**).

2. Though words like *castle, path, fast* are shown as pronounced with an [ah] sound, many speakers use an [a]. Such variations are entirely acceptable and to be assumed by the reader.

3. The letter 'r' in some positions (as in *fern, fear, arm, car,* etc.) is not sounded in the speech of Southern England and elsewhere. However, many speakers in other areas do sound the 'r' in such positions with varying degrees of distinctness. Again such variations are to be assumed, and though the dictionary shows an 'r' in such pronunciations, the reader will sound or not sound the 'r' according to his speech habits.

4. Though the widely received pronunciation of words like *which, why* is with a simple [w] sound and is so shown in the dictionary, many speakers, in Scotland and elsewhere, preserve an aspirated sound: [hw]. Once again this variation is to be assumed.

5. The symbol ə, the schwa, represents the neutral vowel heard in a wide range of unstressed syllables. In some words, however, among some speakers an [i] sound is heard, as in **listless** [list'ləs *or* list'lis].

6. Where a headword is stressed only and not pronounced by respelling, the following values are assumed for certain letters and letter combinations:

Pronunciation

rai'sin	[-ā-]	cord'ial	[-awr-]
carp'et	[-ah-]	board	[-awr-]
laud'able	[-aw-]	aloud'	[-ow-]
fea'ture	[-ē-]	tu'na	[-yōō-]
foam	[-ō-]		

Whenever these letters are pronounced differently, this pronunciation is shown, as:

car'avan [ka'rə-], **caul'iflower** [kol'-], **deaf** [def], **rea'gent** [rē-ā'jənt], **cor'oner** [ko'rə], **cou'gar** [kōō'-], **doub'le** [dub'l], **rou'ble** [rōō'-], **ru'by** [rōō'-].

ABBREVIATIONS USED IN THE DICTIONARY

a.	adjective	m	metre(s)
abbrev.	abbreviation	*masc.*	masculine
adv.	adverb	mm	millimetre(s)
Afr.	Africa (n)	N	North
Amer.	America(n)	*n.*	noun
Aust.	Australia(n)	N.Z.	New Zealand
Brit.	Britain, British	*obs.*	obsolete, obsolescent
Canad.	Canada, Canadian	*offens.*	offensive
cent.	century	oft.	often
cm	centimetre(s)	*orig.*	originally
comb.	combining	*pers.*	person
comp.	comparative	*pert.*	pertaining
conj.	conjunction	*pl.*	plural
cu.	cubic	*pl.n.*	plural noun
dial.	dialect	*poss.*	possessive
dim.	diminutive	*pp.*	past participle
eg	for example	*prep.*	preposition
esp.	especially	*pres.t.*	present tense
fem.	feminine	*pron.*	pronoun
fig.	figuratively	*pr.p.*	present participle
Fr.	French	*pt.*	past tense
g	gram(s)	R.C.	Roman Catholic
Ger.	German	*refl.*	reflexive
Gr.	Greek	S	South
ie	that is	*sing.*	singular
impers.	impersonal	*sl.*	slang
ind.	indicative	Sp.	Spanish
inf.	informal	sq.	square
interj.	interjection	*sup.*	superlative
intr.	intransitive	*tr.*	transitive
It.	Italian	*usu.*	usually
k	kilogram(s)	*v.*	verb
km	kilometre(s)	*v.aux.*	auxiliary verb
l	litre(s)	*vi.*	intransitive verb
Lat.	Latin	*vt.*	transitive verb
lit.	literally		

R	Registered Trade Mark
A	Australian
UK	United Kingdom
US	United States
C	Canadian
SA	South African

A

A (of temperature) absolute; alto; ampere

Å angstrom unit

a are (unit of measure)

a. acre; adjective; answer

a, an a. the indefinite article meaning one; *an* is used before vowels, and sometimes before unaccented syllables beginning with *h* aspirate

AA Alcoholics Anonymous; anti-aircraft, Automobile Association

aard'vark n. S African ant bear

A'asia Australasia

AB able-bodied seaman

aback' adv. —**taken aback** startled

ab'acus n. counting device of beads on wire frame; flat tablet at top of column

abalo'ne [-ō'ni] n. edible shell-fish, yielding mother of pearl

aban'don vt. desert; give up altogether —n. freedom from inhibitions *etc.* —**aban'doned** a. deserted, forsaken; uninhibited; wicked —**aban'donment** n.

abase' vt. humiliate, degrade —**abase'ment** n.

abash' vt. (usu. passive) confuse, make ashamed —**abash'ment** n.

abate' v. make or become less, diminish —**abate'ment** n.

ab'attoir n. slaughterhouse

abb'ey n. dwelling place of community of monks or nuns; church of an abbey

abb'ot n. head of abbey or monastery (**abb'ess** *fem.*) —**ab'bacy** n. office, rights of abbot

abbr., abbrev. abbreviation

abbre'viate vt. shorten, abridge —**abbrevia'tion** n. shortened form of word or phrase

ab'dicate v. formally to give up (throne *etc.*) —**abdica'tion** n.

ab'domen n. belly —**abdom'inal a.**

abduct' vt. carry off, kidnap —**abduc'tion** n.

abeam' adv. abreast, in line

abele' n. white poplar

Ab'erdeen An'gus breed of cattle, *orig.* Scottish

aberra'tion n. deviation from what is normal; flaw; lapse —**aber'rant** a.

abet' vt. assist, encourage, *esp.* in doing wrong —**abett'er, -or** n.

abey'ance n. condition of not being in use or action

abhor' vt. dislike strongly, loathe —**abhor'rence** n. —**abhor'rent** a. hateful

abide' vt. endure, put up with —vi. *obs.* stay, reside (**abode'**, **abi'ded**, **abi'ding**) —**abide by** obey

abil'ity n. competence; power; talent

ab ini'tio [-i-nish'i-ō] *Lat.* from the start

ab'ject a. humiliated, wretched; despicable —**abjec'tion, abjec't-ness** n.

abjure' vt. to give up by oath, renounce —**abjura'tion** n.

ab'lative n. case in (*esp.* Latin) nouns indicating source, agent, instrument of action

ab'laut [-lowt] n. vowel change within word, indicating modification of use, *eg* sink, sank, sunk

ablaze¹ a. burning

a'ble a. capable, competent —**a'bly** adv. —**able-bodied** a.

ablu'tion n. (usu. pl.) act of washing (oneself)

ab'negate vt. give up, renounce —**abnega'tion** n.

abnor'mal a. irregular; not usual or typical; freakish, odd —**abnormal'ity** n. —**abnor'mally** adv.

aboard' adv. on board, on ship, train, or aircraft

abode' n. home; dwelling —pt./pp. of ABIDE

abol'ish vt. do away with —**aboli'tion** n. —**aboli'tionist** n. one who wishes to do away with something, esp. slavery

A-bomb n. atomic bomb

abom'inate vt. detest —**abom'inable** a. —**abom'inably** adv. —**abomina'tion** n. loathing; the object loathed —**abominable snowman** large legendary apelike creature said to inhabit the Himalayas

Aborig'inal a. of, relating to the Aborigines of Aust.; (a-) indigenous, earliest —n. Aborigine

Aborig'ine [-in-ē] n. one of race of people inhabiting Aust. when European settlers arrived; (a-) original inhabitant of country etc.

abort' v. (cause to) end prematurely (esp. pregnancy) —vi. give birth to dead foetus; fail —**abor'tion** n. operation to terminate pregnancy; something deformed —**abor'tionist** n. one who performs abortion, esp. illegally —**abor'tive** a. unsuccessful —**abor'tively** adv.

abound' vi. be plentiful; overflow —**abound'ing** a.

about' adv. on all sides; nearly; up and down; out, astir —prep. round; near; concerning; ready to

—**about turn** reversal, complete change

above' adv. higher up —prep. over; higher than; more than; beyond

ab'racadab'ra n. supposedly magic word

abrade' vt. rub off, scrape away

abra'sion n. place scraped or worn by rubbing (eg on skin); scraping, rubbing —**abra'sive** n. substance for grinding, polishing etc. —a. causing abrasion; grating

abreast' adv. side by side; keeping up with

abridge' vt. cut short, abbreviate —**abridg'(e)ment** n.

abroad' adv. to or in a foreign country; at large

ab'rogate vt. cancel, repeal —**abroga'tion** n.

abrupt' a. sudden; blunt; hasty; steep —**abrupt'ly** adv. —**abrupt'ness** n.

ab'scess [-ses] n. gathering of pus in any part of the body

abscis'sa [-sis'-] n. Math. distance of point from the axis of coordinates (pl. **-sas, -sae** [-sē])

abscond' [-sk-] vi. leave secretly, esp. having stolen something

ab'seil [-āl] vi. descend vertical slope by means of rope

ab'sent a. away; not attentive —vt. [-sent'] keep away —**ab'sence** n. —**absentee'** n. one who stays away esp. habitually —**absentee'ism** n. persistent absence from work etc. —**ab'sently** adv. —**absent-minded** a.

ab'sinth(e) n. potent aniseed flavoured liqueur

ab'solute a. complete; not limited, unconditional; pure (as in absolute alcohol) —n. —**ab'solutely** adv. completely —interj. [-lōōt'-] certainly —**ab'soluteness** n.

absolve' vt. free from, pardon,

acquit —**absolu'tion** n.

absorb' vt. suck up, drink in; engage, occupy (attention etc.); receive impact —**absorb'ent** a. —**absorp'tion** n. —**absorp'tive** a.

abstain' vi. keep from, refrain from drinking alcohol, voting etc. —**abstain'er** n. —**absten'tion** n. —**ab'stinence** n. —**ab'stinent** a.

abste'mious a. sparing in food or esp. drink, temperate —**abste'miously** adv. —**abste'miousness** n.

ab'stract a. existing only in the mind; not concrete; not representational — n. summary, abridgment — vt. [ab-strakt'] draw from, remove; deduct —**abstract'ed** a. preoccupied —**abstrac'tion** n. —**ab'stractly** adv.

abstruse' a. obscure, difficult to understand, profound —**abstruse'ly** adv.

absurd' a. contrary to reason —**absurd'ity** n. —**absurd'ly** adv.

ABTA Association of British Travel Agents

abun'dance n. great amount —**abun'dant** a. plentiful —**abun'dantly** adv.

abuse' [-byōōz'] vt. misuse; address rudely — n. [-byōōs'] misuse; insulting speech —**abu'sive** a. —**abu'sively** adv. —**abu'siveness** n.

abut' vi. adjoin, border on (-**tt**-) —**abut'ment** n. support, esp. of bridge or arch

abuzz' a. noisy, busy with activity etc.

abys'mal [-z'-] a. immeasurable, very great; inf. extremely bad —**abys'mally** adv.

abyss' n. very deep gulf or pit

AC aircraftman; alternating current

A/C account

aca'cia [-kā'shə] n. gum-yielding tree or shrub

acad'emy n. society to advance arts or sciences; institution for specialized training; secondary school —**academ'ic** a. of academy; belonging to University etc.; theoretical —**academ'ically** adv. —**academi'cian** n.

acan'thus n. prickly plant; architectural ornament like its leaf (pl. **-thuses, -thi** [-thī])

ACAS [ā'kas] Advisory Conciliation and Arbitration Service

acc. accompanied; account; accusative

accede' [aks-] vi. agree, consent; attain (office, rank etc.)

accel'erate [aks-] v. (cause to) increase speed, hasten —**accel'era'tion** n. —**accel'erative** a. —**accel'erator** n. mechanism to increase speed, esp. in car

ac'cent [aks'-] n. stress or pitch in speaking; mark to show such stress; local or national style of pronunciation; particular attention or emphasis — vt. [-sent']

accen'tor n. sparrowlike songbird

accent'uate [aks-] vt. stress, emphasize —**accent'ual** a. —**accentua'tion** n.

accept' [aks-] vt. take, receive; admit, believe; agree to —**acceptabil'ity** n. —**accept'able** a. —**accept'ably** adv. —**accept'ance** n. —**accepta'tion** n. common or accepted meaning of word etc. —**accept'er** n.

ac'cess [aks'-] n. act, right, or means of entry —**accessibil'ity** n. —**access'ible** a. easy to approach —**access'ibly** adv.

access'ary n. see ACCESSORY

access'ion n. attaining of office, right etc.; increase, addition

access'ory n. additional or supplementary part of motorcar, woman's dress etc.; person inciting or assisting in crime —a. contributory, assisting

ac'cidence [aks'-] n. the part of

grammar dealing with changes in the form of words

ac'cident [ak's-] *n.* event happening by chance; misfortune or mishap, *esp.* causing injury; nonessential quality —**accident'al** *a.* —**accident'ally** *adv.*

acclaim' *vt.* applaud, praise —*n.* applause —**acclama'tion** *n.* —**acclam'atory** *a.*

accli'matize *vt.* accustom to new climate or environment —**acclimatiza'tion** *n.*

acc'olade *n.* praise, public approval; award, honour; token of award of knighthood

accomm'odate *vt.* supply, *esp.* with board and lodging; oblige; harmonize, adapt —**accom'modating** *a.* obliging —**accommoda'tion** *n.* lodgings

accom'pany *vt.* go with; supplement; occur with; provide a musical accompaniment (-panied, -panying) —**accom'paniment** *n.* that which accompanies, *esp.* in music, part which goes with solos *etc.* —**accom'panist** *n.*

accom'plice [-plis-] *n.* one assisting another in criminal deed

accom'plish *vt.* carry out; finish —**accom'plished** *a.* complete, perfect; proficient —**accom'plishment** *n.* completion; personal ability

accord' *n.* (*esp.* **in accord with**) agreement, harmony —*v.* (cause to) be in accord with —*vt.* grant —**accord'ance** *n.* —**accord'ant** *a.* —**accord'ingly** *adv.* as the circumstances suggest; therefore

accor'dion *n.* portable musical instrument with keys, metal reeds and a bellows —**accor'dionist** *n.* —**piano accordion**

accost' *vi.* approach and speak to, ask question *etc.*

account' *n.* report, description;

importance, value; statement of moneys received, paid, or owed; person's money held in bank; credit available to person at store *etc.* —*vt.* reckon; judge —*vi.* give reason, answer (for) —**accountabil'ity** *n.* —**account'able** *a.* responsible —**account'ancy** *n.* keeping, preparation of business accounts, financial records *etc.* —**account'ant** *n.* one practising accountancy —**account'ing** *n.* skill or practice of keeping and preparing business accounts —*a.*

accou'tre [-ōō'-] *vt.* equip —**accou'trements** [-tro-] *pl.n.* equipment, *esp.* military; trappings

accred'ited *a.* authorized, officially recognized

accre'tion *n.* growth; something added on

accrue' *vi.* be added; result

acct. account

accu'mulate *v.* gather, become gathered in increasing quantity; collect —**accumula'tion** *n.* —**accu'mulator** *n.* type of rechargeable battery, as in car

acc'urate *a.* exact, correct, without errors —**acc'uracy** *n.* —**acc'urately** *adv.*

accurs'ed, accurst' *a.* under a curse; hateful, detestable

accuse' *vt.* charge with wrong doing; blame —**accusa'tion** *n.* —**accu'sative** *n.* grammatical case indicating the direct object —**accu'satory** *a.* —**accu'ser** *n.*

accus'tom *vt.* make used to, familiarize —**accus'tomed** *n.* usual; used (to); in the habit (of)

ace *n.* the one at dice, cards, dominoes; *Tennis* winning serve *esp.* one untouched by opponent; very successful fighter pilot; *inf.* person expert at anything —*a. inf.* excellent

ac'erbate [as'-] *vt.* make worse; make sour, bitter —**acerb'ity** *n.*

severity, sharpness; sour bitterness

ac'etate n. salt of acetic acid —**acetate rayon** synthetic textile fibre

ace'tic a. derived from or having the nature of vinegar

ac'etone [as'-] n. colourless liquid used as a solvent

acet'ylene [-set'-] n. colourless, flammable gas used esp. in welding metals

ache [āk] n. continuous pain —vi. to be in pain —**a'ching** a.

achieve' vt. accomplish, perform successfully; gain —**achieve'ment** n. something accomplished

achromat'ic [ak-] a. free from or not showing colour, as of a lens, colourless

ac'id [as'-] a. sharp, sour —n. sour substance; Chem. one of a class of compounds which combines with bases (alkalis, oxides etc.) to form salts —**acid'ic** a. —**acid'ify** vt. (-fied, -fying) —**acid'ity** n. —**acid'ulate** vt. to make slightly acid —**acid'ulous** a. —**acid rain** rain acidified by atmospheric pollution —**acid test** conclusive test of value

ack-ack n. anti-aircraft guns or gunfire

acknowl'edge [ək-nol'ij] vt. admit, own, recognize; say one has received —**acknowl'edg(e)ment** n.

aclin'ic a. without inclination, said of the magnetic equator, on which the magnetic needle has no dip

ac'me n. highest point

ac'ne n. pimply skin disease

ac'olyte n. follower or attendant, esp. of priest

ac'onite n. genus of plants related to the buttercup, including monkshood; drug, poison obtained from such

a'corn [ā'-] n. nut or fruit of the oak tree

acou'stic a. pert." to sound and to hearing —**acou'stics** pl.n. science of sounds; features of room or building as regards sounds heard within it

acquaint' vt. make familiar, inform —**acquaint'ance** n. person known; personal knowledge —**acquaint'anceship** n.

acquiesce' [a-kwi-es'] vi. agree, consent without complaint —**acquies'cence** n. —**acquies'cent** a.

acquire' vt. gain, get —**acquire'ment** n. —**acquisi'tion** n. act of getting; material gain —**acquis'itive** a. desirous of gaining —**acquis'itiveness** n.

acquit' vt. declare innocent; settle, discharge, as a debt; behave (oneself) (-tt-) —**acquit'tal** n. declaration of innocence in court —**acquit'tance** n. discharge of debts

a'cre [-kər] n. measure of land, 4840 square yards —pl. lands, estates; inf. large area or plenty of —**a'creage** n. the extent of land in acres

ac'rid a. pungent, sharp; irritating —**acrid'ity** n.

ac'rimony n. bitterness of feeling or language —**acrimo'nious** a.

ac'robat n. one skilled in gymnastic feats, esp. as entertainer in circus etc. —**acrobat'ic** a. —**acrobat'ics** pl.n. any activity requiring agility

ac'ronym n. word formed from initial letters of other words eg UNESCO, ANZAC, NATO

acrop'olis n. citadel, esp. in ancient Greece

across' adv./prep. crosswise; from side to side; on or to the other side —**get** (or **put**) it **across** explain, make (something) understood

acros'tic n. word puzzle in which the first, middle, or last letters of each line spell a word or words

acryl'ic [-kril'-] n. variety of synthetic materials, esp. textiles derived from an organic acid

act n. thing done, deed; doing; law or decree; section of a play —v. perform, as in a play —vi. exert force, work, as mechanism; behave —**ac'ting** a. performance of a part —**a.** temporarily performing the duties of —**ac'tion** n. operation; deed; gesture; expenditure of energy; battle; lawsuit —**ac'tionable** a. subject to lawsuit —**ac'tivate** vt. to make active; make radioactive; make chemically active —**activa'tion** n. —**ac'tivator** n. —**ac'tive** a. moving, working; brisk, energetic —**ac'tively** adv. —**ac'tivism** n. —**ac'tivist** n. one who takes (direct) action to achieve political or social ends —**activ'ity** n. —**ac'tor** n. one who acts in a play, film etc. (fem. **-tress**)

ac'tinism n. chemical action of sun's rays —**actin'ic** a.

actin'ium n. radioactive element occurring as decay product of uranium

ac'tual a. existing in the present; real —**actual'ity** n. —**ac'tually** adv. really, indeed

ac'tuary n. statistician who calculates insurance risks, premiums etc. —**actua'rial** a.

ac'tuate vt. activate; motivate —**actua'tion** n.

acu'ity n. keenness, esp. in vision or thought

ac'umen n. sharpness of wit, perception, penetration

ac'upuncture n. orig. Chinese medical treatment involving insertion of needles at various points on the body —**ac'upuncturist** n.

acute' a. keen, shrewd; sharp; severe; less than 90° —n. accent (´) over a letter to indicate the quality or length of its sound eg abbé —**acute'ly** adv. —**acute'ness** n.

AD anno Domini

ad n. abbrev. of ADVERTISEMENT

ad'age n. much used wise saying, proverb

adag'io [-dahzh'-] adv./n. Mus. leisurely, slow (passage)

ad'amant a. very hard, unyielding —**adaman'tine** a.

Adam's apple projecting part at front of the throat, the thyroid cartilage

adapt' vt. alter for new use; fit, modify; change —**adaptabil'ity** n. —**adapt'able** a. —**adapta'tion** n. —**adapt'er, -or** n. esp. appliance for connecting two parts (eg electrical)

add v. join; increase by; say further —**addi'tion** n. —**addi'tional** a. —**ad'ditive** n. something added, esp. to foodstuffs

adden'dum n. thing to be added (pl. **-da**)

add'er n. small poisonous snake

ad'dict n. one who has become dependent on something, eg drugs (a drug addict) —vt. [ə-dikt'] (usu. passive) —**addict'ed** a. —**addic'tion** n. —**addic'tive** a. causing addiction

ad'dle v. make or become rotten, muddled

address' n. direction on letter; place where one lives; speech —pl. courtship —vt. mark destination, as on envelope; speak to; direct; dispatch —**addressee'** n. person addressed

adduce' vt. offer as proof; cite —**addu'cible** a. —**adduc'tion** n.

ad'enoids pl.n. tissue at back of nose —**adenoid'al** a.

adept' a. skilled —n. [ad'-] expert

ad'equate [-kwət] *a.* sufficient, enough, suitable; not outstanding —**ad'equacy** *n.* —**ad'equately** *adv.*

adhere' *vi.* stick to; be firm in opinion *etc.* —**adhe'rent** *n./a.* —**adhe'sion** *n.* —**adhe'sive** *a./n.*

ad hoc' [-hok'] *a./adv.* for a particular occasion only; improvised

adieu' [-dyoo͞'] *interj.* farewell —*n.* act of taking leave (*pl.* **adieus', adieux'**)

ad infini'tum *Lat.* endlessly

ad in'terim *Lat.* for the meantime

ad'ipose *a.* of fat, fatty

ad'it *n.* almost horizontal entrance into a mine

adj. adjective; adjourned; adjutant

adja'cent *a.* lying near, near (to) —**adja'cency** *n.*

ad'jective *n.* word which qualifies or limits a noun —**adjecti'val** *a.* of adjective

adjoin' *v.* be next to; join —**adjoin'ing** *a.* next to, near

adjourn' [ə-jurn'] *v.* postpone temporarily, as meeting; *inf.* move elsewhere —**adjourn'ment** *n.*

adjudge' *vt.* declare; decide; award —**adjudg(e)'ment** *n.*

adju'dicate *v.* try, judge; sit in judgment —**adjudica'tion** *n.* —**adju'dicator** *n.*

ad'junct *a.* joined, added —*n.* person or thing added or subordinate —**adjunc'tive** *a.*

adjure' *vt.* beg, earnestly entreat —**adjura'tion** *n.*

adjust' *vt.* make suitable, adapt; alter slightly, regulate —**adjust'able** *a.* —**adjust'er** *n.* —**adjust'ment** *n.*

ad'jutant *n.* military officer who assists superiors —**ad'jutancy** *n.* his office, rank

ad' lib *v.* improvise and speak

spontaneously —*n.* such speech *etc.* —*a./adv.*

Adm. Admiral; Admiralty

admin'ister *vt.* manage, look after; dispense, as justice *etc.*; apply —**admin'istrate** *vt.* manage business, institution, government department *etc.* —**administra'tion** *n.* —**admin'istrative** *a.* —**admin'istrator** *n.* (*fem.* **-atrix**)

ad'miral *n.* naval officer of highest sea rank —**Admiralty (Board)** department in charge of Royal Navy

admire' *vt.* look on with wonder and pleasure; respect highly —**ad'mirable** *a.* —**ad'mirably** *adv.* —**admira'tion** *n.* —**admi'rer** *n.* —**admi'ringly** *adv.*

admit' *vt.* confess; accept as true; allow; let in (-**tt**-) —**admiss'ible** *a.* —**admiss'ibly** *adv.* —**admis'sion** *n.* permission to enter; entrance fee; confession —**admit'tance** *n.* permission to enter —**admitt'edly** *adv.*

admix'ture *n.* mixture; ingredient —**admix'** *vt.*

admon'ish *vt.* reprove; advise; warn; exhort —**admoni'tion** *n.* —**admon'itory** *a.*

ad naus'eam [nawz'-] *Lat.* to a boring or disgusting extent

ado' [a-doo͞'] *n.* fuss

ado'be [-bi] *n.* sun-dried brick

adoles'cence *n.* period of life just before maturity —**adoles'cent** *n.* a youth —*a.*

Ado'nis *n.* a beautiful youth beloved of Venus

adopt' *vt.* take into relationship, *esp.* as one's child; take up, as principle, resolution —**adop'tion** *n.* —**adop'tive** *a.* that which adopts or is adopted

adore' *vt.* love intensely; worship —**ador'able** *a.* —**adora'tion** *n.* —**ador'er** *n.* lover

adorn' *vt.* beautify, embellish,

deck —**adorn'ment** n. ornament, decoration

ADP automatic data processing

ad rem *Lat.* to the point

adre'nal a. near the kidney —**adrenal gland** —**adren'alin(e)** n. hormone secreted by adrenal glands; this substance used as drug

adrift' a./adv. drifting free; *inf.* detached; *inf.* off course

adroit' a. skilful, expert; clever —**adroit'ly** adv. —**adroit'ness** n. dexterity

adsorb' v. (of gas, vapour) condense and form thin film on surface —**adsorb'ent** a./n. —**ad'sorp'tion** n.

adula'tion [-dyoo-] n. flattery —**ad'ulate** vt. flatter —**ad'ulator** n. —**ad'ulatory** a.

adult' a. grown-up, mature —n. grown-up person; full-grown animal or plant

adul'terate vt. make impure by addition —**adul'terant** n. —**adul'terated** a. —**adultera'tion** n. —**adul'terator** n.

adul'tery n. sexual unfaithfulness of a husband or wife —**adul'terer** n.masc. (**-ess** fem.) —**adul'terous** a.

ad'umbrate vt. outline; give indication of —**adum'brant, -rative** a. —**adumbra'tion** n.

adv. adverb(ial); advertisement

ad valor'em *Lat.* according to the value

advance' [-vah'-] vt. bring forward; suggest; encourage; pay beforehand; *Motoring* to time spark earlier in engine cycle —vi. go forward; improve in position or value —n. movement forward; improvement; a loan —pl. personal approach(es) to gain favour etc. —a. ahead in time or position —**advanced'** a. at a late stage; not elementary;

ahead of the times —**advance'ment** n. promotion

advan'tage n. superiority; more favourable position or state; benefit —**advanta'geous** a. —**advanta'geously** adv.

ad'vent n. a coming, arrival; (**A-**) the four weeks before Christmas —**the Advent** the coming of Christ —**Ad'ventist** n. one of number of Christian sects believing in imminent return of Christ

adventi'tious a. added; accidental, casual

adven'ture n. risk; bold exploit; remarkable happening; enterprise; commercial speculation —v. (take) risk —**adven'turer** n. one who seeks adventures; one who lives on his wits (**-ess** fem.) —**adven'turous** a. —**adven'turously** adv. —**adven'turousness** n.

ad'verb n. word added to verb, adjective, or other adverb to modify meaning —**adverb'ial** a. —**adverb'ially** adv.

ad'verse a. opposed to; hostile; unfavourable, bringing harm —**ad'versary** n. enemy —**adver'sative** a. —**ad'versely** adv. —**ad'versity** n. distress, misfortune

advert'[1] vi. turn the mind or attention to; refer —**advert'ence** n. —**advert'ently** adv.

ad'vert[2] n. *inf.* advertisement

ad'vertise vt. publicize; make known; give notice of, esp. in newspapers etc. —vi. make public request (for) —**advertise'ment** [-iz-] n. —**ad'vertiser** n. —**ad'vertising** a./n.

advice' n. opinion given; counsel; information; (formal) notification

advise' vt. offer advice; recommend a line of conduct; give notice (of) —**advi'sable** a. expedient —**advised'** a. considered,

deliberate, as in **well-advised**
—**advi'sedly** [-li-li] adv. —**advi'ser**, **-or** n. —**advi'sory** a.

ad'vocaat [-cah, -caht] n. liqueur with raw egg base

ad'vocate n. one who pleads the cause of another, esp. in court of law; barrister —vt. uphold, recommend —**ad'vocacy** n. —**advoca'tion** n.

advt. advertisement

adze [adz] n. carpenter's tool, like axe, but with arched blade set at right angles to handle

AEA Atomic Energy Authority

ae'gis [e'jis] n. sponsorship, protection (orig. shield of Zeus)

ae'grotat [l'-] n. in British university, exemption, esp. from final examinations because of illness

Aeo'lian [ē-o'-] a. acted on by the wind, as **Aeolian harp**

ae'on [ē'-] n. age, very long period of time; eternity

a'erate vt. charge liquid with gas, as effervescent drink; expose to air —**aera'tion** n. —**a'erator** n. apparatus for charging liquid with gas

a'erial a. of the air; operating in the air; pertaining to aircraft —n. part of radio etc. receiving or sending radio waves

ae'rie, ae'ry [a'-, l'-] n. see FYRIE

a'ero- (comb. form) air or aircraft as in **aeroengine**

aerobat'ics pl.n. stunt flying

aero'bics pl.n. exercise system designed to increase the amount of oxygen in the blood

a'erodrome n. airfield

aerodynam'ics pl.n. (with sing. v.) study of air flow, esp. round moving solid bodies

a'erofoil n. surfaces of wing etc. of aircraft designed to give lift

a'erogram n. air-mail letter form

a'erolite n. meteoric stone —**aerolit'ic** a.

aerom'etry n. measurement of weight or density of gases

a'eronaut n. pilot or navigator of lighter-than-air craft —**aeronau'tics** pl.n. (with sing. v.) science of air navigation and flying in general —**aeronau'tical** a.

a'eroplane n. heavier-than-air flying machine

a'erosol n. (substance dispensed as fine spray from) pressurized can

a'erospace n. earth's atmosphere and space beyond —a.

aesthet'ic [ēs-] a. relating to principles of beauty, taste and art —**aesthet'ics** pl.n. study of art, taste etc. —**aes'thete** n. one who affects extravagant love of art —**aesthet'ically** adv. —**aes'theticism** n.

aes'tivate [ēs-] vi. spend the summer, esp. in dormant condition —**aestiva'tion** n.

ae'ther see ETHER

aetiol'ogy [ē-ti-] n. study of causes, esp. inquiry into origin of disease —**aetiolog'ical** a.

AEU Amalgamated Engineering Union

AF audio frequency

afar' adv. from, at, or to, a great distance

AFC Air Force Cross; Association Football Club; automatic frequency control

aff'able a. easy to speak to, polite and friendly —**affabil'ity** n. —**aff'ably** adv.

affair' n. thing done or attended to; business; happening; sexual liaison —pl. personal or business interests; matters of public interest

affect' vt. act on, influence; move feelings; make show of;

make pretence; assume; have liking for —**affecta'tion** n. show, pretence —**affect'ed** a. making a pretence; moved; acted upon —**affect'edly** adv. —**affect'ing** — moving the feelings —**affect'ing-ly** adv. —**affec'tion** n. fondness, love —**affec'tionate** a. —**affec'tionately** adv.

aff'erent a. bringing to, esp. describing nerves which carry sensation to the brain

affi'ance vt. betroth —**affi'anced** a./n. (one) promised in marriage

affida'vit n. written statement on oath

affil'iate vt. connect, attach, as society to federation etc.; adopt —**affilia'tion** n.

affin'ity n. natural liking; resemblance; relationship by marriage; chemical attraction —**affin'itive** a.

affirm' v. assert positively, declare; maintain statement; make solemn declaration —**affirma'tion** n. —**affirm'ative** a. asserting —n. word of assent —**affirm'atively** adv.

affix' vt. fasten (to); attach, append —n. [af'-] addition, esp. to word, as suffix, prefix

afflict' vt. give pain or grief to, distress; trouble, vex —**afflic'tion** n. —**afflic'tive** a.

affl'uent a. wealthy; abundant —n. tributary stream —**aff'lu-ence** n. wealth, abundance

afford' vt. to be able to buy; be able to spare the time etc.; produce, yield, furnish

affor'est vt. turn land into forest, plant trees —**afforesta'tion** n.

affray' n. fight, brawl

affront' vt. insult openly —n. insult; offence

afield' adv. away from home; in or on the field

afire' adv. on fire

aflame' adv. burning

afloat' adv. floating; at sea; in circulation

AFM Air Force Medal

afoot' adv. astir; on foot

afore' prep./adv. before, usually in compounds as **afore'said**, **afore'thought**, **afore'time**

afoul [-fowl'] a./adv. into difficulty (with)

Afr. Africa(n)

afraid' a. frightened; regretful

afresh' adv. again, anew

Af'rican a. belonging to Africa —n. native of Africa —**African lily** S Afr. plant with funnel-shaped flowers —**African violet** house plant with pink or purple flowers and hairy leaves

African'der n. breed of hump-backed S Afr. cattle

Afrikaans' [-kahns'] n. language used in S Africa, derived from 17th cent. Dutch —**Afrika'ner** n. white native of S Afr. with Afrikaans as mother tongue

Af'ro n. fuzzy, bushy hair style

aft adv. towards stern of ship

af'ter [ahf'-] adv. later; behind —prep. behind; later than; on the model of; pursuing —conj. at a later time than —a. behind; later; nearer ship's stern —**af'ters** pl.n. course after main course; dessert

af'terbirth n. membrane expelled after a birth

af'tercare n. care, esp. medical, bestowed on person after period of treatment, and esp. after childbirth

af'tereffect n. subsequent effect of deed, event etc.

af'terglow n. light after sunset

af'termath n. result, consequence

afternoon' n. time from noon to evening

af'tershave n. lotion applied to face after shaving

af'terthought n. idea occurring later

af'terward(s) adv. later

Ag Chem. silver

again' adv. once more; in addition; back, in return; besides

against' prep. in opposition to; in contact with; opposite; in readiness for

agape' a./adv. open-mouthed as in wonder etc.

ag'aric n. various fungi, eg mushroom —a. fungoid

ag'ate n. coloured, semiprecious, decorative form of quartz

age [āj] n. length of time person or thing has existed; time of life; period of history; maturity; long time —v. make or grow old —a'ged [ājd or a'jid] a. old —pl.n. [a'jid] old people —a'ge(e)ing n./a. —age'less a. —age-old a.

agen'da [-jen'-] pl.n. (with sing. v.) things to be done; programme of business meeting

a'gent [-j-] n. one authorized to carry on business or affairs for another; person or thing producing effect; cause; natural force —a'gency n. instrumentality; business, place of business, of agent

agent provocateur' [a-zhong'-] Fr. police or secret service spy

agglom'erate v. gather into a mass —n. confused mass; rock consisting of volcanic fragments —a. —agglomera'tion n. —agglom'erative a.

agglu'tinate [-glōō'-] vt. unite with glue etc.; form words into compounds —a. united, as by glue —agglutina'tion n. —agglu'tinative a.

agg'randize vt. make greater in size, power, or rank —agg'gran'dizement n.

agg'ravate vt. make worse or more severe; inf. annoy —ag'gravating a. —aggrava'tion n.

agg'regate vt. gather into mass —a. gathered thus —n. mass, sum total; rock consisting of mixture of minerals; mixture of gravel etc. for concrete —aggrega'tion n.

aggress'ion n. unprovoked attack; hostile activity —aggress' vi. —aggress'ive a. —aggres'siveness n. —aggress'or n.

aggrieve' vt. pain, injure —aggrieved' a.

ag'gro n. sl. aggression

aghast' [-gahst'] a. struck, stupefied with horror or terror

ag'ile [-jīl] a. nimble; active; quick —ag'ilely adv. —agil'ity n.

ag'itate [-j-] vt. disturb, excite; to keep in motion, stir, shake up; trouble —vi. stir up public opinion (for or against) —agita'tion n. —ag'itator n.

aglow' a. glowing

AGM Annual General Meeting

agnos'tic n. one who holds that we know nothing of things outside the material world —a. of this theory —agnos'ticism n.

ag'nus de'i [dā'ī] figure of a lamb emblematical of Christ; part of Mass beginning with these words; the music for it

ago' adv. in the past

agog' a./adv. eager, astir

ag'ony n. extreme suffering of mind or body, violent struggle —ag'onize vi. suffer agony; worry greatly —ag'onizing a. —agony column newspaper or magazine feature offering advice on personal problems; column containing advertisements relating to personal problems

agorapho'bia n. fear of open spaces

agra'rian a. of agriculture, land or its management —**agra'rianism** n.

agree' v. be of same opinion; consent; harmonize; determine, settle; suit (**agreed', agree'ing**) —**agreeabil'ity** n. —**agree'able** a. willing; pleasant —**agree'ableness** n. —**agree'ably** adv. —**agree'ment** n. concord; contract

ag'riculture n. art, practice of cultivating land —**agricul'tural** a. —**agricul'turist** n.

ag'rimony n. yellow-flowered plant with bitter taste

agron'omy n. the study of the management of the land and the scientific cultivation of crops —**agron'omist** n.

aground' adv. (of boat) touching bottom

agt. agent

a'gue [-gyoo] n. obs. periodic fever with shivering

ahead' adv. in front; onwards

ahoy' interj. shout used at sea for hailing

AI artificial insemination; artificial intelligence

AID artificial insemination by donor

aid vt. to help —n. help, support, assistance

aide,   aide'-de-camp' [âd'-də-kong'] n. military officer personally assisting superior (pl. **aides-de-camp**)

AIDS acquired immune (or immuno-) deficiency syndrome

aiguille' [â-gwēl'] n. sharp, slender peak; blasting drill

AIH artificial insemination by husband

ail vt. trouble, afflict, disturb —vi. be ill —**ail'ing** a. sickly —**ail'ment** n. illness

ai'leron [â'-] n. movable section of wing of aircraft which gives lateral control

aim v. give direction to weapon etc.; direct effort towards, try to —n. direction; object, purpose —**aim'less** a. without purpose

ain't nonstandard am not; is not; are not; has not; have not

air n. mixture of gases we breathe, the atmosphere; breeze; tune; manner —pl. affected manners —vt. expose to air to dry or ventilate —**air'ily** adv. —**air'iness** n. —**air'ing** v. time spent in the open air —**air'less** a. stuffy —**air'y** a. —**air bed** —**air'borne** a. flying, in the air —**air brake** brake worked by compressed air; method of slowing down an aircraft —**air'brush** n. atomizer spraying paint by compressed air —**air commodore** —**air-condition** vt. maintain constant stream of clean fresh air in building at correct temperature —**air conditioner** —**air conditioning** —**air'craft** n. collective name for flying machines; aeroplane —**aircraft carrier** —**air cushion** pillow which can be inflated; pocket of air supporting hovercraft —**air'field** n. landing and taking-off area for aircraft —**air force** strength of country in aircraft —**air gun** gun discharged by force of compressed air —**air hostess** stewardess on aircraft —**air letter** air-mail letter, aerogram —**air'lift** n. transport of goods etc. by aircraft —**air'line** n. company operating aircraft —**air'lock** n. air bubble obstructing flow of liquid in pipe; airtight chamber —**air mail** —**air'man** n. —**air'play** n. radio exposure of disc —**air pocket** less dense air where aeroplane drops suddenly —**air'port** n. station for civilian aircraft —**air pump** machine to extract or supply air —**air raid** attack by aircraft —**air'screw** n.

propeller of any aircraft —**air shaft** passage for air into a mine etc. —**air'ship** n. lighter-than-air flying machine with means of propulsion —**air'sickness** n. nausea caused by motion of aircraft in flight —**air'speed** n. speed of aircraft relative to air —**air'strip** n. small airfield with only one runway —**air'tight** a. not allowing passage of air —**air trap** device to prevent escape of foul gases —**air valve** —**air'way** n. regular aircraft route —**air'worthy** a. fit for service in air —**air'worthiness** n.

Aire'dale n. large rough-coated terrier dog

aisle [īl] n. passageway separating seating areas in church, theatre etc.

ajar' adv. partly open

akim'bo adv. with hands on hips and elbows outwards

akin' a. related by blood; alike, having like qualities

Al Chem. aluminium

al'abaster n. soft, white, semi-transparent stone —**alabast'rine** a. of, like this

à la carte Fr. selected freely from the menu

alack' interj. cry of sorrow —**alack-a-day** interj.

alac'rity n. quickness, briskness, readiness

à la mode Fr. in fashion

alarm' n. sudden fright; apprehension; notice of danger; bell, buzzer; call to arms —vt. frighten; warn of danger —**alarm'ing** a. —**alarm'ist** n. one given to prophesying danger or exciting alarm esp. needlessly —**alarm clock** clock which sounds a buzzer or bell at a set time, as to wake someone up

alas' interj. cry of grief

alb n. long white priestly vestment, worn at Mass

al'batross n. large oceanic bird, of petrel family

albe'it [awl-bē'-] conj. although

albi'no [-ē'-] n. person or animal with white skin and hair, and pink eyes, due to lack of colouring matter (pl. -nos) —**al'binism** n.

al'bum n. book of blank leaves, for photographs, stamps, autographs etc.; one or more longplaying gramophone records

al'bumen [-byoo-] n. egg white

al'bumin, -en [-byoo-] n. constituent of animal and vegetable matter, found nearly pure in white of egg —**albu'minous** a.

al'chemy [-k-] n. medieval chemistry, esp. attempts to turn base metals into gold and find elixir of life —**al'chemist** n.

al'cohol n. intoxicating fermented liquor; class of organic chemical substances —**alcohol'ic** a. —n. one addicted to alcoholic drink —**al'coholism** n. disease, alcohol poisoning

al'cove n. recess

al'dehyde n. one of a group of organic chemical compounds

al'der [awl'-] n. tree related to the birch

al'derman [awl'-] n. formerly, member of governing body of a municipality —**alderman'ic** a.

ale n. fermented malt liquor, type of beer, orig. without hops —**ale'house** n. obs. public house

alert' a. watchful; brisk, active —n. warning of sudden attack or surprise —vt. warn, esp. of danger; draw attention to —**alert'ness** n. —**on the alert** watchful

Alexan'drine n. verse of six iambic feet

alfal'fa n. plant used as fodder; a kind of lucerne

alfres'co adv./a. in the open air

alg. algebra

al'gae [-jē] pl.n. (sing. **al'ga** [-gə])

various water plants, including seaweed

al'gebra n. method of calculating, using symbols to represent quantities and to show relations between them, and making a kind of abstract arithmetic —**algebra'i·c(al)** a. —**algebra'ist** n.

ALGOL Computers algorithmic oriented language

al'gorithm n. procedural model for complicated calculations

a'lias adv. otherwise —n. assumed name (pl. **a'liases**)

al'ibi [-bī] n. plea of being somewhere else when crime was committed; inf. excuse

a'lien n. foreign; different in nature; repugnant (to) —n. foreigner —**alienabil'ity** n. —**a'lienable** a. able to be transferred to another owner —**a'lienate** vt. estrange; transfer —**aliena'tion** n.

alight'¹ vi. get down; land, settle

alight'² a. burning; lit up

align' [-līn'] vt. bring into line or agreement —**align'ment** n.

alike' a. like, similar —adv. in the same way

aliment'ary a. of food —**alimentary canal** food passage in body

al'imony n. allowance paid under court order to separated or divorced spouse

A-line a. (of skirt) slightly flared

al'iped a. wing-footed —n. animal, like the bat, whose toes are joined by membrane that serves as wing

al'iquot a. such part of a number as will divide it without remainder

alive' a. living; active; aware; swarming

aliz'arin n. brown to red crystalline solid used as dye

al'kali [-lī] n. substance which

combines with acid and neutralizes it, forming a salt Potash, soda etc. are alkalis (pl. **-li(e)s**) —**al'kaline** a. —**alkalin'ity** n. —**al'kalize** vt. —**al'kaloid** n./a.

all [awl] a. the whole of, every one of —adv. wholly, entirely —n. the whole; everything, everyone —**all fours** hands and feet —**all in** exhausted —**all-in** a. Wrestling no style debarred —**all-rounder** n. person with ability in many fields

Al'lah [-lə] n. Moslem name for the Supreme Deity

allay'¹ vt. lighten, relieve, calm, soothe

allege' vt. state without or before proof; produce as argument —**allega'tion** n. —**alleged'** a. —**alleg'edly** [-lej'id-] adv.

alle'giance n. duty of a subject to his sovereign or state, loyalty

all'egory n. story with a meaning other than literal one; description of one thing under image of another —**allegor'ic(al)** a. —**allegor'ically** adv. —**all'egorist** n. —**all'egorize** vt.

allegrett'o adv./a./n. Mus. lively (passage) but not so quick as allegro

alle'gro [-lā'-] adv./a./n. Mus. fast (passage)

all'ergy n. abnormal sensitivity to some food or substance innocuous to most people —**aller'gen** n. substance capable of inducing an allergy —**aller'gic** a. having or caused by an allergy; inf. having an aversion (to)

alle'viate vt. ease, lessen, mitigate; make light —**allevia'tion** n. —**alle'viator** n.

all'ey n. narrow street; walk, path; enclosure for skittles; fine marble (pl. **-eys**)

alli'ance n. state of being allied; union between families by marriage, and states by treaty; confederation

alli'gator *n.* animal of crocodile family found in America

allitera'tion *n.* beginning of two or more words in close succession with same sound, *eg* Sing a Song of Sixpence —**allit'-erate** *vi.* —**allit'erative** *a.*

all'ocate *vt.* assign as a share; place —**alloca'tion** *n.*

allocu'tion *n.* formal address —**all'ocute** *vi.*

allog'amy *n.* cross-fertilization

allomor'phism *n* variation of form without change in essential nature; variation of crystalline form of chemical compound

allop'athy *n.* orthodox practice of medicine; opposite of homeopathy

allot' *vt.* distribute as shares; give out (-**tt**-) —**allot'ment** *n.* distribution; portion of land rented for cultivation; portion allotted

allot'ropy *n.* property of some elements of existing in more than one form, *eg* carbon in the form of diamond and charcoal —**all'otrope** *n.* —**allotrop'ic** *a.* —**allot'ropism** *n.*

allow' *vt.* permit; acknowledge; set aside —*vi.* (*usu. with* for) take into account —**allow'able** *a.* —**allow'ably** *adv.* —**allow'ance** *n.*

all'oy *n.* mixture of two or more metals —*vt.* [ə-loi'] mix metals, debase

all'spice [awl'-] *n.* pimento or Jamaica pepper

allude' [-lood'] *vi.* mention lightly, hint at, make indirect reference to; refer to —**allu'sion** *n.* —**allu'sive** *a.* —**allu'sively** *adv.*

allure' [-loor'] *vt.* entice, win over, fascinate —*n.* attractiveness —**allure'ment** *n.* —**allu'ring** *a.* charming, seductive —**allu'ringly** *adv.*

allu'vial [-ōōv'-] *a.* deposited by rivers —**allu'vion** *n.* land formed by washed-up deposit —**allu'-vium** *n.* water-borne matter deposited by rivers, floods *etc.* (*pl.* -**viums, -via**)

ally' *vt.* join in relationship by treaty, marriage, or friendship *etc.* (**allied'** [-līd'], **ally'ing**) —**allied'** [*or* al'īd] *a.* —**all'y** *n.* state or sovereign bound to another by treaty; confederate (*pl.* **all'ies**)

al'ma mat'er [-maht'-, -mā'-] *Lat.* one's school, university, or college

al'manac [awl'-] *n.* yearly calendar with detailed information on year's tides, events *etc.*

almi'ghty *a.* having all power, omnipotent; *inf.* very great —**The Almighty** God

alm'ond [ahm'-] *n.* kernel of the fruit of a tree related to the peach; tree that bears it

alm'oner [ahm'-] *n.* in hospitals, formerly, a trained social worker dealing with patients' welfare

al'most [awl'-] *adv.* very nearly, all but

alms [ahmz] *pl.n.* gifts to the poor

al'oe *n.* genus of plants of medicinal value —*pl.* bitter drug made from plant

aloft' *adv.* on high; overhead; in ship's rigging

alone' *a.* single, solitary —*adv.* separately, only

along' *adv.* lengthwise; together (with); forward —*prep.* over the length of —**along'side** *adv./prep.* beside

aloof' *adv.* withdrawn; at a distance; apart —*a.* uninvolved —**aloof'ness** *n.*

alope'cia *n.* baldness

aloud' *adv.* loudly; audibly

alp *n.* high mountain —**Alps** *pl. esp.* mountains of Switzerland —**al'pine** *a.* —*n.* mountain plant

—**al'pinist** n. mountain climber

—**alp'enstock** n. iron-shod staff used by climbers

alpac'a n. Peruvian llama; its wool; cloth made from this

al'phabet n. the set of letters used in writing a language —**alphabet'ic(al)** a. in the standard order of the letters —**alphabet'ically** adv.

alread'y [awl-red'i] adv. before, previously; sooner than expected

Alsa'tian [al-sā'shən] n. large dog of wolflike breed, German shepherd dog

al'so [awl'-] adv. as well, too; besides, moreover

alt. alternate; altitude; alto

al'tar [awl'-] n. raised place, stone etc., on which sacrifices are offered; in Christian church, table on which priest consecrates the Eucharist Forms compounds, as **al'tarcloth** n., **al'tarpiece** n., altar rails

al'ter [awl'-] v. change, make or become different —**alterabil'ity** n. —**al'terable** a. —**al'terably** adv. —**altera'tion** n. —**al'terative** a.

alterca'tion n. dispute, wrangling, controversy —**al'tercate** vi. —**al'tercative** a.

alt'er e'go Lat. second self; close friend

al'ternate [awl'-] v. occur or cause to occur by turns —**alternate** a. one after the other, by turns —**alter'nately** adv. —**alterna'tion** n. —**alter'native** n. one of two choices —a. replacing —**alter'natively** adv. —**al'ternator** n. electric generator for producing alternating current

alt'horn n. a tenor saxhorn

although' [awl-THŌ'] conj. despite the fact that

altim'eter n. instrument for measuring height

al'titude n. height, eminence, elevation, loftiness

al'to n. Mus. male singing voice or instrument above tenor; contralto (pl. -tos)

altogeth'er [awl-] adv. entirely; on the whole; in total

al'truism n. principle of living and acting for good of others —**altruis'tic** a. —**altruis'tically** adv.

al'um n. mineral salt, double sulphate of aluminium and potassium —**alu'minous** [-lōō'-] a.

alumin'ium [-lyoo-], US **alu'minum** n. light nonrusting metal resembling silver —**alu'mina** n. oxide of aluminium —**alu'minous** [-lōō'-] a.

alum'nus n. US graduate of college (pl. -**ni** [-nī])

al'ways [awl'-] adv. at all times; for ever

alys'sum n. garden plant with small yellow or white flowers

AM, am amplitude modulation; ante meridiem

Am. America(n)

am first person sing. pres. ind. of BE

Amad(h)loz'i [am-a-hlo'zi] pl.n. SA ancestral spirits

amal'gam n. compound of mercury and another metal; soft, plastic mixture; combination of elements

amal'gamate v. mix, combine or cause to combine —**amalgama'tion** n.

amanuen'sis n. one who writes to dictation; copyist, secretary (pl. -**ses** [-sēz])

am'aranth n. imaginary purple everlasting flower; genus of flowered plants —**amaran'thine** a. never fading

amaryll'is [-ril'-] n. lilylike plant

amass' v. collect in quantity —**amass'able** a.

am'ateur [-tər] n. one who carries on an art, study, game etc. for the love of it, not for money; unskilled practitioner —**am'a-teurish** a. imperfect, untrained —**am'ateurishly** adv. —**am'a-teurism** n.

am'atol n. high explosive consisting of ammonium nitrate and trinitrotoluene (TNT)

am'atory a. relating to love

amaze' vt. surprise greatly, astound —**amaze'ment** n. —**ama'zing** a. —**ama'zingly** adv.

Am'azon n. female warrior of legend; tall, strong woman —**Amazo'nian** a.

ambass'ador n. senior diplomatic representative sent by one state to another (**ambass'adress** fem.) —**ambassador'ial** a. —**bas'sadorship** n.

am'ber n. yellowish, translucent fossil resin —a. made of, coloured like amber

am'bergris [-grēs] n. waxy substance secreted by the sperm whale, used in making perfumes

ambidex'trous a. able to use both hands with equal ease —**ambidex'terity** n.

am'bience n. atmosphere of a place

am'bient a. surrounding

ambig'uous a. having more than one meaning; obscure —**ambigu'ity** n. —**ambig'uously** adv.

am'bit n. circuit; compass

ambi'tion [-bish'-] n. desire for power, fame, honour; the object of that desire —**ambi'tious** a. —**ambi'tiously** adv. —**ambi'-tiousness** n.

ambiv'alence, ambiv'a-lency n. simultaneous existence of two conflicting desires, opinions etc. —**ambiv'alent** a.

am'ble vi. move along easily and gently; move at an easy pace

—n. this movement or pace —**am'bler** n.

ambro'sia n. Myth. food of the gods; anything smelling, tasting particularly good

am'bulance [-byoo-] n. conveyance for sick or injured

ambuscade' n. a hiding to attack by surprise; ambush

am'bush n. a lying in wait (for) —vt. waylay, attack from hiding, lie in wait for

ame'liorate v. make better, improve —**ameliora'tion** n. —**ame'liorative** a.

amen' [ā-, ah-] interj. surely; so let it be

ame'nable a. easy to be led or controlled; subject to, liable —**amenabil'ity, ame'nableness** n. —**ame'nably** adv.

amend' vi. grow better —vt. correct; improve; alter in detail, as bill in parliament etc. —**amend'ment** n. —**amends'** pl.n. reparation

ame'nity n. (oft. pl.) useful or pleasant facility or service

Amer'ican a. of, relating to, the American continent or the United States of America

am'ethyst n. bluish-violet precious stone

a'miable a. friendly, kindly —**amiabil'ity, a'miableness** n. —**a'miably** adv.

am'icable a. friendly —**amicabil'ity** n. —**am'icably** adv.

amid', amidst' prep. in the middle of, among

amid'ship(s) adv. near, towards, middle of ship

ami'no acid [or -mē'-] organic compound found in protein

amiss' a. wrong —adv. faultily, badly —**take amiss** be offended (by)

am'ity n. friendship

am'meter n. instrument for measuring electric current

ammo'nia n. pungent alkaline gas containing hydrogen and nitrogen —**ammo'niac, ammoni'acal** a. —**ammo'niated** a. —**ammo'nium** n.

amm'onite n. whorled fossil shell like ram's horn

ammuni'tion [-nish'-] n. any projectiles (bullets, rockets *etc.*) that can be discharged from a weapon: also *fig.*

amne'sia n. loss of memory

am'nesty n. general pardon —*vt.* grant this

amniot'ic fluid fluid surrounding baby in womb

amoe'ba [-mē'-] n. microscopic single-celled animal found in ponds *etc.* and able to change its shape (*pl.* -**bas, -bae** [-bē]

amok' *see* AMUCK

among' [-mu-], **amongst'** *prep.* mixed with, in the midst of, of the number of, between

amor'al [a-mor'al] a. nonmoral, having no moral qualities —**amor'alism** n. —**amor'alist** n. —**amoral'ity** n.

am'orous a. inclined to love; in love —**am'orously** adv. —**am'orousness** n.

amorph'ous a. without distinct shape —**amorph'ism** n.

amort'ize vt. pay off a debt by a sinking fund

amount' vi. come, be equal (to) —n. quantity; sum total

amour' [-moor'] n. (illicit) love affair

amour-propre [-prop'r] Fr. self-respect

amp. amperage; ampere(s)

am'pere n. unit of electric current

am'persand n. the sign & (and)

amphet'amine [-mēn] n. synthetic liquid used medicinally as stimulant, a dangerous drug if misused

amphib'ious a. living or operating both on land and in water —**amphib'ian** n. animal that lives first in water then on land; vehicle able to travel on land or water; aircraft that can alight on land or water

am'phitheatre n. building with tiers of seats rising round an arena

am'phora n. two-handled vessel of ancient Greece and Rome

am'ple a. big enough; large, spacious —**am'ply** adv.

am'plify vt. increase; make bigger, louder *etc.* (-**fied, -fying**) —**amplifica'tion** n. —**am'plificatory** a. —**am'plifier** n.

am'plitude n. spaciousness, width

am'poule [-pōōl] n. container for hypodermic dose

am'putate [-pyoo-] vi. cut off (limb *etc.*) —**amputa'tion** n.

amuck', amok' adv. —**run amuck** rush about in murderous frenzy

am'ulet [-yoo-] n. something carried or worn as a charm

amuse' [-myōōz'] vt. divert; occupy pleasantly; cause to laugh or smile —**amuse'ment** n. entertainment, pastime —**amu'sing** a. —**amu'singly** adv.

an *see* A

anabap'tist n. advocate of adult baptism only, hence the rebaptizing of those baptized as infants

anabol'ic ster'oid any of various hormones used by athletes to encourage muscle growth

an'abranch n. stream that leaves a river and enters it further downstream

anach'ronism [-k'-] n. mistake of time, by which something is put in wrong historical period;

something out-of-date —**anachro·nis'tic** a.

anacolu'thon [-lōō'-] n. a sentence or words faulty in grammatical sequence

anacon'da n. large snake which kills by constriction

anae'mia [-nē'-] n. deficiency in number of red blood cells —**anae'mic** a. suffering from anaemia; pale, sickly

anaesthet'ic [-nis-] n./a. (drug) causing loss of sensation —**anaesthe'sia** n. loss of sensation —**anaesthet'ically** adv. —**anaes'thetist** [-nēs'-] n. expert in use of anaesthetics —**anaes'thetize** vt.

Anaglyp'ta [-glip'-] R thick, embossed wallpaper

an'agram n. word or sentence made by arranging in different order the letters of another word or sentence, eg an from tan —**anagrammat'ical** a. —**ana·gram'matist** n.

anal see ANUS

analge'sia n. absence of pain —**analge'sic** a./n. (drug) relieving pain

anal'ogy [-ji] n. agreement or likeness in certain respects; correspondence —**analog'ical** a. —**analog'ically** adv. —**anal'ogist** n. —**anal'ogize** v. explain by analogy —**anal'ogous** [-gəs] a. similar; parallel —**anal'ogously** adv.

anal'ysis n. separation into its elements or components (pl. -yses [-sēz]) —**an'alyse** vt. examine critically; determine the constituent parts —**an'alyst** n. one skilled in analysis, esp. chemical analysis —**analyt'ic(al)** a. —**analyt'ically** adv.

an'ap(a)est n. metrical foot of two short syllables and one long

an'archy [-k-] n. lawlessness; lack of government in a state;

confusion —**anarch'ic(al)** a. —**anar'chically** adv. —**an'archism** n. —**an'archist** n. one who opposes all government

anas'tigmat n. lens corrected for astigmatism

anastomo'sis n. interconnection of veins, arteries etc.

anat. anatomical; anatomy

anath'ema n. anything detested, hateful; ban of the church; curse (pl. -s) —**anath'ematize** vt.

anat'omy n. science of structure of the body; detailed analysis; the body —**anatom'ical** a. —**anatom'ically** adv. —**anat'omist** n. —**anat'omize** vt.

ANC African National Congress

an'cestor n. person from whom another is descended; early type of later form or product —**ances'tral** a. —**an'cestry** n.

an'chor [-ng'k-] n. heavy (usu. hooked) implement dropped on cable, chain etc. to bottom of sea to secure vessel —vt. fasten by or as with anchor —**an'chorage** n. act of, place of anchoring

an'chorite [-ng'k-] n. hermit, recluse (fem. -choress)

an'chovy [-ch-] n. small savoury fish of herring family

anchu'sa [-kyōō'-] n. plant with hairy leaves and blue flowers

an'cient [ān'shənt] a. belonging to former age; old; timeworn —n. one who lived in an earlier age (esp. in pl.) —**an'ciently** adv. —**ancient monument** notable building or site preserved as public property

ancil'lary a. subordinate, subservient, auxiliary

and conj. is a connecting word, used to join words and sentences, to introduce a consequence etc.

andan'te adv. Mus. moderately slow (passage)

and'iron n. iron bar or bracket for supporting logs in a fireplace

an'ecdote n. very short story dealing with single incident —**an'ecdotal** a.

anem'ograph n. instrument recording force and direction of wind

anemom'eter n. wind gauge —**anemomet'ric** a. —**anemom'etry** n.

anem'one [-ni] n. flower related to buttercup —**sea anemone** plantlike sea animal

anent' prep. obs. concerning

an'eroid a. denoting a barometer which measures atmospheric pressure without the use of mercury or other liquid

an'eurism [an'y>-] n. swelling out of a part of an artery

anew' adv. afresh, again

an'gel [an'j-] n. divine messenger; ministering or attendant spirit; person with the qualities of such a spirit, as gentleness, purity etc. —**angel'ic** [an-] a. —**gel'ically** adv.

angel'ica [-j-] n. aromatic plant; its candied stalks used in cookery

An'gelus [-j-] n. devotional service in R.C. Church in memory of the Incarnation, said at morning, noon and sunset

an'ger [-ng'g-] n. strong emotion excited by a real or supposed injury; wrath; rage —vt. excite to wrath; enrage —**an'grily** adv. —**an'gry** a. full of anger; inflamed

angi'na (pec'toris) n. severe pain accompanying heart disease

an'giosperm [-j-] n. plant having a seed vessel

an'gle[1] [ang'gl] vi. fish with hook and line —**an'gler** n. —**an'gling** n.

an'gle[2] [ang'gl] n. meeting of two lines or surfaces; corner; point of view; inf. devious motive —vt. bend at an angle

an'gler (fish) n. sea fish with spiny dorsal fin

An'glican [ang'gli-] a./n. (member) of the Church of England —**An'glicanism** n.

An'glicize [ang'gli-] vt. express in English, turn into English form —**An'glicism** n. English idiom or peculiarity

An'glo- [ang'glō] (comb. form) English, as **Anglo-American**

Anglopho'bia n. dislike of England etc.

ango'ra n. goat with long white silky hair which is used in the making of mohair; cloth or wool made from this hair —**angora cat, rabbit** varieties of cat and rabbit with long, silky fur

angostu'ra [-toor'-] n. bitter tonic, used as flavouring in alcoholic drinks

ang'strom n. unit of length for measuring wavelengths of electromagnetic radiation

an'guish [ang'gw-] n. great mental or bodily pain

an'gular a. (of people) bony, awkward; having angles; measured by an angle —**angular'ity** n.

anhy'drous a. (of chemical substances) free from water

an'iline [-lin, -lēn] n. product of coal tar or indigo, which yields dyes

animadvert' vi. (with (up)on) criticize, pass censure —**animadver'sion** n. criticism, censure

an'imal n. living creature, having sensation and power of voluntary motion; beast —a. of, pert. to animals; sensual —**animal'cule** n. very small animal, esp. one which cannot be seen by naked eye —**animal'cular** a. —**an'imalism** n. —**an'imally** adv.

an'imate vt. give life to; enliven; inspire; actuate; make cartoon film of —**an'imated** a. lively; in form of cartoons —**anima'l-**

tion n. life, vigour; cartoon film —**an'imator** n.

an'imism n. primitive religion, belief that natural effects are due to spirits, that inanimate things have spirits —**an'imist** n. —**animis'tic** a.

animos'ity n. hostility, enmity

an'imus n. hatred; animosity

an'ion [-I-ən] n. ion with negative charge

an'ise [-is] n. plant with aromatic seeds, which are used for flavouring

an'iseed n. the liquorice-flavoured seed of anise

an'kle [ang'kl] n. joint between foot and leg —**an'klet** n. ankle-ornament

ann'als pl.n. historical records of events —**ann'alist** n.

anneal' vt. toughen (metal or glass) by heating and slow cooling; temper —**anneal'ing** n.

ann'elid, annel'idan n. one of class of invertebrate animals, including the earthworm etc.

annex' vt. add, append, attach; take possession of (esp. territory) —**annexa'tion** n.

ann'exe n. supplementary building; something added

anni'hilate [-nī'əl-] vt. reduce to nothing, destroy utterly —**annihila'tion** n. —**anni'hilative** a. —**anni'hilator** n.

anniver'sary n. yearly return of a date; celebration of this

ann'o Dom'ini Lat. in the year of our Lord

ann'otate vt. make notes upon, comment —**annota'tion** n. —**ann'otator** n.

announce' vt. make known, proclaim —**announce'ment** n. —**announ'cer** n. broadcaster who announces items in programme, introduces speakers etc.

annoy' vt. vex; make slightly

angry; tease —**annoy'ance** n.

ann'ual a. yearly; of, for a year —n. plant which completes its life-cycle in a year; book published each year —**ann'ually** adv.

annu'ity n. sum or grant paid every year —**annu'itant** n. holder of annuity

annul' vt. make void, cancel, abolish (-ll-) —**annul'ment** n.

ann'ular a. ring-shaped —**ann'ulated** a. formed in rings —**annula'tion** n. —**ann'ulet** n. small ring or fillet

Annuncia'tion n. angel's announcement to the Virgin Mary; (a-) announcing —**annun'ciate** vt. proclaim, announce

an'ode n. Electricity the positive pole, or point of entry of current —**an'odize** vt. cover a metal object with protective film by using it for an anode in electrolysis

an'odyne a. relieving pain, soothing —n. pain-relieving drug

anoint' vt. smear with oil or ointment; consecrate with oil —**anoint'ment** n. —**the Anointed** the Messiah

anom'alous a. irregular, abnormal —**anom'aly** n. irregularity; deviation from rule

anon' obs. adv. in a short time, soon; now and then

anon. anonymous

anon'ymous a. nameless, esp. without an author's name —**anonym'ity** n. —**anon'ymously** adv.

anoph'eles [-lēz] n. genus of the malarial mosquito

an'orak n. lightweight, warm, waterproof, usu. hooded jacket

anorex'ia n. loss of appetite —**anorexia nervosa** psychological condition characterized by refusal to eat

anoth'er [-uTH'-] pron./a. one other; a different one; one more

ans. answer

an'serine a. of or like a goose; silly

an'swer [ahn'sər] v. reply (to); solve; reply correctly; meet; be accountable (for, to); match; satisfy, suit —n. reply; solution —**an'swerable** a. accountable —**answering machine** apparatus for answering a telephone automatically and recording messages

ant n. small social insect, proverbial for industry —**ant'eater** n. animal which feeds on ants by means of a long, sticky tongue —**ant hill** the mound raised by ants

antag'onist n. opponent, adversary —**antag'onism** n. —**antagonis'tic** a. —**antagonis'tically** adv. —**antag'onize** vt. arouse hostility in

Antarc'tic a. south polar —n. these regions

an'te n. player's stake in poker —vt. stake

ante- (comb. form) before, as in **an'techamber** n. Such words are not given here where the meaning may easily be inferred from the simple word

antece'dent a./n. (thing) going before

antedilu'vian [-loo'-] a. before the Flood; ancient

an'telope n. deer-like ruminant animal, remarkable for grace and speed

antena'tal a. of care etc. during pregnancy

antenn'a n. insect's feeler; aerial (pl. **-ae** [-ē])

ante'rior a. to the front; before

an'them n. song of loyalty, esp. to a country; Scripture passage set to music; piece of sacred music, originally sung in alter- nate parts by two choirs

an'ther n. sac in flower, containing pollen, at top of stamen —**an'theral** a.

anthol'ogy n. collection of poems, literary extracts etc. —**anthol'ogist** n. maker of such —**anthol'ogize** vt. include poem etc. in anthology

an'thracite n. hard coal burning slowly almost without flame or smoke

an'thrax n. malignant disease in cattle, communicable to man; sore caused by this

an'thropoid a. like man —n. ape resembling man

anthropol'ogy n. scientific study of origins, development of human race —**anthropolog'ical** a. —**anthropol'ogist** n.

anthropomor'phize vt. ascribe human attributes to God or an animal —**anthropomorph'ic** a. —**anthropomorph'ism** n.

anti-, ant- (comb. form) against Makes compounds as **anti-aircraft** a. —**antispasmod'ic** a./n. etc. Such words are not given here where meaning may easily be inferred from simple word

antibiot'ic n. any of various chemical, fungal or synthetic substances, esp. penicillin, used against bacterial infection —a.

an'tibody n. substance in, or introduced into, blood serum which counteracts the growth and harmful action of bacteria

antic'ipate [-tis'-] vt. expect; take or consider beforehand; foresee; enjoy in advance —**anticipa'tion** n. —**antic'ipative, antic'ipatory** a.

anticli'max n. sudden descent to the trivial or ludicrous

an'tics pl.n. absurd or grotesque movements or acts

anticy'clone n. system of

winds moving round centre of high barometric pressure

an'tidote n. counteracting remedy

an'tifreeze n. liquid added to water to lower its freezing point, as in car radiators

an'tigen [-j-] n. substance stimulating production of antibodies in the blood

antihis'tamine n. drug used esp. to treat allergies

antimacass'ar n. cover to protect chairs from macassar oil

an'timony n. brittle, bluish-white metal

antip'athy n. dislike, aversion —**antipathet'ic** a.

antiper'spirant n. substance used to reduce sweating

an'tiphon n. composition in which verses, lines are sung alternately by two choirs; anthem —**antiph'onal** a.

antip'odes [-dēz] pl.n. countries, peoples on opposite side of the globe (often refers to Aust. and N Zealand) —**antip'odal, antipode'an** a.

an'tipope n. pope elected in opposition to the one regularly chosen

antipyret'ic n./a. (remedy) effective against fever

antique' [-ēk'] n. relic of former times, usu. a piece of furniture etc. that is collected —a. ancient; old-fashioned —**an'tiquary, antiqua'rian** n. student or collector of old things —**an'tiquated** a. out-of-date —**antiq'uity** n. great age; former times

antirrhi'num [-rī'-] n. genus of plants including snapdragon

anti-Semit'ic a. discriminating against Jews —**anti-Sem'itism** n.

antisep'tic n./a. (substance) preventing infection —a. free from infection

antith'esis n. direct opposite; contrast; opposition of ideas (pl. -eses) —**antithet'ical** a. —**antithet'ically** adv.

antitox'in n. serum used to neutralize disease poisons

antiven'ene, antiven'in n. antitoxin to counteract specific venom, eg of snake or spider

ant'ler n. branching horn of certain deer —**ant'lered** a.

an'tonym n. word of opposite meaning to another eg cold is an antonym of hot

a'nus n. the lower opening of the bowels —**a'nal** a.

an'vil n. heavy iron block on which a smith hammers metal into shape

anx'ious [angk'shəs] a. troubled, uneasy; concerned —**anxi'ety** [ang-zī'-] n. —**anx'iously** adv.

an'y [en'i] a./pron. one indefinitely; some; every —**an'ybody** n. —**an'yhow** adv. —**an'yone** n. —**an'ything** n. —**an'yway** adv. —**an'ywhere** adv.

An'zac n. of Australian-New Zealand Army Corps in WWI (1914-18) —n. soldier of that corps, Gallipoli veteran

AOB any other business

aor'ta [ā-aw'-] n. great artery rising from left ventricle of heart —**aor'tal** a.

apace' adv. swiftly

apart' adv. separately, aside; in pieces

apart'heid [-hīt, -hāt] n. (esp. in S Africa) official government policy of racial segregation

apart'ment n. room; a flat —pl. lodgings

ap'athy n. indifference; lack of emotion —**apathet'ic** a. —**apathet'ically** adv.

ape n. tailless monkey (eg chimpanzee, gorilla); coarse, clumsy person; imitator —vt. imitate —**a'pish** a. —**a'pishly** adv.

ape'rient, aper'itive *a.* mildly laxative —*n.* any such medicine

aperiod'ic [ā-] *a. Electricity* having no natural period or frequency

aper'itif *n.* alcoholic appetizer

ap'erture *n.* opening, hole

a'pex *n.* top, peak; vertex (*pl.* **a'pexes, a'pices**)

APEX Advance Purchase Excursion; Association of Professional, Executive, Clerical and Computer Staff

apha'sia *n.* dumbness, or loss of speech control, due to disease of the brain

aphe'lion *n.* point of planet's orbit farthest from the sun

a'phis *n.* various sap-sucking insects (*pl.* **a'phides** [-dēz]) —**a'phid** *n.* an aphis

aph'orism *n.* maxim, pithy saying —**aph'orist** *n.* —**aphoris'tic** *a.*

aphrodis'iac *a.* exciting sexual desire —*n.* substance which so excites

a'piary *n.* place where bees are kept —**apia'rian, a'pian** *a.* —**a'piarist** *n.* beekeeper —**a'piculture** *n.*

apiece' *adv.* for each

aplomb' [-plom'] *n.* self-possession, coolness, assurance

apoc'alypse *n.* prophetic revelation, *esp.* of St. John, last book of the New Testament —**apocalyp'tic** *a.* —**apocalyp'tically** *adv.*

apoc'rypha *n.* religious writing of doubtful authenticity —**Apoc'rypha** *pl.n.* collective name for 14 books originally in the Old Testament —**apoc'ryphal** *a.* spurious

apod'osis *n.* consequent clause in conditional sentence, as distinct from protasis or *if* clause (*pl.* **-oses** [-sēz])

ap'ogee [-jē] *n.* point of moon's or satellite's orbit farthest from the earth; climax

apol'ogy *n.* acknowledgment of offence and expression of regret; written or spoken defence; poor substitute (*with* for) —**apologet'-ic** *a.* —**apologet'ically** *adv.* —**apologet'ics** *n.* branch of theology charged with defence of Christianity —**apol'ogist** *n.* —**apol'ogize** *vi.*

ap'ophthegm, ap'othegm [-ə-them] *n.* terse saying, maxim —**apothegmat'ic** *a.*

ap'oplexy *n.* loss of sense and often paralysis caused by broken or blocked blood vessel in the brain; a stroke —**apoplec'tic** *a.*

apos'tasy *n.* abandonment of one's religious or other faith —**apos'tate** *n./a.*

a posterio'ri [ā pos-te-ri-aw'ri] *a.* denoting form of inductive reasoning which arrives at causes from effects; empirical

Apos'tle [-sl] *n.* one sent to preach the Gospel, *esp.* one of the first disciples of Jesus; founder of Christian church in a country; (**a-**) leader of reform —**apos'tleship** *n.* —**apostol'ic(al)** *a.*

apos'trophe [-trə-fi] *n.* a mark (') showing the omission of a letter or letters in a word; digression to appeal to someone dead or absent —**apos'trophize** *vt.*

apoth'ecary *n.* old name for one who prepares and sells drugs, *now* chemist

ap'othegm *see* APOPHTHEGM

apotheo'sis *n.* deification, act of raising any person or thing into a god (*pl.* **-ses**)

appal' [-awl'] *vt.* dismay, terrify (**-ll-**) —**appall'ing** *a. inf.* dreadful, terrible

appara'tus *n.* equipment, tools, instruments, for performing any experiment, operation *etc.*; means by which something operates

appar'el [-pa'-] *n.* clothing —*vt.* clothe (**-ll-**)

appar'ent [-pa'-] *a.* seeming; obvious; acknowledged, as in *heir apparent* —**appar'ently** *adv.*

appari'tion [-rish'-] *n.* appearance, *esp.* of ghost

appeal' *vi.* (*with* to) call upon, make earnest request; be attractive; refer to, have recourse to; apply to higher court —*n.* request, reference, supplication —**appeal'able** *a.* —**appeal'ing** *a.* making appeal; pleasant, attractive —**appeal'ingly** *adv.* —**appel'lant** *n.* one who appeals to higher court —**appell'ate** *a.* of appeals

appear' *vi.* become visible or present; seem, be plain; be seen in public —**appear'ance** *n.* an appearing; aspect; pretence

appease' *vt.* pacify, quiet, allay, satisfy —**appeas'able** *a.* —**appease'ment** *n.*

appell'ant *see* APPEAL

appella'tion *n.* name —**appel'lative** *a./n.*

append' *vt.* join on, add —**append'age** *n.*

appendici'tis *n.* inflammation of vermiform appendix

appen'dix *n.* subsidiary addition to book *etc.*; Anatomy projection, *esp.* the small worm-shaped part of the intestine (*pl.* **-dices** [-di-sēz], **-dixes**)

appercep'tion *n.* perception; apprehension; the mind's perception of itself as a conscious agent —**apperceive'** *vt.*

appertain' *vi.* belong, relate to, be appropriate

app'etence, app'etency *n.* desire, craving; sexual appetite —**app'etent** *a.*

app'etite *n.* desire, inclination, *esp.* desire for food —**app'etitive**

a. —**app'etize** *vt.* —**app'etizer** *n.* something stimulating to appetite —**app'etizing** *a.* —**app'etizingly** *adv.*

applaud' *vt.* praise by hand-clapping; praise loudly —**applaud'er** *n.* —**applaud'ing** *a.* —**applaud'ingly** *adv.* —**applause'** *n.* loud approval

ap'ple *n.* round, firm, fleshy fruit; tree bearing it

appli'ance *n.* piece of equipment *esp.* electrical

appli'qué [-plē'kā] *n.* ornaments, embroidery *etc.*, secured to surface of material —*vt.* ornament thus

apply' *vt.* utilize, employ; lay or place on; administer, devote —*vi.* have reference (to); make request (to) (**-lied'**, **-ly'ing**) —**applicabil'ity** *n.* —**app'licable** *a.* relevant —**app'licably** *adv.* —**ap'plicant** *n.* —**applica'tion** *n.* applying something for a particular use; relevance; request for a job *etc.*; concentration, diligence —**applied'** *a.* (of skill, science *etc.*) put to practical use

appoint' *vt.* name, assign to a job or position; fix, settle; equip —**appoint'ment** *n.* engagement to meet; (selection for a) job —*pl.* fittings

appor'tion *vt.* divide out in shares —**appor'tionment** *n.*

app'osite [-zit] *a.* suitable, apt —**app'ositely** *adv.* —**app'positeness** *n.* —**apposi'tion** *n.* proximity; the placing of one word beside another

appraise' *vt.* set price on, estimate value of —**apprais'able** *a.* —**apprais'al** *n.* —**appraise'ment** *n.* —**apprais'er** *n.*

appre'ciate [-shi-] *vt.* value at true worth; be grateful for; understand; enjoy —*vi.* rise in value —**appre'ciable** *a.* estimable; substantial —**appre'ci-**

ably adv. —**apprecia'tion** n. —**appre'ciative**, **appre'ciatory** a. capable of expressing pleasurable recognition —**appre'ciator** n.

apprehend' vt. seize by authority; take hold of; recognize, understand; dread —**apprehensibil'ity** n. —**apprehen'sible** a. —**apprehen'sion** n. dread, anxiety; arrest; conception; ability to understand —**apprehen'sive** a.

appren'tice n. person learning a trade under specified conditions; novice —vt. bind as apprentice —**appren'ticeship** n.

apprise' vt. inform

appro n. inf. approval

approach' v. draw near (to); set about; address request to; approximate to —n. a drawing near; means of reaching or doing; approximation; (oft. pl.) friendly overture(s) —**approachabil'ity** n. —**approach'able** a.

approba'tion n. approval —**ap'probate** vt.

appro'priate vt. take for oneself; put aside for particular purpose —a. suitable, fitting —**appro'priately** adv. —**appro'priateness** n. —**appropria'tion** n. act of setting apart for purpose; parliamentary vote of money —**appro'priative** a. —**appro'priator** n.

approve' vt. think well of, commend; authorize, agree to —**appro'val** n. —**appro'ver** n. —**appro'vingly** adv.

approx. approximate(ly)

approx'imate a. very near, nearly correct; inexact, imprecise —vt. bring close —vi. come near; be almost the same as —**approx'imately** adv. —**approxima'tion** n. —**approx'imative** a.

appur'tenance n. thing which appertains to; accessory

Apr. April

après-ski [ap-rā-] n. social activities after day's skiing

a'pricot n. orange-coloured stone-fruit related to the plum —a. of the colour of the fruit

A'pril n. the fourth month of the year

a priori [ā prī-ōrī] a. denoting deductive reasoning from general principle to expected facts or effects; denoting knowledge gained independently of experience

a'pron n. cloth, piece of leather etc., worn in front to protect clothes, or as part of official dress; in theatre, strip of stage before curtain; on airfield, tarmac area where aircraft stand, are loaded etc.; fig. any of a variety of things resembling these

apropos [-pō'] adv. to the purpose; with reference to —a. apt, appropriate —**apropos of** concerning

apse n. arched recess, esp. in a church —**aps'idal** a.

apt a. suitable; likely; prompt, quick-witted; dexterous —**ap'titude** n. capacity, fitness —**apt'ly** adv. —**apt'ness** n.

aq'ualung n. breathing apparatus used in underwater swimming

aquamarine' n. precious stone, the beryl —a. greenish-blue, sea-coloured

aq'uaplane n. plank or boat towed by fast motor-boat —vi. ride on aquaplane; (of car) be in contact with water on road, not with road surface —**aq'uaplaning** n.

aqua'rium n. tank or pond for keeping water animals or plants (pl. **-riums, -ria**)

Aqua'rius n. (the water-bearer) 11th sign of zodiac, operative c. Jan 20–Feb 18

aquat'ic a. living, growing, done in or on water —**aquat'ics** pl.n. water-sport

aq'uatint n. etching, engraving imitating drawings etc.

aq'ua vi'tae [vē'tī] Lat. obs. brandy

aq'ueduct n. artificial channel for water, esp. one like a bridge; conduit

a'queous a. of, like, containing water

aquile'gia n. columbine

aq'uiline a. relating to eagle; hooked like an eagle's beak

Ar Chem. argon

Ar. Arabic; Aramaic

ar. arrival; arrives

Ar'ab [a-] n. native of Arabia; general term for inhabitants of Middle Eastern countries; Arabian horse —**Ar'abic** n. language of Arabs —a.

arabesque' n. classical ballet position; fanciful painted or carved ornament of Arabian origin —a.

ar'abis [a-] n. low-growing garden plant with white, pink or lilac flowers

ar'able [a-] a. suitable for ploughing or planting crops

arach'nid [-k'-] n. one of the Arachnida (spiders, scorpions, and mites) —**arach'noid** a. —**arachnol'ogy** n.

Ar'an [a-] a. (of sweaters etc.) made with naturally oily, unbleached wool, often with a complicated pattern

ar'biter n. judge, umpire (-**tress** fem.) —**arbi'rament** n. —**ar'bitrarily** adv. —**ar'bitrary** a. not bound by rules, despotic; random —**ar'bitrate** v. decide dispute; submit to, settle by arbitration; act as an umpire —**arbitra'tion** n. hearing, settling of disputes, esp. industrial and legal, by impartial referee(s) —**ar'bitrator** n.

arbor'eal, arbor'eous a. relating to trees —**arbore'tum** n. place for cultivating specimens of trees (pl. -**tums**, -**ta**) —**ar'boriculture** n. forestry, cultivation of trees

arb'our n. leafy glade etc., sheltered by trees

arc n. part of circumference of circle or similar curve; luminous electric discharge between two conductors —**arc lamp** —**arc light**

arcade' n. row of arches on pillars; covered walk or avenue, esp. lined by shops

arcane' a. mysterious; esoteric

arch' n. curved structure in building, supporting itself over open space by pressure of stones one against the other; any similar structure; a curved shape; curved part of sole of the foot —v. form, make into, an arch —**arched** a. —**arch'way** n.

arch² a. chief; experienced, expert; superior, knowing, coyly playful —**arch'ly** adv. —**arch'ness** n.

arch. archaic; architecture

arch- (comb. form) chief, as in **archan'gel** [-k-] n., **archen'emy** n. etc. Such words are not given here where the meaning may easily be inferred from the simple word

archaeol'ogy [-k-] n. study of ancient times from remains of art, implements etc. —**archaeolog'ical** a. —**archaeol'ogist** n.

archa'ic [-k-] a. old, primitive —**archa'ically** adv. —**arch'aism** n. obsolete word or phrase

archbish'op n. chief bishop —**archbish'opric** n.

archdea'con n. chief deacon, clergyman next to bishop —**archdea'conate** n. —**arch-**

dea'conry n. —**archidiac'onal** a.

archduke' n. duke of specially high rank (**archduch'ess** fem.) —**archdu'cal** a. —**archduch'y** n.

arch'ery n. skill, sport of shooting with bow and arrow —**arch'er** n.

arch'etype [-k'-] n. prototype; perfect specimen —**arch'etypal** a.

archiepis'copal [-k-] a. of archbishop —**archiepis'copacy** n. —**archiepis'copate** n.

archipel'ago [-k-] n. group of islands; sea full of small islands, esp. Aegean (pl. **-agoes**) —**archipel'agic** a.

arch'itect [-k'-] n. one qualified to design and supervise construction of buildings; contriver —**architecton'ic** a. —**architec'tural** a. —**arch'itecture** n.

arch'itrave [-k'-] Architecture n. lowest division of the entablature; ornamental band round door or window opening

arch'ives [-kīvz] pl.n. collection of records, documents etc. about an institution, family etc.; place where these are kept —**archi'val** a. —**arch'ivist** n.

Arc'tic a. of northern polar regions; (**a-**) very cold —n. region round north pole

ard'ent a. fiery; passionate —**ard'ency** n. —**ard'ently** adv. —**ard'our** n. enthusiasm; zeal

ard'uous a. laborious, hard to accomplish, difficult, strenuous —**ard'uously** adv. —**ard'uousness** n.

are¹ pres. ind. pl. of BE

are² n. unit of measure, 100 square metres

a'rea n. extent, expanse of any surface; two-dimensional expanse enclosed by boundary (area of square, circle etc.); region; part, section; subject, field of activity; small sunken yard

ar'eca [ă'ri-kə] n. genus of palms, including betel palm

are'na n. enclosure for sports events etc.; space in middle of amphitheatre or stadium; sphere, scene of conflict

ar'gent [-j-] n. silver —a. silver, silvery-white, esp. in heraldry

ar'gon n. a gas, inert constituent of air

ar'gosy n. Poet. large richly-laden merchant ship

arg'ot [-ō] n. slang

ar'gue vi. quarrel, dispute; prove; offer reasons —vt. prove by reasoning; discuss —**ar'guable** a. —**arg'uer** n. —**arg'ument** n. quarrel; reasoning; discussion; theme —**argumenta'tion** n. —**argumen'tative** a.

Arg'us n. fabulous being with a hundred eyes —**Argus-eyed** a. watchful

ar'ia n. air or rhythmical song in cantata, opera etc.

ar'id [-a-] a. parched with heat, dry; dull —**arid'ity** n.

A'ries [-rēz] n. (the ram) 1st sign of zodiac, operative c. Mar 21-Apr 21

aright' adv. rightly

arise' vi. come about; get up; rise (up), ascend (**arose'**, **aris'en**, **ari'sing**)

aristoc'racy n. government by the best in birth or fortune; nobility; upper classes —**ar'istocrat** n. —**aristocrat'ic** a. noble; elegant —**aristocrat'ically** adv.

arith'metic n. science of numbers; art of reckoning by figures —**arithmet'ic(al)** a. —**arithmet'ically** adv. —**arithmeti'cian** n.

ark n. Noah's vessel; (**A-**) coffer containing Jewish Tables of Law

arm¹ n. limb extending from shoulder to wrist; anything projecting from main body, as branch of sea, supporting rail of chair *etc.*; sleeve Compounds as **arm'chair** *n.* —**arm'ful** *n.* —**arm'hole** *n.* —**arm'let** *n.* band worn round arm —**arm'pit** *n.* hollow under arm at shoulder

arm[1] *vt.* supply with weapons, furnish; prepare bomb *etc.* for use —*vi.* take up arms —*n.* weapon; branch of army —*pl.* weapons; war, military exploits; official heraldic symbols —**ar'mament** *n.*

armad'a [-mahd'-] *n.* large number of ships or aircraft

armadill'o *n.* small Amer. animal protected by bands of bony plates (*pl.* **-os**)

arm'ature *n.* part of electric machine, *esp.* revolving structure in electric motor, generator

arm'istice *n.* truce, suspension of fighting

arm'our *n.* defensive covering or dress; plating of tanks, warships *etc.*; armoured fighting vehicles, as tanks —**armor'ial** *a.* relating to heraldic arms —**ar'mourer** *n.* —**arm'oury** *n.*

arm'y *n.* large body of men armed for warfare and under military command; host; great number

arn'ica *n.* Bot. genus of hardy perennials A tincture of *Arnica montana* is used for sprains and bruises

aro'ma *n.* sweet smell; fragrance; peculiar charm —**aromat'ic** *a.* —**aro'matize** *vt.*

arose' *pt.* of ARISE

around' *prep.* on all sides of; somewhere in or near; approximately (of time) —*adv.* on every side; in a circle; here and there, nowhere in particular; *inf.* present in or at some place

arouse' *vt.* awaken, stimulate

arpegg'io [-j'-] *n. Mus.* notes sounded in quick succession, not together; chord so played (*pl.* **-ios**)

arr. arranged; arrival; arrive

arr'ack *n.* coarse spirit distilled from rice *etc.*

arraign' [-ān'-] *vt.* accuse, indict, put on trial —**arraign'er** *n.* —**arraign'ment** *n.*

arrange' *v.* set in order; make agreement; adjust; plan; adapt, as music; settle, as dispute —**arrange'ment** *n.*

arr'ant *a.* downright, notorious —**arr'antly** *adv.*

arr'as *n.* tapestry

array' *n.* order, *esp.* military order; dress; imposing show, splendour —*vt.* set in order; dress, equip, adorn

arrears' *pl.n.* amount unpaid or undone

arrest' *vt.* detain by legal authority; stop; catch attention —*n.* seizure by warrant; making prisoner —**arrest'ing** *a.* attracting attention, striking —**arrest'or** *n.* person who arrests; mechanism to stop or slow moving object

arris' *n.* sharp ridge or edge

arrive' *vi.* reach destination; (with at) reach, attain; *inf.* succeed —**arri'val** *n.*

arr'ogance *n.* aggressive conceit —**arr'ogant** *a.* proud; overbearing —**arr'ogantly** *adv.*

arr'ow *n.* pointed shaft shot from bow —**arr'owhead** *n.* head of arrow; any triangular shape

arr'owroot *n.* nutritious starch from W Indian plant, used as a food

ars'enal *n.* magazine of stores for warfare, guns, ammunition

ars'enic *n.* soft, grey, metallic element; its oxide, a powerful poison —**ars'enate** *n.* —**arsen'ical** *a.* —**arse'nious** *a.*

ars'on *n.* crime of intentionally setting property on fire

art *n.* skill; human skill as opposed to nature; creative skill in painting, poetry, music *etc.*; any of the works produced thus; profession, craft; knack; contrivance, cunning, trick; system of rules —*pl.* certain branches of learning, languages, history *etc.*, as distinct from natural science; wiles —**art'ful** *a.* wily —**art'fully** *adv.* —**art'fulness** *n.* —**art'ist** *n.* one who practises fine art, *esp.* painting; one who makes his craft a fine art —**artiste'** [-tēst'] *n.* professional entertainer, singer, dancer *etc.* —**artis'tic** *a.* —**artis'tically** *adv.* —**art'istry** *n.* —**art'less** *a.* natural, frank —**art'lessly** *adv.* —**art'lessness** *n.* —**art'y** *a.* ostentatiously artistic

art. article; artificial

ar'tefact *n.* something made by man, *esp.* by hand

arteriosclero'sis *n.* hardening of the arteries

ar'tery *n.* one of tubes carrying blood from heart; any main channel of communications —**arte'rial** *a.* pert. to an artery; main, important as **arterial road**

arte'sian *a.* describes deep well in which water rises by internal pressure

Artex R textured finish for ceilings *etc.*

arthri'tis *n.* painful inflammation of joint(s) —**arthrit'ic** *a./n.*

ar'thropod *n.* animal with jointed limbs and segmented body *eg* insect, spider

ar'tichoke *n.* thistle-like perennial, edible flower with **Jerusalem artichoke** sunflower with edible tubers like potato

ar'ticle *n.* item, object; short written piece; paragraph, section; *Grammar* words the, a, an; clause in a contract; rule, condition —*vt.* bind as apprentice

artic'ulate *a.* able to express oneself fluently; jointed; of speech, clear, distinct —*vt.* joint; utter distinctly —*vi.* speak —**artic'ulated** *a.* jointed —**artic'ulately** *adv.* —**artic'ulateness** *n.* —**articula'tion** *n.*

ar'tifice *n.* contrivance, trick, cunning, skill —**artif'icer** *n.* craftsman —**artifi'cial** *a.* manufactured, synthetic; insincere —**artificial'ity** *n.* —**artifi'cially** *adv.* —**artificial intelligence** ability of machines, *esp.* computers, to imitate intelligent human behaviour —**artificial respiration** method of restarting person's breathing after it has stopped

artil'lery *n.* large guns on wheels; the troops who use them

art'isan [-z-] *n.* craftsman, skilled mechanic, manual worker

artiste' *see* ART

a'rum lily plant with large white flower

A'ryan [ă'ri-ən] *a.* relating to Indo-European family of nations and languages

As *Chem.* arsenic

as *adv./conj.* denoting: comparison; similarity; equality; identity; concurrence; reason

asap as soon as possible

asbes'tos *n.* fibrous mineral which does not burn —**asbesto'sis** *n.* lung disease caused by inhalation of asbestos fibre

ascend' [ə-send'] *vi.* climb, rise —*vt.* walk up, climb, mount —**ascend'ancy** *n.* control, dominance —**ascend'ant** *a.* rising —**ascen'sion** *n.* —**ascent'** *n.* rise

ascertain' [as-ər-] *v.* get to know, find out, determine —**ascertain'able** *a.* —**ascertain'ment** *n.*

ascet'ic [-set'-] *n.* one who practises severe self-denial —*a.* rigidly abstinent, austere —**ascet'i-** *n.*

cally *adv.* **—asoct'icism** *n.*
ascor'bic acid vitamin C, present in green vegetables, citrus fruits *etc.*
ascribe' *vt.* attribute, impute, assign **—ascri'bable** *a.* **—ascrip'tion** *n.*
asep'tic *a.* germ-free **—asep'sis** *n.*
asex'ual [-ā-] *a.* without sex
ash[1] *n.* dust or remains of anything burnt **—***pl.* ruins; remains, *eg* of cremated body **—ash'en** *a.* like ashes; pale **—ash'y** *a.* **—The Ashes** symbol of victory in cricket test-match series between England and Australia
ash[2] *n.* deciduous timber tree; its wood **—ash'en** *a.*
ASH Action on Smoking and Health
ashamed' [-āmd'] *a.* affected with shame, abashed
ash'lar *n.* hewn or squared building stone
ashore' *adv.* on shore
Ash Wednesday first day of Lent
A'sian *a.* pert. to continent of Asia **—***n.* native of Asia or descendant of one **—Asiat'ic** *a.*
aside' *adv.* to or on one side; privately **—***n.* words spoken in an undertone not to be heard by some person present
A-side *n.* more important side of disc
as'inine *a.* of or like an ass, silly **—asinin'ity** *n.*
ask [ah-] *vt.* request, require, question, invite **—***vi.* make inquiry or request
askance' *adv.* sideways, awry; with a side look or meaning **—look askance** view with suspicion
askew' *adv.* aside, awry
aslant' [-ahnt'] *adv.* on the slant, obliquely, athwart
asleep' *a./adv.* sleeping, at rest

ASLEF Associated Society of Locomotive Engineers and Firemen
asp *n.* small venomous snake
aspar'agus [-pa'rə-] *n.* plant whose young shoots are a table delicacy
as'pect *n.* look, view, appearance, expression
as'pen *n.* type of poplar tree
asper'ity *n.* roughness; harshness; coldness
asper'sion *n.* (*usu. in pl.*) malicious remarks; slanderous attack
as'phalt *n.* black, hard bituminous substance used for road surfaces *etc.* **—as'phaltic** *a.*
as'phodel *n.* plant with clusters of yellow or white flowers
asphyx'ia *n.* suffocation **—asphyx'iate** *v.* **—asphyx'iated** *a.* **—asphyxia'tion** *n.*
as'pic *n.* jelly used to coat meat, eggs, fish *etc.*; *Bot.* species of lavender
aspidis'tra *n.* plant with broad tapered leaves
aspire' *vi.* desire eagerly; aim at high things; rise to great height **—as'pirant** *n.* one who aspires; candidate **—as'pirate** *vt.* pronounce with full breathing, as "h" **—aspira'tion** *n.* **—aspi'ring** *a.* **—aspi'ringly** *adv.*
as'pirin *n.* (a tablet of) drug used to allay pain and fever
ass *n.* quadruped of horse family; stupid person
ass'agai, ass'egai [-ī] *n.* slender spear of S Afr. tribes
assail' *vt.* attack, assault **—assail'able** *a.* **—assail'ant** *n.*
assas'sin *n.* one who kills, *esp.* prominent person, by treacherous violence; murderer **—assas'sinate** *vt.* **—assassina'tion** *n.*
assault' *n.* attack, *esp.* sudden **—***vt.* attack
assay' *vt.* test, *esp.* proportions of metals in alloy or ore **—***n.*

analysis, *esp.* of metals; trial, test —**assay'er** *n.*

ass'egai *see* ASSAGAI

assem'ble *v.* meet, bring together; collect; put together (of machinery *etc.*) —**assem'blage** *n.* —**assem'bly** *n.* gathering, meeting; assembling —**assembly line** sequence of machines, workers in factory assembling product

assent' *vi.* concur, agree —*n.* acquiescence, agreement, compliance

assert' *vt.* declare strongly, insist upon —**asser'tion** *n.* —**asser'tive** *a.* —**assert'ively** *adv.*

assess' *vt.* fix value; evaluate, estimate, *esp.* for taxation; fix amount (of tax or fine); tax or fine —**assess'able** *a.* —**assess'ment** *n.* —**assess'or** *n.*

ass'et *n.* valuable or useful person, thing —*pl.* property available to pay debts, *esp.* of insolvent debtor

assev'erate *v.* assert solemnly —**assevera'tion** *n.*

assid'uous *a.* persevering, attentive, diligent —**assidu'ity** *n.* —**assid'uously** *adv.*

assign' [-īn'] *vt.* appoint to job *etc.*; allot, apportion, fix; ascribe; transfer —**assign'able** *a.* —**assigna'tion** [-ig-nā'-] *n.* secret meeting; appointment to meet —**assign'ment** *n.* act of assigning; allotted duty —**assign'or** *n.*

assim'ilate *vt.* learn and understand; make similar; absorb into the system —**assim'ilable** *a.* —**assimila'tion** *n.* —**assim'ilative** *a.*

assist' *v.* give help; aid —**assis'tance** *n.* —**assist'ant** *n.* helper

assi'zes *pl.n.* formerly, law court held in each area or county of England and Wales

assn. association

assoc. associated; association

asso'ciate *vt.* link, connect, *esp.* as ideas in mind; join —*vi.* keep company with; combine, unite —*n.* companion, partner; friend, ally; subordinate member of association —*a.* affiliated —**associa'tion** *n.* society, club

ass'onance *n.* likeness in sound; rhyming of vowels only —**ass'onant** *a.*

assort' *vt.* classify, arrange —*n.* match, agree with, harmonize —**assort'ed** *a.* mixed —**assort'ment** *n.*

ASSR Autonomous Soviet Socialist Republic

asst. assistant

assuage' [-sw-] *vt.* soften, pacify; soothe —**assuage'ment** *n.*

assume' *vt.* take for granted; pretend; take upon oneself; claim —**assump'tion** *n.* —**assump'tive** *a.*

assure' *vt.* tell positively, promise; make sure; insure against loss, *esp.* of life; affirm —**assur'ance** *n.* —**assured'** *a.* sure —**assur'edly** [-id-li] *adv.*

AST *US, C* Atlantic Standard Time

astat'ic *a. Physics* having no tendency to take fixed position

as'ter *n.* plant with star-like flowers; Michaelmas daisy

as'terisk *n.* star (*) used in printing —*vt.* mark thus —**as'terism** *n.*

astern' *adv.* in, behind the stern; backwards

as'teroid *n.* small planet —*a.* star-shaped

asth'ma [as'mə] *n.* illness in which one has difficulty in breathing —**asthmat'ic** *a./n.* —**asthmat'ically** *adv.*

astig'matism *n.* inability of lens (*esp.* of eye) to focus properly —**astigmat'ic** *a.*

astil'be [-bi] *n.* plant with ornamental pink or white flowers

astir' adv. on the move; out; in excitement

ASTMS Association of Scientific, Technical, and Managerial Staffs

aston'ish vt. amaze, surprise —**aston'ishing** a. —**aston'ishment** n.

astound' vt. astonish greatly; stun with amazement —**astound'ing** a. startling

astrakhan' [-kan'] n. lambskin with curled wool

as'tral a. of the stars or spirit world —**astral body**

astray' adv. off the right path, wanderingly

astride' adv. with the legs apart, straddling

astrin'gent [-j-] a. severe, harsh; sharp; constricting (body tissues, blood vessels etc.) —n. astringent substance —**astrin'gency** n.

astrol. astrology

astrol'ogy n. foretelling of events by stars; medieval astronomy —**astrol'oger** n. —**astrolog'ical** a.

astrom'etry n. determination of apparent magnitudes of fixed stars

astron. astronomy

as'tronaut n. one trained for travel in space

astron'omy n. scientific study of heavenly bodies —**astron'o-mer** n. —**astronom'ical** a. very large; of astronomy —**astronomical unit** unit of distance used in astronomy equal to the mean distance between the earth and the sun

astrophys'ics n. the science of the chemical and physical characteristics of heavenly bodies —**astrophys'ical** a. —**as-trophys'icist** n.

astute' a. perceptive, shrewd —**astute'ly** adv. —**astute'ness** n.

asun'der adv. apart; in pieces

asy'lum n. refuge, sanctuary, place of safety; old name for home for care of the unfortunate, esp. of mentally ill

asymm'etry n. lack of symmetry —**asymmet'rical** a.

as'ymptote n. straight line that continually approaches a curve, but never meets it

asyn'deton n. omission of conjunctions between parts of sentence —**asyndet'ic** a. without conjunctions or cross references

at prep./adv. denoting: location in space or time; rate; condition or state; amount; direction; cause

at. atmosphere; atomic

atarax'ia n. calmness, emotional tranquillity

at'avism n. appearance of ancestral, not parental, characteristics in human beings, animals or plants —**atavis'tic** a.

atax'ia, atax'y n. lack of muscular coordination

ate [āt or et] pt. of EAT

at'elier [-yā] n. workshop, artist's studio

a'theism [-ā-] n. belief that there is no God —**a'theist** n. —**atheis'tic(al)** a.

ath'lete n. one trained for physical exercises, feats or contests of strength; one good at sports —**athlet'ic** a. —**athlet'ics** pl.n. sports such as running, jumping, throwing etc. —**ath-let'ically** adv. —**athlet'icism** n.

athwart' prep. across —adv. across, esp. obliquely

at'las n. volume of maps

atm. atmosphere; atmospheric

at'mosphere n. mass of gas surrounding heavenly body, esp. the earth; prevailing tone or mood of (place etc.); unit of pressure in cgs system —**atmos-pher'ic** a. —**atmospher'ics** pl.n. noises in radio reception due to electrical disturbance in the atmosphere

at. no. atomic number

at'oll n. ring-shaped coral island enclosing lagoon

at'om n. smallest unit of matter which can enter into chemical combination; any very small particle —**atom'ic** a. of, arising from atoms —**atomic'ity** [-mis'-] n. number of atoms in molecule of an element —**at'omize** vt. reduce to atoms or small particles —**at'omizer** n. instrument for discharging liquids in a fine spray —**atom(ic) bomb** one whose immense power derives from nuclear fission or fusion, nuclear bomb —**atomic energy** nuclear energy —**atomic number** the number of protons in the nucleus of an atom —**atomic reactor** see REACTOR —**atomic weight** the weight of an atom of an element relative to that of carbon 12

atone' vi. make reparation, amends (for); expiate; give satisfaction —**atone'ment** n.

aton'ic a. unaccented

atop' adv. at or on the top; above

atro'cious [-shэs] a. extremely cruel or wicked; horrifying; int. very bad —**atro'ciously** adv. —**atroc'ity** [-tros'-] n. wickedness

at'rophy n. wasting away, emaciation —vi. waste away, become useless (-**phied, -phying**) —**at'rophied** a.

att. attention; attorney

attach' v. (mainly tr.) join, fasten; unite; be connected with; attribute; appoint; seize by law —**attached'** a. (with to) fond of —**attach'ment** n.

attaché [a-tash'ā] n. specialist attached to diplomatic mission (pl. **-s**) —**attaché case** small leather hand-case for papers

attack' vt. take action against (in war, sport etc.); criticize; set

about with vigour; affect adversely —n. attacking action; bout

attain' vt. arrive at; reach, gain by effort, accomplish —**attainabil'ity** n. —**attain'able** a. —**attain'ment** n. esp. personal accomplishment

attain'der n. Hist. loss of rights through conviction of high treason

att'ar n. a fragrant oil made esp. from rose petals

attempt' vt. try, endeavour —n. trial, effort

attend' vt. be present at; accompany —vi. (with to) take care of; give the mind (to), pay attention to —**attend'ance** n. an attending; presence; persons attending —**attend'ant** n./a. —**atten'tion** n. notice; heed; act of attending; care; courtesy; alert position in military drill —**atten'tive** a. —**atten'tively** adv. —**atten'tiveness** n.

atten'uate v. weaken or become weak; make or become thin —**atten'uated** a. —**attenua'tion** n. reduction of intensity

attest' vt. bear witness to, certify —**attesta'tion** n. formal confirmation by oath etc.

att'ic n. space within roof where ceiling follows line of roof —a. of Attica, Athens

attire' vt. dress, array —n. dress, clothing

att'itude n. mental view, opinion; posture, pose; disposition, behaviour —**attitu'dinize** vi. assume affected attitudes

attor'ney [-tur'-] n. one legally appointed to act for another, esp. a lawyer (pl. **-neys**)

attract' v. draw (attention etc.); arouse interest of; cause to come closer (as magnet etc.) —**attrac'tion** n. power to attract; something offered so as to interest, please —**attrac'tive** a. —**attrac'-**

tively adv. —**attrac'tiveness** n.

attrib'ute vt. regard as belonging to or produced by —n. [at'-] quality, property or characteristic of anything —**attrib'utable** a. —attribu'tion n. —attrib'utive a. —attrib'utively adv.

attri'tion [-trish'-] n. wearing away of strength etc.; rubbing away, friction

attune' vt. tune, harmonize; make accordant

at. wt. atomic weight

Au Chem. gold

au'bergine [ō'bər-zhēn] n. eggshaped dark purple fruit, plant bearing it

aubr(i)e'tia n. trailing plant with purple flowers

au'burn a. reddish brown —n. this colour

au courant' [ō-koo-rong'] Fr. up-to-date; acquainted with

auc'tion n. public sale in which bidder offers increase of price over another and what is sold goes to one who bids highest —v. —**auctioneer'** n. —**auction bridge** card game —**Dutch auction** one in which price starts high and is reduced until purchaser is found

auda'cious a. bold; daring, impudent —**audac'ity** n.

au'dible a. able to be heard —**audibil'ity** n. —**au'dibly** adv.

au'dience n. assembly of hearers; act of hearing; judicial hearing; formal interview

au'dio- (comb. form) relating to sound or hearing

audiovis'ual a. (esp. of teaching aids) involving, directed at, both sight and hearing, as film etc.

au'dit n. formal examination or settlement of accounts —vt. examine accounts —**au'ditor** n.

audi'tion n. screen or other test of prospective performer;

hearing —vt. conduct such a test —**auditor'ium** n. place where audience sits; **US, C** hall (pl. **-s, -ia**) —**au'ditory** a. pert. to sense of hearing

au fait' [ō-fā'] Fr. fully informed; expert

auf Wie'dersehen [owf-vē'dər-zā-ən] Ger. goodbye

Aug. August

au'ger n. carpenter's tool for boring holes, large gimlet

aught n. anything —adv. to any extent

augment' v. increase, enlarge —n. [awg'ment] increase —**augmenta'tion** n. —**augment'ative** a. increasing in force

au'gur n. among the Romans, soothsayer —v. be a sign of future events, foretell —**au'gural** a. —**au'gury** n.

august' a. majestic, dignified

Au'gust n. the eighth month

Augus'tan a. of Augustus, the Roman Emperor; hence classic, distinguished, as applied to a period of literature

auk n. northern web-footed seabird with short wings used only as paddles

aunt [ahnt] n. father's or mother's sister, uncle's wife

au pair' [ō-] n. young foreigner who receives free board and lodging in return for housework etc. —a.

au'ra n. quality, air, atmosphere considered distinctive of person or thing; medical symptom warning of impending epileptic fit etc.

au'ral a. of, by ear —**au'rally** adv.

aure'ola, aur'eole n. gold discs round heads in sacred pictures; halo

au revoir' [ō-rə-vwahr'] Fr. goodbye

au'ricle n. outside ear; an upper

cavity of heart —**auric'ular** a. of the auricle; aural

aurif'erous a. gold-bearing

au'rochs [-roks] n. species of wild ox, now extinct

auror'a n. lights in the atmosphere seen radiating from regions of the poles The northern is called **aurora borealis** and the southern, **aurora australis**; dawn (pl. **-ras**)

ausculta'tion n. listening to movement of heart and lungs with stethoscope —**aus'cultator** n. —**auscul'tatory** a.

aus'pice [-pis] n. omen, augury —pl. patronage —**auspi'cious** a. of good omen, favourable —**auspi'ciously** adv.

austere' [-os-] a. harsh, strict, severe; without luxury —**austere'ly** adv. —**auster'ity** n.

aus'tral a. southern

Australa'sian [os-] a./n. (native or inhabitant) of Australasia (Australia, N Zealand and adjacent islands)

Austra'lian [os-] n./a. (native or inhabitant) of Australia

au'tarchy [-ki] n. despotism, absolute power, dictatorship

auth. author; authority; authorized

authen'tic a. real, genuine, true; trustworthy —**authen'tically** adv. —**authen'ticate** vt. make valid, confirm; establish truth, authorship etc. of —**authentica'tion**, **authentic'ity** [-tis'-] n.

au'thor n. writer of book; originator, constructor (-**ess** fem.) —**au'thorship** n.

author'ity [-tho'ri-] n. legal power or right; delegated power; influence; permission; expert; body or board in control, esp. in pl. —**author'itative** a. —**author'itatively** adv. —**authoriza'tion** n. —**auth'orize** vt. empower; permit, sanction

autis'tic a. withdrawn and divorced from reality

auto- (comb. form) self, as in autograph, autosuggestion etc. Such words are not given here where the meaning may easily be inferred from the simple word

autobiog'raphy n. life of person written by himself —**autobiog'rapher** n. —**autobiograph'ical** a. —**autobiograph'ically** adv.

autoch'thon [-ok'-] n. primitive or original inhabitant —**autoch'thonous** a.

au'tocrat n. absolute ruler; despotic person —**autoc'racy** n. —**autocrat'ic** a. —**autocrat'ically** adv.

au'tocross n. motor racing sport over rough course

Au'tocue R electronic television prompting device displaying a speaker's script unseen by the audience

autodestruct' a. likely or able to destroy itself —vi. (of missile etc.) destroy itself

autoer'otism n. self-produced sexual arousal

autog'amy n. self-fertilization

autog'enous [-toj'-] a. self-generated

au'tograph n. a signature; one's own handwriting —vt. sign —**autograph'ic** a.

autogy'ro [-jī'-] n. aircraft like helicopter using horizontal airscrew for vertical ascent and descent

autoimmune' a. (of disease) caused by antibodies produced against substances normally in body

autointoxica'tion n. poisoning of tissues of the body as a result of the absorption of bodily waste

au'tomat n. vending machine

au'tomate vt. make manufacturing process etc. automatic

automat'ic a. operated or controlled mechanically; done without conscious thought —a./n. self-loading (weapon) —**automat'ically** adv. —**automa'tion** n. use of automatic devices in industrial production —**autom'atism** n. involuntary action —**automa'ton** n. self-acting machine, esp. simulating a human being (pl. -ata) —**automatic pilot** device automatically maintaining aircraft on preset course

au'tomobile n. motor car —**automobi'list** [-bē'-] n. motorist

auton'omy n. self-government —**auton'omous** a.

au'topsy n. postmortem examination to determine cause of death; critical analysis

autosugges'tion n. process of influencing the mind (towards health etc.), conducted by the subject himself

au'tumn n./a. (typical of) the season after summer —**autum'nal** a. typical of the onset of winter —**autum'nally** adv.

aux. auxiliary

auxil'iary a. helping, subsidiary —n. helper; something subsidiary, as troops; verb used to form tenses of others

AV Authorized Version (of the Bible)

av. average

avail' v. be of use, advantage, value (to) —n. benefit, as **to be of little avail** etc. —**availabil'ity** n. —**avail'able** a. obtainable; accessible —**avail oneself of** make use of

av'alanche n. mass of snow, ice, sliding down mountain; a sudden overwhelming quantity of anything

avant-garde' [av-ong-] a. markedly experimental or in advance

av'arice [-ris] n. greed for wealth —**avari'cious** a. —**avari'ciously** adv.

avast' [-vah-] interj. stop

avdp. avoirdupois

Ave. Avenue

avenge' vt. take vengeance on behalf of (person) or on account of (thing) —**aven'ger** [-j-] n.

av'enue n. wide, handsome street; an approach; double row of trees

aver' vt. affirm, assert (**-rr-**) —**aver'ment** n.

av'erage n. the mean value or quantity of a number of values or quantities —a. calculated as an average; medium, ordinary —vt. fix or calculate a mean —vi. exist in or form a mean

averse' a. disinclined, unwilling —**aver'sion** n. dislike, person or thing disliked

avert' vt. turn away; ward off

a'viary [āv'yə-ri] n. enclosure for birds —**a'viarist** n.

avia'tion [ā-] n. art of flying aircraft; transport by aircraft —**a'viator** n.

avid' a. keen, enthusiastic; greedy (for) —**avid'ity** n.

avoca'do [-kahd'-] n. tropical tree; its green-skinned edible fruit

avoca'tion n. vocation; employment, business

av'ocet n. wading bird of snipe family with upward-curving bill

avoid' vt. keep away from; refrain from; not allow to happen —**avoid'able** a. —**avoid'ance** n.

avoirdupois' [av-ər-də-poiz'] n./a. system of weights used in many English-speaking countries based on pounds and ounces

avouch' vt. obs. affirm, maintain, attest, own —**avouch'ment** n.

avow' vt. declare; admit —**avow'able** a. —**avow'al** n. —**avowed'** a. —**avow'edly** adv.

await vt. wait or stay for; be in store for

awake, **awa'ken** v. emerge or rouse from sleep; become or cause to become alert (**awoke** or **awaked** [-wākt'], **awa'king**) —a. not sleeping; alert —**awa'kening** n.

award vt. to give formally (esp. a prize or punishment) —n. prize; judicial decision

aware a. informed, conscious —**aware'ness** n.

awash adv. level with the surface of water; filled or overflowing with water

away adv. absent, apart, at a distance —n. Sport game played on opponent's ground

awe n. dread mingled with reverence —**awe'some** a.

aw'ful a. very bad, unpleasant; obs. impressive; inf. very great —**aw'fully** adv. in an unpleasant way; inf. very much

awhile adv. for a time

awk'ward a. clumsy, ungainly; difficult; inconvenient; embarrassed —**awk'wardly** adv. —**awk'wardness** n.

awl n. pointed tool for boring wood, leather etc.

awn'ing n. (canvas) roof or shelter, to protect from weather

awoke pt./pp. of AWAKE

AWOL absent without leave

awry [-rī'] adv. crookedly; amiss; at a slant —a. crooked

axe n. tool with a sharp blade for chopping; inf. dismissal from employment etc. —vt. inf. dismiss, dispense with

ax'iom n. received or accepted principle; self-evident truth —**axiomat'ic** a.

ax'is n. (imaginary) line round which body spins; line or column about which parts are arranged (pl. **ax'es** [-sēz]) —**ax'ial** a. —**ax'ially** adv.

Ax'is n. coalition of Germany, Italy and Japan, 1936–45

ax'le (tree) [ak'sl] n. rod on which wheel turns

ayatoll'ah n. one of a class of Islamic religious leaders

aye adv. yes —n. affirmative answer or vote —pl. those voting for motion

aza'lea n. genus of shrubby flowering plants

az'imuth n. vertical arc from zenith to horizon; angular distance of this from meridian

Az'tec a./n. (member) of race ruling Mexico before Spanish conquest

az'ure [azh'-] n. sky-blue colour; sky —a. sky-blue

B

B bass; Chess bishop; Chem. boron; British

b. Cricket bowled

BA Bachelor of Arts

Ba Chem. barium

bab'ble v. speak foolishly, incoherently, or childishly —n. foolish, confused talk —**bab'bling** n.

babe n. baby; guileless person

ba'bel n. confused uproar

baboon' n. large monkey of Africa and Asia —**baboon'ish** a.

ba'by n. very young child, infant —**ba'byhood** n. —**ba'byish** a. —**baby-sit** vi. —**baby-sitter** n. one who cares for children when parents are out

bacc'arat [-rah] n. gambling card game

bacc'hanal [-k'ən-] n. follower of Bacchus; (participant in) drunken, riotous celebration

bach'elor n. unmarried man; holder of lowest university degree; Hist. young knight

bacill'us [-sil'-] *n.* minute organism sometimes causing disease (*pl.* bacill'**i**) —bacill'**i**form *a.*

back *n.* hinder part of anything, eg human body; part opposite front; part or side of something further away or less used; (position of) player in ball games behind other (forward) players —*a.* situated behind; earlier —*adv.* at, to the back; in, into the past; in return —*vi.* move backwards —*vt.* support; put wager on; provide with back or backing —**back'er** *n.* one supporting another, *esp.* in contest; one betting on horse, *etc.* in race —**back'ing** *n.* support; material to protect the back of something, musical accompaniment, *esp.* for pop singer —**back'ward(s)** *adv.* to the rear; to the past; to worse state —**back'ward** *a.* directed towards the rear; behind in education; reluctant, bashful —**back'wardness** *n.* —**back-bench'er** *n.* Brit., Aust. and Canad. member of Parliament not holding office in government or opposition —**back'bite** *vt.* slander absent person —**back'-biter** *n.* —**back'biting** *n.* —**back'-bone** *n.* spinal column —**back'-chat** *n.* impudent answer —**back'cloth, back'drop** *n.* painted cloth at back of stage —**back-date'** *vt.* make effective from earlier date —**backfire'** *vi.* ignite at wrong time, as fuel in cylinder of internal-combustion engine; (of plan, scheme, *etc.*) fail to work, *esp.* to the cost of the instigator; ignite wrongly, as gas burner *etc.* —**back'gammon** *n.* game played with draughtsmen and dice —**back'ground** *n.* space behind chief figures of picture *etc.*; past history of person —**back'hand** *n.* stroke with hand turned backwards —**back-**

hand'ed *a.* (of compliment *etc.*) with second, uncomplimentary meaning —**back'-hander** *n.* blow with back of hand; *inf.* a bribe —**back'lash** *n.* sudden and adverse reaction —**back'log** *n.* accumulation of work *etc.* to be dealt with —**back'pack** *n.* type of knapsack —*vi.* —**backside'** *n.* rump —**back'slide** *vi.* fall back in faith or morals —**back'stroke** *n.* swimming stroke performed on the back —**back'wash** *n.* water thrown back by ship's propellers *etc.*; a backward current, a reaction —**back'water** *n.* still water fed by back flow of stream —**back'woods** *pl.n.* remote areas

ba'con *n.* cured pig's flesh

bacte'ria *pl.n.* (*sing.* **bacte'rium**) microscopic organisms, some causing disease —**bacte'rial** *a.* —**bacte'ricide** *n.* substance that destroys bacteria —**bacteriol'ogist** *n.* —**bacteriol'ogy** *n.* study of bacteria

bad *a.* of poor quality; faulty; evil; immoral; offensive; severe; rotten, decayed (**worse** *comp.*, **worst** *sup.*) —**bad'ly** *adv.* —**bad'ness** *n.*

bade *pt. of* BID

badge *n.* distinguishing emblem

badg'er *n.* burrowing night animal, about the size of fox —*vt.* pester, worry

bad'inage [-ahzh] *n.* playful talk, banter

bad'minton *n.* game like tennis, played with shuttlecocks over high net

baf'fle *vt.* check, frustrate, bewilder —**baf'fler** *n.* —**baf'fling** *a.* —**baf'fle** (**plate**) *n.* device to regulate or divert flow of liquid, gas, soundwaves *etc.*

bag *n.* sack, pouch; measure of quantity; woman's handbag *offens.* unattractive woman —*pl.* *inf.* lots (of) —*vi.* swell out; bulge;

sag —*vt.* put in bag; kill as game, *etc.* (**-gg-**) —**bagg'ing** *n.* cloth —**bagg'y** *a.* loose, drooping —**bag lady** homeless woman who carries her possessions in shopping bags —**bag'man** *n.* commercial traveller

bagasse' [-gas'] *n.* sugar cane refuse

bagatelle' *n.* trifle; game like pinball played with nine balls and cue on a board

bagg'age *n.* suitcases *etc.*, packed for journey; *offens.* woman

bag'pipes *pl.n.* musical wind instrument, of windbag and pipes —**bag'piper** *n.*

bail¹ *n. Law* security given for person's reappearance in court; one giving such security —*vt.* release, or obtain release of, on security; *inf.* help a person, firm *etc.* out of trouble

bail² *n. Cricket* crosspiece on wicket; bar separating horses in stable

bail³, **bale** *vt.* empty out water from boat —**bail out** leave aircraft by parachute

bai'ley *n.* outermost wall of a castle

Bai'ley bridge bridge composed of prefabricated sections

bai'liff *n.* land steward, agent; sheriff's officer

bai'liwick *n.* jurisdiction of bailiff

bairn *n. Scot.* infant, child

bait *n.* food to entice fish; any lure or enticement —*vt.* set a lure; annoy, persecute

baize *n.* smooth woollen cloth

bake *vt.* cook or harden by dry heat —*vi.* make bread, cakes *etc.*; be scorched or tanned —**ba'ker** *n.* —**ba'kery, bake'-house** *n.* —**ba'king** *n.* —**baking powder** raising agent containing sodium bicarbonate *etc.* used in cooking

Ba'kelite ® hard nonflammable synthetic resin, used for dishes, trays, electrical insulators *etc.*

Balaclav'a [-ahv'ə] *n.* close-fitting woollen helmet, covering head and neck

balalai'ka [-lī'-] *n.* Russian musical instrument, like guitar

bal'ance *n.* pair of scales; equilibrium; surplus; sum due on an account; difference between two sums —*vt.* weigh; bring to equilibrium —**balance sheet** tabular statement of assets and liabilities —**balance wheel** regulating wheel of watch

bal'cony *n.* railed platform outside window; upper seats in theatre

bald [bawld] *a.* hairless; plain; bare —**bald'ing** *a.* becoming bald —**bald'ly** *adv.* —**bald'ness** *n.*

bal'derdash [bawl'-] *n.* idle, senseless talk

bal'dric [bawl'-] *n.* shoulder-belt for sword *etc.*

bale¹ *n.* bundle or package —*vt.* make into bundles or pack into cartons —**ba'ler** *n.* machine which makes bundles

bale² *vt. see* BAIL³

baleen' *n.* whalebone

bale'ful *a.* menacing —**bale'fully** *adv.*

balk [bawk, bawlk] *vi.* swerve, pull up —*vt.* thwart, hinder; shirk —*n.* hindrance; square timber, beam —**balk at** recoil; stop short

ball¹ [bawl] *n.* anything round; globe, sphere, *esp.* as used in games; a ball as delivered; bullet —*vi.* clog, gather into a mass —**ball bearings** steel balls used to lessen friction on bearings —**ball'point (pen)** pen with tiny ball bearing as nib

ball² [bawl] *n.* assembly for

dancing —**ball'room** n.

ball'ad n. narrative poem; simple song

ballade' [-ahd'] n. short poem with refrain and envoy; piece of music

ball'ast n. heavy material put in ship to give steadiness; that which renders anything steady —vt. load with ballast, steady

ball'et [-a] n. theatrical presentation of dancing and miming —**balleri'na** [-e'-] n.

ballis'tic a. moving as, or pertaining to motion of, a projectile —**ballis'tics** pl.n. (with sing. v.) scientific study of ballistic motion

balloon' n. large bag filled with air or gas to make it rise in the air —vi. puff out —**balloon'ing** n. —**balloon'ist** n.

ball'ot n. method of voting secretly, usually by marking ballot paper and putting it into box —v. vote or elicit a vote from —**ballot box**

ball'yhoo n. noisy confusion or uproar; vulgar, exaggerated publicity or advertisement

balm [bahm] n. aromatic substance, healing or soothing ointment; anything soothing —**balm'iness** n. —**balm'y** a.

bal'sa [bawl'-] n. Amer. tree with light but strong wood

bal'sam [bawl'-] n. resinous aromatic substance obtained from various trees and shrubs; soothing ointment —**balsam'ic** a.

bal'uster n. short pillar used as support to rail of staircase etc. —**bal'ustrade** n. row of short pillars surmounted by rail

bamboo' n. large tropical treelike reed (pl. **bamboos'**)

bamboo'zle vt. mystify, hoax

ban vt. prohibit, forbid, outlaw (-**nn**-) —n. prohibition; proclamation —**ban(n)s** pl.n. proclamation of marriage

banal' [-nahl'] a. commonplace, trivial, trite —**banal'ity** n.

banan'a [-nahn'-] n. tropical treelike plant; its fruit

band[1] n. strip used to bind; range of values, frequencies etc., between two limits —**ban'dage** n. strip of cloth for binding wound

band[2] n. company, group; company of musicians —v. bind together —**band'master** n. —**bands'man** n. —**band'stand** n.

bandann'a n. coloured silk or cotton handkerchief

B & B bed and breakfast

band'box n. light box of cardboard for hats etc.

ban'deau [-ō] n. band, ribbon for the hair

ban'dicoot n. ratlike Aust. marsupial

ban'dit n. outlaw; robber, brigand (pl. **ban'dits, bandit'ti**)

bandolier', -leer' n. shoulder belt for cartridges

band'wagon n. —**climb, jump, get on the bandwagon** join something that seems assured of success

ban'dy vt. beat to and fro, toss from one to another (**ban'died, ban'dying**) —**ban'dy, bandy-legged** a. having legs curving outwards

bane n. person or thing causing misery or distress —**bane'ful** a. —**bane'fully** adv.

bang[1] n. sudden loud noise, explosion; heavy blow —vt. make loud noise; beat; strike violently, slam

bang[2] n. fringe of hair cut straight across forehead

ban'gle [bang'gəl] n. ring worn on arm or leg

ban'ish vt. condemn to exile; drive away; dismiss —**ban'ishment** n. exile

ban'isters pl.n. railing and supporting balusters on staircase

ban'jo n. musical instrument like guitar, with circular body (pl. **-jo(e)s**) **—ban'joist** n.

bank[1] n. mound or ridge of earth; edge of river, lake etc.; rising ground in sea —v. enclose with ridge; pile up; (of aircraft) tilt inwards in turning

bank[2] n. establishment for keeping, lending, exchanging etc. money; any supply or store for future use, as a **blood bank** —vt. put in bank —vi. keep with bank **—bank'er** n. **—bank'ing** n. **—bank(er's) card** card guaranteeing payment of cheques by bank up to an agreed amount **—bank clerk** employee of bank **—bank holiday** day(s), usu. public holiday(s), when banks are closed by law **—bank'note** n. written promise of payment **—bank on** rely on

bank[3] n. tier; row of oars

bank'rupt n. one who fails in business, insolvent debtor —a. financially ruined —vt. make, cause to be, bankrupt **—bank'ruptcy** n.

bank'sia n. genus of Aust. shrubs with dense, usually yellow, cylindrical heads of flowers

bann'er n. long strip with slogan etc.; placard; flag used as ensign

banns n. see BAN

ban'quet [bang'kwit] n. feast —vi. feast —vt. treat with feast **—ban'queter** n.

banquette' [-ket'] n. raised firing step behind parapet; US upholstered bench

ban'shee [or -shē'] n. Irish fairy with a wail portending death

ban'tam n. dwarf variety of domestic fowl; very light boxing weight

ban'ter vt. make fun of —n.

light, teasing language

Ban'tu n. collective name for large group of related native tribes in Africa; family of languages spoken by Bantu peoples

ban'tubeer [-tōō-] n. SA malted drink made from sorghum

ban'yan, ban'ian n. Indian fig tree with spreading branches which take root

ba'obab n. Afr. tree with thick trunk and angular branches

Bap'tist n. member of Protestant Christian denomination believing in necessity of baptism by immersion, esp. of adults

baptize' [-īz'] vt. immerse in, sprinkle with water ceremoniously; christen **—bap'tism** n. **—baptis'mal** [-z'-] a. **—baptis'mally** adv. **—bap'tistry** n. place where baptism is performed

bar[1] n. rod or block of any substance; obstacle; bank of sand at mouth of river; rail in law court; body of lawyers; counter where drinks are served, esp. in hotel etc.; unit of music —vt. fasten; obstruct; exclude (**-rr-**) —prep. except **—barring** prep. excepting **—bar code** arrangement of numbers and parallel lines on package, electronically scanned at checkout to give price **—bar'maid** n. **—bar'man** n. **—bar'tender US, C** n.

bar[2] n. unit of pressure

bar. barometer; barrel; barrister

barb n. sharp point curving backwards behind main point of spear, fish hook etc.; cutting remark **—barbed** a. **—barbed wire** fencing wire with barbs at close intervals

bar'barous a. savage, brutal, uncivilized **—barba'rian** n. **—barbar'ic** a. **—bar'barism** n. **—barbar'ity** n. **—bar'barously** adv.

bar'becue n. meal cooked outdoors over open fire; fireplace, grill used for this —*vt.* cook meat *etc.* in this manner

bar'ber *n.* one who shaves beards and cuts hair

barbit'urate *n.* derivative of barbituric acid used as drug —**bar'bitone, bar'bital** *n.*

bar'carole *n.* gondolier's song

bard *n.* Celtic poet; wandering minstrel —**bard'ic** *a.* —**the Bard** Shakespeare

bare *a.* uncovered; naked; plain; scanty —*vt.* make bare —**bare'ly** *adv.* only just, scarcely —**bare'ness** *n.* —**bare'backed** *a.* on unsaddled horse —**bare'faced** *a.* shameless

bar'gain [-gin] *n.* something bought at price favourable to purchaser; contract, agreement —*vi.* haggle, negotiate; make bargain

barge *n.* flat-bottomed freight boat; state or pleasure boat —*vi. inf.* interrupt; *inf.* bump (into), push —**bargee'** *n.*

bar'itone [ba'ri-] *n.* (singer with) second lowest adult male voice —*a.* written for or possessing this vocal range

ba'rium *n.* white metallic element

bark¹ *n.* sharp loud cry of dog *etc.* —*v.* make, utter with such sound —**bark'er** *n.* crier outside fair booth *etc.*

bark² *n.* outer layer of trunk, branches of tree —*vt.* strip bark from; rub off (skin), graze (shins *etc.*)

bark³ *n. see* BARQUE

bar'ley *n.* grain used for food and making malt —**barley sugar** sweet originally made with barley

barm *n. obs.* yeast; froth —**bar'my** *a. inf.* silly, insane

barn *n.* building to store grain, hay *etc.* —**barn dance** (party with) country dancing —**barn'yard** *n.* farmyard

bar'nacle *n.* shellfish which adheres to rocks and ships' bottoms

bar'ney *inf. n.* noisy argument; fight —*vi.* argue or fight

barom'eter *n.* instrument to measure pressure of atmosphere —**baromet'ric** *a.* —**barom'etry** *n.* —**bar'ograph** *n.* recording barometer

bar'on [ba'rən] *n.* member of lowest rank of peerage; powerful businessman (*fem.* **-ess**) —**bar'onage** *n.* —**baro'nial** *a.* —**bar'ony** *n.*

bar'onet [ba'rə-] *n.* lowest British hereditary title, below baron but above knight —**bar'onetage** *n.* —**bar'onetcy** *n.*

baroque' [-ok', -ōk'] *a.* extravagantly ornamented, *esp.* in architecture and art

barouche' [-ōōsh'] *n.* fourwheeled carriage with folding top over rear seat

barque [bahrk] *n.* sailing ship, *esp.* large, three-masted one —**bar'quentine** *n.* small barque

barr'ack¹ *n.* (*usu.* in *pl.*) building for lodging soldiers; huge bare building

barr'ack² *v. inf.* (*usu.* with **for**) encourage by cheering, *esp.* at sporting events; *inf.* criticize loudly; jeer —**barr'acking** *n.*

barracou'ta, barracu'da *n.* large of large, elongated, predatory fish, mostly tropical

barr'age [-ahzh] *n.* heavy artillery fire; continuous and heavy delivery, *esp.* of questions *etc.*; dam across river

barr'atry *n.* fraudulent breach of duty by master of ship; stirring up of law suits —**barr'ator** *n.* —**barr'atrous** *a.*

barr'el *n.* round wooden vessel, made of curved staves bound with hoops; its capacity; anything long and hollow, as tube of gun *etc.* —*vt.* put in barrel (-ll-) —**barr'elled** *a.*

barr'en *a.* unfruitful, sterile; unprofitable; dull —**barr'enness** *n.*

barricade' *n.* improvised fortification, barrier —*vt.* to protect by building barrier; block

barr'ier *n.* fence, obstruction, obstacle, boundary —**barrier reef** coral reef lying parallel to shore

barr'ister *n.* advocate in the higher law courts

barr'ow[1] *n.* small wheeled handcart; wheelbarrow

barr'ow[2] *n.* burial mound; tumulus

bart'er *v.* trade by exchange of goods —*n.*

bar'yon [ba'ri-] *n. Physics* elementary particle of matter

bary'tes [-rī'tēz] *n.* barium sulphate

bas'alt [-awlt] *n.* dark-coloured, hard, compact, igneous rock —**basal'tic** *a.*

bas'cule *n.* lever apparatus; drawbridge on counterpoise principle

base[1] *n.* bottom, foundation; starting point; centre of operations; fixed point; *Chem.* compound that combines with an acid to form a salt; medium into which other substances are mixed —*vt.* found, establish —**base'less** *a.* —**base'ment** *n.* lowest storey of building

base[2] *a.* low, mean; despicable —**base'ly** *adv.* —**base'ness** *n.* —**base'born** *a.* illegitimate

base'ball *n.* game, orig. Amer., played with bat and ball

bash *inf. v.* strike violently —*n.* blow; attempt

bash'ful *a.* shy, modest —**bash'fully** *adv.* —**bash'fulness** *n.*

BASIC *Computers* Beginners'

All-purpose Symbolic Instruction Code

ba'sic *a.* relating to, serving as base; fundamental; necessary

bas'il [baz'-] *n.* aromatic herb

basil'ica [-zil'-] *n.* type of church with long hall and pillars —**basil'ican** *a.*

bas'ilisk [baz'-] *n.* legendary small fire-breathing dragon

ba'sin *n.* deep circular dish; harbour; land drained by river

ba'sis *n.* foundation; principal constituent (*pl.* **-ses** [-sēz])

bask [-ah-] *vi.* lie in warmth and sunshine (*often fig.*)

bask'et [-ah-] *n.* vessel made of woven cane, straw *etc.* —**bas'ketry, bask'etwork** *n.* —**basket-ball** *n.* ball game played by two teams

Basque [bask] *n.* one of race from W Pyrenees; their language

bas-relief' *n.* sculpture with figures standing out slightly from background

bass[1] [bās] *n.* lowest part in music; bass singer or voice —*a.*

bass[2] [bas] *n.* any of large variety of fish, *esp.* sea perch

bass'et *n.* type of smooth-haired dog

bassoon' *n.* woodwind instrument of low tone —**bassoon'ist** *n.*

bas'tard *n.* child born of unmarried parents; *inf.* person, as in **lucky bastard** —*a.* illegitimate; spurious —**bas'tardy** *n.*

baste[1] *vt.* moisten (meat) during cooking with hot fat; beat with stick —**ba'sting** *n.*

baste[2] *vt.* sew loosely, tack

bastina'do *n.* beating with stick, *esp.* on soles of feet —*vt.* (**-does, -doing, -doed**)

bas'tion *n.* projecting part of fortification, tower; strong defence or bulwark

bat[1] *n.* any of various types of club used to hit ball in certain sports, *eg* cricket, baseball —*v.* strike with bat or use bat in sport —**bat'ting** *n.* performance with bat —**bats'man** *n.*

bat[2] *n.* nocturnal mouselike flying animal

bat[3] *vt.* flutter (one's eyelids)

batch *n.* group or set of similar objects, *esp.* cakes *etc.* baked together

ba'ted *a.* —**with bated breath** anxiously

bath [-ah-] *n.* vessel or place to bathe in; water for bathing; act of bathing —*pl.* place for swimming —*vt.* wash

Bath chair invalid chair

bathe [-ATH] *v.* swim; apply liquid; wash; immerse in water (**bathed, ba'thing**) —*n.* —**ba'ther** *n.*

ba'thos *n.* ludicrous descent from the elevated to the ordinary in writing or speech

bath'yscaph, -scaphe [-af], **-scape** *n.* vessel for deep-sea observation

bat'ik *n.* dyeing process using wax

bat'man *n.* military officer's servant

bat'on *n.* stick, *esp.* of policeman, conductor, marshal

batra'chian [-tră'ki-] *n.* any amphibian, *esp.* frog or toad

battal'ion *n.* military unit consisting of three or more companies

batt'en[1] *n.* narrow piece of board, strip of wood —*vt.* (*esp.* with down) fasten, make secure

batt'en[2] *vi.* (*usu.* with on) thrive, *esp.* at someone else's expense

batt'er *vt.* strike continuously —*n.* mixture of flour, eggs, milk, used in cooking

batt'ery *n.* connected group of electrical cells; any electrical cell or accumulator; number of

similar things occurring together; *Law* assault by beating; number of guns; place where they are mounted; unit of artillery; large number of cages for rearing poultry *etc.*

batt'ing *n.* cotton fibre as stuffing

batt'le *n.* fight between armies, combat —*vi.* fight, struggle —**batt'leaxe** *n. inf.* domineering woman

batt'lement *n.* wall, parapet on fortification with openings or embrasures

batt'leship *n.* heavily armed and armoured fighting ship

batt'y *a. inf.* crazy, silly

bau'ble *n.* showy trinket

baulk [bawk] *n. see* BALK —**baulk'line** *n. Billiards* straight line across table behind which cue balls start the game

baux'ite *n.* clay yielding aluminium

bawd *n.* prostitute; brothel keeper —**bawd'y** *a.* obscene, lewd

bawl *vi.* cry; shout —*n.*

bay[1] *n.* wide inlet of sea; space between two columns; recess —**bay window**

bay[2] *n.* bark; cry of hounds in pursuit —*v.* bark **(at) —at bay** cornered; at a distance

bay[3] *n.* laurel tree —*pl.* honorary crown of victory

bay[4] *a.* reddish-brown

bay'onet *n.* stabbing weapon fixed to rifle —*vt.* stab with this **(bay'oneted, bay'oneting)**

bazaar' [-zahr'] *n.* market (*esp.* in Orient); sale of goods for charity

bazoo'ka *n.* antitank rocket launcher

BB Boys' Brigade; (of pencils) double black

BBC British Broadcasting Corporation

BC before Christ; British Columbia

BCG Bacille Calmette-Guérin (antituberculosis vaccine)

B.Com., B.Comm. Bachelor of Commerce

BD Bachelor of Divinity

B/D bank draft

BDS Bachelor of Dental Surgery

BE Bachelor of Engineering

B/E bill of exchange

be *vi.* live; exist; have a state or quality (I **am**, he **is**; we, you, they **are**, *pr. ind.* —**was**, *pl.* **were**, *pt.* —**been** *pp.* —**be'ing** *pr.p.*)

beach *n.* shore of sea —*vt.* run boat on shore —**beach'comber** *n.* one who habitually searches shore debris for items of value —**beach'head** *n.* area on beach captured from enemy; base for operations

beac'on *n.* signal fire; lighthouse, buoy; (radio) signal used for navigation

bead *n.* little ball pierced for threading on string of necklace, rosary *etc.*; drop of liquid; narrow moulding —**bead'ed** *a.* —**bead'ing** *n.* —**bead'y** *a.* small and bright

bead'le *n.* *Hist.* church or parish officer

bea'gle *n.* small hound

beak *n.* projecting horny jaws of bird; anything pointed or projecting; *sl.* magistrate

beak'er *n.* large drinking cup; glass vessel used by chemists

beam *n.* long squared piece of wood; ship's cross timber, cross width; ray of light *etc.*; broad smile; bar of a balance —*vt.* aim light, radio waves *etc.* (to) —*vi.* shine; smile benignly

bean *n.* any of various leguminous plants or their seeds —**full of beans** *inf.* lively —**bean'o** *n.* *inf.* celebration —**bean sprout** edible sprout of newly germi-

nated bean, *esp.* mung bean

bear[1] [bār] *vt.* carry; support; produce; endure; press (upon) (**bore** *pt.*, **born** or **borne** *pp.*, **bear'ing** *pr.p.*) —**bear'er** *n.*

bear[2] [bār] *n.* heavy carnivorous quadruped; other bearlike animals, *eg* Aust. koala bear —**bear'skin** *n.* Guards' tall fur helmet

beard *n.* hair on chin —*vt.* oppose boldly

bear'ing *n.* support or guide for mechanical part, *esp.* one reducing friction; relevance; behaviour; direction; relative position; device on shield

beast *n.* animal; four-footed animal; brutal man —**beast'liness** *n.* —**beast'ly** *a.*

beat *vt.* strike repeatedly; overcome; surpass; stir vigorously with striking action; flap (wings); make, wear (path) —*vi.* throb; sail against wind (**beat** *pt.*, **beat'en** *pp.*) —*n.* stroke; pulsation; appointed course; basic rhythmic unit in piece of music —*a. id.* exhausted —**beat'er** *n.* instrument for beating; one who rouses game for shooters

beat'ify [bē-at'-] *vt.* make happy; *R.C. Church* pronounce in eternal happiness (first step in canonization) (**beat'ified**, **beat'ifying**) —**beatif'ic** *a.* —**beatifica'tion** *n.* —**beat'itude** *n.* blessedness

beau [bō] *n.* suitor (*pl.* **beaux** [bō(z)])

Beau'fort scale system of indicating wind strength (from 0, calm, to 17, hurricane)

beau'ty [byōō'-] *n.* loveliness, grace; beautiful person or thing —**beauti'cian** *n.* one who works in beauty parlour —**beau'teous** *a.* —**beau'tiful** *a.* —**beau'tifully** *adv.* —**beau'tify** *vt.* (**-fied, -fying**) —**beauty parlour** establishment offering hairdressing, manicure *etc.*

bea'ver *n.* amphibious rodent; its fur —**beaver away** work hard

B.Ec. Bachelor of Economics

becalmed' [-kahmd'] *a.* (of ship) motionless through lack of wind

became' *pt. of* BECOME

because' *adv./conj.* by reason of, since

bêche-de-mer' [besh də mer'] *n.* edible sea slug

beck[1] *n.* —**at someone's beck and call** subject to someone's slightest whim

beck[2] *n.* stream

beck'on *v.* summon or lure by silent signal

become' [-kum'] *vi.* come to be —*vt.* suit (**became'** *pt.*, **become'** *pp.*, **becom'ing** *pr.p.*) —**becom'ing** *a.* suitable to; proper

bed *n.* piece of furniture for sleeping on; garden plot; *Architecture etc.* place in which anything rests; bottom of river; layer, stratum —*vt.* lay in a bed; plant (**-dd-**) —**bedd'ing** *n.* —**bed'pan** *n.* container used as lavatory by bedridden people —**bed'ridden** *a.* confined to bed by age or sickness —**bed'rock** *n.* —**bed'room** *n.* —**bed'sitter** *n.* one-roomed flat —**bed'stead** *n.*

bedev'il *vt.* confuse; torment —**bedev'ilment** *n.*

bed'lam *n.* noisy confused scene

Bed'ouin [-oo-in] *n.* member of nomadic Arab race —*a.* nomadic

bedrag'gle *vt.* dirty by trailing in wet or mud —**bedrag'gled** *a.*

Beds. Bedfordshire

bee *n.* insect that makes honey —**bee-eater** *n.* insect-eating bird —**bee'hive** *n.* —**bee'line** *n.* shortest route —**bees'wax** *n.* wax secreted by bees

beech *n.* European tree with smooth greyish bark and small nuts; its wood —**beech'en** *a.* —**beech'y** *a.*

beef *n.* flesh of cattle raised and killed for eating; *inf.* complaint —*vi. inf.* complain —**beeves** *pl.n.* cattle —**beef'y** *a.* fleshy, stolid —**beef'burger** *n. see* HAMBURGER —**beef'eater** *n.* yeoman of the guard; warder of Tower of London

been *pp. of* BE

beep *n.* short, loud sound of car horn *etc.* —*v.* make this sound

beer *n.* fermented alcoholic drink made from hops and malt —**beer'y** *a.*

beet *n.* any of various plants with root used for food or extraction of sugar

bee'tle *n.* class of insect with hard upper-wing cases closed over the back for protection —**beetle-browed** *a.* with prominent brows

befall' [-awl'] *v.* happen (to) (**befell'**, **befall'en**)

befit' *vt.* be suitable to (**-tt-**) —**befit'tingly** *adv.*

befog' *vt.* perplex, confuse (**-gg-**)

before' *prep.* in front of; in presence of; in preference to; earlier than —*adv.* earlier; in front —*conj.* sooner than —**before'hand** *adv.* previously

befoul' *vt.* make filthy

befriend' *vt.* make friend of

beg *vt.* ask earnestly, beseech —*vi.* ask for or live on alms (**-gg-**) —**begg'ar** *n.* —**begg'arly** *a.*

began' *pt. of* BEGIN

beget' *vt.* produce, generate (**begot**, **begat** *pt.*, **begott'en**, **begot'** *pp.*, **begett'ing** *pr.p.*) —**beget'ter** *n.*

begin' *v.* (cause to) start; initiate; originate (**began'**, **begun'**,

beginn'ing) —**beginn'er** n. novice —**beginn'ing** n.

bego'nia n. genus of tropical plant

begot' pt./pp. of BEGET

begrudge' vt. grudge, envy anyone the possession of

beguile' [-gīl'] vt. charm, fascinate; amuse; deceive —**beguil'er** n.

begun' pp. of BEGIN

behalf' [-hahf'] n. favour, benefit, interest, esp. in **on behalf of**

behave' vi. act, function in particular way —**beha'viour** n. conduct —**behave oneself** conduct oneself well

behead' vt. cut off head

beheld' pt./pp. of BEHOLD

behest' n. charge, command

behind' prep. further back or earlier than; in support of —adv. in the rear —**behind'hand** a./adv. in arrears; tardy

behold' [-hō-] vt. watch, see (**beheld'** pt., **beheld'**, **behold'en** pp.) —**behold'er** n.

behold'en a. bound in gratitude

behove' vi. be fit, necessary (only impersonal)

beige [bāzh] n. undyed woollen cloth; its colour

be'ing n. existence; that which exists; creature —pr.p. of BE

bel n. unit for comparing two power levels

bela'bour vt. beat soundly

bela'ted a. late; too late

belay' vt. fasten rope to peg, pin etc.

belch vi. void wind by mouth —vt. eject violently; cast up —n. emission of wind etc.

beleag'uer [-ēg'-] vt. besiege

bel'fry n. bell tower

belie' [-lī'] vt. contradict; misrepresent (**belied'** pt./pp., **bely'ing** pr.p.)

believe' vt. regard as true or

real —vi. have faith —**belief'** n. —**believ'able** a. credible —**believ'er** n. esp. one of same religious faith

Belish'a bea'con [-lēsh'-] flashing light in orange globe marking a pedestrian crossing

belit'tle vt. regard, speak of, as having little worth or value —**belit'tlement** n.

bell n. hollow metal instrument giving ringing sound when struck; electrical device emitting ring or buzz as signal —**bell'boy** n. US, C pageboy in hotel

belladon'na n. deadly nightshade

belle n. beautiful woman, reigning beauty

bell'icose a. warlike

bellig'erent [-ij-] a. hostile, aggressive; making war —n. warring person or nation

bell'ow vi. roar like bull; shout —n. roar of bull; any deep cry or shout

bell'ows pl.n. instrument for creating stream of air

bell'y n. part of body which contains intestines; stomach —v. swell out (**bell'ied, bell'ying**)

belong' vi. be the property or attribute of; be a member or inhabitant of; have an allotted place; pertain to —**belong'ings** pl.n. personal possessions

belov'ed [-luv'id or -luvd'] a. much loved —n. dear one

below' [-ō'] adv. beneath —prep. lower than

belt n. band; girdle; zone or district —vt. surround, fasten with belt; mark with band; inf. thrash

belu'ga [-lōō'-] n. large white sturgeon

BEM British Empire Medal

bemoan' vt. grieve over (loss etc.)

bemuse' v. confuse, bewilder

bench n. long seat; seat or body of judges etc. —vt. provide with benches —**bench mark** fixed point, criterion

bend v. (cause to) form a curve (**bent** pt./pp.) —n. curve —pl. decompression sickness

beneath' prep. under, lower than —adv. below

benedic'tion n. invocation of divine blessing

ben'efit n. advantage, favour, profit, good; money paid by a government etc. to unemployed etc. —vt. do good to —vi. receive good (**ben'efited, ben'efiting**) —**benefac'tion** n. —**ben'efactor** n. one who helps or does good to others; patron (**ben'efactress** fem.) —**ben'efice** n. an ecclesiastical living —**benef'icence** n. —**benef'icent** a. doing good; kind —**benef'icently** adv. —**benefi'cial** a. advantageous, helpful —**benefi'cially** adv. —**benefi'ciary** n.

benev'olent a. kindly, charitable —**benev'olence** n. —**benev'olently** adv.

benight'ed [-nīt'-] a. ignorant, uncultured

benign' [-nīn'-] a. kindly, mild, favourable —**benig'nancy** n. —**benig'nant** a. —**benig'nantly** adv. —**benig'nity** n. —**benign'ly** adv.

bent pt./pp. of BEND —a. curved; resolved (on); inf. corrupt; inf. deviant; inf. crazy —n. inclination, personal propensity

benumb' [-m] vt. make numb, deaden

Ben'zedrine R amphetamine

ben'zene n. one of group of related flammable liquids used in chemistry and as solvents, cleaning agents etc.

bequeath' [-ēTH'] vt. leave property etc. by will —**bequest'** n. bequeathing; legacy

berate' vt. scold harshly

ber'beris n. shrub with red berries

bereave' vt. deprive of, esp. by death (**-reaved', -reft'** pt./pp.) —**bereave'ment** n. loss, esp. by death

ber'et [-rā] n. round, closefitting hat

berg n. large mass of ice; **SA** mountain

ber'gamot n. type of pear with strong flavour; type of orange; perfume, oil produced from this

beriber'i n. tropical disease caused by vitamin B deficiency

Berks. Berkshire

ber'ry n. small juicy stoneless fruit —vi. look for, pick, berries

berserk' a. frenzied

berth n. ship's mooring place; place to sleep in ship or train —vt. to moor

ber'yl n. variety of crystalline mineral including aquamarine and emerald

beseech' vt. entreat, implore (**besought'** pt./pp.)

beset' vt. assail, surround with danger, problems (**beset', beset'ting**)

beside' prep. by the side of, near; distinct from —**besides'** adv./prep. in addition (to)

besiege' vt. surround (with armed forces etc.)

besott'ed a. drunk; foolish; infatuated

besought' pt./pp. of BESEECH

bespeak' vt. engage beforehand (**bespoke'** pt., **bespoke'**, **spo'ken** pp.) —**bespoke'** a. (of garments) made to order; selling such garments

best a./adv. sup. of GOOD or WELL —vt. defeat —**best seller** book or other product sold in great numbers; author of one or more of these

bes'tial _a._ like a beast, brutish —**bestial'ity** _n._

bestir' _vt._ rouse (oneself) to activity

bestow' [-stō'] _vt._ give, confer —**bestow'al** _n._

bestride' _vt._ sit or stand over with legs apart, mount horse (**bestrode'**, **bestridd'en**, **bestri'ding**)

bet _v._ agree to pay money _etc._ if wrong (or win if right) in guessing result of contest _etc._ (**bet** or **bet'ted** _pt./pp._, **bet'ting** _pr.p._) —_n._ money risked in this way

be'tel [bē'tl] _n._ species of pepper —**betel nut** the nut of the areca palm

bête noire [bet-nwahr'] _Fr._ pet aversion

betide' _v._ happen (to)

beto'ken _vt._ be a sign of

bet'ony _n._ plant with reddish-purple flower spike

betray' _vt._ be disloyal to, _esp._ by assisting an enemy; reveal, divulge; show signs of —**betray'al** _n._ —**betray'er** _n._

betroth' [-ŌTH'] _vt._ promise to marry —**betroth'al** _n._ —**betrothed'** _n./a._

bett'er _a./adv. comp._ of GOOD and WELL —_v._ improve —**bett'erment** _n._

between' _prep./adv._ in the intermediate part, in space or time; indicating reciprocal relation or comparison

betwixt' _prep./adv. obs._ between

bev'el _n._ surface not at right angle to another; slant —_vi._ slope, slant —_vt._ cut on slant (**-ll-**) —_a._ slanted

bev'erage _n._ drink

bev'y _n._ flock or group

bewail' _vt._ lament

beware' _vi._ be on one's guard, take care

bewil'der _vt._ puzzle, confuse —**bewil'dering** _a._ —**bewil'deringly** _adv._ —**bewil'derment** _n._

bewitch' _vt._ cast spell over; charm, fascinate —**bewitch'ing** _a._ —**bewitch'ingly** _adv._

beyond' _adv._ farther away; besides —_prep._ on the farther side of; later than; surpassing, out of reach of

B/F brought forward

bhp brake horsepower

Bi _Chem._ bismuth

bi'as _n._ slant; personal inclination or preference; onesided inclination (_pl._ **bi'ases**) —_vt._ influence, affect (**-s-** or **-ss-**) —**bi'ased** _a._ prejudiced

bib _n._ cloth put under child's chin to protect clothes when eating; top of apron or overalls

Bi'ble _n._ the sacred writings of the Christian religion —**bib'lical** _a._ —**bib'licist** _n._

bibliog'raphy _n._ list of books on a subject; history and description of books —**bibliog'rapher** _n._ —**bibliograph'ical** _a._

bib'liophil(e) _n._ lover, collector of books —**biblioph'ily** _n._

bib'ulous _a._ given to drinking

bicar'bonate [-bə-nit] _n._ chemical compound releasing carbon dioxide when mixed with acid

bicente'nary _n._ two hundredth anniversary; its celebration

bi'ceps _n._ two-headed muscle, _esp._ muscle of upper arm

bick'er _vi./n._ quarrel over petty things —**bick'ering** _n._

bi'cycle _n._ vehicle with two wheels, one in front of other, pedalled by rider —**bi'cyclist** _n._

bid _vt._ offer; say; command; invite (**bade**, **bid**, **bidd'en**) —_n._ offer, _esp._ of price; try; _Card Games_ call —**bidd'er** _n._ —**bid'ding** _n._

bide vi. remain; dwell —vt. await —bi'ding n.

bi'det [be'da] n. low basin for washing genital area

bienn'ial [bi-en-] a. happening every two years; lasting two years —n. plant living two years —bienn'ially adv.

bier [ber] n. frame for bearing dead to grave

bifo'cal [bi-] a. having two different focal lengths —bifo'cals pl.n. spectacles having bifocal lenses for near and distant vision

big a. of great or considerable size, height, number, power etc. (bigg'er comp., bigg'est sup.) —big'ness n. —big'head n. inf. conceited person —bighead'ed a. —big shot inf. important or influential person

big'amy n. crime of marrying a person while one is still legally married to someone else —big'amist n. —big'amous a.

bight [bit] n. curve or loop in rope; long curved shoreline or water bounded by it

big'ot n. person intolerant or not receptive to ideas of others (esp. on religion, race etc.) —big'oted a. —big'otry n.

bike n. short for BICYCLE or MOTOR BIKE

biki'ni [-ke'-] n. woman's brief two-piece swimming costume

bilat'eral [bi-] a. two-sided

bil'berry n. small European moorland plant with edible blue berries

bile n. fluid secreted by the liver; anger, ill-temper —bil'ious a. nauseous, nauseating —bil'iousness n.

bilge [-j] n. bottom of ship's hull; dirty water collecting there; inf. nonsense —vi. spring a leak —bilge water

biling'ual [bi-ling'gwəl] a. speaking, or written in, two languages —biling'ualism n.

bill¹ n. written account of charges; draft of Act of Parliament; poster; commercial document —vt. present account of charges; announce by advertisement —bill'ing n. degree of importance (esp. in theatre etc.)

bill² n. bird's beak —vi. touch bills, as doves; caress

bill³ n. tool for pruning; hooked weapon —bill'hook n. hatchet with hook at end of cutting edge

bill'abong n. A pool in intermittent stream

bill'et n. civilian quarters for troops; resting-place —vt. quarter, as troops

billet-doux' [bil-i-dōō'] Fr. love letter

bill'iards n. game played on table with balls and cues

bill'ion n. million millions, 10¹²; US, C thousand millions, 10⁹

bill'ow n. great swelling wave —pl. the sea —vi. surge; swell out

bill'y, bill'ycan n. can with wire handle used for boiling water on open fire

bil'tong n. SA thin strips of meat dried in sun

BIM British Institute of Management

bimonth'ly adv./a. every two months; twice a month

bin n. receptacle for corn, refuse etc.; one particular bottling of wine

bi'nary a. composed of, characterized by, two; dual

bind [-i-] vt. tie fast; tie round; gird; tie together; oblige; seal; constrain; bandage; cohere; unite; put (book) into cover (bound pt./pp.) —bind'er n. one who, or that which binds —bind'ery n. —bind'ing n. cover of book; tape for hem etc. —bind'weed n. convolvulus

binge [-nj] n. inf. excessive indul-

gence in eating or drinking;
spree

bing'o [-ng'gō] *n.* game of chance in which numbers drawn are matched with those on a card

binn'acle *n.* box holding ship's compass

binoc'ular *a.* seeing with, made for both eyes —**binoc'ulars** *pl.n.* telescope made for both eyes

bino'mial [-bī-] *a./n.* (denoting) algebraic expression consisting of two terms

bio- [bī-ō-] *(comb. form)* life, living, as in **biochem'istry** *n.* Such words are not given here where the meaning may easily be inferred from the simple word

biodegra'dable *a.* capable of decomposition by natural means

biog. biographical; biography

biog'raphy [bī-] *n.* story of one person's life —**biog'rapher** *n.* —**biograph'ical** *a.* —**biograph'ically** *adv.*

biol. biological; biology

biol'ogy [bī-] *n.* study of living organisms —**biol'ical** *a.* —**biolog'ically** *adv.* —**biol'ogist** *n.*

bion'ics [bī-] *pl.n.* (*with sing. v.*) study of relation of biological and electronic processes —**bion'ic** *a.* having physical functions controlled, augmented by electronic equipment

bi'opsy *n.* examination of tissue removed surgically from a living body

bi'orhythm *n.* cyclically recurring pattern of physiological states

bi'oscope *n.* SA cinema

bipartisan' [bī-pahrt-i-zan' or -pahrt'-] *a.* consisting of or supported by two political parties

bipart'ite [bī-] *a.* consisting of two parts, parties

bi'ped *n.* two-footed animal —**bi'pe'dal** *a.*

bi'plane *n.* aeroplane with two pairs of wings

birch *n.* tree with silvery bark; rod for punishment, made of birch twigs —*vt.* flog —**birch'en** *a.*

bird *n.* feathered animal; *sl.* young woman or girl

biret'ta *n.* square cap worn by Catholic clergy

Bi'ro R ballpoint pen

birth *n.* bearing, or the being born, of offspring; parentage, origin; noble descent —**birth control** limitation of childbearing usu. by artificial means —**birth'day** *n.* —**birth'mark** *n.* blemish, *usu.* dark, formed on skin before birth

bis'cuit [-kit] *n.* dry, small, thin variety of cake

bisect' [bī-] *vt.* divide into two equal parts —**bisect'or** *n.*

bisex'ual [bī-] *a.* sexually attracted to both men and women; of both sexes

bish'op *n.* clergyman governing diocese; chess piece —**bish'opric** *n.* diocese or office of a bishop

bis'muth [-z-] *n.* reddish-white metal used in medicine *etc.*

bi'son *n.* large wild ox; Amer. buffalo

bi'stro [be'-] *n.* small restaurant

bit [superscript 1] *n.* fragment, piece; biting, cutting part of tool; mouthpiece of horse's bridle

bit [superscript 2] *pt./pp.* of BITE

bit [superscript 3] *n.* Computers smallest unit of information

bitch *n.* female dog, fox or wolf; *offens. sl.* spiteful woman; *inf.* complaint —*vi. inf.* complain —**bitch'y** *a.*

bite *vt.* cut into *esp.* with teeth; grip; rise to bait; corrode (**bit** *pt.*, **bit**, **bitt'en** *pp.*, **bi'ting** *pr.p.*) —*n.*

act of biting; wound so made; mouthful —**bit'ter** n.

bitt'er a. sharp, sour tasting; unpleasant; (of person) angry, resentful; sarcastic —**bitt'erly** adv. —**bitt'erness** n. —**bitt'ers** pl.n. essence of bitter herbs —**bitter end** final extremity

bitt'ern n. wading bird like heron

bit'umen n. viscous substance occurring in asphalt, tar etc.

bi'valve a. having a double shell —n. mollusc with such shell

biv'ouac n. temporary encampment of soldiers, hikers etc. —vi. pass the night in temporary camp (**biv'ouacked, biv'ouacking**)

bizarre' a. unusual, weird

BL Bachelor of Law

blab v. reveal secrets; chatter idly (**-bb-**) —n. telltale; gossip

black a. of the darkest colour; without light; dark; evil; sombre; dishonourable —n. darkest colour; black dye, clothing etc.; (B-) person of dark-skinned race —vt. boycott (specified goods etc.) in industrial dispute —**black'en** vt. —**black'ing** n. substance used for blacking and cleaning leather etc. —**black'ball** vt. vote against, exclude —**black'berry** n. plant with thorny stems and dark juicy berries, bramble —**black'bird** n. common European songbird —**black'board** n. dark-coloured surface for writing on with chalk —**black box** inf. name for FLIGHT RECORDER —**black'cap** n. type of warbler —**black'cock** n. male of the black grouse —**black economy** illegally undeclared income —**black'head** n. dark, fatty plug blocking pore in skin —**black'leg** n. one who works during strike; disease of cattle —**black'list** n. list of people, organizations considered suspicious, untrustworthy etc. —vt. put on blacklist —**Black Mari'a** police van for transporting prisoners —**black market** illegal buying and selling of goods —**black spot** dangerous place, esp. on a road —**black'thorn** n. shrub with black twigs —**black widow** highly poisonous Amer. spider

black'guard [blag'ahrd] n. scoundrel —a. unprincipled, wicked —vt. revile —**black'guardism** n. —**black'guardly** a.

black'mail vt. extort money from (a person) by threats —n. act of blackmailing; money extorted thus —**black'mailer** n.

black'out n. complete failure of electricity supply; sudden cutting off of all stagelights; state of temporary unconsciousness; obscuring of all lights as precaution against night air attack —v.

black'smith n. smith who works in iron

bladd'er n. membranous bag to contain liquid, esp. urinary bladder

blade n. edge, cutting part of knife or tool; leaf of grass etc.; sword; obs. dashing fellow; flat of oar

blain n. inflamed swelling; pimple, blister

blame n. censure; culpability —vt. find fault with; censure —**blam(e)'able** a. —**blame'less** a. —**blame'worthy** a.

blanch [-ah-] v. whiten, bleach, take colour out of; (of foodstuffs) briefly boil or fry; turn pale

blancmange' [blə-monzh'] n. jellylike dessert made with milk

bland a. devoid of distinctive characteristics; smooth in manner

bland'ish vt. coax; flatter —**blan'dishment** n.

blank a. without marks or writing; empty; vacant, confused; (of verse) without rhyme —n. empty space; void; cartridge containing no bullet —**blank'ly** adv.

blank'et n. thick (woollen) covering for bed; concealing cover —vt. cover with blanket; cover, stifle

blare v. sound loudly and harshly —n. such sound

blar'ney n. flattering talk

blasé [blah'zā] a. indifferent through familiarity; bored

blaspheme' v. show contempt for God or sacred things, esp. in speech —**blasphe'mer** n. —**blas'phemous** a. —**blas'phemously** adv. —**blas'phemy** n.

blast [-ahst] n. explosion; high-pressure wave of air coming from an explosion; current of air; gust of wind or air; loud sound; sl. reprimand —vt. blow up; remove, open etc. by explosion; blight; ruin —**blast furnace** furnace for smelting ore, using preheated blast of air

bla'tant a. obvious —**bla'tancy** n.

blaze[1] n. strong fire or flame; brightness; outburst —vi. burn strongly; be very angry

blaze[2] v. (mark trees) to establish trail —n. mark on tree; white mark on horse's face

blaze[3] vt. proclaim, publish (as with trumpet) —n. wide publicity

bla'zer n. type of jacket worn esp. for sports

bla'zon vt. make public, proclaim; describe, depict (arms) —n. coat of arms

bleach v. make or become white —n. bleaching substance

bleak[1] a. cold and cheerless; exposed —**bleak'ly** adv.

bleak[2] n. small, silvery fish

blear'y(-eyed) a. with eyes dimmed, as with tears, sleep

bleat v. cry, as sheep; say, speak, plaintively —n. sheep's cry

bleed vi. lose blood —vt. draw blood or liquid from; extort money from (**bled** pt./pp.)

bleep n. short high-pitched sound —**bleep'er** n. small portable electronic signalling device

blem'ish n. defect; stain —vt. make (something) defective, dirty etc. —**blem'ished** a.

blench vi. start back, flinch

blend v. mix —n. mixture —**blend'er** n. one who, that which blends, esp. electrical kitchen appliance for mixing food

bles'bok n. S Afr. antelope

bless vt. consecrate; give thanks to; ask God's favour for; (usu. passive) endow (with); glorify; make happy (**bless'ed, bless'd** pp.) —**bless'ed** a. —**bless'edness** n. —**bless'ing** n. (ceremony asking for) God's protection, aid; short prayer; approval; welcome event, benefit

bleth'er [-TH-] n. nonsense, gossip —vi. also **blath'er**

blew pt. of BLOW

blight [blīt] n. plant disease; harmful influence —vt. injure as with blight

blight'er [blīt'-] n. inf. fellow, person

blimp n. small, nonrigid airship used for observing

blind [-ī-] a. unable to see; heedless, random; dim; closed at one end; sl. very drunk —vt. deprive of sight —n. something cutting off light; window screen; pretext —**blind'ly** adv. —**blind'ness** n. —**blind flying** navigation of aircraft by use of instruments alone —**blind'fold** vt. cover the eyes of so as to prevent vision —n./a. —**blindman's buff** game in which one player is blindfolded

blink vi. wink; twinkle; shine intermittently —n. gleam —**blink'ers** pl.n. leather flaps to prevent horse from seeing to the side —**blink at** see, know about, but ignore —**on the blink** *inf.* not working (properly)

blip *n.* repetitive sound or visible pulse, eg on radar screen

bliss *n.* perfect happiness —**bliss'ful** *a.* —**bliss'fully** *adv.* —**bliss'fulness** *n.*

blis'ter *n.* bubble on skin; surface swelling, eg on paint —*v.* form blisters (on) —**blis'tering** *a.* (of verbal attack) bitter —**blister pack** package for goods with hard, raised, transparent cover

blithe [blITH] *a.* happy, gay —**blithe'ly** *adv.* —**blithe'ness** *n.*

BLitt Bachelor of Letters

blitz *n.* sudden, concentrated attack

blizz'ard *n.* blinding storm of wind and snow

bloat *v.* puff or swell out —*n.* distension of stomach of cow *etc.* by gas —**bloat'ed** *a.* swollen —**bloat'er** *n.* smoked herring

blob *n.* soft mass, *esp.* drop of liquid; shapeless form

bloc *n.* (political) grouping of people or countries

block *n.* solid (rectangular) piece of wood, stone *etc.*, *esp.* *Hist.* that on which people were beheaded; obstacle; stoppage; pulley with frame; large building of offices, flats *etc.*; group of buildings; area enclosed by intersecting streets —*vt.* obstruct, stop up; shape on block; sketch (in) —**block'age** *n.* obstruction —**block'head** *n.* fool, simpleton —**block letters** written capital letters

blockade' *n.* physical prevention of access, *esp.* to port *etc.* —*vt.*

bloke *n. inf.* fellow, chap

blond *a.* (of hair) light-coloured —*n.* someone with blond hair (**blonde** *fem.*)

blood [blud] *n.* red fluid in veins; race; kindred; good parentage; temperament; passion *v.* initiate (into hunting, war *etc.*) —**blood'ily** *adv.* —**blood'less** *a.* —**blood'y** *a.* covered in blood; slaughterous —*a./adv. sl.* a common intensifier —*v.* make bloody —**blood bank** (institution managing) store of human blood preserved for transfusion —**blood'hound** *n.* breed of large hound noted for keen powers of scent —**blood'shed** *n.* slaughter, killing —**blood'shot** *a.* inflamed (said of eyes) —**blood sport** sport in which animals are killed, eg foxhunting —**blood'sucker** *n.* parasite (eg mosquito) living on host's blood; parasitic person —**blood test** examination of sample of blood —**blood'thirsty** *a.* murderous, cruel —**blood transfusion** transfer of blood from one person to another

bloom *n.* flower of plant; blossoming; prime, perfection; glow; powdery deposit on fruit —*vi.* be in flower; flourish —**bloom'ing** *a.*

bloom'er *n. inf.* ludicrous mistake

bloom'ers *pl.n.* wide, baggy knickers

bloss'om *n.* flower; flower bud —*vi.* flower; develop

blot *n.* spot, stain; disgrace —*vt.* spot, stain; obliterate; detract from; soak up ink *etc.* from (-*tt*-) —**blott'er,** blotting pad —**blotting paper**

blotch *n.* dark spot on skin —*vt.* make spotted —**blotch'y** *a.*

blouse [-owz] *n.* light, loose upper garment

blow[1] [blō] *v.* make a current of air; pant; emit sound —*vt.* drive air upon or into; drive by current of air; sound; spout (of whales); fan; *sl.* squander (**blew, blown**) —*n.* blast; gale —**blow'er**

—**blow-dry** vt. style hair after washing using blast of hot air —n. —**blow'fly** n. fly which infects food etc. —**blow'lamp** n. small burner with very hot flame, for removing paint etc. —**blow'pipe** n. dart tube —**blow-out** n. sudden puncture in tyre; uncontrolled escape of oil, gas, from well; sl. large meal —**blow out** extinguish; (of tyre) puncture suddenly; (of fuse) melt —**blow up** explode; enlarge (photograph); inf. lose one's temper

blow[2] [blō] n. stroke, knock; sudden misfortune, loss

blown pp. of BLOW[1]

blowz'y a. slovenly, sluttish; red-faced

blubb'er vi. weep —n. fat of whales; weeping

bludg'eon [bluj'ən] n. short thick club —vt. strike with one; coerce (someone into)

blue a. of the colour of sky or shades of that colour; livid; depressed; indecent —n. the colour; dye or pigment; indigo powder used in laundering —vt. make blue; dip in blue liquid (**blued** pt./pp.) —**blues** pl.n. inf. (oft. with sing. v.) depression; form of Amer. Negro folk song in slow tempo, employed in jazz music —**blu'ish** a. —**blue baby** baby born with bluish skin caused by heart defect —**blue'bell** n. wild spring flower —**blue'berry** n. N Amer. shrub with blue-black edible berries —**blue blood** royal or aristocratic descent —**blue'bottle** n. blowfly —**blue-collar** a. denoting manual industrial workers —**blue-pencil** vt. alter, delete parts of, esp. to censor —**blue'print** n. copy of drawing; original plan —**blue'stocking** n. scholarly, intellectual woman

bluff[1] n. cliff, steep bank —a.

hearty; blunt; steep; abrupt

bluff[2] vt. deceive by pretence of strength —n. pretence

blun'der n. clumsy mistake —vi. make stupid mistake; act clumsily

blun'derbuss n. obsolete short gun with wide bore

blunt a. not sharp; (of speech) abrupt —vt. make blunt —**blunt'ly** adv. —**blunt'ness** n.

blur v. make, become less distinct (**-rr-**) —n. something vague, indistinct —**blurr'y** a.

blurb n. statement advertising, recommending book etc.

blurt vt. utter suddenly or unadvisedly (usually with out)

blush vi. become red in face; be ashamed; redden —n. this effect —**blush'er** n. cosmetic to give rosy colour to face

blus'ter vi./n. (indulge in) noisy, aggressive behaviour —**blus'tering, blus'tery** a. (of wind etc.) noisy and gusty

BM British Museum

BMA British Medical Association

BMX bicycle motocross; bicycle for such riding

BNFL British Nuclear Fuels Limited

BO inf. body odour; box office

bo'a n. large, nonvenomous snake; long scarf of fur or feathers

boar n. male pig; wild pig

board n. broad, flat piece of wood; sheet of rigid material for specific purpose; table; meals; group of people who administer company; governing body; thick, stiff paper —pl. theatre, stage —vt. cover with planks; supply food daily; enter ship etc. —vi. take daily meals —**board'er** n. —**boarding house** lodging house where meals may be had —**boarding school** school providing living accommodation for pupils —**board'room** n. room where board of company meets —**above board** beyond suspicion —**on board** in or into ship

boast vi. speak too much in praise of oneself, one's possessions —vt. brag of; have to show —n. something boasted of(?) —**boast'er** n. —**boast'ful** a. —**boast'fully** adv. —**boast'fulness** n.

boat n. small open vessel; ship —vi. sail about in boat —**boat'er** n. flat straw hat —**boat'ing** n. —**boat'hook** n. —**boat'house** n. —**boat'man** n. —**boat'swain** [bō'sən] n. ship's officer in charge of boats, sails etc.

bob vi. move up and down —vt. move jerkily; cut (women's) hair short (-bb-) —n. short, jerking motion; short hairstyle; weight on pendulum etc.; inf. formerly, shilling —**bobbed** n.

bobbejaan' [-ə-yahn'] n. SA baboon

bobb'in n. cylinder on which thread is wound

bob'ble n. small, tufted ball for decoration

bobb'y n. inf. policeman

bob'cat n. Amer. wild cat, bay lynx

bob'olink n. Amer. songbird

BOC British Oxygen Company

bode vt. be an omen of

bod'ice [-is] n. upper part of woman's dress

bod'kin n. large blunt needle; tool for piercing holes

bod'y n. whole frame of man or animal; main part of such frame; corpse; main part of anything; substance; mass; person; number of persons united or organized; matter, opposed to spirit —**bod'iless** a. —**bod'ily** a./adv. —**bodyguard** n. escort to protect important person —**body popping**

1980s dance with schematic, mechanical movements (also **robotics, robot dancing**) —**body warmer** quilted jerkin —**bodywork** n. shell of motor vehicle

Boer [boor] n. a S Afr. of Dutch or Huguenot descent —a. —**boer'bul** [-bool] n. SA crossbred mastiff —**boer'ewors** [-rə-vors] n. SA mincemeat sausage —**boer'perd** [-t] n. S Afr. breed of horse

boet(ie) [-oo-] n. SA inf. friend

boff'in n. inf. scientist, technical research worker

bog n. wet, soft ground; sl. lavatory —**bogg'y** a. marshy —**bog down** stick as in a bog

bo'gey n. evil or mischievous spirit; standard golf score for a good player —**bo'geyman** n.

bog'gle vi. stare, be surprised

bo'gie n. low truck on four wheels; pivoted undercarriage, as on railway rolling stock

bo'gus a. sham, false

bohe'mian (also B-) a. unconventional —n. one who leads an unsettled life —**bohe'mianism** n.

boil[1] vi. change from liquid to gas, esp. by heating; become cooked by boiling; bubble; be agitated; seethe; inf. be hot; inf. be angry —vt. cause to boil; cook by boiling —n. boiling state —**boil'er** n. vessel for boiling —**boiler suit** garment covering whole body —**boiling point** temperature at which boiling occurs (100°C for water)

boil[2] n. inflamed suppurating swelling on skin

bois'terous a. wild; noisy; turbulent —**bois'terously** adv. —**bois'terousness** n.

bold a. daring, fearless; presumptuous; striking, prominent —**bold'ly** adv. —**bold'ness** n.

bole n. trunk of a tree

bole'ro [-a'-] n. Spanish dance;

[bol'ə-rō] short loose jacket

boll [-ō] n. seed capsule of cotton, flax etc.

boll'ard n. post on quay or ship to secure mooring lines; short post in road, footpath as barrier or marker

Bol'shevik n. violent revolutionary —**bol'shy, bol'shie** a. inf. rebellious, uncooperative; leftwing

bo'lster vt. support, uphold —n. long pillow; pad, support

bolt [bō-] n. bar or pin (esp. with thread for nut); rush; discharge of lightning; roll of cloth —vt. fasten with bolt; swallow hastily —vi. rush away; break from control

bomb [bom] n. explosive projectile; any explosive device; sl. large amount of money —the **bomb** nuclear bomb —vt. attack with bombs —**bombard'** vt. shell; attack (verbally) —**bombardier'** n. artillery noncommissioned officer —**bombard'ment** n. —**bomb'er** n. aircraft capable of carrying bombs —**bomb'shell** n. shell of bomb; surprise; inf. very attractive girl

bom'bast n. pompous language; pomposity —**bombas'tic** a.

bo'na fi'de [-di] Lat. genuine(ly); sincere(ly) —**bona fides** good faith, sincerity

bonan'za n. sudden good luck or wealth

bond n. that which binds; link, union; written promise to pay money or carry out contract —vt. bind; store goods until duty is paid on them —**bond'ed** a. placed in bond; mortgaged

bond'age n. slavery

bone n. hard substance forming animal's skeleton; piece of this —pl. essentials —vt. take out bone —vi. inf. (with up) study hard —**bone'less** a. —**bo'ny** a.

—**bone'head** n. inf. stupid person

bon'fire n. large outdoor fire

bon'go n. small drum, usu. one of a pair, played with the fingers (pl. **-go(e)s**)

bon'homie [bon'ə-mi] n. Fr. good humour, geniality

bonk'ers a. sl. crazy

bonn'et n. hat with strings; cap; cover of motor vehicle engine

bonn'y a. beautiful, handsome —**bonn'ily** adv.

bon'sai [-sī] n. (art of growing) dwarf trees, shrubs

bon'tebok [-buk] n. S Afr. antelope

bo'nus n. extra (unexpected) payment or gift (pl. **bo'nuses**)

boo interj. expression of disapproval or contempt; exclamation to surprise esp. child —v.

boob n. sl. foolish mistake; female breast

boob'y n. fool; tropical marine bird —**booby trap** harmless-looking object which explodes when disturbed; form of practical joke —**booby prize** mock prize for poor performance

boo'dle n. sl. money

boog'ie-woog'ie n. kind of jazz piano playing, emphasizing a rolling bass in syncopated eighth notes

book n. collection of sheets of paper bound together; literary work; main division of this —vt. reserve room, ticket etc.; charge with legal offence; enter name in book —**book'ing** n. reservation —**book'ish** a. studious, fond of reading —**book'binder** n. —**book'case** n. —**book-keeping** n. systematic recording of business transactions —**book'let** n. —**book'maker** n. one whose work is taking bets (also inf. **book'ie**) —**book'worm** n. great reader

boom[1] n. sudden commercial

activity; prosperity —vi. become active, prosperous

boom[1] vi./n. (make) loud, deep sound

boom[2] n. long spar, as for stretching the bottom of a sail; barrier across harbour; pole carrying overhead microphone etc.

boo'merang n. curved wooden missile of Aust. Aborigines, which returns to the thrower —vi. recoil; return unexpectedly; backfire

boon n. something helpful, favour

boor n. rude person —**boor'ish** a.

boost n. encouragement, help; upward push; increase —vt. —**boost'er** n. person or thing that supports, increases power etc.

boot[1] n. covering for the foot and ankle; luggage receptacle in car; inf. kick —vt. inf. kick —**boot'ed** a. —**boot'ee** n. baby's soft shoe —**boot sale** sale of goods from car boots in car park

boot[2] n. profit, use —**boot'less** a. fruitless, vain —**to boot** in addition

booth [-TH] n. stall; cubicle

boot'leg v. make, carry, sell illicit goods, esp. alcohol —a. —**boot'legger** n.

boo'ty n. plunder, spoil

booze n./vi. inf. (consume) alcoholic drink —**booz'er** n. inf. person fond of drinking; bar or pub —**booz'y** a. inf. —**booze-up** n. inf. drinking spree

bor'ax n. white soluble substance, compound of boron —**bo-ra'cic** a.

bord'er n. margin; frontier; limit; strip of garden —v. provide with border; adjoin

bore[1] vt. pierce, making a hole —n. hole; calibre of gun —**bor'er** n. instrument for making holes; insect which bores holes

bore[2] vt. make weary by repeti-

tion etc. —n. tiresome person or thing —**bore'dom** n. —**bor'ing** a.

bore[3] n. tidal wave which rushes up river estuary

born pt. of BEAR

born pp. of BEAR

bor'on n. chemical element used in hardening steel, etc.

bor'ough [bu'rə] n. town

borr'ow vt. obtain on loan or trust; appropriate —**borr'ower** n.

bor'stal n. reformatory for young criminals

bor'zoi n. breed of tall hound with long, silky coat

bosh n. inf. nonsense

bos'om [booz'-] n. human breast; seat of passions and feelings

boss[1] n. person in charge of or employing others —vt. be in charge of; be domineering over —**boss'y** a. overbearing

boss[2] n. knob or stud; raised ornament —vt. emboss

bot. botanical; botany; bottle

bot'any n. study of plants —**bo-tan'ic(al)** a. —**bot'anist** n.

botch vt. spoil by clumsiness —**botch-up** n. mess

both [bōth] a./pron. the two —adv./conj. as well

both'er [-TH-] vt. pester; perplex —vi./n. fuss, trouble

bot'tle n. vessel for holding liquid; its contents —vt. put into bottle; restrain —**bot'tler** n. —**bot'tlebrush** n. cylindrical brush for cleaning bottle —**bot'tleneck** n. narrow outlet which impedes smooth flow of traffic or production of goods

bott'om n. lowest part of anything; bed of sea, river etc.; buttocks —vt. put bottom to; base (upon); get to bottom of —**bot'tomless** a.

bot'ulism n. kind of food poisoning

bou'clé [boo´klā] *n.* looped yarn giving knobbly effect

bou'doir [boo´dwahr] *n.* lady's private sitting-room; bedroom

bougainvill'(a)ea [boo-gan-vil'i-ə] *n.* (sub)tropical climbing plant with red or purple bracts

bough [bow] *n.* branch of tree

bought *pt./pp. of* BUY

boul'der [bōl-] *n.* large weatherworn rounded stone

boule'vard [bōōl´vahr, -vahrd] *n.* broad street or promenade

bounce *v.* (cause to) rebound (repeatedly) on impact, as a ball —*n.* rebounding; quality in object causing this; *inf.* vitality, vigour —**boun'cer** *n. esp.* one employed to evict undesirables (forcibly) —**boun'cing** *a.* vigorous, robust —**boun'cy** *a.* lively

bound[1] *n./v.* limit —**bound'ary** *n.* —**bound'ed** *a.* —**bound'less** *a.*

bound[2] *vi./n.* spring, leap

bound[3] *a.* on a specified course, as **outward bound**

bound[4] *pt./pp. of* BIND —*a.* committed; certain; tied

boun'ty *n.* liberality; gift; premium —**boun'teous, boun'tiful** *a.* liberal, generous

bouquet' [bōō-kā´] *n.* bunch of flowers; perfume of wine; compliment

bour'bon [bur´-] *n.* US whiskey made from maize

bour'geois [boor´zhwah] *n./a.* (*oft. disparaging*) middle class; smugly conventional (person)

bout *n.* period of time spent doing something; contest, fight

boutique' [bōō-tēk´] *n.* small shop, *esp.* one selling clothes

bo'vine *a.* of the ox or cow; oxlike; stolid, dull

bow[1] [bō] *n.* weapon for shooting arrows; implement for playing violin *etc.*; ornamental knot of ribbon *etc.*; bend, bent line; rainbow —*v.* bend —**bow-legged** *a.*

bandy. —**bow window** one with outward curve

bow[2] [bow] *vi.* bend body in respect, assent *etc.*; submit —*vt.* bend downwards; cause to stoop; crush —*n.*

bow[3] [bow] *n.* fore end of ship; prow; rower nearest bow

bowd'lerize *vt.* expurgate

bow'el *n.* (*oft. pl.*) part of intestine (*esp.* with reference to defecation); inside of anything

bow'er *n.* shady retreat; inner room —**bow'erbird** *n.* Aust. bird that hoards decorative but useless things

bowl[1] [-ō-] *n.* round vessel, deep basin; drinking cup; hollow

bowl[2] [-ō-] *n.* wooden ball —*pl.* game played with such balls —*v.* roll or throw ball in various ways —**bowl'er** *n.* —**bowling alley** —**bowling green**

bowl'er [-ō-] *n.* man's low-crowned stiff felt hat

bow'ser *n.* fuel tanker

bow'sprit [bō´-] *n.* spar projecting from ship's bow

box[1] *n.* (wooden) container, usu. rectangular with lid; its contents; small enclosure; any boxlike cubicle, shelter or receptacle (eg letter box) —*vt.* put in box; confine —**box the compass** make complete turn

box[2] *v.* fight with fists, *esp.* with padded gloves on —*vt.* strike —*n.* blow —**box'er** *n.* one who boxes; breed of large dog resembling bulldog

box[3] *n.* evergreen shrub used for hedges

boy *n.* male child; young man —*interj.* exclamation of surprise —**boy'hood** *n.*

boy'cott *vt.* refuse to deal with or participate in —*n.*

BP British Petroleum; British Pharmacopoeia

BR British Rail

Br *Chem.* bromine

Br. Breton; Britain; British

br. branch; bronze; brother

bra [brah] *n. abbrev. of* BRASSIERE

brace *n.* tool for boring; clasp, clamp; pair, couple; strut, support —*pl.* straps worn over shoulders to hold up trousers —*vt.* steady (oneself) as before a blow; support, make firm —**bra'cing** *a.* invigorating —**brace'let** *n.* ornament for the arm —*pl. sl.* handcuffs

brack'en *n.* large fern

brack'et *n.* support for shelf *etc.*; group —*pl.* marks [ ], ( ) used to enclose words *etc.* —*vt.* enclose in brackets; connect

brack'ish *a.* (of water) slightly salty

bract *n.* small scalelike leaf

brad *n.* small nail —**brad'awl** *n.* small boring tool

brag *vi.* boast (-**gg-**) —*n.* boastful talk —**bragg'art** *n.*

Brah'man, Brah'min *n.* member of priestly Hindu caste; breed of beef cattle

braid *vt.* interweave; trim with braid —*n.* length of anything interwoven or plaited; ornamental tape

braille [brāl] *n.* system of printing for blind, with arrangements of raised dots instead of letters

brain *n.* mass of nerve tissue in head; intellect —*vt.* kill by hitting on head —**brain'less** *a.* —**brain'y** *a.* —**brain'child** *n.* invention —**brain'storm** *n.* sudden mental aberration —**brains trust** group of knowledgeable people who answer questions in panel games, quizzes *etc.* —**brain'wash** *vt.* change, distort a person's ideas or beliefs —**brain'wave** *n.* sudden, clever idea

braise [-āz] *vt.* stew in covered pan

brake[1] *n.* instrument for retard-

ing motion of wheel on vehicle —*vt.* apply brake to

brake[2] *n.* fern; bracken; thicket; brushwood

bram'ble *n.* prickly shrub; blackberry —**bram'bly** *a.*

bram'bling *n.* type of finch

bran *n.* sifted husks of corn

branch [-ah-] *n.* limb of tree; offshoot or subsidiary part of something larger or primary —*vi.* bear branches; diverge; spread —**branched** *a.* —**branch'y** *a.*

brand *n.* trademark; class of goods; particular kind, sort; mark made by hot iron; burning piece of wood; sword; mark of infamy —*vt.* burn with iron; mark; stigmatize —**brand-new** *a.* absolutely new

bran'dish *vt.* flourish, wave (weapon *etc.*)

bran'dy *n.* spirit distilled from wine —**brandy snap** crisp, sweet biscuit

brash *a.* bold, impudent

brass [-ah-] *n.* alloy of copper and zinc; group of brass wind instruments forming part of orchestra or band; *inf.* money; *inf.* (army) officers —*a.* —**brass'y** *a.* showy; harsh

brass'iere *n.* woman's undergarment, supporting breasts

brat *n. contemptuous name for a* child

bravad'o [-vahd'-] *n.* showy display of boldness

brave *a.* bold, courageous; splendid, fine —*n.* warrior —*vt.* defy, meet boldly —**brave'ly** *adv.* —**bra'very** *n.*

bravo[1] [brah-] *interj.* well done!

brawl *vi.* fight noisily —*n.* —**brawl'er** *n.*

brawn *n.* muscle; strength; pickled pork —**brawn'y** *a.* muscular

bray *n.* donkey's cry —*vi.* utter

this; give out harsh, or loud, sounds

braze vt. solder with alloy of brass or zinc

bra'zen a. of, like brass; impudent, shameless —vt. (usu. with out) face, carry through with impudence —**bra'zenness** n. effrontery —**bra'zier** n. brassworker

bra'zier n. pan for burning charcoal or coals

breach n. break; opening; breaking of rule, duty etc.; quarrel —vt. make a gap in

bread [-ed] n. food made of flour or meal baked; food; sl. money —**bread'fruit** n. breadlike fruit found in Pacific Islands —**bread'-winner** n. person supporting dependants by his earnings

breadth [-edth] n. extent across, width; largeness of view, mind

break [brāk] vt. part by force; shatter; burst, destroy; fail to observe; disclose; interrupt; surpass; make bankrupt; relax; mitigate; accustom (horse) to being ridden; decipher (code) —vi. become broken, shattered, divided; open, appear; come suddenly; crack, give way; part, fall out; (of voice) change in tone, pitch (**broke**, **bro'ken**) —n. fracture; gap; opening; separation; interruption; respite; interval; inf. opportunity; dawn; Billiards consecutive series of successful strokes; Boxing separation after a clinch; Cricket deviation of a ball on striking the pitch —**break'able** a. —**break'age** n. —**break'er** n. one that breaks, eg electrical circuit breaker; wave beating on rocks or shore —**break dance** acrobatic dance style of 1980s —**break'down** n. collapse, as nervous breakdown; failure to function effectively; analysis —**break'fast** [brek'-] n.

first meal of the day —**break-in** n. illegal entering of building, esp. by thieves —**break'neck** a. dangerous —**break'through** n. important advance —**break'water** n. barrier to break force of waves

bream n. broad, thin fish

breast [brest] n. human chest; milk-secreting gland on chest of human female; seat of the affections; any protuberance —vt. face, oppose; reach summit of —**breast'stroke** n. stroke in swimming

breath [breth] n. air used by lungs; life; respiration; slight breeze —**breathe** [brēтн] vi. inhale and exhale air from lungs; live; pause, rest —vt. inhale and exhale; utter softly, whisper —**brea'ther** [-тн-] n. short rest —**brea'thing** [-тн-] n. —**breath'less a.** —**breath'taking a.** causing awe or excitement

Breath'alyser R device that estimates amount of alcohol in breath —**breath'alyse** vt.

bred pt./pp. of BREED

breech n. buttocks; hinder part of anything, esp. gun —**breech'es** [brich'iz] pl.n. trousers —**breech'loader** n.

breed vt. generate, bring forth, give rise to; rear —vi. be produced; be with young (**bred** pt./pp.) —n. offspring produced; race, kind —**breed'er** n. —**breed'ing** n. producing; manners; ancestry —**breeder reactor** nuclear reactor producing more fissionable material than it consumes

breeze n. gentle wind —**breez'ily** adv. —**breez'y a.** windy; jovial, lively; casual

breeze block light building brick made of ashes bonded by cement

breth'ren [-тн-] pl. of BROTHER.

obs. except in religious contexts

breve *n.* long musical note

brev'i·ary [or brē'-] *n.* book of daily prayers of R.C. Church

brev'i·ty *n.* conciseness of expression; short duration

brew [-ōō] *vt.* prepare liquor, as beer from malt *etc.*; make drink, as tea, by infusion; plot, contrive —*vi.* be in preparation —*n.* beverage produced by brewing —**brew'er** *n.* —**brew'ery** *n.* —**brew'ing** *n.*

bri'ar[1], **bri'er**[1] *n.* prickly shrub, *esp.* the wild rose

bri'ar[2], **bri'er**[2] *n.* European shrub —**briar pipe** made from its root

bribe *n.* anything offered or given to someone to gain favour, influence —*vt.* influence by bribe —**brib'er** *n.* —**brib'ery** *n.*

bric'-a-brac *n.* miscellaneous small objects, used for ornament

brick *n.* oblong mass of hardened clay used in building —*vt.* build, block *etc.* with bricks —**brick'layer** *n.*

bride *n.* woman about to be, or just, married —**brid'al** *a.* of, relating to, a bride or wedding —**bride'groom** *n.* man about to be, or just, married —**brides'maid** *n.*

bridge[1] *n.* structure for crossing river *etc.*; something joining or supporting other parts; raised narrow platform on ship; upper part of nose; part of violin supporting strings —*vt.* make bridge over, span —**bridge'head** *n.* advanced position established on enemy territory

bridge[2] *n.* card game

bri'dle *n.* headgear of horse harness; curb —*vt.* put on bridle; restrain —*vi.* show resentment —**bridle path** path suitable for riding horses

brief *a.* short in duration; concise; scanty —*n.* summary of case for counsel's use; papal letter; instructions —*pl.* underpants; panties —*vt.* give instructions —**brief'ly** *adv.* —**brief'ness** *n.* —**brief'case** *n.* hand case for carrying papers

bri'er *see* BRIAR

brig *n.* two-masted, square-rigged ship

Brig. Brigade; Brigadier

brigade[1] *n.* subdivision of army; organized band —**brigadier'** *n.* high-ranking army officer, usu. in charge of a brigade

brig'antine *n.* two-masted vessel, with square-rigged foremast and fore-and-aft mainmast

bright [brīt] *a.* shining; full of light; cheerful; clever —**bright'en** *v.* —**bright'ly** *adv.* —**bright'ness** *n.*

brill *n.* European food fish

brill'iant *a.* shining; sparkling; splendid; very clever; distinguished —**brill'iance, brill'iancy** *n.* —**brill'iantly** *adv.*

brim *n.* margin, edge, *esp.* of river, cup, hat —**brimful'** *a.* —**brim'less** *a.* —**brimm'ing** *a.*

brim'stone *n.* sulphur

brin'dle(d) *a.* spotted and streaked

brine *n.* salt water; pickle —**bri'ny** *a.* very salty —*n. inf.* the sea

bring *vt.* fetch; carry with one; cause to come (**brought** *pt./pp.*)

brink *n.* edge of steep place; verge, margin

briquette' [-ket'] *n.* block of compressed coal dust

brisk *a.* active, vigorous —**brisk'ly** *adv.* —**brisk'ness** *n.*

brisk'et *n.* joint of meat from breast of animal

bris'tle [-is'l] *n.* short stiff hair —*vi.* stand erect; show temper —**bris'tliness** *n.* —**bris'tly** *a.*

Brit. Britain; Britannia; British

British thermal unit unit of heat equal to 1055 joules

brit'tle a. easily broken, fragile; curt, irritable —**brit'tleness** n.

broach vt. pierce (cask); open, begin

broad [-aw-] a. wide, spacious, open; plain, obvious; coarse; general; tolerant; (of pronunciation) dialectal —**broad'en** vt. —**broad'ly** adv. —**broad'ness** n. —**broad'cast** vt. transmit by radio or television; make widely known; scatter, as seed —n. radio or television programme —**broad'caster** n. —**broad-minded** a. tolerant; generous —**broad'side** n. discharge of all guns on one side; strong (verbal) attack

brocade' n. rich woven fabric with raised design

brocc'oli n. type of cabbage

bro'chure [-shə] n. pamphlet, booklet

brogue[1] [-ōg] n. stout shoe; dialect, esp. Irish accent

broil[1] n. noisy quarrel

broil[2] vt. cook over hot coals; grill —vi. be heated

broke pt. —**bro'ken** pp. of BREAK —a. inf. penniless

bro'ker n. one employed to buy and sell for others; dealer —**bro'kerage** n. payment to broker

broll'y n. inf. umbrella

bro'mide n. chemical compound used in medicine and photography —**bromide paper** photographic printing paper, treated with silver bromide

bro'mine [-mēn] n. liquid element used in production of chemicals —**bro'mic** a.

bron'chi, -ia [-ng'k-] pl.n. branches of windpipe —**bron'chial** a. —**bronchi'tis** n. inflammation of bronchi

bronc'o n. Amer. half-tamed horse (pl. **-cos**)

brontosau'rus n. very large herbivorous dinosaur

bronze n. alloy of copper and tin —a. made of, or coloured like, bronze —vt. give appearance of bronze to —**bronzed** a. coated with bronze; sunburnt

brooch [-ō-] n. ornamental pin or fastening

brood [-ōō-] n. family of young, esp. of birds; tribe, race —v. sit, as hen on eggs; meditate, fret over —**brood'y** a. moody, sullen

brook[1] [-ōō-] n. small stream —**brook'let** n.

brook[2] [-ōō-] vt. put up with, endure, tolerate

broom [-ōō-] n. brush for sweeping; yellow-flowered shrub —**broom'stick** n. handle of broom

bros. brothers

broth n. thick soup

broth'el n. house of prostitution

broth'er [-uTH'-] n. son of same parents; one closely united with another —**broth'erhood** n. relationship; fraternity, company —**broth'erliness** n. —**broth'erly** a. —**brother-in-law** n. brother of husband or wife; husband of sister

brought pt./pp. of BRING

brow n. ridge over eyes; forehead; eyebrow; edge of hill —**brow'beat** vt. bully (**brow'beat, brow'beaten**)

brown a. of dark colour inclining to red or yellow —n. the colour —v. make, become brown —**browned off** inf. bored, depressed

Brown'ie n. junior Girl Guide —**Brownie point** notional mark to one's credit for being seen to do the right thing

browse vi. look through (book, articles for sale etc.) in a casual manner; feed on shoots and leaves

bruise [-ōōz] vt. injure without breaking skin —n. contusion, discoloration caused by blow —**bruis'er** n. strong, tough person

brum'by n. Aust. wild horse

brunch n. inf. breakfast and lunch combined

brunette' n. woman of dark complexion and hair —a. dark brown

brunt n. shock of attack, chief stress; first blow

brush n. device with bristles, hairs, wires etc. used for cleaning, painting etc.; act, instance of brushing; brief contact; skirmish, fight; bushy tail; brushwood; (carbon) device taking electric current from moving to stationary parts of generator etc. —v. apply, remove, clean, with brush; touch lightly —**brush'off** n. inf. dismissal; refusal; snub; rebuff —**brush'wood** n. broken-off branches; land covered with scrub

brusque [-oosk] a. rough in manner, curt, blunt

brute n. any animal except man; crude, vicious person —a. animal; sensual, stupid; physical —**bru'tal** a. —**brutal'ity** n. —**bru'talize** vt. —**bru'tally** adv. —**bru'tish** a. bestial, gross

bry'ony, bri'ony n. wild climbing hedge plant

BS balance sheet; British Standard

BSC British Steel Corporation; British Sugar Corporation

BSc Bachelor of Science

BSI British Standards Institution

B-side n. less important side of disc

BST British Summer Time

Bt. Baronet

Btu British Thermal Unit

bub'ble n. hollow globe of liquid, blown out with air; something insubstantial, not serious; transparent dome —vi. rise in bubbles; make gurgling sound —**bub'bly** a.

bubon'ic plague [byōō-] n. acute infectious disease characterized by swellings and fever

buccaneer' n. pirate, searover —**buccaneer'ing** n.

buck n. male deer, or other male animal; act of bucking; **US, A** sl. dollar —v. of horse, attempt to throw rider by jumping upwards etc.; resist, oppose (something) —**buck'shot** n. lead shot in shotgun shell —**buck'teeth** pl.n. projecting upper teeth

buck'et n. vessel, round with arched handle, for water etc.; anything resembling this —vt. put, carry, in bucket —**buck'etful** n. —**bucket down** rain very hard —**bucket seat** seat with back shaped to occupier's figure

buck'le n. metal clasp for fastening belt, strap etc. —vt. fasten with buckle —vi. warp, bend —**buck'ler** n. shield —**buckle down** start work

buck'ram n. coarse cloth stiffened with size

Bucks. Buckinghamshire

buckshee' a. sl. free

bucol'ic [byōō-] a. rustic

bud n. shoot or sprout on plant containing unopened leaf, flower etc. —vi. begin to grow —vt. graft (-dd-)

Budd'hism [-d'izm] n. religion founded in India by Buddha —**Budd'hist** a./n.

bud'dleia n. shrub with mauve flower spikes

budd'y n. inf. mate, chum

budge vi. move, stir

budg'erigar n. small Aust. parakeet (also **budg'ie**)

budg'et n. annual financial statement; plan of systematic spending —vi. prepare financial statement; plan financially

buff[1] n. leather made from buffalo or ox hide; light yellow colour; bare skin; polishing pad —vt. polish

buff[2] n. inf. expert on some subject

buff'alo n. any of several species of large oxen (pl. -lo(e)s)

buff'er n. contrivance to lessen shock of concussion

buff'et[1] n. blow, slap; misfortune —vt. strike with blows; contend against —**buff'eting** n.

buff'et[2] [boof'ā] n. refreshment bar; meal at which guests serve themselves; sideboard

buffoon'[1] n. clown; fool —**buffoon'ery** n. clowning

bug n. any small insect; inf. disease, infection; concealed listening device —vt. install secret microphone etc.

bug'bear n. object of needless terror; nuisance

bugg'er n. sodomite; vulg. sl. unpleasant person or thing —sl. vt. tire; (with up) ruin, complicate

bu'gle n. instrument like trumpet —**bu'gler** n.

bu'gloss n. shrub with blue flower clusters

build [bild] v. make, construct, by putting together parts or materials (built pt./pp.) —n. make, form —**build'er** n. —**build'ing** n. —**built-up** a. having many buildings

bulb n. modified leaf bud emitting roots from base, eg onion; anything resembling this; globe surrounding filament of electric light —vi. form bulbs —**bulb'ous** a.

bul'bul n. tropical songbird

bulge n. swelling, protuberance; temporary increase —vi. swell out —**bulg'iness** n. —**bulg'y** a.

bulk n. size; volume; greater

part; cargo —vi. be of weight or importance —**bulk'iness** n. —**bulk'y** a.

bulk'head n. partition in interior of ship

bull[1] n. male of cattle; male of various other animals —**bull'dog** n. thickset breed of dog —**bull'doze** v. —**bull'dozer** n. powerful tractor with blade for excavating etc. —**bu'llock** n. castrated bull —**bull's-eye** middle part of target

bull[2] n. papal edict

bull[3] sl. n. nonsense —v. talk nonsense (to)

bull'et n. projectile discharged from rifle, pistol etc.

bull'etin n. official report

bull'ion n. gold or silver in mass

bull'y n. one who hurts, persecutes, or intimidates weaker people —vt. intimidate, overawe; illtreat (**bull'ied, bull'ying**) —bully beef corned beef

bul'rush n. tall reedlike marsh plant with brown velvety spike

bul'wark n. rampart; any defence or means of security; raised side of ship; breakwater

bum sl. n. buttocks, anus; US loafer, scrounger —vt. get by scrounging —a. useless

bum'ble v. perform clumsily —**bum'bler** n.

bum'blebee n. large bee

bump n. heavy blow, dull in sound; swelling caused by blow; protuberance; sudden movement —vt. strike or push against —**bump'er** n. horizontal bar at front and rear of motor vehicle to protect against damage; full glass —a. full, abundant —bump off sl. murder

bumph, bumf n. inf. useless documents, information etc.

bump'kin n. rustic

bump'tious a. offensively self-assertive

bun *n.* small, round cake; round knot of hair

bunch *n.* number of things tied or growing together; cluster; tuft, knot; group, party —*vt.* put together in bunch —*vi.* gather together —**bunch′y** *a.*

bun′dle *n.* package; number of things tied together; *sl.* lot of money —*vt.* tie in bundle; send (off) without ceremony

bun′du [boon′doo] *n.* **SA** wild uninhabited country

bung *n.* stopper for cask; large cork —*vt.* stop up, seal, close; *inf.* throw, sling —**bung′hole** *n.*

bun′galow [bung′gə-lō] *n.* one-storeyed house

bun′gle [bung′gl] *vt.* do badly from lack of skill, botch —*vt.* act clumsily, awkwardly —*n.* blunder, muddle —**bun′gled** *a.* —**bun′gler** *n.* —**bun′gling** *a.*

bun′ion *n.* inflamed swelling on foot or toe

bunk[1] *n.* narrow, shelflike bed —**bunk bed** one of pair of beds constructed one above the other

bunk[2] *n. sl.* hasty departure —*v.*

bunk[3] *n. see* BUNKUM

bunk′er *n.* large storage container for oil, coal *etc.*; sandy hollow on golf course; (military) underground defensive position

bunk′um *n.* nonsense

bunn′y *inf. n.* rabbit

Bun′sen burn′er gas burner, producing great heat, used for chemical experiments

bun′ting[1] *n.* material for flags

bun′ting[2] *n.* bird with short, stout bill

buoy [boi] *n.* floating marker anchored in sea; lifebuoy —*vt.* mark with buoy; keep from sinking; support —**buoy′ancy** *n.* —**buoy′ant** *a.*

bur(r) *n.* head of plant with prickles or hooks

bur′ble *vi.* gurgle, as stream or baby; talk idly

burd′en[1] *n.* load; weight, cargo; anything difficult to bear —*vt.* load, encumber —**burd′ensome** *a.*

burd′en[2] *n.* chorus of a song; chief theme

bur′dock *n.* plant with prickly burs

bu′reau [-rō] *n.* writing desk; office; government department (*pl.* **-reaus, -reaux**) —**bureau′cracy** [-ok′-] *n.* government by officials; body of officials —**bu′reaucrat** *n.* —**bureaucrat′ic** *a.*

bur′gee [-jē] *n.* small nautical flag

bur′geon [jən] *vi.* bud; develop rapidly

bur′gess [-jis] *n.* inhabitant of borough, *esp.* citizen with full municipal rights

burgh [bur′ə] *n.* Scottish borough —**burgh′er** [ber′gər] *n.* citizen

burg′lar *n.* one who enters building to commit crime, *esp.* theft —**burg′lary** *n.* —**bur′gle** *vt.*

bur′gundy *n.* name of various wines, white and red

bur′lap *n.* coarse canvas

burlesque[1] [-esk′] *n.* (artistic) caricature; ludicrous imitation —*vt.* caricature

bur′ly *a.* sturdy, stout, robust —**bur′liness** *n.*

burn[1] *vi.* destroy or injure by fire —*vi.* be on fire, *lit.* or *fig.*; be consumed by fire (**burned** or **burnt** *pt./pp.*) —*n.* injury, mark caused by fire —**burn′ing** *a.*

burn[2] *n. Scot.* small stream

bur′nish *vt.* make bright by rubbing; polish —*n.* gloss, lustre —**burn′isher** *n.*

burp *v. inf.* belch (*esp.* of baby) —*n.*

burr[1] *n.* soft trilling sound given to letter *r* in some dialects

burr [2] *n.* rough edge left after cutting, drilling *etc.*

burr'o *n.* donkey (*pl.* **-os**)

burr'ow [-rō] *n.* hole dug by rabbit *etc.* —*vt.* make holes in ground; bore; conceal oneself

burs'ar *n.* official managing finances of college, school *etc.* —**burs'ary** *n.* scholarship

burst *vi.* fly asunder; break into pieces; rend; break suddenly into some expression of feeling —*vt.* shatter, break violently —*n.* bursting; explosion; outbreak; spurt

bur'y [ber'i] *vt.* put underground; inter; conceal (**bur'ied, bur'ying**) —**bur'ial** *n./a.*

bus *n.* (*orig.* omnibus) large motor vehicle for passengers —*v.* travel or transport by bus

bus. business

bus'by [-z'-] *n.* tall fur hat worn by certain soldiers

bush [-oo-] *n.* shrub; woodland, thicket; (*Aust., S Afr., Canad. etc.*) uncleared country, backwoods, interior —**bushed** *a.* A lost, bewildered; tired out —**bush'y** *a.* shaggy —**bush'baby** *n.* tree-living, nocturnal Afr. animal —**bush fire** widespread destructive fire in the bush —**bush jacket** shirt-like jacket with patch pockets —**bush'veld** [-felt] *n.* SA bushy countryside

bush'el [-oo-] *n.* dry measure of eight gallons

bus'iness [biz'nis] *n.* profession, occupation; commercial or industrial establishment; commerce, trade; responsibility, affair, matter; work —**bus'inesslike** *a.* —**business park** area designated and landscaped for business of offices, warehouses, *etc.*

busk'er *n.* one who makes money by singing, dancing *etc.* in the street —**busk** *vi.*

bust [1] *n.* sculpture of head and shoulders of human body; woman's breasts

bust [2] *inf.* *v.* burst; make, become bankrupt —*vt.* raid; arrest —*a.* broken; bankrupt —*n.* police raid or arrest

bus'tard *n.* large swift-running bird

bus'tle [1] [-sol] *vi.* be noisily busy, active —*n.* fuss, commotion

bus'tle [2] [-sol] *n. Hist.* pad worn by ladies to support back of the skirt

bus'y [biz'i] *a.* actively employed; full of activity —*vt.* occupy (**bus'ied, bus'ying**) —**bus'ily** *adv.* —**bus'ybody** *n.* meddler —**busy lizzie** house plant

but *prep./conj.* without; except; only; yet; still; besides

bu'tane [byoo-] *n.* gas used for fuel

butch *a./n. sl.* markedly or aggressively masculine (person)

butch'er [-oo-] *n.* one who kills animals for food, or sells meat; bloody, savage man —*vt.* slaughter, murder; spoil work —**butch'ery** *n.*

but'ler *n.* chief male servant

butt [1] *n.* the thick end; target; object of ridicule; bottom or unused end of anything —*v.* lie, be placed end on to

butt [2] *v.* strike with head; push —*n.* blow with head, as of sheep —**butt in** interfere, meddle

butt [3] *n.* large cask

butt'er *n.* fatty substance got from cream by churning —*vt.* spread with butter; flatter

butt'ercup *n.* plant of genus *Ranunculus* with glossy, yellow flowers

butt'erfingers *n.* (*with sing. v.*) *inf.* person who drops things by mistake or fails to catch things —**butt'erfingered** *a.*

butt'erfly *n.* insect with large wings; inconstant person; stroke in swimming —*pl. inf.* tremors in stomach region due to nervousness

butt'ermilk *n.* milk that remains after churning

butt'erscotch *n.* kind of hard, brittle toffee

butt'ery *n.* storeroom for food or wine

butt'ock *n.* rump, protruding hinder part (*usu. pl.*)

butt'on *n.* knob, stud for fastening dress; knob that operates doorbell, machine *etc.* —*vt.* fasten with buttons —**butt'onhole** *n.* slit in garment to pass button through as fastening; flower, spray worn on lapel *etc.* —*vt.* detain (unwilling) person in conversation

butt'ress *n.* structure to support wall; prop —*vt.*

bux'om *a.* full of health, plump, gay; large-breasted

buy [bī] *vt.* get by payment, purchase; bribe (**bought** *pt./pp.*) —**buy'er** *n.*

buzz *vi.* make humming sound —*n.* humming sound of bees; *inf.* telephone call —**buzz'er** *n.* any apparatus that makes buzzing sound —**buzz word** *inf.* word, oft. orig. jargon, that becomes fashionable

buzz'ard *n.* bird of prey of hawk family

by *prep.* near; along; across; past; during; not later than; through use or agency of; in units of —*adv.* near; away, aside; past —**by and by** soon, in the future —**by and large** on the whole; speaking generally —**come by** obtain

by- (*comb. form*) subsidiary, incidental, out-of-the-way, near, as in **by'path, by'product, by'stander**

bye *n. Sport* situation where player, team, wins by default of opponent; *Cricket* run scored off

ball not touched by batsman

by(e)-election parliamentary election caused by death or resignation of member

by(e)law *n.* law, regulation made by local subordinate authority

by'gone *a.* past, former —*n.* (*oft. pl.*) past occurrence; small antique

by'pass *n.* road for diversion of traffic from crowded centres

by'play *n.* diversion, action apart from main action of play

byre [bīr] *n.* cowshed

byte *n. Computers* sequence of bits processed as single unit of information

by'word *n.* a well-known name, saying

C

C *Chem.* carbon; Celsius; Centigrade; Conservative

c. carat; cent; century; circa; copyright

CA chartered accountant

Ca *Chem.* calcium

cab *n.* taxi; driver's enclosed compartment on locomotive, lorry *etc.* —**cab'man, cabb'y** *n.*

cabal' *n.* small group of intriguers; secret plot

cab'aret [-rā] *n.* floor show at a nightclub or restaurant

cabb'age *n.* green vegetable with usu. round head of leaves

ca'ber [kā-] *n.* pole tossed as trial of strength at Highland games

cab'in *n.* hut, shed; small room *esp.* in ship —*vt.* cramp, confine —**cabin boy** —**cabin cruiser** power boat with cabin, bunks *etc.*

cab'inet *n.* piece of furniture with drawers or shelves; outer case of television, radio *etc.*; committee of politicians governing country; *obs.* small room **—cabinet-maker** *n.* craftsman who makes fine furniture

ca'ble *n.* strong rope; wire or bundle of wires conveying electric power, telegraph signals *etc.*; message sent by this; nautical unit of measurement (100-120 fathoms) *—v.* telegraph by cable **—ca'blegram** *n.* cabled message **—cable television** television service conveyed by cable to subscribers

caboo'dle *n. inf.* **—the whole caboodle** the whole lot

caboose' *n.* ship's galley; **US** guard's van on a train

cab'riolet [-lā] *n.* early type of hansom cab

caca'o [-kah'-] *n.* tropical tree from the seeds of which chocolate and cocoa are made

cach'alot [kash'-] *n.* the sperm whale

cache [kash] *n.* secret hiding place; store of food *etc.*

cach'et [kash'ā] *n.* mark, stamp; mark of authenticity; prestige; distinction

cack'le *vi.* make chattering noise, as hen *—n.* cackling noise or laughter; empty chatter **—cack'ler** *n.*

caco'phony *n.* disagreeable sound; discord of sounds **—cacoph'onous** *a.*

cac'tus *n.* spiny succulent plant (*pl.* **cac'tuses, cac'ti** [-tī])

cad *n.* dishonourable, unchivalrous person

cadav'er *n.* corpse **—cadav'erous** *a.* corpselike; sickly-looking; gaunt

cadd'ie, -y *n.* golfer's attendant

cadd'y *n.* small box for tea

ca'dence *n.* fall or modulation of voice in music or verse

caden'za *n. Mus.* elaborate passage for solo instrument or singer

cadet' *n.* youth in training, *esp.* for officer status in armed forces

cadge [kaj] *v.* get (food, money *etc.*) by begging **—cadg'er** *n.* sponger

cad'mium *n.* metallic element

cad're [kahd'ər] *n.* nucleus or framework, *esp.* skeleton of regiment

cae'cum [sē'kəm] *n. Anat.* pouch *esp.* at beginning of large intestine (*pl.* **-ca**)

Caesa'rean section surgical incision through abdominal wall to deliver a baby

caf'é [-ā] *n.* small or inexpensive restaurant serving light refreshments **—cafete'ria** *n.* restaurant designed for self-service

caff'eine [-ēn] *n.* stimulating alkaloid found in tea and coffee plants

caf'tan *n. see* KAFTAN

cage *n.* enclosure, box with bars or wires, *esp.* for keeping animals or birds; place of confinement; enclosed platform of lift, *esp.* in mine *—vt.* put in cage, confine **—ca'gey** *a.* wary, not communicative

cagoule' [kəgōōl'] *n.* lightweight, *usu.* knee-length, anorak

cahoots' *pl.n. sl.* partnership, as **in cahoots with**

cairn *n.* heap of stones, *esp.* as monument or landmark

cairn'gorm *n.* yellow or brownish coloured gem

caisson' [kəsōōn'] *n.* chamber for working under water; apparatus for lifting vessel out of the water; ammunition wagon

cai'tiff [kā'-] *n. obs.* mean, despicable fellow *—a.* base, mean

cajole' *vt.* persuade by flattery, wheedle **—cajole'ment** *n.* **—cajo'ler** *n.* **—cajo'lery** *n.*

cake *n.* baked, sweetened, breadlike food; compact mass —v. make into a cake; harden (as of mud)

cal'amine n. pink powder used medicinally in soothing ointment

calam'ity n. great misfortune; deep distress, disaster —**calam'i-tous** a.

calceola'ria n. Amer. plant with speckled, slipper-shaped flowers

cal'cium n. metallic element, the basis of lime —**calca'reous, -ious** a. containing lime —**cal'ci-fy** v. convert, be converted, to lime —**cal'cine** [-sīn] vt. reduce to quicklime; burn to ashes

cal'culate vt. estimate; compute —vi. make reckonings —**cal'culable** a. —**cal'culating** a. able to perform calculations; shrewd, designing, scheming —**calcula'tion** n. —**cal'culator** n. electronic device for making calculations —**cal'culus** n. branch of mathematics; stone in body (pl. **cal'culi** [-ī])

cal'dron [kawl-] see CAULDRON

cal'endar n. table of months and days in the year; list of events, documents, register —vt. enter in a list; index

calen'dula n. marigold

calf [kahf] n. young of cow and of other animals; leather made of calf's skin (pl. **calves** [kahvz]) —**calve** vi. give birth to calf

calf [kahf] n. fleshy back part of leg below knee (pl. **calves** [kahvz])

cal'ibre [-bər] n. size of bore of gun; capacity, character —**cal'ibrate** vt. mark scale of measuring instrument etc. —**calibra'tion** n.

cal'ico n. cotton cloth

calk see CAULK

call [kawl] vt. speak loudly to attract attention; summon; (oft. with up) telephone; name —vi.

shout; pay visit —n. shout; animal's cry; visit; inner urge, summons, as to be priest etc.; need, demand —**call'er** n. —**call'ing** n. vocation, profession —**call box** kiosk for a public telephone —**call up** summon to serve in army; imagine

callig'raphy n. handwriting, penmanship —**calligraph'ic** a.

cal'liper n. metal splint for leg —pl. instrument for measuring diameters

callisthen'ics [-is-then'-] pl.n. light gymnastic exercises —**callisthen'ic** a.

cal'lous a. hardened, unfeeling —**cal'lously** adv. —**cal'lousness** n.

cal'low a. inexperienced; immature

cal'lus n. area of thick, hardened skin

calm [kahm] a. still, quiet, tranquil —n. stillness; tranquillity; absence of wind —v. become, make, still or quiet —**calm'ly** adv. —**calm'ness** n.

cal'orie, -ory n. unit of heat; unit of energy obtained from foods —**calorif'ic** a. heat-making —**calorim'eter** n.

cal'umet [-yoo-] n. tobacco pipe of N Amer. Indians; pipe of peace

cal'umny n. slander, false accusation —**calum'niate** vt. —**calumnia'tion** n. —**calum'niator** n. —**calum'nious** a.

calyp'so n. (West Indies) improvised song on topical subject

ca'lyx n. covering of bud (pl. **ca'lyxes, ca'lyces** [-sēz])

cam n. device to change rotary to reciprocating motion —**cam'-shaft** n. in motoring, rotating shaft to which cams are fixed to lift valves

camarad'erie [-rahd'-] n. spirit of comradeship, trust

cam'ber n. convexity on upper

surface of road, bridge *etc.*; curvature of aircraft wing

cam'bric *n.* fine white linen or cotton cloth

cam'corder *n.* combined portable video camera and recorder

came *pt.* of COME

cam'el *n.* animal of Asia and Africa, with humped back, used as beast of burden

came'llia *n.* ornamental shrub

cam'eo *n.* medallion, brooch *etc.* with profile head or design carved in relief; single brief scene or appearance in film *etc.* by (well-known) actor

cam'era *n.* apparatus used to make photographs —**cam'eraman** *n.* photographer, *esp.* for television or cinema —**camera obscura** darkened chamber in which views of surrounding country are shown on sheet by means of lenses —**in camera** (of legal proceedings *etc.*) conducted in private

cam'isole *n.* underbodice

c(h)am'omile *n.* aromatic creeping plant, used medicinally

cam'ouflage [-ahzh] *n.* disguise, means of deceiving enemy observation, *eg* by paint, screen —*vt.* disguise

camp *n.* (place for) tents of hikers, army *etc.*; cabins *etc.* for temporary accommodation; group supporting political party *etc.*; *SA* field, pasture —*a.* *inf.* homosexual; consciously artificial —*vi.* form or lodge in a camp —**camp'er** *n.* —**camp'ing** *n.*

campaign' [-pán'] *n.* series of coordinated activities for some purpose, *eg* political or military campaign —*vi.* serve in campaign —**campaign'er** *n.*

campanol'ogy *n.* art of ringing bells musically

campan'ula *n.* plant with blue or white bell-shaped flowers

cam'phor *n.* solid essential oil with aromatic taste and smell —**cam'phorated** *a.* —**camphor'ic** *a.*

cam'pion *n.* white or pink wild flower

cam'pus *n.* grounds of college or university

can[1] *vi.* be able; have the power; be allowed (**could** *pt.*)

can[2] *n.* container, usu. metal, for liquids, foods —*v.* put in can (**-nn-**) —**canned** *a.* preserved in can; (of music, programmes *etc.*) previously recorded —**cann'ery** *n.* factory where food is canned

Canada Day July 1st, anniversary of establishment of Confederation in 1867

Canada goose large greyishbrown N Amer. goose

Cana'dian *n./a.* (native) of Canada

canal' *n.* artificial watercourse; duct in body —**canaliza'tion** *n.* —**can'alize** *vt.* convert into canal; direct (thoughts, energies *etc.*) into one channel

can'apé [-pē] *n.* small piece of toast *etc.* with savoury topping

cana'ry *n.* yellow singing bird

canas'ta *n.* card game played with two packs

can'can *n.* high-kicking (orig. French music-hall) dance

can'cel *vt.* cross out; annul; call off (**-ll-**) —**cancella'tion** *n.*

can'cer *n.* malignant growth or tumour —**can'cerous** *a.*

Can'cer *n.* crab, 4th sign of zodiac, operative c. June 21-July 21; constellation —**tropic of Cancer** parallel of latitude 23° 27′ N of the equator

can'dela *n.* basic SI unit of luminous intensity

can'did *a.* frank, open, impartial —**can'didly** *adv.* —**can'didness, can'dour** *n.* frankness

can'didate *n.* one who seeks

office, appointment *etc.*; person taking examination or test —**can'didature** *n.*

can'dle *n.* stick of wax with wick; light —**candela'brum** [-lahb'-] *n.* large, branched candle holder (*pl.* -**bra**) —**can'dlepower** *n.* unit for measuring light —**can'dlestick** *n.* —**can'dlewick** *n.* cotton fabric with tufted surface

can'dy *n.* crystallized sugar; US confectionery in general —*vt.* preserve with sugar —*vi.* become encrusted with sugar (**can'died, can'dying**) —**can'died** *a.*

can'dytuft *n.* garden plant with clusters of white, pink or purple flowers

cane *n.* stem of small palm or large grass; walking stick —*vt.* beat with cane

ca'nine *a.* like, pert. to, dog —**canine tooth** one of four sharp, pointed teeth, two in each jaw

can'ister *n.* container, *usu.* of metal, *esp.* for storing dry food

cank'er *n.* eating sore; thing that eats away, destroys, corrupts —*vt.* infect, corrupt —*vi.* decay —**cank'ered, cank'erous** *a.* —**cank'erworm** *n.*

cann'a *n.* tropical flowering plant

cann'abis *n.* hemp plant; drug derived from this

cannello'ni *n.* tubular pieces of pasta filled with meat *etc.*

cann'ibal *n.* one who eats human flesh —*a.* relating to this practice —**cann'ibalism** *n.* —**cannibalis'tic** *a.* —**can'nibalize** *vt.* use parts from one machine *etc.* to repair another

cann'on [1] *n.* large gun (*pl.* -**ons** or -**on**) —**cannonade'** *n./v.* attack with cannon —**cann'onball** *n.* —**cannon bone** horse's leg bone

cann'on [2] *n.* billiard stroke, hitting both object balls with one's own —*vi.* make this stroke; rebound, collide

cann'ot negative form of CAN [1]

can'ny *a.* shrewd; cautious; crafty —**cann'ily** *adv.*

canoe' [-nōō'] *n.* very light boat propelled with paddle or paddles (*pl.* -**oes'**) —**canoe'ist** *n.*

can'on [1] *n.* law or rule, *esp.* of church; standard; body of books accepted as genuine; list of saints —**canoniza'tion** *n.* —**can'onize** *vt.* enrol in list of saints

can'on [2] *n.* church dignitary, member of cathedral chapter —**canon'ical** *a.* —**canonis'tic** *a.*

can'opy *n.* covering over throne, bed *etc.*; any overhanging shelter —*vt.* cover with canopy (**-opied, -opying**)

cant [1] *n.* hypocritical speech; whining; language of a sect; technical jargon; slang, *esp.* of thieves —*vi.* use cant

cant [2] *v.* tilt, slope; bevel

can'taloupe, -loup, -lope *n.* variety of musk melon

cantank'erous *a.* ill-natured, quarrelsome

cantat'a [-taht'-] *n.* choral work like, but shorter than, oratorio

canteen' *n.* place in factory, school *etc.* where meals are provided; small shop in military camp; case of cutlery; mess tin

can'ter *n.* easy gallop —*v.* move at, make to canter

Can'terbury bell cultivated campanula

can'ticle *n.* short hymn

can'tilever *n.* beam, girder *etc.* fixed at one end only

can'to [-tō] *n.* division of a poem (*pl.* -**tos**)

can'ton *n.* division of country, *esp.* Swiss federal state

canton'ment [-tōōn'-] *n.* quarters for troops

can'vas n. coarse cloth used for sails, painting on *etc.*; sails of ship; picture

can'vass vt. solicit votes, contributions etc.; discuss, examine —n. solicitation

can'yon n. deep gorge

cap n. covering for head; lid, top, or other covering —vt. put a cap on; outdo; select for a team (-**pp-**)

ca'pable a. able, gifted; competent; having the capacity, power —**capabil'ity** n.

capac'ity [-pas'-] n. power of holding or grasping; room; volume; character; ability, power of mind —**capa'cious** a. roomy —**capac'itance** n. (measure of) ability of system to store electric charge —**capac'itor** n.

capar'ison [-pa'ri-] n. ornamental covering, equipment for horse —vt. adorn thus

cape [1] n. covering for shoulders

cape [2] n. point of land running into sea, headland —**cape pigeon** pied petrel of southern oceans —**Cape salmon SA** the geelbek —**Cape sparrow** common S Afr. bird

ca'per [1] n. skip; frolic; escapade —vi. skip, dance

ca'per [2] n. pickled flower bud of Sicilian shrub

capercail'zie [kap-ər-kā'lyi] n. large black grouse

capill'ary a. hairlike —n. tube with very small bore, *esp.* small blood vessel

cap'ital n. chief town; money, stock, funds; large-sized letter; headpiece of column —a. involving or punishable by death; serious; chief; leading; excellent —**cap'italism** n. economic system which is based on private ownership of industry —**cap'italist** n. owner of capital; supporter of capitalism —a. run by, possessing, capital, as capitalist state

—**cap'italize** v. convert into capital; (*with* on) turn to advantage —**cap'itally** adv.

capita'tion n. tax or grant per head; census

Cap'itol n. U.S. Congress House; a U.S. state legislature building; temple of Jupiter in Rome

capit'ulate vi. surrender on terms, give in —**capitula'tion** n.

ca'pon n. castrated cock fowl fattened for eating —**ca'ponize** vt.

cappucci'no [-chē'-] n. coffee with steamed milk

caprice' [-ēs'] n. whim, freak —**capri'cious** a. —**capri'ciousness** n.

Cap'ricorn n. sea-goat, 10th sign of zodiac, operative c. Dec. 21-Jan. 19; constellation —**tropic of Capricorn** parallel of latitude 23° 27' S of the equator

cap'sicum n. tropical vegetable with mild peppery flavour, sweet pepper

capsize' vt. (of boat) upset —vi. be overturned —**capsi'zal** n.

cap'stan n. machine to wind cable, *esp.* to hoist anchor

cap'sule [-syool] n. gelatin case for dose of medicine or drug; any small enclosed area or container; seed vessel of plant

Capt. Captain

cap'tain [-tin] n. commander of vessel or company of soldiers; leader, chief —vt. be captain of

cap'tion n. heading, title of article, picture etc.

cap'tious [-shəs] a. ready to find fault; critical; peevish —**cap'tiously** adv. —**cap'tiousness** n.

cap'tive n. prisoner —a. taken, imprisoned —**cap'tivate** vt. fascinate —**cap'tivating** a. delightful —**captiv'ity** n.

cap'ture vt. seize, make prisoner —n. seizure, taking —**cap'tor** n.

capybar'a [-bahr'-] *n.* the largest rodent, found in S Amer.

car *n.* self-propelled road vehicle; passenger compartment, as in cable car; railway carriage of specified type —**car park** area, building where vehicles may be left for a time

carafe' [-raf'] *n.* glass water-bottle for the table, decanter

car'amel [ka'rə-] *n.* burnt sugar for cooking; type of confectionery

car'at [ka'rət] *n.* small weight used for gold, diamonds *etc.*; proportional measure of twenty-fourths used to state fineness of gold

car'avan [ka'rə-] *n.* large enclosed vehicle for living in, pulled as trailer by car *etc.*; company of merchants travelling together for safety in the East

car'away [ka'rə-] *n.* plant of which the seeds are used as a spice in cakes *etc.*

carb'ide *n.* compound of carbon with an element, *esp.* calcium carbide

carb'ine *n.* short rifle —**carbineer'** *n.*

carbohy'drate *n.* any of large group of compounds containing carbon, hydrogen and oxygen, *esp.* sugars and starches as components of food

carbol'ic (acid) disinfectant derived from coal tar

carb'on *n.* nonmetallic element, substance of pure charcoal, found in all organic matter —**car'bonate** *n.* salt of carbonic acid —**carbon'ic** *a.* —**carbonif'erous** *a.* —**carb'onize** *vt.* —**carbonic acid** carbon dioxide; compound formed by carbon dioxide and water —**carbon dioxide** colourless gas exhaled in respiration of animals —**carbon paper** paper coated with a dark, waxy pigment, used for duplicating written or typed matter, producing **carbon copy**

carborun'dum *n.* artificial silicate of carbon

car'boy *n.* large glass jar protected by wicker casing

car'buncle *n.* inflamed ulcer, boil or tumour; fiery-red precious stone

carburett'or [-byoo-] *n.* device for vaporizing and mixing petrol with air in internal combustion engine

carc'ass, carc'ase *n.* dead animal body; *orig.* skeleton

carcin'ogen [-sin'-] *n.* substance producing cancer

carcino'ma [-sin-] *n.* a cancer

card[1] *n.* thick, stiff paper; piece of this giving identification *etc.*; illustrated card sending greetings *etc.*; one of the 52 playing cards making up a pack; *inf.* any card game —**card'board** *n.* thin, stiff board made of paper pulp —**card index** index in which each entry is made on separate card

card[2] *n.* instrument for combing wool *etc.* —*vt.* comb —**card'er** *n.*

car'diac *a.* pert. to the heart —*n.* heart stimulant —**car'dioid** *a.* heart-shaped —**car'diograph** *n.* instrument which records movements of the heart —**car'diogram** *n.* graph of such

card'igan *n.* knitted woollen jacket, waistcoat

card'inal *a.* chief, principal —*n.* highest rank, next to the Pope in R.C. church —**car'dinalate** *n.* —**cardinal numbers** 1, 2, 3, *etc.* —**cardinal points** N, S, E, W

care *vi.* be anxious; have regard or liking (for); look after; be disposed to —*n.* attention; pains; heed; charge, protection; anxiety; caution —**care'free** *a.* —**care'ful**

a. —**care'fully** *adv.* —**care'ful-ness** *n.* —**care'less** *a.* —**care'lessness** *n.* —**care'taker** *n.* person in charge of premises —*a.* temporary, interim

careen' *vt.* lay ship over on her side for cleaning and repair —*vi.* keel over; sway dangerously

career' *n.* course through life; profession; rapid motion —*vi.* run or move at full speed

caress' *vt.* fondle, embrace, treat with affection —*n.* act or expression of affection

car'et [ka'rit] *n.* mark (‸) showing where to insert something omitted

car'go *n.* load, freight, carried by ship, plane *etc.* (*pl.* -**goes**)

car'ibou [ka'ri-bōō] *n.* N Amer. reindeer

car'icature [ka'ri-] *n.* likeness exaggerated or distorted to appear ridiculous —*vt.* portray in this way

ca'ries [kā'ri-ēz] *n.* decay of tooth or bone

carill'on [-yən *or* ka'-] *n.* set of bells *usu.* hung in tower and played by set of keys, pedals *etc.*; tune so played

car'minative *n.* medicine to remedy flatulence —*a.* acting as this

car'mine *n.* brilliant red colour (prepared from cochineal) —*a.* of this colour

carn'age *n.* slaughter

carn'al *a.* fleshly, sensual; worldly —**carn'alism** *n.* —**carn'ality** *n.* —**carn'ally** *adv.*

carna'tion *n.* cultivated flower; flesh colour

carn'ival *n.* festive occasion; travelling fair; show or display for amusement

carniv'orous *a.* flesh-eating —**carn'ivore** *n.*

car'ob [ka'rɔb] *n.* Mediterranean tree with edible pods

car'ol [ka'rəl] *n.* song or hymn of joy or praise (*esp.* Christmas carol) —*vi.* sing (carols) (-**ll**-)

carouse' [-owz'] *vi.* have merry drinking spree —*n.* —**carous'al** *n.* —**carous'er** *n.*

carousel' [-rə-sel'] *n.* US merry-go-round

carp[1] *n.* freshwater fish

carp[2] *vi.* complain about small faults or errors; nag —**carp'er** *n.* —**carp'ing** *a.* —**carp'ingly** *adv.*

carp'enter *n.* worker in timber as in building *etc.* —**carp'entry** *n.* this art

carp'et *n.* heavy fabric for covering floor —*vt.* cover floor; call up for censure —**carp'etbag** *n.* travelling bag —**carp'etbagger** *n.* political adventurer

carr'iage [-ij] *n.* railway coach; bearing, conduct; horse-drawn vehicle; act, cost, of carrying —**carr'iageway** *n.* part of a road along which traffic passes in a single line

carr'iole *n.* small open carriage for one

carr'ion *n.* rotting dead flesh —**carrion crow**

carr'ot *n.* plant with orange-red edible root; inducement —**carr'oty** *a.* red, reddish

carr'y *vt.* convey; transport; capture, win; effect; behave —*vi.* (of projectile, sound) reach (**carr'ied**, **carr'ying**) —*n.* range —**carr'ier** *n.* one that carries goods; one who, himself immune, communicates a disease to others; aircraft carrier; kind of pigeon —**carry on** continue; *inf.* fuss unnecessarily

cart *n.* open (two-wheeled) vehicle, *esp.* pulled by horse —*vt.* convey in cart; carry with effort —**cart'age** *n.* —**cart'er** *n.* —**cart'horse** *n.* —**cart'wheel** *n.* large, spoked wheel; sideways somersault —**cart'wright** n. maker of carts

carte blanche' [blahnch'] Fr. complete discretion or authority

cartel' n. industrial combination for the purpose of fixing prices, output etc.; alliance of political parties etc. to further common aims

Carte'sian a. pert. to the French philosopher René Descartes (1596-1650) or his system of coordinates —n. an adherent of his philosophy

cart'ilage n. firm elastic tissue in the body; gristle —**cartilag'inous** [-aj'-] a.

cartog'raphy n. map making —**cartog'rapher** n.

cart'on n. cardboard or plastic container

cartoon' n. drawing, esp. humorous or satirical; sequence of drawings telling story; preliminary design for painting —**cartoon'ist** n.

cart'ridge n. case containing charge for gun; container for film, magnetic tape etc.; unit in head of gramophone pick-up —**cartridge paper** strong, thick paper

carve vt. cut; hew; sculpture; engrave; cut in pieces or slices (meat) —**carv'er** n. —**carv'ing** n.

caryat'id [karē-] n. supporting column in shape of female figure

cascade' n. waterfall; anything resembling this —vi. fall in cascades

case¹ n. instance; event, circumstance; question at issue; state of affairs, condition; arguments supporting particular action etc.; Med. patient under treatment; law suit; grounds for suit; grammatical relation of words in sentence

case² n. box, sheath, covering; receptacle; box and contents —vt. put in a case —**case-harden** vt. harden by carbonizing the surface of (esp. iron) by converting into steel; make hard, callous

ca'sein [kā'sē-in] n. protein in milk and its products —**ca'seous** a. like cheese

case'ment [kās'-] n. window opening on hinges

cash n. money, banknotes and coin —vt. turn into or exchange for money —**cashier'** n. one in charge of receiving and paying of money —**cash'book** n. —**cash dispenser** computerized device outside a bank for supplying cash —**cash'book** n. —**cash register** till that records amount of money put in

cashier' vt. dismiss from office or service

cash'mere n. fine soft fabric; shawl made from goat's wool

casi'no [-sē-] n. building, institution for gambling (pl. **-os**)

cask [-ah-] n. barrel; container for wine

cask'et [-ah-] n. small case for jewels etc.; US coffin

cassat'a [-saht'-] n. ice cream, esp. containing fruit and nuts

cass'erole n. fireproof cooking and serving dish; kind of stew cooked in this dish

cassette' n. plastic container for film, magnetic tape etc.

cass'ock n. long tunic worn by clergymen

cast [kah-] v. throw or fling; shed; throw down; deposit (a vote); allot, as parts in play; mould, as metal —n. throw; distance thrown; squint; mould; that which is shed or ejected; set of actors; type or quality —**cast'ing** n. —**cast'away** n. shipwrecked person —**casting vote** decisive vote

castanets' pl.n. (in Spanish dancing) two small curved

pieces of wood *etc.* clicked together in hand

caste [kah-] *n.* section of society in India; social rank

cast'er sugar [kah-] finely powdered sugar (also **castor sugar**)

cas'tigate *vt.* punish, rebuke severely, correct; chastise —**castiga'tion** *n.* —**cas'tigator** *n.* —**castiga'tory** *a.*

cas'tle [kahs'l] *n.* fortress; country mansion; chess piece

cast'or [kah-] *n.* bottle with perforated top; small swivelled wheel on table leg *etc.*

castor oil vegetable medicinal oil

castrate' *vt.* remove testicles, deprive of power of generation —**castra'tion** *n.*

cas'ual [-z'-] *a.* accidental; unforeseen; occasional; unconcerned; informal —**cas'ually** *adv.* —**cas'ualty** *n.* person killed or injured in accident, war *etc.*; thing lost, destroyed, in accident *etc.* (*pl.* **-ties**)

cas'uist [-z'-] *n.* one who studies and solves moral problems; quibbler —**casuis'tical** *a.* —**cas'uistry** *n.*

cat *n.* any of various feline animals, including, *eg* small domesticated furred animal, and lions, tigers *etc.* —**catt'y** *a.* spiteful —**cat'call** *n.* derisive cry —**cat'fish** *n.* mainly freshwater fish with catlike whiskers —**cat'kin** *n.* drooping flower spike —**cat'mint** *n.* scented plant —**cat'nap** *vi./n.* doze —**Cat's'eye** R glass reflector set in road to indicate traffic lanes —**cat'walk** *n.* narrow, raised path or plank

catab'olism *n.* breaking down of complex molecules, destructive metabolism

cat'aclysm [-kli-zəm] *n.* (disastrous) upheaval; deluge —**cataclys'mal** *a.*

cat'acomb [-kōōm, -kōm] *n.* underground gallery for burial —*pl.* series of underground tunnels and caves

cat'alepsy *n.* condition of unconsciousness with rigidity of muscles —**catalep'tic** *a.*

cat'alogue [-log] *n.* descriptive list —*vt.* make such list of; enter in catalogue

cat'alyst *n.* substance causing or assisting a chemical reaction without taking part in it —**cat'alyse** *vt.* —**catal'ysis** *n.*

catamaran' *n.* type of sailing boat with twin hulls; raft of logs

cat'apult *n.* small forked stick with elastic sling used for throwing stones; *Hist.* engine of war for hurling arrows, stones *etc.*; launching device —*vt.*

cat'aract *n.* waterfall; downpour; disease of eye

catarrh' *n.* inflammation of a mucous membrane —**catarrh'al** *a.*

catas'trophe [-fi] *n.* great disaster, calamity; culmination of a tragedy —**catastroph'ic** *a.*

catch *vt.* take hold of, seize, understand; hear; contract disease; be in time for; surprise, detect —*vi.* be contagious; get entangled; begin to burn (**caught** *pt./pp.*) —*n.* seizure; thing that holds, stops *etc.*; what is caught; *inf.* snag, disadvantage; form of musical composition; thing, person worth catching —**catch'er** *n.* —**catch'ing** *a.* —**catch'y** *a.* pleasant, memorable; tricky —**catch'penny** *a.* worthless; made to sell quickly —**catch'word** *n.* popular phrase or idea —**catch 22** inescapable dilemma —**catchment area** area in which rainfall collects to form the supply of river *etc.*; area from which people are allocated to a particular school, hospital *etc.*

cat'echize [-kīz] *vt.* instruct by question and answer; question —**catechet'ical** [-go'ri-] *a.* —**cat'echism** *n.* —**cat'echist** *n.* —**catechu'men** *n.* one under instruction in Christianity

cat'egory *n.* class, order, division —**categor'ical** [-go'ri-] *a.* positive; of category —**categor'ically** *adv.* —**cat'egorize** *vt.*

catena'tion *n.* chain, or series as links of chain

ca'ter *vi.* provide what is required or desired, *esp.* food *etc.* —**ca'terer** *n.*

cat'erpillar *n.* hairy grub of moth or butterfly; type of tractor fitted with caterpillar wheels —**caterpillar wheel** articulated belt revolving round two or more wheels to propel heavy vehicle over difficult ground

cat'erwaul *vi.* wail, howl

cathe'dral *n.* principal church of diocese —*a.* pert. to, containing cathedral

cath'ode *n.* negative electrode —**cathode rays** stream of electrons

cath'olic *a.* universal; including whole body of Christians; (**C-**) relating to R.C. Church —*n.* (**C-**) adherent of R.C. Church —**Cathol'icism** *n.* —**catholic'ity** [-lis'-] *n.* —**cathol'icize** *vt.*

cat'tle *pl.n.* beasts of pasture, *esp.* oxen, cows —**cat'tleman** *n.* —**cattle-grid** *n.* heavy grid over ditch in road to prevent passage of livestock

Cau'casoid *a.* of, pert. to, light-complexioned racial group of mankind

cau'cus *n.* group, meeting, *esp.* of members of political party, with power to decide policy *etc.*

caught *pt./pp.* of CATCH

caul'dron *n.* large pot used for boiling

caul'iflower [kol'-] *n.* variety of cabbage with edible white flowering head

caulk [kawk] *vt.* stop up cracks (*orig.* of ship) with waterproof filler —**caulk'er** *n.* —**caulk'ing** *n.*

cause [-z] *n.* that which produces an effect; reason; origin; motive, purpose; charity, movement; lawsuit —*vt.* bring about, make happen —**caus'al** *a.* —**causal'ity** *n.* —**causa'tion** *n.* —**cause'less** *a.* groundless

cause célè'bre [-sə-leb'rə] *Fr.* famous case

cause'way [-z-] *n.* raised way over marsh *etc.*; paved street

caus'tic *a.* burning; bitter, severe —*n.* corrosive substance —**caus'tically** *adv.*

cau'terize *vt.* burn with caustic or hot iron —**cauteriza'tion** *n.* —**cau'tery** *n.*

cau'tion *n.* heedfulness, care; warning —*vt.* warn —**cau'tionary** *a.* containing warning or precept —**cau'tious** *a.* —**cau'tiously** *adv.* —**cau'tiousness** *n.*

cavalcade' *n.* column or procession of riders

cavalier' *a.* careless, disdainful —*n.* courtly gentleman; *obs.* horseman; (**C-**) adherent of Charles I in English Civil War —**cavalier'ly** *adv.*

cav'alry *n.* mounted troops

cave *n.* hollow place in the earth; den —**cav'ern** *n.* deep cave —**cav'ernous** *a.* —**cav'ernously** *adv.* —**ca'ving** *n.* sport of exploring caves —**cav'ity** *n.* hollow —**cave'man** *n.* prehistoric cave dweller —**cave in** fall in; submit; give in

caviar(e)' *n.* salted sturgeon roe

cav'il *vi.* find fault without sufficient reason, make trifling objections (-**ll**-) —**cav'illing** n. —**cav'-iller** n.

cavort' vi. prance, frisk

ca'vy n. small S Amer. rodent

caw n. crow's cry —vi. cry so

cayenne' (pepper) [kā-] n. pungent red pepper

CB Companion of the Order of the Bath; Citizens' Band

CBE Commander of the British Empire

CBI Confederation of British Industry

cc cubic centimetre(s)

Cd Chem. cadmium

CD compact disc —**CD-ROM** compact disc storing written information to be displayed on VDU

cease v. bring or come to an end —**cease'less** a. —**cease'lessly** adv.

ce'dar n. large evergreen tree; its wood

cede vt. yield, give up, transfer, esp. of territory

cedill'a n. hooklike mark placed under a letter c to show the sound of s

Ceefax R BBC teletext service

cei'lidh [kā'li] n. informal social gathering for singing and dancing esp. in Scotland

cei'ling [sē'-] n. inner, upper surface of a room; maximum price, wage etc.; Aviation lower level of clouds; limit of height to which aircraft can climb —**cei**l vt. line (room), esp. with plaster

celan'dine n. yellow wild flower

cel'ebrate v. rejoice or have festivities to mark (happy day, event etc.) —vt. observe (birthday etc.); perform (religious ceremony etc.); praise publicly —**cel'ebrant** n. —**cel'ebrated** a. famous —**celebra'tion** n. —**ce-leb'rity** n. famous person; fame

celer'ity n. swiftness

cel'ery n. vegetable with long juicy edible stalks

celes'tial a. heavenly; divine; of the sky

cel'ibacy n. single life, unmarried state —**cel'ibate** n.

cell n. small room, esp. in prison; small cavity; minute, basic unit of living matter; device converting chemical energy into electrical energy; small local group operating as nucleus of larger political or religious organization —**cell'ular** a. —**cell'ule** n. small cell

cell'ar n. underground room for storage; stock of wine —**cell'arage** n. —**cell'arer** n.

cell'o [ch-] n. stringed instrument of violin family

cell'ophane n. transparent wrapping

cell'uloid [-yoo-] n. synthetic plastic substance with wide range of uses; coating of photographic film; cinema film

cell'ulose [-yoo-] n. substance of vegetable cell wall; group of carbohydrates; varnish

Cel'sius a./n. (of) scale of temperature from 0° (melting point of ice) to 100° (boiling point of water)

Cel'tic [kel'tik or sel'-] n. branch of language including Gaelic and Welsh —a. of, or relating to the Celtic peoples or languages

cement' n. fine mortar; adhesive, glue —vt. unite with cement; join firmly

cem'etery n. burial ground, esp. other than churchyard

cen'otaph n. monument to one buried elsewhere

cen'ser n. pan in which incense is burned —**cense** vt.

cen'sor n. one authorized to examine films, books etc. and suppress all or part if considered morally or otherwise unacceptable —vt. —**censor'ial** a. of censor —**censor'ious** a. fault-finding —**censor'iousness** n. —**cen'sorship** n.

cen'sure n. blame; harsh criticism —vt. blame; criticize harshly

cen'sus n. official counting of people, things etc.

cent n. hundredth part of dollar etc.

cen'taur n. mythical creature, half man, half horse

cente'nary n. 100 years; celebration of hundredth anniversary —a. pert. to a hundred —**centena'rian** n. one a hundred years old —**centenn'ial** a. lasting, happening every hundred years

cent'igrade a. another name for Celsius; having one hundred degrees

cent'imetre n. hundredth part of metre

cent'ipede n. small segmented animal with many legs

CENTO Central Treaty Organization

cen'tre n. midpoint; pivot, axis; point to or from which things move or are drawn; place for specific organization or activity —**cen'tral** a. —**central'ity** n. —**centraliza'tion** n. —**cen'tralize** vt. bring to a centre; concentrate under one control —**cen'trally** adv. —**cen'tric** a. —**cen'trifugal** a. tending from centre —**centrip'etal** a. tending towards centre —**central heating** central heating of building from one central source —**central processing unit** Computers part of a computer that performs logical and arithmetical operations

centu'rion n. Roman commander of 100 men

cen'tury n. 100 years; any set of 100

ceram'ic n. hard brittle material of baked clay; object made of this —pl. (with sing. v.) art, techniques of making ceramic objects; such objects —a.

ce'real n. any edible grain, eg wheat, rice etc.; (breakfast) food made from grain —a.

cer'ebral a. pert. to brain

cer'emony n. formal observance; sacred rite; courteous act —**ceremo'nial** a./n. —**ceremonially** adv. —**ceremo'nious** a. —**ceremo'niously** adv. —**ceremo'niousness** n.

cerise' [sə-rez'] n./a. clear, pinkish red

cert n. inf. something certain, esp. in a **dead cert**

cert'ain a. sure; settled, inevitable; some, one; of moderate (quantity, degree etc.) —**cer'tainly** adv. —**cert'ainty** n. —**cer'titude** n. confidence

cert'ify vt. declare formally; endorse, guarantee; declare legally insane (-**fied, -fying**) —**cer'tificate** n. written declaration —vt. give written declaration —**certifica'tion** n. —**cert'ifier** n.

ceru'lean [-roo-] a. sky-blue

cer'vix n. neck, esp. of womb —**cer'vical** a.

cessa'tion n. ceasing or stopping, pause

cess'ion n. yielding up

cess'pool n. pit in which filthy water collects, receptacle for sewage

cf. confer (Lat., compare)

c/f carried forward

cg centigram

cgs units metric system of units based on centimetre, gram, second

ch. chapter; church

chafe vt. make sore or worn by rubbing; make warm by rubbing; vex, irritate

chaff [-ah-] n. husks of corn;

worthless matter; banter —v. tease good-naturedly

chaff'er vi. haggle, bargain —n. bargaining

chaff'inch n. small songbird

chag'rin [sh-] n. vexation, disappointment —vt. embarrass; annoy; disappoint

chain n. series of connected links or rings; thing that binds; connected series of things or events; surveyor's measure Makes compound nouns as **chain armour, chain mail, chain reaction, chain smoker, chain stitch, chain store** etc. —vt. fasten with a chain; confine; restrain

chair n. movable seat, with back, for one person; seat of authority; professorship; iron support for rail on railway —vt. preside over; carry in triumph —**chair'lift** n. series of chairs fixed to cable for conveying people (esp. skiers) up mountain —**chair'man** n. one who presides over meeting —**chair'manship** n.

chaise [shāz] n. light horse-drawn carriage —**chaise longue** [-long] sofa

chalced'ony [kal-sed'-] n. whitish, bluish-white variety of quartz

chal'et [shal'ā] n. Swiss wooden house

chal'ice n. Poet. cup or bowl; communion cup

chalk [chawk] n. white substance, carbonate of lime; crayon —v. rub, draw, mark with chalk —**chalk'iness** n. —**chalk'y** a.

chall'enge vt. call to fight or account; dispute; stimulate; object to; claim —n. —**chall'enger** n. —**chall'enging** a. difficult but stimulating

cham'ber n. room for assembly; assembly, body of men; compartment; cavity; obs. room —pl. office or apartments of barrister; lodgings —**cha'mberlain** n. official at court of a monarch having charge of domestic and ceremonial affairs —**cha'mbermaid** n. servant with care of bedrooms —**chamber music** music for performance by a few instruments —**chamber (pot)** vessel for urine

chame'leon [kə-] n. small lizard famous for its power of changing colour

cham'fer vt. groove; bevel; flute —n. groove

cham'ois [sham'wah] n. goatlike mountain antelope; [sham'i] a soft pliable leather

champ[1] v. munch (food) noisily, as horse; be nervous, impatient

champ[2] n. short for CHAMPION

champagne' [sham-pān'] n. light, sparkling white wine of several varieties

cham'pion n. one that excels all others; defender of a cause; one who fights for another; hero —vt. fight for, maintain —**cham'pionship** n.

chance [-ah-] n. unpredictable course of events; fortune, luck; opportunity; possibility; risk; probability —vt. risk —vi. happen —a. casual, unexpected —**chan'cy** a. risky

chan'cel [-ah-] n. part of a church where altar is

chan'cellor [-ah-] n. high officer of state; head of university —**chan'cellorship** n. —**chan'cellery, -ory** n.

Chan'cery [-ah-] n. division of British High Court of Justice

chandelier' [sh-] n. hanging frame with branches for holding lights

chand'ler [-ah-] n. dealer in ropes, ships' supplies etc.

change v. alter, make or become different; put on (different clothes, fresh coverings) —vt.

put or give for another; exchange, interchange —n. alteration, variation; variety; conversion of money; small money, coins; balance received on payment —**changeabil'ity** n. —**change'able** a. —**change'ably** adv. —**change'ful** a. —**change'less** a. —**change'ling** n. child believed substituted for another by fairies

chann'el n. bed of stream; strait; deeper part of strait, bay, harbour; groove; means of passing or conveying; band of radio frequencies; television broadcasting station —vt. groove, furrow; guide, convey

chant [-ah-] n. simple song or melody; rhythmic or repetitious slogan —v. sing or utter chant; speak monotonously or repetitiously

chanticleer' n. cock

chant'y [ch-, sh-] n. see SHANTY[2]

cha'os [ka'-] n. disorder, confusion; state of universe before Creation —**chaot'ic** a.

chap[1] v. of skin, become dry, raw and cracked, esp. by exposure to cold and wind (-**pp**-) —**chapped** a.

chap[2] n. inf. fellow, man

chap'el n. private church; subordinate place of worship; division of church with its own altar; Nonconformist place of worship; association of printers

chap'eron(e) [sh-] n. one who attends young unmarried lady in public as protector —vt. attend in this way

chap'lain [-lin] n. clergyman attached to chapel, regiment, warship, institution etc. —**chap'laincy** n. his office

chaps pl.n. cowboy's leggings of thick leather

chap'ter n. division of book; section, heading; assembly of

clergy, bishop's council etc.; organized branch of society, fraternity —**chap'terhouse** n.

char[1] vt. scorch, burn to charcoal (-**rr**-) —**charred** a.

char[2] inf. n. charwoman —v. act as charwoman

char[3] n. troutlike small fish

char[4] n. sl. tea

char'acter [ka-] n. nature; total of qualities making up individuality; moral qualities; reputation of possessing them; statement of qualities of person; an eccentric; personality in play or novel; letter, sign, or any distinctive mark; essential feature —**characteris'tic** a. —**characteris'tically** adv. —**characteriza'tion** n. —**char'acterize** vt. mark out, distinguish; describe by peculiar qualities —**char'acterless** a.

charade' [shə-rahd'] n. absurd act; travesty —pl. word-guessing parlour game with syllables of word acted

char'coal n. black residue of wood, bones etc., produced by smothered burning; charred wood —**charcoal-burner** n.

charge vt. ask as price; bring accusation against; lay task on; command; attack; deliver injunction; fill with electricity; fill, load —vi. make onrush, attack —n. cost, price; accusation; attack; onrush; command, exhortation; accumulation of electricity —pl. expenses —**charge'able** a. —**char'ger** n. strong, fast battle horse; that which charges, esp. electrically

char'iot [cha-] n. two-wheeled vehicle used in ancient fighting; state carriage —**charioteer'** n.

charis'ma [kə-riz'-] n. special power of individual to inspire fascination, loyalty etc. —**charismat'ic** a.

char'ity [cha-] n. the giving of

help, money *etc.* to those in need; organization for doing this; the money *etc.* given; love, kindness; disposition to think kindly of others —**char'itable** *a.* —**char'itably** *adv.*

charl'atan [sh-] *n.* quack, impostor —**charl'atanry** *n.*

charles'ton *n.* fast, rhythmic dance of 1920s

char'lie *inf. n.* fool

charm *n.* attractiveness; anything that fascinates; amulet; magic spell —*vt.* bewitch; delight, attract —**charmed** *a.* —**charm'er** *n.* —**charm'ing** *a.*

charn'el house vault for bones of the dead

chart *n.* map of sea; diagram or tabulated statement —*vt.* map; represent on chart

chart'er *n.* document granting privileges *etc.*; patent —*vt.* let or hire; establish by charter

char'woman, -lady *n.* woman paid to clean office, house *etc.*

cha'ry *a.* cautious, sparing —**cha'rily** *adv.* —**cha'riness** *n.* caution

chase[1] *vt.* hunt, pursue; drive from, away, into *etc.* —*n.* pursuit, hunting; the hunted; hunting ground —**cha'ser** *n.* drink of beer, soda *etc.*, taken after neat spirit

chase[2] *vt.* engrave —**cha'ser** *n.* —**cha'sing** *n.*

chasm [kazm] *n.* deep cleft, fissure; abyss

chassé [shas'ā] *n.* rapid gliding step used in dancing —*vi.* perform the step

chass'is [shas'i] *n.* framework, wheels and machinery of motor vehicle excluding body and coachwork; underframe of aircraft

chaste *a.* virginal; pure; modest; virtuous —**chaste'ly** *adv.* —**chas'tity** *n.*

cha'sten [-sən] *vt.* correct by punishment; restrain, subdue —**cha'stened** *a.* —**chastise'** [chas-tīz'] *vt.* inflict punishment on —**chas'tisement** [-tiz-] *n.*

chas'uble [-z'-] *n.* priest's long sleeveless outer vestment

chat[1] *vi.* talk idly or familiarly (-tt-) —*n.* familiar idle talk —**chat'tily** *adv.* —**chatt'y** *a.* —**chat show** television or radio programme in which guests are interviewed informally

chat[2] *n.* any of various European songbirds, Amer. warblers, Aust. wrens

chat'eau [shat'ō] *n.* (*esp.* in France) castle, country house (*pl.* -teaux [-tō] *or* -teaus)

chatt'el *n.* any movable property (*usu. in pl.*)

chatt'er *vi.* talk idly or rapidly; rattle teeth —*n.* idle talk —**chatt'erer** *n.* —**chatt'ering** *n.* —**chatt'erbox** *n.* one who chatters incessantly

chauff'eur [shō'fər] *n.* paid driver of motorcar (**chauffeuse** *fem.*)

chau'vinism [shō'-] *n.* aggressive patriotism; smug sense of superiority

cheap *a.* low in price; inexpensive; easily obtained; of little value or estimation; mean, inferior —**cheap'en** *vt.* —**cheap'ly** *adv.* —**cheap'ness** *n.*

cheat *vt.* deceive, defraud, swindle, impose upon —*vi.* practise deceit to gain advantage —*n.* fraud

check *vt.* stop; restrain; hinder; repress; control; examine for accuracy, quality *etc.* —*n.* repulse; stoppage; restraint; brief examination for correctness or accuracy; pattern of squares on fabric; threat to king at chess —**check'mate** *n. Chess* final winning move; any overthrow, defeat

—vt. Chess make the movement ending game; defeat —**check'out** n. counter in supermarket where customers pay —**check'up** n. examination (esp. medical) to see if all is in order

checked a. having pattern of small squares

check'er see CHEQUER

Ched'dar n. smooth hard cheese

cheek n. side of face below eye; inf. impudence —vt. inf. address impudently —**cheek'y** a.

cheep vi./n. (utter) high-pitched cry, as of young bird

cheer vt. comfort; gladden; encourage by shouts —vi. shout applause —n. shout of approval; happiness, good spirits; mood; obs. rich food —**cheer'ful** a. —**cheer'fully** adv. —**cheer'fulness** n. —**cheer'ily** adv. —**cheer'less** a. —**cheer'lessness** n. —**cheer'y** a.

cheese n. curd of milk coagulated, separated from the whey and pressed —**chees'iness** n. —**chees'y** a. —**cheese'cloth** n. loosely woven cotton cloth —**cheese'paring** a. mean

chee'tah n. large, swift, spotted feline animal

chef [sh-] n. head cook, esp. in restaurant

chef-d'oeu'vre [shā-dur'vr] Fr. masterpiece

chem. chemical; chemistry

chem'istry [k-] n. science concerned with properties of substances and their combinations and reactions —**chem'ical** n./a. —**chem'ically** adv. —**chem'ist** n. qualified dispenser of prescribed medicines; shop that sells medicines etc.; one trained in chemistry

chemother'apy [k-] n. treatment of disease by chemical means

chem'urgy [k-] n. branch of applied chemistry devoted to the development of agricultural products —**chemur'gic(al)** a.

chenille' [shə-nēl'] n. soft cord, fabric of silk or worsted

cheong'sam [chawng'-] n. (Chinese) straight dress with slit in one side of skirt

cheque [-ek] n. written order to banker to pay money from one's account; printed slip of paper used for this —**cheque'book** n. book of cheques —**cheque card** banker's card

chequ'er [-ər] n. marking as on chessboard; marble, peg etc. used in games, eg Chinese chequers —pl. squares like those of chessboard; another name for draughts —vt. mark in squares; variegate —**chequ'ered** a. marked in squares; uneven, varied

cher'ish vt. treat with affection; protect; foster

cheroot' [sh-] n. cigar with both ends open

cherr'y n. small red fruit with stone; tree bearing it —a. ruddy, bright red

cher'ub n. winged creature with human face; angel (pl. **cher'ubim, cher'ubs**) —**cheru'bic** a.

cher'vil n. a herb

chess n. game of skill played by two with 32 pieces on chequered board of 64 squares —**chess'board** n. —**chess'men** pl.n. pieces used in chess

chest n. upper part of trunk of body; large, strong box —**chest of drawers** piece of furniture containing drawers

chest'erfield n. padded sofa

chest'nut [-s'n-] n. large reddish-brown nut growing in prickly husk; tree bearing it; inf. old joke —a. reddish-brown

chev'ron [sh-] *n.* Mil. V-shaped band of braid worn on sleeve to designate rank

chew [-ᴏᴏ] *v.* grind with teeth —*n.* —**chew'y** *a.* firm, sticky when chewed —**chewing gum**

chian'ti [ki-] *n.* It. wine

chic [shēk] *a.* stylish, elegant —*n.*

chica'nery [shi-] *n.* quibbling; trick, artifice

chick, chick'en *n.* young of birds, *esp.* of hen; *sl.* girl, young woman —**chicken feed** trifling amount (of money) —**chicken-hearted** *a.* cowardly —**chick'en-pox** *n.* infectious disease, *esp.* of children —**chick'pea** *n.* dwarf pea —**chick'weed** *n.* weed with small white flowers

chic'ory *n.* salad plant of which the root is ground and used with, or instead of, coffee

chide *vt.* scold, reprove, censure (**chid** *pt.*, **chidd'en, chid** *pp.*, **chi'ding** *pr.p.*)

chief *n.* head or principal person —*a.* principal, foremost, leading —**chief'ly** *adv.* —**chief'tain** *n.* leader, chief of clan or tribe

chiff'chaff *n.* common European warbler

chiff'on [sh-] *n.* thin gauzy material —**chiffonier'** *n.* ornamental cupboard

chi'gnon [shē'nyon] *n.* roll, knot, of hair worn at back of head

chihua'hua [chi-wah'wah] *n.* breed of tiny dog, *orig.* from Mexico

chil'blain *n.* inflamed sore on hands, legs *etc.*, due to cold

child [-ī-] *n.* young human being; offspring (*pl.* **child'ren** [-i-]) —**child'ish** *a.* of or like a child; silly; trifling —**child'ishly** *adv.* —**child'less** *a.* —**child'like** *a.* of or like a child; innocent; frank; docile —**child'bed** *n.* state of giving birth to child —**child'-**

birth *n.* —**child'hood** *n.* period between birth and puberty —**child's play** very easy task

chill *n.* coldness; cold with shivering; anything that damps, discourages —*v.* make, become cold (*esp.* food, drink) —**chilled** *a.* —**chill'iness** *n.* —**chill'y** *a.*

chill'i *n.* small red hot-tasting seed pod; plant producing it

chime *n.* sound of bell; harmonious, ringing sound —*vi.* ring harmoniously; agree —*vt.* strike (bells) —**chime in** come into conversation with agreement

chim(a)e'ra [kī-mē'-] *n.* fabled monster, made up of parts of various animals; wild fancy —**chimer'ic(al)** *a.* fanciful

chim'ney *n.* a passage for smoke; narrow vertical cleft in rock (*pl.* **-neys**)

chimpanzee' *n.* gregarious, intelligent ape of Africa

chin *n.* part of face below mouth

chi'na *n.* fine earthenware, porcelain; cups, saucers *etc.* collectively

chincherinchee' *n.* S Afr. plant with white or yellow flower spikes

chinchill'a *n.* S Amer. rodent with soft, grey fur

chine *n.* backbone; joint of meat; ridge or crest of land

Chinese lantern Asian plant cultivated for its orange-red inflated calyx

chink[1] *n.* cleft, crack

chink[2] *n.* light metallic sound —*v.* (cause to) make this sound

chintz *n.* cotton cloth printed in coloured designs

chip *n.* splinter; place where piece has been broken off; thin strip of potato, fried; tiny wafer of silicon forming integrated circuit in computer *etc.* —*vt.* chop into small pieces; break small pieces from; shape by cutting off pieces —vi. break off (**-pp-**) —**chip in** interrupt; contribute

chip'munk n. small, striped N Amer. squirrel

chipolat'a [-lah'-] n. small sausage

chirog'raphy [kï-] n. calligraphy

chirop'odist [ki-] n. one who treats disorders of feet —**chirop'ody** n.

chi'ropractor [kï'-] n. one skilled in treating bodily disorders by manipulation, massage etc. —**chiroprac'tic** n.

chirp, chirr'up n. short, sharp cry of bird —vi. make this sound —**chirp'y** a. inf. happy

chis'el [-z'-] n. cutting tool, usu. bar of steel with edge across main axis —vt. cut, carve with chisel; sl. cheat (**-ll-**)

chit[1] n. informal note, memorandum

chit[2] n. child, young girl

chiv'alry [sh-] n. bravery and courtesy; medieval system of knighthood —**chiv'alrous** a. —**chiv'alrously** adv.

chive n. herb with mild onion flavour

chlor'ine [kl-] n. nonmetallic element, yellowish-green poison gas —**chlor'ate** n. salt of chloric acid —**chlor'ic** a. —**chlor'ide** n. compound of chlorine; bleaching agent —**chlor'inate** vt. disinfect; purify with chlorine

chlor'oform [kl-] n. volatile liquid formerly used as anaesthetic —vt. render insensible with it

chlor'ophyll [kl-] n. green colouring matter in plants

chock n. block or wedge to prevent heavy object rolling or sliding —**chock-full, chock-a-block** a. packed full

choc'olate n. paste from ground cacao seeds; confect-

ery, drink made from this —a. dark brown

choice n. act or power of choosing; alternative; thing or person chosen —a. select, fine, worthy of being chosen —**choice'ly** adv.

choir [kwïr] n. band of singers, esp. in church; part of church set aside for them

choke vt. hinder, stop the breathing of; smother, stifle; obstruct —vi. suffer choking —n. act, noise of choking; device in carburettor to increase richness of petrol-air mixture —**choked** a. —**choke'bore** n. gun with bore narrowed towards muzzle —**choke'damp** n. carbon dioxide gas in coal mines

chol'er [k-] n. bile, anger —**chol'eric** a. bad-tempered

chol'era [k-] n. deadly infectious disease marked by vomiting and diarrhoea

choles'terol [kol-] n. substance found in animal tissue and fat

chomp v. chew noisily

choose vt. pick out, select; take by preference —vi. decide, think fit (**chose, cho'sen, choo'sing**) —**choo'ser** n. —**choo'sy** a. fussy

chop[1] vt. cut with blow; hack (**-pp-**) —n. hewing blow; slice of meat containing rib or other bone —**chopp'er** n. short axe; inf. helicopter; inf. large motorbike —**chopp'y** a. (of sea) having short, broken waves

chop[2] vt. exchange, bandy, eg **chop logic, chop and change** (**-pp-**)

chops pl.n. inf. jaws, cheeks

chop'sticks pl.n. implements used by Chinese for eating food

chop su'ey [-soo'-] a kind of rich Chinese stew with rice

chor'al [k-] a. of, for, sung by, a choir

chorale' [-rahl'] n. slow, stately hymn tune

chord [k-] n. emotional response, esp. of sympathy; simultaneous sounding of musical notes; straight line joining ends of arc

chore n. (unpleasant) task; odd job

choreog'raphy [ko-ri-] n. art of arranging dances, esp. ballet; art, notation of ballet dancing —**choreog'rapher** n. —**choreograph'ic** a.

chorog'raphy [ko-] n. art of describing and making maps of particular regions —**chorograph'ic** a.

chorol'ogy [kə-] n. the science of geographical distribution of plants and animals —**chorol'ogist** n.

chor'tle vi. chuckle happily —n.

chor'us [k-] n. band of singers; combination of voices singing together; refrain —vt. sing or say together —**chor'ic** [kor'-] a. —**chor'ister** [kori'-] a.

chose pt. —**cho'sen** pp. of CHOOSE

chough [chuf] n. large black bird of crow family

chow[1] n. inf. food

chow[2] n. thick-coated dog with curled tail, orig. from China

Christ [krīst] n. Jesus of Nazareth, regarded by Christians as the Messiah

Chris'tian [kris'chən] n. follower of Christ —a. following Christ; relating to Christ or his religion —**christ'en** [kris'n] vt. baptize, give name to —**Chris'tendom** [-s'n-] n. all the Christian world —**Christian'ity** n. religion of Christ —**christ'ianize** vt. —**Christian name** name given at baptism —**Christian Science** religious system founded by Mrs. Eddy in U.S.A.

Christ'mas [kris'-] n. festival of birth of Christ —**Christmas box** tip, present given at Christmas —**Christmas card** —**Christmas tree**

chromat'ic [krə-] a. of colour; Mus. of scale proceeding by semitones

chro'matin [krō'-] n. part of protoplasmic substance in nucleus of cells which takes colour in staining tests

chrome, chro'mium [krō'-] n. metal used in alloys and for plating

chro'mosome [krō'-] n. microscopic gene-carrying body in the tissue of a cell

chro'mosphere [krō'-] n. layer of incandescent gas surrounding the sun

Chron. Chronicles

chron'ic [kr-] a. lasting a long time; habitual; inf. serious; inf. of bad quality

chron'icle [kr-] n. record of events in order of time; account —vt. record —**chron'icler** n.

chronol'ogy [kr-] n. determination of sequence of past events; arrangement in order of occurrence —**chronolog'ical** a. arranged in order of time —**chronolog'ically** adv. —**chronol'ogist** n.

chronom'eter [kr-] n. instrument for measuring time exactly; watch —**chronomet'rical** a. —**chronom'etry** n.

chrys'alis [kris'-] n. resting state of insect between grub and butterfly etc.; case enclosing it (pl. **chrys'alises, chrysal'ides** [-idēz])

chrysan'themum [kri-] n. garden flower of various colours

chubb'y a. plump

chuck[1] inf. vt. throw; pat affectionately (under chin); give up, reject

chuck[2] n. cut of beef; device for gripping, adjusting bit in power drill etc.

chuck'le vi. laugh softly —n. such laugh

chukk'er n. period of play in game of polo

chum n. inf. close friend —**chum'my** a.

chunk n. thick, solid piece —**chunk'y** a.

church n. building for Christian worship; (C-) whole body or sect of Christians; clergy —**church'man** n. —**churchward'en** n. officer who represents interests of parish; long clay pipe —**church'yard** n.

churl n. rustic; ill-bred fellow —**churl'ish** a. —**churl'ishly** adv. —**churl'ishness** n.

churn n. large container for milk; vessel for making butter —v. shake up, stir (liquid) violently

chute [shoot] n. slide for sending down parcels, coal etc.; channel; narrow passageway, eg for spraying, counting cattle, sheep etc.; inf. short for PARACHUTE

chut'ney n. pickle of fruit, spices etc.

CIA US Central Intelligence Agency

cica'da [si-kah'-] n. cricketlike insect

cic'atrix [sik'-] n. scar of healed wound —**cic'atrize** v. heal —**cicatriza'tion** n.

CID Criminal Investigation Department

ci'der n. fermented drink made from apples

cigar' n. roll of tobacco leaves for smoking —**cigarette'** n. finely-cut tobacco rolled in paper for smoking

C-in-C Commander-in-Chief

cinch n. inf. easy task, certainty

cin'der n. remains of burned coal

cine camera [sin'i] camera for taking moving pictures —**cine film**

cin'ema n. building used for showing of films; films generally or collectively —**cinemat'ograph** n. combined camera, printer and projector —**cinematog'raphy** n.

cinera'ria n. garden plant with daisylike flowers

cin'erary a. pert. to ashes

cinn'amon n. spice got from bark of Asian tree; the tree —a. light-brown colour

cinque'foil [singk'-] n. plant with five-lobed leaves

ci'pher, cy'pher n. secret writing; arithmetical symbol; person of no importance; monogram —vt. write in cipher

cir'ca Lat. about, approximately

cir'cle n. perfectly round figure; ring; Theatre section of seats above main level of auditorium; group, society with common interest; spiritualist seance; class of society —vt. surround —vi. move round —**cir'cular** a. round; moving round —n. letter sent to several persons —**cir'culate** vi. move round; pass from hand to hand or place to place —vt. send round —**circula'tion** n. flow of blood from, and back to, heart; act of moving round; extent of sale of newspaper etc. —**cir'culatory** a.

cir'cuit [-k'it] n. complete round or course; area; path of electric current; round of visitation, esp. of judges; series of sporting events; district —**circu'itous** a. roundabout, indirect —**circu'itously** adv. —**cir'cuitry** n. electrical circuit(s)

cir'cumcise [-z] vt. cut off foreskin of —**circumcis'ion** n.

circum'ference n. boundary line, esp. of circle

cir'cumflex n. accent (ˆ) over

vowel to indicate length of its sound

circumlocu'tion *n.* roundabout speech

circumnav'igate *vt.* sail or fly right round —**circumnaviga'tion** *n.* —**circumnav'igator** *n.*

circ'umscribe [*or* -skrīb'] *vt.* confine, bound, limit, hamper

circ'umspect *a.* watchful, cautious, prudent —**cir'cumspectly** *adv.* —**circumspec'tion** *n.*

circ'umstance *n.* detail; event; matter of fact —*pl.* state of affairs; condition in life, *esp.* financial; surroundings or things accompanying an action —**circumstan'tial** *a.* depending on detail or circumstances; detailed; minute; incidental —**circumstantial'ity** *n.* —**circumstan'tially** *adv.* —**circumstan'tiate** *vt.* prove by details; describe exactly

circumvent' *vt.* outwit, evade, get round —**circumven'tion** *n.*

circ'us *n.* (performance of) travelling group of acrobats, clowns, performing animals *etc.*; circular structure for public shows; circular space in town where roads converge (*pl.* **-es**)

cirrho'sis [si-rō'-] *n.* any of various chronic progressive diseases of liver —**cirrhot'ic** *a.*

cir'rus *n.* high wispy cloud (*pl.* **cir'ri** [-ī])

cis'tern *n.* water tank

cit'adel *n.* fortress in, near, or commanding a city

cite *vt.* quote; bring forward as proof —**cita'tion** *n.* quoting; commendation for bravery *etc.*

cit'izen *n.* naturalized member of state, nation *etc.*; inhabitant of city —**cit'izenship** *n.*

cit'ron *n.* fruit like a lemon; the tree —**cit'ric** *a.* of the acid of

lemon or citron —**citrus fruit** citrons, lemons, limes, oranges *etc.*

cit'y *n.* a large town

civ'et *n.* strong, musky perfume —**civet-cat** *n.* catlike animal producing it

civ'ic *a.* pert. to city or citizen —**civ'ics** *pl.n.* (*with sing. v.*) study of the rights and responsibilities of citizenship

civ'il *a.* relating to citizens of state; not military; refined, polite; *Law* not criminal —**civil'ian** *n.* nonmilitary person —**civil'ity** *n.* —**civ'illy** *adv.* —**civil service** service responsible for the public administration of the government of a country

civ'ilize *vt.* bring out of barbarism; refine —**civiliza'tion** *n.* —**civ'ilized** *a.*

civ'vy *sl. n.* civilian —*pl.* civilian clothing

Cl *Chem.* chlorine

cl centilitre

clack *n.* sound, as of two pieces of wood striking together —*v.*

clad *pt./pp. of* CLOTHE

cladd'ing *n.* material used for outside facing of building *etc.*

claim *vt.* demand as right; assert; call for —*n.* demand for thing supposed due; right; thing claimed; plot of mining land marked out by stakes as required by law —**claim'ant** *n.*

clairvoy'ance [-voi'-] *n.* power of seeing things not present to senses, second sight —**clairvoy'ant** *n./a.*

clam *n.* edible mollusc

clam'ber *vi.* to climb with difficulty or awkwardly

clamm'y *a.* moist and sticky —**clamm'iness** *n.*

clam'our *n.* loud shouting, outcry, noise —*vi.* shout, call noisily (for) —**clam'orous** *a.* —**clam'orously** *adv.*

clamp n. tool for holding or compressing —vt. fasten, strengthen with or as with clamp

clan n. tribe or collection of families under chief and of common ancestry; faction, group —**clan'nish** a. —**clan'nishly** adv. —**clann'ishness** n.

clandes'tine a. secret; sly

clang v. (cause to) make loud ringing sound —n. loud ringing sound —**clang'er** n. inf. conspicuous mistake; that which clangs

clank n. short sound as of pieces of metal struck together —v. cause, move with, such sound

clap' v. (cause to) strike with noise; strike (hands) together; applaud —vt. pat; place or put quickly (-pp-) —n. hard, explosive sound; slap —**clapp'er** n. —**clapp'ing** n. —**clap'trap** n. empty words

clap' n. sl. gonorrhoea

clar'et [kla'rət] n. a dry dark red wine of Bordeaux

clar'ify [kla'ri-] v. make or become clear, pure, or more easily understood (-fied, -fying) —**clarifica'tion** n. —**clar'ity** n. clearness

clarinet' n. woodwind musical instrument

clar'ion [kla'ri-] n. clear-sounding trumpet; rousing sound

cla'ry n. herb

clash n. loud noise, as of weapons striking; conflict, collision —vi. make clash; come into conflict; (of events) coincide; (of colours) look ugly together —vt. strike together to make clash

clasp [-ah-] n. hook or other means of fastening; embrace —vt. fasten; embrace, grasp —**clasp knife**

class [-ah-] n. any division, order, kind, sort; rank; group of school pupils etc. taught together; division by merit; quality; inf. excellence or elegance —vt. assign to proper division —**class'ify** [klas'-] vt. arrange methodically in classes (-fied, -fying) —**classifica'tion** n. —**class'ified** a. arranged in classes; secret; (of advertisements) arranged under headings in newspapers —**class'y** [-ah-] a. inf. stylish, elegant

class'ic a. of first rank; of highest rank generally; of art; refined; typical; famous —n. (literary) work of recognized excellence —pl.n. ancient Latin and Greek literature —**clas'sical** a. of Greek and Roman literature, art, culture; of classic quality; Mus. of established standards of form, complexity etc. —**class'ically** adv. —**class'icism** n. —**class'icist** n.

clatt'er n. rattling noise; noisy conversation —v. (cause to) make clatter

clause [-z] n. part of sentence, containing verb; article in formal document as treaty, contract etc.

claustropho'bia n. abnormal fear of confined spaces

clav'ichord [-k-] n. musical instrument with keyboard, forerunner of piano

clav'icle n. collarbone —**clavic'ular** a. pert. to this

claw n. sharp hooked nail of bird or beast; foot of bird of prey; clawlike article —vt. tear with claws; grip

clay n. fine-grained earth, plastic when wet, hardening when baked; earth —**clay'ey** a.

clay'more n. ancient Highland two-edged sword

clean a. free from dirt, stain, or defilement; pure; guiltless; trim, shapely —adv. so as to leave no dirt; entirely —vt. free from dirt —**clean'er** n. —**clean'liness** [klen'-] n. —**clean'ly** [klen'-] adv.

—*a.* [klēn'-] clean —**clean'ness** [klēn'-] *n.* —**cleanse** [klenz] *vt.* make clean —**come clean** *inf.* confess

clear *a.* pure, undimmed, bright; free from cloud; transparent; plain, distinct; without defect or drawback; unimpeded —*adv.* brightly; wholly, quite —*vt.* make clear; acquit; pass over or through; make as profit; free from obstruction, difficulty; free by payment of dues —*vi.* become clear, bright, free, transparent —**clear'ance** *n.* making clear; removal of obstructions, surplus stock *etc.*; certificate that ship has been cleared at custom house; space for moving part, vehicle, to pass within, through or past something —**clear'ing** *n.* land cleared of trees —**clear'ly** *adv.* —**clear'ness** *n.* —**clear-sighted** *a.* discerning —**clear'way** *n.* stretch of road on which motorists may stop only in an emergency

cleat *n.* wedge; piece of wood or iron with two projecting ends round which ropes are made fast

cleave[1] *vt.* split asunder —*vi.* crack, part asunder (**clove, cleft** *pt.* **clo'ven, cleft** *pp.* **cleav'ing** *pr.p.*) —**cleav'age** *n.* —**cleav'er** *n.* short chopper

cleave[2] *vi.* stick, adhere; be loyal (**cleaved, cleav'ing**)

clef *n.* *Mus.* mark to show pitch of stave

cleft *n.* crack, fissure, chasm; opening made by cleaving —*pt./pp.* of CLEAVE[1]

cleg *n.* horsefly

clem'atis [*or* -ā'tis] *n.* flowering climbing perennial plant

clem'ent *a.* merciful; gentle; mild —**clem'ency** *n.* —**clem'ently** *adv.*

clench [-ch, -sh] *vt.* set firmly together; grasp, close (fist)

cler'gy *n.* body of appointed ministers of Christian church —**cler'gyman** *n.*

cler'ic [kler'ik] *n.* clergyman —**cler'icalism** *n.*

cler'ical [kler'ik-] *a.* of clergy; of, connected with, office work

clerk [-ark, US -erk] *n.* subordinate who keeps files *etc.* in an office; officer in charge of records, correspondence *etc.*, of department or corporation *etc.*, of **US** shop assistant —**clerk'ly** *a.* —**clerk'ship** *n.*

clev'er *a.* intelligent; able, skilful, adroit —**clev'erly** *adv.* —**clev'erness** *n.*

cli'ché [klē'shā] *n.* stereotyped hackneyed phrase (*pl.* **-s**)

click[1] *n.* short, sharp sound, as of latch in door; catch —*vi.* make this sound

click[2] *vi.* *sl.* be a success; *inf.* become clear; *inf.* strike up friendship

cli'ent *n.* customer; one who employs professional person —**clientele**[1] [klē-on-tel'] *n.* body of clients

cliff *n.* steep rock face —**cliff'-hanger** *n.* tense situation, *esp.* in film *etc.*

cli'mate *n.* condition of country with regard to weather; prevailing feeling, atmosphere —**cli-mat'ic** *a.* of climate

cli'max *n.* highest point, culmination; point of greatest excitement, tension in story *etc.* —**cli-mac'tic** *a.*

climb [klīm] *v.* go up or ascend; progress with difficulty; creep up, mount; slope upwards —**climb'er** *n.* —**climb'ing** *n.*

clime *n.* region, country; climate

clinch *vt.* *see* CLENCH; settle, conclude (an agreement) —**clinch'er** *n.* *inf.* something decisive

cling *vi.* adhere; be firmly attached to; be dependent (**clung** *pt./pp.*) —**cling'film** *n.* thin polythene wrapping material

clin'ic *n.* place for medical examination, advice, or treatment —**clin'ical** *a.* relating to clinic, care of sick *etc.*; objective, unemotional; bare, plain —**clin'ically** *adv.* —**clinical thermometer** used for taking body temperature

clink[1] *n.* sharp metallic sound —*v.* (cause to) make this sound

clink[2] *n. sl.* prison

clink'er *n.* fused coal residues from fire or furnace; hard brick

clinker-built *a.* (of boat) with outer boards or plates overlapping

clip[1] *vt.* cut with scissors; cut short (**-pp-**) —*n. inf.* sharp blow —**clipp'er** *n.*

clip[2] *n.* device for gripping or holding together, *esp.* hair, clothing *etc.*

clipp'er *n.* fast sailing ship

clique [-ēk] *n.* small exclusive set; faction, group of people —**clique'ish** *a.*

clit'oris *n.* small erectile part of female genitals

cloak *n.* loose outer garment; disguise, pretext —*vt.* cover with cloak; disguise, conceal —**cloak'room** *n.* place for keeping coats, hats, luggage

clobb'er *inf. vt.* beat, batter; defeat utterly —*n.* belongings

cloche [klosh] *n.* cover to protect young plants; woman's close-fitting hat

clock *n.* instrument for measuring time; device with dial for recording or measuring —**clock'wise** *adv./a.* in the direction that the hands of a clock rotate —**clock'work** *n.* mechanism similar to that of a clock, as in a wind-up toy —**clock in** *or* **on, out**

or **off** record arrival or departure on automatic time recorder

clod *n.* lump of earth; blockhead —**clodd'ish** *a.*

clog *vt.* hamper, impede, choke up (**-gg-**) —*n.* obstruction, impediment; wooden-soled shoe —**clog dance**

cloisonn'é [klwah-zon'ā] *n.* enamel decoration in compartments formed by small fillets of metal —*a.*

clois'ter *n.* covered pillared arcade; monastery or convent —**clois'tered** *a.* confined, secluded, sheltered

clone *n.* group of organisms, cells of same genetic constitution as another, derived by asexual reproduction, as graft of plant *etc.* —*v.*

clop *vi.* move, sound, as horse's hooves

close[1] [-s] *a.* adjacent, near; compact; crowded; affectionate; intimate; almost equal; careful, searching; confined; secret; unventilated, stifling; reticent; niggardly; strict, restricted —*adv.* nearly; tightly —*n.* shut-in place; precinct of cathedral —**close'ly** *adv.* —**close'ness** *n.* —**close-fisted** *a.* mean; avaricious —**close season** when it is illegal to kill certain kinds of game and fish —**close'up** *n.* close view, *esp.* portion of cinema film

close[2] [-z] *vt.* shut; stop up; prevent access to; finish —*vi.* come together; grapple —*n.* end

closed shop place of work in which all workers must belong to a trade union

clos'et [-oz'-] *n. US, C* cupboard; small private room; water closet, lavatory —*vt.* shut up in private room, *esp.* for conference

clo'sure [-zh-] *n.* act of closing; ending of debate by majority vote or other authority

clot *n.* mass or lump; *inf.* fool; *Med.* coagulated mass of blood —*vt.* form into lumps —*vi.* coagulate (**-tt-**)

cloth [-TH] *n.* woven fabric —**clothes** [-TH-] *pl.n.* dress; bed coverings —**clothe** *vt.* put clothes on (**clothed** [klŏTHd] *or* **clad** *pt./pp.*) —**clo'thier** *n.* —**clo'thing** *n.*

cloud *n.* condensed water vapour floating in air; state of gloom; multitude —*vt.* overshadow, dim, darken —*vi.* become cloudy —**cloud'less** *a.* —**cloud'y** *a.*

clout *n. inf.* blow; short, flatheaded nail; influence, power —*vt.* strike

clove[1] *n.* dried flower bud of tropical tree, used as spice; one of small bulbs making up compound bulb

clove[2] *pt.* —**clo'ven** *pp.* of CLEAVE[1]

clo'ver *n.* low-growing forage plant, trefoil —**be in clover** be in luxury

clown *n.* comic entertainer in circus; jester, fool —**clown'ish** *a.*

cloy *vt.* weary by sweetness, sameness *etc.*

club *n.* thick stick; bat, stick used in some games; association for pursuance of common interest; building used by such association; one of the suits at cards —*vt.* strike with club —*vi.* join for a common object (**-bb-**)

club foot deformed foot

cluck *vi./n.* (make) noise of hen

clue *n.* indication, *esp.* of solution of mystery or puzzle —**not have a clue** be ignorant or incompetent

clump[1] *n.* cluster of trees or plants; compact mass

clump[2] *vi.* walk, tread heavily —*n.*

clum'sy [-z-] *a.* awkward, un-

wieldy, ungainly; badly made or arranged —**clums'ily** *adv.* —**clum'siness** *n.*

clung *pt./pp.* of CLING

clunk *n.* (sound of) blow or something falling

clus'ter *n.* group, bunch —*v.* gather, grow in cluster

clutch[1] *v.* grasp eagerly; snatch (at) —*n.* grasp, tight grip; device enabling two revolving shafts to be connected and disconnected at will

clutch[2] *n.* set of eggs hatched at one time; brood of chickens

clutt'er *v.* strew; crowd together in disorder —*n.* disordered, obstructive mass of objects

cm centimetre(s)

CND Campaign for Nuclear Disarmament

Co Commanding Officer

Co *Chem.* cobalt

Co. Company; County

c/o care of; carried over

coach *n.* long-distance or touring bus; large four-wheeled carriage; railway carriage; tutor, instructor —*vt.* instruct —**coach'man** *n.*

coag'ulate *v.* curdle, clot, form into a mass; congeal, solidify —**coagula'tion** *n.*

coal *n.* mineral consisting of carbonized vegetable matter, used as fuel; glowing ember —*v.* supply with or take in coal —**coal'field** *n.* district in which coal is found

coalesce' [-les'] *vi.* unite, merge —**coales'cence** *n.*

coal'fish *n.* food fish with dark-coloured skin

coali'tion *n.* alliance, *esp.* of political parties

coarse *a.* rough, harsh; unrefined; indecent —**coarse'ly** *adv.* —**coarse'ness** *n.*

coast *n.* sea shore —*v.* move under momentum; proceed without making much effort; sail by the coast —**coast'er** n. small ship; that which, one who, coasts; small table mat for glasses etc.

coat n. sleeved outer garment; animal's fur or feathers; covering layer —vt. cover with layer; clothe —**coat of arms** armorial bearings

coax [kōks] vt. wheedle, cajole, persuade, force gently

coax'ial [kō-aks'-] a. having the same axis —**coax'ially** adv.

cob n. short-legged stout horse; male swan; head of corn; round loaf of bread

co'balt n. metallic element; blue pigment from it

cob'ble vt. patch roughly; mend shoes —n. round stone —**cob'bler** n. shoe mender

co'bra n. venomous, hooded snake of Asia and Africa

cob'web n. spider's web

Coca-Cola R carbonated soft drink

cocaine' [-kān'-] n. addictive narcotic drug used medicinally as anaesthetic

cochineal' n. scarlet dye from Mexican insect

cock n. male bird, esp. of domestic fowl; tap for liquids; hammer of gun; its position drawn back —vt. draw back (gun hammer) to firing position; raise, turn in alert or jaunty manner —**cock'erel** n. young cock —**cock'eye(d)** a. crosseyed; with a squint; askew —**cock'fight** n. staged fight between roosters

cockade' n. rosette, badge for hat

cockatoo' n. Aust., New Guinea, crested parrot

cock'atrice n. fabulous animal similar to basilisk

cock'chafer n. large, flying beetle

cock'le [1] n. shellfish

cock'le [2] v. wrinkle; pucker

Cock'ney [-ni] n. native of London (pl. **-neys**)

cock'pit n. pilot's seat, compartment in small aircraft; driver's seat in racing car; orig. enclosure for cockfighting

cock'roach n. kind of insect, household pest

cock'tail n. short drink of spirits with flavourings etc.; appetizer

cock'y a. conceited, pert

co'coa [-kō] n. powder made from seed of cacao (tropical) tree; drink made from the powder

co'conut n. tropical palm; very large, hard nut from this palm

cocoon' n. sheath of insect in chrysalis stage; any protective covering

co'copan n. SA small truck on rails used esp. in mines

COD cash on delivery

cod n. large sea fish of northern hemisphere

co'da n. Mus. final part of musical composition

cod'dle vt. overprotect, pamper

code n. system of letters, symbols and rules for their association to transmit messages secretly or briefly; scheme of conduct; collection of laws —**co'dify** vt. (-fied, -fying) —**codifica'tion** n.

co'deine [-dēn] n. alkaline sedative, analgesic drug

co'dex n. ancient manuscript volume, esp. of Bible etc. (pl. **co'dices** [-sēz])

codg'er n. inf. man, esp. old

cod'icil n. addition to will —**codicil'lary** a.

coeduca'tional a. of education of boys and girls together in mixed classes —**co-ed** n. coeducational school etc. —a.

coeffi'cient [-fish'-] n. Maths.

numerical or constant factor

coe'liac [se͞e'-] *a.* pert. to the belly

coerce' [kō-ers'] *vt.* compel, force —**coer'cive, coer'cible** *a.* —**coer'cion** *n.* forcible compulsion or restraint

coe'val [kō-ē'-] *a.* of same age or generation

coexist' *vi.* exist together —**coexis'tence** *n.* —**coexis'tent** *a.*

C of E Church of England

coff'ee *n.* seeds of tropical shrub; drink made from roasting and grinding these

coff'er *n.* chest for valuables; treasury, funds

coff'er(dam) *n.* watertight structure enabling construction work to be done under water

coff'in *n.* box for corpse

cog *n.* one of series of teeth on rim of wheel; person, thing forming small part of big process, organization *etc.* —**cog'wheel** *n.*

co'gent *a.* convincing, compelling, persuasive —**co'gency** *n.* —**co'gently** *adv.*

cog'itate [koj'-] *vi.* think, reflect, ponder —**cogita'tion** *n.* —**cog'itative** *a.*

cog'nac [kon'yak] *n.* French brandy

cog'nate *a.* of same stock, related, kindred —**cogna'tion** *n.*

cogni'tion [-nish'-] *n.* act or faculty of knowing —**cogni'tional** *a.*

cog'nizance [*or* kon'-] *n.* knowledge, perception —**cog'nizable** *a.* —**cog'nizant** *a.*

cogno'men *n.* surname, nickname (*pl.* **cogno'mens**)

cognoscen'ti [kon-yŏ-shen'ti] *pl.n.* people with knowledge in particular field, *esp.* arts

cohab'it *vi.* live together as husband and wife

coheir' [kō-ār'] *n.* a joint heir (**coheir'ess** *fem.*) —**coher'itor** *n.* a coheir

cohere' *vi.* stick together, be consistent —**cohe'rence** *n.* —**cohe'rent** *a.* capable of logical speech, thought; connected, making sense; sticking together —**cohe'rently** *adv.* —**cohe'sion** *n.* cohering —**cohe'sive** *a.*

co'hort *n.* troop; associate

COHSE Confederation of Health Service Employees

coiffeur' [kwah-fer'] *n.* hairdresser

coiffure' [kwah-fyoor'] *n.* hairstyle

coil *vt.* lay in rings; twist into winding shape —*vi.* twist, take up a winding shape or spiral —*n.* series of rings; device in vehicle *etc.* to transform low tension current to higher voltage for ignition purposes; contraceptive device inserted in womb

coin *n.* piece of money; money —*vt.* make into money, stamp; invent —**coin'age** *n.* coining; coins collectively —**coin'er** *n.* maker of counterfeit money

coincide' [kō-in-] *vi.* happen together; agree exactly —**coin'cidence** *n.* —**coin'cident** *a.* coinciding —**coinciden'tal** *a.*

coir *n.* fibre of coconut husk

coit'ion [kō-ish'-] *n.* sexual intercourse (*also* **co'itus** [kō'it-])

coke [1] *n.* residue left from distillation of coal, used as fuel

coke [2] *sl. n.* Coca-Cola; cocaine

col *n.* high mountain pass

Col. Colonel; Colossians

co'la *n.* tropical tree; its nut, used to flavour drink

col'ander, cull'ender *n.* culinary strainer perforated with small holes

cold *a.* lacking heat; indifferent, unmoved, apathetic; dispiriting; reserved or unfriendly; (of colours) giving an impression of coldness —n. lack of heat; illness, marked by runny nose etc. —**cold'ly** adv. —**cold'ness** n. —**cold-blooded** a. lacking pity, mercy; having body temperature that varies with that of the surroundings —**cold chisel** toughened steel chisel —**cold feet** sl. fear —**cold storage** method of preserving perishable foods etc. by keeping them at artificially reduced temperature —**cold war** economic, diplomatic but nonmilitary hostility

cole'slaw n. salad dish based on shredded cabbage

co'leus [kō′li-əs] n. plant cultivated for its variegated leaves (pl. **-es**)

col'ic n. severe pains in the intestines —**coli'tis** n. inflammation of the colon

collab'orate vi. work with another on a project —**collabora'-tion** n. —**collab'orator** n. one who works with another, esp. one who aids an enemy in occupation of his own country

collage' [-ahzh′] n. (artistic) composition of bits and pieces stuck together on background

collapse' vi. fall; give way; lose strength, fail —n. act of collapsing; breakdown —**collaps'ible**, **-able** a.

coll'ar n. band, part of garment, worn round neck —vt. seize by collar; inf. capture, seize —**coll'arbone** n. bone from shoulder to breastbone

collate' vt. compare carefully; place in order (as printed sheets for binding) —**colla'tion** n. collating; light meal

collat'eral n. security pledged for repayment of loan —a. accompanying; side by side; of same stock but different line; subordinate

coll'eague [-ēg] n. associate,

companion in office or employment, fellow worker

collect'[1] vt. gather, bring together —vi. come together; inf. receive money —**collec'ted** a. calm; gathered —**collec'tion** n. —**collec'tive** a. factory, farm etc., run on principles of collectivism —a. —**collec'tively** adv. —**collec'tivism** n. theory that the State should own all means of production —**collec'tor** n.

coll'ect[2] n. short prayer

coll'ege [-lij] n. place of higher education; society of scholars; association —**colle'giate** a. —**colle'gian** n. student

collide' vi. strike or dash together; come into conflict —**colli'sion** [-lizh′ən] n. colliding

coll'ie n. silky-coated breed of sheepdog

coll'ier n. coal miner; coal ship —**coll'iery** n. coal mine mine

coll'ocate vt. group, place together —**colloca'tion** n.

collo'dion n. chemical solution used in photography and medicine

coll'oid n. suspension of particles in a solution

collo'quial a. pert. to, or used in, informal conversation —**collo'quialism** n. —**coll'oquy** [-kwi] n. conversation; dialogue

collu'sion [-lōō′-] n. secret agreement for a fraudulent purpose, esp. in legal proceedings —**collu'sive** a.

cologne' [kə-lōn′] n. perfumed liquid

co'lon[1] n. mark (:) indicating break in a sentence

co'lon[2] n. part of large intestine from caecum to rectum

colonel [kur′nəl] n. commander of regiment or battalion —**colo'nelcy** [kur′-] n.

colonnade' n. row of columns

col'ony n. body of people who

settle in new country but remain subject to parent state; country so settled; distinctive group living together —**colo'nial** a. of colony —**col'onist** n. —**coloniza'tion** n. —**col'onize** vt.

col'ophon n. publisher's imprint or device

coloss'us n. huge statue; something, somebody very large (pl. **coloss'i** [-ȷ], **-suses**) —**coloss'al** a. huge, gigantic

col'our [kul'ər] n. hue, tint; complexion; paint; pigment; fig. semblance, pretext; timbre, quality; mood —pl. flag; Sport distinguishing badge, symbol —vt. stain, dye, paint, give colour to; disguise; influence or distort —vi. become coloured; blush —**colora'tion** n. —**col'oured** a. non-White; in S Africa, of mixed descent —**col'ourful** a. with bright or varied colours; distinctive —**col'ourway** n. one of several colour combinations for wallpaper or fabric pattern

colt [-ō-] n. young male horse

colts'foot n. wild plant with heart-shaped leaves and yellow flowers

col'umbine n. flower with five spurred petals

col'umn [-m] n. long vertical cylinder, pillar; support; division of page; body of troops —**colum'nar** a. —**col'umnist** n. journalist writing regular feature for newspaper

co'ma n. state of unconsciousness —**co'matose** a.

comb [kōm] n. toothed instrument for tidying, arranging, ornamenting hair; cock's crest; mass of honey cells —vt. use comb on; search with great care

com'bat vt./n. fight, contest —**com'batant** n. —**com'bative** a.

combine' v. join together; ally —n. [kom'-] trust, syndicate, esp.

of businesses, trade organizations etc. —**combina'tion** n. —**com'binative** a. —**combine harvester** machine to harvest and thresh grain in one operation

combus'tion n. process of burning —**combustibil'ity** n. —**combus'tible** a.

come [kum] vi. approach, arrive, move towards; reach; happen to; occur; be available; originate (from); become; turn out to be (**came, come, com'ing**) —**come'-back** n. inf. return to active life after retirement; inf. retort —**come'down** n. setback; descent in social status

com'edy n. dramatic or other work of light, amusing character; humour —**come'dian** n. entertainer who tells jokes etc.; actor in comedy (**comedienne'** fem.)

come'ly [kum'-] a. fair, pretty, good-looking —**come'liness** n.

comest'ible n. (usu. pl.) food

com'et n. luminous heavenly body consisting of diffuse head, nucleus and long tail —**com'etary** a.

com'fit [kum'-] n. sweet

com'fort [kum'-] n. wellbeing; ease; consolation; means of consolation or satisfaction —vt. soothe; cheer, gladden, console —**com'fortable** a. free from pain etc.; inf. well-off financially —**com'fortably** adv. —**com'forter** n. one who comforts; baby's dummy; woollen scarf

com'frey [kum'-] n. wild plant with hairy leaves

com'ic a. relating to comedy; funny, laughable —n. comedian; magazine consisting of strip cartoons —**com'ical** a. —**com'ically** adv.

Comm. Commonwealth; Communist

comm'a n. punctuation mark (,)

separating short parts of sentence

command' [-mahnd'] vt. order; rule; compel; have in one's power; overlook, dominate —vi. exercise rule —n. order; power of controlling, ruling, dominating, overlooking; knowledge, mastery; post of one commanding; district commanded, jurisdiction —**comm'andant** n. —**commandeer'** vt. seize for military use, appropriate —**command'er** n. —**command'ing** a. in command; with air of authority —**command'ment** n.

comman'do [-mahn'dō] n. (member of) special military unit trained for airborne, amphibious attack (pl. **-dos**)

commem'orate vt. celebrate, keep in memory by ceremony; be a memorial of —**commemora'tion** n. —**commem'orative** a.

commence' v. begin —**commence'ment** n.

commend' vt. praise; commit, entrust —**commend'able** a. —**commend'ably** adv. —**commenda'tion** n. —**commend'atory** a.

commen'surate a. equal in size or length of time; in proportion, adequate

comm'ent n. remark, criticism; gossip; note, explanation —vi. remark, note; annotate, criticize —**comm'entary** n. explanatory notes or comments; spoken accompaniment to film etc. —**comm'entate** vi. —**comm'entator** n. author, speaker of commentary

comm'erce n. buying and selling; dealings; trade —**commer'cial** a. of, concerning, business, trade, profit etc. —n. advertisement, esp. on radio or television

commis'erate [-miz'-] vt. pity, condole, sympathize with —**commisera'tion** n.

comm'issar n. official of Communist Party responsible for political education

commissa'riat n. military department of food supplies and transport

commiss'ion [-sh'-] n. something entrusted to be done; delegated authority; body entrusted with some special duty; payment by percentage for doing something; warrant, esp. royal warrant, giving authority; document appointing soldier, sailor or airman to officer's rank; doing, committing —vt. charge with duty or task; Mil. confer a rank; give order for —**commiss'ioner** n. one empowered to act by commission or warrant; member of commission or government board

commissionaire' n. messenger, porter, doorkeeper (usu. uniformed)

commit' vt. entrust, give in charge; perpetrate, be guilty of; pledge, promise; compromise, entangle; send for trial (-**tt**-) —**commit'ment** n. —**committ'al** n.

committ'ee n. body appointed, elected for special business usu. from larger body

commode' n. chest of drawers; stool containing chamber pot

commo'dious a. roomy

commod'ity n. article of trade; anything useful

comm'odore n. naval officer, senior to captain; president of yacht club; senior captain in convoy of merchant ships

comm'on a. shared by or belonging to all, or to several; public, general; ordinary, usual, frequent; inferior; vulgar —n. land belonging to community

—*pl.* ordinary people; (C-) lower House of British Parliament, House of Commons —**com'monalty** *n.* general body of people —**com'oner** *n.* one of the common people, *ie* not of the nobility —**com'only** *adv.* —**Common Market** *see* EUROPEAN ECONOMIC COMMUNITY —**com'monplace** *a.* ordinary, everyday —*n.* trite remark; anything occurring frequently —**common sense** sound, practical understanding —**com'monwealth** *n.* republic; (C-) federation of self-governing states

commo'tion *n.* stir, disturbance, tumult

commune'[1] [-myōō-] *vi.* converse together intimately —**commu'nion** *n.* sharing of thoughts, feelings *etc.*; fellowship; body with common faith; (C-) participation in sacrament of the Lord's Supper; (C-) that sacrament, Eucharist

comm'une[2] *n.* group of families, individuals living together and sharing property, responsibility *etc.* —**comm'unal** *a.* for common use

commu'nicate *vt.* impart, convey; reveal —*vi.* give or exchange information; have connecting passage, door; receive Communion —**commu'nicable** *a.* —**commu'nicant** *n.* one who receives Communion —**communica'tion** *n.* act of giving, *esp.* information; information, message; (*usu. pl.*) passage (road, railway *etc.*), or means of exchanging messages (radio, post *etc.*) between places —*pl.* connections between military base and front —**commu'nicative** *a.* free with information

commu'niqué [-ni-kā] *n.* official announcement

comm'unism *n.* doctrine that all goods, means of production *etc.*, should be property of community —**comm'unist** *n./a.* —**communis'tic** *a.*

commu'nity *n.* body of people with something in common, *eg* district of residence, religion *etc.*; society, the public; joint ownership; similarity, agreement —**community centre** building for communal activities

commute'[1] [-myōō-] *vi.* travel daily some distance to work —*vt.* exchange; change (punishment *etc.*) into something less severe; change (duty *etc.*) for money payment —**commuta'tion** *n.* —**com'mutator** *n.* device to change alternating electric current into direct current —**commu'ter** *n.* one who travels some distance daily to work

compact'[1] *a.* neatly arranged or packed; solid, concentrated; terse —*v.* make, become compact; compress —**compact'ly** *adv.* —**compact'ness** *n.* —**compact disc** small disc on which sound is recorded as series of metallic pits enclosed in PVC and played back by optical scanning by laser

com'pact[2] *n.* small case to hold face powder, powder puff and mirror

com'pact[3] *n.* agreement, covenant, treaty, contract

compan'ion[1] *n.* mate, fellow, comrade, associate; person employed to live with another —**compan'ionable** *a.* —**compan'ionship** *n.*

compan'ion[2] *n.* raised cover over staircase from deck to cabin of ship; deck skylight —**compan'ionway** *n.* staircase from deck to cabin

com'pany [kum'-] *n.* gathering of persons; companionship, fellowship; guests; business firm;

division of regiment under captain; crew of ship; actors in play

compare' vt. notice or point out likenesses and differences of things; liken; make comparative and superlative of adjective or adverb —vi. be like; compete with —**comparabil'ity** n. —**com'parable** a. —**compar'ative** [-pa'r∂-] a. that may be compared; not absolute; relative, partial; Grammar denoting form of adjective, adverb, indicating 'more' —n. —**compar'atively** adv. —**compar'ison** [-pa'ri-] n. act of comparing

compart'ment n. division or part divided off, eg in railway carriage; section

com'pass [kum'-] n. instrument for showing the north; (usu. pl.) instrument for drawing circles; circumference; measurement round; space, area; scope, reach —vt. surround; comprehend; attain, accomplish

compass'ion [-sh'-] n. pity, sympathy —**compass'ionate** a. —**compass'ionately** adv.

compat'ible a. capable of harmonious existence; consistent, agreeing with —**compatibil'ity** n. —**compat'ibly** adv.

compat'riot n. fellow countryman —a.

com'peer n. equal, associate, companion

compel' vt. force, oblige; bring about by force (-ll-)

compend'ium n. collection of different games; abridgment, summary (pl. -s, -ia) —**compen'dious** a. brief but inclusive —**compen'diously** adv.

com'pensate vt. make up for; recompense suitably; reward —**compensa'tion** n.

com'père [kom'per] n. one who presents artists in cabaret, television shows etc. —vt.

compete' vi. (oft. with with) strive in rivalry, contend for, vie with —**competi'tion** n. —**compet'itive** a. —**compet'itor** n.

com'petent a. able, skilful; properly qualified; proper, due, legitimate; suitable, sufficient —**com'petence** n. efficiency —**com'petently** adv.

compile' vt. make up (eg book) from various sources or materials; gather, put together —**compila'tion** n. —**compil'er** n.

compla'cent a. self-satisfied; pleased or gratified —**compla'cence, -cency** n. —**compla'cently** adv.

complain' vi. grumble; bring charge, make known a grievance; (with of) make known that one is suffering from —**complaint'** n. statement of a wrong, grievance; ailment, illness —**complain'ant** n.

complai'sant [-lā'z-] a. obliging, willing to please, compliant —**complai'sance** n. act of pleasing; affability

com'plement n. something making up a whole; full allowance, equipment etc. —vt. add to, make complete —**complemen'tary** a.

complete' a. full, perfect; finished, ended; entire; thorough —vt. make whole, perfect; finish —**complete'ly** adv. —**complete'ness** n. —**comple'tion** n.

com'plex a. intricate, compound, involved —n. complicated whole; group of related buildings; psychological abnormality, obsession —**complex'ity** n.

complex'ion [-ek'sh∂n] n. look, colour, of skin, esp. of face, appearance; aspect, character; disposition

compli'ant see COMPLY

com'plicate vt. make intri-

cate, involved, difficult, mix up
—**complica'tion** n.

complic'ity [-plis'-] n. partnership in wrongdoing

com'pliment n. expression of regard, praise; flattering speech —pl. expression of courtesy, formal greetings —vt. praise, congratulate —**complimen'tary** a. expressing praise; free of charge

com'plin(e) n. last service of day in R.C. Church

comply' vi. consent, yield, do as asked (**complied'**, **comply'ing**) —**compli'ance** n. —**compli'ant** a.

compo'nent n. part, element, constituent of whole —a. composing, making up

comport' v. agree; behave

compose' vt. arrange, put in order; write, invent; make up; calm; settle, adjust —**composed'** a. calm —**compo'ser** n. one who composes, esp. music —**compo'site** a. made up of distinct parts —**composi'tion** n. —**compos'itor** n. typesetter, one who arranges type for printing —**compo'sure** n. calmness

com'pos men'tis Lat. of sound mind

com'post n. fertilizing mixture of decayed vegetable matter for soil

com'pote [-pōt] n. fruit stewed or preserved in syrup

com'pound[1] n. mixture, joining; substance, word, made up of parts —a. not simple; composite, mixed —vt. [kəm-pownd'] mix, make up, put together; intensify, make worse; compromise, settle debt by partial payment; Law agree not to prosecute in return for a consideration

com'pound[2] n. (fenced or walled) enclosure containing houses etc.

comprehend' vt. understand, take in; include, comprise —**com-**

prehen'sible a. —**comprehen'-sion** n. —**comprehen'sive** a. wide, full; taking in much —**comprehen'sively** adv. —**comprehen'siveness** n. —**comprehensive school** secondary school for children of all abilities

compress' vt. squeeze together; make smaller in size, bulk —n. [kom'-] pad of lint applied to wound, inflamed part etc. —**compress'ible** a. —**compress'ion** [-sh'-] n. in internal combustion engine, squeezing of explosive charge before ignition, to give additional force —**compress'or** n. esp. machine to compress air, gas

comprise' vt. include, contain —**compri'sable** a.

com'promise [-īz] n. meeting halfway, coming to terms by giving up part of claim; middle course —v. settle (dispute) by making concessions —vt. expose to risk or suspicion

Comptom'eter R a calculating machine

comptro'ller [kən-trō'-] n. controller (in some titles)

compul'sion n. act of compelling; irresistible impulse —**compul'sive** a. —**compul'sorily** adv. —**compuls'ory** a. not optional

compunc'tion n. regret for wrongdoing

compute' [-pyōō] vt. reckon, calculate, esp. using computer —**computa'tion** n. reckoning, estimate —**compu'ter** n. electronic machine for storing, retrieving information and performing calculations —**compu'terize** v. equip with, perform by computer

com'rade n. mate, companion, friend —**com'radeship** n.

con[1] v. inf. (short for confidence trick) swindle, defraud

con[2] n. abbrev. of contra, against

—**pros and cons** (arguments) for and against

con[3] *vt.* direct steering of ship (-**nn**-) —**conn'er** *vt.*

concat'enate *vt.* link together —**concatena'tion** *n.* connected chain (as of circumstances)

concave' [*or* -kāv'] *a.* hollow, rounded inwards —**concav'ity** *n.*

conceal' [-sēl'] *vt.* hide, keep secret —**conceal'ment** *n.*

concede' [-sēd'] *vt.* admit, admit truth of; grant, allow, yield

conceit' [-sēt'] *n.* vanity, overweening opinion of oneself; farfetched comparison —**conceit'ed** *a.*

conceive' [-sēv'] *v.* think of, imagine; believe; form in the mind; become pregnant —**conceiv'able** *a.* —**conceiv'ably** *adv.*

con'centrate *vt.* focus (one's efforts *etc.*); increase in strength; reduce to small space —*vi.* devote all attention; come together —*n.* concentrated material or solution —**concentra'tion** *n.* —**concentration camp** prison camp, *esp.* one in Nazi Germany

concen'tric *a.* having the same centre

con'cept *n.* abstract idea; mental expression —**concep'tual** *a.* —**concep'tualize** *v.*

concep'tion *n.* idea, notion; act of conceiving

concern' *vt.* relate, apply to; interest, affect, trouble; (*with* in *or* with) involve (oneself) —*n.* affair; regard, worry; importance; business, enterprise —**concerned'** *a.* connected with; interested; worried; involved —**concern'ing** *prep.* respecting, about

con'cert *n.* musical entertainment; harmony, agreement —*vt.* [kən-sert'] arrange, plan together —**concert'ed** *a.* mutually arranged, planned; determined

—**concerti'na** [-sər-tē'-] *n.* musical instrument with bellows and keys —*vi.* fold, collapse, as bellows —**concert'o** [-cher'-] *n.* musical composition for solo instrument and orchestra (*pl.* -**tos**)

concess'ion [-sh'-] *n.* act of conceding; thing conceded; grant; special privilege —**concess'ive** *a.*

conch [kongk *or* konch] *n.* seashell —**con'choid** [-k-] *n.* shell-like curve —**conchol'ogy** [kong-kol'-] *n.* study, collection of shells and shellfish

concierge' [kon-si-erzh'] *n.* in France, caretaker, doorkeeper

concil'iate *vt.* pacify, win over from hostility —**concilia'tion** *n.* —**concil'iator** *n.* —**concil'iatory** *a.*

concise' [-sīs'] *a.* brief, terse —**concise'ly** *adv.* —**concise'ness** *n.* —**concl'sion** [-si'zh-] *n.*

con'clave *n.* private meeting; assembly for election of Pope

conclude' [-ōōd'] *vt.* end, finish; deduce; settle —*vi.* come to end; decide —**conclu'sion** *n.* —**conclu'sive** *a.* decisive, convincing —**conclu'sively** *adv.*

concoct' *vt.* make mixture, prepare with various ingredients; make up; contrive, plan —**concoc'tion** *n.*

concom'itant *a.* accompanying —**concom'itance** *n.* existence

con'cord *n.* agreement; harmony —*vi.* [-kord'] agree —**concord'ance** *n.* agreement; index to words of book (*esp.* Bible) —**concord'ant** *a.*

con'course *n.* crowd; large, open place in public area

con'crete *n.* mixture of sand, cement *etc.*, used in building —*a.* made of concrete; particular, specific; perceptible, actual; solid —**con'cretely** *adv.* —**concre'tion** *n.* mass of compressed particles;

stonelike growth in body

conc'ubine [-ngk'yoo-] n. woman living with man as his wife, but not married to him; 'secondary' wife of inferior legal status —**concu'binage** n.

concu'piscence n. lust

concur' vi. agree, express agreement; happen together; coincide (-**rr**-) —**concur'rence** n. —**concur'rent** a. —**concur'rently** adv. at the same time

concuss' vt. injure brain by blow, fall etc. —**concuss'ion** n. brain injury; physical shock

condemn' vt. blame; find guilty; doom; find, declare unfit for use —**condemna'tion** n. —**condem'natory** a.

condense' vt. concentrate, make more solid; turn from gas into liquid; pack into few words —vi. turn from gas to liquid —**condensa'tion** n. —**conden'ser** n. Electricity apparatus for storing electrical energy, a capacitor; apparatus for reducing vapours to liquid form; a lens or mirror for focusing light

condescend' vi. treat graciously one regarded as inferior; do something below one's dignity —**condescend'ing** a. —**condescen'sion** n.

con'diment n. relish, seasoning for food

condi'tion [-dish'-] n. state or circumstances of anything; thing on which statement or happening or existing depends; stipulation, prerequisite; health, physical fitness; rank —vt. accustom; regulate; make fit, healthy; be essential to happening or existence of; stipulate —**condi'tional** a. dependent on circumstances or events —n. Grammar form of verbs —**conditioned reflex** in psychology and physiology, automatic response induced by stimulus repeatedly applied

condole' vi. grieve with, offer sympathy; commiserate with —**condo'lence** n.

con'dom n. sheathlike rubber contraceptive device worn by man

condomin'ium n. joint rule by two or more states

condone' vt. overlook, forgive, treat as not existing

con'dor n. large vulture found in the Andes

conduce' [-dyōōs'] vi. help, promote; tend towards —**condu'cive** a.

con'duct n. behaviour; management —vt. [kən-dukt'] escort, guide; lead, direct; manage; transmit (heat, electricity) —**conduc'tion** n. —**conduc'tive** a. —**conductiv'ity** n. —**conduc'tor** n. person in charge of bus etc., who collects fares; director of orchestra; one who leads, guides; substance capable of transmitting heat, electricity etc.; US official in charge of passenger train

con'duit [-dit] n. channel or pipe for conveying water, electric cables etc.

cone n. solid figure with circular base, tapering to a point; fruit of pine, fir etc. —**con'ic(al)** a.

confab'ulate vi. chat —**con'fab** n. inf. shortened form of **confabula'tion** n. confidential conversation

confec'tion n. prepared delicacy, esp. something sweet —**confec'tioner** n. dealer in fancy cakes, pastries, sweets etc. —**confec'tionery** n. sweets, cakes etc.

confed'erate [-rit] n. ally; accomplice —v. [-rāt] unite —**confed'eracy** n. —**confedera'tion** n. alliance of political units

confer' vt. grant, give; bestow;

award —*vi.* talk with, take advice (**-rr-**) —**con'ference** *n.* meeting for consultation or deliberation —**confer'ment** *n.*

confess' *vt.* admit, own; (of priest) hear sins of —*vi.* acknowledge; declare one's sins orally to priest —**confes'sion** *n.* —**confes'sional** *n.* confessor's stall or box —**confes'sor** *n.* priest who hears confessions

confet'ti *pl.n.* small bits of coloured paper for throwing at weddings

confide' *vi.* (**with** in) tell secrets, trust —*vt.* entrust —**confi'dant'** *n.* one entrusted with secrets (**-e** *fem.*) —**con'fidence** *n.* trust; boldness, assurance; intimacy; something confided, secret —**con'fident** *a.* —**confiden'tial** *a.* private; secret; entrusted with another's confidences —**confiden'tially** *adv.* —**con'fidently** *adv.* —**confidence trick** swindle in which victim entrusts money *etc.*, to thief, believing him honest

configura'tion *n.* shape, aspect, conformation, arrangement

confine' *vt.* keep within bounds, keep in house, bed *etc.*; shut up, imprison —**con'fines** *pl.n.* boundaries, limits —**confine'ment** *n.* esp. childbirth

confirm' *vt.* make sure, verify; strengthen, settle; make valid, ratify; administer confirmation to —**confirma'tion** *n.* making strong, certain; rite administered by bishop to confirm vows made at baptism —**confirm'ative, confirm'atory** *a.* tending to confirm or establish; corroborative —**confirmed'** *a.* (of habit *etc.*) long-established

con'fiscate *vt.* seize by authority —**confisca'tion** *n.* —**confis'catory** *a.*

conflagra'tion *n.* great destructive fire

conflate' *vt.* combine, blend to form whole

con'flict *n.* struggle, trial of strength; disagreement —*vi.* [-flikt'] be at odds with, be inconsistent with; clash

con'fluence, con'flux *n.* union of streams; meeting place —**con'fluent** *a.*

conform' *v.* comply with accepted standards, conventions *etc.*; adapt to rule, pattern, custom *etc.* —**conform'able** *a.* —**conform'ably** *adv.* —**conforma'tion** *n.* structure, adaptation —**conform'ist** *n.* one who conforms, *esp.* excessively —**conform'ity** *n.* compliance

confound' *vt.* baffle, perplex; confuse; defeat —**confound'ed** *a. esp. inf.* damned

confront' [-unt'] *vt.* face; bring face to face with —**confronta'tion** *n.*

confuse' [-fyōō-] *vt.* bewilder; jumble; make unclear; mistake (one thing) for another; disconcert —**confu'sion** *n.*

confute' [-fyōō-] *vt.* prove wrong; disprove —**confuta'tion** *n.*

con'ga [-ng'g-] *n.* Latin American dance performed by number of people in single file

congeal' [-j-] *v.* solidify by cooling or freezing —**congela'tion** *n.*

conge'nial [-jē'-] *a.* pleasant, to one's liking; of similar disposition, tastes *etc.* —**congenial'ity** *n.* —**conge'nially** *adv.*

congen'ital [-jen'-] *a.* existing at birth; dating from birth

con'ger [-ng'g-] *n.* variety of large, voracious, sea eel

conge'ries [-jē'-] *n. sing. and pl.* collection or mass of small bodies, conglomeration

congest' [-jest'] *v.* overcrowd or

clog —**conges'tion** n. abnormal accumulation, overcrowding —**congest'ed** a.

conglom'erate n. thing, substance (*esp.* rock) composed of mixture of other, smaller elements or pieces; business organization comprising many companies —v. gather together —a. —**conglomera'tion** n.

conglu'tinate [-gloō-] v. glue or grow together; heal by uniting

congrat'ulate vt. express pleasure at good fortune, success *etc.* —**congratula'tion** n. —**congrat'ulatory** a.

con'gregate [-ng'gr-] v. assemble; collect, flock together —**congrega'tion** n. assembly, *esp.* for worship —**congrega'tional** a. —**Congrega'tionalism** n. system in which each separate church is self-governing —**congrega'tionalist** n.

con'gress [-ng'gr-] n. meeting; formal assembly for discussion; legislative body —**congress'ional** a. —**con'gressman** n. member of the U.S. Congress

con'gruent [-ng'gr-] a. suitable, accordant; fitting together, *esp.* triangles —**con'gruence** n. —**congru'ity** n. —**con'gruous** a.

con'ic see CONE

co'nifer [or kon'-] n. conebearing tree, as fir, pine *etc.* —**conif'erous** a.

conjec'ture n. guess, guesswork —v. guess, surmise —**conjec'tural** a.

conjoin' vt. combine —vi. come, or act, together —**conjoint'** a. concerted, united —**conjoint'ly** adv.

con'jugal a. relating to marriage; between married persons —**conjugal'ity** n.

con'jugate v. inflect verb in its various forms (past, present *etc.*) —**conjuga'tion** n.

conjunc'tion n. union; simultaneous happening; part of speech joining words, phrases *etc.* —**conjunc'tive** a. —**conjunc'tive** n.

conjuncti'va n. mucous membrane lining eyelid —**conjunctivi'tis** n. inflammation of this

con'jure [kun'jər] v. produce magic effects; perform tricks by jugglery *etc.*; invoke devils; [kən'joor'] implore earnestly —**conjura'tion** n. —**con'jurer, -or** n.

conk inf. vt. strike (*esp.* on head) —vi. (*oft.* with out) break down

con'ker n. inf. horse chestnut

connect' v. join together, unite; associate in the mind —**connec'tion, connex'ion** n. association; train, *etc.* timed to enable passengers to transfer from another; family relation —**connec'tive** a. —**connecting rod** that part of engine which transfers motion from piston to crankshaft

conning tower armoured control position in submarine, battleship, *etc.*; see CON[3]

connive' vi. plot, conspire; assent, refrain from preventing or forbidding —**conni'vance** n.

connoisseur' [kon-i-sur'] n. critical expert in matters of taste, *esp.* fine arts; competent judge

connote' vt. imply, mean in addition to primary meaning —**connota'tion** n.

connu'bial a. of marriage

con'quer [kong'kər] vt. win by force of arms, overcome; defeat —vi. be victorious —**con'queror** n. —**con'quest** [kon'kwest] n.

Cons. Conservative

consanguin'ity n. kinship —**consanguin'eous** a.

con'science [-shəns] n. sense of right or wrong governing person's words and actions —**conscien'tious** a. scrupulous; obedient to the dictates of conscience —**conscien'tiously** adv. —**conscientious objector** one who refuses military service on moral or religious grounds

con'scious [-shəs] a. aware; awake to one's surroundings and identity; deliberate, intentional —**con'sciously** adv. —**con'sciousness** n. being conscious

con'script n. one compulsorily enlisted for military service —**conscript'** vt. —**conscrip'tion** n.

con'secrate vt. make sacred —**consecra'tion** n.

consec'utive a. in unbroken succession —**consec'utively** adv.

consen'sus n. widespread agreement, unanimity

consent' vi. agree to, comply —n. acquiescence; permission; agreement —**consen'tient** a.

con'sequence n. result, effect, outcome; that which naturally follows; significance, importance —**con'sequent** a. —**consequen'tial** a. important —**con'sequently** adv. therefore, as a result

conservatoire ['-twahr'] n. school for teaching music

conserve' vt. keep from change or decay; preserve; maintain —n. [also kon'-] jam, preserved fruit etc. —**conserva'tion** n. protection, careful management of natural resources and environment —**conserva'tionist** n./a. —**conserv'ative** a. tending, or wishing to conserve; moderate —n. Politics one who desires to preserve institutions of his country against change and innovation; one opposed to hasty changes or innovations —**conserv'atism** n. —**conserv'atory** n. greenhouse

consid'er vt. think over; examine; make allowance for; be of opinion that; discuss —**consid'er-**

able a. important; somewhat large —**consid'erably** adv. —**consid'erate** a. thoughtful for others' feelings, careful —**consid'erately** adv. —**considera'tion** n. deliberation; point of importance; thoughtfulness; bribe, recompense

consign' [-īn'] vt. commit, hand over; entrust to carrier —**consignee'** n. —**consign'ment** n. goods consigned —**consign'or** n.

consist' vi. be composed of; (with in) have as basis; agree with, be compatible —**consist'ency, consist'ence** n. agreement; harmony; degree of firmness —**consist'ent** a. unchanging, constant; agreeing (with) —**consist'ently** adv.

consis'tory n. ecclesiastical court or council, esp. of Pope and Cardinals

console'[1] vt. comfort, cheer in distress —**consola'tion** n. —**consol'atory** a.

con'sole[2] n. bracket supporting shelf; keyboard, stops etc., of organ; cabinet for television, radio etc.

consol'idate vt. combine into connected whole; make firm, secure —**consolida'tion** n.

consommé [-ā] n. clear meat soup

con'sonant n. sound making a syllable only with vowel; nonvowel —a. agreeing with, in accord —**con'sonance** n.

consort' vi. associate, keep company with —n. [kon'-] husband, wife, esp. of ruler; ship sailing with another —**consor'tium** n. association of banks, companies etc.

conspec'tus n. a comprehensive view or survey of subject; synopsis

conspic'uous a. striking, noticeable, outstanding; prominent;

eminent —**conspic'uously** adv.

conspire' vi. combine for evil purpose; plot, devise —**conspir'acy** n. —**conspir'ator** n. —**conspirato'rial** a.

con'stable [kun'-] n. policeman of the lowest rank; *Hist.* officer of the peace —**constab'ulary** n. police force

con'stant a. fixed, unchanging; steadfast; always duly happening or continuing —n. quantity that does not vary —**con'stancy** n. steadfastness; loyalty —**con'stantly** adv.

constella'tion n. group of stars

consterna'tion n. alarm, dismay, panic —**con'sternate** v.

constipa'tion n. difficulty in emptying bowels —**con'stipate** vt. affect with this disorder

constit'uent a. going towards making up whole; having power to make, alter constitution of state; electing representative —n. component part; element; elector —**constit'uency** n. body of electors; parliamentary division

con'stitute vt. compose, set up, establish, form; make into, found, give form to —**constitu'tion** n. structure, composition; health; character, disposition; principles on which state is governed —**constitu'tional** a. pert. to constitution; in harmony with political constitution —n. walk taken for health's sake —**constitu'tionally** adv.

constrain' vt. force, compel —**constraint'** n. compulsion; restraint; embarrassment, tension

constric'tion n. compression, squeezing together —**constrict'** vt. —**constrict'ive** a. —**constric'tor** n. that which constricts; *see also* BOA

construct' vt. make, build, form; put together; compose —**con'struct** n. —**construc'tion** n. —**construc'tive** a. serving to improve; positive —**construc'tively** adv.

construe' vt. interpret; deduce; analyse grammatically

con'sul n. officer appointed by a government to represent it in a foreign country; in ancient Rome, one of the chief magistrates —**con'sular** [-syoo-] a. —**con'sulate** n. —**con'sulship** n.

consult' v. seek counsel, advice, information from —**consul'tant** n. specialist, expert; senior hospital physician or surgeon —**consulta'tion** n. consulting; appointment to seek professional advice, *esp.* of doctor, lawyer —**consul'tative** a. having privilege of consulting, but not of voting; advisory

consume' [-syōom'] vt. eat or drink; engross, possess; use up; destroy —**consu'mer** n. buyer or user of commodity; one who consumes —**consump'tion** n. using up; destruction; wasting disease, *esp.* tuberculosis of the lungs —**consump'tive** a./n. —**consump'tiveness** n.

con'summate vt. perfect; fulfil; complete (*esp.* marriage by sexual intercourse) —a. [-sum'-] of greatest perfection or completeness —**consumm'ately** adv. —**consumma'tion** n.

cont. continued

con'tact n. touching; being in touch; junction of two or more electrical conductors; useful acquaintance —vt. —**contact lens** lens fitting over eyeball to correct defect of vision

conta'gion [-jən] n. passing on of disease by touch, contact; contagious disease; harmful physical or moral influence

—**conta'gious** a. communicable by contact, catching

contain' vt. hold; have room for; include, comprise; restrain (oneself) —**contain'er** n. box etc. for holding; large cargo-carrying standard-sized receptacle for different modes of transport

contam'inate vt. stain, pollute, infect; make radioactive —**contamina'tion** n. pollution

con'template vt. reflect, meditate on; gaze upon; intend —**contempla'tion** n. thoughtful consideration; spiritual meditation —**con'templative** [or -tem'-] a./n. (one) given to contemplation

contem'porary a. existing or lasting at same time; of same age; present-day —n. one existing at same time as another —**contempora'neous** a.

contempt' n. feeling that something is worthless, despicable etc.; expression of this feeling; state of being despised, disregarded; wilful disrespect of authority

contend' vi. strive, fight; dispute —vt. maintain (that) —**conten'tion** n. strife; debate; subject matter of dispute —**conten'tious** a. quarrelsome; causing dispute —**conten'tiously** adv.

con'tent' n. that contained; holding capacity —pl. that contained; index of topics in book

content' [¹] ² a. satisfied; willing (to) —vt. satisfy —n. satisfaction —**content'ed** a. —**content'ment** n.

conter'minous, conter'minal a. of the same extent (in time etc.); meeting along a common boundary; meeting end to end

con'test n. competition; conflict —vt. [-test'] dispute, debate; fight or compete for —**contest'able** a.

—**contest'ant** n. —**contesta'tion** n.

con'text n. words coming before, after a word or passage; conditions and circumstances of event, fact etc. —**context'ual** a.

contig'uous a. touching, near —**contigu'ity** n.

con'tinent' [¹] n. large continuous mass of land —**continent'al** a.

con'tinent² a. able to control one's urination and defecation; sexually chaste —**con'tinence** n.

contin'gent [-j-] a. depending (on); possible; accidental —n. group (of troops, sportsmen etc.) part of or representative of a larger group —**contin'gency** n. —**contin'gently** adv.

contin'ue v. remain, keep in existence; carry on, last, go on; resume; prolong —**contin'ual** a. —**contin'ually** adv. —**continua'tion** n. extension, extra part; resumption; constant succession, prolongation —**continu'ity** n. logical sequence; state of being continuous —**contin'uous** a. —**contin'uously** adv.

contort' vt. twist out of normal shape —**contor'tion** n. —**contor'tionist** n. one who contorts his body to entertain

con'tour [-oor] n. outline, shape, esp. mountains, coast etc. —con-tour line line on map drawn through places of same height —contour map

contra- (comb. form) against, as in contradistinc'tion, contraposi'tion etc. Such words are omitted where the meaning may easily be inferred from the simple word

con'traband n. smuggled goods; illegal traffic in such goods —a. prohibited by law

contracep'tion n. prevention of conception usu. by artificial means, birth control —**contra-cep'tive** *a./n.*

contract' *v.* make or become smaller, shorter; [*or* kon'-] enter into agreement; agree upon —*vt.* incur, become affected by —*n.* [kon'-] bargain, agreement; formal document recording agreement; agreement enforceable by law —**contract'ed** *a.* drawn together —**contract'ile** *a.* tending to contract —**contrac'tion** *n.* —**contrac'tor** *n.* one making contract, *esp.* builder —**contract'ual** *a.*

contradict' *vt.* deny; be at variance or inconsistent with —**contradic'tion** *n.* —**contradic'tious** *a.* —**contradic'tor** *n.* —**contradic'tory** *a.*

con'traflow *n.* two-way traffic on one carriageway of motorway

contral'to *n.* lowest of three female voices (*pl.* -s)

contrap'tion *n.* gadget; device; construction, device often overelaborate or eccentric

contrapun'tal *a. Mus.* pert. to counterpoint

con'trary *a.* opposed; opposite, other; [kən-trār'-] perverse, obstinate —*n.* something the exact opposite of another —*adv.* in opposition —**contrari'ety** *n.* —**contra'rily** *adv.* —**con'trariwise** *adv.* conversely

contrast' [-ah—] *vt.* bring out differences; set in opposition for comparison —*vi.* show great difference —*n.* [kon'-] striking difference; *Television* sharpness of image

contravene' *vt.* transgress, infringe; conflict with; contradict —**contraven'tion** *n.*

con'tretemps [kon'trə-tahn] *n.* unexpected and embarrassing event or mishap

contrib'ute *v.* give, pay to common fund; help to occur;

write for the press —**contribu'tion** *n.* —**contrib'utive** *a.* —**contrib'utor** *n.* one who writes articles for newspapers *etc.*; one who donates —**contrib'utory** *a.* partly responsible; giving to pension fund *etc.*

con'trite [*or* -trīt'] *a.* remorseful for wrongdoing, penitent —**con'tritely** *adv.* —**contri'tion** *n.*

contrive' *vt.* manage; devise, invent, design —**contri'vance** *n.* artifice or device —**contrived'** *a.* obviously planned, artificial —**contri'ver** *n.*

control' [-ōl'] *vt.* command, dominate; regulate; direct, check, test (-ll-) —*n.* power to direct or determine; curb, check; standard of comparison in experiment —*pl.n.* system of instruments to control car, aircraft *etc.* —**controll'able** *a.* —**controll'er** *n.* one who controls; official controlling expenditure —**control tower** tower in airfield from which take-offs and landings are directed

con'troversy [*or* -trov'-] *n.* dispute, debate, *esp.* over public issues —**controver'sial** *a.* —**controver'sialist** *n.* —**con'trovert** *vt.* deny; argue —**controvert'ible** *a.*

con'tumacy [-tyoo-] *n.* stubborn disobedience —**contuma'cious** *a.*

con'tumely [-tyoom-i-li] *n.* insulting language or treatment —**contume'lious** *a.* abusive, insolent

contu'sion [-yoo'zh-] *n.* bruise —**contuse'** *vt.* bruise

conun'drum *n.* riddle, *esp.* with punning answer

conurba'tion *n.* densely populated urban sprawl formed by spreading of towns

convalesce' [-es'] *vi.* recover health after illness, operation *etc.* —**convales'cence** *n.* —**convales'cent** *a./n.*

convec'tion *n.* transmission, *esp.* of heat, by currents in liquids or gases —**convec'tor** *n.*

convene' *vt.* call together, assemble, convoke —**conven'tion** *n.* assembly; treaty, agreement; rule; practice based on agreement; accepted usage —**conven'tional** *a.* (slavishly) observing customs of society; customary; (of weapons, war *etc.*) not nuclear —**conventional'ity** *n.* —**conven'tionally** *adv.*

conve'nient *a.* handy; favourable to needs, comfort; well-adapted to one's purpose —**conve'nience** *n.* ease, comfort, suitability; a (public) lavatory —*a.* (of food) quick to prepare —**conve'niently** *adv.*

con'vent *n.* religious community, *esp.* of nuns; their building —**conven'tual** *a.*

converge' *vi.* approach, tend to meet —**conver'gence, -gency** *n.* —**conver'gent** *a.*

conver'sant *a.* acquainted, familiar (with), versed in

conversa'tion *see* CONVERSE[1]

converse'[1] *vi.* talk (with) —*n.* [kon'-] talk —**conversa'tion** *n.* —**conversa'tional** *a.* —**conversa'tionalist** *n.*

con'verse[2] *a.* opposite, turned round, reversed —*n.* the opposite, contrary

convert' *vt.* apply to another purpose; change; transform; cause to adopt (another) religion, opinion; *Rugby* make a conversion —*n.* [kon'-] converted person —**conver'sion** *n.* change of state; unauthorized appropriation; change of opinion, religion, or party; *Rugby* score made after a try by kicking ball over crossbar —**convert'er** *n.* one who, that which converts; electrical ma-

chine for changing alternating current into direct current; vessel in which molten metal is refined —**conver'tible** *n.* car with folding roof —*a.*

con'vex [*or* -veks'] *a.* curved outwards; of a rounded form —**convex'ity** *n.*

convey' *vt.* carry, transport; impart, communicate; *Law* make over, transfer —**convey'ance** *n.* carrying; vehicle; act by which title to property is transferred —**convey'ancer** *n.* one skilled in legal forms of transferring property —**convey'ancing** *n.* this work —**conveyor belt** continuous moving belt for transporting things, *esp.* in factory

convict' *vt.* prove or declare guilty —*n.* [kon'-] person found guilty of crime; criminal serving prison sentence —**convic'tion** *n.* verdict of guilty; being convinced, firm belief, state of being sure

convince' *vt.* firmly persuade, satisfy by evidence or argument —**convin'cing** *a.* capable of compelling belief, effective

conviv'ial *a.* sociable, festive, jovial —**convivial'ity** *n.*

convoke' *vt.* call together —**convoca'tion** *n.* calling together, assembly, *esp.* of clergy, university graduates *etc.*

con'volute [-lōot] *vt.* twist, coil, tangle —**con'voluted** *a.* —**convolu'tion** *n.*

convol'vulus *n.* genus of plants with twining stems

con'voy *n.* party (of ships, troops, lorries *etc.*) travelling together for protection —*vt.* escort for protection

convulse' *vt.* shake violently; affect with violent involuntary contractions of muscles —**convul'sion** *n.* violent upheaval —*pl.* spasms; fits of laughter or hysteria —**convul'sive** a. —**convul'sively** adv.

co'n(e)y n. rabbit

coo n. cry of doves —vi. make such cry (**cooed** [kōōd], **coo'ing**)

cook vt. prepare (food) for table, esp. by heat; inf. falsify (accounts etc.) —vi. undergo cooking; act as cook —n. one who prepares food for table —**cook'er** n. cooking apparatus; cooking apple —**cook'ery** n. —**cook'ie** n. (esp. US) biscuit —**cook up** inf. invent, plan; prepare meal

cool a. moderately cold; unexcited, calm; lacking friendliness or interest; inf. calmly insolent; inf. sophisticated, elegant —v. make, become cool —n. cool time, place etc.; inf. calmness, composure —**cool'ant** n. fluid used for cooling tool, machinery etc. —**cool'er** n. vessel in which liquids are cooled; sl. prison —**cool'ly** adv.

cool'ie n. (oft. offens.) cheaply hired oriental unskilled labour

coomb [kōōm] n. valley

coon n. sl. offens. coloured person

coop[1] n. cage or pen for fowls —vt. shut up in a coop; confine

co'op[2], **co-op** [kō'op] n. co-operative society or shop run by one

coop'er n. one who makes casks

coop'erate [kō-op'-] vi. work together —**coopera'tion** n. —**coop'erative** a. willing to cooperate; (of an enterprise) owned collectively and managed for joint economic benefit (also n.) —**coop'erator** n.

coopt'[1] [kō-opt'] vt. bring on (committee etc.) as member, colleague, without election by larger body choosing first members

coord'inate [kō-awrd'-] vt. bring into order as parts of whole; place in same rank; put into harmony —n. Maths any of set of numbers defining location of point —a. equal in degree, status etc. —**coordina'tion** n. —**coord'inative** a.

coot n. small black water fowl; sl. silly (old) person

cop sl. vt. catch; (usu. with it) be punished —n. policeman; a capture

co'pal n. resin used in varnishes

copart'ner n. joint partner —**copart'nership** n.

cope[1] vi. deal successfully (with)

cope[2] n. ecclesiastical vestment like long cloak

Coper'nican a. pert. to Copernicus, Polish astronomer (1473–1543), or to his system

co'ping n. top course of wall, usu. sloping to throw off rain

co'pious a. abundant; plentiful; full, ample —**co'piously** adv. —**co'piousness** n.

copp'er[1] n. reddish-brown malleable ductile metal; bronze money, coin; large washing vessel —vt. cover with copper —**copper beech** tree with reddish leaves —**copper-bottomed** a. reliable, esp. financially —**copp'erplate** n. plate of copper for engraving, etching; print from this; copybook writing; first-class handwriting —**copp'ersmith** n. one who works with copper

copp'er[2] n. sl. policeman

copp'ice, **copse** n. wood of small trees

cop'ra n. dried coconut kernels

cop'ula n. word, esp. verb acting as connecting link in sentence; connection, tie (pl. **-las**)

cop'ulate vi. unite sexually —**copula'tion** n. —**cop'ulative** a.

cop'y n. imitation; single specimen of book; matter for printing —vt. make copy of, imitate; transcribe; follow an example

(cop'ied, cop'ying) —cop'yist n.
—cop'yright n. legal exclusive
right to print and publish book,
article, work of art etc. —vt.
protect by copyright —cop'y-
writer n. one who composes
advertisements

coquette' [-ket'] n. woman who
flirts —co'quetry n. —coquet'-
tish a.

cor'acle [ko'rə-] n. boat of wicker covered with skins

cor'al [ko'rəl] n. hard substance
made by sea polyps and forming
growths, islands, reefs; ornament
of coral —a. made of coral; of
deep pink colour —cor'alline a.

cor ang'lais [kor-ong'lā] n.
oboe set a fifth lower than ordinary oboe

corb'el n. stone or timber projection from wall to support
something

cord n. thin rope or thick string;
rib on cloth; ribbed fabric —vt.
fasten with cord —cord'age n.

cord'ate a. heart-shaped

cord'ial a. hearty, sincere,
warm —n. sweet, fruit-flavoured
drink —cordial'ity n. —cor'dial-
ly adv.

cor'dite n. explosive compound

cord'on n. chain of troops or
police; fruit tree grown as single
stem —vt. form cordon around

cordon bleu' [-blə'] a. (esp. of
food preparation) of highest
standard

cor'duroy [-də-] n. cotton fabric
with velvety, ribbed surface

core n. horny seed case of apple
and other fruits; central or inner-
most part of anything —vt. take
out the core

co-respond'ent n. one cited
in divorce case, alleged to have
committed adultery with the re-
spondent

cor'gi n. a small Welsh dog

coria'ceous a. of, like leather

corian'der n. herb

Corin'thian [-th-] a. of Corinth;
of Corinthian order of architecture, ornate Greek

cork n. bark of an evergreen
Mediterranean oak tree; piece of
it or other material, esp. used as
stopper for bottle etc. —vt. stop
up with cork —cork'age n.
charge for opening wine bottles
in restaurant —cork'er n. sl.
something, someone outstanding
—cork'screw n. tool for pulling
out corks

corm n. underground stem like a
bulb, but more solid

cor'morant n. large voracious
sea bird

corn¹ n. grain, fruit of cereals;
grain of all kinds; US maize;
oversentimental, trite quality in
play, film etc. —vt. preserve
(meat) with salt —corn'y a. inf.
trite, oversentimental, hackneyed —corn'crake n. brown
bird with harsh call, land rail
—corn'flakes pl.n. breakfast cereal —corn'flour n. finely ground
maize —corn'flower n. blue flower growing in cornfields

corn² n. painful horny growth
on foot or toe

cor'nea n. transparent membrane covering front of eye

corne'lian n. precious stone,
kind of chalcedony

cor'ner n. part of room where
two sides meet; remote or humble place; point where two walls,
streets etc. meet; angle, projection; Business buying up of whole
existing stock of commodity;
Sport free kick or shot from
corner of field —vt. drive into
position of difficulty, or leaving
no escape; establish monopoly
—vi. move round corner —cor'-
nered a. —corn'erstone n. indispensable part, basis

cor'net n. trumpet with valves;

cone-shaped ice cream wafer

corn'ice n. projection near top of wall; ornamental, carved moulding below ceiling

cornuco'pia n. symbol of plenty, consisting of goat's horn, overflowing with fruit and flowers

coroll'a n. flower's inner envelope of petals

coroll'ary n. inference from a preceding statement; deduction; result

coro'na n. halo around heavenly body; flat projecting part of cornice; top or crown (pl. -s, -nae [-nē]) —**cor'onal** [ko'r∂] a.

cor'onary [ko'r∂] a. of blood vessels surrounding heart —n. coronary thrombosis —**coronary thrombosis** disease of the heart

corona'tion n. ceremony of crowning a sovereign

cor'oner [ko'r∂] n. officer who holds inquests on bodies of persons supposed killed by violence, accident etc. —**cor'onership** n.

cor'onet [ko'r∂] n. small crown

corp'oral[1] a. of the body; material, not spiritual —**corporal punishment** (flogging etc.) of physical nature

corp'oral[2] n. noncommissioned officer below sergeant; Navy petty officer under a master-at-arms

corpora'tion n. association, body of persons legally authorized to act as an individual; authorities of town or city —**cor'porate** a.

corpor'eal a. of the body, material; tangible

corps [kawr] n. military force, body of troops; any organized body of persons (pl. **corps** [kawrz])

corpse n. dead body

corp'ulent a. fat —**corp'ulence** n.

cor'pus n. collection or body of

works, esp. by single author; main part or body of something

corp'uscle [-usl] n. minute organism or particle, esp. red and white corpuscles of blood

corral' [-rahl'] n. US enclosure for cattle, or for defence

correct' vt. set right; indicate errors in; rebuke, punish; counteract, rectify —a. right, exact, accurate; in accordance with facts or standards —**correc'tion** n. —**correct'ive** n./a. —**correct'ly** adv. —**correct'ness** n.

corr'elate vt. bring into reciprocal relation —n. either of two things or words necessarily implying the other —**correla'tion** n. —**corr'elative** a./n.

correspond' vi. be in agreement with, be consistent with; be similar (to); exchange letters —**respond'ence** n. agreement, corresponding; similarity; exchange of letters; letters received —**correspond'ent** n. writer of letters; one employed by newspaper etc. to report on particular topic, country etc.

corr'idor n. passage in building, railway train etc.; strip of territory (or air route) not under control of state through which it passes

corrigen'dum [-jen'-] n. thing to be corrected (pl. **-da**)

corrob'orate vt. confirm, support (statement etc.) —**corrobora'tion** n. —**corrob'orative** a.

corrode' vt. eat, wear away, eat into (by chemical action, disease etc.) —**corro'sion** n. —**corro'sive** a.

corr'ugate v. wrinkle, bend into wavy ridges —**corr'ugated** a. —**corruga'tion** n.

corrupt' a. lacking integrity; open to, or involving, bribery; wicked; spoilt by mistakes, altered for the worse (of words, literary passages *etc*.) —*vt*. make evil, pervert; bribe; make rotten —**corruptibil'ity** *n*. —**corrup'tible** *a*. —**corrup'tion** *n*. —**corrupt'ly** *adv*.

corsage¹ [-sahzh'] *n*. (flower, spray, worn on) bodice of woman's dress

cors'air *n*. pirate (ship)

cors'et *n*. close-fitting undergarment stiffened to give support or shape to the body

cors(e)'let *n*. piece of armour to cover the trunk

cortege¹ [-tāzh'] *n*. formal (funeral) procession

cor'tex *n. Anat.* outer layer; bark; sheath (*pl.* **cor'tices** [-tisēz]) —**cor'tical** *a*.

cor'tisone *n*. synthetic hormone used in the treatment of a variety of diseases

corun'dum *n*. native crystalline aluminium oxide, used as abrasive

corvette¹ *n*. lightly armed warship for escort and antisubmarine duties

cosh *n*. blunt weapon —*vt*. strike with one

co'sine *n*. in a right-angled triangle, the ratio of a side adjacent to a given angle and the hypotenuse

cosmet'ic [-z-] *n*. preparation to beautify or improve skin, hair *etc*. —*a*. designed to improve appearance only

cos'mic [koz'-] *a*. relating to the universe; of the vastness of the universe —**cosmog'rapher** *n*. —**cosmograph'ic** *a*. —**cosmog'raphy** *n*. description or mapping of the universe —**cosmolog'ical** *a*. —**cosmol'ogy** *n*. the science or study of the universe

cosmic rays high-energy electromagnetic rays from space

cos'monaut [-z'-] *n*. Soviet astronaut

cosmopol'itan [-z-] *n*. person who has lived and travelled in many countries; familiar with many countries; sophisticated; free from national prejudice —**cosmopol'itanism** *n*. —**cosmop'olite** *n*.

cos'mos¹ [-z'-] *n*. the world or universe considered as an ordered system

cos'mos² [-z'-] *n*. plant cultivated for brightly coloured flowers (*pl.* -**mos, -moses**)

Coss'ack *n*. member of tribe in SE Russia

coss'et *vt*. pamper, pet

cost *n*. price; expenditure of time, labour *etc*. —*pl.* expenses of lawsuit —*vt*. have as price; entail payment, or loss, or sacrifice of —**cost'ing** *n*. system of calculating cost of production —**cost'liness** *n*. —**cost'ly** *a*. valuable; expensive —**cost (price)** price at which article is bought by one intending to resell it

cos'tal *a*. pert. to side of body or ribs —**cos'tate** *a*. ribbed

cos'tume *n*. style of dress of particular place or time, or for particular activity; theatrical clothes —**costu'mier** [-mi-ər] *n*. dealer in costumes —**costume jewellery** artificial jewellery

co'sy [-z-] *a*. snug, comfortable, sheltered —*n*. covering to keep teapot *etc*. hot —**co'sily** *adv*.

cot *n*. child's bed usu. with barred sides; swinging bed on ship —**cot death** unexplained death of baby while asleep

cote *n*. shelter, shed for animals or birds, *eg* dovecot(e)

co'terie *n*. exclusive group of people with common interests; social clique

cotill'(i)on [-til'yən] *n. Hist.* lively dance

cotoneas'ter [-tō-ni-as'-] *n*. garden shrub with red berries

cott'age n. small house —**cottage cheese** mild, soft cheese —**cottage industry** industry in which workers work in their own homes

cott'er n. pin, wedge etc. to prevent relative motion of two parts of machine etc.

cott'on n. plant; white downy fibrous covering of its seeds; thread or cloth made of this —**cotton on** to understand (idea etc.)

cotyle'don [kot-i-lē'-] n. primary leaf of plant embryos

couch n. piece of furniture for reclining on by day, sofa —vt. put into (words), phrase; cause to lie down —**couch'ant** a. Heraldry lying down

couch grass [or -ōō-] type of creeping grass

cou'gar [kōō'-] n. puma

cough [kof] vi. expel air from lungs with sudden effort and noise, often to remove obstruction —n. act of coughing

could pt. of CAN[1]

cou'lomb [kōō'lom] n. unit of quantity of electricity

coul'ter [-ō-] n. sharp blade or disc at front of plough

coun'cil n. deliberative or administrative body; one of its meetings; local governing authority of town etc. —**coun'cillor** n. member of council

coun'sel n. advice, deliberation or debate; barrister or barristers; plan, policy —vt. advise, recommend (-ll-) —**coun'sellor** n. adviser —**keep one's counsel** keep a secret

count[1] vt. reckon, calculate, number; include; consider to be —vi. be reckoned in; depend (on); be of importance —n. reckoning; total number reached by counting; item in list of charges or indictment; act of counting

—**count'less** a. too many to be counted —**counting house** room or building for book-keeping

count[3] n. nobleman corresponding to British earl —**count'ess** n. fem. wife or widow of count or earl

count'enance n. face, its expression; support, approval —vt. give support, approve

count'er[1] n. horizontal surface in bank, shop etc., on which business is transacted; disc, token used for counting or scoring, esp. in board games

count'er[2] adv. in opposite direction; contrary —vi. oppose, contradict; Fencing parry —n. parry

counter- (comb. form) reversed, opposite, rival, retaliatory, as in **count'erclaim** n. —**counterir'ritant** n. —**count'ermarch** vi. —**count'ermine** vi. —**counter-revolu'tion** n. etc. Such words are not given here where the meaning may be inferred from the simple word

counteract' vt. neutralize or hinder —**counterac'tion** n.

count'erattack v./n. attack after enemy's advance

count'erbalance n. weight balancing or neutralizing another

count'erfeit [-fit] a. sham, forged —n. imitation, forgery —vi. imitate with intent to deceive; forge —**count'erfeiter** n. —**count'erfeitly** adv.

count'erfoil n. part of cheque, receipt, postal order, kept as record

countermand' [-mahnd'] vt. cancel (previous order)

count'erpane n. top cover for bed

count'erpart n. thing so like another as to be mistaken for it; something complementary to or correlative of another

count'erpoint n. melody added as accompaniment to given melody; art of so adding melodies

Counter-Reforma'tion n. reform movement in Catholic Church in 16th and early 17th cent.

count'ersign [-sīn] vt. sign document already signed by another; ratify

count'ersink v. enlarge upper part of hole (drilled in timber etc.) to take head of screw, bolt etc. below surface

count'ess n. see COUNT²

coun'try [kun'-] n. region, district; territory of nation; land of birth, residence etc.; rural districts as opposed to town; nation —**coun'trified** a. rural in manner or appearance —**coun'tryman** n. rustic; compatriot —**country music** popular music based on Amer. White folk music —**coun'tryside** n. rural district; its inhabitants

coun'ty n. division of country; shire

coup [kōō] n. successful stroke, move or gamble; (short for **coup d'état**) sudden, violent seizure of government

cou'pé [kōō'pā] n. sporty style of motor car, usu. with two seats

coup'le [kup'l] n. two, pair; brace; husband and wife; any two persons —vt. connect, fasten together; associate, connect in the mind —vi. join, associate —**coup'ler** n. —**coup'let** n. two lines of verse, esp. rhyming and of equal length —**coup'ling** n. connection esp. chain between railway wagons

cou'pon [kōō'-] n. ticket or voucher entitling holder to discount, gift etc.; detachable slip used as order form; (in betting etc.) printed form on which to forecast results

cour'age [ku-] n. bravery, boldness —**coura'geous** a. —**coura'geously** adv.

courgette [-zhet'] n. type of small vegetable marrow

cour'ier [koor-] n. express messenger; person who looks after, guides travellers

course [-aw-] n. movement in space or time; direction of movement; successive development, sequence; line of conduct or action; series of lectures, exercises etc.; any of successive parts of meal; continuous line of masonry at particular level in building; area where golf is played; track or ground on which a race is run —vt. hunt —vi. run swiftly, gallop about; (of blood) circulate —**cours'er** n. Poet. swift horse

court [-aw-] n. space enclosed by buildings, yard; area marked off or enclosed for playing various games; retinue and establishment of sovereign; body with judicial powers, place where it meets, one of its sittings; attention, homage, flattery —vt. woo, try to win or attract; seek, invite —**court'ier** n. one who frequents royal court —**court'liness** n. —**court'ly** a. ceremoniously polite; characteristic of a court —**court card** king, queen or jack at cards —**court martial** court of naval or military officers for trying naval or military offences (pl. **court martials, courts martial**) —**court shoe** woman's low-cut shoe without straps or laces —**court'yard** n. paved space enclosed by buildings or walls

courtesan' [kawr-ti-zan'] obs. n. court mistress; high-class prostitute

cour'tesy [kur'-] n. politeness, good manners; act of civility

—**court'eous** [kurt'-] *a.* polite
—**cour'teously** *adv.* —**courtesy** title title accorded by usage to which one has no valid claim

court'ship [-aw-] *n.* wooing

cous'in [kuz'n] *n.* son or daughter of uncle or aunt; formerly, any kinsman —**cous'inly** *adv.*

cove [1] *n.* small inlet of coast, sheltered bay

cove [2] *n. sl.* fellow, chap

cov'en [ku-] *n.* gathering of witches

cov'enant [ku-] *n.* contract, mutual agreement; compact —*v.* agree to a covenant —**cov'enanter** *n.*

cov'er [ku-] *vt.* place or spread over; extend, spread; bring upon (oneself); screen, protect; travel over; include; be sufficient; *Journalism etc.* report; point a gun at —*n.* lid, wrapper, envelope, binding, screen, anything which covers —**cov'erage** *n.* amount, extent covered —**cov'erlet** *n.* top covering of bed

cov'ert [ku-] *a.* secret, veiled, concealed, sly —*n.* thicket, place sheltering game —**cov'ertly** *adv.*

cov'et [ku-] *vt.* long to possess, *esp.* what belongs to another —**cov'etous** *a.* avaricious —**cov'etousness** *n.*

cov'ey [ku-] *n.* brood of partridges or quail (*pl.* **-eys**)

cow [1] *n.* the female of the bovine and of certain other animals (*eg* elephant, whale) (*pl.* **cows**) —**cow'boy** *n.* herdsman in charge of cattle on western plains of U.S.; *inf.* ruthless or unscrupulous operator in business *etc.* —**cow'pox** *n.* disease of cows, source of vaccine

cow [2] *vt.* frighten into submission, overawe, subdue

cow'ard *n.* one who lacks courage, shrinks from danger —**cow'ardice** *n.* —**cow'ardly** *a.*

cow'er *vi.* crouch, shrink in fear

cowl *n.* monk's hooded cloak; its hood; hooded top for chimney, ship's funnel *etc.*

cowl'ing *n.* covering for aircraft engine

cow'rie *n.* brightly-marked sea shell

cow'slip *n.* wild species of primrose

cox'comb *n. obs.* one given to showing off

cox'swain [kok'sən], **cox** *n.* steersman of boat —**cox** *v.* act as cox

coy *a.* (pretending to be) shy, modest —**coy'ly** *adv.* —**coy'ness** *n.*

coyo'te [-ō'ti] *n.* N Amer. prairie wolf

coy'pu [-pōo] *n.* aquatic rodent, orig. from S Amer., yielding nutria fur

coz'en [ku-] *vt.* flatter in order to cheat, beguile

CP Cape Province; Communist Party

Cpl. Corporal

Cr *Chem.* chromium

crab *n.* edible crustacean with ten legs, noted for sidelong and backward walk; type of louse —*vi.* catch crabs; move sideways —**crabb'ed** *a.* of handwriting, hard to read —**crabb'y** *a.* bad-tempered —**catch a crab** *Rowing* dig oar too deeply for clean retrieval

crab apple wild sour apple

crack *vt.* break, split partially; break with sharp noise; cause to make sharp noise; of whip, rifle *etc.*; break down, yield; *inf.* tell (joke); solve, decipher —*vi.* make sharp noise; split, fissure; of the voice, lose clearness when changing from boy's to man's —*n.* sharp explosive noise; split, fissure; flaw; *inf.* joke, *esp.* sarcastic; chat; *sl.* pure, highly addictive form of cocaine —a. inf. special, smart, of great reputation for skill or fashion —**crack'er** n. decorated paper tube, pulled apart with a bang, containing paper hat, motto, toy etc.; explosive firework; thin dry biscuit —**crack'ers** a. sl. unbalanced, crazy —**crack'le** n. sound of repeated small cracks —vi. make this sound —**crack'ling** n. crackle; crisp skin of roast pork —**cracks'man** n. burglar, esp. safe-breaker

cra'dle n. infant's bed (on rockers); fig. earliest resting-place or home; supporting framework —vt. hold or rock as in a cradle; cherish —**cra'dling** n.

craft[1] [-ah-] n. skill, ability, esp. manual ability; cunning; skilled trade; members of a trade —**craft'ily** adv. —**craft'y** a. cunning, shrewd —**crafts'man** n. —**crafts'manship** n.

craft[1] [-ah-] n. vessel; ship

crag n. steep rugged rock —**crag'gy** a. rugged

crake n. any of various birds of rail family

cram vt. fill quite full; stuff, force; pack tightly; feed to excess; prepare quickly for examination (-**mm**-) —n.

cramp n. painful muscular contraction; clamp for holding masonry, timber etc. together —vt. restrict or hamper; hem in, keep within too narrow limits

cramp'on n. spike in shoe for mountain climbing esp. on ice

cran'berry n. edible red berry of dwarf evergreen shrub

crane n. wading bird with long legs, neck, and bill; machine for moving heavy weights —vi. stretch neck to see

crane fly insect with long spindly legs

cranes'bill n. plant with pink or purple flowers and beaked fruits

craniom'etry [krā-] n. the study of the measurements of the human head

cra'nium n. skull (pl. -niums, -nia) —**cra'nial** a.

crank n. arm at right angles to axis, for turning main shaft, changing reciprocal into rotary motion etc.; inf. eccentric person, faddist —v. start (engine) by turning crank —**crank'y** a. eccentric; US, C bad-tempered; shaky —**crank'shaft** n. principal shaft of engine

crann'y n. small opening, chink —**crann'ied** a.

crap, craps US n. gambling game played with two dice

crape n. crepe, esp. when used for mourning clothes

crash v. (cause to) make loud noise; (cause to) fall with crash —vi. break, smash; collapse, fail, esp. financially; cause (aircraft) to hit land or water; collide with (another car etc.); move noisily or violently —n. loud, violent fall or impact; collision, esp. between vehicles; sudden, uncontrolled descent of aircraft to land; sudden collapse or downfall; bankruptcy —a. requiring, using, great effort to achieve results quickly —**crash helmet** helmet worn by motor-cyclists etc. to protect head —**crash-land** v. land aircraft in emergency, esp. with damage to craft

crass a. grossly stupid —**crass'ness** n. —**crass'ly** adv.

crate n. large (usu. wooden) container for packing goods

cra'ter n. mouth of volcano; bowl-shaped cavity, esp. one made by explosion of large shell, bomb, mine etc.

cravat' n. man's neckcloth

crave v. have very strong desire

for, long for —vt. ask humbly; beg —**cra'ving** n.

cra'ven a. cowardly, abject, spineless —n. coward

craw n. bird's or animal's stomach; bird's crop

crawl vi. move on belly or on hands and knees; move very slowly; ingratiate oneself, cringe; swim with crawl-stroke; be overrun (with) —n. crawling motion; very slow walk; racing stroke at swimming —**crawl'er** n.

cray'fish, craw'fish n. edible freshwater crustacean like lobster

cray'on n. stick or pencil of coloured chalk, wax etc.

craze n. short-lived current fashion; strong desire or passion, mania; madness —**crazed** a. demented; (of porcelain) having fine cracks —**cra'zy** a. insane; very foolish; madly eager (for) —**crazy paving** paving made with flat irregularly shaped slabs of stone

creak n. harsh grating noise —vi. make creaking sound

cream n. fatty part of milk; various foods, dishes, resembling cream; cosmetic etc. with cream-like consistency; yellowish-white colour; best part of anything —vt. take cream from; take best part from; beat to creamy consistency —**cream'y** a.

crease [-s] n. line made by folding; wrinkle; Cricket line defining bowler's and batsman's positions; superficial bullet wound —v. make, develop creases

create' [krē-āt'] vt. bring into being; give rise to; make —vi. inf. make a fuss —**crea'tion** n. —**crea'tive** a. —**crea'tor** n.

creat'ure [krēch'-] n. living being; thing created; dependant

—**creature comforts** bodily comforts

crèche [kresh, krāsh] n. day nursery for very young children

cre'dence n. belief, credit; side-table for elements of the Eucharist before consecration

creden'tials pl.n. testimonials; letters of introduction, esp. those given to ambassador

cred'ible a. worthy of belief; trustworthy —**credibil'ity** n. —**cred'ibly** adv.

cred'it n. commendation, approval; source, cause, of honour; belief, trust; good name; influence, honour or power based on trust of others; system of allowing customers to take goods for later payment; money at one's disposal in bank etc.; side of book on which such sums are entered; reputation for financial reliability —pl. list of those responsible for production of film —vt. attribute, believe that person has; believe; put on credit side of account —**cred'itable** a. bringing honour —**cred'itably** adv. —**cred'itor** n. one to whom debt is due

cred'ulous a. too easy of belief, easily deceived or imposed on, gullible —**credu'lity** n. —**cred'ulousness** n.

creed n. formal statement of Christian beliefs; statement, system of beliefs or principles

creek n. narrow inlet on seacoast

creel n. angler's fishing basket

creep vi. make way along ground, as snake; move with stealthy, slow movements; crawl; act in servile way; of skin or flesh, feel shrinking, shivering sensation, due to fear or repugnance (**crept** pt./pp.) —n. creeping; sl. repulsive person —pl. feeling of fear or repugnance

—**creep'er** n. creeping or climbing plant, eg ivy —**creep'y** inf. a. uncanny, unpleasant; causing flesh to creep

crema'tion n. burning as means of disposing of corpses —**cremate'** vt. —**cremator'ium** n. place for cremation

cren'ellated a. having battlements

cre'ole n. hybrid language; (C-) native born W Indian, Latin American, of European descent

cre'osote [krez'-] n. oily antiseptic liquid distilled from coal or wood tar, used for preserving wood —vt. coat or impregnate with creosote

crepe [krāp] n. fabric with crimped surface; crape —**crepe rubber** rough-surfaced rubber used for soles of shoes

crept pt./pp. of CREEP

Cres. Crescent

crescen'do [-sh-] n. gradual increase of loudness, esp. in music —a./adv.

cres'cent [krez'ənt] n. (shape of) moon as seen in first or last quarter; any figure of this shape; row of houses built on curve

cress n. various plants with edible pungent leaves

crest n. comb or tuft on bird's or animal's head; plume on top of helmet; top of mountain, ridge, wave etc.; badge above shield of coat of arms, also used separately on seal, plate etc. —vi. crown —vt. reach top of —**crest'fallen** a. cast down by failure, dejected

creta'ceous [-shəs] a. chalky

cret'in n. person afflicted with cretinism; inf. stupid person —**cret'inism** n. deficiency in thyroid gland causing physical and mental retardation

cretonne' n. unglazed cotton cloth printed in coloured patterns

crevasse' n. deep open chasm, esp. in glacier

crev'ice [-is] n. cleft, fissure, chink

crew [-ōō] n. ship's, boat's or aircraft's company, excluding passengers; inf. gang or set —v. serve as crew —**crew cut** man's closely cropped haircut

crew'el [krōō'-] n. fine worsted yarn, used in fancy work and embroidery

crib n. child's cot; barred rack used for fodder; plagiarism; translation used by students, sometimes illicitly —vt. confine in small space; copy unfairly (-bb-)

cribb'age n. card game for two, three, or four players

crick n. spasm or cramp in muscles, esp. in neck

crick'et[1] n. chirping insect

crick'et[2] n. outdoor game played with bats, ball and wickets by teams of eleven a side —**crick'eter** n.

crime n. violation of law (usu. a serious offence); wicked or forbidden act; inf. something to be regretted —**crim'inal** a./n. —**criminal'ity** n. —**crim'inally** adv. —**criminol'ogy** n. study of crime and criminals

crimp vt. pinch into tiny parallel pleats; wrinkle

crim'son [-z-] a./n. (of) rich deep red —v. turn crimson

cringe vi. shrink, cower; behave obsequiously

crin'kle [-ng·k-] v./n. wrinkle

crin'oline [-lin] n. hooped petticoat or skirt

crip'ple n. one not having normal use of limbs, disabled or deformed person —vt. maim, disable, impair; weaken, lessen efficiency of

cri'sis n. turning point or decisive moment, esp. in illness; time of acute danger or difficulty (*pl.* **cri'ses** [-sēz])

crisp *a.* brittle but firm; brisk, decided; clear-cut; fresh, invigorating; crackling; of hair, curly —*n.* very thin, fried slice of potato, eaten cold —**crisp'er** *n.* refrigerator compartment for storing salads *etc.* —**crisp'ly** *a.* —**crisp'bread** *n.* thin, dry biscuit

crite'rion [krī-] *n.* standard of judgment (*pl.* **-ria**)

crit'ical *a.* fault-finding; discerning; skilled in or given to judging; of great importance, crucial, decisive —**crit'ic** *n.* one who passes judgment; writer expert in judging works of literature, art *etc.* —**crit'ically** *adv.* —**crit'icism** *n.* —**crit'icize** *vt.* —**critique'** [-ēk'] *n.* critical essay, carefully written criticism

croak *v.* utter deep hoarse cry, as raven, frog; talk dismally —*vi. sl.* die —*n.* deep hoarse cry —**croak'er** *n.* —**croak'y** *a.* hoarse

cro'chet [-shā] *n.* kind of handicraft like knitting, done with small hooked needle —*v.* do, make such work

crock *n.* earthenware jar or pot; broken piece of earthenware; *inf.* old broken-down thing or person; *inf.* cripple —**crock'ery** *n.* earthenware dishes, utensils *etc.*

croc'odile [krok'-] *n.* large amphibious reptile; line of children walking two by two —**crocodil'ian** *a.* —**crocodile tears** insincere grief

cro'cus *n.* small bulbous plant with yellow, white or purple flowers (*pl.* **-cuses**)

croft *n.* (*esp.* in *Scot.*) small piece of arable land, smallholding —**crof'ter** *n.* one who works croft

croissant [krwahs'ong] *n.*

crescent-shaped roll of yeast dough like pastry

crom'lech [-lek] *n.* prehistoric structure, monument of flat stone resting on two upright ones

crone *n.* witchlike old woman

cro'ny *n.* intimate friend

crook *n.* hooked staff; any hook, bend, sharp turn; *inf.* swindler, criminal —**crook'ed** *a.* bent, twisted; deformed; dishonest

croon *v.* hum, sing in soft, low tone —**croon'er** *n.*

crop *n.* produce of cultivation of any plant or plants; harvest, *lit.* or *fig.*; pouch in bird's gullet; stock of whip; hunting whip; short haircut —*v.* cut short; raise, produce or occupy land with crop; (of animals) bite, eat down; poll or clip (**-pp-**) —**crop'per** *inf. n.* heavy fall; disastrous failure —**crop-dusting** *n.* spreading fungicide *etc.* on crops from aircraft —**crop up** *inf.* happen unexpectedly

cro'quet [-kā] *n.* lawn game played with balls, wooden mallets and hoops

croquette' [-ket'] *n.* fried ball of minced meat, fish *etc.*

cro'sier, cro'zier [-zhər] *n.* bishop's or abbot's staff

cross *n.* structure or symbol of two intersecting lines or pieces (at right angles); such a structure of wood as means of execution by tying or nailing victim to it; symbol of Christian faith; any thing or mark in the shape of cross; misfortune, annoyance, affliction; intermixture of breeds, hybrid —*v.* move or go across (something); intersect; meet and pass —*vt.* mark with lines across; (*with* out) delete; place or put in form of cross; make sign of cross on or over; modify breed of animals or plants by intermixture; thwart; oppose —*a.* out of temper, angry; peevish, perverse; transverse; intersecting; contrary; adverse —**cross'ing** *n.* intersection of roads, rails *etc.*; part of street where pedestrians are expected to cross —**cross'ly** *adv.* —**cross'wise** *adv./a.* —**cross'bill** *n.* bird whose mandibles cross when closed —**cross'bow** *n.* bow fixed across wooden shoulder stock —**cross'breed** *n.* breed produced from parents of different breeds —**cross country** long race held over open ground —**cross-examine** *vt.* examine witness already examined by other side —**cross-eyed** *a.* having eye(s) turning inward —**cross-fertilization** *n.* fertilization of one plant by pollen of another —**cross-grained** *a.* perverse —**cross-ply** *a.* (of tyre) having fabric cords in outer casing running diagonally —**cross-reference** *n.* reference within text to another part of text —**cross'roads** *n.* —**cross section** transverse section; group of people fully representative of a nation, community *etc.* —**cross-word puzzle** puzzle built up of intersecting words, of which some letters are common, the words being indicated by clues —**The Cross** cross on which Jesus Christ was executed; model or picture of this

crotch *n.* angle between legs, genital area; fork

crotch'et *n.* musical note, equal to half the length of a minim

crotch'ety *a.* peevish; irritable

crouch *vi.* bend low; huddle down close to ground; stoop servilely, cringe —*n.*

croup[1] [-ōō-] *n.* throat disease of children, with cough

croup[2] [-ōō-] *n.* hindquarters of horse; place behind saddle

croup'ier [-ōō-] *n.* person dealing cards, collecting money *etc.* at gambling table

crow[1] [-ō] *n.* large black carrion-eating bird —**crow's-foot** *n.* wrinkle at corner of eye —**crow's-nest** *n.* lookout platform high on ship's mast

crow[2] [-ō] *vi.* utter cock's cry; boast one's happiness or superiority —*n.* cock's cry

crow'bar [-ō-] *n.* iron bar, usu. beaked, for levering

crowd *n.* throng, mass —*vi.* flock together —*vt.* cram, force, thrust, pack; fill with people —**crowd out** exclude by excess already in

crown *n.* monarch's headdress; wreath for head; monarch; monarchy; royal power; formerly, British coin of five shillings; various foreign coins; top of head; summit, top; completion or perfection of thing —*vt.* put crown on; confer title; occur as culmination of series of events; *inf.* hit on head —**crown land** public land —**crown prince** heir to throne

cru'cial [krōō'shəl] *a.* decisive, critical; *inf.* very important

cru'ciate [-ōō-] *a.* cross-shaped

cru'cible [-ōō-] *n.* small melting-pot

cru'cify [-ōō-] *vt.* put to death on cross; treat cruelly; *inf.* ridicule (**cru'cified, cru'cifying**) —**cru'cifix** *n.* cross; image of (Christ on the) Cross (*pl.* **-es**) —**crucifix'ion** *n.* —**cru'ciform** *a.*

crude [-ōō-] *a.* lacking taste, vulgar; in natural or raw state, unrefined; rough, unfinished —**crude'ly** *adv.* —**cru'dity** *n.*

cru'el [-ōō-] *a.* delighting in others' pain; causing pain or suffering —**cru'elly** *adv.* —**cru'elty** *n.*

cru'et [-ōō-] *n.* small container for salt, pepper, vinegar, oil *etc.*; stand holding set of these

cruise [-ōōz] *vi.* travel about in a

ship for pleasure *etc.*; (of vehicle, aircraft) travel at safe, average speed —*n.* cruising voyage, *esp.* organized for holiday purposes —**cruis'er** *n.* ship that cruises; warship lighter and faster than battleship —**cruise missile** subsonic missile guided throughout its flight —**cruis'erweight** *n.* Boxing light-heavyweight

crumb [krum] *n.* small particle, fragment, *esp.* of bread —*vt.* reduce to, break into, cover with crumbs —**crumb'y** *a.*

crum'ble *v.* break into small fragments, disintegrate, crush; perish, decay —*vi.* fall apart or away —*n.* pudding covered with crumbly mixture —**crum'bly** *a.*

crumm'y *a. sl.* inferior, contemptible

crump *vi.* thud, explode with dull sound —*n.*

crum'pet *n.* flat, soft cake eaten with butter; *sl.* sexually desirable woman or women

crum'ple *v.* (cause to) collapse; make or become crushed, wrinkled, creased —**crum'pled** *a.*

crunch *n.* sound made by chewing crisp food, treading on gravel, hard snow *etc.*; *inf.* critical moment or situation —*v.* make crunching sound

crupp'er *n.* strap holding back of saddle in place by passing round horse's tail; horse's hindquarters

crusade[1] *n.* medieval Christian war to recover Holy Land; campaign against something believed to be evil; concerted action to further a cause —*vi.* —**crusa'der** *n.*

cruse [-ōōz] *n.* small earthenware jug or pot

crush[1] *vt.* compress so as to break, bruise, crumple; break to small pieces; defeat utterly, over-

throw —*n.* act of crushing; crowd of people *etc.*

crush[2] *n. inf.* infatuation

crust *n.* hard outer part of bread; similar hard outer casing on anything —*v.* cover with, form, crust —**crust'ily** *adv.* —**crust'y** *a.* having, or like, crust; short-tempered

crusta'cean [-shən] *n.* hard-shelled animal, *eg* crab, lobster —**crusta'ceous** [-shəs] *a.*

crutch *n.* staff with crosspiece to go under armpit of lame person; support; groin, crotch

crux *n.* that on which a decision turns; anything that puzzles very much (*pl.* **crux'es**, **cru'ces** [krōō'sēz])

cry *vi.* weep; wail; utter call; shout; clamour or beg (for) —*vt.* utter loudly, proclaim (**cried**, **cry'ing**) —*n.* loud utterance; scream, wail, shout; call of animal; fit of weeping; watchword

cryogen'ics [-jen'-] *n.* branch of physics concerned with phenomena at very low temperatures —**cryogen'ic** *a.*

crypt [kript] *n.* vault, *esp.* under church —**cryp'tic** *a.* secret, mysterious —**cryp'tically** *adv.* —**cryp'togram** *n.* piece of writing in code —**cryptog'raphy** *n.* art of writing, decoding ciphers

cryp'togam *n.* nonflowering plant, *eg* fern, moss *etc.*

crys'tal *n.* clear transparent mineral; very clear glass; cut-glass ware; characteristic form assumed by many substances, with definite internal structure and external shape of symmetrically arranged plane surfaces —**crys'talline**, **crys'talloid** *a.* —**crystalliza'tion** *n.* —**crys'tallize** *v.* form into crystals; become definite —**crystallog'rapher** *n.* —**crystallog'raphy** *n.* science of the structure, forms and properties of crystals

CSE Certificate of Secondary Education

CST US, C Central Standard Time

Cu *Chem.* copper

cu. cubic

cub *n.* young of fox and other animals; C-) Cub Scout —*v.* bring forth cubs (**-bb-**) —**Cub Scout** member of junior branch of the Scout Association

cubb'yhole *n.* small, enclosed space or room

cube [kyōōb] *n.* regular solid figure contained by six equal square sides; cube-shaped block; product obtained by multiplying number by itself twice —*vt.* multiply thus —**cu'bic(al)** *a.* —**cu'bism** *n.* style of art in which objects are presented as assemblage of geometrical shapes —**cu'bist** *n./a.*

cu'bicle *n.* partially or totally enclosed section of room, as in dormitory

cu'bit *n.* old measure of length, about 18 inches

cuck'old *n.* man whose wife has committed adultery —*vt.*

cuck'oo [kook'ōō] *n.* migratory bird which deposits its eggs in the nests of other birds; its call —*a. sl.* crazy

cu'cumber *n.* plant with long fleshy green fruit; the fruit, used in salad

cud *n.* food which ruminant animal brings back into mouth to chew again —**chew the cud** reflect, meditate

cud'dle *vt.* hug —*vi.* lie close and snug, nestle —*n.*

cudd'y *n.* small cabin in boat

cudg'el *n.* short thick stick —*vt.* beat with cudgel (**-ll-**)

cue[1] [kyōō] *n.* last words of actor's speech *etc.* as signal to another to act or speak; signal,

hint, example for action

cue[2] [kyōō] *n.* long tapering rod used in billiards; pigtail

cuff[1] *n.* ending of sleeve; wristband —**off the cuff** *inf.* without preparation

cuff[2] *vt.* strike with open hand —*n.* blow with hand

cuirass' [kwi-] *n.* metal or leather armour of breastplate and backplate

cuisine' [kwi-zēn'] *n.* style of cooking; menu, food offered by restaurant *etc.*

cul'-de-sac *n.* street, lane open only at one end; blind alley (*pl.* **culs-de-sac**)

cul'inary *a.* of, for, suitable for, cooking or kitchen

cull *vt.* gather, select; take out selected animals from herd —*n.* act of culling

cul'minate *vi.* reach highest point; come to climax, to a head —**culmina'tion** *n.*

culottes' [kyōō-] *pl.n.* flared trousers (*esp.* for women) cut to look like skirt

cul'pable *a.* blameworthy —**culpabil'ity** *n.* —**cul'pably** *adv.*

cul'prit *n.* one guilty of usu. minor offence

cult *n.* system of religious worship; pursuit of, devotion to, some person, thing, or activity

cul'tivate *vt.* till and prepare (ground) to raise crops; develop, improve, refine; devote attention to, cherish; practise; foster —**cultiva'tion** *n.* —**cul'tivator** *n.*

cul'ture *n.* state of manners, taste, and intellectual development at a time or place; cultivating; artificial rearing; set of bacteria so reared —**cul'tural** *a.* —**cul'tured** *a.* refined, showing culture —**cultured pearl** pearl artificially induced to grow in oyster shell

cul'vert *n.* tunnelled drain for

passage of water under road, railway *etc.*

cum *Lat.* with

cum'bersome *a.* awkward, unwieldy

cum(m)'in *n.* herb

cumm'erbund *n.* broad sash worn round waist

cum'quat [-kwot] *n.* see KUMQUAT

cu'mulative [-iv] *a.* becoming greater by successive additions; representing the sum of many items

cu'mulus *n.* cloud shaped in rounded white woolly masses (*pl.* **cu'muli**)

cu'neiform [kyōō'ni-] *a.* wedge-shaped, *esp.* of ancient Babylonian writing

cunn'ing *a.* crafty, sly; ingenious —*n.* skill in deceit or evasion; skill, ingenuity —**cunn'ingly** *adv.*

cup *n.* small drinking vessel with handle at one side; any small drinking vessel; contents of cup; various cup-shaped formations, cavities, sockets *etc.*; cup-shaped trophy as prize; portion or lot; iced drink of wine and other ingredients —*vt.* shape as cup (hands *etc.*) —**cup'ful** *n.* (*pl.* **cup'fuls**) —**cup'board** [kub'ərd] *n.* piece of furniture, recess in room, with door, for storage

cu'pel *n.* small vessel used in refining metals

Cu'pid *n.* god of love

cupid'ity *n.* greed for possessions; covetousness

cu'pola *n.* dome

cu'preous, cu'pric, cu'prous *a.* of, containing, copper

cur *n.* dog of mixed breed; surly, contemptible, or mean person

cu'raçao [kyoor'ə-sō] *n.* liqueur flavoured with bitter orange peel

curar'e, curar'i *n.* poisonous resin of S Amer. tree, now used

as muscle relaxant in medicine

cu'rate [kyoor'ət] *n.* parish priest's appointed assistant —**cu'racy** *n.* his office

cu'rative [kyoor'-] *a.* tending to cure disease —*n.*

cura'tor [kyoo-rā'-] *n.* custodian, *esp.* of museum, library *etc.* —**curato'rial** *a.* —**cura'torship** *n.*

curb *n.* check, restraint; chain or strap passing under horse's lower jaw and giving powerful control with reins —*vt.* restrain; apply curb to

curd *n.* coagulated milk —**cur'dle** *v.* turn into curd, coagulate —**curd'y** *a.* —**blood'curdling** *a.* terrifying, making blood appear to curdle

cure [kyoor] *vt.* heal, restore to health; remedy; preserve (fish, skins *etc.*) —*n.* remedy; course of medical treatment; successful treatment, restoration to health —**curabil'ity** *n.* —**cu'rable** *a.* —**cure of souls** care of parish or congregation

curet(te)' [kyoor-] *n.* surgical instrument for removing dead tissue *etc.* from some body cavities —**curettage'** [-tahzh'] *n.*

cur'few *n.* official regulation restricting or prohibiting movement of people, *esp.* at night; time set as deadline by such regulation

cu'rie [kyoor'-] *n.* standard unit of radium emanation

cu'rio [kyoor'-] *n.* rare or curious thing or thing sought for collections (*pl.* **cu'rios**)

cu'rious [kyoor'-] *a.* eager to know, inquisitive; prying; puzzling, strange, odd —**curios'ity** *n.* eagerness to know; inquisitiveness; strange or rare thing —**cu'riously** *adv.*

cu'rium *n.* element produced from plutonium

curl *vi.* take spiral or curved shape or path —*vt.* bend into spiral or curved shape —*n.* spiral lock of hair; spiral, curved state, form or motion —**curl'ing** *n.* game like bowls, played with large rounded stones on ice —**curl'y** *a.* —**curling tongs** heated, metal, scissor-like device for curling hair

cur'lew *n.* large long-billed wading bird

curmudg'eon *n.* surly or miserly person

curr'ach, curr'agh [kur'əh] *n.* Scots, Irish name for coracle

curr'ant *n.* dried type of grape; fruit of various plants allied to gooseberry; the plants

curr'ent *a.* of immediate present, going on; up-to-date, not yet superseded; in circulation or general use —*n.* body of water or air in motion; tendency, drift; transmission of electricity through conductor —**curr'ency** *n.* money in use; state of being in use; time during which thing is current —**curr'ently** *adv.*

curric'ulum *n.* specified course of study (*pl.* **-lums, -la**)

curr'y[1] *n.* highly-flavoured, pungent condiment, preparation of turmeric; dish flavoured with it —*vt.* prepare, flavour dish with curry (**curr'ied, curr'ying**)

curr'y[2] *vt.* groom (horse) with comb; dress (leather) (**curr'ied, curr'ying**) —**curry comb** metal comb for grooming horse —**curry favour** try to win favour unworthily, ingratiate oneself

curse *n.* profane or obscene expression of anger *etc.*; utterance expressing extreme ill will towards some person or thing; affliction, misfortune, scourge —*v.* utter curse, swear (at); afflict —**curs'ed** *a.* hateful; wicked; deserving of, or under, a curse

—**curs'edly** *adv.* —**curs'edness** *n.*

curs'ive *a.* written in running script, with letters joined

curs'ory *a.* rapid, hasty, not detailed, superficial —**curs'orily** *adv.*

curt *a.* short, rudely brief, abrupt —**curt'ly** *adv.* —**curt'ness** *n.*

curtail[1] *vt.* cut short, diminish —**curtail'ment** *n.*

cur'tain [-tən] *n.* hanging drapery at window *etc.*; cloth hung as screen; screen separating audience and stage in theatre; end to act or scene *etc.* —*vt.* provide, cover with curtain —**curtain call** return to stage by performers to acknowledge applause —**curtain-raiser** *n.* short play coming before main one; any preliminary event

curt'(e)y *n.* woman's bow or respectful gesture made by bending knees and lowering body —*vi.*

curve *n.* line of which no part is straight; bent line or part —*v.* bend into curve —**curva'ceous** *a. inf.* shapely —**curv'ature** *n.* a bending; bent shape —**curvilin'ear** *a.* of bent lines

cush'ion [-oo-] *n.* bag filled with soft stuffing or air, to support or ease body; any soft pad or support; resilient rim of billiard table —*vt.* provide, protect with cushion; lessen effects of

cush'y [-oo-] *a. inf.* soft, comfortable, pleasant, light, well-paid

cusp *n.* pointed end, *esp.* of tooth —**cus'pid** *n.* pointed tooth —**cus'pidal** *a.* ending in point; of, or like, cusp

cus'pidor *n.* spittoon

cus'tard *n.* dish made of eggs and milk; sweet sauce of milk and cornflour

cus'tody *n.* safe-keeping, guardianship, imprisonment

—cus**to'dian** n. keeper, caretaker, curator

cus'tom n. habit; practice; fashion, usage; business patronage; toll, tax —pl. duties levied on imports; government department which collects these; area in airport etc. where customs officials examine baggage for dutiable goods —cus'tomarily adv. —cus'tomary a. usual, habitual —cus'tomer n. one who enters shop to buy, esp. regularly; purchaser —customs duties taxes laid on imported or exported goods —customs house building where customs are collected

cut vt. sever, penetrate, wound, divide, or separate with pressure of edge or edged instrument; pare, detach, trim, or shape by cutting; divide; intersect; reduce, decrease; abridge; inf. ignore (person); strike (with whip etc.); hit cricket ball to point's left; inf. deliberately stay away from (cut, cutt'ing) —n. act of cutting; stroke; blow, wound (of knife, whip etc.); reduction, decrease; fashion, shape; incision; engraving; piece cut off; division; inf. share, esp. of profits —cutt'er n. one who, that which, cuts; warship's rowing and sailing boat; small sloop-rigged vessel with straight running bowsprit —cutt'ing n. act of cutting, thing cut off or out, esp. excavation (for road, canal etc.) through high ground; shoot, twig of plant; piece cut from newspaper etc. —a. sarcastic, unkind —cut'throat a. merciless —n. murderer —cut dead refuse to recognize an acquaintance —cut in drive in front of another's vehicle so as to affect his driving; interrupt (in conversation); intrude

cuta'neous [kyoō-] a. of skin

cute [kyoōt] a. appealing, attractive, pretty

cu'ticle n. dead skin, esp. at base of fingernail

cut'lass n. short broad-bladed sword

cut'lery n. knives, forks, spoons etc. —cut'ler n. one who makes, repairs, deals in knives and cutting implements

cut'let n. small piece of meat grilled or fried

cut'tle n. sea mollusc like squid

CV curriculum vitae (outline of person's educational and professional history)

Cwlth. Commonwealth

cwt. hundredweight

cy'anide [sī-] n. extremely poisonous chemical compound —cyan'ogen n. poisonous gas composed of nitrogen and carbon

cyano'sis [sī-] n. blueness of the skin

cybernet'ics [sī-] pl.n. (with sing. v.) comparative study of control mechanisms of electronic and biological systems

cyc'lamen [sik'-] n. plant with flowers having turned-back petals

cy'cle [sī-] n. recurrent series or period; rotation of events; complete series or period; development following course of stages; series of poems etc.; bicycle —vi. move in cycles; ride bicycle —cy'clic(al) a. —cy'clist n. bicycle rider —cyclom'eter n. instrument for measuring circles or recording distance travelled by wheel, esp. of bicycle

cy'clone [sī-] n. system of winds moving round centre of low pressure; circular storm —cyclon'ic a.

cyclope'dia see ENCYCLOPEDIA

cy'clostyle [sī-] vt. produce (pamphlets etc.) in large numbers for distribution —a./n. (of) machine, method for doing this

cy'clotron [sī'-] *n.* powerful apparatus which accelerates the circular movement of subatomic particles in a magnetic field, used for work in nuclear disintegration *etc.*

cyg'net [sig'-] *n.* young swan

cyl'inder [sil'-] *n.* roller-shaped solid or hollow body, of uniform diameter; piston-chamber of engine —**cylin'drical** *a.* —**cyl'indroid** *a.*

cym'bal [sim'-] *n.* one of pair of two brass plates struck together to produce ringing or clashing sound in music

Cym'ric [kim'-] *a.* Welsh

cyn'ic [sin'-] *n.* one who expects, believes, the worst about people, their motives, or outcome of events —**cyn'ical** *a.* —**cyn'icism** *n.* being cynical

cyn'osure [sin'əz-yoor *or* sīn'-] *n.* centre of attraction

cy'pher *see* CIPHER

cy'press *n.* coniferous tree with very dark foliage

cyst [si-] *n.* sac containing liquid secretion or pus —**cys'tic** *a.* of cysts; of the bladder —**cysti'tis** *n.* inflammation of bladder

cytol'ogy [sī-] *n.* study of plant and animal cells

Czar, Tzar, Tsar [zahr] *n.* emperor, king, *esp.* of Russia 1547-1917 —**Czari'na** [-rē'-], **Czarit'sa, Tsarit'sa, Tzarit'sa** *n.* wife of Czar

Czech [chek] *n.* member of western branch of Slavs

D

D Democratic; *Chem.* deuterium

d *Physics* density

d. day; denarius (*Lat.*, penny); departs; died

dab[1] *vt.* apply with momentary pressure, *esp.* anything wet and soft; strike feebly —*n.* smear; slight blow or tap; small mass —**dab'chick** *n.* small grebe —**dab hand** *inf.* someone good at something

dab[2] *n.* small flatfish

dab'ble *vi.* splash about; be desultory student or amateur (in)

dace *n.* small freshwater fish

dachs'hund [daks'hoond] *n.* short-legged long-bodied dog

dac'tyl *n.* metrical foot of one long followed by two short syllables

dad, dad'dy *n. inf.* father —**daddy-longlegs** *n. inf.* crane fly

da'do [dā'dō] *n.* lower part of room wall when lined or painted separately (*pl.* **-do(e)s**)

daff'odil *n.* spring flower, yellow narcissus

daft [-ah-] *a.* foolish, crazy

dag, dag'lock *n.* dung-caked locks of wool around hindquarters of sheep —**dag** *n.* **A, NZ** *sl.* eccentric character

dagg'a [-H-] *n.* **SA** hemp smoked as narcotic

dagg'er *n.* short, edged stabbing weapon

da'go *n. offens.* Italian or other Latin (*pl.* **-(e)s**)

daguerre'otype [-ger'-] *n.* early photographic process; photograph by it

dahl'ia [dāl'-] *n.* garden plant of various colours

Dáil, Dáil Éir'eann [doil-ā'rən] *n.* lower chamber of

parliament in the Irish Republic

dail'y a. done, occurring, published every day —adv. every day —n. daily newspaper; charwoman

dain'ty a. delicate; elegant, choice; pretty and neat; fastidious —n. delicacy —**dain'tily** adv. —**dain'tiness** n.

dair'y n. place for processing milk and its products —**dair'ying** n. —**dair'ymaid** n. —**dair'yman** n.

da'is [dā'-] n. raised platform, usually at end of hall

dais'y [-z-] n. flower with yellow centre and white petals

Dal'ai Lam'a [-l-lahm'-] n. head of Buddhist hierarchy in Tibet

dale n. valley —**dales'man** n. native of dale, esp. of N England

dall'y vi. trifle, spend time in idleness or amusement; toy (**dall'ied, dall'ying**) —**dall'iance** n.

Dalma'tian n. large dog, white with black spots

dam[1] n. barrier to hold back flow of waters; water so collected —vt. hold with or as with dam (**-mm-**)

dam[2] n. female parent (used of animals)

dam'age n. injury, harm, loss —pl. sum claimed or adjudged in compensation for injury —vt. harm

dam'ask n. figured woven material of silk or linen, esp. white table linen with design shown up by light; colour of damask rose, velvety red —**dam'ascene, dam'askeen** vt. decorate (steel etc.) with inlaid gold or silver

dame n. obs. lady; (D-) title of lady in Order of the British Empire; sl. woman

damn [-m] vt. condemn to hell; be the ruin of; give hostile recep-

tion to —vi. curse (**damned** [damd], **damn'ing** [dam'ing]) —interj. expression of annoyance, impatience etc. —**damnable** a. deserving damnation; hateful, annoying —**damna'tion** n. —**damn'atory** a.

damp a. moist; slightly moist —n. diffused moisture; in coal mines, dangerous gas —vt. make damp; (often with down) deaden, discourage —**damp'en** v. make, become damp —vt. stifle, deaden —**damp'er** n. anything that discourages or depresses; plate in a flue to control draught

dam'sel [-z-] n. obs. girl

dam'son [-z-] n. small darkpurple plum; tree bearing it; its colour

Dan. Daniel

dance [-ah-] vi. move with measured rhythmic steps, usu. to music; be in lively movement; bob up and down —vt. perform (dance); cause to dance —n. lively, rhythmical movement; arrangement of such movements; tune for them; social gathering for the purpose of dancing —**danc'er** n. —**danseuse'** [-sэz'] n. female dancer (pl. **-s**)

D & C dilation and curettage (of womb)

dan'delion n. yellow-flowered wild plant

dan'der n. inf. temper, fighting spirit

dan'druff n. dead skin in small scales among the hair

dan'dy n. man excessively concerned with smartness of dress —a. inf. excellent —**dan'dyism** n.

dan'ger [dān'j-] n. liability or exposure to harm; risk, peril —**dan'gerous** a. —**dan'gerously** adv.

dan'gle [-ng'gəl] v. hang loosely and swaying; hold suspended; tempt with

dank a. unpleasantly damp and chilly —**dank'ness** n.

daph'ne n. ornamental shrub with bell-shaped flowers

dap'per a. neat and precise, esp. in dress, spruce

dap'ple v. mark with spots —**dap'pled** a. spotted; mottled; variegated —**dapple-grey** a. (of horse) grey marked with darker spots

dare [dâr] vt. venture, have courage (to); challenge —n. challenge —**da'ring** a. bold —n. adventurous courage —**dare'devil** a./n. reckless (person)

dark a. without light; gloomy; deep in tint; dim, secret; unenlightened; wicked —n. absence of light or colour or knowledge —**dark'en** v. —**dark'ly** adv. —**dark'ness** n. —**dark horse** somebody, something, esp. competitor in race, about whom little is known —**dark'room** n. darkened room for processing film

dar'ling a./n. much loved or very lovable (person)

darn[1] vt. mend by filling (hole) with interwoven yarn —n. place so mended —**darn'ing** n.

darn[2] interj. mild expletive

dart n. small light pointed missile; darting motion; small seam or intake in garment —pl. indoor game played with numbered target and miniature darts —vt. cast, throw rapidly (dart glance etc.) —vi. go rapidly or abruptly

Darwin'ian a. pert. to Charles Darwin or his theory of evolution

dash vt. smash, throw, thrust, send with violence; cast down; tinge, flavour, mix —vi. move, go with great speed or violence —n. rush; vigour; smartness; small quantity, tinge; stroke (-) between words —**dash'ing** a. spirited, showy —**dash'board** n. in car

etc., instrument panel in front of driver

dass'ie n. SA hyrax

das'tard n. obs. contemptible, sneaking coward —**das'tardly** a.

dat. dative

da'ta pl.n. (oft. with sing. v.) series of observations, measurements, or facts; information —**data base** systematized collection of data that can be manipulated by data-processing system for specific purpose —**data pen** device for scanning magnetically coded data on labels, packets, etc. —**data processing** handling of data by computer

date[1] n. day of the month; statement on document of its time of writing; time of occurrence; period of work of art etc.; engagement, appointment —vt. mark with date; refer to date; reveal age of; inf. accompany on social outing —vi. exist (from); betray time or period of origin, become old-fashioned —**date'less** a. without date; immemorial

date[2] n. sweet, single-stone fruit of palm; the palm

Da'tel R Post Office service transmitting data over telephone or telex

da'tive [-tiv] n. noun case indicating indirect object etc.

da'tum n. thing given, known, or assumed as basis for reckoning, reasoning etc. (da'ta pl.)

daub vt. coat, plaster, paint coarsely or roughly —n. rough picture; smear —**daub'er** n.

daught'er [dawt'-] n. one's female child —**daught'erly** a. —**daughter-in-law** n. son's wife

daunt vt. frighten, esp. into giving up purpose —**daunt'less** a. intrepid, fearless

dau'phin [daw'fin] n. formerly (1349–1830) eldest son of French king

dav'enport n. small writing table with drawers; US large couch or settee

dav'it n. crane, usu. one of pair, at ship's side for lowering and hoisting boats

Davy Jones's locker sea, considered as sailors' grave

Da'vy lamp miner's safety lamp

daw n. obs. jackdaw

daw'dle vi. idle, waste time, loiter —**dawd'ler** n.

dawn n. first light, daybreak; first gleam or beginning of anything —vi. begin to grow light; appear, begin; (begin to) be understood —**dawn'ing** n.

day n. period of 24 hours; time when sun is above horizon; point or unit of time; daylight; part of day occupied by certain activity, time period; special or designated day —**day'book** n. book in which day's sales etc. are entered for later transfer to ledger —**day'break** n. dawn —**day centre** place providing meals etc. where the elderly, handicapped etc. may spend the day —**day'dream** n. idle fancy —vi. —**day'light** n. natural light; dawn —**day'lights** pl.n. consciousness, wits —**daylight saving** in summer, time set one hour ahead of local standard time, giving extra daylight in evenings —**day release** system of releasing employees for part-time education —**day'spring** n. dawn —**day'star** n. morning star —**day'time** n. time between sunrise and sunset

daze vt. stupefy, stun, bewilder —n. stupefied or bewildered state —**dazed** a.

daz'zle vt. blind, confuse or overpower with brightness, light, brilliant display or prospects —n. brightness that dazzles the vision —**daz'zlement** n.

dB decibel(s)

DBE Dame Commander of the British Empire

DBS Direct Broadcasting by Satellite

DC direct current

DCM Distinguished Conduct Medal

DD Doctor of Divinity

D-day day selected for start of something, esp. Allied invasion of Europe in 1944

D.D.T. n. hydrocarbon compound used as an insecticide

de- (comb. form) removal of, from, reversal of, as in **delouse, desegregate** Such words are omitted where their meaning may easily be inferred from the simple word

dea'con [dē'kən] n. one in lowest degree of holy orders; one who superintends secular affairs of presbyterian church (**dea'coness** fem.)

dead [ded] a. no longer alive; obsolete; numb, without sensation; no longer functioning, extinguished; lacking lustre or movement or vigour; sure, complete —n. dead person or persons (oft. in pl., the dead) —adv. utterly —**dead'en** vt. —**dead'ly** a. fatal; deathlike —adv. as if dead —**dead-and-alive** a. dull —**dead'beat** n. inf. lazy, useless person —**dead'head** n. US, C log sticking out of water as hindrance to navigation —**dead heat** race in which competitors finish exactly even —**dead letter** law no longer observed; letter which post office cannot deliver —**dead'line** n. limit of time allowed —**dead'lock** n. standstill —**deadly nightshade** plant with poisonous black berries —**dead'pan** a. expressionless —**dead reckoning** calculation of ship's position from log and compass, when observations cannot be taken —**dead set** absolutely; resolute attack —**dead of night** time of greatest stillness and darkness

deaf [def] *a.* wholly or partly without hearing; unwilling to listen —**deaf'en** *vt.* make deaf —**deaf'ness** *n.*

deal[1] *vt.* distribute, give out; inflict —*vi.* act; treat; do business (with, in) (dealt *pt./pp.*) —*n.* agreement; treatment; share; business transaction —**deal'er** *n.* one who deals (*esp.* cards); trader —**deal'ings** *pl.n.* transactions or relations with others —**deal with** handle, act towards

deal[2] *n.* (plank of) fir or pine wood

dean *n.* university or college official; head of cathedral chapter —**dean'ery** *n.* cathedral dean's house or appointment

dear *a.* beloved; precious; costly, expensive —*n.* beloved one —*adv.* at a high price —**dear'ly** *adv.* —**dear'ness** *n.*

dearth [derth] *n.* scarcity

death [deth] *n.* dying; end of life; end, extinction; annihilation; (D-) personification of death, as skeleton —**death'less** *a.* immortal —**death'ly** *a./adv.* like death —**death duty** tax on property left at death —**death mask** cast of person's face taken after death —**deathwatch beetle** beetle that bores into wood

debac'le [dā-bahk'l] *n.* utter collapse, rout, disaster

debar' *vt.* shut out from; stop; prohibit; preclude (-**rr**-)

debark' *v.* disembark

debase' *vt.* lower in value, quality or character; adulterate coinage —**debase'ment** *n.*

debate' *v.* argue, discuss, *esp.* in a formal assembly; consider —*n.* discussion; controversy —**deba't'able** *a.* —**deba'ter** *n.*

debauch' [-bawch'] *vt.* lead into a life of depraved self-indulgence —*n.* bout of sensual indulgence —**debauchee'** *n.* dissipated person —**debauch'ery** *n.*

deben'ture *n.* bond of company or corporation

debil'ity *n.* feebleness, *esp.* of health; languor —**debil'itate** *vt.* weaken, enervate

deb'it *Accounting* —*n.* entry in account of sum owed; side of book in which such sums are entered —*vt.* charge, enter as due

debonair' *a.* suave, genial, affable

debouch' *vi.* move out from narrow place to wider one —**debouch'ment** *n.*

debrief' *v.* of soldier *etc.*, report to superior on result of mission

de'bris [dā'brē, deb'-] *n. sing. and pl.* fragments, rubbish

debt [det] *n.* what is owed; state of owing —**debt'or** *n.*

debunk' *vt.* expose falseness, pretentiousness of, *esp.* by ridicule

de'but [dā'byoo] *n.* first appearance in public —**deb'utante** *n.* girl making official debut into society

Dec. December

deca- (*comb. form*) ten, as in **dec'alitre**

dec'ade *n.* period of ten years; set of ten

dec'adent *a.* declining, deteriorating; morally corrupt —**dec'adence** *n.*

decaff'einated [-in-āt-əd] *a.* (of coffee) with the caffeine removed

dec'agon *n.* figure of 10 angles —**decag'onal** *a.*

decahe'dron *n.* solid of 10 faces —**decahe'dral** *a.*

decal'cify *vt.* deprive of lime, as bones or teeth of their calcareous matter (**-fied, -fying**)

Dec'alogue [-log] *n.* the Ten Commandments

decamp' *vi.* make off, break camp, abscond

deca'nal *a.* of dean, deanery

decant' *vt.* pour off (liquid, as wine) to leave sediment —**decant'er** *n.* stoppered bottle for wine or spirits

decap'itate *vt.* behead —**decapita'tion** *n.* —**decap'itator** *n.*

decar'bonize *vt.* remove deposit of carbon, as from motor cylinder —**decarboniza'tion** *n.*

dec'asyllable *n.* ten-syllabled line —**decasyllab'ic** *a.*

decath'lon [-kath-] *n.* athletic contest with ten events

decay' *v.* rot, decompose; fall off, decline —*n.* rotting; a falling away, break up

decease' [-sēs'] *n.* death —*vi.* die —**deceased'** *a.* dead —*n.* person lately dead

deceive' [-sēv'] *vt.* mislead, delude, cheat —**deceit'** *n.* fraud; duplicity —**deceit'ful** *a.* —**deceiv'er** *n.*

decel'erate [-sel'-] *vi.* slow down

Decem'ber *n.* twelfth and last month of year

decenn'ial [-sen'-] *a.* of period of ten years —**decenn'ially** *adv.*

de'cent *a.* respectable; fitting, seemly; not obscene; adequate; *inf.* kind —**de'cency** *n.* —**de'cently** *adv.*

decen'tralize *vt.* divide (government, organization) among local centres

decep'tion *n.* deceiving; illusion; fraud; trick —**decep'tive** *a.* misleading; apt to mislead

dec'ibel [des'-] *n.* unit for measuring intensity of a sound

decide' *vt.* settle, determine, bring to resolution; give judgment —*vi.* come to a decision, conclusion —**deci'ded** *a.* unmistakable; settled; resolute —**deci'dedly** *adv.* certainly, undoubtedly —**deci'sion** [-zhon] *n.* —**deci'sive** *a.* —**deci'sively** *adv.*

decid'uous *a.* of trees, losing leaves annually; of antlers, teeth *etc.* being shed at the end of a period of growth

dec'imal [des'-] *a.* relating to tenths; proceeding by tens —*n.* decimal fraction —**decimaliza'tion** *n.* —**dec'imalize'** *vt.* convert into decimal fractions or system —**decimal system** system of weights and measures, or coinage, in which value of each denomination is ten times the one below it —**dec'igram** *n.* tenth of gram —**dec'ilitre** *n.* tenth of litre —**dec'imetre** *n.* tenth of metre

dec'imate *vt.* destroy or kill a tenth of, large proportion of —**decima'tion** *n.* —**dec'imator** *n.*

deci'pher *vt.* make out meaning of; decode —**deci'pherable** *a.*

deck *n.* platform or floor, *esp.* one covering whole or part of ship's hull; turntable of record player; part of tape recorder supporting tapes —*vt.* array, decorate —**deck chair** folding chair made of canvas suspended in wooden frame

declaim' *v.* speak dramatically, rhetorically or passionately; protest loudly —**declama'tion** *n.* —**declam'atory** *a.*

declare' *vt.* announce formally; state emphatically; show; name (as liable to customs duty) —*vi.* take sides (for); *Cricket* bring innings to an end before last wicket has fallen —**declara'tion** *n.* —**declar'ative, declar'atory** *a.* —**decla'rer** *n.* *Bridge* person who names trumps or calls "No trumps"

decline' *vi.* refuse; slope, bend

or sink downwards; deteriorate gradually; grow smaller, diminish; list the case endings of nouns —n. gradual deterioration; movement downwards; diminution; downward slope —**declen'sion** n. group of nouns; falling off; declining —**decli'nable** a. —**declina'tion** n. sloping away, deviation; angle

decliv'ity n. downward slope —**decliv'itous** a.

declutch' vt. disengage clutch of car etc.

decoc'tion n. extraction of essence by boiling down; such essence —**decoct'** vt. boil down

decode' vt. put in intelligible terms a message in code or secret alphabet

décolle·té [dā-kol'tā] a. (of women's garment) having a low-cut neckline

decommiss'ion vt. dismantle (nuclear reactor, industrial plant) sufficiently to abandon safely

decompose' [-ōz'] v. separate into elements; rot —**decomposi'tion** n. decay

decompress' vt. free from pressure; return to condition of normal atmospheric pressure —**decompres'sion** n.

decongest'ant [-j-] a./n. (drug) relieving (esp. nasal) congestion

decontam'inate vt. free from contamination eg from poisons, radioactive substances —**decontamina'tion** n.

decontrol' vt. release from state control (-ll-)

dé'cor, de'cor [dā'-] n. decorative scheme of a room etc.; stage decoration, scenery

dec'orate vt. beautify by additions; paint or wallpaper room etc.; to invest (with an order, medal etc.) —**decora'tion** n.

—**dec'orative** a. —**dec'orator** n.

decor'um n. seemly behaviour, propriety, decency —**dec'orous** a. —**dec'orously** adv.

de'coy n. something used to entrap others or to distract their attention; bait, lure —v. [di-koi'] lure, be lured as with decoy

decrease' v. diminish, lessen —n. [dē'-] lessening

decree' n. order having the force of law; edict —v. determine judicially; order

dec'rement n. act or state of decreasing; quantity lost by decrease

decrep'it a. old and feeble; broken down, worn out —**decrep'itude** n.

decry' vt. disparage (**decried'**, **decry'ing**)

ded'icate vt. commit wholly to special purpose or cause; inscribe or address (book etc.) devote to God's service —**dedica'tion** n. —**ded'icatory** a. —**ded'icator** n.

deduce' vt. draw as conclusion from facts —**deduct'** vt. take away, subtract —**deduct'ible** a. —**deduc'tion** n. deducting; amount subtracted; conclusion deduced; inference from general to particular —**deduc'tive** a. —**deduc'tively** adv.

deed n. action or fact; exploit; legal document

deem vt. judge, consider, regard

deep a. extending far down, in or back; at, of given depth; profound; heartfelt; hard to fathom; cunning; engrossed, immersed; of colour, dark and rich; of sound, low and full —n. deep place; the sea —adv. far down etc. —**deep'en** vt. —**deep'ly** adv. —**deep field** Cricket position behind bowler, near boundary —**deepfreeze'** n. refrigerator storing frozen food

deer n. family of ruminant animals typically with antlers in male (*pl.* **deer**) —**deer'hound** *n.* large rough-coated dog —**deer'-stalker** *n.* one who stalks deer; kind of cloth hat with peaks

deface' *vt.* spoil or mar surface; disfigure —**deface'ment** *n.*

de fac'to [dā-fak'tō] *Lat.* existing in fact, whether legally recognized or not

defame' *vt.* speak ill of, dishonour by slander or rumour —**defama'tion** *n.* —**defam'atory** *a.*

default' *n.* failure, neglect to act, appear or pay —*v.* fail (to pay) —**default'er** *n. esp.* soldier guilty of military offence —**in default of** in the absence of

defeat' *vt.* overcome, vanquish; thwart —*n.* overthrow; lost battle or encounter; frustration —**defeat'ism** *n.* attitude tending to accept defeat —**defeat'ist** *n./a.*

def'ecate *vt.* empty the bowels; clear of impurities —**defeca'tion** *n.*

de'fect [*or* -fekt'] *n.* lack, blemish, failing —*vi.* [-fekt'] desert one's country, cause *etc., esp.* to join opponents —**defec'tion** *n.* abandonment of duty or allegiance —**defect'ive** *a.* incomplete; faulty

defend' *vt.* protect, ward off attack; support by argument, evidence; (try to) maintain (title *etc.*) against challenger —**defence'** *n.* —**defend'ant** *n.* person accused in court —**defend'er** *n.* —**defensibil'ity** *n.* —**defens'ible** *a.* —**defens'ive** *a.* serving for defence —*n.* position or attitude of defence

defer'[1] *vt.* put off, postpone (-**rr**-) —**defer'ment** *n.*

defer'[2] *vi.* submit to opinion or judgment of another (-**rr**-) —**def'erence** *n.* respect for another inclining to accept his

views *etc.* —**deferen'tial** *a.* —**deferen'tially** *adv.*

defi'ance *n.*, **defi'ant** *a. see* DEFY

defi'cient [-ish'ənt] *a.* lacking or falling short in something, insufficient —**defi'ciency** *n.* —**def'icit** *n.* amount by which sum of money is too small

defile'[1] *vt.* make dirty, pollute, soil; sully; desecrate —**defile'-ment** *n.*

de'file[2] *n.* narrow pass or valley —*vi.* march in file

define' *vt.* state contents or meaning of; show clearly the form; lay down clearly, fix; mark out —**defin'able** *a.* —**defini'tion** *n.* —**def'inite** [-it] *a.* exact, defined; clear, specific; certain, sure —**def'initely** *adv.* —**defin'itive** *a.* conclusive, to be looked on as final —**defin'itively** *adv.*

deflate' *v.* (cause to) collapse by release of gas from; take away (person's) self-esteem; *Economics* cause deflation —**defla'tion** *n.* deflating; *Economics* reduction of economic and industrial activity —**defla'tionary** *a.*

deflect' *v.* (cause to) turn from straight course —**deflec'tion, deflex'ion** *n.*

deflow'er *vt.* deprive of virginity, innocence *etc.* —**deflora'tion** *n.*

defo'liate *v.* (cause to) lose leaves, *esp.* by action of chemicals —**defo'liant** *n.* —**defolia'tion** *n.*

defor'est *vt.* clear of trees —**deforesta'tion** *n.*

deform' *vt.* spoil shape of; make ugly; disfigure —**deforma'tion** *n.* —**deformed'** *a.* —**deform'ity** *n.*

defraud' *vt.* cheat, swindle

defray' *vt.* provide money for (expenses *etc.*)

defrock' *vt.* deprive (priest,

minister) of ecclesiastical status

defrost' v. make, become free of frost, ice; thaw

deft a. skilful, adroit —**deft'ly** adv. —**deft'ness** n.

defunct' a. dead, obsolete

defuse' vt. remove fuse of bomb, etc.; remove tension (from situation etc.)

defy' vt. challenge, resist successfully; disregard (**defied'**, **defy'ing**) —**defi'ance** n. resistance —**defi'ant** a. openly and aggressively hostile; insolent —**defi'antly** adv.

degauss' vt. equip (ship) with apparatus which prevents it detonating magnetic mines

degen'erate vi. deteriorate to lower mental, moral, or physical level —a. fallen away in quality —n. degenerate person —**degen'eracy** n. —**degenera'tion** n. —**degen'erative** a.

degrade' vt. dishonour; debase; reduce to lower rank —vi. decompose chemically —**degra'dable** a. capable of chemical, biological decomposition —**degra'ded** a. shamed, humiliated —**degrada'tion** n.

degree' n. step, stage in process, scale, relative rank, order, condition, manner, way; university rank; unit of measurement of temperature or angle —**third degree** severe, lengthy examination, esp. of accused person by police, to extract information, confession

dehis'cent [-his'ənt] a. opening, as capsule of plant —**dehisce'** vi. burst open —**dehis'cence** n.

dehumid'ify vt. to extract moisture from

dehy'drate vt. remove moisture from —**dehydra'tion** n.

de-ice' vt. to dislodge ice from (eg windscreen) or prevent its forming

de'ify [or dā'-] vt. make god of, treat, worship as god (**de'ified**, **de'ifying**) —**deifica'tion** n. —**de'iform** a. godlike in form

deign [dān] vt. condescend, stoop; think fit

de'ism [or dā'-] n. belief in god but not in revelation —**de'ist** n. —**deis'tic** a. —**de'ity** n. divine status or attributes; a god

déjà vu' [dā-zha-vōō'] Fr. experience of perceiving new situation as if it had occurred before

deject' vt. dishearten, cast down, depress —**deject'ed** a. —**dejec'tion** n.

de jur'e [dā-joor'ä] Lat. in law, by right

dekk'o n. sl. look

delay' vt. postpone, hold back —vi. be tardy, linger (**delayed'**, **delay'ing**) —n. act or instance of delaying; interval of time between events

delect'able a. delightful —**delecta'tion** n. pleasure

del'egate n. person chosen to represent another —vt. send as deputy; commit (authority, business etc.) to a deputy —**del'egacy** n. —**delega'tion** n.

delete' vt. remove, cancel, erase —**dele'tion** n.

delete'rious a. harmful, injurious

delib'erate [-it] a. intentional; well-considered; without haste, slow —v. [-āt] consider, debate —**delib'erately** adv. —**delibera'tion** n. —**delib'erative** a.

del'icate a. exquisite; not robust, fragile; sensitive; requiring tact; deft —**del'icacy** n. —**del'icately** adv.

delicatess'en n. shop selling esp. imported or unusual foods

deli'cious [-ish'əs] a. delightful, pleasing to senses, esp. taste —**deli'ciously** adv.

delight' vt. please greatly —vi.

take great pleasure (in) —*n.* great pleasure —**delight'ful** *a.* charming

delimita'tion *n.* assigning of boundaries —**delim'it** *vt.*

delin'eate *vt.* portray by drawing or description —**delinea'tion** *n.* —**delin'eator** *n.*

delin'quent *n.* someone, esp. young person, guilty of delinquency —*a.* —**delin'quency** *n.* (minor) offence or misdeed

deliquesce' [-kwes'] *vi.* become liquid —**deliques'cence** *n.* —**deliques'cent** *a.*

delir'ium *n.* disorder of the mind, esp. in feverish illness; violent excitement —**delir'ious** *a.* raving; light-headed, wildly excited

deliv'er *vt.* carry (goods *etc.*) to destination; hand over; release; give birth or assist in birth (of); utter or present (speech *etc.*) —**deliv'erance** *n.* rescue —**deliv'erer** *n.* —**deliv'ery** *n.*

dell *n.* wooded hollow

Del'phic *a.* pert. to Delphi or to the oracle of Apollo

delphin'ium *n.* garden plant with tall spikes of usu. blue flowers

del'ta *n.* alluvial tract where river at mouth breaks into several streams; Greek letter (Δ); shape of this letter

delude' [-ōōd'] *vt.* deceive; mislead —**delu'sion** *n.* —**delu'sive** *a.*

del'uge *n.* flood, great flow, rush, downpour, cloudburst —*vt.* flood, overwhelm

de luxe [-looks'] *a.* rich, sumptuous; superior in quality

delve *v.* (with into) search intensively; dig

demag'netize *vt.* deprive of magnetic polarity

dem'agogue [-og] *n.* mob leader or agitator —**demagog'ic** *a.* —**dem'agogy** *n.*

demand' [-ah-] *vt.* ask as giving an order; ask as by right; call for as due, right or necessary —*n.* urgent request, claim, requirement; call for (specific commodity) —**deman'ding** *a.* requiring great skill, patience *etc.*

de'marcate *vt.* mark boundaries or limits of —**demarca'tion** *n.*

démarche [dā-mahsh'] *n.* step or manoeuvre, esp. in diplomacy

demean' *vt.* degrade, lower, humiliate

demean'our *n.* conduct, bearing, behaviour

dement'ed *a.* mad, crazy; beside oneself —**demen'tia** [-shə] *n.* form of insanity

demera'ra *n.* kind of brown cane sugar

demer'it *n.* bad point; undesirable quality

demesne' [-ān', -ēn'] *n.* estate, territory; sphere of action —**hold in demesne** have unrestricted possession of

demi- (comb. form) half, as in **demigod** Such words are not given here where meaning may be inferred from the simple word

dem'ijohn *n.* large (wicker-cased) bottle

demil'itarize *vt.* prohibit military presence or function in (an area) —**demilitariza'tion** *n.*

demimonde' *n.* class of women of doubtful reputation

demise' [-īz'] *n.* death; conveyance by will or lease; transfer of sovereignty on death or abdication —*vt.* convey to another by will; lease

dem'iurge [dem'i-ərj] *n.* name given in some philosophies (esp. Platonic) to the creator of the world and man

dem'o *n.* inf. short for DEMONSTRATION

demob' *vt.* inf. demobilize

demo'bilize vt. disband (troops); discharge (soldier) —demobiliza'tion n.

democ'racy n. government by the people or their elected representatives; state so governed —dem'ocrat n. advocate of democracy —democrat'ic a. connected with democracy; favouring popular rights —democrat'ically adv. —democratiza'tion n. —democ'ratize vt.

demog'raphy n. study of population statistics, as births, deaths, diseases —demog'rapher n. —demograph'ic a.

demol'ish vt. knock to pieces; destroy utterly; overthrow —demoli'tion n.

de'mon n. devil, evil spirit; very cruel or malignant person; person very good at or devoted to a given activity —demo'niac n. one possessed with a devil —demoni'acal a. —demon'ic a. of the nature of a devil —demonol'ogy n. study of demons

dem'onstrate vt. show by reasoning, prove; describe, explain by specimens or experiments —vi. make exhibition of support, protest etc. by public parade, rally; make show of armed force —demon'strable a. —demon'strably adv. —demonstra'tion n. making clear, proving by evidence; exhibition and description; organized expression of public opinion; display of armed force —demon'strative a. expressing feelings, emotions easily and unreservedly; pointing out; conclusive —dem'onstrator n. one who demonstrates equipment, products etc.; one who takes part in a public demonstration; professor's assistant in laboratory etc.

demor'alize vt. deprive of courage and discipline; under-mine morally —demoraliza'tion n.

demote' vt. reduce in status or rank —demo'tion n.

demur' [-mur] vi. make difficulties, object (-rr-) —n. raising of objection; objection raised —demur'rer n. Law exception taken to opponent's point

demure' [-myoor'] a. reserved, quiet —demure'ly adv.

demurr'age n. charge for keeping ship etc. beyond time agreed for unloading

den n. cave or hole of wild beast; lair; small room, esp. study; site, haunt

denat'ionalize vt. return (an industry) from public to private ownership —denationaliza'tion n.

dena'ture vt. deprive of essential qualities, adulterate —denatured alcohol spirit made undrinkable

dene n. valley

den'gue [deng'gi] n. an infectious tropical fever

deni'al see DENY

den'ier n. unit of weight of silk, rayon and nylon yarn

den'igrate vt. belittle or disparage character of

den'im n. strong cotton drill for trousers, overalls etc.

den'izen n. inhabitant

denom'inate vt. give name to —denomina'tion n. distinctly named church or sect; name, esp. of class or group —denomina'tional a. —denom'inator n. divisor in vulgar fraction

denote' vt. stand for, be the name of; mark, indicate, show —denota'tion n.

denoue'ment [dā-nōō'mon] n. unravelling of dramatic plot; final solution of mystery

denounce' vt. speak violently against; accuse; terminate (treaty) —denuncia'tion n. denouncing —denun'ciatory a.

dense a. thick, compact; stupid —dense'ly adv. —dens'ity n. mass per unit of volume

dent n. hollow or mark left by blow or pressure —vt. make dent in; mark with dent

dent'al a. of, pert. to teeth or dentistry; pronounced by applying tongue to teeth —dent'ate a. toothed —dent'ifrice [-is] n. powder, paste, or wash for cleaning teeth —dent'ist n. surgeon who attends to teeth —dent'istry n. art of dentist —denti'tion [-ish'ən] n. teething; arrangement of teeth —dent'ure n. (usu. pl.) set of false teeth —dental floss soft thread, oft. waxed, for cleaning teeth

dent'ine [-ēn] n. the hard bonelike part of a tooth

denude' vt. strip, make bare; expose (rock) by erosion of plants, soil etc. —denuda'tion n.

denuncia'tion see DENOUNCE

deny' vt. declare untrue; contradict; reject, disown; refuse to give; refuse; (reflex.) abstain from (denied', deny'ing) —deni'able a. —deni'al n.

deo'dorize vt. rid of smell or mask smell of —deo'dorant n. —deodoriza'tion n. —deo'dorizer n.

deontol'ogy n. the science of ethics and moral obligations —deontol'ogist n.

De'o volen'te [dā'ō-vo-len'ti] Lat. God willing

deox'idize vt. deprive of oxygen —deoxidiza'tion n.

DEP Department of Employment and Productivity

dep. depart(s); departure; deposed; deposit; deputy

depart' vi. go away; start out, set forth; deviate, vary; die —depar'ture n.

depart'ment n. division; branch; province —departmen'tal a. —department'ally adv. —department store large shop selling all kinds of goods

depend' vi. (usu. with on) rely entirely; live; be contingent, await settlement or decision —depend'able a. reliable —depend'ant n. one for whose maintenance another is responsible —depend'ent a. depending on —depend'ence n. —depend'ency n. subject territory

depict' vt. give picture of; describe in words —depic'tion n. —depic'tor n.

depil'atory n. substance that removes hair —a.

deplete' vt. empty; reduce; exhaust —deple'tion n.

deplore' vt. lament, regret; deprecate, complain of —deplor'able a. lamentable; disgraceful

deploy' v. of troops, ships, (cause to) adopt battle formation; arrange —deploy'ment n.

depo'larize vt. deprive of polarity —depolariza'tion n.

depo'nent a. of verb, having passive form but active meaning —n. deponent verb; one who makes statement on oath; deposition

depop'ulate v. (cause to) be reduced in population —depopula'tion n.

deport' vt. expel from foreign country, banish —deporta'tion n.

deport'ment n. behaviour, conduct, bearing —deport' v. behave, carry (oneself)

depose' vt. remove from office, esp. of sovereign —vi. make statement on oath, give evidence —depo'sable a. —depo'sal n. removal from office; statement made on oath

depos'it [-poz'-] vt. set down, esp. carefully; give into safe keeping, *esp.* in bank; let fall (as sediment) —*n.* thing deposited; money given in part payment or as security; sediment —**depos'itary** *n.* person with whom thing is deposited —**deposi'tion** *n.* statement written and attested; act of deposing or depositing —**depos'itor** *n.* —**depos'itory** *n.* place for safe-keeping

dep'ot [-ō] *n.* storehouse; building for storage and servicing of buses, railway engines *etc.*; US [dē'pō] railway station

deprave' *vt.* make bad, corrupt, pervert —**deprav'ity** *n.* wickedness, viciousness

dep'recate *vt.* express disapproval of; advise against —**depreca'tion** *n.* —**dep'recatory** *a.*

depre'ciate [-shi-] *vt.* lower price, value or purchasing power of; belittle —*vi.* fall in value —**deprecia'tion** *n.* —**depre'cia- tor** *n.* —**depre'ciatory** *a.*

depreda'tion *n.* plundering, pillage —**dep'redate** *vt.* plunder, despoil —**dep'redator** *n.*

depress' *vt.* affect with low spirits; lower, in level or activity —**depress'ion** *n.* hollow; low spirits, dejection, despondency; low state of trade, slump —**depres'sant** *n.* —**depres'sive** *a.*

deprive' *vt.* strip, dispossess —**depriva'tion** *n.* —**deprived'** *a.* lacking adequate food, care, amenities *etc.*

dept. department

depth *n.* (degree of) deepness; deep place, abyss; intensity (of colour, feeling); profundity (of mind) —**depth charge** bomb for use against submarines

depute' [-pyōōt'] *vt.* allot; appoint as an agent or substitute —*a./n.* [dep'-] in Scotland assistant —**deputa'tion** *n.* persons to speak for others —**dep'u- tize** *vi.* act for another —*vt.*

depute —**dep'uty** *n.* assistant; substitute, delegate

derail' *v.* (cause to) go off the rails, as train *etc.* —**derail'ment** *n.*

derail'leur [-yər] *a./n.* (of) gear-change mechanism for bicycles

derange' *vt.* put out of place, out of order; upset; make insane —**derange'ment** *n.*

der'by [dah'-] *n.* horserace, *esp.* (D-) famous horserace at Epsom, England; contest between local teams; [der'-] US bowler hat

dereg'ulate *vt.* remove regulations or controls from

der'elict *a.* abandoned, forsaken; falling into ruins, dilapidated —*n.* social outcast, vagrant; abandoned property, ship *etc.* —**derelic'tion** *n.* neglect (of duty); abandoning

deride' *vt.* speak of or treat with contempt, ridicule —**deri'- sion** [-zh-] *n.* ridicule —**deri'sive** *a.* —**deri'sory** *a.* mocking, ridiculing

de rigueur [-gər'] *Fr.* required by etiquette or fashion

derive' *vt.* deduce, get from; show origin of —*vi.* issue, be descended (from) —**deriva'tion** *n.* —**deriv'ative** *a./n.*

dermati'tis *n.* inflammation of skin

dermatol'ogy *n.* science of skin —**dermatol'ogist** *n.* physician specializing in skin diseases

derog'atory *a.* disparaging, belittling, intentionally offensive

derr'ick *n.* hoisting machine; framework over oil well *etc.*

derr'ing-do *n.* (act of) spirited bravery, boldness

derr'inger [-j-] *n.* small pistol with large bore

derv *n.* diesel oil for road vehicles (*d*iesel *e*ngine *r*oad *v*ehicle)

der'vish *n.* member of Muslim

ascetic order, noted for frenzied, whirling dance

des'cant n. Mus. decorative variation sung as accompaniment to basic melody —vi. [-kant'] talk about in detail; dwell (on) at length

descend' [-send'] vi. come or go down; slope down; stoop, condescend; spring from (ancestor etc.); pass to heir, be transmitted; swoop on or attack —vt. go or come down —**descend'ant** n. person descended from an ancestor —**descent'** n.

describe' vt. give detailed account; pronounce or label; trace out (geometrical figure etc.) —**descrip'tion** n. detailed account; marking out; kind, sort, species —**descrip'tive** a.

descry' vt. make out, catch sight of, esp. at a distance, espy (descried', descry'ing)

des'ecrate vt. violate sanctity of; profane; convert to evil use —**desecra'tion** n.

deselect' vt. refuse to select (existing MP) for re-election

des'ert¹ [-z-] n. uninhabited and barren region —a. barren, uninhabited, desolate

desert² [-z-] vt. abandon, forsake, leave —vi. run away from service, esp. of soldiers etc. —**desert'er** n. —**deser'tion** n.

desert³ [-z-] n. (usu. pl.) what is due as reward or punishment; merit, virtue

deserve' [-z-] vt. show oneself worthy of; have by conduct a claim to —**deserv'edly** [-id-li] adv. —**deserv'ing** a. worthy (of reward etc.)

deshabille¹ [dá-za-bēl'] n. see DISHABILLE

des'iccate v. dry; dry up —**desicca'tion** n.

desiderat'um [-raht'-] n. something lacked and wanted

design' [-zīn'] vt. make working drawings for; sketch; plan out; intend, select for —n. outline sketch; working plan; art of making decorative patterns etc.; project, purpose, mental plan —**design'edly** [-id-li] adv. on purpose —**design'er** n. esp. one who draws designs for manufacturers —**design'ing** a. crafty, scheming

des'ignate [dez'ig-] vt. name, pick out, appoint to office —a. appointed but not yet installed —**designa'tion** n. name, appellation

desire' [-zīr'] vt. wish, long for; ask for, entreat —n. longing, craving; expressed wish, request; sexual appetite; something wished for or requested —**desirabil'ity** n. —**desi'rable** a. worth desiring —**desi'rous** a. filled with desire

desist' [-zist'] vi. cease, stop

desk n. table or other piece of furniture designed for reading or writing; counter; editorial section of newspaper etc. covering specific subject

des'olate a. uninhabited; neglected, ruinous; solitary; dreary, dismal, forlorn —vt. depopulate, lay waste; overwhelm with grief —**desola'tion** n.

despair' vi. lose hope —n. loss of all hope; cause of this; despondency

despatch' see DISPATCH

des'perate a. reckless from despair; difficult or dangerous; frantic; hopelessly bad; leaving no room for hope —**despera'do** [-rahd'-] n. reckless, lawless person (pl. **-do(e)s**) —**des'perately** adv. —**despera'tion** n.

despise' [-īz'] vt. look down on as contemptible, inferior —**des'picable** [or -spik'-] a. base, contemptible, vile —**des'picably** adv.

despite[1] *prep.* in spite of

despoil[1] *vt.* plunder, rob, strip of —**despolia'tion** *n.*

despond'ent *a.* dejected, depressed —**despond'** *vi.* —**despond'ency** *n.* —**despond'ently** *adv.*

des'pot *n.* tyrant, oppressor —**despot'ic** *a.* —**despot'ically** *adv.* —**des'potism** *n.* autocratic government, tyranny

despu'mate *vi.* throw off impurities; form scum

des'quamate *vi.* (of skin) come off in scales —**desquama'tion** *n.*

dessert' [-z-] *n.* sweet course, or fruit, served at end of meal

destina'tion *n.* place a person or thing is bound for; goal; purpose

des'tine [-tin] *vt.* ordain or fix beforehand; set apart, devote

des'tiny *n.* course of events or person's fate; the power which foreordains

des'titute *a.* in absolute want; in great need, devoid (of); penniless —**destitu'tion** *n.*

destroy' *vt.* ruin; pull to pieces; undo; put an end to; demolish; annihilate —**destroy'er** *n.* one who destroys; small, swift, heavily armed warship —**destruct'** *v.* destroy (one's own missile *etc.*) for safety —**destruct'ible** *a.* —**destruc'tion** *n.* ruin, overthrow; death —**destruct'ive** *a.* destroying; negative, not constructive —**destruct'ively** *adv.* —**destruct'or** *n.* that which destroys, *esp.* incinerator

desu'etude [-syooi-tyood] *n.* disuse, discontinuance

des'ultory *a.* passing, changing fitfully from one thing to another; aimless; unmethodical

detach' *vt.* unfasten, disconnect, separate —**detach'able** *a.* —**detached'** *a.* standing apart, isolat-

ed; impersonal, disinterested —**detach'ment** *n.* aloofness; detaching; a body of troops detached for special duty

de'tail *n.* particular; small or unimportant part; treatment of anything item by item; party or man assigned for duty in army —*vt.* relate in full; appoint for duty

detain' *vt.* keep under restraint; hinder; keep waiting —**deten'tion** *n.* confinement; arrest; detaining

detect' *vt.* find out or discover existence, presence, nature or identity of —**detec'tion** *n.* —**detec'tive** *n.* policeman or private agent employed in detecting crime —*a.* employed in detection —**detect'or** *n.* *esp.* mechanical sensing device or device for detecting radio signals

détente [dā-tahnt'] *n.* lessening of tension in political or international affairs

deten'tion *n.* see DETAIN

deter' *vt.* discourage, frighten; hinder, prevent (-rr-) —**deter'rent** *a./n.*

deter'gent *n.* cleansing, purifying substance —*a.* having cleansing power —**deterge'** *vt.*

dete'riorate *v.* become or make worse —**deteriora'tion** *n.*

deter'mine *vt.* make up one's mind; resolve; fix as known; bring to a decision; be deciding factor in; *Law* end —*vi.* come to an end; come to a decision —**determi'nable** *a.* —**deter'minant** *a./n.* —**deter'minate** *a.* fixed in scope or nature —**determina'tion** *n.* determining; firm or resolute conduct or purpose; resolve —**deter'mined** *a.* resolute —**deter'minism** *n.* theory that human action is settled by forces independent of will —**deter'minist** *n./a.*

detest' vt. hate, loathe —**detest'able** a. —**detest'ably** adv. —**detesta'tion** n.

dethrone' vt. remove from throne, depose —**dethrone'ment** n.

det'onate v. of bomb, mine, explosives etc., (cause to) explode —**detona'tion** n. —**det'onator** n. mechanical, electrical device, or small amount of explosive, used to set off main explosive charge

de'tour n. course which leaves main route to rejoin it later; roundabout way —vi.

detract' v. take away (a part) from, diminish —**detrac'tion** n. —**detrac'tive** a. —**detrac'tor** n.

det'riment n. harm done, loss, damage —**detrimen'tal** a. damaging, injurious —**detrimen'tally** adv.

detri'tus n. worn-down matter such as gravel, or rock debris —**detri'tal** a. —**detri'tion** [-trish'-] n. wearing away from solid bodies by friction

de trop [də-trō'] Fr. not wanted, superfluous

detrude' vt. to thrust down —**detru'sion** n.

deuce [dyōōs] n. two; card with two spots; Tennis forty all; in exclamatory phrases, the devil —**deu'ced** a. inf. excessive

Deut. Deuteronomy

deute'rium [dyōō-] n. form of hydrogen twice as heavy as the normal gas —**deu'teron** n. nucleus of this gas

Deut'sche Mark [doi'chə-] monetary unit of W Germany

deut'zia [dyōōt'sih-ə] n. shrub with white or pink flower clusters

deval'ue, deval'uate v. (of currency) reduce or be reduced in value; reduce the value or worth of —**devalua'tion** n.

dev'astate vt. lay waste; ravage; inf. overwhelm —**devasta'tion** n.

devel'op vt. bring to maturity; elaborate; bring forth, bring out; evolve; treat photographic plate or film to bring out image; improve value or change use of (land) by building etc. —vi. grow to maturer state (**devel'oped, devel'oping**) —**devel'oper** n. one who develops land; chemical for developing film —**devel'opment** n.

de'viate vi. leave the way, turn aside, diverge —**de'viant** n./a. (person) deviating from normal esp. in sexual practices —**devia'tion** n. —**de'viator** n. —**de'vious** a. deceitful, underhand; roundabout, rambling; erring

device' n. contrivance, invention; apparatus; stratagem; scheme, plot; heraldic or emblematic figure or design

dev'il n. personified spirit of evil; superhuman evil being; person of great wickedness, cruelty etc.; inf. fellow; inf. something difficult or annoying; energy, dash, unconquerable spirit; inf. rogue, rascal; one who devils for lawyer or author —vt. to do work that passes for employer's, as for lawyer or author; grill with hot condiments —**dev'ilish** a. like, of the devil; evil —adv. inf. very, extremely —**dev'ilment** n. wickedness; wild and reckless mischief, revelry, high spirits —**dev'ilry** n. —**devil-may-care** a. happy-go-lucky —**devil's advocate** one who advocates opposing, unpopular view, usu. for sake of argument; RC Church one appointed to state disqualifications of person whom it is proposed to make a saint

de'vious a. see DEVIATE

devise' [-īz'] vt. plan, contrive;

invent; plot; leave by will —**devisee**[1] n. —**devi'sor** n.

devitrifica'tion n. loss of glassy or vitreous condition —**devit'rify** vt. deprive of character or appearance of glass (**-fied, -fying**)

devoid[1] a. (usu. with of) empty, lacking, free from

devolve[1] vi. pass or fall (to, upon) —vt. throw (duty etc.) on to another —**devolu'tion** [-loo-] n. devolving, esp. transfer of authority from central to regional government

devote[1] vt. set apart, give up exclusively (to person, purpose etc.) —**devo'ted** a. loving, attached —**devotee'** n. ardent enthusiast; zealous worshipper —**devo'tion** n. deep affection, loyalty; dedication; religious earnestness —pl. prayers, religious exercises —**devo'tional** a.

devour[1] vt. eat greedily; consume, destroy; read, gaze at eagerly —**devour'er** n.

devout[1] a. earnestly religious, pious; sincere, heartfelt —**devout'ly** adv.

dew n. moisture from air deposited as small drops on cool surface between nightfall and morning; any beaded moisture —vt. wet with or as with dew —**dew'iness** n. —**dew'y** a. —**dew'claw** n. partly developed inner toe of dogs —**dew'lap** n. fold of loose skin hanging from neck —**dewy-eyed** a. naive, innocent

dew'berry n. bramble with blue-black fruits

dexter'ity n. manual skill, neatness, deftness, adroitness —**dex'ter** a. Heraldry on the bearer's right-hand side of a shield —**dex'terous** a. showing dexterity, skilful

dex'trose n. white, soluble, sweet-tasting crystalline solid,

occurring naturally in fruit, honey, animal tissue

DF Defender of the Faith

DFC Distinguished Flying Cross

DFM Distinguished Flying Medal

dg decigram

d(h)ow n. lateen-rigged Arab sailing vessel

DHSS Department of Health and Social Security

dia- [dī-a-] (comb. form) through

diabe'tes [-bē'tēz] n. various disorders characterized by excretion of abnormal amount of urine, esp. **d. melli'tus**, in which body fails to store and utilize glucose —**diabet'ic** n./a.

diabol'ic(al) a. devilish; inf. very bad —**diabol'ically** adv. —**diab'olism** n. devil-worship

diab'olo n. game in which top is spun into air from string attached to two sticks

diac'onal a. pert. to deacon —**diac'onate** n. office, rank of deacon; body of deacons

diacrit'ic n. sign above letter or character indicating special phonetic value etc. —**diacrit'ic(al)** a. of a diacritic; showing a distinction

di'adem n. a crown

diaer'esis see DIERESIS

diagno'sis n. identification of disease from symptoms (pl. **diagno'ses**) —**di'agnose** vt. —**diagnos'tic** a.

diag'onal a. from corner to corner; oblique —n. line from corner to corner —**diag'onally** adv.

di'agram n. drawing, figure in lines, to illustrate something being expounded —**diagrammat'ic** a. —**diagrammat'ically** adv.

di'al n. face of clock etc.; plate marked with graduations on which a pointer moves (as on a meter, weighing machine etc.);

numbered disc on front of telephone; *sl.* face —*vt.* operate telephone; indicate on dial (**-ll-**)

di'alect *n.* characteristic speech of district; local variety of a language —**dialect'al** *a.*

dialect'ic *n.* art of arguing —**dialect'ic(al)** *a.* —**dialec'tically** *adv.* —**dialecti'cian** *n.* logician; reasoner

di'alogue *n.* conversation between two or more (persons); representation of such conversation in drama, novel *etc.*; discussion between representatives of two states, countries *etc.*

dial'ysis *n. Med.* filtering of blood through membrane to remove waste products

diaman'té *n.* (fabric covered with) glittering particles —**diaman'tine** *a.* like diamond

diam'eter *n.* (length of) straight line from side to side of figure or body (*esp.* circle) through centre; thickness —**diamet'rical** *a.* opposite —**diamet'rically** *adv.*

di'amond *n.* very hard and brilliant precious stone, also used in industry; rhomboid figure; suit at cards; playing field in baseball —**diamond jubilee, wedding** 60th (sometimes 75th) anniversary

dian'thus *n.* genus of herbaceous flowers, *eg* pinks and carnations

diapa'son [-pā'z-] *n.* fundamental organ stop; compass of voice or instrument

di'aper *n. US* baby's napkin; fabric with small diamond pattern; pattern of that kind —**di'apered** *a.*

diaph'anous *a.* transparent

diaphoret'ic *n.* drug promoting perspiration —*a.*

di'aphragm [-am] *n.* muscular partition dividing two cavities of body, midriff; plate or disc wholly or partly closing tube or opening; any thin dividing or covering membrane —**diaphragmat'ic** [-frag-] *a.*

diarrhoe'a [-rē'ə] *n.* excessive looseness of the bowels —**diarrhoe'al** *a.*

di'ary *n.* daily record of events or thoughts; book for this; book for noting engagements, memoranda *etc.* —**di'arist** *n.* writer of diary

di'astase [-as-tās] *n.* enzyme that converts starch into sugar

dias'tole [-tə-li] *n.* dilation of the chambers of the heart

di'athermy *n.* heating of body tissues with electric current for medical or surgical purposes

di'atom *n.* one of order of microscopic algae —**diatom'ic** *a.* of two atoms

diaton'ic *a. Mus.* pert. to regular major and minor scales; (of melody) composed in such a scale

di'atribe *n.* violently bitter verbal attack, invective, denunciation

dibb'er, dib'ble *n.* pointed tool for making holes in soil for seeds or plants

dice *pl.n.* (*also* functions *as sing.*, *orig. sing.* **die**) cubes each with six sides marked one to six for games of chance —*vi.* gamble with dice —*vt. Cookery* cut vegetables into small cubes —**di'cer** *n.* —**di'cey** *a. inf.* dangerous, risky

diceph'alous [dī-sef'-] *a.* two-headed

dichot'omy [-kot'-] *n.* division into two parts

di'chroism [-krō-] *n.* property possessed by some crystals of exhibiting different colours when viewed from different directions —**dichro'ic** *a.*

dick *sl.* *n.* fellow, person; detective

dick'y [1], **dick'ey** *n.* detachable false shirt front (*pl.* **dick'ies**, **dick'eys**) —**dick'ybird** *n.* *inf.* small bird

dick'y [2] *a.* *sl.* shaky, unsound

Dic'taphone *n.* R tape recorder, used *esp.* for dictation

dictate' *v.* say or read for another to transcribe; prescribe, lay down; impose (as terms) —*n.* [dik'-] bidding —**dicta'tion** *n.* —**dicta'tor** *n.* absolute ruler —**dictator'ial** *a.* despotic; overbearing —**dictator'ially** *adv.* —**dicta'torship** *n.*

dic'tion *n.* choice and use of words; enunciation

dic'tionary *n.* book setting forth, alphabetically, words of language with meanings *etc.*; reference book with items in alphabetical order

dic'tum *n.* pronouncement, saying, maxim (*pl.* **dic'ta**)

did *pt.* of DO

didac'tic *a.* designed to instruct; (of people) opinionated, dictatorial —**didac'ticism** *n.*

did'dle *vt.* *inf.* cheat

die [1] [dī] *vi.* cease to live; come to an end; stop functioning; *inf.* be nearly overcome (with laughter *etc.*); *inf.* look forward (to) (**died, dy'ing**) —**die'hard** *n.* one who resists (reform *etc.*) to the end

die [2] [dī] *see* DICE

die [3] [dī] *n.* shaped block of hard material to form metal in forge, press *etc.*; tool for cutting thread on pipe *etc.*

dielec'tric [dī-ə-lek'-] *n.* substance through or across which electric induction takes place; nonconductor; insulator

dier'esis, diaer'esis [dī-er'-] *n.* mark (¨) placed over vowel to show that it is sounded separately from preceding one (*eg* in

Noël) (*pl.* **di(a)er'eses**)

die'sel [dē'zl] *a.* pert. to internal-combustion engine using oil as fuel —*n.* this engine; vehicle powered by it; the fuel

di'et [1] *n.* restricted or regulated course of feeding; kind of food lived on; food —*vi.* follow a dietary regimen, as to lose weight —**di'etary** *a.* relating to diet —*n.* a regulated diet; system of dieting —**dietet'ic** *a.* —**dietet'ics** *pl.n.* science of diet —**dietl'cian, -tian** [-tish'-] *n.* one skilled in dietetics —**dietary fibre** fibrous substances in fruit and vegetables, consumption of which aids digestion (*also* **roughage**)

di'et [2] *n.* parliament of some countries; formal assembly

diff'er *vi.* be unlike; disagree —**diff'erence** *n.* unlikeness; degree or point of unlikeness; disagreement; remainder left after subtraction —**diff'erent** *a.* unlike —**diff'erently** *adv.*

differen'tial *a.* varying with circumstances; special; *Math.* pert. to an infinitesimal change in variable quantity; *Physics etc.* relating to difference between sets of motions acting in the same direction or between pressures *etc.* —*n.* *Math.* infinitesimal difference between two consecutive states of variable quantity; mechanism in car *etc.* allowing back wheels to revolve at different speeds when rounding corner; difference between rates of pay for different types of labour —**differen'tially** *adv.* —**differen'tiate** *vt.* serve to distinguish between, make different —*vi.* discriminate —**differentia'tion** *n.* —**differential calculus** method of calculating relative rate of change for continuously varying quantities

diff'icult a. requiring effort, skill etc. to do or understand, not easy; obscure —**diff'iculty** n. being difficult; difficult task, problem; embarrassment; hindrance; obscurity; trouble

diff'ident a. lacking confidence, timid, shy —**diff'idence** n. shyness —**diff'idently** adv.

diffract' vi. break up, esp. of rays of light, sound-waves —**diffrac'tion** n. deflection of ray of light, electromagnetic wave caused by an obstacle

diffuse' [-fyōoz'] vt. spread abroad —a. [-fyōos'] widely spread; loose, verbose, wordy —**diffuse'ly** adv. loosely; wordily —**diffu'sible** a. —**diffu'sion** n. —**diffu'sive** a. —**diffu'sively** adv.

dig vi. work with spade; search, investigate —vt. turn up with spade; hollow out, make hole in; excavate; thrust into; discover by searching (**dug, dig'ging**) —n. piece of digging; (archaeological) excavation; thrust; jibe, taunt —pl. inf. lodgings (also **dig'gings**) —**dig'ger** n. one who digs; gold-miner; Aust. or N.Z. soldier (oft. term of address)

digest' [-j-] vt. prepare (food) in stomach etc. for assimilation; bring into handy form by sorting, tabulating, summarizing; reflect on, absorb —vi. of food, undergo digestion —n. [dī'-] methodical summary, esp. of laws; magazine containing condensed version of articles etc. already published elsewhere —**digest'ible** a. —**diges'tion** n. digesting —**digest'ive** a.

dig'it [-j-] n. finger or toe; any of the numbers 0 to 9 —**dig'ital** a. of, resembling digits; performed with fingers; displaying information (time etc.) by numbers rather than by pointer on dial —**dig'itate(d)** a. having separate

fingers, toes —**digital recording** sound recording process that converts audio signals into pulses corresponding to voltage level

digit'alis, -lin [-j-] n. drug made from foxglove

dig'nity n. stateliness, gravity; worthiness, excellence, repute; honourable office or title —**dig'nify** vt. give dignity to (**-fied, -fying**) —**dig'nified** a. stately, majestic —**dig'nitary** n. holder of high office

digress' [dī-] vi. turn from main course, esp. to deviate from subject in speaking or writing —**digres'sion** n. —**digres'sive** a.

dihe'dral [dī-] a. having two plane faces or sides

dik'-dik n. small Afr. antelope

dike see DYKE

dik'tat n. arbitrary decree

dilap'idated a. in ruins; decayed —**dilapida'tion** n.

dilate' [dī-] vt. widen, expand —vi. expand; talk or write at length (on) —**dil(at)a'tion** n.

dil'atory a. tardy, slow, belated —**dil'atorily** adv. —**dil'atoriness** n. delay

dilemm'a n. position in fact or argument offering choice only between unwelcome alternatives; predicament

dilettan'te [-tahn'ti] n. person with taste and knowledge of fine arts as pastime; dabbler (pl. **dilettan'ti**) —a. amateur, desultory —**dilettan'tism** n.

dil'igent a. unremitting in effort, industrious, hard-working —**dil'igence** n.

dill n. yellow-flowered herb with medicinal seeds

dilly-dall'y vi. inf. loiter; vacillate

dilute' [-lōot'] vt. reduce (liquid) in strength, esp. by adding water; thin; reduce in force, effect etc. —a. weakened thus —**dil'uent**

[-yoo-] *a./n.* —**dilu'tion** *n.*

dilu'vial, -vian [-lōō'-] *a.* of, connected with, a deluge or flood, *esp.* the Flood of the Book of Genesis

dim *a.* indistinct, faint, not bright; mentally dull; unfavourable (**dimm'er** *comp.*, **dimm'est** *sup.*) —*v.* make, grow dim (**-mm-**) —**dim'ly** *adv.* —**dim'mer** *n.* device for dimming electric lights —**dim'ness** *n.*

dime *n.* 10-cent piece, coin of US and Canada

dimen'sion *n.* measurement, size; aspect —**dimen'sional** *a.* —**fourth dimension** *Physics* time; supranatural, fictional dimension additional to those of length, breadth, thickness

dimin'ish *v.* lessen —**diminu'tion** *n.* —**dimin'utive** *a.* very small —*n.* derivative word, affix implying smallness

diminuen'do *a./adv. Mus.* of sound, dying away

dim'ity *n.* strong cotton fabric

dim'ple *n.* small hollow in surface of skin, *esp.* of cheek; any small hollow —*v.* mark with, show dimples

din *n.* continuous roar of confused noises —*vt.* repeat to weariness, ram (fact, opinion *etc.*) into (**-nn-**)

dine *vi.* eat dinner —*vt.* give dinner to —**di'ner** *n.* one who dines; small *usu.* cheap restaurant —**dining car** railway restaurant-car —**dining room**

ding *v.* ring (*esp.* with tedious repetition); make (imitation of) sound of bell —*n.* this sound

din'ghy [ding'gi] *n.* small open boat; collapsible rubber boat

din'gle [ding'gəl] *n.* dell

din'go [-ng'gō] *n.* Aust. wild dog

din'gy [-j-] *a.* dirty-looking, dull —**din'giness** *n.*

dinn'er *n.* chief meal of the day; official banquet

di'nosaur *n.* extinct reptile, often of gigantic size —**dino'saur'ian** *a.*

dint *n.* dent, mark —**by dint of** by means of

di'ocese [dī'ə-sis] *n.* district, jurisdiction of bishop —**dioc'esan** [-os'-] *a.* —*n.* bishop, clergyman, people of diocese

di'ode *n. Electronics* device for converting alternating current to direct current

diop'tre [dī-] *n.* unit for measuring refractive power of lens —**di-op'trics** *pl.n.* (*with sing. v.*) that part of the science of optics which deals with refraction of light

diora'ma [dī-ə-rahm'ə] *n.* miniature three-dimensional scene, *esp.* as museum exhibit

diox'ide [dī-] *n.* oxide with two parts of oxygen to one of the other constituents

diox'in [dī-] *n.* extremely toxic byproduct of the manufacture of certain herbicides and bactericides

dip *vt.* put partly or for a moment into liquid; immerse, involve; lower and raise again; take up in ladle, bucket *etc.*; direct headlights of vehicle downwards —*vi.* plunge partially or temporarily; go down, sink; slope downwards (**-pp-**) —*n.* act of dipping; bathe; liquid chemical in which livestock are immersed to treat insect pests *etc.*; downward slope; hollow; creamy (savoury) mixture in which crisps *etc.* are dipped before being eaten; lottery —**dip into** glance at

diphthe'ria [dip-the'-] *n.* infectious disease of throat with membranous growth —**diphtherit'ic** *a.*

diph'thong [dif'-] *n.* union of two vowel sounds in single compound sound

diplo'ma *n.* document vouching for person's proficiency; title to degree, honour *etc.*

diplo'macy *n.* management of international relations; skill in negotiation; tactful, adroit dealing —**dip'lomat** *n.* one engaged in official diplomacy —**diplomat'ic** *a.* —**diplomat'ically** *adv.* —**diplo'matist** *n.* diplomat; tactful person

diplo'pia *n.* double vision

dipo'lar [dī-] *a.* having two poles

di'pole *n.* type of radio and television aerial

dipp'er *n.* a ladle, bucket, scoop; bird (water ouzel)

dipsoma'nia *n.* uncontrollable craving for alcohol —**dipsoma'niac** *n.* victim of this

dip'tych [-ik] *n.* ancient tablet hinged in the middle, folding together like a book; painting, carving on two hinged panels

dire *a.* terrible; urgent

direct' *vt.* control, manage, order; point out the way; aim, point, turn; address (letter *etc.*); supervise actors *etc.* in play or film —*a.* frank, straightforward; straight; going straight to the point; immediate; lineal —**direc'tion** *n.* directing; aim, course of movement; address, instruction —**direct'ive** *a./n.* —**direct'ly** *adv.* —**direct'ness** *n.* —**direct'or** *n.* one who directs, *esp.* a film; member of board managing company (**direct'ress** *fem.*) —**direc'torate** *n.* body of directors; office of director —**direct'orship** *n.* —**direct'ory** *n.* book of names, addresses, streets *etc.*; (**D-**) French revolutionary government 1795–9 —**direction finder** radio receiver that determines the direction of incoming waves

dirge *n.* song of mourning

dir'igible [-ij-] *a.* steerable —*n.* balloon or airship

dirk *n.* short dagger orig. carried by Scottish clansmen

dirn'dl [durn'-] *n.* full, gathered skirt

dirt *n.* filth; soil, earth; obscene material; contamination —**dirt'iness** *n.* —**dirt'y** *a.* unclean, filthy; obscene; unfair; dishonest —**dirt track** loose-surfaced track (*eg* for motorcycle racing)

dis- (*comb. form*) negation, opposition, deprivation; in many verbs indicates undoing of a

disapproba'tion	disembark'
disappro'val	disengage'
disapprove'	disengage'ment
disarrange'	disentang'le
disasso'ciate	disentang'lement
disavow'	disestab'lish
disband'	disestab'lishment
disbelief'	disfa'vour
discompose'	disfran'chise
discompo'sure	dishar'mony
disconnect'	disheart'en
discontent'	dishon'est
discontent'ment	dishon'esty
discontin'ue	dishon'ourable
discourt'eous	disinter'
discourt'esy	disjoin'
disloy'al	
disloy'alty	
dismount'	
disorganiza'tion	
disor'ganize	
dispropor'tion	
disprove'	
disrep'utable	
disrepute'	
disrespect'(ful)	
dissatisfac'tion	
dissat'isfy	
dissim'ilar	
dissimilar'ity	
dissymm'etry	
distrust'	

action of simple verb In the list below, the meaning may be inferred from the word to which dis- is prefixed

disa'ble vt. make unable; cripple, maim —**disabil'ity** n. incapacity; drawback

disabuse' [-byōōz'] vt. undeceive, disillusion; free from error

disadvant'age [-vahnt'-] n. drawback; hindrance; detriment —vt. handicap —**disadvant'aged** a. deprived, discriminated against, underprivileged —**disadvanta'geous** a.

disaffec'ted a. ill-disposed, alienated, estranged —**disaffec'tion** n.

disagree' vi. be at variance; conflict; (of food etc.) have bad effect on —**disagree'ment** n. difference of opinion; discord; discrepancy —**disagree'able** a. unpleasant

disallow' vt. reject as untrue or invalid —**disallow'ance** n.

disappear' vi. vanish; cease to exist; be lost —**disappear'ance** n.

disappoint' vt. fail to fulfil (hope), frustrate —**disappoint'ment** n.

disarm' v. deprive of arms or weapons; reduce country's war weapons; win over —**disarm'ament** n. —**disarm'ing** a. removing hostility, suspicion

disarray' vt. throw into disorder, derange —n. disorderliness, esp. of clothing

disas'ter [-zahs'-] n. calamity, sudden or great misfortune —**disas'trous** a. calamitous

disbar' vt. Law expel from the bar

disbud' vt. remove superfluous buds, shoots from

disburse' vt. pay out money —**disburse'ment** n.

disc n. thin, flat, circular object like a coin; gramophone record

—**disc harrow, plough** harrow or plough which cuts the soil with inclined discs —**disc jockey** announcer playing records, oft. on radio

discard' v. reject; give up; cast off, dismiss

discern' [-sern'] vt. make out; distinguish —**discern'ible** a. —**discern'ing** a. discriminating, penetrating —**discern'ment** n. insight

discharge' vt. release; dismiss; emit; perform (duties) fulfil (obligations); let go; fire off; unload; pay —n. discharging; being discharged; release; matter emitted; document certifying release, payment etc.

disci'ple [-sī'-] n. follower, one who takes another as teacher and model —**disci'pleship** n.

dis'cipline [-si-plin] n. training that produces orderliness, obedience, self-control; result of such training in order, conduct etc.; system of rules, etc. —vt. train; punish —**disciplina'rian** n. one who enforces rigid discipline **dis'ciplinary** a.

disclaim' vt. deny, renounce —**disclaim'er** n. repudiation, denial

disclose' [-ōz'-] vt. allow to be seen; make known —**disclo'sure** [-zhə] n. revelation

dis'co n. short for DISCOTHEQUE

discol'our [-kul-] vt. alter colour of, stain —**discolo(u)ra'tion** n.

discom'fit [-um'-] vt. embarrass, disconcert, baffle —**discom'fiture** n.

discommode' vt. put to inconvenience; disturb —**disconmo'dious** a.

disconcert' vt. ruffle, confuse, upset, embarrass

discon'solate a. unhappy, downcast, forlorn

dis'cord n. strife; difference; dissension; disagreement of sounds —**discord'ance** n. —**discord'ant** a. —**discord'antly** adv.

dis'cotheque [-tek] n. club etc. for dancing to recorded music; mobile equipment for providing music for dancing

dis'count [or -kount'] vt. consider as possibility but reject as unsuitable, inappropriate etc.; deduct (amount, percentage) from usual price; sell at reduced price —n. [dis'-] amount deducted from cost, expressed as cash amount or percentage

discount'enance vt. abash; discourage; frown upon

discour'age [-kur'-] vt. reduce confidence of; deter; show disapproval of —**discour'agement** n.

dis'course n. conversation; speech, treatise, sermon —vi. [-kaws'] speak, converse, lecture

discov'er [-kuv'-] vt. (be the first to) find out, light upon; make known —**discov'erable** a. —**discov'erer** n. —**discov'ery** n.

discred'it vt. damage reputation of; cast doubt on; reject as untrue —n. disgrace; doubt —**discred'itable** a.

discreet' a. prudent, circumspect —**discreet'ly** adv. —**discreet'ness** n.

discrep'ancy n. conflict, variation, as between figures —**discrep'ant** a.

discrete' a. separate, disunited, discontinuous

discre'tion [-kresh'ǝn] n. quality of being discreet; prudence; freedom to act as one chooses —**discre'tionary** a.

discrim'inate vi. single out for special favour or disfavour; distinguish between; be discerning —**discrimina'tion** n.

discur'sive a. passing from subject to subject, rambling

dis'cus n. disc-shaped object thrown in athletic competition

discuss' vt. exchange opinions about; debate —**discuss'ion** n.

disdain' n. scorn, contempt —vt. scorn —**disdain'ful** a. —**disdain'fully** adv.

disease' n. illness; disorder of health —**diseased'** a.

disembod'ied a. (of spirit) released from bodily form

disembow'el vt. take out entrails of

disenchant'ed [-ah-] a. disillusioned

disfig'ure vt. mar appearance of —**disfigura'tion** n. —**disfig'urement** n. blemish, defect

disgorge' vt. vomit; give up —**disgorge'ment** n.

disgrace' n. shame, loss of reputation, dishonour —vt. bring shame or discredit upon —**disgrace'ful** a. shameful —**disgrace'fully** adv.

disgrun'tled a. vexed; put out

disguise' [-gīz'] vt. change appearance of, make unrecognizable; conceal, cloak; misrepresent —n. false appearance; device to conceal identity

disgust' n. violent distaste, loathing, repugnance —vt. affect with loathing

dish n. shallow vessel for food; portion or variety of food; contents of dish; sl. attractive person —vt. put in dish; serve (up)

dishabille' [di-sa-bēl'] n. state of being partly or carelessly dressed

dishev'elled a. [-sh-] with disordered hair; ruffled, untidy, unkempt

disillu'sion [-lōō'-] vt. destroy ideals, illusions, or false ideas of —n.

disinfect'ant n. substance that prevents or removes infection —**disinfect'** vt.

disinforma'tion n. false information intended to deceive or mislead

disingen'uous a. not sincere or frank

disinher'it vt. to deprive of inheritance

disin'tegrate v. break up, fall to pieces —**disintegra'tion** n.

disin'terest n. freedom from bias or involvement —**disin'terested** a.

disjoint' vt. put out of joint; break the natural order or logical arrangement of —**disjoint'ed** a. (of discourse) incoherent, disconnected

disk see DISC

dis'locate vt. put out of joint; disrupt, displace —**disloca'tion** n.

dislodge' vt. drive out or remove from hiding place or previous position —**dislodge'ment** n.

dis'mal [-z-] a. depressing; depressed; cheerless, dreary, gloomy —**dis'mally** adv.

disman'tle vt. take apart —**disman'tlement** n.

dismay' vt. dishearten, daunt —n. consternation, horrified amazement; apprehension

dismem'ber vt. tear or cut limb from limb; divide, partition —**dismem'berment** n.

dismiss' vt. remove, discharge from employment; send away; reject —**dismiss'al** n.

disobey' [-bā'] v. refuse or fail to obey —**disobe'dience** n. —**disobe'dient** a.

disoblige' vt. disregard the wishes, preferences of

disor'der n. disarray, confusion, disturbance; upset of health, ailment —vt. upset order of; disturb health of —**disor'derly** a. untidy; unruly

disor'ientate vt. cause (someone) to lose his bearings, confuse

disown' vt. refuse to acknowledge

dispar'age [-pa'rij] vt. speak slightingly of; belittle —**dispar'agement** n.

dis'parate a. essentially different, unrelated —**dispar'ity** n. inequality; incongruity

dispass'ionate a. unswayed by passion; calm, impartial

dispatch', **despatch'** vt. send off to destination or on an errand; send off; finish off, get done with speed; inf. eat up; kill —n. sending off; efficient speed; official message, report

dispel' vt. clear, drive away, scatter (**-ll-**)

dispense' vt. deal out; make up (medicine); administer (justice); grant exemption from —**dispen'sable** a. —**dispen'sary** n. place where medicine is made up —**dispensa'tion** n. act of dispensing; licence or exemption; provision of nature or providence —**dispens'er** n. —**dispense with** do away with; manage without

disperse' vt. scatter —**dispersed'** a. scattered; placed here and there —**dispers'al**, **disper'sion** n.

dispir'ited a. dejected, disheartened —**dispir'itedly** adv. —**dispir'iting** a.

displace' vt. move from its place; remove from office; take place of —**displace'ment** n. displacing; weight of liquid displaced by a solid in it —**displaced person** person forced from his home country, esp. by war etc.

display' vt. spread out for show; show, expose to view —n. displaying; parade; show, exhibition; ostentation

displease' v. offend; annoy —**displeas'ure** n. anger, vexation

disport *v.refl.* gambol, amuse oneself, frolic

dispose' [-ōz'] *vt.* arrange; distribute; incline; adjust —*vi.* determine —**dispo'sable** *a.* designed to be thrown away after use —**dispo'sal** *n.* —**disposi'tion** *n.* inclination; temperament; arrangement; plan —**dispose of** sell, get rid of; have authority over, deal with

dispossess' *vt.* cause to give up possession (of)

dispute' *vi.* debate, discuss —*vt.* call in question; debate; argue; oppose, contest —**dispu'table** *a.* —**dispu'tant** *n.* —**disputa'tion** *n.* —**disputa'tious** *a.* argumentative; quarrelsome

disqual'ify *vt.* make ineligible, unfit for some special purpose

disqui'et *n.* anxiety, uneasiness —*vt.* cause (someone) to feel this

disquisi'tion [-zish'ən] *n.* learned or elaborate treatise, discourse or essay

disrepair' *n.* state of bad repair, neglect

disrobe' *v.* undress; divest of robes

disrupt' *vt.* interrupt; throw into turmoil or disorder —**disrup'tion** *n.* —**disrup'tive** *a.*

dissect' *vt.* cut up (body, organism) for detailed examination; examine or criticize in detail —**dissec'tion** *n.* —**dissect'or** *n.* anatomist

dissem'ble *v.* conceal, disguise (feelings *etc.*); act the hypocrite —**dissem'bler** *n.*

dissem'inate *vt.* spread abroad, scatter —**dissemina'tion** *n.* —**dissem'inator** *n.*

dissent' *vi.* differ in opinion; express such difference; disagree with doctrine *etc.* of established church —*n.* such disagreement —**dissen'sion** *n.* —**dissent'er** *n.* —**dissen'tient** *a./n.*

disserta'tion *n.* written thesis; formal discourse —**dis'sertate** *vi.* hold forth

disser'vice *n.* ill turn, wrong, injury

dis'sident *n./a.* (one) not in agreement, *esp.* with government —**dis'sidence** *n.* dissent; disagreement

dissim'ulate *v.* pretend not to have; practise deceit —**dissimula'tion** *n.* —**dissim'ulator** *n.*

dis'sipate *vt.* scatter; waste, squander —**dis'sipated** *a.* indulging in pleasure without restraint, dissolute; scattered, wasted —**dissipa'tion** *n.* scattering; frivolous, dissolute way of life

disso'ciate *v.* separate, sever; disconnect —**dissocia'tion** *n.*

diss'olute *a.* lax in morals

dissolu'tion [-lōō'-] *n.* break up; termination of parliament, meeting or legal relationship; destruction; death

dissolve' [-z-] *vt.* absorb or melt in fluid; break up, put an end to, annul —*vi.* melt in fluid; disappear, vanish; break up, scatter —**dissol'vable, dissol'uble** *a.* capable of being dissolved —**dissol'vent** *n.* thing with power to dissolve

diss'onant *a.* jarring, discordant —**diss'onance** *n.*

dissuade' [-sw-] *vt.* advise to refrain, persuade not to —**dissua'sion** *n.* —**dissua'sive** *a.*

dissyll'able, disyll'able [dī-] *n.* word or metrical foot having two syllables —**dis(s)yllab'ic** *a.*

dis'taff [-ahf] *n.* cleft stick to hold wool *etc.*, for spinning —**dis'taff side** maternal side; female line

dis'tance *n.* amount of space between two things; remoteness; aloofness, reserve —*vt.* hold or place at distance —**dis'tant** *a.* far off, remote; haughty, cold —**dis¹·tantly** adv.

distaste¹ n. dislike of food or drink; aversion, disgust —**distaste¹ful** a. unpleasant, displeasing to feelings —**distaste¹fully** adv. —**distaste¹fulness** n.

distem¹per n. disease of dogs; method of painting on plaster without oil; paint used for this —vt. paint with distemper

distend¹ v. swell out by pressure from within, inflate —**disten¹sible** a. —**disten¹sion** n.

dis¹tich [-ik] n. couplet

distil¹ vt. vaporize and recondense a liquid; purify, separate, concentrate liquids by this method; fig. extract quality of —vi. trickle down (-ll-) —**dis¹tillate** n. distilled liquid, esp. as fuel for some engines —**distill¹er** n. one who distils, esp. manufacturer of alcoholic spirits —**distill¹ery** n.

distinct¹ a. clear, easily seen; definite; separate, different —**distinc¹tion** n. point of difference; act of distinguishing; eminence, repute, high honour, high quality —**distinct¹ive** a. characteristic —**distinct¹ly** adv. —**distinct¹ness** n.

distin¹guish [-ng'gw-] vt. make difference in; recognize, make out; honour; make prominent or honoured (usu. refl.); class —vi. (usu. with between or among) draw distinction, grasp difference —**distin¹guishable** a. —**distin¹guished** a. noble, dignified; famous, eminent

distort¹ vt. put out of shape, deform; misrepresent; garble, falsify —**distor¹tion** n.

distract¹ vt. draw attention of (someone) away from work etc.; divert; perplex, bewilder, drive mad —**distrac¹tion** n.

distraint¹ n. legal seizure of goods to enforce payment —**dis-train¹** vt. —**distrain¹ment** n.

distrait¹ [-trā¹] a. absent-minded; abstracted

distraught¹ [-awt¹] a. bewildered, crazed with grief; frantic, distracted

distress¹ n. severe trouble, mental pain; severe pressure of hunger, fatigue or want; Law distraint —vt. afflict, give mental pain —**distress¹ful** a.

distrib¹ute vt. deal out, dispense; spread, dispose at intervals; classify —**distribu¹tion** n. —**distrib¹utive** a. —**distrib¹utor** n. rotary switch distributing electricity in car engine

dis¹trict n. region, locality; portion of territory

disturb¹ vt. trouble, agitate, unsettle, derange —**disturb¹ance** n. —**disturb¹er** n.

disuse¹ [-s¹] n. state of being no longer used —**disused¹** [-zd¹] a.

disyll¹able [dī-] n. see DISSYLLABLE

ditch n. long narrow hollow dug in ground for drainage etc. —v. make, repair ditches; run car etc. into ditch —vt. sl. abandon, discard

dith¹er vi. be uncertain or indecisive —n. this state

dith¹yramb [-i-ram] n. ancient Greek hymn sung in honour of Dionysus —**dithyram¹bic** a.

ditt¹any n. aromatic plant native to Greece

ditt¹o n. It. same, aforesaid (used to avoid repetition in lists etc.) —do. dittmarks.

ditt¹y n. simple song

diuret¹ic [dī-yoo-] a. increasing the discharge of urine —n. substance with this property

diur¹nal [dī-ur¹-] a. daily; in or of daytime; taking a day

diva¹lent [dī-] a. capable of combining with two atoms of hydrogen or their equivalent

divan' n. bed, couch without back or head; low cushioned seat by wall

dive vi. plunge under surface of water; descend suddenly; disappear; go deep down into; reach quickly —n. act of diving; sl. disreputable bar or club —**di'ver** n. one who descends into deep water; kinds of diving bird —**dive bomber** aircraft which attacks after diving steeply

diverge' [dī-] vi. get farther apart; separate —**diver'gence** n. —**diver'gent** a.

di'vers [-z] a. obs. some, various

diverse' [dī-] a. different, varied —**divers'ify** vt. make diverse or varied; give variety to (-ified, -ifying) —**diverse'ly** adv. —**diversifica'tion** n. —**divers'ity** n.

divert' [dī-] vt. turn aside, ward off; amuse, entertain —**diver'sion** n. a diverting; official detour for traffic when main route is closed; amusement —**divert'ing** a.

divest' [dī-] vt. unclothe, strip; dispossess, deprive

divide' vt. make into two or more parts, split up, separate; distribute, share; diverge in opinion; classify —vi. become separated, part into two groups for voting —n. watershed —**div'idend** n. share of profits, of money divided among creditors etc.; number to be divided by another —**divi'ders** pl.n. measuring compasses

divine' a. of, pert. to, proceeding from, God; sacred; heavenly —n. theologian; clergyman —v. guess; predict, foresee, tell by inspiration or magic —**divina'tion** n. divining —**divine'ly** adv. —**divi'ner** n. —**divin'ity** n. quality of being divine; god; theology —**divining rod** (forked) stick said to move when held over ground where water is present

divis'ion [-vizh'-] n. act of dividing; part of whole; barrier; section; political constituency; difference in opinion etc.; Math. method of finding how many times one number is contained in another; army unit; separation, disunion —**divis'ible** a. capable of division —**divis'ional** a. —**divi'sive** a. causing disagreement —**divi'sor** n. Math. number which divides dividend

divorce' n. legal dissolution of marriage; complete separation, disunion —vt. dissolve marriage; separate; sunder —**divorcee'** n.

div'ot n. piece of turf

divulge' [dī-] vt. reveal, let out (secret) —**divul'gence** n.

divv'y inf. vt. (esp. with up) divide and share —n. dividend

dix'ie n. inf. (military) cooking utensil or mess tin; (D-) southern states of USA

DIY do-it-yourself

dizz'y a. feeling dazed, unsteady, as if about to fall; causing or fit to cause dizziness, as speed etc.; inf. silly —vt. make dizzy (dizz'ied, dizz'ying) —**dizz'ily** adv. —**diz'ziness** n.

DJ dinner jacket; disc jockey

dl decilitre

dm decimetre

DNA n. abbrev. for **deoxyribonucleic acid**, main constituent of the chromosomes of all organisms

do¹ [dōō] vt. perform, effect, transact, bring about, finish; work at; work out, solve; suit; cover (distance); provide, prepare; sl. cheat, swindle; frustrate; look after —vi. act; manage; work; fare; serve, suffice; happen —v. aux. makes negative and interrogative sentences and expresses emphasis (**did, done, do'ing**) —n. inf. celebration, festivity —**do away with** destroy —**do up** fasten; renovate —**do with** need; make use of —**do without** deny oneself

do[2] *see* DOH

do. ditto

do'cile *a.* willing to obey, submissive —**docil'ity** *n.*

dock[1] *n.* artificial enclosure near harbour for loading or repairing ships —*v.* of vessel, put or go into dock; of spacecraft, link or be linked together in space —**dock'er** *n.* one who works at docks, *esp.* loading *etc.* cargoes —**dock'yard** *n.* enclosure with docks, for building or repairing ships

dock[2] *n.* solid part of tail; cut end, stump —*vt.* cut short, *esp.* tail; curtail, deduct (an amount) from

dock[3] *n.* enclosure in criminal court for prisoner

dock[4] *n.* coarse weed

dock'et *n.* piece of paper sent with package *etc.* with details of contents, delivery instructions *etc.* —*vt.* fix docket to

doc'tor *n.* medical practitioner; one holding university's highest degree in any faculty —*vt.* treat medically; repair, mend; falsify (accounts *etc.*); *inf.* castrate or spay —**doc'toral** *a.* —**doc'torate** *n.*

doc'trine [-in] *n.* what is taught; teaching of church, school, or person; belief, opinion, dogma —**doctrinaire'** *a.* stubbornly insistent on applying theory without regard for circumstances —*n.* —**doctri'nal** *a.*

doc'udrama *n.* TV dramatization of true events

doc'ument *n.* piece of paper *etc.* providing information or evidence —*vt.* furnish with proofs, illustrations, certificates —**documen'tary** *a./n. esp.* (of) type of film dealing with real life, not fiction —**documenta'tion** *n.*

dodd'er *vi.* totter or tremble, as with age —**dodd'erer** *n.* feeble or inefficient person

dodge [doj] *v.* avoid or attempt to avoid (blow, discovery *etc.*) as by moving quickly; evade questions by cleverness —*n.* trick, artifice; ingenious method; act of dodging —**dodg'er** *n.* shifty person —**dodg'y** *inf.* a. dangerous; unreliable; tricky

Dodg'em [doj'-] **R** car used for bumping other cars in rink at funfair

do'do *n.* large extinct bird (*pl.* **do'do(e)s**)

doe [dō] *n.* female of deer, hare, rabbit

doek [dook] *n.* **SA** *inf.* head cloth worn *esp.* by Afr. women

does [duz] *third pers. sing., pres. ind.* active of DO

doff *vt.* take off (hat, clothing); discard, lay aside

dog *n.* domesticated carnivorous four-legged mammal; male of wolf, fox and other animals; person (in contempt, abuse or playfully); name given to various mechanical contrivances acting as holdfasts; device with tooth which penetrates or grips object and detains it; andiron or firedog —*vt.* follow steadily or closely (**-gg-**) —**dogg'ed** *a.* persistent, resolute, tenacious —**dogg'ly** *a.* —**dog'like** *a.* —**dog'cart** *n.* open vehicle with crosswise back-to-back seats —**dog days** hot season of the rising of Dog Star; period of inactivity —**dog-ear** *n.* turneddown corner of page in book —*vt.* turn down corners of pages —**dog-end** *inf.* n. cigarette end; rejected piece of anything —**dog'fight** *n.* skirmish between fighter planes; savage contest characterized by disregard of rules —**dog'fish** n. very small species of shark —**doggy bag** bag in which diner may take leftovers for dog —**dog'house** n. US kennel; inf. disfavour, as **in the doghouse** —**dog'leg** n. sharp bend or angle —**dog rose** wild rose —**dogs'body** n. inf. drudge —**Dog Star** star Sirius —**dog'watch** n. in ships, short half-watch, 4–6, 6–8 p.m. —**dog'wood** n. any of various shrubs having red shoots in winter —**go to the dogs** degenerate —**the dogs** greyhound race meeting

doge [dōj] n. formerly, chief magistrate in Venice

dogg'erel n. slipshod, unpoetic or trivial verse

doggo adv. —**lie doggo** inf. keep quiet, still, hidden

do'gie, do'g(e)y [-gi] n. US, C motherless calf (pl. **-gies** or **-geys**)

dog'ma n. article of belief, esp. one laid down authoritatively by church; body of beliefs (pl. **-s**, **-ata**) —**dogmat'ic** a. asserting opinions with arrogance; relating to dogma —**dogmat'ically** adv. —**dog'matism** n. arrogant assertion of opinion —**dog'matist** n. —**dog'matize** vi.

doh, do n. first sol-fa note

doi'ly, doy'l(e)y n. small cloth, paper, piece of lace to place under cake, dish etc.

Dol'by R system used in tape recording to reduce unwanted noise

dol'ce [-chā] a. Mus. sweet

dol'drums pl.n. state of depression, dumps; region of light winds and calms near the equator

dole n. charitable gift; inf. payment under unemployment insurance —vt. (usu. with out) deal out sparingly

dole'ful a. dreary, mournful —**dole'fully** adv.

doll n. child's toy image of human being; sl. attractive girl or woman —v. dress (up) in latest fashion or smartly

doll'ar n. standard monetary unit of many countries, esp. USA and (since 1966) Aust.

doll'op n. inf. semisolid lump

doll'y n. doll; wheeled support for film, TV camera; various metal devices used as aids in hammering, riveting

dol'men n. kind of cromlech; stone table

dol'omite n. a type of limestone

dol'our n. grief, sadness, distress —**dol'orous** a. —**dol'orously** adv.

dol'phin n. sea mammal, smaller than whale, with beaklike snout —**dolphina'rium** n. pool for dolphins, esp. where they give public displays

dolt [-ō-] n. stupid fellow —**dolt'ish** a.

domain' n. lands held or ruled over; sphere, field of influence; province

dome n. a rounded vault forming a roof; something of this shape

Domes'day Book [dōōmz'-] record of survey of England in 1086

domes'tic a. of, in the home; homeloving; (of animals) tamed, kept by man; of, in one's own country, not foreign —n. house servant —**domes'ticate** vt. tame (animals); accustom to home life; adapt to an environment —**domestica'tion** n. —**domestic'ity** [-tis'-] n.

dom'icile n. person's regular place of abode —**dom'iciled** a. living —**domicil'iary** a. of a dwelling place

dom'inate vt. rule, control, sway; of heights, overlook —vi. control, be the most powerful or influential member or part of something —**dom'inant** a. —**domina'tion** n. —**domineer'** vi. act imperiously, tyrannize

dom'inee n. **SA** minister of Dutch Reformed Church

Domin'ican n. friar or nun of the order of St. Dominic —a. pert. to this order

domin'ion n. sovereignty; rule; territory of government

Dominion Day see CANADA DAY

dom'inoes pl.n. game played with 28 oblong flat pieces marked on one side with 0 to 6 spots on each half of the face —sing. one of these pieces; cloak with eye mask for masquerading

don[1] vt. put on (clothes) (**-nn-**)

don[2] n. fellow or tutor of college; Spanish title, Sir

donate' [dō-] vt. give —**dona'-tion** n. gift to fund —**do'nor** n. —**donor card** card specifying organs that may be used for transplant after card-holder's death

done pp. of DO

don'ga [-ŋgɔ] n. **SA** deep gully

don'jon see DUNGEON

donk'ey n. ass (pl. **-eys**) —**don-key engine** auxiliary engine —**donkey-work** n. drudgery

donned pt./pp. of DON

doo'dle vi. scribble absent-mindedly —n.

doom n. fate, destiny; ruin; judicial sentence, condemnation; the Last Judgment —vt. sentence, condemn; destine to destruction or suffering —**dooms'day** n. the day of the Last Judgment

door [dawr] n. hinged or sliding barrier to close any entrance —**door'way** n. entrance with or without door

dope n. kind of varnish; drug, esp. illegal, narcotic drug; inf. information; inf. stupid person

—vt. drug (esp. of racehorses) —**do'p(e)y** a. inf. foolish; drugged; half-asleep

Dor'ic [do'rik] n. dialect of Dorians; style of Greek architecture; rustic dialect —a. —**Dor'ian** [dawr-] a./n. (member) of early Greek race

dorm'ant a. not active, in state of suspension; sleeping —**dor'mancy** n.

dorm'er n. upright window set in sloping roof

dorm'itory n. sleeping room with many beds —**dormitory town** town whose inhabitants travel elsewhere to work

dor'mouse n. small hibernating mouselike rodent

dorp n. **SA** small town

dor'sal a. of, on back

dor'y n. deep-bodied type of fish, esp. John Dory

dose n. amount (of drug etc.) administered at one time; inf. instance or period of something unpleasant, esp. disease —vt. give doses to —**do'sage** n.

doss inf. n. temporary bed —vi. sleep in dosshouse; sleep —**doss'-house** n. cheap lodging house

doss'ier [-i-ā, -yɔ] n. set of papers on some particular subject or event

dot[1] n. small spot, mark —vt. mark with dots; sprinkle; sl. hit —**dott'y** a. sl. crazy; sl. extremely fond of; marked with dots

dot[2] n. dowry

dote vi. (with on or upon) be passionately fond of; be silly or weak-minded —**do'tage** n. senility —**do'tard** n. —**do'ting** a. blindly affectionate

dott'erel n. kind of plover

doub'le [dub'l] a. of two parts, layers etc., folded; twice as much or many; of two kinds; designed for two users; ambiguous; deceitful —adv. twice; to twice the amount or extent; in a pair —*n*. person or thing exactly like, or mistakable for, another; quantity twice as much as another; sharp turn; running pace —*v*. make, become double; increase twofold; fold in two; turn sharply; get round, sail round —**doub'ly** *adv*. —**double agent** spy employed simultaneously by two opposing sides —**double bass** largest and lowest-toned instrument in violin form —**double-cross** *v*. work for two sides at once, cheating each to betray another's trust —**double-crosser** *n*. —**double-dealing** *n*. artifice, duplicity —**double Dutch** *inf*. incomprehensible talk, gibberish —**double glazing** two panes of glass in a window to insulate against cold, sound *etc*. —**double knitting** medium thickness of knitting wool —**double-knitting** *a*. —**double-quick** *a./adv*. very fast —**double take** delayed reaction to a remark, situation *etc*.

double enten'dre [dub-ɔl-ahn-tahn'-drɔ] *n*. word or phrase with two meanings, one usu. indelicate

doub'let [dub'-] *n*. close-fitting body garment formerly worn by men; one of two words from same root but differing in form and usu. in meaning, as *warden* and *guardian*; false gem of thin layer of gemstone fused onto base of glass *etc*.

doubloon' [dub-] *n*. ancient Spanish gold coin

doubt [dowt] *vt*. hesitate to believe; call in question; suspect —*vi*. be wavering or uncertain in belief or opinion —*n*. uncertainty, wavering in belief; state of affairs giving cause for uncertainty —**doubt'er** *n*. —**doubt'ful** *a*. —**doubt'fully** *adv*. —**doubt'less** *adv*.

douche [doosh] *n*. jet or spray of water applied to (part of) body —*vt*. give douche to

dough [dō] *n*. flour or meal kneaded with water; *sl*. money —**dough'y** *a*. —**dough'nut** *n*. sweetened and fried ball or ring-shaped piece of dough

dough'ty [dowt'-] *a*. valiant —**dough'tily** *adv*. —**dough'tiness** *n*. boldness

dour [door] *a*. grim, stubborn, severe

douse [dows] *vt*. thrust into water; extinguish (light)

dove [duv] *n*. bird of pigeon family; person opposed to war —**dove'cot(e)** *n*. house for doves —**dove'tail** *n*. joint made with fan-shaped tenon —*v*. fit closely, neatly, firmly together

dow'ager [-j-] *n*. widow with title or property derived from deceased husband

dow'dy *a*. unattractively or shabbily dressed —*n*. woman so dressed

dow'el *n*. wooden, metal peg, *esp*. joining two adjacent parts

dow'er *n*. widow's share for life of husband's estate —*vt*. endow —**dow'ry** property wife brings to husband at marriage; any endowment

down' *adv*. to, in, or towards, lower position; below the horizon; (of payment) on the spot, immediate —*prep*. from higher to lower part of; at lower part of; along —*a*. depressed, miserable —*vt*. knock, pull, push down; *inf*. drink, *esp*. quickly —**down'ward** *a./adv*. —**down'wards** *adv*. —**down'cast** *a*. dejected; looking down —**down'pour** *n*. heavy fall of rain —**down'right** *a*. plain, straightforward —*adv*. quite, thoroughly —**down'stage** *a./adv*. at, to front of stage —**down-and-out** finished, defeated —**down**

under *inf.* Australia and New Zealand —**have a down on** *inf.* have grudge against

down² *n.* soft underfeathers, hair or fibre; fluff —**down'y** *a.*

down'land *n.* open high land: also **downs** *pl.n.*

dow'ry see DOWER

dowse *vi.* use divining rod —**dow'ser** *n.* water diviner

doxol'ogy *n.* short hymn of praise to God

doy'en *n.* senior member of a body or profession (-**enne'** *fem.*)

doy'ley see DOILY

doz. dozen

doze *vi.* sleep drowsily, be half-asleep —*n.* nap —**do'zy** *a.* drowsy; *inf.* stupid

doz'en [duz'-] *n.* (set of) twelve

DPP Director of Public Prosecutions

Dr. Doctor; Drive

drab *a.* dull, monotonous; of a dingy brown colour —*n.* mud colour

drachm [dram] *n.* unit of weight, 1/8 of fluid ounce, 1/16 of avoirdupois ounce

drach'ma [-k-] *n.* monetary unit of Greece (*pl.* -**mas** *or* -**mae** [-mē])

Draco'nian *a.* (*also* d-) like the laws of Draco; very harsh, cruel

draft¹ [-ah-] *n.* design, sketch; rough copy of document; order for money; detachment of men, *esp.* troops, reinforcements —*vt.* make sketch, plan, or rough design of; make rough copy (of writing *etc.*); send detached party

draft² US *vt.* select for compulsory military service; *see* DRAUGHT —*n.*

drag *vt.* pull along with difficulty or friction; trail, go heavily; sweep with net or grapnels; protract —*vi.* lag, trail; be tediously protracted (**-gg-**) —*n.* check on

progress; checked motion; iron shoe to check wheel; type of carriage; lure for hounds to hunt; kind of harrow; sledge, net, grapnel, rake; *inf.* tedious person or thing; *sl.* women's clothes worn by (transvestite) man —**drag'ster** *n.* car designed, modified for drag racing —**drag'net** *n.* fishing net to be dragged along sea floor; comprehensive search, *esp.* by police for criminal *etc.* —**drag race** motor car race where cars are timed over measured distance

dragée¹ [-zhā'] *n.* sugar-coated sweet, nut or pill

drag'on *n.* mythical fire-breathing monster, like winged crocodile; type of large lizard —**drag'onfly** *n.* long-bodied insect with gauzy wings

dragoon' *n.* cavalryman of certain regiments —*vt.* oppress; coerce

drain *vt.* draw off (liquid) by pipes, ditches *etc.*; dry; drink to dregs; empty, exhaust —*vi.* flow off or away; become void of liquid —*n.* channel for removing liquid; sewer; depletion, strain —**drain'age** *n.*

drake *n.* male duck

Dra'lon [-ā-] R acrylic fibre fabric, used *esp.* for upholstery

dram *n.* small draught of strong drink; drachm

dram'a [-ahm'-] *n.* stage play; art or literature of plays; playlike series of events —**dramat'ic** *a.* pert. to drama; suitable for stage representation; with force and vividness of drama; striking; tense; exciting —**dram'atist** *n.* writer of plays —**dramatiza'tion** *n.* —**dram'atize** *vt.* adapt novel for acting

dram'aturgy *n.* the technique of writing and producing plays

—**dram'aturgist** n. a playwright
—**dramatur'gic** a.

drape vt. cover, adorn with
cloth; arrange in graceful folds
—**dra'per** n. dealer in cloth, linen
etc. —**dra'pery** n.

dras'tic a. extreme, forceful;
severe

draught, US draft [drahft] n.
current of air between apertures
in room etc.; act or action of
drawing; dose of medicine; act of
drinking; quantity drunk at once;
inhaling; depth of ship in water;
the drawing in of, or fish taken
in, net; (now usu. **draft**) preliminary plan or layout for work to
be executed —pl. game played
on chessboard with flat round
"men" —a. for drawing; drawn
—vt. see DRAFT —**draught'y** a.
full of air currents —**draught
horse** horse for vehicles carrying
heavy loads —**draughts'man** n.
one who makes drawings, plans
etc. —**draughts'manship** n.

draw vt. pull, pull along, haul;
inhale; entice; delineate, portray
with pencil etc.; frame, compose,
draft, write; attract; bring (upon,
out etc.); get by lot; of ship,
require (depth of water); take
from (well, barrel etc.); receive
(money); bend (bow) —vi. pull,
shrink; attract; make, admit current of air; make pictures with
pencil etc.; finish game with
equal points, goals etc., tie; write
orders for money; come, approach (near) (**drew** pt., **drawn**
pp.) —n. act of drawing; casting
of lots; unfinished game, tie
—**draw'able** a. —**draw'er** n. one
who or that which draws; sliding
box in table or chest —pl. two-legged undergarment —**draw'ing** n. art of depicting in line;
sketch so done; action of verb
—**draw'back** n. anything that
takes away from satisfaction;

snag —**draw'bridge** n. hinged
bridge to pull up —**drawing
room** living room, sitting room
—**draw near** approach —**draw
out** lengthen —**draw up** arrange;
stop

drawl v. speak slowly —n. such
speech —**drawl'ingly** adv.

drawn pp. of DRAW

dray n. low cart without sides for
heavy loads

dread [dred] vt. fear greatly —n.
awe, terror —a. feared, awful
—**dread'ful** a. disagreeable,
shocking or bad —**dread'locks**
pl.n. Rastafarian hairstyle of long
matted or tightly curled strands
—**dread'nought** n. large battle-ship mounting heavy guns

dream [drēm] n. vision during
sleep; fancy, reverie, aspiration;
very pleasant idea, person, thing
—vi. have dreams —vt. see, imagine in dreams; think of as
possible (**dreamt** [dremt] or
dreamed [drēmd] pt./pp.)
—**dream'er** n. —**dream'less** a.
—**dream'y** a. given to daydreams, unpractical, vague; inf.
wonderful —**dream'time** n. Golden Age of long ago, in mythology
of some Aust. Aboriginal tribes

drear'y a. dismal, dull —**drear**
a. —**drear'ily** adv. —**drear'iness**
n. gloom

dredge[1] v. bring up mud etc.,
from sea bottom; deepen channel
by dredge; search for, produce
obscure, remote, unlikely material —n. form of scoop or grab
—**dredg'er** n. ship for dredging

dredge[2] vt. sprinkle with flour
etc. —**dredg'er** n.

dregs pl.n. sediment, grounds;
worthless part

drench vt. wet thoroughly, soak;
make (an animal) take dose of
medicine —n. soaking; dose for
animal

dress vt. clothe; array for show;

trim, smooth, surface of; prepare (food) for table; put dressing on (wound); align (troops) —vi. put on one's clothes; form in proper line —n. one-piece garment for woman; clothing; clothing for ceremonial evening wear —**dress'er** n. one who dresses, esp. actors or actresses; surgeon's assistant; kitchen sideboard —**dress'ing** n. something applied to something else, as sauce to food, ointment to wound, manure to land, stiffening to linen etc.; inf. scolding, as in **dressing down** —**dress'y** a. stylish; fond of dress —**dress circle** first gallery in theatre —**dress coat** cutaway coat worn by men as evening dress —**dressing gown** —**dressing room** —**dressing table** —**dress'maker** n.

dress'age [-ahzh] n. method of training horse in special manoeuvres to show obedience

drew pt. of DRAW

drey n. squirrel's nest

drib'ble v. flow in drops, trickle; run at the mouth; Football work ball forward with short kicks —n. trickle, drop —**drib'let** n. small portion or instalment

drift vi. be carried as by current of air, water; move aimlessly or passively —n. process of being driven by current; slow current or course; deviation from course; tendency; speaker's meaning; wind-heaped mass of snow, sand etc.; material driven or carried by water —**drift'er** n. one who, that which drifts; inf. aimless person with no fixed job etc. —**drift'wood** n. wood washed ashore by sea

drill[1] n. boring tool or machine; exercise of soldiers or others in handling of arms and manoeuvres; routine teaching —vt. bore,

pierce hole; exercise in military and other routine —vi. practise routine

drill[2] n. machine for sowing seed; small furrow for seed; row of plants —vt. sow seed in drills or furrows

drill[3] n. coarsely woven twilled fabric

drill[4] n. W Afr. monkey

drink v. swallow liquid; absorb; take intoxicating liquor, esp. to excess (**drank** pt., **drunk** pp.) —n. liquid for drinking; portion of this; act of drinking; intoxicating liquor; excessive use of it —**drink'able** a. —**drink'er** n. —**drink to, drink the health of** express good wishes etc. by drinking a toast to

drip v. fall or let fall in drops (-**pp**-) —n. act of dripping; drop; Med. intravenous administration of solution; inf. dull, insipid person —**drip'ping** n. melted fat that drips from roasting meat —a. very wet —**drip-dry** a. (of fabric) drying free of creases if hung up while wet —**drip'stone** n. projection over window or door to stop dripping of water

drive v. urge in some direction; make move and steer (vehicle, animal etc.); urge, impel; fix by blows, as nail; chase; convey in vehicle; hit a ball with force as in golf, tennis —vi. keep machine, animal, going, steer it; be conveyed in vehicle; rush, dash, drift fast (**drove, driv'en, driv'ing**) —n. act, action of driving; journey in vehicle; private road leading to house; capacity for getting things done; united effort, campaign; energy; forceful stroke in cricket, golf, tennis —**driv'er** n. one that drives; golf club —**driving belt** belt that communicates motion to machinery

driv'el vi. run at the mouth or

nose; talk nonsense —n. silly nonsense —**driv'eller** n.

driz'zle vi. rain in fine drops —n. fine, light rain

drogue [drōg] n. any funnel-like device, esp. of canvas, used as sea anchor; small parachute; wind indicator; windsock towed behind target aircraft; funnel-shaped device on end of refuelling hose of tanker aircraft to receive probe of aircraft being refuelled

droll [-ō-] a. funny, odd, comical —**droll'ery** n. —**droll'y** adv.

drom'edary n. one-humped camel bred esp. for racing

drone n. male of honey bee; lazy idler; deep humming; bass pipe of bagpipe; its note —v. hum; talk in monotonous tone

dron'go [-ng-g-] n. black, tropical bird

drool vi. to slaver, drivel

droop vi. hang down; wilt, flag —vt. let hang down —n. drooping condition —**droop'y** a.

drop n. globule of liquid; very small quantity; fall, descent; distance through which thing falls; thing that falls, as gallows platform —vt. let fall; let fall in drops; utter casually; set down, unload; discontinue —vi. fall; fall in drops; lapse; come or go casually (-**pp-**) —**drop'let** n. —**drop'pings** pl.n. dung of rabbits, sheep, birds etc. —**drop'out** n. person who fails to complete course of study or one who rejects conventional society

drop'sy n. disease causing watery fluid to collect in the body —**drop'sical** a.

dross n. scum of molten metal; impurity, refuse; anything of little or no value

drought [-owt] n. long spell of dry weather

drove[1] pt. of DRIVE

drove[2] n. herd, flock, crowd, esp. in motion —v. drive cattle etc., esp. a long distance —**drov'er** n. driver of cattle

drown v. die or be killed by immersion in liquid; get rid of as by submerging in liquid; make sound inaudible by louder sound

drow'sy [-z-] a. half-asleep; lulling; dull —**drowse** vi. —**drow'sily** adv. —**drow'siness** n.

drub vt. thrash, beat (-**bb-**) —**drub'bing** n. beating

drudge vi. work at menial or distasteful tasks, slave —n. one who drudges, hack —**drudg'ery** n.

drug n. medical substance; narcotic; commodity which is unsaleable because of overproduction —vt. mix drugs with; administer drug to, esp. one inducing unconsciousness (-**gg-**) —**drug'store** n. US, C pharmacy where wide variety of goods is available

drugg'et n. coarse woollen fabric, esp. for carpeting

dru'id [-ōō-] n. (also D-) member of ancient order of Celtic priests; Eisteddfod official —**dru'id'ic(al)** a. —**dru'idism** n.

drum n. percussion instrument of skin stretched over round hollow frame, played by beating with sticks; various things shaped like drum; part of ear —v. play drum; tap, thump continuously (-**mm-**) —**drumm'er** n. one who plays drum —**drum'fire** n. heavy continuous rapid artillery fire —**drum'head** n. part of drum that is struck —**drumhead court-martial** summary one held at war front —**drum major** leader of military band —**drum'stick** n. stick for beating drum; lower joint of cooked fowl's leg —**drum out** expel from club etc.

drunk a. overcome by strong drink; fig. under influence of strong emotion —*pp. of* DRINK —**drunk'ard** *n.* one given to excessive drinking —**drunk'en** *a.* drunk; caused by, showing intoxication —*archaic pp. of* DRINK —**drunk'enness** *n.*

dry *a.* without moisture; rainless; not yielding milk, or other liquid; cold, unfriendly; caustically witty; having prohibition of alcoholic drink; uninteresting; needing effort to study; lacking sweetness (as wines) —*vt.* remove water, moisture —*vi.* become dry; evaporate (**dried, dry'ing**) —**dri'ly** *adv.* —**dry'ness** *n.* —**dry'er, dri'er** *n.* person or thing that dries; apparatus for removing moisture —**dry bat'tery** electric battery without liquid —**dry-clean** *v.* clean clothes with solvent other than water —**dry-cleaner** *n.* —**dry farming** methods of producing crops in areas of low rainfall —**dry ice** solid carbon dioxide —**dry point** needle for engraving without acid; engraving so made —**dry rot** fungoid decay in wood —**dry run** practice, rehearsal in simulated conditions

dry'ad *n.* wood nymph

DSC Distinguished Service Cross

DSc Doctor of Science

DSO Distinguished Service Order

D.T.'s *inf. short for* **delir'ium tre'mens**, disordered mental state produced by advanced alcoholism

du'al *a.* twofold; of two, double, forming pair —**du'alism** *n.* recognition of two independent powers or principles, *eg* good and evil, mind and matter —**dual'ity** *n.*

dub *vt.* confer knighthood on; give title to; provide film with soundtrack not in original language; smear with grease, dubbin (**-bb-**) —**dubb'in, dubb'ing** *n.*

grease for making leather supple

du'bious *a.* causing doubt, not clear or decided; of suspect character —**dubi'ety** *n.* uncertainty, doubt

du'cal *a.* of, like a duke

duc'at [duk'-] *n.* former gold coin of Italy *etc.*

duch'ess *n.* duke's wife or widow

duch'y *n.* territory of duke, dukedom

duck[1] *n.* common swimming bird (**drake** *masc.*); *Cricket* batsman's score of nothing —*v.* plunge (someone) under water; bob down —**duck'ling** *n.* —duckbilled platypus *see* PLATYPUS —**duck'weed** *n.* plant that floats on ponds *etc.*

duck[2] *n.* strong linen or cotton fabric —*pl.* trousers of it

duck[3], **DUKW** *n.* amphibious vehicle used in World War II

duct *n.* channel, tube —**duct'ile** *a.* capable of being drawn into wire; flexible and tough; docile —**ductil'ity** *n.* —**duct'less** *a.* (of glands) secreting directly certain substances essential to health

dud *n.* futile, worthless person or thing; shell that fails to explode —*a.* worthless

dude US *n.* tourist, *esp.* in ranch district —**dude ranch** ranch serving as guesthouse and showplace

dudg'eon [-j'ən] *n.* anger, indignation, resentment

duds *pl.n. inf.* clothes

due *a.* owing; proper to be given, inflicted *etc.*; adequate, fitting; under engagement to arrive; be present; timed for —*adv.* (with points of compass) exactly —*n.* person's right; (*usu. pl.*) charge, fee *etc.* —**du'ly** *adv.* properly; fitly; rightly; punctually —**due** to attributable to; caused by

du'el *n.* arranged fight with deadly weapons, between two persons; keen two-sided contest —vi. fight in duel (-ll-) —du'ellist n.

duenn'a [dyōō-] n. Spanish lady-in-waiting; elderly governess, guardian, chaperon

duet' [dyōō] n. piece of music for two performers —duett'ist n.

duff[1] n. kind of boiled pudding

duff[2] vt. manipulate, alter article so as to make it look like new; mishit, esp. at golf —a. sl. bad, useless

duff'el, duff'le n. coarse woollen cloth; coat of this

duff'er n. stupid inefficient person

dug[1] pt./pp. of DIG

dug[2] n. udder, teat of animal

du'gong n. whalelike mammal of tropical seas

dug'out n. covered excavation to provide shelter for troops etc.; canoe of hollowed-out tree; Sport covered bench for players when not on the field

dui'ker, duy'ker [dī'-] n. small Afr. antelope

duke n. peer of rank next below prince; sovereign of small state called duchy (duch'ess fem.) —duke'dom n.

dukes pl.n. sl. fists

dul'cet [-sit] a. (of sounds) sweet, melodious

dul'cimer [-sim-] n. stringed instrument played with hammers, ancestor of piano

dull a. stupid; insensible; sluggish; tedious; lacking liveliness or variety; gloomy, overcast —v. make or become dull —dull'ard n. —dull'y adv.

du'ly see DUE

dumb [dum] a. incapable of speech; silent; inf. stupid —dumb'ly adv. —dumb'ness n. —dumb'bell n. weight for exercises —dumbfound' vt. confound

into silence —dumb show acting without words

dum'dum n. soft-nosed expanding bullet

dumm'y n. tailor's or dressmaker's model; imitation object; Cards hand exposed on table and played by partner; Sports feigned move or pass; baby's dummy teat —a. sham, bogus —dummy run practice or rehearsal

dump vt. throw down in mass; deposit; unload; send (low-priced goods) for sale abroad —n. rubbish heap; inf. dirty, unpleasant place; temporary depot of stores or munitions —pl. low spirits, dejection —dump'ling n. small round pudding of dough, often fruity —dump'y a. short, stout —dumpy level surveyor's levelling instrument

dun[1] vt. persistently demand payment of debts (-nn-) —n. one who duns

dun[2] n. dull greyish brown —n. this colour; dun horse

dunce n. slow learner, stupid pupil

dun'derhead n. blockhead —dun'derheaded a.

dune n. sandhill on coast or desert

dung n. excrement of animals; manure —vt. manure (ground)

dungaree' n. coarse cotton fabric —pl. overalls of this material

dun'geon [-jon] n. underground cell or vault for prisoners, donjon; formerly, tower or keep of castle

dunk vt. dip bread etc. in liquid before eating it; submerge

dun'lin n. small sandpiper

dunn'age n. material for packing cargo

dunn'ock n. hedge sparrow

du'o n. pair of performers

duodec'imal [-des'-] a. computed by twelves; twelfth —**duo-de'nary** a. twelvefold

duodec'imo [-des'-] n. size of book in which each sheet is folded into 12 leaves; book of this size (pl. **-mos** [-mōz]) —a. of this size

duode'num n. upper part of small intestine —**duode'nal** a.

dupe n. victim of delusion or sharp practice —vt. deceive for advantage, impose upon

du'plex a. twofold

du'plicate vt. make exact copy of; double —a. double; exactly the same as something else —n. exact copy —**duplica'tion** n. —**du'plicator** n. machine for making copies —**duplic'ity** [-plis'-] n. deceitfulness, double-dealing, bad faith

du'rable a. lasting, resisting wear —**durabil'ity** n. —**du'rably** adv.

du'rance n. obs. imprisonment

dura'tion n. time thing lasts

duress' [dyoo-] n. compulsion by use of force or threats

du'ring prep. throughout, in the time of, in the course of

durst obs. pt. of DARE

dusk n. darker stage of twilight; partial darkness —**dusk'ily** adv. —**dusk'y** a. dark; dark-coloured

dust n. fine particles, powder of earth or other matter, lying on surface or blown along by wind; ashes of the dead —vt. sprinkle with powder; rid of dust —**dust'-er** n. cloth for removing dust —**dust'y** a. covered with dust —**dust'bin** n. large, usu. cylindrical container for household rubbish —**dust'bowl** n. area in which dust storms have carried away the top soil

Dutch a. pert. to the Netherlands, its inhabitants, its language —**Dutch courage** drunken bravado —**Dutch treat** one where each person pays his own share

du'ty n. moral or legal obligation; that which is due; tax on goods; military service; one's proper employment —**du'teous** a. —**du'tiable** a. liable to customs duty —**du'tiful** a.

du'vet [dōō'vā] n. quilt filled with down or artificial fibre

dux [duks] n. head pupil of school or class, leader

DV Deo volente

dwarf n. very undersized person; mythological, small, manlike creature (pl. **dwarfs**, **dwarves**) —a. unusually small, stunted —vt. make seem small by contrast; make stunted —**dwarf'ish** a.

dwell vi. live, make one's abode (in); fix one's attention, write or speak at length (on) (**dwelt** pt./pp.) —**dwell'er** n. —**dwell'ing** n. house

dwin'dle vi. grow less, waste away, decline

dye [dī] vt. impregnate (cloth etc.) with colouring matter; colour thus (**dyed**, **dye'ing** [dī'ing]) —n. colouring matter in solution or which may be dissolved for dyeing; tinge, colour —**dy'er** n.

dyke n. embankment to prevent flooding; ditch

dynam'ics [dī-] pl.n. (with sing. v.) branch of physics dealing with force as producing or affecting motion; physical forces —**dynam'ic** a. of, relating to motive force, force in operation; energetic and forceful —**dynam'ical** a. —**dynam'ically** adv.

dy'namite n. high explosive mixture —vt. blow up with this —**dy'namiter** n.

dy'namo n. machine to convert mechanical into electrical energy, generator of electricity (pl.

-mos) —**dynamom'eter** n. instrument to measure energy expended

dyn'asty [din'-] n. line, family, succession of hereditary rulers —**dyn'ast** n. —**dynast'ic** a. of dynasty

dyne n. cgs unit of force

dys'entery [dis-] n. infection of intestine causing severe diarrhoea

dysfunc'tion [dis-] n. abnormal, impaired functioning, esp. of bodily organ

dyslex'ia [dis-] n. impaired ability to read, caused by brain disorder —**dyslex'ic** a.

dyspep'sia [dis-] n. indigestion —**dyspep'tic** a./n.

dys'trophy n. wasting of body tissues, esp. muscles

E

E Earl; East; Eastern; English

each a./pron. every one taken separately

ea'ger [ē'-] a. having a strong wish (for something); keen, impatient —**ea'gerly** adv. —**ea'gerness** n.

ea'gle [ē'-] n. large bird with keen sight which preys on small birds and animals; Golf score of two strokes under par for a hole —**ea'glet** n. young eagle

ear [1] n. organ of hearing, esp. external part of it; sense of hearing; sensitiveness to sounds; attention —**ear'ache** n. acute pain in ear —**ear'mark** vt. assign, reserve for definite purpose; make identification mark on ear of sheep etc. —n. this mark —**ear'phone** n. receiver for radio etc. held to or put in ear —**ear'ring** n. ornament for lobe of the ear —**ear'shot** n. hearing

distance —**ear'wig** n. small insect with pincer-like tail

ear [2] n. spike, head of corn

earl [erl] n. British nobleman ranking next below marquis —**earl'dom** n. his domain, title

ear'ly [erl'-] a./adv. before expected or usual time; in first part, near or nearer beginning of some portion of time

earn [ern] vt. obtain by work or merit; gain —**earn'ings** pl.n.

earn'est [1] [ern'-] a. serious, ardent, sincere —**earn'estly** adv. —**in earnest** serious, determined

earn'est [2] [ern'-] n. money paid over in token to bind bargain, pledge; foretaste

earth [er-] n. planet or world we live on; ground, dry land; mould, soil, mineral; fox's hole; wire connecting electrical apparatus to earth —vt. cover with earth; connect electrically with earth —**earth'en** a. made of clay or earth —**earth'ly** a. possible, feasible —**earth'ly** a. of earth; uninhibited; vulgar —**earth'enware** n. (vessels of) baked clay —**earth'quake** n. convulsion of earth's surface —**earth'work** n. bank of earth in fortification —**earth'worm** n.

ease [ēz] n. comfort; freedom from constraint, annoyance, awkwardness, pain or trouble; idleness —v. reduce burden; give bodily or mental ease to; slacken; (cause to) move carefully or gradually; relieve of pain —**ease'ment** n. Law right of way etc., over another's land —**eas'ily** adv. —**eas'y** a. not difficult; free from pain, care, constraint or anxiety; compliant; characterized by low demand; fitting loosely; inf. having no preference for any particular course of action —**easy-going** a. not fussy; indolent

eas'el [ēz'l] *n.* frame to support picture *etc.*

east *n.* part of horizon where sun rises; eastern lands, orient —*a.* on, in, or near, east; coming from east —*adv.* from, or to, east —**east'erly** *a./adv.* from, or to, east —**east'ern** *a.* of, dwelling in, east —**east'erner** *n.* —**east'ing** *n.* distance eastwards of a point from a given meridian —**east'ward** *a./n.* —**east'ward(s)** *adv.*

East'er *n.* movable festival of the Resurrection of Christ

eas'y *see* EASE

eat *v.* chew and swallow; consume, destroy; gnaw; wear away (ate *pt.*, eat'en *pp.*) —**eat'able** *a.*

eau de Cologne [ō-də-kə-lōn'] *Fr.* a light perfume

eaves [ēvz] *pl.n.* overhanging edges of roof —**eaves'drop** *v.* listen secretly —**eaves'dropper** *n.* —**eaves'dropping** *n.*

ebb *vi.* flow back; decay —*n.* flowing back of tide; decline, decay —**ebb tide**

eb'ony *n.* hard black wood —*a.* made of, black as ebony —**eb'onite** *n.* vulcanite —**eb'onize** *vt.* make colour of ebony

ebull'ient *a.* exuberant; boiling —**ebull'ience** *n.* —**ebull'ition** *n.* boiling; effervescence; outburst

eccen'tric [eks-] *a.* odd, unconventional; irregular; not placed, or not having axis placed, centrally; not circular (in orbit) —*n.* odd, unconventional person; mechanical contrivance to change circular into to-and-fro movement —**eccen'trically** *adv.* —**eccentri'city** [-is'-] *n.*

Eccles. Ecclesiastes

ecclesias'tic [-klēz-] *n.* clergyman —*a.* of, relating to the Christian Church —**ecclesias'tical** *a.* —**ecclesiol'ogy** *n.* science of church building and decoration

eccrinol'ogy *n.* branch of physiology that relates to bodily secretions

ECG electrocardiogram; electrocardiograph

ech'elon [esh'-] *n.* level, grade, of responsibility or command; formation of troops, planes *etc.* in parallel divisions each slightly to left or right of the one in front

ech'o [ek'ō] *n.* repetition of sounds by reflection; close imitation (*pl.* ech'oes) —*vt.* repeat as echo, send back the sound of; imitate closely —*vi.* resound; be repeated (**ech'oed, ech'oing**) —**echo sounder** —**echo sounding** system of ascertaining depth of water by measuring time required to receive an echo from sea bottom or submerged object

éclair' [ā-klār'] *n.* finger-shaped, iced cake filled with cream

éclat' [ā-klah'] *n.* splendour, renown, acclamation

eclec'tic *a.* selecting; borrowing one's philosophy from various sources; catholic in views or taste —*n.* —**eclec'ticism** *n.*

eclipse' *n.* blotting out of sun, moon *etc.* by another heavenly body; obscurity —*vt.* obscure, hide; surpass —**eclip'tic** *a.* of eclipse —*n.* apparent path of sun

ec'logue [-og] *n.* short poem, *esp.* pastoral dialogue

ecol'ogy *n.* science of plants and animals in relation to their environment —**ecolog'ical** *a.* —**ecol'ogist** *n.* specialist in or advocate of ecological studies

econ'omy *n.* careful management of resources to avoid unnecessary expenditure or waste; sparing, restrained or efficient use; system of interrelationship of money, industry and employment in a country —**econom'ic** *a.* of economics; profitable; economical —**econom'ical** *a.* not

wasteful of money, time, effort
etc.; frugal —**econom'ically** *adv.*
—**econom'ics** *pl.n.* (*with sing. v.*)
study of economies of nations;
(*used as pl.*) financial aspects
—**econ'omist** *n.* specialist in economics —**econ'omize** *v.* limit or
reduce expense, waste *etc.*

ec'ru [ek'rōō, ā'-] *n./a.* (of) colour of unbleached linen

ec'stasy *n.* exalted state of
feeling, mystic trance; frenzy
—**ecstat'ic** *a.* —**ecstat'ically**
adv.

ec'toplasm *n.* in spiritualism,
supposedly a semiluminous plastic substance which exudes from
medium's body

ecumen'ic(al) [ē-kyoo-] *a.* of
the Christian Church throughout
the world, *esp.* with regard to its
unity —**ecumen'icism** *n.*

ec'zema *n.* skin disease

E'dam *n.* round Dutch cheese
with red rind

Edd'a *n.* collection of old Ice-
landic myths

edd'y *n.* small whirl in water,
smoke *etc.* —*vi.* move in whirls
(**edd'ied, edd'ying**)

e'delweiss [ā'dl-vīs] *n.* white-
flowered alpine plant

E'den *n.* garden in which Adam
and Eve were placed at the
Creation; any delightful, happy
place or state

edge *n.* border, boundary; cutting side of blade; sharpness;
advantage; acrimony, bitterness
—*vt.* sharpen, give edge or border to; move gradually —*vi.* advance sideways or gradually
—**edge'ways,** US, C **edge'wise**
adv. —**edg'ing** *n.* —**edg'y** *a.* irritable, sharp or keen in temper
—**on edge** nervy, irritable; excited

ed'ible *a.* eatable, fit for eating
—**edibil'ity** *n.*

e'dict *n.* order proclaimed by
authority, decree

ed'ifice [-fis] *n.* building, *esp.* big
one

ed'ify *vt.* improve morally, instruct (**-fied, -fying**) —**edifica'-
tion** *n.* improvement of the mind
or morals

ed'it *vt.* prepare book, film, tape
etc. for publication or broadcast
—**edi'tion** *n.* form in which something is published; number of
copies of new publication printed
at one time —**ed'itor** *n.* —**edito'-
rial** *a.* of editor —*n.* article
stating opinion of newspaper *etc.*

ed'ucate *vt.* provide schooling
for; teach; train mentally and
morally; train; improve, develop
—**educa'tion** *n.* —**educa'tional** *a.*
—**educa'tionally** *adv.* —**educa'-
tion(al)ist** *n.* one versed in theory and practice of education
—**ed'ucative** *a.* —**ed'ucator** *n.*

educe' *vt.* bring out, elicit, develop; infer, deduce —**edu'cible**
a. —**educ'tion** *n.*

EEC European Economic Community

EEG electroencephalogram

eel *n.* snakelike fish

ee'rie, ee'ry *a.* weird, uncanny; causing superstitious fear

efface' *vt.* wipe or rub out
—**efface'able** *a.* —**efface'ment**
n.

effect' *n.* result, consequence;
efficacy; impression; condition of
being operative —*pl.* property;
lighting, sounds *etc.* to accompany film, broadcast *etc.* —*vt.* bring
about, accomplish —**effect'ive** *a.*
having power to produce effects;
in effect, operative; serviceable;
powerful; striking —**effect'ively**
adv. —**effect'ual** *a.* successful in
producing desired effect; satisfactory; efficacious —**effect'ually** *adv.* —**effect'uate** *vt.*

effem'inate *a.* womanish, unmanly —**effem'inacy** n.

eff'erent a. conveying outward or away

effervesce' [-es'] vi. give off bubbles; be in high spirits —**efferves'cence** n. —**efferves'cent** a.

effete' a. worn-out, feeble

effica'cious a. producing or sure to produce desired effect; effective; powerful; adequate —**eff'icacy** n. potency; force; efficiency

effi'cient [-fish'ont] a. capable, competent, producing effect —**effi'ciency** n. —**effi'ciently** adv.

eff'igy n. image, likeness

effloresce' [-es'] vt. burst into flower —**efflores'cence** n. —**efflores'cent** a.

eff'luent n. liquid discharged as waste; stream flowing from larger stream, lake etc. —a. flowing out —**eff'luence** n. —**efflu'vium** n. something flowing out invisibly, esp. affecting lungs or sense of smell (pl. -**ia**) —**eff'lux** n.

eff'ort n. exertion, endeavour, attempt or something achieved —**eff'ortless** a.

effront'ery [-un-] n. brazen impudence

efful'gent a. radiant, shining brightly —**efful'gence** n.

effu'sion n. (unrestrained) outpouring —**effuse'** vt. pour out, shed —**effu'sive** a. gushing, demonstrative —**effu'sively** adv. —**effu'siveness** n.

EFTA European Free Trade Association

Eftpos, EFTPOS electronic funds transfer at point of sale

e.g. exempli gratia (Lat., for example)

egalita'rian a. believing that all people should be equal; promoting this ideal —n. —**egalita'rianism** n.

egg[1] n. oval or round object produced by female of bird etc., from which young emerge, esp. egg of domestic hen, used as food —**egg cup** —**egg'plant** n. see AUBERGINE

egg[2] vt. —**egg on** encourage, urge; incite

eg'lantine n. sweet brier

eg'o [or ē'-] n. the self; one's conscious thinking subject; one's image of oneself; morale —**e'goism** n. systematic selfishness; theory that bases morality on self-interest —**eg'oist** n. —**egoistic(al)** a. —**eg'otism** n. selfishness; self-conceit —**eg'otist** n. —**egotis'tic(al)** a. —**egocen'tric** a. self-centred; egoistic; centred in the ego

egre'gious [-jəs] a. outstandingly bad, blatant; absurdly obvious, esp. of mistake etc.

e'gress n. way out; departure

e'gret n. lesser white heron; down of dandelion

ei'der [ī'-] n. Arctic duck —**ei'derdown** n. its breast feathers; quilt (stuffed with feathers)

eight [āt] n. cardinal number one above seven; eight-oared boat; its crew —a. —**eight'een'** a./n. eight more than ten —**eight'eenth'** a./n. —**eight'eenth'ly** adv. —**eighth** [āt-th] a./n. ordinal number —**eighth'ly** adv. —**eight'ieth** a./n. —**eight'y** a./n. ten times eight —**figure of eight** a skating figure; any figure shaped as 8

Ei're [ā'rə] n. the Republic of Ireland

eistedd'fod [ī-stedh'fəd] n. annual congress of Welsh bards; local gathering for competition in music and other performing arts

ei'ther [ī'-, ē'-] a./pron. one or the other; one of two; each —adv./conj. bringing in first of alternatives or strengthening an added negation

ejac'ulate v. eject (semen); exclaim, utter suddenly —**ejacula'tion** n. —**ejac'ulatory** a.

eject' vt. throw out; expel, drive out —**ejec'tion** n. —**eject'ment** n. —**eject'or** n.

eke out make (supply) last, esp. by frugal use; supply deficiencies of; make with difficulty (a living etc.)

elab'orate [-it] a. carefully worked out, detailed; complicated —vi. [-at] expand (upon) —vt. work out in detail; take pains with —**elabora'tion** n. —**elab'orator** n.

élan' [ā-lahn'] n. dash; ardour; impetuosity

e'land n. largest S Afr. antelope, resembling elk

elapse' vi. of time, pass

elas'tic a. resuming normal shape after distortion, springy; flexible —n. tape, fabric, containing interwoven strands of flexible rubber —**elas'ticated** a. —**elastic'ity** [-is'-] n.

ela'tion n. high spirits; pride —**elate'** vt. (usu. passive be elated etc.) raise the spirits of; make happy; exhilarate

el'bow [-bō] n. joint between fore and upper parts of arm (esp. outer part of it); part of sleeve covering this —vt. shove, strike with elbow —**elbow grease** hard work —**elbow'room** n. sufficient room

el'der [1] a. older, senior —comp. of OLD —n. person of greater age; old person; official of certain churches —**el'derly** a. growing old —**el'dest** a. oldest —sup. of OLD

el'der [2] n. white-flowered tree

El Dorad'o [-ahd'-] n. fictitious country rich in gold

eld'ritch a. hideous; weird; uncanny; haggish

elect' vt. choose by vote; choose —a. appointed but not yet in office; chosen, select, choice —**elec'tion** n. choosing, esp. by voting —**electioneer'** vi. busy oneself in political elections —**elec'tive** a. appointed, filled, or chosen by election —**elec'tor** n. one who elects —**elec'toral** a. —**elec'torate** n. body of electors —**elec'torship** n.

electric'ity [-is'-] n. form of energy associated with stationary or moving electrons or other charged particles; electric current or charge; science dealing with electricity —**elec'tric** a. derived from, produced by, producing, transmitting or powered by electricity; excited, emotionally charged —**elec'trical** a. —**elec'trician** n. one trained in installation etc. of electrical devices —**electrifica'tion** n. —**elec'trify** vt. (-**fied, -fying**) —**electric chair** US chair in which criminals sentenced to death are electrocuted —**electric organ** Mus. organ in which sound is produced by electric devices instead of wind

electro- (comb. form) by, caused by electricity, as in **electrother'apy** n. Such words are not given here where the meaning may easily be inferred from the simple word

electrocar'diograph n. instrument for recording electrical activity of heart —**electrocar'diogram** n. tracing produced by this

elec'trocute vt. execute, kill by electricity —**electrocu'tion** n.

elec'trode n. conductor by which electric current enters or leaves electric battery, vacuum tube etc.

electrodynam'ics n. dynamics of electricity

electroenceph'alograph n. [-sef'-] instrument for recording electrical activity of brain —**electroenceph'alogram** n. tracing produced by this

elec'trolyse vt. decompose by electricity —**electrol'ysis** n.

elec'trolyte n. solution, molten substance that conducts electricity

electromag'net n. magnet containing coil of wire through which electric current is passed —**electromagnet'ic** a.

elec'tron n. one of fundamental particles of matter identified with unit of charge of negative electricity and essential component of the atom —**electron'ic** a. of electrons or electronics; using devices, such as semiconductors, transistors or valves, dependent on action of electrons —**electron'ics** pl.n. (with sing. v.) technology concerned with development of electronic devices and circuits; science of behaviour and control of electrons —**electron volt** unit of energy used in nuclear physics

elec'troplate vt. coat with silver etc. by electrolysis —n. articles electroplated

elec'troscope n. instrument to show presence or kind of electricity

elec'trotype n. art of producing copies of type etc., by electric deposition of copper upon mould; copy so produced

elec'trum n. alloy of gold and silver used in jewellery etc.

eleemos'ynary [el-é-mos'i-] a. charitable; dependent on charity

el'egant a. graceful, tasteful; refined —**el'egance** n.

el'egy [-ji] n. lament for the dead in poem or song —**elegi'ac** a.

suited to elegies; plaintive —**elegi'acs** pl.n. elegiac verses

el'ement n. substance which cannot be separated into other substances by ordinary chemical techniques; component part; small amount, trace; heating wire in electric kettle, stove etc.; proper abode or sphere —pl. powers of atmosphere; rudiments, first principles —**el'emental** a. fundamental; of powers of nature —**element'ary** a. rudimentary, simple

el'ephant n. huge four-footed, thick-skinned animal with ivory tusks and long trunk —**elephanti'asis** n. disease with hardening of skin and enlargement of legs etc. —**elephant'ine** a. unwieldy, clumsy, heavily big

el'evate vt. raise, lift up, exalt —**eleva'tion** n. raising; height, esp. above sea level; angle above horizon, as of gun; drawing of one side of building etc. —**el'evator** n. US lift

elev'en n. number next above 10; team of 11 persons —a. —**elev'enfold** a./adv. —**elev'enses** pl.n. inf. light mid-morning snack —**elev'enth** a. the ordinal number —**eleventh hour** latest possible time

elf n. fairy; woodland sprite (pl. elves) —**elf'in, elf'ish, elv'ish, elf'like** a. roguish, mischievous

elic'it [-is'-] vt. draw out, evoke; bring to light

elide' vt. omit in pronunciation a vowel or syllable —**eli'sion** [-izh'ən] n.

el'igible a. fit or qualified to be chosen; suitable, desirable —**eligibil'ity** n.

elim'inate vt. remove, get rid of, set aside —**elimina'tion** n. —**elim'inator** n. one who, that which, eliminates

eli'sion see ELIDE

elite' [i-lēt', ā-] n. choice or select body; the pick or best part of society; typewriter typesize (12 letters to inch) —a. —**elit'ism** n.

elix'ir [-ik'sə] n. preparation sought by alchemists to change base metals into gold, or to prolong life; sovereign remedy

elk n. large deer

ellipse' n. oval —**ellip'tic(al)** a. —**ellip'tically** adv.

ellip'sis n. Grammar omission of parts of word or sentence (pl. -ses [sēz])

elm n. tree with serrated leaves; its wood

elocu'tion n. art of public speaking, voice management —**elocu'tionist** n. teacher of this; specialist in verse speaking

e'longate vt. lengthen, extend, prolong —**elonga'tion** n.

elope' vi. run away from home with lover —**elope'ment** n.

el'oquence n. fluent, powerful use of language —**el'oquent** a. —**el'oquently** adv.

else adv. besides, instead; otherwise —**elsewhere'** adv. in or to some other place

elu'cidate [-loo'-] vt. throw light upon, explain —**elucida'tion** n. —**elu'cidatory** a.

elude' [-lood'] vt. escape, slip away from, dodge; baffle —**elu'sion** n. act of eluding; evasion —**elu'sive** a. difficult to catch hold of, deceptive —**elus'ively** adv. —**elu'sory** a.

el'ver n. young eel

elves, elv'ish see ELF

em n. Printing the square of any size of type

em- prefix see EN-

ema'ciate v. make or become abnormally thin —**emacia'tion** n.

em'anate vi. issue, proceed from, originate —**emana'tion** n. —**em'anative** a.

eman'cipate vt. set free —**emancipa'tion** n. act of setting free, esp. from social, legal restraint; state of being set free —**emancipa'tionist** n. advocate of emancipation of slaves, women etc. —**eman'cipator** n. —**eman'cipatory** a.

emas'culate vt. castrate; enfeeble, weaken —**emascula'tion** n. —**emas'culative** a.

embalm' vt. preserve corpse from decay by use of chemicals, herbs etc. —**embalm'ment** n.

embank'ment n. artificial mound carrying road, railway, or serving to dam water

embar'go n. order stopping movement of ships; suspension of commerce; ban (pl. **-goes**) —vt. put under embargo; requisition

embark' v. put, go, on board ship, aircraft etc.; (with on or upon) commence new project, venture etc. —**embarka'tion** n.

embarr'ass vt. perplex, disconcert; abash; confuse; encumber —**embarr'assment** n.

em'bassy n. office, work or official residence of ambassador; deputation

embed', imbed' vt. fix fast in something solid

embell'ish vt. adorn, enrich —**embell'ishment** n.

em'ber n. glowing cinder —pl. red-hot ashes

Ember days days appointed by Church for fasting in each quarter

embez'zle vt. divert fraudulently, misappropriate (money in trust etc.) —**embezz'lement** n. —**embezz'ler** n.

embitt'er vt. make bitter —**embitt'erment** n.

embla'zon vt. to adorn richly, esp. heraldically

em'blem n. symbol; badge, device —**emblemat'ic** a. —**emblemat'ically** adv.

embod'y vt. give body, concrete expression to; represent, include, be expression of (**embod'ied, embod'ying**) —**embod'iment** n.

embold'en vt. make bold

em'bolism n. Med. obstruction of artery by blood clot or air bubble

emboss' vt. mould, stamp or carve in relief

embrace' vt. clasp in arms, hug; seize, avail oneself of, accept; comprise —n.

embra'sure [-zhə] n. opening in wall for cannon; bevelling of wall at sides of window

embroca'tion n. lotion for rubbing limbs etc. to relieve pain —**em'brocate** vt.

embroi'der vt. ornament with needlework; embellish, exaggerate (story) —**embroi'dery** n.

embroil' vt. bring into confusion; involve in hostility —**embroil'ment** n.

em'bryo [-bri-ō] n. unborn or undeveloped offspring, germ; undeveloped thing (pl. **-os**) —**embryol'ogist** n. —**embryol'ogy** n. —**embryon'ic** a.

embus' v. (esp. of troops) put into, mount bus (**-ss-**)

emend' vt. to remove errors from, correct —**emenda'tion** n. —**e'mendator** n. —**emen'datory** a.

em'erald n. bright green precious stone —a. of the colour of emerald

emerge' vi. come up, out; rise to notice; come into view; come out on inquiry —**emer'gence** n. —**emer'gent** a.

emer'gency n. sudden unforeseen thing or event needing prompt action; difficult situation; exigency, crisis

emer'itus a. retired, honourably discharged but retaining one's title (eg professor) on honorary basis

em'ery n. hard mineral used for polishing —**emery paper** stiff paper coated with finely powdered emery

emet'ic n./a. (medicine) causing vomiting

em'igrate vt. go and settle in another country —**em'igrant** n. —**emigra'tion** n. —**em'igratory** a.

émigré [em'i-grā] n. emigrant, esp. one forced to leave his country for political reasons (pl. **-s**)

em'inent a. distinguished, notable —**em'inence** n. distinction; height; rank; fame; rising ground; (E-) title of cardinal —**em'inently** adv.

em'issary n. agent, representative (esp. of government) sent on mission

emit' vt. give out, put forth (**-tt-**) —**emis'sion** n. —**emitt'er** n.

emoll'ient a. softening, soothing —n. ointment or other softening application

emol'ument n. salary, pay, profit from work

emo'tion n. mental agitation, excited state of feeling, as joy, fear etc. —**emo'tional** a. given to emotion; appealing to the emotions —**emo'tive** a. tending to arouse emotion

em'pathy n. power of understanding, imaginatively entering into, another's feelings

em'peror n. ruler of an empire (**em'press** fem.)

em'phasis n. importance attached; stress on words; vigour of speech, expression (pl. **-ses** [-sēz]) —**em'phasize** vt. —**emphat'ic** a. forceful, decided; stressed —**emphat'ically** adv.

em'pire n. large territory, esp. aggregate of states under supreme ruler, supreme control

empir'ical *a.* relying on experiment or experience, not on theory —**empir'ic** *a.* empirical —*n.* one who relies solely on experience and observation —**empir'ically** *adv.* —**empir'icism** [-s-] *n.*

emplace'ment *n.* putting in position; gun platform

employ' *vt.* provide work for (a person) in return for money, hire; keep busy; use (**employed', employ'ing**) —**employ'ee** *n.* —**employ'er** *n.* —**employ'ment** *n.* an employing, being employed; work, trade; occupation

empor'ium *n.* large general shop; centre of commerce (*pl.* **-riums, -ria**)

empow'er *vt.* enable, authorize

em'press *see* EMPEROR

emp'ty *a.* containing nothing; unoccupied; senseless; vain, foolish —*v.* make, become devoid of content; discharge (contents) into (**emp'tied, emp'tying**) —**emp'ties** *pl.n.* empty boxes, bottles *etc.* —**emp'tiness** *n.*

EMS European Monetary System

e'mu [ē'myōō] *n.* large Aust. flightless bird like ostrich

em'ulate *vt.* strive to equal or excel; imitate —**emula'tion** *n.* rivalry; competition —**em'ulative** *a.* —**em'ulator** *n.* —**em'ulous** *a.* eager to equal or surpass another or his deeds

emul'sion *n.* light-sensitive coating of film; milky liquid with oily or resinous particles in suspension; paint *etc.* in this form —**emul'sifier** *n.* —**emul'sify** *vt.* (**emul'sified, emul'sifying**) —**emul'sive** *a.*

en *n.* Printing unit of measurement, half an em

en- (*also* **em-** *before labials*) (*comb. form*) put in, into, on, as

enrage' *vt.* Such words are not given here where the meaning may easily be inferred from the simple word

ena'ble *vt.* make able, authorize, empower, supply with means (to do something)

enact' *vi.* make law; act part —**enact'ment** *n.*

enam'el *n.* glasslike coating applied to metal *etc.* to preserve surface; coating of teeth; any hard outer coating —*vt.* (**-ll-**)

enam'our *vt.* inspire with love; charm; bewitch

en bloc' [on-blok'] *Fr.* in a lump or block; all together

encamp' *v.* set up (in) camp —**encamp'ment** *n.* camp

encap'sulate *vt.* enclose in capsule; put in concise or abridged form

encaus'tic [-kos'-] *a.* with colours burnt in —*n.* art of ornament by burnt-in colours

enceph'alogram [-sef'-] *n.* X-ray photograph of brain

enchant' [-ah-] *vt.* bewitch, delight —**enchant'er** *n.* (**-tress** *fem.*) —**enchant'ment** *n.*

encir'cle *vt.* surround; enfold; go round so as to encompass —**encir'clement** *n.*

en'clave *n.* portion of territory entirely surrounded by foreign land

enclit'ic *a.* pronounced as part of (another word) —*n.*

enclose' *vt.* shut in; surround; envelop; place in with something else (in letter *etc.*) —**enclo'sure** [-zho] *n.* —**enclosed order** Christian religious order whose members do not go into the outside world

enco'mium *n.* formal praise; eulogy —**enco'miast** *n.* one who composes encomiums —**encomias'tic** *a.* —**encomias'tically** *adv.*

encom'pass vt. surround, en-circle, contain

en'core [ong'kawr] interj. again, once more —n. call for repetition of song etc.; the repetition —vt. ask to repeat

encoun'ter vt. meet unexpectedly; meet in conflict; be faced with (difficulty) —n.

encour'age [-kur'-] vt. hearten, animate, inspire with hope; embolden —**encour'agement** n.

encroach' vi. intrude (on) as usurper; trespass —**encroach'ment** n.

encrust', incrust' v. cover with or form a crust, or hard covering

encum'ber vt. hamper; burden —**encum'brance** n. impediment, burden

ency'clical [-sik'-] a. sent to many persons or places —n. circular letter, esp. from Pope to all R.C. bishops

encyclop(a)e'dia [-pēd'-] n. book, set of books of information on all subjects, or on every branch of subject, usu. arranged alphabetically —**encyclop(a)e'dic** a. —**encyclop(a)e'dist** n.

end n. limit; extremity; conclusion, finishing; fragment; latter part; death; event, issue; purpose, aim; Sport either of the defended areas of a playing field etc. —v. put an end to; come to an end, finish —**end'ing** n. —**end'less** a. —**end'ways** adv. —**end'papers** pl.n. blank pages at beginning and end of book

endear' vt. to make dear or beloved —**endear'ing** a. —**endear'ingly** adv. —**endear'ment** n. loving word; tender affection

endeav'our [-dev'ər] vi. try, strive after —n. attempt, effort

endem'ic a. regularly occurring in a country or district —n. endemic disease

end'ive n. curly-leaved chicory used as salad

endo- (comb. form) within, as in endocardium, endocrine etc. Such words are not given here where the meaning may easily be inferred from the simple word

endocar'dium n. lining membrane of the heart

en'docrine [-In] a. of those glands (thyroid, pituitary etc.) which secrete hormones directly into bloodstream

endorse' vt. sanction; confirm; write (esp. sign name) on back of; record conviction on driving licence —**endorse'ment** n.

endow' vt. provide permanent income for; furnish (with) —**endow'ment** n.

endue' vt. invest, furnish (with quality etc.)

endure' vt. undergo; tolerate; bear —vi. last —**endur'able** a. —**endur'ance** n. act or power of enduring

en'ema n. medicine, liquid injected into rectum

en'emy n. hostile person; opponent; armed foe; hostile force

en'ergy n. vigour, force, activity; source(s) of power, as oil, coal etc.; capacity of machine, battery etc. for work or output of power —**energet'ic** a. —**energet'ically** adv. —**en'ergize** vt. give vigour to

en'ervate vt. weaken, deprive of vigour —**enerva'tion** n. lassitude, weakness

enfee'ble vt. weaken, debilitate —**enfee'blement** n.

enfilade' [-lād'] n. fire from artillery, sweeping line from end to end

enforce' vt. compel obedience to; impose (action) upon; drive home —**enforce'able** a. —**enforce'ment** n.

enfran'chise vt. give right of

voting to; give parliamentary representation to; set free —**enfran'chisement** n.

Eng. England; English

engage' [-gāj'] vt. employ; reserve, hire; bind by contract or promise; pledge oneself; betroth; undertake; attract; occupy; bring into conflict; interlock —vi. employ oneself (in); promise; begin to fight —**engaged'** a. betrothed; in use; occupied, busy —**engage'ment** n. —**engag'ing** a. charming

engen'der [-jen'-] vt. give rise to; beget; rouse

en'gine [-jin] n. any machine to convert energy into mechanical work, as steam or petrol engine; railway locomotive; fire engine —**engineer'** n. one who is in charge of engines, machinery etc. or construction work (eg roads, bridges) or installation of plant; one who originates, organizes something —vt. construct as engineer; contrive —**engineer'ing** n.

Eng'lish [ing'gl-] n. the language of Britain, the U.S., most parts of the Commonwealth and certain other countries; the people of England —a. relating to England

engraft' [-ah-] vt. graft on; plant deeply; incorporate

engrain' vt. see INGRAIN

engrave' vt. cut in lines on metal for printing; carve, incise; impress deeply —**engra'ver** n. —**engra'ving** n. copy of picture printed from engraved plate

engross' [-ō-] vt. absorb (attention); occupy wholly; write out in large letters or in legal form; corner —**engross'ment** n.

engulf' vt. swallow up

enhance' [-ah-] vt. heighten, intensify, increase value or attractiveness —**enhance'ment** n.

enig'ma n. puzzling thing or person; riddle —**enigmat'ic(al)** a. —**enigmat'ically** adv.

enjamb'ment [-zham'-] n. in verse, continuation of sentence beyond end of line

enjoin' vt. command; impose, prescribe

enjoy' vt. delight in; take pleasure in; have use or benefit of —v. refl. be happy —**enjoy'able** a. —**enjoy'ment** n.

enlarge' vt. make bigger; reproduce on larger scale, as photograph —vi. grow bigger; talk, write about, in greater detail; be capable of reproduction on larger scale —**enlarge'able** a. —**enlarge'ment** n. —**enlar'ger** n. optical instrument for enlarging photographs

enlight'en vt. give information to; instruct, inform, shed light on —**enlight'enment** n.

enlist' v. engage as soldier or helper —**enlist'ment** n.

enli'ven vt. brighten, make more lively, animate

en masse [on-mas'] adv. in a group, body; all together

enmesh' vt. entangle

en'mity n. ill will, hostility

enno'ble vt. make noble, elevate —**enno'blement** n.

ennui [on'wē] n. boredom —**en'nuied, ennuyé** a.

enor'mous a. very big, vast —**enor'mity** n. a gross offence; great wickedness; inf. great size

enough' [i-nuf'] a. as much or as many as need be; sufficient —n. sufficient quantity —adv. (just) sufficiently

enounce' vt. state; enunciate, proclaim —**enounce'ment** n.

en passant [on-pa-song'] Fr. in passing, by the way

enquire' vt. see INQUIRE

enrap'ture vt. delight excessively; charm —**enrapt'**, **enrap'-tured** a. entranced

enrich' vt. make rich; add to —**enrich'ment** n.

enrol' [-ōl'] vt. write name of on roll or list; engage, enlist, take in as member; enter, record (-**ll**-) —vi. become member —**enrol'ment** n.

en route' [on-rōōt'] Fr. on the way

ensconce' vt. place snugly; establish in safety

ensem'ble [on-som'bəl] n. whole; all parts taken together; woman's complete outfit; company of actors, dancers etc.; Mus. group of soloists performing together; Mus. concerted passage; general effect

enshrine' vt. set in shrine, preserve with great care and sacred affection

en'sign [-sīn] n. naval or military flag; badge

en'silage see SILAGE

enslave' vt. make into slave —**enslave'ment** n. bondage —**ensla'ver** n.

ensnare' vt. capture in snare or trap; trick into false position; entangle

ensue' vi. follow, happen after

en suite' [on-swēt'] adv. forming a set or single unit

ensure' vt. make safe or sure; make certain to happen; secure

entail' vt. involve as result, necessitate; Law restrict ownership of property to designated line of heirs

entan'gle vt. ensnare; perplex —**entan'glement** n.

entente' [on-tont'] n. friendly understanding between nations

en'ter vt. go, come into; penetrate; join; write in, register —vi. go, come in, join, begin —**en'trance** n. going, coming in; door, passage to enter; right to

enter; fee paid for this —**en'trant** n. one who enters, esp. contest —**en'try** n. entrance; entering; item entered, eg in account, list

enter'ic a. of or relating to the intestines —**enteri'tis** n. bowel inflammation

en'terprise n. bold or difficult undertaking; bold spirit; force of character in launching out; business, company —**en'terprising** a.

entertain' vt. amuse, divert; receive as guest; maintain; consider favourable, take into consideration —**entertain'er** n. —**entertain'ment** n.

enthral' vt. captivate, thrill, hold spellbound (-**ll**-) —**enthral'-ment** n.

enthu'siasm n. ardent eagerness, zeal —**enthuse'** v. (cause to) show enthusiasm —**enthu'siast** n. ardent supporter of —**enthusias'tic** a. —**enthusias'tically** adv.

entice' vt. allure, attract, inveigle, tempt —**entice'ment** n. —**entic'ing** a. alluring

entire' a. whole, complete, unbroken —**entire'ly** adv. —**enti'rety** n.

enti'tle vt. give claim to; qualify; give title to; style

en'tity n. thing's being or existence; reality; thing having real existence

entomol'ogy n. study of insects —**entomolog'ical** a. —**entomol'ogist** n. —**entomol'ogize** vi.

entourage' [on-too-rahzh'] n. associates, retinue; surroundings

entozo'on n. internal parasite (pl. **entozo'a**) —**entozo'ic** a.

en'trails pl.n. bowels, intestines; inner parts

en'trance'¹ see ENTER

entrance'² [-ah-] vt. delight; throw into a trance

entreat' vt. ask earnestly; beg,

implore —**entreat'y** n. earnest request

en'trée [on'trā] n. (dish served before) main course of meal; right of access, admission

entrench' vt. establish in fortified position with trenches; establish firmly —**entrench'ment** n.

entrepreneur' [on-trə-prə-nur'] n. person who attempts to profit by risk and initiative

en'tropy n. unavailability of the heat energy of a system for mechanical work; measurement of this

entrust' vt. commit, charge with; put into care or protection of

entwine' vt. plait, interweave; wreathe with; embrace

E number any of series of numbers prefixed by E indicating specific food additive recognized by EEC

enu'merate vt. mention one by one; count —**enumera'tion** n. —**enu'merative** a. —**enu'merator** n.

enun'ciate vt. state clearly; proclaim; pronounce —**enuncia'tion** n. —**enun'ciative** a. —**enun'ciator** n.

envel'op vt. wrap up, enclose, surround; encircle —**envel'opment** n.

en'velope n. folded, gummed cover of letter; covering, wrapper

enven'om vt. put poison, venom in; embitter

envi'ron vt. surround —**envi'ronment** n. surroundings; conditions of life or growth —**environmen'tal** a. —**environmen'talist** n. ecologist —**envi'rons** pl.n. districts round (town etc.), outskirts

envis'age [-z'-] vt. conceive as possibility; visualize

en'voy n. messenger; diplomatic

minister of rank below ambassador

en'vy vt. grudge another's good fortune, qualities or success; feel jealous of (**en'vied, en'vying**) —n. bitter contemplation of another's good fortune; jealousy; object of this feeling —**en'viable** a. arousing envy —**en'vious** a. full of envy

en'zyme [-zīm] n. any of group of complex proteins produced by living cells and acting as catalysts in biochemical reactions

EOC Equal Opportunities Commission

e'olith [ē'ō-] n. early flint implement —**eolith'ic** a. of the period before stone age

ep-, eph-, epi- (comb. form) upon, during, as in ephemeral, epitaph, epoch etc. Such words are not given here where the meaning may easily be inferred from the simple word

ep'aulette n. shoulder ornament on uniform

Eph. Ephesians

ephem'eral a. short-lived, transient —**ephem'eron** n. ephemeral thing (pl. **-rons, -ra**) Also **ephem'era** (pl. **-ras, -rae**) —**ephem'erous** a.

ep'ic n. long poem or story telling of achievements of hero or heroes; film etc. about heroic deeds —a. of, like, an epic; impressive, grand

ep'icene [-sēn] a. common to both sexes

ep'icentre n. focus of earthquake —**epicen'tral** a.

ep'icure n. one delighting in eating and drinking —**epicure'an** [-ē'-] a. of Epicurus, who taught that pleasure, in the shape of practice of virtue, was highest good; given to refined sensuous enjoyment —n. such person or philosopher —**epicure'anism** n. —**ep'icurism** n.

ep'icycle n. circle whose centre moves on circumference of greater circle

epidem'ic a. (esp. of disease) prevalent and spreading rapidly; widespread —n. —**epidem'ical** a.

epider'mis n. outer skin

epidur'al [-dyoor-] n./a. (of) spinal anaesthetic used for relief of pain during childbirth

epiglott'is n. cartilage that covers opening of larynx in swallowing —**epiglott'ic** a.

ep'igram n. concise, witty poem or saying —**epigrammat'ic(al)** a. —**epigrammat'ically** adv. —**epigramm'atist** n.

ep'igraph n. inscription

ep'ilepsy n. disorder of nervous system causing fits and convulsions —**epilep'tic** n. sufferer from this —a. of, subject to, this

ep'ilogue [-og] n. short speech or poem at end, esp. of play

Epiph'any [-pif'-] n. festival of the announcement of Christ to the Magi, celebrated 6 Jan.

epis'copal a. of bishop; ruled by bishops —**epis'copacy** n. government by body of bishops —**Episcopa'lian** a. of branch of Anglican church —n. member, adherent of Episcopalian church —**epis'copate** n. bishop's office, see, or duration of office; body of bishops

ep'isode n. incident; section of (serialized) book, television programme etc. —**episod'ic(al)** a.

epistemol'ogy n. study of source, nature and limitations of knowledge —**epistemolog'ical** a. —**epistemol'ogist** n.

epis'tle [-sl] n. letter, esp. of apostle; poem in letter form —**epis'tolary** a. —**epis'toler** n.

ep'itaph n. memorial inscription on tomb

ep'ithet n. additional, descriptive word or name —**epithet'ic(al)** a.

epit'ome [-ə-mi] n. typical example; summary (pl. -s) —**epit'omist** n. —**epit'omize** vt. typify

EPNS electroplated nickel silver

e'poch [-ok] n. beginning of period; period, era, esp. one of notable events —**e'pochal** a.

ep'ode n. third, or last, part of lyric ode

EPOS electronic point of sale

e'quable a. even-tempered, placid; uniform, not easily disturbed —**equabil'ity** n. —**eq'uably** adv.

e'qual a. the same in number, size, merit etc.; identical; fit or qualified; evenly balanced —n. one equal to another —vt. be equal to —**equal'ity** [-ol'-] n. state of being equal; uniformity —**equaliza'tion** n. —**e'qualize** v. make, become, equal —**e'qually** adv. —**equal opportunity** nondiscrimination as to sex, race etc. in employment, pay etc.

equanim'ity n. calmness, composure, steadiness

equate' vt. make equal; bring to a common standard —**equa'tion** n. equating of two mathematical expressions; balancing

equa'tor n. imaginary circle round earth equidistant from the poles —**equator'ial** a.

equerr'y n. officer in attendance on sovereign; officer in royal household in charge of horses

eques'trian a. of, skilled in, horse-riding; mounted on horse —n. rider

equi- (comb. form) equal, at equal, as in **equidis'tant** a. Such words are not given here where the meaning can easily be inferred from the simple word

equian'gular a. having equal angles

equilat'eral a. having equal sides

equilib'rium n. state of steadiness, equipoise or stability (pl. -riums, -ria)

eq'uine a. of, like a horse

e'quinox n. time when sun crosses equator and day and night are equal —pl. points at which sun crosses equator —equinoc'tial a.

equip' vt. supply, fit out, array (-pp-) —eq'uipage n. carriage, horses and attendants; obs. outfit, requisites —equip'ment n.

eq'uipoise n. perfect balance; counterpoise; equanimity —vt. counterbalance

eq'uity n. fairness; use of principles of justice to supplement law; system of law so made —eq'uitable a. fair, reasonable, just —eq'uitably adv.

equiv'alent a. equal in value; having the same meaning or result; tantamount; corresponding —equiv'alence n. —equiv'alency n.

equiv'ocal a. of double or doubtful meaning; questionable; liable to suspicion —equivocal'ity n. —equiv'ocate vi. use equivocal words to mislead —equivoca'tion n. —equiv'ocator n.

ER Elizabeth Regina

e'ra n. system of time in which years are numbered from particular event; time of the event; memorable date, period

erad'icate vt. wipe out, exterminate; root out —erad'icable a. —eradica'tion n. —erad'icative a./n. —erad'icator n.

erase' vt. rub out; remove, eg recording from magnetic tape —era'ser n. —era'sure n.

ere [âr] prep./conj. Poet. before; sooner than

erect' a. upright —vt. set up; build —erec'tile a. —erec'tion n. esp. an erect penis —erect'or n.

erg n. cgs unit of work or energy

ergonom'ics pl.n. (with sing. v.) study of relationship between workers and their environment —ergon'omist n.

er'got n. disease of grain; diseased seed used as drug —er'gotism n. disease caused by eating ergot-infested bread

er'ica n. genus of plants including heathers

er'mine [-min] n. stoat in northern regions, esp. in winter; its white winter fur

Ern'ie n. computer that randomly selects winning numbers of Premium Bonds (Electronic Random Number Indicating Equipment)

erode' vt. wear away; eat into —ero'sion n. —ero'sive a.

erog'enous [-j-] a. sensitive to sexual stimulation

erot'ic a. relating to, or treating of, sexual pleasure —erot'ica pl.n. sexual literature or art —erot'icism n.

err vi. make mistakes; be wrong; sin —errat'ic a. irregular in movement, conduct etc. —errat'ically adv. —errat'um [- aht'-] n. printing mistake noted for correction (pl. -ta) —erro'neous a. mistaken, wrong —err'or n. mistake; wrong opinion; sin

err'and n. short journey for simple business; the business, mission of messenger; purpose —errand boy

err'ant a. wandering in search of adventure; erring —err'ancy n. erring state or conduct —er'rantry n. state or conduct of knight errant

er'satz [-zats] a. substitute; imitation

erst, erst'while adv. of old, formerly

er'udite a. learned —**erudi'tion** n. learning

erupt' vi. burst out —**erup'tion** n. bursting out, esp. volcanic outbreak; rash on the skin —**erup'tive** a.

erysip'elas n. acute skin infection

erythe'ma n. patchy inflammation of skin —**erythemat'ic, erythe'matous** a.

es'calate v. increase, be increased, in extent, intensity etc.

es'calator n. moving staircase

escall'op see SCALLOP

escape' vi. get free; get off safely; go unpunished; find way out —vt. elude; be forgotten by —n. escaping —**es'capade** [or -pād] n. wild (mischievous) adventure —**esca'pism** n. taking refuge in fantasy to avoid facing disagreeable facts —**escapol'ogist** n. entertainer specializing in freeing himself from confinement

escarp' n. steep bank under rampart —**escarp'ment** n. steep hillside, escarp

eschatol'ogy [-k-] n. study of death, judgment and last things —**eschatolog'ical** a.

eschew' vt. avoid, abstain from, shun

eschschol'tzia [is-kol'shə] n. garden plant with bright flowers, California poppy

es'cort n. armed guard for traveller etc.; person or persons accompanying another —**escort'** vt.

escritoire' [-twah'] n. type of writing desk

es'culent a. edible

escutch'eon [-kuch'ən] n. shield with coat of arms; ornamental plate round keyhole etc.

Es'kimo n. one of aboriginal race inhabiting N Amer., Greenland etc.; their language (pl. -mos)

esoter'ic [-ō-] a. abstruse, obscure; secret; restricted to initiates

ESP extrasensory perception

espal'ier [-yə] n. shrub, (fruit) tree trained to grow flat, as against wall etc.; trellis for this

espar'to n. kind of grass yielding fibre used for making rope etc.

espec'ial [is-pesh'əl] a. preeminent, more than ordinary; particular —**espec'ially** adv.

Esperan'to n. artificial language designed for universal use —**Esperant'ist** n. one who uses Esperanto

es'pionage [-nahzh'] n. spying; use of secret agents

esplanade' n. level space, esp. one used as public promenade

espouse' [-owz'] vt. support, embrace (cause etc.); obs. marry —**espous'al** n.

espress'o n. strong coffee made by forcing steam through ground coffee beans

esprit' [-prē'] n. spirit; animation —**esprit de corps** [-kawr'] attachment, loyalty to the society etc., one belongs to

espy' vt. catch sight of (**espied', espy'ing**) —**espi'al** n. observation

Esq. Esquire

esquire' n. gentleman's courtesy title used on letters; formerly, a squire

ess'ay n. prose composition; short treatise; attempt —**essay'** vt. try, attempt; test (**essayed', essay'ing**) —**ess'ayist** n.

ess'ence n. all that makes thing what it is; existence, being; entity, reality; extract got by distillation —**essen'tial** a. necessary, indispensable; inherent; of, constituting essence of thing —n. indispensable element; chief point —**essential'ity** n.

EST C, US Eastern Standard Time

estab'lish vt. make secure; set up; settle; prove —**estab'lishment** n. permanent organized body, full number of regiment etc.; household; business; public institution —**Established Church** church officially recognized as national institution —**the Establishment** n. group, class of people holding authority within a society

estate' n. landed property; person's property; area of property development, esp. of houses or factories; class as part of nation; rank, state, condition of life —**estate agent** one who sells houses etc. for others —**estate car** car with rear door and luggage space behind rear seats

esteem' vt. think highly of; consider; n. favourable opinion, regard, respect

es'ter n. Chem. organic compound produced by reaction between acid and alcohol

es'timate vt. form approximate idea of (amounts, measurements etc.); form opinion of; quote approximate price for —n. approximate judgment of amounts etc.; amount etc., arrived at; opinion; price quoted by contractor —**es'timable** a. worthy of regard —**estima'tion** n. opinion, judgment, esteem

estrange' vt. lose affection of; alienate —**estrange'ment** n.

es'tuary n. tidal mouth of river, inlet —**es'tuarine** a.

ETA estimated time of arrival

etc., &c. et cetera

et cet'era [-set'-] Lat. and the rest, and others, and so on (abbrevs. etc., &c.)

etch vt. make engraving by eating away surface of metal plate with acids etc.; imprint vividly —**etch'er** n. —**etch'ing** n.

eter'nal a. without beginning or end; everlasting; changeless —**eter'nally** adv. —**eter'nity** n.

e'ther [-th-] n. colourless volatile liquid used as anaesthetic; intangible fluid formerly supposed to fill all space; the clear sky, region above clouds —**ethe'real** a. light, airy; heavenly, spiritlike —**ethereal'ity** n.

eth'ic(al) a. relating to morals —**eth'ically** adv. —**eth'ics** pl.n. science of morals; moral principles, rules of conduct

eth'nic a. of race or relating to classification of humans into social, cultural etc., groups —**ethnograph'ic** a. —**ethnog'raphy** n. description of races of men —**ethnolog'ical** a. —**ethnol'ogy** n. the study of human races

e'thos n. distinctive character, spirit etc. of people, culture etc.

eth'yl [or e'thīl] n. (C₂H₅) radical of ordinary alcohol and ether —**eth'ylene** n. poisonous gas used as anaesthetic and fuel

et'iquette [-ket] n. conventional code of conduct or behaviour

é'tude [ā'- or -tyōōd'] n. short musical composition, study, intended often as technical exercise

etymol'ogy n. tracing, account of, formation of word's origin, development; science of this —**etymolog'ical** a. —**etymolog'ically** adv. —**etymol'ogist** n.

eu-, ev- (comb. form) well, as in eugenic, euphony, evangelist etc.

eu'calypt, eucalyp'tus n. mostly Aust. genus of tree, the gum tree, yielding timber and oil, used medicinally from leaves

Eu'charist [-k-] *n.* Christian sacrament of the Lord's Supper; the consecrated elements —**Eucharis'tic** *a.*

eugen'ic [-j-] *a.* relating to, or tending towards, production of fine offspring —**eugen'icist** *n.* —**eugen'ics** *pl.n.* (with *sing. v.*) this science

eu'logy *n.* speech or writing in praise of person; praise —**eu'logist** *n.* —**eulogis'tic** *a.* —**eulogis'tically** *adv.* —**eu'logize** *vt.*

eu'nuch [-k] *n.* castrated man, *esp.* formerly one employed in harem

eu'phemism *n.* substitution of mild term for offensive or hurtful one; instance of this —**eu'phemist** *n.* —**euphemis'tic** *a.* —**euphemis'tically** *adv.* —**eu'phemize** *vt.*

eu'phony *n.* pleasantness of sound —**euphon'ic** *a.* —**eupho'nious** *a.* pleasing to ear —**eupho'nium** *n.* brass musical instrument, bass-tenor tuba

euphor'ia *n.* sense of wellbeing or elation —**euphor'ic** [-o'-] *a.*

eu'phuism *n.* affected highflown manner of writing, *esp.* in imitation of Lyly's *Euphues* (1580) —**euphuis'tic** *a.*

Eura'sian *a.* of mixed European and Asiatic descent; of Europe and Asia —*n.* one of this descent

eure'ka [yoo-rē'-] *interj.* exclamation of triumph at finding something

Europe'an *n./a.* (native) of Europe —**European Economic Community** association of a number of European nations for trade

Eusta'chian tube passage leading from pharynx to middle ear

euthana'sia *n.* gentle, painless death; putting to death in this way, *esp.* to relieve suffering

euthen'ics *pl.n.* (with *sing. v.*) science of the relation of environment to human beings

evac'uate *vt.* empty; withdraw from; discharge —**evacua'tion** *n.* —**evacuee'** *n.* person moved from danger area *esp.* in time of war

evade' *vt.* avoid, escape from; elude —**eva'sion** *n.* subterfuge; excuse; equivocation —**eva'sive** *a.* elusive, not straightforward —**eva'sively** *adv.*

eval'uate *vt.* find or judge value of —**evalua'tion** *n.*

evanesce' [-es'] *vi.* fade away —**evanes'cence** *n.* —**evanes'cent** *a.* fleeting, transient

evangel'ical [-jel'-] *a.* of, or according to, gospel teaching; of Protestant sect which maintains salvation by faith —*n.* member of evangelical sect —**evangel'icalism** *n.* —**evan'gelism** *n.* —**evan'gelist** *n.* writer of one of the four gospels; ardent, zealous preacher of the gospel; revivalist —**evangeliza'tion** *n.* —**evan'gelize** *vt.* preach gospel to; convert

evap'orate *vi.* turn into, pass off in, vapour —*vt.* turn into vapour —**evapora'tion** *n.* —**evap'orator** *n.*

eva'sion *see* EVADE

eve [ēv] *n.* evening before (festival *etc.*); time just before (event *etc.*); *obs.* evening —**e'ven** *n. obs.* evening —**e'vensong** *n.* evening prayer

e'ven *a.* flat, smooth; uniform in quality, equal in amount, balanced; divisible by two; impartial —*vt.* make even; smooth; equalize —*adv.* equally; simply; notwithstanding; (used to express emphasis)

e'vening [-vn-] *n.* the close of

day or early part of night; decline, end

event[1] *n.* happening; notable occurrence; issue, result; any one
contest in series in sporting programme —**event'ful** *a.* full of
exciting events —**event'ing** *n.*
sport of competing in equestrian
events consisting of dressage,
cross country and showjumping
—**event'ual** *a.* resulting in the
end; ultimate; final —**eventual'-
ity** *n.* possible event —**even'tually** *adv.* —**even'tuate** *vi.* turn out;
happen

ev'er *adv.* always; constantly; at
any time —**ev'ergreen** *n./a.*
(tree or shrub) bearing foliage
throughout year —**evermore'**
adv.

ev'ery [-vri] *a.* each of all; all
possible —**ev'erybody** *n.*
—**ev'eryday** *a.* usual, ordinary
—**ev'eryone** *n.* —**ev'erything** *n.*
—**ev'erywhere** *adv.* in all places

evict[1] *vt.* expel by legal process,
turn out —**evic'tion** *n.* —**evic'tor**
n.

ev'ident *a.* plain, obvious
—**ev'idence** *n.* ground of belief;
sign, indication; testimony —*vt.*
indicate, prove —**eviden'tial** *a.*
—**ev'idently** *adv.* —**in evidence**
conspicuous

e'vil *a.* bad, harmful —*n.* what is
bad or harmful; sin —**e'villy** *adv.*
—**e'vildoer** *n.* sinner

evince[1] *vt.* show, indicate

evoke[1] *vt.* draw forth; call to
mind —**evoca'tion** *n.* —**evoc'a-
tive** *a.*

evolve[1] *v.* develop or cause to
develop gradually —*vi.* undergo
slow changes in process of
growth —**evolu'tion** [-lōō-] *n.*
evolving; development of species
from earlier forms —**evolu'tion-
al** *a.* —**evolu'tionary** *a.* —**evolu'-
tionist** *n.* —**ev'olutive** *a.*

ewe [yōō] *n.* female sheep

ew'er [yōō-] *n.* pitcher, water
jug for washstand

ex [eks] *n. inf.* ex-wife, ex-
husband *etc.*

ex. example; except(ed); extra

ex-, e-, ef- (*comb. form*) out
from, from, out of, formerly, as in
exclaim, evade, effusive, exodus
Such words are not given here
where the meaning may easily
be inferred from the simple word

exac'erbate [ig-zas'-] *vt.* aggra-
vate, embitter, make worse —**ex-
acerba'tion** *n.*

exact[1] [igz-] *a.* precise, accurate,
strictly correct —*vt.* demand,
extort; insist upon; enforce —**exact'ing** *a.* making rigorous or
excessive demands —**exac'tion**
n. act of exacting; that which is
exacted, as excessive work *etc.*;
oppressive demand —**exac'ti-
tude** *n.* —**exact'ly** *adv.* —**exact'-
ness** *n.* accuracy; precision —**exac'tor** *n.*

exagg'erate [ig-zaj'-] *vt.* mag-
nify beyond truth, overstate; enlarge; overestimate —**exaggera'-
tion** *n.* —**exagg'erative** *a.* —**ex-
ag'gerator** *n.*

exalt[1] [igz-awlt'] *vt.* raise up;
praise; make noble, dignify —**ex-
alta'tion** *n.* an exalting; elevation
in rank, dignity or position; rap-
ture

exam[1] *n. short for* examination

exam'ine [-gz-] *vt.* investigate;
look at closely; ask questions of;
test knowledge or proficiency of;
inquire into —**examina'tion** *n.*
—**examinee'** *n.* —**exam'iner** *n.*

exam'ple [ig-zahm'-] *n.* thing
illustrating general rule; specimen; model; warning, precedent,
instance

exas'perate [ig-zahs'-] *vt.* irritate, enrage; intensify, make
worse —**exaspera'tion** *n.*

ex'cavate *vt.* hollow out; make

hole by digging; unearth —**exca·va'tion** n. —**ex'cavator** n.

exceed' vt. be greater than; do more than authorized; go beyond; surpass —**exceed'ingly** adv. very; greatly

excel' vt. surpass, be better than —vi. be very good, pre-eminent (-ll-) —**ex'cellence** n. —**ex'cellency** n. title borne by viceroys, ambassadors —**ex'cellent** a. very good

except' prep. not including; but —conj. obs. unless —vt. leave or take out; exclude —**except'ing** prep. not including —**excep'tion** n. thing excepted, not included in a rule; objection —**excep'tionable** a. open to objection —**excep'tional** a. not ordinary, esp. much above average —**excep'tionally** adv.

ex'cerpt n. quoted or extracted passage from book etc. —**excerpt'** vt. extract, quote (passage from book etc.) —**excerp'tion** n.

excess' n. an exceeding; amount by which things exceeds; too great amount; intemperance or immoderate conduct —**exces'sive** a. —**excess'ively** adv.

exchange' vt. give (something) in return for something else; barter —n. giving one thing and receiving another; giving or receiving coin, bills etc., of one country for those of another; thing given for another; building where merchants meet for business; central telephone office where connections are made etc. —**exchangeabil'ity** n. —**exchange'able** a.

exche'quer [-k'ər] n. government department in charge of revenue

ex'cise' [-iz] n. duty charged on home goods during manufacture or before sale

excise'² [-iz'] vt. cut out, cut

away —**exci'sion** [-si'zhən] n.

excite' vt. arouse to strong emotion, stimulate; rouse up, set in motion; Electricity magnetize poles of —**excitabil'ity** n. —**ex'citable** a. —**ex'citably** adv. —**excita'tion** n. —**excite'ment** n. —**exci'ting** a. thrilling; rousing to action

exclaim' v. speak suddenly, cry out —**exclama'tion** n. —**exclam'atory** a.

exclude' vt. shut out; debar from; reject, not consider —**exclu'sion** n. —**exclu'sive** a. excluding; inclined to keep out (from society etc.); sole, only; select —n. something exclusive, esp. story appearing only in one newspaper —**exclu'sively** adv.

excommu'nicate vt. to cut off from the sacraments of the Church —**excommunica'tion** n.

ex'crement n. waste matter from body, esp. from bowels; dung —**excre'ta** pl.n. (usu. used as sing.) excrement —**excrete'** vi. discharge from the system —**excre'tion** n. —**excre'tory** a.

excres'cent a. growing out of; redundant —**excres'cence** n. unnatural outgrowth

excru'ciate [-krōō'shi-] vt. torment acutely, torture in body or mind —**excru'ciating** a. —**excrucia'tion** n.

ex'culpate vt. free from blame, acquit —**exculpa'tion** n. —**excul'patory** a.

excur'sion n. journey, ramble, trip for pleasure; digression —**excur'sus** n. digression (pl. -es, -sus rare)

excuse' [-skyōō'] vt. forgive, overlook; try to clear from blame; gain exemption; set free, remit —n. [-skyōōs'] that which serves to excuse; apology —**excu'sable** [-z-] a.

ex'ecrable a. abominable, hatefully bad

ex'ecute vt. inflict capital punishment on, kill; carry out, perform; make, produce; sign (document) —**exec'utant** n. performer, esp. of music —**execu'tion** n. —**execu'tioner** n. one employed to execute criminals —**exec'utive** n. person in administrative position; executive body; committee carrying on business of society etc. —a. carrying into effect, esp. of branch of government enforcing laws —**exec'utor** n. person appointed to carry out provisions of a will (**exec'utrix** fem.)

exege'sis [-jē'-] n. explanation, esp. of Scripture (pl. **-ge'ses** [-sēz]) —**exeget'ic(al)** a.

exem'plar n. model type —**exem'plarily** adv. —**exem'plary** a. fit to be imitated, serving as example; commendable; typical

exem'plify vt. serve as example of; illustrate; exhibit; make attested copy of (-**fied**, -**fying**) —**exemplifica'tion** n.

exempt' [igz-] vt. free from; excuse —a. freed from, not liable for; not affected by —**exemp'tion** n.

ex'equies [-kwiz] pl.n. funeral rites or procession

ex'ercise [-z] vt. use, employ; give exercise to; carry out, discharge; trouble, harass —vi. take exercise —n. use of limbs for health; practice for training; task for training; lesson; employment; use (of limbs, faculty etc.)

exert' [igz-] vt. apply (oneself) diligently, make effort; bring to bear —**exer'tion** n. effort, physical activity

ex'eunt Theatre they leave the stage: stage direction

exfo'liate v. peel in scales, layers

ex gra'tia [-grā'shə] adj. given as favour, esp. where no legal obligation exists

exhale' v. breathe out; give, pass off as vapour

exhaust' [ig-zawst'] vt. tire out; use up; empty; draw off; treat, discuss thoroughly —n. used steam or fluid from engine; waste gases from internal combustion engine; passage for, or coming out of this —**exhaustibil'ity** n. —**exhaust'ible** a. —**exhaus'tion** n. state of extreme fatigue; limit of endurance —**exhaus'tive** a. comprehensive

exhib'it [igz-] vt. show, display; manifest; show publicly (often in competition) —n. thing shown, esp. in competition or as evidence in court —**exhibi'tion** [eks-] n. display, act of displaying; public show (of works of art etc.) —**exhibi'tionist** n. one with compulsive desire to draw attention to himself or to expose genitals publicly —**exhib'itor** n. one who exhibits, esp. in show —**exhib'itory** a.

exhil'arate [igz-] vt. enliven, gladden —**exhilara'tion** n. high spirits, enlivenment

exhort' [igz-] vt. urge, admonish earnestly —**exhorta'tion** n. —**exhort'er** n.

exhume' [-hyōōm'] vt. unearth what has been buried, disinter —**exhuma'tion** n.

ex'igent [-j-] a. exacting; urgent, pressing —**ex'igence, ex'igency** n. pressing need; emergency —**ex'igible** a. liable to be exacted or demanded

exig'uous [ig-zig'-] a. scanty, meagre

ex'ile [egz'-] n. banishment, expulsion from one's own country; long absence abroad; one banished or permanently living away from his home or country —*vt.* banish, expel

exist' [igz-] *vi.* be, have being, live —**exist'ence** *n.* —**exist'ent** *a.*

existen'tialism [egz-] *n.* philosophy stressing importance of personal responsibility and the free agency of the individual in a seemingly meaningless universe

ex'it *n.* way out; going out; death; actor's departure from stage —*vi.* go out

ex li'bris [-le'-] *Lat.* from the library of

ex'ocrine [-in] *a.* of gland (*eg* salivary, sweat) secreting its products through ducts

ex'odus *n.* departure, *esp.* of crowd; (**E-**) second book of Old Testament

ex offic'io [-fish'-] *Lat.* by right of position or office

exon'erate *vt.* free, declare free, from blame; exculpate; acquit —**exonera'tion** *n.* —**exon'erative** *a.*

exorb'itant [igz-] *a.* very excessive, inordinate, immoderate —**exorb'itance** *n.* —**exorb'itantly** *adv.*

ex'orcise [-z] *vt.* cast out (evil spirits) by invocation; free person of evil spirits —**ex'orcism** *n.* —**ex'orcist** *n.*

exord'ium *n.* introductory part of a speech or treatise (*pl.* **-s, -ia**) —**exord'ial** *a.*

exoter'ic [-ō-te'rik] *a.* understandable by the many; ordinary, popular

exot'ic [igz-] *a.* brought in from abroad, foreign; rare, unusual, having strange or bizarre allure —*n.* exotic plant *etc.* —**exot'ica** *pl.n.* (*usu.* with *sing. v.*) (collection of) exotic objects —**exot'icism** *n.*

expand' *v.* increase, spread out, dilate, develop —**expand'able, -ible** *a.* —**expanse'** *n.* wide space;

open stretch of land —**expan'sibil'ity** *n.* —**expan'sible** *a.* —**expan'sion** *n.* —**expan'sive** *a.* wide; extensive; friendly, talkative

expa'tiate [-shi-] *vi.* speak or write at great length (on); enlarge (upon) —**expatia'tion** *n.*

expat'riate *vt.* banish; exile; withdraw (oneself) from one's native land —*a./n.* —**expatria'tion** *n.*

expect' *vt.* regard as probable; look forward to; await, hope —**expect'ancy** *n.* state or act of expecting; that which is expected; hope —**expect'ant** *a.* looking or waiting for, *esp.* for birth of child —**expect'antly** *adv.* —**expecta'tion** *n.* act or state of expecting; prospect of future good; what is expected; promise; value of something expected —*pl.* prospect of fortune or profit by will

expect'orate *v.* spit out (phlegm *etc.*) —**expectora'tion** *n.*

expe'dient *a.* fitting, advisable; politic; suitable; convenient —*n.* something suitable, useful, *esp.* in emergency —**expe'diency** *n.* —**expe'diently** *adv.*

ex'pedite [-īt] *vt.* help on, hasten; dispatch —**expedi'tion** [-ish'-] *n.* journey for definite (often scientific or military) purpose; people, equipment comprising expedition; excursion; promptness —**expedi'tionary** *a.* —**expedi'tious** *a.* prompt, speedy

expel' *vt.* drive, cast out; exclude; discharge (**-ll-**) —**expul'sion** *n.* —**expul'sive** *a.*

expend' *vt.* spend, pay out; use up —**expend'able** *a.* likely, or meant, to be used up or destroyed —**expend'iture** *n.* —**expense'** *n.* cost; (cause of) spending —*pl.* charges, outlay incurred —**expens'ive** *a.*

expe'rience n. observation of facts as source of knowledge; being affected consciously by event; the event; knowledge, skill, gained from life, by contact with facts and events —vt. undergo, suffer, meet with —**expe'rienced** a. skilled, expert, capable —**experien'tial** a.

exper'iment [-peri-] n. test, trial, something done in the hope that it may succeed, or to test theory —vi. make experiment —**experiment'al** a. —**experimen'talist** n. —**experiment'ally** adv.

ex'pert n. one skilful, knowledgeable, in something; authority —a. practised, skilful —**expertise'** [-tēz'] n.

ex'piate vt. pay penalty for; make amends for —**expia'tion** n. —**ex'piator** n. —**ex'piatory** a.

expire' vi. come to an end; give out breath; die —vt. breathe out —**expira'tion** n. —**expi'ratory** a. —**expi'ry** n. end

explain' vt. make clear, intelligible; interpret; elucidate; give details of; account for —**explana'tion** n. —**explan'atory**, **explan'ative** a.

exple'tive n. exclamation; oath —a. serving only to fill out sentence etc.

explic'able [or ex'-] a. explainable —**ex'plicate** vt. develop, explain —**explic'ative** a. —**explic'atory** a.

explic'it [-is'-] a. stated in detail; stated, not merely implied; outspoken; clear, plain; unequivocal

explode' vi. go off with bang; burst violently; (of population) increase rapidly —vt. make explode; discredit; expose (a theory etc.) —**explo'sion** n. —**explo'sive** a./n.

ex'ploit n. brilliant feat, deed —vt. [-ploit'] turn to advantage; make use of for one's own ends —**exploita'tion** n. —**exploit'er** n.

explore' vt. investigate; examine; scrutinize; examine (country etc.) by going through it —**explora'tion** n. —**explo'ratory** [-plo'-] a. —**explor'er** n.

explo'sion see EXPLODE

ex'po n. inf. exposition, large international exhibition

expo'nent see EXPOUND

export' vt. send (goods) out of the country —**ex'port** n./a. —**exporta'tion** n. —**export'er** n.

expose' [-ōz'] vt. exhibit; disclose, reveal; lay open (to); leave unprotected; expose photographic plate or film to light —**expo'sure** n.

expo'sé [-zā] n. newspaper article etc., disclosing scandal, crime etc.

exposi'tion see EXPOUND

expos'tulate vi. remonstrate; reason with (in a kindly manner) —**expostula'tion** n. —**expos'tulatory** a.

expound' vt. explain, interpret —**expo'nent** n. one who expounds or promotes (idea, cause etc.); performer, executant; Math. small, raised number showing the power of a factor —**exponen'tial** a. —**exposi'tion** n. explanation, description; exhibition of goods etc. —**expos'itor** n. one who explains, interpreter —**expos'itory** a. explanatory

express' vt. put into words; make known or understood by words, behaviour etc.; squeeze out —a. definitely stated; specially designed; clear; positive; speedy; of messenger, specially sent off; of train, fast and making few stops —adv. specially; on purpose; with speed —n. express train or messenger; rapid parcel delivery service —**express'ible** a. —**expression** n. expressing;

word, phrase; look, aspect; feeling; utterance —**express'ionism** n. theory that art depends on expression of artist's creative self, not on mere reproduction —**express'ive** a. —**express'ly** adv.

expro'priate vt. dispossess; take out of owner's hands —**expropria'tion** n. —**expro'priator** n.

expulsion see EXPEL

expunge' vt. strike out, erase —**expunc'tion** n.

ex'purgate vt. remove objectionable parts (from book etc.), purge —**expurga'tion** n. —**ex'purgator** n. —**expurg'atory** a.

exquis'ite [-kwiz'- or eks'-] a. of extreme beauty or delicacy; keen, acute; keenly sensitive —**exquis'itely** adv.

extant' a. still existing

extem'pore [-pə-ri] a./adv. without previous thought or preparation —**extempora'neous** a. —**extem'porary** a. —**extempora'tion** n. —**extem'porize** v. speak without preparation; devise for the occasion

extend' vt. stretch out, lengthen; prolong in duration; widen in area, scope; accord, grant —vi. reach; cover area; have range or scope; become larger or wider —**exten'dible, -dable, exten'sible** a. that can be extended —**exten'sion** n. stretching out, prolongation or enlargement; expansion; continuation, additional part, as of telephone etc. —**exten'sive** a. wide, large, comprehensive —**exten'sor** n. straightening muscle —**ex-tent'** n. space or degree to which thing is extended; size; compass; volume

exten'uate vt. make less blameworthy, lessen; mitigate

—**extenua'tion** n. —**exten'uatory** a.

exte'rior n. the outside; outward appearance —a. outer, outward, external

exterm'inate vt. destroy utterly, annihilate, root out, eliminate —**extermina'tion** n. —**exterm'inator** n. destroyer

extern'al a. outside, outward —**extern'ally** adv.

extinct' a. having died out or come to an end; no longer existing; quenched; no longer burning —**extinc'tion** n.

exting'uish [-ng'gw-] vt. put out, quench; wipe out —**extin'guishable** a. —**extin'guisher** n. device, esp. spraying liquid or foam, used to put out fires

ex'tirpate vt. root out, destroy utterly —**extirpa'tion** n. —**ex'tirpator** n.

extol' [-tōl'] vt. praise highly (-ll-)

extort' vt. get by force or threats; wring out; exact —**extor'tion** n. —**extor'tionate** a. of prices etc., excessive, exorbitant —**extor'tioner** n.

ex'tra a. additional; larger, better, than usual —adv. additionally; more than usually —n. extra thing; something charged as additional; Cricket run not scored off bat; Films actor hired for crowd scenes

extra- (comb. form) beyond, as in extradition, extramural, extra-territorial etc. Such words are not given here where the meaning may easily be inferred from the simple word

extract' vt. take out, esp. by force; obtain against person's will; get by pressure, distillation etc.; deduce, derive; copy out, quote —n. [eks'-] passage from book, film etc.; matter got by distillation; concentrated solution

—**extrac'tion** n. extracting, esp. of tooth; ancestry —**extract'or** n.

extradi'tion [-dish'-] n. delivery, under treaty, of foreign fugitive from justice to authorities concerned —**ex'tradite** vt. give or obtain such delivery —**extradi'table** a.

extramur'al [-myoor'-] a. connected with but outside normal courses etc. of university or college; situated outside walls or boundaries of a place

extra'neous a. not essential; irrelevant; added from without, not belonging

extraor'dinary [-trawd'-] a. out of the usual course; additional; unusual, surprising, exceptional —**extraord'inarily** adv.

extrap'olate vt. infer something not known from known facts; Maths. estimate a value beyond known values

extrasen'sory a. of perception apparently gained without use of known senses

extraterrest'rial a. of, or from outside the earth's atmosphere

extrav'agant a. wasteful; exorbitant; wild, absurd —**extrav'agance** n. —**extrav'agantly** adv. —**extravagan'za** n. elaborate, lavish, entertainment; display etc.

ex'travert see EXTROVERT

extreme' a. of high or highest degree; severe; going beyond moderation; at the end; outermost —n. utmost degree; thing at one end or the other, first and last of series —**extreme'ly** adv. —**extre'mist** n. advocate of extreme measures —**extrem'ity** n. end —pl. hands and feet; utmost distress; extreme measures

ex'tricate vt. disentangle, unravel, set free —**ex'tricable** a. —**extrica'tion** n.

extrin'sic a. accessory, not belonging, not intrinsic —**extrin'sically** adv.

ex'trovert n. one who is interested in other people and things rather than his own feelings —**extrover'sion** n.

extrude' vt. squeeze, force out; (esp. of molten metal or plastic etc.) shape by squeezing through suitable nozzle or die

exu'berant [ig-zyōō'-] a. highspirited, vivacious, prolific, abundant, luxurious —**exu'berance** n. —**exu'berantly** adv.

exude' [ig-zyōōd'] vi. ooze out —vt. give off (moisture) —**exuda'tion** n. —**exu'dative** a.

exult' [igz-] vi. rejoice, triumph —**exult'ancy** n. —**exult'ant** a. triumphant —**exulta'tion** n.

eye [ī] n. organ of sight; look, glance; attention; aperture; view; judgment; watch; vigilance; thing, mark resembling eye; slit in needle for thread —vt. look at; observe —**eye'less** a. —**eye'ball** n. ball of eye —**eye'brow** n. fringe of hair above eye —**eye'glass** n. glass to assist sight; monocle —**eye'lash** n. hair fringing eyelid —**eye'let** n. small hole for rope etc. to pass through —**eye'lid** n. lid or cover of eye —**eye'opener** n. surprising news; revealing statement —**eye shadow** coloured cosmetic put on around the eyes —**eye'sore** n. ugly object; thing that annoys one to see —**eye'tooth** n. canine tooth —**eye'wash** inf. n. deceptive talk etc., nonsense —**eye'witness** n. one who saw something for himself

ey'rie [er'-, īr'-] n. nest of bird of prey, esp. eagle; high dwelling place

F

F Fahrenheit; farad; Fellow; *Chem.* fluorine

f. feminine; folio; following; *Mus.* forte

fa *see* FAH

FA Football Association

fa'ble *n.* short story with moral, *esp.* one with animals as characters; tale; legend; fiction or lie —*vt.* invent, tell fables about —**fab'ulist** *n.* writer of fables —**fab'ulous** *a.* amazing; *inf.* extremely good; told of in fables; unhistorical

Fab'lon R adhesive-backed plastic material used to cover and decorate shelves *etc.*

fab'ric *n.* cloth; texture; frame, structure —**fab'ricate** *vt.* build; frame; construct; invent (lie *etc.*); forge (document) —**fabrica'tion** *n.* —**fab'ricator** *n.*

façade [fɔ-sahd'] *n.* front of building; *fig.* outward appearance

face [fās] *n.* front of head; distorted expression; outward appearance; front, upper surface, or chief side of anything; dial or clock *etc.*; dignity —*vt.* look or front towards; meet (boldly); give a covering surface —*vi.* turn —**fac'et** [fas'-] *n.* one side of many-sided body, *esp.* cut gem; one aspect —**fa'cial** [fā'shl] *a.* pert. to face —*n.* cosmetic treatment for face —**fa'cings** *pl.n.* lining for decoration or reinforcement, sewn on collar, cuff *etc.*; collar, cuffs *etc.* of uniform —**face'less** *a.* without a face; anonymous —**face-lifting** *n.* operation to tighten skin of face to remove wrinkles

face'tious [fɔ-sē'shɔs] *a.* (sarcastically) witty; humorous, given to jesting, *esp.* at inappropriate time

fa'cia [-sh-] *see* FASCIA

fac'ile [fas'-] *a.* easy; working easily; easy-going; superficial, silly —**facil'itate** [-sil'-] *vt.* make easy, help —**facilita'tion** *n.* —**facil'itator** *n.* —**facil'ity** *n.* easiness, dexterity —*pl.* opportunities, good conditions; means, equipment for doing something

facsim'ile [fak-sim'i-li] *n.* an exact copy

fact *n.* thing known to be true; deed; reality —**fac'tual** *a.*

fac'tion[1] *n.* (dissenting) minority group within larger body; dissension —**fac'tious** *a.* of or producing factions

fac'tion[2] *n.* novel, film or TV programme presenting dramatized version of actual events

facti'tious [-ish'-] *a.* artificial; specially made up; unreal

fac'tor *n.* something contributing to a result; one of numbers which multiplied together give a given number; agent, dealer —**facto'tum** *n.* man-of-all-work —**factor 8** protein that participates in clotting of blood

fac'tory *n.* building where things are manufactured

fac'ulty *n.* inherent power; power of the mind; ability, aptitude; department of university; members of profession; authorization —**fac'ultative** *a.* optional, contingent

fad *n.* short-lived fashion; whim —**fadd'ish** *a.* —**fadd'ism** *n.* —**fadd'ist** *n.* —**fadd'y** *a.*

fade *vi.* lose colour, strength; wither; grow dim; disappear gradually —*vt.* cause to fade —**fade'less** *a.* —**fade-in, -out** *n. Radio* variation in strength of signals; *TV, Cinema* gradual appearance and disappearance of picture

fae'ces [fe'sēz] pl.n. excrement, waste matter —**fae'cal** [fē'kəl] a.

fag n. inf. boring task; sl. cigarette; US sl. homosexual (abbrev. of FAGGOT) —v. inf. (esp. with out) tire; do menial tasks for a senior boy in school (-**gg**-) —**fag end** last part, inferior remnant

fagg'ot n. bundle of sticks for fuel etc.; ball of chopped liver etc.; US sl. male homosexual

fah, fa n. fourth sol-fa note

Fah'renheit [fa'rən-hīt] a. measured by thermometric scale with freezing point of water 32°, boiling point 212°

faïence' [fī-ahns'] n. glazed earthenware or china

fail vi. be unsuccessful; stop operating or working; be below the required standard; be insufficient; run short; be wanting when in need; lose power; die away; become bankrupt —vt. disappoint, give no help to; neglect, forget to do; judge (candidate) to be below required standard —**fail'ing** n. deficiency; fault —prep. in default of —**fail'ure** n. —**fail-safe** a. of device ensuring safety or remedy of malfunction in machine, weapon etc. —**without fail** in spite of every difficulty; certainly

fain obs. a. glad, willing, constrained to —adv. gladly

faint a. feeble, dim, pale; weak; dizzy, about to lose consciousness —vi. lose consciousness temporarily

fair [1] a. just, impartial; according to rules, legitimate; blond; beautiful; ample; of moderate quality or amount; unblemished; plausible; middling; (of weather) favourable —adv. honestly —**fair'ing** n. Aviation streamline casing, or any part so shaped that it provides streamline form —**fair'ish** a. —**fair'ly** adv. —**fair'ness** n. Golf trimmed turf between rough

fair [2] n. navigable channel; **fair'way** n. navigable channel; Golf trimmed turf between rough

fair [3] n. travelling entertainment with sideshows, amusements etc.; large exhibition of commercial or industrial products; periodical market often with amusements —**fair'ground** n.

fair'y n. imaginary small creature with powers of magic; sl. male homosexual —a. of fairies; like fairy, beautiful and delicate, imaginary —**fairy lamp** small coloured lamp for decorations —**fair'yland** n. —**fairy ring** circle of darker colour in grass —**fairy-tale** a. of or like fairy tale —**fairy tale** story of imaginary beings and happenings, esp. as told to children

fait accom'pli [fe-ta-kon'plē] Fr. something already done that cannot be altered

faith n. trust; belief; belief without proof; religion; promise; loyalty, constancy —**faith'ful** a. constant, true —**faith'fully** adv. —**faith'less** a.

fake vt. conceal defects of by artifice; touch up; counterfeit —n. fraudulent object, person, act —a. —**fa'ker** n. one who deals in fakes; swindler

fa'kir n. member of Islamic religious order; Hindu ascetic

fal'chion [fawl'chən] n. a broad curved medieval sword

fal'con [fawl'-, faw'-] n. small bird of prey, esp. trained in hawking for sport —**fal'coner** n. one who keeps, trains, or hunts with, falcons —**fal'conry** n. hawking

fall [fawl] vi. drop, come down freely; become lower; decrease; hang down; come to the ground, cease to stand; perish; collapse; be captured; revert; lapse; be uttered; become; happen (**fell** pt., **fall'en** pp.) —n. falling; amount that falls; amount of descent; decrease; collapse; ruin; drop; (oft. pl.) cascade; cadence; decline to temptation; **US** autumn; rope of hoisting tackle —**fall'out** n. radioactive particles spread as result of nuclear explosion —**fall for** inf. fall in love with; inf. be taken in by

fall'acy [fal'-] n. incorrect, misleading opinion or argument; flaw in logic; illusion —**falla'cious** a. —**fallibil'ity** n. —**fal'lible** a. liable to error —**fall'ibly** adv.

fall'en pp. of FALL

Fallo'pian tube either of a pair of tubes through which egg cells pass from ovary to womb

fall'ow[1] [fal'ō] a. ploughed and harrowed but left without crop; uncultivated; neglected

fall'ow[2] a. brown or reddish yellow —**fallow deer** deer of this colour

false [-aw-] a. wrong, erroneous; deceptive; faithless; sham, artificial —**false'ly** adv. —**false'ness** n. faithlessness —**falsifica'tion** n. —**fal'sify** vt. alter fraudulently; misrepresent; disappoint (hopes etc.) (**fal'sified, fal'sifying**) —**fal'sity** n. —**false'hood** n. lie

falsett'o n. forced voice above natural range (pl. **-os**)

Falstaff'ian [fawl-stahf'-] a. like Shakespeare's Falstaff; fat; convivial; boasting

fal'ter [-aw-] vi. hesitate; waver; stumble —**fal'teringly** adv.

fame n. reputation; renown —**famed** a. —**fa'mous** a. widely known; excellent

famil'iar a. well-known; frequent; customary; intimate; closely acquainted; unceremonious; impertinent, too friendly —n. familiar friend; familiar demon —**familiar'ity** n. —**familiariza'tion** n. —**famil'iarize** vt. —**famil'iarly** adv.

fam'ily n. group of parents and children, or near relatives; person's children; all descendants of common ancestor; household; group of allied objects —**famil'ial** a.

fam'ine [-in] n. extreme scarcity of food; starvation —**fam'ish** vi. be very hungry

fa'mous see FAME

fan[1] n. instrument for producing current of air, esp. for ventilating or cooling; folding object of paper etc., used, esp. formerly, for cooling the face; outspread feathers of a bird's tail —vt. blow or cool with fan —v. spread out like fan (**-nn-**) —**fan'light** n. (fan-shaped) window over door

fan[2] inf. devoted admirer; an enthusiast, particularly for sport etc.

Fan'agalo n. SA pidgin language of Zulu, English and Afrikaans

fanat'ic a. filled with abnormal enthusiasm, esp. in religion —n. fanatic person —**fanat'ical** a. —**fanat'ically** adv. —**fanat'icism** n. —**fanat'icize** v.

fan'cy a. ornamental, not plain; of whimsical or arbitrary kind —n. whim, caprice; liking, inclination; imagination; mental image —vt. imagine; be inclined to believe; inf. have a liking for (**fan'cied, fan'cying**) —**fan'cier** n. one with liking and expert knowledge (respecting some specific thing) —**fan'ciful** a. —**fan'cifully** adv.

fandan'go n. lively Spanish dance with castanets; music for this dance (pl. **-goes**)

fan'fare n. a flourish of trumpets or bugles; ostentatious display

fang n. snake's poison tooth; long, pointed tooth

fan'tail n. kind of bird (*esp.* pigeon) with fan-shaped tail

fan'tasy n. power of imagination, *esp.* extravagant; mental image; fanciful invention or design —**fanta'sia** [-z-] n. fanciful musical composition —**fan'tasize** v. —**fantas'tic** a. quaint, grotesque, extremely fanciful; wild; *inf.* very good; *inf.* very large —**fantas'tically** adv.

far adv. at or to a great distance, or advanced point; at or to a remote time; by very much (**far'ther**, **fur'ther** comp., **far'thest**, **fur'thest** sup.) —a. distant; more distant —**far-fetched** a. incredible —**Far North** Arctic and sub-Arctic regions

far'ad [fa'rəd] n. unit of electrical capacity —**farada'ic** a.

farce n. comedy of boisterous humour; absurd and futile proceeding —**far'cical** a. ludicrous —**far'cically** adv.

fare n. charge for passenger's transport; passenger; food —vi. get on; happen; travel, progress —**farewell'** interj. goodbye —n. leave-taking

farina'ceous a. mealy, starchy

farm n. tract of land for cultivation or rearing livestock; unit of land, water, for growing or rearing a particular crop, animal etc. —v. cultivate (land); rear livestock (on farm) —**farm'er** n. —**farm'house** n. —**farm'stead** [-sted] n. —**farm'yard** n. —**farm out** send (work) to be done by others; put into care of others

fa'ro n. card game

farrag'o [-rahg'-] n. medley, hotchpotch (pl. **-gos**)

farr'ier n. one who shoes, cares for, horses —**farr'iery** n. his art

farr'ow n. litter of pigs —v. produce this

fart vulg. n. (audible) emission of gas from anus —vi.

far'ther [-TH-] adv./a. further; comp. of FAR —**far'thest** adv./a. furthest; sup. of FAR

far'thing [-TH-] n. formerly, coin worth a quarter of a penny

far'thingale [-TH-] n. Hist. hoop worn under skirts

fas'ces [fas'ēz] pl.n. bundle of rods bound together round axe, forming Roman badge of authority; emblem of Italian fascists

fas'cia, fa'cia [-sh-] n. flat surface above shop window; *Architecture* long flat surface between mouldings under eaves; face of wood or stone in a building; dashboard (pl. **fa'(s)-ciae** [-ē])

fas'cinate vt. attract and delight by rousing interest and curiosity; render motionless, as with a fixed stare —**fascina'tion** n.

fas'cism [-sh'-] n. authoritarian political system opposed to democracy and liberalism; behaviour (*esp.* by those in authority) supposedly typical of this system —**fas'cist** a./n.

fash'ion n. (latest) style, *esp.* of dress *etc.*; manner, mode; form, type —vt. shape, make —**fash'ionable** a. —**fash'ionably** adv.

fast¹ [-ah-] a. (capable of) moving quickly; permitting, providing, rapid progress; ahead of true time; *obs.* dissipated; firm, steady; permanent —adv. rapidly; tightly —**fast'ness** n. fast state; fortress, stronghold —**fast'back** n. car with back forming continuous slope from roof to rear —**fast food** food, *esp.* hamburgers, etc., prepared and served very quickly

fast² [-ah-] vi. go without food, or

some kinds of food —*n.* —**fast'-ing** *n.*

fast'en [fahs'n] *vt.* attach, fix, secure —*vi.* become joined; seize (upon)

fastid'ious *a.* hard to please; discriminating; particular

fat *n.* oily animal substance; fat part —*a.* having too much fat; containing fat, greasy; profitable; fertile (**fatt'er** *comp.*, **fatt'est** *sup.*) —*vt.* feed (animals) for slaughter (**-tt-**) —**fat'ness** *n.* —**fatt'en** *v.* —**fatt'y** *a.* —**fat'head** *n. inf.* dolt, idiot

fate *n.* power supposed to predetermine events; goddess of destiny; destiny; person's appointed lot or condition; death or destruction —*vt.* preordain —**fa'tal** *a.* deadly, ending in death; destructive; disastrous; inevitable —**fa'talism** *n.* belief that everything is predetermined; submission to fate —**fa'talist** *n.* —**fatalis'tic** *a.* —**fatalis'tically** *adv.* —**fatal'ity** *n.* accident resulting in death; person killed in war, accident **fa'tally** *adv.* —**fate'ful** *a.* fraught with destiny; prophetic

fath'er [fahTH'-] *n.* male parent; forefather, ancestor; (**F-**) God; originator, early leader; priest, confessor; oldest member of a society —*vt.* beget; originate; pass as father or author of; act as father to —**fath'erhood** *n.* —**fa'therless** *a.* —**fath'erly** *a.* —**father-in-law** *n.* husband's or wife's father

fath'om [faTH'-] *n.* measure of six feet of water —*vt.* sound (water); get to bottom of, understand —**fath'omable** *a.* —**fath'omless** *a.* too deep to fathom

fatigue' [-têg'] *n.* weariness; toil; weakness of metals *etc.*, subjected to stress; soldier's nonmilitary duty —*vt.* weary

fat'uous *a.* very silly, idiotic —**fatu'ity** *n.*

fau'cet [faw'sit] *n.* US tap

fault *n.* defect; flaw; misdeed; blame, culpability; blunder; mistake; *Tennis* ball wrongly served; *Geology* break in strata —*v.* find fault in; (cause to) undergo or commit fault —**fault'ily** *adv.* —**fault'less** *a.* —**fault'lessly** *adv.* —**faulty** *a.*

faun *n.* mythological woodland being with tail and horns

fau'na *n.* animals of region or period collectively (*pl.* **s, ae** [-ē])

faux pas' [fō-pah'] *n.* social blunder or indiscretion

fa'vour [-vər] *n.* goodwill; approval; especial kindness; partiality; badge or knot of ribbons —*vt.* regard or treat with favour; oblige; treat with partiality; aid; support; resemble —**fa'vourable** *a.* —**fa'vourably** *adv.* —**fa'vourite** [-it] *n.* favoured person or thing; horse *etc.* expected to win race —*a.* chosen, preferred —**fa'vouritism** *n* practice of showing undue preference

fawn[1] *n.* young deer —*a.* light yellowish brown

fawn[2] *vi.* of person, cringe, court favour servilely; *esp.* of dog, show affection by wagging tail and grovelling

FBI US Federal Bureau of Investigation

FC Football Club

FD Fidei Defensor

Fe *Chem.* iron

fe'alty *n.* fidelity of vassal to his lord; loyalty

fear *n.* dread, alarm, anxiety, unpleasant emotion caused by coming evil or danger —*vi.* have this feeling, be afraid —*vt.* regard with fear; hesitate, shrink from, revere —**fear'ful** *a.* —**fear'fully** *adv.* —**fear'less** *a.*

intrepid —**fear'lessly** adv. —**fear'some** a.

fea'sible [-z-] a. able to be done; likely —**feasibil'ity** n. —**fea'sibly** adv.

feast n. banquet, lavish meal; religious anniversary; something very pleasant, sumptuous —vi. partake of banquet, fare sumptuously —vt. regale with feast; provide delight for —**feast'er** n.

feat n. notable deed; surprising or striking trick

feath'er [feTH'-] n. one of the barbed shafts which form covering of birds; anything resembling this —vt. provide, line with feathers —vi. grow feathers —v. turn (oar) edgeways —**feath'ery** a. —**feath'erweight** n. very light person or thing —**feather one's nest** enrich oneself —**the white feather** cowardice

fea'ture n. (usu. pl.) part of face; characteristic; notable part of anything; main or special item —vt. portray; Cinema present in leading role in a film; give prominence to —vi. be prominent (in) —**fea'tureless** a. without striking features

Feb. February

fe'brile a. of fever

Feb'ruary n. second month of year (normally containing 28 days; in leap year, 29)

feck'less a. spiritless, weak, irresponsible

fec'ulent a. full of sediment, turbid —**fec'ulence** n.

fe'cund [or fek'-] a. fertile, fruitful, fertilizing —**fe'cundate** vt. fertilize, impregnate —**fecunda'tion** n. —**fecund'ity** [fi-] n.

fed pt./pp. of FEED —**fed up** bored, dissatisfied

fed'eral a. of, or like, the government of states which are united but retain internal independence —**fed'eralism** n.

—**fed'eralist** n. —**fed'erate** v. form into, become, a federation —**federa'tion** n. league; federal union

fee n. payment for professional and other services

fee'ble a. weak; lacking strength or effectiveness; insipid —**fee'bly** adv.

feed vt. give food to; supply, support —vi. take food (**fed** pt./pp.) —n. feeding; fodder, pasturage; allowance of fodder; material supplied to machine; part of machine taking in material —**feed'er** n. one who or that which feeds; child's bib —**feed'back** n. return of part of output of electrical circuit or loudspeakers; information received in response to enquiry etc. —**feed'lot** n. area, building where cattle are fattened for market

feel v. perceive, examine by touch; experience; proceed, find (one's way) cautiously; be sensitive to; show emotion (for); believe, consider (**felt** pt./pp.) —n. act or instance of feeling; quality or impression of something perceived by feeling; sense of touch —**feel'er** n. special organ of touch in some animals; proposal put forward to test others' opinion; that which feels —**feel'ing** n. sense of touch; ability to feel; physical sensation; emotion; sympathy, tenderness; conviction or opinion not solely based on reason —pl. susceptibilities —a. sensitive, sympathetic, heartfelt —**feel like** have an inclination for

feet see FOOT

feign [fān] v. pretend, sham

feint [fānt] n. sham attack or blow meant to deceive opponent; semblance, pretence —vi. make feint

felic'ity [-is'-] n. great happiness, bliss; appropriateness of wording —**felic'itate** vt. congratulate —**felicita'tion** n. (usu. in pl.) —**felic'itous** a. apt, well-chosen; happy

fe'line a. of cats; catlike —**felin'ity** n.

fell[1] pt. of FALL

fell[2] vt. knock down; cut down (tree) —**fell'er** n.

fell[3] a. obs. fierce, terrible

fell[4] n. skin or hide with hair

fell[5] n. mountain, stretch of moorland, esp. in N of England

fell'oe [-ō], **fell'y** n. outer part (or section) of wheel

fell'ow n. inf. man, boy; person; comrade, associate; counterpart; like thing; member of (society, college etc.) —a. of the same class, associated —**fell'owship** n. fraternity; friendship; (in university etc.) research post or special scholarship

fel'on n. one guilty of felony —**felo'nious** a. —**fel'ony** n. serious crime

fel(d)'spar n. crystalline mineral found in granite etc. —**fel(d)spath'ic** a.

felt[1] pt./pp. of FEEL

felt[2] n. soft, matted fabric made by bonding fibres chemically and by pressure; thing made of this —vt. make into, or cover with, felt —vi. become matted like felt —**felt-tip pen** pen with writing point made from pressed fibres

fem. feminine

fe'male a. of sex which bears offspring; relating to this sex —n. one of this sex

fem'inine [-in] a. of women; womanly; class or type of grammatical inflection in some languages —**fem'inism** n. advocacy of equal rights for women —**fem'inist** n./a. —**feminin'ity** n.

fem'oral a. of the thigh

fe'mur [fē'mə] n. thigh-bone

fen n. tract of marshy land, swamp —**fenn'y** a.

fence n. structure of wire, wood etc. enclosing an area; (machinery) guard, guide; sl. dealer in stolen property —v. erect fence; enclose; fight (as sport) with swords; avoid question etc.; sl. deal in stolen property —**fen'cing** n. art of swordplay

fend vt. ward off, repel —vi. provide (for oneself etc.) —**fend'er** n. low metal frame in front of fireplace; name for various protective devices; frame; edge; buffer; US mudguard of car

fenestra'tion n. arrangement of windows in a building

fenn'el n. yellow-flowered fragrant herb

fe'ral[1] a. wild, uncultivated

fe'ral[2] a. obs. funereal, gloomy

fe'ria n. Eccles. ordinary week-day, not festival or fast day

fer'ment n. leaven, substance causing thing to ferment; excitement, tumult —v. [-ment'] (cause to) undergo chemical change with effervescence, liberation of heat and alteration of properties, eg process set up in dough by yeast; (cause to) become excited —**fermenta'tion** n.

fern n. plant with feathery fronds —**fern'ery** n. place for growing ferns —**fern'y** a. full of ferns

fero'cious [-shəs] a. fierce, savage, cruel —**feroc'ity** n.

ferr'et n. tamed animal like weasel, used to catch rabbits, rats etc. —vt. drive our with ferrets; search out —vi. search about, rummage

ferr'ic, ferr'(e)ous a. pert. to, containing, iron —**ferrif'erous** a. yielding iron —**ferru'ginous** [-ŏŏ'-] a. containing iron; reddish-brown —**ferrocon'crete**

n. concrete strengthened by framework of metal

ferr'is wheel in fairground, large, vertical wheel with seats for riding

ferr'ule *n.* metal cap to strengthen end of stick *etc.*

ferr'y *n.* boat *etc.* for transporting people, vehicles, across body of water, *esp.* as repeated or regular service; place for ferrying —*v.* carry, travel, by ferry (**ferr'ied, ferr'ying**) —**ferr'yman** *n.*

fer'tile *a.* (capable of) producing offspring, bearing crops *etc.*; fruitful, producing abundantly; inventive —**fertil'ity** *n.* —**fertiliza'tion** *n.* —**fer'tilize** *vt.* make fertile —**fer'tilizer** *n.*

fer'vent, fer'vid *a.* ardent, vehement, intense —**fer'vency** *n.* —**fer'vently** *adv.* —**fer'vour** [-vər] *n.*

fes'cue *n.* grass used as pasture, with stiff narrow leaves

fes'tal *a.* of feast or holiday; merry, gay —**fes'tally** *adv.*

fes'ter *v.* (cause to) form pus —*vi.* rankle; become embittered

fes'tival *n.* day, period, set aside for celebration, *esp.* of religious feast; organized series of events, performances *etc.* usu. in one place —**fes'tive** *a.* joyous, merry; of feast —**festiv'ity** *n.* gaiety, mirth; rejoicing —*pl.* festive proceedings

festoon' *n.* chain of flowers, ribbons *etc.* hung in curve between two points —*vt.* form, adorn with festoons

fetch *vt.* go and bring; draw forth; be sold for; attract —*n.* trick —**fetch'ing** *a.* attractive —**fetch up** *inf.* arrive at; run onto, into

fete, fête [fāt] *n.* gala, bazaar *etc.*, *esp.* one held out of doors; festival, holiday; celebration —*vt.*

feast; honour with festive entertainment

fet'id, foet'id [-ē-] *a.* stinking

fet'ish *n.* (inanimate) object believed to have magical powers; excessive attention to something; object, activity, to which excessive devotion is paid

fet'lock *n.* projection behind and above horse's hoof, or tuft of hair on this

fett'er *n.* chain or shackle for feet; check, restraint —*pl.* captivity —*vt.* chain up; restrain, hamper

fet'tle *n.* condition, state of health

fe'tus *see* FOETUS

feu [fyōō] *n.* in Scotland, tenure of land in return for fixed annual payment

feud [fyōōd] *n.* bitter, lasting, mutual hostility, *esp.* between two families or tribes; vendetta —*vi.* carry on feud

feu'dal [fyōō-] *a.* of, like, medieval social and economic system based on holding land from superior in return for service; *inf.* very old-fashioned —**feu'dalism** *n.*

fe'ver *n.* condition of illness with high body temperature; intense nervous excitement —**fe'vered** *a.* —**fe'verish** *a.* having fever; accompanied by, caused by, fever; in a state of restless excitement —**fe'verishly** *adv.* —**fever pitch** very fast pace; intense excitement

few *a.* not many —*n.* small number —**good few, quite a few** several

fey [fā] *a.* clairvoyant, visionary; *esp.* Scottish, fated to die

fez *n.* red, brimless, orig. Turkish tasselled cap (*pl.* **fezz'es**)

ff *Mus.* fortissimo

ff. folios; following

fian'cé [-on'sā] *n.* man engaged

to be married (**fian'cée** *fem.*)

fias'co *n.* breakdown, total failure (*pl.* **-co(e)s**)

fi'at *n.* decree; official permission

fib *n.* trivial lie, falsehood —*vt.* tell fib (**-bb-**) —**fibb'er** *n.*

fi'bre *n.* filament forming part of animal or plant tissue; substance that can be spun (*eg* wool, cotton) —**fibrosi'tis** *n.* inflammation of tissues of muscle sheaths —**fi'brous** *a.* made of fibre —**fi'breboard** *n.* building material of compressed plant fibres —**fi'breglass** *n.* material made of fine glass fibres —**fibre optics** *pl.n.* (*with sing. v.*) use of bundles of long transparent glass fibres in transmitting light

fib'rin *n.* insoluble protein in blood, causing coagulation

fib'ula *n.* slender outer bone of lower leg —**fib'ular** *a.*

fic'kle *a.* changeable, inconstant —**fic'kleness** *n.*

fic'tion *n.* prose, literary works of the imagination; invented statement or story —**fic'tional** *a.* —**ficti'tious** *a.* not genuine, false; imaginary; assumed

fid'dle *n.* violin; triviality; *inf.* illegal, fraudulent arrangement —*vi.* play fiddle; make idle movements, fidget, trifle —*v. sl.* cheat, contrive —**fidd'ling** *a.* trivial —**fid'dly** *a.* small, awkward to handle —**fid'dlesticks** *interj.* nonsense

fi'dei defen'sor [fī'di-] *Lat.* defender of the faith

fidel'ity *n.* faithfulness; quality of sound reproduction

fidg'et *vi.* move restlessly; be uneasy —*n.* (*oft. pl.*) nervous restlessness, restless mood; one who fidgets —**fidg'ety** *a.*

fidu'ciary [-sh-] *a.* held, given in trust; relating to trustee —*n.* trustee

fief [fēf] *n. Hist.* land held of a superior in return for service

field *n.* area of (farming) land; enclosed piece of ground; tract of land rich in specified product (*eg goldfield*); players in a game or sport collectively; all competitors but the favourite; battlefield; area over which electric, gravitational, magnetic force can be exerted; surface of shield, coin *etc.*; sphere of knowledge; range, area of operation —*v. Cricket etc.*, stop and return ball; send player, team, on to sportsfield —**field'er** *n.* —**field day** day of manoeuvres, outdoor activities; important occasion —**field events** throwing and jumping events in athletics —**field'fare** *n.* type of thrush with pale grey head and rump —**field glasses** binoculars —**field hockey** US, C hockey played on field, as distinct from ice hockey —**field marshal** army officer of highest rank —**field'work** *n.* research, practical work, conducted away from the classroom, laboratory *etc.* —**field of view** area covered in telescope, camera *etc.*

fiend *n.* demon, devil; wicked person; person very fond of or addicted to something *eg* **fresh-air fiend, drug fiend** —**fiend'ish** *a.* wicked, difficult, unpleasant

fierce *a.* savage, wild, violent; rough; severe; intense —**fierce'ly** *adv.* —**fierce'ness** *n.*

fi'ery *a.* consisting of fire; blazing, glowing, flashing; irritable; spirited (**fi'erier** *comp.*, **fi'eriest** *sup.*) —**fi'erily** *adv.*

fies'ta *n.* (religious) celebration, carnival

fife *n.* high-pitched flute —*v.* play on fife —**fif'er** *n.*

fif'teen, fifth, fif'ty *see* FIVE

fig *n.* soft, pear shaped fruit; tree bearing it —**full fig** full dress

fight [fɪt] v. contend with in battle or in single combat; maintain against opponent; settle by combat (**fought** pt./pp.) —n. —**fight'er** n. one who fights; Mil. aircraft designed for destroying other aircraft —a.

fig'ment n. invention, purely imaginary thing

fig'ure [-ər] n. numerical symbol; amount, number; form, shape; bodily shape; appearance, esp. conspicuous appearance; space enclosed by lines, or surfaces; diagram, illustration; likeness; image; pattern, movement in dancing, skating, etc.; abnormal form of expression for effect in speech, eg metaphor —v.t. calculate, estimate; represent by picture or diagram; ornament —v.i. (oft. with in) show, appear, be conspicuous, be included —**figurative** a. metaphorical; full of figures of speech —**fig'uratively** adv. —**figurine'** [-ēn'] n. statuette —**figurehead** n. nominal leader; ornamental figure under bowsprit of ship

fil'ament n. fine wire in electric light bulb and radio valve which is heated by electric current; threadlike body

filch v.t. steal, pilfer

file[1] n. box, folder, clip etc. holding papers for reference; papers so kept; information about specific person, subject; orderly line, as of soldiers, one behind the other —v.t. arrange (papers etc.) and put them away for reference; Law place on records of a court; bring suit in lawcourt —v.i. march in file —**fi'ling** n. —**single** (or **Indian**) **file** single line of people one behind the other

file[2] n. roughened tool for smoothing or shaping —v.t. apply file to, smooth, polish —**fi'ling** n.

action of using file; scrap of metal removed by file

fil'ial a. of, befitting, son or daughter —**fil'ially** adv.

fil'ibuster n. US process of obstructing legislation by using delaying tactics —v.i.

fil'igree n. fine tracery or openwork of metal, usu. gold or silver wire

fill v.t. make full; occupy completely; hold, discharge duties of; stop up; satisfy; fulfil —v.i. become full —n. full supply; as much as desired; soil etc., to bring area of ground up to required level —**fill'ing** n. —**filling station** garage selling oil, petrol etc. —**fill the bill** inf. supply all that is wanted

fill'et n. boneless slice of meat, fish; narrow strip —v.t. cut into fillets, bone —**fill'eted** a.

fill'ip n. stimulus; sudden release of finger bent against thumb; snap so produced —v.t. stimulate; give fillip to

fill'y n. female horse under four years old

film n. sequence of images projected on screen, creating illusion of movement; story etc. presented thus, and shown in cinema or on television; sensitized celluloid roll used in photography, cinematography; thin skin or layer; dimness on eyes; slight haze —a. connected with cinema —v.t. photograph with cine camera; make cine film of (scene, story etc.) —v. cover, become covered, with film —**film'y** a. membraneous; gauzy —**film star** popular cinema actor or actress

fil'ter n. cloth or other material, or a device, permitting fluid to pass but retaining solid particles; anything performing similar function —v. act as filter, or as if passing through filter —v.i. pass slowly (through) —**fil'trate** n. filtered gas or liquid

filth [-th] n. disgusting dirt; pollution; obscenity —**filth'ily** adv. —**filth'iness** n. —**filth'y** a. unclean; foul

fin n. propelling or steering organ of fish; anything like this, eg stabilizing plane of aeroplane

fi'nal a. at the end; conclusive —n. game, heat, examination etc., coming at end of series —**final'e** [fi-nahl'i] n. closing part of musical composition, opera etc.; termination —**final'ity** n. —**fi'nalize** v. —**fi'nally** adv.

finance' [fi-, fī-, or fī'-] n. management of money; money resources (also pl.) —vt. find capital for —**finan'cial** a. of finance —**finan'cially** adv. —**finan'cier** n.

finch n. one of family of small singing birds

find [fī-] vt. come across; light upon; obtain; recognize; experience, discover; discover by searching; ascertain; supply (as funds); Law give a verdict (**found** pt./pp.) —n. finding; (valuable) thing found —**find'er** n. —**find'ing** n. judicial verdict

fine[1] a. choice, of high quality; delicate, subtle; pure; in small particles; slender; excellent; handsome; showy; inf. healthy, at ease, comfortable; free from rain —vt. make clear or pure; refine; thin —**fine'ly** adv. —**fine'ness** n. —**fi'nery** n. showy dress —**finesse'** [fin-] n. elegant, skilful management —**fine art** art produced for its aesthetic value —**fine-tune** vt. to make fine adjustments for optimum performance

fine[2] n. sum fixed as penalty —vt. punish by fine —**in fine** in conclusion; in brief

fin'ger [-ng'g-] n. one of the jointed branches of the hand; various things like this —vt. touch or handle with fingers —**fin'gering** n. manner or act of touching; choice of fingers, as in playing musical instrument; indication of this —**fin'gerboard** n. part of musical instrument on which fingers are placed —**fin'gerprint** n. impression of tip of finger, esp. as used for identifying criminals —**fin'gerstall** n. cover to protect finger

fi'nial n. Architecture ornament at apex of gables, spires etc.

fin'icking, fin'icky a. fastidious, fussy; too fine

fin'is Lat. end, esp. of book

fin'ish v. (mainly tr.) bring, come to an end, conclude; complete; perfect; kill —n. end; way in which thing is finished, as an oak finish, of furniture; final appearance —**fin'isher** n.

fi'nite a. bounded, limited

fiord see FJORD

fir n. kind of coniferous resinous tree; its wood

fire n. state of burning, combustion, flame, glow; mass of burning fuel; destructive burning, conflagration; device for heating a room etc.; ardour, keenness, spirit; shooting of firearms —vt. discharge (firearm); propel from firearm; inf. dismiss from employment; bake; make burn; supply with fuel; inspire; explode —vi. discharge firearm; begin to burn; become excited —**fire'arm** n. gun, rifle, pistol etc. —**fire'brand** n. burning piece of wood; energetic (troublesome) person —**fire'break** n. strip of cleared land to arrest progress of bush or grass fire —**fire brigade** organized body of men and appliances to put out fires and rescue those in danger —**fire'bug** n. inf. person who intentionally sets fire to buildings *etc.* —**fire'crest** *n.* small European warbler —**fire'-damp** *n.* explosive hydrocarbon gas forming in mines —**fire drill** rehearsal of procedures for escape from fire —**fire engine** vehicle with apparatus for extinguishing fires —**fire escape** means, *esp.* stairs, for escaping from burning buildings —**fire'fly** *n.* insect giving off phosphorescent glow —**fire'guard, fire screen** protective grating in front of fire —**fire irons** tongs, poker and shovel —**fire'man** *n.* member of fire brigade; stoker; assistant to locomotive driver —**fire'place** *n.* recess in room for fire —**fire ship** burning vessel sent drifting against enemy ships —**fire station** building housing fire brigade —**fire'work** *n.* (*oft.* *pl.*) device to give spectacular effects by explosions and coloured sparks —*pl.* outburst of temper, anger —**firing party, firing squad** detachment sent to fire volleys at military funeral, or to shoot criminal

fir'kin *n.* small cask; *UK* measure of 9 gallons

firm *a.* solid, fixed, stable; steadfast; resolute; settled —*v.* make, become firm —*n.* commercial enterprise; partnership

firm'ament *n.* expanse of sky, heavens

first *a.* earliest in time or order; foremost in rank or position; most excellent; highest, chief —*n.* beginning; first occurrence of something; first-class honours degree at university —*adv.* before others in time, order *etc.* —**first'ly** *adv.* —**first aid** first help given to injured person before arrival of doctor —**first-hand** *a.* obtained directly from the first source —**first mate, first officer** officer of merchant vessel immediately below captain —**first-rate** *a.* of highest class or quality —**first-strike** *a.* (of a nuclear missile) for use in an opening attack to destroy enemy nuclear weapons

firth, frith *n.* (*esp.* in Scotland) arm of the sea, river estuary

fis'cal *a.* of government finances

fish *n.* vertebrate cold-blooded animal with gills, living in water; its flesh as food (*pl.* **fish, fish'es**) —*v.* (attempt to) catch fish; search (for); try to get information indirectly —**fish'er** *n.* —**fish'ery** *n.* business of fishing; fishing ground —**fish'y** *a.* of, like, or full of fish; dubious, open to suspicion; unsafe —**fish'erman** *n.* one who catches fish for a living or for pleasure —**fish'fin'ger** *n.* small piece of fish covered in breadcrumbs —**fish'monger** [-mung-] *n.* seller of fish —**fish'wife** *n.* coarse, scolding woman

fish'plate *n.* piece of metal holding rails together

fiss'ure [-sh'-] *n.* cleft, split, cleavage —**fiss'ile** [fis'-] *a.* capable of splitting; tending to split —**fiss'ion** *n.* splitting; reproduction by division of living cells with two parts, each of which becomes complete organism; splitting of atomic nucleus with release of large amount of energy —**fiss'ionable** *a.* capable of undergoing nuclear fission —**fiss'iparous** *a.* reproducing by fission

fist *n.* clenched hand —**fist'i-cuffs** *pl.n.* fighting

fist'ula *n.* pipelike ulcer (*pl.* **-las, -lae** [-lē])

fit *vt.* be suited to; be properly adjusted to; arrange, adjust, apply, insert; supply, furnish —*vi.* be correctly adjusted or adapted; be of right size (**-tt-**) —*a.* well-suited, worthy; qualified; proper, becoming; ready; in good condition or health (**fitt'er** *comp.*, **fitt'est** *sup.*) —*n.* way something fits, its style; adjustment —**fit'ly** *adv.* —**fit'ment** *n.* piece of furniture —**fit'ness** *n.* —**fitt'er** *n.* one who, that which, makes fit; one who supervises making and fitting of garments; mechanic skilled in fitting up metal work —**fitt'ing** *a.* appropriate, suitable; proper —*n.* fixture; apparatus; action of fitting

fit[2] *n.* seizure with convulsions, spasms, loss of consciousness *etc.*, as of epilepsy, hysteria *etc.*; sudden passing attack of illness; passing state, mood —**fit'ful** *a.* spasmodic, capricious —**fit'fully** *adv.*

five *a./n.* cardinal number after four —**fifth** *a./n.* ordinal number —**fifth'ly** *adv.* —**fives** *pl.n.* (with *sing. v.*) ball game played with hand or bat in a court —**fif'teen** *a./n.* ten plus five —**fif'teenth** *a./n.* —**fif'tieth** *a./n.* —**fif'ty** *a./n.* five tens —**fifth column** organization spying for enemy within country at war —**five-a-side** *n.* football with teams of five

fix *vt.* fasten, make firm or stable; set, establish; appoint, assign, determine; make fast; repair; *inf.* influence the outcome of unfairly or by deception; bribe; *sl.* give someone just deserts —*vi.* become firm or solidified; determine —*n.* difficult situation; position of ship, aircraft ascertained by radar, observation *etc.*; *sl.* dose of narcotic drug —**fixa'tion** *n.* act of fixing; preoccupation, obsession; situation of being set in some way of acting or thinking —**fix'ative** *a.* capable of, or tending to fix —*n.* —**fix'edly** [-id-li] *adv.* intently —**fix'ity** *n.* —**fix'ture** *n.* thing fixed in posi-

tion; thing attached to house; date for sporting event; the event —**fix up** arrange —**fix (someone) up** attend to person's needs

fizz *vi.* hiss, splutter —*n.* hissing noise; effervescent liquid as soda water, champagne —**fiz'zle** *vi.* splutter weakly —*n.* fizzling noise; fiasco —**fizzle out** *inf.* come to nothing, fail

fjord, fiord [fyord] *n.* (*esp.* in Norway) long, narrow inlet of sea

flabb'ergast [-gahst] *vt.* overwhelm with astonishment

flabb'y *a.* hanging loose, limp; out of condition, too fat; feeble; yielding —**flab** *n. inf.* unsightly fat on the body —**flabb'iness** *n.*

flacc'id [flas'-, flak'-] *a.* flabby, lacking firmness —**flaccid'ity** *n.*

flag[1] *n.* banner, piece of bunting attached to staff or halyard as standard or signal; small paper emblem sold on flag days —*vt.* inform by flag signals (**-gg-**) —**flag day** day on which small flags or emblems are sold in streets for charity —**flag'ship** *n.* admiral's ship; most important ship of fleet —**flag'staff** *n.* pole for flag

flag[2] *n.* water plant with sword-shaped leaves, *esp.* the iris —**flag'gy** *a.*

flag[3] *n.* flat slab of stone —*pl.* pavement of flags —*vt.* (**-gg-**) —**flag'stone** *n.*

flag[4] *vi.* droop, fade; lose vigour (**-gg-**)

flag'ellate [-aj'-] *vt.* scourge, flog —**flag'ellant** *n.* one who scourges himself, *esp.* in religious penance —**flagella'tion** *n.* —**flag'ellator** *n.*

flageolet' [flaj-ə-let'] *n.* small flutelike instrument

flag'on *n.* large bottle of wine *etc.*

fla'grant *a.* glaring, scandalous,

blatant —**fla'grancy** n. —**fla'-grantly** adv.

flail n. instrument for threshing corn by hand —v. beat with, move as, flail

flair n. natural ability; elegance

flak n. anti-aircraft fire; inf. adverse criticism

flake n. small, thin piece, esp. particle of snow; piece chipped off —v. (cause to) peel off in flakes —**fla'ky** a. —**flake out** inf. collapse, sleep from exhaustion

flamboy'ant a. florid, gorgeous, showy; exuberant, ostentatious

flame n. burning gas, esp. above fire; visible burning; passion, esp. love; inf. sweetheart —vi. give out flames, blaze; shine; burst out

flamen'co n. Spanish dance to guitar

flamin'go [-ng'g-] n. large pink bird with long neck and legs (pl. -s, -es)

flamm'able a. liable to catch fire

flan n. open sweet or savoury tart

flange [-anj] n. projecting flat rim, collar, or rib —v. provide with or take form of flange

flank n. part of side between hips and ribs; side of anything, eg body of troops —vt. guard or strengthen on flank; attack or take in flank; be at, move along either side of

flann'el n. soft woollen fabric for clothing, esp. trousers; small piece of cloth for washing face and hands; inf. insincere talk —**flannelette'** n. cotton fabric imitating flannel —**flann'elly** a.

flap v. move (wings, arms etc.) as bird flying; (cause to) sway; strike with flat object; inf. be agitated, flustered (-**pp**-) —n. act of flapping; broad piece of anything hanging from hinge or loosely from one side; movable part of aircraft wing; inf. state of excitement or panic

flare [-ār] vi. blaze with unsteady flame; inf. (with up) suddenly burst into anger; spread outwards, as bottom of skirt —n. instance of flaring; signal light

flash n. sudden burst of light or flame; sudden short blaze; very short time; brief news item; ribbon or badge; display —vi. break into sudden flame; gleam; burst into view; move very fast; appear suddenly; sl. expose oneself indecently —vt. cause to gleam; emit (light etc.) suddenly —**flash, flash'y** a. showy, sham —**flash'-er** n. something which flashes; sl. someone who indecently exposes himself —**flash'back** n. break in continuity of book, play or film, to introduce what has taken place previously —**flash point** temperature at which a vapour ignites

flask [-ah-] n. long-necked bottle for scientific use; pocket bottle; vacuum flask

flat[1] a. level; spread out; at full length; smooth; downright; dull, lifeless; Mus. below true pitch; (of tyre) deflated, punctured; (of battery) fully discharged, dead (**flatt'er** comp., **flatt'est** sup.) —n. what is flat; Mus. note half tone below natural pitch —**flat'ly** adv. —**flat'ness** n. —**flatt'en** vt. —**flat'fish** n. type of fish which swims along sea floor on one side of body with both eyes on uppermost side —**flat race** race over level ground with no jumps —**flat rate** the same in all cases —**flat out** at, with maximum speed or effort

flat[2] n. suite of rooms in larger building

flatt'er vt. fawn on; praise insincerely; inspire unfounded belief;

gratify (senses); represent too favourably —**flatt'erer** n. —**flatt'ery** a.

flat'ulent a. suffering from, generating (excess) gases in intestines; pretentious —**flat'ulence** n. flatulent condition; verbosity, emptiness

flaunt v. show off; wave proudly —**flaunt'y** a.

flaut'ist n. flute player

flaves'cent a. yellowish, turning yellow

fla'vour [-vər] n. mixed sensation of smell and taste; distinctive taste, savour; undefinable characteristic, quality of anything —vt. give flavour to; season —**fla'vouring** n.

flaw n. crack; defect, blemish —vt. make flaw in —**flaw'less** a. perfect

flax n. plant grown for its textile fibre and seeds; its fibres, spun into linen thread —**flax'en** a. of flax; light yellow or straw-coloured

flay vt. strip skin off; criticize severely

flea [-ē] n. small, wingless, jumping, blood-sucking insect —**flea'bag** n. unkempt person, horse etc. —**flea'bite** n. insect's bite; trifling injury; trifle —**flea-bitten** a. bitten by flea; mean, worthless; scruffy —**flea market** market for cheap goods

fleck n. small mark, streak, or particle —vt. mark with flecks

fled pt./pp. of FLEE

fledged a. (of birds) able to fly; experienced, trained —**fledge(e)'ling** n. young bird; inexperienced person

flee v. run away from (**fled, flee'ing**)

fleece n. sheep's wool —vt. rob —**flee'cy** a.

fleet[1] n. number of warships organized as unit; number of

ships, cars etc. operating together

fleet[1] a. swift, nimble —**fleet'ing** a. passing, transient —**fleet'ingly** adv.

flense vt. strip (esp. whale) of flesh

flesh n. soft part, muscular substance, between skin and bone; in plants, pulp; fat; sensual appetites —**flesh'ily** adv. —**flesh'ly** a. carnal, material —**flesh'y** a. plump, pulpy —**flesh'pots** pl.n. (places catering for) self-indulgent living —**in the flesh** in person, actually present

fleur-de-lis' [flur-də-lē'] n. heraldic lily with three petals; iris (pl. **fleurs-de-lis**)

flew pt. of FLY

flex n. flexible insulated electric cable —v. bend, be bent —**flexibil'ity** n. —**flex'ible** a. easily bent; manageable; adaptable —**flex'ibly** adv. —**flex'ion, flec'tion** n. bending; bent state —**flex'(i)time** n. system permitting variation in starting and finishing times of work, providing an agreed number of hours is worked over a specified period

flibb'ertigibb'et n. flighty, gossiping person

flick vt. strike lightly, jerk —n. light blow; jerk —pl. sl. cinema

flick'er vi. burn, shine, unsteadily; waver, quiver —n. unsteady light or movement

flight [-īt] n. act or manner of flying through air; number flying together, as birds; journey in aircraft; Air Force unit of command; power of flying; swift movement or passage; sally; distance flown; stairs between two landings; running away —**flight recorder** electronic device in aircraft storing information about its flight

flight'y a. frivolous, erratic

flim'sy [-zi] a. frail, weak, thin; easily destroyed —**flim'sily** adv.

flinch vi. shrink, draw back, wince

fling v. (mainly tr.) throw, send, move, with force (**flung** pt./pp.) —n. throw; hasty attempt; spell of indulgence; vigorous dance

flint n. hard steel-grey stone; piece of this; hard substance used (as flint) for striking fire —**flint'ily** adv. —**flint'y** a. like or consisting of flint; hard, cruel

flip v. throw or flick lightly; turn over (-**pp**-) —n. instance, act, of flipping; drink with beaten egg —**flipp'ancy** n. —**flipp'ant** a. treating serious things lightly —**flip'pantly** adv. —**flip'per** n. limb, fin for swimming —pl. fin-shaped rubber devices worn on feet to help in swimming

flirt vi. toy, play with another's affections; trifle, toy (with) —n. person who flirts —**flirta'tion** n. —**flirta'tious** a.

flit vi. pass lightly and rapidly; dart; inf. go away hastily, secretly (-**tt**-)

flitch n. side of bacon

float vi. rest, drift on surface of liquid; be suspended freely; move aimlessly —vt. of liquid, support, bear alone; in commerce, get (company) started; obtain loan —n. anything small that floats (esp. to support something else, eg fishing net); small delivery vehicle, esp. one powered by batteries; motor vehicle carrying tableau etc., in parade; sum of money used to provide change —pl. footlights —**floata'tion** n. act of floating, esp. floating of company

flocc'ulent a. like tufts of wool

flock[1] n. number of animals of one kind together; fig. body of people; religious congregation —vi. gather in a crowd

flock[2] n. lock, tuft of wool etc.; wool refuse for stuffing cushions etc. —**flock'y** a.

floe [-ō] n. sheet of floating ice

flog vt. beat with whip, stick etc.; sl. sell (-**gg**-)

flood [flud] n. inundation, overflow of water; rising of tide; outpouring; flowing water —vt. inundate; cover, fill with water; arrive, move etc. in great numbers —**flood'gate** n. gate, sluice for letting water in or out —**flood'light** n. broad, intense beam of artificial light —**flood'lit** a. —**flood tide** the rising tide; fig. peak of prosperity

floor [flawr] n. lower surface of room; set of rooms on one level, storey; flat space; (right to speak in) legislative hall —vt. supply with floor; knock down; confound —**floor'ing** n. material for floors —**floor show** entertainment in nightclub etc.

flop vi. bend, fall, collapse loosely, carelessly; fall flat on floor, on water etc.; inf. go to sleep; inf. fail (-**pp**-) —n. flopping movement or sound; inf. failure —**flop'pily** adv. —**flopp'iness** n. —**flopp'y** a. limp, unsteady —**floppy disk** Computers flexible magnetic disk that stores information

flor'a n. plants of a region; list of them (pl. -**ras**, -**rae** [-rē]) —**flo'ral** a. of flowers —**flores'cence** n. state or time of flowering —**flor'et** n. small flower forming part of composite flower —**floribun'da** n. type of rose whose flowers grow in large clusters —**floricul'tural** a. —**flor'iculture** n. cultivation of flowers —**floricul'turist** n. —**flor'ist** [-o-] n. dealer in flowers

flor'id [-o-] a. with red, flushed complexion; ornate

flor'in [-o-] n. formerly, British

silver two-shilling piece

floss *n.* mass of fine, silky fibres, eg of cotton, silk; fluff —**floss'y** *a.* light and downy

flota'tion *see* FLOAT

flotill'a *n.* fleet of small vessels; group of destroyers

flot'sam *n.* floating wreckage; discarded waste objects

flounce[1] *vi.* go, move abruptly and impatiently —*n.* fling, jerk of body or limb

flounce[2] *n.* ornamental gathered strip on woman's garment

floun'der[1] *vi.* plunge and struggle, *esp.* in water or mud; proceed in bungling, hesitating manner —*n.* act of floundering

floun'der[2] *n.* flatfish

flour *n.* powder prepared by sifting and grinding wheat *etc.*; fine soft powder —*vt.* sprinkle with flour —**flour'iness** *n.* —**flour'y** *a.*

flour'ish [flu'-] *vi.* thrive; be in the prime —*vt.* brandish, display; wave about —*n.* ornamental curve; showy gesture in speech *etc.*; waving of hand, weapon *etc.*; fanfare (of trumpets)

flout *vt.* show contempt for, mock; defy

flow [flō] *vi.* glide along as stream; circulate, as the blood; move easily; move in waves; hang loose; be present in abundance —*n.* act, instance of flowing; quantity that flows; rise of tide; ample supply —**flow chart** diagram showing sequence of operations in industrial *etc.* process

flow'er *n.* coloured (not green) part of plant from which fruit is developed; bloom, blossom; ornamentation; choicest part, pick —*pl.* chemical sublimate —*vi.* produce flowers; bloom; come to prime condition —*vt.* ornament with flowers —**flow'eret** *n.* small

flower —**flow'ery** *a.* abounding in flowers; full of fine words, ornamented with figures of speech —**flower girl** girl selling flowers

flown [-ō-] *pp. of* FLY

fl. oz. fluid ounce(s)

flu *n. short for* INFLUENZA

fluc'tuate *v.* vary, rise and fall, undulate —**fluctua'tion** *n.*

flue [flōō] *n.* passage or pipe for smoke or hot air, chimney

flu'ent [flōō'-] *a.* speaking, writing a given language easily and well; easy, graceful

fluff *n.* soft, feathery stuff; down; *inf.* mistake —*v.* make or become soft, light; *inf.* make mistake —**fluff'y** *a.*

flu'id [flōō'-] *a.* flowing easily, not solid —*n.* gas or liquid —**flu-id'ity** *n.* —**fluid ounce** unit of capacity 1/20 of pint

fluke[1] [flōōk] *n.* flat triangular point of anchor —*pl.* whale's tail

fluke[2] [flōōk] *n.* stroke of luck, accident —*vt.* gain, make, hit by accident or by luck —**flu'ky** *a.* uncertain, got by luck

fluke[3] [flōōk] *n.* flatfish; parasitic worm

flume [flōōm] *n.* narrow (artificial) channel for water

flumm'ery *n.* nonsense, idle talk, humbug; dish of milk, flour, eggs *etc.*

flumm'ox *vt.* bewilder, perplex

flung *pt./pp. of* FLING

flunk'ey *n.* servant, *esp.* liveried manservant; servile person

fluor'(spar) [flōōr'] *n.* mineral containing fluorine —**fluor'ide** *n.* salt containing fluorine, *esp.* as added to domestic water supply as protection against tooth decay —**fluor'idate** *vt.* —**fluorida'tion** *n.* —**fluor'ine** *n.* nonmetallic element, yellowish gas

fluores'cence *n.* emission of light or other radiation from substance when bombarded by particles (electrons *etc.*) or other radiation, as in fluorescent lamp —**fluoresce**[1] *vi.* —**fluores'cent** *a.*

flurr'y *n.* squall, gust; bustle, commotion; death-struggle of whale; fluttering (as of snow-flakes) —*vt.* agitate, bewilder, fluster (**flur'ried, flur'rying**)

flush[1] *vi.* blush; of skin, redden; flow suddenly or violently; be excited —*vt.* cleanse (eg toilet) by rush of water; excite —*n.* reddening, blush; rush of water; excitement; elation; glow of colour; freshness, vigour —*a.* full, in flood; well supplied; level with surrounding surface

flush[2] *v.* (cause to) leave cover and take flight

flush[3] *n.* set of cards all of one suit

flus'ter *v.* make or become nervous, agitated —*n.*

flute [floot] *n.* wind instrument of tube with holes stopped by fingers or keys and blowhole in side; groove, channel —*vi.* play on flute —*vt.* make grooves in —**flu'ted** *a.* —**flu'ting** *n.*

flutt'er *v.* flap (as wings) rapidly without flight or in short flights; quiver; be or make excited, agitated —*n.* flapping movement; nervous agitation; *inf.* modest wager

flu'vial [floo'-] *a.* of rivers

flux *n.* discharge; constant succession of changes; substance mixed with metal to clean, aid adhesion in soldering *etc.*; measure of strength in magnetic field

fly[1] *v.* move through air on wings or in aircraft; pass quickly (through air); float loosely; spring, rush; flee, run away —*vt.* operate aircraft; cause to fly; set flying —*vi.* run from (**flew** *pt.*, **flown** *pp.*) —*n.* (zip or buttons fastening) opening in trousers;

flap in garment or tent; flying —**fly'ing** *a.* hurried, brief —**fly'fish** *v.* fish with artificial fly as lure —**flying boat** aeroplane fitted with floats instead of landing wheels —**flying buttress** *Architecture* arched or slanting structure attached at only one point to a mass of masonry —**flying colours** conspicuous success —**flying doctor** (*esp.* Aust.) doctor visiting patients in outback areas by aircraft —**flying fish** fish with winglike fins used for gliding above the sea —**flying fox** large fruit-eating bat —**flying saucer** unidentified (disc-shaped) flying object, supposedly from outer space —**flying squad** special detachment of police, soldiers *etc.*, ready to act quickly —**fly'leaf** *n.* blank leaf at beginning or end of book (*pl.* **-leaves**) —**fly'over** *n.* road passing over another by bridge —**fly'wheel** *n.* heavy wheel regulating speed of machine

fly[2] *n.* two-winged insect, *esp.* common housefly —**fly'blown** *a.* infested with larvae of blowfly —**fly'catcher** *n.* small insect-eating songbird

fly[3] *a. sl.* sharp and knowing

FM Field Marshal; frequency modulation

FO Flying Officer

foal *n.* young of horse, ass *etc.* —*v.* bear (foal)

foam *n.* collection of small bubbles on liquid; froth of saliva or sweat; light cellular solid used for insulation, packing *etc.* —*v.* (cause to) produce foam; be very angry —**foam'y** *a.*

fob[1] *n.* short watch chain; small pocket in waistband of trousers or waistcoat

fob off ignore, dismiss someone or something in offhand (insulting) manner; dispose of (**-bb-**)

foc'sle [fōk'səl] *n.* contracted form of FORECASTLE

fo'cus *n.* point at which rays meet after being reflected or refracted; state of optical image when it is clearly defined; state of instrument producing such image; point of convergence; point on which interest, activity is centred (*pl.* **fo'cuses, fo'ci** [-sī]) —*vt.* bring to focus, adjust; concentrate —*vi.* come to focus; converge (**fo'cused, fo'cusing**) —**fo'cal** *a.* of, at focus

fod'der *n.* bulk food for livestock

foe [fō] *n.* enemy

FoE, FOE Friends of the Earth

foe'tus, fe'tus [-ē-] *n.* fully-developed young in womb or egg —**foe'tal** *a.*

fog *n.* thick mist; dense watery vapour in lower atmosphere; cloud of anything reducing visibility —*vt.* cover in fog; puzzle (**-gg-**) —**fogg'y** *a.* —**fog'horn** *n.* instrument to warn ships in fog

fo'g(e)y *n.* old-fashioned person

foi'ble *n.* minor weakness, idiosyncrasy

foil[1] *vt.* baffle, defeat, frustrate —*n.* blunt sword, with button on point for fencing —**foil'able** *a.* —**foil'er** *n.*

foil[2] *n.* metal in thin sheet; anything which sets off another thing to advantage

foist *vt.* (*usu. with off or on*) sell, pass off inferior or unwanted thing as valuable

fold[1] [-ō-] *vt.* double up, bend part of; interlace (arms); wrap up; clasp (in arms); *Cooking* mix gently —*vi.* become folded; admit of being folded; *inf.* fail —*n.* folding; coil; winding; line made by folding; crease; foldlike geological formation —**fold'er** *n.* binder, file for loose papers

fold[2] [-ō-] *n.* enclosure for sheep; body of believers, church

fo'liage *n.* leaves collectively, leafage —**folia'ceous** [-shəs] *a.* of or like leaf —**fo'liate** *a.* leaflike, having leaves

fo'lio *n.* sheet of paper folded in half to make two leaves of book; book of largest common size made up of such sheets; page numbered on one side only; page number (*pl.* **fo'lios**)

folk [fōk] *n.* people in general; family, relatives; race of people —**folk dance** —**folk'lore** *n.* tradition, customs, beliefs popularly held —**folk song** music originating among a people

foll'icle *n.* small sac; seed vessel —**follic'ular** *a.*

foll'ow *v.* go or come after —*vt.* accompany, attend on; keep to (path *etc.*); take as guide, conform to; engage in; have a keen interest in; be consequent on; grasp meaning of —*vi.* come next; result —**foll'ower** *n.* disciple, supporter —**foll'owing** *a.* about to be mentioned —*n.* body of supporters —**follow-through** *n.* in ball games, continuation of stroke after impact with ball —**follow-up** *n.* something done to reinforce initial action

foll'y *n.* foolishness; foolish action *etc.*; useless, extravagant structure

foment' *vt.* foster, stir up; bathe with hot lotions —**fomenta'tion** *n.*

fond *a.* tender, loving; *obs.* credulous; *obs.* foolish —**fond'ly** *adv.* —**fond'ness** *n.* —**fond of** having liking for

fon'dant *n.* soft sugar mixture for sweets; sweet made of this

fon'dle *vt.* caress

fon'due [-dyoō] *n.* Swiss dish of sauce (*esp.* cheese) into which pieces of bread *etc.* are dipped

font *n.* bowl for baptismal water usu. on pedestal

fontanel(le)[1] *n.* soft, membraneous gap between bones of baby's skull

food [-ōō-] *n.* solid nourishment; what one eats; mental or spiritual nourishment —**food additive** natural or synthetic substance added to commercially processed food as preservative or to add colour, flavour *etc.* —**food processor** electric domestic appliance for automatic chopping, blending *etc.* of foodstuffs —**food'stuff** *n.* food

fool [-ōō-] *n.* silly, empty-headed person; dupe; simpleton; *Hist.* jester, clown; dessert of puréed fruit mixed with cream *etc.* —*vt.* delude; dupe —*vi.* act as fool —**fool'ery** *n.* habitual folly; act of playing the fool; absurdity —**fool'hardiness** *n.* —**fool'hardy** *a.* foolishly adventurous —**fool'ish** *a.* ill-considered, silly, stupid —**fool'ishly** *adv.* —**fool'proof** *a.* proof against failure —**fool's cap** jester's or dunce's cap; this as watermark —**fools'cap** *n.* size of paper which formerly had this mark

foot [-oo-] *n.* lowest part of leg, from ankle down; lowest part of anything, base, stand; end of bed *etc.*; infantry; measure of twelve inches; division of verse (*pl.* **feet**) —*v.* (usu. *tr.*) dance; walk (*esp.* **foot it**); pay cost of (*esp.* in **foot the bill**) —**foot'age** *n.* length in feet; length, extent, of film used —**foot'ie, foot'y** *n. sl.* football —**foot'ing** *n.* basis, foundation; firm standing, relations, conditions —*pl.* (concrete) foundations for walls of buildings —**foot-and-mouth disease** infectious viral disease in sheep, cattle *etc.* —**foot'ball** *n.* game played with large blown-up ball; the ball

—**foot'baller** *n.* —**football pools** form of gambling on results of football matches —**foot brake** brake operated by pressure on foot pedal —**foot fault** *Tennis* fault of overstepping base line while serving —**foot'hold** *n.* place affording secure grip for the foot; secure position from which progress may be made —**foot'lights** *pl.n.* lights across front of stage —**foot'loose** *a.* free from any ties —**foot'man** *n.* liveried servant —**foot'note** *n.* note of reference or explanation printed at foot of page —**foot'plate** *n.* platform for driver and fireman of locomotive —**foot-pound** *n.* unit of measurement of work in fps system —**foot'print** *n.* mark left by foot —**foot'slog** *vi.* walk, go on foot —**foot'slogger** *n.*

fop *n.* man excessively concerned with fashion —**fopp'ery** *n.* —**fopp'ish** *a.* —**fopp'ishly** *adv.*

for *prep.* intended to reach, directed or belonging to; because of; instead of; towards; on account of; in favour of; respecting; during; in search of; in payment of; in the character of; in spite of —*conj.* because —**for it** *inf.* liable for punishment or blame

for- (*comb. form*) from, away, against, as in **forswear**, **forbid** Such words are not given here where the meaning may easily be inferred from the simple word

for'age [fo'rij] *n.* food for cattle and horses —*vi.* collect forage; make roving search —**forage cap** soldier's undress cap

forasmuch' *conj.* (*with* as) as, seeing that, since

for'ay [fo'rā] *n.* raid, inroad —*v.* make one —**for'ayer** *n.*

for(e)'bear [-bār] *n.* ancestor

forbear' [-bār'] *v.* (*esp.* *with* from) cease; refrain (from); be patient (**forbore'** *pt.*, **forborne'**

pp.) —**forbear'ance** n. self-control, patience —**forbear'ing** a.

forbid' vt. prohibit; refuse to allow (**forbade'** [-bad] pt., **forbid'den** pp., **forbid'ding** pr.p.) —**forbid'ding** a. uninviting, threatening

force n. strength, power; compulsion; that which tends to produce a change in a physical system; mental or moral strength; body of troops, police etc.; group of people organized for particular task or duty; effectiveness, operative state; violence —vt. constrain, compel; produce by effort, strength; break open; urge, strain; drive; hasten maturity of —**forced** a. accomplished by great effort; compulsory; unnatural; strained; excessive —**force'ful** a. powerful, persuasive —**for'cible** a. done by force; efficacious, compelling, impressive; strong —**for'cibly** adv.

for'ceps pl.n. surgical pincers

ford n. shallow place where river may be crossed —vt. —**ford'able** a.

fore[1] a. in front (**form'er, fur'ther** comp., **fore'most, first, fur'thest** sup.) —n. front part

fore[2] interj. golfer's warning

fore- (comb. form) previous, before, front

fore-and-aft a. placed in line from bow to stern of ship

fore'arm n. arm between wrist and elbow —vt. [-arm'] arm beforehand

forebode' vt. indicate in advance —**forebo'ding** n. anticipation of evil

fore'cast vt. estimate beforehand (esp. weather); prophesy —n. prediction

fore'castle [fōk'səl] n. forward raised part of ship; sailors' quarters

foreclose' vt. take away power of redeeming (mortgage); prevent, shut out, bar —**foreclo'sure** n.

fore'court n. courtyard, open space, in front of building

fore'father n. ancestor

fore'finger n. finger next to thumb

foregath'er see FORGATHER

forego[1] vt. precede in time, place (-**went** pt., -**gone** pp., -**go'ing** pr.p.) —**forego'ing** a. going before, preceding —**fore'gone** a. determined beforehand; preceding —**foregone conclu'sion** result that might have been foreseen

forego[2] see FORGO

fore'ground n. part of view, esp. in picture, nearest observer

fore'hand a. of stroke in racquet games made with inner side of wrist leading

fore'head [or fo'rid] n. part of face above eyebrows and between temples

for'eign [fo'rin] a. not of, or in, one's own country; relating to, or connected with other countries; irrelevant; coming from outside; unfamiliar, strange —**for'eigner** n.

fore'lock n. lock of hair above forehead

fore'man n. one in charge of work; leader of jury

fore'mast n. mast nearest bow

fore'most a./adv. first in time, place, importance etc.

fore'noon n. morning

foren'sic a. of courts of law —**forensic medicine** application of medical knowledge in legal matters

fore'play n. sexual stimulation before intercourse

fore'runner n. one who goes before, precursor

foresee' vt. see beforehand (-saw' pt., -seen' pp.)

foreshad'ow vt. show, suggest beforehand, be a type of

fore'shore n. part of shore between high and low tide marks

foreshort'en vt. draw (object) so that it appears shortened; make shorter

fore'sight n. foreseeing; care for future

fore'skin n. skin that covers the glans penis

for'est [fo'rist] n. area with heavy growth of trees and plants; these trees; fig. something resembling forest (in an area) —**for'ester** n. one skilled in forestry —**for'estry** n. study, management of forest planting and maintenance

forestall' vt. anticipate; prevent, guard against in advance

fore'taste n. anticipation; taste beforehand

foretell' vt. prophesy (foretold' pt./pp.)

fore'thought n. thoughtful consideration of future events

forev'er adv. always; eternally; inf. for a long time

forewarn' vt. warn, caution in advance

forewent' see FOREGO[1]

fore'word n. preface

for'feit [-fit] n. thing lost by crime or fault; penalty, fine —a. lost by crime or fault —vt. lose by penalty —**for'feiture** n.

for(e)gath'er [-TH-] vi. meet together, assemble, associate

forge[1] [-j] n. place where metal is worked, smithy; furnace, workshop for melting or refining metal —vt. shape (metal) by heating in fire and hammering; make, shape, invent; make a fraudulent imitation of thing; counterfeit —**for'ger** n. —**for'gery** n. forged document, banknote etc.; the making of it

forge[2] [-j] vi. advance steadily

forget' vt. lose memory of, neglect, overlook (forgot' pt., forgot'ten or US, obs. forgot' pp., forgett'ing pr.p.) —**forget'ful** a. liable to forget —**forget'fully** adv. —**forget-me-not** n. plant with small blue flower

forgive' [-giv'] v. cease to blame or hold resentment against; pardon —**forgive'ness** n.

forgo' vt. go without; give up (-went' pt., -gone' pp., -go'ing pr.p.)

forgot', forgott'en see FORGET

fork n. pronged instrument for eating food; pronged tool for digging or lifting; division into branches; point of this division; one of the branches —vi. branch —vt. dig, lift, throw, with fork; make forkshaped —**fork out** inf. pay (reluctantly)

forlorn' a. forsaken; desperate —**forlorn hope** anything undertaken with little hope of success

form n. shape, visible appearance; visible person or animal; structure; nature; species, kind; regularly drawn up document, esp. printed one with blanks for particulars; condition; good condition; class in school; customary way of doing things; set order of words; long seat without back, bench; hare's nest; esp. US sp. of FORME —vt. shape, mould, arrange, organize; train, shape in the mind, conceive; go to make up, make part of —vi. come into existence or shape —**forma'tion** n. forming; thing formed; structure, shape, arrangement; military order —**for'mative** a. of, relating to, development; serving or tending to form; used in forming —**form'less** *a.*

for'mal *a.* ceremonial, according to rule; of outward form or routine; of, for, formal occasions; according to rule that does not matter; precise; stiff —**for'malism** *n.* quality of being formal; exclusive concern for form, structure, technique in an activity, *eg* art —**for'malist** *n.* —**formal'ity** *n.* observance required by custom or etiquette; condition or quality of being formal; conformity to custom; conventionality, mere form; in art, precision, stiffness, as opposed to originality —**for'mally** *adv.*

formal'dehyde *n.* colourless, poisonous, pungent gas, used in making antiseptics and in chemistry —**form'alin** *n.* solution of formaldehyde in water, used as disinfectant, preservative *etc.*

for'mat *n.* size and shape of book; organization of television show *etc.*

forme *n. Printing* frame for type

for'mer *a.* earlier in time; of past times; first named —*pron.* first named thing or person or fact —**for'merly** *adv.* previously

Formi'ca R type of laminated sheet used to make heat-resistant surfaces

for'mic acid acid found in insects (*esp.* ants) and some plants

for'midable *a.* to be feared; overwhelming, terrible, redoubtable; likely to be difficult, serious —**for'midably** *adv.*

for'mula [-myoo-] *n.* set form of words setting forth principle, method or rule for doing, producing something; substance so prepared; specific category of car in motor racing; recipe; *Science, Math.* rule, fact expressed in

symbols and figures (*pl.* **-ulae** [-ē], **-s**) —**for'mulary** *n.* collection of formulas —**for'mulate** *vt.* reduce to, express in formula, or in definite form; devise —**formula'tion** *n.* —**for'mulator** *n.*

fornica'tion *n.* sexual intercourse outside marriage —**for'nicate** *vi.*

forsake' *vt.* abandon, desert; give up (**forsook'**, **forsa'ken**, **forsa'king**)

forsooth' *adv. obs.* in truth

forswear' *vt.* renounce, deny —*refl.* perjure (**-swore'** *pt.*, **-sworn'** *pp.*)

forsy'thia *n.* widely cultivated shrub with yellow flowers

fort *n.* fortified place, stronghold

forte[1] [or for'tā] *n.* one's strong point, that in which one excels

for'te[2] [-ti] *adv. Mus.* loudly —**fortiss'imo** *sup.*

forth *adv.* onwards, into view —**forthcom'ing** *a.* about to come; ready when wanted; willing to talk, communicative —**forthwith'** *adv.* at once, immediately

forth'right *a.* direct; outspoken

for'tieth see FOUR

for'tify *vt.* strengthen; provide with defensive works (**for'tified**, **for'tifying**) —**fortifica'tion** *n.*

for'titude *n.* courage in adversity or pain, endurance

fort'night [-nīt] *n.* two weeks —**fort'nightly** *adv.*

FORTRAN *Computers* a programming language for mathematical and scientific purposes

fort'ress *n.* fortified place, *eg* castle, stronghold

fortu'itous *a.* accidental, by chance —**fortu'itously** *adv.* —**fortu'ity** *n.*

for'tune *n.* good luck, prosperity; wealth; stock of wealth; chance, luck —**for'tunate** *a.* —**for'tunately** *adv.* —**fortunehunter** *n.* person seeking fortune, *esp.* by marriage —**fortune-teller** *n.* one who predicts a person's future

for'ty *see* FOUR

for'um *n.* (place or medium for) meeting, assembly for open discussion or debate

for'ward *a.* lying in front of; onward; presumptuous, impudent; advanced, progressive; relating to the future —*n.* player placed in forward position in various team games, *eg* football —*adv.* towards the future; towards the front, to the front, into view; at, in fore part of ship; onward, so as to make progress —*vt.* help forward; send, dispatch —**for'wardly** *adv.* pertly —**for'wardness** *n.* —**for'wards** *adv.*

forwent' *see* FORGO

fosse *n.* ditch or moat

foss'il *n.* remnant or impression of animal or plant, *esp.* prehistoric one, preserved in earth; *inf.* person, idea *etc.* that is outdated and incapable of change —*a.* —**foss'ilize** *v.* turn into fossil; petrify

fos'ter *vt.* promote growth or development of; bring up child, *esp.* not one's own —**foster brother** one related by upbringing not blood; thus, —**foster father, mother, parent, child**

fought [fawt] *pt./pp. of* FIGHT

foul *a.* loathsome, offensive; stinking; dirty; unfair; wet, rough; obscene, disgustingly abusive; charged with harmful matter, clogged, choked —*n.* act of unfair play; the breaking of a rule —*adv.* unfairly —*v.* (*mainly tr.*) make, become foul; jam; collide with —**foul'ly** *adv.*

found[1] *pt./pp. of* FIND

found[2] *vt.* establish, institute; lay base of; base, ground —**founda'tion** *n.* basis; base, lowest part of building; founding; endowed institution *etc.* —**found'er** *n.* (**found'ress** *fem.*) —**foundation stone** one of stones forming foundation of building, *esp.* stone laid with public ceremony

found[3] *vt.* melt and run into mould; cast —**found'er** *n.* —**found'ry** *n.* place for casting; art of this

found'er *vi.* collapse; sink; become stuck as in mud *etc.*

found'ling *n.* deserted infant

fount *n.* fountain; assortment of printing type of one size

foun'tain [-in] *n.* jet of water, *esp.* ornamental one; spring; source —**foun'tainhead** *n.* source —**fountain pen** pen with ink reservoir

four [-aw-] *n./a.* cardinal number next after three —**fourth** *a.* the ordinal number —**fourth'ly** *adv.* —**for'tieth** *a.* —**for'ty** *n./a.* four tens —**four'teen** *n./a.* four plus ten —**four'teenth** *a.* —**fourposter** *n.* bed with four posts for curtains *etc.* —**four'some** *n.* group of four people; game or dance for four people —*a.* —**four'square** *a.* firm, steady —**four-stroke** *n.* internal-combustion engine firing once every four strokes of piston —**on all fours** on hands and knees

fowl *n.* domestic cock or hen; bird, its flesh —*vi.* hunt wild birds —**fowl'er** *n.* —**fowling piece** light gun

fox *n.* red bushy-tailed animal; its fur; cunning person —*vt.* perplex; discolour (paper) with brown spots; mislead —*vi.* act craftily; sham —**fox'y** *a.* —**fox'glove** *n.* tall flowering plant —**fox'hole** *n.* *sl.* in war, small trench giving protection —**fox'hound** *n.* dog bred for hunting foxes —**fox terrier** small dog now mainly kept as a pet —**fox'trot** *n.* (music for) ballroom dance —*v.*

foy'er [-ā] n. entrance-hall in theatres, hotels *etc.*

fps feet per second; foot-pound-second

Fr. Father; Frater (*Lat.* brother); French; Friday

frac'as [-k'ah] n. noisy quarrel; uproar, brawl

frac'tion n. numerical quantity not an integer; fragment, piece —**frac'tional** a. constituting a fraction; forming but a small part; insignificant —**frac'tionary** a.

frac'tious [-shəs] a. unruly, irritable

frac'ture n. breakage, part broken; breaking of bone; breach, rupture —v. break

frag'ile [-aj'-] a. breakable; frail; delicate —**fragil'ity** n.

frag'ment n. piece broken off; small portion, incomplete part —v. [-ment'] —**frag'mentary** a.

fra'grant a. sweet-smelling —**fra'grance** n. scent —**fra'grantly** adv.

frail a. fragile, delicate; infirm; in weak health; morally weak —**frail'ly** adv. —**frail'ty** n.

frame n. that in which thing is set, as square of wood round picture *etc.*; structure; build of body; constitution; mood; individual exposure on strip of film —vt. put together, make; adapt; put into words; put into frame; bring false charge against —**frame-up** n. *sl.* plot, manufactured evidence —**frame'work** n. structure into which completing parts can be fitted; supporting work

franc [-angk] n. monetary unit of France, Switzerland and other countries

fran'chise n. right of voting; citizenship; privilege or right, *esp.* right to sell certain goods

Francis'can n. monk or nun of the order founded by St. Francis of Assisi —a.

fran'colin [-ng-] n. African or Asian partridge

frangipan'i [-ji-pahn'i] n. tropical American shrub

frank a. candid, outspoken; sincere —n. official mark on letter either cancelling stamp or ensuring delivery without stamp —vt. mark letter thus —**frank'ly** adv. candidly —**frank'ness** n.

Frank'enstein's monster [-īn-] creation or monster that brings disaster and is beyond the control of its creator

frank'furter n. smoked sausage

frank'incense n. aromatic gum resin burned as incense

fran'tic a. distracted with rage, grief, joy *etc.*; frenzied —**fran'tically** adv.

frater'nal a. of brother, brotherly —**frater'nally** adv. —**frater'nity** n. brotherliness; brotherhood; US college society —**frater'nize** vi. to associate, make friends —**fratrici'dal** a. —**frat'ricide** [-sīd] n. killing, killer of brother or sister

fraud n. criminal deception; swindle, imposture —**fraud'ulence** n. —**fraud'ulent** a.

fraught [-awt] a. filled (with), involving

fray[1] n. fight; noisy quarrel

fray[2] v. wear through by rubbing; make, become ragged at edge

fraz'zle inf. v. make or become exhausted; make or become irritated —n. exhausted state

freak n. abnormal person, animal, thing —a. —**freak'ish**, (inf.) **freak'y** a. —**freak out** inf. (cause to) hallucinate, be wildly excited *etc.*

freck'le n. light brown spot on skin, *esp.* caused by sun; any small spot —v. bring, come out in freckles —**freck'led** a.

free a. able to act at will, not under compulsion or restraint; not restricted or affected by; not subject to cost or tax; independent; not exact or literal; generous; not in use; (of person) not occupied, having no engagement; loose, not fixed —vt. set at liberty; remove (obstacles, pain etc.); rid (of) (**freed, free'ing**) —**free'dom** n. —**free'ly** adv. —**free-for-all** n. brawl —**free'hand** a. drawn without guiding instruments —**free'hold** n. tenure of land without obligation of service or rent; land so held —**free house** public house not bound to sell only one brewer's products —**free'lance** [-ah-] a./n. (of) self-employed, unattached person —**Free'mason** n. member of secret fraternity for mutual help —**free-range** a. kept, produced in natural, nonintensive conditions —**free space** region that has no gravitational and electromagnetic fields —**free speech** right to express opinions publicly —**free'think'er** n. sceptic who forms his own opinions, esp. in religion —**free trade** international trade free of protective tariffs —**free'way** n. US major road

free'sia [-zi-ə] n. plant with fragrant, tubular flowers

freeze v. change (by reduction of temperature) from liquid to solid, as water to ice —vt. preserve (food etc.) by extreme cold, as in freezer; fix (prices etc.) —vi. feel very cold; become rigid as with fear; stop (**froze, fro'zen, free'zing**) —**free'zer** n. insulated cabinet for long-term storage of perishable foodstuffs —**fro'zen** a. of credits etc., unrealizable —**freezing point** tem-

perature at which liquid becomes solid

freight [-at] n. commercial transport (esp. by railway, ship); cost of this; goods so carried —vt. send as or by freight —**freight'age** n. money paid for freight —**freight'er** n. —**freight'liner** n. goods train, lorry carrying containers

French n. language spoken by people of France —a. of, pertaining to France —**French dressing** salad dressing —**French horn** musical wind instrument —**French leave** unauthorized leave —**French polish** varnish for wood made from shellac dissolved in alcohol —**French window** window extended to floor level and used as door

frenet'ic a. frenzied

fren'zy n. violent mental derangement; wild excitement —**fren'zied** a.

fre'quent a. happening often; common; numerous —vt. [-kwent'] go often to —**fre'quency** n. rate of occurrence; in radio etc. cycles per second of alternating current —**frequent'ative** a. expressing repetition —**fre'quently** adv.

fres'co n. method of painting in water colour on plaster of wall before it dries; painting done thus (pl. **-co(e)s**)

fresh a. not stale; new; additional; different; recent; inexperienced; pure; not pickled, frozen etc.; not faded or dimmed; not tired; of wind, strong; inf. impudent; arrogant —**fresh'en** v. —**fresh'et** n. rush of water at river mouth; flood of river water —**fresh'ly** adv. —**fresh'man, fresh'er** n. first-year student —**fresh'ness** n.

fret [1] v. be irritated, worry (**-tt-**)

—*n.* irritation —**fret'ful** *a.* irritable, (easily) upset

fret[2] *n.* repetitive geometrical pattern; small bar on fingerboard of guitar *etc.* —*vt.* ornament with carved pattern (**-tt-**) —**fret saw** saw with narrow blade and fine teeth, used for fretwork —**fret'-work** *n.* carved or open woodwork in ornamental patterns and devices

Freu'dian [-oi'-] *a.* pert. to Austrian psychologist Sigmund Freud, or his theories

fri'able *a.* easily crumbled —**friabil'ity, fri'ableness** *n.*

fri'ar *n.* member of mendicant religious order —**fri'ary** *n.* house of friars

fricassee' [*or* frik'-] *n.* dish of pieces of chicken or meat, fried or stewed and served with rich sauce —*vt.* cook thus

fric'tion *n.* rubbing; resistance met with by body moving over another; clash of wills *etc.*, disagreement —**fric'tional** *a.*

Fri'day *n.* the sixth day of the week —**Good Friday** the Friday before Easter

fridge *n. inf.* refrigerator

fried *pt./pp. of* FRY

friend [frend] *n.* one well known to another and regarded with affection and loyalty; intimate associate; supporter; (**F-**) Quaker —**friend'less** *a.* —**friend'liness** *n.* —**friend'ly** *a.* having disposition of a friend, kind; favourable —**friend'ship** *n.*

frieze[1] [frēz] *n.* ornamental band, strip (on wall)

frieze[2] [frēz] *n.* kind of coarse woollen cloth

frig'ate *n.* old (sailing) warship corresponding to modern cruiser; fast destroyerlike warship equipped for escort and antisubmarine duties —**frigate bird** bird

of tropical and subtropical seas, with wide wingspan

fright [frīt] *n.* sudden fear; shock; alarm; grotesque or ludicrous person or thing —*vt. obs.* frighten —**fright'en** *vt.* cause fear, fright in —**fright'ful** *a.* terrible, calamitous; shocking; *inf.* very great, very large —**fright'fully** *adv. inf.* terribly; very —**fright'fulness** *n.*

frig'id [-ij'-] *a.* formal, dull; (sexually) unfeeling; cold —**frigid'ity** *n.* —**frig'idly** *adv.*

frill *n.* fluted strip of fabric gathered at one edge; ruff of hair, feathers around neck of dog, bird *etc.*; fringe; unnecessary words, politeness; superfluous thing; adornment —*vt.* make into, decorate with frill

fringe *n.* ornamental edge of hanging threads, tassels *etc.*; anything like this; hair cut in front and falling over brow; edge, limit —*vt.* adorn with, serve as, fringe —*a.* (of theatre *etc.*) unofficial, unconventional, extra

fripp'ery *n.* finery; trivia

frisk *vi.* move, leap, playfully —*vt.* wave briskly; *inf.* search (person) for concealed weapons *etc.* —*n.* —**frisk'ily** *adv.* —**frisk'y** *a.*

fritill'ary *n.* plant with purple or white bell-shaped flowers

fritt'er[1] *vt.* waste —**fritter away** throw away, waste

fritt'er[2] *n.* piece of food fried in batter

friv'olous *a.* not serious, unimportant; flippant —**frivol'ity** *n.*

frizz *vt.* crisp, curl into small curls —*n.* frizzed hair —**frizz'y** *a.* crimped

friz'zle *v.* fry, toast or grill with sizzling sound

fro *adv.* away, from (*only in* **to and fro**)

frock *n.* woman's dress; various

similar garments —vt. invest with office of priest

frog[1] n. tailless amphibian animal developed from tadpole —**frog'man** n. swimmer equipped for swimming, working, underwater —**frog'march** n. any method of moving person against his will

frog[2] n. military-style coat fastening of button and loop; attachment to belt to carry sword

frol'ic n. merrymaking —vi. behave playfully (**frol'icked, frol'icking**) —**frol'icsome** a.

from prep. expressing point of departure, source, distance, cause, change of state etc.

frond n. plant organ consisting of stem and foliage, usually with fruit forms, esp. in ferns

front [-unt] n. fore part; position directly before or ahead; seaside promenade; battle line or area; Meteorology dividing line between two air masses of different characteristics; outward aspect, bearing; inf. something serving as a respectable cover for another, usu. criminal, activity; field of activity; group with common goal —v. look, face; inf. be a cover for —a. of, at, the front —**front'age** n. façade of building; extent of front —**front'al** a. —**fron'tier** n. part of country which borders on another —**fron'tispiece** n. illustration facing title page of book

frost n. frozen dew or mist; act or state of freezing; weather in which temperature falls below point at which water turns to ice —v. cover, be covered with frost or something similar in appearance; give slightly roughened surface —**frost'ily** adv. —**frost'y** a. accompanied by frost; chilly; cold; unfriendly —**frost'bite** n.

destruction by cold of tissue, esp. of fingers, ears etc.

froth [-th] n. collection of small bubbles, foam; scum; idle talk —v. (cause to) foam —**froth'ily** adv. —**froth'y** a.

frown vi. wrinkle brows —n.

frow'zy a. dirty, unkempt

froze pt. —**fro'zen** pp. of FREEZE

FRS Fellow of the Royal Society

fruc'tify v. (cause to) bear fruit (**fruc'tified, fruc'tifying**) —**fructifica'tion** n.

fru'gal [frōō'-] a. sparing; thrifty, economical; meagre —**frugal'ity** n. —**fru'gally** adv.

fruit [-ōō-] n. seed and its envelope, esp. edible one; vegetable product; (usu. in pl.) result, benefit —vi. bear fruit —**fruit'erer** n. dealer in fruit —**fruit'ful** a. —**frui'tion** [-ōō-ish'-] n. enjoyment; realization of hopes —**fruit'less** a. —**fruit'y** a. —**fruit machine** gambling machine operated by coins

frump n. dowdy woman —**frump'ish, frump'y** a.

frustrate' vt. thwart, balk; baffle, disappoint —**frustra'tion** n.

fry[1] vt. cook with fat —vi. be cooked thus (**fried, fry'ing**) —n. fried meat; dish of anything fried

fry[2] n. young fishes —**small fry** young or insignificant beings

ft. feet; foot; fort

fu'chsia [fyōō'shə] n. ornamental shrub with purple-red flowers

fud'dle v. (cause to) be intoxicated, confused —n. this state

fudd'y-dudd'y n. inf. (elderly) dull person

fudge[1] n. soft, variously flavoured sweet

fudge[2] vt. make, do carelessly or dishonestly; fake

fu'el n. material for burning as source of heat or power; something which nourishes —vt. provide with fuel

fug n. stuffy indoor atmosphere —**fugg′y** a.

fu′gitive n. one who flees, esp. from arrest or pursuit —a. fleeing, elusive

fugue [fyoog] n. musical composition in which themes are repeated in different parts

Füh′rer [fyoor′-] n. leader, title of German dictator, esp. Hitler

ful′crum n. point on which a lever is placed for support (pl. **ful′cra**)

fulfil′ [fool-] vi. satisfy; carry out; obey; satisfy (desire etc.) (**-ll-**) —**fulfil′ment** n.

full [fool] a. containing as much as possible; abundant; complete; ample; plump; (of garment) of ample cut —adv. very; quite; exactly —**full′y** adv. —**full′ness, ful′ness** n. —**ful′some** a. excessive —**fullblown′** a. fully developed —**full stop** punctuation mark (.) at end of sentence

ful′mar [fool′-] n. Arctic sea bird

ful′minate vi. (esp. with against) criticize harshly —n. chemical compound exploding readily —**fulmina′tion** n.

fulsome see FULL

fum′ble v. grope about; handle awkwardly —n. awkward attempt

fume [fyoom] vi. be angry; emit smoke or vapour —n. smoke; vapour —**fu′migate** vt. apply fumes or smoke to, esp. for disinfection —**fumiga′tion** n. —**fu′migator** n.

fu′mitory n. plant with spurred flowers

fun n. anything enjoyable, amusing etc. —**funn′ily** adv. —**funn′y** a. comical; odd; difficult to explain

func′tion [-ngk′-] n. work a thing is designed to do; (large) social event; duty; profession; Math. quantity whose value depends on varying value of another —vi. operate, work —**func′tional** a. having a special purpose; practical, necessary; capable of operating —**func′tionary** n. official

fund n. stock or sum of money; supply, store —pl. money resources —vt. (in financial, business dealings) provide or obtain fund(s) in various ways

fundament′al a. of, affecting, or serving as, the base; essential, primary —n. basic rule or fact —**fund′ament** n. buttocks; foundation —**fundament′alism** n. —**fundamen′talist** n. one laying stress on belief in literal and verbal inspiration of Bible and other traditional creeds

fu′neral n. (ceremony associated with) burial or cremation of dead —**fune′real** [-nē-] a. like a funeral; dark; gloomy

fun′gus [-ng′g-] n. plant without leaves, flowers, or roots, as mushroom, mould (pl. **-gi** [-jī, -gī, -ji], **-guses**) —**fun′gal, fun′gous** a. —**fun′gicide** n. fungus destroyer

funic′ular [fyoō-] n. cable railway on mountainside with two counterbalanced cars

funk n. panic (esp. **blue funk**)

funn′el n. cone-shaped vessel or tube; chimney of locomotive or ship; ventilating shaft —v. (cause to) move as through funnel; concentrate, focus

funn′y see FUN

fur n. soft hair of animal; garment etc. of dressed skins with such hair; furlike coating —vt. cover with fur (**-rr-**) —**furr′ier** n. dealer in furs —**furr′y** a. of, like fur

fur′bish vt. clean up

fur′cate(d) a. forked, branching

fur′ious [fyoor′-] a. extremely

angry; violent —**fur'iously** adv. —**fur'iousness** n.

furl vt. roll up and bind (sail, umbrella etc.)

fur'long n. eighth of mile

fur'lough [-lō] n. US leave of absence, esp. to soldier

fur'nace n. apparatus for applying great heat to metals; closed fireplace for heating boiler etc.; hot place

fur'nish vt. fit up house with furniture; equip; supply, yield —**fur'niture** n. movable contents of a house or room

furor'e [fyoo-] n. public outburst, esp. of protest; sudden enthusiasm

furr'ow [-ō] n. trench as made by plough; groove —vt. make furrows in

fur'ther [-TH-] adv. more; in addition; at or to a greater distance or extent —a. more distant; additional —comp. of FAR, FORE[1] —vt. help forward; promote —**fur'therance** n. —**fur'therer** n. —**fur'thermore** adv. besides —**fur'thest** a. sup. of FAR, FORE[1] —adv. —**fur'thermost** n.

fur'tive a. stealthy, sly, secret —**fur'tively** adv.

fur'y [fyoor'-] n. wild rage, violent anger; violence of storm etc.; (usu. pl.) snake-haired avenging deity

furze n. prickly shrub, gorse

fus'cous [-kəs] a. dark-coloured

fuse [fyooz] v. blend by melting; melt with heat; amalgamate; (cause to) fail as a result of blown fuse —n. soft wire, with low melting point, used as safety device in electrical systems; device (orig. combustible cord) for igniting bomb etc. —**fu'sible** a. —**fu'sion** n. melting; state of being melted; union of things, as atomic nuclei, as if melted together

fu'selage [-ahzh] n. body of aircraft

fusilier[1] [fyoo-zi-] n. soldier of certain regiments —**fusillade**[1] n. continuous discharge of firearms

fuss n. needless bustle or concern; complaint; objection —vi. make fuss —**fuss'ily** adv. —**fuss'iness** n. —**fuss'y** a. particular; faddy; overmeticulous; overelaborate

fus'tian n. thick cotton cloth; inflated language

fus'ty a. mouldy; smelling of damp; old-fashioned —**fus'tily** adv. —**fus'tiness** n.

fu'tile a. useless, ineffectual, trifling —**futil'ity** n.

fu'ton [foo-] n. Japanese padded quilt, laid on floor as bed

fu'ture n. time to come; what will happen; tense of verb indicating this; likelihood of development —a. that will be; of, relating to, time to come —**fu'turism** n. movement in art marked by revolt against tradition —**fu'turist** n./a. —**futuris'tic** a. ultramodern —**futur'ity** n.

fuze US see FUSE

fuzz n. fluff; fluffy or frizzed hair; blur; sl. police(man) —**fuzz'y** a. fluffy, frizzy; blurred, indistinct

fwd. forward

G

g gram(s); (acceleration due to) gravity

gab'ble v. talk, utter inarticulately or too fast (**gab'bled, gab'bling**) —n. such talk —**gab** inf. n./v. talk, chatter —**gift of the gab** talkative —**gift of the gab** eloquence, loquacity

gab'erdine, **gab'ardine** [-ēn] n. fine twill cloth like serge used *esp.* for raincoats; *Hist.* loose upper garment worn by Jews

ga'ble *n.* triangular upper part of wall at end of ridged roof —**gable end**

gad *vi.* (*esp.* with about) go around in search of pleasure (**-dd-**) —**gad'about** *n.* pleasure-seeker

gad'fly *n.* cattle-biting fly; worrying person

gadg'et *n.* small mechanical device; object valued for its novelty or ingenuity —**gadg'etry** *n.*

Gael [gāl] *n.* one who speaks Gaelic —**Gae'lic** *n.* language of Ireland and Scottish Highlands —*a.* of Gaels, their language or customs

gaff *n.* stick with iron hook for landing fish; spar for top of fore-and-aft sail —*vt.* seize (fish) with gaff

gaffe *n.* blunder; tactless remark

gaff'er *n.* old man; *inf.* foreman, boss

gag[1] *vt.* stop up (person's mouth) with cloth *etc.* —*vi. sl.* retch, choke (**-gg-**) —*n.* cloth *etc.* put into, tied across mouth

gag[2] *n.* joke, funny story, gimmick

ga'ga [gah'gah] *sl. a.* senile; crazy

gage[1] [gāj] *n.* pledge, thing given as security; challenge, or something symbolizing one

gage[2] [gāj] *see* GAUGE

gag'gle *n.* flock of geese; *inf.* disorderly crowd

gai'ety *see* GAY

gain *vt.* obtain, secure; obtain as profit; win; earn; reach —*vi.* increase, improve; get nearer; (of watch, machine *etc.*) operate too fast —*n.* profit; increase, improvement —**gain'fully** *adv.* profitably; for a wage, salary

gainsay[1] *vt.* deny, contradict

(**gainsaid, gainsaying**)

gait [gāt] *n.* manner of walking; pace

gait'er *n.* covering of leather, cloth *etc.* for lower leg

Gal. Galatians

gal'a [gahl'ə] *n.* festive occasion; show; competitive sporting event

galah' *n.* Aust. grey cockatoo with reddish breast

gal'axy *n.* system of stars bound by gravitational forces; splendid gathering, *esp.* of famous people —**galac'tic** *a.*

gale *n.* strong wind; *inf.* loud outburst, *esp.* of laughter

gale'na *n.* sulphide of, and principal ore of lead

gal(l)'ivant, gal'avant *vi.* gad about

gall[1] [gawl] *n. inf.* impudence; bitterness —**gall bladder** sac attached to liver, reservoir for bile —**gall'stone** *n.* hard secretion in gall bladder or ducts leading from it

gall[2] [gawl] *n.* painful swelling, *esp.* on horse; sore caused by chafing —*vt.* make sore by rubbing; vex, irritate

gall[3] [gawl] *n.* abnormal outgrowth on trees *etc.*

gall'ant *a.* fine, stately, brave; [*also* -lant'] chivalrous, very attentive to women —*n.* [*also* -lant'] lover, suitor; dashing, fashionable young man —**gall'antly** *adv.* —**gall'antry** *n.*

gall'eon *n.* large, high-built sailing ship of war

gall'ery *n.* covered walk with side openings, colonnade; platform or projecting upper floor in church, theatre *etc.*; group of spectators; long, narrow platform on outside of building; room or rooms for special purposes, *eg* showing works of art; passage in wall, open to interior of building; horizontal passage in mining

gall'ey n. one-decked vessel with sails and oars, usu. rowed by slaves or criminals; kitchen of ship or aircraft; large rowing boat; printer's tray for composed type —**galley proof** printer's proof in long slip form —**galley slave** one condemned to row in galley; drudge

Gall'ic a. of ancient Gaul; French —**gall'icism** n. French word or idiom

gall'ium n. soft, grey metal of great fusibility

gall'on n. liquid measure of eight pints (4.55 litres)

gall'op v. go, ride at gallop; move fast —n. horse's fastest pace with all four feet off ground together in each stride; ride at this pace —**gall'oper** n. —**gall'oping** a. at a gallop; speedy, swift

gall'ows [-ōz] n. structure, usu. of two upright beams and crossbar, esp. for hanging criminals

Gall'up poll n. method of finding out public opinion by questioning a cross section of the population

galoot' n. inf. silly, clumsy person

galore' adv. in plenty

galosh'es pl.n. waterproof overshoes

galvan'ic a. of, producing, concerning electric current, esp. when produced chemically; inf. resembling effect of electric shock, startling —**gal'vanize** vt. stimulate to action; excite, startle; cover (iron etc.) with protective zinc coating

gam'bit n. Chess opening involving offer of a pawn; any opening manoeuvre, comment etc. intended to secure an advantage

gam'ble vi. play games of chance to win money; act on expectation of something —n. risky undertaking; bet, wager —**gam'bler** n.

gamboge' [-ōzh'] n. gum resin used as yellow pigment

gam'bol vi. skip, jump playfully (-ll-) —n.

game[1] n. diversion, pastime; jest; contest for amusement; scheme, strategy; animals or birds hunted; their flesh —a. brave; willing —vi. gamble —**game'ster** n. gambler —**game'cock** n. fowl bred for fighting —**game'keeper** n. man employed to breed game, prevent poaching

game[2], **gamm'y** a. lame, crippled

gam'ete [-ēt] n. Biology a sexual cell that unites with another for reproduction or the formation of a new individual

gamm'a n. third letter of the Greek alphabet —**gamma ray** a very penetrative electromagnetic ray

gamm'on n. cured or smoked ham; bottom piece of flitch of bacon

gamm'y a. see GAME[2]

gamp n. inf. large umbrella, usu. clumsy or very worn

gam'ut n. whole range or scale (orig. of musical notes)

gan'der n. male goose; inf. a quick look

gang n. (criminal) group; organized group of workmen —vi. (esp. with **together**) form gang —**gang'er** n. foreman of a gang of labourers —**gang up (on)** inf. combine against

gan'gling [-ng'g-] a. lanky, awkward in movement

gan'glion [-ng'g-] n. nerve nucleus

gang'plank n. portable bridge for boarding or leaving vessel

gan'grene [-ng'g-] n. death or

decay of body tissue as a result of disease or injury —**gan'grenous** a.

gang'ster n. member of criminal gang; notorious or hardened criminal

gang'way n. bridge from ship to shore; anything similar; passage between row of seats —interj. make way, please!

gann'et n. predatory sea bird

gan'oid a./n. (fish) with smooth, hard, enamelled, bony scales, eg sturgeon

ga(u)n'try n. structure to support crane, railway signals etc.; framework beside rocket on launching pad

gaol [jāl] n. see JAIL.

gap n. breach, opening, interval; cleft; empty space

gape vi. stare in wonder; open mouth wide, as in yawning; be, become wide open —n.

gar'age [ga'rahzh, -rij] n. (part of) building to house cars; refuelling and repair centre for cars —vt. leave car in garage

garb n. dress; fashion of dress —vt. dress, clothe

gar'bage [-ij] n. rubbish

gar'ble vt. jumble or distort story, account etc.

gar'den n. ground for growing flowers, fruit, or vegetables —vi. cultivate garden —**gar'dener** n. —**gar'dening** n. —**garden centre** place selling plants, tools etc. for gardening

garde'nia [-ē-] n. (sub)tropical shrub, with fragrant white or yellow flowers

gar'(fish) n. elongated bony fish

gargan'tuan a. immense, enormous, huge

gar'gle vi. wash throat with liquid kept moving by the breath —vt. wash (throat) thus —n.

gargling; preparation for this purpose

gar'goyle n. carved (grotesque) face on waterspout, esp. on Gothic church

gar'ish a. showy; gaudy

gar'land n. wreath of flowers worn or hung as decoration —vt. decorate with garlands

gar'lic n. (bulb of) plant with strong smell and taste, used in cooking and seasoning

gar'ment n. article of clothing —pl. clothes

gar'ner vt. store up, collect, as if in granary

gar'net n. red semiprecious stone

gar'nish vt. adorn, decorate (esp. food) —n. material for this

gar'ret n. room on top floor, attic

gar'rison n. troops stationed in town, fort etc.; fortified place —vt. furnish or occupy with garrison

garrotte' n. Spanish capital punishment by strangling; apparatus for this —vt. execute, kill thus —**garrott'er** n.

garr'ulous a. (frivolously) talkative —**garru'lity** n. loquacity

garryow'en n. Rugby high kick forwards followed by a charge to where it lands

gar'ter n. band worn round leg to hold up sock or stocking

gas n. air-like substance, esp. one that does not liquefy or solidify at ordinary temperatures; fossil fuel in form of gas, used for heating or lighting; gaseous anaesthetic; poisonous or irritant substance dispersed through atmosphere in warfare etc.; inf. (esp. US) petrol; inf. idle, boastful talk (pl. -es) —vt. project gas over; poison with gas —vi. inf. talk idly, boastfully (-ss-) —**gas'eous** a. of, like gas —**gass'y** a. —**gas'bag** n. sl. person who talks idly —**gas mask** mask with chemical filter to guard against poisoning by gas —**gasom'eter** n. tank for storing coal gas etc.

gash n. gaping wound, slash —vt. cut deeply

gas'ket n. rubber, asbestos etc. used as seal between metal faces, esp. in engines

gas'oline, -ene [-ēn] n. US petrol

gasp [-ah-] vi. catch breath with open mouth, as in exhaustion or surprise —n. convulsive catching of breath

gas'tric a. of stomach —**gastronom'ical** a. —**gastron'omy** n. art of good eating

gastroenteri'tis n. inflammation of stomach and intestines

gas't(e)ropod n. mollusc, eg snail, with dorsal-like organ of locomotion on ventral surface

gate n. opening in wall, fence etc.; barrier for closing it; sluice; any entrance or way out; (entrance money paid by) those attending sporting event —**gatecrash** v. enter meeting, social function etc. uninvited

gât'eau [-ō] n. elaborate, rich cake (pl. -x)

gath'er [GATH'-] v. (cause to) assemble; increase gradually; draw together —vt. collect; learn, understand; draw material into small tucks or folds —**gath'ering** n. assembly

gauche [gōsh] a. tactless, blundering —**gauch'erie** n. awkwardness, clumsiness

gauch'o [gowch'-] n. S Amer. cowboy

gaud [-aw-] n. showy ornament —**gaud'ily** adv. —**gaud'iness** n. —**gaud'y** a. showy in tasteless way

gauge [gāj] n. standard measure, as of diameter of wire, thickness of sheet metal etc.; distance between rails of railway; capacity, extent; instrument for measuring such things as wire, rainfall, height of water in boiler etc. —vt. measure; estimate

gaunt [-aw-] a. lean, haggard

gaunt'let [-aw-] n. armoured glove; glove covering part of arm —**run the gauntlet** formerly, run as punishment between two lines of men striking at runner with sticks etc.; be exposed to criticism or unpleasant treatment; undergo ordeal —**throw down the gauntlet** offer challenge

gaun'try [-aw-] see GANTRY

gauss [gows] n. unit of density of magnetic field

gauze [-aw-] n. thin transparent fabric of silk, wire etc. —**gauz'y** a.

gave pt. of GIVE

gav'el n. mallet of presiding officer or auctioneer

gavotte' n. lively dance; music for it

gawk vi. stare stupidly —**gaw'ky** a. clumsy, awkward

gawp v. sl. stare stupidly; gape

gay a. merry; lively; cheerful; bright; light-hearted; showy; given to pleasure; inf. homosexual —**gai'ety** n. —**gai'ly** adv.

gaze vi. look fixedly —n.

gaze'bo [-ē-] n. summer-house, turret on roof, with extensive view

gazelle' n. small graceful antelope

gazette' n. official newspaper for announcements of government appointments etc.; newspaper title —vt. publish in gazette —**gazetteer'** n. geographical dictionary

gazump' v. raise the price of something, esp. a house, after agreeing it with a prospective buyer

GB Great Britain

GC George Cross

GCE General Certificate of Education

GCSE general certificate of secondary education

GDP gross domestic product

GDR German Democratic Republic

gean [gēn] n. white-flowered tree with red fruit, wild cherry

gear n. set of wheels working together, esp. by engaging cogs; connection by which engine, motor etc. is brought into work; arrangement by which driving wheel of cycle, car etc. performs more or fewer revolutions relative to pedals, pistons etc.; equipment; clothing; goods, utensils; apparatus, tackle, tools; rigging; harness —vt. adapt (one thing) so as to conform with another; provide with gear; put in gear —**gear'box** n. case protecting gearing of bicycle, car etc. —**in gear** connected up and ready for work —**out of gear** disconnected, out of working order; upset

geel'bek [chēl'-] n. edible S Afr. marine fish

geese pl. of GOOSE

gee'zer n. inf. (old, eccentric) man

Gei'ger counter [gī'-] n. instrument for detecting radioactivity, cosmic radiation and charged atomic particles

gei'sha [gā'-] n. in Japan, professional female companion for men

gel [jel] n. jelly-like substance; such substance applied to hair before styling to retain shape —vi. form a gel (-ll-) Also **jell**

gel'atin(e) [jel'-] n. substance prepared from animal bones etc., producing edible jelly; anything resembling this —**gelat'inous** a. like gelatin or jelly

geld vt. castrate —**geld'ing** n. castrated horse

gel'id [jel'-] a. very cold

gel'ignite [jel'-] n. powerful explosive consisting of dynamite in gelatin form

gem n. precious stone, esp. when cut and polished; treasure —vt. adorn with gems

gem'inate vt. double, pair, repeat —**gemina'tion** n.

Gemi'ni n. (the twins) 3rd sign of the zodiac, operative May 21–June 20

gems'bok [-buk] n. S Afr. oryx

Gen. General; Genesis

gen [j-] n. inf. information

gen. gender; general; genitive; genus

gendarme' [zhon-] n. policeman in France

gen'der [j-] n. sex, male or female; grammatical classification of nouns, according to sex (actual or attributed)

gene [jēn] n. biological factor determining inherited characteristics

geneal'ogy [jē-] n. account of descent from ancestors; pedigree; study of pedigrees —**genealog'ical** a. —**geneal'ogist** n.

gen'era [j-] pl. of GENUS

gen'eral [j-] a. common, widespread; not particular or specific; applicable to all or most; not restricted to one department; usual, prevalent; miscellaneous; dealing with main element only; vague, indefinite —n. army officer of rank above colonel —**gen'eral'ity** n. general principle; vague statement; indefiniteness —**generaliza'tion** n. general conclusion from particular instance; inference —**gen'eralize** vt. reduce to general laws —vi. draw general conclusions —**gen'erally**

adv. —**general practitioner** non-specialist doctor with practice serving particular local area

gen'erate [-j-] *vt.* bring into being; produce —**genera'tion** *n.* bringing into being; all persons born about same time; average time between two such generations (about 30 years) —**genera'tive** *a.* —**gen'erator** *n.* apparatus for producing (steam, electricity *etc.*); begetter

gener'ic [ji-ne'rik] *a.* belonging to, characteristic of class or genus —**gener'ically** *adv.*

gen'erous [-j-] *a.* liberal, free in giving; abundant —**generos'ity** *n.* —**gen'erously** *adv.*

gen'esis [-j-] *n.* origin; mode of formation; (G-) first book of Bible (*pl.* **-eses**)

gen'et [-j-] *n.* catlike mammal of Afr. and S Europe

genet'ics [-j-] *pl.n.* (*with sing. v.*) scientific study of heredity and variation in organisms —**genet'ic** *a.*

ge'nial [je'-] *a.* cheerful, warm in behaviour; mild, conducive to growth —**genial'ity** *n.* —**ge'nially** *adv.*

ge'nie [je'-] *n.* in fairy tales, servant appearing by, and working, magic (*pl.* **ge'nii**)

gen'ital [-j-] *a.* relating to sexual organs or reproduction —**gen'itals** *pl.n.* the sexual organs

gen'itive [-j-] *a./n.* possessive (case) —**geniti'val** *a.*

ge'nius [je'-] *n.* (person with) exceptional power or ability, esp. of mind; distinctive spirit or nature (of nation *etc.*)

gen'ocide [-j-] *n.* murder of a nationality or ethnic group

genre [zhahn'rə] *n.* kind; sort; style; painting of homely scene

gent [-j-] *inf.* for **gentleman** —*pl.* men's public lavatory

genteel' [-j-] *a.* well-bred; stylish; affectedly proper —**genteel'ly** *adv.*

gen'tian [jen'shən] *n.* plant, usu. with blue flowers

gen'tile [-j-] *a.* of race other than Jewish; heathen —*n.*

gen'tle [-j-] *a.* mild, quiet, not rough or severe; soft and soothing; courteous; moderate; gradual; noble; well-born —**gentil'ity** *n.* noble birth; respectability, politeness —**gen'tleness** *n.* quality of being gentle; tenderness —**gen'tly** *adv.* —**gen'try** *n.* people of social standing next below nobility —**gen'tleman** *n.* chivalrous well-bred man; man of good social position; man (used as a mark of politeness) —**gen'tlemanly**, —**gen'tlemanlike** *a.* —**gentleman's agreement** agreement binding by honour but not valid in law —**gen'tlewoman** *n.*

gen'uflect [-j-] *vi.* bend knee, *esp.* in worship —**genuflec'tion**, **genuflex'ion** *n.*

gen'uine [-j-] *a.* real, true, not sham, authentic; sincere; pure

ge'nus [je'-] *n.* class, order, group (*esp.* of insects, animals *etc.*) with common characteristics usu. comprising several species (*pl.* **gen'era**)

geocen'tric [jē-ō-sen'-] *a.* Astronomy measured, seen from the earth; having the earth as centre —**geocen'trically** *adv.*

ge'ode [je'-] *n.* cavity lined with crystals; stone containing this

geodes'ic [jē-] *a.* of geometry of curved surfaces —**geodesic dome** light but strong hemispherical construction formed from set of polygons

geod'esy [ji-od'-] *n.* science of measuring the earth's surface

geog'raphy [-j-] *n.* science of earth's form, physical features, climate, population *etc.* —**geog'rapher** *n.* —**geograph'ic(al)** *adj.*

—**geograph'ically** adv.

geol'ogy [-j-] n. science of earth's crust, rocks, strata etc. —**geolog'ical** a. —**geolog'ically** adv. —**geol'ogist** n.

geom'etry [-j-] n. science of properties and relations of lines, surfaces etc. —**geomet'rical** a. —**geomet'rically** adv. —**geometri'cian** n.

geophys'ics [-j-] n. science dealing with physics of the earth —**geophys'ical** a. —**geophys'icist** n.

georgette' [jawr-jet'] n. fine, silky, semitransparent fabric

Geor'gian [jawrj'-] a. of the times of the four George's (1714-1830) or of George V (1910-36)

georg'ic [jawrj'-] n. poem on rural life, esp. one by Virgil

geosta'tionary a. (of satellite) in orbit around earth so it remains over same point on surface

gera'nium [-j-] n. common cultivated plant with red, pink or white flowers, pelargonium; strong pink colour

ger'bil [-j-] n. burrowing, desert rodent of Asia and Africa

ger'ent [jer'-] n. ruler, governor, director

geria'trics, gerontol'ogy [-j-] n. branch of science dealing with old age and its illnesses —**geriat'ric** a./n. old (person)

germ [-j-] n. microbe, esp. causing disease; elementary thing; rudiment of new organism, of animal or plant —**germici'dal** a. —**germ'icide** n. substance for destroying disease germs

Ger'man [-j-] n./a. (language or native) of Germany —**German measles** rubella, mild disease with symptoms like measles

ger'man [-j-] a. of the same parents; closely akin (only in brother-, sister-, cousin-german)

germane' [-j-] a. relevant, pertinent

germ'inate [-j-] v. (cause to) sprout or begin to grow —**germina'tion** n.

gerr'ymander [-j-] vt. manipulate constituency so as to favour one side —n.

ger'und [jer'-] n. noun formed from verb, eg living

Gestap'o [-ahp'o] n. secret state police in Nazi Germany

gesta'tion [-j-] n. carrying of young in womb between conception and birth; this period

gestic'ulate [-j-] vi. use expressive movements of hands and arms when speaking —**gesticula'tion** n.

ges'ture [-j-] n. movement to convey meaning; indication of state of mind —vi. make such a movement

get vt. obtain, procure; contract; catch; earn; cause to go or come; bring into position or state; induce; engender; be in possession of, have (to do); inf. understand —vi. succeed in coming or going; reach, attain; become (**got, get'ting**) —**get'away** n. escape —**get across** be understood —**get at** gain access to; annoy; criticize; influence —**get (one's) goat** sl. make (one) angry, annoyed

ge'um [jee'-] n. garden plant with orange, yellow or white flowers

gey'ser [gee'z-] n. hot spring throwing up spout of water from time to time; apparatus for heating water and delivering it from a tap

ghast'ly [gah-] a. inf. unpleasant; deathlike, pallid; inf. unwell; horrible —adv. sickly

gher'kin [ger'-] n. small cucumber used in pickling

ghett'o [get'-] n. densely populated (*esp.* by one racial group) slum area (*pl.* -**tos**)

g(h)ill'ie *n.* in Scotland, attendant for hunting or fishing

ghost [gō-] *n.* spirit, dead person appearing again; spectre; semblance; faint trace; one who writes work to appear under another's name —*v.* write another's work, speeches *etc.* —**ghost'ly** *a.*

ghoul [gool] *n.* malevolent spirit; person with morbid interests; fiend —**ghoul'ish** *a.* of or like ghoul; horrible

GHQ General Headquarters

G.I. *short for* **Government Issue**, stamped on US military equipment —*n. inf.* US soldier

gi'ant [jī-] *n.* mythical being of superhuman size; very tall person, plant *etc.* —*a.* huge —**gigan'tic** *a.* enormous, huge

gibb'er [j-] *vi.* make meaningless sounds with mouth, jabber, chatter —**gibb'erish** *n.* meaningless speech or words

gibb'et [j-] *n.* gallows; post with arm on which executed criminal was hung; death by hanging —*vt.* hang on gibbet; hold up to scorn

gibb'on *n.* type of ape

gibe [j-], **jibe** *v.* utter taunts; mock; jeer —*n.*

gib'lets [-] *pl.n.* internal edible parts of fowl, as liver, gizzard *etc.*

gidd'y *a.* dizzy, feeling as if about to fall; liable to cause this feeling; flighty, frivolous —**gid'dily** *adv.* —**gidd'iness** *n.*

gift *n.* thing given, present; faculty, power —*vt.* present (with); endow, bestow —**gift'ed** *a.* talented

gig *n.* light, two-wheeled carriage; *inf.* single booking of musicians to play at concert *etc.*; cluster of fish-hooks

gigan'tic [jī-] *see* GIANT

gig'gle *vi.* laugh nervously, fool-

ishly —*n.* such a laugh; joke

gig'olo [zhig-'] *n.* man kept, paid, by (older) woman to be her escort, lover

gild¹ *vt.* put thin layer of gold on; make falsely attractive (**gilded** *pt.* —**gilt** *or* **gilded** *pp.*) —**gilt** *a.* gilded —*n.* thin layer of gold put on; superficial appearance

gild² *see* GUILD

gill¹ [g-] *n.* breathing organ in fish (*usu. pl.*)

gill² [j-] *n.* liquid measure, quarter of pint (0.142 litres)

gill'yflower *n.* fragrant flower

gim'bals [j-] *pl.n.* pivoted rings, for keeping things, *eg* compass, horizontal at sea

gim'let [-] *n.* boring tool, usu. with screw point

gimm'ick *n.* clever device, stratagem *etc.*, *esp.* designed to attract attention or publicity

gimp *n.* narrow fabric or braid used as edging or trimming

gin¹ [j-] *n.* spirit flavoured with juniper berries

gin² [j-] *n.* primitive engine in which vertical shaft is turned to drive horizontal beam in a circle; machine for separating cotton from seeds; snare, trap

gin'ger [j-] *n.* plant with hot-tasting spicy root used in cooking *etc.*; the root; *inf.* spirit, mettle; light reddish-yellow colour —*vt.* stimulate —**gin'gery** *a.* of, like ginger; hot; high-spirited; reddish —**ginger ale** ginger-flavoured soft drink —**ginger beer** effervescing beverage made by fermenting ginger —**gin'gerbread** *n.* cake flavoured with ginger —**ginger group** group within a party, association *etc.* that enlivens or radicalizes its parent body

gin'gerly [j-] *adv.* cautiously, warily, reluctantly —*a.*

ging'ham [-ng'əm] *n.* cotton

cloth, usu. checked, woven from dyed yarn

gink'go, ging'go n. ornamental Chinese tree (pl. **-oes**)

gin'seng n. (root of) plant believed to have tonic and energy-giving properties

Gip'sy n. see GYPSY

giraffe' [ji-rahf'] n. Afr. ruminant animal, with spotted coat and very long neck and legs

gird vt. put belt round; fasten clothes thus; equip with, or belt on, a sword; prepare (oneself); encircle (**girt, gird'ed** pt./pp) —**gird'er** n. large beam, esp. of steel

gir'dle n. corset; waistband; anything that surrounds, encircles; griddle —vt. surround, encircle

girl n. female child; young (unmarried) woman —**girl'hood** n. —**girl'ish** a.

gi'ro [jī'-] n. system operated by banks and post offices which provides for the transfer of money between accounts or by giro cheque

girt pt./pp. of GIRD

girth n. measurement round thing; leather or cloth band put round horse to hold saddle etc. —vt. surround, secure, with girth

gist [j-] n. substance, main point (of remarks etc.)

give [giv] vt. bestow, confer ownership of, make present of; deliver; impart; assign; yield, supply; utter; emit; be host of (party etc.); make over; cause to have —vi. yield, give way, move (**gave, giv'en, giv'ing**) —n. yielding, elasticity —**give up** acknowledge defeat; abandon

gizz'ard n. part of bird's stomach

gla'brous, gla'brate a. smooth; without hairs or any unevenness

glac'é [glas'i] a. crystallized, candied, iced; glossy

glac'ier [-as'-, -si'-] n. river of ice, slow-moving mass of ice formed by accumulated snow in mountain valleys —**gla'cial** a. of ice, or of glaciers; very cold —**gla'ciated** a. —**glacia'tion** n.

glad a. pleased; happy, joyous; giving joy —**gladd'en** vt. make glad —**glad'ly** adv. —**glad'ness** n. —**glad'rags** pl.n. sl. clothes for special occasions

glade n. clear, grassy space in wood or forest

glad'iator n. trained fighter in Roman arena

gladio'lus n. kind of iris, with sword-shaped leaves —**glad** inf. gladiolus

Glad'stone (bag) n. travelling bag

glair n. white of egg; sticky substance —vt. smear with white of egg —**glair'y** a.

glam'our n. alluring charm, fascination —**glam'orize** vt. make appear glamorous —**glam'orous** a.

glance [-ah-] vi. look rapidly or briefly; allude; touch; glide off something struck; pass quickly —n. brief look; flash; gleam; sudden (deflected) blow

gland n. one of various small organs controlling different bodily functions by chemical means —**gland'ers** n. contagious horse disease —**gland'ular** a.

glare [-ār] vi. look fiercely; shine brightly, intensely; be conspicuous —n. —**gla'ring** a.

glass [-ah-] n. hard transparent substance made by fusing sand, soda, potash etc.; things made of it; tumbler; its contents; lens; mirror; telescope; barometer; microscope —pl. spectacles —**glass'ily** adv. —**glass'iness** n. —**glass'y** a. like glass; expressionless —**glass'house** n. greenhouse; inf. army prison —**glass wool** insulating fabric

glauco'ma n. eye disease

glaze vt. furnish with glass; cover with glassy substance —vi. become glassy —n. transparent coating; substance used for this; glossy surface —**gla'zier** n. one who glazes windows

gleam n. slight or passing beam of light; faint or momentary show —vi. give out gleams

glean v. pick up (facts etc.); gather, pick up (orig.) after reapers in cornfields —**glean'er** n.

glebe n. land belonging to parish church or benefice

glee n. mirth, merriment; musical composition for three or more voices —**glee'ful** a. —**glee'fully** adv.

glen n. narrow valley, usu. wooded and with a stream, esp. in Scotland

glengarr'y n. Scottish woollen boat-shaped cap with ribbons hanging down back

glib a. fluent but insincere or superficial; plausible —**glib'ly** adv. —**glib'ness** n.

glide vi. pass smoothly and continuously; of aeroplane, move without use of engines —n. smooth, silent movement; Mus. sounds made in passing from tone to tone —**gli'der** n. aircraft without engine which moves in air currents —**gli'ding** n. sport of flying gliders

glimm'er vi. shine faintly, flicker —n. —**glimm'ering** n. faint gleam of light; faint idea, notion

glimpse n. brief or incomplete view —vt. catch glimpse of

glint v. flash, glance, glitter; reflect —n.

glissade' [-ahd'] n. gliding dance step; slide, usu. on feet down slope of ice —vi.

glis'ten [-is'n] vi. gleam by reflecting light

glitt'er vi. shine with bright quivering light, sparkle; be showy —n. lustre; sparkle

gloa'ming [-o-] n. evening twilight

gloat vi. regard, dwell on with smugness or malicious satisfaction

glob n. soft lump or mass

globe n. sphere with map of earth or stars; heavenly sphere, esp. the earth; ball, sphere —**glo'bal** a. of globe; relating to whole world —**glob'ular** a. globeshaped —**glob'ule** n. small round particle; drop —**glob'ulin** n. kind of simple protein —**globe'trotter** n. (habitual) worldwide traveller

glock'enspiel [-spēl] n. percussion instrument of metal bars which are struck with hammers

gloom n. darkness; melancholy, depression —**gloom'ily** adv. —**gloom'y** a.

glory n. renown, honourable fame; splendour; exalted or prosperous state; heavenly bliss —vi. take pride (in) (**glor'ied, glory'ing**) —**glorifica'tion** n. —**glor'ify** vt. make glorious; invest with glory (**-ified, -ifying**) —**glor'ious** a. illustrious; splendid; excellent; delightful —**glor'iously** adv. —**glory hole** inf. untidy cupboard, room or receptacle for storage

Glos. Gloucestershire

gloss [1] n. surface shine, lustre —vt. put gloss on; (esp. with over) (try to) cover up, pass over (fault, error) —**gloss'iness** n. —**gloss'y** a. smooth, shiny —n. magazine printed on shiny paper

gloss [2] n. marginal interpretation of word; comment, explanation —vt. interpret; comment; explain away —**gloss'ary** n. dictionary, vocabulary of special words

glott'is *n.* human vocal apparatus, larynx —**glott'al, glott'ic** *a.*

glove [-uv] *n.* covering for the hand —*vt.* cover with, or as with glove —**glove box, compartment** small storage area in dashboard of car —**the gloves** boxing gloves; boxing

glow [-ō] *vi.* give out light and heat without flames; shine; experience feeling of wellbeing or satisfaction; be or look hot; burn with emotion —*n.* shining heat; warmth of colour; feeling of wellbeing; ardour —**glow-worm** *n.* female insect giving out green light

glow'er [-ow'-] *vi.* scowl

gloxin'ia *n.* tropical plant with large bell-shaped flowers

glu'cose [glōō'-] *n.* type of sugar found in fruit *etc.*

glue [-ōō] *n.* any natural or synthetic adhesive; any sticky substance —*vt.* fasten with glue —**glu'ey** *a.* —**glue-sniffing** *n.* practice of inhaling fumes of glue for intoxicating or hallucinatory effects —**glue-sniffer** *n.*

glum *a.* sullen, moody, gloomy

glut *n.* surfeit, excessive amount —*vt.* feed, gratify to the full or to excess; overstock (**-tt-**)

glu'ten [glōō'-] *n.* protein present in cereal grain —**glu'tinous** *a.* sticky, gluey

glutt'on[1] *n.* greedy person; one with great liking or capacity for something —**glutt'onous** *a.* like glutton, greedy —**glutt'ony** *n.*

glutt'on[2] *n.* wolverine

glyc'erin(e), **glyc'erol** [glis'-] *n.* colourless sweet liquid with wide application in chemistry and industry

glyp'tic *a.* pert. to carving, *esp.* on precious stones

GM George Medal

gm gram

GMT Greenwich Mean Time

gnarled [narld] *a.* knobby, rugged, twisted

gnash [n-] *v.* grind (teeth) together as in anger or pain

gnat [n-] *n.* small, biting, two-winged fly

gnaw [n-] *v.* bite or chew steadily; (*esp.* **with** at) cause distress to

gneiss [nīs] *n.* coarse-grained metamorphic rock

gnome [n-] *n.* legendary creature like small old man; international financier

gno'mic [nō'-] *a.* of or like an aphorism

gnos'tic [n-] *a.* of, relating to knowledge, *esp.* spiritual knowledge

GNP Gross National Product

gnu [nōō] *n.* S Afr. antelope somewhat like ox

go *vi.* move along, make way; be moving; depart; function; make specified sound; fail, give way, break down; elapse; be kept; put; be able to be put; result; contribute to result; tend to; be accepted, have force; become (**went** *pt.*, **gone** *pp.*) —*n.* going; energy, vigour; attempt; turn —**go-go dancer** dancer, *usu.* scantily dressed, who performs rhythmic and oft. erotic modern dance routines, *esp.* in nightclub —**go-slow** *n.* deliberate slackening of the rate of production as form of industrial protest

goad *n.* spiked stick for driving cattle; anything that urges to action; incentive —*vt.* urge on; torment

goal *n.* end of race; object of effort; posts through which ball is to be driven in football *etc.*; the score so made

goat *n.* four-footed animal with long hair, horns and beard —**goat'ee** *n.* beard like goat's

—**goat'-herd** n. —**get (someone's) goat** sl. annoy (someone)

gob n. lump; sl. mouth —**gobb'et** n. lump (of food) —**gob'ble** vt. eat hastily, noisily or greedily

gob'ble n. throaty, gurgling cry of the turkey-cock —vi. make such a noise

gob'bledegook, gob'bledygook n. pretentious language, esp. as used by officials

gob'let n. drinking cup

gob'lin n. Folklore small, usu. malevolent being

god n. superhuman being worshipped as having supernatural power; object of worship, idol; (G-) in monotheistic religions, the Supreme Being, creator and ruler of universe (**godd'ess** fem.) —**god'like** a. —**god'liness** n. —**god'ly** a. devout, pious —**god'child** n. one considered in relation to godparent n. —**god'father** n. sponsor at baptism (fem. **god'mother**) —**god-fearing** a. religious, good —**god'forsaken** a. hopeless, dismal —**god'head** n. divine nature or deity —**god'send** n. something unexpected but welcome

gode'tia [-shə] n. annual garden plant

god'wit n. large shore bird of N regions

gogg'a [ʜoʜ'ə] n. SA inf. insect, creepy-crawly

gog'gle vi. (of eyes) bulge; stare —pl.n. protective spectacles

goi'tre [-tə] n. neck swelling due to enlargement of thyroid gland

go-kart (or **cart**) n. miniature, low-powered racing car

gold [-ō-] n. yellow precious metal; coins of this; wealth; beautiful or precious thing; colour of gold —a. of, like gold —**gold'en** a. —**gold'crest** n. small bird with yellow crown —**gold-digger** n. woman skilful in extracting mon-

ey from men —**golden mean** middle way between extremes —**goldenrod'** n. tall plant with golden flower spikes —**golden rule** important principle —**golden wedding** fiftieth wedding anniversary —**gold'field** n. place where gold deposits are known to exist —**gold'finch** n. bird with yellow feathers —**gold'fish** n. any of various ornamental pond or aquarium fish —**gold standard** financial arrangement whereby currencies of countries accepting it are expressed in fixed terms of gold

golf n. outdoor game in which small hard ball is struck with clubs into a succession of holes —vi. play this game —**golf'er** n.

goll'iwog n. black-faced doll

gon'ad n. gland producing gametes

gon'dola n. Venetian canal boat —**gondolier'** n. rower of gondola

gone [gon] pp. of GO

gong n. metal plate with turned rim which resounds as bell when struck with soft mallet; anything used thus

gonorrhoe'a [-rē'ə] n. a venereal disease

good a. commendable; right; proper; excellent; beneficial; well-behaved; virtuous; kind; safe; adequate; sound; valid (**bet'ter** comp., **best** sup.) —n. benefit; wellbeing; profit —pl. property; wares —**good'ly** a. large, considerable —**good'ness** n. —**good sort** inf. agreeable person —**good will** kindly feeling, heartiness; value of a business in reputation etc. over and above its tangible assets

goodbye' interj./n. form of address on parting

goo'ey a. inf. sticky, soft

goof inf. n. mistake; stupid per-

son —vi. make mistake —goof'y
a. silly, sloppy

goo'gly n. Cricket ball which
changes direction unexpectedly
on the bounce

goon n. inf. stupid fellow

goosan'der n. type of duck

goose n. web-footed bird; its
flesh; simpleton (pl. geese)
—goose flesh bristling of skin
due to cold, fright —goose step
formal parade step

goose'berry [gooz'-] n. thorny
shrub; its hairy fruit; inf. unwelcome third party

go'pher n. various species of
Amer. burrowing rodents

gore¹ n. (dried) blood from
wound —go'rily adv. —go'ry a.

gore² vt. pierce with horns

gore³ n. triangular piece inserted to shape garment —vt. shape
thus

gorge [-j] n. ravine; disgust, resentment —vi. feed greedily
—gor'get [-jit] n. armour, ornamentation or clothing for throat

gor'geous [-jəs] a. splendid,
showy, dazzling; inf. extremely
pleasing

gor'gon n. terrifying or repulsive woman

gorill'a n. largest anthropoid
ape, found in Afr.

gor'mandize vt. eat hurriedly
or like a glutton

gorm'less a. inf. stupid

gorse n. prickly shrub

gory see GORE¹

gos'hawk n. large hawk

gos'ling [-z-] n. young goose

gos'pel n. unquestionable truth;
(G-) any of first four books of
New Testament

goss'amer n. filmy substance
like spider's web; thin gauze or
silk fabric

goss'ip n. idle (malicious) talk
about other persons, esp. regard-

less of fact; one who talks thus
—vi. engage in gossip; chatter

got see GET

Goth'ic a. Architecture of the
pointed arch style common in
Europe from twelfth-sixteenth
century; of Goths; barbarous;
gloomy; grotesque; (of type) German black letter

gouge [gowj] vt. scoop out; force
out —n. chisel with curved cutting edge

gou'lash [goō-] n. stew of meat
and vegetables seasoned with
paprika

gourd [goord] n. trailing or
climbing plant; its large fleshy
fruit; its rind as vessel

gour'mand [goor'-] n. glutton

gour'met [goor'mā] n. connoisseur of wine, food; epicure

gout [-ow-] n. disease with inflammation, esp. of joints
—gout'y a.

Gov. Government; Governor

gov'ern [guv-] vt. rule, direct,
guide, control; decide or determine; be followed by (grammatical case etc.) —gov'ernable a.
—gov'ernance n. act of governing —gov'erness n. woman
teacher, esp. in private household —gov'ernment n. exercise
of political authority in directing
a people, state etc.; system by
which community is ruled; body
of people in charge of government of state; ministry; executive power; control; direction;
exercise of authority —govern-
men'tal a. —gov'ernor n. one
who governs, esp. one invested
with supreme authority in state
etc.; chief administrator of an
institution; member of committee responsible for an organization or institution; regulator for
speed of engine

gown n. loose flowing outer
garment; woman's (long) dress;

official robe, as in university *etc.*

goy *n. sl.* derogatory Jewish term for a non-Jew (*pl.* **goy'im, goys**)

GP General Practitioner

GPO General Post Office

grab *vt.* grasp suddenly; snatch (**-bb-**) —*n.* sudden clutch; quick attempt to seize; device or implement for clutching

grace *n.* charm, elegance; accomplishment; goodwill, favour; sense of propriety; postponement granted; short thanksgiving before or after meal; title of duke or archbishop —*vt.* add grace to, honour —**grace'ful** *a.* —**grace'fully** *adv.* —**grace'less** *a.* shameless, depraved —**gra'cious** *a.* favourable; kind; pleasing; indulgent, beneficent, condescending —**gra'ciously** *adv.* —**grace note** *Mus.* melodic ornament

grade *n.* step, stage; degree of rank *etc.*; class; mark, rating; slope —*vt.* arrange in classes; assign grade to; level ground, move earth with grader —**gra-da'tion** *n.* series of degrees or steps; each of them; arrangement in steps; in painting, gradual passing from one shade *etc.* to another —**gra'der** *n. esp.* machine with wide blade used in road making —**make the grade** succeed

gra'dient *n.* (degree of) slope

grad'ual *a.* taking place by degrees; slow and steady; not steep —**grad'ually** *adv.*

grad'uate *vi.* take university degree —*vt.* divide into degrees; mark, arrange according to scale —*n.* holder of university degree —**gradua'tion** *n.*

graffi'ti [-fē'tē] *pl.n.* (*sing.* **graffi'to**) (*oft.* obscene) writing, drawing on walls

graft[1] [-ah-] *n.* shoot of plant set in stalk of another; the process; surgical transplant of skin, tissue —*vt.* insert (shoot) in another stalk; transplant (living tissue in surgery)

graft[2] [-ah-] *inf. n.* hard work; self-advancement, profit by unfair means, *esp.* through official or political privilege; bribe; swindle —**graft'er** *n.*

grail *n.* (*usu.* **Holy Grail**) cup or dish used by Christ at the Last Supper

grain *n.* seed, fruit of cereal plant; wheat and allied plants; small hard particle; unit of weight, 1/7000th of pound avoirdupois (0.0648 gram); texture; arrangement of fibres; any very small amount; natural temperament or disposition —**grain'y** *a.*

gram(me) *n.* unit of weight in metric system, one thousandth of a kilogram

gramm'ar *n.* science of structure and usages of language; book on this; correct use of words —**gramma'rian** *n.* —**grammat'ical** *a.* according to grammar —**grammat'ically** *adv.* —**grammar school** *esp.* formerly, state-maintained secondary school providing education with strong academic bias

gram'ophone *n.* record player

gram'pus *n.* type of dolphin; person who huffs, breathes heavily

gran, grann'y *n. inf.* grandmother —**granny flat** flat in or added to house (for elderly parent)

gran'ary *n.* storehouse for grain; rich grain growing region

grand *a.* imposing; magnificent; majestic; noble; splendid; eminent; lofty; chief, of chief importance; final (total) —**gran'deur** [-jə] *n.* nobility; magnificence; dignity —**grandil'oquence** *n.* —**grandil'oquent** *a.* pompous in speech —**grandil'oquently** *adv.*

—**grand'iose** a. imposing; affectedly grand; striking —**grand'child** [-n'ch-] n. child of one's child (**grand'son** or **grand'daughter**) —**grand'parent** [-n(d)'-] n. parent of parent (**grand'father** or **grand'mother**) —**grand piano** large harp-shaped piano with horizontal strings —**grand'stand** [-n(d)'-] n. structure with tiered seats for spectators

grange [-j] n. country house with farm buildings

gran'ite [-it] n. hard crystalline igneous rock —**granit'ic** a.

graniv'orous a. feeding on grain or seeds

grant [-ah-] vt. consent to fulfil (request); permit; bestow; admit —n. sum of money provided by government for specific purpose, as education; gift; allowance, concession —**grantee'** n. —**grantor'** n.

gran'ule n. small grain —**gran'ular** a. of or like grains —**gran'ulate** vt. form into grains —vi. take form of grains —**granula'tion** n.

grape n. fruit of vine —**grape hyacinth** plant with clusters of small, rounded blue flowers —**grape'shot** n. bullets scattering when fired —**grape'vine** n. grape-bearing vine; inf. unofficial means of conveying information

grape'fruit n. subtropical citrus fruit

graph n. drawing depicting relation of different numbers, quantities etc.

graph'ic a. vividly descriptive; of, in, relating to, writing, drawing, painting etc. —**graph'icacy** n. ability to understand and use maps, plans etc. —**graph'ically** adv. —**graph'ite** n. form of carbon (used in pencils) —**graphol'ogy** n. study of handwriting

grap'nel n. hooked iron instrument for seizing anything; small anchor with several flukes

grap'ple v. come to grips with, wrestle; cope or contend —n. grappling; grapnel

grasp [-ah-] v. (try, struggle to) seize hold; understand —n. act of grasping; grip; comprehension —**grasp'ing** a. greedy, avaricious

grass [-ah-] n. common type of plant with jointed stems and long narrow leaves (including cereals, bamboo etc.); such plants grown as lawn; pasture; sl. marijuana; sl. informer, esp. criminal who betrays others to police —vt. cover with grass; inform (on) —**grass'hopper** n. jumping, chirping insect —**grass roots** fundamentals —**grass'roots** a. coming from ordinary people, the rank-and-file —**grass widow** wife whose husband is absent

grate¹ n. framework of metal bars for holding fuel in fireplace —**gra'ting** n. framework of parallel or latticed bars covering opening

grate² vt. rub into small bits on rough surface —vi. rub with harsh noise; have irritating effect —**gra'ter** n. utensil with rough surface for reducing substance to small particles —**gra'ting** a. harsh; irritating

grate'ful a. thankful; appreciative; pleasing —**grate'fully** adv. —**grate'fulness** n. —**grat'itude** n. sense of being thankful for favour

grat'ify vt. satisfy; please; indulge —**gratifica'tion** n.

gratin' [gra-tan'] n. method of cooking to form light crust; dish so cooked

gra'tis [-a'-, -a'-, -ah'-] adv./a. free, for nothing

gratu'itous a. given free; uncalled for —**gratu'itously** adv.

—gratu'ity n. gift of money for services rendered; donation

grave[1] n. hole dug to bury corpse; death —**grave'stone** n. monument on grave —**grave'yard** n.

grave[2] a. serious, weighty; dignified, solemn; plain, dark in colour; deep in note —**grave'ly** adv.

grave[3] [-ah-] n. accent (`) over vowel to indicate special sound quality

grave[4] vt. clean (ship's bottom) by scraping (**graved** pt./pp.) —**graving dock** dry dock

grav'el n. small stones; coarse sand —vt. cover with gravel —**grav'elly** a.

gra'ven a. carved, engraved

grav'itate vi. move by gravity; tend (towards) centre of attraction; sink, settle down —**gravita'tion** n.

grav'ity n. force of attraction of one body for another, esp. of objects to the earth; heaviness; importance; seriousness; staidness

gra'vy n. juices from meat in cooking; sauce for food made from these

gray a. alt., esp. US, spelling of GREY —**gray'ling** n. fish of salmon family

graze[1] v. feed on grass, pasture —**gra'zier** n. one who raises cattle for market

graze[2] vt. touch lightly in passing, scratch, scrape —n. grazing; abrasion

grease [-ēs] n. soft melted fat of animals; thick oil as lubricant —vt. [or -ēz] apply grease to —**greas'er** n. one who greases; inf. mechanic; sl. unpleasant, dirty person —**grea'sily** adv. —**grea'siness** n. —**grea'sy** a. —**grease gun** appliance for injecting oil or grease into machin-

ery —**grease monkey** inf. mechanic —**grease'paint** n. theatrical make-up

great [-āt] a. large, big; important; pre-eminent, distinguished; inf. excellent —prefix indicates a degree further removed in relationship, eg **great-grand'father** n. —**great'ly** adv. —**great'ness** n. —**great'coat** n. overcoat, esp. military —**Great Dane** breed of very large dog

greave n. armour for leg below knee

grebe n. aquatic bird

Gre'cian a. of (ancient) Greece

greed n. excessive consumption of, desire for, food, wealth —**greed'y** a. gluttonous; eagerly desirous; voracious; covetous —**greed'ily** adv. —**greed'iness** n. voracity of appetite

Greek n. native language of Greece —a. of Greece or Greek

green a. of colour between blue and yellow; grass-coloured; emerald; unripe; uncooked (esp. prawns); (of bacon) unsmoked; inexperienced; gullible; envious —n. colour; area of grass, esp. for playing bowls etc. —pl. green vegetables —**green'ery** n. vegetation —**green belt** area of farms, open country around a town —**green'finch** n. European finch with dull green plumage in male —**green fingers** talent for gardening —**green'fly** n. aphid, small green garden pest —**green'gage** n. kind of plum —**green'grocer** n. dealer in vegetables and fruit —**green'grocery** n. —**green'horn** n. inexperienced person, newcomer —**green'house** n. glasshouse for rearing plants —**green'room** n. room for actors when offstage —**green'shank** n. large European sandpiper —**green'stone** n.

New Zealand jade —**green'-sward** n. turf

greet vt. meet with expressions of welcome; accost, salute; receive —**greet'ing** n.

grega'rious a. fond of company, sociable; living in flocks —**grega'riousness** n.

grem'lin n. imaginary being blamed for mechanical and other troubles

grenade' n. explosive shell or bomb, thrown by hand or shot from rifle —**grenadier'** n. soldier of Grenadier Guards; formerly, grenade thrower

grenadine' [-ēn'] n. syrup made from pomegranate juice, for sweetening and colouring drinks

grew [grōō] pt. of GROW

grey [grā] a. between black and white, as ashes or lead; clouded; dismal; turning white; aged; intermediate, indeterminate —n. grey colour; grey or white horse

grey'hound n. swift slender dog used in coursing and racing

grid n. network of horizontal and vertical lines, bars etc.; any interconnecting system of links; national network of electricity supply

grid'dle, gir'dle n. flat iron plate for cooking

grid'iron n. frame of metal bars for grilling; (field of play for) American football

grief [-ēf] n. deep sorrow —**grie'vance** n. real or imaginary ground of complaint —**grieve** vi. feel grief —vt. cause grief to —**grie'vous** a. painful, oppressive; very serious

griff'in, griff'on, gryph'on n. fabulous monster with eagle's head and wings and lion's body

grill n. device on cooker to radiate heat downwards; food cooked under grill; gridiron —v. cook (food) under grill; subject to severe questioning —**grill'ing** a. very hot —n. severe cross-examination —**grill'room** n. where grilled food is served

grill(e) n. grating, crosswork of bars over opening

grim a. stern; of stern or forbidding aspect, relentless; joyless —**grim'ly** adv.

grimace' n. wry face —vi. pull wry face

grime n. ingrained dirt, soot —vt. soil; dirty; blacken —**gri'my** a.

grin vi. show teeth, as in laughter (-**nn**-) —n. grinning smile

grind [-ī-] vt. crush to powder; oppress; make sharp, smooth; grate —vi. perform action of grinding; inf. work (esp. study) hard; grate (**ground** pt./pp.) —n. inf. hard work; action of grinding —**grind'er** n. —**grind'stone** n. stone used for grinding

grin'go [-ng'g-] n. in Mexico, contemptuous name for foreigner, esp. Englishman or Amer. (pl. -**s**)

grip n. firm hold, grasp; grasping power; mastery; handle; suitcase or travelling bag —vt. grasp or hold tightly; hold interest or attention of (-**pp**-)

gripe vi. inf. complain (persistently) —n. intestinal pain (esp. in infants); inf. complaint

gris'ly [-z-] a. grim, causing terror, ghastly

grist n. corn to be ground —**grist for one's mill** something which can be turned to advantage

gris'tle [gris'l] n. cartilage, tough flexible tissue

grit n. rough particles of sand; coarse sandstone; courage —pl. wheat etc. coarsely ground —v. clench, grind (teeth) (-**tt**-)

—**gritt'iness** n. —**gritt'y** a.

griz'zle[1] v. make, become grey —**griz'zled** a. —**griz'zly** (**bear**) large Amer. bear

griz'zle[2] inf. vi. grumble, whine, complain —**griz'zly** a.

groan vi. make low, deep sound of grief or pain; be in pain or overburdened —n.

groat Hist. n. fourpenny piece; orig. various European coins

gro'cer n. dealer in foodstuffs —**gro'ceries** pl.n. commodities sold by a grocer —**gro'cery** n. trade, premises of grocer

grog n. spirit (esp. rum) and water —**grog'gy** a. inf. unsteady, shaky, weak

groin n. fold where legs meet abdomen; euphemism for genitals; edge made by intersection of two vaults —vt. build with groins

groom n. person caring for horses; bridegroom; officer in royal household —vt. tend or look after; brush or clean (esp. horse); train (someone for something) —**grooms'man** n. friend attending bridegroom —**well-groomed** a. neat, smart

groove n. narrow channel, hollow, esp. cut by tool; rut, routine —vt. cut groove in —**groo'vy** a. sl. fashionable, exciting

grope vi. feel about, search blindly

gro'per [grō'-] n. see GROUPER

gros'beak [grōs'-] n. finch with large powerful bill

gross [-ōs] a. very fat; total, not net; coarse; indecent; flagrant; thick, rank —n. twelve dozen —**gross'ly** adv.

grotesque' [-tesk'] a. (horribly) distorted; absurd —n. decorative style using distorted human, animal and plant forms; grotesque person, thing —**grotesque'ly** adv.

grott'o n. cave (pl. -o(e)s)

grott'y a. inf. dirty, untidy, unpleasant

grouch inf. n. persistent grumbler; discontented mood —vi. grumble, be peevish

ground[1] n. surface of earth; soil, earth; reason, motive; coating to work on with paint; background, main surface worked on in painting, embroidery etc.; special area; bottom of sea —pl. dregs; enclosed land round house —vt. establish; instruct (in elements); place on ground —vi. run ashore —**groun'ded** a. of aircraft, unable or not permitted to fly —**ground'ing** n. basic general knowledge of a subject —**ground'less** a. without reason —**ground'nut** n. earthnut; peanut —**ground'sheet** n. waterproof sheet on ground under tent etc. —**ground'speed** n. aircraft's speed in relation to ground

ground[2] pt./pp. of GRIND

ground'sel n. yellow flowered plant

group [-ōō-] n. number of persons or things near together, or placed or classified together; small musical band of players or singers; class; two or more figures forming one artistic design —v. place, fall into group

group'er [-ōō-] n. large, edible sea fish

grouse[1] [-ows] n. game bird; its flesh (pl. **grouse**)

grouse[2] [-ows] vi. grumble, complain —n. complaint —**grous'er** n. grumbler

grout n. thin fluid mortar —vt. fill up with grout

grove n. small group of trees; road lined with trees

grov'el vi. abase oneself; lie face down (-ll-)

grow [-ō] vi. develop naturally; increase in size, height etc.; be produced; become by degrees

—*vt.* produce by cultivation (grew *pt.*, grown *pp.*) —**growth** *n.* growing; increase; what has grown or is growing —**grow bag** plastic bag containing sufficient growing medium and nutrients to enable plant, as tomato, to grow to full size in it —**grown-up** *a./n.* adult

growl *vi.* make low guttural sound of anger; rumble; murmur, complain —*n.*

groyne *n.* wall or jetty built out from riverbank or shore to control erosion

grub *vt.* dig superficially; root up —*vi.* dig, rummage; plod (**-bb-**) —*n.* larva of insect; *sl.* food —**grub'by** *a.* dirty

grudge *vt.* be unwilling to give, allow —*n.* ill will

gru'el [groo'-] *n.* food of oatmeal *etc.*, boiled in milk or water —**gru'elling** *a./n.* exhausting, severe (experience)

grue'some [groo'-] *a.* fearful, horrible, grisly —**grue'someness** *n.*

gruff *a.* rough in manner or voice, surly —**gruff'ly** *adv.*

grum'ble *vi.* complain; rumble, murmur; make growling sounds —*n.* complaint; low growl —**grum'bler** *n.*

grump'y *a.* ill-tempered, surly —**grump'ily** *adv.*

grunt *vi.* make sound characteristic of pig —*n.* pig's sound; gruff noise

gryph'on *n. see* GRIFFIN

gry'sbok *n.* small Afr. antelope

G-string *n.* very small covering for genitals; *Mus.* string tuned to G

GT gran turismo, touring car, used of (sports) car capable of high speed

guan'o [gwahn'-] *n.* sea bird manure (*pl.* **-nos**)

guarantee'¹ [ga-] *n.* formal assurance (*esp.* in writing) that product *etc.* will meet certain standards, last for given time *etc.* —*vt.* give guarantee of, for something; secure (against risk *etc.*) (**guaranteed'**, **guarantee'ing**) —**guarantor'** *n.* one who undertakes fulfilment of another's promises

guard [gah-] *vt.* protect, defend —*vi.* be careful, take precautions (against) —*n.* person, group that protects, supervises, keeps watch; sentry; soldiers protecting anything; official in charge of train; protection; screen for enclosing anything dangerous; protector; posture of defence —*pl.* (G-) certain British regiments —**guard'ian** *n.* keeper, protector; person having custody of infant *etc.* —**guard'ianship** *n.* care —**guard'house, -room** *n.* place for stationing those on guard or for prisoners —**Guards'man** *n.* soldier in Guards

guav'a [gwahv'-] *n.* tropical tree with fruit used to make jelly

gudg'eon¹ *n.* small freshwater fish

gudg'eon² *n.* pivot bearing; socket for rudder; kind of connecting pin

guelder-rose [gel-] *n.* shrub with clusters of white flowers

guer'don [gur'-] *n.* reward

guer(r)ill'a [gə-] *n.* member of irregular armed force, *esp.* fighting established force, government *etc.* —*a.*

guern'sey [gurn'-] *n.* breed of cattle; close-fitting knitted jumper

guess [ges] *vt.* estimate without calculation; conjecture, suppose; *US* consider, think —*vi.* form conjectures —*n.*

guest [gest] *n.* one entertained at another's house; one living in hotel —**guest'house** *n.* boarding house, usu. without alcoholic licence

guff n. sl. silly talk

guffaw' n. burst of boisterous laughter —vi.

guide [gīd] n. one who shows the way; adviser; book of instruction or information; contrivance for directing motion —vt. lead, act as guide to; arrange —**gui'dance** n. —**Girl Guide** member of Girl Guides' Association, organization for girls similar to that of Scouts —**guided missile** missile whose flight path is controlled by radio or preprogrammed homing mechanism

g(u)ild [gi-] n. organization, club; society for mutual help, or with common object; Hist. society of merchants or tradesmen —**guild'hall** n. meeting place of guild or corporation

guile [gīl] n. cunning, deceit —**guile'ful** a. —**guile'fully** adv. —**guile'less** a.

guill'emot [gil'i-] n. species of sea bird

guill'otine [gil'ə-tēn] n. machine for beheading; machine for cutting paper; in parliament etc. method of restricting length of debate by fixing time for taking vote —vt. behead; use guillotine on; limit debate by guillotine

guilt [gilt] n. fact, state of having done wrong; responsibility for criminal or moral offence —**guilt'iness** n. —**guilt'ily** adv. —**guilt'less** a. innocent —**guilt'y** a. having committed an offence

guin'ea [gin'i] n. formerly, sum of 21 shillings; gold coin of this value —**guinea fowl** bird allied to pheasant —**guinea pig** rodent originating in S Amer.; inf. person or animal used in experiments

guise [gīz] n. external appearance, esp. one assumed

guitar' [git-] n. 6-stringed instrument played by plucking or strumming strings; part or player of the guitar —**guitar'ist** n. player of the guitar

gulch n. ravine; gully

gulf n. large inlet of the sea; chasm; large gap

gull[1] n. long-winged web-footed sea bird

gull[2] n. dupe, fool —vt. dupe, cheat —**gullibil'ity** n. —**gull'ible** a. easily imposed on, credulous

gull'et n. food passage from mouth to stomach

gull'y n. channel or ravine worn by water

gulp vt. swallow eagerly —vi. gasp, choke —n.

gum[1] n. firm flesh in which teeth are set —**gumm'y** a. toothless

gum[2] n. sticky substance issuing from certain trees; an adhesive; chewing gum; gumtree, eucalypt —vt. stick with gum (-mm-) —**gum'my** a. —**gum'boots** pl.n. boots of rubber —**gum'tree** n. any species of eucalypt —**gum up the works** inf. impede progress —**up a gum tree** sl. in a difficult position

gump'tion n. resourcefulness; shrewdness, sense

gun n. weapon with metal tube from which missiles are discharged by explosion; cannon, pistol etc. —v. shoot; pursue, as with gun; race engine (of car) —**gunn'er** n. —**gunn'ery** n. use or science of large guns —**gun'boat** n. small warship —**gun dog** (breed of) dog used to retrieve etc. game —**gun'man** n. armed criminal —**gun'metal** n. alloy of copper and tin or zinc, formerly used for guns —**gun'powder** n. explosive mixture of saltpetre, sulphur, charcoal —**gun'room** n. in warship, mess room of junior officers —**gun'shot** n. shot or range of gun —a. caused by missile from gun —**gun'wale** [gun'əl], **gunn'el** n. upper edge of ship's side

gunge n. inf. any sticky, unpleasant substance

gunk n. inf. any dirty, oily matter

gunn'y n. strong, coarse sacking made from jute

gupp'y n. small colourful aquarium fish

gur'gle n. bubbling noise —vi. utter, flow with gurgle

gur'nard, **gur'net** n. spiny armour-headed sea fish

gur'u [goo'roo] n. a spiritual teacher, esp. in India

gush vi. flow out suddenly and copiously, spurt —n. sudden and copious flow; effusiveness —**gush'er** n. gushing person; oil well

guss'et n. triangle or diamond-shaped piece of material let into garment —**guss'eted** a.

gust n. sudden blast of wind; burst of rain, anger, passion etc. —**gust'y** a.

gust'o n. enjoyment, zest

gut n. (oft. pl.) entrails, intestines; material made from guts of animals, eg for violin strings etc. —pl. inf. essential, fundamental part; courage —vt. remove guts from (fish etc.); remove, destroy contents of (house) —**gut'sy** a. inf. greedy; courageous

gutta-percha n. (tropical tree producing) whitish rubber substance

gutt'er n. shallow trough for carrying off water from roof or side of street —vt. make channels in —vi. flow in streams; (of candle, melt away by wax forming channels and running down —**gutter press** journalism that relies on sensationalism —**gutt'ersnipe** n. neglected slum child; mean vindictive person

gutt'ural a. of, relating to, or produced in, the throat —n. guttural sound or letter

guy[1] [gī] n. effigy of Guy Fawkes burnt on Nov. 5th; inf. person (usu. male) —vt. make fun of; ridicule —**wise guy** inf., usu. disparaging clever person

guy[2] [gī] n. rope, chain to steady, secure something, eg tent —vt. keep in position by guy —**guy'rope** n.

guz'zle v. eat or drink greedily —n

gybe [jīb] v. (of boom of fore-and-aft sail) swing over to other side with following wind; alter course thus

gym [jim] n. short for GYMNASIUM or GYMNASTICS

gymkhan'a [jim-kahn'-] n. competition or display of horse riding

gymna'sium [jim-] n. place equipped for muscular exercises, athletic training (pl. -s, -na'sia) —**gym'nast** n. expert in gymnastics —**gymnas'tics** pl.n. muscular exercises, with or without apparatus, eg parallel bars

gynaecol'ogy [gīn-] n. branch of medicine dealing with functions and diseases of women —**gynaecol'ogical** a. —**gynaecol'ogist** n.

gypsoph'ila [jip-] n. garden plant with small white or pink flowers

gyp'sum [jip'-] n. crystalline sulphate of lime, a source of plaster

Gyp'sy [jip'-] n. one of wandering race originally from NW India, Romany

gyrate' [jī-] vi. move in circle, spirally, revolve —**gyra'tion** n. —**gyra'tional** a. —**gy'ratory** a. revolving, spinning

gyr'falcon, **ger'falcon**

[jer-] *n.* large, rare falcon

gy'rocompass [jī-] *n.* compass using gyroscope

gy'roscope [jī-] *n.* disc or wheel so mounted as to be able to rotate about any axis, *esp.* to keep disc (with compass *etc.*) level despite movement of ship *etc.* —**gyroscop'ic** *a.*

gyrosta'bilizer [jī-] *n.* gyroscopic device to prevent rolling of ship or aeroplane

H

H (of pencils) hard; *Chem.* hydrogen

ha'beas cor'pus [hā'bi-əs-] *n.* writ issued to produce prisoner in court

hab'erdasher *n.* dealer in articles of dress, ribbons, pins, needles *etc.* —**hab'erdashery** *n.*

habil'iments *pl.n.* dress

hab'it *n.* settled tendency or practice; constitution; customary apparel *esp.* of nun or monk; woman's riding dress —**habit'ual** *a.* formed or acquired by habit; usual, customary —**habit'ually** *adv.* —**habit'uate** *vt.* accustom —**habitua'tion** *n.* —**habit'ué** [-yoo-ā] *n.* constant visitor

hab'itable *a.* fit to live in —**hab'itat** *n.* natural home (of animal *etc.*) —**habita'tion** *n.* dwelling place

hacien'da [ha-si-en'-] *n.* ranch or large estate in Sp. Amer.

hack[1] *vt.* cut, chop (at) violently; *Sport* foul by kicking the shins; *inf.* utter harsh, dry cough —*n.* —**hack'er** *n. sl.* computer fanatic who through personal computer breaks into computer system of company or government

hack[2] *n.* horse for ordinary riding; drudge, *esp.* writer of inferior literary works —**hack work** dull, repetitive work

hac'kle *n.* neck feathers of turkey *etc.* —*pl.* hairs on back of neck of dog and other animals which are raised in anger

hack'ney *n.* harness horse, carriage, coach kept for hire (*pl.* -**neys**)

hack'neyed *a.* (of words *etc.*) stale, trite because of overuse

hack'saw *n.* handsaw for cutting metal

had *pt./pp.* of HAVE

hadd'ock *n.* large, edible seafish

ha'dedah [hah'di-dah] *n.* S Afr. ibis

Ha'des [hā'dēz] *n.* abode of the dead; underworld; hell

haema-, **haemo-** (*comb. form*) blood

hae'matite [hē'-] *n.* ore of iron

haemoglo'bin [hē-] *n.* colouring and oxygen-bearing matter of red blood corpuscles

haemophil'ia [hē-] *n.* hereditary tendency to intensive bleeding as blood fails to clot —**haemophil'iac** *n.*

haem'orrhage [hem'ə-rij] *n.* profuse bleeding

haem'orrhoids [hem'ə-roidz] *pl.n.* swollen veins in rectum (*also called* piles)

haft [-ah-] *n.* handle (of knife *etc.*) —*vt.* fit with handle

hag *n.* ugly old woman; witch —**hag-ridden** *a.* troubled, careworn

hagg'ard *a.* wild-looking; anxious, careworn —*n.* Falconry untamed hawk

hagg'is *n.* Scottish dish made from sheep's heart, lungs, liver, chopped with oatmeal, suet, onion *etc.*, and boiled in the stomach-bag

hag'gle *vi.* bargain, wrangle over price —*n.*

hagiol'ogy [hag-] *n.* literature of the lives of saints —**hagiog'rapher** *n.* —**hagiog'raphy** *n.* writing of this

hail[1] *n.* (shower of) pellets of ice; intense shower, barrage —*v.* pour down as shower of hail —**hail'stone** *n.*

hail[2] *vt.* greet (*esp.* enthusiastically); acclaim, acknowledge; call —*vi.* come (from)

hair *n.* filament growing from skin of animal, as covering of man's head; such filaments collectively —**hair'iness** *n.* —**hair'y** *a.* —**hair'do** *n.* way of dressing hair —**hair'dresser** *n.* one who attends to and cuts hair, *esp.* women's hair —**hair'grip** *n.* small, tightly bent metal hairpin —**hair'line** *a./n.* very fine (line) —**hair'pin** *n.* pin for keeping hair in place —**hairpin bend** U-shaped turn of road —**hair'splitting** *n.* making of over-fine distinctions —**hair'spring** *n.* very fine, delicate spring in timepiece —**hair trigger** trigger operated by light touch

hake *n.* edible fish of the cod family

hal'berd *n.* combined spear and battleaxe

hal'cyon [-si-ən] *n.* bird fabled to calm the sea and to breed on floating nest, kingfisher —**halcyon days** time of peace and happiness

hale *a.* robust, healthy, *esp.* in **hale and hearty**

half [hahf] *n.* either of two equal parts of thing (*pl.* **halves** [hahvz]) —*a.* forming half —*adv.* to the extent of half —**half'back** *n. Football* man behind forwards —**half-baked** *a.* underdone; *inf.* immature, silly —**half-breed**, **half-caste** *n.* person with parents of different races —**half-brother**, **-sister** *n.* brother (sister) by one parent only —**half-cocked** *a.* illprepared —**half-hearted** *a.* unenthusiastic —**half-life** *n.* time taken for half the atoms in radioactive material to decay —**halfnelson** *n.* hold in wrestling —**half'penny** [hā'pni] *n.* formerly, half British penny; half British new penny (*pl.* **-pence** *or* **-pennies**) *Also inf.* **half** —**half-time** *n. Sport* rest period between two halves of a game —**half'tone** *n.* illustration printed from relief plate, showing lights and shadows by means of minute dots —**half volley** striking of a ball the moment it bounces —**half-wit** *n.* mentally-retarded person; stupid person —**half seas over** *inf.* drunk

hal'ibut *n.* large edible flatfish

halito'sis *n.* bad-smelling breath

hall [hawl] *n.* (entrance) passage; large room or building belonging to particular group or used for particular purpose *esp.* public assembly

hallelu'jah [-loo'yə] *n./interj.* exclamation of praise to God

hall'mark *n.* mark used to indicate standard of tested gold and silver; mark of excellence; distinguishing feature

hallo[1] *interj. see* HELLO

halloo' *n.* call to spur on hunting dogs —*v.* shout loudly to

hall'ow [-ō] *vt.* make, or honour as holy —**Hallowe'en**[1] *n.* the evening of Oct. 31st, the day before All Hallows' or All Saints' day

hallu'cinate [-loo'si-] *vi.* suffer illusions —**hallucina'tion** *n.* illusion —**hallu'cinatory** *a.* —**hallu'cinogen** *n.* drug inducing hallucinations

ha'lo *n.* circle of light round

moon, sun *etc.*; disc of light round saint's head in picture; ideal glory attaching to person (*pl.* **-lo(e)s**) —*vt.* surround with halo

halt [hawlt] *n.* interruption or end to progress *etc.* (*esp.* as command to stop marching); minor railway station without station buildings —*v.* (cause to) stop

halt² [hawlt] *vi.* falter, fail —**halt'ing** *a.* hesitant, lame

hal'ter [hawl't-] *n.* rope or strap with headgear to fasten horses or cattle; low-cut dress style with strap passing behind neck; noose for hanging person —*vt.* put halter on, fasten with one

halve [hahv] *vt.* cut in half; reduce to half; share

hal'yard, hall'iard *n.* rope for raising sail, signal flags *etc.*

ham *n.* meat (*esp.* salted or smoked) from thigh of pig; actor adopting exaggerated, unconvincing style (*also a. and v.*); amateur radio enthusiast —**ham'fisted, -handed** *a.* clumsy —**ham'string** *n.* tendon at back of knee —*vt.* cripple by cutting this

ham'burger *n.* fried cake of minced beef, *esp.* served in bread roll

ham'let *n.* small village

hamm'er *n.* tool usu. with heavy head at end of handle, for beating, driving nails *etc.*; machine for same purposes; contrivance for exploding charge of gun; auctioneer's mallet; metal ball on wire thrown in sports —*v.* strike with, or as with, hammer —**hamm'erhead** *n.* shark with wide, flattened head —**hamm'ertoe** *n.* deformed toe —**hammer out** solve problem by full investigation of difficulties

hamm'ock *n.* bed of canvas *etc.*, hung on cords

hamp'er¹ *n.* large covered basket; large parcel, box *etc.* of food, wines *etc.*, *esp.* one sent as Christmas gift

hamp'er² *vt.* impede, obstruct movements of

ham'ster *n.* type of rodent, sometimes kept as pet

ham'strung *a.* crippled; thwarted

hand *n.* extremity of arm beyond wrist; side, quarter, direction; style of writing; cards dealt to player; measure of four inches; manual worker; sailor; help, aid; pointer on dial; applause —*v.* pass; deliver; hold out —**hand'ful** *n.* small quantity or number; *inf.* person, thing causing problems (*pl.* **-fuls**) —**hand'ily** *adv.* —**hand'iness** *n.* dexterity; state of being near, available —**hand'y** *a.* convenient; clever with the hands —**hand'bag** *n.* woman's bag for personal articles; bag for carrying in hand —**hand'bill** *n.* small printed notice —**hand'book** *n.* small reference or instruction book —**hand'cuff** *n.* fetter for wrist, usu. joined in pair —*vt.* secure thus —**hand'icraft** *n.* manual occupation or skill —**hand'iwork** *n.* thing done by particular person —**hand'kerchief** [hang'kə-chif] *n.* small square of fabric carried in pocket for wiping nose *etc.*; neckerchief —**hand-out** *n.* money, food *etc.* given free; pamphlet giving news, information *etc.* —**hands-on** *a.* involving practical experience of equipment —**hand'stand** *n.* act of supporting body in upside-down position by hands alone —**hand'writing** *n.* way person writes —**hand'yman** *n.* man employed to do various tasks; man skilled in odd jobs —**hand in glove** very intimate

hand'icap *n.* something that hampers or hinders; race, contest in which chances are equalized by starts, weights carried *etc.*; condition so imposed; any physical disability —*vt.* hamper; impose handicaps on (-**pp-**)

han'dle *n.* part of thing to hold it by —*vi.* touch, feel with hands; manage; deal with; trade —**han'dlebars** *pl.n.* curved metal bar used to steer bicycle, motorbike *etc.*

hand'some [han's-] *a.* of fine appearance; generous; ample —**hand'somely** *adv.*

han'epoot [-ə-port] *n.* SA type of grape

hang *vt.* suspend; kill by suspension by neck (**hanged** *pt./pp.*); attach, set up (wallpaper, doors *etc.*) —*vi.* be suspended, cling (**hung** *pt./pp.*) —**hang'er** *n.* frame on which clothes *etc.* can be hung —**hang'dog** *a.* sullen, dejected —**hang-glider** *n.* glider like large kite, with pilot hanging in frame below —**hang-gliding** *n.* —**hang'man** *n.* executioner —**hang'over** *n.* after-effects of too much drinking —**hang out** *inf.* reside, frequent —**hang-up** *n.* *inf.* persistent emotional problem

hang'ar *n.* large shed for aircraft

hank *n.* coil, skein, length, *esp.* as measure of yarn

hank'er *vi.* crave

hank'y, hank'ie *n.* short for HANDKERCHIEF

hank'y-pank'y *inf.* *n.* trickery; illicit sexual relations

Han'sard *n.* official printed record of speeches, debates *etc.* in Brit., Aust., Canad. and other parliaments

han'som *n.* two-wheeled horse-drawn cab for two to ride inside with driver mounted up behind

Hants. Hampshire

haphaz'ard *a.* random, careless

hap'less *a.* unlucky

happ'en *vi.* come about, occur; chance to do —**happ'ening** *n.* occurrence, event

happ'y *a.* glad, content; lucky, fortunate; apt —**happ'ily** *adv.* —**happ'iness** *n.* —**happy-go-lucky** *a.* casual, lighthearted

harakir'i *n.* in Japan, ritual suicide by disembowelling

harangue' [-ang'] *n.* vehement speech; tirade —*v.*

har'ass [ha'rəs] *vt.* worry, trouble, torment —**har'assment** *n.*

harb'inger [-j-] *n.* one who announces another's approach; forerunner, herald

har'bour [-bər] *n.* shelter for ships; shelter —*v.* give shelter, protection to; maintain (secretly) *esp.* grudge *etc.*

hard *a.* firm, resisting pressure; solid; difficult to understand; harsh, unfeeling; difficult to bear; practical, shrewd; heavy; strenuous; of water, not making lather well with soap; of drugs, highly addictive —*adv.* vigorously; with difficulty; close —**hard'en** *v.* —**hard'ly** *adv.* unkindly, harshly; scarcely, not quite; only just —**hard'ness** *n.* —**hard'ship** *n.* ill-luck; severe toil, suffering; instance of this —**hard'board** *n.* thin stiff sheet made of compressed sawdust and woodchips —**hard-boiled** *a.* boiled so long as to be hard; *inf.* of person, experienced, unemotional, unsympathetic —**hard court** tennis court made of asphalt, concrete *etc.*, instead of grass —**hard-headed** *a.* shrewd —**hard shoulder** surfaced verge at motorway edge for emergency stops —**hard'ware** *n.* tools, implements; necessary (parts of) machinery; *Computers* mechanical and electronic parts —**hard'wood** *n.* wood from deciduous trees —**hard of**

hearing rather deaf —**hard up** very short of money

har'dy a. robust, vigorous; bold; of plants, able to grow in the open all the year round —**har'di-hood** n. extreme boldness, audacity —**hard'ily** adv. —**hard'iness** n.

hare n. animal like large rabbit, with longer legs and ears, noted for speed —**hare'bell** n. round-leaved bell-flower —**hare'brained** a. rash, wild —**hare'lip** n. fissure of upper lip —**hare and hounds** paperchase

ha'rem [or hah-rēm'] n. women's part of Mohammedan dwelling; one man's wives

har'icot [ha'ri-kō] n. type of French bean that can be dried

hark vi. listen —**hark back** return to previous subject of discussion

har'lequin n. stock comic character, esp. masked clown in diamond-patterned costume —**harlequinade'** n. scene in pantomime; buffoonery

har'lot n. whore, prostitute —**har'lotry** n.

harm n. damage, injury —vt. cause harm to —**harm'ful** a. —**harm'fully** adv. —**harm'less** a. unable or unlikely to hurt —**harm'lessly** adv.

harm'ony n. agreement; concord; peace; combination of notes to make chords; melodious sound —**harmon'ic** a. of harmony —n. tone or note whose frequency is a multiple of its pitch —**harmon'ics** pl.n. science of musical sounds; harmonious sounds —**harmon'ica** n. various musical instruments, but esp. mouth organ —**harmo'nious** a. —**harmo'niously** adv. —**har'monist** n. —**harmo'nium** n. small organ —**harmoniza'tion** n. —**har'monize** vt. bring into har-

mony; cause to agree; reconcile —vi. be in harmony

harn'ess n. equipment for attaching horse to cart, plough etc.; any such equipment —vt. put on, in harness; utilize energy or power of (waterfall etc.)

harp n. musical instrument of strings played by hand —vi. play on harp; dwell on continuously —**harp'er, harp'ist** n. —**harp'si-chord** n. stringed instrument like piano

harpoon' n. barbed spear with rope attached for catching whales —vt. catch, kill with this —**harpoon'er** n. —**harpoon gun** gun for firing harpoon in whaling

harp'y n. monster with body of woman and wings and claws of bird; cruel, grasping person

harr'idan n. shrewish old woman, hag

harr'ier n. hound used in hunting hares; falcon

harr'ow [-ō] n. implement for smoothing, levelling or stirring up soil —vt. draw harrow over; distress greatly —**harr'owing** a. heart-rending; distressful

harr'y vt. harass; ravage (**harr'-ied, harr'ying**)

harsh a. rough, discordant; severe; unfeeling —**harsh'ly** adv.

hart n. male deer —**harts'horn** n. material made from harts' horns, formerly the chief source of ammonia

hart'beest n. African antelope Also **harte'beest**

ha'rum-sca'rum a. reckless, wild; giddy

harv'est n. (season for) gathering in grain; gathering; crop; product of action —vt. reap and gather in —**harv'ester** n.

has third person sing. pres. indicative of HAVE

hash n. dish of hashed meat etc.;

inf. short for HASHISH —*vt.* cut up small, chop; mix up

hash'ish [-ĕsh], **hash'eesh** *n.* resinous extract of Indian hemp, *esp.* used as hallucinogen

hasp [-ah-] *n.* clasp passing over a staple for fastening door *etc.* —*vt.* fasten, secure with hasp

has'sle *inf. n.* quarrel; a lot of bother, trouble —*v.*

hass'ock *n.* kneeling-cushion; tuft of grass

hast *obs. second person sing. pres. indicative of* HAVE

haste [hāst] *n.* speed, quickness, hurry —*vi.* hasten —**ha'sten** [-sən] *v.* (cause to) hurry, increase speed —**ha'stily** *adv.* —**ha'sty** *a.*

hat *n.* head-covering, usu. with brim —**hatt'er** *n.* dealer in, maker of hats —**hat trick** any three successive achievements, *esp.* in sport

hatch[1] *v.* of young, *esp.* of birds, (cause to) emerge from egg; contrive, devise —**hatch'ery** *n.*

hatch[2] *n.* hatchway; trapdoor over it; opening in wall or door, as service hatch, to facilitate service of meals *etc.*, between two rooms; lower half of divided door —**hatch'back** *n.* car with single lifting door in rear —**hatch'way** *n.* opening in deck of ship *etc.*

hatch[3] *vt.* engrave or draw lines on for shading; shade with parallel lines

hatch'et *n.* small axe —**hatchet job** malicious verbal or written attack —**hatchet man** *inf.* person carrying out unpleasant assignments for another —**bury the hatchet** make peace

hate *vt.* dislike strongly; bear malice towards —*n.* this feeling; that which is hated —**hate'ful** *a.* detestable —**hate'fully** *adv.*

—**ha'tred** *n.* extreme dislike, active ill will

haughty [hawt'-] *a.* proud, arrogant —**haught'ily** *adv.* —**haugh'tiness** *n.*

haul *vt.* pull, drag with effort —*vi.* of wind, shift —*n.* hauling; what is hauled; catch of fish; acquisition; distance (to be) covered —**haul'age** *n.* carrying of loads; charge for this —**haul'ier** *n.* firm, person that transports goods by road

haunch *n.* human hip or fleshy hindquarter of animal; leg and loin of venison

haunt *vt.* visit regularly; visit in form of ghost; recur to —*n. esp.* place frequently visited —**haunt'ed** *a.* frequented by ghosts; worried

hauteur[1] [ō-tur'] *n.* haughty spirit

Havan'a, Havann'ah *n.* fine quality of cigar

have [hav] *vt.* hold, possess; be possessed, affected with; be obliged (to do); cheat, outwit; engage in, obtain; contain; allow; cause to be done; give birth to; (as auxiliary, forms perfect and other tenses) (*pres. tense:* I *have,* thou *hast,* he *has,* we, you, they *have*) (**had, hav'ing**)

ha'ven *n.* place of safety

hav'ersack *n.* canvas bag for provisions *etc.* carried on back or shoulder when hiking *etc.*

hav'oc *n.* devastation, ruin; *inf.* confusion, chaos

haw'finch *n.* uncommon European finch

hawk[1] *n.* bird of prey smaller than eagle; supporter, advocate, of warlike policies —*vi.* hunt with hawks; attack like hawk

hawk[2] *vt.* offer (goods) for sale, as in street —**hawk'er** *n.*

hawk[3] *vi.* clear throat noisily

hawse [-z] n. part of ship's bows with holes for cables

haw'ser [-z-] n. large rope or cable

haw'thorn n. thorny shrub or tree

hay n. grass mown and dried —**hay'box** n. box filled with hay in which heated food is left to finish cooking —**hay fever** allergic reaction to pollen, dust etc. —**hay'stack** n. large pile of hay —**hay'wire** a. crazy; disorganized

haz'ard n. chance; risk, danger —vt. expose to risk; run risk of —**haz'ardous** a. risky

haze n. mist, often due to heat; obscurity —**ha'zy** a. misty; obscured; vague

ha'zel n. bush bearing nuts; yellowish-brown colour of the nuts —a. light brown

H bomb short for HYDROGEN BOMB

HE high explosive; His Eminence; His (or Her) Excellency

He Chem. helium

he pron. (third person masculine pronoun) person, animal already referred to; (comb. form) male, as **he-goat**

head [hed] n. upper part of man's or animal's body, containing mouth, sense organs and brain; upper part of anything; chief of organization, school etc.; chief part; aptitude, capacity; crisis; leader; section of chapter; title; headland; person, animal considered as unit; white froth on beer etc.; inf. headache —a. chief, principal; of wind, contrary —vt. be at the top, head of; lead, direct; provide with head; hit (ball) with head —vi. make for; form a head —**head'er** n. plunge headfirst; brick laid with end in face of wall; action of striking ball with head —**head'ing** n. title —**heads** adv. inf. with obverse side (of coin) uppermost —**head'y** a. apt to intoxicate or excite —**head'ache** [-ak] n. continuous pain in head; worrying circumstance —**head-banger** n. sl. person, esp. teenager, who shakes his head violently to beat of heavy-metal music —**head'board** n. vertical board at head of bed —**head'land** n. promontory —**head'light** n. powerful lamp carried on front of locomotive, motor vehicle etc. —**head'line** n. news summary, in large type in newspaper —**head'long** adv. head foremost, in rush —**head'quarters** pl.n. residence of commander-in-chief; centre of operations —**head'stone** n. gravestone —**head'strong** a. self-willed —**head'way** n. advance, progress

heal v. make or become well —**health** [helth] n. soundness of body; condition of body; toast drunk in person's honour —**health'ily** adv. —**health'iness** n. —**health'y** a. of strong constitution; of or producing good health, wellbeing etc.; vigorous —**health food** vegetarian food, organically grown, eaten for dietary value

heap n. pile of things lying one on another; great quantity —vt. pile, load with

hear vt. perceive by ear; listen to; Law try (case); heed —vi. perceive sound; learn (**heard** [herd] pt./pp.) —**hear'er** n. —**hear'ing** n. ability to hear; earshot; judicial examination —**hear! hear!** interj. exclamation of approval, agreement —**hear'say** n. rumour —a.

hear'ken [hahr'-] vi. listen

hearse [hurs] n. funeral carriage for coffin

heart [-ah-] n. organ which makes blood circulate; seat of emotions and affections; mind, soul, courage; central part; playing card marked with figure of heart; one of these marks —**heart'en** v. make, become cheerful —**heart'ily** adv. —**heart'less** a. unfeeling —**heart'y** a. friendly; vigorous; in good health; satisfying the appetite —**heart attack** sudden severe malfunction of heart —**heart'burn** n. pain in higher intestine —**heart'free** a. with the affections free or disengaged —**heart-rending** a. overwhelming with grief; agonizing —**hearts'ease** n. wild pansy —**heart-throb** n. sl. object of infatuation —**by heart** by memory

hearth [-ah-] n. part of room where fire is made; home

heat n. hotness; sensation of this; hot weather or climate; warmth of feeling, anger etc.; sexual excitement caused by readiness to mate in female animals; one of many races etc. to decide persons to compete in finals —v. make, become hot —**heat'ed** a. esp. angry —**heat'edly** adv.

heath n. tract of waste land; low-growing evergreen shrub

hea'then [-TH-] a. not adhering to a religious system; pagan; barbarous; unenlightened —n. heathen person (pl. **hea'thens**, **hea'then**) —**hea'thendom** n. —**hea'thenish** a. of or like heathen; rough; barbarous —**hea'thenism** n.

heath'er [heTH'-] n. shrub growing on heaths and mountains —**heath'ery** a.

heave vt. lift with effort; throw (something heavy); utter (sigh) —vi. swell, rise; feel nausea —n.

heav'en [hev'n] n. abode of God; place of bliss; sky (also pl.) —**heav'enly** a. lovely, delightful;

divine; beautiful; of or like heaven

heav'y [hev'-] a. weighty, striking, falling with force; dense; sluggish; difficult, severe; sorrowful; serious; dull —**heav'ily** adv. —**heav'iness** n. —**heavy industry** basic, large scale industry producing metal, machinery etc. —**heavy metal** rock music with strong beat and amplified instrumental effects —**heavy water** deuterium oxide, water in which normal hydrogen content has been replaced by deuterium

Heb. Hebrew, Hebrews

He'brew n. member of an ancient Semitic people; their language; its modern form, used in Israel —a.

hec'kle [hek'l] v. interrupt or try to annoy (speaker) by questions, taunts etc.

hect-, hecto- (comb. form) one hundred, esp. in metric system, as in **hec'tolitre**, **hec'tometre**

hec'tare [-tahr] n. one hundred ares or 10 000 square metres (2.471 acres)

hec'tic a. rushed, busy

hec'tor v. bully, bluster —n. blusterer

hed'dle n. Weaving one of set of frames of vertical wires

hedge n. fence of bushes —vt. surround with hedge; obstruct; hem in; bet on both sides —vi. make or trim hedges; be evasive; secure against loss —**hedge'hog** n. small animal covered with spines —**hedge'row** n. bushes forming hedge —**hedge sparrow** small brownish songbird

he'donism n. doctrine that pleasure is the chief good —**he'donist** n. —**hedonis'tic** a.

heed vt. take notice of, care for —**heed'ful** a. —**heed'less** a. careless

heel[1] n. hinder part of foot; part of shoe supporting this; sl. undesirable person —vt. supply with heel; touch ground, ball, with heel

heel[2] v. of ship, (cause) to lean to one side —n. heeling, list

hef'ty a. bulky; weighty; strong

hegem'ony n. leadership, political domination —**hegemon'ic** a.

heif'er [hef-] n. young cow

height [hīt] n. measure from base to top; quality of being high; elevation; highest degree; (oft. pl.) hilltop —**height'en** vt. make higher; intensify —**height of land** US, C watershed

hei'nous [hā-] a. atrocious, extremely wicked, detestable

heir [ār] n. person entitled to inherit property or rank (**heir'ess** fem.) —**heir'loom** n. thing that has been in family for generations

held pt./pp. of HOLD

hel'ical a. spiral

hel'icopter n. aircraft made to rise vertically by pull of airscrew revolving horizontally —**hel'iport** n. airport for helicopters

helio- (comb. form) sun

he'liograph n. signalling apparatus employing a mirror to reflect sun's rays

he'liostat n. astronomical instrument used to reflect the light of the sun in a constant direction

heliother'apy [hē-] n. therapeutic use of sunlight

he'liotrope n. plant with purple flowers; colour of the flowers —**heliotrop'ic** a. growing, turning towards source of light

he'lium n. very light, nonflammable gaseous element

hell n. abode of the damned; abode of the dead generally; place or state of wickedness, or misery, or torture —**hell'ish** a.

hell'ebore n. plant with white flowers that bloom in winter, Christmas rose

Hellen'ic a. pert. to inhabitants of Greece —**Hell'enist** n.

hello[1] (also **hallo**[1], **hullo**[1]) interj. expression of greeting or surprise

helm n. tiller, wheel for turning ship's rudder

helm'et n. defensive or protective covering for head Also **helm**

help vt. aid, assist; support; succour; remedy, prevent —n. —**help'er** n. —**help'ful** a. —**help'ing** n. single portion of food taken at a meal —**help'less** a. useless, incompetent; unaided; unable to help —**help'lessly** adv. —**help'mate, -meet** n. helpful companion; husband or wife

hel'ter-skel'ter adv./a./n. (in) hurry and confusion —n. high spiral slide at fairground

hem n. border of cloth, esp. one made by turning over edge and sewing it down —vt. sew thus; confine, shut in (-mm-) —**hem'stitch** n. ornamental stitch —vt.

hemi- (comb. form) half

hem'isphere n. half sphere; half of celestial sphere; half of the earth —**hemispher'ical** a.

hem'istich [-ik] n. half a line of verse

hem'lock n. poisonous plant; poison extracted from it; US evergreen of pine family

hemp n. Indian plant; its fibre used for rope etc.; any of several narcotic drugs made from varieties of hemp —**hemp'en** a. made of hemp or rope

hen n. female of domestic fowl and others —**hen'peck** vt. (of a woman) harass (a man, esp. husband) by nagging

hence adv. from this point; for this reason —**hencefor'ward,**

hence'forth adv. from now onwards

hench'man n. trusty follower

hen'na n. flowering shrub; reddish dye made from it

henothe'ism n. belief in one god (of several) as special god of one's family, tribe etc.

hen'ry n. SI unit of electrical inductance

hepat'ic a. pert. to the liver —**hepati'tis** n. inflammation of the liver

hepta- (comb. form) seven

hept'agon n. figure with seven angles —**heptag'onal** a.

hept'archy [-ki] n. rule by seven

her a. objective and possessive case of SHE —**hers** pron. of her —**herself'** pron.

her'ald [he'rəld] n. messenger, envoy; officer who makes royal proclamations, arranges ceremonies, regulates armorial bearings etc. —vt. announce; proclaim approach of —**herald'ic** a. —**her'aldry** n. study of (right to have) heraldic bearings

herb n. plant with soft stem which dies down after flowering; plant of which parts are used in cookery or medicine —**herba'ceous** [-shəs] a. of, like herbs; perennial flowering —**herb'age** n. herbs; grass; pasture —**herb'al** a. of herbs —**herb'alist** n. writer on herbs; dealer in medicinal herbs —**herba'rium** n. collection of dried plants (pl. **-iums, -ia**) —**herb'icide** n. chemical which destroys plants —**herbiv'orous** a. feeding on plants

Her'cules [-kyoo-lēz] n. mythical hero noted for strength —**hercule'an** a. requiring great strength, courage

herd n. company of animals, usu. of same species, feeding or traveling together; herdsman —v. crowd together —vt. tend (herd) —**herds'man** n.

here adv. in this place; at or to this point —**hereaf'ter** adv. in time to come —n. future existence —**heretofore'** adv. before

hered'ity n. tendency of organism to transmit its nature to its descendants —**heredit'ament** n. Law property that can be inherited —**hered'itarily** adv. —**hered'itary** a. descending by inheritance; holding office by inheritance; that can be transmitted from one generation to another

her'esy [he'rə-] n. opinion contrary to orthodox opinion or belief —**her'etic** n. one holding opinions contrary to orthodox faith —**heret'ical** a. —**heret'ically** adv.

her'itage [her-i-] n. what may be or is inherited; anything from past, esp. owned or handed down by tradition —**her'itable** a. that can be inherited

hermaph'rodite n. person, animal with characteristics, or reproductive organs, of both sexes

hermet'ic a. sealed so as to be airtight —**hermet'ically** adv.

her'mit n. one living in solitude, esp. from religious motives —**her'mitage** n. his abode

hern'ia n. projection of (part of) organ through lining encasing it (pl. **-ias, -iae** [-i-ē]) —**hern'ial** a.

he'ro n. one greatly regarded for achievements or qualities; principal character in poem, play, story; illustrious warrior; demigod (pl. **he'roes** —**her'oine** fem.) —**hero'ic** [hi-] a. of, like hero; courageous, daring —**hero'ically** adv. —**hero'ics** pl.n. extravagant behaviour —**her'oism** [he'rō-] n. qualities of hero; courage, boldness —**hero worship** admiration of heroes or of great men; excessive admiration of others

her'oin [her-ō-] n. white crystalline derivative of morphine, a highly addictive narcotic

her'on [her'ən] n. long-legged wading bird —**her'onry** n. place where herons breed

her'pes [-pēz] n. any of several skin diseases, including shingles and cold sores

herr'ing n. important food fish of northern hemisphere

herr'ingbone n. stitch, or pattern of zigzag lines

Herts. Hertfordshire

hertz n. SI unit of frequency (pl. **hertz**)

hes'itate [hez'-] vi. hold back; feel, or show indecision; be reluctant —**hes'itancy**, **hesita'tion** n. wavering; doubt; stammering —**hes'itant** a. undecided, pausing —**hes'itantly** adv.

hess'ian n. coarse jute cloth

hest n. behest, command

hetero- (comb. form) other or different

het'erodox a. not orthodox —**het'erodoxy** n.

heteroge'neous a. composed of diverse elements —**heterogene'ity** n.

heterosex'ual n. person sexually attracted to members of the opposite sex —**heterosexual'ity** n.

heu'chera [hoi'kə-rə] n. plant with ornamental foliage

heuris'tic [hyoo-] a. serving to find out or to stimulate investigation

hew v. chop, cut with axe (**hewn**, **hewed** pp.) —**hew'er** n.

hex-, hexa- (comb. form) six

hex'agon n. figure with six angles —**hexag'onal** a.

hexam'eter n. line of verse of six feet

hey'day n. bloom, prime

HF high frequency

Hg Chem. mercury

HGV heavy goods vehicle

HH His (or Her) Highness; His Holiness

hia'tus [hī-ā'-] n. break or gap where something is missing (pl. **hia'tuses**, **hia'tus**)

hi'bernate vi. pass the winter, esp. in a torpid state —**hiberna'tion** n. —**hi'bernator** n.

Hiber'nian a./n. Irish (person)

hibis'cus n. flowering (sub-) tropical shrub

hicc'up, hicc'ough [hik'up] n. spasm of the breathing organs with an abrupt cough-like sound —vi. have this

hick a. US, C inf. rustic; unsophisticated —n. person like this

hick'ory n. N Amer. nut-bearing tree; its tough wood

hide[1] vt. put, keep out of sight; conceal, keep secret —vi. conceal oneself (**hid** pt., **hidd'en** or **hid** pp., **hi'ding** pr.p.) —n. place of concealment eg for birdwatcher —**hide-out** n. hiding place

hide[2] n. skin of animal —**hi'ding** n. sl. thrashing —**hide'bound** a. restricted, esp. by petty rules etc.; narrow-minded; (of tree, having bark so close that it impedes growth

hid'eous a. repulsive, revolting —**hid'eously** adv.

hie [hī] v. obs. hasten (**hied** [hīd] pt./pp., **hy'ing** or **hie'ing** pr.p.)

hi'erarchy [-ki] n. system of persons or things arranged in graded order —**hierarch'ical** a.

hieroglyph'ic a. of a system of picture writing, as used in ancient Egypt —n. symbol representing object, concept or sound; symbol, picture, difficult to decipher —**hi'eroglyph** n.

hi'-fi [hī'fī] a. short for

HIGH-FIDELITY —*n.* high-fidelity equipment

hig'gledy-pig'gledy *adv./a.* in confusion

high [hī] *a.* tall, lofty; far up; of roads, main; of meat, tainted; of season, well advanced; of sound, acute in pitch; expensive; of great importance, quality, or rank; *inf.* in state of euphoria, *esp.* induced by drugs; *inf.* bad-smelling —*adv.* far up; strongly, to a great extent; at, to a high pitch; at a high rate —**high'ly** *adv.* —**high'ness** *n.* quality of being high, (H-) title of prince and princess —**high'brow** *n. sl.* intellectual, *esp.* intellectual snob —*a.* intellectual; difficult; serious —**High Church** party within Church of England emphasizing authority of bishops and importance of sacraments, rituals and ceremonies —**high-fidelity** *a.* of high-quality sound reproducing equipment —**high-flown** *a.* extravagant, bombastic —**high-handed** *a.* domineering, dogmatic —**high'land(s)** *n.(pl.)* relatively high ground —**High'land** *a.* of, from the Highlands of Scotland —**high'light** *n.* lightest or brightest area in painting, photograph *etc.*; outstanding feature —*vt.* bring into prominence —**highly strung** excitable, nervous —**high-rise** *a.* of building that has many storeys —**high-sounding** *a.* pompous, imposing —**high tea** early evening meal with *usu.* cooked course followed by cakes *etc.* with tea to drink —**high tech** interior design using features of industrial equipment —**high-tech** *a.* —**high time** latest possible time —**high'way** *n.* main road; ordinary route —**Highway Code** regulations and recommendations applying to all road users —**high'wayman** *n.* (formerly)

robber on road, *esp.* mounted

hi'jack *vt.* divert or wrongfully take command of a vehicle (*esp.* aircraft) or its contents; rob —**hi'jacker** *n.*

hike *vi.* walk a long way (for pleasure) in country —*vt.* pull (up), hitch —*n.* —**hi'ker** *n.*

hilar'ity [-la'ri-] *n.* cheerfulness, gaiety —**hila'rious** *a.*

hill *n.* natural elevation, small mountain; mound —**hill'ock** *n.* little hill —**hill'y** *a.* —**hill'billy** *n.* unsophisticated (country) person

hilt *n.* handle of sword *etc.*

him *pron.* objective case of pronoun HE —**himself'** *pron.* emphatic form of HE

hind¹ [hīnd] *n.* female of deer

hind² [hīnd], **hind'er** *a.* at the back, posterior

hin'der *vt.* obstruct, impede, delay —**hin'drance** *n.*

Hin'di *n.* language of N central India —**Hin'du** [-ōō] *n.* person who adheres to **Hinduism**, the dominant religion of India

hinge [-j] *n.* movable joint, as that on which door hangs —*vt.* attach with, or as with, hinge —*vi.* turn, depend on

hint *n.* slight indication or suggestion —*v.* give hint of

hint'erland *n.* district lying behind coast, or near city, port *etc.*

hip *n.* either side of body below waist and above thigh; angle formed where sloping sides of roof meet; fruit of rose, *esp.* wild

hipp'ie, -y *n.* (young) person whose behaviour, dress *etc.* implies rejection of conventional values

hipp'odrome *n.* music hall; variety theatre; circus

hipp'ogriff, hipp'ogryph *n.* griffin-like creature with horse's body

hippopot'amus *n.* large Afr.

animal living in rivers (*pl.* -amuses, -amí [-mí])

hire *vt.* obtain temporary use of by payment; engage for wage —*n.* hiring or being hired; payment for use of thing —**hire'ling** *n.* one who serves for wages —**hire-purchase** *n.* system by which thing becomes hirer's after stipulated number of payments

hir'sute [-syōōt] *a.* hairy

his *pron./a.* belonging to him

his'pid *a.* rough with bristles or minute spines; bristly, shaggy —**hispid'ity** *n.*

hiss *vi.* make sharp sound of letter S, *esp.* in disapproval —*vt.* express disapproval, deride thus —*n.* —**hiss'ing** *n.*

hist'amine [-ēn] *n.* substance released by body tissues, sometimes creating allergic reactions

histog'eny [-toj'-] *n.* formation and development of organic tissues

histol'ogy *n.* science that treats of minute structure of organic tissues —**histol'ogist** *n.*

his'tory *n.* record of past events; study of these; train of events, public or private; course of life or existence; systematic account of phenomena —**histor'ian** *n.* writer of history —**histor'ic** [-to'rik] *a.* noted in history —**histor'ical** *a.* of, based on, history; belonging to past —**histor'ically** *adv.* —**historic'ity** [-ris'-] *n.* historical authenticity —**historiog'rapher** *n.* official historian; one who studies historical method

histrion'ic *a.* excessively theatrical, insincere, artificial in manner —**histrion'ics** *pl.n.* behaviour like this

hit *vt.* strike with blow or missile; affect injuriously; find —*vi.* strike; light (upon) (**hit, hitt'ing**)

—*n.* blow; success —**hitt'er** *n.* —**hit man** *sl.* hired assassin —**hit it off** get along with (person) —**hit or miss** haphazard(ly) —**hit the hay** *sl.* go to bed —**hit the trail, hit the road** *inf.* proceed on journey; leave

hitch *vt.* fasten with loop *etc.*; raise, move with jerk —*vi.* be caught or fastened —*n.* difficulty; knot, fastening; jerk —**hitch'-(hike)** *vi.* travel by begging free rides

hith'er [hiTH'-] *adv.* to or towards this place —*a.* situated on this side —**hitherto'** *adv.* up to now or to this time

hive *n.* structure in which bees live or are housed; *fig.* place swarming with busy occupants —*v.* gather, place bees, in hive —**hive away** store, keep —**hive off** transfer; dispose of

hives *pl.n.* eruptive skin disease

HM His (*or* Her) Majesty

HMS His (*or* Her) Majesty's Service *or* Ship

HMSO His (*or* Her) Majesty's Stationery Office

hoard [-aw] *n.* stock, store, *esp.* hidden away —*vt.* amass and hide away; store

hoard'ing [-aw-] *n.* large board for displaying advertisements; temporary wooden fence round building or piece of ground

hoarse [-aw-] *a.* rough, harsh sounding, husky —**hoarse'ly** *adv.* —**hoarse'ness** *n.*

hoar'y [hawr'-] *a.* grey with age; greyish-white; of great antiquity; venerable —**hoar'frost** *n.* frozen dew

hoax [hōks] *n.* practical joke; deceptive trick —*vt.* play trick upon; deceive —**hoax'er** *n.*

hob *n.* flat-topped casing of fireplace; top area of cooking stove —**hob'nail** *n.* large-headed nail for boot soles

hob'ble vi. walk lamely —vt. tie legs together (of horse etc.) —n. straps or ropes put on an animal's legs to prevent it straying; limping gait

hob'bledehoy n. obs. rough, ill-mannered clumsy youth

hobb'y n. favourite occupation as pastime; small falcon —**hobb'yhorse** n. toy horse; favourite topic, preoccupation

hobgob'lin n. mischievous fairy

hob'nob vi. drink together; be familiar (with) (**-bb-**)

ho'bo n. US, C shiftless, wandering person (pl. **-bo(e)s**)

hock[1] n. backward-pointing joint on leg of horse etc., corresponding to human ankle —vt. disable by cutting tendons of hock

hock[2] n. dry white wine

hock'ey n. team game played on a field with ball and curved sticks; US, C ice hockey

ho'cus-po'cus n. trickery; mystifying jargon

hod n. small trough on a staff for carrying mortar, bricks etc.; tall, narrow coal scuttle

hoe n. tool for weeding, breaking ground etc. —vt. (**hoed, hoe'ing**)

hog n. pig, esp. castrated male for fattening; greedy, dirty person —vt. inf. eat, use (something) selfishly —**hogs'head** n. large cask; liquid measure of 52½ or 54 imperial gallons —**hog'wash** n. nonsense; pig food

Hogmanay' n. in Scotland, last day of year

hoi polloi' n. the common mass of people; the masses

hoist vt. raise aloft, raise with tackle etc.

hold[1] [-ō-] vt. keep fast, grasp; support in or with hands etc.; maintain in position; have capacity for; own, occupy; carry on; detain; celebrate; keep back; be- lieve —vi. cling; not to give away; abide (by); keep (to); last, proceed, be in force; occur (**held** pt./pp.) —n. grasp; influence —**hold'er** n. —**hold'ing** n. (oft. pl.) property, as land or stocks and shares —**hold'all** n. valise or case for carrying clothes etc. —**hold'fast** n. clamp —**hold'up** n. armed robbery; delay

hold[2] [-ō-] n. space in ship or aircraft for cargo

hole n. hollow place, cavity; perforation; opening; inf. unattractive place; inf. difficult situation —v. make holes in, go into a hole; drive into a hole —**ho'ley** a.

hol'iday n. day or other period of rest from work etc., esp. spent away from home

holl'and n. linen fabric —**hol'lands** n. spirit, gin

holl'ow [-ō-] a. having a cavity, not solid; empty; false; insincere; not full-toned —n. cavity, hole, valley —vt. make hollow, make hole in; excavate

holl'y n. evergreen shrub with prickly leaves and red berries

holl'yhock n. tall plant bearing many large flowers

holm oak evergreen Mediterranean oak tree

hol'ocaust n. great destruction of life, esp. by fire

hol'ograph n. document wholly written by the signer

holog'raphy n. science of using lasers to produce a photographic record (**hologram**) which can reproduce a three-dimensional image

hol'ster [hōl'-] n. leather case for pistol, hung from belt etc.

holt [-ō-] n. wood, wooded hill

ho'ly a. belonging, devoted to God; free from sin; divine; consecrated —**ho'lily** adv. —**ho'liness** n. sanctity; (**H-**) Pope's title —**holy day** day of religious festival —**Holy Communion** service of the Eucharist —**Holy Week** that before Easter

hom'age n. tribute, respect, reverence; formal acknowledgment of allegiance

home n. dwelling-place; residence; native place; institution for the elderly, infirm etc. —a. of, connected with, home; native —adv. to, at one's home; to the point —v. direct or be directed onto a point or target —**home'less** a. —**home'ly** a. unpretentious; warm and domesticated; **US, C** plain —**home'ward** a./adv. —**home'wards** adv. —**homebrew** n. alcoholic drink made at home —**home'sick** a. depressed by absence from home —**home'sickness** n. —**home'spun** a. domestic; simple —n. cloth made of homespun yarn —**home'stead** [-sted] n. house with outbuildings, esp. on farm; **US, C** house and land occupied by owner and exempt from seizure and forced sale for debt —**home'steader** n. —**home'work** n. school work done usu. at home —**bring home to** impress deeply upon —**home and dry** safe or successful

hom'icide n. killing of human being; killer —**homici'dal** a.

hom'ily n. sermon; religious discourse —**homilet'ic** a. of sermons —**homilet'ics** pl.n. art of preaching

Ho'mo n. genus to which modern man belongs

homo- (comb. form) same, as in homeopathy, homosexual etc. Such words are not given here where the meaning may easily be inferred from the simple word

hom(o)eop'athy [hŏ-mi-op'-] n. treatment of disease by small doses of what would produce symptoms in healthy person —**ho'meopath** n. one who be-

lieves in or practises homoeopathy —**homoeopath'ic** a. —**homoeopath'ically** adv.

homoge'neous [-j-] a. formed of uniform parts; similar, uniform; of the same nature —**homogene'ity** n. —**homog'enize** vt. break up fat globules in milk and cream to distribute them evenly

homol'ogous a. having the same relation, relative position etc. —**hom'ologue** n. homologous thing

hom'onym n. word of same form as another, but of different sense —**homon'ymous** a.

homosex'ual n. person sexually attracted to members of the same sex —a. —**homosexual'ity** n. —**homopho'bia** n. hate or fear of homosexuals and homosexuality —**ho'mophobe** n.

Hon. Honourable; (also **h-**) honorary

hone n. whetstone —vt. sharpen on one

hon'est [on'-] a. not cheating, lying, stealing etc.; genuine; without pretension —**hon'estly** adv. —**hon'esty** n. quality of being honest; plant with silvery seed pods

hon'ey [hun'i] n. sweet fluid made by bees —**hon'eycomb** n. wax structure in hexagonal cells in which bees place honey, eggs etc. —vt. fill with cells or perforations —**hon'eydew** n. sweet sticky substance found on plants; type of sweet melon —**hon'eymoon** n. holiday taken by newly-wedded pair —**hon'eysuckle** n. climbing plant

honk n. call of wild goose; any sound like this, esp. sound of motor-horn —vi. make this sound

hon'our [on'-] n. personal integrity; renown; reputation; sense of what is right or due; chastity;

high rank or position; source, cause of honour; pleasure, privilege —*pl.* mark of respect; distinction in examination —*vt.* respect highly; confer honour on; accept or pay (bill *etc.*) when due —**hon'ourable** *a.* —**hon'ourably** *adv.* —**honora'rium** *n.* a fee (*pl.* **-ria**) —**hon'orary** *a.* conferred for the sake of honour only; holding position without pay or usual requirements; giving services without pay —**hon'orif'ic** *a.* conferring honour

hood[1] *n.* covering for head and neck, often part of cloak or gown; hood-like thing as (adjustable) top of motor-car, perambulator *etc.*; **US** car bonnet —**hood'ed** *a.* covered with or shaped like a hood —**hood'wink** *vt.* deceive

hood[2] *n. sl.* hoodlum

hood'lum [-ōō-] *n.* gangster, bully

hoo'doo *n.* cause of bad luck

hoof [-ōō-] *n.* horny casing of foot of horse *etc.* (*pl.* **hoofs** or **hooves**) —**on the hoof** (of livestock) alive

hoo'-ha [hōō-] *n.* needless fuss, bother *etc.*

hook *n.* bent piece of metal *etc.*, for catching hold, hanging up *etc.*; something resembling hook in shape or function; curved cutting tool; *Boxing* blow delivered with bent elbow —*vt.* grasp, catch, hold, as with hook; fasten with hook; *Golf* drive (ball) widely to the left; *Cricket* hit off ball to leg —**hooked** *a.* shaped like hook; caught; *sl.* addicted to —**hook'er** *n.* **US** *sl.* prostitute; *Rugby* player who uses feet to get ball in scrum —**hook-up** *n.* linking of radio, television stations —**hook'worm** *n.* parasitic worm infesting humans and animals

hook'ah *n.* oriental pipe in which smoke is drawn through water and long tube

hoo'ligan *n.* violent, irresponsible (young) person —**hoo'liganism** *n.*

hoop [-ōō-] *n.* rigid circular band of metal, wood *etc.*; such a band used for binding barrel *etc.*, for use as a toy, or for jumping through as in circus acts —*vt.* bind with hoops; encircle —**go through the hoop(s)** *inf.* go through an ordeal or test

hoop'la [hōō'lah] *n.* game played at fairs *etc.* by throwing rings at objects for prizes

hoop'oe [hōō'pō] *n.* bird with large crest

hoot [-ōō-] *n.* owl's cry or similar sound; cry of disapproval or derision; *inf.* funny person or thing —*vi.* utter hoot (*esp.* in derision); sound motor horn; *inf.* laugh —**hoot'er** *n.* device (*eg* horn) to emit hooting sound; *sl.* nose

Hoo'ver [hōō'-] **R** vacuum cleaner —*v.* (**h-**) vacuum

hop[1] *vi.* spring on one foot; *inf.* move quickly (**-pp-**) —*n.* leap, skip; one stage of journey —**hop'scotch** *n.* children's game of hopping in pattern drawn on ground

hop[2] *n.* climbing plant with bitter cones used to flavour beer *etc.* —*pl.* the cones

hope *n.* expectation of something desired; thing that gives, or object of, this feeling —*v.* feel hope (for) —**hope'ful** *a.* —**hope'fully** *adv.* (*esp.* now) *inf.* it is hoped —**hope'less** *a.* —**young hopeful** promising boy or girl

hopp'er *n.* one who hops; device for feeding material into mill or machine or grain into railway truck *etc.*; mechanical hoppicker; **SA** *see* COCOPAN

hor'al, hor'ary *a. obs.* pert. to an hour; hourly

horde n. large crowd (esp. moving together)

hore'hound n. plant with bitter juice formerly used medicinally

hori'zon n. boundary of part of the earth seen from any given point; lines where earth and sky seem to meet; boundary of mental outlook —**horizon'tal** a. parallel with horizon, level —**horizon'tally** adv.

hor'mone n. substance secreted by certain glands which stimulates organs of the body; synthetic substance with same effect

horn n. hard projection on heads of certain animals, eg cows; substance made of, or resembling it; wind instrument orig. made of a horn; device (esp. in car) emitting sound as alarm, warning etc. —**horned** a. having horns —**horn'y** a. —**horn'beam** n. tree with smooth grey bark —**horn'bill** n. type of bird with horny growth on large bill —**horn'pipe** n. lively dance, esp. associated with sailors

horn'blende n. mineral consisting of silica, with magnesia, lime, or iron

horn'et n. large insect of wasp family

hor'ologe [hor_ə-loj] n. any timepiece —**horol'ogy** n. art or science of clock-making and measuring time

hor'oscope [horə-] n. observation of, or scheme showing disposition of planets etc., at given moment, esp. birth, by which character and abilities of individual are predicted; telling of person's fortune by this method

horren'dous a. horrific

horr'or n. terror; loathing, fear of; its cause —**horr'ible** a. exciting horror, hideous, shocking —**horr'ibly** adv. —**horr'id** a. unpleasant, repulsive; inf. unkind —**horr'ify** vt. move to horror (-ified, -ifying) —**horrif'ic** a. particularly horrible

hors d'oeu'vre [aw-dur'vr] n. small dish served before main meal

horse n. four-footed animal used for riding and draught; cavalry; vaulting-block; frame for support etc., esp. for drying clothes —vt. provide with horse or horses —**hors'y** a. having to do with horses; devoted to horses or horse racing —**horse chestnut** tree with conical clusters of white or pink flowers and large nuts —**horse'fly** n. large, bloodsucking fly —**horse laugh** harsh boisterous laugh —**horse'man** n. (**horse'woman** fem.) rider on horse —**horse'power** n. unit of power of engine etc. 550 footpounds per second —**horse'radish** n. plant with pungent root —**horse'shoe** n. protective U-shaped piece of iron nailed to horse's hoof; thing so shaped —**horse'tail** n. green flowerless plant with erect, jointed stem —**horse about** (or **around**) inf. play roughly, boisterously

hor'ticulture n. art or science of gardening —**horticul'tural** a. —**horticul'turist** n.

Hos. Hosea

hosann'a [-z-] n. cry of praise, adoration

hose n. flexible tube for conveying liquid or gas; stockings —vt. water with hose —**ho'sier** n. dealer in stockings etc. —**ho'siery** n. stockings etc.

hos'pice [-is] n. obs. traveller's house of rest kept by religious order

hos'pital n. institution for care of sick —**hospitaliza'tion** n.

—**hos'pitalize** *vt.* to place for care in a hospital

hospital'ity *n.* friendly and liberal reception of strangers or guests —**hos'pitable** *a.* welcoming, kindly —**hos'pitably** *adv.*

host[1] [hō-] *n.* (**host'ess** *fem.*) one who entertains another; innkeeper; compere of show; animal, plant on which parasite lives —*vt.* act as a host

host[2] [hō-] *n.* large number

Host [hō-] *n.* consecrated bread of the Eucharist

hos'ta *n.* garden plant with large ornamental leaves

hos'tage *n.* person taken or given as pledge or security

hos'tel *n.* building providing accommodation at low cost for particular category of people, as students, or the homeless —**hos'telry** *n. obs.* inn

hos'tile *a.* opposed, antagonistic; warlike; of an enemy; unfriendly —**hostil'ity** *n.* enmity —*pl.* acts of warfare

hot *a.* of high temperature, very warm, giving or feeling heat; angry; severe; recent, new; much favoured; spicy; *sl.* good, quick, smart; *sl.* stolen (**hott'er** *comp.*, **hott'est** *sup.*) —**hot'ly** *adv.* —**hot'ness** *n.* —**hot air** *inf.* boastful, empty talk —**hot'bed** *n.* bed of earth heated by manure and grass for young plants; any place encouraging growth —**hot'-blooded** *a.* passionate, excitable —**hot dog** hot sausage (*esp.* frankfurter) in split bread roll —**hot'foot** *v./adv.* (go) quickly —**hot'head** *n.* hasty, intemperate person —**hot'house** *n.* forcing house for plants; heated building for cultivating tropical plants in cold or temperate climates —**hot line** direct communication link between heads of governments *etc.* —**hot'plate** *n.* heated plate on electric cooker; portable device for keeping food warm

hotch'potch *n.* medley; dish of many ingredients

hotel' [hō-] *n.* commercial establishment providing lodging and meals —**hotel keeper**, **hotel'ier** [-yā] *n.*

Hott'entot *n.* member of a native S Afr. race, now nearly extinct

hough [hok] *n. same as* HOCK[1]

hound *n.* hunting dog —*vt.* chase, urge, pursue

hour [owr] *n.* twenty-fourth part of day; sixty minutes; time of day; appointed time —*pl.* fixed periods for work, prayers *etc.*; book of prayers —**hour'ly** *adv.* every hour; frequently —*a.* frequent; happening every hour —**hour'glass** *n.* sand-glass running an hour

hou'ri [hoor'i] *n.* beautiful nymph of the Muslim paradise (*pl.* -ris)

house [-s] *n.* building for human habitation; building for other specified purpose; legislative, or other assembly; family; business firm; theatre audience, performance —*vt.* [-z] give or receive shelter, lodging or storage; cover or contain —**hous'ing** *n.* (providing of) houses; part or structure designed to cover, protect, contain —**house'boat** *n.* boat for living in on river *etc.* —**house'breaker** *n.* burglar —**house'coat** *n.* woman's long loose garment for casual wear at home —**house'hold** *n.* inmates of house collectively —**house'holder** *n.* occupier of house as his dwelling; head of household —**house'keeper** *n.* person managing affairs of household —**house'keeping** *n.* (money for) running household —**house'maid** *n.* maidservant who cleans rooms *etc.*

—**house-warming** n. party to celebrate entry into new house
—**house'wife** n. woman who runs a household —**housey-housey** n. gambling game, bingo

hov'el n. mean dwelling

hov'er vi. hang in the air (of bird etc.); loiter; be in state of indecision —**hov'ercraft** n. type of craft which can travel over both land and sea on a cushion of air

how adv. in what way; by what means; in what condition; to what degree; (in direct or dependent question) —**howbe'it** adv. obs. nevertheless —**however** conj. nevertheless —adv. in whatever way, degree; all the same

how'dah n. (canopied) seat on elephant's back

how'itzer n. short gun firing shells at high elevation

howl vi. utter long loud cry —n. such cry —**howl'er** n. one that howls; inf. stupid mistake

hoy'den, hoi'den n. wild, boisterous girl, tomboy

HP high pressure; hire purchase; (also **hp**) horsepower

HQ headquarters

HRH His (or Her) Royal Highness

HRT hormone replacement therapy

hub n. middle part of wheel, from which spokes radiate; central point of activity

hubb'ub n. confused noise of many voices; uproar

huck'ster n. person using aggressive or questionable methods of selling —vt. sell goods thus

hud'dle n. crowded mass; inf. impromptu conference —v. heap, crowd together; hunch

hue [hyōō] n. colour, complexion

hue and cry public uproar,

outcry; loud outcry usually in pursuit of wrongdoer

huff n. passing mood of anger —v. make or become angry, resentful —vi. blow, puff heavily —**huff'ily** adv. —**huff'y** a.

hug vt. clasp tightly in the arms; cling; keep close to (-**gg**-) —n. fond embrace

huge a. very big —**huge'ly** adv. very much

hu'la [hŌO-] n. native dance of Hawaii

Hula-Hoop R hoop of plastic etc. swung round body by wriggling hips

hulk n. body of abandoned vessel; offens. large, unwieldy person or thing —**hulk'ing** a. unwieldy, bulky

hull n. frame, body of ship; calyx of strawberry, raspberry, or similar fruit; shell, husk —vt. remove shell, hull; send shot into hull

hullabaloo' n. uproar, clamour, row

hum vi. make low continuous sound as bee; sl. smell unpleasantly; sl. be very active —vt. sing with closed lips (-**mm**-) —n. humming sound; sl. smell; sl. great activity; in radio, disturbance affecting reception —**humm'ing-bird** n. very small bird whose wings make humming noise

hu'man a. of man, relating to, characteristic of, man's nature —**humane'** a. benevolent, kind; merciful —**hu'manism** n. belief in human effort rather than religion; interest in human welfare and affairs; classical literary culture —**hu'manist** n. —**humanita'rian** n. philanthropist —a. —**human'ity** n. human nature; human race; kindliness —pl. study of literature, philosophy, the arts —**hu'manize** vt. make human; civilize —**hu'manly** adv.

—hu'mankind n. whole race of man

hum'ble a. lowly, modest **—vt.** bring low, abase, humiliate **—hum'bly** adv.

hum'bug n. impostor; sham, nonsense, deception; sweet of boiled sugar **—vt.** deceive; defraud (**-gg-**)

hum'dinger n. sl. excellent person or thing

hum'drum a. commonplace, dull, monotonous

hu'meral a. of shoulder **—hu'merus** n. long bone of upper arm (pl. **-eri** [-ī])

hu'mid a. moist, damp **—humid'ifier** n. device for increasing amount of water vapour in air in room etc. **—humid'ify** vt. **—humid'ity** n.

humil'iate [hyoō-] vt. lower dignity of, abase, mortify **—humilia'tion** n.

humil'ity [hyoō-] n. state of being humble; meekness

humm'ock n. low knoll, hillock; ridge of ice

hu'mour n. faculty of saying or perceiving what excites amusement; state of mind, mood; temperament; obs. fluids of body **—vt.** gratify, indulge **—hu'morist** n. person who acts, speaks, writes humorously **—hu'morous** a. funny; amusing **—hu'morously** adv.

hump n. normal or deforming lump, esp. on back; hillock; inf. dejection **—vt.** make humpshaped; sl. carry or heave **—hump'back** n. person with hump **—hump'backed** a. having a hump

hu'mus n. decayed vegetable and animal mould

hunch n. inf. intuition or premonition; hump **—vt.** thrust, bend into hump **—hunch'back** n. humpback

hun'dred n./a. cardinal number, ten times ten **—hun'dredth** a. the ordinal number **—hun'dredfold** a./adv. **—hun'dredweight** n. weight of 112 lbs. (50.8 kg), 20th part of ton

hung pt./pp. of HANG **—a.** (of jury etc.) unable to decide; not having majority **—hung-over** a. inf. suffering from after-effects of excessive drinking **—hung up** inf. delayed; inf. emotionally disturbed

hun'ger n. discomfort, exhaustion from lack of food; strong desire **—vi.** **—hung'rily** adv **—hun'gry** a. having keen appetite **—hunger strike** refusal of all food, as a protest

hunk n. thick piece

hunt v. seek out to kill or capture for sport or food; search (for) **—n.** chase, search; track of country hunted over; (party organized for) hunting; pack of hounds; hunting district or society **—hunt'er** n. one who hunts (**hunt'ress** fem.); horse, dog bred for hunting **—hunter-killer** a. denoting submarine designed to pursue and destroy enemy craft **—hunts'man** n. man in charge of pack of hounds

hur'dle n. portable frame of bars for temporary fences or for jumping over; obstacle **—pl.** race over hurdles **—vi.** race over hurdles **—hurd'ler** n. one who races over hurdles

hur'dy-gur'dy n. mechanical (musical) instrument, eg barrel organ

hurl vt. throw violently **—hurly-burly** n. loud confusion

hur'ling, hur'ley n. Irish game like hockey

hurrah', hurray' interj. exclamation of joy or applause

hurr'icane n. very strong, potentially destructive wind or storm —**hurricane lamp** lamp with glass covering round flame

hurr'y v. (cause to) move or act in great haste (**hurr'ied, hurr'ry-ing**) —n. undue haste; eagerness —**hurr'iedly** adv.

hurt vt. injure, damage, give pain to, wound feelings of; distress —vi. inf. feel pain (**hurt** pt./pp.) —n. wound, injury, harm —**hurt'ful** a.

hur'tle vi. move rapidly; rush violently; whirl

hus'band [-z-] n. married man —vt. economize; use to best advantage —**hus'bandry** n. farming; economy

hush v. make or be silent —n. stillness; quietness —**hush'hush** a. inf. secret —**hush up** suppress rumours, information, make secret

husk n. dry covering of certain seeds and fruits; worthless outside part —vt. remove husk from —**husk'y** a. rough in tone; hoarse; dry as husk, dry in the throat; inf. big, full of husks; inf. big and strong

hus'ky n. Arctic sledgedog

hussar' [-z-] n. light armed cavalry soldier

huss'y n. cheeky girl or young woman

hust'ings pl.n. platform from which parliamentary candidates were nominated; political campaigning

hus'tle [hus'l] v. push about, jostle, hurry —vi. US, C sl. solicit —n. —**hus'tler** n.

hut n. any small house or shelter, usu. of wood or metal

hutch n. box-like pen for rabbits etc.

hy'acinth n. bulbous plant with bell-shaped flowers, esp. purple-blue; this blue; orange gem jacinth

hy(a)e'na [hi-ē'nə] n. wild animal related to dog

hy'aline [-lin] a. clear, translucent

hy'brid n. offspring of two plants or animals of different species; mongrel —a. crossbred —**hy'bridism** n. —**hy'bridize** v. make hybrid; cross-breed

hy'datid a./n. (of) watery cyst, resulting from development of tapeworm larva causing serious disease (in man)

hy'dra n. fabulous many-headed water serpent; any persistent problem; a freshwater polyp —**hydra-headed** a. hard to root out

hydrang'ea [-rānj'ə] n. ornamental shrub with pink, blue, or white flowers

hy'drant n. water-pipe with nozzle for hose

hydraul'ic a. concerned with, operated by, pressure transmitted through liquid in pipe —**hy-drau'lics** pl.n. science of mechanical properties of liquid in motion

hydro- (comb. form) water, as hydroelectric; presence of hydrogen, as hydrocarbon

hydrocar'bon n. compound of hydrogen and carbon

hydrochlor'ic acid [-klo'-] strong colourless acid used in many industrial and laboratory processes

hydrodynam'ics n. science of the motions of system wholly or partly fluid

hydroelec'tric a. pert. to generation of electricity by use of water

hy'drofoil n. fast, light vessel with hull raised out of water at speed by vanes in water

hy'drogen n. colourless gas which combines with oxygen to form water —**hydrogen bomb**

atom bomb of enormous power in which hydrogen nuclei are converted into helium nuclei —**hydrogen peroxide** colourless liquid used as antiseptic and bleach

hydrog'raphy n. description of waters of the earth —**hydrog'rapher** n. —**hydrograph'ic** a.

hydrol'ysis n. decomposition of chemical compound reacting with water

hydrom'eter n. device for measuring relative density of liquid

hydropho'bia n. aversion to water, esp. as symptom of rabies

hy'drophone n. instrument for detecting sound through water

hy'droplane n. light skimming motor-boat; seaplane; vane controlling motion of submarine etc.

hydropon'ics pl.n. science of cultivating plants in water without using soil

hydrother'apy n. Med. treatment of disease by external application of water

hy'drous a. containing water

hy'giene [hrjēn] n. principles and practice of health and cleanliness; study of these principles —**hygie'nic** a. —**hygie'nically** adv. —**hy'gienist** n.

hygrom'eter n. instrument for measuring humidity of air

hygroscop'ic a. readily absorbing moisture from the atmosphere

hy'men n. membrane partly covering vagina of virgin; (H-) Greek god of marriage

hymn [him] n. song of praise, esp. to God —vt. praise in song —**hym'nal** a. of hymns —n. book of hymns Also **hymn book** —**hym'nodist** n. —**hym'nody** n. singing or composition of hymns

hype[1] sl. n. hypodermic syringe;

drug addict —v. (with up) inject (oneself) with drug

hype[2] sl. n. deception, racket; intensive publicity —v. promote (a product) using intensive publicity

hyper- (comb. form) over, above, excessively, as in **hyperac'tive** etc. Such words are not given here where the meaning may easily be inferred from the simple word

hyper'bola n. curve produced when cone is cut by plane making larger angle with the base than the side makes

hyper'bole [-bə-li] n. rhetorical exaggeration —**hyperbol'ic(al)** a.

hyperbor'ean a./n. (inhabitant) of extreme north

hypercrit'ical a. too critical —**hypercrit'icism** n.

hy'permarket n. huge self-service store

hypersen'sitive a. unduly vulnerable emotionally or physically

hyperten'sion n. abnormally high blood pressure

hy'phen n. short line (-) indicating that two words or syllables are to be connected —**hy'phenate** vt. —**hy'phenated** a. joined by a hyphen

hypno'sis [hip-] n. induced state like deep sleep in which subject acts on external suggestion —**hypnot'ic** a. of hypnosis or of the person or thing producing it —**hyp'notism** n. —**hyp'notist** n. —**hyp'notize** vt. affect with hypnosis

hy'po n. short for hyposulphite (sodium thiosulphate), used as fixer in developing photographs

hypo-, hyph-, hyp- (comb. forms) under, below, less, as in hypocrite, hyphen etc. Such words are not given here where meaning may easily be inferred from simple word

hypoallergen'ic a. (of cosmetics etc.) not likely to cause allergic reaction

hy'pocaust n. ancient Roman underfloor heating system

hypochon'dria [hī-pō-kon'-] n. morbid depression, without cause, about one's own health —**hypochon'driac** a./n. —**hypochondri'acal** a.

hypoc'risy [hip-] n. assuming of false appearance of virtue; insincerity —**hyp'ocrite** n. —**hypocrit'ical** a. —**hypocrit'ically** adv.

hypoderm'ic [hī-] a. introduced, injected beneath the skin —n. hypodermic syringe or needle

hypogas'tric [hī-] a. relating to, situated in, lower part of abdomen

hypot'enuse [hī-] n. side of a right-angled triangle opposite the right angle

hypother'mia n. condition of having body temperature reduced to dangerously low level

hypoth'esis [hī-] n. suggested explanation of something; assumption as basis of reasoning (pl. -eses [-sēz]) —**hypothet'ical** a. —**hypothet'ically** adv. —**hypoth'esize** v.

hypso- (comb. form) height, as in hypsometry

hypsog'raphy n. branch of geography dealing with altitudes

hypsom'eter n. instrument for measuring altitudes —**hypsom'etry** n. science of measuring altitudes

hy'rax n. genus of hoofed but rodent-like animals

hyss'op [his'-] n. small aromatic herb

hysterec'tomy [his-] n. surgical operation for removing the uterus

hystere'sis [his-] n. Physics lag or delay in changes in variable property of a system

hyste'ria [his-] n. mental disorder with emotional outbursts; any frenzied emotional state; fit of crying or laughing —**hyster'ical** [-te'ri-] a. —**hyster'ically** adv. —**hyster'ics** pl.n. fits of hysteria

Hz hertz

I

I Chem. iodine

I pron. the pronoun of the first person singular

iam'bus, i'amb [ī-] n. metrical foot of short and long syllable (pl. -uses, -bi [-bī], i'ambs) —**iam'bic** a.

IATA International Air Transport Association

iat'ric, iat'rical [ī-] a. of medicine or physicians, esp. as suffix -iatrics, -iatry, as in paediatrics, psychiatry

IBA Independent Broadcasting Authority

Ibe'rian [ī-] a. of Iberia, ie Spain and Portugal

i'bex n. wild goat with large horns (pl. i'bexes, ib'ices [-sēz])

ibid' short for ibidem (Lat. in the same place)

i'bis n. storklike bird

IBM International Business Machines Corporation

i/c in charge

ICBM intercontinental ballistic missile

ice n. frozen water; frozen confection, ice cream —v. cover, become covered with ice; cool with ice; cover with icing —**i'ci-**

cle n. tapering spike of ice hanging where water has dripped —i'cily adv. —i'ciness n. —i'cing n. mixture of sugar and water etc. used to decorate cakes —i'cy a. covered with ice; cold; chilling —ice'berg n. large floating mass of ice —ice cream sweetened frozen dessert made from cream, eggs etc. —ice floe sheet of floating ice —ice hockey team game played on ice with puck —ice lolly ice cream, flavoured on stick

ichneu'mon [ik-nyoo'-] n. greyish brown mongoose —**ichneumon fly** insect laying its eggs on larvae of other insects

ichthyol'ogy [ik-thi-] n. scientific study of fish —**ichthyosaur'us** n. a prehistoric marine animal (pl. **-i**)

ICI Imperial Chemical Industries

i'cicle see ICE

i'con n. image, representation, esp. of religious figure —**icon'oclasm** n. —**icon'oclast** n. one who attacks established principles etc.; breaker of icons —**iconoclas'tic** a. —**iconog'raphy** n. icons collectively; study of icons

id n. Psychoanalysis the mind's instinctive energies

ide'a n. notion in the mind; conception; vague belief; plan, aim —**ide'al** n. conception of something that is perfect; perfect person or thing —a. perfect; visionary; existing only in idea —**ide'alism** n. tendency to seek perfection in everything; philosophy that mind is the only reality —**ide'alist** n. one who holds doctrine of idealism; one who strives after the ideal; impractical person —**idealis'tic** a. —**idealiza'tion** n. —**ide'alize** vt. portray as ideal —**ide'ally** adv.

i'dem Lat. the same

ident'ity n. individuality; being the same, exactly alike —**iden'tical** a. very same —**ident'ically** adv. —**ident'ifiable** a. —**identifica'tion** n. —**ident'ify** v. establish identity of; associate (oneself) with; treat as identical (**ident'ified, ident'ifying**) —**ident'ikit** R set of pictures of parts of faces that can be built up to form likeness of person sought by police etc.

id'eograph n. picture, symbol, figure etc., suggesting an object without naming it Also **id'eogram** —**ideog'raphy** n. representation of things by ideographs

ideol'ogy [I-di-] n. body of ideas, beliefs of group, nation etc. —**ideolog'ical** a.

ides [Idz] pl.n. the 15th of March, May, July and Oct. and the 13th of other months of the Ancient Roman calendar

id'iocy see IDIOT

id'iom n. way of expression natural or peculiar to a language or group; characteristic style of expression —**idiomat'ic** a. using idioms; colloquial —**idiomat'ically** adv.

idiosyn'crasy n. peculiarity of mind, temper or disposition in a person

id'iot n. mentally deficient person; foolish, senseless person —**id'iocy** n. —**idiot'ic** a. utterly senseless or stupid —**idiot'ically** adv.

i'dle a. unemployed; lazy; useless, vain, groundless —vi. be idle; (of engine) run slowly with gears disengaged —vt. (esp. with away) waste —**i'dleness** n. —**i'dler** n. —**i'dly** adv.

i'dol n. image of deity as object of worship; object of excessive devotion —**idol'ater** n. worshipper of idols (**idol'atress** fem.) —**idol'atrous** a. —**idol'atry** n.

—i'dolize vt. love or venerate to excess; make an idol of

id'yll n. short descriptive poem of picturesque or charming scene or episode, esp. of rustic life —idyll'ic a. of, like, idyll; delightful —idyll'ically adv.

i.e. Lat. id est, that is

if conj. on condition or supposition that; whether; although —n. uncertainty or doubt (esp. in ifs and buts) —iff'y a. inf. dubious

ig'loo n. dome-shaped Eskimo house of snow and ice

ig'neous a. esp. of rocks, formed as molten rock cools and hardens

ignite' v. (cause) to burn —ig-ni'tion n. act of kindling or setting on fire; in internal-com-bustion engine, means of firing explosive mixture, usu. electric spark

igno'ble a. mean, base; of low birth —igno'bly adv.

ig'nominy n. dishonour, dis-grace; shameful act —ignomin'i-ous a. —ignomin'iously adv.

ignore' vt. disregard, leave out of account —ignora'mus n. igno-rant person (pl. -muses) —ig'no-rance n. lack of knowledge —ig'-norant a. lacking knowledge; un-educated; unaware —ig'norantly adv.

iguan'a [i-gwahn'ə] n. large tropical American lizard

iguan'odon [gwahn'-] n. gigan-tic extinct herbivorous reptile

il— (comb. form) for in- before l: see IN- and listed words

il'eum n. lower part of small intestine —il'eac a.

ilk n. same —of that ilk of the same type or class

ill a. not in good health; bad, evil; faulty; unfavourable —n. evil, harm; mild disease —adv. badly; hardly, with difficulty —ill'ness n. —ill-advised a. imprudent; in-

judicious —ill-fated a. unfortu-nate —ill-favoured a. ugly, de-formed —ill-gotten a. obtained dishonestly —ill-mannered a. boorish, uncivil —ill-omened a. unlucky, inauspicious —ill-timed a. inopportune —ill-treat vt. treat cruelly —ill will unkind feeling, hostility

ill. illustrated; illustration

illegit'imate [-jit'-] a. born out of wedlock; unlawful; not regular —n. bastard —illegit'imacy n.

illic'it [-lis'-] a. illegal; prohibit-ed, forbidden

illim'itable a. that cannot be limited, boundless, unrestricted, infinite —illim'itableness n.

illit'erate a. not literate; un-able to read or write —n. illiter-ate person —illit'eracy n.

illu'minate [-loo'-] vt. light up; clarify; decorate with lights; decorate with gold and colours —illu'minant n. agent of lighting —illumina'tion n. —illu'mina-tive a. —illu'mine vt. Poet. illu-minate

illu'sion [-loo'-] n. deceptive ap-pearance or belief —illu'sionist n. conjuror —illu'sive a. false —illu'sory a.

ill'ustrate vt. provide with pic-tures or examples; exemplify —illustra'tion n. picture, dia-gram; example; act of illustrating —ill'ustrative a. providing ex-planation —ill'ustrator n.

illus'trious a. famous; distin-guished; exalted

im— (comb. form) for in- before m, b, and p: see IN- and listed words

im'age n. representation or like-ness of person or thing; optical counterpart, as in mirror; double, copy; general impression; mental picture created by words, esp. in literature —vt. make image of; reflect —im'agery n. images collectively, *esp.* in literature

imag'ine [-maj'-] *vt.* picture to oneself; think; conjecture —**im- ag'inable** *a.* —**imag'inary** *a.* existing only in fancy —**imagina'- tion** *n.* faculty of making mental images of things not present; fancy —**imag'inative** *a.* —**im- ag'inatively** *adv.*

ima'go *n.* last, perfected state of insect life; image (*pl.* **-es, ima'gi- nes** [i-maj'ə-nēz])

imam' [-mahm'] *n.* Islamic minister or priest

imbal'ance *n.* lack of balance proportion

im'becile [-sēl] *n.* idiot —*a.* idiotic —**imbecil'ity** *n.*

imbibe' *vt.* drink in; absorb —*vi.* drink

im'bricate(d) *a.* lying over each other in regular order, like tiles or shingles on roof —**imbri- ca'tion** *n.*

imbrogl'io [-brōl'yō] *n.* complicated situation, plot (*pl.* **-ios**)

imbrue' *vt.* stain (*esp.* with blood); permeate —**imbrue'ment** *n.*

imbue' [-byoo'] *vt.* inspire; imbue, saturate, dye

IMF International Monetary Fund

im'itate *vt.* take as model; mimic, copy —**im'itable** *a.* —**imita'- tion** *n.* act of imitating; copy of original; likeness; counterfeit —**im'itative** *a.* —**im'itator** *n.*

immac'ulate *a.* spotless; pure; unsullied

imm'anent *a.* abiding in, inherent —**imm'anence** *n.*

immate'rial *a.* unimportant, trifling; not consisting of matter; spiritual

imme'diate *a.* occurring at once; direct, not separated by others —**imme'diacy** *n.* —**im- me'diately** *adv.*

immemor'ial *a.* beyond

memory —**immemor'ially** *adv.*

immense' *a.* huge, vast —**im- mense'ly** *adv.* —**immen'sity** *n.* vastness

immerse' *vt.* dip, plunge, into liquid; involve; engross —**im- mer'sion** *n.* immersing —**im- mersion heater, immer'ser** *n.* electric appliance for heating liquid in which it is immersed

imm'igrate *vi.* come into country as settler —**imm'igrant** *n./a.* —**immigra'tion** *n.*

imm'inent *a.* liable to happen soon; close at hand —**im'mi- nence** *n.* —**imm'inently** *adv.*

imm'olate *vt.* kill, sacrifice —**immola'tion** *n.*

immor'al [-mo'ral] *a.* corrupt; promiscuous; indecent; unethical —**immoral'ity** *n.*

immor'tal *a.* deathless; famed for all time —*n.* immortal being; god; one whose fame will last —**immortal'ity** *n.* —**immor'tal- ize** *vt.*

immune' [-myōōn'] *a.* proof (against a disease *etc.*); secure, exempt —**immu'nity** *n.* state of being immune; freedom from prosecution, tax *etc.* —**immuni- za'tion** *n.* process of making immune to disease —**imm'unize** *vt.* make immune —**immunol'- ogy** *n.* branch of biology concerned with study of immunity

immure' *vt.* imprison, wall up

immu'table *a.* unchangeable

imp *n.* little devil; mischievous child

imp. imperative; imperfect

im'pact *n.* collision; profound effect —**impact'** *vt.* drive, press

impair' *vt.* weaken, damage —**impair'ment** *n.*

impa'la [-pah'-] *n.* antelope of Southern Africa

impale' *vt.* pierce with sharp instrument; combine (two coats of arms) by placing them side by side with line between —**im-pale'ment** n.

impart' vt. communicate (information etc.); give

impar'tial a. not biased or prejudiced; fair —**impartial'ity** n.

impass'able a. not capable of being passed; blocked, as mountain pass

impasse' [-pahs'] n. deadlock; place, situation, from which there is no outlet

impass'ioned [-sh-] a. deeply moved, ardent

impass'ive a. showing no emotion; calm —**impassiv'ity** n.

impeach' vt. charge with crime; call to account; denounce —**impeach'able** a. —**impeach'-ment** n.

impecc'able a. without flaw or error —**impeccabil'ity** n.

impecu'nious a. poor —**impecunios'ity** n.

impede' vt. hinder —**impe'd-ance** n. Electricity measure of opposition offered to flow of alternating current —**imped'i-ment** n. obstruction; defect

impel' vt. induce, incite; drive, force (-ll-) —**impel'ler** n.

impend' vi. threaten; be imminent; hang over —**impen'ding** a.

imper'ative [-pe'rə-] a. necessary; peremptory; expressing command —n. imperative mood —**imper'atively** adv.

impe'rial a. of empire, or emperor; majestic; denoting weights and measures established by law in Brit. —**impe'rialism** n. extension of empire; belief in colonial empire —**impe'rialist** n. —**imperialis'tic** a.

imper'il [-pe'ril] vt. bring into peril, endanger (-ll-)

impe'rious a. domineering; haughty; dictatorial

imper'sonal a. objective, having no personal significance; devoid of human warmth, personality etc.; (of speech) without personal subject —**impersonal'ity** n.

imper'sonate vt. pretend to be (another person); play the part of —**impersona'tion** n. —**imper'sonator** n.

impert'inent a. insolent, rude —**impert'inence** n. —**imper'ti-nently** adv.

impertur'bable a. calm, not excitable —**impertur'bably** adv.

imper'vious a. not affording passage; impenetrable (to feeling, argument etc.) —**imper'vi-ously** adv. —**imper'viousness** n.

impeti'go [-tī'-] n. contagious skin disease

impet'uous a. likely to act without consideration, rash —**impet'uously** adv. —**impetuos'ity** n.

im'petus n. force with which body moves; impulse

impinge' vi. encroach (upon); collide (with) —**impinge'ment** n.

im'pious a. irreverent, profane, wicked

implac'able a. not to be appeased; unyielding —**implac-abil'ity** n.

implant' [-ah-] vt. insert, fix

im'plement n. tool, instrument, utensil —vt. carry out (instructions etc.); put into effect

im'plicate vt. involve, include; entangle; imply —**implica'tion** n. something implied —**implic'it** [-plis'-] a. implied but not expressed; absolute and unreserved —**implic'itly** adv.

implore' vt. entreat earnestly —**implor'ingly** adv.

imply' vt. indicate by hint, suggest; mean (**implied'**, **imply'ing**)

import' vt. bring in, introduce (esp. goods from foreign country); imply —n. [im'-] thing imported; meaning; importance

—**import'able** a. —**importa'tion** n. —**import'er** n.

import'ant a. of great consequence; momentous; pompous —**impor'tance** n. —**import'antly** adv.

impor'tune vt. request, demand persistently —**impor'tunate** a. persistent —**impor'tunately** adv. —**importu'nity** n.

impose' vt. levy (tax, duty etc., upon) —vi. take advantage (of), practise deceit on —**impos'ing** a. impressive —**imposi'tion** n. that which is imposed; tax; burden; deception —**im'post** n. duty, tax on imports

imposs'ible a. incapable of being done or experienced; absurd; unreasonable —**impossibil'ity** n. —**imposs'ibly** adv.

impos'tor n. deceiver, one who assumes false identity —**impos'ture** n.

im'potent a. powerless; (of males) incapable of sexual intercourse —**im'potence** n. —**im'potently** adv.

impound' vt. take legal possession of and, often, place in a pound (cars, animals etc.); confiscate

impov'erish vt. make poor or weak —**impov'erishment** n.

impreca'tion n. invoking of evil; curse —**im'precate** vt.

impreg'nable a. proof against attack; unassailable; unable to be broken into —**impregnabil'ity** n. —**impreg'nably** adv.

im'pregnate vt. saturate, infuse; make pregnant —**impregna'tion** n.

impresar'io n. organizer of public entertainment; manager of opera, ballet etc. (pl. **-s**)

impress'[1] vt. affect deeply, usu. favourably; imprint, stamp; fix —n. [im'-] act of impressing; mark impressed —**impressibil'-**

ity n. —**impress'ible** a. —**impres'sion** n. effect produced, esp. on mind; notion, belief; imprint; a printing; total of copies printed at once; printed copy —**impressionabil'ity** n. —**impress'ionable** a. susceptible to external influences —**impres'sionism** n. art style that renders general effect without detail —**impres'sionist** n. —**impressionis'tic** a. —**impres'sive** a. making deep impression

impress'[2] vt. press into service —**impress'ment** n.

imprest' vt. advance on loan by government —n. money advanced by government

imprima'tur n. licence to print book etc.

im'print n. mark made by pressure; characteristic mark —vt. [im-print'] produce mark; stamp; fix in mind

impris'on n. [-z'-] put in prison —**impris'onment** n.

impromp'tu [-tyōō] adv./a. extempore; unrehearsed —n. improvisation

improve' [-ōōv'] v. make or become better in quality, standard, value etc. —**improv'able** a. —**improve'ment** n. —**improv'er** n.

improv'ident a. thriftless; negligent; imprudent —**improv'idence** n.

im'provise v. make use of materials at hand; compose, utter without preparation —**improvisa'tion** n.

im'pudent [-pyoo-] a. disrespectful, impertinent —**im'pudence** n. —**im'pudently** adv.

impugn' [-pyōōn'] vt. call in question, challenge

im'pulse n. sudden inclination to act; sudden application of force; motion caused by it; stimulation of nerve moving muscle

—**impul'sion** n. impulse, usu. in the first sense —**impul'sive** a. given to acting without reflection, rash —**impul'sively** adv.

impu'nity n. freedom, exemption from injurious consequences or punishment

impute' vt. ascribe, attribute to —**imputabil'ity** n. —**imputa'tion** n. that which is imputed as a charge or fault; reproach, censure

in prep. expresses inclusion within limits of space, time, circumstance, sphere etc. —adv. in or into some state, place etc.; inf. in vogue etc. —a. inf. fashionable

in. inch(es)

in- (comb. form) with its forms **il-, im-, ir-** negatives the idea of the simple word: also forms compounds with the meaning of in, into, upon, as inter, impend, irrigate. The list below contains some compounds that will be understood if not or lack of is used with the meaning of the simple word

inadvert'ent a. not attentive; negligent; unintentional —**inadvert'ence, inadvert'ency** n. —**inadvert'ently** adv.

inane' a. foolish, silly, vacant

—**inani'tion** n. exhaustion; silliness —**inan'ity** n.

inan'imate a. lacking qualities of living beings; appearing dead; lacking vitality

inasmuch' adv. seeing that (only in inasmuch as)

inaug'urate [-yoo-rāt] vt. begin, initiate the use of, esp. with ceremony; admit to office —**inaug'ural** a. —**inaug'urally** adv. —**inaugura'tion** n. act of inaugurating; ceremony to celebrate the initiation or admittance of

inauspi'cious [-spish'-] a. not auspicious; unlucky; unfavourable —**inauspi'ciously** adv.

in'board a. inside hull or bulwarks

in'born a. existing from birth; inherent

inbreed' vt. breed from union of closely related individuals (**inbred'** pp.) —**inbred'** a. produced as result of inbreeding; inborn, ingrained —**inbreed'ing** n.

inc. inclusive; incorporated; increase

incal'culable a. beyond calculation; very great

in cam'era in secret or private session

incandes'cent a. glowing

ille'gal	impure'	indeci'sive	insincere'
illeg'ible	inabil'ity	indef'inite	insol'vent
illog'ical	inac'curate	indirect'	insuffic'ient
immature'	inad'equate	indiscreet'	intan'gible
immo'bile	inappro'priate	ineffic'ient	intol'erable
immod'erate	inca'pable	inexpen'sive	inval'id
immod'est	incom'parable	inexper'ienced	inva'riable
immov(e)'able	incompat'ible	infer'tile	invis'ible
impa'tient	incom'petent	infor'mal	invul'nerable
impercep'tible	incomplete'	infre'quent	irra'tional
imper'fect	inconsid'erate	ingrat'itude	irreg'ular
impolite'	inconsist'ent	inhospit'able	irrel'evant
imprac'ticable	inconve'nience	inoffen'sive	irreplace'able
imprac'tical	incorrect'	insan'itary	irresist'ible
improb'able	incu'rable	insen'sitive	irres'olute
impropri'ety	inde'cent	insignif'icant	irrespon'sible

with heat, shining; of artificial light, produced by glowing filament —**incandesce'** vi. glow —**incandes'cence** n.

incanta'tion n. magic spell or formula, charm

incapac'itate [-pas'-] vt. disable; make unfit; disqualify —**incapac'ity** n.

incar'cerate vt. imprison —**incarcera'tion** n. —**incar'cerator** n.

incar'nate vt. embody in flesh, esp. in human form —a. embodied in flesh, in human form; typified —**incarna'tion** n.

incen'diary a. of malicious setting on fire of property; creating strife, violence etc.; designed to cause fires —n. fire raiser; agitator; bomb filled with inflammatory substance —**incen'diarism** n.

incense'[1] vt. enrage

in'cense[2] n. gum, spice giving perfume when burned; its smoke —vt. burn incense to; perfume with it

incen'tive n. something that arouses to effort or action; stimulus

incep'tion n. beginning —**incep'tive** a. —**incep'tor** n.

incess'ant a. unceasing

in'cest n. sexual intercourse between two people too closely related to marry —**incest'uous** a.

inch n. one twelfth of foot, or 0.0254 metre —v. move very slowly

incho'ate [-kō'-] a. just begun; undeveloped

in'cident n. event, occurrence —a. naturally attaching to; striking, falling (upon) —**in'cidence** n. degree, extent or frequency of occurrence; a falling on, or affecting —**incident'al** a. occurring as a minor part or an inevitable accompaniment or by chance —**incident'ally** adv. by chance; by the way —**inciden'tals** pl.n. accompanying items

incin'erate vt. burn up completely; reduce to ashes —**incinera'tion** n. —**incin'erator** n.

incip'ient a. beginning

incise' [-sīz'] vt. cut into; engrave —**inci'sion** [-sizh'-] n. —**inci'sive** a. keen or biting (of remark etc.); sharp —**inci'sor** n. cutting tooth

incite' vt. urge, stir up —**incita'tion, incite'ment** n.

inclem'ent a. of weather, stormy, severe, cold —**inclem'ency** n.

incline' v. lean, slope; (cause to) be disposed; bend or lower (the head etc.) —n. [in'-] slope —**inclina'tion** n. liking, tendency or preference; sloping surface; degree of deviation

include' [-klōōd'] vt. have as (part of) contents; comprise; add in; take in —**inclu'sion** n. —**inclu'sive** a. including (everything) —**inclu'sively** adv.

incog'nito [-nē- or in-kog'-] adv./a. under assumed identity —n. assumed identity (pl. -**tos**)

incohe'rent a. lacking clarity, disorganized; inarticulate —**incohe'rence** n. —**incohe'rently** adv.

in'come n. amount of money, esp. annual, from salary, investments etc.; receipts —**income tax** personal tax levied on annual income

in'coming a. coming in; about to come into office; next

incommode' vt. trouble, inconvenience; disturb —**incommo'dious** a. cramped; inconvenient

incommunicad'o [-kahd'ō] a./adv. deprived (by force or by choice) of communication with others

incon'gruous [-ng'g-] a. not

appropriate; inconsistent, absurd —**incongru'ity** n. —**incon'gruously** adv.

incon'sequent, inconsequen'tial a. illogical; irrelevant, trivial

incontrover'tible a. undeniable; indisputable

incor'porate vt. include; unite into one body; form into corporation —**incorpora'tion** n.

incor'rigible a. beyond correction or reform; firmly rooted —**incorrigibil'ity** n.

increase' v. make or become greater in size, number etc. —n. [in'-] growth, enlargement, profit —**increas'ingly** adv. more and more

incred'ible a. unbelievable; inf. marvellous, amazing

incred'ulous a. unbelieving —**incredu'lity** n.

in'crement n. increase, esp. one of a series

incrim'inate vt. imply guilt of; charge with crime —**incrim'inatory** a.

incrust' see ENCRUST

in'cubate [-kyoo-] vt. provide (eggs, embryos, bacteria etc.) with heat or other favourable condition for development —vi. develop in this way —**incuba'tion** n. —**in'cubator** n. apparatus for artificially hatching eggs, for rearing premature babies

in'cubus [-kyoo-] n. nightmare or obsession; (orig.) demon believed to afflict sleeping person (pl. **-bi** [-bi], **-buses**)

in'culcate vt. impress on the mind —**inculca'tion** n. —**in'culcator** n.

incum'bent a. lying, resting (on) —n. holder of office, esp. church benefice —**incum'bency** n. obligation; office or tenure of incumbent —**it is incumbent on** it is the duty of

incur' vt. fall into, bring upon oneself (-**rr**-) —**incur'sion** n. invasion, penetration

incuse' vt. impress by striking or stamping —a. hammered —n. impression made by stamping

ind. independent; index; indicative

inda'ba [-dah'-] n. SA meeting, discussion; problem

indebt'ed [-det'-] a. owing gratitude for help, favours etc.; owing money —**indebt'edness** n.

indeed' adv. in truth; really; in fact; certainly —interj. denoting surprise, doubt etc.

indefat'igable a. untiring —**indefat'igably** adv.

indefeas'ible [-fēz'-] a. that cannot be lost or annulled —**indefeasibil'ity** n.

indefen'sible a. not justifiable or defensible —**indefen'sibly** adv.

indel'ible a. that cannot be blotted out, effaced or erased; producing such a mark —**indelibil'ity** n. —**indel'ibly** adv.

indel'icate a. coarse, embarrassing, tasteless

indem'nity n. compensation; security against loss —**indemnifica'tion** n. —**indem'nify** vt. give indemnity to; compensate (**indem'nified, indem'nifying**)

indent' v. set in (from margin etc.); make notches, holes in; draw up document in duplicate; make an order (upon someone for); place order for by indent —n. [in'-] notch; order, requisition —**indenta'tion** n. —**inden'ture** n. indented document; contract, esp. one binding apprentice to master —vt. bind thus

indepen'dent a. not subject to others; self-reliant; free; valid in itself; politically of no party —**indepen'dence, indepen'dency** n. being independent; self-reliance;

self-support —indepen'dently adv.

indescri'bable a. beyond description; too intense etc. for words —indescri'bably adv.

indeterm'inate a. uncertain; inconclusive; incalculable

in'dex n. alphabetical list of references, usu. at end of book; pointer, indicator; Math. exponent; forefinger (pl. in'dexes, Math. in'dices [-sēz]) —vt. provide book with index; insert in index

In'dian n. native of India; aboriginal American —a —Indian hemp cannabis —Indian ink very dark black (drawing) ink

India rubber rubber, eraser

in'dicate vt. point out; state briefly; signify —indica'tion n. sign; token; explanation —in-dic'ative a. pointing to; Grammar stating fact —in'dicator n. one who, that which, indicates; on vehicle, flashing light showing driver's intention to turn

indict' [-dīt'] vt. accuse, esp. by legal process —indict'able a. —indict'ment n.

indiff'erent a. uninterested; unimportant; neither good nor bad; inferior; neutral —indiff'erence n. —indiff'erently adv.

indig'enous [-dij-] a. born in or natural to a country —in'digene n. aborigine; native

in'digent [-j-] a. poor, needy —in'digence n. poverty

indiges'tion [-jest'-] n. (discomfort, pain caused by) difficulty in digesting food —indigest'ible a.

indig'nant a. moved by anger and scorn; angered by sense of injury or injustice —indig'nantly adv. —indigna'tion n. —indig'nity n. humiliation, insult, slight

in'digo n. blue dye obtained from plant; the plant (pl. -go(e)s) —a. deep blue

indiscrim'inate a. lacking discrimination; jumbled

indispens'able a. necessary; essential

indisposi'tion [-zish'-] n. sickness; disinclination —indispose' vt. —indisposed' a. unwell, not fit; disinclined

indissol'uble a. permanent

in'dium n. soft silver-white metallic element

individ'ual a. single; characteristic of single person or thing; distinctive —n. single person or thing —individ'ualism n. principle of asserting one's independence —individ'ualist n. —individualis'tic a. —individ'ual'ity n. distinctive character; personality —individ'ualize vt. make (or treat as) individual —individ'ually adv. singly

indoc'trinate vt. implant beliefs in the mind of

in'dolent a. lazy —in'dolence n. —in'dolently adv.

indom'itable a. unyielding —indom'itably adv.

in'door a. within doors; under cover —indoors' adv.

indorse' see ENDORSE

indu'bitable a. beyond doubt; certain —indu'bitably adv.

induce' vt. persuade; bring on; cause; produce by induction —induce'ment n. incentive, attraction

induct' vt. install in office —induc'tion n. an inducting; general inference from particular instances; production of electric or magnetic state in body by its being near (not touching) electrified or magnetized body; in internal combustion engine, part of the piston's action which draws gas from carburettor —induc'tance n. —induc'tive a. —induc'tively adv. —induc'tor n.

indulge' vt. gratify; give free

course to; pamper; spoil —**indul'gence** n. an indulging; extravagance; something granted as a favour or privilege; *RC Ch.* remission of temporal punishment due after absolution —**indul'gent** a. —**indul'gently** adv.

indun'a [-doon'ə] n. *SA* headman, overseer

in'dustry n. manufacture, processing *etc.* of goods; branch of this; diligence; habitual hard work —**indus'trial** a. of industries, trades —**indus'trialize** vt. —**indus'trious** a. diligent

ine'briate vt. make drunk; intoxicate —a. drunken —n. habitual drunkard —**inebria'tion, inebri'ety** n. drunkenness

ined'ible a. not eatable; unfit for food —**inedibil'ity** n.

ined'ucable a. incapable of being educated, *esp.* through mental retardation

ineff'able a. too great or sacred for words; unutterable —**ineffabil'ity** n. —**ineff'ably** adv.

inel'igible [-ji-] a. not fit or qualified (for something) —**ineligibil'ity** n.

inept' a. absurd; out of place; clumsy —**inept'itude** n.

inert' a. without power of action or resistance; slow, sluggish; chemically unreactive —**iner'tia** [-shə] n. inactivity; property by which matter continues in its existing state of rest or motion in straight line, unless that state is changed by external force —**inert'ly** adv. —**inert'ness** n.

ines'timable a. too good, too great, to be estimated

inev'itable a. unavoidable; sure to happen —**inevitabil'ity** n. —**inev'itably** adv.

inex'orable a. relentless —**inex'orably** adv.

inexplic'able a. impossible to explain

in extre'mis *Lat.* at the point of death

inf. infinitive; information

infall'ible a. unerring; not liable to fail; certain, sure —**infallibil'ity** n. —**infall'ibly** adv.

in'famous a. notorious; shocking —**in'famously** adv. —**in'famy** n.

in'fant n. very young child —**in'fancy** n. —**in'fanticide** n. murder of newborn child; person guilty of this —**in'fantile** a. childish

in'fantry n. foot soldiers

infat'uate vt. inspire with folly or foolish passion —**infat'uated** a. foolishly enamoured —**infatua'tion** n.

infect' vt. affect (with disease); contaminate —**infec'tion** n. —**infec'tious** a. catching, spreading, pestilential

infer' vt. deduce, conclude (-rr-) —**in'ference** n. —**inferen'tial, infer'able** a. deduced

infe'rior a. of poor quality; lower —n. one lower (in rank *etc.*) —**inferior'ity** n. —**inferiority complex** *Psychoanalysis* repressed sense of inferiority

infern'al a. devilish; hellish; irritating, confounded —**infer'nally** adv.

infer'no n. region of hell; conflagration

infest' vt. inhabit or overrun in dangerously or unpleasantly large numbers —**infesta'tion** n.

infidel'ity n. unfaithfulness; religious disbelief; disloyalty; treachery —**in'fidel** n. unbeliever —a.

in'filtrate v. trickle through; cause to pass through pores; gain access surreptitiously —**infiltra'tion** n.

in'finite [-it] a. boundless —**in'finitely** adv. exceedingly —**infinites'imal** a. extremely, infinitely small —**infin'ity** *n.* unlimited and endless extent

infin'itive *a. Grammar* in mood expressing notion of verb without limitation of tense, person, or number —*n.* verb in this mood; the mood

infirm' *a.* physically weak; mentally weak; irresolute —**infir'mary** *n.* hospital, sickquarters —**infirm'ity** *n.*

inflame' *v.* rouse to anger, excitement; cause inflammation in; become inflamed —**inflammabil'ity** *n.* —**inflamm'able** *a.* easily set on fire; excitable —**inflamma'tion** *n.* infection of part of the body, with pain, heat, swelling, and redness —**inflam'matory** *a.*

inflate' *v.* blow up with air, gas; swell; cause economic inflation; raise price, *esp.* artificially —**infla'table** *a.* —**infla'tion** *n.* increase in prices and fall in value of money —**infla'tionary** *a.*

inflect' *vt.* modify (words) to show grammatical relationships; bend inwards —**inflec'tion, inflex'ion** *n.* modification of word; modulation of voice

inflex'ible *a.* incapable of being bent; stern —**inflexibil'ity** *n.* —**inflex'ibly** *adv.*

inflict' *vt.* impose, deliver forcibly —**inflic'tion** *n.* inflicting; punishment

inflores'cence *n.* the unfolding of blossoms; botanical term for arrangement of flowers on stem

in'fluence *n.* effect of one person or thing on another; power of person or thing having an effect; thing, person exercising this —*vt.* sway; induce; affect —**influen'tial** *a.* —**influen'tially** *adv.*

influen'za *n.* contagious feverish catarrhal virus disease

in'flux *n.* a flowing in; inflow

in'fo *n. inf.* information

inform' *vt.* tell; animate —*vi.* give information (about) —**inform'ant** *n.* one who tells —**informa'tion** *n.* what is told, knowledge —**inform'ative** *a.* —**inform'er** *n.*

in'fra *adv.* below; under; after —**infra dig** *inf.* beneath one's dignity —**infrared'** *a.* denoting rays below red end of visible spectrum

infrac'tion *n. see* INFRINGE

in'frastructure *n.* basic structure or fixed capital items of an organization or economic system

infringe' *vt.* transgress, break —**infringe'ment** *n.* —**infrac'tion** *n.* breach; violation

infur'iate [-fyoor'-] *vt.* enrage

infuse' *v.* soak to extract flavour *etc.*; instil, charge —**infu'sion** *n.* an infusing; liquid extract obtained

inge'nious [-jē'-] *a.* clever at contriving; cleverly contrived —**inge'niously** *adv.* —**ingenu'ity** *n.*

ingénue' [an-zhā-nyōō'] *n.* artless girl or young woman; actress playing such a part

ingen'uous [-jen'-] *a.* frank; naïve, innocent —**ingen'uously** *adv.*

ingest'ion [-jest'-] *n.* act of introducing food into the body

in'glenook [ing'-] *n.* corner by a fireplace

in'got [ing'g-] *n.* brick of cast metal, *esp.* gold

ingrain', engrain' *vt.* implant deeply; *obs.* dye, infuse deeply —**ingrained', engrained'** *a.* deep-rooted; inveterate

ingra'tiate *v. refl.* get (oneself) into favour —**ingra'tiatingly** *adv.*

ingre'dient n. component part of a mixture

in'gress n. entry, means, right of entrance

inhab'it vt. dwell in —**inhab'itable** a. —**inhab'itant** n. —**inhabita'tion** n.

inhale' v. breathe in (air etc.) —**inhala'tion** n. esp. medical preparation for inhaling —**inha'ler** n. device producing, and assisting inhalation of therapeutic vapours

inhere' vi. of qualities, exist (in); of rights, be vested (in person) —**inhe'rence, inhe'rency** n. —**inhe'rent** a. existing as an inseparable part —**inhe'rently** adv.

inher'it [-he'rit] vt. receive as heir; derive from parents —vi. succeed as heir —**inher'itance** n. —**inher'itor** n. heir; one who inherits (-**ress, -rix** fem.)

inhe'sion n. inherence

inhib'it vt. restrain (impulse, desire etc.); hinder (action); forbid —**inhibi'tion** n. repression of emotion, instinct; a stopping or retarding —**inhib'itory** a.

inhu'man a. cruel, brutal; not human —**inhuman'ity** n.

inhume' [-hyōōm'] vt. bury, inter —**inhuma'tion** n.

inim'ical a. unfavourable (to); unfriendly; hostile

inim'itable a. defying imitation —**inim'itably** adv.

iniq'uity n. gross injustice; wickedness, sin —**iniq'uitous** a. unfair, sinful, unjust; inf. outrageous

ini'tial [-ish'-] a. of, occurring at the beginning —n. initial letter, esp. of person's name —vt. mark, sign with one's initials (-**ll**-)

ini'tiate [-ish'-] vt. originate; begin; admit into closed society; instruct in elements (of) —n. initiated person —**initia'tion** n.

ini'tiative n. first step, lead; ability to act independently —a. originating —**ini'tiatory** a.

inject' vt. introduce (esp. fluid, medicine etc. with syringe) —**injec'tion** n. —**inject'or** n.

injunc'tion n. judicial order to restrain; authoritative order

in'jury n. physical damage or harm; wrong —**in'jure** vt. do harm or damage to —**injur'ious** a. —**injur'iously** adv.

injus'tice n. want of justice; wrong; injury; unjust act

ink n. fluid used for writing or printing —vt. mark with ink; cover, smear with it —**ink'er** n. —**ink'y** a. —**ink'well** n. vessel for holding ink —**ink'stand** n.

ink'ling n. hint, slight knowledge or suspicion

inko'si [-kor'si] n. **SA** chief, leader

inlaid' see INLAY

in'land n. interior of country —a. in this; away from the sea; within a country —adv. in or towards the inland

in'-law n. relative by marriage

inlay' vt. embed; decorate with inset pattern (**inlaid'** pt./pp.) —n. [in'-] inlaid piece or pattern

in'let n. entrance; mouth of creek; piece inserted

in lo'co paren'tis Lat. in place of a parent

in'mate n. occupant, esp. of prison, hospital etc.

in'most a. most inward, deepest —sup. of IN

inn n. public house providing food and accommodation; hotel —**inn'keeper** n. —**Inns of Court** four societies admitting to English Bar; their buildings

inn'ards (orig. **in'wards**) pl.n. inf. internal organs or working parts

innate' a. inborn; inherent

inn'er a. lying within —n. ring

next to the bull's-eye on target —**inn'ermost** a. —**inner tube** rubber air tube of pneumatic tyre

inn'ings n. Sport player's or side's turn of batting; spell, turn

inn'ocent a. pure; guiltless; harmless; —n. innocent person, esp. young child —**inn'ocence** n. —**inn'ocently** adv.

innoc'uous a. harmless —**innoc'uously** adv.

inn'ovate vt. introduce changes, new things —**innova'tion** n. —**inn'ovator** n.

innuen'do n. allusive remark, hint; indirect accusation (pl. -does)

innu'merable a. countless; very numerous —**innu'merably** adv.

inoc'ulate vt. immunize by injecting vaccine —**inocula'tion** n.

inop'erable a. unworkable; Med. that cannot be operated on —**inop'erative** a. not operative; ineffective

inopp'ortune a. badly timed

inord'inate a. excessive

inorgan'ic a. not having structure or characteristics of living organisms; of substances without carbon —**inorgan'ically** adv.

in'patient n. patient that stays in hospital

in'put n. act of putting in; that which is put in, as resource needed for industrial production etc.; data etc. fed into a computer

in'quest n. legal or judicial inquiry presided over by a coroner; detailed inquiry or discussion

inquire', enquire' vi. seek information —**inqui'rer, enqui'rer** n. —**inqui'ry, enqui'ry** n. question; investigation

inquisi'tion [-zish'-] n. searching investigation, official inquiry; Hist. (I-) tribunal for suppression

of heresy —**inquis'itor** n. —**inquisito'rial** a.

inquis'itive a. curious; prying —**inquis'itively** adv.

in'road n. incursion

ins. inches; insurance

insane' a. mentally deranged; crazy, senseless —**insane'ly** adv. like a lunatic, madly; excessively —**insan'ity** n.

insa'tiable a. incapable of being satisfied

inscribe' vt. write, engrave (in or on something); mark; dedicate; trace (figure) within another —**inscrip'tion** n. inscribing; words inscribed on monument etc.

inscru'table a. mysterious, impenetrable; affording no explanation —**inscrutabil'ity** n. —**inscru'tably** adv.

in'sect n. small invertebrate animal with six legs, usu. segmented body and two or four wings —**insect'icide** n. preparation for killing insects —**insec'tivorous** a. insect-eating

insecure' [-kyoor'] a. not safe or firm, anxious, not confident

insem'inate vt. implant semen into —**artificial insemination** impregnation of the female by artificial means

insen'sate a. without sensation, unconscious; unfeeling

insen'sible a. unconscious; without feeling; not aware; not perceptible —**insensibil'ity** n. —**insen'sibly** adv. imperceptibly

insert' vt. introduce; place or put (in, into, between) —n. [in'-] something inserted —**inser'tion** n.

in'set n. something extra inserted esp. as decoration —**inset'** vt.

in'shore adv./a. near shore

inside' [or in'-] n. inner side, surface, or part —a. of, in, or on the inside —adv. in or into the inside;

sl. in prison —*prep.* within, on inner side

insid'ious *a.* stealthy, treacherous; unseen but deadly —**insid'iously** *adv.*

in'sight [-sīt] *n.* mental penetration, discernment

insig'nia *pl.n.* badges, emblems of honour or office

insin'uate *vt.* hint; work oneself into favour; introduce gradually or subtly —**insinua'tion** *n.*

insip'id *a.* dull, tasteless, spiritless —**insipid'ity** *n.*

insist' *vi.* demand persistently; maintain; emphasize —**insist'ence** *n.* —**insist'ent** *a.* —**insist'ently** *adv.*

in si'tu [-yōō] *Lat.* in its original position

in'solent *a.* arrogantly impudent —**in'solence** *n.* —**in'solently** *adv.*

insom'nia *n.* sleeplessness —**insom'niac** *a./n.*

insomuch' *adv.* to such an extent

insou'ciant [-sōō'si-] *a.* indifferent, careless, unconcerned —**insou'ciance** *n.*

inspan' *vt.* SA harness, yoke (-nn-)

inspect' *vt.* examine closely or officially —**inspec'tion** *n.* —**inspec'tor** *n.* one who inspects; high-ranking police officer —**inspecto'rial** *a.*

inspire' *vt.* animate, invigorate; arouse, create feeling, thought; give rise to; breathe in, inhale —**inspira'tion** *n.* good idea; creative influence or stimulus

inspir'it *vt.* animate, put spirit into, encourage

inst. (*instant*) of the current month

instal(l) [-awl'] *vt.* have (apparatus) put in; establish; place (person in office *etc.*) with ceremony —**installa'tion** *n.* act of installing; that which is installed

instal'ment [-awl'-] *n.* payment of part of debt; any of parts of a whole delivered in succession

in'stance *n.* example; particular case; request; stage in proceedings —*vt.* cite

in'stant *n.* moment, point of time —*a.* immediate; urgent; (of foods) requiring little preparation —**instanta'neous** *a.* happening in an instant —**instanta'neously** *adv.* —**instan'ter** *adv.* Law at once —**in'stantly** *adv.* at once

instead' [-ed'] *adv.* in place (of); as a substitute

in'step *n.* top of foot between toes and ankle

in'stigate *vt.* incite, urge; bring about —**instiga'tion** *n.* —**in'stigator** *n.*

instil' *vt.* implant; inculcate (-ll-) —**instilla'tion** *n.* —**instil'ment** *n.*

in'stinct *n.* inborn impulse or propensity; unconscious skill; intuition —**instinct'ive** *a.* —**instinc'tively** *adv.*

in'stitute *vt.* establish, found; appoint; set going —*n.* society for promoting some public object, *esp.* scientific; its building —**institu'tion** *n.* an instituting; establishment for care or education, hospital, college *etc.*; an established custom or law or (*inf.*) figure —**institu'tional** *a.* of institutions; routine —**institu'tionalize** *vt.* subject to (adverse) effects of confinement in institution; place in an institution; make or become an institution —**in'stitutor** *n.*

instruct' *vt.* teach; inform; order; brief (solicitor, barrister) —**instruc'tion** *n.* teaching; order —*pl.* directions —**instruc'tive** *a.* informative; useful —**instruc'-**

tively adv. —**instruc'tor** n. (**instruc'tress** fem.)

in'strument n. tool, implement, means, person, thing used to make, do, measure etc.; mechanism for producing musical sound; legal document —**instrumen'tal** a. acting as instrument or means; helpful; belonging to, produced by musical instruments —**instrument'alist** n. player of musical instrument —**instrumental'ly** adv. —**instrumental'ity** n. agency, means —**instrumenta'tion** n. arrangement of music for instruments

insubor'dinate a. not submissive; mutinous, rebellious —**insubordina'tion** n.

in'sular [-syoo-] a. of an island; remote, detached; narrow-minded or prejudiced —**insular'ity** n.

in'sulate [-syoo-] vt. prevent or reduce transfer of electricity, heat, sound etc.; isolate, detach —**insula'tion** n. —**in'sulator** n.

in'sulin [-syoo-] n. pancreatic hormone used in treating diabetes

insult' vt. behave rudely to; offend —n. [in'-] offensive remark; affront —**insult'ing** a. —**insult'ingly** adv.

insu'perable [-sōō-] a. that cannot be got over or surmounted; unconquerable —**insuperabil'ity** n. —**insu'perably** adv.

insure' v. contract for payment in event of loss, death etc., by payment of premiums; make such contract about; make safe (against) —**insur'able** a. —**insur'ance** n. —**insur'er** n. —**insurance policy** contract of insurance

insur'gent a. in revolt —n. rebel —**insur'gence, insurrec'tion** n. revolt

int. interest; interior; internal; international

intact' a. untouched; uninjured

intagl'io [-tahl'-] n. engraved design; gem so cut (pl. **-los, -i** [-yē]) —**intagl'iated** a.

in'take n. what is taken in; quantity taken in; opening for taking in; in car, air passage into carburettor

in'teger [-j-] n. whole number; whole of anything

in'tegral [-g-] a. constituting an essential part of a whole —**in'tegrate** vt. combine into one whole; unify diverse elements (of community etc.) —**integra'tion** n. —**integral calculus** branch of mathematics of changing quantities which calculates total effects of the change —**integrated circuit** tiny electronic circuit, usu. on silicon chip

integ'rity n. honesty; original perfect state

integ'ument n. natural covering, skin, rind, husk

in'tellect n. power of thinking and reasoning —**intellec'tual** a. of, appealing to intellect; having good intellect —n. one endowed with intellect and attracted to intellectual things —**intellectual'ity** n.

intell'igent a. having, showing good intellect; quick at understanding; informed —**intell'igence** n. quickness of understanding; mental power or ability; intellect; information, news, esp. military information —**intell'igently** adv. —**intelligent'sia** n. intellectual or cultured classes —**intelligibil'ity** n. —**intell'igible** a. understandable —**intell'igibly** adv.

intemp'erate a. drinking alcohol to excess; immoderate; unrestrained —**intemp'erance** n.

intend' vt. propose, mean (to

do, say *etc.*) —**intend'ed** *a.* planned, future —*n. inf.* proposed spouse

intense' *a.* very strong or acute; emotional —**intensifica'tion** *n.* —**intens'ify** *v.* make or become stronger; increase (**intens'ified, intens'ifying**) —**inten'sity** *n.* intense quality; strength —**inten'sive** *a.* characterized by intensity or emphasis on specified factor —**intens'ively** *adv.*

intent' *n.* purpose —*a.* concentrating (on); resolved, bent; preoccupied, absorbed —**inten'tion** *n.* purpose, aim —**inten'tional** *a.* —**inten'tly** *adv.* —**intent'ness** *n.*

inter' *vt.* bury (**-rr-**) —**inter'ment** *n.*

inter- (*comb. form*) between, among, mutually *eg* **intergla'cial, interrela'tion** Such words are not given here where the meaning may easily be inferred from the simple word

interact' *vi.* act on each other —**interac'tion** *n.*

in'ter a'lia *Lat.* among other things

interbreed' *v.* breed within a related group

intercede' *vi.* plead in favour of, mediate —**intercess'ion** *n.* —**intercess'or** *n.*

intercept' *vt.* cut off; seize, stop in transit —**intercep'tion** *n.* —**intercept'or, -er** *n.* one who, that which intercepts; fast fighter plane, missile *etc.*

interchange' *v.* (cause to) exchange places —*n.* [in'-] motorway junction —**interchange'able** *a.* able to be exchanged in position or use

inter-cit'y *a./n.* (denoting) fast train or rail service between main towns

in'tercom *n.* internal telephonic system

intercontinen'tal *a.* con-

necting continents; (of missile) able to reach one continent from another

in'tercourse *n.* mutual dealings; communication; sexual joining of two people; copulation

in'terdict *n.* decree of Pope restraining clergy from performing divine service; formal prohibition —**interdict'** *vt.* prohibit, forbid; restrain —**interdic'tion** *n.* —**interdict'ory** *a.*

in'terest *n.* concern, curiosity; thing exciting this; sum paid for use of borrowed money (*also fig.*); legal concern; right, advantage, share —*vt.* excite, cause to feel interest —**in'teresting** *a.* —**in'terestingly** *adv.*

in'terface *n.* area, surface, boundary linking two systems

interfere' *vi.* meddle, intervene; clash —**interfe'rence** *n.* act of interfering; *Radio* interruption of reception by atmospherics or by unwanted signals

interfe'ron *n.* a cellular protein that stops the development of an invading virus

in'terim *n.* meantime —*a.* temporary, intervening

inte'rior *a.* inner; inland; indoors —*n.* inside; inland region

interject' *vt.* interpose (remark *etc.*) —**interjec'tion** *n.* exclamation; interjected remark

interlace' *vt.* unite, as by lacing together —**interlace'ment** *n.*

interlard' *v.* intersperse

interleave' *vt.* insert, as blank leaves in book, between other leaves —**in'terleaf** *n.* extra leaf

interlock' *v.* lock together firmly —*a.* knitted with close, small stitches

interloc'utor *n.* one who takes part in conversation —**interlocu'tion** *n.* dialogue —**interloc'utory** *a.*

in'terloper *n.* one intruding in

in'terlude n. interval (in play etc.); something filling an interval

intermarr'y vi. (of families, races, religions) become linked by marriage; marry within one's family —**intermarr'iage** n.

interme'diate a. coming between; interposed —**interme'diary** n.

intermezz'o [-mets'-] n. short performance between acts of play or opera (pl. **-os**, **-mezz'i** [-e])

interm'inable a endless in ter'minably adv.

intermit' v. stop for a time (-tt-) —**intermiss'ion** n. —**intermit'tent** a. occurring at intervals

intern' vt. confine to special area or camp —**intern'ment** n.

inter'nal a. inward; interior; within (a country, organization) —**inter'nally** adv. —**internal combustion** process of exploding mixture of air and fuel in piston-fitted cylinder

interna'tional [-nash'-] a. of relations between nations —n. game or match between teams of different countries —**Interna'tionale** n. socialist hymn —**interna'tionally** adv.

interne'cine a. mutually destructive; deadly

in'ternode n. space between two nodes or leaf joints —**interno'dal** a.

inter'pellate vt. interrupt business of the day to demand explanation from (minister) —**interpella'tion** n.

interplan'etary a. of, linking planets

in'terplay n. action and reaction of two things, sides etc., upon each other; interaction; reciprocation

inter'polate vt. insert new

(esp. misleading) matter (in book etc.); interject (remark); Maths. estimate a value between known values —**interpola'tion** n.

interpose' vt. insert; say as interruption; put in the way —vi. intervene; obstruct —**interposi'tion** n.

inter'pret vt. explain; translate, esp. orally; Art render, represent —**interpreta'tion** n. —**inter'preter** n.

interreg'num n. interval between reigns; gap in continuity (pl. **-na**, **-nums**)

interr'ogate vt. question, esp. closely or officially —**interroga'tion** n. —**interrog'ative** a. questioning —n. word used in asking question —**interr'ogator** n. —**interrog'atory** a. of inquiry —n. question, set of questions

interrupt' v. break in (upon); stop the course of; block —**interrup'tion** n.

intersect' vt. divide by passing across or through —vi. meet and cross —**intersec'tion** n. point where lines, roads cross

intersperse' vt. sprinkle (something with or something among or in) —**interspers'ion** n.

in'terstate a. US between, involving two or more states

interstell'ar a. (of the space) between stars

inter'stice n. chink, gap, crevice —**intersti'tial** a.

intertwine' v. twist together, entwine

in'terval n. intervening time or space; pause, break; short period between parts of play, concert etc.; difference (of pitch)

intervene' vi. come into a situation in order to change it; be, come between or among; occur in meantime; interpose —**interven'tion** n.

in'terview n. meeting, esp. formally arranged and involving questioning of a person —vt. have interview with —**inter'viewee'** n. —**in'terviewer** n.

intest'ate a. not having made a will —n. person dying intestate —**intes'tacy** n.

intest'ine n. (usu. pl.) lower part of alimentary canal between stomach and anus —**intes'tinal** a. of bowels

in'timate [-it] a. closely acquainted, familiar; private; extensive; having sexual relations (with) —n. intimate friend —**in'timacy** n.

in'timate [-āt] vt. announce; imply —**intima'tion** n. notice

intim'idate vt. frighten into submission; deter by threats —**intimida'tion** n. —**intim'idator** n.

in'to prep. expresses motion to a point within; indicates change of state; indicates coming up against, encountering; indicates arithmetical division

intone' vt. chant; recite in monotone —**intona'tion** n. modulation of voice; intoning; accent

intox'icate vt. make drunk; excite to excess —**intox'icant** a./n. intoxicating (liquor) —**intoxica'tion** n.

intra- (comb. form) within

intract'able a. difficult to influence; hard to control

intran'sigent a. uncompromising, obstinate

intrau'terine [-ə-yōō'-] a. within the womb: see IUD

intrave'nous a. into a vein

intrep'id a. fearless, undaunted —**intrepid'ity** n.

in'tricate a. involved, puzzlingly entangled —**in'tricacy** n. —**in'tricately** adv.

intrigue' [-trēg'] n. underhand plot; secret love affair —vi. carry

on intrigue —vt. interest, puzzle —**intri'guer** n.

intrin'sic a. inherent, essential —**intrin'sically** adv.

intro- (comb. form) into, within, as in introduce, introvert, etc.

introduce' vt. make acquainted; present; bring in; bring forward; bring into practice; insert —**introduc'tion** n. an introducing; presentation of one person to another; preliminary section or treatment —**introduc'tory** a. preliminary

in'troit n. Eccles. anthem sung as priest approaches altar

introspec'tion n. examination of one's own thoughts —**introspec'tive** a. —**introspec'tively** adv.

in'trovert n. Psychoanalysis one who looks inward rather than at the external world —**introver'sible** a. —**introver'sion** n. —**introver'sive** a. —**in'troverted** a.

intrude' v. thrust (oneself) in uninvited —**intru'der** n. —**intru'sion** n. —**intru'sive** a.

intui'tion [-ish'-] n. immediate mental apprehension without reasoning; immediate insight —**intu'it** v. —**intu'itive** a. —**intu'itively** adv.

In'uit [in'yōō-it] n. C Eskimo of N Amer. or Greenland

in'undate vt. flood; overwhelm —**inunda'tion** n.

inure' vt. accustom, esp. to hardship, danger etc.

invade' vt. enter by force with hostile intent; overrun; pervade —**inva'der** n. —**inva'sion** n.

in'valid [-lēd] n. one suffering from chronic ill health —a. ill, suffering from sickness or injury —v. become an invalid; retire from active service because of illness etc.

inval'uable a. priceless

In'var n. R steel containing 30 per cent nickel, with low coefficient of expansion

inva'sion see INVADE

inveigh' [-vā'] vi. speak violently (against) —**invec'tive** n. abusive speech or writing, vituperation

invei'gle [-vē'-, -vā'-] vt. entice, seduce, wheedle —**invei'glement** n.

invent' vt. devise, originate; fabricate (falsehoods etc.) —**inven'tion** n. that which is invented; ability to invent; contrivance; deceit; lie —**inven'tive** a. resourceful; creative —**inven'tively** adv. —**invent'or** n.

in'ventory n. detailed list of goods etc. —vt. make list of

invert' vt. turn upside down; reverse position, relations of —**inverse'** [or in'-] a. inverted; opposite —n. —**inverse'ly** adv. —**inver'sion** n.

inver'tebrate n. animal having no vertebral column —a. spineless

invest' vt. lay out (money, time, effort etc.) for profit or advantage; install; endow; obs. clothe; Poet. cover as with garment —**invest'iture** n. formal installation of person in office or rank —**invest'ment** n. investing; money invested; stocks and shares bought —**invest'or** n.

inves'tigate vt. inquire into; examine —**investiga'tion** n. —**inves'tigator** n.

invet'erate a. deep-rooted; long established, confirmed —**invet'eracy** n.

invid'ious a. likely to cause ill will or envy —**invid'iously** adv.

invig'ilate [-vij'-] vi. supervise examination candidates

invig'orate vt. give vigour to, strengthen

invin'cible a. unconquerable —**invincibil'ity** n.

invi'olable a. not to be profaned; sacred; unalterable —**invi'olate** a. unhurt; unprofaned; unbroken

invite' vt. request the company of; ask courteously; ask for; attract, call forth —n. inf. [in'-] invitation —**invita'tion** n.

in'voice n. a list of goods or services sold, with prices —vt. make or present an invoice

invoke' vt. call on; appeal to; ask earnestly for; summon —**invoca'tion** n.

invol'untary a. not done voluntarily; unintentional; instinctive —**invol'untarily** adv.

in'volute a. complex; coiled spirally; rolled inwards (also **invo'luted**) —n. Maths. a type of curve —**involu'tion** n.

involve' vt. include; entail; implicate (person); concern; entangle —**involu'tion** n. —**involved'** a. complicated; concerned (in)

in'ward a. internal; situated within; spiritual; mental —adv. (also **in'wards**) towards the inside; into the mind —pl.n. see INNARDS —**in'wardly** adv. in the mind; internally

i'odine [-ēn] n. nonmetallic element found in seaweed and used in antiseptic tincture, photography, and dyeing —**i'odize** vt. treat or react with iodine —**io'doform** n. antiseptic

i'on n. electrically charged atom or group of atoms —**ion'ic** a. —**ioniza'tion** n. —**i'onize** vt. change into ions —**ion'osphere** n. region of atmosphere 60 to 100 km above earth's surface

Ion'ic [ī-] a. Architecture distinguished by scroll-like decoration on columns

io'ta [ī-ō'-] n. the Greek letter i;

(*usu. with* not) very small amount

I.O.U. *n.* signed paper acknowledging debt

IPA International Phonetic Alphabet

ipecacuan'ha [-an'ɔ] *n.* S Amer. plant yielding an emetic (**ip'ecac**)

ip'so fac'to *Lat.* by that very fact

IQ intelligence quotient

ir- (*comb. form*) for *in-* before *r. see* IN- and listed words

IRA Irish Republican Army

ire *n.* anger, wrath —**irascibil'ity** [i-] *n.* —**iras'cible** *a.* hottempered —**iras'cibly** *adv.* —**irate'** [i-] *a.* angry

irides'cent *a.* exhibiting changing colours like those of the rainbow —**irides'cence** *n.*

irid'ium *n.* very hard, corrosion-resistant metal

i'ris *n.* circular membrane of eye containing pupil; plant with sword-shaped leaves and showy flowers

irk *vt.* irritate, vex —**irk'some** *a.* tiresome

i'ron *n.* metallic element, much used for tools *etc.*, and the raw material of steel; tool *etc.*, of this metal; appliance used, when heated, to smooth cloth; metalheaded golf club —*pl.* fetters —*a.* of, like, iron; inflexible, unyielding; robust —*v.* smooth, cover, fetter *etc.*, with iron or an iron —**iron age** era of iron implements —**i'ronclad** *a.* protected with or as with iron —**iron curtain** any barrier that separates communities or ideologies —**iron lung** apparatus for administering artificial respiration —**i'ronmonger** *n.* dealer in hardware —**i'ronmongery** *n.* his wares —**i'ronwood** *n.* various S Afr. trees

i'rony *n.* (*usu.* humorous or mildly sarcastic) use of words to mean the opposite of what is said; event, situation opposite of that expected —**iron'ic(al)** *a.* of, using, irony

irra'diate *vt.* treat by irradiation; shine upon, throw light upon, light up —**irradia'tion** *n.* impregnation by X-rays, light rays

irrefrang'ible *a.* inviolable; in optics, not susceptible to refraction

irref'utable *a.* that cannot be refuted, disproved

irreg. irregular(ly)

irrep'arable *a.* not able to be repaired or remedied

irrespec'tive *a.* without taking account (of)

irrev'ocable *a.* not able to be changed, undone, altered

irr'igate *vt.* water by artificial channels, pipes *etc.* —**irriga'tion** *n.* —**irr'igator** *n.*

irr'itate *vt.* annoy; inflame; stimulate —**irr'itable** *a.* easily annoyed —**irr'itably** *adv.* —**irr'itant** *a./n.* (person or thing) causing irritation —**irrita'tion** *n.*

irrupt' *vi.* enter forcibly; increase suddenly —**irrup'tion** *n.*

Is. Isaiah

is third person singular, *present indicative of* BE

ISBN International Standard Book Number

i'singlass ['zing-glahs] *n.* kind of gelatin obtained from some freshwater fish

Is'lam [iz'lahm] *n.* Mohammedan faith or world —**Islam'ic** *a.*

i'sland ['īlɔnd] *n.* piece of land surrounded by water; anything like this, as raised piece for pedestrians in middle of road —**i'slander** *n.* inhabitant of island

isle [īl] *n.* island —**i'slet** [ī'lit] *n.* little island

i'sobar *n.* line on map connecting places of equal mean barometric pressure —**isobar'ic** *a.*

i'solate *vt.* place apart or alone —**isola'tion** *n.* —**isola'tionism** *n.* policy of not participating in international affairs —**isola'tionist** *n.*

i'somer *n.* substance with same molecules as another but different atomic arrangement —**isomer'ic** *a.* —**isom'erism** *n.*

isomet'ric *a.* having equal dimensions; relating to muscular contraction without movement —**isomet'rics** *pl.n.* system of isometric exercises

isos'celes [ī-sos'i-lēz] *a.* of triangle, having two sides equal

i'sotherm *n.* line on map connecting points of equal mean temperature

i'sotope *n.* atom of element having a different nuclear mass and atomic weight from other atoms in same element —**isotop'ic** *a.* —**isot'opy** *n.* existence in the form of isotopes

iss'ue [i'shyōō] *n.* sending or giving out officially or publicly; number or amount so given out; discharge; offspring; children; topic of discussion; question, dispute; outcome, result —*vi.* go out; result in; arise (from) —*vt.* emit, give out, send out; distribute, publish

isth'mus [is'məs] *n.* neck of land between two seas

it *pron.* neuter pronoun of the third person —**its** *a.* belonging to it —**it's** *contraction of* it is —**it-self'** *pron.* emphatic form of *it*

IT information technology

ital. italic (type)

Ital'ian *n.* language or native of Italy —*a.* of Italy

ital'ic *a.* of type, sloping —**ital'-**
ics *pl.n.* this type, now used for emphasis *etc.* —**ital'icize** *vt.* put in italics

itch *vi./n.* (feel) irritation in the skin —**itch'y** *a.*

i'tem *n.* single thing in list, collection *etc.*; piece of information; entry in account *etc.* —*adv.* also —**i'temize** *vt.*

it'erate *vt.* repeat —**itera'tion** *n.* —**it'erative** *a.*

itin'erant [i-, ī-] *a.* travelling from place to place; working for a short time in various places; travelling on circuit —**itin'eracy** *n.* —**itin'erary** *n.* record, line of travel; route; guidebook

ITV Independent Television

IUD intrauterine device (for contraception)

i'vory *n.* hard white substance of the tusks of elephants *etc.* —**ivory tower** seclusion, remoteness

i'vy *n.* climbing evergreen plant —**i'vied** *a.* covered with ivy

J

jab *vt.* poke roughly; thrust, stab abruptly (**-bb-**) —*n.* poke; *inf.* injection

jabb'er *v.* chatter; utter, talk rapidly, incoherently —**jabb'er-wocky** *n.* nonsense, *esp.* in verse

jab'ot [zhab'ō] *n.* frill, ruffle at throat or breast of garment

jacaran'da *n.* S Amer. tree with fernlike leaves and pale purple flowers

jac'inth [jas'-] *n.* reddish-orange precious stone

jack *n.* fellow, man; *inf.* sailor; male of some animals; device for lifting heavy weight, *esp.* motor car; various mechanical appliances; lowest court card, with picture of pageboy; *Bowls* ball aimed at; socket and plug connection in electronic equipment; small flag, *esp.* national, at sea —*vt.* (*usu.* with **up**) lift (an object) with a jack

jack'al [-awl] *n.* wild, gregarious animal of Asia and Africa closely allied to dog

jack'ass *n.* the male of the ass; blockhead —**laughing jackass** the Aust. kookaburra

jack'boot *n.* large riding boot coming above knee

jack'daw *n.* small kind of crow

jack'et *n.* outer garment, short coat; outer casing, cover

jack'hammer *n.* hand-held hammer drill

jack'knife *n.* clasp knife; dive with sharp bend at waist in midair —*v.* bend sharply, *eg* an articulated lorry forming a sharp angle with its trailer

jack'pot *n.* large prize, accumulated stake, as pool in poker

jack rabbit US hare

Jacobe'an [-be'ən] *a.* of the reign of James I

Jac'obite *n.* adherent of Stuarts after overthrow of James II

Jac'quard [zhak'ard] *n.* fabric in which design is incorporated into the weave

Jacu'zzi [jə-kōō'zi] R device that swirls water in a bath; bath with this device

jade¹ *n.* ornamental semi-precious stone, *usu.* dark green; this colour

jade² *n.* sorry or worn-out horse; *obs. offens.* woman —**ja'ded** *a.* tired; off colour

jag *n.* sharp or ragged projection —**jagg'ed** *a.*

jag'uar *n.* large S Amer. spotted animal of cat tribe

jail *n.* building for confinement of criminals or suspects —*vt.* send to, confine in prison —**jail'er** *n.*

—**jail'bird** *n.* hardened criminal

jalop'y *n. inf.* old car

jam *vt.* pack together; (cause to) stick together and become unworkable; apply fiercely; squeeze; *Radio* block (another station) with impulses of equal wavelength (**-mm-**) —*n.* fruit preserved by boiling with sugar; crush; hold-up of traffic; awkward situation —**jam-packed** *a.* filled to capacity —**jam session** (improvised) jazz session

jamb [jam] *n.* side post of door, fireplace *etc.*

jamboree' *n.* large gathering or rally of Boy Scouts; spree, celebration

Jan. January

jan'gle [-ng-gl] *v.* (cause to) sound harshly, as bell; (of nerves) irritate —*n.* harsh sound

jan'itor *n.* caretaker, cleaner (**jan'itress** *fem.*)

Jan'uary *n.* first month

japan' *n.* very hard *usu.* black varnish —*vt.* cover with this (**-nn-**)

jape *n./vi.* joke

japon'ica *n.* shrub with red flowers

jar¹ *n.* round vessel of glass, earthenware *etc.*; *inf.* glass of *esp.* beer

jar² *v.* (cause to) vibrate suddenly, violently; have disturbing, painful effect on (**-rr-**) —*n.* jarring sound; shock *etc.*

jardinière' [zhah-din-yār'] *n.* ornamental pot for growing plants

jar'gon *n.* specialized language concerned with particular subject; pretentious or nonsensical language

Jas. James

jas'min(e), jess'amin(e) *n.* flowering shrub

jas'per *n.* red, yellow, dark green or brown quartz

jaun'dice n. disease marked by yellowness of skin; bitterness, ill humour; prejudice —v. make, become prejudiced, bitter etc.

jaunt n. short pleasure excursion —vi. make one

jaunt'y a. sprightly; brisk; smart, trim —**jaunt'ily** adv.

jav'elin n. spear, esp. for throwing in sporting events

jaw n. one of bones in which teeth are set —pl. mouth; fig. narrow opening of a gorge or valley; gripping part of vice etc. —vi. sl. talk lengthily

jay n. noisy bird of brilliant plumage —**jay'walker** n. careless pedestrian —**jay'walk** vi.

jazz n. syncopated music and dance —**jazz'y** a. flashy, showy —**jazz up** play as jazz; make more lively, appealing

JCB R construction machine with shovel at front and excavator at rear

jeal'ous (jel'-) a. distrustful of the faithfulness (of); envious; suspiciously watchful —**jeal'ously** adv. —**jeal'ousy** n.

jeans pl.n. casual trousers, esp. of denim

Jeep R light four-wheel drive motor utility vehicle

jeer v. scoff, deride —n. scoff, taunt, gibe

Jeho'vah (jiho'va) n. God

jejune' (ji-jōōn') a. simple, naive; meagre

jell v. congeal; inf. assume definite form

jell'y n. semitransparent food made with gelatin, becoming softly stiff as it cools; anything of the consistency of this —**jell'y-fish** n. jellylike small sea animal

jemm'y n. short steel crowbar, pinchbar

jenn'y n. female ass; female wren

jeop'ardy [jep'-] n. danger

—**jeop'ardize** vt. endanger

Jer. Jeremiah

jerbo'a n. small Afric. burrowing rodent animal resembling a mouse; desert rat

jerepi'go n. a sweet S Afr. wine

jerk n. sharp, abruptly stopped movement; twitch; sharp pull; sl. stupid person —v. move or throw with a jerk —**jerk'ily** adv. —**jerk'iness** n. —**jerk'y** a. uneven, spasmodic

jer'kin n. sleeveless jacket, esp. of leather

jerr'y-built a. of flimsy construction with bad materials —**jerry-builder** n.

jer'sey [-z-] n. knitted jumper; machine-knitted fabric; (J-) breed of cow

jess'amine see JASMINE

jest n./vi. joke —**jest'er** n. joker, esp. Hist. court fool

Jes'uit [jez-] n. member of Society of Jesus, Order founded by Ignatius Loyola in 1534 —**Jesuit'ical** a. of Jesuits

jet[1] n. stream of liquid, gas etc., esp. shot from small hole; the small hole; spout; nozzle; aircraft driven by jet propulsion —v. throw out; shoot forth (-tt-) —**jet lag** fatigue caused by crossing time zones in jet aircraft —**jet propulsion** propulsion by thrust provided by jet of gas or liquid —**jet-propelled** a.

jet[2] n. hard black mineral capable of brilliant polish —**jet-black** a. glossy black

jet'sam n. goods thrown out to lighten ship and later washed ashore —**jett'ison** vt. abandon; throw overboard

jett'y n. small pier, wharf

Jew n. one of Hebrew religion or ancestry; offens. inf. miser —**Jew'ess** n.fem. —**Jew'ish** a. —**Jew'ry** n. the Jews —**jew's-harp** n. small musical instrument held between teeth and played by finger

jew'el *n.* precious stone; ornament containing one; precious thing —**jew'eller** *n.* dealer in jewels —**jew'ellery** *n.*

jew'fish *n.* large fish of tropical and temperate waters

jib *n.* triangular sail set forward of mast; projecting arm of crane or derrick —*vi.* object to proceeding; of horse, person, stop and refuse to go on (-**bb**-) —**jib'ber** *n.* —**jib boom** spar from end of bowsprit

jibe *see* GYBE *and* GIBE

jiff'y *n. inf.* very short period of time

Jiff'y bag R large padded envelope

jig *n.* lively dance; music for it; small mechanical device; guide for cutting *etc.*; *Angling* any of various lures —*vi.* dance jig; make jerky up-and-down movements —**jig'er** *n.* —**jig'saw** *n.* machine fretsaw —**jigsaw puzzle** picture stuck on board and cut into interlocking pieces with jigsaw

jigg'er *n.* small glass for spirits

jigg'ery-po'kery *n. inf.* trickery, nonsense

jig'gle *v.* move (up and down *etc.*) with short jerky movements

jilt *vt.* cast off (lover)

jin'gle [-ng'gl] *n.* mixed metallic noise, as of shaken chain; catchy, rhythmic verse, song *etc.* —*v.* (cause to) make jingling sound

jin'goism [-ng'g-] *n.* chauvinism —**jingoist'ic** *a.*

jinks *pl.n.* —**high jinks** boisterous merrymaking

jinx *n.* force, person, thing bringing bad luck —*v.*

jitt'ers *pl.n.* worried nervousness, anxiety —**jitt'ery** *a.* nervous

jiu'jitsu *n. see* JUJUTSU

jive *n.* (dance performed to) rock and roll music, *esp.* of 1950's —*vi.*

job *n.* piece of work, task; post, office; difficult task; *inf.* crime, *esp.* robbery —**jobb'er** *n.* stockjobber —**jobb'ing** *a.* doing single, particular jobs for payment —**job'less** *a./pl.n.* unemployed (people) —**job centre** government office in town centre providing information about vacant jobs —**job lot** assortment sold together; miscellaneous collection

jock'ey *n.* professional rider in horse races (*pl.* **-eys**) —*v.* (*esp.* *with* for) manoeuvre (**jock'eyed, jock'eying**)

jocose' *a.* waggish, humorous —**jocose'ly** *adv.* —**jocos'ity** *n.* —**joc'ular** *a.* joking; given to joking —**jocular'ity** *n.*

joc'und *a.* merry, cheerful —**jocun'dity** *n.*

jodh'purs [jod'pərz] *pl.n.* tight-legged riding breeches

jog *vi.* run slowly or move at trot, *esp.* for physical exercise —*vt.* jar, nudge; remind, stimulate (-**gg**-) —*n.* jogging —**jogg'er** *n.* —**jogg'ing** *n.* —**jog trot** slow regular trot

jog'gle *v.* move to and fro in jerks; shake —*n.*

John *n.* name —**John Bull** typical Englishman —**John Dory** *see* DORY

joie de vi'vre [zhwad vēv'r] *Fr.* enjoyment of life, ebullience

join *vt.* put together, fasten, unite; become a member (of) —*vi.* become united, connected; (*with* up) enlist; take part in —*n.* joining; place of joining —**join'er** *n.* maker of finished woodwork; one who joins —**join'ery** *n.* joiner's work

joint *n.* arrangement by which two things fit together, rigidly or loosely; place of this; meat for roasting, oft. with bone; *inf.* house, place *etc.*; *sl.* disreputable bar or nightclub; *sl.* marijuana cigarette —*a.* common; shared by two or more —*vt.* connect by joints; divide at the joints —**joint'ly** *adv.* —**out of joint** dislocated; disorganized

join'ture *n.* property settled on wife for her use after husband's death

joist *n.* one of the parallel beams stretched from wall to wall on which to fix floor or ceiling —**joist'ed** *a.*

juke *n.* thing said or done to cause laughter; something not in earnest, or ridiculous —*v.* make jokes —**jo'ker** *n.* one who jokes; *sl.* fellow; extra card in pack, counting as highest card in some games

joll'y *a.* jovial; festive, merry —*vt.* (*esp. with* along) (try to) make person, occasion *etc.* happier (**joll'ied, joll'ying**) —**jollifi-ca'tion** *n.* merrymaking —**joll'ity** *n.*

Joll'y Rog'er pirates' flag, black, with white skull and cross-bones

jolt [-ō-] *n.* sudden jerk; bump; shock —*v.* move, shake with jolts —**jolt'y** *a.*

jon'quil *n.* fragrant yellow or white narcissus —*a.* pale yellow

joss *n.* Chinese idol —**joss house** Chinese temple —**joss stick** stick of Chinese incense

jos'tle [-sl] *v.* knock or push against

jot *n.* small amount, whit —*vt.* write briefly; make note of (-**tt-**) —**jott'er** *n.* notebook —**jott'ing** *n.* memorandum

joule [jōōl] *n. Electricity* unit of work or energy

jour'nal [jur'nəl] *n.* daily newspaper or other periodical; daily record; logbook; part of axle or shaft resting on the bearings —**journalese'** *n.* journalist's jargon; high-flown style, full of clichés —**jour'nalism** *n.* editing, writing in periodicals —**jour'nalist** *n.* —**journalis'tic** *a.*

jour'ney [jur'-] *n.* going to a place, excursion; distance travelled —*vi.* travel

jour'neyman *n.* craftsman or artisan employed by another

joust *Hist.* *n.* encounter with lances between two mounted knights —*vi.* engage in joust

jo'vial *a.* convivial, merry, gay —**jovial'ity** *n.*

jowl *n.* cheek, jaw; outside of throat when prominent

joy *n.* gladness, pleasure, delight; cause of this —**joy'ful** *a.* —**joy'less** *a.* —**joy ride** trip *esp.* in stolen car —**joy'stick** *n.* *inf.* control column of aircraft

JP Justice of the Peace

Jr. Junior

ju'bilate *vi.* rejoice —**ju'bilant** *a.* exultant —**ju'bilantly** *adv.* —**jubila'tion** *n.*

ju'bilee *n.* time of rejoicing, *esp.* 25th or 50th anniversary

Jud. Judges

Juda'ic [jōō-] *a.* Jewish —**Ju'daism** *n.* —**Ju'daize** [-dā-īz] *vt.* make Jewish; follow Jewish custom

Ju'das tree small tree with pinkish-purple flowers

judd'er *vi.* shake, vibrate —*n.*

judge [juj] *n.* officer appointed to try cases in law courts; one who decides in a dispute, contest *etc.*; one able to form a reliable opinion, arbiter; umpire; in Jewish history, ruler —*vi.* act as judge —*vt.* act as judge of; try, estimate; decide —**judg(e)'ment** *n.* faculty of judging; sentence of court; opinion; misfortune regarded as sign of divine displeasure

ju'dicature n. administration of justice; body of judges —**judi'cial** [-ish'-] a. of, by, a court or judge; proper to a judge; discriminating —**judi'cially** adv. —**judi'ciary** n. system of courts and judges —**judi'cious** a. well-judged, sensible, prudent —**judi'ciously** adv.

ju'do n. modern sport derived from jujitsu

jug n. vessel for liquids, with handle and small spout; its contents; sl. prison —vt. stew (esp. hare) in jug (-**gg**-)

jugg'ernaut n. large heavy lorry; any irresistible, destructive force

jugg'ins n. inf. silly fellow

jug'gle v. throw and catch (several objects) so most are in the air simultaneously; manage, manipulate (accounts etc.) to deceive —n. —**jugg'ler** n. —**jug'glery** n.

jug'ular vein one of three large veins of the neck returning blood from the head

juice [joos] n. liquid part of vegetable, fruit, or meat; inf. electric current; inf. petrol; vigour, vitality —**juic'y** a. succulent

jujit'su, jujut'su, jiujit'su n. the Japanese art of wrestling and self-defence

ju'jube n. lozenge of gelatin, sugar etc.; a fruit; shrub producing it

juke'box n. automatic, coin-operated record-player

ju'lep n. sweet drink; medicated drink

Ju'lian a. of Julius Caesar —**Julian calendar** calendar as adjusted by Julius Caesar in 46 B.C., in which the year was made to consist of 365 days, 6 hours, instead of 365 days

julienne' n. kind of clear soup

July' n. the seventh month

jum'ble vt. mingle, mix in confusion —n. confused heap, muddle; articles for jumble sale —**jumble sale** sale of miscellaneous, usu. secondhand, items

jum'bo inf. n. elephant; anything very large

jump v. (cause to) spring, leap (over); move hastily; pass or skip (over) —vi. move hastily; rise steeply; parachute from aircraft; start, jerk (with astonishment etc.); of faulty film etc., make abrupt movements —vt. come off (tracks, rails etc.); inf. attack without warning —n. act of jumping; obstacle to be jumped; distance, height jumped; sudden nervous jerk or start; sudden rise in prices —**jump'er** n. one who, that which jumps; sweater, pullover —**jump'y** a. nervous —**jump leads** electric cables to connect discharged car battery to external battery to aid starting of engine —**jump suit** one-piece garment of trousers and top

junc'tion n. railway station etc. where lines, routes join; place of joining; joining

junc'ture n. state of affairs

June [joon] n. the sixth month

jun'gle [-ng'gl] n. tangled vegetation of equatorial forest; land covered with it; tangled mass; condition of intense competition, struggle for survival —**jun'gly** a.

ju'nior a. younger; of lower standing —n. junior person

ju'niper n. evergreen shrub with berries yielding oil of juniper, used for medicine and gin making

Junk[1] n. discarded, useless objects; inf. nonsense; sl. narcotic drug —**junk'ie, junk'y** n. sl. drug addict —**junk food** food, oft. of low nutritional value, eaten in addition to or instead of regular meals

junk² n. Chinese sailing vessel

junk'et n. curdled milk flavoured and sweetened —vi. feast, picnic —**junk'eting** n.

jun'ta n. group of military officers holding power in a country

Ju'piter n. Roman chief of gods; largest of the planets

jurisdic'tion [joor-] n. administration of justice; authority; territory covered by it —**jurispru'dence** n. science of, skill in, law —**ju'rist** n. one skilled in law —**juris'tic** a. —**juris'tical** a.

jur'y [joor'i] n. body of persons sworn to render verdict in court of law; body of judges of competition —**jur'or, jur'yman** n. one of jury —**jury box**

just a. fair; upright, honest; proper, right, equitable —adv. exactly; barely; at this instant; merely, only; really —**just'ice** [-s] n. quality of being just; fairness; judicial proceedings; judge, magistrate —**just'ify** vt. prove right, true or innocent; vindicate; excuse (-**ified, ifying**) —**just'ifiable** a. —**just'ifiably** adv. —**justifica'tion** n. —**just'ly** adv.

jut vi. project, stick out (-**tt**-) —n. projection

jute n. fibre of certain plants, used for rope, canvas etc.

ju'venile a. young; of, for young children; immature —n. young person, child —**juvenes'cence** n. —**juvenes'cent** a. becoming young —**juveni'lia** pl.n. works produced in author's youth —**juveni'lity** n. —**juvenile court** court dealing with young offenders or children in need of care —**juvenile delinquent** young person guilty of some offence, anti-social behaviour etc.

juxtapose' [-pōz'] vt. put side by side —**juxtaposi'tion** n. contiguity, being side by side

K

K Kelvin; Chess king; Chem. potassium

k knit

Kaf(f)ir [kaf'ər] n. obs. offens. SA any black African —**Kaf'firboom** n. S Afr. flowering tree —**Kaffir corn** S Afr. variety of sorghum

kaf'tan n. long coatlike Eastern garment; imitation of it, esp. as woman's long, loose dress with sleeves

kai [kī] n. in New Zealand and S Sea islands, food —**kai'-kai** n. feasting

kale, kail n. type of cabbage

kalei'doscope [-lī'-] n. optical toy for producing changing symmetrical patterns by multiple reflections of coloured glass chips etc., in inclined mirrors enclosed in tube; any complex, frequently changing pattern —**kaleidoscop'ic** a. swiftly changing

kamikaz'e [-kahz'-] n. suicidal attack, esp. as in World War II, by Japanese pilots

kangaroo' n. Aust. marsupial with very strongly developed hind legs for jumping —v. inf. (of car) move forward with sudden jerks —**kangaroo court** irregular, illegal court

ka'olin n. a fine white clay used for porcelain and medicinally

ka'pok n. tropical tree; fibre from its seed pods used to stuf f cushions etc.

kaput' a. inf. ruined, broken, no good

karat'e [-raht'-] n. Japanese system of unarmed combat using feet, hands, elbows *etc.* as weapons in a variety of ways

kar'ma *n.* Buddhism & Hinduism person's actions affecting his fate for his next reincarnation

karoo' *n.* SA high, arid plateau

kaross' *n.* SA cloak made of skins

katab'olism *n. see* CATABOLISM

kau'ri [-ow'-] *n.* large N.Z. pine giving valuable timber

kav'a [-ah-] *n.* the beverage derived from a Polynesian plant of the pepper family

kay'ak [kī'-] *n.* Eskimo canoe made of sealskins stretched over frame; any canoe of this design

kazoo' *n.* cigar-shaped musical instrument producing nasal sound

KB Knight of the Bath

KBE Knight Commander (of the Order) of the British Empire

KC King's Counsel

KCB Knight Commander (of the Order) of the Bath

kebab' *n.* dish of small pieces of meat, tomatoes *etc.* grilled on skewers (*also* **shish kebab**)

kedge *n.* small anchor —*vt.* move (ship) by cable attached to kedge

kedg'eree *n.* dish of fish cooked with rice, eggs *etc.*

keel *n.* lowest longitudinal support on which ship is built —**keel'haul** *vt.* formerly, punish by hauling under keel of ship; rebuke severely —**keel'son** [kel'-] *n.* line of timbers or plates bolted to keel —**keel over** turn upside down; *inf.* collapse suddenly

keen[1] *a.* sharp; acute; eager; shrewd, strong; (of price) competitive —**keen'ly** *adv.* —**keen'ness** *n.*

keen[2] *n.* funeral lament —*vi.* wail over the dead

keep *vt.* retain possession of, not lose; store; cause to continue; take charge of; maintain, detain; provide upkeep; reserve —*vi.* remain good; remain; continue (**kept** *pt./pp.*) —*n.* living or support; charge or care; central tower of castle, stronghold —**keep'er** *n.* —**keep'ing** *n.* harmony, agreement; care, charge, possession —**keep fit** exercises designed to promote physical fitness —**keep'sake** *n.* thing treasured for sake of giver

keg *n.* small barrel; metal container for beer

kelp *n.* large seaweed; its ashes, yielding iodine

Kel'vin *a.* of thermometric scale starting at absolute zero (−273.15° Celsius) —*n.* SI unit of temperature

ken *n.* range of knowledge —*vt.* (in Scotland) know

ken'do *n.* Japanese form of fencing, using wooden staves

kenn'el *n.* house, shelter for dog —*pl.* place for breeding, boarding dogs —*vt.* put into kennel (-ll-)

kent'ledge *n.* Naut. scrap metal used as ballast

kept *pt./pp.* of KEEP

kerb *n.* stone edging to footpath —**kerb crawling** driving slowly beside pavement soliciting

ker'chief [-chif] *n.* head-cloth; handkerchief

kerfuf'fle *n.* *inf.* commotion, disorder

kerm'es [-iz] *n.* an insect used for red dyestuff

kern'el *n.* inner seed of nut or fruit stone; central, essential part

ker'osene *n.* paraffin oil distilled from petroleum or coal and shale

kes'trel *n.* small falcon

ketch *n.* two-masted sailing vessel

ketch'up *n.* sauce of vinegar, tomatoes *etc.*

ket'tle *n.* metal vessel with spout and handle, *esp.* for boiling water —**ket'tledrum** *n.* musical instrument made of membrane stretched over copper hemisphere —**a fine kettle of fish** awkward situation, mess

key *n.* instrument for operating lock, winding clock *etc.*; something providing control, explanation, means of achieving an end *etc.*; *Mus.* set of related notes; operating lever of typewriter, piano, organ *etc.*; spanner; mode of thought —*vt.* provide symbols on map *etc.* to assist identification of positions on it; scratch plaster surface to provide bond for plaster or paint —*a.* vital; most important —**key'board** *n.* set of keys on piano *etc.* —**key'note** *n.* dominant idea; basic note of musical key —**key'pad** *n.* small keyboard with push buttons —**key'stone** *n.* central stone of arch which locks all in position

kg kilogram(s)

khak'i [kahk'-] *a.* dull yellowish-brown —*n.* khaki cloth; military uniform

Khmer [kmer] *n.* member of a people of Kampuchea

kHz kilohertz

kib'ble *vt.* grind into small pieces

kibbutz' [-oo-] *n.* Jewish communal agricultural settlement in Israel

ki'bosh *n. sl.* —**to put the kibosh on** silence; get rid of; defeat

kick *vi.* strike out with foot; score with a kick; be recalcitrant; recoil —*vt.* strike or hit with foot; *inf.* free oneself of (habit *etc.*) —*n.* foot blow; recoil; excitement, thrill —**kick'back** *n.* strong reaction; money paid il-

legally for favours done *etc.* —**kick off** *v.* start game of football; *inf.* begin (discussion *etc.*) —**kick-start** *v.* start motorcycle engine by pedal that is kicked downwards

kid *n.* young goat; leather of its skin; *inf.* child —*vt. inf.* tease, deceive —*vi. inf.* behave, speak in fun (**-dd-**)

kid'nap *vt.* seize and hold to ransom (**-pp-**) —**kid'napper** *n.*

kid'ney *n.* either of the pair of organs which secrete urine; animal kidney used as food; nature, kind (*pl.* **-neys**) —**kidney bean** dwarf French bean; scarlet runner

kill *vt.* deprive of life; destroy; neutralize; pass (time); weaken or dilute; *inf.* exhaust; *inf.* cause to suffer pain; *inf.* quash, defeat, veto —*n.* act or time of killing; animals *etc.* killed in hunt —**kill'er** *n.* one who, that which, kills —**kill'ing** *inf. a.* very tiring; very funny —*n.* sudden success, *esp.* on stock market

kiln *n.* furnace, oven

ki'lo [kee'-] *n. short for* KILOGRAM

kilo- (*comb. form*) one thousand, as in **kil'olitre** *n.*, **kil'ometre** [or **-lom'-**] *n.*

kil'ogram(me) *n.* weight of 1000 grams

kil'ohertz *n.* one thousand cycles per second

kil'owatt *n. Electricity* one thousand watts

kilt *n.* short, usu. tartan, skirt, deeply pleated, worn orig. by Scottish Highlanders —**kilt'ed** *a.*

kimo'no *n.* loose, wide-sleeved Japanese robe, fastened with sash; European garment like this

kin *n.* family, relatives —*a.* related by blood —**kin'dred** *n.* relationship; relatives —*a.* similar; related —**kins'folk** *n.* —**kin'ship**

n. —**kins'man** *n.* (**kins'woman** *fem.*)

kind [kīnd] *n.* genus, sort, class —*a.* sympathetic, considerate; good, benevolent; gentle —**kind'liness** *n.* —**kind'ly** *a.* kind, genial —*adv.* —**kind'ness** *n.* —**kind'hearted** *a.* —**in kind** (of payment) in goods rather than money; with something similar

kin'dergarten *n.* class, school for children of about four to six years old

kin'dle *vt.* set on fire; inspire, excite —*vi.* catch fire —**kind'ling** *n.* small wood to kindle fires

kine *obs. pl. of* COW

kinemat'ic [ki-] *a.* of motion without reference to mass or force —**kinemat'ics** *pl.n.* science of this —**kinemat'ograph** *see* CINEMATOGRAPH

kinet'ic *a.* of motion in relation to force —**kinet'ics** *pl.n.* science of this

king *n.* male sovereign ruler of independent state; monarch; piece in game of chess; highest court card, with picture of a king; *Draughts* two pieces on top of one another, allowed freedom of movement —**king'ly** *a.* royal; appropriate to a king —**king'ship** *n.* —**king'dom** *n.* state ruled by king; realm; sphere —**king'fisher** *n.* small bird with bright plumage which dives for fish —**king'pin** *n.* swivel pin; central or front pin in bowling; *inf.* chief thing or person —**king post** beam in roof framework rising from tie beam to the ridge —**king-size(d)** *a. inf.* large; larger than standard size

king'klip *n.* S Afr. marine fish

kink *n.* tight twist in rope, wire, hair *etc.*; crick, as of neck; *inf.* eccentricity —*v.* make, become kinked; put, make kink in; twist —**kink'y** *a.* full of kinks; *inf.*

eccentric, *esp.* given to deviant (sexual) practices

ki'osk [kē-'] *n.* small, sometimes movable booth selling drinks, cigarettes, newspapers *etc.*; public telephone box

kip *n./vi. inf.* sleep

kipp'er *vt.* cure (fish) by splitting open, rubbing with salt, and drying or smoking —*n.* kippered fish

kirk *n.* in Scotland, church

kirsch *n.* brandy made from cherries

kis'met [kiz'-] *n.* fate, destiny

kiss *n.* touch or caress with lips; light touch —*v.* —**kiss'er** *n.* one who kisses; *sl.* mouth or face —**kiss'agram** *n.* greetings service in which messenger kisses person celebrating —**kiss of life** mouth-to-mouth resuscitation

kist *n.* large wooden chest

kit *n.* outfit, equipment; personal effects, *esp.* of traveller; set of pieces of equipment sold ready to be assembled —**kit'bag** *n.* bag for holding soldier's or traveller's kit

kitch'en *n.* room used for cooking —**kitchenette'** *n.* small room (or part of larger room) used for cooking —**kitchen garden** garden for raising vegetables, herbs *etc.* —**kitchen sink** sink in kitchen —*a.* sordidly domestic

kite *n.* light papered frame flown in wind; *sl.* aeroplane; large hawk —**Kite mark** official mark on articles approved by Brit. Standards Institution

kith *n.* acquaintance, kindred (*only in* **kith and kin**)

kitsch [kitch] *n.* vulgarized, pretentious art, literature *etc.*, usu. with popular, sentimental appeal

kitt'en *n.* young cat

kitt'iwake *n.* type of seagull

kitt'y *n. short for* KITTEN; in

some card games, pool; communal fund

ki'wi [kē'-] *n.* any N.Z. flightless bird of the genus *Apteryx*; *inf.* New Zealander —**kiwi fruit** fuzzy fruit of Asian climbing plant, the Chinese gooseberry

klax'on *n.* formerly, a powerful electric motor horn

kleptoma'nia *n.* compulsive tendency to steal for the sake of theft —**kleptoma'niac** *n.*

klip'springer *n.* small agile Afr. antelope

kloof *n.* SA mountain pass

km kilometre(s)

knack [n-] *n.* acquired facility or dexterity; trick; habit

knack'er [n-] *n.* buyer of worn-out horses *etc.*, for killing —**knack'ered** *a. sl.* exhausted

knap'sack [n-] *n.* soldier's or traveller's bag to strap to the back, rucksack

knave [nā-] *n.* jack at cards; *obs.* rogue —**kna'very** *n.* villainy —**kna'vish** *a.*

knead [nē-] *vt.* work (flour) into dough; work, massage —**knead'er** *n.*

knee [n-] *n.* joint between thigh and lower leg; part of garment covering knee; lap —*vt.* strike, push with knee —**knee'cap** *n.* bone in front of knee —**knees-up** *n. inf.* party, oft. with dancing

kneel [n-] *vi.* fall, rest on knees (**knelt** *pt./pp.*)

knell [n-] *n.* sound of a bell, *esp.* at funeral or death; portent of doom

knew *pt. of* KNOW

knick'erbockers [n-] *pl.n.* loose-fitting breeches gathered in at knee

knick'ers [n-] *pl.n.* woman's undergarment for lower half of body

knick'knack [nik'nak] *n.* trifle, trinket

knife [n-] *n.* cutting blade, *esp.* one in handle, used as implement or weapon —*vt.* cut or stab with knife —**knife edge** critical, possibly dangerous situation

knight [nīt] *n.* man of rank below baronet, having right to prefix *Sir* to his name; member of medieval order of chivalry; champion; piece in chess —*vt.* confer knighthood on —**knight'-hood** *n.* —**knight'ly** *a.*

knit [n-] *v.* form (garment *etc.*) by putting together series of loops in wool, or other yarn; draw together; unite (**knitt'ed, knit** *pt./pp.* —**knitt'ing** *pr.p.*) —**knitt'er** *n.* —**knitt'ing** *n.* knitted work; act of knitting

knob [n-] *n.* rounded lump, *esp.* at end or on surface of anything —**knobb'(l)y** *a.*

knock [n-] *vt.* strike, hit; *inf.* disparage; rap audibly; (of engine) make metallic noise, pink —*n.* blow, rap —**knock'er** *n.* metal appliance for knocking on door; who or what knocks —**knock-kneed** *a.* having incurved legs —**knocked up** *inf.* exhausted, tired, worn out —**knock off** *inf.* cease work; *inf.* make something hurriedly; *inf.* kill; *inf.* steal —**knock out** *inf.* render opponent unconscious; overwhelm, amaze —**knock'out** *n.* blow *etc.* that renders unconscious; *inf.* person or thing overwhelmingly attractive

knoll [nōl] *n.* small rounded hill, mound

knot [n-] *n.* fastening of strands by looping and pulling tight; cockade, cluster; small closely knit group; tie, bond; hard lump, *esp.* of wood where branch joins or has joined in; measure of ship's speed, *eg* **ten knots** means ten nautical miles per hour; difficulty —*vt.* tie with knot, in knots

(-tt-) —**knott'y** a. full of knots; puzzling, difficult —**knot'hole** n. hole in wood where knot has been

knot[2] n. small northern sandpiper with grey plumage

know [nō] vt. be aware of, have information about, be acquainted with, recognize, have experience, understand —vi. have information or understanding (knew pt., known pp.) —**know'able** a. —**know'ing** a. cunning, shrewd —**know'ingly** adv. shrewdly; deliberately —**knowl'edge** [nol-] n. knowing; what one knows; learning —**knowl'edg(e)able** a. intelligent, well-informed —**know-how** n. inf. practical knowledge, experience, aptitude —**in the know** inf. informed

knuc'kle [nuk'l] n. bone at finger joint; knee joint of calf or pig —vt. strike with knuckles —**knuckle-duster** n. metal appliances worn on knuckles to add force to blow —**knuckle down** get down to (work) —**knuckle under** yield, submit —**near the knuckle** inf. approaching indecency

knur, nur [n-] n. knot in wood; hard lump

knurled [n-] a. serrated; gnarled

KO knockout

koal'a [kō-ahl'ə] n. marsupial Aust. animal, native bear

kohl [kōl] n. powdered antimony used orig. in Eastern countries for darkening the eyelids

kohlra'bi [kōl-rah'bi] n. type of cabbage with edible stem

ko'la n. see COLA

kook'aburra n. large Aust. kingfisher with cackling cry (also called **laughing jackass**)

ko'pe(c)k, co'peck n. Soviet monetary unit, one hundredth of rouble

kop'je, kopp'ie [kop'i] n. SA small hill

Koran' [-ahn'] n. sacred book of Muslims

ko'sher a. permitted, clean, good, as of food etc., conforming to the Jewish dietary law; inf. legitimate, authentic —n. kosher food

kow'tow n. former Chinese custom of touching ground with head in respect; submission —vi. (esp. with to) prostrate oneself; be obsequious, fawn on

kraal [-ah-] n. S Afr. village with fence; corral

krak'en [-ah-] n. mythical Norwegian sea monster

krans [-ah-] n. SA cliff

kraut [-owt] n. a./n. sl. offens. German

Krem'lin n. central government of Soviet Union

krill n. small shrimplike marine animal (pl. krill)

kryp'ton [krip'-] n. rare gaseous element, present in atmosphere

ku'dos [kyōō'-] n. fame; credit

ku'du [kōō'-dōō] n. Afr. antelope with spiral horns

kuk'ri [koo-] n. heavy, curved Gurkha knife

ku'ku, kuku'pa n. New Zealand fruit-eating pigeon

ku'lak [kōō'-] n. independent well-to-do Russian peasant

ku'mara, ku'mera n. NZ sweet potato

küm'mel n. cumin flavoured German liqueur

kum'quat [-kwot] n. small Chinese tree; its round orange fruit

kung fu [fōō] n. Chinese martial art combining techniques of judo and karate

kW kilowatt

ky'mograph [kī'-] n. instrument for recording on graph

pressure, oscillations, sound waves

L

L Latin; Learner (driver)

l litre

l. lake; left; line

la *see* LAH

laa'ger [lah'-] *n.* **SA** encampment surrounded by wagons

lab *n. inf.* short for LABORATORY

la'bel *n.* slip of paper, metal *etc.*, fixed to object to give information about it; brief, descriptive phrase or term —*vt.* (**-ll-**)

la'bial *a.* of the lips; pronounced with the lips —*n.*

labor'atory [-bo'-] *n.* place for scientific investigations or for manufacture of chemicals

la'bour [lā'bər] *n.* exertion of body or mind; task; workers collectively; effort, pain, of childbirth or time taken for this —*vi.* work hard; strive; maintain normal motion with difficulty; (esp. of ship) be tossed heavily —*vt.* elaborate; stress to excess —**la'-boured** *a.* uttered, done, with difficulty —**la'bourer** *n.* one who labours, esp. man doing manual work for wages —**labor'ious** *a.* tedious —**labor'iously** *adv.*

lab'rador *n.* breed of large, smooth-coated retriever dog

labur'num *n.* tree with yellow hanging flowers

lab'yrinth *n.* network of tortuous passages, maze; inexplicable difficulty; perplexity —**labyrin'-thine** [-th-] *a.*

lac¹ *n.* resinous substance secreted by some insects

lac², **lakh** *n.* one hundred thousand (of rupees)

lace *n.* fine patterned openwork fabric; cord, usu. one of pair, to draw edges together, *eg* to tighten shoes *etc.*; ornamental braid —*vt.* fasten with laces; flavour with spirit —**lac'y** *a.* fine, like lace

la'cerate [las'-] *vt.* tear, mangle; distress —**lacera'tion** *n.* —**lac'erable** *a.*

lac'hrymal, lac'rimal [lak'ri-] *a.* of tears —**lac'hryma-tory** *a.* causing tears or inflammation of eyes —**lac'hrymose** *a.* tearful

lack *n.* deficiency, need —*vt.* need, be short of —**lack'lustre** *a.* lacking brilliance or vitality

lackadai'sical [-dā'z-] *a.* languid, listless; lazy, careless

lack'ey *n.* servile follower; footman (*pl.* **-eys**) —*vt.* be, or play, the lackey; to wait upon

lacon'ic [lə-kon'-] *a.* using, expressed in few words; brief, terse; offhand, not caring —**la-con'ically** *adv.* —**lacon'icism** *n.*

lac'quer [lak'ər] *n.* hard varnish —*vt.* coat with this

lacrosse' *n.* ball game played with long-handled racket or crosse

lac'tic, lac'teal *a.* of milk —**lac'tate** *vi.* secrete milk —**lac-ta'tion** *n.* —**lacto'meter** *n.* instrument for measuring purity and density of milk —**lac'tose** *n.* white crystalline substance occurring in milk

lacu'na [-kyōō'-] *n.* gap, missing part, esp. in document or series (*pl.* **-nae** [-nē], **-nas**)

lad *n.* boy, young fellow

ladd'er *n.* frame of two poles connected by cross-bars called rungs, used for climbing; flaw in stockings, jumpers *etc.*, caused by running of torn stitch

lade *vt.* load; ship; burden; weigh down (**la'den** *pp.*) —**la'ding** *n.* cargo, freight

la'dle *n.* spoon with long handle and large bowl —*vt.* serve out liquid with a ladle

la'dy *n.* female counterpart of gentleman; *polite term for a woman*; title of some women of rank —**la'dybird** *n.* small beetle, usu. red with black spots —**Lady Day** Feast of the Annunciation, 25th March —**la'dylike** *a.* gracious; well-mannered —**la'dyship** *n.* title of a lady —**Our Lady** the Virgin Mary —**lady's finger** species of small banana —**lady's-slipper** *n.* orchid with reddish or purple flowers

lag[1] *vi.* go too slowly, fall behind (**-gg-**) —*n.* lagging, interval of time between events —**lagg'ard** *n.* one who lags —**lagg'ing** *a.* loitering, slow

lag[2] *vt.* wrap boiler, pipes *etc.* with insulating material —**lag'ging** *n.* this material

lag[3] *n. sl.* convict (*esp. old lag*)

lag'er [lahg'-] *n.* a light-bodied type of beer

lagoon[1] *n.* saltwater lake, enclosed by atoll, or separated by sandbank from sea

lah, la *n.* sixth sol-fa note

la'ic *a.* secular, lay —**la'icize** *vt.* render secular or lay —**laiciza'tion** *n.*

laid *pt./pp.* of LAY —**laid-back** *a. inf.* relaxed

lain *pp.* of LIE

lair *n.* resting place, den of animal

laird *n.* Scottish landowner —**laird'ship** *n.* estate

laissez-faire[1] [les-â-fer'] *n.* principle of nonintervention, *esp.* by government in commercial affairs; indifference

la'ity *n.* laymen, the people as opposed to clergy

lake[1] *n.* expanse of inland water —**lake'let** *n.*

lake[2] *n.* red pigment

lam *vt. sl.* beat, hit (**-mm-**) —**lam'ming** *n.* beating, thrashing

Lam. Lamentations

la'ma [lahm'-] *n.* Buddhist priest in Tibet or Mongolia —**la'masery** *n.* monastery of lamas

lamb [lam] *n.* young of the sheep; its meat; innocent or helpless creature —*vi.* (of sheep) give birth to lamb —**lamb'like** *a.* meek, gentle

lambast(e)[1] [-bâst'] *vt.* beat, reprimand

lam'bent *a.* (of flame) flickering softly; glowing

lame *a.* crippled in a limb, *esp.* leg; limping; (of excuse *etc.*) unconvincing —*vt.* cripple —**lame duck** disabled, weak person or thing

lam'é [lahm'â] *n./a.* (fabric) interwoven with gold or silver thread

lamell'a *n.* thin plate or scale (*pl.* **-ae** [-ē]) —**lamell'ar, -ate** *a.*

lament' *v.* feel, express sorrow (for) —*n.* passionate expression of grief; song of grief —**lam'entable** *a.* deplorable —**lamenta'tion** *n.*

lam'ina *n.* thin plate, scale, flake (*pl.* **-nae** [-nē], **-nas**) —**lam'inate** *v.* make (sheet of material) by bonding together two or more thin sheets; split, beat, form into thin sheets; cover with thin sheet of material —*n.* laminated sheet —**lamina'tion** *n.*

Lamm'as *n.* 1st August, formerly a harvest festival

lammerg'ei'er, lammergey'er [-gī'-] *n.* type of rare vulture

lamp *n.* any of various appliances (*esp.* electrical) that produce light, heat, radiation *etc.*; formerly, vessel holding oil burned by wick for lighting —**lamp'black** *n.* pigment made from soot —**lamp'light** *n.*

—**lamp'post** n. post supporting lamp in street —**lamp'shade** n.

lampoon' n. satire ridiculing person, literary work etc. —vt. satirize, ridicule —**lampoo'ner, -ist** n.

lamp'rey n. fish like an eel with a sucker mouth

lance' [-ah-] n. horseman's spear —vt. pierce with lance or lancet —**lan'ceolate** a. lance-shaped, tapering —**lan'cer** n. formerly, cavalry soldier armed with lance —**lan'cet** n. pointed two-edged surgical knife —**lance corporal, lance sergeant** n. noncommissioned officer in army

Lancs. Lancashire

land n. solid part of earth's surface, ground, soil; country; property consisting of land —pl. estates —vi. come to land, disembark; bring an aircraft from air to land or water; alight, step down; arrive on ground —vt. bring to land; come or bring to some point or condition; inf. obtain; catch; inf. strike —**land'ed** a. possessing, consisting of lands —**land'ing** n. act of landing; platform between flights of stairs; a landing stage —**land'ward** a./adv. —**land'wards** adv. —**land'fall** n. ship's approach to land at end of voyage —**land'-locked** a. enclosed by land —**land'lord** n., **land'lady** fem. person who lets land or houses etc.; master or mistress of inn, boarding house etc. —**land'lub-ber** n. person ignorant of the sea and ships —**land'mark** n. boundary mark, conspicuous object, as guide for direction etc.; event, decision etc. considered as important stage in development of something —**land'scape** n. piece of inland scenery; picture of it; prospect —v. create, arrange, garden, park etc. —**land-**scape gardening —**landscape painter** —**land'slide, land'slip** n. falling of soil, rock etc. down mountainside; overwhelming electoral victory —**landing stage** platform for embarkation and disembarkation

lan'dau [-daw] n. four-wheeled carriage with folding top

lane n. narrow road or street; specified route followed by shipping or aircraft; area of road for one stream of traffic

lan'guage [lang'gwij] n. system of sounds, symbols etc. for communicating thought; specialized vocabulary used by a particular group; style of speech or expression

lan'guish [-ng-gw-] vi. be or become weak or faint; be in depressing or painful conditions; droop, pine —**lan'guid** a. lacking energy, interest; spiritless, dull —**lan'guidly** adv. —**lan'guor** [-gər] n. want of energy or interest; faintness; tender mood; softness of atmosphere —**lan'guorous** a.

lan'iary a. lacerating or tearing (esp. of teeth)

lank a. lean and tall; greasy and limp —**lank'y** a.

lan'olin n. grease from wool used in ointments etc.

lanta'na n. tropical shrub

lan'tern n. transparent case for lamp or candle; erection on dome or roof to admit light —**lant'horn** n. obs. lantern

lan'thanum n. silvery-white ductile metallic element

lan'yard n. short cord for securing knife or whistle; short nautical rope; cord for firing cannon

lap' n. the part between waist and knees of a person when sitting; fig. place where anything lies securely; single circuit of racecourse, track; stage or part of journey; single turn of wound thread *etc.* —*vt.* enfold, wrap round; overtake opponent to be one or more circuits behind (**-pp-**) —**lapʹpet** *n.* flap, fold —**lapʹdog** *n.* small pet dog

lap [2] *vt.* drink by scooping up with tongue; (of waves *etc.*) beat softly (**-pp-**)

lapel *n.* part of front of a coat folded back towards shoulders

lapʹidary *n.* of stones; engraved on stone *-a.* cutter, engraver of stones

lapʹis lazʹuli [-yoo-lī] *n.* bright blue stone or pigment

lapse *n.* fall (in standard, condition, virtue *etc.*); slip; mistake; passing (of time *etc.*) —*vi.* fall away; end, *esp.* through disuse

lapʹwing *n.* type of plover

larʹboard *n./a.* old term for port (side of ship)

larʹceny *n.* theft

larch *n.* deciduous coniferous tree

lard *n.* prepared pig's fat —*vt.* insert strips of bacon in (meat); intersperse, decorate (speech with strange words *etc.*) —**lardʹy** *a.*

lardʹer *n.* storeroom for food

large *a.* broad in range or area; great in size, number *etc.*; liberal; generous —*adv.* in a big way —**largeʹly** *adv.* —**largessʹe** [n] *n.* bounty; gift; donation —**at large** free, not confined; in general; fully

larʹgo *adv. Mus.* in a slow dignified manner

larʹiat [laʹri-] *n.* lasso

lark [1] *n.* small, brown singing-bird, skylark —**larkʹspur** *n.* plant with spikes of blue, pink, or white flowers

lark [2] *n.* frolic, spree —*vi.* indulge in lark —**larkʹy** *a.*

larʹva *n.* insect in immature but

active stage (*pl.* **-ae** [-ē]) —**larʹval** *a.*

larʹynx [laʹringks] *n.* part of throat containing vocal cords (*pl.* **larynʹges** [-jēz]) —**laryngiʹtis** *n.* inflammation of this

lasagʹne [lə-zanʹyə] *n.* pasta formed in wide, flat sheets

lasʹcar *n.* E Indian seaman

lasciʹvious [lə-sivʹ-] *a.* lustful

laʹser [lāʹz-] *n.* device for concentrating electromagnetic radiation or light of mixed frequencies into an intense, narrow, concentrated beam

lash [1] *n.* stroke with whip; flexible part of whip; eyelash —*vt.* strike with whip, thong *etc.*; dash against (as waves); attack verbally, ridicule; flick, wave sharply to and fro —*vi.* (*with* out) hit, kick

lash [2] *vt.* fasten or bind tightly with cord *etc.*

lashʹings *pl.n. inf.* abundance

lass, lassʹie *n.* girl

lassʹitude *n.* weariness

lasso [-ōō] *n.* rope with noose for catching cattle *etc.* (*pl.* **lasso(e)s**) —*vt.* (**lassoed** [lə-sōōd], **lassoʹing**)

last [1] [-ah-] *a./adv.* after all others, coming at the end; most recent(ly) —*a.* only remaining —*sup.* of LATE —*n.* last person or thing —**lastʹly** *adv.* finally

last [2] [-ah-] *vi.* continue, hold out, remain alive or unexhausted, endure

last [3] [-ah-] *n.* model of foot on which shoes are made, repaired

last [4] [-ah-] *n.* large measure of quantity

latch *n.* fastening for door, consisting of bar, catch for it, and lever to lift it; small lock with spring action —*vt.* fasten with latch

late *a.* coming after the appointed time; delayed; that was recently but now is not; recently dead; recent in date; of late stage of development (**la'ter** *comp.*, **la'test, last** *sup.*) —*adv.* after proper time; recently; at, till late hour —**late'ly** *adv.* not long since

lateen' (sail) *a.* triangular sail on long yard hoisted to head of mast

la'tent *a.* existing but not developed; hidden

lat'eral *a.* of, at, from the side —**lat'erally** *adv.*

lat'erite *n.* brick-coloured rock or clay formed by weathering of rock in tropical regions

la'tex *n.* sap or fluid of plants, *esp.* of rubber tree —**laticif'erous** [lat-i-sif'-] *a.* bearing or containing latex or

lath [lahth] *n.* thin strip of wood (*pl.* **-s**) —**lath'y** *a.* like a lath; tall and thin —**lath'ing** *n.*

lathe [lāTH] *n.* machine for turning object while it is being shaped

lath'er [lahTH'-] *n.* froth of soap and water; frothy sweat —*v.* make frothy; *inf.* beat

Lat'in *n.* language of ancient Romans —*a.* of ancient Romans, of, in their language; speaking a language descended from theirs —**Lat'inism** *n.* word, idiom imitating Latin —**Latin'ity** *n.* manner of writing Latin; Latin style

lat'itude *n.* angular distance on meridian reckoned N or S from equator; deviation from a standard; freedom from restriction; scope —*pl.* regions —**latitud'inal** *a.* —**latitudinar'ian** *a.* claiming, showing latitude of thought, *esp.* in religion —**latitudinar'ianism** *n.*

latrine' [-ēn'] *n.* in army *etc.*, lavatory

latt'er *a.* second of two; later; more recent —**latt'erly** *adv.*

latt'ice *n.* structure of strips of wood, metal *etc.* crossing with

spaces between; window so made —**latt'iced** *a.*

laud *n.* praise, song of praise —*vt.* —**laudabil'ity** *n.* —**laud'able** *a.* praiseworthy —**laud'ably** *adv.* —**lauda'tion** *n.* praise; honour paid —**laud'atory** *a.* expressing, containing, praise

laud'able *a.* praiseworthy

laud'anum *n.* tincture of opium

laugh [lahf] *vi.* make sounds instinctively expressing amusement, merriment, or scorn —*n.* —**laugh'able** *a.* ludicrous **laugh'ably** *adv.* —**laugh'ter** *n.* —**laughing gas** nitrous oxide as anaesthetic —**laughing hyena** spotted hyena, so called from its cry —**laughing jackass** *see* KOOKABURRA —**laughing stock** object of general derision

launch' *vt.* set afloat; set in motion; begin; propel (missile, spacecraft) into space; hurl, send —*vi.* enter on course —**launch'er** *n.* installation, vehicle, device for launching rockets, missiles *etc.*

launch' *n.* large power-driven boat

laun'dry *n.* place for washing clothes, *esp.* as a business; clothes *etc.* for washing —**laun'der** *vt.* wash and iron —**Laundrette'** [-dret'] R shop with coin-operated washing, drying machines

lau'reate [law'ri-ət] *a.* crowned with laurels —**poet laureate** poet with appointment to Royal Household, nominally to compose verses on occasions of national importance —**lau'reateship** *n.* his post

lau'rel [lo'-] *n.* glossy-leaved shrub, bay tree —*pl.* its leaves, emblem of victory or merit

lav'a [lahv'-] *n.* molten matter thrown out by volcanoes, solidifying as it cools

lav'atory n. toilet, water closet

lave vt. wash, bathe

lav'ender n. shrub with fragrant flowers; colour of the flowers, pale lilac

lav'ish a. giving or spending profusely; very, too abundant —vt. spend, bestow, profusely

law n. rule binding on community; system of such rules; legal science; knowledge, administration of it; inf. (member of) police force; general principle deduced from facts; invariable sequence of events in nature —**law'ful** a. allowed by law —**law'fully** adv. —**law'less** a. ignoring laws; violent —**law'lessly** adv. —**law'yer** n. professional expert in law —**law-abiding** a. obedient to laws; well-behaved —**law'giver** n. one who makes laws —**law'suit** n. prosecution of claim in court

lawn[1] n. stretch of carefully tended turf in garden etc. —**lawn mower** —**lawn tennis** tennis played on grass court

lawn[2] n. fine linen

lawyer see LAW

lax a. not strict; lacking precision; loose, slack —**lax'ative** a. having loosening effect on bowels —n. —**lax'ity, lax'ness** n. slackness; looseness of (moral) standards —**lax'ly** adv.

lay[1] pt. of LIE —**lay'about** n. lazy person, loafer

lay[2] vt. deposit, set, cause to lie (**laid, lay'ing**) —**lay'er** n. single thickness of some substance, as stratum or coating on surface; laying hen; shoot of plant pegged down or partly covered with earth to encourage root growth —vt. propagate plants by making layers —**lay-by** n. stopping place for traffic beside road —**lay'out** n. arrangement, esp. of matter for printing —**lay off** dismiss

staff during slack period (**lay-off** n.) —**lay on** provide, supply; apply; strike —**lay out** display; expend; prepare for burial; plan copy for printing; sl. knock out —**lay waste** devastate

lay[3] n. minstrel's song

lay[4] a. not clerical or professional; of, or done, by persons not clergymen —**lay'man** n. ordinary person

layette[1] n. clothes for newborn child

lay figure jointed figure of the body used by artists; nonentity

laz'ar n. leper

la'zy a. averse to work, indolent —**laze** vi. indulge in laziness —**la'zily** adv. —**la'ziness** n.

lb. pound

l.b.w. leg before wicket

lea [lē] n. Poet. piece of meadow or open ground

lead[1] [lēd] vt. guide, conduct; persuade; direct; conduct people —vi. be, go, play first; result; give access to (**led, lead'ing**) —n. leading; that which leads or is used to lead; example; front or principal place, role etc.; cable bringing current to electric instrument —**lead'er** n. one who leads; article in newspaper expressing editorial views (also **leading article**) —**lead'ership** n. —**leading case** legal decision used as precedent —**leading question** question worded to prompt answer desired —**lead time** time between design of product and its production

lead[2] [led] n. soft heavy grey metal; plummet, used for sounding depths of water; graphite —pl. lead-covered roof; strips of lead used to widen spaces in printing etc. —vt. cover, weight or space with lead (**lead'ed, lead'ing**) —**lead'en** a. of, like lead; heavy; dull —**leads'-**

man *n.* sailor who heaves the lead

leaf *n.* organ of photosynthesis in plants, consisting of a flat, usu. green blade on stem; two pages of book *etc.*; thin sheet; flap, movable part of table *etc.* (*pl.* **leaves**) —*vt.* turn through (pages *etc.*) cursorily —**leaf′less** *a.* —**leaf′let** *n.* small leaf; single sheet, often folded, of printed matter for distribution, handbill —**leaf′y** *a.*

league[1] [lēg] *n.* agreement for mutual help; parties to it; federation of clubs *etc.*; *inf.* class, level —*vi.* form an alliance; combine in an association —**leag′uer** *n.* member of league

league[2] [lēg] *n. obs.* measure of distance, about three miles

leak *n.* hole, defect, that allows escape or entrance of liquid, gas, radiation *etc.*; disclosure —*vi.* let fluid *etc.* in or out; (of fluid *etc.*) find its way through leak —*vt.* let escape —*v.* (allow to) become known little by little —**leak′age** *n.* leaking; gradual escape or loss —**leak′y** *a.*

lean[1] *a.* lacking fat; thin; meagre; (of mixture of fuel and air) with too little fuel —*n.* lean part of meat, mainly muscular tissue

lean[2] *v.* rest against; bend, incline; tend (towards); depend, rely (on) (**leaned** [lēnd] or **leant** [lent] *pt./pp.*) —**lean′ing** *n.* tendency —**lean-to** *n.* room, shed built against existing wall

leap *vi.* spring, jump —*vt.* spring over (**leaped** [lēpt] or **leapt** [lept] *pt./pp.*) —*n.* jump —**leap′frog** *n.* game in which player vaults over another bending down —**leap year** year with February 29th as extra day, occurring every fourth year

learn [lern] *vt.* gain skill, knowledge by study, practice or teach-ing —*vi.* gain knowledge; be taught; find out (**learnt, learned** [lernd] *pt./pp.*) —**learn′ed** *a.* erudite, deeply read; showing much learning —**learn′edly** *adv.* —**learn′er** *n.* —**learn′ing** *n.* knowledge got by study

lease *n.* contract by which land or property is rented for stated time by owner to tenant —*vt.* let, rent by, take on lease —**lease′-hold** *a.* held on lease

leash *n.* thong for holding a dog; set of three animals held in leash —*vt.* hold in leash

least *a.* smallest —*sup. of* LITTLE —*n.* smallest one —*adv.* in small-est degree

leath′er [leTH′-] *n.* prepared skin of animal —**leath′ery** *a.* like leather, tough —**leath′erjacket** *n.* crane fly grub —**leath′erwood** *n.* N Amer. tree with tough, leathery bark

leave[1] *vt.* go away from; deposit; allow to remain; depart from; entrust; bequeath —*vi.* go away, set out (**left, lea′ving**)

leave[2] *n.* permission; permission to be absent from work, duty; period of such absence; formal parting

leav′en [lev′-] *n.* yeast; *fig.* transforming influence —*vi.* raise with leaven; taint; influence; modify

lech′er *n.* man given to lewd-ness —**le(t)ch** *vi. inf.* behave lecherously —**lech′erous** *a.* lewd; provoking lust; lascivious —**lech′erously** *adv.* —**lech′er-ousness** *n.* —**lech′ery** *n.*

lec′tern *n.* reading desk, *esp.* in church

lec′tion *n.* difference in copies of manuscript or book; reading —**lec′tionary** *n.* book, list of scripture lessons for particular days —**lec′tor** *n.* reader

lec′ture *n.* instructive discourse; speech of reproof —*vi.* deliver discourse —*vt.* reprove —**lec'turer** *n.* —**lec'tureship** *n.* appointment as lecturer

LED light-emitting diode

ledge *n.* narrow shelf sticking out from wall, cliff *etc.*; ridge, rock below surface of sea

ledg'er *n.* book of debit and credit accounts, chief account book of firm; flat stone —**ledger line** *Mus.* short line, above or below stave

lee *n.* shelter; side of anything, *esp.* ship, away from wind —**lee'ward** *a./n.* (on) lee side —*adv.* towards this side —**lee'way** *n.* leeward drift of ship; room for free movement within limits; loss of progress

leech[1] *n.* species of blood-sucking worm; *Hist.* physician

leech[2] *n.* edge of a sail

leek *n.* plant like onion with long bulb and thick stem; Welsh emblem

leer *vi.* glance with malign, sly, or lascivious expression —*n.* such glance

lees [-z] *pl.n.* sediment of wine *etc.*; dregs of liquor

leet *n.* in Scotland, selected list of candidates for office

left[1] *a.* denotes that side that faces west when the front faces north; opposite to the right —*n.* the left hand or part; *Politics* reforming or radical party (also **left wing**) —*adv.* on or towards the left —**left'ist** *n./a.* (person) of the political left

left[2] *pt./pp. of* LEAVE

leg *n.* one of limbs on which person or animal walks, runs, stands; part of garment covering leg; anything which supports, as leg of table; stage of journey; *Cricket* part of field away from the striker's bat —**leg'gings** *pl.n.* covering of leather or other ma-

terial for legs —**leg'gy** *a.* long-legged; (of plants) straggling —**leg'warmer** *n.* one of pair of long knitted footless socks worn over tights when exercising

leg'acy *n.* anything left by will, bequest; thing handed down to successor

le'gal *a.* of, appointed or permitted by, or based on, law —**legal'ity** *n.* —**legaliza'tion** *n.* —**le'galize** *vt.* make legal —**le'gally** *adv.*

le'gate *n.* ambassador, *esp.* papal —**leg'ateship** *n.* —**lega'tion** *n.* diplomatic minister and his staff; his residence

legatee' *n.* recipient of legacy

lega'to [-gah'tō] *adv. Mus.* smoothly

leg'end [lej'-] *n.* traditional story or myth; traditional literature; famous, renowned, person or event; inscription —**leg'endary** *a.*

leg'erdemain [lej'-] *n.* juggling, conjuring, sleight of hand, trickery

leg'horn *n.* kind of straw; hat made of it; [le-gorn'] breed of fowls

leg'ible [lej'-] *a.* easily read —**legibil'ity** *n.* —**leg'ibly** *adv.*

le'gion [lē'jan] *n.* body of infantry in Roman army; various modern military bodies; association of veterans; large number —**le'gionary** *a./n.* —**legionnaire's disease** serious bacterial disease similar to pneumonia

leg'islator [lej'-] *n.* maker of laws —**leg'islate** *vi.* make laws —**legisla'tion** *n.* act of legislating; laws which are made —**leg'islative** *a.* —**leg'islature** *n.* body that makes laws of a state

legit'imate [-j-] *a.* born in wedlock; lawful, regular; fairly deduced —**legit'imacy** *n.* —**legit'imate**, **legit'imize** *vt.* make legitimate —**legit'imateness** *n.* —**le-**

gitima'tion n. —**legit'imism** n. —**legit'imist** n. supporter of hereditary title to monarchy

Leg'o R construction toy of plastic bricks fitted together by studs

legu'uan [-oo-ahn] n. large S Afr. lizard

legu'minous [-gyōō-] a. (of plants) pod-bearing

lei [lā] n. garland of flowers

Leics. Leicestershire

lei'sure [lezh'ər] n. freedom from occupation; spare time —**lei'surely** a. deliberate, unhurried —adv. slowly —**lei'sured** a. with plenty of spare time

leit'motif [līt'mō-tēf] n. Mus. recurring theme associated with some person, situation, thought

lemm'ing n. rodent of arctic regions

lem'on n. pale yellow acid fruit; tree bearing it; its colour; sl. useless or defective person or thing —**lemonade'** n. drink made from lemon juice —**lemon curd** creamy spread made of lemons, butter etc.

le'mur [lē'mər] n. nocturnal animal like monkey

lend vt. give temporary use of; let out for hire or interest; give, bestow (**lent, lend'ing**) —**lend'er** n. —**lends itself to** is suitable for

length n. quality of being long; measurement from end to end; duration; extent; piece of a certain length —**length'en** v. make, become, longer; draw out —**length'ily** adv. —**length'wise** a./adv. —**length'y** a. (over)long —**at length** in full detail; at last

le'nient a. mild, tolerant, not strict —**le'nience, le'niency** n. —**le'niently** adv.

len'itive n. soothing or mildly laxative drug

len'ity n. mercy; clemency

le'no n. thin linen or cotton cloth like muslin

lens [-z] n. piece of glass or similar material with one or both sides curved, used to converge or diverge light rays in cameras, spectacles, telescopes etc. (pl. **lens'es**)

lent pt./pp. of LEND

Lent n. period of fasting from Ash Wednesday to Easter Eve —**Lent'en** a. of, in, or suitable to Lent

lent'il n. edible seed of leguminous plant —**lentic'ular** a. like lentil

len'to adv. Mus. slowly

Le'o n. (the lion) 5th sign of the zodiac, operative c. July 22–Aug. 21

le'onine a. like a lion

leop'ard [lep'-] n. large, spotted, carnivorous animal of cat family, like panther (**leop'ardess** fem.)

le'otard [lē'ō-] n. tight-fitting garment covering most of body, worn by acrobats, dancers etc.

lep'er n. one suffering from leprosy; person ignored or despised —**lep'rosy** n. disease attacking nerves and skin resulting in loss of feeling in affected parts —**lep'rous** a.

lepidop'tera pl.n. order of insects with four wings covered with fine gossamer scales, as moths, butterflies —**lepidop'terous** a.

lep'rechaun [-kawn] n. mischievous elf of Irish folklore

les'bian n. a homosexual woman —**les'bianism** n.

lèse-majesté [lāz-maj'es-tā] Fr. n. treason; taking of liberties

le'sion n. injury, injurious change in texture or action of an organ of the body

less a. comp. of LITTLE; not so much —n. smaller part, quantity; a lesser amount —adv. to a smaller extent or degree —prep. after deducting, minus —**less'en**

vt. diminish; reduce —**less'er** *a.* less; smaller; minor

lessee' *n.* one to whom lease is granted

les'son *n.* instalment of course of instruction; content of this; experience that teaches; portion of Scripture read in church

less'or *n.* grantor of a lease

lest *conj.* in order that not; for fear that

let [1] *vt.* allow, enable, cause; allow to escape; grant use of for rent, lease —*vi.* be leased —*v. aux.* used to express a proposal, command, threat, assumption (**let, lett'ing**)

let [2] *n.* hindrance; in some games, minor infringement or obstruction of ball requiring replaying of point

le'thal [lē'-] *a.* deadly

leth'argy *n.* apathy, want of energy or interest; unnatural drowsiness —**lethar'gic** *a.* —**lethar'gically** *adv.*

lett'er *n.* alphabetical symbol; written message; strict meaning, interpretation —*pl.* literature, knowledge of books —*vt.* mark with, in, letters —**lett'ered** *a.* learned —**lett'erpress** *n.* printed matter as distinct from illustrations *etc.* —**letters patent** document under seal of state, granting exclusive right, privilege

lett'uce [-tis] *n.* plant grown for use in salad

leu'cocyte [lyōō'kō-sīt] *n.* one of white blood corpuscles

leuco'ma [lyōō-kō'-] *n.* disorder of the eye, characterized by opacity of the cornea

leukae'mia [lyōō-kē'-] *n.* a progressive blood disease

Lev. Leviticus

lev'ee [1] *n.* British sovereign's reception for men only; *Hist.* reception held by sovereign on rising

lev'ee [2] *n.* river embankment, natural or artificial; landing-place

lev'el *a.* horizontal; even in surface; consistent in style, quality *etc.* —*n.* horizontal line or surface; instrument for showing, testing horizontal plane; position on scale; standard, grade; horizontal passage in mine —*vt.* make level; bring to same level; knock down; aim (gun, or, *fig.*, accusation *etc.*) —*vi. inf.* (*esp. with* with) be honest, frank —**lev'eller** *n.* advocate of social equality —**level crossing** point where railway line and road intersect —**level-headed** *a.* not apt to be carried away by emotion

le'ver *n.* rigid bar pivoted about a fulcrum to transfer a force with mechanical advantage; handle pressed, pulled *etc.* to operate something —*vt.* prise, move, with lever —**le'verage** *n.* action, power of lever; influence; power to accomplish something; advantage

lev'eret *n.* young hare

levi'athan *n.* sea monster; anything huge or formidable

lev'igate *Chem. vt.* smooth; grind to fine powder

levita'tion *n.* the power of raising a solid body into the air supernaturally —**lev'itate** *v.* (cause to) do this

lev'ity *n.* inclination to make a joke of serious matters, frivolity; facetiousness

lev'y *vt.* impose (tax); raise (troops) (**lev'ied, lev'ying**) —*n.* imposition or collection of taxes; enrolling of troops; amount, number levied

lewd *a.* lustful; indecent —**lewd'ly** *adv.* —**lewd'ness** *n.*

lex'icon *n.* dictionary —**lex'ical** *a.* —**lexicog'rapher** *n.* writer of dictionaries —**lexicog'raphy** n.

li'able a. answerable; exposed (to); subject (to); likely (to) —**lia-bil'ity** n. state of being liable, obligation; hindrance, disadvantage —pl. debts

liai'son [lē-ā'zon] n. union; connection; intimacy, esp. secret —**liaise'** vi. —**liaison officer** officer who keeps units of troops in touch

lian'a, liane' [-ah-] n. climbing plant in tropical forests

liar n. one who tells lies

Lib. Liberal

lib n. inf. short for LIBERATION

liba'tion [lī-] n. drink poured as offering to the gods

li'bel n. published statement falsely damaging person's reputation —vt. defame falsely (-ll-) —**li'bellous** a. defamatory

lib'eral a. (also L-) of political party favouring democratic reforms or favouring individual freedom; generous; tolerant; abundant; (of education) designed to develop general cultural interests —n. one who has liberal ideas or opinions —**lib'eralism** n. principles of Liberal party —**liberal'ity** n. munificence —**lib'eralize** vt. —**lib'erally** adv.

lib'erate vt. set free —**libera'tion** n. —**lib'erator** n.

libertar'ian n. believer in freedom of thought etc., or in free will —a. —**libertar'ianism** n.

lib'ertine [-ēn] n. morally dissolute person —a. dissolute —**lib'ertinism** n.

lib'erty n. freedom —pl. rights, privileges —**at liberty** free; having the right —**take liberties (with)** to be presumptuous

libi'do [-bē'-] n. life force; emotional craving, esp. of sexual origin —**libid'inous** a. lustful

Li'bra [lī'-] n. (the balance) 7th sign of the zodiac, operative c. Sept. 22-Oct. 22; Hist. a pound weight

li'brary n. room, building where books are kept; collection of books, gramophone records etc.; reading, writing room in house —**librar'ian** n. keeper of library —**librar'ianship** n.

li'brate v. vibrate as scales before attaining balance; quiver, oscillate; poise —**libra'tion** n. —**li'bratory** a. vibrating

libret'to n. words of an opera (pl. -os, -i) —**libret'tist** n.

Libr'ium R drug used as tranquillizer

lice pl.n. see LOUSE

li'cence, US li'cense n. (document, certificate, giving) leave, permission; excessive liberty; dissoluteness; writer's, artist's transgression of rules of his art (often **poetic licence**) —**li'cense** vt. grant licence to —**licensee'** n. holder of licence —**li'centiate** n. one licensed to practise art, profession

licen'tious [lī-] a. dissolute; sexually immoral —**licen'tiously** adv.

li'chen [līk'-, lich'-] n. small flowerless plants forming crust on rocks, trees etc. —**li'chened** a. —**lichenol'ogy** n.

lich'gate, lych'gate n. roofed gate of churchyard

lick vt. pass the tongue over; touch lightly; sl. defeat; sl. flog, beat —n. act of licking; small amount (esp. of paint etc.); block or natural deposit of salt or other chemical licked by cattle etc.; inf. speed —**lick'ing** n. sl. beating

lic'orice n. see LIQUORICE

lid n. movable cover; cover of the eye; sl. hat

li'do [lē'-] n. pleasure centre with swimming and boating

lie[1] *vi.* be horizontal, at rest; be situated; remain, be in certain state or position; exist, be found; recline (**lay, lain, lying**) —*n.* state of affairs *etc.*; direction

lie[2] *vi.* make false statement (**lied, ly'ing**) —*n.* deliberate falsehood —**li'ar** *n.* person who tells lies —**white lie** untruth said without evil intent —**give the lie to** disprove

liege [lēj] *a.* bound to render or receive feudal service; faithful —*n.* lord; vassal, subject

li'en [lē'ən] *n.* right to hold another's property until claim is met

lieu [lyōō] *n.* place —**in lieu of** instead of

lieuten'ant [lef-] *n.* deputy; *Army* rank below captain; *Navy* [lə-ten'-] rank below commander; *US* [lōō-ten'-] police officer

life *n.* active principle of existence of animals and plants, animate existence; time of its lasting; history of such existence; way of living; vigour, vivacity (*pl.* **lives**) —**life'less** *a.* dead; inert; dull —**life'long** *a.* lasting a lifetime —**life belt, jacket** buoyant device to keep afloat person in danger of drowning —**life style** particular attitudes, habits *etc.* of person or group —**life-support** *a.* of equipment or treatment necessary to keep a person alive —**life'time** *n.* length of time person, animal, or object lives or functions

lift *vt.* raise in position, status, mood, volume *etc.*; take up and remove; exalt spiritually; *inf.* steal —*vi.* rise —*n.* raising apparatus; cage raised and lowered in vertical shaft to transport people or goods; act of lifting; ride in car *etc.*, as passenger; air force acting at right angles on aircraft wing, so lifting it; *inf.* feeling of cheerfulness, uplift

lig'ament *n.* band of tissue joining bones —**lig'ature** *n.* anything which binds; thread for tying up artery

light[1] [līt] *a.* of, or bearing, little weight; not severe; gentle; easy, requiring little effort; trivial; (of industry) producing small, usu. consumer goods, using light machinery —*adv.* in light manner —*vi.* alight (from vehicle *etc.*); come by chance (upon) (**light'ed, lit** *pt./pp.*) —**light'en** *vt.* reduce, remove (load *etc.*) —**light'ly** *adv.* —**light'ness** *n.* —**lights** *pl.n.* lungs of animals —**light-headed** *a.* dizzy, inclined to faint; delirious —**light-hearted** *a.* carefree —**light-minded** *a.* frivolous —**light'weight** *n./a.* (person) of little weight or importance

light[2] [līt] *n.* electromagnetic radiation by which things are visible; source of this, lamp; window; mental vision; light part of anything; means or act of setting fire to; understanding —*pl.* traffic lights —*a.* bright; pale, not dark —*vt.* set burning; give light to —*vi.* take fire; brighten (**light'ed** or **lit** *pt./pp.*) —**light'en** *vt.* give light to —**light'ing** *n.* apparatus for supplying artificial light —**light'ning** *n.* visible discharge of electricity in atmosphere —**light'house** *n.* tower with a light to guide ships —**light year** *Astronomy* distance light travels in one year, about six million million miles

light'er *n.* device for lighting cigarettes *etc.*; flat-bottomed boat for unloading ships

lig'neous *a.* of, or of the nature of, wood —**lig'nite** *n.* woody or brown coal

lig'nin *n.* organic substance which forms characteristic part of all woody fibres

lig'num vi'tae [vī'ti] *Lat.*

tropical tree; its extremely hard wood

like[1] a. resembling; similar; characteristic of —adv. in the manner of —pron. similar thing —**like'lihood** n. probability —**like'ly** a. probable; hopeful, promising —adv. probably —**li'ken** vt. compare —**like'ness** n. resemblance; portrait —**like'wise** adv. in like manner

like[2] vt. find agreeable, enjoy, love —**like'able** a. —**lik'ing** n. fondness; inclination; taste

li'lac n. shrub bearing pale mauve or white flowers, pale mauve colour —a. of lilac colour

Lilliput'ian a. diminutive —n. midget, pygmy

Li'lo R inflatable rubber mattress (pl. **-los**)

lilt v. sing merrily; move lightly —n. rhythmical effect in music, swing —**lilt'ing** a.

lil'y n. bulbous flowering plant —**lily-white** a. —**lily of the valley** small garden plant with fragrant, white bell-like flowers

limb[1] [lim] n. arm or leg; wing; branch of tree

limb[2] [lim] n. edge of sun or moon; edge of sextant

lim'ber[1] n. detachable front of gun carriage

lim'ber[2] a. pliant, lithe —**limber up** loosen stiff muscles by exercises

lim'bo[1] n. supposed region intermediate between Heaven and Hell for the unbaptized; intermediate, indeterminate place or state (pl. **-bos**)

lim'bo[2] n. West Indian dance in which dancers pass under a bar (pl. **-bos**)

lime[1] n. any of certain calcium compounds used in making fertilizer, cement —vt. treat (land) with lime —**lime'light** n. formerly, intense white light obtained

by heating lime; glare of publicity —**lime'stone** n. sedimentary rock used in building

lime[2] n. small acid fruit like lemon —**lime-juice** n. juice of lime prepared as drink

lime[3] n. tree, the linden

lim'erick n. self-contained, nonsensical, humorous verse of five lines

li'mey n. US sl. term used for British person

lim'it n. utmost extent or duration; boundary —vt. restrict, restrain, bound —**limita'tion** n. —**lim'itable** a. —**lim'itless** a. —**limited company** one whose shareholders' liability is restricted

limn [lim] vt. paint, depict, draw —**lim'ner** n.

lim'ousine [-zēn] n. large, luxurious car

limp[1] a. without firmness or stiffness —**limp'ly** adv.

limp[2] vi. walk lamely —n. limping gait

lim'pet n. shellfish which sticks tightly to rocks

lim'pid a. clear; translucent —**limpid'ity** n. —**lim'pidly** adv.

linch'pin n. pin to hold wheel on its axle; essential person or thing

linc'tus n. syrupy cough medicine

lind'en n. deciduous tree, with fragrant flowers; the lime

line n. long narrow mark; stroke made with pen etc.; continuous length without breadth; row; series, course; telephone connection; progeny; province of activity; shipping company; railway track; any class of goods; cord; string; wire; advice, guidance; inf. medical certificate —vt. cover inside; mark with lines; bring into line; be, form border, edge —**lin'eage** [-i-ij] n. descent from, descendants of an ancestor —**lin'eal** a. of lines; in direct line of descent —**lin'eament** [-i-ə-mənt] n. feature —**lin'ear** a. of, in lines —**li'ner** n. large ship or aircraft of passenger line —**lines'man** n. in some sports, official who helps referee, umpire —**get a line on** obtain all relevant information about

lin'en a. made of flax —n. cloth made of flax; linen articles collectively; sheets, tablecloths etc., or shirts (orig. made of linen)

ling[1] n. slender food fish

ling[2] n. heather

lin'ger [-ng'g-] vi. delay, loiter; remain long

lin'gerie [lan'zhə-rē] n. women's underwear or nightwear

ling'o n. inf. language, speech esp. applied to dialects

lin'gua fran'ca It. language used for communication between people of different mother tongues

lin'gual [-ng'gw-] a. of the tongue or language —n. sound made by the tongue, as d, l, t —**lin'guist** n. one skilled in languages or language study —**linguis'tic** a. of languages or their study —**linguis'tics** pl.n. (with sing. v.) study, science of language

lin'iment n. embrocation

li'ning n. covering for the inside of garment etc.

link n. ring of a chain; connection; measure, 1-100th part of chain —vt. join with, as with, link; intertwine —vi. be so joined —**link'age** n.

links pl.n. golf course

linn'et n. songbird of finch family

li'no n. short for LINOLEUM

li'nocut n. design cut in relief on block of linoleum; print from this

lino'leum n. floor covering of hessian with smooth, hard, decorative coating of powdered cork, linseed oil etc.

li'notype n. typesetting machine which casts lines of words in one piece

lin'seed n. seed of flax plant

lint n. soft material for dressing wounds

lin'tel n. top piece of door or window

li'on n. large animal of cat family (**li'oness** fem.) —**li'onize** vt. treat as celebrity —**lion-hearted** a. brave

lip n. either edge of the mouth; edge or margin; sl. impudence —**lip gloss** cosmetic to give lips sheen —**lip-reading** n. method of understanding spoken words by interpreting movements of speaker's lips —**lip salve** ointment for the lips —**lip service** insincere tribute or respect —**lip'stick** n. cosmetic preparation in stick form, for colouring lips

liqueur[1] [li-kyoor'] n. alcoholic liquor flavoured and sweetened

liq'uid a. fluid, not solid or gaseous; flowing smoothly; (of assets) in form of money or easily converted into money —n. substance in liquid form —**lique-faction** n. —**liq'uefy, liq'uidize** v. make or become liquid (**liq'uefied, liq'uefying**) —**liques'cence** n. —**liques'cent** a. tending to become liquid —**liquid'ity** n. state of being able to meet financial obligations —**liq'uidizer** n. —**liquid air, gas** air, or gas, reduced to liquid state on application of increased pressure at low temperature —**liquid fuel** petrol, paraffin oil etc., carried in liquid form and vaporized for combustion

liq'uidate vt. pay (debt); arrange affairs of, and dissolve (company); wipe out, kill —**liquida'tion** n. process of clearing up financial affairs; state of being bankrupt —**liq'uidator** n. official appointed to liquidate business

liq'uor [lik'ər] n. liquid, esp. an alcoholic one

liq'uorice [-kər-is], also, esp. US, **lic'orice** n. black substance used in medicine and as a sweet; plant, its root from which it is obtained

lir'a [lē-] n. monetary unit of Italy and Turkey (pl. **-re, -ras**)

lisle [līl] n. fine hand-twisted cotton thread

lisp v. speak with faulty pronunciation of 's' and 'z'; speak falteringly —n.

liss'om a. supple, agile

list¹ n. inventory, register; catalogue; edge of cloth —pl. field for combat —vt. place on list

list² vi. (of ship) lean to one side —n. inclination of ship

list'en [lis'ən] vi. try to hear, attend to —**list'ener** n.

list'less a. indifferent, languid —**list'lessly** adv.

lit pt./pp. of LIGHT

lit'any n. prayer with responses from congregation

lit'eral a. according to sense of actual words, not figurative; exact in wording; of letters —**lit'erally** adv.

lit'erate a. able to read and write; educated —n. literate person —**lit'eracy** n. —**litera'ti** [-ah'-] pl.n. scholarly, literary people

lit'erature n. books and writings of a country, period or subject —**lit'erary** a. of or learned in literature —**lit'erarily** adv.

lithe [līTH] a. supple, pliant —**lithe'some** a. lissom, supple

lith'ium n. one of the lightest alkaline metals

lithog'raphy n. method of printing from metal or stone block using the antipathy of grease and water —**lith'ograph** n. print so produced —vt. print thus —**lithog'rapher** n. —**lithograph'ic** a.

lit'igant n./a. (person) conducting a lawsuit —**litiga'tion** n. lawsuit

lit'igate vt. contest in law —vi. carry on a lawsuit —**lit'igant** n./a. (person) conducting a lawsuit —**litiga'tion** n. lawsuit —**liti'gious** [-tij-] a. given to engaging in lawsuits; disputatious

lit'mus n. blue dye turned red by acids and restored to blue by alkali —**litmus paper**

li'totes [lī'tō-tēz] n. ironical understatement for rhetorical effect

li'tre [lē'tər] n. measure of volume of fluid, one cubic decimetre, about 1.75 pints

litt'er n. untidy refuse; odds and ends; young of animal produced at one birth; straw etc. as bedding for animals; portable couch; kind of stretcher for wounded —vt. strew with litter; bring forth

lit'tle a. small, not much (**less, least**) —n. small quantity —adv. slightly

litt'oral a. pert. to the seashore —n. coastal district

lit'urgy n. prescribed form of public worship —**litur'gical** a.

live¹ [liv] v. have life; pass one's life; continue in life; continue, last; dwell; feed —**liv'able** a. suitable for living in; tolerable —**liv'ing** n. action of being in life; people now alive; way of living; means of living; church benefice

live² [līv] a. living, alive, active, vital; flaming; (of rail etc.) carrying electric current; (of broadcast) transmitted during the actual performance —**live'ly** a.

brisk, active, vivid —**live'liness** n. —**li'ven** vt. (esp. with up) make (more) lively —**live-axle** n. driving shaft in car's back axle —**live'stock** n. domestic animals —**live wire** wire carrying electric current; able, very energetic person

live'lihood n. means of living; subsistence, support

live'long [liv-] a. lasting throughout the whole day

liv'er n. organ secreting bile; animal liver as food —**liv'erish** a. unwell, as from liver upset; cross, touchy, irritable

liv'ery n. distinctive dress of person or group, esp. servant(s); allowance of food for horses; US a livery stable —**liv'eryman** n. member of a London guild —**livery stable** where horses are kept at a charge or hired out

liv'id a. of a bluish pale colour; discoloured, as by bruising. inf. angry, furious

liz'ard n. four-footed reptile

LJ Lord Justice

LL Lord Lieutenant

llam'a [lahm'ɔ] n. woolly animal used as beast of burden in S Amer.

LL.B. Bachelor of Laws

loach n. carplike freshwater fish

load n. burden; amount usu. carried at once; actual load carried by vehicle; resistance against which engine has to work; amount of electrical energy drawn from a source —vt. put load on or into; charge (gun); weigh down —**load'ed** a. carrying a load; (of dice) dishonestly weighted; biased; (of question) containing hidden trap or implication; sl. wealthy; sl. drunk

load'star, -stone n. see LODE

loaf [1] n. mass of bread as baked; shaped mass of food (pl. **loaves**)

loaf [2] vi. idle, loiter —**loaf'er** n. idler

loam n. fertile soil

loan n. act of lending; thing lent; money borrowed at interest; permission to use —vt. lend, grant loan of

lo(a)th [-th] a. unwilling, reluctant (to) —**loath'ly** a./adv. —**loathe** [-TH] vt. hate, abhor —**loath'ing** n. disgust; repulsion —**loath'some** a. disgusting

lob n. in tennis etc., shot pitched high in air —v. throw, pitch shot thus (**-bb-**)

lobb'y n. corridor into which rooms open; passage or room in legislative building, esp. houses of parliament of Britain and Aust., to which the public has access; group which tries to influence members of law-making assembly —**lobb'ying** n. frequenting lobby to collect news or influence members

lobe n. any rounded projection; subdivision of body organ; soft, hanging part of ear —**lobed** a. —**lobot'omy** n. surgical incision into lobe of organ, esp. brain

lobe'lia [lō-bē'-] n. garden plant with blue, red or white flowers

lob'ster n. shellfish with long tail and claws, turning red when boiled

lob'worm n. lugworm

lo'cal a. of, existing in particular place; confined to a definite spot, district or part of the body; of place —n. person belonging to a district; (nearby) pub —**lo'cale** [-ahl'] n. scene of event —**local'ity** n. place, situation; district —**lo'calize** vt. assign, restrict to definite place —**lo'cally** adv. —**local anaesthetic** anaesthetic which produces insensibility in one part of body

locate' vt. attribute to a place; find the place of; situate —**loca'-**

tion *n.* placing; situation; site of film production away from studio; **SA** black Afr. or coloured township —**loc'ative** *a./n.* grammatical case denoting "place where"

loch¹ [loн, lok] *n.* Scottish lake or long narrow bay

lock¹ *n.* appliance for fastening door, lid *etc.*; mechanism for firing gun; enclosure in river or canal for moving boats from one level to another; extent to which vehicle's front wheels will turn; appliance to check the revolution of a wheel, interlocking; block, jam —*vt.* fasten, make secure with lock; place in locked container; join firmly; cause to become immovable; embrace closely —*vi.* become fixed or united; become immovable —**lock'er** *n.* small cupboard with lock —**lock'jaw** *n.* tetanus —**lock'nut** *n.* second nut used on top of first on bolt to prevent it shaking loose —**lock'out** *n.* exclusion of workmen by employers as means of coercion —**lock'smith** *n.* one who makes and mends locks —**lock'up** *n.* prison; garage, storage area away from main premises

lock² *n.* tress of hair

lock'et *n.* small hinged pendant for portrait *etc.*

lo'co cita'to *Lat.* at the place quoted (*usu. loc. cit.*)

locomo'tive [lō-] *n.* engine for pulling carriages on railway tracks —*a.* having power of moving from place to place —**loco-mo'tion** *n.* action, power of moving

lo'cum te'nens *Lat.* (*usu. shortened to* **lo'cum**) substitute, *esp.* for doctor or clergyman during absence —**lo'cum te'nency**

lo'cus *n.* exact place or locality; curve made by all points satisfying certain mathematical condition, or by point, line or surface moving under such condition (*pl.* **lo'ci** [-sī])

lo'cust *n.* destructive winged insect —**locust tree** false acacia; the carob —**locust bean** its bean-shaped fruit

locu'tion *n.* a phrase; speech; mode or style of speaking

lode *n.* a vein of ore —**lode'star** *n.* Pole Star —**lode'stone** *n.* magnetic iron ore

lodge *n.* house, cabin used seasonally or occasionally, *eg* for hunting, skiing; gatekeeper's house; meeting place of branch of Freemasons *etc.*; the branch —*vt.* house; deposit; bring (a charge *etc.*) against someone —*vi.* live in another's house at fixed charge; come to rest (in, on) —**lodg'er** *n.* —**lodge(e)'ment, lodg'ment** *n.* lodging, being lodged —**lodg'ings** *pl.n.* rented room(s) in another person's house

loft *n.* space between top storey and roof; gallery in church *etc.* —*vt.* send (golf ball *etc.*) high —**loft'ily** *adv.* haughtily —**loft'iness** *n.* —**loft'y** *a.* of great height; elevated; haughty

log¹ *n.* portion of felled tree stripped of branches; detailed record of voyages, time travelled *etc.* of ship, aircraft *etc.*; apparatus used formerly for measuring ship's speed —*vt.* keep a record of; travel (specified distance, time) (**-gg-**) —**logg'er** *n.* —**log'ging** *n.* **US** cutting and transporting logs to river —**log'book** *n.*

log² *n.* logarithm

lo'ganberry *n.* trailing prickly plant, cross between raspberry and blackberry; its purplish-red fruit

log'arithm [-тнəm] *n.* one of series of arithmetical functions tabulated for use in calculation —**logarith'mic** a.

logg'erhead n. —**at logger-heads** quarrelling, disputing

lo'ggia [lō'jə] n. covered, arcaded gallery (pl. **lo'ggias, lo'gge**)

log'ic [loj'-] n. art or philosophy of reasoning; reasoned thought or argument; coherence of various facts, events etc. —**log'ical** a. of logic; according to reason; reasonable; apt to reason correctly —**log'ically** adv. —**logi'cian** n.

logis'tics pl.n. (with sing. or pl. v.) the transport, housing and feeding of troops; organization of any project, operation —**logis'tical** a.

lo'go n. company emblem or similar device

Log'os n. the Divine Word incarnate, Christ

loin n. part of body between ribs and hip; cut of meat from this —pl. hips and lower abdomen —**loin'cloth** n. garment covering loins only

loi'ter vi. dawdle, hang about; idle —**loi'terer** n.

loll vi. sit, lie lazily; (esp. of the tongue) hang out —vt. hang out (tongue)

loll'ipop n. boiled sweet etc., esp. on small wooden stick

loll'y n. inf. lollipop or ice lolly; sl. money

lone a. solitary —**lone'ly** a. sad because alone; unfrequented; solitary, alone —**lone'liness** n. —**lo'ner** n. inf. one who prefers to be alone —**lone'some** a.

long [1] a. having length, esp. great length, in space or time; extensive; protracted —adv. for a long time —**long'hand** n. writing of words, letters etc. in full —**long'playing** a. (of record) lasting for 10 to 30 minutes

because of its fine grooves —**long-range** a. of the future; able to travel long distances without refuelling; (of weapons) designed to hit distant target —**long shot** competitor, undertaking, bet etc. with small chance of success —**long ton** the imperial ton (2240 lb) —**long-winded** a. tediously loquacious

long [2] vi. have keen desire, yearn (for) —**long'ing** n. yearning

lon'geron [-jər-] n. long spar running fore and aft in body of aircraft

longev'ity [-j-] n. long existence or life —**longe'val** a.

lon'gitude [-j-] n. distance east or west from standard meridian —**longitu'dinal** a. of length or longitude; lengthwise

long'shoreman n. US wharf labourer

loo n. inf. lavatory

loo'fah n. pod of plant used as sponge; the plant

look vi. direct, use eyes; face; seem; search (for); hope (for); (with after) take care of —n. looking; view; search; (oft. pl.) appearance —**good looks** beauty —**look'alike** n. person who is double of another —**looking glass** mirror —**look'out** n. guard; place for watching; prospect; watchman; inf. worry, concern —**look after** tend —**look down on** despise

loom [1] n. machine for weaving; middle part of oar

loom [2] vi. appear dimly; seem ominously close; assume great importance

loon n. inf. stupid, foolish person —**loo'ny** a./n. —**loony bin** inf. mental hospital

loop n. figure made by curved line crossing itself; similar rounded shape in cord or rope etc.

crossed on itself; contraceptive coil; aerial manoeuvre in which aircraft describes complete circle —*v.* form loop —**loop line** *n.* railway line which leaves, then rejoins, main line

loop'hole *n.* means of escape, of evading rule without infringing it; vertical slit in wall, *esp.* for defence

loose *a.* not tight, fastened, fixed, or tense; slack; vague; dissolute —*vt.* free; unfasten; slacken —*vi.* (with off) shoot, let fly —**loose'ly** *adv.* —**loos'en** *vt.* make loose —**loose'ness** *n.* —**on the loose** free; *inf.* on a spree

loot *n./vt.* plunder

lop[1] *vt.* cut away twigs and branches; chop off (-**pp-**)

lop[2] *vi.* hang limply (-**pp-**) —**lop'eared** *a.* having drooping ears —**lop'sided** *a.* with one side lower than the other, badly balanced

lope *vi.* run with long, easy strides

loqua'cious *a.* talkative —**lo-quac'ity** [-kwas'-] *n.*

lo'quat [lō'kwot] *n.* Japanese plum tree; its fruit

lord *n.* British nobleman, peer of the realm; feudal superior; one ruling others; owner; God —*vt.* domineer —**lord'liness** *n.* —**lord'ly** *a.* imperious, proud; fit for a lord —**lord'ship** *n.* rule, ownership; domain; title of some noblemen

lore *n.* learning; body of facts and traditions

lorgnette' [lor-nyet'] *n.* pair of spectacles mounted on long handle

lor'ikeet *n.* small parrot

lor'is *n.* tree-dwelling, nocturnal Asian animal

lorn *a. poet.* abandoned; desolate

lor'ry *n.* motor vehicle for transporting loads by road, truck

lose [lōōz] *vt.* be deprived of, fail to retain or use; let slip; fail to get; (of clock *etc.*) run slow (by specified amount); be defeated in —*vi.* suffer loss (**lost** *pt./pp.* —**los'ing** [lōōz'ing] *pr.p.*) —**loss** *n.* a losing; what is lost; harm or damage resulting from losing —**lost** *a.* unable to be found; unable to find one's way; bewildered; not won; not utilized

lot *pron.* great number —*n.* collection; large quantity; share; fate; destiny; item at auction; one of a set of objects used to decide something by chance, as in **to cast lots**; area of land —*pl. inf.* great numbers or quantity —*adv. inf.* a great deal

loth *see* LOATH

lo'tion *n.* liquid for washing wounds, improving skin *etc.*

lott'ery *n.* method of raising funds by selling tickets and prizes by chance; gamble

lott'o *n.* game of chance like bingo

lo'tus *n.* legendary plant whose fruits induce forgetfulness when eaten; Egyptian water lily —**lo-tus position** seated cross-legged position used in yoga *etc.*

loud *a.* strongly audible; noisy; obtrusive —**loud'ly** *adv.* —**loud-speak'er** *n.* instrument for converting electrical signals into sound audible at a distance

lough [loH, lok] *n.* in Ireland, loch

lounge *vi.* sit, lie, walk, or stand in a relaxed manner —*n.* living room of house; general waiting, relaxing area in airport, hotel *etc.* —**loung'er** *n.* loafer —**lounge suit** man's suit for daytime wear

lour *see* LOWER

lour'ie *n.* S Afr. bird with bright plumage

louse [lows] *n.* a parasitic insect

(*pl.* **lice**) —**lous'y** [-z'-] *a.* nasty, unpleasant; *sl.* (too) generously provided, thickly populated (with); *sl.* bad, poor; having lice

lout *n.* crude, oafish person —**lout'ish** *a.*

lou'vre [lōō'vər] *n.* one of a set of boards or slats set parallel and slanted to admit air but not rain; ventilating structure of these

love [luv] *n.* warm affection; benevolence; charity; sexual passion; sweetheart; *Tennis etc.* score of nothing —*vt.* admire passionately; delight in —*vi.* be in love —**lov'(e)able** *a.* —**love'less** *a.* —**love'lorn** *a.* forsaken by, pining for a lover —**love'liness** *n.* —**love'ly** *a.* beautiful, delightful —**lov'er** *n.* —**lov'ing** *a.* affectionate; tender —**lov'ingly** *adv.* —**love'bird** *n.* small parrot —**love-in-a-mist** *n.* plant with pale-blue flowers —**love letter** *n.* —**love-lies-bleeding** *n.* plant with long, drooping red flowers —**loving cup** bowl formerly passed round at banquet —**make love (to)** have sexual intercourse (with)

low¹ [lō] *a.* not tall, high or elevated; humble; commonplace; coarse, vulgar; dejected; ill; not loud; moderate; cheap —**low'er** *vt.* cause, allow to descend; move down; diminish, degrade —*a.* below in position or rank; at an early stage, period of development —**low'liness** *n.* —**low'ly** *a.* modest, humble —**low'brow** *n.* one with no intellectual or cultural interests —*a.* —**Low Church** section of Anglican Church stressing evangelical beliefs and practices —**low'down** *n. inf.* inside information —**low-down** *a. inf.* mean, shabby, dishonourable —**low frequency** in electricity any frequency of alternating current from about 30 to 10,000

cycles; frequency within audible range —**low-key** *a.* subdued, restrained, not intense —**low'land** *n.* low-lying country —**Low'lands** *pl.n.* less mountainous parts of Scotland —**Low'lander** *n.* —**low-tension** *a.* carrying, operating at low voltage

low² [lō] *vi.* of cattle, utter their cry, bellow —*n.* cry of cattle, bellow

low'er, lour [low'ər] *vi.* look gloomy or threatening, as sky; scowl —*n.* scowl, frown

loy'al *a.* faithful, true to allegiance —**loy'alist** *n.* —**loy'ally** *adv.* —**loy'alty** *n.*

loz'enge *n.* small sweet or tablet of medicine; rhombus, diamond figure

LP long-playing (record)

LPG liquefied petroleum gas

L-plate *n.* sign on car driven by learner driver

LSD lysergic acid diethylamide (hallucinogenic drug); librae, solidi, denarii (*Lat.*, pounds, shillings, pence)

Lt. Lieutenant

Ltd. Limited (Liability)

lubb'er *n.* clumsy fellow; unskilled seaman

lu'bricate [lōō'-] *vt.* oil, grease; make slippery —**lu'bricant** *n.* substance used for this —**lubrica'tion** *n.* —**lu'bricator** *n.* —**lubric'ity** [-bris'-] *n.* slipperiness, smoothness; lewdness

lu'cent [lōō'-] *a.* bright, shining

lucerne¹ [lōō'-] *n.* fodder plant like clover, alfalfa

lu'cid [lōō'sid] *a.* clear; easily understood; sane —**lucid'ity, lu'cidness** *n.* —**lu'cidly** *adv.*

Lu'cifer [lōō'-] *n.* Satan; Venus as the morning star; *obs.* match

luck *n.* fortune, good or bad; good fortune; chance —**luck'ily** *adv.* fortunately —**luck'less** *a.*

having bad luck —**luck'y** a. having good luck

lu'cre [lōō'kər] n. (usu. facetious) money, wealth —**lu'crative** a. very profitable —**filthy lucre** inf. money

lu'dicrous [lōō'-] a. absurd, laughable, ridiculous

lu'do [lōō'-] n. game played with dice and counters on board

luff n. the part of fore-and-aft sail nearest mast —v. sail (ship) into wind so that sails flap; (of sails) flap

lug [1] vt. drag with effort —vi. pull hard ('**-gg-**')

lug [2] n. projection, tag serving as handle or support; inf. ear

lugg'age n. traveller's trunks and other baggage

lugg'er n. working boat (eg fishing, prawning lugger) orig. fitted with lugsail

lug'sail n. oblong sail fixed on yard which hangs slanting on mast

lugu'brious [lōō-gōō'-] a. mournful, doleful, gloomy —**lugu'briously** adv.

lug'worm n. large worm used as bait, lobworm

luke'warm [lōōk'-] a. moderately warm, tepid; indifferent

lull vt. soothe, sing to sleep; make quiet —vi. become quiet, subside —n. brief time of quiet in storm etc. —**lull'aby** [-bī] n. lulling song, esp. for children

lum'bar a. relating to body between lower ribs and hips —**lumba'go** n. rheumatism in the lower part of the back

lum'ber n. disused articles, useless rubbish; sawn timber —vi. move heavily —vt. inf. burden with something unpleasant —**lum'berjack** n. **US**, **C** man who fells trees and prepares logs for transport to mill

lu'men n. SI unit of luminous

flux (pl. **-mens**, **-mina**)

lu'minous [lōō'-] a. bright; shedding light; glowing; lucid —**lu'minary** n. learned person; heavenly body giving light —**lumines'cence** n. emission of light at low temperatures by process (eg chemical) not involving burning —**luminos'ity** n.

lump n. shapeless piece or mass; swelling; large sum —vt. throw together in one mass or sum —vi. move heavily —**lump'ish** a. clumsy; stupid —**lump'y** a. full of lumps; uneven —**lump it** inf. put up with

lu'nar [lōō'-] a. relating to the moon

lu'natic [lōō'-] a. insane —n. insane person —**lu'nacy** n. —**lunatic fringe** extreme, radical section of group etc.

lunch n. meal taken in the middle of the day —v. eat, entertain to lunch —**lunch'eon** [-shən] n. a lunch

lung n. one of the two organs of respiration in vertebrates —**lung'fish** n. type of fish with air-breathing lung —**lung'worm** n. parasitic worm infesting lungs of some animals —**lung'wort** n. flowering plant

lunge vi. thrust with sword etc. —n. such thrust; sudden movement of body, plunge

lu'pin [lōō'-] n. leguminous plant with tall spikes of flowers

lu'pine [lōō'-] a. like a wolf

lu'pus [lōō'-] n. skin disease

lurch n. sudden roll to one side —vi. stagger —**leave in the lurch** leave in difficulties

lurch'er n. crossbred dog trained to hunt silently

lure [lyōōr] n. something which entices; bait; power to attract —vt. entice; attract

lu'rid a. vivid in shocking detail, sensational; pale, wan; lit with unnatural glare —**lu'ridly** adv.

lurk vi. lie hidden —**lurk'ing** a. (of suspicion) not definite

lus'cious [-shəs] a. sweet, juicy; extremely pleasurable or attractive

lush[1] a. (of grass etc.) luxuriant and juicy, fresh

lush[2] n. US sl. heavy drinker; alcoholic —**lush'y** a.

lust n. strong desire for sexual gratification; any strong desire —vi. have passionate desire —**lust'ful** a. —**lust'ily** adv. —**lust'y** a. vigorous, healthy

lustra'tion n. purification by sacrifice —**lus'trate** vt. —**lus'tral** a. used in lustration

lus'tre n. gloss, sheen; splendour; renown; glory; glossy material; metallic pottery glaze —**lus'trous** a. shining, luminous

lute[1] [loot] n. old stringed musical instrument played with the fingers —**lu'tenist, lu'tist** n.

lute[2], [loot] n. composition to make joints airtight (also **lu'ting**) —vt. close with lute

lux n. SI unit of illumination (pl. **lux**)

lux'ury n. possession and use of costly, choice things for enjoyment; enjoyable but not necessary thing; comfortable surroundings —**luxu'riance** n. abundance, proliferation —**luxu'riant** a. growing thickly; abundant —**luxu'riantly** adv. —**luxu'riate** vi. indulge in luxury; flourish profusely; take delight (in) —**luxu'rious** a. fond of luxury; self-indulgent; sumptuous —**luxu'riously** adv.

lyce'um [lī-sē'-] n. public building for concerts etc.

lych'gate see LICHGATE

lyd'dite n. powerful explosive used in shells

lye n. water made alkaline with wood ashes etc. for washing

ly'ing pr.p. of LIE

lymph n. colourless bodily fluid, mainly of white blood cells —**lymphat'ic** a. of lymph; flabby, sluggish —n. vessel in the body conveying lymph

lynch vt. put to death without trial —**lynch law** procedure of self-appointed court trying and executing accused

lynx n. animal of cat family

lyre [līr] n instrument like harp —**lyr'ic(al)** [lir'-] a. of short personal poems expressing emotion; of lyre; meant to be sung —**lyr'ic** n. lyric poem —pl. words of popular song —**lyr'icist** n. —**lyr'ist** n. [līr'-] lyric poet; [lī'-] player on lyre —**lyre'bird** n. Aust. bird, the male of which displays tail shaped like a lyre —**wax lyrical** express great enthusiasm

M

M Medieval; Monsieur; Motorway

m metre(s)

m. male; married; masculine; mile; minute

MA Master of Arts

macab're [-kahb'ər] a. gruesome, ghastly

macad'am n. road surface made of pressed layers of small broken stones —**macad'amize** vt. pave road with this

macaro'ni n. pasta in long, thin tubes (pl. **-ni(e)s**)

macaroon' n. small cake, biscuit containing almonds

macaw' n. kind of parrot

mace[1] n. staff with metal head; staff of office

mace[2] n. spice made of the husk of the nutmeg

mac'erate [mas'-] vt. soften by

soaking; cause to waste away —**macera'tion** n.

Mach (number) [mah, mak] n. the ratio of the air speed of an aircraft to the velocity of sound under given conditions

machet'e [mə-shet'i] n. broad, heavy knife used for cutting or as a weapon

Machiavell'ian [mak-] a. politically unprincipled, crafty, perfidious, subtle, deep-laid

machina'tion [-kin-] n. (usu. pl.) plotting, intrigue —**mach'inate** vi. lay, devise plots; conspire

machine' [-shēn'] n. apparatus combining action of several parts to apply mechanical force; controlling organization; mechanical appliance; vehicle —vt. sew, print, shape etc. with machine —**machin'ery** n. parts of machine collectively; machines —**machin'ist** n. one who makes or works machines —**machine gun** gun firing repeatedly and continuously with an automatic loading and firing mechanism

machis'mo [-kiz-] n. strong or exaggerated masculine pride or masculinity —**mach'o** [-chō] a. denoting or exhibiting such pride in masculinity —n. (pl. -**os**)

mack'erel n. edible sea fish with blue and silver stripes

mack'intosh n. waterproof raincoat of rubberized cloth; any raincoat

macram'é [-krahm'i] n. ornamental work of knotted cord

macrobiot'ics pl.n. (with sing. v.) dietary system advocating grain and vegetables grown without chemical additives

mac'rocosm n. the universe; any large, complete system

mad a. suffering from mental disease, insane; wildly foolish; very enthusiastic (about); excited; inf. furious, angry —**madd'en** vt. make mad —**mad'ly** adv. —**mad'man** n. —**mad'ness** n. insanity; folly

mad'am n. polite form of address to a woman; inf. precocious or conceited girl

mad'cap n. reckless person —a.

madd'er n. climbing plant; its root; red dye made from this

made pt./pp. of MAKE

Madeir'a [-dēr'ə] n. rich sherry wine —**Madeira cake** rich sponge cake

Madonn'a n. the Virgin Mary; picture or statue of her

madrepore' n. kind of coral

mad'rigal n. unaccompanied part song; short love poem or song

mael'strom [māl'-] n. great whirlpool; turmoil

mae'nad [mē'-] n. Class. Literature frenzied female worshipper of Dionysus

maesto'so [mī-stō'zō] adv. Mus. grandly, in majestic manner

mae'stro [mī'-] n. outstanding musician, conductor; man regarded as master of any art

Mae West [mā] sl. inflatable life jacket

Maf'ia n. international secret criminal organization, orig. Italian

magazine' [-zēn'] n. periodical publication with stories and articles by different writers; appliance for supplying cartridges automatically to gun; storehouse for explosives or arms

magen'ta [-j-] a./n. (of) deep purplish-red colour

magg'ot n. grub, larva —**mag'goty** a. infested with maggots

Ma'gi [mā'jī] pl.n. priests of ancient Persia; the wise men from the East at the Nativity

mag'ic [-j'-] n. art of supposedly

mag'istrate [maj'-] *n.* civil officer administering law; justice of the peace —**magiste'rial** *a.* of, referring to magistrate; dictatorial —**mag'istracy** *n.* office of magistrate; magistrates collectively

mag'ma *n.* paste, suspension; molten rock inside earth's crust

magnan'imous *a.* noble, generous, not petty —**magnanim'ity** *n.*

mag'nate *n.* influential or wealthy person

magne'sium *n.* metallic element —**magne'sia** *n.* white powder compound of this used in medicine

mag'net *n.* piece of iron, steel having properties of attracting iron, steel and pointing north and south when suspended; lodestone —**magnet'ic** *a.* with properties of magnet; exerting powerful attraction —**magnet'ically** *adv.* —**mag'netism** *n.* magnetic phenomena; science of this; personal charm or power of attracting others —**magnetiza'tion** *n.* —**mag'netize** *vt.* make into a magnet; attract as if by magnet; fascinate —**magne'to** *n.* apparatus for ignition in internal combustion engine (*pl.* **-tos**) —**magnetom'eter** *n.* instrument used to measure magnetic force —**magnetic tape** long coated plastic strip for recording sound or video signals

Magnif'icat *n.* hymn of Virgin Mary in *Luke* 1. 46-55, used as canticle

magnif'icent *a.* splendid; stately, imposing; excellent —**magnif'icence** *n.* —**magnif'icently** *adv.*

mag'nify [-ft] *vt.* increase apparent size of, as with lens; exaggerate; make greater (**-fied, -fying**) —**magnifica'tion** *n.*

magnil'oquent *a.* speaking pompously; grandiose —**magnil'oquence** *n.*

mag'nitude *n.* importance; greatness, size

magno'lia *n.* shrub or tree with large white, sweet-scented flowers

mag'num *n.* large wine bottle (approx. 52 fluid ounces)

mag'pie *n.* black-and-white bird

Mag'yar *n.* member of prevailing race in Hungary; native speech of Hungary —*a.* pert. to Magyars; *Dressmaking* cut with sleeves and bodice of garment in one piece

mahara'jah [mah-ə-rah'-] *n.* former title of some Indian princes (**mahara'nee** *fem.*)

mahari'shi [mah-hah-rē'-] *n.* Hindu religious teacher or mystic

mahat'ma *n. Hinduism* man of saintly life with supernatural powers; one endowed with great wisdom and power

mahjong(g)' *n.* Chinese table game for four, played with pieces called tiles

mahl'stick *n. see* MAULSTICK

mahog'any *n.* tree yielding reddish brown wood

maid'en *n. Literary* young unmarried woman *a.* unmarried; of, suited to maiden; first; having blank record —**maid** *n. Literary* young unmarried woman; woman servant —**maid'enly** *a.* modest —**maid'enhair** *n.* fern with

delicate stalks and fronds
—**maid'enhead** n. virginity
—**maid'enhood** n. —**maiden
name** woman's surname before
marriage —**maiden over** Cricket
over in which no runs are scored

mail[1] n. letters etc. transported
and delivered by the post office;
letters etc. conveyed at one time;
the postal system; train, ship etc.
carrying mail —vt. send by post
—**mail order** referring to goods
ordered through post

mail[1] n. armour of interlaced
rings or overlapping plates
—**mailed** a. covered with mail

maim vt. cripple, mutilate

main a. chief, principal, leading
—n. principal pipe, line carrying
water, electricity etc.; chief part;
strength, power; obs. open sea
—**main'ly** adv. for the most part,
chiefly —**main force** physical
strength —**main'frame** Computers a. denoting a high-speed
general-purpose computer —n.
such a computer; the central
processing unit of a computer
—**main'land** n. stretch of land
which forms main part of a
country —**main'mast** n. chief
mast in ship —**main'sail** n. lowest sail of mainmast —**main'-
spring** n. chief spring of watch or
clock; chief cause or motive
—**main'stay** n. rope from mainmast; chief support

maintain' vt. carry on; preserve; support; sustain; keep up;
keep supplied; affirm; support by
argument; defend —**maintain'-
able** a. —**main'tenance** n. maintaining; means of support; upkeep of buildings etc.; provision
of money for separated or divorced spouse

maisonette' [mā-zon-et'] n.
part of house usu. on two floors
fitted as self-contained dwelling

maître d'hôtel' [met-rə

dō-tel'] Fr. restaurant manager

maize n. type of corn

maj'esty n. stateliness; sovereignty; grandeur —**majes'tic** a.
splendid; regal —**majes'tically**
adv.

ma'jor n. army officer ranking
next above captain; scale in music; US principal field of study at
university etc. (also vi.); person
of legal majority —a. greater in
number, quality, extent; significant, serious —**major'ity** n.
greater number; larger party
voting together; excess of the
vote on one side; coming of age;
rank of major —**major-do'mo** n.
house-steward (pl. **-s**)

make vt. construct; produce;
create; establish; appoint;
amount to; cause to do something; accomplish; reach; earn
—vi. tend; contribute (**made,
ma'king**) —n. brand, type, or
style —**ma'king** n. creation —pl.
necessary requirements or qualities —**make'shift** n. temporary
expedient —**make-up** n. cosmetics; characteristics; layout
—**make'weight** n. trifle added to
make something stronger or better —**make up** compose; compile; complete; compensate; apply cosmetics; invent —**on the
make** inf. intent on gain

mak'o [mahk'ō] n. type of shark

mal-, male- (comb. form) ill,
badly, as in **malforma'tion** n.,
malfunc'tion n./vi.

malacc'a n. brown cane used
for walking-stick

mal'achite [-kīt] n. green mineral

maladjust'ed a. Psychol. unable to meet the demands of
society; badly adjusted —**maladjust'ment** n.

maladministra'tion n. inefficient or dishonest administra-

maladroit' a. clumsy, awkward

mal'ady n. disease

malaise' [-āz'] n. vague, unlocated feeling of bodily discomfort

mal'apropism n. ludicrous misuse of word

malapropos' [-pō'] a./adv. inappropriate(ly)

mala'ria n. infectious disease caused by bite of some mosquitoes —**mala'rial** a.

Malay' n. native of Malaysia or Indonesia; language of this people —**Malay'an** a./n.

mal'content a. actively discontented —n. malcontent person

male a. of sex producing gametes which fertilize female gametes; of men or male animals —n. male person or animal

malediction n. curse

mal'efactor n. criminal

malef'icent a. harmful, hurtful —**malef'icence** n.

malev'olent a. full of ill will —**malev'olence** n.

malfea'sance [-fē'z-] n. illegal action; official misconduct —**malfea'sant** a./n.

mal'ice n. ill will; spite —**mali'cious** a. intending evil or unkindness; spiteful; moved by hatred —**mali'ciously** adv.

malign' [-līn'] a. evil in influence or effect —vt. slander, misrepresent —**malig'nancy** n. —**malig'nant** a. feeling extreme ill will; (of disease) resistant to therapy —**malig'nantly** adv. —**malig'nity** n. malignant disposition

maling'er [-ng'g-] vi. feign illness to escape duty —**malin'gerer** n.

mall [mawl, mal] n. level, shaded walk; street, shopping area closed to vehicles

mall'ard n. wild duck

mall'eable a. capable of being hammered into shape; adaptable —**malleabil'ity** n.

mall'et n. (wooden) hammer; croquet or polo stick

mall'ow n. wild plant with purple flowers

malm'sey [mahm'zi] n. strong sweet wine

malnutri'tion [-trish'-] n. inadequate nutrition

malo'dorous a. evil-smelling

malprac'tice n. immoral, illegal or unethical conduct

malt [mawlt] n. grain used for brewing —vt. make into malt —**malt'ster** n. maker of malt

maltreat' vt. treat badly, handle roughly —**maltreat'ment** n.

mam'ba n. deadly S Afr. snake

mam'bo n. Latin Amer. dance like rumba

mamm'al n. animal of type that suckles its young —**mamma'lian** a.

mamm'ary a. of, relating to breast or milk-producing gland

mamm'on n. wealth regarded as source of evil; (M-) false god of covetousness —**mamm'onism** n. —**mamm'onist** n.

mamm'oth n. extinct animal like an elephant —a. colossal

man n. human being; person; human race; adult male; **SA** sl. any person; manservant; piece used in chess etc. (pl. **men**) —vt. supply (ship etc.) with necessary men; fortify (-**nn**-) —**man'ful** a. brave, vigorous —**man'fully** adv. —**man'like** a. —**man'liness** n. —**man'ly** a. —**mann'ish** a. like a man —**man'handle** vt. treat roughly —**man'hole** n. opening through which man may pass to a drain, sewer etc. —**man'hood** n. —**mankind'** n. human beings in general —**man(n)'ikin** n. little man; model of human body; lay figure —**man'power** n. power of human effort; available number of workers —**man'slaughter** n. culpable homicide without malice aforethought

man'acle n. fetter, handcuff —vt. shackle

man'age vt. be in charge of, administer; succeed in doing; control; handle, cope with; conduct, carry on; persuade —**man'ageable** a. —**man'agement** n. those who manage, as board of directors etc.; administration; skilful use of means; conduct —**man'ager** n. (**manageress'** fem.) one in charge of business, institution, actor etc.; one who manages efficiently —**manage'rial** a. —**man'aging** a. having administrative control

manatee' n. large, plant-eating aquatic mammal

man'ciple n. steward who buys provisions for college etc.

manda'mus n. writ from superior court to inferior, conveying order

man'darin n. Hist. Chinese high-ranking bureaucrat; fig. any high government official; Chinese variety of orange

man'date n. command of, or commission to act for, another; commission from United Nations to govern a territory; instruction from electorate to representative or government —**man'dated** a. committed to a mandate —**man'datory, -tary** n. holder of a mandate —**man'datory** a. compulsory

man'dible n. lower jawbone; either part of bird's beak —**mandib'ular** a. of, like mandible

man'dolin(e) n. stringed musical instrument

man'drake, mandrag'ora n. narcotic plant

man'drel n. axis on which material is supported in a lathe; rod

round which metal is cast or forged

man'drill n. large blue-faced baboon

mane n. long hair on neck of horse, lion etc. —**maned** a.

man'ganese [-ng'g-] n. metallic element; black oxide of this

mange [mānj] n. skin disease of dogs etc. —**ma'ngy** a. scruffy, shabby

man'gelwurzel [mang'gəl-] n. variety of beet used as cattle food: also **man'goldwurzel**

man'ger [mān'jər] n. eating trough in stable

man'gle [mang'gəl] n. machine for rolling clothes etc. to remove water —vt. press in mangle

man'gle [mang'gəl] vt. mutilate, spoil, hack

man'go [-ng'gō] n. tropical fruit; tree bearing it (pl. **-go(e)s**)

man'grove n. tropical tree which grows on muddy banks of estuaries

ma'nia n. madness; prevailing craze —**ma'niac, mani'acal, man'ic** a. affected by mania —**ma'niac** inf. n. mad person; crazy enthusiast

man'icure n. treatment and care of fingernails and hands —vt. apply such treatment —**man'icurist** n. one doing this professionally

man'ifest a. clearly revealed, visible, undoubted —vt. make manifest —n. list of cargo for customs —**manifesta'tion** n. —**man'ifestly** adv. clearly —**manifes'to** n. declaration of policy by political party, government, or movement (pl. **-to(e)s**)

man'ifold a. numerous and varied —n. in internal combustion engine, pipe with several outlets —vt. make copies of (document)

man(n)ikin *see* MAN

manil(l)'a *n.* fibre used for ropes; tough paper

manip'ulate *vt.* handle; deal with skilfully; manage; falsify —**manipula'tion** *n.* act of manipulating, working by hand; skilled use of hands —**manip'ulative** *a.* —**manip'ulator** *n.*

man'ito(u) *n.* spirit of good or evil among Amer. Indians

man'na *n.* food of Israelites in the wilderness; nourishment

mann'equin [-i-kin] *n.* woman who models clothes, *esp.* at fashion shows

mann'er *n.* way thing happens or is done; sort, kind; custom; style —*pl.* social behaviour —**man'nerism** *n.* person's distinctive habit, trait —**mann'erly** *a.* polite

manoeu'vre [-ōō'vər] *n.* contrived, complicated, perhaps deceptive plan or action; skilful management —*v.* employ stratagems, work skilfully; (cause to) perform manoeuvres

manom'eter *n.* gauge of gas pressure

man'or *n. Hist.* land belonging to a lord; feudal unit of land —**mano'rial** *a.* —**manor house** residence of lord of manor

man'sard roof roof with break in its slope, lower part being steeper than upper

manse *n.* house of minister in some religious denominations

man'sion *n.* large house

man'tel *n.* structure round fireplace —**mantel shelf, man'telpiece** *n.* shelf at top of mantel

mantill'a *n.* in Spain, (lace) scarf worn as headdress

man'tis *n.* genus of insects including the stick-insects and leaf insects (*pl.* **man'tes** [-tēz])

man'tle *n.* loose cloak; covering; incandescent gauze round gas jet —*vt.* cover; conceal

man'ual *a.* of, or done with, the hands; by human labour, not automatic —*n.* handbook; textbook; organ keyboard

manufac'ture *vt.* process, make (materials) into finished articles; produce (articles); invent, concoct —*n.* making of articles, materials, *esp.* in large quantities; anything produced from raw materials —**manufac'turer** *n.* owner of factory

manumit' *vt.* free from slavery (-tt-) —**manumiss'ion** *n.*

manure' *vt.* enrich land —*n.* dung or chemical fertilizer used to enrich land

man'uscript *n.* book, document, written by hand; copy for printing —*a.* handwritten

Manx *a.* of Isle of Man —*n.* Manx language —**Manx'man** *n.* —**Manx** cat tailless breed of cat

man'y [men'i] *a.* numerous (**more** *comp.,* **most** *sup.*) —*n.* large number

Mao'ism [mow'-] *n.* form of Marxism advanced by Mao Tse-Tung in China —**Mao'ist** *n./a.*

Mao'ri [mow'ri] *n.* New Zealand native race; their language

map *n.* flat representation of the earth or some part of it, or of the heavens —*vt.* make a map of, (*with* out) plan (-pp-)

ma'ple *n.* tree of the sycamore family, a variety of which yields sugar

ma'quis [ma'kē] *n.* scrubby undergrowth of Mediterranean countries; name adopted by French underground resistance movement in WWII

mar *vt.* spoil, impair (-rr-)

Mar. March

mar'abou [ma-] *n.* kind of stork; its soft white lower tail feathers, used to trim hats *etc.*; kind of silk

marac'a [-ak'-] *n.* percussion instrument of gourd containing dried seeds *etc.*

maraschi'no [mar-ə-skē'-] *n.* liqueur made from cherries

mar'athon [ma-] *n.* long-distance race; endurance contest

maraud' *v.* make raid for plunder; pillage —**maraud'er** *n.*

mar'ble *n.* kind of limestone capable of taking polish; slab of, sculpture in this; small ball used in children's game —**mar'bled** *a.* having mottled appearance, like marble —**mar'bly** *a.*

March *n.* third month

march[1] *vi.* walk with military step; go, progress —*vt.* cause to march —*n.* action of marching; distance marched in day; tune to accompany marching

march[2] *n.* border or frontier —*vi.* border

mar'chioness [-shən-] *n.* wife, widow of marquis

Mar'di Gras' [-grah'] *n.* festival of Shrove Tuesday; revelry celebrating this

mare *n.* female horse —**mare's nest** supposed discovery which proves worthless

mar'garine [-j-, -g-] *n.* butter substitute made from vegetable fats (*inf.* **marge** [-j])

mar'gin [-j-] *n.* border, edge; space round printed page; amount allowed beyond what is necessary —**mar'ginal** *a.*

marguerite' [-ēt'] *n.* large daisy

mar'igold [ma-] *n.* plant with yellow flowers

marijua'na, marihua'na [mar-i-hwah'nə] *n.* dried flowers and leaves of hemp plant, used as narcotic

mari'na [-rē'-] *n.* mooring facility for yachts and pleasure boats

marinade' *n.* seasoned, flavoured liquid used to soak fish, meat *etc.* before cooking —**mar'inate** *vt.*

marine' [-ēn'] *a.* of the sea or shipping; used at, found in sea —*n.* shipping, fleet; soldier trained for land or sea combat —**mar'iner** *n.* sailor

marionette' [ma-] *n.* puppet worked with strings

mar'ital [ma'-] *a.* relating to a husband or to marriage

mar'itime [ma'-] *a.* connected with seafaring; naval; bordering on the sea

mar'joram *n.* aromatic herb

mark[1] *n.* line, dot, scar *etc.*; sign, token; inscription; letter, number showing evaluation of schoolwork *etc.*; indication; target —*vt.* make a mark on; be distinguishing mark of; indicate; notice; watch; assess, *eg* examination paper; stay close to sporting opponent to hamper his play —*vi.* take notice —**mark'er** *n.* one who, that which keeps score at games; counter used at card playing *etc.* —**marks'man** *n.* skilled shot

mark[2] *n.* German coin

mark'et *n.* assembly, place for buying and selling; demand for goods; centre for trade —*vt.* offer or produce for sale —**mark'etable** *a.*

marl *n.* clayey soil used as fertilizer —*vt.* fertilize with it

mar'line [-in] *n.* two-strand cord —**mar'linespike** *n.* pointed hook *esp.* for unravelling rope to be spliced

mar'malade *n.* preserve usually made of oranges, lemons *etc.*

marmor'eal *a.* of or like marble

mar'moset *n.* small bushy-tailed monkey

mar'mot *n.* burrowing rodent

maroon[1] *n.* brownish-crimson; firework —*a.* of the colour

maroon[1,2] *vt.* leave (person) on deserted island or coast; isolate, cut off by any means

marquee[-kē'] *n.* large tent

mar'quetry [-kit-] *n.* inlaid work, wood mosaic

mar'quis, -quess *n.* nobleman of rank below duke —**mar'quisate** *n.*

marr'am grass various grasses that grow on sandy shores

marr'ow [-rō] *n.* fatty substance inside bones; vital part; vegetable marrow —**marr'owy** *a.* —**marr'owfat** *n.* large pea

marr'y *v.* join as husband and wife; unite closely (**married, marr'ying**) —**marr'iage** [-ij] *n.* state of being married; wedding —**marr'iageable** *a.*

Mars *n.* Roman god of war; planet nearest but one to earth —**Mar'tian** *n.* supposed inhabitant of Mars —*a.* of Mars

Marsal'a [-sahl'-] *n.* a sweet wine

Marseillaise[1] [mah-sā-yāz'] *n.* the French national anthem

marsh *n.* low-lying wet land —**marsh'y** *a.* —**marshmall'ow** *n.* spongy sweet orig. made from root of **marsh mallow**, shrubby plant growing near marshes

mar'shal *n.* high officer of state; **US** law enforcement officer —**field marshal** military officer of the highest rank (**air marshal** in RAF) —*vt.* arrange in due order; conduct with ceremony —**marshalling yard** railway depot for goods trains

marsu'pial *n.* animal that carries its young in pouch, *eg* kangaroo —*a.*

mart *n.* place of trade; market

martell'o tow'er round fort, for coast defence

mar'ten *n.* weasellike animal; its fur

mar'tial [-shəl] *a.* relating to war; warlike, brave —**court martial** *see* COURT —**martial law** law enforced by military authorities in times of danger or emergency

mar'tin *n.* species of swallow

martinet' *n.* strict disciplinarian —**martinet'ish** *a.*

mar'tingale [-ng-g-] *n.* strap to prevent horse from throwing up its head

marti'ni [-tē'-] *n.* cocktail containing *esp.* vermouth, gin, bitters; (**M-**) **R** Italian vermouth

Mar'tinmas *n.* feast of St. Martin, 11th November

mart'let *n. Heraldry* bird without feet

mar'tyr [-tər] *n.* one put to death for his beliefs; one who suffers in some cause; one in constant suffering —*vt.* make martyr of —**mar'tyrdom** *n.* —**martyrol'ogy** *n.* list, history of Christian martyrs

mar'vel *vi.* wonder (**-ll-**) —*n.* wonderful thing —**mar'vellous** *a.* amazing; wonderful

Marx'ism [marks'izm] *n.* state socialism as conceived by Karl Marx —**Marx'ian** *a.* —**Marx'ist** *n./a.*

mar'zipan *n.* paste of almonds, sugar *etc.* used in sweets, cakes *etc.*

masc. masculine

mascar'a *n.* cosmetic for darkening eyelashes

mas'cot *n.* thing supposed to bring luck

mas'culine [-lin] *a.* relating to males; manly; of the grammatical gender to which names of males belong

mash *n.* meal mixed with warm water; warm food for horses *etc.*; *inf.* mashed potatoes —*vt.* make into a mash; crush into soft mass or pulp

mash'ie *n. Golf* iron club with

deep sloping blade for lob shots

mask [-ah-] *n.* covering for face; *Surgery* covering for nose and mouth; disguise, pretence —*vt.* cover with mask; hide, disguise

mas'ochism [-kizm] *n.* abnormal condition where pleasure (*esp.* sexual) is derived from pain, humiliation *etc.* —**mas'ochist** *n.* —**masochis'tic** *a.*

ma'son *n.* worker in stone; (M-) Freemason —**Mason'ic** *a.* of Freemasonry —**ma'sonry** *n.* stonework; (M-) Freemasonry

masque [mahsk] *n. Hist.* form of theatrical performance —**masquerade'** *n.* masked ball —*vi.* appear in disguise

Mass *n.* service of the Eucharist, *esp.* in R.C. Church

mass *n.* quantity of matter; dense collection of this; large quantity or number —*v.* form into a mass —**mass've** *a.* large and heavy —**mass'y** *a.* solid, weighty —**mass-produce** *vt.* produce standardized articles in large quantities —**mass produc'tion** —**the masses** the populace

mass'acre [-kǝr] *n.* indiscriminate, large-scale killing, *esp.* of unresisting people —*vt.* kill indiscriminately

mass'age [-ahzh] *n.* rubbing and kneading of muscles *etc.* as curative treatment —*vt.* apply this treatment to —**masseur'** *n.* one who practises massage (**masseuse'** *fem.*)

massé' [-sā'] *n. Billiards* stroke with cue upright

mas'sif [-sēf] *n.* compact group of mountains

mast [-ah-] *n.* pole for supporting ship's sails; tall upright support for aerial *etc.*

mast *n.* fruit of beech, oak *etc.* used as pig fodder

mastec'tomy *n.* surgical removal of a breast

mas'ter [mah'-] *n.* one in control; employer; head of household; owner; document *etc.* from which copies are made; captain of merchant ship; expert; great artist; teacher —*vt.* overcome; acquire knowledge of or skill in —**mas'terful** *a.* imperious, domineering —**mas'terly** *a.* showing great competence —**mas'tery** *n.* full understanding (of); expertise; authority; victory —**master key** one that opens many different locks —**mas'termind** *vt.* plan, direct —*n.* —**mas'terpiece** *n.* outstanding work

mas'tic *n.* gum got from certain trees; puttylike substance

mas'ticate *vt.* chew —**mastica'tion** *n.* —**mas'ticatory** *a.*

mas'tiff *n.* large dog

mas'toid *a.* nipple-shaped —*n.* prominence on bone behind human ear —**mastoidi'tis** *n.* inflammation of this area

mas'turbate *v.* stimulate (one's own) genital organs —**masturba'tion** *n.*

mat *n.* small rug; piece of fabric to protect another surface or to wipe feet on *etc.*; thick tangled mass —*v.* form into such mass (**-tt-**) —**on the mat** *inf.* called up for reprimand

mat *a.* dull, lustreless, not shiny

mat'ador *n.* man who slays bull in bullfights

match *n.* contest, game; equal; person, thing exactly corresponding to another; marriage; person regarded as eligible for marriage —*vt.* get something corresponding to (colour, pattern *etc.*); oppose, put in competition (with); join (in marriage) —*vi.* correspond —**match'less** *a.* unequalled —**match'board** *n.* boards fitted into each other by tongue and groove —**match'maker** *n.* one who schemes to bring about a marriage

match[2] *n.* small stick with head which ignites when rubbed; fuse —**match'box** *n.* —**match'lock** *n.* early musket fired by fuse —**match'wood** *n.* small splinters

mate[1] *n.* comrade; husband, wife; one of pair; officer in merchant ship; *inf.* common Brit. and Aust. term of address, *esp.* between males —*v.* marry; pair —**ma'tey** *a. inf.* friendly, sociable

mate[2] *n./vt.* Chess checkmate

mate'rial *n.* substance from which thing is made; cloth, fabric —*a.* of matter or body; affecting physical wellbeing; unspiritual; important, essential —**mate'rialism** *n.* excessive interest in, desire for money and possessions; doctrine that nothing but matter exists, denying independent existence of spirit —**mate'rialist** *a./n.* —**materialis'tic** *a.* —**mate'rialize** *vi.* come into existence or view —*vt.* make material —**mate'rially** *adv.* appreciably

mater'nal *a.* of, related through mother —**mater'nity** *n.* motherhood

mathemat'ics *pl.n.* (*with sing. v.*) science of number, quantity, shape and space —**mathemat'ical** *a.* —**mathemat'ically** *adv.* —**mathemati'cian** [-tish'-] *n.*

maths *n. inf.* mathematics

mat'inée [-nā] *n.* afternoon performance in theatre

mat'ins *pl.n.* morning prayers

ma'triarch [-k] *n.* mother as head and ruler of family —**ma'triarchal** *a.* —**ma'triarchy** *n.* society with matriarchal government and descent reckoned in female line

mat'ricide *n.* the crime of killing one's mother; one who does this

matric'ulate *v.* enrol, be enrolled in a college or university —**matricula'tion** *n.*

mat'rimony *n.* marriage —**matrimo'nial** *a.*

ma'trix *n.* substance, situation in which something originates, takes form, or is enclosed; mould for casting; *Math.* rectangular array of elements set out in rows and columns (*pl.* **ma'trices** [-sēz])

ma'tron *n.* married woman; *former name for* NURSING OFFICER; woman who superintends domestic arrangements of public institution, boarding school *etc.* —**ma'tronly** *a.* sedate

Matt. Matthew

matt *see* MAT[1]

matt'er *n.* substance of which thing is made; physical or bodily substance; affair, business; cause of trouble; substance of book *etc.*; pus —*vi.* be of importance, signify

matt'ock *n.* tool like pick with ends of blades flattened for cutting, hoeing

matt'ress *n.* stuffed flat case, often with springs, or foam rubber pad, used as part of bed; underlay

mature' *a.* ripe, completely developed; grown-up —*v.* bring, come to maturity —*vi.* (of bill) fall due —**matura'tion** *n.* process of maturing —**matu'rity** *n.* full development

maud'lin *a.* weakly or tearfully sentimental

maul *vt.* handle roughly; beat or bruise —*n.* heavy wooden hammer; *Rugby* loose scrum

maul'stick *n.* light stick with ball at one end, held in left hand to support right hand while painting

maun'der *vi.* talk, act aimlessly, dreamily

maun'dy *n.* foot-washing ceremony on Thursday before Easter (cf. *John* xiii, 14); royal alms given on that day

mausole'um *n.* stately building as a tomb (*pl.* **-le'ums, -le'a**)

mauve [mōv] *a./n.* (of) pale purple colour

mav'erick *n.* US unbranded steer, strayed cow; independent, unorthodox person

maw *n.* stomach, crop

mawk'ish *a.* weakly sentimental, maudlin; sickly

maxill'a *n.* jawbone —**maxill'lary** *a.* of the jaw

max'im *n.* general truth, proverb; rule of conduct, principle

max'imum *n.* greatest size or number; highest point —*a.* greatest —**max'imize** *vt.*

May *n.* fifth month; (m-) hawthorn or its flowers —**may'fly** *n.* short-lived flying insect, found near water —**may'pole** *n.* pole set up for dancing round on **May Day**, first day of May

may *v. aux.* expresses possibility, permission, opportunity *etc.* (**might** *pt.*) —**may'be** *adv.* perhaps; possibly

May'day *n.* international radiotelephone distress signal

may'hem *n.* depriving person by violence of limb, member or organ, or causing mutilation of body; any violent destruction; confusion

mayonnaise' *n.* creamy sauce of egg yolks *etc.*, esp. for salads

mayor [mār] *n.* head of municipality —**mayor'al** *a.* —**mayor'alty** *n.* (time of) office of mayor —**mayor'ess** *n.* mayor's wife; lady mayor

maze *n.* labyrinth; network of paths, lines; state of confusion

maz(o)ur'ka *n.* lively Polish dance like polka; music for it

MB Bachelor of Medicine

MBE Member of the Order of the British Empire

MC Master of Ceremonies; Military Cross

MCC Marylebone Cricket Club

MCP male chauvinist pig

MD Doctor of Medicine

me[1] *pron.* objective case singular of first personal pronoun I

me[2], **mi** *n.* third sol-fa note

me'a cul'pa [mā'ah-kul'pah] *Lat.* my fault

mead *n.* alcoholic drink made from honey

mead'ow [med'-] *n.* piece of grassland —**mead'owsweet** *n.* plant with dense heads of small fragrant flowers

mea'gre [mē'gər] *a.* lean, thin, scanty, insufficient

meal[1] *n.* occasion when food is served and eaten; the food

meal[2] *n.* grain ground to powder —**meal'y** *a.* —**mealy-mouthed** *a.* euphemistic, insincere in what one says

meal'ie *n.* SA maize

mean[1] *vt.* intend; signify —*vi.* have a meaning; have the intention of behaving (**meant** [ment] *pt./pp.*, **mean'ing** *pr.p.*) —**mean'ing** *n.* sense, significance —*a.* expressive —**mean'ingful** *a.* of great meaning or significance —**mean'ingless** *a.*

mean[2] *a.* ungenerous, petty; miserly, niggardly; unpleasant; callous; shabby; ashamed —**mean'ly** *adv.* —**mean'ness** *n.*

mean[3] *n.* thing which is intermediate; middle point —*pl.* that by which thing is done; money; resources —*a.* intermediate in time, quality *etc.*; average —**means test** enquiry into person's means to decide eligibility for pension, grant *etc.* —**mean'time, mean'while** *adv./n.* (during) time between one happening and another —**by all means** certainly —**by no means** not at all

meand'er [mē-and'-] *vi.* flow windingly; wander aimlessly

meas'les [mēz'lz] *n.* infectious disease producing rash of red spots —**meas'ly** *a. inf.* poor, wretched, stingy; of measles

meas'ure [mezh'ər] *n.* size, quantity; vessel, rod, line *etc.* for ascertaining size or quantity; unit of size or quantity; course, plan of action; law; practical rhythm; musical time; *Poet.* tune; *obs.* dance —*vt.* ascertain size, quantity of; be (so much) in size or quantity; indicate measurement of; estimate; bring into competition (against) —**meas'urable** *a.* —**meas'ured** *a.* determined by measure; steady; rhythmical; carefully considered —**meas'urement** *n.* measuring; size —*pl.* dimensions

meat *n.* animal flesh as food; food —**meat'y** *a.* (tasting) of, like meat; brawny; full of import or interest

Mecc'a *n.* holy city of Islam; place that attracts visitors

mechan'ic [-k-] *n.* one employed in working with machinery; skilled workman —*pl.* scientific theory of motion —**mechan'ical** *a.* concerned with machines or operation of them; worked, produced (as though) by machine; acting without thought —**mechan'ically** *adv.* —**mechani'cian** [-nish'-] *n.*

mech'anism [mek'-] *n.* structure of machine; piece of machinery —**mechaniza'tion** *n.* —**mech'anize** *vt.* equip with machinery; make mechanical, automatic; *Mil.* equip with armoured vehicles —**mech'anized** *a.*

med. medical; medicine; medieval; medium

med'al *n.* piece of metal with inscription *etc.* used as reward or memento —**medall'ion** *n.* large

medal; various things like this in decorative work —**med'allist** *n.* winner of a medal; maker of medals

med'dle *vi.* interfere, busy oneself with unnecessarily —**med'dlesome** *a.*

me'dia *n., pl. of* MEDIUM, used *esp.* of the mass media, radio, television *etc.* —**media event** event staged for or exploited by mass media

mediae'val *see* MEDIEVAL

me'dial *a.* in the middle; pert. to a mean or average —**me'dian** *a./n.* middle (point or line)

me'diate *vi.* intervene to reconcile —*vt.* bring about by mediation —*a.* depending on mediation —**media'tion** *n.* intervention on behalf of another; act of going between —**me'diator** *n.*

med'icine [-sin] *n.* drug or remedy for treating disease; science of preventing, diagnosing, alleviating, or curing disease —**med'ical** *a.* —**med'ically** *adv.* —**medic'ament** *n.* remedy —**med'icate** *vt.* impregnate with medicinal substances —**medica'tion** *n.* —**med'icative** *a.* healing —**medic'inal** *a.* curative —**medicine ball** heavy ball for physical training —**medicine man** witch doctor

medie'val, mediae'val *a.* of Middle Ages —**medie'valism** *n.* spirit of Middle Ages; cult of medieval ideals —**medie'valist** *n.* student of the Middle Ages

medio'cre [mē-dē-ō'kər] *a.* neither bad nor good, ordinary, middling; second-rate —**medioc'rity** *n.*

med'itate *vi.* be occupied in thought; reflect deeply on spiritual matters —*vt.* think about; plan —**medita'tion** *n.* thought; absorption in thought; religious contemplation —**med'itative** *a.* thoughtful; reflective —**med′itatively** adv.

me′dium a. between two qualities, degrees etc., average —n. middle quality, degree; intermediate substance conveying force; means, agency of communicating news etc. to public, as radio, newspapers etc.; person through whom communication can supposedly be held with spirit world; surroundings; environment (pl. **me′diums, me′dia**) —**medium waves** Radio waves between 100-1000 metres

med′lar n. tree with fruit like small apple; the fruit, eaten when decayed

med′ley n. miscellaneous mixture (pl. **′-leys**)

medull′a n. marrow, pith, inner tissue —**medull′ary** a.

Medu′sa [-dyŏō′zə] n. Myth. Gorgon whose head turned beholders into stone; (m-) jellyfish (pl. **-sae** [-zē])

meek a. submissive, humble —**meek′ly** adv. —**meek′ness** n.

meer′kat n. S Afr. mongoose

meer′schaum [-shəm] n. white substance like clay; tobacco pipe bowl of this

meet[1] vt. come face to face with, encounter; satisfy; pay —vi. come face to face; converge at specified point; assemble; come into contact (met pt./pp.) —n. meeting, esp. for sports —**meet′ing** n. assembly; encounter

meet[2] a. obs. fit, suitable

meg′abit n. Computers one million bits; 2^{20} bits

meg′aflop n. Computers measure of processing speed consisting of one million floating-point operations a second

meg′alith n. great stone —**megalith′ic** a.

megaloma′nia n. desire for, delusions of grandeur, power etc.

—megaloma′niac a./n.

meg′aphone n. cone-shaped instrument to amplify voice

meg′aton n. one million tons; explosive power of 1 000 000 tons of TNT

meg′ohm n. Electricity one million ohms

mel′ancholy [-k-] n. sadness, dejection, gloom —a. gloomy, dejected —**melancho′lia** n. mental disease accompanied by depression —**melanchol′ic** a.

melange[1] [-lahnzh′] n. mixture

mel′anin n. dark pigment found in hair, skin etc. of man

mêl′ée [mel′ā] n. mixed fight, or crowd

me′liorate v. improve —**meliora′tion** n. —**me′liorism** n. doctrine that the world may be improved by human effort —**me′liorist** n.

mellif′luous, -luent a. (of sound) smooth, sweet —**mellif′luence** n.

mell′ow a. ripe; softened by age, experience; soft, not harsh; genial, gay —v. make, become mellow

mel′odrama n. play full of sensational and startling situations, often highly emotional; overdramatic behaviour, emotion —**melodramat′ic** a.

mel′ody n. series of musical notes which make tune; sweet sound —**melo′dious** a. pleasing to the ear; tuneful —**mel′odist** n. singer; composer

mel′on n. large, fleshy, juicy fruit

melt v. (cause to) become liquid by heat; dissolve; soften; waste away; blend (into); disappear (**melt′ed** pt./pp., **mol′ten** [mōl′tən] pp.) —**melt′ing** a. softening; languishing; tender —**melt′down** n. in nuclear reactor, melting of fuel rods, with possible release of radiation

mem'ber n. any of individuals making up body or society; limb; any part of complex whole —**mem'bership** n.

mem'brane n. thin flexible tissue in plant or animal body

memen'to n. thing serving to remind, souvenir (pl. -to(e)s)

mem'o n. short for MEMORANDUM

mem'oir [-wahr] n. autobiography, personal history, biography; record of events

mem'ory n. faculty of recollecting, recalling to mind; recollection; thing remembered; length of time one can remember; commemoration; part or faculty of computer which stores information —**memor'ial** a. of, preserving memory —n. thing, esp. a monument, which serves to keep in memory —**mem'orable** a. worthy of remembrance, noteworthy —**mem'orably** adv. —**memoran'dum** n. note to help the memory etc.; informal letter; note of contract (pl. -dums, -da) —**memor'ialist** n. —**memo'rialize** vt. commemorate —**mem'orize** vt. commit to memory

men n. pl. of MAN

men'ace n. threat —vt. threaten, endanger

ménage' [me-nahzh', mā-] n. persons of a household

menag'erie [-j-] n. exhibition, collection of wild animals

mend vt. repair, patch; reform, correct, put right —vi. improve, esp. in health —n. repaired breakage, hole —**on the mend** regaining health

menda'cious a. untruthful —**mendac'ity** n. (tendency to) untruthfulness

mend'icant a. begging —n. beggar —**mend'icancy, mendic'ity** n. begging

men'hir n. single, upright monumental stone, monolith

me'nial a. of work requiring little skill; of household duties or servants; servile —n. servant; servile person

meningi'tis [-jī'-] n. inflammation of the membranes of the brain

menis'cus n. curved surface of liquid; curved lens

men'opause n. final cessation of menstruation

menstrua'tion n. approximately monthly discharge of blood and cellular debris from womb of nonpregnant woman —**men'strual** a. —**men'struate** vi.

mensura'tion [-shə-rā'-] n. measuring, esp. of areas

men'tal a. of, done by the mind; inf. feeble-minded, mad —**men'tality** n. state or quality of mind —**men'tally** adv.

men'thol n. organic compound found in peppermint, used medicinally

men'tion vt. refer to briefly, speak of —n. acknowledgment; reference to or remark about (person or thing) —**men'tionable** a. fit or suitable to be mentioned

men'tor n. wise, trusted adviser, guide

men'u n. list of dishes to be served, or from which to order

MEP Member of the European Parliament

mer'cantile [-k-] a. of, engaged in trade, commerce

Merca'tor projection method of map making with all parallels and meridians as straight lines

mer'cenary [-s-] a. influenced by greed; working merely for reward —n. hired soldier

mer'cer n. esp. formerly, dealer in fabrics —**mer'cery** n. his trade, goods

mer'cerize vt. give lustre to cotton fabrics by treating with chemicals —**mer'cerized** a.

mer'chant n. one engaged in trade; wholesale trader —**mer'chandise** n. his wares —**mer'chantman** n. trading ship —**merchant navy** ships engaged in a nation's commerce

mer'cury [-kyoor-] n. silvery metal, liquid at ordinary temperature, quicksilver; (M-) Roman god of eloquence; planet nearest to sun —**mercu'rial** a. relating to, containing mercury; lively, changeable

mer'cy n. refraining from infliction of suffering by one who has right, power to inflict it, compassion —**mer'ciful** a. —**mer'ciless** a.

mere[1] [mēr] a. only; not more than; nothing but —**mere'ly** adv.

mere[2] [mēr] n. obs. lake

meretric'ious [-ish-] a. superficially or garishly attractive; insincere

morgan'ser n. large, crested diving duck

merge v. (cause to) lose identity or be absorbed —**mer'ger** [-j-] n. combination of business firms into one; absorption into something greater

merid'ian n. circle of the earth passing through poles; imaginary circle in sky passing through celestial poles; highest point reached by star etc.; period of greatest splendour —a. of meridian; at peak of something

meringue' [mɔ-rang'] n. baked mixture of white of eggs and sugar; cake of this

meri'no [-ē'-] n. breed of sheep originating in Spain (pl. -os)

mer'it n. excellence, worth; quality of deserving reward —pl.

excellence —vt. deserve —**merito'rious** a. deserving praise

mer'lin n. small falcon

mer'maid n. imaginary sea creature with upper part of woman and lower part of fish

merr'y a. joyous, cheerful —**mer'rily** adv. —**merr'iment** n. —**merry-go-round** n. roundabout

mesembryan'themum n. [miz-] low-growing plant with daisylike flowers of various colours

mesh n. (one of the open spaces of, or wires etc. forming) network, net —v. entangle, become entangled; (of gears) engage —vi. coordinate (with)

mes'merism [-z-] n. former term for HYPNOTISM —**mesmer'ic** a. —**mes'merist** n. —**mes'merize** vt. hypnotize; fascinate, hold spellbound

me'son [-z-] n. elementary atomic particle

mess n. untidy confusion; trouble, difficulty; group in armed services who regularly eat together; place where they eat —vi. make mess, potter (about); Mil. eat in a mess —vt. muddle —**mess'y** a.

mess'age n. communication sent; meaning, moral; errand —**mess'enger** n. bearer of message

Messi'ah n. Jews' promised deliverer; Christ —**messian'ic** a.

Messrs. [mes'ɔz] pl. of Mr.

Met a./n. inf. Meteorological (Office in London)

met pt./pp. of MEET

meta- (comb. form) change, as in metamorphose, metathesis etc.

metab'olism n. chemical process of living being —**metabol'ic** a. —**metab'olize** vt.

met'al n. mineral substance, opaque, fusible and malleable, capable of conducting heat and electricity; broken stone for macadamized roads —**metall'ic** a. —**metall'urgist** n. —**metall'urgy** n. scientific study of extracting, refining metals, and their structure and properties

metamor'phosis n. change of shape, character etc. (pl. -**phoses** [-ēz]) —**metamor'phic** a. (esp. of rocks) changed in texture, structure by heat, pressure etc. —**metamor'phose** vt. transform

met'aphor n. figure of speech in which term is transferred to something it does not literally apply to; instance of this —**metaphor'ical** [-fo'ri-] a. figurative —**metaphor'ically** adv.

metaphys'ics pl.n. (with sing. v.) branch of philosophy concerned with being and knowing —**metaphys'ical** a. —**metaphysi'cian** n.

metath'esis n. transposition, esp. of letters in word, eg Old English *bridd* gives modern *bird* (pl. -**eses** [-ēz])

mete vt. measure —**mete out** distribute; allot as punishment

me'teor n. small, fast-moving celestial body, visible as streak of incandescence if it enters earth's atmosphere —**meteor'ic** [-o'rik] a. of, like meteor; brilliant but short-lived —**me'teorite** n. fallen meteor

meteorol'ogy n. study of earth's atmosphere, esp. for weather forecasting —**meteorolog'ical** a. —**meteorol'ogist** n.

me'ter n. that which measures; instrument for recording consumption of gas, electricity etc.

me'thane n. inflammable gas, compound of carbon and hydrogen

meth'anol n. colourless, poisonous liquid used as solvent and fuel (also called **methyl alcohol**)

methinks' v. impers. obs. it seems to me (**methought'** pt.)

meth'od n. way, manner; technique; orderliness, system —**method'ical** a. orderly —**meth'odize** vt. reduce to order —**methodol'ogy** n. particular method or procedure

Meth'odist n. member of any of the churches originated by Wesley and his followers —a. —**Meth'odism** n.

meths n. inf. methylated spirits

meth'yl [meth'-, mē'-] n. (compound containing) a saturated hydrocarbon group of atoms —**meth'ylate** vt. combine with methyl; mix with methanol —**methylated spirits** alcoholic mixture denatured with methanol

metic'ulous a. (over)particular about details

mét'ier [māt'yā] n. profession, vocation; one's forte

meton'ymy n. figure of speech in which thing is replaced by another associated with it, eg 'the Crown' for 'the king' —**metonym'ical** a.

me'tre n. unit of length in decimal system; SI unit of length; rhythm of poem —**met'ric** a. of system of weights and measures in which metre is a unit —**met'rical** a. of measurement of poetic metre

met'ronome n. instrument which marks musical time by means of ticking pendulum

metrop'olis n. chief city of a country, region (pl. -**lises**) —**metropol'itan** a. of metropolis —n. bishop with authority over other bishops of a province

met'tle n. courage, spirit —**met'tlesome** a. high-spirited

mew n. cry of cat, gull —vi. utter this cry

mews *pl.n.* (used as sing.) yard, street orig. of stables, now oft. converted to houses

mezz'anine [met's*ə*-nēn, mez'*ə*-] *n.* intermediate storey, balcony between two main storeys, *esp.* between first and second floors

mezz'o-sopra'no [met'sō-] *n.* voice, singer between soprano and contralto (*pl.* -nos)

mezz'otint [met'sō-] *n.* method of engraving by scraping roughened surface; print so made

Mg *Chem.* magnesium

mg milligram(s)

M.Glam Mid Glamorgan

MHz megahertz

mi *see* ME[1]

MI Military Intelligence

mias'ma [-z-] *n.* unwholesome or foreboding atmosphere (*pl.* -mata, -mas) —**miasmat'ic** *a.*

mi'ca *n.* mineral found as glittering scales, plates

Mich'aelmas [mik'*ə*l-] *n.* feast of Archangel St. Michael, 29th September —**Michaelmas daisy** common garden flower of aster family

mi'crobe *n.* minute organism; disease germ —**micro'bial** *a.*

mi'crochip *n.* small wafer of silicon *etc.* containing electronic circuits, chip

microcompu'ter *n.* computer having a central processing unit contained in one or more silicon chips

mi'crocopy *n.* minute photographic replica useful for storage because of its small size

mi'crocosm *n.* miniature representation, model *etc.* of some larger system; man as epitome of universe —**microcos'mic** *a.*

mi'crodot *n.* extremely small microcopy

mi'crofiche [-fēsh] *n.* microfilm in sheet form

mi'crofilm *n.* miniaturized recording of manuscript, book on roll of film

mi'crogroove *n.* narrow groove of long-playing gramophone record —*a.*

mi'crolight *n.* small, light, private aircraft used in pleasure flying and racing

microm'eter [mī-] *n.* instrument for measuring very small distances or angles

mi'cron *n.* unit of length, one millionth of a metre

microor'ganism [-ō-or'-] *n.* organism of microscopic size

mi'crophone *n.* instrument for amplifying, transmitting sounds

micropro'cessor *n.* integrated circuit acting as central processing unit in small computer

mi'croscope *n.* instrument by which very small body is magnified and made visible —**microscop'ic** *a.* of microscope; very small —**micros'copy** *n.* use of microscope

mi'crowave *n.* electromagnetic wave with wavelength of a few centimetres, used in radar, cooking *etc.*

mid *a.* intermediate, in the middle of —**mid'day** *n.* noon —**mid'land** *n.* middle part of country —*pl.* central England —**mid'night** *n.* twelve o'clock at night —**mid'shipman** *n.* naval officer of lowest commissioned rank —**midsum'mer** *n.* summer solstice; middle of summer —**mid'way** *a./adv.* halfway —**midwin'ter** *n.*

midd'en *n.* dunghill; rubbish heap

mid'dle *a.* equidistant from two extremes; medium, intermediate —*n.* middle point or part —**mid'dling** *a.* mediocre; moderate —*adv.* —**Middle Ages** period from end of Roman Empire to Renaissance, roughly A.D. 500-1500 —**middle class** social class of businessmen, professional people *etc.* —**middle-class** a. —**mid'dleman** n. trader between producer and consumer

Middx Middlesex

midge n. gnat or similar insect

midg'et [mij'it] n. very small person or thing

mid'riff n. middle part of body

midst prep. in the middle of —n. middle —**in the midst of** surrounded by, among

mid'wife n. trained person who assists at childbirth —**mid'wifery** [-wif-ǝri] n. art, practice of this

mien [mēn] n. person's bearing, demeanour or appearance

might[1] [mīt] *see* MAY

might[2] [mīt] n. power, strength —**might'ily** adv. strongly; powerfully —**might'y** a. of great power; strong; valiant; important —adv. inf. very

mignonette[1] [min-yǝn-] n. grey-green plant with sweet-smelling flowers

mi'graine [mē'grān] n. severe headache, often with nausea and other symptoms

migrate[1] [mī-] vi. move from one place to another —**mi'grant** n./a. —**migra'tion** n. act of passing from one place, condition to another; number migrating together —**mi'gratory** a. of, capable of migration; (of animals) changing from one place to another according to season

mike n. inf. microphone

milch a. giving, kept for milk

mild [-ī-] a. not strongly flavoured; gentle, merciful; calm or temperate —**mild'ly** adv. —**mild'ness** n.

mil'dew n. destructive fungus on plants or things exposed to

damp —v. become tainted, affect with mildew

mile n. measure of length, 1760 yards, 1.609 km —**mile'age** n. distance in miles; travelling expenses per mile; miles travelled (per gallon of petrol) —**mile'stone** n. stone marker showing distance; significant event, achievement

mil'foil n. yarrow

mil'lieu [mēl'yǝ] n. environment, condition in life

mil'itary a. of, for, soldiers, armies or war —n. armed services —**mil'itancy** n. —**mil'itant** a. aggressive, vigorous in support of cause; prepared, willing to fight —**mil'itarism** n. enthusiasm for military force and methods —**mil'itarist** n. —**mil'itarize** vt. convert to military use —**mili'tia** [-ish'ǝ] n. military force of citizens for home service

mil'itate vi. (*esp. with* against) have strong influence, effect on

milk n. white fluid with which mammals feed their young; fluid in some plants —vt. draw milk from —**milk'y** a. containing, like milk; (of liquids) opaque, clouded —**milk bar** snack bar specializing in milk drinks —**milk'maid** n. *esp.* formerly, woman working with cows or in dairy —**milk'sop** n. effeminate fellow —**milk teeth** first set of teeth in young mammals —**Milky Way** luminous band of stars *etc.* stretching across sky, the galaxy

mill n. factory; machine for grinding, pulverizing corn, paper *etc.* —vt. put through mill; cut fine grooves across edges of (*eg* coins) —vi. move in confused manner, as cattle or crowds of people —**mill'er** n. —**mill'race** n. current of water driving mill wheel —**mill'stone** n. flat circular stone for grinding

millenn'ium n. period of a thousand years during which some claim Christ is to reign on earth; period of a thousand years; period of peace, happiness (pl. **-iums, -ia**)

mill'epede, mill'ipede n. small animal with jointed body and many pairs of legs

mill'et n. a cereal grass

milli- (comb. form) thousandth, as in **mill'igram** n. thousandth part of a gram **—mill'ilitre** n. **—mill'imetre** n.

mill'ibar n. unit of atmospheric pressure

mill'iner n. maker of, dealer in women's hats, ribbons etc. **—mill'inery** n. his goods or work

mill'ion n. 1000 thousands **—millionaire'** n. owner of a million pounds, dollars etc.; very rich man **—mill'ionth** a./n.

mil(e)om'eter n. device that records number of miles vehicle has travelled

milt n. spawn of male fish

mime n. acting without the use of words **—v.** act in mime

mim'ic vt. imitate (person, manner etc.) esp. for satirical effect (**mim'icked, mim'icking**) **—n.** one who, or animal which does this, or is adept at it **—a.** **—mim'icry** n. mimicking

mimo'sa n. genus of plants with fluffy, yellow flowers and sensitive leaves

min. minim; minimum; minute

minaret' n. tall slender tower of mosque

mince vt. cut, chop small; soften or moderate (words etc.) **—vi.** walk, speak in affected manner **—n.** minced meat **—min'cer** n. **—min'cing** a. affected in manner **—mince'meat** n. mixture of currants, spices, suet etc. **—mince pie** pie containing mincemeat or mince

mind [-ī-] n. thinking faculties as distinguished from the body, intellectual faculties; memory, attention; intention; taste; sanity **—vt.** take offence at; care for; attend to; be cautious, careful about (something); be concerned, troubled about **—vi.** be careful; heed **—mind'ful** a. heedful; keeping in memory **—mind'less** a. stupid, careless

mine[1] pron. belonging to me

mine[2] n. deep hole for digging out coal, metals etc.; in war, hidden deposit of explosive to blow up ship etc., profitable source **—vt.** dig from mine; make mine in or under; place explosive mines in, on **—vi.** make, work in mine **—mi'ner** n. one who works in a mine **—mine'field** n. area of land or sea containing mines **—mine'layer** n. ship for laying mines **—mine'sweeper** n. ship for clearing away mines

min'eral n. naturally occurring inorganic substance, esp. as obtained by mining **—a.** **—min'eralist** n. **—mineralog'ical** a. **—mineral'ogy** n. science of minerals **—mineral water** water containing some mineral, esp. natural or artificial kinds for drinking

minestro'ne [-ō'ni] n. type of soup containing pasta

min'gle [-ng'g-] v. mix, blend, unite, merge

min'i n. something small or miniature; short skirt **—a.**

min'iature [-it-] n. small painted portrait; anything on small scale **—a.** small-scale, minute **—min'iaturist** n.

min'ibus n. small bus for about ten passengers

min'im n. unit of fluid measure, one sixtieth of a drachm; Mus. note half the length of semibreve

min'imize vt. bring to, esti-

mate at smallest possible amount —**min'imal** a. —**min'imum** n. lowest size or quantity —a. least possible (pl. **-mums, -ma**) —**minimum lending rate** minimum rate of interest at which the Bank of England lends money

min'ion n. favourite; servile dependant

min'iseries n. TV programme in several parts, shown on consecutive days

min'ister n. person in charge of department of State; diplomatic representative; clergyman —vi. attend to needs of, take care of —**ministe'rial** a. —**ministe'rialist** n. supporter of government —**minis'trant** a./n. —**ministra'tion** n. rendering help, esp. to sick —**min'istry** n. office of clergyman; body of ministers forming government; act of ministering

min'iver n. a white fur used in ceremonial costumes

mink n. variety of weasel; its (brown) fur

minn'ow [-ō] n. small freshwater fish

mi'nor a. lesser; under age —n. person below age of legal majority; scale in music —**minor'ity** n. lesser number; smaller party voting together; ethical or religious group in a minority in any state; state of being a minor

Mi'notaur [-tawr] n. fabled monster, half bull, half man

min'ster n. Hist. monastery church; cathedral, large church

min'strel n. medieval singer, musician, poet —pl. performers of negro songs —**min'strelsy** n. art, body of minstrels; collection of songs

mint' n. place where money is coined —vt. coin, invent

mint' n. aromatic plant

minuet' n. stately dance; music for it

mi'nus prep./a. less, with the deduction of, deprived of; lacking; negative —n. the sign of subtraction (-)

minute' [mī-nyōōt'] a. very small; precise —**minute'ly** adv. —**minu'tiae** [-shi-ē] pl.n. trifles, precise details

min'ute² [min'it] n. 60th part of hour or degree; moment; memorandum —pl. record of proceedings of meeting etc. —vt. make minute of; record in minutes

minx n. bold, flirtatious woman

mir'acle n. supernatural event; marvel —**mirac'ulous** a. —**mirac'ulously** adv. —**miracle play** drama (esp. medieval) based on sacred subject

mir'age [-ahzh] n. deceptive image in atmosphere, eg of lake in desert

mire n. swampy ground, mud —vt. stick in, dirty with mud

mirr'or n. glass or polished surface reflecting images —vt. reflect

mirth n. merriment, gaiety —**mirth'ful** a. —**mirth'less** a.

mis-¹ (comb. form) wrong(ly), bad(ly), as in the following

> misbehave'
> miscal'culate
> miscon'duct
> mis'deed
> misfor'tune
> misinform'
> misjudge'
> misman'agement
> misplace'
> mis'print
> mispronounce'
> missha'pen
> misspell'
> misspent'
> misunderstand'
> misuse'

misadven'ture n. unlucky chance

mis'anthrope, misan'thropist n. hater of mankind —**misanthrop'ic** a. —**misan'thropy** n.

misappro'priate vt. put to dishonest use; embezzle —**misappropria'tion** n.

miscarr'y vi. bring forth young prematurely; go wrong, fail —**miscar'riage** n.

miscast' v. distribute acting parts wrongly; assign to unsuitable role —a.

miscella'neous a. mixed, assorted —**miscell'any** n. collection of assorted writings in one book; medley

mischance' n. unlucky event

mis'chief [-chif] n. annoying behaviour; inclination to tease, disturb; harm; source of harm or annoyance —**mis'chievous** a. of a child, full of pranks; disposed to mischief; having harmful effect

mis'cible a. capable of mixing

misconcep'tion n. wrong idea, belief

mis'creant n. wicked person, evildoer, villain

misdemea'nour n. formerly, offence less grave than a felony; minor offence

mi'ser n. hoarder of money; stingy person —**mi'serliness** n. —**mi'serly** a. avaricious; niggardly

mis'erable [-z-] a. very unhappy, wretched; causing misery; worthless; squalid —**mis'ery** n. great unhappiness; distress; poverty

misfire' vi. fail to fire, start, function successfully

mis'fit n. esp. person not suited to his environment or work

misgiv'ing n. (oft. pl.) feeling of fear, doubt etc.

misgui'ded a. foolish, unreasonable

mis'hap n. minor accident

mislay' vt. put in place which cannot later be remembered

mislead' vt. give false information to; lead astray (**misled'** pp.) —**mislead'ing** a. deceptive

misno'mer n. wrong name or term; use of this

misog'amy [-og-] n. hatred of marriage —**misog'amist** n.

misog'yny [-oj-] n. hatred of women —**misog'ynist** n.

misrepresent' vt. portray in wrong or misleading light

Miss n. title of unmarried woman; (m-) girl

miss vt. fail to hit, reach, find, catch, or notice; not to be in time for; omit; notice or regret absence of; avoid —vi. (of engine) misfire —n. fact, instance of missing —**miss'ing** a. lost; absent

miss'al n. book containing prayers etc. of the Mass

miss'ile n. that which may be thrown, shot, homed to damage, destroy —**guided missile** see GUIDE

miss'ion [mish'ən] n. specific task or duty; calling in life; delegation; sending or being sent on some service; those sent —**miss'ionary** n. one sent to a place, society to spread religion —a.

miss'ive [-iv] n. letter

mist n. water vapour in fine drops —**mist'ily** adv. —**mis'ty** a. full of mist; dim; obscure

mistake' n. error, blunder —vt. fail to understand; form wrong opinion about; take (person or thing) for another —vi. be in error

mis'ter n. title of courtesy to man (abbrev. **Mr.**)

mis'tletoe [mis'əl-] n. evergreen parasitic plant with white berries which grows on trees

mis'tral n. strong, dry, N wind in France

mis'tress n. object of man's illicit love; woman with mastery or control; woman owner; woman teacher; obs. title given to married woman (abbrev. **Mrs.** [mis'iz])

mite n. very small insect; anything very small; small but well-meant contribution

mit'igate vt. make less severe —**mitiga'tion** n.

mi'tre [-tər] n. bishop's headdress; joint between two pieces of wood etc. meeting at right angles —vt. join with, shape for a mitre joint; put mitre on

mitt n. glove leaving fingers bare; baseball catcher's glove; sl. hand

mitt'en n. glove with two compartments, one for thumb and one for fingers

mix vt. put together, combine, blend, mingle —vi. be mixed; associate —**mixed** a. composed of different elements, races, sexes etc. —**mix'ture** n. —**mixed-up** a. inf. confused —**mix-up** n. confused situation

miz(z)'en n. lowest fore-and-aft sail on aftermost mast of ship —**miz(z)'enmast** n. aftermost mast on full-rigged ship

mks units metric system of units based on the metre, kilogram and second

ml millilitre(s)

mm millimetre(s)

Mn Chem. manganese

mnemon'ic [n-] a. helping the memory —n. something intended to help the memory

MO Medical Officer

mo [mō] n. inf. short for MOMENT

moan n. low murmur, usually of pain —v. utter with moan, lament

moat n. deep wide ditch esp. round castle —vt. surround with moat

mob n. disorderly crowd of people; mixed assembly —vt. attack in mob, hustle or ill-treat (**-bb-**)

mo'bile a. capable of movement; easily moved or changed —n. hanging structure of card, plastic etc. designed to move in air currents —**mobil'ity** n.

mo'bilize v. (of armed services) prepare for military service —vt. organize for a purpose —**mobiliza'tion** n. in war time, calling up of men and women for active service

mocc'asin n. Amer. Indian soft shoe, usu. of deerskin

mo'cha [mok'-] n. type of strong, dark coffee; this flavour

mock vt. make fun of, ridicule; mimic —vi. scoff —n. act of mocking; laughing stock —a. sham, imitation —**mock'er** n. —**mock'ery** n. derision; travesty —**mocking bird** N Amer. bird which imitates songs of others —**mock orange** shrub with white fragrant flowers —**mock-up** n. scale model —**put the mockers on** inf. ruin chances of success of

mod. moderate; modern

mode n. method, manner; prevailing fashion —**mo'dish** a. in the fashion

mod'el n. miniature representation; pattern; person or thing worthy of imitation; person employed by artist to pose, or by dress designer to display clothing —vt. make model of; mould; display (clothing) for dress designer (**-ll-**)

mod'erate [-ər-it] a. not going to extremes, temperate, medium —n. person of moderate views —v. [-ər-āt] make, become less violent or excessive; preside over meeting etc. —**modera'tion** n.

—**mod'erator** n. mediator; president of Presbyterian body; arbitrator

mod'ern a. of present or recent times; in, of current fashion —n. person living in modern times —**mod'ernism** n. (support of) modern tendencies, thoughts etc. —**mod'ernist** n. —**modern'ity** n. —**moderniza'tion** n. —**mod'ernize** vt. bring up to date

mod'est a. not overrating one's qualities or achievements; shy; moderate, not excessive; decorous, decent —**mod'estly** adv. —**mod'esty** n.

mod'icum n. small quantity

mod'ify [-fī] v. (mainly tr.) change slightly; tone down (-**fied, -fying**) —**modifica'tion** n. —**mod'ifier** n. esp. word qualifying another

mod'ulate vt. regulate; vary in tone —vi. change key of music —**modula'tion** n. modulating; Electronics superimposing signals on to high-frequency carrier —**mod'ulator** n.

mod'ule n. (detachable) unit, section, component with specific function

mo'dus operan'di Lat. method of operating, tackling task

mo'gul n. important or powerful person

MOH Medical Officer of Health

mo'hair n. fine cloth of goat's hair; hair of Angora goat

Mohamm'ed n. prophet and founder of Islam —**Moham'medan** a./n. Muslim

mohi'can [mōhē'-] n. punk hairstyle with shaved sides and stiff central strip of hair, oft. brightly coloured

moi'ety n. a half

moist a. damp, slightly wet —**mois'ten** [moi'sən] v. —**mois'ture** n. liquid, esp. diffused or in drops —**moist'urize** vt. add, restore moisture to (skin etc.)

moke n. sl. donkey

mo'lar a. (of teeth) for grinding —n. molar tooth

molass'es [-iz] n. syrup, byproduct of process of sugar refining

mole[1] n. small dark protuberant spot on the skin

mole[2] n. small burrowing animal; spy, informer

mole[3] n. pier or breakwater; causeway; harbour within this

mole[4] n. SI unit of amount of substance

mol'ecule n. simplest freely existing chemical unit, composed of two or more atoms; very small particle —**molec'ular** a. of, inherent in molecules

molest' vt. pester, interfere with so as to annoy or injure —**molesta'tion** n.

moll sl. n. gangster's female accomplice; prostitute

moll'ify vt. calm down, placate, soften (-**fied, -fying**) —**mollifica'tion** n.

moll'usc [-əsk] n. soft-bodied, usu. hard-shelled animal, eg snail, oyster

moll'ycoddle v. pamper

Mol'otov cock'tail incendiary petrol bomb

molten see MELT

molyb'denum [-lib'-] n. silverwhite metallic element

mo'ment n. very short space of time; (present) point in time —**mo'mentarily** adv. —**mo'mentary** a. lasting only a moment

momen'tous a. of great importance

momen'tum n. force of a moving body; impetus gained from motion (pl. **-ta, -tums**)

mon'arch [-k] n. sovereign ruler of a state —**monarch'ic** a. —**mon'archist** n. supporter of monarchy —**mon'archy** n. state ruled by sovereign; his rule

mon'astery n. house occupied by a religious order —**monas'tic** a. relating to monks, nuns, or monasteries — n. monk, recluse —**monas'ticism** n.

Mon'day [mun'di] n. second day of the week, or first of working week

mon'ey [mun'i] n. banknotes, coin etc., used as medium of exchange (pl. **-eys, -ies**) —**mon'etarism** n. theory that inflation is caused by increase in money supply —**mon'etarist** n./a. —**mon'etary** a. —**monetiza'tion** n. —**mon'etize** vt. make into, recognize as money —**mon'eyed, mon'ied** a. rich

mon'golism [-ng'g-] n. form of physical and mental retardation —**mon'gol** n./a. (one) afflicted with this

mon'goose [-ng'g-] n. small animal of Asia and Africa noted for killing snakes (pl. **-gooses**)

mon'grel [mung'g-] n. animal, esp. dog, of mixed breed; hybrid — a.

mon'itor n. person or device which checks, controls, warns or keeps record of something; pupil assisting teacher with odd jobs in school; television set used in a studio for checking programme being transmitted; type of large lizard —vt. watch, check on —**moni'tion** n. warning —**mon'itory** a.

monk [mungk] n. one of a religious community of men living apart under vows —**monk'ish** a. —**monks'hood** n. poisonous plant with hooded flowers

monk'ey [mungk'i] n. long-tailed primate; mischievous child —vi. meddle, fool (with) —**monkey puzzle** coniferous tree with sharp stiff leaves —**monkey**

wrench spanner with movable jaw

mono- (comb. form) single, as in **monosyllab'ic** a.

mon'ochrome n. representation in one colour —a. of one colour —**monochromat'ic** a.

mon'ocle n. single eyeglass

monoc'ular a. one-eyed

monog'amy n. custom of being married to one person at a time

mon'ogram n. design of letters interwoven

mon'ograph n. short book on single subject

mon'olith n. monument consisting of single standing stone

mon'ologue [-log] n. dramatic composition with only one speaker; long speech by one person

monoma'nia n. excessive preoccupation with one thing

mon'oplane n. aeroplane with one pair of wings

monop'oly n. exclusive possession of trade, privilege etc. —**monop'olist** n. —**monop'olize** vt. claim, take exclusive possession of

mon'orail n. railway with cars running on or suspended from single rail

mon'otheism n. belief in only one God —**mon'otheist** n.

mon'otone n. continuing on one note —**monot'onous** a. lacking in variety, dull, wearisome —**monot'ony** n.

Mon'otype R type set as individual letters

monsoon' n. seasonal wind of SE Asia; very heavy rainfall season

mon'ster n. fantastic imaginary beast; misshapen animal or plant; very wicked person; huge person, animal or thing —a. huge —**monstros'ity** n. monstrous being; deformity; distortion —**mon'-**

strous a. of, like monster; unnatural; enormous; horrible —**mon'strously** adv.

mon'strance n. R.C.Ch. vessel in which consecrated Host is exposed for adoration

montage' [-ahzh'] n. elements of two or more pictures imposed upon a single background to give a unified effect; method of editing a film

montbre'tia [mon-brē'sha] n. plant with orange flowers on long stems

month [munth] n. one of twelve periods into which the year is divided; period of moon's revolution —**month'ly** a. happening or payable once a month —adv. once a month —n. magazine published every month

mon'ument n. anything that commemorates, esp. a building or statue —**monument'al** a. vast, lasting; of or serving as monument

moo n. cry of cow —vi. make this noise, low

mooch vi. sl. loaf, slouch

mood[1] n. state of mind and feelings —**mood'y** a. gloomy, pensive; changeable in mood

mood[2] n. Grammar form indicating function of verb

moon n. satellite which takes lunar month to revolve round earth; any secondary planet —vi. go about dreamily —**moon'light** n. —**moon'shine** n. whisky illicitly distilled; nonsense —**moon'stone** n. transparent semiprecious stone —**moon'struck** a. deranged

Moor n. member of race in Morocco and adjoining parts of N W Africa

moor[1] n. tract of open uncultivated land, often hilly and heather-clad —**moor'hen** n. water bird

moor[2] v. secure (ship) with chains or ropes —**moor'age** n. place, charge for mooring —**moor'ings** pl.n. ropes etc. for mooring; something providing stability, security

moose n. N Amer. deer, like elk

moot a. that is open to argument, debatable —vt. bring for discussion —n. meeting

mop n. bundle of yarn, cloth etc. on end of stick, used for cleaning; tangle (of hair etc.) —vt. clean, wipe with mop or other absorbent stuff (-**pp**-)

mope vi. be gloomy, apathetic

mo'ped n. light motorized bicycle

moraine' n. accumulated mass of debris, earth, stones etc., deposited by glacier

mor'al [mo'-] a. pert. to right and wrong conduct; of good conduct —n. practical lesson, eg of fable —pl. habits with respect to right and wrong, esp. in matters of sex —**mor'alist** n. teacher of morality —**moral'ity** n. good moral conduct; moral goodness or badness; kind of medieval drama, containing moral lesson —**mor'alize** vi. write, think about moral aspect of things —vt. interpret morally —**mor'ally** adv. —**moral victory** triumph that is psychological rather than practical

morale' [-ahl'] n. degree of confidence, hope of person or group

morass' n. marsh; mess

morator'ium n. act authorizing postponement of payments etc.; delay (pl. **-ria**)

mor'ay [mo'-] n. large, voracious eel

mor'bid a. unduly interested in death; gruesome; diseased

mord'ant a. biting; corrosive; scathing —n. substance that fixes dyes

more a. greater in quantity or number —comp. of MANY and MUCH —adv. to a greater extent; in addition —pron. greater or additional amount or number —**moreo'ver** adv. besides, further

morganat'ic marr'iage marriage of king or prince in which wife does not share husband's rank or possessions and children do not inherit from father

mor'gen n. **SA** land unit, approx. two acres (0.8 hectare)

morgue [mawrg] n. mortuary

mor'ibund [mo'ri-] a. dying; stagnant

Mor'mon n. member of religious sect founded in U.S.A. —**Mor'monism** n.

mor'nay a. denoting cheese sauce used in various dishes

morn'ing n. early part of day until noon —**morn** n. Poet. morning —**morning-glory** n. plant with trumpet-shaped flowers which close in late afternoon

morocc'o n. goatskin leather

mor'on n. mentally deficient person; inf. fool —**moron'ic** a.

morose' [-ōs'] a. sullen, moody

morph'ia, morph'ine n. narcotic extract of opium; drug used to induce sleep and relieve pain

morphol'ogy n. science of structure of organisms; form and structure of words of a language —**morpholog'ical** a.

morr'is dance n. English folk dance

morr'ow [mo'rō] n. Poet. next day

Morse n. system of telegraphic signalling in which letters of alphabet are represented by combinations of dots and dashes, or short and long flashes

mor'sel n. fragment, small piece

mor'tal a. subject to death; causing death —n. mortal creature —**mortal'ity** n. state of being mortal; great loss of life; death rate —**mor'tally** adv. fatally; deeply, intensely —**mortal sin** R.C.Ch. sin meriting damnation

mor'tar n. mixture of lime, sand and water for holding bricks and stones together; small cannon firing over short range; vessel in which substances are pounded —**mor'tarboard** n. square academic cap

mort'gage [mawr'gij] n. conveyance of property as security for debt with provision that property be reconveyed on payment within agreed time —vt. convey by mortgage; pledge as security —**mortgagee'** n. —**mort'gagor, -ger** n.

mort'ify vt. humiliate; subdue by self-denial —vi. (of flesh) be affected with gangrene (-**fied, -fying**) —**mortifica'tion** n.

mor'tise [-tis] n. hole in piece of wood etc. to receive the tongue (tenon) and end of another piece —vt. make mortise in; fasten by mortise and tenon —**mortise lock** one embedded in door

mor'tuary n. building where corpses are kept before burial —a. of, for burial

Mosa'ic [mō-zā'ik] a. of Moses

mosa'ic [mō-zā'ik] n. picture or pattern of small bits of coloured stone, glass etc.; this process of decoration

Moselle' [mō-zel'] n. light white wine

Mos'lem n. see MUSLIM

mosque [mosk] n. Muslim temple

mosqui'to [-kē'tō] n. various kinds of flying, biting insects (pl. **-toes**)

moss *n.* small plant growing in masses on moist surfaces; peat bog, swamp —**moss'y** *a.* covered with moss —**moss agate** agate with mosslike markings

moss'ie *n.* **SA** Cape sparrow

most [mōst] *a.* greatest in size, number, or degree —*sup.* of MUCH and of MANY —*n.* greatest number, amount, or degree —*adv.* in the greatest degree; **US** *abbrev.* of ALMOST —**most'ly** *adv.* for the most part, generally, on the whole

MOT Ministry of Transport —**MOT test** compulsory annual test of the roadworthiness of vehicles over a certain age

motel[1] [mō-] *n.* roadside hotel with accommodation for motorists and vehicles

motet[1] [mō-] *n.* short sacred vocal composition

moth *n.* usu. nocturnal insect like butterfly; its grub —**moth'y** *a.* infested with moths —**moth'-ball** *n.* small ball of camphor or naphthalene to repel moths from stored clothing *etc.* —*vt.* put in mothballs; store, postpone *etc.* —**moth'eaten** *a.* eaten, damaged by grub of moth; decayed, scruffy

moth'er [muTH'-] *n.* female parent; head of religious community of women —*a.* natural, native, inborn —*vt.* act as mother to —**moth'erhood** *n.* —**moth'erly** *a.* —**mother-in-law** *n.* mother of one's wife or husband —**mother of pearl** iridescent lining of certain shells

motif[1] [mō-tēf'] *n.* dominating theme; recurring design

mo'tion *n.* process or action or way of moving; proposal in meeting; application to judge; evacuation of bowels —*vt.* direct by sign —**mo'tionless** *a.* still, immobile

mo'tive *n.* that which makes person act in particular way; inner impulse —*a.* causing motion —**mo'tivate** *vt.* instigate; incite —**motiva'tion** *n.*

mot'ley *a.* miscellaneous, varied; multicoloured —*n.* motley colour or mixture; jester's particoloured dress

mo'tocross *n.* motorcycle race over rough course

mo'tor *n.* that which imparts movement; machine to supply motive power; motorcar —*vi.* travel by car —**mo'toring** *n.* —**mo'torist** *n.* user of motorcar —**mo'torize** *vt.* equip with motor; provide with motor transport —**mo'torbike, mo'torcycle, mo'torboat, mo'torcar, motor scooter** *n.* vehicles driven by motor —**mo'torway** *n.* main road for fast-moving traffic, with limited access

mot'tle *vt.* mark with blotches, variegate —*n.* arrangement of blotches; blotch on surface

mott'o *n.* saying adopted as rule of conduct; short inscribed sentence; word or sentence on heraldic crest (*pl.* **-es**)

mou'f(f)lon [mōō'-] *n.* wild mountain sheep

mould[1] [mōld] *n.* hollow object in which metal *etc.* is cast; pattern for shaping; character; shape, form —*vt.* shape or pattern —**mould'ing** *n.* moulded object; ornamental edging; decoration

mould[2] [mōld] *n.* fungoid growth caused by dampness —**mould'y** *a.* stale, musty

mould[3] [mōld] *n.* loose or surface earth —**mould'er** *vi.* decay into dust

moult [mōlt] *v.* cast or shed fur, feathers *etc.* —*n.* moulting

mound *n.* heap of earth or stones; small hill

mount *vi.* rise; increase; get on

horseback —vt. get up on; frame (picture); fix, set up; provide with horse —n. that on which thing is supported or fitted; horse; hill

moun'tain n. hill of great size; surplus —**mountaineer'** n. one who lives among or climbs mountains —**mountaineer'ing** n. —**moun'tainous** a. very high, rugged

moun'tebank [-ti-] n. charlatan, fake

Mount'ie n. inf. member of Royal Canadian Mounted Police

mourn [-aw-] v. feel, show sorrow (for) —**mourn'er** n. —**mourn'ful** a. sad; dismal —**mourn'fully** adv. —**mourn'ing** n. grieving; conventional signs of grief for death; clothes of mourner

mouse n. small rodent (pl. mice) —vi. catch, hunt mice; prowl —**mous'er** n. cat used for catching mice —**mous'y** a. like mouse, esp. in colour; meek, shy

mousse [moos] n. sweet dish of flavoured cream whipped and frozen

moustache' [mə-stahsh'] n. hair on the upper lip

mouth [-th; pl. -THz] n. opening in head for eating, speaking etc.; opening into anything hollow; outfall of river; entrance to harbour etc. —vt. [-TH] declaim, esp. in public; form (words) with lips without speaking; take, move in mouth —**mouth'piece** n. end of anything placed between lips, eg pipe; spokesman

move [moov] vt. change position of; stir emotions of; incite; propose for consideration —vi. change places; change one's dwelling etc.; take action —n. a moving; motion towards some goal —**mov(e)'able** a./n. —**move'ment** n. process, action of moving; moving parts of machine; division of piece of music

mo'vie [moo-] US inf. n. film —pl. cinema

mow [mō] v. cut (grass etc.) (**mown** pp.) —**mow'er** n. man or machine that mows

MP Member of Parliament; Military Police; Mounted Police

mpg miles per gallon

mph miles per hour

Mr. mister

Mrs. title of married woman

Ms [miz] title used instead of Miss or Mrs.

MS(S) manuscript(s)

MSc Master of Science

MST US, C Mountain Standard Time

Mt. Mount

much a. existing in quantity (**more** comp., **most** sup.) —n. large amount; a great deal; important matter —adv. in a great degree; nearly

mu'cilage n. gum, glue

muck n. cattle dung; unclean refuse —**muck'y** a. dirty; messy; unpleasant

mu'cus n. viscid fluid secreted by mucous membrane —**mucos'ity** n. —**mu'cous** a. resembling mucus; secreting mucus; slimy —**mucous membrane** lining of canals and cavities of the body

mud n. wet and soft earth; inf. slander —**mudd'y** a. —**mud'guard** n. cover over wheel to prevent mud, water etc. being splashed —**mud'pack** n. cosmetic paste to improve complexion

mud'dle vt. (esp. with up) confuse; bewilder; mismanage —n. confusion; tangle

mues'li [myōōz'-] n. mixture of grain, dried fruit etc. eaten with milk

muezz'in [myōō-ez'-] n. crier who summons Muslims to prayer

muff[1] n. tube-shaped covering

to keep the hands warm

muff[1] *vt.* miss, bungle, fail in

muff'in *n.* round, spongy, flat scone

muf'fle *vt.* wrap up, esp. to deaden sound —**muff'ler** *n.* scarf

muf'ti *n.* plain clothes as distinguished from uniform, *eg* of soldier

mug[1] *n.* drinking cup

mug[2] *n. sl.* face; *sl.* fool, simpleton, one easily imposed upon —*vt.* rob violently —**mugg'er** *n.*

mug[3] *vi. inf.* (*esp. with up*) study hard

mugg'ins *n. inf.* fool, simpleton

mugg'y *a.* damp and stifling

mulatt'o [myōō-] *n.* child of one European and one Negro parent (*pl.* **-o(e)s**)

mul'berry *n.* tree whose leaves are used to feed silkworms; its purplish fruit

mulch *n.* straw, leaves *etc.*, spread as protection for roots of plants —*vt.* protect thus

mulct *vt.* defraud; fine

mule *n.* animal which is cross between horse and ass; hybrid; spinning machine —**muleteer'** [myōō-li-] *n.* mule driver —**mu'lish** *a.* obstinate

mull *vt.* heat (wine) with sugar and spices; think (over), ponder

mull'ah *n.* Muslim theologian

mull'e(i)n [-lin] *n.* plant with tall spikes of yellow flowers

mull'et *n.* edible sea fish

mulligataw'ny *n.* soup made with curry powder

mull'ion *n.* upright dividing bar in window —**mull'ioned** *a.*

multi-, mult- (*comb. form*) many, as in **multira'cial** *a.*, **multisto'rey** *a.* Such words are omitted where the meaning may easily be found from the simple word

multifa'rious *a.* of various

kinds or parts —**multifa'riously** *adv.*

mul'tiple *a.* having many parts —*n.* quantity which contains another an exact number of times —**multiplicand'** *n. Math.* number to be multiplied —**multiplica'tion** *n.* —**multiplic'ity** [-plis'-] *n.* variety, greatness in number —**mul'tiply** *v.* (cause to) increase in number, quantity, or degree —*vt.* combine (two numbers or quantities) by multiplication —*vi.* increase in number by reproduction (-**plied, -plying**)

mul'tiplex *a. Telecommunications* capable of transmitting numerous messages over same wire or channel

mul'titude *n.* great number; great crowd; populace —**multitu'dinous** *a.* very numerous

mum, mummy[1] *n. inf.* mother

mum'ble *v.* speak indistinctly, mutter

mumm'er *n.* actor in dumb show —**mum** *a.* silent —**mum(m)** *v.* act in mime (-**mm-**) —**mum'mery** *n.* dumb show acting

mumm'y[2] *n.* embalmed body —**mumm'ify** *vt.* (-**fied, -fying**)

mumps *pl.n.* infectious disease marked by swelling in the glands of the neck

munch *v.* chew noisily and vigorously; crunch

mundane' *a.* ordinary, everyday; belonging to this world, earthly

munic'ipal [myōō-nis'-] *a.* belonging to affairs of city or town —**municipal'ity** *n.* city or town with local self-government; its governing body

munif'icent [myōō-] *a.* very generous —**munif'icence** *n.* bounty

mu'niments *pl.n.* title deeds, documents verifying ownership

muni'tion [myoo-nish'-] *n.* (*usu. pl.*) military stores

mur'al [myoor'-] *n.* painting on a wall —*a.* of or on a wall

mur'der *n.* unlawful premeditated killing of human being —*vt.* kill thus —**mur'derer** *n.* (**mur'deress** *fem.*) —**mur'derous** *a.*

murk *n.* thick darkness —**murk'y** *a.* gloomy

mur'mur *n.* low, indistinct sound —*vi.* make such a sound; complain —*vt.* utter in a low voice

murr'ain [-in] *n.* cattle plague

mus. museum; music(al)

mus'cat *n.* musk-flavoured grape; raisin —**muscatel'** *n.* muscat; strong wine made from it

mus'cle [mus'al] *n.* part of body which produces movement by contracting; system of muscles —**mus'cular** *a.* with well-developed muscles; strong; of, like muscle —**muscle-bound** *a.* with muscles stiff through over-development —**muscular dystrophy** [dis'trə-fi] *disease* with wasting of muscles —**muscle in** *inf.* force one's way into

Muse [myooz] *n.* one of the nine goddesses inspiring learning and the arts

muse [myooz] *vi.* ponder; consider meditatively; be lost in thought —*n.* state of musing or abstraction; reverie

muse'um [myoo-ze'-] *n.* (place housing) collection of natural, artistic, historical or scientific objects

mush *n.* soft pulpy mass; *inf.* cloying sentimentality —**mush'y** *a.*

mush'room *n.* fungoid growth, typically with stem and cap structure, some species edible —*vi.* shoot up rapidly; expand

mu'sic [-z-] *n.* art form using melodious and harmonious combination of notes; laws of this; composition in this art —**mu'sical** *a.* of, like music; interested in, or with instinct for, music; pleasant to ear —*n.* show, film in which music plays essential part —**mu'sically** *adv.* —**musi'cian** [-zish'ən] *n.* —**musicol'ogist** *n.* —**musicol'ogy** *n.* scientific study of music —**musical comedy** light dramatic entertainment of songs, dances *etc.* —**music hall** variety theatre

musk *n.* scent obtained from gland of **musk deer**; various plants with similar scent —**mus'ky** *a.* —**musk ox** ox of Arctic Amer. —**musk'rat** *n.* N Amer. rodent found near water; its fur

mus'ket *n. Hist.* infantryman's gun —**musketeer'** *n.* —**mus'ketry** *n.* (use of) firearms

Mus'lim *n.* follower of religion of Islam —*a.* of religion, culture *etc.* of Islam

mus'lin [-z-] *n.* fine cotton fabric —**mus'lined** *a.*

mus'quash *n.* muskrat

muss'el *n.* bivalve shellfish

must[1] *v. aux.* be obliged to, or certain to —*n.* something one must do

must[2] *n.* newly-pressed grape juice; unfermented wine

mus'tang *n.* wild horse

mus'tard *n.* powder made from the seeds of a plant, used in paste as a condiment; the plant —**mustard gas** poisonous gas causing blistering

mus'ter *v.* assemble —*n.* assembly, *esp.* for exercise, inspection

must'y *a.* mouldy, stale —**must'ness** *n.*

mutate' [myoo-] *v.* (cause to) undergo mutation —**mu'table** *a.* liable to change —**mu'tant** *n.* mutated animal, plant *etc.* —**muta'tion** *n.* change, *esp.* genetic change causing divergence from kind or racial type

mute a. dumb; silent —n. dumb person; *Mus.* contrivance to soften tone of instruments —**mu'ted** a. (of sound) muffled; (of light) subdued —**mute'ly** adv.

mu'ti [moo'-] n. **SA** (herbal) medicine

mu'tilate vt. deprive of a limb or other part; damage; deface —**mutila'tion** n. —**mu'tilator** n.

mu'tiny n. rebellion against authority, esp. against officers of disciplined body —vi. commit mutiny (**mu'tinied, mu'tinying**) —**mutineer'** n. —**mu'tinous** a. rebellious

mutt inf. n. stupid person; dog

mutt'er vi. speak with mouth nearly closed, indistinctly; grumble —vt. utter in such tones —n. act of muttering

mutt'on n. flesh of sheep used as food —**mutton bird** migratory seabird —**mutt'onhead** n. sl. fool

mu'tual a. done, possessed etc., by each of two with respect to the other; reciprocal; inf. common to both or all —**mu'tually** adv.

Mu'zak R recorded light music played in shops etc.

muz'zle n. mouth and nose of animal; cover for these to prevent biting; open end of gun —vt. put muzzle on; silence, gag

muzz'y a. indistinct, confused, muddled

MV motor vessel

MW megawatt(s)

mW milliwatt(s)

my a. belonging to me —**myself'** pron. emphatic or reflexive form of I or ME

myal'gia n. pain in a muscle

mycol'ogy n. science of fungi

my'na(h) n. Indian bird related to starling

myo'pia n. short-sightedness —**myop'ic** a.

myoso'tis n. kinds of small plant with blue, pink or white flowers, eg. forget-me-not

myr'iad [mir'-] a. innumerable —n. large indefinite number

myrrh [mer] n. aromatic gum, formerly used as incense

myr'tle [mer'-] n. flowering evergreen shrub

myself' see MY

mys'tery [mis'-] n. obscure or secret thing; anything strange or inexplicable; religious rite; in Middle Ages, biblical play —**myste'rious** a. —**myste'riously** adv.

mys'tic [mis'-] n. one who seeks divine, spiritual knowledge, esp by prayer, contemplation etc. —a. of hidden meaning, esp. in religious sense —**myst'ical** a. —**myst'icism** n.

mys'tify [mis'-] vt. bewilder, puzzle (-**fied, -fying**) —mystifica'tion n.

mystique' [mis-tēk'] n. aura of mystery, power etc.

myth [.mith] n. tale with supernatural characters or events; invented story; imaginary person or object —**myth'ical** a. —**mytholog'ical** a. —**mythol'ogist** n. —**mythol'ogy** n. myths collectively; study of them

myxomato'sis [miks-] n. contagious, fatal disease of rabbits caused by a virus

N

N Chess knight; Chem. nitrogen; Physics newton; north(ern)

n. neuter; noun; number

Na Chem. sodium

Naaf'i [naf'-] n. organization providing canteens etc. for the services (*Navy, Army and Air Force Institutes*)

naar'tjie [nahr'chè] *n.* **SA** tangerine

nab *inf. vt.* arrest criminal; catch suddenly (**-bb-**)

NACODS National Association of Colliery Overmen, Deputies and Shotfirers

na'cre [-kər] *n.* mother-of-pearl; shellfish

na'dir *n.* point opposite the zenith; lowest point

naeve, nae'vus [nēv'-] *n.* congenital mark on skin; birthmark, mole

naff *a. sl.* inferior or useless

nag [*v.* scold or annoy constantly; cause pain to constantly (**-gg-**) —*n.* nagging; one who nags

nag [*n. inf.* horse; small horse for riding

nai'ad [nī-] *n.* water nymph

nail [nāl] *n.* horny shield at ends of fingers, toes; claw; small metal spike for fixing wood *etc.* —*vt.* fix, stud with nails; *inf.* catch

naive', naïve' [nah-ēv', nī-] *a.* simple, unaffected, ingenuous —**naiveté', naïve'ty** *n.*

na'ked *a.* without clothes; exposed, bare; undisguised —**na'kedly** *adv.* —**na'kedness** *n.* —**naked eye** the eye unassisted by any optical instrument

NALGO National and Local Government Officers' Association

nam'by-pam'by *a.* weakly; sentimental; insipid —*n.*

name *n.* word by which person, thing *etc.* is denoted; reputation; title; credit; family; famous person —*vt.* give name to; call by name; entitle; appoint; mention; specify —**name'less** *a.* without a name; indescribable; too dreadful to be mentioned; obscure —**name'ly** *adv.* that is to say —**name'sake** *n.* person with

same name as another

nann'y *n.* child's nurse —**nanny goat** she-goat

nap [*vi.* take short sleep, *esp.* in daytime (**-pp-**) —*n.* short sleep

nap [*n.* downy surface on cloth made by projecting fibres

nap [*n.* card game

na'palm [nā'pahm, nap'-] *n.* jellied petrol, highly inflammable, used in bombs *etc.*

nape *n.* back of neck

naph'tha [naf'-, nap'-] *n.* inflammable oil distilled from coal *etc.* —**naph'thalene** *n.* white crystalline product distilled from coal tar, used in disinfectants, mothballs *etc.*

nap'kin *n.* cloth, paper for wiping fingers or lips at table, serviette; small towel; nappy

napp'y *n.* towelling cloth or other material placed around waist, between legs, of baby to absorb its excrement

narciss'us *n.* genus of bulbous plants including daffodil, jonquil, *esp.* one with white flowers (*pl.* **-ciss'i** [-ī]) —**nar'cissism** *n.* abnormal love and admiration of oneself —**nar'cissist** *n.*

narcot'ic *n.* any of a group of drugs, including morphine and opium, producing numbness and stupor, used medicinally but addictive —*a.* —**narco'sis** *n.* effect of narcotic

nark *vt. sl.* annoy, irritate

narrate' *vt.* relate, recount, tell (story) —**narra'tion** *n.* —**narra'tive** *n.* account, story —*a.* relating —**narra'tor** *n.*

narr'ow [-ō] *a.* of little breadth, *esp.* in comparison to length; limited; barely adequate or successful —*v.* make, become narrow —**narr'ows** *pl.n.* narrow part of straits —**narr'owly** *adv.* —**narr'owness** *n.* —**narrow-minded** *a.* illiberal; bigoted

—**narrow-mindedness** n. prejudice, bigotry

nar'whal n. arctic whale with long spiral tusk

NASA US National Aeronautics and Space Administration

na'sal [-z-] a. of nose —n. sound partly produced in nose —**na'salize** vt. make nasal in sound —**na'sally** adv.

nas'cent a. just coming into existence; springing up

nastur'tium [-shəm] n. genus of plants which includes the watercress; trailing garden plant with red or orange flowers

nas'ty [nah-] a. foul, disagreeable, unpleasant —**nas'tily** adv. —**nas'tiness** n.

NAS/UWT National Association of Schoolmasters/Union of Women Teachers

nat. national; native; natural

na'tal a. of birth

na'tant a. floating

na'tion [-shən] n. people or race organized as a state —**na'tional** [nash'-] a. belonging or pert. to a nation; public, general —n. member of a nation —**na'tionalism** n. loyalty, devotion to one's country; movement for independence of state, people, ruled by another —**na'tionalist** n./a. —**national'ity** n. national quality or feeling; fact of belonging to particular nation —**nationaliza'tion** n. acquisition and management of industries by the State —**na'tionalize** vt. convert (private industry, resources etc.) to state control —**na'tionally** adv. —**National Health Service** system of medical services financed mainly by taxation —**national insurance** state insurance scheme providing payments to the unemployed, sick etc.

na'tive a. inborn; born in particular place; found in pure state;

that was place of one's birth —n. one born in a place; member of indigenous race of a country; species of plant, animal etc. originating in a place

nativ'ity n. birth; time, circumstances of birth; (N-) birth of Christ

NATO North Atlantic Treaty Organization

NATSOPA National Society of Operative Printers and Assistants

natt'er vi. inf. talk idly

natt'y a. neat and smart; spruce —**natt'ily** adv.

na'ture n. innate or essential qualities of person or thing; class, sort; life force; (oft. N-) power underlying all phenomena in material world; material world as a whole; natural unspoilt scenery or countryside, and plants and animals in it; disposition; temperament —**nat'ural** a. of, according to, occurring in, provided by, nature; inborn; normal; unaffected; illegitimate —n. something, somebody well suited for something; Mus. character (♮) used to remove effect of sharp or flat preceding it —**nat'uralist** n. student of natural history —**naturalis'tic** a. of or imitating nature in effect or characteristics —**naturaliza'tion** n. —**nat'uralize** vt. admit to citizenship; accustom to new climate —**nat'urally** adv. of or according to nature; by nature; of course —**na'turism** n. nature-worship; nudism —**na'turist** n. —**natural history** study of animals and plants

naught [nawt] n. obs. nothing; nought —**set at naught** defy, disregard

naught'y a. disobedient, not behaving well; inf. mildly indecent —**naught'ily** adv.

nau'sea [-si-ə, -zi-ə] *n.* feeling that precedes vomiting —**nau'seate** *vt.* sicken —**nau'seous** *a.* disgusting; causing nausea

nau'tical *a.* of seamen or ships; marine —**nautical mile** 1852 metres

nau'tilus *n.* univalvular shellfish (*pl.* **-tiluses, -till** [-I])

na'val *see* NAVY

nave[1] *n.* main part of church

nave[2] *n.* hub of wheel

na'vel *n.* umbilicus, small scar, depression in middle of abdomen where umbilical cord was attached

nav'igate *v.* plan, direct, plot path or position of ship *etc.*; travel —**nav'igable** *a.* —**naviga'tion** *n.* science of directing course of seagoing vessel, or of aircraft in flight; shipping —**nav'igator** *n.* one who navigates

navv'y *n.* labourer employed on roads, railways *etc.*

na'vy *n.* fleet; warships of country with their crews and organization —*a.* navy-blue —**na'val** *a.* of the navy —**navy-blue** *a.* very dark blue

nay *adv. obs.* no

Na'zi [naht'si] *n.* member of the National Socialist political party in Germany, 1919–45; one who thinks, acts, like a Nazi —*a.* —**Na'zi(i)ism** *n.* Nazi doctrine

NB nota bene

Nb *Chem.* niobium

NCB National Coal Board

NCO noncommissioned officer

NE northeast(ern)

Ne *Chem.* neon

Nean'derthal [ni-an'dər-tahl] *a.* of a type of primitive man

neap *a.* low —**neap tide** low tide at the first and third quarters of the moon

near *prep.* close to —*adv.* at or to a short distance —*a.* close at hand; closely related; narrow, so as barely to escape; stingy; (of vehicles, horses *etc.*) left —*v.* approach —**near'by** *a.* adjacent —**near'ly** *adv.* closely; almost —**near'ness** *n.*

neat *a.* tidy, orderly; efficient; precise, deft; cleverly worded; undiluted; simple and elegant —**neat'ly** *adv.* —**neat'ness** *n.*

neb'ula *n. Astronomy* diffuse cloud of particles, gases (*pl.* **-ulae** [-lē]) —**neb'ulous** *a.* cloudy; vague, indistinct

NEC National Executive Committee

nec'essary [nes'-] *a.* needful, requisite, that must be done; unavoidable, inevitable —**nec'essarily** *adv.* —**necess'itate** *vt.* make necessary —**necess'itous** *a.* poor, needy, destitute —**neces'sity** *n.* something needed, requisite; constraining power or state of affairs; compulsion; poverty

neck *n.* part of body joining head to shoulders; narrower part of a bottle *etc.*; narrow piece of anything between wider parts —*vi. sl.* embrace, cuddle —**neck'erchief** [-chif] *n.* kerchief for the neck —**neck'lace** *n.* ornament round the neck —**neck'let** *n.* neck ornament, piece of fur *etc.*

nec'romancy *n.* magic, *esp.* by communication with dead —**nec'romancer** *n.* wizard

necrop'olis *n.* cemetery (*pl.* **-olises, -oleis** [-lǝs])

nec'tar *n.* honey of flowers; drink of the gods —**nec'tary** *n.* honey gland of flower

nec'tarine [-rin] *n.* variety of peach

NEDC National Economic Development Council

née, nee [nā] *a.* indicating maiden name of married woman

need vt. want, require —n. (state, instance of) want; requirement; necessity; poverty —**need'ful** a. necessary, requisite —**need'less** a. unnecessary —**needs** adv. of necessity (esp. in **needs must** or **must needs**) —**need'y** a. poor, in want

nee'dle n. pointed pin with an eye and no head, for sewing; long, pointed pin for knitting; pointer of gauge, dial; magnetized bar of compass; stylus for record player; leaf of fir or pine; obelisk; inf. hypodermic syringe —vt. inf. goad, provoke —**nee'dlecord** n. corduroy fabric with narrow ribs —**nee'dlework** n. embroidery, sewing

ne'er [nâr] adv. Literary never —**ne'er-do-well** n. worthless person

nefar'ious [-âr'-] a. wicked

negate' vt. deny, nullify —**nega'tion** n. contradiction, denial

neg'ative a. expressing denial or refusal; lacking enthusiasm, energy, interest; not positive; of electrical charge having the same polarity as the charge of an electron —n. negative word or statement; Photography picture made by action of light on chemicals in which lights and shades are reversed —vt. disprove, reject

neglect' vt. disregard, take no care of; fail to do; omit through carelessness —n. fact of neglecting or being neglected —**neglect'ful** a.

neg'ligee, -gé(e) [-zhā] n. woman's light, gauzy nightdress or dressing gown

neg'ligence [-jɒns] n. neglect; carelessness —**neg'ligent** a. —**neg'ligible** a. able to be disregarded; very small or unimportant

nego'tiate vi. discuss with view to mutual settlement —vt. arrange by conference; transfer (bill, cheque etc.); get over, past, around (obstacle) —**nego'tiable** a. —**negotia'tion** n. treating with another on business; discussion; transference (of bill, cheque etc.) —**nego'tiator** n.

Ne'gro n. member of black orig. Afr. race (pl. -es, fem. **Ne'gress**) —**Ne'groid** a. of or like Negro

neigh [nā] n. cry of horse —vi. utter this cry

neigh'bour [nā'bər] n. one who lives near another —**neigh'bourhood** n. district; people of a district; region round about —**neigh'bouring** a. situated nearby —**neigh'bourly** a. as or befitting a good or friendly neighbour; friendly; sociable; helpful

nei'ther [nī'-, nē'-] a./pron. not the one or the other —adv. not on the one hand; not either —conj. not yet

nem. con. (Lat., nemine contradicente) unanimously

neme'sia n. garden plant with flowers of various colours

Nem'esis n. retribution; the goddess of vengeance

ne'o- (comb. form) new, later, revived in modified form, based upon

neolith'ic a. of the later Stone Age

neol'ogism [-j-] n. new-coined word or phrase —**neol'ogize** vi.

ne'on n. one of the inert constituent gases of the atmosphere, used in illuminated signs and lights

ne'ophyte n. new convert; beginner, novice

neph'ew [nev'-, nef'-] n. brother's or sister's son

nephri'tis [-frī'-] n. inflammation of a kidney

nep'otism n. undue favouritism towards one's relations

Nep'tune n. god of the sea; planet second farthest from sun

neptu'nium n. synthetic metallic element

nerve n. sinew, tendon; fibre or bundle of fibres conveying feeling, impulses to motion etc. to and from brain and other parts of body; assurance; coolness in danger; audacity —pl. irritability, unusual sensitiveness to fear, annoyance etc. —vt. give courage or strength to —**nerve'less** a. without nerves; useless; weak; paralysed —**nerv'ous** a. excitable; timid, apprehensive, worried; of the nerves —**nerv'ously** adv. —**nerv'ousness** n. —**nerv'y** a. nervous, jumpy, irritable; on edge —**nervous breakdown** condition of mental, emotional disturbance, disability

nes'cient [-si-ənt] a. ignorant; agnostic —**nes'cience** n.

ness n. headland, cape

nest n. place in which bird lays and hatches its eggs; animal's breeding place; snug retreat —vi. make, have a nest —**nest egg** (fund of) money in reserve

nes'tle [-sl] vi. settle comfortably, usu. pressing in or close to something

nest'ling n. bird too young to leave nest

net n. openwork fabric of meshes of cord etc.; piece of it used to catch fish etc. —vt. cover with, or catch in, net (-tt-) —**nett'ing** n. string or wire net —**net'ball** n. game in which ball has to be thrown through elevated horizontal ring, from which hangs short piece of netting

net(t) a. left after all deductions; free from deduction —vt. gain, yield as clear profit

neth'er [-TH-] a. lower

net'suke [-soo-ki] n. carved wooden or ivory toggle or button worn in Japan

net'tle n. plant with stinging hairs on the leaves —vt. irritate, provoke

net'work n. system of intersecting lines, roads etc.; interconnecting group of people or things; in broadcasting, group of stations connected to transmit same programmes simultaneously

neu'ral [nyoo'-] a. of the nerves

neural'gia [nyoor-] n. pain in, along nerves, esp. of face and head —**neural'gic** a.

neuri'tis [nyoor-] n. inflammation of nerves

neurol'ogy [nyoor-] n. science, study of nerves —**neurol'ogist** n.

neuro'sis [nyoor-] n. relatively mild mental disorder —**neurot'ic** a. suffering from nervous disorder; abnormally sensitive —n. neurotic person

neut'er [nyoo'-] a. neither masculine nor feminine —n. neuter word; neuter gender —vt. castrate, spay (domestic animals)

neu'tral [nyoo'-] a. taking neither side in war, dispute etc.; without marked qualities; belonging to neither of two classes —n. neutral nation or a subject of one; neutral gear —**neutral'ity** n. —**neu'tralize** vt. make ineffective; counterbalance —**neutral gear** in vehicle, position of gears that leaves transmission disengaged

neu'tron [nyoo'-] n. electrically neutral particle of the nucleus of an atom —**neutron bomb** nuclear bomb designed to destroy people but not buildings

nev'er adv. at no time —**nev'ertheless'** adv. for all that, notwithstanding

never-never n. inf. hire-purchase

new *a.* not existing before, fresh; that has lately come into some state or existence; unfamiliar, strange —*adv.* (*usu.* **new'ly**) recently, fresh —**new'ly** *adv.* —**new'ness** *n.* —**new'comer** *n.* recent arrival —**new'fang'led** [-ng'gld] *a.* of new fashion

new'el *n.* central pillar of winding staircase; post at top or bottom of staircase rail

news *n.* report of recent happenings, tidings; interesting fact not previously known —**news'y** *a.* full of news —**news'agent** *n.* shopkeeper who sells and distributes newspapers —**news'cast** *n.* news broadcast —**news'caster** *n.* —**news'flash** *n.* brief news item, *oft.* interrupting programme —**news'paper** *n.* periodical publication containing news —**news'print** *n.* paper of the kind used for newspapers *etc.* —**news'reel** *n.* cinema or television film giving news —**news'room** *n.* room where news is received and prepared for publication or broadcast —**news'worthy** *a.* sufficiently interesting or important to be reported as news

newt *n.* small, tailed amphibious creature

new'ton *n.* SI unit of force

next *a./adv.* nearest; immediately following —**next-of-kin** *n.* nearest relative

nex'us *n.* tie; connection, link (*pl.* **nex'us**)

NFU National Farmers' Union

NHS National Health Service

Ni *Chem.* nickel

nib *n.* (split) pen point; bird's beak —*pl.* crushed cocoa beans

nib'ble *v.* take little bites of —*n.* little bite

nibs *n.* mock title of respect, as **his nibs**

nice *a.* pleasant; friendly; kind; attractive; subtle; fine; careful;

exact; difficult to decide —**nice'ly** *adv.* —**ni'cety** [-si-ti] *n.* minute distinction or detail; subtlety; precision

niche [nich, nēsh] *n.* recess in wall; suitable place in life, public estimation *etc.*

nick *vt.* make notch in, indent; *sl.* steal —*n.* notch; exact point of time; *sl.* prison —**in good nick** *inf.* in good condition

nick'el *n.* silver-white metal much used in alloys and plating; **US, C** five cent piece

nickelo'deon US *n. Hist* cheap cinema; jukebox

nick'name *n.* familiar name added to or replacing an ordinary name

nic'otine [-ēn] *n.* poisonous oily liquid in tobacco —**nic'otinism** *n.* tobacco poisoning

niece *n.* brother's or sister's daughter

nif'ty *inf.* *a.* neat, smart; quick

nigg'ard *n.* mean, stingy person —**nigg'ardly** *a./adv.*

nigg'er *n.* offens. Negro

nig'gle *vi.* find fault continually; annoy —**nig'gling** *a.* petty; irritating and persistent

nigh [nī] *a./adv./prep.*, *obs.* or *Poet.* near

night [nīt] *n.* time of darkness between sunset and sunrise; end of daylight; dark —**night'ie, night'y** *n.* woman's nightdress —**night'ly** *a.* happening, done every night; of the night —*adv.* every night; by night —**night'cap** *n.* cap worn in bed; late-night (alcoholic) drink —**night'club** *n.* establishment for dancing, music *etc.* opening late at night —**night'dress** *n.* woman's loose robe worn in bed —**night'ingale** [-ng-g-] *n.* small bird which sings *usu.* at night —**night'jar** *n.* nocturnal bird with harsh cry —**night'mare** *n.* very bad dream;

terrifying experience **—night'-shade** n. various plants of potato family, some of them with very poisonous berries **—night-time** n.

ni'hilism [nʰil-] n. rejection of all religious and moral principles; opposition to all constituted authority, or government **—ni'-hilist** n. **—nihilist'ic** a.

nil n. nothing, zero

nim'ble a. agile, active, quick, dexterous **—nim'bly** adv.

nim'bus n. rain or storm cloud; cloud of glory, halo (pl. **-bi** [-bi'], **-buses**)

nin'compoop n. fool, simpleton

nine a./n. cardinal number next above eight **—ninth** [-1-] a. **—ninth'ly** adv. **—nine'teen'** a./ ₙ.ᵢ nine'more, than ten ' **—nine'-teenth'** a. **—nine'ty** a./n. nine tens **—nine'tieth** a. **—nine'pins** pl.n. game where wooden pins are set up to be knocked down by rolling ball, skittles

ninn'y n. fool, simpleton

nip vt. pinch sharply; detach by pinching, bite; check growth (of plants) **—**sl. steal **—**vi. inf. hurry (**-pp-**) **—**n. pinch; check to growth; sharp coldness of weather; short drink **—nipp'er** n. thing (eg crab's claw) that nips; inf. small child **—**pl. pincers **—nipp'y** inf. a. cold; quick

nip'ple n. point of a breast, teat; anything like this

Nipp'on n. Japan

NIREX Nuclear Industry Radioactive Waste Executive

nirvan'a [-vahn'ə] n. Buddhism absolute blessedness; Hinduism merging of individual in supreme spirit

ni'si a. (of decree) coming into effect within a certain time, unless cause is shown for rescinding it (esp. in divorce cases)

Niss'en hut temporary military building of corrugated sheet steel

nit n. egg of louse or other parasite; inf. short for nitwit **—nit-picking** a. inf. overconcerned with detail, esp. to find fault **—nit'wit** n. inf. fool **—nitty-gritty** n. inf. basic facts, details

ni'trogen n. one of the gases making up the air **—ni'trate** n. compound of nitric acid and an alkali **—ni'tric, ni'trous** a. **—nitrog'enous** [-j-] a. of, containing nitrogen **—nitrogly'cerin(e)** [-s-] n. explosive liquid

nix n. sl. nothing

NNE north-northeast

NNW north-northwest

no a. not any, not a; not at all **—**adv. expresses negative reply to question or request **—**n. refusal; denial; negative vote or voter (pl. **noes**) **—no-one, no one** nobody **—no-go** area district barricaded off, which police, army can only enter by force **—no-man's-land** waste or unclaimed land; contested land between two opposing forces

no. number

nob sl. n. member of upper classes; the head

nob'ble sl. vt. disable (esp. racehorse with drugs); secure dishonestly; catch criminal; cheat, swindle

nobe'lium n. synthetic element produced from curium

No'bel Prize prize awarded annually since 1901 for outstanding achievement in various fields

no'ble a. of the nobility; showing, having high moral qualities; impressive, excellent **—**n. member of the nobility **—nobil'ity** n. class holding special rank, usu. hereditary, in state; being noble **—no'bleman** n. **—no'bly** adv.

no'body n. no person; person of no importance

noc'turnal a. of, in, by, night; active by night

noc'turne n. dreamy piece of music; night scene

nod v. bow head slightly and quickly in assent, command etc.; let head droop with sleep (-dd-) —n. act of nodding —**nodding acquaintance** slight knowledge of person or subject —**nod off** inf. fall asleep

nod'dle n. inf. the head

node n. knot or knob; point at which curve crosses itself —**no'dal** a. —**nod'ical** a.

nod'ule n. little knot; rounded irregular mineral mass

Noel', Nowel(l)' [nō-el'] n. Christmas; Christmas carol

nog n. peg or block; stump —**nog'ging** n. horizontal timber member in framed construction

nogg'in n. small amount of liquor; small mug; inf. head

noise n. any sound, esp. disturbing one; clamour, din; loud outcry; talk or interest —vt. rumour —**noise'less** a. without noise, quiet, silent —**nois'ily** adv. —**nois'y** a. making much noise; clamorous

noi'some a. disgusting

no'mad n. member of tribe with no fixed dwelling place; wanderer —**nomad'ic** a.

nom de plume Fr. writer's

assumed name; pen name; pseudonym

nomen'clature n. terminology of particular science etc.

nom'inal a. in name only; (of fee etc.) small, insignificant; of a name or names —**nom'inally** adv. in name only; not really

nom'inate vt. propose as candidate; appoint to office —**nomina'tion** n. —**nom'inative** a./n. (of) case of nouns, pronouns when subject of verb —**nomina'tor** n. —**nominee'** n. candidate

non- (comb. form) negatives the idea of the simple word, as in list below

nonagena'rian [nōn-] a. aged between ninety and ninety-nine —n. person of such age

non'agon n. plane figure of nine sides

nonaligned' a. (of states etc.) not part of a major alliance or power bloc

nonce n. —**for the nonce** for the occasion only; for the present

non'chalant [-sh-] a. casually unconcerned, indifferent, cool —**non'chalance** n. —**non'chalantly** adv.

noncom'batant n. civilian during war; member of army who does not fight eg doctor

noncommiss'ioned offic'er Mil. subordinate officer, risen from the ranks

nonaggress'ion	nonexist'ent	nonselec'tive
nonalcohol'ic	nonfic'tion	nonshrink'able
nonbeliev'er	noninterven'tion	nonslip'
nonbreak'able	noni'ron	nonsmo'ker
noncombust'ible	nonmem'ber	nonstan'dard
noncompet'itive	non-nego'tiable	nonstart'er
nonconduc'tive	nonpart'y	nonstick'
noncontrib'utory	nonpay'ment	nonstop'
noncontrover'sial	non-profit-making	nontax'able
nondenomina'tional	nonread'er	nontech'nical
nondrink'er	nonres'ident	nontox'ic
nonevent'	nonreturn'able	nonvi'olent

noncommitt'al a. avoiding definite preference or pledge

non com'pos men'tis Lat. of unsound mind

nonconform'ist n. dissenter, esp. from Established Church —**nonconform'ity** n.

non'descript a. lacking distinctive characteristics, indeterminate

none [nun] pron. no-one, not any —a. no —adv. in no way —**none'theless'** adv. despite that, however

nonen'tity n. insignificant person, thing; nonexistent thing

nonflamm'able a. incapable of burning; not easily set on fire

non'pareil [-rəl] a. unequalled, matchless —n. person or thing unequalled or unrivalled

nonplus' vt. disconcert, confound, or bewilder completely (-ss-)

non'sense n. lack of sense; absurd language; absurdity; silly conduct —**nonsen'sical** a. ridiculous; meaningless; without sense

non se'quitur [-sek'wit-] Lat. statement with little or no relation to what preceded it

noo'dle[1] n. strip of pasta served in soup etc.

noo'dle[2] n. simpleton, fool

nook n. sheltered corner, retreat —**nook'y** a.

noon [-ōō-] n. midday, twelve o'clock —**noon'day** n. noon —**noon'tide** n. the time about noon

noose [-ōō-] n. running loop; snare —vt. catch, ensnare in noose, lasso

nor conj. and not

Nor'dic a. pert. to peoples of Germanic stock

norm n. average level of achievement; rule or authoritative standard; model; standard type or pattern —**nor'mal** a.

ordinary; usual; conforming to type —n. Geom. perpendicular —**normal'ity** n. —**nor'mally** adv.

north [-th] n. direction to the right of person facing the sunset; part of the world, of country etc. towards this point —adv. towards or in the north —a. to, from, or in the north —**nor'therly** [-TH-] a. —n. wind from the north —**nor'thern** a. —**nor'therner** n. person from the north —**north'wards** adv.

Northants. Northamptonshire

Northd. Northumberland

nos. numbers

nose n. organ of smell, used also in breathing; any projection resembling a nose, as prow of ship, aircraft etc. —v. (cause to) move forward slowly and carefully —vt. touch with nose; smell, sniff —vi. smell; pry —**no'se(y)** a. inf. inquisitive —**nose dive** downward sweep of aircraft —**nose'gay** n. bunch of flowers

nosh sl. n. food —v. eat

nostal'gia [-j-] n. longing for return of past events; homesickness —**nostal'gic** a.

nos'tril n. one of the two external openings of the nose

nos'trum n. quack medicine; secret remedy

not adv. expressing negation, refusal, denial

no'ta be'ne [-ni] Lat. note well

no'table a. worthy of note, remarkable —n. person of distinction —**notabil'ity** n. an eminent person —**no'tably** adv.

no'tary n. person authorized to draw up deeds, contracts

nota'tion n. representation of numbers, quantities, by symbols; set of such symbols

notch n. V-shaped cut or indentation; inf. step, grade —vt. make notches in

note n. brief comment or record;

short letter; banknote; symbol for musical sound; single tone; sign; indication, hint; fame; notice; regard —*pl.* brief jottings written down for future reference —*vt.* observe, record; heed —**no'ted** *a.* well-known —**note'book** *n.* small book with blank pages for writing —**note'worthy** *a.* worth noting, remarkable

noth'ing [nuth'-] *n.* no thing, not anything, nought —*adv.* not at all, in no way —**noth'ingness** *n.*

no'tice [-tis] *n.* observation; attention, consideration; warning, intimation, announcement; advance notification of intention to end a contract *etc.*, as of employment; review —*vt.* observe, mention; give attention to —**no'ticeable** *a.* conspicuous; attracting attention; appreciable

no'tify *vt.* report; give notice of or to (-**fied, -fying**) —**notifi'able** *a.* —**notifica'tion** *n.*

no'tion *n.* concept; opinion; whim —**no'tional** *a.* speculative, imaginary, abstract

notor'ious *a.* known for something bad; well-known —**notori'ety** *n.* discreditable publicity

Notts. Nottinghamshire

notwithstand'ing *prep.* in spite of —*adv.* all the same —*conj.* although

nou'gat [nōō'gah, nug'ət] *n.* chewy sweet containing nuts, fruit *etc.*

nought [nawt] *n.* nothing; cipher 0

noun [nown] *n.* word used as name of person, idea, or thing, substantive

nour'ish [nu'-] *vt.* feed; nurture; tend; encourage —**nour'ishment** *n.*

nous [nows] *n.* mind, intellect; common sense

nouvelle cuisine [nōōvel'] *Fr.* style of preparing and pre-

senting food with light sauces and unusual combinations of flavours

Nov. November

no'va *n.* star that suddenly becomes brighter then loses brightness through months or years (*pl.* -**vae** [-vē], -**vas**)

nov'el[1] *n.* fictitious tale in book form —**novelette'** *n.* short novel —**nov'elist** *n.* writer of novels

nov'el[2] *a.* new, recent; strange —**nov'elty** *n.* newness; something new or unusual; small ornament, trinket

Novem'ber *n.* the eleventh month

nove'na [nō-vē'-] *n.* R.C. Church prayers, services, lasting nine consecutive days

nov'ice *n.* one new to anything; beginner; candidate for admission to religious order —**novi'tiate, novi'ciate** [-vish'-] *n.* probationary period; part of religious house for novices; novice

now *adv.* at the present time; immediately; recently (*oft. with* just) —*conj.* seeing that, since —**now'adays** *adv.* in these times, at present

now'el *n.* inner part of large mould used for castings

Nowel(l)[1] *n.* see NOEL

no'where *adv.* not in any place or state

no'wise *adv.* not in any manner or degree

nox'ious [-k'shəs] *a.* poisonous, harmful

noz'zle *n.* pointed spout, *esp.* at end of hose

NSPCC National Society for the Prevention of Cruelty to Children

NT National Trust; New Testament

nuance' [nyōō-ahns', nyōō'-] *n.* delicate shade of difference, in colour, tone of voice *etc.*

nub n. small lump; main point (of story etc.)

nu'bile a. marriageable

nu'cleus n. centre, kernel; beginning meant to receive additions; core of the atom (pl. **-lei** [-li-I]) —**nu'clear** [-i-ər] a. of, pert. to atomic nucleus —**nucleon'ics** pl.n. (with sing. v.) branch of physics dealing with applications of nuclear energy —**nuclear energy** energy released by nuclear fission —**nuclear fission** disintegration of the atom —**nuclear reaction** change in structure and energy content of atomic nucleus by interaction with another nucleus, particle —**nuclear reactor** see REACTOR —**nuclear winter** period of extremely low temperatures and little light after nuclear war

nude [nyōōd] n. state of being naked; (picture, statue etc. of) naked person —a. naked —**nu'dism** n. practice of nudity —**nu'dist** n. —**nu'dity** n.

nudge vt. touch slightly with elbow —n. such touch

nu'gatory a. trifling, futile

nugg'et n. rough lump of native gold

nui'sance [nyōō'-] n. something or someone harmful, offensive, annoying or disagreeable

NUJ National Union of Journalists

nuke [nyōōk] vt. sl. attack or destroy with nuclear weapons

null a. of no effect, void —**null'ify** vt. cancel; make useless or ineffective (**-fied, -fying**) —**null'ity** n. state of being null and void

NUM National Union of Mineworkers

Num. Numbers

numb [num] a. deprived of feeling, esp. by cold —vt. make numb; deaden

num'ber n. sum or aggregate; word or symbol saying how many; single issue of a paper etc., issued in regular series; classification as to singular or plural; song, piece of music; performance; company, collection; identifying number, as of particular house, telephone etc.; sl. measure, correct estimation of —vt. count; class, reckon; give a number to; amount to —**num'berless** a. countless —**number crunching** Computers large-scale processing of numerical data —**num'berplate** n. plate on front and rear of car with registration number

nu'meral n. sign or word denoting a number —**nu'merate** a. able to use numbers in calculations —vt. count —**numera'tion** n. —**nu'merator** n. top part of fraction, figure showing how many of the fractional units are taken —**numer'ical** a. of, in respect of, number or numbers —**nu'merous** a. many

numismat'ic [nyōō-miz-] a. of coins —**numismat'ics** pl.n. (with sing. v.) the study of coins —**numis'matist** n.

num'skull n. dolt, dunce

nun n. woman living in (convent) under religious vows —**nunn'ery** n. convent of nuns

NUPE National Union of Public Employees

nup'tial a. of, relating to marriage —**nup'tials** pl.n. marriage; wedding ceremony

NUR National Union of Railwaymen

nurse n. person trained for care of sick or injured; woman tending another's child —vt. act as nurse to; suckle; pay special attention to; harbour (grudge etc.) —**nur'sery** n. room for children; rearing place for plants —**nur'seryman** n. one who raises plants for sale —**nursery slope** gentle slope for beginners in skiing —**nursing officer** administrative head of nursing staff of hospital

nur'ture n. bringing up; education; rearing; nourishment —vt. bring up; educate

NUT National Union of Teachers

nut n. fruit consisting of hard shell and kernel; hollow metal collar into which a screw fits; inf. head; inf. eccentric or crazy person (also **nutt'er**) —vi. gather nuts (-tt-) —**nutt'y** a. of, like nut; pleasant to taste and bite; sl. insane, crazy (also **nuts**) —**nut'hatch** n. small songbird —**nut'meg** n. aromatic seed of Indian tree

nu'tria n. fur of coypu

nu'trient a. nourishing —n. something nutritious

nu'triment n. nourishing food —**nutri'tion** [-trish'-] n. receiving foods; act of nourishing —**nutri'tious, nu'tritive** a. nourishing; promoting growth

nux vom'ica n. seed of tree which yields strychnine

nuz'zle vi. burrow, press with nose; nestle

NW northwest(ern)

ny'lon n. synthetic material used for fabrics, bristles, ropes etc. —pl. stockings made of this

nymph n. legendary semidivine maiden of sea, woods, mountains etc.

nymph'et n. sexually precocious young girl

nymphoma'nia n. abnormally intense sexual desire in women

NZ New Zealand

O

O Chem. oxygen

oaf n. lout; dolt

oak n. common, deciduous forest tree —**oak'en** a. of oak —**oak apple** round gall on oak trees

oak'um n. loose fibre got by unravelling old rope

OAP old age pensioner

oar n. wooden lever with broad blade worked by the hands to propel boat; oarsman —v. row —**oars'man** n. —**oars'manship** n. skill in rowing

oa'sis [ō-ā'-] n. fertile spot in desert (pl. **oa'ses** [-sēz])

oast n. kiln for drying hops

oat n. (usu. pl.) grain of cereal plant; the plant —**oat'meal** n.

oath n. confirmation of truth of statement by naming something sacred; curse

OAU Organization of African Unity

ob'durate a. stubborn, unyielding —**ob'duracy** n.

OBE Officer of the Order of the British Empire

obe'dience n. submission to authority —**obe'dient** a. willing to obey; compliant; dutiful —**obe'diently** adv.

obeis'ance [-bās'-, -bēs'-] n. a bow or curtsey

ob'elisk n. tapering rectangular stone column, with pyramidal apex

obese' a. very fat, corpulent —**obe'sity** n.

obey' [-bā'] vt. do the bidding of; act in accordance with —vi. do as ordered; submit to authority

ob'fuscate vt. perplex; darken

obit'uary n. notice, record of death; biographical sketch of deceased person, esp. in newspaper (also inf. **ob'it**) —obit**uarist** n.

obj. object; objective

ob'ject [1] n. material thing; that to which feeling or action is directed; end or aim; *Grammar* word dependent on verb or preposition —**object lesson** lesson with practical and concrete illustration —**no object** not an obstacle or hindrance

object [2] vt. state in opposition —vi. feel dislike or reluctance to something —**objec'tion** n. —**objec'tionable** a. disagreeable; justly liable to objection —**objec'tor** n.

objec'tive a. external to the mind; impartial —n. thing or place aimed at —**objectiv'ity** n.

objure' vt. charge under oath —**objura'tion** n.

ob'jurgate vt. scold, reprove —**objurga'tion** n.

ob'late a. of a sphere, flattened at the poles

obla'tion n. offering —**ob'late** n. person dedicated to religious work —**obla'tional** a.

ob(b)liga'to [-ah'-] n. an essential part of a musical score (pl. **-tos**)

oblige' vt. bind morally or legally to do service to; compel —**ob'-ligate** vt. bind esp. by legal contract; put under obligation —**obliga'tion** n. binding duty, promise; debt of gratitude —**oblig'atory** a. required; binding —**obli'ging** a. ready to serve others, civil, helpful, courteous

oblique' [-lēk'] a. slanting, indirect —**oblique'ly** adv. —**obliq'uity** [-lik'wit-i] n. slant; dishonesty —**oblique angle** one not a right angle

oblit'erate vt. blot out, efface, destroy completely —**oblitera'tion** n.

obliv'ion n. forgetting or being

forgotten —**obliv'ious** a. forgetful; unaware

ob'long a. rectangular, with adjacent sides unequal —n. oblong figure

ob'loquy [-kwi] n. reproach, abuse; disgrace; detraction

obnox'ious [-nok'shəs] a. offensive, disliked, odious

o'boe [-bō] n. woodwind instrument, hautboy —**o'boist** n.

obscene' a. indecent, lewd, repulsive —**obscen'ity** n.

obscure' a. unclear, indistinct; unexplained; dark, dim; humble —vt. make unintelligible; dim; conceal —**obscu'rant** n. one who opposes enlightenment or reform —**obscurant'ism** n. —**obscu'rity** n. indistinctness; lack of intelligibility; darkness; obscure, esp. unrecognized, place or position; retirement

ob'secrate vt. beseech

ob'sequies [-iz] pl.n. funeral rites —**obse'quial** a.

obse'quious a. servile, fawning

observe' [-z-] vt. notice, remark; watch; note systematically; keep, follow —vi. make a remark —**observ'able** a. —**observ'ably** adv. —**observ'ance** n. paying attention; keeping —**observ'ant** a. quick to notice —**observa'tion** n. action, habit of observing; noticing; remark —**observ'atory** n. place for watching stars etc. —**observ'er** n.

obsess' vt. haunt, fill the mind —**obses'sion** n. fixed idea; domination of the mind by one idea —**obsess'ive** a.

obsid'ian n. fused volcanic rock, forming hard, dark, natural glass

ob'solete a. disused, out of date —**obsoles'cent** [-ənt] a. going out of use

ob'stacle n. hindrance; impediment, barrier, obstruction

obstet'rics pl.n. (with sing. v.) branch of medicine concerned with childbirth and care of women before and after childbirth —**obstet'ric** a. —**obstetri'cian** n.

ob'stinate a. stubborn; self-willed; unyielding; hard to overcome or cure —**ob'stinacy** n. —**ob'stinately** adv.

obstrep'erous a. unruly, noisy, boisterous

obstruct' vt. block up; hinder; impede —**obstruc'tion** n. —**obstruc'tionist** n. one who deliberately opposes transaction of business —**obstruc'tive** a.

obtain' vt. get; acquire; procure by effort —vi. be customary —**obtain'able** a. procurable

obtrude' vt. thrust forward unduly —**obtru'sion** n. —**obtru'sive** a. forward, pushing —**obtru'sively** adv.

obtuse' [-tyōōs'] a. dull of perception; stupid; greater than right angle; not pointed —**obtuse'ly** adv.

ob'verse n. a fact, idea etc. which is the complement of another; side of coin, medal etc. that has the principal design —a.

ob'viate vt. remove, make unnecessary

ob'vious a. clear, evident; wanting in subtlety

ocari'na [-rē'-] n. small, egg-shaped wind instrument made of terracotta

occa'sion n. time when thing happens; reason, need; opportunity; special event —vt. cause —**occa'sional** a. happening, found now and then; produced for some special event, as occasional music —**occa'sionally** adv. sometimes, now and then

Oc'cident [ok'si-] n. the West —**Occident'al** a.

oc'ciput [ok'si-] n. back of head —**occip'ital** a.

occlude' [-klōōd'] vt. shut in or out —**occlu'sion** n. —**occlu'sive** a. serving to occlude

occult' a. secret, mysterious; supernatural —n. esoteric knowledge —vt. hide from view —**occulta'tion** n. eclipse —**occult'ism** n. study of supernatural —**occult'ness** n. mystery

occ'upy vt. inhabit, fill; employ; take possession of (-**pied**, -**pying**) —**occ'upancy** n. fact of occupying; residing —**occ'upant** n. —**occupa'tion** n. employment; pursuit; fact of occupying; seizure —**occupa'tional** a. pert. to occupation, esp. of diseases arising from a particular occupation; pert. to use of occupations, eg craft, hobbies etc. as means of rehabilitation —**occ'upier** n. tenant

occur' vi. happen; come to mind (-**rr**-) —**occurr'ence** n. happening

o'cean [ō'shən] n. great body of water; large division of this; the sea —**ocean'ic** [ō-shi-, ō-si-] a. —**oceanol'ogy** n. branch of science which relates to ocean

o'celot [ō'si-, os'i-] n. Amer. leopard

och'e [ok'i] n. Darts mark on the floor behind which a player must stand

o'chre [ō'kər] n. various earths used as yellow or brown pigments —**o'chr(e)ous** a.

o'clock' adv. by the clock

oct-, octa-, octo- (comb. form) eight

oc'tagon n. plane figure with eight angles —**octag'onal** a.

octahe'dron n. solid figure with eight sides

oc'tane n. ingredient of motor fuel —**octane rating** measure of quality or type of petrol

oc'tant *n.* the eighth part of a circle; instrument for measuring angles having arc of 45°

oc'tave *n. Mus.* eighth note above or below given note; this space; eight lines of verse

octa'vo *n.* book in which each sheet is folded three times forming eight leaves (*pl.* **-vos**)

octenn'ial *a.* lasting, happening every eight years

octet' *n.* group of eight; music for eight instruments or singers

Octo'ber *n.* the tenth month (Roman eighth)

octogena'rian *n.* person aged between eighty and ninety —*a.*

oc'topus *n.* mollusc with eight arms covered with suckers —**oc'topod** *n./a.* (mollusc) with eight feet

oc'tosyllable *n.* word, line of verse of eight syllables

OCTU Officer Cadets' Training Unit

oc'ular *a.* of eye or sight —**oc'ularly** *adv.*

OD *Med.* overdose

odd *a.* strange, queer; incidental; random; that is one in addition when the rest have been divided into equal groups; not even; not part of a set —**odds** *pl.n.* advantage conceded in betting; likelihood —**odd'ity** *n.* odd person or thing; quality of being odd —**odd'ments** *pl.n.* remnants; trifles —**odds and ends** odd fragments or scraps

ode *n.* lyric poem on particular subject

o'dium *n.* hatred, widespread dislike —**o'dious** *a.* hateful, repulsive, obnoxious

odontol'ogy *n.* science of dentistry

o'dour *n.* smell —**odorif'erous** *a.* spreading an odour —**o'dorize** *vt.* fill with scent —**o'dorous** *a.* fragrant; scented —**o'dourless** *a.*

Od'yssey *n.* Homer's epic describing Odysseus' return from Troy; any long adventurous journey

OECD Organization for Economic Cooperation and Development

oede'ma [i-dē'-] *n.* swelling in body tissues, due to accumulation of fluid

oesoph'agus [ē-] *n.* canal from mouth to stomach, gullet (*pl.* **-gi** [-gī]) —**oesophage'al** *a.*

oes'trogen [ēs'-] *n.* hormone in females *esp.* controlling changes, cycles in reproductive organs

of *prep.* denotes removal, separation, ownership, attribute, material, quality

off *adv.* away —*prep.* away from —*a.* not operative; cancelled or postponed; bad, sour *etc.*; distant; of horses, vehicles *etc.*, right; *Cricket* to bowler's left —**off'ing** *n.* part of sea visible to observer on ship or shore —**off colour** slightly ill —**offhand'** *a./adv.* without previous thought; curt —**off-licence** *n.* place where alcoholic drinks are sold for consumption elsewhere —**off'set** *n.* that which counterbalances, compensates; method of printing —**offset'** *vt.* —**off'spring** *n.* children, issue —**in the offing** likely to happen soon

off. office; officer; official

off'al *n.* edible entrails of animal; refuse

offend' *vt.* hurt feelings of, displease —*vi.* do wrong —**offence'** *n.* wrong; crime; insult —**offend'er** *n.* —**offen'sive** *a.* causing displeasure; aggressive —*n.* position or movement of attack

off'er *vt.* present for acceptance or refusal; tender; propose; attempt —*vi.* present itself —*n.* offering, bid —**off'erer** *n.* —**of'fertory** *n.* offering of the bread and wine at the Eucharist; collection in church service

off'ice n. room(s), building, in which business, clerical work etc. is done; commercial or professional organization; official position; service; duty; form of worship —pl. task; service —**off'icer** n. one in command in army, navy, ship etc.; official

offic'ial [-fish'-] a. with, by, authority —n. one holding office, esp. in public body —**offic'ialdom** n. officials collectively, or their attitudes, work, usu. in contemptuous sense —**Official Receiver** officer who manages estate of bankrupt

offic'iate [-fish'-] vi. perform duties of office; perform ceremony

offic'ious [-fish'əs] a. importunate in offering service; interfering

offside' a./adv. Sport illegally forward

of'ten [of'n] adv. many times, frequently (Poet. oft)

o'gee arch pointed arch with S-shaped curve on both sides

o'gle v. stare, look (at) amorously —n. this look —**o'gler** n.

o'gre [-gər] n. Folklore man-eating giant; monster (**o'gress** fem.)

oh [ō] interj. exclamation of surprise, pain etc.

ohm n. unit of electrical resistance —**ohm'meter** n. —**ohm'ic** a.

OHMS On His (or Her) Majesty's Service

oil n. any of a number of viscous liquids with smooth, sticky feel and wide variety of uses; petroleum; any of variety of petroleum derivatives, esp. as fuel or lubricant —vt. lubricate with oil; apply oil to —**oil'y** a. —**oil'skin** n. cloth treated with oil to make it

waterproof —**well oiled** sl. drunk

oint'ment n. greasy preparation for healing or beautifying the skin

o.k., okay! inf. a./adv. all right —n. approval —vt. approve

okap'i [-kahp'-] n. Afr. animal like short-necked giraffe

old [ōld] a. aged, having lived or existed long; belonging to earlier period (**old'er, eld'er** comp., **old'est, eld'est** sup.) —**old'en** a. old —**old'ish** a. —**old-fashioned** a. in style of earlier period, out of date; fond of old ways —**old maid** elderly spinster

oleag'inous [ō-lē-aj'-] a. oily, producing oil; unctuous, fawning —**oleag'inousness** n.

olean'der [ō-lē-an'-] n. evergreen flowering shrub, poisonous, esp. to cattle

oleas'ter [ō-lē-as'-] n. wild olive; yellow-flowered shrubs like it

olfac'tory a. of smelling

ol'igarchy [-ki] n. government by a few —**ol'igarch** n. —**oligarch'ic** a.

ol'ive [-iv] n. evergreen tree; its oil-yielding fruit; its wood —a. greyish-green

Olym'piad n. four-year period between Olympic Games

OM Order of Merit

om'budsman [-boodz-] n. official who investigates citizens' complaints against government etc.

o'mega [ō'-] n. last letter of Greek alphabet; end

om'elet(te) n. dish of eggs beaten up and fried with seasoning

o'men n. prophetic object or happening —**om'inous** a. boding evil, threatening

omit' vt. leave out, neglect; leave undone (-tt-) —**omiss'ion** n. —**omiss'ive** a.

omni- (comb. form) all

om'nibus n. large road vehicle travelling on set route and taking passengers at any stage (also **bus**); book containing several works —a. serving, containing several objects

omnidirec'tional a. in radio, denotes transmission, reception in all directions

omnip'otent a. all-powerful —**omnip'otence** n.

omnipres'ent a. present everywhere —**omnipres'ence** n.

omnis'cient [-nis'i-ənt] a. knowing everything —**omnis'cience** n.

omniv'orous a. devouring all foods; not fastidious

on prep. above and touching, at, near, towards etc.; attached to; concerning; performed upon; during; taking regularly —a. operating; taking place; Cricket denoting part of field to left of right-handed batter, and to right of bowler —adv. so as to be on; forwards; continuously etc.; in progress

on- (comb. form) on, as **on'-looker**

on'ager [-j-] n. wild ass (pl. -gri [-grī], -gers)

o'nanism n. masturbation

once [wuns] adv. one time; formerly; ever —**once-over** n. inf. quick examination —**at once** immediately; simultaneously

on'cogene [ong'kōjen] n. any of several genes that when abnormally activated can cause cancer

one [wun] a. lowest cardinal number; single; united; only, without others; identical —n. number or figure 1; unity; single specimen —pron. particular but not stated person; any person —**one'ness** n. unity; uniformity; singleness —**oneself'** pron. —**one-sided** a. partial; uneven

—one-way a. denotes system of traffic circulation in one direction only

on'erous a. burdensome

on'ion [un'yən] n. edible bulb of pungent flavour

on'ly [ō-] a. being the one specimen —adv. solely, merely, exclusively —conj. but then, excepting that

onomas'tics pl.n. study of proper names

onomatopoe'ia [-pē'ə] n. formation of a word by using sounds that resemble or suggest the object or action to be named —**onomatopoe'ic**, **onomatopoet'ic** [-pō-et'-] a.

on'set n. violent attack; assault; beginning

on'slaught [-slawt] n. attack

on'to prep. on top of; aware of

ontol'ogy n. science of being or reality —**ontolog'ical** a. —**ontol'ogist** n.

o'nus n. responsibility, burden

on'ward a. advanced or advancing —adv. in advance, ahead, forward —**on'wards** adv.

on'yx [on'iks] n. variety of chalcedony

oo'dles pl.n. inf. abundance

ool'ogy [ō-ol'-] n. study of eggs, of birds during the nesting season

ooze vi. pass slowly out, exude (moisture) —n. sluggish flow; wet mud, slime —**ooz'y** a.

op. opera; operation; opus

o'pal n. glassy gemstone displaying variegated colours —**opales'cent** a.

opaque' [ō-pāk'] a. not allowing the passage of light, not transparent —**opac'ity** [-pas'-] n.

op. cit. (Lat. opere citato) in the work cited

OPEC Organization of Petroleum Exporting Countries

o'pen a. not shut or blocked up; without lid or door; bare; undisguised; not enclosed, covered or exclusive; spread out, accessible; frank, sincere —vt. set open, uncover, give access to; disclose, lay bare; begin; make a hole in —vi. become open; begin —n. clear space, unenclosed country; Sport competition in which all may enter —o'pening n. hole, gap; beginning; opportunity —a. first; initial —o'penly adv. without concealment —o'pencast a. of coal, mined from the surface, not underground —open-handed a. generous —open-hearted a. frank, magnanimous —openminded a. unprejudiced —open prison one without restraints to prevent absconding —open verdict coroner's verdict not stating cause (of death) —o'penwork n. pattern with interstices

op'era n. musical drama —operat'ic a. of opera —operett'a n. light, comic opera

opera'tion n. working, way things work; scope; act of surgery; military action —op'erate vt. cause to function; effect —vi. work; produce an effect; perform act of surgery; exert power —opera'tional a. of operation(s); working —op'erative a. working —n. worker, esp. with a special skill —op'erator n.

oper'culum [ō-per'-] n. lid or cover (pl. -lums, -la)

ophid'ian [ō-fid'-] a./n. (reptile) of the order including snakes

ophthal'mic [of-thal'-] a. of eyes —ophthalmol'ogist n. —ophthalmol'ogy n. study of eye and its diseases —ophthal'moscope n. instrument for examining interior of eye —ophthalmic optician one qualified to prescribe spectacles etc.

o'piate see OPIUM

opin'ion n. what one thinks about something; belief, judgment —opine' vt. think; utter opinion —opin'ionated a. stubborn in one's opinions; dogmatic

o'pium n. sedative-narcotic drug made from poppy —o'piate n. drug containing opium; narcotic —a. inducing sleep; soothing

oposs'um n. small Amer. and Aust. marsupial animal

oppo'nent n. adversary, antagonist

opp'ortune a. seasonable, well-timed —opportu'nism n. policy of doing what is expedient at the time regardless of principle —opportu'nist n./a. —opportu'nity n. favourable time or condition; good chance

oppose' [-z] vt. resist, withstand; contrast; set against —oppo'ser n. —opp'osite [-zit] a. contrary; facing; diametrically different; adverse —n. the contrary —prep./adv. facing; on the other side —opposi'tion [-ish'-] n. antithesis; resistance; obstruction; hostility; group opposing another; party opposing that in power

oppress' vt. govern with tyranny; weigh down —oppress'ion n. act of oppressing; severity; misery —oppress'ive a. tyrannical; hard to bear; heavy; hot and tiring (of weather) —oppres'sively adv. —oppress'or n.

oppro'brium n. disgrace —oppro'brious a. reproachful; shameful; abusive

oppugn' [ə-pyōōn'] vt. call into question, dispute

op'sonin n. substance in blood assisting destruction of invading bacteria —opsonic index a. standard by which the power of resistance to disease is estimated

opt vi. make a choice —op'tative a. expressing wish or desire —n. mood of verb expressing wish

opt. optical; optional

op'tic a. of eye or sight —n. eye —pl. (with sing. v.) science of sight and light —**op'tical** a. —**op'tician** [-ish'-] n. maker of, dealer in spectacles, optical instruments

op'timism n. disposition to look on the bright side; doctrine that good must prevail in the end; belief that the world is the best possible world —**op'timist** n. —**optimis'tic** a. —**optimis'tically** adv.

op'timum a./n. the best, the most favourable

op'tion n. choice; preference; thing chosen; in business, purchased privilege of either buying or selling things at specified price within specified time —**op'tional** a. leaving to choice

optom'etrist n. person usu. not medically qualified, testing eyesight, prescribing corrective lenses etc. —**optom'etry** n.

op'ulent a. rich; copious —**op'ulence** n. riches, wealth

o'pus n. work; musical composition (pl. **op'era**)

or conj. introduces alternatives; if not

or'acle [or'ə-] n. divine utterance, prophecy, oft. ambiguous, given at shrine of god; the shrine; wise or mysterious adviser; (O-)R ITV teletext service —**orac'ular** a. of oracle; prophetic; authoritative; ambiguous

or'al a. spoken; by mouth —n. spoken examination —**or'ally** adv.

or'ange [o'rinj] n. bright reddish-yellow round fruit; tree bearing it; fruit's colour

orang-outang', **orang-utan'** n. large E. Indian ape

or'ator [or'ə-] n. maker of speech; skilful speaker —**ora'tion** n. formal speech —**orator'ical** a. of orator or oration —**or'a-**

tory n. speeches; eloquence; small private chapel

orato'rio n. semi-dramatic composition of sacred music (pl. **-rios**)

orb n. globe, sphere —**orbic'ular** a.

orb'it n. track of planet, satellite, comet etc., around another heavenly body; field of influence, sphere; eye socket —v. move in, or put into, an orbit

orch'ard n. area for cultivation of fruit trees; the trees

or'chestra [-k-] n. band of musicians; place for such band in theatre etc. —**orches'tral** a. —**or'chestrate** vt. compose or arrange music for orchestra; organize, arrange —**orchestra'tion** n.

or'chid, **or'chis** [-k-] n. genus of various flowering plants

ordain' vt. admit to Christian ministry; confer holy orders upon; decree, enact; destine —**ordina'tion** n.

ordeal' n. severe, trying experience; Hist. form of trial by which accused underwent severe physical test

or'der n. regular or proper arrangement or condition; sequence; peaceful condition of society; rank, class; group; command; request for something to be supplied; mode of procedure; instruction; monastic society —vt. command; request (something) to be supplied or made; arrange —**or'derliness** n. —**or'derly** a. tidy; methodical; well-behaved —n. hospital attendant; soldier following officer to carry orders —**or'dinal** a. showing position in a series —n. ordinal number

or'dinance n. decree, rule; rite, ceremony

or'dinary a. usual, normal;

common; plain; commonplace —*n.* bishop in his province —**or'dinarily** *adv.*

ord'nance *n.* big guns, artillery; military stores —**ordnance survey** official geographical survey of Britain

or'dure *n.* dung; filth

ore *n.* naturally occurring mineral which yields metal

oreg'ano [o-ri-gahn'ō] *n.* herb, variety of marjoram

or'gan *n.* musical wind instrument of pipes and stops, played by keys; member of animal or plant carrying out particular function; means of action; medium of information, *esp.* newspaper —**organ'ic** *a.* of, derived from, living organisms; of bodily organs; affecting bodily organs; having vital organs; *Chem.* of compounds formed from carbon; grown with fertilizers derived from animal or vegetable matter; organized, systematic —**organ'ically** *adv.* —**or'ganist** *n.* organ player

or'gandie *n.* light, transparent muslin

or'ganize *vt.* give definite structure; get up, arrange; put into working order; unite in a society —**or'ganism** *n.* organized body or system; plant, animal —**organiza'tion** *n.* act of organizing; body of people; society —**or'ganizer** *n.*

or'gasm *n.* sexual climax

or'gy [-ji] *n.* drunken or licentious revel, debauch; act of immoderation, overindulgence

or'iel *n.* projecting part of an upper room with a window; the window

or'ient *n.* (O-) East; lustre of best pearls —*a.* rising; (O-) Eastern —*vt.* place so as to face East; take bearings; determine one's position (*lit.* or *fig.*) —**orien'tal** *a./n.* —**orien'talist** *n.* expert in Eastern languages and history —**orien'tate** *vt.* orient —**orienta'tion** *n.* —**orientee'ring** *n.* competitive sport involving compass and map-reading skills

or'ifice [o'ri-] *n.* opening, mouth of a cavity, *eg* pipe

origam'i [o-ri-gahm'i] *n.* Japanese art of paper folding

or'igin [o'ri-j-] *n.* beginning; source; parentage

orig'inal [-j-] *a.* primitive, earliest; new, not copied or derived; thinking or acting for oneself; eccentric —*n.* pattern, thing from which another is copied; unconventional or strange person —**original'ity** *n.* power of producing something individual to oneself —**orig'inally** *adv.* at first; in the beginning

orig'inate *v.* come or bring into existence, begin —**origina'tion** *n.* —**orig'inator** *n.*

or'iole *n.* tropical thrushlike bird

Ori'on *n.* bright constellation

or'ison [o'ri-zən] *n.* prayer

ur'molu [-lōō] *n.* gilded bronze; gold-coloured alloy; articles of these

or'nament *n.* any object used to adorn or decorate; decoration —*vt.* adorn —**ornament'al** *a.* —**ornamenta'tion** *n.*

ornate' *a.* highly decorated or elaborate

ornithol'ogy *n.* science of birds —**ornitholog'ical** *a.* —**ornithol'ogist** *n.*

orog'raphy, orol'ogy *n.* geography of mountains

or'otund [o'rō-] *a.* full, clear, and musical; pompous

or'phan *n.* child bereaved of one or both parents —**or'phanage** *n.* institution for care of orphans —**or'phanhood** *n.*

orr'ery *n.* mechanical model of

solar system to show revolutions, planets *etc.*

orr'is, orr'ice *n.* kind of iris —**orris root** violet-scented perfume from root of kinds of iris

ortho- *(comb. form)* right, correct

or'thodox *a.* holding accepted views; conventional —**or'thodoxy** *n.*

orthog'raphy *n.* correct spelling

orthopaed'ic [-pēd'-] *a.* for curing deformity, disorder of bones

orthop'tics *n.* the science and study of correcting ocular deviation, by exercising the eye muscles —**orthop'tist** *n.*

ort'olan *n.* a small bird, *esp.* as table delicacy

or'yx *n.* large Afr. antelope

os'cillate *vi.* swing to and fro; waver; fluctuate (regularly) —**os'cilla'tion** *n.* —**os'cillator** *n.* —**os'cillatory** *a.* —**oscill'oscope** *n.* electronic instrument producing visible representation of rapidly changing quantity

o'sier [-z-] *n.* species of willow used for basketwork

os'mium [oz'-] *n.* heaviest known of metallic elements

osmo'sis [oz-] *n.* percolation of fluids through porous partitions —**osmot'ic** *a.*

os'prey *n.* fishing hawk; plume

oss'eous *a.* of, like bone; bony —**ossifica'tion** *n.* —**oss'ify** *v.* turn into bone; grow rigid (**-fied, -fying**)

osten'sible *a.* apparent; professed —**osten'sibly** *adv.*

ostenta'tion *n.* show, pretentious display —**ostenta'tious** *a.* given to display; showing off —**ostenta'tiously** *adv.*

osteop'athy *n.* art of treating disease by removing structural derangement by manipulation, *esp.* of spine —**os'teopath** *n.* one

skilled in this art, bonesetter

os'tler [-sl-] *n. Hist.* stableman at an inn

os'tracize *vt.* exclude, banish from society, exile —**os'tracism** *n.* social boycotting

os'trich *n.* large swift-running flightless Afr. bird

OTC Officers' Training Corps

oth'er [UTH'-] *a.* not this; not the same; alternative, different —*pron.* other person or thing —**oth'erwise** *adv.* differently; in another way —*conj.* else, if not

o'tiose *a.* superfluous; useless

OTT over the top

ott'er *n.* furry aquatic fish-eating animal

Ott'oman *a.* Turkish —*n.* Turk; (**o-**) cushioned, backless seat, storage box

ou [ō] *SA. sl.* man —**ou'baas** *n.* man in authority

oubliette' *n.* dungeon entered by trapdoor

ouch *interj.* exclamation of sudden pain

ought [awt] *v. aux.* expressing duty or obligation or advisability; be bound

oui'ja [wē'-] *n.* board with letters and symbols used to obtain messages at seances

ou'ma [ō'mah] *n. SA* grandmother; elderly woman

ounce *n.* a weight, sixteenth of avoirdupois pound (28.4 grams), twelfth of troy pound (31.1 grams)

ou'pa [ō'pah] *n. SA* grandfather; elderly man

our *a.* belonging to us —**ours** *pron.* —**ourself'** *pron.* myself, used in regal, or formal style —**ourselves'** *pl.pron.* emphatic or reflexive form of WE

oust *vt.* put out, expel

out *adv.* from within, away; wrong; on strike —*a.* not worth considering; not allowed; unfashionable; unconscious; not in use, operation *etc.*; at an end; not burning; *Sport* dismissed —**out'er** *a.* away from the inside —**out'ermost, out'most** *a.* on extreme outside —**out'ing** *n.* pleasure excursion —**out'ward** *a./adv.* —**out'wardly** *adv.* —**out'wards** *adv.*

out- (*comb. form*) beyond, in excess, as **outclass'** *vt.*, **outdis'tance** *vt.*, **out'size** *n.* Such compounds are not given here where the meaning may easily be inferred from the simple word

out'back *n.* A remote, sparsely populated country

outbal'ance *vt.* outweigh; exceed in weight

out'board *a.* of boat's engine, mounted on, outside stern

out'break *n.* sudden occurrence, *esp.* of disease or strife

out'burst *n.* bursting out, *esp.* of violent emotion

out'cast *n.* someone rejected —*a.*

outclass' *vt.* excel, surpass

out'come *n.* result

out'crop *n. Geology* rock coming out of stratum to the surface —*vi.* come out to the surface (**-pp-**)

outdoors' *adv.* in the open air —**out'door** *a.*

out'fall *n.* mouth of river

out'fit *n.* equipment; clothes and accessories; *inf.* group or association regarded as a unit —**out'fitter** *n.* one who deals in outfits

outflank' *vt.* to get beyond the flank (of enemy army); circumvent

out'going *n.* departing; friendly, sociable

outgrow' *vt.* become too large or too old for; surpass in growth (**outgrew'**, **outgrown'**, **outgrow'ing**)

out'house *n.* shed *etc.* near main building

outland'ish *a.* queer, extravagantly strange

out'law *n.* one beyond protection of the law; exile, bandit —*vt.* make (someone) an outlaw; ban —**out'lawry** *n.*

out'lay *n.* expenditure

out'let *n.* opening, vent; means of release or escape; market for product or service

out'line *n.* rough sketch; general plan; lines enclosing visible figure —*vt.* sketch; summarize

out'look *n.* point of view; probable outcome; view

out'lying *a.* distant, remote

outmo'ded *a.* no longer fashionable or accepted

out'put *n.* quantity produced; *Computers* information produced

out'rage *n.* violation of others' rights; gross or violent offence or indignity; anger arising from this —*vt.* offend grossly; insult; injure, violate —**outra'geous** *a.*

ou'tré [ŌŌ'trā] *a.* extravagantly odd; bizarre

out'rigger *n.* frame, *esp.* with float attached, outside boat's gunwale; frame on rowing boat's side with rowlock; boat with one

out'right *a.* undisputed; downright; positive —*adv.* completely; once for all; openly

out'set *n.* beginning

outside' *n.* exterior —*adv.* not inside; in the open air —*a.* on exterior; remote, unlikely; greatest possible, probable —**outsid'er** *n.* person outside specific group; contestant thought unlikely to win

out'skirts *pl.n.* outer areas, districts, *esp.* of city

out'span *n. SA* unyoking of oxen; area for rest

outspo'ken *a.* frank, candid

outstand'ing *a.* excellent; remarkable; unsettled, unpaid

outstrip' *vt.* outrun, surpass

out-take *n.* unreleased take from recording, film or television programme

outwit' *vt.* get the better of by cunning

out'work *n.* part of fortress outside main wall

ou'zel, ou'sel [ōō'-] *n.* type of thrush; kind of diving bird

o'val *a.* egg-shaped, elliptical —*n.* something of this shape

o'vary *n.* female egg-producing organ —**ova'rian** *a.*

ova'tion *n.* enthusiastic burst of applause

ov'en [uv'-] *n.* heated chamber for baking in

o'ver *adv.* above, above and beyond, going beyond, in excess, too much, past, finished, in repetition, across, downwards *etc.* —*prep.* above; on, upon; more than, in excess of, along *etc.* —*a.* upper, outer —*n.* Cricket delivery of agreed number of balls from one end (usu. 6, formerly in Aust. 8)

over- (*comb. form*) too, too much, in excess, above, as in

overawe'	overlap'
overbal'ance	overlord'
o'vercoat	overpow'er
overcrowd'	overreact'
overdo'	overrule'
o'verdose	overrun'
o'verdue	overshoot'
o'verflow	overspill'

o'verall *n.* loose garment worn as protection against dirt *etc.* (*also pl.*) —*a.* total

overbear'ing *a.* domineering

overblown' *a.* excessive, bombastic

o'verboard *adv.* from a vessel into the water

o'vercast *a.* covered over, *esp.* by clouds

overcome' *vt.* conquer; surmount; make powerless

o'verdraft *n.* withdrawal of money in excess of credit balance on bank account

overhaul' *vt.* examine and set in order, repair; overtake —*n.* [ō'-] thorough examination, *esp.* for repairs

overhead' *a.* over one's head, above —*adv.* aloft, above —**o'verheads** *pl.n.* expenses of running a business, over and above cost of manufacturing and of raw materials

o'verkill *n.* capacity, advantage greater than required

o'verland *a./adv.* by land

overlook' *vt.* fail to notice; disregard; look over

override' *vt.* set aside, disregard; cancel; trample down

o'verseas *a.* foreign —*a./adv.* to, from place over the sea

o'verseer *n.* supervisor —**oversee'** *vt.* supervise

o'versight *n.* failure to notice; mistake

o'vert *a.* open, unconcealed —**o'vertly** *adv.*

overtake' *vt.* move past (vehicle, person) travelling in same direction; come up with in pursuit; catch up

overtax' *vt.* tax too heavily; impose too great a strain on

overthrow' *vt.* upset, overturn; defeat (**overthrew'**, **overthrown'**, **overthrow'ing**) —*n.* [ō'-] ruin; defeat; fall

o'vertime *n.* time at work, outside normal working hours; payment for this time

o'vertone *n.* additional meaning, nuance

o'verture *n.* Mus. orchestral introduction; opening of negotiations; formal offer

overween'ing a. thinking too much of oneself

overwhelm' vt. crush; submerge, engulf —**overwhelm'ing** a. decisive; irresistible —**overwhelm'ingly** adv.

overwrought' a. overexcited; too elaborate

o'viform a. egg-shaped

o'vine [-ī-] a. of, like, sheep

ovip'arous a. laying eggs

o'void a. egg-shaped

ov'ule n. unfertilized seed —**ov'ulate** vi. produce, discharge (egg) from ovary —**ovula'tion** n.

o'vum n. female egg-cell, in which development of foetus takes place (pl. **o'va**)

owc [ō] vt. be bound to repay, be indebted for —**ow'ing** a. owed, due —**owing to** caused by, as result of

owl n. night bird of prey —**owl'et** n. young owl —**owl'ish** a. solemn and dull

own [ōn] a. emphasizes possession —vt. possess; acknowledge —vi. to confess —**own'er** n. —**own'ership** n. possession

ox n. large cloven-footed and usu. horned farm animal; bull or cow (pl. **ox'en**) —**ox'bow** n. U-shaped harness collar of ox; lake formed from deep bend of river —**ox'eye** n. daisylike plant

oxal'is n. genus of plants —**oxal'ic acid** poisonous acid derived from oxalis

Ox'fam Oxford Committee for Famine Relief

ox'ide n. compound of oxygen and one other element —**oxidiza'tion** n. —**ox'idize** v. (cause to) combine with oxide, rust

Oxon. Oxfordshire

ox'ygen n. gas in atmosphere essential to life, combustion etc. —**ox'ygenate, ox'ygenize** vt. combine or treat with oxygen —**oxyacet'ylene** a. denoting

flame used for welding produced by mixture of oxygen and acetylene

oxymor'on n. figure of speech in which two ideas of opposite meaning are combined to form an expressive phrase or epithet, eg "cruel kindness"

oyez' [ō-yes'] n. call, uttered three times by public crier or court official

oy'ster [oi'-] n. edible bivalve mollusc or shellfish —**oy'stercatcher** n. shore bird

oz. ounce

o'zone n. form of oxygen with pungent odour —**o'zonize** vt.

P

P (car) park; Chess pawn; Chem. phosphorus; pressure

p page; pence; penny; Mus. piano (softly)

PA public-address system

p.a. per annum

pace n. step; its length; rate of movement; walk, gait —vi. step —vt. set speed for; cross, measure with steps —**pa'cer** n. one who sets the pace for another —**pace'maker** n. esp. electronic device surgically implanted in those with heart disease

pach'yderm [pak'-] n. thick-skinned animal, eg elephant —**pachyder'matous** a. thick-skinned, stolid

pac'ify [pas'-] vt. calm; establish peace —**-ified, -ifying**) —**pacif'ic** a. peaceable; calm, tranquil —**pacifica'tion** n. —**pacifica'tory** a. tending to make peace —**pac'ifism** n. —**pac'ifist** n. advocate of abolition of war; one who refuses to help in war

pack n. bundle; band of animals;

large set of people or things; set of, container for, retail commodities; set of playing cards; mass of floating ice —*vt.* put together in suitcase *etc.*; make into a bundle; press tightly together, cram; fill with things; fill (meeting *etc.*) with one's own supporters; order off —**pack'age** *n.* parcel; set of items offered together —*vt.* —**pack'et** *n.* small parcel; small container (and contents); *sl.* large sum of money —**pack'et (boat)** *n.* mail-boat —**pack'horse** *n.* horse for carrying goods —**pack ice** loose floating ice which has been compacted together —**pack saddle** one to carry goods

pact *n.* covenant, agreement, compact —**pac'tional** *a.*

pad[1] *n.* piece of soft stuff used as a cushion, protection *etc.*; block of sheets of paper; foot or sole of various animals; place for launching rockets; *sl.* residence —*vt.* make soft, fill in, protect *etc.*, with pad or padding (**-dd-**) —**padd'ing** *n.* material used for stuffing; literary matter put in simply to increase quantity

pad[2] *vi.* walk with soft step; travel slowly (**-dd-**) —*n.* sound of soft footstep

pad'dle[1] *n.* short oar with broad blade at one or each end —*v.* move by, as with, paddles; row gently —**paddle wheel** wheel with crosswise blades striking water successively to propel ship

pad'dle[2] *vt.* walk with bare feet in shallow water —*n.*

padd'ock *n.* small grass field or enclosure

padd'y[1] *n.* rice growing or in the husk —**paddy field** field where paddy is grown

padd'y[2] *n. inf.* temper

pad'lock *n.* detachable lock with hinged hoop to go through staple or ring —*vt.* fasten thus

pad're [pahd'ri] *n.* chaplain with the armed forces

pae'an [pē'-] *n.* song of triumph or thanksgiving

paediat'rics [pē-] *pl.n.* branch of medicine dealing with diseases and disorders of children (*also US* **pediat'rics**) —**paediatri'cian** *n.*

pa'gan *a./n.* heathen —**pa'ganism** *n.*

page[1] *n.* one side of leaf of book *etc.*

page[2] *n.* boy servant or attendant —*v.* summon by loudspeaker announcement

pag'eant [paj'ənt] *n.* show of persons in costume in procession, dramatic scenes *etc.*, usu. illustrating history; brilliant show —**pag'eantry** *n.*

pag'inate [paj'-] *vt.* number pages of —**pagina'tion** *n.*

pago'da *n.* pyramidal temple or tower of Chinese or Indian type

paid *pt./pp. of* PAY —**put paid to** *inf.* end, destroy

pail *n.* bucket —**pail'ful** *n.*

paill'asse *n. see* PALLIASSE

pain *n.* bodily or mental suffering; penalty or punishment —*pl.* trouble, exertion —*vt.* inflict pain upon —**pain'ful** *a.* —**pain'fully** *adv.* —**pain'less** *a.* —**pain'lessly** *adv.* —**pain'killer** *n.* drug, as aspirin, that reduces pain —**pains'taking** *a.* diligent, careful

paint *n.* colouring matter spread on a surface with brushes, roller, spray gun *etc.* —*vt.* portray, colour, coat, or make picture of, with paint; apply make-up; describe —**paint'er** *n.* —**paint'ing** *n.* picture in paint

paint'er *n.* line at bow of boat for tying it up

pair *n.* set of two, *esp.* existing or

generally used together —v. arrange in twos; group or be grouped in twos

pais'ley [páz'-] n. pattern of small curving shapes

pajam'as pl.n. US see PYJAMAS

pal n. inf. friend

pal'ace n. residence of king, bishop etc.; stately mansion —**pala'tial** a. like a palace; magnificent —**pal'atine** a. with royal privileges

pal'adin n. Hist. knight errant

palaeog'raphy [-li-og'-] n. study of ancient writings

palaeolith'ic [pal-i-ō-] a. of the old Stone Age

palaeontol'ogy [-li-on-] n. study of past geological periods and fossils —**palaeontolog'ical** a.

pal'ate n. roof of mouth; sense of taste —**pal'atable** a. agreeable to eat —**pal'atal, pal'atine** a. of the palate; made by placing tongue against palate —n. palatal sound

pala'tial, pal'atine see PALACE

palav'er [-ahv'-] n. fuss; conference, discussion

pale [1] a. wan, dim, whitish —v. whiten; lose superiority or importance

pale [2] n. stake, boundary —**pa'ling** n. upright plank making up fence

pal'ette n. artist's flat board for mixing colours on

pal'indrome n. word, verse or sentence that is the same when read backwards or forwards

palisade' [1] n. fence of stakes —vt. to enclose or protect with one

pall [1] [pawl] n. cloth spread over a coffin; depressing, oppressive atmosphere —**pall'bearer** n. one carrying, attending coffin at funeral

pall [2] [pawl] vi. become tasteless or tiresome; cloy

pall'et [1] n. straw mattress; small bed

pall'et [2] n. portable platform for storing and moving goods

pall'iasse [pal'i-as] n. straw mattress

pall'iate vt. relieve without curing; excuse —**pallia'tion** n. —**pall'iative** a. giving temporary or partial relief —n. that which excuses, mitigates or alleviates

pall'id a. pale, wan, colourless —**pall'or** n. paleness

palm [pahm] n. inner surface of hand; tropical tree; leaf of the tree as symbol of victory —vt. conceal in palm of hand; pass off by trickery —**palm'ist** n. —**palm'istry** n. fortune-telling from lines on palm of hand —**palm'y** a. flourishing, successful —**Palm Sunday** Sunday before Easter

palomi'no [-mē'-] n. golden horse with white mane and tail

pal'pable a. obvious; certain; that may be touched or felt —**pal'pably** adv.

pal'pate vt. Med. examine by touch

pal'pitate vi. throb; pulsate violently —**palpita'tion** n. throbbing; violent, irregular beating of heart

pal'sy [pawl'zi] n. paralysis —**pal'sied** a. affected with palsy

pal'try [pawl'-] a. worthless, contemptible, trifling

pam'pas pl.n. vast grassy treeless plains in S Amer.

pam'per vt. overindulge, spoil by coddling

pamph'let n. thin unbound book usu. on some topical subject —**pamphleteer'** n. writer of these

pan [1] n. broad, shallow vessel; bowl of lavatory; depression in ground, *esp.* where salt forms —*vt.* wash gold ore in pan; *inf.* criticize harshly (-**nn**-) —**pan'tile** *n.* curved roofing tile —**pan out** *vi.* result

pan[1] *v.* move film camera slowly while filming to cover scene, follow moving object *etc.* (-**nn**-)

pan-, pant-, panto- (*comb. form*) all, as in panacea, pantomime Such words are not given here where the meaning may easily be inferred from simple word

panace'a [-sē'ə] *n.* universal remedy, cure for all ills

panache' [-ash'] *n.* dashing style

panama' [-mah'] *n.* straw hat

pan'cake *n.* thin cake of batter fried in pan; flat cake or stick of compressed make-up —*vi. Aviation* make flat landing by dropping in a level position

panchromat'ic *a. Photography* sensitive to light of all colours

pan'creas [-ng'-kri-əs] *n.* digestive gland behind stomach —**pancreat'ic** *a.*

pan'da *n.* large black and white bearlike mammal of China —**panda car** police patrol car

pandem'ic *a.* (of disease) occurring over wide area

pandemo'nium *n.* scene of din and uproar

pan'der *v.* (*esp. with* to) give gratification to (weakness or desires) —*n.* pimp

P & O Peninsular and Oriental (Steamship Company)

p & p postage and packing

pane *n.* single piece of glass in a window or door

panegyr'ic [-i-jir'-] *n.* speech of praise —**panegyr'ical** *a.* laudatory —**panegyr'ist** *n.*

pan'el *n.* compartment of surface, usu. raised or sunk, *eg* in door; any distinct section of

something, *eg* of car body; strip of material inserted in garment; group of persons as team in quiz game *etc.*; list of jurors, doctors *etc.*; thin board with picture on it —*vt.* adorn with panels (-**ll**-) —**pan'elling** *n.* panelled work —**pan'ellist** *n.* member of panel —**panel beater** one who repairs damage to car body

pang *n.* sudden pain, sharp twinge; compunction

pan'ic *n.* sudden and infectious fear; extreme fright; unreasoning terror —*a.* of fear *etc.* —*v.* feel or cause to feel panic (-**icked**, -**icking**) —**pan'icky** *a.* inclined to panic; nervous —**panic button** button or switch that operates safety device, for use in emergency —**pan'icmonger** *n.* one who starts panic —**panic-stricken, -struck** *a.*

pann'ier *n.* basket carried by beast of burden, bicycle, or on person's shoulders

pann'ikin *n. obs.* small metal drinking cup

pan'oply *n.* complete, magnificent array —**pan'oplied** *a.*

panoram'a [-ahm'-] *n.* wide or complete view; picture arranged round spectator or unrolled before him —**panoram'ic** [-ram'-] *a.*

pan'sy [-zi] *n.* flower, species of violet; *inf.* effeminate man

pant *vi.* gasp for breath; yearn; long; throb —*n.* gasp

pantaloon' *n.* in pantomime, foolish old man who is the butt of clown —*pl. inf.* baggy trousers

pantech'nicon [-tek'-] *n.* large van, *esp.* for carrying furniture

pan'theism *n.* identification of God with the universe —**pan'theist** *n.* —**panthe'istic** *a.* —**pan'theon** *n.* temple of all gods

pan'ther *n.* variety of leopard

pan'ties *pl.n.* women's undergarment

pan'tihose n. see TIGHTS

pan'tograph n. instrument for copying maps etc., to any scale —**pantograph'ic** a.

pan'tomime n. theatrical show, usu. produced at Christmas time, often founded on a fairy tale; dramatic entertainment in dumbshow

pan'try n. room for storing food or utensils

pants pl.n. undergarment for lower trunk; **US** trousers

pap[1] n. soft food for infants, invalids etc.; pulp, mash; **SA** maize porridge

pap[2] n. breast; nipple

pa'pacy n. office of Pope; papal system —**pa'pal** a. of, relating to, the Pope —**pa'pist** n. —**papist'ic** a.

paparaz'zo [pap͟ərat'sō] n. freelance photographer specializing in candid camera shots of famous people (pl. -raz'zi [-rat'sē])

pa'paw [paw'paw] n. tree bearing melon-shaped fruit; its fruit (also papay'a [pə-pī'ə])

pa'per n. material made by pressing pulp of rags, straw, wood etc., into thin, flat sheets; printed sheet of paper; newspaper; article, essay; set of examination questions —pl. documents etc. —vt. cover, decorate with paper —**pa'perback** n. book with flexible covers

papier-mâch'é [papyā-mash'ā] n. pulp from rags or paper mixed with size, shaped by moulding and dried hard

papoose' n. N Amer. Indian child

pap'rika n. (powdered seasoning prepared from) type of red pepper

papy'rus n. species of reed; (manuscript written on) kind of paper made from this plant (pl. papy'ri [-rī])

par n. equality of value or standing; face value (of stocks and shares); Golf estimated standard score —**par'ity** [par'i-] n. equality; analogy

par. paragraph; parallel; parenthesis

par'a-, par-, pa- (comb. form) beside, beyond, as in paradigm, parallel, parody

par'able [pa'rə-] n. allegory, story with a moral lesson

parab'ola [pə-] n. section of cone cut by plane parallel to the cone's side

parace'tamol n. mild drug used as alternative to aspirin

par'achute [pa'rə-shoot] n. apparatus extending like umbrella used to retard the descent of a falling body —v. land or cause to land by parachute —**par'achutist** n.

parade' n. display; muster of troops; parade ground; public walk —v. march; display

par'adigm [pa'rə-dīm] n. example; model —**paradigmat'ic** [-digmat'-] a.

par'adise [pa'rə-] n. Heaven; state of bliss; Garden of Eden

par'adox [pa'rə-] n. statement that seems absurd or self-contradictory but may be true —**paradox'ical** a.

par'affin [pa'rə-] n. waxlike or liquid hydrocarbon mixture used as fuel, solvent, in candles etc.

par'agliding n. sport of cross-country gliding using a specially designed parachute

par'agon [pa'rə-] n. pattern or model of excellence

par'agraph [pa'rə-] n. section of chapter or book; short notice, as in newspaper —vt. arrange in paragraphs —**paragraph'ic** a.

par'akeet [pa'rэ] *n.* small kind of parrot

par'allax [pa'rэ] *n.* apparent difference in object's position or direction as viewed from different points

par'allel [pa'rэ] *a.* continuously at equal distances; precisely corresponding —*n.* line equidistant from another at all points; thing exactly like another; comparison; line of latitude —*vt.* represent as similar, compare —**par'allelism** *n.* —**paral'lel'ogram** [pa'rэ] four-sided plane figure with opposite sides parallel

paral'ysis *n.* incapacity to move or feel, due to damage to nervous system (*pl.* -yses [-sēz]) —**par'alyse** [pa'rэ] *vt.* affect with paralysis; cripple; make useless or ineffectual —**paralyt'ic** *a./n.* (person) affected with paralysis —**infantile paralysis** poliomyelitis

paramed'ical *a.* of persons working in various capacities in support of the medical profession

param'eter *n.* any constant limiting factor

paramil'itary *a.* of civilian group organized on military lines or in support of the military

par'amount [pa'rэ] *a.* supreme, eminent, pre-eminent, chief

par'amour [pa'rэ] *n. esp.* formerly, illicit lover, mistress

par'ang *n.* heavy Malay knife

paranoi'a [pa'rэ] *n.* mental disease with delusions of fame, grandeur, persecution —**paranoi'ac** *a./n.* —**par'anoid** *a.* of paranoia; *inf.* exhibiting fear of persecution *etc.* —*n.*

par'apet [pa'rэ] *n.* low wall, railing along edge of balcony, bridge *etc.*

parapherna'lia *pl.n.* (*used as sing.*) personal belongings; odds

and ends of equipment

par'aphrase [pa'rэ] *n.* expression of meaning of passage in other words; free translation —*vt.* put into other words

paraple'gia [-j-] *n.* paralysis of lower half of body —**paraple'gic** *n./a.*

parapsychol'ogy *n.* study of subjects pert. to extrasensory perception, *eg* telepathy

Par'aquat [pa'rэ] R very poisonous weedkiller

par'asite [pa'rэ] *n.* animal or plant living in or on another; self-interested hanger-on —**parasit'ic** *a.* of the nature of, living as, parasite —**par'asitism** *n.* —**parasitol'ogy** *n.* study of animal and vegetable parasites, *esp.* as causes of disease

par'asol [pa'rэ] *n.* sunshade

paratax'is *n.* arrangement of sentences which omits connecting words

par'atroops, -troopers [pa'rэ] *pl.n.* troops trained to descend by parachute

paraty'phoid *n.* an infectious disease similar to but distinct from typhoid fever

par'boil *vt.* boil until partly cooked

par'cel *n.* packet of goods, *esp.* one enclosed in paper; quantity dealt with at one time; piece of land —*vt.* wrap up; divide into parts (-ll-)

parch *v.* dry by heating; make, become hot and dry; scorch; roast slightly

parch'ment *n.* sheep, goat, calf skin prepared for writing; manuscript of this

par'don *vt.* forgive, excuse —*n.* forgiveness; release from punishment —**par'donable** *a.* —**par'donably** *adv.*

pare *vt.* trim, cut edge or surface of; decrease bit by bit

—**pa'ring** n. piece pared off, rind

pa'rent n. father or mother —**pa'rentage** n. descent, extraction —**parent'al** a. —**pa'renthood** n.

paren'thesis n. word or sentence inserted in passage independently of grammatical sequence and usu. marked off by brackets, dashes, or commas —**paren'theses** [-sēz] pl.n. round brackets, (), used for this —**parenthet'ical** a.

par'get [-jit] n. rough plaster; gypsum —vt. cover with plaster

pari'ah n. social outcast

pari'etal a. of the walls of bodily cavities, eg skull

par'ish [pa'-] n. district under one clergyman; subdivision of county —**parish'ioner** n. inhabitant of parish

par'ity see PAR

park n. large area of land in natural state preserved for recreational use; large enclosed piece of ground, usu. with grass or woodland, attached to country house or for public use; space in camp for storing military supplies —vt. leave for a short time; manoeuvre (car) into a suitable space; arrange or leave in a park

park'a n. warm waterproof coat, often with hood

park'y a. inf. chilly, cold

parl'ance n. way of speaking, conversation; idiom

parl'ey n. meeting between leaders or representatives of opposing forces to discuss terms (pl. **-leys**) —vi. hold discussion about terms

parl'iament n. the legislature of the United Kingdom; any similar legislative assembly —**parliamenta'rian** n. member of parliament —**parliament'ary** a.

parl'our n. sitting room, room for receiving company in small house; place for milking cows; US room or shop as business premises, esp. hairdresser etc.

parl'ous a. obs. perilous

Parmesan' n. hard dry Italian cheese

paro'chial [-k-] a. narrow, provincial; of a parish —**paro'chialism** n.

par'ody [pa'rə-] n. composition in which author's style is made fun of by imitation; travesty —vt. write parody of (**-odied, -odying**) —**par'odist** n.

parole' [-rōl'] n. early freeing of prisoner on condition he is of good behaviour; word of honour —vt. place on parole

par'oxysm [pa'roks-] n. sudden violent attack of pain, rage, laughter

par'quet [-kā] n. flooring of wooden blocks arranged in pattern —vt. lay a parquet —**par'quetry** [-kit-] n.

parr'akeet n. see PARAKEET

parr'icide n. murder or murderer of a parent

parr'ot n. bird with short hooked beak, some varieties of which can imitate speaking; unintelligent imitator

parr'y vt. ward off, turn aside (**par'ried, par'rying**) —n. act of parrying, esp. in fencing

parse [-z] vt. describe (word); analyse (sentence) in terms of grammar

par'sec n. unit of length used in expressing distance of stars

par'simony n. stinginess; undue economy —**parsimo'nious** a. sparing

par'sley n. herb used for seasoning, garnish etc.

par'snip n. edible yellow root vegetable

par'son n. clergyman of parish or church; clergyman —**par'sonage** n. parson's house

part n. portion, section, share; division; actor's role; duty; (oft. pl.) region; interest —v. divide; separate —**part'ing** n. division between sections of hair on head; separation; leave-taking —**part'ly** adv. in part —**part song** song for several voices singing in harmony

partake' v. take or have share in; take food or drink (**partook', ta'ken, ta'king**)

parterre' [-târ'] n. ornamental arrangement of beds in a flower garden; the pit of a theatre

par'tial [-shəl] a. not general or complete; prejudiced; fond of —**partial'ity** n. favouritism; fondness for —**par'tially** adv. partly

partic'ipate [-tis'-] v. share in; take part in —**partic'ipant** n. —**participa'tion** n. —**partic'ipator** n.

part'iciple n. adjective made by inflection from verb and keeping verb's relation to dependent words —**particip'ial** a.

part'icle n. minute portion of matter; least possible amount; minor part of speech in grammar, prefix, suffix

par'ti-coloured a. differently coloured in different parts, variegated

partic'ular a. relating to one, not general; distinct; minute; very exact; fastidious —n. detail, item —pl. detailed account; items of information —**particular'ity** n. —**partic'ularize** vt. mention in detail —**partic'ularly** adv.

partisan' [-zan'] n. adherent of a party; guerilla, member of resistance movement —a. adhering to faction; prejudiced

parti'tion [-tish'-] n. division; interior dividing wall —vt. divide, cut into sections

part'ner n. ally or companion; a member of a partnership; one

that dances with another; a husband or wife; Golf, Tennis etc. one who plays with another against opponents —v. (cause to) be a partner of —**part'nership** n. association of persons for business etc.

part'ridge n. game bird of the grouse family

parturi'tion [-yoo-rish'-] n. act of bringing forth young; childbirth

part'y n. social assembly; group of persons travelling or working together; group of persons united in opinion; side; person —a. of, belonging to, a party or faction —**party line** telephone line serving two or more subscribers; policies of political party —**party wall** common wall separating adjoining premises

par'venu [-nyōo] n. one newly risen into position of notice, power, wealth; upstart

pas'cal n. SI unit of pressure

pas'chal [-kəl] a. of the Passover or Easter

pass [-ah-] vt. go by, beyond, through etc.; exceed; be accepted by; undergo successfully; spend; transfer; exchange; disregard —v. go; be transferred from one state or person to another; elapse; undergo examination successfully; bring into force, sanction a parliamentary bill etc. —n. way, esp. a narrow and difficult way; permit, licence, authorization; successful result from test; condition; Sport transfer of ball —**pass'able** a. (just) acceptable —**pass'ing** a. transitory; cursory; casual —**pass up** ignore, neglect, reject

pass'age n. channel, opening; way through, corridor; part of book etc.; journey, voyage, fare; enactment of law by parliament etc.; conversation, dispute

pass'é [pas'-, pahs'-] *a.* out-of-date; past the prime

pass'enger *n.* traveller, *esp.* by public conveyance; one of a team who does not pull his weight

pass'erine *a.* of the order of perching birds

pass'im *Lat.* everywhere, throughout

pass'ion [-sh'-] *n.* ardent desire, *esp.* sexual; any strongly felt emotion; suffering (*esp.* that of Christ) —**pass'ionate** *a.* (easily) moved by strong emotions —**pass'ionflower** *n.* tropical Amer. plant —**passion fruit** edible fruit of passionflower

pass'ive *a.* unresisting; submissive; inactive; denoting grammatical mood of verb in which the action is suffered by the subject —**passiv'ity** *n.* —**passive smoking** inhalation of smoke from other's cigarettes by non-smoker

Pass'over [-ah-] *n.* Jewish spring festival

pass'port [-ah-] *n.* official document granting permission to pass, travel abroad *etc.*

pass'word [-ah-] *n.* word, phrase, to distinguish friend from enemy; countersign

past [-ah-] *a.* ended; gone by; elapsed —*n.* bygone times —*adv.* by; along —*prep.* beyond; after

pas'ta *n.* any of several variously shaped edible preparations of dough, eg spaghetti

paste *n.* soft composition, as toothpaste; soft plastic mixture or adhesive; fine glass to imitate gems —*vt.* fasten with paste —**pa'sty** *a.* like paste; white; sickly —**paste'board** *n.* stiff thick paper

pas'tel *n.* coloured crayon; art of drawing with crayons; pale, delicate colour —*a.* delicately tinted

pas'teurize *vt.* sterilize by heat —**pasteuriza'tion** *n.*

pastiche' [-tēsh'] *n.* literary, musical, artistic work composed of parts borrowed from other works and loosely connected together; work imitating another's style

pas'til(le) [-ah-] *n.* lozenge; aromatic substance burnt as fumigator

pas'time [-ah-] *n.* that which makes time pass agreeably; recreation

pas'tor [-ah-] *n.* clergyman in charge of a congregation —**pas'toral** *a.* of, or like, shepherd's or rural life; of office of pastor —*n.* poem describing rural life —**pas'torate** *n.* office, jurisdiction of pastor

pa'stry *n.* article of food made chiefly of flour, fat and water

pas'ture [-ah-] *n.* grass for food of cattle; ground on which cattle graze —*v.* (cause to) graze —**pas'turage** *n.* (right to) pasture

pas'ty *n.* small pie of meat and crust, baked without a dish

pat¹ *vt.* tap (-**tt**-) —*n.* light, quick blow; small mass, as of butter, beaten into shape

pat² *adv.* exactly; fluently; opportunely; glib; exactly right

pat. patent(ed)

patch *n.* piece of cloth sewed on garment; spot; plot of ground; protecting pad for the eye; small contrasting area; short period —*vt.* mend; repair clumsily —**patch'y** *a.* of uneven quality; full of patches —**patch'work** *n.* work composed of pieces sewn together; jumble

patchou'li [-choo'-] *n.* Indian herb; perfume from it

pate *n.* head; top of head

pât'é [pat'ā] *n.* spread of finely minced liver *etc.*

patell'a *n.* kneecap (*pl.* patell'-lae [-ē]) —**patell'ar** *a.*

pat'en n. plate for bread in the Eucharist

pat'ent n. deed securing to person exclusive right to invention —a. open; evident; manifest; open to public perusal, as **letters patent** —vt. secure a patent —**patentee'** n. one that has a patent —**pa'tently** adv. obviously —**patent leather** (imitation) leather processed to give hard, glossy surface

paterfamil'ias [pā-] n. father of a family (pl. **patresfamil'ias** [pā-trēz-])

pater'nal a. fatherly; of a father —**pater'nalism** n. authority exercised in a way that limits individual responsibility —**paternalis'tic** a. —**pater'nity** n. relation of a father to his offspring; fatherhood

paternos'ter n. Lord's Prayer; beads of rosary; type of lift

path [-ah-] n. way or track; course of action

pathet'ic a. affecting or moving tender emotions; distressingly inadequate —**pathet'ically** adv.

pathogen'ic [-jen'-] a. producing disease —**patho'geny** n. mode of development of disease

pathol'ogy n. science of diseases —**patholog'ical** a. of the science of disease; due to disease; inf. compulsively motivated —**pathol'ogist** n.

pa'thos n. power of exciting tender emotions

pa'tient [-shənt] a. bearing trials calmly —n. person under medical treatment —**pa'tience** n. quality of enduring; card game for one

pat'ina n. fine layer on a surface; sheen of age on woodwork

pat'io n. paved area adjoining house

pat'ois [-wah] n. regional dialect

pa'triarch [-k-] n. father and ruler of family, esp. Biblical —**patriarch'al** a. venerable

patri'cian [-rish-] n. noble of ancient Rome; one of noble birth —a. of noble birth

pat'ricide n. murder or murderer of father

pat'rimony n. property inherited from ancestors

pa'triot [or pat'-] n. one that loves his country and maintains its interests —**patriot'ic** [pat-] a. inspired by love of one's country —**pat'riotism** n. love of, loyalty to one's country

patrol' [-ōl'] n. regular circuit by guard; person, small group patrolling; unit of Boy Scouts or Girl Guides —v. go round on guard, or reconnoitring (-ll-)

pa'tron n. one who sponsors or aids artists, charities etc.; protector; regular customer; guardian saint; one that has disposition of church living etc. —**pat'ronage** n. support given by, or position of, a patron —**pat'ronize** vt. assume air of superiority towards; frequent as customer; encourage

patronym'ic n. name derived from that of parent or an ancestor

patt'en n. Hist. wooden clog, shoe, on raised platform

patt'er vi. make noise, as sound of quick, short steps; tap in quick succession; pray; talk rapidly —n. quick succession of taps; inf. glib, rapid speech

patt'ern n. arrangement of repeated parts; design; shape to direct cutting of cloth etc.; model; specimen —vt. (with on, after) model; decorate with pattern

patt'y n. a little pie

pau'city n. scarcity; smallness of quantity; fewness

paunch n. belly

pau'per n. poor person, esp.

formerly, one supported by the public —**pau'perism** n. destitution; extreme poverty —**pauperi-za'tion** n. —**pau'perize** vt. reduce to pauperism

pause vi. cease for a time —n. stop or rest

pave vt. form surface with stone or brick —**pave'ment** n. paved floor, footpath; material for paving

pavil'ion n. clubhouse on playing field etc.; building for housing exhibition etc.; large ornate tent

paw n. foot of animal —v. scrape with forefoot; handle roughly; stroke with the hands

pawn[1] vt. deposit (article) as security for money borrowed —n. article deposited —**pawn'-broker** n. lender of money on goods pledged

pawn[2] n. piece in chess; fig. person used as mere tool

pay vt. give money etc., for goods or services rendered; compensate; give or bestow; be profitable to; (with out) release bit by bit, as rope —vi. be remunerative; be profitable; (with out) spend; (**paid, pay'ing**) —n. wages; paid employment —**pay'-able** a. justly due; profitable —**payee'** n. person to whom money is paid or due —**pay'ment** n. discharge of debt —**pay'load** n. part of cargo earning revenue; explosive power of missile etc. —**paying guest** boarder, lodger, esp. in private house

P.A.Y.E. pay as you earn

Pb Chem. lead

PC Police Constable; Privy Councillor

p.c. per cent; postcard

PE physical education

pea n. fruit, growing in pods, of climbing plant; the plant —**pea-green** a. of shade of green like

colour of green peas —**peasoup'-er** n. inf. thick fog

peace n. freedom from war; harmony; quietness of mind; calm; repose —**peace'able** a. disposed to peace —**peace'ably** adv. —**peace'ful** a. free from war, tumult; mild; undisturbed —**peace'fully** adv.

peach n. stone fruit of delicate flavour; inf. anything very pleasant; pinkish-yellow colour —**peach'y** a. like peach; inf. fine, excellent

pea'cock n. male of bird (**pea'-fowl**) with fan-like tail, brilliantly coloured (**pea'hen** fem.) —vt. strut about or pose, like a peacock

peak n. pointed end of anything, esp. hill's sharp top; point of greatest development etc.; sharp increase; projecting piece on front of cap —v. (cause) to form, reach peaks —**peaked, peak'y** a. like, having a peak; sickly, wan, drawn

peal n. loud sound or succession of loud sounds; changes rung on set of bells; chime —vi. sound loudly

pea'nut n. pea-shaped nut that ripens underground —pl. inf. trifling amount of money

pear [pâr] n. tree yielding sweet, juicy fruit; the fruit —**pear-shaped** a. shaped like a pear, heavier at the bottom than the top

pearl [purl] n. hard, lustrous structure found in several molluscs, esp. pearl oyster and used as jewel —**pearl'y** a. like pearls —**pearl barley** barley with skin ground off

peas'ant [pez'-] n. member of low social class, esp. in rural district —**peas'antry** n. peasants collectively

peat n. decomposed vegetable

substance found in bogs; turf of it used for fuel

peb'ble n. small roundish stone; pale, transparent rock crystal; grainy, irregular surface —vt. pave, cover with pebbles —**pebble dash** finish for exterior walls with small stones in plaster

pecan' n. N Amer. tree, species of hickory, allied to walnut; its edible nut

pecc'able a. liable to sin —**pecc'ancy** n. —**pecc'ant** a. sinful; offensive

peccadill'o n. slight offence; petty crime (pl. **-es**, **-s**)

pecc'ary n. vicious Amer. animal allied to pig

peck[1] n. fourth part of bushel, 2 gallons; great deal

peck[2] v. pick, strike with or as with beak; nibble; inf. kiss quickly —n. —**peck'ish** a. inf. hungry

pec'tin n. gelatinizing substance obtained from ripe fruits —**pec'tic** a. congealing; denoting pectin

pec'toral a. of the breast —n. chest medicine; breastplate

pec'ulate v. embezzle; steal —**pecula'tion** n. —**pec'ulator** n.

pecu'liar a. strange; particular; belonging to —**peculiar'ity** n. oddity; characteristic; distinguishing feature

pecu'niary a. relating to, or consisting of, money

ped'agogue [-gog] n. schoolmaster; pedant —**pedagog'ic** a.

ped'al n. something to transmit motion from foot; foot lever to modify tone or swell of musical instrument; Mus. note, usu. bass, held through successive harmonies —a. of a foot —v. propel bicycle by using its pedals; use pedal (**-ll-**)

ped'ant n. one who overvalues, or insists on, petty details of book-learning, grammatical rules etc. —**pedant'ic** a. —**ped'antry** n.

ped'dle vt. go round selling goods —**pedd'ler** n. one who sells narcotic drugs

ped'erast n. man who has homosexual relations with boy —**ped'erasty** n.

ped'estal n. base of column, pillar

pedes'trian n. one who walks on foot —a. going on foot; commonplace; dull, uninspiring —**pedes'trianism** n. the practice of walking —**pedestrian crossing** place marked where pedestrians may cross road —**pedestrian precinct** area for pedestrians only to shop etc.

pediat'rics n. see PAEDIATRICS

ped'icel [-s-] n. small, short stalk of leaf, flower or fruit

ped'icure n. medical or cosmetic treatment of feet

ped'igree n. register of ancestors; genealogy

ped'iment n. triangular part over Greek portico etc. —**pedimen'tal** a.

ped'lar n. one who sells; hawker

pedom'eter n. instrument which measures the distance walked

pedun'cle n. flower stalk; stalk-like structure

peek vi./n. peep, glance

peel vt. strip off skin, rind or any form of covering —vi. come off, as skin, rind —n. rind, skin —**peeled** a. inf. of eyes, watchful —**peel'ings** pl.n.

peep[1] vi. look slyly or quickly —n. such a look

peep[2] vi. cry, as chick; chirp —n. such a cry

peer[1] n. nobleman (**peer'ess** fem.); one of the same rank —**peer'age** n. body of peers; rank of peer —**peer'less** a. without match or equal

peer[2] *vi.* look closely and intently

peeved *a. inf.* sulky, irritated

peev'ish *a.* fretful; irritable —**peev'ishly** *adv.* —**peev'ishness** *n.* annoyance

pee'wit *n.* lapwing

peg *n.* nail or pin for joining, fastening, marking *etc.*; (mark of) level, standard *etc.* —*vt.* fasten with pegs; stabilize (prices); *inf.* throw —*vi.* (*with away*) persevere (**-gg-**) —**peg out** *sl.* die

pei'gnoir [pā'nwahr] *n.* lady's dressing gown, jacket, wrapper

pejor'ative [pi-jo'rə- *or* pē'jər-] *a.* (of words *etc.*) with unpleasant, disparaging connotation

Pekin(g)ese' [-ēz'] *n.* small Chinese dog

pela'gian, pelag'ic *a.* of the deep sea

pelargo'nium *n.* plant with red, white or pink flowers

pel'ican *n.* large, fish-eating waterfowl with large pouch beneath its bill

pel'let *n.* little ball, pill

pell'icle *n.* thin skin, film

pell'-mell' *adv.* in utter confusion, headlong

pellu'cid [-lōō'-] *a.* translucent; clear —**pellucid'ity** *n.*

pel'met *n.* ornamental drapery or board, concealing curtain rail

pelt[1] *vt.* strike with missiles —*vi.* throw missiles; rush; fall persistently, as rain

pelt[2] *n.* raw hide or skin

pel'vis *n.* bony cavity at base of human trunk (*pl.* **pel'vises, -ves** [-vēz]) —**pel'vic** *a.* pert. to pelvis

pen[1] *n.* instrument for writing —*vt.* compose; write (**-nn-**) —**pen name** author's pseudonym

pen[2] *n.* small enclosure, as for sheep —*vt.* put, keep in enclosure (**-nn-**)

pen[3] *n.* female swan

pe'nal *a.* of, incurring, inflicting, punishment —**pe'nalize** *vt.* impose penalty on; handicap —**pen'alty** *n.* punishment for crime or offence; forfeit; *Sports* handicap or disadvantage imposed for infringement of rule *etc.*

pen'ance *n.* suffering submitted to as expression of penitence; repentance

pence *n. pl.* of PENNY

pen'chant [*or* pahn'shahn] *n.* inclination, decided taste

pen'cil *n.* instrument as of graphite, for writing *etc.*; *Optics* narrow beam of light —*vt.* paint or draw; mark with pencil (**-ll-**)

pend'ant *n.* hanging ornament —**pend'ent** *a.* suspended; hanging; projecting

pend'ing *prep.* during, until —*a.* awaiting settlement; undecided; imminent

pend'ulous *a.* hanging, swinging —**pend'ulum** *n.* suspended weight swinging to and fro, *esp.* as regulator for clock

pen'etrate *vt.* enter into; pierce; arrive at the meaning of —**penetrabil'ity** *n.* quality of being penetrable —**pen'etrable** *a.* capable of being entered or pierced —**pen'etrating** *a.* sharp; easily heard; subtle; quick to understand —**penetra'tion** *n.* insight, acuteness —**pen'etrative** *a.* piercing; discerning —**pen'etrator** *n.*

pen'guin *n.* flightless, shortlegged swimming bird

penicill'in [-sil'-] *n.* antibiotic drug effective against a wide range of diseases, infections

penin'sula *n.* portion of land nearly surrounded by water —**penin'sular** *a.*

pe'nis *n.* male organ of copulation (and of urination) in man and many mammals (*pl.* **pe'-nises, pe'nes** [-nēz])

pen'itent *a.* affected by sense of guilt —*n.* one that repents of sin —**pen'itence** *n.* sorrow for sin; repentance —**peniten'tial** *a.* of, or expressing, penitence —**peniten'tiary** *a.* relating to penance, or to the rules of penance —*n.* US prison

penn'ant *n.* long narrow flag

penn'on *n.* small pointed or swallow-tailed flag

penn'y *n.* Brit. bronze coin, now 100th part of pound (*pl.* **pence, penn'ies**) —**penn'iless** *a.* having no money; poor

penol'ogy [pē-] *n.* study of punishment and prevention of crime

pen'sion[1] *n.* regular payment to old people, retired public officials, soldiers *etc.* —*vt.* grant pension to —**pen'sioner** *n.*

pension'[1][2] [pahn-syon'] *n.* continental boarding house; (full) board

pen'sive *a.* thoughtful with sadness; wistful

pent *a.* shut up, kept in —**pent-up** *a.* not released, repressed

pent'agon *n.* plane figure having five angles —**pentag'onal** *a.*

Pent'agon *n.* military headquarters in USA

pentam'eter *n.* verse of five metrical feet

Pent'ateuch [-tyōōk] *n.* first five books of Old Testament

pentath'lon *n.* athletic contest of five events

Pent'ecost *n.* Whitsuntide; Jewish harvest festival on 50th day after Passover

pent'house *n.* apartment, flat or other structure on top, or top floor, of building

pen'tode *n.* Electronics five-electrode thermionic valve, having anode, cathode and three grids

pentste'mon *n.* bright-flowered garden plant

pen'ult [*or* -nult'] *n.* last syllable but one of word —**penul'timate** *a.* next before the last

penum'bra *n.* imperfect shadow; in an eclipse, the partially shadowed region which surrounds the full shadow —**penum'bral** *a.*

pen'ury *n.* extreme poverty; extreme scarcity —**penu'rious** *a.* niggardly, stingy; poor, scanty

pe'ony *n.* plant with showy red, pink, or white flowers

peo'ple [pē'pl] *pl.n.* persons generally; community, nation; race; family —*vt.* stock with inhabitants; populate

pep *n. inf.* vigour; energy; enthusiasm —*vt.* impart energy to; speed up (-**pp**-)

pepp'er *n.* fruit of climbing plant, which yields pungent aromatic spice; various slightly pungent vegetables *eg* capsicum —*vt.* season with pepper; sprinkle, dot; pelt with missiles —**pepp'ery** *a.* having the qualities of pepper; irritable —**pepp'ercorn** *n.* dried pepper berry; something trifling —**pepp'ermint** *n.* plant noted for aromatic pungent liquor distilled from it; a sweet flavoured with this —**pepper tree** ornamental, evergreen tree

pep'tic *a.* relating to digestion or digestive juices

per *prep.* for each; by; in manner of

per-, par-, pel-, pil- (*comb. form*) through, thoroughly, as in *perfect, pellucid*

peram'bulate *vt.* walk through or over; traverse —*vi.* walk about —**peram'bulator** *n.* pram

per ann'um *Lat.* by the year

percale' n. woven cotton used esp. for sheets

perceive' vt. obtain knowledge of through senses; observe; understand —**perceiv'able** a. —**perceptibil'ity** n. —**percep'tible** a. discernible, recognizable —**percep'tion** n. faculty of perceiving; intuitive judgment —**percep'tive** a.

percent'age n. proportion or rate per hundred —**per cent** in each hundred

percep'tion n. see PERCEIVE

perch' n. freshwater fish

perch² n. resting place, as for bird; formerly, measure of 5½ yards —vt. place, as on perch —vi. alight, settle on fixed body; roost; balance on

perchance' adv. obs. perhaps

percip'ient a. having faculty of perception; perceiving —n. one who perceives

per'colate v. pass through fine mesh as liquor; permeate; filter —**percola'tion** n. —**per'colator** n. coffeepot with filter

percuss'ion [-sh'-] n. collision; impact; vibratory shock —**percussion instrument** one played by being struck, eg drum, cymbals etc.

perdi'tion [-ish'-] n. spiritual ruin

per'egrinate [pe'ri-] vi. travel about; roam —**peregrina'tion** n.

per'egrine [pe'ri-] n. type of falcon

peremp'tory a. authoritative, imperious; forbidding debate; decisive

perenn'ial a. lasting through the years; perpetual, unfailing —n. plant lasting more than two years —**perenn'ially** adv.

per'fect a. complete; finished; whole; unspoilt; faultless; correct, precise; excellent; of highest quality —n. tense denoting a complete act —vt. [-fekt'] improve; finish; make skilful —**perfect'ible** a. capable of becoming perfect —**perfec'tion** n. state of being perfect; faultlessness —**per'fectly** adv.

per'fidy n. treachery, disloyalty —**perfid'ious** a.

per'forate vt. make holes in, penetrate —**perfora'tion** n. hole(s) made through thing

perforce' adv. of necessity

perform' vt. bring to completion; accomplish; fulfil; represent on stage —vi. function; act part; play, as on musical instrument —**perform'ance** n. —**perform'er** n.

per'fume n. agreeable scent; fragrance —vt. [-fyōom'] imbue with an agreeable odour; scent —**perfu'mer** n. —**perfu'mery** n. perfumes in general

perfunc'tory a. superficial; hasty; done indifferently

per'gola n. area covered by plants growing on trellis; the trellis

perhaps' adv. possibly

peri- (comb. form) round, as in perimeter, period, periphrasis

pericar'dium n. membrane enclosing the heart —**pericar'di-ac, -dial** a. —**pericardi'tis** n. inflammation of this

perihe'lion n. point in orbit of planet or comet nearest to sun (pl. -lia)

per'il [pe'r-] n. danger; exposure to injury —**per'ilous** a. full of peril, hazardous

perim'eter n. outer boundary of an area; length of this

pe'riod n. particular portion of time; a series of years; single occurrence of menstruation; cycle; conclusion; full stop (.) at the end of a sentence; complete sentence —a. of furniture, dress, play etc., belonging to particular

peripatetic [pe'ri-] *n.* instrument used *esp.* in submarines, for giving view of objects on different level —**periscop'ic** *a.*

time in history —**period'ic** *a.* recurring at regular intervals —**period'ical** *a./n.* (of) publication issued at regular intervals —*a.* of a period; periodic —**perio-dic'ity** *n.*

peripatet'ic *a.* itinerant; walking, travelling about

periph'ery *n.* circumference; surface, outside —**periph'eral** *a.* minor, unimportant; of periphery

periph'rasis *n.* roundabout speech or phrase; circumlocution —**periphras'tic** *a.*

per'iscope [pe'ri-] *n.* instrument used *esp.* in submarines, for giving view of objects on different level —**periscop'ic** *a.*

per'ish [pe'ri-] *vi.* die, waste away; decay, rot —**perishabil'ity** *n.* —**per'ishable** *a.* that will not last long —*pl.n.* perishable food

per'istyle [pe'ri-] *n.* range of pillars surrounding building, square *etc.*; court within this

peritone'um *n.* membrane lining internal surface of abdomen (*pl.* **-ne'a**) —**peritoni'tis** *n.* inflammation of it

per'iwig [pe'ri-] *n. Hist.* wig

per'iwinkle [pe'ri-] *n.* flowering plant; small edible shellfish (*also* winkle)

per'jure *vt.* be guilty of perjury —**per'jury** *n.* crime of false testimony on oath; false swearing

perk *n. inf. short for* PERQUISITE

per'ky *a.* lively, cheerful, jaunty, gay —**perk up** make, become cheerful

per'mafrost *n.* permanently frozen ground

per'manent *a.* continuing in same state; lasting —**per'manence, per'manency** *n.* fixedness —**permanent wave** (*abbrev.* perm) *n.* (treatment of hair producing) long-lasting style

permang'anate *n.* salt of an acid of manganese

per'meate *vt.* pervade, saturate; pass through pores of —**per'meable** *a.* admitting of passage of fluids

permit' *vt.* allow; give leave to (*-tt-*) —*n.* [per'-] warrant or licence to do something; written permission —**permiss'ible** *a.* allowable —**permiss'ion** *n.* authorization; leave, liberty —**permiss'ive** *a.* (too) tolerant, lenient, *esp.* sexually

permute' *vt.* interchange —**permuta'tion** *n.* mutual transference; *Maths.* arrangement of a number of quantities in every possible order

perni'cious [-nish'-] *a.* wicked or mischievous; extremely hurtful; having quality of destroying or injuring

pernick'ety *a. inf.* fussy; fastidious about trifles

perora'tion *n.* concluding part of oration —**per'orate** *vi.*

perox'ide *n.* oxide of a given base containing greatest quantity of oxygen; *short for* HYDROGEN PEROXIDE

perpendic'ular *a.* at right angles to the plane of the horizon; at right angles to given line or surface; exactly upright —*n.* line falling at right angles on another line or plane

per'petrate *vt.* perform or be responsible for (something bad) —**perpetra'tion** *n.* —**per'petrator** *n.*

perpet'ual *a.* continuous; lasting for ever —**perpet'ually** *adv.* —**perpet'uate** *vt.* make perpetual; not to allow to be forgotten —**perpetua'tion** *n.* —**perpetu'ity** *n.*

perplex' *vt.* puzzle; bewilder; make difficult to understand —**perplex'ity** *n.* puzzled or tangled state

per'quisite [-it] *n.* any incidental benefit from a certain type of employment; casual payment in addition to salary

perr'y n. fermented drink made from pears

per se [-sā'] *Lat.* by or in itself

per'secute vt. oppress because of race, religion *etc.*; subject to persistent ill-treatment —**persecu'tion** n. —**per'secutor** n.

persevere' vi. persist, maintain effort —**perse'verance** n. persistence

per'siflage [-flahzh] n. idle talk; frivolous style of treating subject

persimm'on n. Amer. tree; its hard wood; its fruit

persist' vi. continue in spite of obstacles or objections —**persis'tence, persist'ency** n. —**persis'tent** a. persisting; steady; persevering; lasting

per'son n. individual (human) being; body of human being; *Grammar* classification, or one of the classes, of pronouns and verb forms according to the person speaking, spoken to, or spoken of —**perso'na** n. assumed character —**per'sonable** a. good-looking —**per'sonage** n. notable person —**per'sonal** a. individual, private, or one's own; of, relating to grammatical person —**personal'ity** n. distinctive character; a celebrity —**per'sonally** adv. in person —**per'sonalty** n. personal property —**per'sonate** vt. pass oneself off as —**persona'tion** n. —**personal property** Law all property except land and interests in land that pass to heir

person'ify vt. represent as person; typify (-**ified, -ifying**) —**personifica'tion** n.

personnel' n. staff employed in a service or institution

perspec'tive [-iv] n. mental view; art of drawing on flat surface to give effect of solidity and relative distances and sizes; drawing in perspective

Per'spex R transparent acrylic substitute for glass

perspica'cious a. having quick mental insight —**perspicac'ity** [-kas'-] n.

perspic'uous a. clearly expressed; lucid; plain; obvious —**perspicu'ity** n.

perspire' v. sweat —**perspira'tion** n. sweating

persuade' [-sw-] vt. bring (one to do something) by argument, charm *etc.*, convince —**persua'sion** n. act of persuading; way of thinking or belief —**persua'sive** a.

pert a. forward, saucy

pertain' vi. belong, relate, have reference (to); concern

pertina'cious [-shəs] a. obstinate, persistent —**pertinac'ity** [-as'-] n. doggedness, resolution

pert'inent a. to the point —**pert'inence** n. relevance

perturb' vt. disturb greatly; alarm —**perturb'able** a. —**perturba'tion** n. agitation of mind

peruke' [-ōōk'] n. *Hist.* wig

peruse' [-ōōz'] vt. read, *esp.* in slow and careful, or leisurely, manner —**peru'sal** n.

pervade' vt. spread through; be rife among —**perva'sion** n. —**perva'sive** a.

pervert' vt. turn to wrong use; lead astray —n. [per'-] one who shows unhealthy abnormality, *esp.* in sexual matters —**perverse'** a. obstinately or unreasonably wrong; self-willed; headstrong; wayward —**perverse'ly** adv. —**perver'sion** n. —**perver'sity** n.

per'vious a. permeable; penetrable, giving passage

pese'ta n. Sp. monetary unit

pess'ary n. instrument used to

support mouth and neck of uterus; appliance to prevent conception; medicated suppository

pess'imism n. tendency to see the worst side of things; theory that everything turns to evil —**pess'imist** n. —**pessimist'ic** a.

pest n. troublesome or harmful thing, person or insect; plague —**pest'icide** n. chemical for killing pests, esp. insects —**pestif'erous** a. troublesome; bringing plague

pest'er vt. trouble or vex persistently; harass

pes'tilence n. epidemic disease esp. bubonic plague —**pes'tilent** a. troublesome; deadly —**pestilen'tial** a.

pes'tle [pes'al] n. instrument with which things are pounded in a mortar —v.

Pet. Peter

pet n. animal or person kept or regarded with affection —vt. make pet of; inf. hug, embrace, fondle (-**tt**-)

pet'al n. white or coloured leaf-like part of flower —**pet'alled** a.

petard' n. formerly, an explosive device

pe'ter vi. —**peter out** inf. disappear, lose power gradually

pe'tersham n. thick corded ribbon used to stiffen belts etc.

pet'it [-i] a. Law small, petty

petite' [-tēt'] a. small, dainty

peti'tion [-ish-] n. entreaty, request, esp. one presented to sovereign or parliament —vt. present petition to —**peti'tionary** a. —**peti'tioner** n.

pet'rel n. sea bird

pet'rify vt. turn to stone; fig. make motionless with fear; make dumb with amazement (-**ified**, -**ifying**) —**petrifac'tion**, **petrifica'tion** n.

petro'leum n. mineral oil —**pet'rol** n. refined petroleum used in motorcars etc. —**petrol bomb** home-made incendiary device consisting of bottle filled with petrol

petrol'ogy n. study of rocks and their structure

pett'icoat n. women's undergarment worn under skirts, dresses etc.

pett'ifogger n. low-class lawyer; one given to mean dealing in small matters —**pett'ifog** vi. be, act like pettifogger

petty' a. unimportant, trivial; small-minded, mean; on a small scale —**petty cash** cash kept by firm to pay minor incidental expenses —**petty officer** non-commissioned officer in Navy

pet'ulant a. given to small fits of temper; peevish —**pet'ulance** n. peevishness

petu'nia n. plant with funnel-shaped purple or white flowers

pew n. fixed seat in church; inf. chair, seat

pe'wit see PEEWIT

pew'ter n. alloy of tin and lead; ware of this

phalan'ger n. any of various Aust. tree-dwelling marsupials, the Aust. possum

phal'anx n. body of men formed in close array (pl. **phal'anxes**, **phalan'ges** [-jēz])

phal'arope n. small wading bird

phall'us n. penis; symbol of it used in primitive rites —**phall'icism** n. —**phall'ic** a.

phan'tasm n. vision of absent person; illusion —**phantasmago'ria** n. crowd of dim or unreal figures; exhibition of illusions —**phantas'mal** a. —**phan'tasy** n. see FANTASY

phan'tom n. apparition; spectre, ghost; fancied vision

Pha'raoh [fā'rō] n. title of ancient Egyptian kings

phar'isee [fa'ri-] n. sanctimonious person; hypocrite —**pharisa'ic(al)** a.

pharmaceut'ic [-syoot'-] a. of pharmacy —**pharmaceut'ics** pl.n. science of pharmacy —**pharmaceu'tical** a. —**phar'macist** n. person qualified to dispense drugs —**pharmacol'ogy** n. study of drugs —**pharmacopoe'ia** [-pē'-] n. official book with list and directions for use of drugs —**phar'macy** n. preparation and dispensing of drugs; dispensary

phar'ynx [fa'ringks] n. cavity forming back part of mouth and terminating in gullet (pl. **pharyn'ges** [-jēz]) —**pharyn'geal** a. —**pharyngi'tis** [-jī'-] n. inflammation of pharynx

phase [-z] n. any distinct or characteristic period or stage in a development or chain of events —vt. arrange, execute in stages or to coincide with something else

PhD Doctor of Philosophy

pheas'ant [fez'-] n. game bird with bright plumage

phenac'etin [-nas'-] n. drug to relieve fever, used for headache etc.

phenobarb'itone [fē-nō-] n. drug inducing sleep

phe'nol n. carbolic acid

phenom'enon n. anything appearing or observed; remarkable person or thing (pl. **phenom'ena**) —**phenom'enal** a. relating to phenomena; remarkable; recognizable or evidenced by senses

phi'al n. small bottle for medicine etc.

Phil. Philippians

phil- (comb. form) loving, as in philanthropy, philosophy

philan'der vi. (of man) flirt with women

philan'thropy n. practice of doing good to one's fellow men; love of mankind —**philanthrop'ic** a. loving mankind; benevolent —**philan'thropist** n.

philat'ely n. stamp collecting —**philatel'ic** a. —**philat'elist** n.

philharmon'ic a. musical (only for titles of societies)

philis'tine n. ignorant, smug person —a. —**phil'istinism** n.

philoden'dron n. widely cultivated tropical Amer. climbing plant

philol'ogy n. science of structure and development of languages —**philolog'ical** a. —**philol'ogist** n.

philos'ophy n. pursuit of wisdom; study of realities and general principles; system of theories on nature of things or on conduct; calmness of mind —**philos'opher** n. one who studies, possesses, or originates philosophy —**philosoph'ic(al)** a. of, like philosophy; wise, learned; calm, stoical —**philos'ophize** vi. reason like philosopher; theorize; moralize

phil'tre [-tər] n. love potion

phlebi'tis n. inflammation of a vein

phlegm [flem] n. viscid substance formed by mucous membrane and ejected by coughing etc.; calmness, sluggishness —**phlegmat'ic** [fleg-] a. not easily agitated; composed

phlox n. flowering plant

pho'bia n. fear or aversion; unreasoning dislike

phoe'nix [fē'-] n. legendary bird; unique thing

phone n./a./vi. inf. telephone —**phone'card** n. public telephone operated by special card; card itself

phonet'ic a. of, or relating to, vocal sounds —**phonet'ics** pl.n.

science of vocal sounds —**pho-neti'cian** n.

pho'ney inf. a. counterfeit, sham, fraudulent; suspect

phono- (comb. form) sounds, as in phonology

pho'nograph n. instrument recording and reproducing sounds —**phonograph'ic** a.

phonol'ogy n. study of speech sounds and their development; system of sounds in a language —**phonolog'ic(al)** a. —**phonol'o-gist** n.

phos'gene [foz'jēn] n. lung-irritant poison gas used in warfare

phos'phorus n. toxic, flammable, nonmetallic element which appears luminous in the dark —**phos'phate** n., **phos'phide** n., **phos'phite** n. compounds of phosphorus —**phosphores'cence** n. faint glow in the dark

pho'to n. inf. short for PHOTOGRAPH —**photo finish** photo taken at end of race to show placing of contestants

photo- (comb. form) light, as in photometer, photosynthesis

photochem'istry n. study of chemical action of light

pho'tocopy n. photographic reproduction —vt.

photoelectric'ity n. electricity produced or affected by action of light

photoelec'tron n. electron liberated from metallic surface by action of beam of light

photogen'ic a. capable of being photographed attractively

pho'tograph n. picture made by chemical action of light on sensitive film —vt. take photograph of —**photog'rapher** n. —**photograph'ic** a. —**photog'ra-phy** n.

photogravure' n. process of etching, product of photography;

picture so reproduced

photolithog'raphy n. art of printing from photographs transferred to stone or metal plate —**photolithograph'ic** a.

photom'eter n. instrument for measuring light's intensity —**photom'etry** n.

Pho'tostat R apparatus for obtaining direct, facsimile, photographic reproductions of documents, manuscripts, drawings etc., without printing from negatives —vt. take photostat copies of

photosyn'thesis n. process by which green plant uses sun's energy to build up carbohydrate reserves

phrase [-z] n. group of words; pithy expression; mode of expression —vt. express in words —**phraseol'ogy** [frāz-i-] n. manner of expression, choice of words —**phrasal verb** phrase consisting of verb and preposition, often with meaning different to the parts (eg take in)

phrenol'ogy n. (formerly) study of skull's shape; theory that character and mental powers are indicated by shape of skull —**phrenolog'ical** a. —**phrenol'o-gist** n.

phut n. dull, heavy sound —**go phut** collapse

phylac'tery n. leather case containing religious texts worn by Jewish men

phys'ic [-iz'-] n. medicine, esp. cathartic —pl. science of properties of matter and energy —**phys'ical** a. bodily, as opposed to mental or moral; material; of physics of body —**phys'ically** adv. —**physi'cian** n. qualified medical practitioner —**phys'icist** n. one skilled in, or student of, physics

physiog'nomy [-on'-] n. judging character by face; face; outward appearance of something

physiog'raphy n. science of the earth's surface —**physiog'rapher** n.

physiol'ogy n. science of normal function of living things —**physiol'ogist** n.

physiother'apy n. therapeutic use of physical means, as massage etc. —**physiother'apist** n.

physique' [-ēk'] n. bodily structure, constitution and development

pi n. Maths. ratio of circumference of circle to its diameter

pian'o [-a'tɔ] (orig. pianofor'te) musical instrument with strings which are struck by hammers worked by keyboard (pl. **pian'os**) —a./adv. Mus. softly —**pi'anist** [pē'-] n. performer on piano —**Piano'la** R mechanically played piano

piazz'a [-at'sɔ] n. square, marketplace

pi'broch [pē'broH] n. form of bagpipe music

pic n. inf. picture; illustration (pl. **pics, pix**)

pi'ca n. printing type of 6 lines to the inch; size of type, 12 point; typewriter typesize (10 letters to inch)

pic'ador n. mounted bullfighter with lance

picaresque' [-esk'] a. of fiction, esp. episodic and dealing with the adventures of rogues

pic'caninny n. offens. small negro child —**picc'anin** n. SA male Afr. child

picc'olo n. small flute (pl. **-los**)

pick¹ vt. choose, select carefully; pluck, gather; peck at; pierce with something pointed; find occasion for —n. act of picking; choicest part —**pick'ings** pl.n. gleanings; odds and ends of profit

—**pick'lock** n. instrument for opening locks —**pick-me-up** inf. n. tonic; stimulating drink —**pick'pocket** n. one who steals from another's pocket —**pick-up** n. device for conversion of mechanical energy into electric signals, as in record player etc.; small truck —**pick on** find fault with —**pick up** raise, lift; collect; improve, get better; accelerate

pick² n. tool with curved iron crossbar and wooden shaft, for breaking up hard ground or masonry —**pick'axe** n. pick

pick'aback n. ride on the back of man or animal, given to child

pick'erel n. young pike

pick'et n. prong, pointed stake; party of trade unionists posted to deter would-be workers during strike —vt. post as picket; beset with pickets; tether to peg —**picket fence** fence of pickets

pic'kle [pik'l] n. food preserved in brine, vinegar etc.; liquid used for preserving; awkward situation; mischievous child —pl. pickled vegetables —vt. preserve in pickle —**pick'led** a. inf. drunk

pic'nic n. pleasure excursion including meal out of doors —vi. take part in picnic (**pic'nicked, pic'nicking**)

pic'ric acid powerful acid used in dyeing, medicine, and as ingredient in certain explosives

Pict n. member of ancient race of NE Scotland —**Pict'ish** a.

pic'ture n. drawing or painting; mental image; beautiful or picturesque object —pl. cinema —vt. represent in, or as in, a picture —**pictor'ial** a. of, in, with, painting or pictures; graphic —n. newspaper with pictures —**picto'rially** adv. —**picturesque'** [-esk'] a. such as would be effective in picture; striking, vivid

pidg'in n. language, not a mother tongue, made up of elements of two or more other languages

pie n. baked dish of meat, fruit etc., usu. with pastry crust; obs. magpie

pie'bald a. irregularly marked with black and white; motley —n. piebald horse or other animal —**pied** a. piebald; variegated

piece [pēs] n. bit, part, fragment; single object; literary or musical composition etc.; sl. young woman; small object used in draughts, chess etc. —vt. mend, put together —**piece'meal** adv. by, in, or into pieces, a bit at a time —**piece'work** n. work paid for according to quantity produced

pièce de résistance [pyes-də-re-zis-tahns'] Fr. principal item

pie-eyed a. sl. drunk

pier n. structure running into sea as landing stage; piece of solid upright masonry, esp. supporting bridge

pierce vt. make hole in; make a way through —**pierc'ing** a. keen; penetrating

pier'rot [pēr'ō] n. pantomime character, clown

pi'ety n. godliness; devoutness, goodness; dutifulness

pif'fle n. inf. rubbish, twaddle, nonsense, trash

pig n. wild or domesticated mammal killed for pork, ham, bacon; inf. greedy, dirty person; derogatory sl. policeman; oblong mass of smelted metal —vi. of sow, produce litter (-**gg**-) —**pigg'ery** n. place for keeping, breeding pigs; greediness —**pigg'ish, pig'gy** a. dirty; greedy; stubborn —**pig-headed** a. obstinate —**pig'tail** n. plait of hair hanging from back or either side of head

pig'eon [pij'in] n. bird of many wild and domesticated varieties, often trained to carry messages; inf. concern, responsibility —**pig'eonhole** n. compartment for papers in desk etc. —vt. defer; classify —**pigeon-toed** a. with feet, toes turned inwards

pigg'yback n. see PICKABACK

pig'ment n. colouring matter, paint or dye

pig'my see PYGMY

pike[1] n. various types of large, predatory freshwater fish

pike[2] n. spear formerly used by infantry

pike'let n. various small cakes, esp. one of fried sweet batter

pilas'ter n. square column, usu. set in wall

pilau [-low], **pil'af(f)** n. Oriental dish of meat or fowl boiled with rice, spices etc.

pil'chard n. small sea fish like the herring

pile[1] n. heap; great mass of building —vt. heap (up), stack load —vi. (with in, out, off etc.) move in a group —**atomic pile** nuclear reactor

pile[2] n. beam driven into the ground, esp. as foundation for building in water or wet ground —**pile'driver** n. machine for driving down piles

pile[3] n. nap of cloth, esp. of velvet, carpet etc.; down

piles pl.n. tumours of veins of rectum, haemorrhoids

pil'fer v. steal in small quantities —**pil'ferage** n. —**pil'ferer** n.

pil'grim n. one who journeys to sacred place; wanderer, wayfarer —**pil'grimage** n.

pill n. small ball of medicine swallowed whole; anything disagreeable which has to be endured —**the pill** oral contraceptive —**pill'box** n. small box for pills; small concrete fort

pill'age v. plunder, ravage, sack

—*n.* seizure of goods, *esp.* in war; plunder

pill'ar *n.* slender, upright structure, column; prominent supporter

pill'ion *n.* seat, cushion, for passenger behind rider of motorcycle or horse

pill'ory *n.* frame with holes for head and hands in which offender was confined and exposed to public abuse and ridicule —*vt.* expose to ridicule and abuse; set in pillory (**pill'oried, pill'orying**)

pill'ow *n.* cushion for the head, *esp.* in bed —*vt.* lay on, or as on, pillow

pi'lot *n.* person qualified to fly an aircraft or spacecraft; one qualified to take charge of ship entering or leaving harbour, or where knowledge of local water is needed; steersman; guide —*a.* experimental and preliminary —*vt.* act as pilot to; steer —**pi'lotage** *n.* work, fee of pilot —**pilot fish** small fish which accompanies sharks, larger fish —**pilot light** small auxiliary flame lighting main one in gas appliance *etc.*; small electric light as indicator

Pils'(e)ner *n.* type of pale beer

pill'ule *n.* small pill

pimen'to *n.* allspice; sweet red pepper: *also* **pimien'to** (*pl.* -**tos**)

pimp *n.* one who solicits for prostitute —*vi.* act as pimp

pim'pernel *n.* plant with small scarlet, blue, or white flowers closing in dull weather

pim'ple *n.* small pus-filled spot on the skin —**pim'ply** *a.*

pin *n.* short thin piece of stiff wire with point and head, for fastening; wooden or metal peg or rivet —*vt.* fasten with pin; seize and hold fast (-**nn**-) —**pin'ball** *n.* electrically operated table game, where small ball is shot

through various hazards —**pin money** trivial sum —**pin'point** *vt.* mark exactly

pin'afore *n.* apron; dress with a bib top

pince-nez [pans'nā] *sing. n.* eyeglasses kept on nose by spring

pin'cers *pl.n.* tool for gripping, composed of two limbs crossed and pivoted; claws of lobster *etc.*

pinch *vt.* nip, squeeze; stint; *inf.* steal; *inf.* arrest —*n.* nip; as much as can be taken up between finger and thumb; stress, emergency —**pinch'bar** *n.* jemmy

pinch'beck *n.* zinc and copper alloy —*a.* counterfeit, flashy

pine[1] *n.* evergreen coniferous tree; its wood —**pine marten** type of marten

pine[2] *vi.* yearn; waste away with grief *etc.*

pin'eal *a.* shaped like pine cone —**pineal gland** small cone-shaped gland situated at base of brain

pine'apple *n.* tropical plant with spiny leaves bearing large edible fruit; the fruit

ping *n.* device that makes ringing sound, *esp.* timer

Ping'-Pong *n.* R table tennis

pin'ion[1] *n.* bird's wing —*vt.* disable or confine by binding wings, arms *etc.*

pin'ion[2] *n.* small cogwheel

pink *n.* pale red colour; garden plant; best condition, fitness —*a.* of colour pink —*vt.* pierce; ornament with perforations or scalloped, indented edge —*vi.* of engine, knock

pinn'acle *n.* highest pitch or point; mountain peak; pointed turret on buttress or roof

pint [ɪ-] *n.* liquid measure, half a quart, 1/8 gallon (.568 litre)

pin'tail *n.* type of duck

pin'tle *n.* pivot pin

pin'-up *n.* picture of sexually attractive person, *esp.* (partly) naked

pioneer' [pī-ə-] *n.* explorer; early settler; originator; one of advance party preparing road for troops —*vi.* act as pioneer or leader

pi'ous *a.* devout; righteous

pip[1] *n.* seed in fruit

pip[2] *n.* high-pitched sound used as time signal on radio; spot on playing cards, dice, or dominoes; *inf.* star on junior officer's shoulder showing rank

pip[3] *n.* disease of fowl —**give someone the pip** *sl.* annoy someone

pipe *n.* tube of metal or other material; tube with small bowl at end for smoking tobacco; musical instrument, whistle; wine cask —*pl.* bagpipes —*v.* play on pipe; utter in shrill tone; convey by pipe; ornament with a piping or fancy edging —**pi'per** *n.* player on pipe or bagpipes —**pi'ping** *n.* system of pipes; decoration of icing on cake; fancy edging or trimming on clothes; act or art of playing on pipe, *esp.* bagpipes —**pipe dream** fanciful, impossible plan *etc.* —**pipe'line** *n.* long pipe for transporting oil, water *etc.*; means of communications —**in the pipeline** yet to come; in process of completion *etc.*

pipette' *n.* slender glass tube to transfer fluids from one vessel to another

pip'it *n.* bird like lark

pipp'in *n.* kinds of apple

pi'quant [pē'kənt] *a.* pungent; stimulating —**pi'quancy** *n.*

pique [pēk] *n.* feeling of injury, baffled curiosity or resentment —*vt.* hurt pride of; irritate; stimulate

pi'qué [pē'kā] *n.* stiff ribbed cotton fabric

piquet' [pi-ket', -kā'] *n.* card game for two

piran'ha [-rahn'yə] *n.* small voracious freshwater fish of tropical Amer.

pi'rate *n.* sea robber; publisher who infringes copyright —*n./a.* (person) broadcasting illegally —*vt.* use or reproduce (artistic work *etc.*) illicitly —**pi'racy** *n.* —**pirat'ical** *a.* —**pirat'ically** *adv.*

pirouette' [pi-roo-] *n.* spinning round on the toe —*vi.* do this

Pi'sces [pī'sēz] *pl.n.* the Fishes, 12th sign of zodiac, operative *c.* Feb. 19–Mar. 20 —**pis'catory, piscato'rial** *a.* of fishing or fishes

pistach'io [-tahsh'-] *n.* small hard-shelled, sweet-tasting nut; tree producing it (*pl.* **-os**)

pist'il *n.* seed-bearing organ of flower

pist'ol *n.* small firearm for one hand —*vt.* shoot with pistol (**-ll-**)

pist'on *n.* in internal combustion engine, steam engine *etc.*, cylindrical part propelled to and fro in hollow cylinder by pressure of gas *etc.* to convert reciprocating motion to rotation

pit *n.* deep hole in ground; mine or its shaft; depression; part of theatre occupied by orchestra; enclosure where animals were set to fight; servicing, refuelling area on motor-racing track —*vt.* set to fight, match; mark with small dents or scars (**-tt-**) —**pit'fall** *n.* any hidden danger; covered pit for catching animals or men

pitch[1] *vt.* cast or throw; set up; set the key of (a tune) —*vi.* fall headlong; of ship, plunge lengthwise —*n.* act of pitching; degree, height, intensity; slope; distance airscrew advances during one revolution; distance between threads of screw, teeth of saw etc.; acuteness of tone; part of ground where wickets are set up; *Sport* field of play; station of street vendor etc.; *inf.* persuasive sales talk —**pitch'er** n. *US Base-ball* player who delivers ball to batter —**pitch'fork** n. fork for lifting hay etc. —vt. throw with, as with pitchfork

pitch[2] n. dark sticky substance obtained from tar or turpentine —vt. coat with this —**pitch'y** a. covered with pitch; black as pitch —**pitch-black, -dark** a. very dark —**pitch pine** resinous kind of pine

pitch'blende n. mineral composed largely of uranium oxide, yielding radium

pitch'er n. large jug

pith n. tissue in stems and branches of certain plants; essential substance, most important part —**pith'ily** adv. —**pith'less** adj. —**pith'y** a. terse, cogent, concise; consisting of pith

pitt'ance n. small allowance; inadequate wages

pitu'itary a. of, pert. to, the endocrine gland at base of brain

pit'y n. sympathy, sorrow for others' suffering; regrettable fact —vt. feel pity for (**pit'ied, pit'y-ing**) —**pit'eous** a. deserving pity; sad, wretched —**pit'iable** a. —**pit'iably** adv. —**pit'iful** a. woeful; contemptible —**pit'iless** a. feeling no pity; hard, merciless

piv'ot n. shaft or pin on which thing turns —vt. furnish with pivot —vi. hinge on one —**piv'ot-al** a. of, acting as, pivot; of crucial importance

pix'y, pix'ie n. fairy

pizz'a [pēt'sə] n. dish, (orig. It.) of baked disc of dough covered with wide variety of savoury toppings —**pizzeri'a** [-rē'ə] n. place selling pizzas

pizzazz' [pə-] n. *inf.* sparkle, vitality, glamour

pizzicat'o [pit-si-caht'ō] a./n. *Mus.* note, passage played by plucking string of violin etc., with finger

pl. place; plate; plural

plaas [-ah-] n. *SA* farm

plac'ard n. paper or card with notice on one side for posting up or carrying, poster —vt. post placards on; advertise, display on placards

placate' vt. conciliate, pacify, appease —**plac'atory** [or -kā'-] a.

place n. locality, spot; position; stead; duty; town, village, residence, buildings; office, employment; seat, space —vt. put in particular place; set; identify; make (order, rank) etc.

place'bo n. sugar pill etc. given to unsuspecting patient as active drug

placen'ta [-sen'-] n. organ formed in uterus during pregnancy, providing nutrients for foetus; afterbirth (pl. **-tas, -tae** [-tē]) —**placen'tal** a.

plac'id [plas'-] a. calm; equable —**placid'ity** n. mildness, quiet

plack'et n. opening at top of skirt etc. fastened with buttons, zip

pla'giarism [-jə-] n. taking ideas, passages etc. from an author and presenting them, unacknowledged, as one's own —**pla'giarize** v.

plague [plāg] n. highly contagious disease, *esp.* bubonic plague; *inf.* nuisance; affliction —vt. trouble, annoy —**pla'guily** adv. —**pla'gue(y)** [plā'gi] a. *inf.* tiresome; annoying

plaice n. flat fish

plaid [plad, plād] n. long Highland cloak or shawl; checked or tartan pattern

plain a. flat, level; unobstructed,

not intricate; clear, obvious; easily understood; simple; ordinary; without decoration; not beautiful —n. tract of level country —adv. clearly —**plain'ly** adv. —**plain'ness** n. —**plain clothes** civilian dress, as opposed to uniform —**plain sailing** unobstructed course of action —**plain speaking** frankness, candour

plaint n. Law statement of complaint; obs. lament —**plaint'iff** n. Law one who sues in court —**plain'tive** a. sad, mournful, melancholy

plait [plat] n. braid of hair, straw etc. —vt. form or weave into plaits

plan n. scheme; way of proceeding; project, design; drawing of horizontal section; diagram, map —vt. make plan of; arrange beforehand (-**nn**-)

plan'chet [-ahn'-] n. disc of metal from which coin is stamped

planchette' [plahn-shet'] n. small board used in spiritualism

plane¹ n. smooth surface; a level; carpenter's tool for smoothing wood —vt. make smooth with one —a. perfectly flat or level —**pla'ner** n. planing machine

plane² v. of aeroplane, glide; of boat, rise and partly skim over water —n. wing of aeroplane; aeroplane

plane³ n. tree with broad leaves

plan'et n. heavenly body revolving round the sun —**plan'etary** a. of planets

planeta'rium n. an apparatus that shows the movement of sun, moon, stars and planets by projecting lights on the inside of a dome; building in which the apparatus is housed

plan'gent [-j-] a. resounding

plank n. long flat piece of sawn timber —vt. cover with planks

plank'ton n. minute animal and vegetable organisms floating in ocean

plant [-ah-] n. living organism feeding on inorganic substances and without power of locomotion; such an organism that is smaller than tree or shrub; equipment or machinery needed for manufacture; building and equipment for manufacturing purposes; heavy vehicles used for road building etc. —vt. set in ground, to grow; support, establish; stock with plants; sl. hide, esp. to deceive or observe —**plant'er** n. one who plants; ornamental pot or stand for house plants

plan'tain¹ [-tin] n. low-growing herb with broad leaves

plan'tain² [-tin] n. tropical plant like banana; its fruit

planta'tion n. estate for cultivation of tea, tobacco etc.; wood of planted trees; formerly, colony

plaque [plak] n. ornamental plate, tablet; plate of clasp or brooch; filmy deposit on surfaces of teeth, conducive to decay

plas'ma [-az'-] n. clear, fluid portion of blood —**plas'mic** a.

plast'er [-ah-] n. mixture of lime, sand etc. for coating walls etc.; piece of fabric spread with medicinal or adhesive substance —vt. apply plaster to; apply like plaster —**plast'erer** n.

plast'ic n. any of a group of synthetic products derived from casein, cellulose etc. which can be readily moulded into any form and are extremely durable —a. made of plastic; easily moulded, pliant; capable of being moulded; produced by moulding —**plastic'ity** [-s'-] n. ability to be moulded —**plastic bullet** solid PVC cylinder fired by police in riot control —**plastic surgery** repair or reconstruction of missing or malformed parts of the body for medical or cosmetic reasons

Plasticine R a modelling material like clay

plate n. shallow round dish; flat thin sheet of metal, glass etc.; utensils of gold or silver; device for printing; illustration in book; device used by dentists to straighten children's teeth; set of false teeth —vt. cover with thin coating of gold, silver, or other metal —**plate'ful** n. —**pla'ter** n. —**plate glass** kind of thick glass used for mirrors, windows etc. —**plate tecton'ics** Geol. study of structure of earth's crust, esp. movement of layers of rocks

plat'eau [-ō] n. tract of level high land, tableland; period of stability

plat'en n. Printing plate by which paper is pressed against type; roller in typewriter

plat'form n. raised level surface or floor, stage; raised area in station from which passengers board trains; political programme

plat'inum n. white heavy malleable metal

plat'itude n. commonplace remark —**platitu'dinous** a.

Platon'ic a. of Plato or his philosophy; (p-) (of love) purely spiritual, friendly

platoon' n. body of soldiers employed as unit

platt'eland [-ɔ-lant] n. SA rural district

platt'er n. flat dish

plat'ypus n. small Aust. egg-laying amphibious mammal, with dense fur, webbed feet and duck-like bill; also **duck-billed platypus** (pl. -**puses**)

plau'dit n. act of applause, hand clapping

plau'sible [-z-] a. apparently fair or reasonable; fair-spoken —**plausibil'ity** n.

play [plā] vi. amuse oneself; take part in game; behave carelessly; act a part on the stage; perform on musical instrument; move with light or irregular motion, flicker etc. —vt. contend with in game; take part in (game); trifle; act the part of; perform (music); perform on (instrument); use, work (instrument) —n. dramatic piece or performance; sport; amusement; manner of action or conduct; activity; brisk or free movement; gambling —**play'er** n. —**play'ful** a. lively —**play'group** n. group of young children playing regularly under adult supervision —**play'house** n. theatre —**playing card** one of set of 52 cards used in card games —**playing fields** extensive piece of ground for open-air games —**play'thing** n. toy —**play'wright** n. author of plays

plaz'a [-ahz'ɔ] n. open space or square; complex of shops etc.

PLC, plc Public Limited Company

plea [plē] n. entreaty; statement of prisoner or defendant; excuse —**plead** vi. make earnest appeal; address court of law —vt. bring forward as excuse or plea (**plead'ed** or US, Scots **pled**, **plead'ing**)

please [-z] vt. be agreeable to; gratify; delight —vi. like; be willing —adv. word of request —**pleas'ance** [plez'-] n. secluded part of garden —**pleas'ant** a. pleasing, agreeable —**pleas'antly** adv. —**pleas'antry** n. joke, humour —**pleas'urable** a. giving pleasure —**pleas'ure** n. enjoyment; satisfaction, will, choice

pleat n. any of various types of fold made by doubling material back on itself —*vi.* make, gather into pleats

plebe'ian [-bē'ən] *a.* belonging to the common people; low or rough —*n.* one of the common people; *also offens. sl.* **pleb**

pleb'iscite *n.* decision by direct voting of the electorate

plec'trum *n.* small implement for plucking strings of guitar *etc.*

pledge *n.* promise; thing given over as security; toast —*vt.* promise formally; bind or secure by pledge; give over as security

plei'stocene [plī'stə-sēn] *a.* glacial period of formation

ple'nary *a.* complete, without limitations, absolute; of meeting *etc.*, with all members present

plenipoten'tiary *a./n.* (envoy) having full powers

plen'itude *n.* completeness, abundance, entirety

plen'ty *n.* abundance; quite enough —**plent'eous** *a.* ample; rich; copious —**plent'iful** *a.* abundant

ple'num *n.* space as considered to be full of matter (opposed to vacuum); condition of fullness

ple'onasm *n.* use of more words than necessary —**pleonas'tic** *a.* redundant

pleth'ora *n.* oversupply —**pletho'ric** [-o'rik] *a.*

pleur'isy [ploor'-] *n.* inflammation of pleura, membrane lining the chest and covering the lungs

plex'us *n.* network of nerves, or fibres (*pl.* **plex'us**)

pli'able *a.* easily bent or influenced —**pliabil'ity** *n.* —**pli'ancy** *n.* —**pli'ant** *a.* pliable

pli'ers *pl.n.* tool with hinged arms and jaws for gripping

plight[1] [plīt] *n.* distressing state; predicament

plight[2] [plīt] *vt.* promise, engage oneself to

Plim'soll line mark on ships

indicating maximum draught permitted when loaded

plim'solls *pl.n.* rubber-soled canvas shoes

plinth *n.* slab as base of column *etc.*

pli'ocene *n. Geol.* the most recent tertiary deposits

PLO Palestine Liberation Organization

plod *vi.* walk or work doggedly (-**dd**-)

plonk[1] *v.* drop, fall suddenly and heavily —*n.*

plonk[2] *n. inf.* alcoholic drink, *esp.* (cheap) wine

plop *n.* sound of object falling into water without splash —*v.*

plot[1] *n.* secret plan, conspiracy; essence of story, play *etc.* —*vt.* devise secretly; make position of; make map of —*vi.* conspire (-**tt**-)

plot[2] *n.* small piece of land

plough, US plow [plow] *n.* implement for turning up soil; similar implement for clearing snow *etc.* —*vt.* turn up with plough, furrow —*vi.* work at slowly —**plough'man** *n.* —**plough'share** *n.* blade of plough

plov'er [pluv'-] *n.* various shore birds, typically with round head, straight bill and long pointed wings

ploy *n.* stratagem; occupation; prank

pluck *vt.* pull, pick off; strip from; sound strings of (guitar *etc.*) with fingers, plectrum —*n.* courage; sudden pull or tug —**pluck'ily** *adv.* —**pluck'y** *a.* courageous

plug *n.* thing fitting into and filling a hole; *Electricity* device connecting appliance to electricity supply; tobacco pressed hard; *inf.* recommendation, advertisement —*vt.* stop with plug; *inf.* advertise anything by constant repetition; *sl.* punch; *sl.* shoot —*vi. inf.* (with away) work hard (-gg-) —**plug in** connect (electrical appliance) with power source by means of plug

plum *n.* stone fruit; tree bearing it; choicest part, piece, position *etc.*; dark reddish-purple colour —*a.* choice; plum-coloured

plu'mage *see* PLUME

plumb [-m] *n.* ball of lead (**plumb bob**) attached to string used for sounding, finding the perpendicular *etc.* —*a.* perpendicular —*adv.* perpendicularly; exactly; **US** *inf.* downright; honestly; exactly —*vt.* set exactly upright; find depth of; reach, undergo; equip with, connect to plumbing system —**plumb'er** *n.* worker who attends to water and sewage systems —**plumb'ing** *n.* trade of plumber; system of water and sewage pipes —**plumb'line** *n.* cord with plumb attached

plume [ploom] *n.* feather; ornament of feathers or horsehair —*vt.* furnish with plumes; pride oneself —**plu'mage** *n.* bird's feathers collectively

plumm'et *vi.* plunge headlong —*n.* plumbline

plump[1] *a.* of rounded form, moderately fat, chubby —*v.* make, become plump

plump[2] *vi.* sit, fall abruptly; choose, vote only for —*vt.* drop, throw abruptly —*adv.* suddenly; heavily; directly

plun'der *vt.* take by force; rob systematically —*vi.* rob —*n.* pillage; booty, spoils

plunge *vt.* put forcibly (into) —*vi.* throw oneself (into); enter, rush with violence; descend very suddenly —*n.* dive —**plun'ger** *n.* rubber suction cap to unblock drains; pump piston —**take the plunge** *inf.* embark on risky enterprise; *inf.* get married

plunk *v.* pluck (string of banjo *etc.*); drop suddenly

pluper'fect *a./n.* (tense) expressing action completed before past point of time

plur'al [ploor'-] *a.* of, denoting more than one person or thing —*n.* word in its plural form —**plur'alism** *n.* holding of more than one appointment, vote *etc.*; coexistence of different social groups *etc.*, in one society —**plu'ralist** *n./a.* —**plural'ity** *n.* majority of votes *etc.*

plus *prep.* with addition of (*usu.* indicated by the sign $+$) —*a.* to be added; positive

plush *n.* fabric with long nap, long-piled velvet —*a.* luxurious

Plu'to *n.* Greek god of the underworld; farthest planet from the sun

plutoc'racy [ploo-] *n.* government by the rich; state ruled thus; wealthy class —**plu'tocrat** *n.* wealthy man —**plutocrat'ic** *a.*

Pluto'nian *a.* pert. to Pluto or the infernal regions, dark

pluto'nium *n.* radioactive metallic element used *esp.* in nuclear reactors and weapons

plu'vial [ploo-] *a.* of, caused by the action of rain

ply[1] *vt.* wield; work at; supply pressingly; urge; keep busy —*vi.* go to and fro, run regularly (**plied, ply'ing**)

ply[2] *n.* fold or thickness; strand of yarn —**ply'wood** *n.* board of thin layers of wood glued together with grains at right angles

PM paymaster; postmaster; prime minister

pm, PM post meridiem (*Lat.,* after noon); post mortem

PMG Postmaster General('s Department)

PMS premenstrual syndrome

PMT premenstrual tension

pneumat'ic [nyoo-] a. of, worked by, inflated with wind or air

pneumo'nia [nyoo-] n. inflammation of the lungs

PO Petty Officer; postal order; Post Office

poach[1] vt. take (game) illegally; trample, make swampy or soft —vi. trespass for this purpose; encroach —**poach'er** n.

poach[2] vt. simmer (eggs, fish etc.) gently in water etc. —**poach'er** n.

po'chard n. various diving ducks

pock n. pustule, as in smallpox etc. —**pock'marked** a.

pock'et n. small bag inserted in garment; cavity filled with ore etc.; socket, cavity, pouch or hollow; mass of water or air differing from that surrounding it; isolated group or area; **SA** bag of vegetables, fruit —vt. put into one's pocket; appropriate, steal —a. small —**pocket money** small, regular allowance given to children by parents; allowance for small, occasional expenses

pod n. long seed vessel, as of peas, beans etc. —vi. form pods —vt. shell (-dd-)

podg'y a. short and fat

po'dium n. small raised platform

po'em n. imaginative composition in rhythmic lines —**po'et** n. writer of poems (**po'etess** fem.) —**po'etry** n. art or work of poet, verse —**po'esy** [-zi] n. poetry —**poet'ic(al)** a. —**poet'ically** adv. —**poetast'er** n. would-be or inferior poet

pog'rom n. organized persecution and massacre, esp. of Jews

poign'ant [poin'yənt] a. moving; biting, stinging; vivid; pungent —**poign'ancy** n.

poincian'a [-ahn'-] n. tropical tree with scarlet flowers

poinsett'ia n. orig. Amer. shrub, widely cultivated for its clusters of scarlet leaves, resembling petals

point n. dot, mark; punctuation mark; item, detail; unit of value; position, degree, stage; moment; gist of an argument; purpose; striking or effective part or quality; essential object or thing; sharp end; single unit in scoring; headland; one of direction marks of compass; movable rail changing train to other rails; fine kind of lace; act of pointing; power point; printing unit, one twelfth of a pica —pl. electrical contacts in distributor of engine —vi. show direction or position by extending finger; direct attention; (of dog) indicate position of game by standing facing it —vt. aim, direct; sharpen; fill up joints with mortar; give value to (words etc.) —**point'ed** a. sharp; direct, telling —**point'edly** adv. —**point'er** n. index; indicating rod etc., used for pointing; indication; dog trained to point —**point'less** a. blunt; futile, irrelevant —**point-blank** a. aimed horizontally; plain, blunt —adv. with level aim (there being no necessity to elevate for distance); at short range —**point duty** police regulation of traffic —**point-to-point** n. steeplechase usu. for amateur riders only

poise n. composure; self-possession; balance, equilibrium, carriage (of body etc.) —v. (cause to be) balanced or suspended —vt. hold in readiness

poi'son [-z-] n. substance which kills or injures when introduced into living organism —vt. give poison to; infect; pervert, spoil —**poi'soner** n. —**poi'sonous** a.

—**poison-pen letter** malicious anonymous letter

poke[1] vt. push, thrust with finger, stick etc.; thrust forward —vi. make thrusts; pry —n. act of poking —**po'ker** n. metal rod for poking fire —**po'ky** a. small, confined, cramped

poke[2] —**pig in a poke** something bought etc. without previous inspection

po'ker n. card game

po'lar a. see POLE[2]

Po'laroid R type of plastic which polarizes light; camera that develops print very quickly inside itself

pol'der [or pŏl'-] n. land reclaimed from the sea

pole[1] n. long rounded piece of wood etc. —vt. propel with pole —**up the pole** inf. slightly mad; in error, confused

pole[2] n. each of the ends of axis of earth or celestial body; each of opposite ends of magnet, electric cell etc. —**po'lar** a. pert. to the N and S pole, or to magnetic poles; directly opposite in tendency, character etc. —**polar'ity** n. —**polariza'tion** n. —**po'larize** vt. give polarity to; affect light in order to restrict vibration of its waves to certain directions —**polar bear** white Arctic bear

pole'axe n. battle-axe —vt. hit, fell as with poleaxe

pole'cat n. small animal of weasel family

polem'ic n. controversial —n. war of words, argument —**polem'ical** a. —**polem'icize** vt.

police' [pэ-lēs'] n. the civil force which maintains public order —vt. keep in order —**police'man** n. member of police force (**police'woman** fem.)

pol'icy[1] n. course of action adopted, esp. in state affairs; prudence

pol'icy[2] n. insurance contract

poliomyeli'tis [-mī-ə-lī'tis] n. disease of spinal cord characterized by fever and possibly paralysis (abbrev. **po'lio**)

pol'ish vt. make smooth and glossy; refine —n. shine; polishing; substance for polishing; refinement

polite' a. showing regard for others in manners, speech etc. refined, cultured —**polite'ly** adv. —**polite'ness** n. courtesy

pol'itic a. wise, shrewd, expedient, cunning —**pol'itics** pl.n. art of government; political affairs or life —**polit'ical** a. of the state or its affairs —**politi'cian** n. one engaged in politics **pol'ity** n. form of government; organized state; civil government —**political economy** former name for economics

pol'ka n. lively dance in 2/4 time; music for it —**polka dot** one of pattern of bold spots on fabric etc.

poll [pōl] n. voting; counting of votes; number of votes recorded; canvassing of sample of population to determine general opinion; (top of) head —vt. receive (votes); take votes of; lop, shear; cut horns from animals —vi. vote —**poll, polled** a. hornless —**poll'ster** n. one who conducts polls —**polling booth** voting place at election —**poll tax** (esp. formerly) tax on each person

poll'ack n. type of food fish

poll'ard n. hornless animal of normally horned variety; tree on which a close head of young branches has been made by polling —vt. make a pollard of

poll'en n. fertilizing dust of flower —**poll'inate** vt.

pollute' [-lōōt'] vt. make foul; corrupt; desecrate —**pollu'tant** n. —**pollu'tion** n.

po'lo n. game like hockey played by teams of 4 players on horseback —**water polo** game played similarly by swimmers seven-a-side

polonaise' [-nāz'] n. Polish dance; music for it

pol'tergeist [-gīst] n. noisy mischievous spirit

poltroon' n. abject coward

pol'y n. inf. polytechnic

poly- (comb. form) many, as in **polysyllab'ic** a.

polyan'dry n. polygamy in which woman has more than one husband

polyan'thus n. cultivated primrose

pol'ychrome a. many coloured —n. work of art in many colours —**polychromat'ic** a.

polyes'ter n. any of large class of synthetic materials used as plastics, textile fibres etc.

polyg'amy [-lig'-] n. custom of being married to several persons at a time —**polyg'amist** n.

pol'yglot n. speaking, writing in several languages

pol'ygon n. figure with many angles or sides —**polyg'onal** a.

polyg'yny [-lij'-] n. polygamy in which one man has more than one wife

polyhe'dron n. solid figure contained by many faces

pol'ymer n. compound, as polystyrene, that has large molecules formed from repeated units —**polymeriza'tion** n. —**pol'ymerize** vt.

pol'yp n. sea anemone, or allied animal; (also **pol'ypus**) tumour with branched roots

pol'yphase a. of alternating current of electricity, possessing number of regular sets of alternations

polysty'rene n. synthetic material used esp. as white rigid foam for packing etc.

polytech'nic n. college dealing mainly with various arts and crafts —a.

pol'ytheism n. belief in many gods —**pol'ytheist** n. —**polytheis'tic** a.

pol'ythene n. tough thermoplastic material

polyunsat'urated a. of group of fats that do not form cholesterol in blood

polyur'ethane [-yoor'-] n. class of synthetic materials, often in foam or flexible form

polyva'lent a. having more than one valency

poman'der n. (container for) mixture of sweet-smelling herbs etc.

pom'egranate n. tree; its fruit with thick rind containing many seeds in red pulp

Pomera'nian n. breed of small dog

pomm'el n. front of saddle; knob of sword hilt —vt. see PUMMEL

pomp n. splendid display or ceremony

pom'pon, pom'pom n. tuft of ribbon, wool, feathers etc., decorating hat, shoe etc.

pomp'ous a. self-important; ostentatious; of language, inflated, stilted —**pompos'ity** n.

ponce sl. n. effeminate man; pimp

pon'cho n. loose circular cloak with hole for head (pl. -s)

pond n. small body, pool or lake of still water —**pond'weed** n. various water plants

pon'der v. muse, meditate, think over; consider, deliberate on

pond'erous a. heavy, unwieldy; boring —**pond'erable** a. able to be evaluated or weighed

pong *inf. n.* strong (unpleasant) smell —*vi.*

pon'iard [-yəd] *n.* dagger —*vt.* stab with one

pon'tiff *n.* Pope; high priest; bishop —**pontif'ical** *a.* —**pontif'icate** *n.* dignity or office of pontiff —**pon'tify, pontif'icate** *vi.* speak bombastically; act as pontiff

pontoon'[1] *n.* flat-bottomed boat or metal drum for use in supporting temporary bridge

pontoon'[2] *n.* gambling card game (*also* **twenty-one**)

po'ny *n.* horse of small breed; very small glass —**po'nytail** *n.* long hair tied in one bunch at back of head

poo'dle *n.* pet dog with long curly hair often clipped fancifully

poof *n. sl.* homosexual man

Pooh'-Bah' *n.* pompous official

pool[1] [-oo-] *n.* small body of still water; deep place in river or stream; puddle; swimming pool

pool[2] [-oo-] *n.* common fund or resources; group of people, *eg* typists, any of whom can work for any of several employers; collective stakes in various games; cartel; variety of billiards —*pl. see* FOOTBALL POOLS —*vt.* put in common fund

poop [-oo-] *n.* ship's stern

poor *a.* having little money; unproductive; inadequate, insignificant; needy; miserable, pitiable; feeble; not fertile —**poor'ly** *adv./a.* not in good health —**poor'ness** *n.*

poort *n. SA* narrow mountain pass

pop[1] *vi.* make small explosive sound; *inf.* go or come unexpectedly or suddenly —*vt.* cause to make small explosive sound; put or place suddenly (**-pp-**) —*n.* small explosive sound; *inf.* nonalcoholic fizzy drink —**pop'corn** *n.*

any kind of maize that puffs up when roasted; the roasted product

pop[2] *inf. n.* father; old man

pop[3] *n.* music of general appeal, *esp.* to young people —*a. short for* popular

pop. popular; population

Pope *n.* bishop of Rome and head of R.C. Church —**po'pery** *n. offens.* papal system, doctrines

pop'lar *n.* tree noted for its slender tallness

pop'lin *n.* corded fabric *usu.* of cotton

popp'adom *n.* thin, round, crisp Indian bread

popp'y *n.* bright-flowered plant yielding opium

pop'ulace *n.* the common people; the masses

pop'ular *a.* finding general favour; of, by the people —**popular'ity** *n.* state or quality of being generally liked —**populariza'tion** *n.* —**pop'ularize** *vt.* make popular —**pop'ularly** *adv.*

pop'ulate *vt.* fill with inhabitants —**popula'tion** *n.* inhabitants; their number —**pop'ulous** *a.* thickly populated or inhabited

por'beagle *n.* kind of shark

por'celain [-slin] *n.* fine earthenware, china —**porcelain clay** kaolin

porch *n.* covered approach to entrance of building

por'cine [-sin] *a.* of, like pig

por'cupine *n.* rodent covered with long, pointed quills

pore[1] *vi.* fix eye or mind upon; study closely

pore[2] *n.* minute opening, *esp.* in skin —**poros'ity** *n.* —**por'ous** *a.* allowing liquid to soak through; full of pores

pork *n.* pig's flesh as food —**pork'er** *n.* pig raised for food —**pork'y** *a.* fleshy, fat

porn, por'no n. inf. short for
PORNOGRAPHY

pornog'raphy n. indecent literature, films etc. —**pornog'rapher** n. —**pornograph'ic** a.
—**pornograph'ically** adv.

porph'yry n. reddish stone
with embedded crystals

por'poise [-pos] n. blunt-nosed
sea mammal like dolphin

porr'idge n. soft food of oatmeal etc. boiled in water; sl.
imprisonment

port[1] n. harbour, haven; town
with harbour

port[2] n. larboard or left side of
ship —vt. turn to left side of a
ship

port[3] n. strong red wine

port[4] n. opening in side of ship
—**port'hole** n. small opening or
window in side of ship

port[5] vt. Mil. carry rifle, etc.
diagonally across body —n. this
position

port'able n./a. (something)
easily carried

port'age n. (cost of) transport

port'al n. large doorway or
imposing gate

portcull'is n. defence grating
to raise or lower in front of castle
gateway

portend' vt. foretell; be an
omen of —**port'ent** n. omen,
warning; marvel —**portent'ous**
a. ominous; threatening; pompous

port'er n. person employed to
carry burden, eg on railway;
door-keeper —**port'erage** n.
(charge for) carrying of supplies

portfo'lio n. flat portable case
for loose papers; office of minister of state (pl. **-s**)

por'tico n. colonnade; covered
walk (pl. **-os**)

portiere' [-ti-ār'] n. heavy door
curtain

por'tion n. part, share, helping;

destiny, lot —vt. divide into
shares —**por'tionless** a.

port'ly a. bulky, stout

portman'teau [-tō] n. leather
suitcase, esp. one opening into
two compartments (pl. **-s, -x**
[-ōz])

portray' vt. make pictures of,
describe —**por'trait** [-trit] n. likeness of (face of) individual
—**por'traiture** n. —**portray'al** n.
act of portraying

Portuguese' [-gēz] a. pert. to
Portugal or its inhabitants —**Portuguese man-of-war** kind of
jellyfish

pose vt. place in attitude; put
forward —vi. assume attitude,
affect or pretend to be a certain
character —n. attitude, esp. one
assumed for effect —**poseur'** n.
one who assumes affected attitude to create impression

po'ser n. puzzling question

posh a. inf. smart, elegant, stylish

pos'it [poz'-] vt. lay down as
principle

posi'tion [-zish'-] n. place; situation; location, attitude; status;
state of affairs; employment;
strategic point —vt. place in
position

pos'itive [poz'-] a. certain; sure;
definite, absolute, unquestionable; utter; downright; confident;
not negative; greater than zero;
Electricity having deficiency of
electrons —n. something positive; Photog. print in which lights
and shadows are not reversed
—**pos'itively** adv. —**pos'itivism**
n. philosophy recognizing only
matters of fact and experience
—**pos'itivist** n. believer in this

pos'itron [poz'-] n. positive electron

poss'e n. US body of men, esp.
for maintaining law and order

possess' [-zes'] vt. own; (of evil

spirit *etc.*) have mastery of —**posses'sion** *n.* act of possessing; thing possessed; ownership —**posses'sive** *a.* of, indicating possession; with excessive desire to possess, control —*n.* possessive case in grammar —**posses'sor** *n.* owner

poss'ible *a.* that can, or may, be, exist, happen or be done; worthy of consideration —*n.* possible candidate —**possibil'ity** *n.* —**poss'ibly** *adv.* perhaps

poss'um *n. see* OPOSSUM —**play possum** pretend to be dead, asleep *etc.* to deceive opponent

post [pōst] *n.* upright pole of timber or metal fixed firmly, usu. to support or mark something —*vt.* display; stick up (on notice board *etc.*) —**post'er** *n.* large advertising bill; one who posts bills —**poster paints, colours** lustreless paints suited for posters

post [pōst] *n.* official carrying of letters or parcels; collection or delivery of these; office; situation; point, station, place of duty; place where soldier is stationed; place held by body of troops; fort —*vt.* put into official box for carriage by post; supply with latest information; station (soldiers *etc.*) in particular spot; transfer (entries) to ledger —*adv.* in haste —**post'age** *n.* charge for carrying letter —**post'al** *a.* —**postal order** written order, available at post office, for payment of sum of money —**post'card** *n.* stamped card sent by post —**post'code** *n.* system of letters and numbers used to aid sorting of mail —**post'man** *n.* man who collects or delivers post —**post'mark** *n.* official mark with name of office *etc.* stamped on letters —**post'master, post'mistress** *n.* official in charge of **post office**,

place where postal business is conducted

post- (*comb. form*) after, behind, later than, *eg* **post'war** *a.* Such compounds are not given here where the meaning can easily be found from the simple word

postdate' *vt.* give date later than actual date

poste' restante' [post'ri-stant'] *Fr.* department of post office where traveller's letters are kept till called for

poste'rior [pos-] *a.* later, hinder —*n.* the buttocks

poster'ity [-te'ri-] *n.* later generations; descendants

pos'tern *n.* private entrance; small door, gate

postgrad'uate *a.* carried on after graduation —*n.*

pos'thumous [-tyoo-] *a.* occurring after death; born after father's death; published after author's death —**pos'thumously** *adv.*

postill'ion *n. Hist.* man riding one of pair of horses drawing a carriage

postmor'tem *n.* medical examination of dead body —*a.* taking place after death

post-o'bit *a.* taking effect after death

postpone' *vt.* put off to later time, defer —**postpone'ment** *n.*

postpran'dial *a.* after dinner

post'script *n.* addition to letter, book

pos'tulant *n.* candidate for admission to religious order

pos'tulate *vt.* take for granted; lay down as self-evident; stipulate —*n.* proposition assumed without proof; prerequisite —**postula'tion** *n.*

pos'ture *n.* attitude, position of body —*v.* pose

po'sy *n.* bunch of flowers

pot *n.* round vessel; cooking vessel; trap, *esp.* for crabs, lobsters; *sl.* cannabis —*pl. inf.* a lot —*vt.* put into, preserve in pot (-tt-) —**pott'ed** *a.* preserved in a pot; *inf.* abridged —**pot'hole** *n.* pitlike cavity in rocks, usu. limestone, produced by faulting and water action; hole worn in road —**pot'luck**[1] *n.* whatever is to be had (to eat) —**pot'sherd** *n.* broken fragment of pottery —**pot shot** easy or random shot

po'table *a.* drinkable —**pota'tion** *n.* drink; drinking

pot'ash *n.* alkali used in soap *etc.*; crude potassium carbonate

potass'ium *n.* white metallic element

pota'to *n.* plant with tubers grown for food (*pl.* -es) —**sweet potato** trailing plant; its edible sweetish tubers

poteen' *n.* illicitly distilled Irish alcoholic liquor

po'tent *a.* powerful, influential; (of male) capable of sexual intercourse —**po'tency** *n.* physical or moral power; efficacy —**po'tently** *adv.*

po'tentate *n.* ruler

poten'tial *a.* latent, that may or might but does not now exist or act —*n.* possibility; amount of potential energy; *Electricity* level of electric pressure —**potential'ity** *n.*

po'tion *n.* dose of medicine or poison

potpourri' [pō-poor'i] *n.* mixture of rose petals, spices *etc.*; musical, literary medley

pott'age *n.* soup or stew

pott'er[1] *n.* maker of earthenware vessels —**pott'ery** *n.* earthenware; where it is made; art of making it

pott'er[2] *vi.* work, act in feeble, unsystematic way

pott'y *a. inf.* (of person) mad; (of thing) silly, trivial

pouch *n.* small bag; pocket —*vt.* put into one

pouf(fe) [pōōf] *n.* large solid cushion

poult'ice [pōlt'is] *n.* soft composition of mustard, kaolin *etc.*, applied hot to sore or inflamed parts of the body

poul'try [pōl'-] *n.* domestic fowls —**poul'terer** *n.* dealer in poultry

pounce[1] *vi.* spring upon suddenly, swoop (upon) —*n.* swoop or sudden descent

pounce[2] *n.* fine powder used to prevent ink from spreading on unsized paper or in pattern making

pound[1] *vt.* beat, thump; crush to pieces or powder; walk, run heavily

pound[2] *n.* unit of troy weight; unit of avoirdupois weight equal to 0.454 kg; monetary unit in U.K.

pound[3] *n.* enclosure for stray animals or officially removed vehicles; confined space

pound'al *n.* a unit of force in the foot-pound-second system

pour [pawr] *vi.* come out in a stream, crowd *etc.*; flow freely; rain heavily —*vt.* give out thus; cause to run out

pout[1] *v.* thrust out (lips), look sulky —*n.* act of pouting —**pout'er** *n.* pigeon with power of inflating its crop

pout[2] *n.* type of food fish

pov'erty *n.* state of being poor; poorness; lack of means; scarcity

POW prisoner of war

pow'der *n.* solid matter in fine dry particles; medicine in this form; gunpowder; facepowder *etc.* —*vt.* apply powder to; reduce to powder —**pow'dery** *a.*

pow'er *n.* ability to do or act; strength; authority; control; person or thing having authority; mechanical energy; electricity supply; rate of doing work; product from continuous multiplication of number by itself —**pow'ered** a. having or operated by mechanical or electrical power —**pow'erful** a. —**pow'erless** a. —**pow'erhouse, power station** n. installation for generating and distributing electric power —**power point** socket on wall for plugging in electrical appliance

pow'wow n. conference —vi. confer

pox n. one of several diseases marked by pustular eruptions of skin; inf. syphilis

pp pages

PR proportional representation; public relations

pr. pair; present; price; pronoun

prac'tical a. given to action rather than theory; relating to action or real existence; useful; in effect though not in name; virtual —**prac'tically** adv. —**practicabil'ity** n. —**prac'ticable** a. that can be done, used etc. —**practi'tioner** n. one engaged in a profession

prac'tise, US prac'tice vt. do repeatedly, work at to gain skill; do habitually; put into action —vi. exercise oneself; exercise profession —**prac'tice** n. habit; mastery or skill; exercise of art or profession; action, not theory

pragmat'ic a. concerned with practical consequence; of the affairs of state —**pragmat'ical** a. —**prag'matism** n. —**prag'matist** n.

prair'ie n. large treeless tract of grassland —**prairie dog** small Amer. rodent allied to marmot —**prairie oyster** cocktail

praise n. commendation; fact, state of being praised —vt. express approval, admiration of; speak well of; glorify —**praise'worthy** a.

pral'ine [prahl'ēn] n. sweet composed of nuts and sugar

pram n. carriage for baby, perambulator

prance [-ah-] vi. swagger; caper; walk with bounds —n. prancing

pran'dial a. of dinner

prang v./n. inf. crash, damage, wreck

prank n. mischievous trick or escapade, frolic

prase n. light green translucent chalcedony

prate vi. talk idly, chatter —n.

prat'incole n. swallowlike shore bird

prat'tle vi. talk like child —n. trifling, childish talk —**prat'tler** n. babbler

prawn n. edible sea crustacean like a shrimp but larger

prax'is n. practice, esp. as opposed to theory

pray vi. ask earnestly; entreat —vi. offer prayers esp. to God —**prayer** [prâr] n. action, practice of praying to God; earnest entreaty

pre- (comb. form) before, beforehand eg **prena'tal** a., **prerecord'** vt., **preshrunk'** a. Such compounds are not given here where the meaning can easily be found from the simple word

preach vi. deliver sermon; give moral, religious advice —vt. set forth in religious discourse; advocate —**preach'er** n.

pream'ble n. introductory part of story etc.

preb'end n. stipend of canon or member of cathedral chapter —**preb'endary** n. holder of this

preca'rious a. insecure, unstable, perilous

precau'tion n. previous care to prevent evil or secure good; preventive measure —**precau'tionary** a.

precede' v. go, come before in

rank, order, time *etc.* —**prec'-edence** [*or* prē-sē'-] *n.* priority in position, rank, time *etc.* —**prec'edent** *n.* previous case or occurrence taken as rule

precent'or *n.* leader of singing choir or congregation

pre'cept *n.* rule for conduct, maxim —**precept'or** *n.* instructor —**precepto'rial** *a.*

precess'ion [-sesh'-] *n.* act of preceding; motion of spinning body (*eg* top, planet) wobbling so that axis of rotation marks out a cone

pre'cinct *n.* enclosed, limited area; **US** administrative area of city —*pl.* environs

precious [presh'əs] *a.* beloved, cherished; of great value, highly valued; rare —**precios'ity** *n.* overrefinement in art or literature —**prec'iously** *adv.* —**pre'ciousness** *n.*

prec'ipice [pres'-] *n.* very steep cliff or rockface —**precip'itous** *a.* sheer

precip'itant *a.* hasty, rash; abrupt —**precip'itance, -ancy** *n.*

precip'itate [-āt] *vt.* hasten happening of; throw headlong; *Chem.* cause to be deposited in solid form from solution —*a.* [-it] too sudden; rash, impetuous —*n.* [-āt] substance chemically precipitated —**precip'itately** *adv.* —**precipita'tion** *n.* *esp.* rain, snow *etc.*

pré'cis [prā'sē] *n.* abstract, summary (*pl.* **pré'cis** [-sēz])

precise' *a.* definite; particular; exact, strictly worded; careful in observance; punctilious, formal —**precise'ly** *adv.* —**preci'sion** *n.* accuracy

preclude' *vt.* prevent from happening; shut out

preco'cious *a.* developed, matured early or too soon —**preco'city** [-os'-], **preco'ciousness** *n.*

preconceive' *vt.* form an idea beforehand —**preconcep'tion** *n.*

precondi'tion *n.* necessary or required condition

precur'sor *n.* forerunner —**precur'sive, precur'sory** *a.*

pred'atory *a.* hunting, killing other animals *etc.* for food; plundering —**pred'ator** *n.* predatory animal

pre'decessor *n.* one who precedes another in an office or position; ancestor

predes'tine [-tin] *vt.* decree beforehand, foreordain —**predestina'tion** *n.*

predic'ament *n.* perplexing, embarrassing or difficult situation

pred'icate *vt.* affirm, assert; base (on or upon) —*n.* that which is predicated; *Grammar* statement made about a subject —**predica'tion** *n.* —**predic'ative** *a.*

predict' *vt.* foretell, prophesy —**predict'able** *a.* —**predic'tion** *n.*

pre'dikant *n.* in S Afr., minister in Dutch Reformed Church

predilec'tion *n.* preference, liking, partiality

predispose' *vt.* incline, influence someone (towards); make susceptible (to)

predom'inate *vi.* be main or controlling element —**predom'inance** *n.* —**predom'inant** *a.* chief

pre-em'inent *a.* excelling all others, outstanding —**pre-em'inence** *n.* —**pre-em'inently** *adv.*

pre-empt' *vt.* acquire in advance or act in advance of or to exclusion of others —**pre-emp'tion** *n.* —**pre-emp'tive** *a.*

preen *vt.* trim (feathers) with beak, plume; smarten oneself

pref. preface; preference; prefix

prefab'ricate *vt.* manufacture

buildings *etc.* in shaped sections, for rapid assembly on the site —**pre'fab** *n.* house so made

pref'ace [-is] *n.* introduction to book *etc.* —*vt.* introduce —**pref'atory** *a.*

pre'fect *n.* person put in authority; schoolchild in position of limited power over others —**pre'fecture** *n.* office, residence, district of a prefect

prefer' *vt.* like better; promote (-rr-) —**pref'erable** *a.* more desirable —**pref'erably** *adv.* —**pref'erence** *n.* —**preferen'tial** *a.* giving, receiving preference —**prefer'ment** *n.* promotion, advancement

prefig'ure *vt.* exhibit, suggest by previous types, foreshadow —**prefig'urative** *a.*

pre'fix *n.* preposition or particle put at beginning of word or title —*vt.* [-fiks'] put as introduction; put before word to make compound

preg'nant *a.* carrying foetus in womb; full of meaning, significance; inventive —**preg'nancy** *n.*

prehen'sile *a.* capable of grasping —**prehensil'ity** *n.*

prehistor'ic [-to'rik] *a.* before period in which written history begins —**prehis'tory** *n.*

prej'udice [-is] *n.* preconceived opinion; bias, partiality; injury likely to happen to person or his rights as a result of others' action or judgment —*vt.* influence; bias; injure —**prejudi'cial** *a.* injurious; disadvantageous

prel'ate *n.* bishop or other church dignitary of equal or higher rank —**prel'acy** *n.* his office —**prelat'ical** *a.*

prelim'inary *a.* preparatory, introductory —*n.* introductory, preparatory statement, action

prel'ude *n.* Mus. introductory movement; performance, event *etc.* serving as introduction —*v.* serve as prelude, introduce

premar'ital *a.* occurring before marriage

premature' [or prem'-] *a.* happening, done before proper time

premed'itate *vt.* consider, plan beforehand —**premedita'tion** *n.*

prem'ier *n.* prime minister; head of government of Aust. state —*a.* chief, foremost; first —**prem'iership** *n.* office of premier

première' [-mi-Ar'] *n.* first performance of a play, film *etc.*

prem'ise [-is] *n.* Logic proposition from which inference is drawn —*pl.* house, building with its belongings; *Law* beginning of deed —**premise'** [-īz'] *vt.* state by way of introduction —**prem'iss** *n.* (logical) premise

pre'mium *n.* bonus; sum paid for insurance; excess over nominal value; great value or regard (*pl.* -**iums**) —**premium savings bond** bond issued by government on which no interest is paid but cash prizes can be won

premoni'tion [-nish'-] *n.* presentiment, foreboding

preocc'upy [-pī] *vt.* occupy to the exclusion of other things —**preoccupa'tion** *n.* mental concentration or absorption

prep. preparation; preparatory; preposition

prepare' *vt.* make ready; make —*vi.* get ready —**prepara'tion** *n.* making ready beforehand; something that is prepared, as a medicine; at school, (time spent) preparing work for lesson —**prepar'atory** [-pa'rǝ-] *a.* serving to prepare; introductory —**prepar'edness** *n.* state of being prepared

prepay' *vt.* pay in advance (**prepaid', prepay'ing**)

prepond'erate *vi.* be of greater weight or power —**prepon'-derance** n. superiority of power, numbers etc.

preposi'tion [-zish'-] n. word marking relation between noun or pronoun and other words —**preposi'tional** a.

prepossess' [prē-] vt. impress, esp. favourably, beforehand; possess beforehand —**prepossess'-ing** a. inviting favourable opinion, attractive, winning —**pre-posses'sion** n.

prepos'terous a. utterly absurd, foolish

prep'uce n. retractable fold of skin covering tip of penis, foreskin

prereq'uisite n./a. (something) required as prior condition

prerog'ative n. peculiar power or right, esp. as vested in sovereign —a. privileged

Pres. President

pres'age n. omen, indication of something to come —vt. foretell

presbyo'pia n. progressively diminishing ability of the eye to focus, esp. on near objects, longsightedness

pres'byter [prez'bi-tər] n. elder in early Christian church; priest; member of a presbytery —**Presby-te'rian** a./n. (member) of Protestant church governed by lay elders —**Presbyte'rianism** n. —**pres'bytery** n. church court composed of all ministers within a certain district and one ruling elder from each church; R.C.Ch. priest's house

pres'cience n. foreknowledge —**pres'cient** a.

prescribe' v. set out rules for; order; ordain; order use of (medicine) —**prescrip'tion** n. prescribing; thing prescribed; written statement of it —**prescrip'tive** a.

pres'ent[1] [-z-] a. that is here; now existing or happening —n.

present time or tense —**pres'-ence** n. being present; appearance, bearing —**pres'ently** adv. soon; US at present

present'[2] [-z-] vt. introduce formally; show; give; offer; point, aim —**pres'ent** n. gift —**present'able** a. fit to be seen —**presenta'tion** n. —**present'er** n. person introducing TV or radio show, compere —**present'ment** n.

present'iment [-z-] n. sense of something (esp. evil) about to happen

preserve' [-z-] vt. keep from harm, injury or decay; maintain; pickle —n. special area; that which is preserved, as fruit etc.; place where game is kept for private fishing, shooting —**pres-erva'tion** n. —**preserv'ative** n. chemical put into perishable foods, drinks etc. to keep them from going bad —a. tending to preserve; having quality of preserving

preside' [-z-] vi. be chairman; superintend —**pres'ident** n. head of society, company, republic etc. —**pres'idency** n. —**presiden'tial** a.

press[1] vt. subject to push or squeeze; smooth by pressure or heat; urge steadily, earnestly —vi. bring weight to bear; throng; hasten —n. a pressing; machine for pressing, esp. printing machine; printing house; its work or art; newspapers collectively; reporters, journalists; crowd; stress; large cupboard —**press'ing** a. urgent; persistent —**press agent** person employed to advertise and secure press publicity for any person, enterprise etc. —**press'man** n. printer who attends to the press; journalist

press[2] vt. force to serve in navy

or army —**press gang** formerly, body of men employed to press men into naval service —*vt.* force (someone to do something)

press'ure [presh'-] *n.* act of pressing; influence; authority; difficulties; *Physics* thrust per unit area —**pressuriza'tion** *n.* in aircraft, maintenance of normal atmospheric pressure at high altitudes —**press'urize** *vt.* —**pressure cooker** vessel like saucepan which cooks food rapidly by steam under pressure —**pressure group** organized group which exerts influence on policies, public opinion *etc.*

Pres'tel R Post Office viewdata service

prestige' [-ēzh'] *n.* reputation; influence depending on it —**prestig'ious** [-tij'-] *a.*

pres'to *adv.* *Mus.* quickly

prestressed' *a.* (of concrete) containing stretched steel cables for strengthening

presume' [-zyōōm'] *vt.* take for granted —*vi.* take liberties —**presu'mably** *adv.* probably; doubtlessly —**presump'tion** *n.* forward, arrogant opinion or conduct; strong probability —**presump'tive** *a.* that may be assumed as true or valid until contrary is proved —**presump'tuous** *a.* forward, impudent, taking liberties —**presump'tuously** *adv.* —**heir presumptive** heir whose right may be defeated by birth of nearer relative

presuppose' *vt.* assume or take for granted beforehand —**presupposi'tion** *n.* previous supposition

pretend' *vt.* claim or allege (something untrue); make believe, as in play —*vi.* lay claim (to) —**pretence'**, US **pretense'** *n.* simulation; pretext —**pretend'er** *n.* claimant (to throne) —**pre-**

ten'sion *n.* —**preten'tious** *a.* making claim to special merit or importance; given to outward show

preter- (*comb. form*) beyond, more than

pret'erite [-it] *a.* past; expressing past state or action —*n.* past tense

preternat'ural [prē-] *a.* out of ordinary way of nature; abnormal, supernatural

pre'text *n.* excuse; pretence

prett'y [prit'i] *a.* having beauty that is attractive rather than imposing; charming *etc.* —*adv.* fairly, moderately —**prett'ily** *adv.* —**prett'iness** *n.*

pret'zel [-sol] *n.* small, brittle, savoury biscuit

prevail' *vi.* gain mastery; triumph; be in fashion, generally established —**prevail'ing** *a.* widespread; predominant —**prev'alence** *n.* —**prev'alent** *a.* extensively existing, rife

prevar'icate [-va'ri-] *vi.* make evasive or misleading statements; quibble —**prevarica'tion** *n.* —**prevar'icator** *n.*

prevent' *vt.* stop, hinder —**prevent'able** *a.* —**preven'tion** *n.* —**preven'tive** *a./n.*

pre'view *n.* advance showing; a showing of scenes from a forthcoming film

pre'vious *a.* earlier; preceding; happening before; *inf.* hasty —**pre'viously** *adv.*

prey *n.* that is hunted and killed by carnivorous animals; victim —*vi.* seize for food; treat as prey; afflict, obsess (*with* upon)

price *n.* that for which thing is bought or sold; cost; value; reward; odds in betting —*vt.* fix, ask price for —**price'less** *a.* invaluable; *inf.* very funny —**pri'c(e)y** *a.* *inf.* expensive

prick *vt.* pierce slightly with

sharp point; cause to feel mental pain; mark by prick; erect (ears) —*n.* slight hole made by pricking; pricking or being pricked; sting; remorse; that which pricks; sharp point —**prick'le** *n.* thorn, spike —*vi.* feel tingling or pricking sensation —**prick'ly** *a.* —**prickly heat** inflammation of skin with stinging pains

pride *n.* too high an opinion of oneself, inordinate self-esteem; worthy self-esteem; feeling of elation or great satisfaction; something causing this; group (of lions) —*v.refl.* take pride

priest *n.* official minister of religion, clergyman (**-ess** *fem.*) —**priest'hood** *n.* —**priest'ly** *a.*

prig *n.* self-righteous person who professes superior culture, morality *etc.* —**prig'gery** *n.* —**prig'gish** *a.* —**prig'gism** *n.*

prim *a.* very restrained, formally prudish

pri'ma [prē'-] *a.* first —**prima donna** principal female singer in opera; *inf.* temperamental person (*pl.* **donnas**)

pri'macy *n.* state of being first in rank, grade *etc.*; office of archbishop

pri'ma fa'cie [-shi] *Lat.* at first sight

pri'mal *a.* of earliest age; first, original —**pri'marily** *adv.* —**pri'mary** *a.* chief; of the first stage, decision *etc.*; elementary

pri'mate[1] *n.* archbishop

pri'mate[2] *n.* one of order of mammals including monkeys and man

prime[1] *a.* fundamental; original; chief; best —*n.* first, best part of anything; youth; full health and vigour —*vt.* prepare (gun, engine, pump *etc.*) for use; fill up, *eg* with information, liquor —**pri'ming** *n.* powder mixture used for priming gun —**Prime**

Minister leader of government

prime[2] *vt.* prepare for paint with preliminary coating of oil, size *etc.* —**pri'mer** *n.* paint *etc.* for priming

pri'mer *n.* elementary school book or manual

prim(a)e'val *a.* of the earliest age of the world

prim'itive *a.* of an early undeveloped kind, ancient; crude, rough

primogen'iture *n.* rule by which real estate passes to the first born son —**primogen'ital** *a.*

primor'dial *a.* existing at or from the beginning

prim'rose *n.* pale yellow spring flower; this colour —*a.* of this colour

prim'ula *n.* genus of plants, including primrose

Pri'mus R portable cooking stove, used *esp.* by campers (*pl.* **-ses**)

prince *n.* son or (in Britain) grandson of king or queen; ruler; chief (**princess**[1] *fem.*) —**prince'ly** *a.* generous, lavish; stately; magnificent

prin'cipal *a.* chief in importance —*n.* person for whom another is agent; head of institution, *esp.* school or college; sum of money lent and yielding interest; chief actor —**principal'ity** *n.* territory, dignity of prince

prin'ciple *n.* moral rule; settled reason of action; uprightness; fundamental truth or element

print *vt.* reproduce (words, pictures *etc.*), by pressing inked types on blocks to paper *etc.*; produce thus; write in imitation of this; impress; *Photog.* produce pictures from negatives; stamp (fabric) with coloured design —*n.* printed matter; printed lettering; written imitation of printed type; photograph; impression, mark left on surface by thing that has pressed against it; printed cotton fabric —**print'er** n. one engaged in printing —**printed circuit** electronic circuit with wiring printed on an insulating base —**print-out** n. printed information from computer, teleprinter *etc.* —**out of print** no longer available from publisher

pri'or a. earlier —n. chief of religious house or order (**-ess** *fem.*) —**prior'ity** [-o'ri-] n. precedence; something given special attention —**pri'ory** n. monastery, nunnery under prior, **prioress** —**prior to** before, earlier

prise vt. force open by levering; obtain (information *etc.*) with difficulty

prism [-zəm] n. transparent solid usu. with triangular ends and rectangular sides, used to disperse light into spectrum or refract it in optical instruments *etc.* —**prismat'ic** a. of prism shape; (of colour) such as is produced by refraction through prism, rainbowlike, brilliant

pris'on [-iz'-] n. jail —**pris'oner** n. one kept in prison; captive

priss'y a. *inf.* fussy, prim

pris'tine a. original, primitive, unspoiled, good

pri'vate a. secret, not public; reserved for, or belonging to, or concerning, an individual only; personal; secluded; denoting soldier of lowest rank; not part of National Health Service; not controlled by State —n. private soldier —**pri'vacy** [*or* priv'-] n. —**pri'vately** adv.

privateer' *Hist.* n. privately owned armed vessel authorized by government to take part in war; captain of such ship —**privateer'ing** n./a.

priva'tion n. want of comforts or necessaries; hardship; act of depriving —**priv'ative** a. of privation or negation

priv'et n. bushy evergreen shrub used for hedges

priv'ilege [-lij] n. advantage or favour that only a few obtain; right, advantage belonging to person or class —**priv'ileged** a. enjoying special right or immunity

priv'y a. admitted to knowledge of secret —n. lavatory, *esp.* outhouse; *Law* person having interest in an action —**priv'ily** adv. —**privy council** council of state of monarch

prize[1] n. reward given for success in competition; thing striven for; thing won, *eg* in lottery *etc.* —a. winning or likely to win a prize —vt. value highly —**prize'-fight** n. boxing match for money —**prize'fighter** n. professional boxer

prize[2] n. ship, property captured in (naval) warfare

pro[1] a./adv. in favour of

pro[2] n. professional; prostitute —a. professional

pro- (*comb. form*) for, instead of, before, in front, as in *proconsul, pronoun, project* Such compounds are not given here where the meaning may easily be found from the simple word

prob'able a. likely —**probabil'ity** n. likelihood; anything that has appearance of truth —**prob'ably** adv.

pro'bate n. proving of authenticity of will; certificate of this

proba'tion n. system of releasing law breakers, *esp.* juvenile ones, but placing them under supervision for stated period; testing of candidate before admission to full membership —**proba'tioner** n. person on probation

probe vt. search into, examine,

question closely —*n.* that which probes, or is used to probe; thorough inquiry

pro'bity *n.* honesty, uprightness, integrity

prob'lem *n.* matter *etc.* difficult to deal with or solve; question set for solution; puzzle —**problemat'ic(al)** *a.* questionable: uncertain; disputable

probos'cis [-sis] *n.* trunk or long snout, *eg* of elephant (*pl.* **probos'cides** [-si-dēz])

proceed' *vi.* go forward, continue; be carried on; go to law —**pro'ceeds** *pl.n.* price or profit —**proce'dural** *a.* —**proce'dure** *n.* act, manner of proceeding; conduct —**proceed'ing** *n.* act or course of action; transaction —*pl.* minutes of meeting; methods of prosecuting charge, claim *etc.*

pro'cess *n.* series of actions or changes; method of operation; state of going on; action of law; outgrowth —*vt.* handle, treat, prepare by special method of manufacture *etc.* —**proces'sion** *n.* regular, orderly progress; train of persons in formal order —**proces'sional** *a.* —**proces'sor** *n.*

proclaim' *vt.* announce publicly, declare —**proclama'tion** *n.*

procliv'ity *n.* inclination, tendency

procon'sul *n. Hist.* governor of province

procras'tinate *vi.* put off, delay —**procrastina'tion** *n.* —**pro-cras'tinator** *n.*

pro'create *vt.* produce offspring, generate —**procrea'tion** *n.*

Procrust'ean *a.* compelling uniformity by violence

proc'tor *n.* university official with disciplinary powers

procure' *vt.* obtain, acquire;

provide; bring about —*vi.* act as pimp —**procu'rable** *a.* —**procura'tion** *n.* —**proc'urator** *n.* one who manages another's affairs —**procure'ment** *n.* —**procu'rer** *n.* one who procures; pimp (**procu'ress** *fem.*)

prod *vt.* poke with something pointed (**-dd-**) —*n.* prodding; goad; pointed instrument

prod'igal *a.* wasteful; extravagant —*n.* spendthrift —**prodigal'ity** *n.* reckless extravagance

prod'igy [-ji] *n.* person with some marvellous gift; thing causing wonder —**prodig'ious** *a.* very great, immense; extraordinary —**prodig'iously** *adv.*

produce' *vt.* bring into existence; yield; make; bring forward; manufacture; exhibit; present on stage, film, television; *Geom.* extend in length —*n.* [prod'-] that which is yielded or made —**produ'cer** *n.* person who produces, *esp.* play, film *etc.* —**prod'uct** *n.* result of process of manufacture; number resulting from multiplication —**produc'tion** *n.* producing; things produced —**produc'tive** *a.* fertile; creative; efficient —**productiv'ity** *n.*

Prof. Professor

profane' *a.* irreverent, blasphemous; not sacred —*vt.* pollute, desecrate —**profana'tion** *n.* —**profan'ity** *n.* profane talk or behaviour, blasphemy

profess' *vt.* affirm belief in; confess publicly; assert; claim, pretend —**profess'edly** [-id-li] *adv.* avowedly —**profes'sion** *n.* calling or occupation, *esp.* learned, scientific or artistic; a professing; vow of religious faith on entering religious order —**profes'sional** *a.* engaged in a profession; engaged in a game or sport for money —*n.* paid player —**profes'sor** *n.* teacher of highest rank in university —**profes-so'rial** a. —**professor'iate** n. body of university professors —**profes'sorship** n.

proff'er vt./n. offer

profi'cient [-ish'-] a. skilled; expert —**profi'ciency** n.

pro'file n. outline, esp. of face, as seen from side; brief biographical sketch

prof'it n. money gained; benefit obtained —v. benefit —**prof'it-able** a. yielding profit —**profi-teer'** n. one who makes excessive profits at the expense of the public —vi. do this —**prof'itless** a.

prof'ligate a. dissolute; reckless, wasteful —n. dissolute person —**prof'ligacy** n.

pro for'ma Lat. prescribing a set form

profound' a. very learned; deep —**profun'dity** n.

profuse' [-fyōōs'] a. abundant, prodigal —**profu'sion** n.

prog'eny [proj'-] n. children —**progen'itor** n. ancestor

progest'erone [-jest'-] n. hormone which prepares uterus for pregnancy and prevents further ovulation

progna'thous a. with projecting lower jaw

progno'sis n. art of foretelling course of disease by symptoms; forecast —**prognost'ic** a. of, serving as prognosis —n. —**prognos'-ticate** vt. foretell —**prognostica'-tion** n.

pro'gramme n. plan, detailed notes of intended proceedings; broadcast on radio or television —**pro'gram** n. detailed instructions for a computer —vt. feed program into (computer); arrange detailed instructions for computer (-mm-) —**pro'gram-mer** n.

pro'gress n. onward move-

ment; development —vi. [-gres'] go forward; improve —**progres'-sion** n. moving forward; advance, improvement; increase or decrease of numbers or magnitudes according to fixed law; Mus. regular succession of chords —**progres'sive** a. progressing by degrees; favouring political or social reform

prohib'it vt. forbid —**prohibi'-tion** [-bish'-] n. act of forbidding; interdict; interdiction of supply and consumption of alcoholic drinks —**prohib'itive** a. tending to forbid or exclude; (of prices) very high —**prohib'itory** a.

proj'ect n. plan, scheme; design —vt. [-jekt'] plan; throw; cause to appear on distant background —vi. stick out, protrude —**pro-jec'tile** n. heavy missile, esp. shell or ball —a. for throwing —**projec'tion** n. —**projec'tionist** n. operator of film projector —**projec'tor** n. apparatus for projecting photographic images, films, slides on screen; one that forms scheme or design

pro'lapse, prolap'sus n. falling, slipping down of part of body from normal position

pro'late a. having polar diameter greater than the equatorial diameter

prolegom'ena pl.n. introductory remarks prefixed to a book, preface

proleta'riat n. lowest class of community, working class —**prole-ta'rian** a./n.

prolif'erate v. grow or reproduce rapidly —**prolifera'tion** n.

prolif'ic a. fruitful; producing much

pro'lix a. wordy, long-winded —**prolix'ity** n.

pro'logue [-log] n. preface, esp. speech before a play

prolong' vt. lengthen; protract —**prolonga'tion** n.

prom n. short for PROMENADE (CONCERT)

promenade' [-ahd'] n. leisurely walk; place made or used for this —vi. take leisurely walk; go up and down —**promenade concert** concert at which audience stands rather than sits

prom'inent a. sticking out; conspicuous; distinguished —**prom'inence** n.

promis'cuous a. indiscriminate, esp. in sexual relations; mixed without distinction —**promiscu'ity** n.

prom'ise [-is] v. give undertaking or assurance —vi. be likely to —n. undertaking to do or not to do something; potential —**prom'ising** a. showing good signs, hopeful —**prom'issory** a. containing promise —**promissory note** written promise to pay sum to person named, at specified time

prom'ontory n. point of high land jutting out into the sea, headland

promote' vt. help forward; move up to higher rank or position; work for; encourage sale of —**promo'ter** n. —**promo'tion** n. advancement; preferment

prompt a. done at once; acting with alacrity; punctual; ready —v. urge, suggest; help out (actor or speaker) by reading or suggesting next words —**prompt'er** n. —**prompt'itude, prompt'ness** n. —**prompt'ly** adv.

prom'ulgate vt. proclaim, publish —**promulga'tion** n. —**prom'ulgator** n.

pron. pronoun; pronunciation

prone a. lying face or front downwards; inclined (to) —**prone'ness** n.

prong n. one spike of fork or similar instrument

prong'horn n. Amer. antelope

pro'noun n. word used to replace noun —**pronom'inal** a. pert. to, like pronoun

pronounce' vt. utter formally; form with organs of speech; speak distinctly; declare —vi. give opinion or decision —**pronounce'able** a. —**pronounced'** a. strongly marked, decided —**pronounce'ment** n. declaration —**pronuncia'tion** n. way word etc. is pronounced; articulation

pron'to adv. inf. at once, immediately, quickly

proof n. evidence; thing which proves; test, demonstration; trial impression from type or engraved plate; Photog. print from a negative; standard of strength of alcoholic drink —a. giving impenetrable defence against; of proved strength —**proof'read** v. read and correct proofs —**proof'reader** n. —**proof'reading** n.

prop[1] vt. support, sustain, hold up (-pp-) —n. pole, beam etc. used as support

prop[2] n. short for PROPELLER

prop[3] n. short for (theatrical) PROPERTY

propagand'a n. organized dissemination of information to assist or damage political cause etc. —**propagan'dist** n.

prop'agate vt. reproduce, breed, spread by sowing, breeding etc.; transmit —vi. breed, multiply —**propaga'tion** n. —**prop'agative** a.

pro'pane n. colourless, flammable gas from petroleum

propel' vt. cause to move forward (-ll-) —**propell'ant, -ent** n. something causing propulsion, eg rocket fuel —**propell'er** n. revolving shaft with blades for driving ship or aircraft —**pro-**

pul'sion n. act of driving forward —**propul'sive, propul'sory** a. tending, having power to propel; urging on

propen'sity n. inclination or bent; tendency; disposition

prop'er a. appropriate; correct; conforming to etiquette, decorous; strict; (of noun) denoting individual person or place —**prop'erly** adv.

prop'erty n. that which is owned; estate whether in lands, goods, or money; quality, attribute of something; article used on stage in play etc.

proph'et n. inspired teacher or revealer of Divine Will; foreteller of future (**-tess** fem.) —**proph'ecy** [-si] n. prediction, prophetic utterance —**proph'esy** [-sī] vi. foretell —**proph'etic** a. —**prophet'ically** adv.

prophylac'tic n./a. (something) done or used to ward off disease; condom —**prophylax'is** n.

propin'quity n. nearness, proximity, close kinship

propi'tiate [-ish'-] vt. appease, gain favour of —**propitia'tion** n. —**propi'tiatory** a. —**propi'tious** a. favourable, auspicious

propo'nent n. one who advocates something

propor'tion n. relative size or number; comparison; due relation between connected things or parts; share; relation —pl. dimensions —vt. arrange proportions of —**propor'tionable** a. —**propor'tional, propor'tionate** a. having a due proportion; corresponding in size, number etc. —**propor'tionally** adv.

propose' vt. put forward for consideration; nominate; intend —vi. offer marriage —**propo'sal** n. —**propo'ser** n. —**proposi'tion** n. offer; statement, assertion;

theorem; suggestion of terms; inf. thing to be dealt with

propound' vt. put forward for consideration or solution

propri'etor n. owner (**-tress, -trix** fem.) —**propri'etary** a. belonging to owner; made by firm with exclusive rights of manufacture

propri'ety n. properness, correct conduct, fitness

propul'sion see PROPEL

pro rat'a [-raht'-] Lat. in proportion

prorogue' [-rōg'] vt. dismiss (parliament) at end of session without dissolution

prosa'ic a. commonplace, unromantic —**prosa'ical** a.

prosce'nium [-sē'-] n. arch or opening framing stage (pl. **-nia**)

proscribe' vt. outlaw, condemn —**proscrip'tion** n.

prose n. speech or writing not verse —**pro'sily** adv. —**pro'siness** n. —**pro'sy** a. tedious, dull

pros'ecute vt. carry on, bring legal proceedings against —**prosecu'tion** n. —**pros'ecutor** n. (**-trix** fem.)

pros'elyte n. convert —**pros'elytize** vt. —**pros'elytism** n.

pros'ody n. system, study of versification —**pros'odist** n.

pros'pect n. expectation, chance for success; view, outlook; likely customer or subscriber; mental view —v. [or -pekt'] explore, esp. for gold —**prospec'tive** a. anticipated; future —**prospec'tively** adv. —**prospect'or** n. —**prospec'tus** n. circular describing company, school etc.

pros'per v. (cause to) do well —**prosper'ity** [-pe'ri-] n. good fortune, wellbeing —**pros'perous** a. doing well, successful; flourishing, rich, well-off —**pros'perously** adv.

pros'tate n. gland accessory to

male generative organs

pros'thesis n. (replacement of part of body with) artificial substitute

pros'titute n. one who offers sexual intercourse in return for payment —vt. make a prostitute of; put to unworthy use —**prostitu'tion** n.

pros'trate a. lying flat; crushed, submissive, overcome —vt. [-trāt'] throw flat on ground; reduce to exhaustion —**prostra'tion** n.

protag'onist n. leading character; principal actor; champion of a cause

prot'asis n. introductory clause of conditional sentence

pro'tea [-ti-ə] n. showy Afric. shrub

prote'an a. variable; versatile

protect' vt. defend, guard, keep from harm —**protec'tion** n. —**protec'tionist** n. one who advocates protecting industries by taxing competing imports —**protec'tive** a. —**protect'or** n. one who protects; regent —**protec'torate** n. relation of state to territory it protects and controls; such territory; office, period of protector of a state

pro'tégé [-ti-zhā] n. one under another's care, protection or patronage (**-ée** fem.)

pro'tein [-tēn] n. kinds of organic compound which form most essential part of food of living creatures

pro tem'pore [-pə-ri] Lat. for the time being: also **pro tem**

pro'test n. declaration or demonstration of objection —vi. [-test'] make declaration against; assert formally —**protesta'tion** n. strong declaration

Prot'estant a. belonging to any branch of the Western Church outside the Roman Catholic Church —n. member of such church —**Prot'estantism** n.

prothalam'ium, -ion n. bridal song

pro'tium n. most common isotope of hydrogen

proto-, prot- (comb. form) first, as in prototype

pro'tocol n. diplomatic etiquette; draft of terms signed by parties as basis of formal treaty

pro'ton n. positively charged particle in nucleus of atom

pro'toplasm n. substance that is living matter of all animal and plant cells —**protoplas'mic** a.

pro'totype n. original, or model, after which thing is copied; pattern

protozo'an n. minute animal of lowest and simplest class

protract' vt. lengthen; prolong; delay; draw to scale —**protract'ed** a. long drawn out; tedious —**protrac'tion** n. —**protract'or** n. instrument for measuring angles on paper

protrude' v. stick out, project —**protru'sion** n. —**protru'sive** a. thrusting forward —**protru'sively** adv. —**protru'siveness** n. —**protru'sile** a.

protu'berant a. bulging out —**protu'berance** n. bulge, swelling

proud a. feeling or displaying pride; arrogant; gratified; noble; self-respecting; stately —**proud'ly** adv. —**proud flesh** flesh growing around healing wound

Prov. Proverbs

prove [proov] vt. establish validity of; demonstrate, test —vi. turn out (to be etc.); (of dough) rise in warm place before baking (**proved, pro'ven** [proo'-] pp.) —**pro'ven** [proo'-] a. proved

prov'enance n. place of origin, source

prov'ender n. fodder

prov'erb n. short, pithy, traditional saying in common use —**prover'bial** a.

provide' vi. make preparation —vt. supply, equip, prepare; furnish, give —**provi'der** n. —**provided that** on condition that

prov'ident a. thrifty; showing foresight —**prov'idence** n. kindly care of God or nature; foresight; economy —**providen'tial** a. strikingly fortunate, lucky —**providen'tially** adv.

prov'ince n. division of a country, district; sphere of action —pl. any part of country outside capital —**provin'cial** a. of a province; unsophisticated; narrow in outlook —n. unsophisticated person; inhabitant of province —**provin'cialism** n. narrowness of outlook; lack of refinement; idiom peculiar to province

provi'sion [-vizh'-] n. a providing, esp. for the future; thing provided —pl. food; Law articles of instrument or statute —vt. supply with food —**provi'sional** a. temporary; conditional —**provi'sionally** adv.

provi'so n. condition (pl. -os)

provoke' vt. irritate; incense; arouse; excite; cause —**provoca'tion** n. —**provoc'ative** a.

prov'ost n. one who superintends or presides; head of certain colleges; administrative head of Scottish burgh —**provost marshal** [prə-vō'] head of military police

prow n. bow of vessel

prow'ess n. bravery, fighting capacity; skill

prowl vi. roam stealthily, esp. in search of prey or booty —n. —**prowl'er** n.

prox'imate a. nearest, next, immediate —**proxim'ity** n. —**prox'imo** adv. in the next month

prox'y n. authorized agent or substitute; writing authorizing one to act as this

prude' n. one who affects excessive modesty or propriety —**pru'dery** n. —**pru'dish** a.

pru'dent a. careful, discreet; sensible —**pru'dence** n. habit of acting with careful deliberation; wisdom applied to practice —**pruden'tial** a.

prune[1] n. dried plum

prune[2] vt. cut out dead parts, excessive branches etc.; shorten, reduce —**pruning hook**

pru'rient [proor'-] a. given to, springing from lewd thoughts; having unhealthy curiosity or desire —**prur'ience, prur'iency** n.

pry vi. make furtive or impertinent inquiries; look curiously; US force open (**pried, pry'ing**)

PS postscript

Ps. Psalm(s)

psalm [sahm] n. sacred song; (**P-**) one of the sacred songs making up the Book of Psalms in the Bible —**psalm'ist** n. writer of psalms —**psalm'ody** n. art, act of singing sacred music —**Psal'ter** [sawl'-] n. book of psalms; copy of the Psalms as separate book —**psal'tery** n. obsolete stringed instrument like lyre

PSBR public sector borrowing requirement

psephol'ogy [se-] n. statistical study of elections

pseu'd(o) [syōō'-] n./a. inf. (something, somebody) sham, fake

pseudo- (comb. form) sham, as in pseudo-Gothic, pseudomodern etc. Such compounds are not given here where the meaning may easily be inferred from the simple word

pseu'donym [syōō'-] n. false, fictitious name; pen name —**pseudon'ymous** a.

psitt'acine [sĭt'ə-sīn] a. pert. to, like parrots —**psittaco'sis** [-kō'-] n. dangerous infectious disease, germ of which is carried by parrots

PST US, C Pacific Standard Time

psychedel'ic a. of or causing hallucinations; like intense colours etc. experienced during hallucinations

psy'chic [sī'kĭk] a. sensitive to phenomena lying outside range of normal experience; of soul or mind; that appears to be outside region of physical law —**psy'chical** a. psychic —**psychi'atry** n. medical treatment of mental diseases —**psychoanal'ysis** n. method of studying and treating mental disorders —**psychoan'alyst** n. —**psycholog'ical** a. of psychology; of the mind —**psychol'ogist** n. —**psychol'ogy** n. study of mind; inf. person's mental make-up —**psychom'etry** n. measurement, testing of psychological processes; supposed ability to divine unknown person's qualities by handling object used or worn by him —**psy'chopath** n. person afflicted with severe mental disorder causing him to commit antisocial, often violent acts —**psychopath'ic** a. —**psycho'sis** n. severe mental disorder in which person's contact with reality becomes distorted —**psychosomat'ic** a. of physical disorders thought to have psychological causes —**psychother'apy** n. treatment of disease by psychological, not physical, means

psych up [sīk] prepare (oneself or another) psychologically for action, performance etc.

PT physical therapy; physical training

Pt Chem. platinum

Pt. Point; Port

pt. part; pint; point

PTA Parent-Teacher Association

ptar'migan [t-] n. bird of grouse family which turns white in winter

Pte. Private (soldier)

pterodact'yl [t-] n. extinct flying reptile with batlike wings

PTO please turn over

pto'maine [t-] n. kinds of poisonous alkaloid found in decaying matter

Pu Chem. plutonium

pub n. public house, building with bar(s) and licence to sell alcoholic drinks

pu'berty n. sexual maturity —**pu'bertal** a.

pu'bic a. of the lower abdomen

pub'lic a. of or concerning the public as a whole; not private; open to general observation or knowledge; accessible to all; serving the people —n. the community or its members —**pub'lican** n. keeper of public house —**pub'licly** adv. —**public house** see PUB —**public relations** promotion of good relations of an organization or authority with the general public —**public school** private independent fee-paying school in England; in some Canadian provinces, a local elementary school —**public service** government employment —**public spirit** interest in and devotion to welfare of community

pub'licist n. writer on public concerns; journalist —**public'ity** [-lĭs'-] n. process of attracting public attention; attention thus gained —a. pert. to advertisement —**pub'licize** vt. advertise

pub'lish vt. prepare and issue for sale (books, music etc.); make generally known; proclaim —**publica'tion** n. —**pub'lisher** n.

puce *a./n.* purplish-brown (colour)

puck *n.* rubber disc used instead of ball in ice hockey

Puck *n.* mischievous sprite —**puck'ish** *a.*

puck'er *v.* gather into wrinkles —*n.* crease, fold

pud'ding [pood'-] *n.* sweet, cooked dessert, often made from suet, flour *etc.*; sweet course of meal; soft savoury dish with pastry or batter; kind of sausage

pud'dle *n.* small muddy pool; rough cement for lining ponds *etc.* —*vt.* line with puddle; make muddy —**pudd'ling** *n.* method of converting pig iron to wrought iron by oxidizing the carbon

pu'dency *n.* modesty; chastity —**pu'dic** *a.*

puer'ile [pyoor'-] *a.* childish; foolish; trivial

puerpe'rium [pyoor-] *n.* period of about six weeks after childbirth —**puer'peral** [pyoo-er'-] *a.*

puff *n.* short blast of breath, wind *etc.*; its sound; type of pastry, laudatory notice or advertisement —*vi.* blow abruptly; breathe hard —*vt.* send out in a puff; blow out, inflate; advertise; smoke hard —**puff'y** *a.* short-winded; swollen —**puff'ball** *n.* ball-shaped fungus

puff'in *n.* sea bird with large brightly-coloured beak

pug *n.* small snub-nosed dog; *sl.* boxer —**pug nose** snub nose

pu'gilist [-j-] *n.* boxer —**pu'gilism** *n.* —**pugilis'tic** *a.*

pugna'cious *a.* given to fighting —**pugnac'ity** *n.*

pu'issant *a. Poet.* powerful, mighty —**pu'issance** [or pwē'-] *n.* show jumping competition over very high fences; *obs.* power —**puiss'antly** *adv.*

puke [pyōōk] *vi. sl.* vomit —*n. sl.* vomiting

pul'chritude *n.* beauty

pule [pyōōl] *vi.* whine; whimper

pull [pool] *vt.* exert force on object to move it towards source of force; strain or stretch; tear; propel by rowing —*n.* act of pulling; force exerted by it; draught of liquor; *inf.* power, influence —**pull in** (of train) arrive; (of car *etc.*) drawn in to side of road or stop; attract; *sl.* arrest —**pull off** *inf.* carry through to successful issue —**pull out** withdraw; extract; (of train) depart; (of car *etc.*) move away from side of road or move out to overtake —**pull (someone's) leg** *inf.* make fun of —**pull up** tear up; recover lost ground; improve; come to a stop; halt; reprimand

pull'et [-oo-] *n.* young hen

pull'ey [-oo-] *n.* wheel with groove in rim for cord, used to raise weights by downward pull

Pull'man car railway saloon car

pull'over *n.* jersey, sweater without fastening, to be pulled over head

pul'monary *a.* of lungs

pulp *n.* soft, moist, vegetable or animal matter; flesh of fruit; any soft soggy mass —*vt.* reduce to pulp

pul'pit [-oo-] *n.* (enclosed) platform for preacher

pul'sar *n.* small dense star emitting radio waves

pulse[1] *n.* movement of blood in arteries corresponding to heartbeat, discernible to touch, *eg* in wrist; any regular beat or vibration —**pulsate'** *vi.* throb, quiver —**pulsa'tion** *n.*

puise[2] *n.* edible seeds of pod-bearing plants, *eg* beans

pul'verize *vt.* reduce to powder; smash or demolish —**pul·veriza'tion** n.

pu'ma n. large Amer. feline carnivore, cougar

pum'ice [-is] n. light porous variety of lava

pumm'el vt. strike repeatedly (-ll-)

pump[1] n. appliance in which piston and handle are used for raising water, or putting in or taking out air or liquid etc. —vt. raise, put in, take out etc. with pump; empty by means of a pump; extract information from —vi. work pump; work like pump —**pump iron** sl. do body-building exercises

pump[2] n. light shoe

pump'kin n. varieties of gourd, eaten esp. as vegetable

pun n. play on words —vi. make one (-nn-) —**pun'ster** n.

punch[1] n. tool for perforating or stamping; blow with fist; inf. vigour —vt. stamp, perforate with punch; strike with fist —**punch-drunk**, inf. **punch'y** a. dazed, as by repeated blows

punch[2] n. drink of spirits or wine with fruit juice, spice etc.

Punchinell'o n. clown and chief character of Italian puppet show —**Punch** n. same character in English puppet show, called **Punch and Judy show**

punctil'ious a. making much of details of etiquette; very exact, particular

punc'tual a. in good time, not late, prompt —**punctual'ity** n. —**punc'tually** adv.

punc'tuate vt. put in punctuation marks; interrupt at intervals —**punctua'tion** n. marks, eg commas, colons etc. put in writing to assist in making sense clear

punc'ture n. small hole made by sharp object, esp. in tyre; act

of puncturing —vt. prick hole in, perforate

pun'dit n. self-appointed expert

pun'gent [-j-] a. biting; irritant; piercing; tart; caustic —**pun'gency** n.

pun'ish vt. cause to suffer for offence; inflict penalty on; use or treat roughly —**pun'ishable** a. —**pun'ishment** n. —**pu'nitive** a. inflicting or intending to inflict punishment

punk a./n. inferior, rotten, worthless (person or thing); petty (hoodlum); (of) style of rock music

punn'et n. small (wooden) basket for fruit

punt[1] n. flat-bottomed square-ended boat, propelled by pushing with pole —vt. propel thus

punt[2] vt. Sport kick ball before it touches ground, when let fall from hands —n. such a kick

punt[3] vi. gamble, bet —**punt'er** n. one who punts; professional gambler

pu'ny a. small and feeble

pup n. young of certain animals, eg dog, seal

pu'pa n. stage between larva and adult in metamorphosis of insect, chrysalis (pl. **pu'pae** [-pē]) —**pu'pal** a.

pu'pil n. person being taught; opening in iris of eye

pupp'et n. small doll or figure of person etc. controlled by operator's hand —**puppeteer**[1] n. —**pupp'etry** n. —**puppet show** show with puppets worked by hidden showman

pupp'y n. young dog

pur'blind a. dim-sighted

pur'chase vt. buy —n. buying; what is bought; leverage, grip —**pur'chaser** n.

pur'dah [-də] n. Muslim, Hindu custom of keeping women in seclusion; screen, veil to achieve this

pure [pyoor] a. unmixed, untainted; simple; spotless; faultless; innocent; concerned with theory only —**pure'ly** adv. —**purifica'tion** n. —**pur'ificatory** a. —**pu'rify** vt. make, become pure, clear or clean (**-ified, -ifying**) —**pur'ism** n. excessive insistence on correctness of language —**pur'ist** n. —**pur'ity** n. state of being pure

pur'ée [pyoor'ā] n. pulp of cooked fruit or vegetables —vt.

pur'fle, pur'fling n. ornamental border on edges of furniture, garments etc.

purg'atory n. place or state of torment, pain or distress, esp. temporary —**purgator'ial** a.

purge [-j] vt. make clean, purify; remove, get rid of; clear out —n. act, process of purging; removal of undesirable members from political party, army etc. —**purga'tion** [-gā'-] n. —**pur'gative** a./n.

Pur'itan [pyoor'-] n. Hist. member of extreme Protestant party; (p-) person of extreme strictness in morals or religion —**puritan'ic(al)** a. strict in the observance of religious and moral duties; overscrupulous —**pu'ritanism** n.

purl' n. stitch that forms ridge in knitting —vi. knit in purl

purl' vi. flow with burbling sound, swirl, babble

pur'lieus [-lyōōz] pl.n. outlying parts, outskirts

purloin' vt. steal; pilfer

pur'ple n./a. (of) colour between crimson and violet

purport' vt. claim to be (true etc.); signify, imply —n. [pur'-] meaning; apparent meaning; significance

pur'pose [-pos] n. reason, object; design; aim, intention —vt.

intend —**pur'posely** adv. —**on purpose** intentionally

purr n. pleased noise which cat makes —vi. utter this

purse n. small bag for money; resources; money as prize —vt. pucker in wrinkles —vi. become wrinkled and drawn in —**pur'ser** n. ship's officer who keeps accounts

pursue' [-syōō'] vt. run after; chase; aim at; engage in; continue; follow —vi. go in pursuit; continue —**pursu'ance** n. carrying out —**pursu'ant** adv. accordingly —**pursu'er** n. —**pursuit'** [-syōōt'] n. running after, attempt to catch; occupation

pur'suivant [-siv-] n. officer of College of Arms below herald

pur'ulent a. see PUS

purvey' vt. supply (provisions) —**purvey'ance** n. —**purvey'or** n.

pur'view n. scope, range

pus n. yellowish matter produced by suppuration —**pur'ulence** n. —**pur'ulent** [pyoor'-] a. forming, discharging pus; septic

push [-oo-] vt. move, try to move away by pressure; drive or impel; inf. sell (esp. narcotic drugs) illegally —vi. make thrust; advance with steady effort —n. thrust; persevering self-assertion; big military advance; sl. dismissal —**push'er** n. —**push'ing, inf. push'y** a. given to pushing oneself —**push'chair** n. (collapsible) chair-shaped carriage for baby

pusillan'imous [pyōō-] a. cowardly —**pusillanim'ity** n.

puss [poos] n. cat: also **puss'y**

puss'yfoot inf. vi. move stealthily; act indecisively, procrastinate

pust'ule n. pimple containing pus —**pust'ular** a.

put [poot] vt. place; set; express; throw (esp. shot) (**put, putt'ing**) —n. throw —**put across** express, carry out successfully —**put off** postpone; disconcert; repel —**put up** erect; accommodate; nominate

pu'tative a. reputed, supposed —**pu'tatively** adv.

pu'trid a. decomposed; rotten —**pu'trefy** v. make or become rotten (**-efied, -efying**) —**putrefac'tion** n. —**putres'cence** n. —**putres'cent** a. becoming rotten —**putrid'ity** n.

putsch [pooch] n. surprise attempt to overthrow the existing power, political revolt

putt [put] vt. strike (golf ball) along ground in direction of hole —**putt'er** n. golf club for putting

putt'ee n. strip of cloth wound round leg like bandage, serving as gaiter

putt'y n. paste of whiting and oil as used by glaziers; jeweller's polishing powder —vt. fix, fill with putty (**-ied, -ying**)

puz'zle v. perplex or be perplexed —n. bewildering, perplexing question, problem or toy —**puz'zlement** n.

PVC polyvinyl chloride, synthetic thermoplastic material

pyae'mia [pī-ē'-] n. form of blood poisoning —**pyae'mic** a.

pyg'my, pig'my n. abnormally undersized person; (**P-**) member of one of dwarf peoples of Equatorial Africa —a. undersized

pyjam'as [pə-jahm'-] pl.n. sleeping suit of trousers and jacket

py'lon n. towerlike erection esp. to carry electric cables

pyorrhoe'a [-rē'ə] n. inflammation of the gums with discharge of pus and loosening of teeth

pyr'amid n. solid figure with sloping sides meeting at apex; structure of this shape, esp. ancient Egyptian; group of persons or things highest in the middle —**pyram'idal** a.

pyre n. pile of wood for burning a dead body

pyre'thrum [pī-rē'-] n. type of cultivated chrysanthemum; insecticide made from it

Py'rex R glassware resistant to heat

pyri'tes n. sulphide of a metal, esp. iron pyrites

pyrogen'ic, pyrog'enous a. produced by or producing heat; causing or resulting from fever

pyroma'niac n. person with uncontrollable desire to set things on fire

pyrom'eter n. instrument for measuring very high temperature —**pyrom'etry** n.

pyrotech'nics [-k-] n. manufacture, display of fireworks —**pyrotech'nist** n.

Pyr'rhic victory [pi'rik] one won at high cost

py'thon n. large nonpoisonous snake that crushes its prey —**py'thon'ic** a.

pyx [piks] n. box in Brit. Royal Mint holding specimen coins kept to be tested for weight; vessel in which consecrated Host is preserved

Q

Q Chess Queen; Question

q. quart; quarter; quarto; question

QC UK Queen's Counsel

QED (Lat., quod erat demonstrandum) which was to be proved

QM Quartermaster

qr. quarter; quire

qt. quart; quantity

qua [kwā] prep. in the capacity of

quack n. harsh cry of duck;

pretender to medical or other skill —vi. (of duck) utter cry

quad [kwod] short for quadrangle; quadrant; quadraphonic; quadruplet

quadr-, quadri- (comb. form) four

Quadrages'ima [kwod-rə-jes'-] n. forty days of fast before Easter; Lent

quad'rangle [kwod'-] n. four-sided figure; four-sided courtyard in a building —**quadrang'ular** a.

quad'rant [kwod'-] n. quarter of circle; instrument for taking angular measurements —**quadrate** vt. make square —**quadrat'ic** a. of equation, involving square of unknown quantity

quadraphon'ic [kwod-] a. of a sound system using four independent speakers

quadrilat'eral [kwod-] a. four-sided —n. four-sided figure

quadrille' [kwod-] n. square dance; music played for it; old card game

quadrill'ion [kwod-] n. fourth power of million

quadru'manous [kwod roo'-] a. of apes etc. having four feet which can be used as hands

quad'ruped [kwod'-] n. four-footed animal —**quadru'pedal** [-roo'-] a.

quad'ruple [kwod'-] a. fourfold —v. make, become four times as much —**quadru'plicate** a. fourfold

quad'ruplet [kwod'-] n. one of four offspring born at one birth

quaff [-o-, -ah-] v. drink heartily or in one draught

quag, quag'mire n. bog, swamp

quagg'a n. recently extinct member of horse family

quail[1] n. small bird of partridge family

quail[2] vi. flinch; cower

quaint a. interestingly old-fashioned or odd; curious; whimsical —**quaint'ly** adv. —**quaint'ness** n.

quake vi. shake, tremble

Qua'ker n. member of Christian sect, the **Society of Friends** (**Qua'keress** fem.)

qual'ify vi. make oneself competent —vt. moderate; limit; make competent; ascribe quality to; describe (**-fied, -fying**) —**qualifica'tion** n. thing that qualifies, attribute; restriction; qualifying

qual'ity [kwol'-] n. attribute, characteristic, property; degree of excellence; rank —**qual'ita-tive** a. depending on quality

qualm [kwahm] n. misgiving; sudden feeling of sickness —**qualm'ish** a.

quan'dary [kwon'-] n. state of perplexity, puzzling situation, dilemma

quan'go n. quasi-autonomous national (or non)government(al) organization (pl. **-gos**)

quan'tity [kwon'-] n. size, number, amount; specified or considerable amount —**quant'ify** vt. discover, express quantity of —**quan'titative** a. —**quan'tum** n. desired or required amount (pl. **-ta**) —**quantity surveyor** one who estimates cost of materials, labour for building job —**quantum theory** theory that in radiation, energy of electrons is discharged not continuously but in discrete units or quanta

quar'antine [kwo'rən-tēn] n. isolation to prevent spreading of infection —vt. put, keep in quarantine

quark n. Physics any of several hypothetical particles thought to be fundamental units of matter

quarr'el [kwo'r-] n. angry dispute; argument —vi. argue; find fault with (**-ll-**) —**quarr'elsome** a.

quarr'el [kwo'r-] n. crossbow arrow; diamond-shaped pane

quarr'y[1] [kwo'ri] n. object of hunt or pursuit; prey

quarr'y[2] [kwo'ri] n. excavation where stone etc. is got from ground for building etc. —v. get from quarry (**quarr'ied, quarr'ying**)

quart [kwort] n. liquid measure, quarter of gallon or 2 pints (1.1 litres)

quart'er [kwort'-] n. fourth part; US, C 25 cents; unit of weight, 28 lb; region, district; mercy —pl. lodgings —vt. divide into quarters; lodge —**quart'erly** a. happening, due etc. each quarter of year —n. quarterly periodical —**quartet'** n. group of four musicians; music for four performers —**quart'o** n. size of book in which sheets are folded into four leaves (pl. **-os**) —a. of this size —**quarter day** any of four days in the year when certain payments become due —**quart'erdeck** n. after part of upper deck used esp. for official, ceremonial purposes —**quarter horse** small, powerful breed of horse —**quart'ermaster** n. officer responsible for stores —**quart'erstaff** n. long staff for fighting

quartz [kworts] n. stone of pure crystalline silica —**quartz'ite** n. quartz rock —**quartz timepiece** watch or clock operated by a vibrating quartz crystal

qua'sar [-z-] n. extremely distant starlike object emitting powerful radio waves

quash [kwosh] vt. annul; reject; subdue forcibly

qua'si- [kwā'zī, kwahz'ī] (comb. form) seemingly, resembling but not actually being, as in **quasi-scientific**

quass'ia [kwosh'ə] n. tropical Amer. tree

quater'nary a. of the number four; having four parts; Geology (**Q-**) of most recent period after Tertiary

quatrain' [kwot-] n. four-line stanza, esp. rhymed alternately

qua'ver vt. say or sing in quavering tones —vi. tremble, shake, vibrate —n. musical note half length of crotchet; quavering trill

quay [kē] n. solid, fixed landing stage; wharf

queas'y a. inclined to, or causing, sickness

queen n. king's wife; female sovereign; piece in chess; fertile female bee, wasp etc.; court card with picture of a queen, ranking between king and jack; inf. male homosexual —**queen'ly** adv.

queer a. odd, strange; inf. homosexual (also n.) —vt. inf. spoil; interfere with

quell vt. crush, put down; allay; pacify

quench vt. slake; extinguish, put out, suppress

quern n. stone hand mill

quer'ulous [kwe'roo-] a. fretful, peevish, whining

que'ry n. question; mark of interrogation —vt. question, ask (**que'ried, que'rying**)

quest n./vi. search

ques'tion [-chən] n. sentence seeking for answer; that which is asked; interrogation; inquiry; problem; point for debate; debate, strife —vt. ask questions of, interrogate; dispute; doubt —**ques'tionable** a. doubtful, esp. not clearly true or honest —**questionnaire'** n. list of questions drawn up for formal answer

queue [kyōō] n. line of waiting persons, vehicles —vi. wait in queue (with **up**)

quib'ble n. trivial objection —v. make this

quiche [kēsh] n. open savoury tart

quick a. rapid, swift; keen; brisk; hasty —n. part of body sensitive to pain; sensitive flesh; obs. (the) living people —adv. rapidly —quick'en v. make, become faster or more lively —quick'ie n. inf. a quick one —quick'ly adv. —quick'lime n. calcium oxide —quick'sand n. loose wet sand easily yielding to pressure and engulfing persons, animals etc. —quick'silver n. mercury —quick'step n. ballroom dance —vi. —quick-tempered a. irascible

quid n. inf pound (sterling)

quid pro quo Lat. something given in exchange

quies'cent [kwi-es'-] a. at rest, inactive, inert; silent —quies'cence, quies'cency n.

qui'et a. with little or no motion or noise; undisturbed; not showy or obtrusive —n. state of peacefulness, absence of noise or disturbance —v. make, become quiet —qui'eten v. make, become quiet —qui'etly adv. —qui'etness, qui'etude n.

qui'etism n. passive attitude to life, esp. as form of religion —qui'etist n.

quill n. large feather; hollow stem of this; pen, plectrum made from feather; spine of porcupine

quilt n. padded coverlet —vt. stitch (two pieces of cloth) with pad between

quin n. short for QUINTUPLET

quince n. acid pear-shaped fruit; tree bearing it

quinine' [-ēn'] n. bitter drug made from bark of tree, used to treat fever, and as tonic

Quinquages'ima [-jes'-] n. Sunday 50 days before Easter

quinquenn'ial a. occurring once in, or lasting, five years

quin'sy [-zi] n. inflammation of throat or tonsils

quintess'ence n. purest form, essential feature; embodiment —quintessen'tial a.

quintet' n. set of five singers or players; composition for five voices, or instruments

quin'tuplet [-tyoo-] n. one of five offspring born at one birth

quip n./v. (utter) witty saying

quire n. 24 sheets of writing paper

quirk n. Individual peculiarity of character; unexpected twist or turn

quis'ling [-iz'-] n. traitor who aids occupying enemy force

quit vi. stop doing a thing; depart —vt. leave, go away from; cease from (quit or quitt'ed pt./pp.) —a. free, rid —quits a. on an equal or even terms by repayment etc. —quitt'ance n. discharge; receipt —quitt'er n. one lacking perseverance

quite adv. wholly, completely; very considerably, somewhat, rather —interj. exactly, just so

quiv'er[1] vi. shake or tremble —n. quivering; vibration

quiv'er[2] n. carrying case for arrows

quixot'ic a. unrealistically and impractically optimistic, idealistic, chivalrous

quiz n. entertainment in which general or specific knowledge of players is tested by questions; examination, interrogation —vt. question, interrogate (-zz-) —quiz'zical a. questioning; mocking

quod n. sl. prison

quoin n. external corner of building; small wedge for locking printing type into the forme

quoit n. ring for throwing at peg

as a game —*pl.* (*with sing. v.*) the game

quor'um *n.* least number that must be present in meeting to make its transactions valid

quo'ta *n.* share to be contributed or received; specified number, quantity, which may be imported or admitted (*pl.* **-s**)

quote *vt.* copy or repeat passages from; refer to, *esp.* to confirm view; state price for —**quo'table** *a.* —**quota'tion** *n.*

quoth [-ō] *obs.* said

quotid'ian *a.* daily; everyday, commonplace

quo'tient [-shənt] *n.* number resulting from dividing one number by another

q.v. *quod vide* (*Lat.*, which see)

qwert'y *n.* standard typewriter keyboard layout

R

R radius; ratio; Regina (*Lat.* Queen); Rex (*Lat.* King); river; *Chess* rook

RA Rear Admiral; Royal Academy; Royal Artillery

Ra *Chem.* radium

rabb'i [-ī] *n.* Jewish learned man, spiritual leader (*pl.* **rabb'is** [-īz]) —**rabbin'ical** *a.* —**rab'binism** *n.*

rabb'it *n.* small burrowing mammal —*vi.* hunt rabbits —**rabbit punch** sharp blow to back of neck

rab'ble *n.* crowd of vulgar, noisy people; mob

rab'id *a.* relating to or having rabies; furious; mad; fanatical —**rab'idly** *adv.* —**rab'idness** *n.*

ra'bies *n.* acute infectious viral disease transmitted by dogs *etc.*

RAC Royal Automobile Club

raccoon' *n.* small N Amer. mammal

race' *n.* contest of speed, as in running, swimming *etc.*; contest, rivalry; strong current of water, *esp.* leading to water wheel —*pl.* meeting for horse racing —*vt.* cause to run rapidly —*vi.* run swiftly; of engine, pedal *etc.*, to move rapidly and erratically, *esp.* on removal of resistance —**ra'cer** *n.* person, vehicle, animal that races

race' *n.* group of people of common ancestry with distinguishing physical features (skin colour *etc.*); species; type —**ra'cial** *a.* —**ra'cialism, ra'cism** *n.* belief in innate superiority of particular race; antagonism towards members of different race based on this belief —**ra'cialist, ra'cist** *a./n.*

raceme' *n.* cluster of flowers along a central stem, as in the foxglove

rack' *n.* framework for displaying or holding baggage, books, hats, bottles *etc.*; *Mechanics* straight bar with teeth on its edge, to work with pinion; instrument of torture by stretching —*vt.* stretch on rack or wheel; torture; stretch, strain —**rack'ing** *a.* agonizing (pain)

rack' *n.* destruction *esp.* in **rack and ruin**

rack' *n.* thin, flying clouds

rack' *vt.* clear wine, beer *etc.* by drawing off from dregs

rack' *n.* neck or rib section of mutton, lamb, pork

rack'et' *n.* loud noise, uproar; occupation by which money is made illegally —**racketeer'** *n.* one making illegal profits —**racketeer'ing** *n.* —**rack'ety** *a.* noisy

rack'et' *n.* bat used in tennis

etc. —*pl.* ball game played in paved, walled court

raconteur' [-kon-] *n.* skilled storyteller

rac'quet *see* RACKET²

ra'cy *a.* spirited; lively; having strong flavour; spicy; piquant —**ra'cily** *adv.* —**ra'ciness** *n.*

ra'dar *n.* device for finding range and direction by ultrahigh frequency point-to-point radio waves, which reflect back to their source and reveal position and nature of objects sought

ra'dial *see* RADIUS

ra'diate *v.* emit, be emitted in rays; spread out from centre —**ra'diance** *n.* brightness; splendour —**ra'diant** *a.* beaming; shining; emitting rays —*n. Geometry* straight line from point about which it is imagined to revolve —**radia'tion** *n.* transmission of heat, light *etc.* from one body to another; particles, rays, emitted in nuclear decay; act of radiating —**ra'diator** *n.* that which radiates, *esp.* heating apparatus for rooms; cooling apparatus of car engine

rad'ical *a.* fundamental, thorough; extreme; of root —*n.* person of extreme (political) views; radicle; number expressed as root of another; group of atoms of several elements which remain unchanged in a series of chemical compounds —**rad'icalism** *n.*

rad'icle *n.* root

ra'dio *n.* use of electromagnetic waves for broadcasting, communication *etc.*; device for receiving, amplifying radio signals; broadcasting, content of radio programmes —*vt.* transmit message *etc.* by radio

radio- (*comb. form*) of rays, of radiation, of radium, as in *radiology*

radioact'ive *a.* emitting invisible rays that penetrate matter —**radioactiv'ity** *n.*

radiog'raphy *n.* production of image on film or plate by radiation —**radiog'rapher** *n.*

radiol'ogy *n.* science of use of rays in medicine —**radiol'ogist** *n.*

radiother'apy *n.* diagnosis and treatment of disease by x-rays

rad'ish *n.* pungent root vegetable

ra'dium *n.* radioactive metallic element

ra'dius *n.* straight line from centre to circumference of circle; outer of two bones in forearm (*pl.* **ra'dii** [-di-ī], **ra'diuses**) —**ra'dial** *a.* arranged like radii of circle; of ray or rays; of radius

ra'don *n.* radioactive gaseous element

RAF Royal Air Force

raff'ia *n.* prepared palm fibre for making mats *etc.*

raff'ish *a.* disreputable

raf'fle *n.* lottery in which an article is assigned by lot to one of those buying tickets —*vt.* dispose of by raffle

raft [-ah-] *n.* floating structure of logs, planks *etc.*

raft'er [-ah-] *n.* one of the main beams of a roof

rag¹ *n.* fragment of cloth; torn piece; *inf.* newspaper *etc.*, *esp.* one considered worthless; piece of ragtime music —*pl.* tattered clothing —**ragg'ed** *a.* shaggy; torn; clothed in torn clothes; lacking smoothness —**rag'bag** *n.* confused assortment —**rag'time** *n.* style of jazz piano music —**rag trade** *inf.* clothing industry, trade

rag² *vt.* tease; torment; play practical jokes on —*n.* period of carnival with procession *etc.* organized by students to raise money for charities

rag'amuffin n. ragged, dirty person or boy

rage n. violent anger or passion; fury —vi. speak, act with fury; proceed violently and without check (as storm, battle etc.); be widely and violently prevalent —**all the rage** very popular

rag'lan a. of sleeves that continue to the neck so that there are no shoulder seams

ragout' [-gōō'] n. highly seasoned stew of meat and vegetables

raid n. rush, attack; foray —vt. make raid on —**raid'er** n.

rail[1] n. horizontal bar, esp. as part of fence, track etc. —**rail'ing** n. fence, barrier made of rails supported by posts —**rail'head** n. farthest point to which railway line extends —**rail'way, US rail'road** n. track of iron rails on which trains run; company operating railway (also pl.) —**off the rails** inf. astray; on wrong track; in error; leading reckless, dissipated life

rail[2] vi. utter abuse; scoff; scold; reproach —**rail'lery** n. banter

rail[3] n. kinds of marsh bird

rai'ment [rā'-] n. obs. clothing

rain n. moisture falling in drops from clouds; fall of such drops —vi. fall as rain —vt. pour down like rain —**rain'y** a. —**rain'bow** n. arch of prismatic colours in sky —**rain'coat** n. light water-resistant overcoat —**rain gauge** instrument for measuring rainfall

raise [-z] vt. lift up; set up; build; increase; elevate; promote; heighten, as pitch of voice; breed into existence; levy, collect; end (siege) —**raise Cain** inf. be riotous, angry etc.

rai'sin [-z-] n. dried grape

raison d'être[1] [rā-zon-detr'] Fr. reason or justification for existence

raj [rahj] n. rule, sway, esp. in India —**raj'ah** n. Indian prince or ruler

rake[1] n. tool with long handle and crosspiece with teeth for gathering hay, leaves etc. —vt. gather, smooth with rake; sweep, search over; sweep with shot —**rake-off** n. inf. monetary commission, esp. illegal

rake[2] n. dissolute or dissipated man

rake[3] n. slope, esp. backwards, of ship's funnel etc. —v. incline from perpendicular —**ra'kish** a. appearing dashing or speedy

rall'y vt. bring together, reunite; bring back together, as routed army or dispersed troops —vi. come together; regain health or strength, revive (**rall'ied, rall'ying**) —n. act of rallying; assembly, esp. outdoor, of any organization; Tennis lively exchange of strokes

ram n. male sheep; hydraulic machine; battering engine —vt. force, drive; strike against with force; stuff; strike with ram (**-mm-**)

Ramadan' [-dahn'] n. 9th Mohammedan month; strict fasting observed during this time

ram'ble vi. walk without definite route; wander; talk incoherently; spread in random fashion —n. rambling walk —**ram'bler** n. climbing rose; one who rambles

rambu'tan [-bōō'-] n. SE Asian tree; its bright red edible fruit

ram'ekin n. small fireproof dish; savoury food baked in it

ram'ify v. spread in branches, subdivide; become complex (**-ified, -ifying**) —**ramifica'tion** n. branch, subdivision; process of branching out; consequence

ra'mose a. branching

ramp n. gradual slope joining two level surfaces

rampage' vi. dash about violently —n. [ram'-] angry or destructive behaviour —**rampa'geous** a.

ram'pant a. violent; rife; rearing

ram'part n. mound, wall for defence —vt. defend with one

ram'shackle a. tumbledown, rickety, makeshift

ran pt. of RUN

ranch [-ah-] n. Amer. cattle farm —vi manage one **ranch'er** n.

ran'cid a. smelling or tasting offensively, like stale fat —**ran-cid'ity** n.

ran'cour [rang'kər] n. bitter, inveterate hate —**ran'corous** a. malignant; virulent

rand n. monetary unit of S Africa

ran'dom a. made or done by chance, without plan —**at random** haphazard(ly)

rand'y a. sl. sexually aroused

rang pt. of RING[2]

range n limits; row; scope, sphere; distance missile can travel; distance of mark shot at; place for shooting practice or rocket testing; rank; kitchen stove —vt. set in row; classify; roam —vi. extend; roam; pass from one point to another; fluctuate (as prices) —**rang'er** n. official in charge of or patrolling park etc.; (**R-**) member of senior branch of Guides —**rang'y** [rānˈji] a. with long, slender limbs; spacious —**range'finder** n. instrument for finding distance away of given object

rank[1] n. row, line; place where taxis wait; order; social class; status; relative place or position —pl. common soldiers; great mass or majority of people (also

rank and file) —vt. draw up in rank, classify —vi. have rank, place; have certain distinctions

rank[1] a. growing too thickly, coarse; offensively strong; rancid; vile; flagrant —**rank'ly** adv.

ran'kle [-ng'kl] vi. fester, continue to cause anger, resentment or bitterness

ran'sack vt. search thoroughly; pillage, plunder

ran'som n. release from captivity by payment; amount paid —vt. pay ransom for —**ran'som-er** n.

rant vi. rave in violent, high-sounding language —n. noisy, boisterous speech; wild gaiety —**rant'er** n.

ranun'culus n. kinds of plant, eg buttercup

rap[1] n. smart slight blow —v. give rap to —vt. utter abruptly —vi. perform rhythmic monologue to music (-pp-) —**take the rap** sl. suffer punishment (for) whether guilty or not

rap[1] n. —**not care a rap** inf. not care at all

rapa'cious a. greedy; grasping —**rapac'ity** [-pas'-] n.

rape[1] vt. force (woman) to submit unwillingly to sexual intercourse —n. act of raping; any violation or abuse —**ra'pist** n.

rape[2] n. plant with oil-yielding seeds, also used as fodder

rap'id a. quick, swift —n. (esp. in pl.) part of river with fast, turbulent current —**rapid'ity** n. —**rap'idly** adv.

ra'pier n. fine-bladed sword for thrusting only

rap'ine n. plunder

rapport' [-pawr'] n. harmony, agreement

rapproche'ment [-prosh'-mong] n. re-establishment of friendly relations, esp. between nations

rapscall'ion *n.* rascal, rogue

rapt *a.* engrossed, spellbound —**rap'ture** *n.* ecstasy —**rap'turous** *a.*

raptor'ial *a.* predatory; of the order of birds of prey

rare[1] [rãr] *a.* uncommon; infrequent; of uncommon quality; of atmosphere, having low density, thin —**rare'ly** *adv.* seldom —**ra'rity** *n.* anything rare; rareness

rare[2] [rãr] *a.* (of meat) lightly cooked

rare'bit [rãr'-] *n.* savoury cheese dish

ra'refy *v.* make, become thin, rare, or less dense; refine (-**fied**, -**fying**) —**rarefaction** *n.*

ra'ring *a.* enthusiastically willing, ready

ras'cal *n.* rogue; naughty (young) person —**rascal'ity** *n.* roguery, baseness —**ras'cally** *a.*

rash[1] *a.* hasty, reckless, incautious —**rash'ly** *adv.*

rash[2] *n.* skin eruption; outbreak, series of (unpleasant) occurrences

rash'er *n.* thin slice of bacon or ham

rasp [-ah-] *n.* harsh, grating noise; coarse file — *v.* scrape with rasp; make scraping noise; speak in grating voice; grate upon; irritate

rasp'berry [rahz'b-] *n.* red, juicy edible berry; plant which bears it; *inf.* spluttering noise with tongue and lips to show contempt

Rastafa'rian (*oft. shortened to* **Ras'ta**) *n.* member of Jamaican cult regarding Haile Selassie as God — *a.*

rat *n.* small rodent; *inf.* contemptible person, *esp.* deserter, informer *etc.* — *vi.* inform (on); betray; desert, abandon; hunt rats (-**tt**-) —**ratt'y** *sl. a.* mean, ill-

tempered, irritable —**rat-catcher** *n.* —**rat race** continual hectic competitive activity

ratafi'a [-fē'ə] *n.* liqueur made from fruit; almond-flavoured biscuit

rat'chet *n.* set of teeth on bar or wheel allowing motion in one direction only

rate[1] *n.* proportion between two things; charge; degree of speed *etc.* — *pl.* local tax on property — *vt.* value; estimate value of; assess for local taxation —**rat(e)'able** *a.* that can be rated; liable to pay rates —**rate'-payer** *n.*

rate[2] *vt.* scold, chide

rath'er [rahTH'-] *adv.* to some extent; preferably; more willingly

rat'ify *vt.* confirm (-**ified**, -**ifying**) —**ratifica'tion** *n.*

ra'ting *n.* valuing or assessing; fixing a rate; classification, *esp.* of ship; sailor (**naval rating**); angry rebuke

ra'tio [-shi-ō] *n.* proportion; quantitative relation

ratioc'inate [-ti-os'-] *vi.* reason —**ratiocina'tion** *n.*

ra'tion [rash'ən] *n.* fixed allowance of food *etc.* — *vt.* supply with, limit to certain amount

ra'tional [rash'ən-] *a.* reasonable, sensible; capable of thinking, reasoning —**rationale'** [-ahl'] *n.* reasons given for actions *etc.* —**ra'tionalism** *n.* philosophy which regards reason as only guide or authority —**ra'tionalist** *n.* —**rational'ity** *n.* —**rationaliza'tion** *n.* —**ra'tionalize** *vt.* justify by plausible reasoning; reorganize to improve efficiency *etc.* —**ra'tionally** *adv.*

rattan' *n.* climbing palm with jointed stems; cane of this

rat'tle *vi.* give out succession of short sharp sounds; clatter — *vt.*

shake briskly causing a sharp clatter of sounds; *inf.* confuse, fluster —*n.* such sound; instrument for making it; set of horny rings in rattlesnake's tail —**rat'tlesnake** *n.* poisonous snake

rau'cous [-aw'-] *a.* hoarse; harsh

raunch'y *a. sl.* earthy, sexy

rav'age *vt.* lay waste, plunder —*n.* destruction

rave *vi.* talk wildly in delirium or enthusiastically —*n.*

rav'el *vt.* entangle; fray out; disentangle (-**ll**-)

ra'ven[1] *n.* black bird like crow

rav'en[2] *v.* seek prey, plunder —**rav'enous** *a.* very hungry

ravine' [-ēn'] *n.* narrow steep-sided valley worn by stream, gorge

ravio'li *pl.n.* small, thin pieces of dough filled with highly seasoned, chopped meat and cooked

rav'ish *vt.* enrapture; commit rape upon —**rav'ishing** *a.* lovely, entrancing

raw *a.* uncooked; not manufactured or refined; skinned; inexperienced, unpractised, as recruits, sensitive; chilly —**raw deal** unfair or dishonest treatment —**raw'hide** *n.* untanned hide; whip of this

ray[1] *n.* single line or narrow beam of light, heat *etc.*; any of set of radiating lines —*vi.* come out in rays; radiate

ray[2] *n.* marine fish, often very large, with winglike pectoral fins and whiplike tail

ray[3], **re** *n.* second sol-fa note

ray'on *n.* (fabric of) synthetic fibre

raze *vt.* destroy completely; wipe out, delete; level

ra'zor *n.* sharp instrument for shaving or for cutting hair —**ra'zorbill** *n.* N Atlantic auk

RC Red Cross; Roman Catholic

Rd. Road

RE religious education

re[1] *see* RAY[3]

re[2] *prep.* with reference to, concerning

re-, red-, ren- (*comb. form*) again In the list below, the meaning may be inferred from the word to which *re-* is prefixed

reach *vt.* arrive at; extend; succeed in touching; attain to —*vi.* stretch out hand; extend —*n.* act of reaching; power of touching; grasp, scope; range; stretch of river between two bends

react[1] *vi.* act in return, opposition or towards former state —**reac'tance** *n. Electricity* resistance in coil, apart from ohmic resistance, due to current reacting on itself —**reac'tion** *n.* any action resisting another; counter or backward tendency; *inf.* response; chemical or nuclear change, combination or decomposition —**reac'tionary** *n./a.* (person) opposed to change, *esp.* in politics *etc.* —**reac'tive** *a.* chemically active —**reac'tor** *n.* apparatus in which nuclear reaction is maintained and controlled to produce nuclear energy

read [rēd] *vt.* look at and understand written or printed matter;

readmiss'ion	rediscov'er
reappear'	re-ech'o
rearm'	re-elect'
rearrange'	refill'
rebuild'	re-form'
recap'ture	reheat'
reconnect'	remarr'y
reconsid'er	reo'pen
reconstruct'	reprint'
reconvene'	reroute'
re-cov'er	reset'
re-create'	reshuf'fle
redec'orate	reunite'
redevel'op	rewind'

learn by reading; interpret mentally; read and utter; interpret; study; understand any indicating instrument; (of instrument) register —vi. be occupied in reading; find mentioned in reading (**read** [red] *pt./pp.*) —**readabil'ity** *n.* —**read'able** *a.* that can be read, or read with pleasure —**read'er** *n.* one who reads; university lecturer; school textbook; one who reads manuscripts submitted to publisher; one who reads printer's proofs —**read'ing** *n.*

read'y [red'i] *a.* prepared for use or action; willing, prompt —**read'ily** *adv.* promptly; willingly —**read'iness** *n.*

rea'gent [rē-ā'jǝnt] *n.* chemical substance that reacts with another and is used to detect presence of the other —**rea'gency** *n.*

real *a.* existing in fact; happening; actual; genuine; (of property) consisting of land and houses —**re'alism** *n.* regarding things as they are; artistic treatment with this outlook —**re'alist** *n.* —**realis'tic** *a.* —**real'ity** *n.* real existence —**re'ally** *adv.* —**re'alty** *n.* real estate —**real estate** landed property —**real ale** beer allowed to ferment in the barrel and served without using carbon dioxide

re'alize *vt.* apprehend, grasp significance of; make real; convert into money —**realiza'tion** *n.*

realm [relm] *n.* kingdom, province, domain, sphere

ream[1] *n.* twenty quires of paper, generally 480 sheets —*pl. inf.* large quantity of written matter

ream[2] *vt.* enlarge, bevel out, as hole in metal —**ream'er** *n.* tool for this

reap *v.* cut and gather harvest; receive as fruit of previous activity —**reap'er** *n.*

rear[1] *n.* back part; part of army, procession *etc.* behind others —**rear admiral** lowest flag rank in certain navies —**rear'guard** *n.* troops protecting rear of army —**rear'most** *a.*

rear[2] *vt.* care for and educate (children); breed; erect —*vi.* rise, *esp.* on hind feet

reas'on [rēz'-] *n.* ground, motive; faculty of thinking; sanity; sensible or logical thought or view —*vi.* think logically in forming conclusions —*vt.* (*usu.* with **with**) persuade by logical argument into doing *etc.* —**reas'onable** *a.* sensible, not excessive; suitable; logical

reassure' *vt.* restore confidence to

re'bate[1] *n.* discount, refund —*vt.* [-bāt'] deduct

re'bate[2] *n.* recess, groove cut into piece of timber to join with matching piece —*vt.* cut rebate in

rebel' *vi.* revolt, resist lawful authority, take arms against ruling power (-**ll**-) —*n.* [reb'-] one who rebels; insurgent —*a.* in rebellion —**rebell'ion** *n.* organized open resistance to authority, revolt —**rebell'ious** *a.* —**rebel'liously** *adv.*

re'bore, rebor'ing *n.* boring of cylinder to regain true shape

rebound' *vi.* spring back; misfire, *esp.* so as to hurt perpetrator (of plan, deed *etc.*) —*n.* [rē'-] act of springing back or recoiling; return

rebuff' *n.* blunt refusal; check —*vt.* repulse, snub

rebuke' *vt.* reprove, reprimand, find fault with —*n.*

re'bus *n.* riddle in which names of things *etc.* are represented by pictures standing for syllables *etc.* (*pl.* **-es**)

rebut' *vt.* refute, disprove (-tt-) —**rebut'tal** *n.*

recal'citrant *a./n.* wilfully disobedient (person) —**recal'citrance** *n.*

recall' *vt.* recollect, remember; call, summon, order back; annul, cancel; revive, restore —*n.* summons to return; ability to remember

recant' *vt.* withdraw statement, opinion *etc.* —**recanta'tion** *n.*

re'cap *v./n.* short for RECAPITULATE, RECAPITULATION

recapit'ulate *vt.* state again briefly; repeat —**recapitula'tion** *n.*

recede' *vi.* go back; become distant; slope backwards; start balding

receipt' [-sēt'] *n.* written acknowledgement of money received; receiving or being received —*vt.* acknowledge payment of in writing

receive' [-sēv'] *vt.* take, accept, get; experience; greet (guests) —**receiv'able** *a.* —**receiv'er** *n.* officer appointed to take public money; one who takes stolen goods knowing them to have been stolen; equipment in telephone, radio or television that converts electrical signals into sound and light

re'cent *a.* that has lately happened; new —**re'cently** *adv.*

recep'tacle *n.* vessel, place or space, to contain anything

recep'tion *n.* receiving; manner of receiving; welcome; formal party; area for receiving guests, clients *etc.*; in broadcasting, quality of signals received —**recep'tionist** *n.* person who receives guests, clients *etc.*

recep'tive *a.* able, quick, willing to receive new ideas, suggestions *etc.* —**receptiv'ity** *n.*

recess' *n.* niche, alcove; hollow;

secret, hidden place; remission or suspension of business; vacation, holiday

reces'sion [-sesh'-] *n.* period of reduction in trade; act of receding —**reces'sive** *a.* receding

reces'sional *n.* hymn sung while clergy retire

recher'ché [-sher'shā] *a.* of studied elegance; exquisite; choice

recid'ivist *n.* one who relapses into crime

rec'ipe [res'i-pi] *n.* directions for cooking a dish; prescription; expedient

recip'ient *a.* that can or does receive —*n.* one who, that which receives —**recip'ience** *n.*

recip'rocal *a.* complementary; mutual; moving backwards and forwards; alternating —**recip'rocally** *adv.* —**recip'rocate** *vt.* give and receive mutually; return —*vi.* move backwards and forwards —**reciproca'tion** *n.* —**reciproc'ity** [-os'-] *n.*

recite' *vt.* repeat aloud, *esp.* to audience —**recit'al** *n.* musical performance, usu. by one person; act of reciting; narration of facts *etc.*; story; public entertainment of recitations *etc.* —**recita'tion** *n.* recital, usu. from memory, of poetry or prose; recountal —**recitative'** [-ēv'] *n.* musical declamation —**recit'er** *n.*

reck'less *a.* heedless, incautious —**reck'lessness** *n.*

reck'on *v.* count; include; consider; think, deem; make calculations —**reck'oner** *n.*

reclaim' *vt.* make fit for cultivation; bring back; reform; demand the return of —**reclaim'able** *a.* —**reclama'tion** *n.*

recline' *vi.* sit, lie back or on one's side

recluse' [-klōōs'] *n.* hermit —*a.* living in complete retirement

—reclu'sive a. **—reclu'sion** n.

rec'ognize vt. know again; treat as valid; notice, show appreciation of **—recogni'tion** n. **—recogni'zable** a. **—recog'nizance** n. avowal; bond by which person undertakes before court to observe some condition; obs. recognition

recoil' vi. draw back in horror etc.; go wrong so as to hurt the perpetrator; rebound (esp. of gun when fired) **—**n. [or re'-] backward spring; retreat; recoiling

recollect' vt. call back to mind, remember **—recollec'tion** n.

recommend' vt. advise, counsel; praise, commend; make acceptable **—recommenda'tion** n.

rec'ompense vt. reward; compensate, make up for **—**n. compensation; reward; requital

rec'oncile vt. bring back into friendship; adjust, settle, harmonize **—rec'oncilable** a. **—reconcile'ment** n. **—reconcilia'tion** n.

recon'dite a. obscure, abstruse, little known

recondi'tion [-dish-] vt. restore to good condition, working order

reconnoi'tre [-tər] vt. make preliminary survey of; survey position of enemy **—**vi. make reconnaissance **—recon'naissance** n. examination or survey for military or engineering purposes; scouting

recon'stitute vt. restore (food) to former state esp. by addition of water to a concentrate

rec'ord n. being recorded; document or other thing that records; disc with indentations which gramophone transforms into sound; best recorded achievement; known facts about person's past **—**vt. [-kord'] put in writing; register **—**v. preserve (sound, TV programmes etc.) on plastic disc, magnetic tape etc. for reproduction on playback device **—record'er** n. one who, that which records; type of flute; judge in certain courts **—record'ing** n. process of making records from sound; something recorded, eg radio or TV programme **—record player** instrument for reproducing sound on discs **—off the record** not for publication

recount' vt. tell in detail **—recount'al** n.

recoup' vt. recompense, compensate; recover what has been expended or lost

recourse' n. (resorting to) source of help; Law right of action or appeal

recov'er [-kuv'-] vt. regain, get back **—**vi. get back health **—recov'erable** a. **—recov'ery** n.

rec'reant a. cowardly, disloyal **—**n. recreant person; renegade **—rec'reancy** n.

recrea'tion n. agreeable or refreshing occupation, relaxation, amusement **—rec'reative** a.

recrim'inate vi. make countercharge or mutual accusation **—recrimina'tion** n. mutual abuse and blame **—recrim'inative, recrim'inatory** a.

recrudesce' [-krōō-des'] vi. break out again **—recrudes'cence** n. **—recrudes'cent** a.

recruit' [-ōōt'] n. newly-enlisted soldier; one newly joining society etc. **—**vt. enlist fresh soldiers etc. **—recruit'ment** n.

rect'angle n. oblong four-sided figure with four right angles **—rectang'ular** a. shaped thus

rect'ify vt. put right, correct, remedy, purify (**-fied, -fying**) **—rectifica'tion** n. act of setting right; refining by repeated distillation; Electricity conversion of alternating current into direct current —**rect'ifier** n. thing that rectifies

rectilin'eal, rectilin'ear a. in straight line; characterized by straight lines

rect'itude n. moral uprightness; honesty of purpose

rect'o n. right-hand page of book, front of leaf

rec'tor n. clergyman with care of parish; head of certain institutions, chiefly academic —**rec'torship** n. —**rec'tory** n. rector's house

rect'um n. final section of large intestine (pl. **·ta**) —**rec'tal** a.

recum'bent a. lying down —**recum'bency** n.

recu'perate [-kōō'-] v. restore, be restored from illness, losses etc.; convalesce —**recupera'tion** n.

recur' vi. happen again; return again and again; go or come back in mind (**-rr-**) —**recur'rence** n. repetition —**recurr'ent** a.

rec'usant n. one who refused to conform to rites of Established Anglican Church —a. obstinate in refusal

recy'cle vt. reprocess a manufactured substance for use again; reuse

red a. of colour varying from crimson to orange and seen in blood, rubies, glowing fire etc. —n. the colour; inf. communist —**redd'en** v. make red; become red; flush —**redd'ish** a. —**red-blooded** a. vigorous; virile —**red'breast** n. robin —**red'brick** a. of provincial and relatively new university —**red'coat** n. obs. soldier —**Red Cross** international humanitarian organization providing medical care for war casualties, famine relief etc. —**red'fish** n. various types of fish —**red flag** emblem of communist party; (**R- F-**) their song; danger signal —**red-handed** a. inf. (caught) in the act —**red herring** topic introduced to divert attention from main issue —**red-hot poker** garden plant with tall spikes of red or orange flowers —**Red Indian** N Amer. Indian —**red'shank** n. large European sandpiper —**red tape** excessive adherence to official rules —**red'wood** n. giant coniferous tree of California —**in the red** inf. in debt —**see red** inf. be angry

redeem' vt. buy back; set free; free from sin; make up for —**redemp'tion** n. —**redeem'able** a. —**The Redeemer** Jesus Christ

Rediffu'sion R system by which radio, TV programmes are relayed to subscribers from a central receiver

red'olent a. smelling strongly, fragrant; reminiscent (of) —**red'olence** n.

redou'ble [-dub'-] v. increase, multiply, intensify; double a second time

redoubt' [-dowt'] n. detached outwork in fortifications

redoubt'able [-dowt'-] a. dreaded, formidable

redound' vt. contribute (to); recoil

redress' vt. set right; make amends for —n. compensation, amends

reduce' vt. bring down, lower; lessen, weaken; bring by force or necessity to some state or action; slim; simplify; dilute; Chem. separate substance from others with which it is combined —**reduc'ible** a. —**reduc'tion** n. —**reduc'ing agent** substance used to deoxidize or lessen density of another substance

redun'dant a. superfluous; (of worker) deprived of job because no longer needed —**redun'dancy** n.

reed n. various marsh or water plants; tall straight stem of one; *Mus.* vibrating cane or metal strip of certain wind instruments —**reed'y** a. full of reeds; like reed instrument, harsh and thin in tone —**reed'buck** n. S Afr. antelope with buff coat

reef n. ridge of rock or coral near surface of sea; vein of ore; part of sail which can be rolled up to reduce area —vt. take in a reef of —**reef'er** n. sailor's jacket; sl. hand-rolled cigarette, esp. with cannabis

reek n. strong (unpleasant) smell —vi. emit fumes; smell

reel n. spool on which film is wound; *Cinema* portion of film; winding apparatus; bobbin; thread wound on this; lively dance; music for it; act of staggering —vt. wind on reel; draw (in) by means of reel —vi. stagger, sway, rock —**reel off** recite, write fluently, quickly

reeve[1] n. *Hist.* manorial steward or official

reeve[2] vt. pass (rope) through hole, in block etc.

reeve[3] n. female of ruff (bird)

ref. referee; reference; reformed

refec'tory n. room for meals in college etc. —**refec'tion** n. meal

refer[1] vi. relate (to), allude —vt. send to for information; trace, ascribe to; submit for decision (-rr-) —**refer(r)'able** a. —**refer'ral** n. act, instance of referring —**referee'** n. arbitrator; person willing to testify to someone's character etc.; umpire —v. act as referee —**ref'erence** n. act of referring; citation or direction in book; appeal to judgment of another; testimonial; one to whom inquiries as to character etc. may be made —**referen'dum** n.

submitting of question to electorate (pl. **-dums, -da**)

refine[1] vt. purify —**refine'ment** n. subtlety; improvement, elaboration; fineness of feeling, taste or manners —**refi'ner** n. —**refi'nery** n. place where sugar, oil etc. is refined

refla'tion n. (steps taken to produce) increase in economic activity of country etc.

reflect[1] vt. throw back, esp. rays of light; cast (discredit etc.) upon —vi. meditate —**reflec'tion, reflex'ion** n. act of reflecting; return of rays of heat, light, or waves of sound, from surface; image of object given back by mirror etc.; conscious thought; meditation; expression of thought —**reflect'ive** a. meditative, quiet, contemplative; throwing back images —**reflec'tor** n. polished surface for reflecting light etc.

re'flex n. reflex action; reflected image; reflected light, colour etc. —a. (of muscular action) involuntary; reflected; bent back —**reflex'ive** a. *Grammar* describes verb denoting agent's action on himself —**reflex action** involuntary response to (nerve) stimulation

re'flux n. flowing back, ebb —**ref'luence** n. —**ref'luent** a. returning, ebbing

reform[1] v. improve; abandon evil practices; reconstruct —n. improvement —**reforma'tion** n. —**reform'atory** n. institution for reforming juvenile offenders —a. reforming —**reform'er** n.

refract[1] vi. change course of light etc. passing from one medium to another —**refrac'tion** n. —**refract'ive** a.

refrac'tory a. unmanageable; difficult to treat or work; *Med.* resistant to treatment; resistant to heat

refrain[1] *vi.* abstain (from)

refrain[2] *n.* chorus

refran'gible *a.* that can be refracted —**refrangibil'ity** *n.*

refresh' *vt.* give freshness to; revive; renew; brighten; provide with refreshment —**refresh'er** *n.* that which refreshes —**refresh'ment** *n.* that which refreshes, *esp.* food, drink; restorative

refrig'erate [-frij-] *vt.* freeze; cool —**refrig'erant** *n.* refrigerating substance —*a.* —**refrigera'tion** *n.* —**refrig'erator** *n.* apparatus in which foods, drinks are kept cool

ref'uge *n.* shelter, protection, retreat, sanctuary —**refugee'** *n.* one who seeks refuge, *esp.* in foreign country

reful'gent [-j-] *a.* shining, radiant —**reful'gence** *n.* —**reful'gency** *n.* splendour

refund' *vt.* pay back —*n.* [rē'-]

refur'bish *vt.* furbish, furnish or polish anew

refuse[1] [-z] *v.* decline, deny, reject —**refu'sal** *n.* denial of anything demanded or offered; option

ref'use[2] [-yōōs] *n.* rubbish, useless matter

refute' *vt.* disprove —**refu'table** *a.* —**refuta'tion** *n.*

re'gal[1] *a.* of, like a king —**rega'lia** *pl.n.* insignia of royalty, as used at coronation *etc.*; emblems of high office, an order *etc.* —**regal'ity** *n.* —**re'gally** *adv.*

regale' *vt.* give pleasure to; feast —**regale'ment** *n.*

regard' *vt.* look at; consider; relate to; heed —*n.* look; attention; particular respect; esteem —*pl.* expression of good will —**regard'ful** *a.* heedful, careful —**regard'less** *a.* heedless —*adv.* in spite of everything

regatt'a *n.* meeting for yacht or boat races

regen'erate [-jen'-] *v.* cause spiritual rebirth; reform morally; reproduce, re-create; reorganize —*a.* born anew —**regenera'tion** *n.* —**regen'erative** *a.* —**regen'erator** *n.*

re'gent *n.* ruler of kingdom during absence, minority *etc.*, of its monarch —*a.* ruling —**re'gency** *n.* status, (period of) office of regent

regg'ae [-gā] *n.* style of popular West Indian music with strong beat

reg'icide [rej'-] *n.* one who kills a king; this crime

regime[1] [rā-zhēm'] *n.* system of government, administration

reg'imen [rej'-] *n.* prescribed system of diet *etc.*; rule

reg'iment [rej'-] *n.* organized body of troops as unit of army —*vt.* discipline, organize rigidly or too strictly —**regiment'al** *a.* of regiment —**regiment'als** *pl.n.* uniform

re'gion [-jan] *n.* area, district; stretch of country; part of the body; sphere, realm; (*oft.* **R-**) administrative division of a country —**re'gional** *a.*

reg'ister [rej'-] *n.* list; catalogue; roll; device for registering; written record; range of voice or instrument —*v.* show, be shown on meter, face *etc.* —*vt.* enter in register; record; show; set down in writing; *Printing, Photography* cause to correspond precisely —**registrar'** *n.* keeper of a register; senior hospital doctor, junior to consultant —**registra'tion** *n.* —**reg'istry** *n.* registering; place where registers are kept, *esp.* of births, marriages, deaths —**registration number** sequence of numbers and letters displayed on motor vehicle to identify it

re'gius [-j-] *a.* appointed by crown, *esp.* applied to professor holding university chair founded by crown

reg'nal a. pert. to reign of a sovereign —**reg'nancy** n. rule; predominance —**reg'nant** a. reigning

regorge' v. vomit up

regress' vi. return, revert to former place, condition etc. —n. [re'-] —**regression** n. act of returning; retrogression —**regressive** a. falling back —**regressively** adv.

regret' vt. feel sorry, distressed for loss of or on account of (-tt-) —n. sorrow, distress for thing done or left undone or lost —**regret'ful** a. —**regrett'able** a.

reg'ular a. normal; habitual; done, occurring, according to rule; periodical; straight; level; living under rule; belonging to standing army —n. regular soldier; inf. regular customer —**regular'ity** n. —**reg'ularize** vt.

reg'ulate vt. adjust; arrange; direct; govern; put under rule —**regula'tion** n. —**reg'ulator** n. contrivance to produce uniformity of motion, as fly wheel, governor etc.

regur'gitate [-gur'ji-] v. vomit; bring back (swallowed food) into mouth —**regurgita'tion** n.

rehabil'itate [- he-] vt. help (person) to readjust to society after a period of illness, imprisonment etc.; restore to reputation or former position; make fit again; reinstate —**rehabilita'tion** n.

rehash' vt. rework, reuse —n. old materials presented in new form

rehearse' [-hurs'] vt. practise (play etc.); repeat aloud; say over again; train, drill —**rehears'al** n.

reign [ran] n. period of sovereign's rule —vi. be sovereign; be supreme

reimburse' [re-im-] vt. refund; pay back —**reimburse'ment** n.

rein [ran] n. narrow strap attached to bit to guide horse; instrument for governing —vt. check, manage with reins; control —**give rein to** remove restraints

reincarna'tion [re-in-] n. rebirth of soul in successive bodies; one of series of such transmigrations —**rein'carnate** vt.

rein'deer [ran'-] n. deer of cold regions, eg Lapland

reinforce' [re-in-] vt. strengthen with new support, material, force; strengthen with additional troops, ships etc. —**reinforce'ment** n. —**reinforced concrete** concrete strengthened internally by steel bars; ferroconcrete

reinstate' [re-in-] vt. replace, restore, re-establish —**reinstate'ment** n.

reit'erate [re-it'-] vt. repeat again and again —**reitera'tion** n. repetition —**reit'erative** a.

reject' vt. refuse to accept; put aside; discard; renounce —n. [re'-] person or thing rejected as not up to standard —**rejec'tion** n. refusal

rejig' vt. re-equip (factory, plant); rearrange (-gg-)

rejoice' v. make or be joyful, merry; gladden; exult

rejoin' vt. reply; join again —**rejoin'der** n. answer, retort

reju'venate vt. restore to youth —**rejuvena'tion** n. —**rejuvenes'cence** n. process of growing young again —**rejuvenes'cent** a.

relapse' vi. fall back into evil, illness etc. —n.

relate' vt. narrate, recount; establish relation between; have reference or relation to —vi. (with) to) form sympathetic relationship

rela'tion *n.* relative quality or condition; connection by blood or marriage; connection between things; act of relating; narrative —**rela'tionship** *n.* —**rel'ative** *a.* dependent on relation to something else, not absolute; having reference or relation (to) —*n.* one connected by blood or marriage; relative word or thing —**rel'atively** *adv.* —**relativ'ity** *n.* state of being relative; subject of two theories of Albert Einstein, dealing with relationships of space, time and motion, and acceleration and gravity

relax' *vt.* make loose or slack —*vi.* become loosened or slack; ease up from effort or attention; become more friendly, less strict —**relaxa'tion** *n.* relaxing recreation; alleviation; abatement

re'lay *n.* fresh set of people or animals relieving others; *Electricity* device for making or breaking local circuit; *Radio, Television* broadcasting station receiving programmes from another station —*vt.* [-lā'] pass on, as message (**relayed', re'laying**) —**relay race** race between teams of which each runner races part of distance

release' *vt.* give up, surrender, set free; permit public showing of (film *etc.*) —*n.* setting free; releasing; written discharge; permission to show publicly; film, record *etc.* newly issued

rel'egate *vt.* banish, consign; demote —**relega'tion** *n.*

relent' *vi.* give up harsh intention, become less severe —**relent'less** *a.* pitiless; merciless

rel'evant *a.* having to do with the matter in hand, to the point —**rel'evance** *n.*

reli'able, reli'ance *see* RELY

rel'ic *n.* thing remaining, *esp.* as memorial of saint; memento —*pl.* remains, traces; *obs.* dead body —**rel'ict** *n. obs.* widow

relief' *n.* alleviation, end of pain, distress *etc.*; money, food given to victims of disaster, poverty *etc.*; release from duty; one who relieves another; bus, plane *etc.* that carries passengers when a scheduled service is full; freeing of besieged city *etc.*; projection of carved design from surface; distinctness, prominence —**relieve'** *vt.* bring or give relief to —**relief map** map showing elevations and depressions of country in relief

relig'ion [-lij'-] *n.* system of belief, in worship of a supernatural power or god —**relig'ious** *a.* pert. to religion; pious; conscientious —**relig'iously** *adv.* in religious manner; scrupulously; conscientiously

relin'quish *vt.* give up, abandon —**relin'quishment** *n.*

rel'iquary [-kwər-i] *n.* case or shrine for holy relics

rel'ish *v.* enjoy, like —*n.* liking, gusto; savoury taste; taste or flavour

reluct'ant *a.* unwilling, loath, disinclined —**reluct'ance** *n.*

rely' *vi.* depend (on); trust (**relied', rely'ing**) —**reliabil'ity** *n.* —**reli'able** *a.* trustworthy, dependable —**reli'ance** *n.* trust; confidence; dependence —**reli'ant** *a.* confident

remain' *vi.* stay, be left behind; continue; abide; last —**remains'** *pl.n.* relics, traces of ancient buildings; dead body —**remain'der** *n.* rest, what is left after subtraction —*vt.* offer (end of consignment of goods, material *etc.*) at reduced prices

remand' *vt.* send back, *esp.* into custody —**remand home** place of detention for young delinquents

remark' vi. make casual comment (on) —vt. comment, observe; say; take notice of —n. observation, comment —**remark'able** a. noteworthy, unusual —**remark'ably** adv. exceedingly; unusually

rem'edy n. means of curing, counteracting or relieving disease, trouble etc. —vt. put right (-edied, -edying) —**reme'diable** a. —**reme'dial** a. designed, intended to correct specific disability, handicap etc.

remem'ber vt. retain in, recall to memory —vi. have in mind —**remem'brance** n. memory; token; souvenir; reminiscence

remind' [-mīnd'] vt. cause to remember; put in mind (of) —**mind'er** n.

reminisce' [-is'] vi. talk, write of past times, experiences etc. —**reminis'cence** n. remembering; thing recollected —pl. memoirs —**reminis'cent** a. reminding or suggestive (of)

remiss' a. negligent, careless —**remiss'ly** adv.

remit' vt. send money for goods, services etc., esp. by post; refrain from exacting; give up; restore, return; slacken; obs. forgive —n. [rē'-] area of competence, authority —**remiss'ible** a. —**remiss'ion** n. abatement; reduction in length of prison term; pardon, forgiveness —**remitt'ance** n. sending of money; money sent

rem'nant n. fragment or small piece remaining; oddment

rem'onstrate vi. protest, reason with, argue —**remon'strance** n.

remorse' n. regret and repentance —**remorse'ful** a. —**remorse'fully** adv. —**remorse'less** a. pitiless

remote' a. far away, distant; aloof; slight —**remote'ly** adv.

—**remote control** control of apparatus from a distance by electrical device

re'mould n. see RETREAD

remove' [-mōōv'] vt. take away or off; transfer; withdraw —vi. go away, change residence —n. degree of difference —**remo'vable** a. —**remo'val** [-ōō-] n.

remu'nerate vt. reward, pay —**remunera'tion** n. —**remu'nerative** a.

renais'sance [-nā'səns] n. revival, rebirth, esp. (R-) revival of learning in 14th to 16th centuries (also **renas'cence**)

re'nal a. of the kidneys

renas'cent a. springing up again into being

rend v. tear, wrench apart; burst, break, split (**rent, rend'ing**)

rend'er vt. submit, present; give in return, deliver up; cause to become; portray, represent; melt down; cover with plaster

rend'ezvous [rond'i-vōō] n. meeting place; appointment; haunt; assignation —vi. meet, come together

rendi'tion [-dish'-] n. performance; translation

ren'egade n. deserter; outlaw; rebel —a.

reneg(u)e' [-nēg'] vi. (usu. with on) go back on (promise etc.)

renew' vt. begin again; reaffirm; make valid again; make new; revive; restore to former state; replenish —vi. be made new; grow again —**renewabil'ity** n. quality of being renewable —**renew'able** a. —**renew'al** n. revival, restoration; regeneration

renn'et n. preparation for curdling milk

renounce' vt. give up, cast off, disown; abjure; resign, as title or claim —**renuncia'tion** n.

ren'ovate vt. restore, repair,

renew, do up —**renova'tion** n.

renown' n. fame

rent' n. payment for use of land, buildings, machines etc. —vt. hold by lease; hire; let —**rent'al** n. sum payable as rent

rent' n. tear; fissure —pt./pp. of REND

renuncia'tion see RENOUNCE

rep' n. fabric with corded surface for upholstery also **repp**

rep' a./n. short for REPERTORY (COMPANY)

rep' n. short for REPRESENTATIVE

repaid' pt./pp. of REPAY

repair' vt. make whole, sound again; mend; patch; restore —n. —**repair'able** a. —**repara'tion** n. repairing; amends, compensation

repair' vi. resort (to), go

repartee' n. witty retort; interchange of them

repast' [-ah-] n. meal

repat'riate vt. send (someone) back to his own country —**repatria'tion** n.

repay' vt. pay back, refund; make return for (**repaid'**, re-**pay'ing**) —**repay'able** a. —**repay'ment** n.

repeal' vt. revoke, annul, cancel —n. act of repealing

repeat' vt. say, do again; reproduce; recur —vi. recur —n. act, instance of repeating, esp. TV show broadcast again —**repeat'-edly** [-id-li] adv. again and again; frequently —**repeat'er** n. firearm that may be discharged many times without reloading; watch that strikes hours —**repeti'tion** n. act of repeating; thing repeated; piece learnt by heart and repeated —**repeti'tious** a. repeated unnecessarily —**re-pet'itive** a. repeated

repel' vt. drive back, ward off, refuse; be repulsive to (-ll-) —**re-pel'lent** a. distasteful; resisting water etc. —n. that which repels, esp. chemical to repel insects

repent' vi. wish one had not done something; feel regret for deed or omission —vt. feel regret for —**repent'ance** n. contrition —**repent'ant** a.

repercuss'ion [-kush'-] n. indirect effect, oft. unpleasant; recoil; echo

rep'ertory n. repertoire, collection; store —**reper'toire** [-twahr'] n. stock of plays, songs etc. that player or company can give —**repertory (theatre, company, group)** (theatre etc. with) permanent company producing succession of plays

repeti'tion, repeti'tious, repet'itive see REPEAT

repine' vi. fret, complain

replace' vt. substitute for; put back —**replace'ment** n.

re'play n. immediate reshowing on T.V. of incident in sport, esp. in slow motion (also **action replay**); replaying of a match —vt. [-pla']

replen'ish vt. fill up again —**replen'ishment** n.

replete' a. filled, gorged —**reple'tion** n. complete fullness

rep'lica n. exact copy; facsimile, duplicate —**rep'licate** vt. make, be a copy of

reply' v. answer (**replied'**, re-**ply'ing**) —n.

report' n. account, statement; written statement of child's progress at school; rumour; repute; bang —vt. announce, relate; make, give account of; take down in writing; complain about —vi. make report; act as reporter; present oneself (to) —**report'er** n. one who reports, esp. for newspaper

repose' n. peace; composure; sleep —vi. rest —vt. lay at rest; place; rely, lean (on) —**repos'itory** n. place where valuables are deposited for safekeeping; store

repouss'é [rə-pōos'ā] a. embossed; hammered into relief from reverse side —n. metal work so produced

reprehend' vt. find fault with —**reprehen'sible** a. deserving censure; unworthy —**reprehen'sion** n. censure

represent' [-zent'] vt. stand for; deputize for; act, play; symbolize; make out to be; call up by description or portrait —**representa'tion** n. —**represent'ative** n. one chosen to stand for group; (travelling) salesman —a. typical

repress' vt. keep down or under, quell, check —**repress'ion** n. restraint —**repress'ive** a.

reprieve' vt. suspend execution of (condemned person); give temporary relief (to) —n. postponement or cancellation of punishment; respite; last-minute intervention

rep'rimand [-mahnd] n. sharp rebuke —vt. rebuke sharply

repri'sal [-zəl] n. retaliation

reproach' vt. blame, rebuke —n. scolding, upbraiding; expression of this; thing bringing discredit —**reproach'ful** a.

rep'robate a. depraved; cast off by God —n. depraved or disreputable person —vt. disapprove of, reject —**reproba'tion** n.

reproduce' [-rē-] vt. produce copy of; bring new individuals into existence; re-create, produce anew —v. propagate; generate —**reprodu'cible** a. —**reproduc'tion** n. process of reproducing; that which is reproduced; facsimile, as of painting etc. —**reproduc'tive** a.

reprove' [-ōōv'] vt. censure, rebuke —**reproof'** n.

rep'tile n. cold-blooded, air breathing vertebrate with horny scales or plates, as snake, tortoise etc. —**reptil'ian** a.

repub'lic n. state without monarch in which supremacy of people or their elected representatives is formally acknowledged —**repub'lican** a./n. —**repub'licanism** n.

repu'diate vt. reject authority or validity of; cast off, disown —**repudia'tion** n.

repug'nant a. offensive; distasteful; contrary —**repug'nance** n. dislike, aversion; incompatibility

repulse' vt. drive back; rebuff; repel —n. driving back, rejection, rebuff —**repul'sion** n. distaste, aversion; Physics force separating two objects —**repul'sive** a. loathsome, disgusting

repute' vt. reckon, consider —n. reputation, credit —**rep'utable** a. of good repute; respectable —**reputa'tion** n. estimation in which person is held; character; good name

request' n. asking; thing asked for —vt. ask

Re'quiem [rek'wi-əm] n. Mass for the dead; music for this

require' vt. want, need; demand —**require'ment** n. essential condition; specific need; want

req'uisite [-zit] a. necessary; essential —n.

requisi'tion [-zish'-] n. formal demand, eg for materials or supplies —vt. demand (supplies); press into service

requite' vt. repay —**requi'tal** n.

rere'dos [rēr'dos] n. ornamental screen behind altar

rescind' [-sind'] vt. cancel, annul —**rescis'sion, rescind'ment** n.

res'cue vt. save, deliver, extricate —n. —**res'cuer** n. —**res'cuing** n.

research' n. investigation, esp.

scientific study to discover facts —*v.* carry out investigations (on, into) —**research'er** *n.*

resem'ble [-z-] *vt.* be like; look like —**resem'blance** *n.*

resent' [-z-] *vt.* show, feel indignation at; retain bitterness about —**resent'ful** *a.* —**resent'ment** *n.*

reserve' [-z-] *vt.* hold back, set aside, keep for future use —*n.* (also *pl.*) something, *esp.* money, troops *etc.* kept for emergencies; area of land reserved for particular purpose or for use by particular group of people *etc.* (also **reserva'tion**); reticence, concealment of feelings or friendliness —**reserva'tion** *n.* reserving; thing reserved; doubt; exception or limitation —**reserved'** *a.* not showing feelings, lacking cordiality —**reserv'ist** *n.* one serving in reserve

res'ervoir [rez'ər-vwahr] *n.* enclosed area for storage of water, *esp.* for community supplies; receptacle for liquid, gas *etc.*; place where anything is kept in store

reside' [-z-] *vi.* dwell permanently —**res'idence** *n.* home; house —**res'idency** *n.* official dwelling *esp.* formerly of British government agent —**res'ident** *a./n.* —**residen'tial** *a.* (of part of town) consisting mainly of residences; of, connected with residence; providing living accommodation

res'idue [rez'-] *n.* what is left, remainder —**resid'ual** *n.* —**sid'uary** *a.*

resign' [-zīn'] *vt.* give up —*vi.* give up office, employment *etc.*; reconcile (oneself) to —**resigna'tion** [-zig-nā'-] *n.* resigning; being resigned, submission —**resigned'** *a.* content to endure

resil'ient [-z-] *a.* capable of returning to normal after stretching *etc.*, elastic; (of person) recovering quickly from

shock *etc.* —**resil'ience, -ency** *n.*

res'in [rez'-] *n.* sticky substance formed in and oozing from plants, *esp.* firs and pines —**res'inous** *a.* of, like resin

resist' [-z-] *v.* withstand, oppose —**resist'ance** *n.* act of resisting; opposition; hindrance; *Electricity* opposition offered by circuit to passage of current through it —**resist'ant** *a.* —**resist'ible** *a.* —**resistiv'ity** *n.* measure of electrical resistance —**resist'or** *n.* component of electrical circuit producing resistance

res'olute [rez'ə-loot] *a.* determined —**res'olutely** *adv.* —**reso-lu'tion** *n.* resolving; firmness; purpose or thing resolved upon; decision of court, or vote of assembly

resolve' [-z-] *vt.* make up one's mind; decide with effort of will; form by resolution of vote; separate component parts of; make clear —*n.* resolution; fixed purpose —**resolv'able** *a.* —**resol'vent** *a./n.* —**resolv'er** *n.*

res'onance [rez'-] *n.* echoing, *esp.* in deep tone; sound produced by body vibrating in sympathy with neighbouring source of sound —**res'onant** *a.* —**res'onate** *vi.* —**res'onator** *n.*

resort' [-z-] *vi.* have recourse; frequent —*n.* place of recreation *eg* beach; recourse; frequented place; haunt

resound' [-z-] *vi.* echo, ring, go on sounding —**resound'ing** *a.* echoing; thorough

resource' [-zawrs', -sawrs'] *n.* capability, ingenuity; that to which one resorts for support; expedient —*pl.* source of economic wealth; stock that can be drawn on; means of support, funds —**resource'ful** *a.* —**resource'fully** *adv.* —**resource'ful-ness** *n.*

respect' n. deference, esteem; point or aspect; reference, relation —vt. treat with esteem; show consideration for —**respectabil'ity** n. —**respect'able** a. worthy of respect, decent; fairly good —**respect'er** n. —**respect'ful** a. —**respect'ing** prep. concerning —**respect'ive** a. relating separately to each of those in question; several, separate —**respec'tively** adv.

respire' v. breathe —**respir'able** a. —**respira'tion** n. —**res'pirator** n. apparatus worn over mouth and breathed through as protection against dust, poison gas etc. or to provide artificial respiration —**res'piratory** a.

res'pite n. pause; interval; suspension of labour; delay; reprieve

resplend'ent a. brilliant, splendid; shining —**resplend'ence, -ency** n.

respond' vi. answer; act in answer to any stimulus; react —**respond'ent** a. replying —n. one who answers; defendant —**response'** n. answer —**respon'sive** a. readily reacting to some influence —**respon'siveness** n.

respon'sible a. liable to answer for; accountable; dependable; involving responsibility; of good credit or position —**responsibil'ity** n. state of being answerable; duty; charge; obligation

rest[1] n. repose; freedom from exertion etc.; that on which anything rests or leans; pause, esp. in music; support —vi. take rest; be supported —vt. give rest to; place on support —**rest'ful** a. —**rest'less** a.

rest[2] n. remainder; others —vi. remain; continue to be

rest'aurant [-tɔ-rong, -ront] n. commercial establishment serving food —**restaurateur'** n. keeper of one

restitu'tion n. giving back or making up; reparation, compensation

rest'ive a. restless; resisting control, impatient

restore' vt. build up again, repair, renew; re-establish; give back —**restora'tion** n. —**restor'ative** a. restoring —n. medicine to strengthen etc. —**restor'er** n.

restrain' vt. check, hold back; prevent; confine —**restraint'** n. restraining, control, esp. self-control

restrict' vt. limit, bound —**restric'tion** n. limitation; restraint; rule —**restrict'ive** a. —**restricted area** area in which speed limit for vehicles applies

result' [-z-] vi. follow as consequence; happen; end —n. effect, outcome —**result'ant** a. arising as result

resume' [-z-] vt. begin again —**rés'umé** [rez'yoo-mā] n. summary, abstract —**resump'tion** [-z-] n. resuming; fresh start —**resump'tive** a.

resur'gence n. rising again —**resur'gent** a.

resurrect' vt. restore to life, resuscitate; use once more (something discarded etc.) —**resurrec'tion** n. rising again (esp. from dead); revival

resus'citate vt. revive to life, consciousness —**resuscita'tion** n.

re'tail n. sale in small quantities —adv. by retail —v. sell, be sold, retail; [-tāl'] recount —**re'tailer** n.

retain' vt. keep; engage services of —**retain'er** n. fee to retain professional adviser, esp. barrister; Hist. follower of nobleman etc. —**reten'tion** n. —**re-**

ten'tive *a.* capable of retaining, remembering

retal'iate *v.* repay in kind; revenge —**retalia'tion** *n.* —**retal'iatory** *a.*

retard' *vt.* make slow or late; keep back; impede development of —**retarda'tion** *n.* —**retard'ed** *a.* underdeveloped, *esp.* mentally

retch *vi.* try to vomit

ret'icent *a.* reserved in speech; uncommunicative —**ret'icence** *n.*

retic'ulate [-lit], **retic'ular** *a.* made or arranged like a net —**retic'ulate** [-lāt] *v.* make, be like net —**reticula'tion** *n.*

ret'ina *n.* light-sensitive membrane at back of eye

ret'inue *n.* band of followers or attendants

retire' *vi.* give up office or work; go away; withdraw; go to bed —*vt.* cause to retire —**tired'** *a.* that has retired from office etc. —**retire'ment** *n.* —**reti'ring** *a.* unobtrusive, shy

retort' *vt.* reply; repay in kind, retaliate; hurl back (charge etc.) —*vi.* reply with counidercharge —*n.* vigorous reply or repartee; vessel with bent neck used for distilling

retouch' *vt.* touch up, improve by new touches, *esp.* of paint etc.

retrace' *vt.* go back over (a route etc.) again

retract' *v.* draw back, recant —**retract'able, -ible** *a.* —**retrac'tion** *n.* drawing or taking back, *esp.* of statement etc. —**retrac'tor** *n.* muscle; surgical instrument

retread' [-tred] *vt.* renovate worn rubber tyre —*n.* [rē'-] renovated tyre

retreat' *vi.* move back from any position; retire —*n.* act of, or military signal for, retiring; withdrawal; place to which anyone

retires; refuge; sunset call on bugle

retrench' *vt.* reduce expenditure, *esp.* by dismissing staff; cut down —**retrench'ment** *n.*

retribu'tion *n.* recompense, *esp.* for evil deeds; vengeance —**retrib'utive** *a.*

retrieve' *vt.* fetch back again; restore; rescue from ruin; recover, *esp.* information from computer; regain —**retriev'able** *a.* —**retriev'al** *n.* —**retriev'er** *n.* dog trained to retrieve game

ret'roact *vi.* react; act in opposite direction —**retroac'tive** *a.* applying or referring to the past —**retroac'tively** *adv.*

ret'roflex *a.* bent, curved backwards

ret'rograde *a.* going backwards, reverting; reactionary —**retrogres'sion** *n.* —**retrogres'sive** *a.*

ret'rorocket *n.* rocket engine to slow or reverse spacecraft etc.

ret'rospect *n.* looking back, survey of past —**retrospec'tion** *n.* —**retrospec'tive** *a.*

retrousse' [-trōōs'ā] *a.* turned upwards, pug

retsi'na [-sē'-] *n.* Greek wine

return' *vi.* go, come back —*vt.* give, send back; report officially; elect —*n.* returning, being returned; profit; official report; return ticket —**returning officer** one conducting election —**return ticket** one allowing passenger to travel to and from a place

reun'ion *n.* gathering of people who have been apart

Rev. Revelation(s); Reverend

rev *inf.* *n.* revolution (of engine) —*v.* (*oft.* with up) increase speed of revolution (of engine)

reval'ue *v.* adjust exchange value of currency upwards —**revalua'tion** *n.*

revamp' *vt.* renovate, restore

reveal' vt. make known; show —**revela'tion** n.

reveill'e [-val'i] n. morning bugle call etc. to waken soldiers

rev'el vi. take pleasure (in); make merry (-ll-) —n. (usu. pl.) merrymaking —**rev'eller** n. —**rev'elry** n. festivity

rev'enant n. something, esp. ghost, that returns

revenge' n. retaliation for wrong done; act that satisfies this; desire for this —vt. avenge; make retaliation for —v.refl. avenge oneself —**revenge'ful** a. vindictive; resentful

rev'enue n. income, esp. of state, as taxes etc. —**Inland Revenue** government department that administers and collects direct taxes eg income tax

rever'berate v. echo, resound, throw back (sound etc.) —**reverbera'tion** n.

revere' [-vēr'] vt. hold in great regard or religious respect —**rev'erence** n. revering; awe mingled with respect and esteem; veneration —**rev'erend** a. (esp. as prefix to clergyman's name) worthy of reverence —**rev'erent** a. showing reverence —**reveren'tial** a. marked by reverence

rev'erie n. daydream, absent-minded state

revers' [-vēr'] n. part of garment which is turned back, eg lapel

reverse' v. (of vehicle) (cause to) move backwards —vt. turn upside down or other way round; change completely —n. opposite, contrary; side opposite, obverse; defeat; reverse gear —a. opposite, contrary —**rever'sal** n. —**rever'sible** a. —**reverse charge** telephone call made at recipient's expense —**reverse gear** mechanism enabling vehicle to move backwards

revert' vi. return to former state; come back to subject; refer to a second time; turn backwards —**rever'sion** n. (of property) rightful passing to owner or designated heir etc. —**revert'ed** a. —**revert'ible** a.

revet'ment n. facing of stone, sand bags etc. for wall

review' [-vyōō'] vt. examine; look back on; reconsider; hold, make, write review of —n. general survey; critical notice of book etc.; periodical with critical articles; inspection of troops —**review'er** n. writer of reviews

revile' vt. be viciously scornful of, abuse —**revi'ler** n.

revise' [-vīz'] vt. look over and correct; restudy (work done previously) in preparation for an examination; change, alter —**revi'ser** n. —**revi'sion** n. re-examination for purpose of correcting; revising of notes, subject for an examination; revised copy

revive' v. bring, come back to life, vigour, use etc. —**revi'val** n. reviving, esp. of religious fervour —**revi'valist** n. organizer of religious revival

revoke' vt. take back, withdraw; cancel —**rev'ocable** a. —**revoca'tion** n. repeal

revolt' [-ō-] n. rebellion —vi. rise in rebellion; feel disgust —vt. affect with disgust —**revolt'ing** a. disgusting, horrible

revolve' vi. turn round, rotate; be centred on —vt. rotate —**revolu'tion** [-lōō'-] n. violent overthrow of government; great change; complete rotation, turning or spinning round —**revolu'tionary** a./n. —**revolu'tionize** vt. change considerably; bring about revolution in

revol'ver n. repeating pistol with revolving magazine

revue' n. theatrical entertainment with topical sketches and songs

revul'sion n. sudden violent change of feeling; marked repugnance or abhorrence

reward' vt. pay, make return for service, conduct etc. —n. —**reward'ing** a. giving personal satisfaction, worthwhile

RFC Rugby Football Club

rhap'sody n. enthusiastic or high-flown (musical) composition or utterance —**rhapsod'ic** a. —**rhap'sodist** n. —**rhap'sodize** v.

rhe'a n. S Amer. three-toed ostrich

rhe'buck n. brownish-grey S Afr. antelope

rheol'ogy n. science of the study of the deformation and flow of matter —**rheol'ogist** n.

rhe'ostat n. instrument for regulating the value of the resistance in an electric circuit

rhe'sus n. small, long-tailed monkey of S Asia —**rhesus factor** (also **Rh factor**) feature distinguishing different types of human blood

rhet'oric n. art of effective speaking or writing; artificial or exaggerated language —**rhetor'ical** [-o'ri-] a. —**rhetor'ical** [-o'ri-] a. (of question) not requiring an answer —**rhetori'cian** n.

rheum [room] n. watery discharge, mucus; catarrh —**rheum'y** a.

rheum'atism [room'-] n. painful inflammation of joints or muscles —**rheumat'ic** a./n. —**rheu'matoid** a. of, like rheumatism

Rh factor see RHESUS

rhinoc'eros [-os'-] n. large thick-skinned animal with one or two horns on nose

rho'dium n. hard metal like platinum —**rho'dic** a.

rhododen'dron n. evergreen flowering shrub

rhom'bus, rhomb [rom] n. equilateral but not right-angled parallelogram, diamond-shaped figure —**rhom'boid** a.

rhon'chus [-kəs] n. rattling or wheezing sound, as of disordered respiration

rhu'barb n. garden plant of which the fleshy stalks are cooked and eaten as fruit; laxative from root of allied Chinese plant

rhyme, rime n. identity of sounds at ends of lines of verse, or in words; word or syllable identical in sound to another; verse marked by rhyme —vt. make rhymes —**rhy'mer, ri'mer** n.

rhythm [riTH'əm] n. measured beat or flow, esp. of words, music etc. —**rhyth'mic(al)** a. —**rhyth'mically** adv.

RI religious instruction

rib' n. one of curved bones springing from spine and forming framework of upper part of body; cut of meat including rib(s); curved timber or framework of boat; raised series of rows in knitting etc. —vt. furnish, mark with ribs; knit to form a rib pattern (**-bb-**) —**ribb'ing** n.

rib' vt. inf. tease, ridicule

rib'ald a. irreverent, scurrilous; indecent —n. ribald person —**rib'aldry** n. vulgar, indecent talk

ribb'on n. narrow band of fabric used for trimming, tying etc.; long strip or line of anything —**ribbon development** building of houses along main road leading out of town etc.

ribofla'vin [rī-] n. form of vitamin B

rice n. Eastern cereal plant; its seeds as food —**rice paper** fine, edible Chinese paper

rich a. wealthy; fertile; abounding; valuable; (of food) containing much fat or sugar; mellow; amusing —n. the wealthy classes —**rich'es** pl.n. wealth —**rich'ly** adv.

rick [1] n. stack of hay etc.

rick [2] vt./n. sprain, wrench

rick'ets n. disease of children marked by softening of bones, bow legs etc., caused by vitamin D deficiency —**rick'ety** a. shaky, insecure, unstable; suffering from rickets

rick'shaw n. light two-wheeled man-drawn Asian vehicle

ric'ochet [-shā] vi. (of bullet) rebound or be deflected by solid surface or water —n. bullet or shot to which this happens

rid vt. clear, relieve of; free; deliver (**rid**, **ridd'ing**) —**rid'dance** n. clearance; act of ridding; deliverance; relief

ridd'en pp. of RIDE —a. (in combination) afflicted, affected, as **disease-ridden**

rid'dle [1] n. question made puzzling to test one's ingenuity; enigma; puzzling thing, person —vi. speak in, make riddles

rid'dle [2] vt. pierce with many holes —n. coarse sieve for gravel etc. —**riddled with** full of, esp. holes

ride v. sit on and control or propel (horse, bicycle etc.); be carried on or across —vi. go on horseback or in vehicle; lie at anchor —vt. travel over (**rode**, **ridd'en**, **ri'ding**) —n. journey on horse etc., or in any vehicle; riding track —**ri'der** n. one who rides; supplementary clause; addition to a document; mathematical problem on given proposition —**ri'derless** a

ridge n. long narrow hill; long, narrow elevation on surface; line of meeting of two sloping surfaces —vt. form into ridges

ridic'ulous a. deserving to be laughed at, absurd, foolish —**rid'icule** n. treatment of person or thing as ridiculous —vt. laugh at, deride

ri'ding n. former administrative district of Yorkshire

ries'ling [rēz'-] n. dry white wine; type of grape used to make it

rife a. prevalent, common

rif'fle v. flick through (pages etc.) quickly

riff'raff n. rabble, disreputable people

ri'fle vt. search and rob; ransack; make spiral grooves in (gun barrel etc.) —n. firearm with long barrel —**ri'fling** n. arrangement of grooves in gun barrel; pillaging

rift n. crack, split, cleft

rig vt. provide (ship) with spars, ropes etc.; equip; set up, esp. as makeshift; arrange in dishonest way (**-gg-**) —n. way ship's masts and sails are arranged; apparatus for drilling for oil and gas; **US** articulated lorry; style of dress —**rigg'er** n. —**rigg'ing** n. ship's spars and ropes

right [rīt] a. just; in accordance with truth and duty; true; correct; proper; of side that faces east when front is turned to north; *Politics* conservative or reactionary (also **right wing**); straight; upright; of outer or more finished side of fabric —vt. bring back to vertical position; do justice to —vi. come back to vertical position —n. claim, title etc. allowed or due; what is right, just or due; conservative political party; punch, blow with right hand —adv. straight; properly; very; on or to right side —**right'ful** a. —**right'ly** adv. —**right angle** angle of 90 degrees —**right of way**

Law right to pass over someone's land; path used

right'eous [rī'chəs] *a.* just, upright; godly; virtuous; good; honest —**right'eousness** *n.*

rig'id [rij'-] *a.* inflexible; harsh, stiff —**rigid'ity** *n.*

rig'marole *n.* meaningless string of words; long, complicated procedure

ri'gor [*or* rig'-] *n.* sudden coldness attended by shivering —**rigor mortis** stiffening of body after death

rig'our *n.* harshness, severity, strictness; hardship —**rig'orous** *a.* stern, harsh, severe

rile *vt. inf.* anger, annoy

rill *n.* small stream

rim *n.* edge, border, margin; outer ring of wheel —**rimmed** *a.* bordered, edged

rime *n.* hoarfrost —**ri'my** *a.*

ri'mu [rē'moō] *n.* tall N.Z. tree, red pine; its valuable cabinet wood

rind [-ī-] *n.* outer coating of fruits *etc.*

rin'derpest *n.* malignant infectious disease of cattle

ring[1] *n.* circle of gold *etc.*, *esp.* for finger; any circular band, coil, rim *etc.*; circle of persons; enclosed area, *esp.* roped-in square for boxing *etc.*; any ring round; mark (bird *etc.*) with ring —**ring'er** *n.* one who rings bells; *sl.* (*esp.* in **dead ringer**) person, thing apparently identical to another —**ring'bark** *vt.* kill tree by cutting bark round trunk —**ring'leader** *n.* instigator of mutiny, riot *etc.* —**ring'let** *n.* curly lock of hair —**ring road** main road that bypasses a town (centre) —**ring'worm** *n.* fungal skin disease in circular patches

ring[2] *vi.* give out clear resonant sound, as bell; resound —*vt.* cause (bell) to sound; telephone

(**rang** *pt.*, **rung** *pp.*) —*n.* a ringing; telephone call

rink *n.* sheet of ice for skating or curling; floor for roller skating

rink'hals [-hows] *n.* S Afr. ring-necked cobra

rinse [-s] *vt.* remove soap (from washed clothes, hair *etc.*) by applying clean water; wash lightly —*n.* a rinsing; liquid to tint hair

ri'ot *n.* tumult, disorder; loud revelry; disorderly, unrestrained disturbance; profusion —*vi.* make, engage in riot —**ri'otous** *a.* unruly, rebellious, wanton —**riot shield** rectangular shield used by police or servicemen during a riot

RIP requiescat in pace (*Lat.*, rest in peace)

rip[1] *vt.* cut, tear away, slash, rend (-**pp-**) —*n.* rent, tear —**rip'cord** *n.* cord pulled to open parachute —**rip'saw** *n.* handsaw with coarse teeth (used for cutting wood along grain) —**rip off** *sl.* steal; *sl.* overcharge —**rip off** *n. sl.* act of stealing, overcharging *etc.*

rip[2] *n.* strong current, *esp.* one moving away from the shore

ripa'rian [rī-] *a.* of, on banks of river

ripe *a.* ready to be reaped, eaten *etc.*; matured; (of judgment *etc.*) sound —**ri'pen** *v.* grow ripe; mature

riposte' *n.* verbal retort; counterstroke; *Fencing* quick lunge after parry

rip'ple *n.* slight wave, ruffling of surface; sound like ripples of water —*vi.* flow, form into little waves; (of sounds) rise and fall gently —*vt.* form ripples on

rise [rīz] *vi.* get up; move upwards; appear above horizon; reach higher level; increase in value or price; rebel; adjourn;

have its source (**rose, ris'en, ri'sing**) —n. rising; upslope; increase, esp. of wages —**ri'ser** n. one who rises, esp. from bed; vertical part of step —**ri'sing** n. revolt —a. increasing in rank, maturity

ris'ible [riz'-] a. inclined to laugh; laughable —**risibil'ity** n.

risk n. chance of disaster or loss —vt. venture; put in jeopardy; take chance of —**risk'ily** adv. —**risk'y** a. dangerous; hazardous

risott'o [-zot'-] n. dish of rice cooked in stock with various other ingredients

ris'qué [-kā] a. suggestive of indecency

riss'ole n. dish of fish or meat minced, coated with egg and breadcrumbs and fried

rite n. formal practice or custom, esp. religious —**rit'ual** n. prescribed order or book of rites; regular, stereotyped action or behaviour —a. concerning rites —**rit'ualism** n. practice of ritual —**rit'ualist** n.

ri'val n. one that competes with another for favour, success etc. —vt. vie with (**-ll-**) —a. in position of rival —**ri'valry** n. keen competition

riv'en a. split

riv'er n. large natural stream of water; copious flow

riv'et n. bolt for fastening metal plates, the end being put through holes and then beaten flat —vt. fasten with rivets; cause to be fixed or held firmly, esp. (fig.) in surprise, horror etc. —**riv'eter** n.

riv'ulet n. small stream

RL Rugby League

rly. railway

RN Royal Navy

RNLI Royal National Lifeboat Institution

RNZAF Royal New Zealand Air Force

RNZN Royal New Zealand Navy

roach n. freshwater fish

road n. track, way prepared for passengers, vehicles etc.; direction, way; street —**road'ie** n. inf. person who transports and sets up equipment for band or group —**road'block** n. barricade across road to stop traffic for inspection etc. —**road hog** selfish, aggressive driver —**road'house** n. public house, restaurant on country route —**road metal** broken stones used in macadamizing roads —**road sense** sound judgment in driving road vehicles —**road'side** n./a. —**road'ster** n. obs. touring car; kind of bicycle —**road'works** pl.n. repairs to road, esp. blocking part of road —**road'worthy** a. (of vehicle) mechanically sound

roam v. wander about, rove —**roam'er** n.

roan a. (of horses) having coat in which main colour is thickly interspersed with another, esp. bay, sorrel or chestnut mixed with white or grey —n. roan horse

roar [rawr] v. make or utter loud deep hoarse sound as of lion, thunder, voice in anger etc. —n. such a sound —**roar'ing** a. inf. brisk and profitable —adv. noisily

roast v. bake, cook in closed oven; cook by exposure to open fire; make, be very hot —n. roasted joint —a. roasted —**roast'ing** n. esp. inf. severe criticism, scolding

rob vt. plunder, steal from; pillage, defraud (**-bb-**) —**robb'er** n. —**robb'ery** n.

robe n. long outer garment, often denoting rank or office —vt. dress —vi. put on robes, vestments

rob'in *n.* small brown bird with red breast

ro'bot *n.* automated machine, *esp.* performing functions in human manner; person of machine-like efficiency; SA traffic lights —**robot'ics** *n.* science of designing and using robots; robot dancing, body popping

robust' *a.* sturdy, strong —**robust'ness** *n.*

roc [rok] *n.* monstrous bird of Arabian mythology

roch'et *n.* garment like surplice, with tight sleeves, worn by bishops

rock¹ *n.* stone; large rugged mass of stone; hard sweet in sticks —**rock'ery** *n.* mound or grotto of stones or rocks for plants in a garden —**rock'y** *a.* having rocks; rugged —**rock bottom** lowest possible level —**rock rabbit** SA dassie, hyrax

rock² *v.* (cause to) sway to and fro —*n.* style of pop music derived from rock-and-roll —**rock'er** *n.* curved piece of wood *etc.* on which thing may rock; rocking chair —**rock-and-roll** *n.* popular dance rhythm —**off one's rocker** *inf.* insane

rock'et¹ *n.* self-propelling device powered by burning of explosive contents (used as firework, for display, signalling, line carrying, weapon *etc.*); vehicle propelled by rocket engine, as weapon or carrying spacecraft —*vi.* move fast, *esp.* upwards, as rocket —**rock'etry** *n.*

rock'et² *n.* kinds of flowering plant

roco'co [rə-kō'kō] *a.* of furniture, architecture *etc.* having much conventional decoration in style of early 18th cent. work in France; tastelessly florid

rod *n.* slender straight bar, stick; cane; old measure (5½ yards)

rode *pt. of* RIDE

ro'dent *n.* gnawing animal, *eg* rat

ro'deo [*or* -dā'ō] *n.* US, A display of skills, competition, with bareback riding, cattle handling techniques *etc.*

roe¹ *n.* small species of deer

roe² *n.* mass of eggs in fish

roent'gen [ront'-] *n.* measuring unit of radiation dose

Roga'tion Days three days preceding Ascension day

rogue [rōg] *n.* rascal, knave, scoundrel; mischief-loving person or child; wild beast of savage temper, living apart from herd —**ro'guish** [-gish] *a.* —**ro'guery** *n.*

rois'ter *vi.* be noisy, boisterous, bragging —**rois'terer** *n.* reveller

role, rôle *n.* actor's part; specific task or function

roll [rōl] *v.* move by turning over and over —*vt.* wind round; smooth out with roller —*vi.* move, sweep along; undulate; of ship, swing from side to side; of aircraft, turn about a line from nose to tail in flight —*n.* act of lying down and turning over and over or from side to side; piece of paper *etc.* rolled up; any object thus shaped, as *meat roll, Swiss roll, etc.*; list, catalogue; bread baked into small oval or round; continuous sound, as of drums, thunder *etc.* —**roll'er** *n.* cylinder of wood, stone, metal *etc.* used for pressing, crushing, smoothing, supporting thing to be moved, winding thing on *etc.*; long wave of sea —**roll call** act, time of calling over list of names, as in schools or army —**rolled gold** metal coated with a thin layer of gold —**roller bearings** bearings of hardened steel rollers —**roller skate** skate with wheels instead of runner —**roller skating** —**roller towel** loop of towel on roller —**rolling pin** cylindrical roller for pastry or dough —**rolling stock** locomotives, carriages *etc.* of railway —**roll-top** *a./n.* in desk, flexible lid sliding in grooves —**roll up** *inf.* appear, turn up

rol'licking *a.* boisterously jovial and merry

ro'ly-po'ly *n.* pudding of suet pastry covered with jam and rolled up —*a.* round, plump

ROM *Computers* read only memory

Rom. Romans

Ro'man *a.* of Rome or Church of Rome —**Roman Catholic** member of that section of Christian Church which acknowledges supremacy of the Pope —**Roman numerals** letters I, V, X, L, C, D, M used to represent numbers in manner of Romans —**roman type** plain upright letters, ordinary style of printing

Romance[1] *a.* of vernacular language of certain countries, developed from Latin, as French, Spanish *etc.* —*n.*

romance[1] *n.* love affair, *esp.* intense and happy one; mysterious or exciting quality; tale of chivalry; tale with scenes remote from ordinary life; literature like this; picturesque falsehood —*vi.* exaggerate, fantasize —**roman'cer** *n.* —**roman'tic** *a.* characterized by romance; of or dealing with love; of literature *etc.*, preferring passion and imagination to proportion and finish —*n.* —**roman'ticism** *n.* —**roman'ticist** *n.* —**roman'ticize** *vi.*

romanesque' [-esk'] *a./n.* (in) style of round-arched vaulted architecture of period between Classical and Gothic

Rom'any *n.* gypsy; gypsy language —*a.* gypsy

romp *vi.* run, play wildly, joyfully —*n.* spell of romping —**rom'pers** *pl.n.* child's overall —**romp home** win easily

ronda'vel [-dah'-] *n.* **SA** circular building, oft. thatched

ron'deau [-dō] *n.* short poem with opening words used as refrain (*pl.* **-x**) —**ron'del** *n.* extended rondeau —**ron'delet** *n.* short rondeau

ron'do *n.* piece of music with leading theme to which return is continually made

Ro'neo R duplicating machine —*v.* duplicate letters *etc.* by this means

rönt'gen *n. see* ROENTGEN

rood [rōōd] *n.* the Cross; crucifix; quarter of acre —**rood screen** one separating nave from choir

roof [rōōf] *n.* outside upper covering of building; top, covering part of anything —*vt.* put roof on, over

rooi'bos [roi'-] *n.* S Afr. redleafed tree

rooi'kat [roi'-] *n.* S Afr. lynx

rook[1] *n.* bird of crow family —*vt. sl.* swindle, cheat —**rook'ery** *n.* colony of rooks

rook[2] *n.* piece at chess (*also* castle)

rook'ie *n. inf.* recruit, *esp.* in army

room [rōōm] *n.* space; space enough; division of house; scope, opportunity —*pl.* lodgings —**room'y** *a.* spacious

roost [-ōō-] *n.* perch for fowls —*vi.* perch —**roost'er** *n.* **US** domestic cock

root[1] [rōōt] *n.* part of plant that grows down into earth and conveys nourishment to plant; plant with edible root, *eg* carrot; vital part; source, origin, original cause of anything; *Anatomy* embedded portion of tooth, nail, hair *etc.*; primitive word from which other words are derived; factor of a quantity which, when multiplied by itself the number of times indicated, gives the quantity —*v.* (cause to) take root; pull by roots; dig, burrow

root[2] [root] *vi. inf.* cheer; applaud; encourage —**root'er** *n.*

rope *n.* thick cord —*vt.* secure, mark off with rope —**ro'piness** *n.* —**ro'py** *a. inf.* inferior, inadequate; *inf.* not well; (of liquid) sticky and stringy

ro'sary *n.* series of prayers; string of beads for counting these prayers as they are recited; rose garden

rose[1] *n.* shrub, climbing plant *usu.* with prickly stems and fragrant flowers; the flower; perforated flat nozzle for hose *etc.*; pink colour —*a.* of this colour —**ro'seate** *a.* rose-coloured, rosy —**rosette'** *n.* rose-shaped bunch of ribbon; rose-shaped architectural ornament —**ro'sy** *a.* flushed; hopeful, promising —**rose-coloured** *a.* having colour of rose; unwarrantably optimistic —**rose window** circular window with series of mullions branching from centre —**rose'wood** *n.* fragrant wood —**rose of Sharon** low, spreading shrub with yellow flowers

rose[1] *pt. of* RISE

ro'sé [-zā] *n.* pink wine

rose'mary *n.* evergreen fragrant flowering shrub

Rosicru'cian [rōz-] *n.* member of secret order devoted to occult law —*a.* —**Rosicru'cianism** *n.*

ros'in [roz'-] *n.* resin

ros'ter *n.* list or plan showing turns of duty

ros'trum *n.* platform, stage, pulpit; beak or bill of a bird (*pl.* **-trums, -tra**)

rot *v.* decompose naturally; corrupt (**-tt-**) —*n.* decay, putrefaction; any disease producing decomposition of tissue; *inf.* nonsense —**rott'en** *a.* decomposed, putrid; corrupt

ro'ta *n.* roster, list

ro'tary *a.* (of movement) circular; operated by rotary movement —**rotate'** *v.* (cause to) move round centre or on pivot —**rota'tion** *n.* rotating; regular succession —**ro'tatory** *a.* —**Rotary Club** one of international association of businessmen's clubs —**Rota'rian** *n.* member of such

rote *n.* mechanical repetition —**by rote** by memory

rotiss'erie *n.* (electrically driven) rotating spit for cooking meat

ro'tor *n.* revolving portion of a dynamo motor or turbine

rott'en *see* ROT

rotund' *a.* round; plump; sonorous —**rotund'ity** *n.*

rou'ble [roō-] *n.* Russian monetary unit

rouge [roōzh] *n.* red powder, cream used to colour cheeks —*v.* colour with rouge

rough [ruf] *a.* not smooth, of irregular surface; violent, stormy, boisterous; rude; uncivil; lacking refinement; approximate; in preliminary form —*vt.* make rough; plan out approximately; (*with* it) live without usual comforts *etc.* —*n.* rough state or area; sketch —**rough'en** *vt.* —**rough'ly** *adv.* —**rough'age** *n.* unassimilated portion of food promoting proper intestinal action —**rough'cast** *a.* coated with mixture of lime and gravel —*n.* such mixture —*vt.* coat with it —**rough diamond** trustworthy but unsophisticated person —**rough-hew** *vt.* shape roughly —**rough'house** *n./v. sl.* fight, row

roulette¹ [rōō-] *n.* game of chance played with revolving wheel and ball

round [-ow-] *a.* spherical, cylindrical, circular, curved; full, complete; roughly correct; large, considerable; plump; positive —*adv.* with circular or circuitous course —*n.* thing round in shape; recurrent duties; stage in competition; customary course, as of milkman; game (of golf); one of several periods in boxing match *etc.*; cartridge for firearm; rung; movement in circle —*prep.* about; on all sides of —*v.* make, become round —*vt.* move round —**round'ers** *pl.n.* ball game —**round'ly** *adv.* plainly; thoroughly —**round'about** *n.* revolving circular platform on which people ride for amusement; road junction at which traffic passes round a central island —*a.* not straightforward —**round robin** petition signed with names in circle to conceal order —**round up** drive (cattle) together; collect and arrest criminals

round'el [-ow-] *n.* rondeau; small disc —**round'elay** *n.* simple song with refrain

rouse [rowz] *vt.* wake up, stir up, excite to action; cause to rise —*vi.* waken —**roust'about** [rowst-] *n.* labourer on oil rig

rout [rowt] *n.* overwhelming defeat, disorderly retreat; noisy rabble —*vt.* scatter and put to flight

route [rōōt] *n.* road, chosen way —**route'march** *n.* long march undertaken for training purposes

routine¹ [rōō-tēn¹] *n.* regularity of procedure, unvarying round; regular course —*a.* ordinary, regular

roux [rōō] *n.* fat and flour cooked together as basis for sauces

rove *v.* wander, roam —**ro'ver** *n.* one who roves; pirate

row¹ [rō] *n.* number of things in a straight line; rank; file; line

row² [rō] *v.* propel boat by oars —*n.* spell of rowing —**rowing boat**

row³ *inf. n.* dispute; disturbance —*vi.* quarrel noisily

row'an [or rō'-] *n.* native British tree producing bright red berries, mountain ash

rowd'y *a.* disorderly, noisy and rough —*n.* person like this

row'el *n.* small wheel with points on spur

row'lock [rol'ək] *n.* appliance on gunwale of a boat serving as point of leverage for oar

roy'al *a.* of, worthy of, befitting, patronized by, king or queen; splendid —**roy'alist** *n.* supporter of monarchy —**roy'alty** *n.* royal dignity or power; royal persons; payment to owner of land for right to work minerals, or to inventor for use of his invention; payment to author depending on sales

RPI retail price index

rpm revolutions per minute

RSPCA Royal Society for the Prevention of Cruelty to Animals

RSVP répondez s'il vous plaît (*Fr.* please reply)

RU Rugby Union

rub *vt.* apply pressure to with circular or backwards and forwards movement; clean, polish, dry, thus; pass hand over; abrade, chafe; remove by friction —*vi.* come into contact accompanied by friction; become frayed or worn by friction (**-bb-**) —*n.* rubbing; impediment

rubb'er¹ *n.* coagulated sap of rough, elastic consistency, of certain tropical trees; piece of rubber *etc.* used for erasing; thing for rubbing; person who rubs —*a.*

of rubber —**rubb'erize** vt. coat, impregnate, treat with rubber —**rubb'ery** a. —**rubber stamp** device for imprinting dates etc.; automatic authorization

rubb'er[2] n. series of odd number of games or contests at various games; two out of three games won

rubb'ish n. refuse, waste material; anything worthless; trash, nonsense —**rubb'ishy** a. valueless

rub'ble n. fragments of stone etc.; builders' rubbish

rubell'a n. mild contagious viral disease, German measles

ru'bicund [rōō'-] a. ruddy

ru'bric [rōō'-] n. title, heading; direction in liturgy; instruction

ru'by [rōō'-] n. precious red gem; its colour —a. of this colour

ruck[1] n. crowd; common herd; rank and file; Rugby loose scrummage or maul

ruck[2] n. crease —v. make, become wrinkled

ruck'sack n. pack carried on back, knapsack

ruck'us n. inf. uproar, disturbance

ruc'tion n. inf. noisy disturbance

rudd'er n. flat piece hinged to boat's stern or rear of aircraft to steer by

rudd'y a. of fresh or healthy red colour; rosy; florid

rude a. impolite; coarse; vulgar; primitive; roughly made; uneducated; sudden, violent —**rude'ly** adv.

ru'diments [rōō'-] pl.n. elements, first principles —**rudi-men'tary** a.

rue[1] [rōō] v. grieve for; regret; deplore; repent —n. obs. repentance —**rue'ful** a. sorry; regretful; dejected; deplorable —**rue'fully** adv.

rue[2] [rōō] n. plant with evergreen bitter leaves

ruff[1] n. starched and frilled collar; natural collar of feathers, fur etc. on some birds and animals; type of shore bird —**ruf'fle** vt. rumple, disorder; annoy, put out; frill, pleat —n. frilled trimming

ruff[2] n./v. Cards trump

ruff'ian n. violent, lawless person —**ruff'ianism** n. —**ruff'ianly** a.

rug n. small, oft. shaggy or thick-piled floor mat; thick woollen wrap, coverlet

rug'by n. form of football in which the ball may be carried in the hands (also inf. **rugg'er**)

rugg'ed a. rough; broken; unpolished; harsh, austere

ru'in [rōō'-] n. decay, destruction; downfall; fallen or broken state; loss of wealth, position etc. —pl. ruined buildings etc. —vt. reduce to ruins; bring to decay or destruction; spoil; impoverish —**ru-ina'tion** n. —**ru'inous** a. causing or characterized by ruin or destruction —**ru'inously** adv.

rule n. principle; precept; authority; government; what is usual; control; measuring stick —vt. govern; decide; mark with straight lines; draw (line) —**ru'ler** n. one who governs; stick for measuring or ruling lines

rum n. spirit distilled from sugar cane

rum'ba n. rhythmic dance, orig. Cuban; music for it

rum'ble vi. make noise as of distant thunder, heavy vehicle etc. —n. such noise

rumbust'ious a. boisterous, unruly

ru'minate [rōō'-] vi. chew cud; ponder over; meditate —**ru'mi-nant** a./n. cud-chewing (animal) —**rumina'tion** n. quiet meditation and reflection —**ru'minative** a.

rumm'age v. search thoroughly —n.

rumm'y n. card game

ru'mour [roo'mə] n. hearsay, common talk, unproved statement —vt. put round as, by way of, rumour

rump n. tail end; buttocks

rum'ple v./n. crease, wrinkle

rum'pus n. disturbance; noise and confusion

run vi. move with more rapid gait than walking; go quickly; flow; flee; compete in race, contest, election; revolve; continue; function; travel according to schedule; fuse; melt; spread over; have certain meaning —vt. cross by running; expose oneself (to risk etc.); cause to run; (of newspaper) print, publish; land and dispose of (smuggled goods); manage; operate (**ran** pt., **run** pp., **runn'ing** pr.p.) —n. act, spell of running; rush; tendency; course; period; sequence; heavy demand; enclosure for domestic fowls, animals; ride in car; series of unravelled stitches, ladder; score of one at cricket; steep snow-covered course for skiing —**runn'er** n. racer; messenger; curved piece of wood on which sleigh slides; any similar appliance; slender stem of plant running along ground forming new roots at intervals; strip of cloth, carpet —**running** a. continuous, consecutive; flowing; discharging; effortless; entered for race; used for running —n. act of moving or flowing quickly; management —**runn'y** a. tending to flow or exude moisture —**run'down** n. summary —**run-down** a. exhausted —**run down** stop working; reduce; exhaust; denigrate —**run'way** n. level stretch where aircraft take off and land —**in the running** having fair chance in competition

rune n. character of earliest Germanic alphabet; magic sign —**ru'nic** a.

rung 1 n. crossbar or spoke, esp. in ladder

rung 2 pp. of RING 1

runn'el n. gutter; small brook or rivulet

running see RUN

runt n. small animal, below usual size of species; offens. undersized person

rupee' n. monetary unit of India and Pakistan

rup'ture n. breaking, breach; hernia —v. break; burst, sever

rur'al [roor'-] a. of the country; rustic —**rur'alize** v.

rus'bank [roos'-] n. SA wooden bench, settle

ruse [-z] n. stratagem, trick

rush 1 vt. impel, carry along violently and rapidly; take by sudden assault —vi. cause to hurry; move violently or rapidly —n. rushing, charge; hurry; eager demand for; heavy current (of air, water etc.) —a. done with speed; characterized by speed —**rush hour** period at beginning and end of day when many people are travelling to and from work

rush 2 n. marsh plant with slender pithy stem; the stems as material for baskets —**rush'y** a. full of rushes

rusk n. kind of biscuit, esp. used for feeding babies

russ'et a. reddish-brown —n. the colour

rust n. reddish-brown coating formed on iron by oxidation; disease of plants —v. contract, affect with rust —**rust'y** a. coated with rust, of rust colour; out of practice —**rust'proof** a.

rust'ic *a.* of, or as of, country people; rural; of rude manufacture; made of untrimmed branches —*n.* countryman, peasant —**rust'icate** *vt.* banish from university —*vi.* live a country life —**rustica'tion** *n.* —**rustic'ity** *n.*

rus'tle[1] [-sl] *vi.* make sound as of blown dead leaves *etc.* —*n.* this sound

rus'tle[2] [-sl] *vt.* US steal (cattle) —**rus'tler** *n.* US cattle thief

rut[1] *n.* furrow made by wheel; settled habit or way of living; groove —**rutt'y** *a.*

rut[2] *n.* periodic sexual excitement among animals —*vi.* be under influence of this (-tt-)

ruth'less [rōōth'-] *a.* pitiless, merciless —**ruth'lessly** *adv.*

rye *n.* grain used for fodder and bread; plant bearing it; whisky made from rye

rye-grass *n.* kinds of grass cultivated for fodder

S

S Saint; South(ern); *Chem.* sulphur

s second(s); shilling; singular

SA Salvation Army; South Africa; South Australia

Sabb'ath *n.* Saturday, devoted to worship and rest from work in Judaism and certain Christian Churches; Sunday, observed by Christians as day of worship and rest —**sabbat'ical** *a./n.* (denoting) leave granted to university staff *etc.* for study

sa'ble *n.* small weasellike Arctic animal; its fur; black —*a.* black

sab'ot [-bō] *n.* shoe made of wood, or with wooden sole

sab'otage [-tahzh] *n.* intentional damage done to roads, machines

etc., *esp.* secretly in war —*v.* —**saboteur'** *n.*

sa'bre [-bər] *n.* curved cavalry sword

sac *n.* pouchlike structure in an animal or vegetable body

sacc'harin [sak'ə-] *n.* artificial sweetener —**sacc'harine** *a.* *lit./fig.* excessively sweet

sacerdo'tal [sas-] *a.* of priests

sach'et [sash'ā] *n.* small envelope or bag, *esp.* one holding liquid, as shampoo

sack *n.* large bag, *orig.* of coarse material; pillaging; *inf.* dismissal; *sl.* bed —*vt.* pillage (captured town); *inf.* dismiss —**sack'ing** *n.* material for sacks —**sack'cloth** *n.* coarse fabric used for sacks

sac'rament *n.* one of certain ceremonies of Christian Church *esp.* Eucharist —**sacramen'tal** *a.*

sa'cred *a.* dedicated, regarded as holy; set apart, reserved; inviolable; connected with, intended for religious use —**sa'credly** *adv.*

sac'rifice *n.* giving something up for sake of something else; act of giving up; thing so given up; making of offering to a god; thing offered —*vt.* offer as sacrifice; give up; sell at very cheap price —**sacrifi'cial** [-fish-] *a.*

sac'rilege [-lij] *n.* misuse, desecration of something sacred —**sacrileg'ious** *a.* profane; desecrating

sac'ristan *n.* official in charge of vestments and sacred vessels of church —**sac'risty** *n.* room where sacred vessels *etc.* are kept

sac'rosanct *a.* preserved by religious fear against desecration or violence; inviolable —**sacrosanc'tity** *n.*

sa'crum *n.* five vertebrae forming compound bone at base of spinal column

sad a. sorrowful; unsatisfactory, deplorable —**sadd'en** vt. make sad —**sad'ly** adv. —**sad'ness** n.

sad'dle n. rider's seat to fasten on horse, bicycle etc.; anything resembling a saddle; joint of mutton or venison; ridge of hill —vt. put saddle on; lay burden, responsibility on —a. resembling a saddle, as in **sadd'leback** —**sadd'ler** n. maker of saddles etc. —**sadd'lery** n.

sa'dism n. form of (sexual) perversion marked by love of inflicting pain —**sa'dist** n. —**sa·dis'tic** a.

s.a.e. stamped addressed envelope

safar'i n. (party making) overland (hunting) journey, esp. in Africa —**safari park** park where lions etc. may be viewed by public from cars

safe a. secure, protected; uninjured, out of danger; not involving risk; trustworthy; sure, reliable; cautious —n. strong lockable container; ventilated cupboard for meat etc. —**safe'ly** adv. —**safe'ty** n. —**safe-conduct** n. passport, permit to pass somewhere —**safe'guard** n. protection —vt. protect —**safety glass** unsplinterable glass

saff'lower n. thistlelike plant with flowers used for dye, oil

saff'ron n. crocus; orange coloured flavouring obtained from it; the colour —a. orange

sag vi. sink in middle; hang sideways; curve downwards under pressure; give way; tire; (of clothes) hang loosely (**-gg-**) —n. droop

sag'a [sahg'ə] n. legend of Norse heroes; any long (heroic) story

saga'cious a. wise —**saga'ciously** adv. —**sagac'ity** [-gas'-] n.

sage[1] n. very wise man —a. wise —**sage'ly** adv.

sage[2] n. aromatic herb

Sagitta'rius [saj-] n. (the Archer) 9th sign of zodiac, operative c. Nov. 22-Dec. 20

sa'go n. starchy cereal from powdered pith of sago palm

said [sed] pt./pp. of SAY

sail n. piece of fabric stretched to catch wind for propelling ship etc.; act of sailing; journey upon the water; ships collectively; arm of windmill —vi. travel by water; move smoothly; begin voyage —vt. navigate —**sail'or** n. seaman; one who sails —**sail'board** n. craft used for windsurfing like surfboard with mast and single sail

saint n. (title of) person formally recognized (esp. by R.C. Church) after death, as having gained by holy deeds a special place in heaven; exceptionally good person —**saint'ed** a. canonized; sacred —**saint'liness** n. holiness —**saint'ly** a. —**saintpau'lia** n. African violet

saithe n. coalfish

sake[1] n. cause, account; end, purpose —**for the sake of** on behalf of; to please or benefit

sak'e[2] [sahk'i] n. Japanese alcoholic drink made of fermented rice

salaam' [-lahm'] n. bow of salutation, mark of respect in East —vt. salute

sala'cious a. excessively concerned with sex, lewd —**salac'ity** n.

sal'ad n. mixed vegetables, or fruit, used as food without cooking —a. —**salad dressing** oil, vinegar, herbs etc. mixed together as sauce for salad

sal'amander n. variety of lizard; mythical lizardlike fire spirit

salam'i [-lahm'-] n. variety of highly-spiced sausage

sal'ary n. fixed regular payment to persons employed usu. in nonmanual work —**sal'aried** a.

sale n. selling; selling of goods at unusually low prices; auction —**sale'able** a. capable of being sold —**sales'man** n. shop assistant; one travelling to sell goods, esp. as representative of firm —**sales'manship** n. art of selling or presenting goods in most effective way

sal'icin n. substance obtained from poplars and used in medicine —**salicyl'ic** a.

sa'lient a. prominent, noticeable; jutting out —n. salient angle, esp. in fortification —**sa'lience** n. —**sa'liently** adv.

sa'line a. containing, consisting of a chemical salt, esp. common salt; salty —**salin'ity** n.

sali'va n. liquid which forms in mouth, spittle —**sal'ivary** a. —**sal'ivate** v.

Salk vaccine [sawlk] vaccine against poliomyelitis

sall'ow[1] a. of unhealthy pale or yellowish colour

sall'ow[2] n. tree or low shrub allied to the willow

sall'y n. rushing out, esp. by troops; outburst; witty remark —vi. rush; set out (**sall'ied, sall'ying**)

salm'on [sam'-] n. large silvery fish with orange-pink flesh valued as food; colour of its flesh —a. of this colour

salmonell'a pl.n. bacteria causing disease (esp. food poisoning)

sal'on n. (reception room for) guests in fashionable household; commercial premises of hairdressers, beauticians etc.

saloon' n. principal cabin or sitting room in passenger ship; public room for specified use, eg billiards; closed car with 2 or 4 doors and 4-6 seats —**saloon bar**

first-class bar in hotel etc.

salpigloss'is n. plant with bright funnel-shaped flowers

sal'sify [-fi] n. purple-flowered plant with edible root

SALT Strategic Arms Limitation Talks

salt [sawlt] n. white powdery or granular crystalline substance consisting mainly of sodium chloride, used to season or preserve food; chemical compound of acid and metal; wit —vt. season, sprinkle with, preserve with salt —**salt'less** a. —**salt'ness** n. —**salt'y** a. of, like salt —**old salt** sailor —**salt'cellar** n. small vessel for salt at table —**salt lick** deposit, block of salt licked by game, cattle etc. —**salt'pan** n. depression encrusted with salt after draining away of water —**saltpe'tre** [-tǝr] n. potassium nitrate used in gunpowder —**salt'water** n. —**with a pinch, grain, of salt** allowing for exaggeration —**worth one's salt** efficient

sal'tant a. leaping; dancing —**sal'tatory** a. —**salta'tion** n.

salu'brious [-lōō'-] a. favourable to health, beneficial —**salu'brity** n.

Salu'ki n. tall hound with silky coat

sal'utary a. wholesome, resulting in good —**sal'utarily** adv.

salute' [-lōōt'] vt. greet with words or sign; acknowledge with praise —vi. perform military salute —n. word, sign by which one greets another; motion of arm as mark of respect to superior etc. in military usage; firing of guns as military greeting of honour —**saluta'tion** [-yoo-tā'-] n.

sal'vage n. act of saving ship or other property from danger of loss; property so saved —vt.

salva'tion n. fact or state of

being saved, *esp.* of soul

salve [*or* sahv] *n.* healing ointment —*vt.* anoint with such, soothe

sal'ver *n.* (silver) tray for presentation of food, letters *etc.*

sal'via *n.* plant with blue or red flowers

sal'vo *n.* simultaneous discharge of guns *etc.* (*pl.* **-vo(e)s**)

sal volat'ile [-il-i] *n.* preparation of ammonia used to revive persons who faint *etc.*

SAM surface-to-air missile

Sam. Samuel

Samar'itan [-ma'ri-] *n.* native of ancient Samaria; benevolent person

sam'ba *n.* dance of S Amer. origin; music for it

same *a.* identical, not different, unchanged; uniform; just mentioned previously —**same'ness** *n.* similarity, sameness

sam'ite *n.* rich silk cloth

sam'ovar *n.* Russian tea urn

Samoyed' *n.* dog with thick white coat and tightly curled tail

samp *n.* SA crushed maize used for porridge

sam'pan *n.* small oriental boat

sam'phire *n.* herb found on rocks by seashore

sam'ple [sah'-] *n.* specimen —*vt.* take, give sample of; try; test; select —**sam'pler** *n.* beginner's exercise in embroidery —**sam'pling** *n.* the taking of samples; sample

sam'urai [-oo-rī] *n.* member of ancient Japanese warrior caste

sanator'ium *n.* hospital, *esp.* for chronically ill; health resort (*pl.* **-riums, -ria**) —**san'atory,** **san'ative** *a.* curative

sanc'tify *vt.* set apart as holy; free from sin (**-fied, -fying**) —**sanctifica'tion** *n.* —**sanc'tity** *n.* saintliness; sacredness; inviolability —**sanc'tuary** *n.* holy

place; part of church nearest altar; place where fugitive was safe from arrest or violence; place protected by law where animals *etc.* can live without interference —**sanc'tum** *n.* sacred place or shrine; person's private room

sanctimo'nious *a.* making a show of piety, holiness —**sanc'timony, sanctimo'niousness** *n.*

sanc'tion *n.* permission, authorization; penalty for breaking law —*pl.* boycott or other coercive measure *esp.* by one state against another regarded as having violated a law, right *etc.* —*vt.* allow, authorize, permit

sand *n.* substance consisting of small grains of rock or mineral, *esp.* on beach or in desert —*pl.* stretches or banks of this, usually forming seashore —*vt.* polish, smooth with sandpaper; cover, mix with sand —**sand'er** *n.* power tool for smoothing surfaces —**sand'y** *a.* like sand; sandcoloured; consisting of, covered with sand —**sand'bag** *n.* bag filled with sand or earth, used as protection against gunfire, floodwater *etc.* and as weapon —*vt.* beat, hit with sandbag —**sand'blast** *n.* jet of sand blown from a nozzle under pressure for cleaning, grinding *etc.* —*vt.* —**sand'paper** *n.* paper with sand stuck on it for scraping or polishing wood *etc.* —**sand'piper** *n.* various kinds of shore birds —**sand'pit** *n.* quantity of sand for children to play in —**sand'shoe** *n.* canvas shoe for beach wear *etc.* —**sand'stone** *n.* rock composed of sand

san'dal *n.* shoe consisting of sole attached by straps

san'dalwood *n.* sweet-scented wood

sand'wich [san'wij] *n.* two

slices of bread with meat or
other substance between —vt.
insert between two other things

sane a. of sound mind; sensible,
rational —**san'ity** n.

San'forize R preshrink (fabric)
using a patented process

sang pt. of SING

sang-froid' [sahn-frwah'] n.
composure; indifference; self-
possession

san'guine [-ng'gwin] a. cheerful, confident; ruddy in complexion —**san'guinary** a. accompanied by bloodshed; bloodthirsty
—**san'guinely** adv. hopefully,
confidently

san'itary a. helping protection
of health against dirt etc. —**sani-
ta'tion** n. measures, apparatus
for preservation of public health

sank pt. of SINK

San'skrit, San'scrit n. ancient language of India

sap[1] n. moisture which circu-
lates in plants; energy —v. drain
off sap —**sap'less** a. —**sap'ling** n.
young tree

sap[2] v. undermine; destroy insidiously; weaken —n. trench dug
in order to approach or under-
mine enemy position —**sap'per**
n. soldier in engineering unit

sap[3] n. inf. foolish, gullible person —**sapp'y** a.

sa'pient a. (usu. ironical) wise;
discerning; shrewd; knowing
—**sa'pience** n.

Sapph'ic [saf'-] a. of Sappho, a
Grecian poetess; denoting a kind
of verse —n. Sapphic verse
—**sap'phism** n. lesbianism

sapph'ire [saf-] n. (usu. blue)
precious stone; deep blue —a.

sar'aband(e) [sa'rə-] n. slow,
stately Spanish dance; music for
it

Sar'acen [sa'rə-] n. Arabian; adherent of Mohammedanism in

Syria and Palestine; infidel
—**Saracen'ic** a.

sar'casm n. bitter or wounding
ironic remark; such remarks;
taunt; sneer; irony; use of such
expressions —**sarcas'tic** a.
—**sarcas'tically** adv.

sarcoph'agus [-kof'-] n. stone
coffin

sard n. precious stone, variety of
chalcedony

sardine' [-dēn'] n. small fish of
herring family, usu. preserved in
oil

sardon'ic a. characterized by
irony, mockery or derision

sar'donyx [-də-niks] n. gemstone, variety of chalcedony

sargass'um, sargass'o n.
gulfweed, type of floating seaweed

sar'i n. Hindu woman's robe

sarong' n. skirtlike garment
worn in Asian and Pacific countries

sarsaparill'a n. (flavour of)
drink, orig. made from root of
plant

sartor'ial a. of tailor, tailoring,
or men's clothes

SAS Special Air Service

sash[1] n. decorative belt, ribbon,
wound around the body

sash[2] n. wooden window frame
opened by moving up and down
in grooves

sass'afras n. laurellike tree
with aromatic bark used medicinally

sat pt./pp. of SIT

Sa'tan n. the devil —**satan'ic(al)** a. devilish, fiendish —**satan'ically** adv.

sat'chel n. small bag, esp. for
school books

sate vt. satisfy a desire or appetite fully or excessively

sat'ellite n. celestial body or
man-made projectile orbiting

planet; person, country *etc.* dependent on another

sa'tiate [-shi-āt] *vt.* satisfy to the full; surfeit —**sa'tiable** *a.* —**satia'tion** *n.* —**sati'ety** [sə-tī'-] *n.* feeling of having had too much

sat'in *n.* fabric (of silk, rayon *etc.*) with glossy surface on one side —**sat'iny** *a.* of, like satin —**sat'inwood** *n.* various tropical trees yielding hard satiny wood

sat'ire *n.* composition in which vice, folly or foolish person is held up to ridicule; use of ridicule or sarcasm to expose vice and folly —**satir'ic(al)** [-tir'i-] *a.* of nature of satire; sarcastic; bitter —**sat'irist** *n.* —**sat'irize** *vt.* make object of satire; censure thus

sat'isfy *vt.* content, meet wishes of; pay; fulfil, supply adequately; convince (**-fied, -fying**) —**sat'isfac'tion** *n.* —**satisfac'tory** *a.*

satsu'ma [-sŏŏ'-] *n.* kind of small orange

sat'urate *vt.* soak thoroughly; cause to absorb maximum amount; *Chem.* cause substance to combine to its full capacity with another; shell or bomb heavily —**satura'tion** *n.* act, cause of saturating

Sat'urday *n.* seventh day of week, after Friday

Sat'urn *n.* Roman god; one of planets —**sat'urnine** *a.* gloomy; sluggish in temperament, dull, morose —**Saturna'lia** *n.* ancient festival of Saturn; (*also* **s-**) noisy revelry, orgy

sat'yr [-ər] *n.* woodland deity, part man, part goat; lustful man —**satyr'ic** [-ti'rik] *a.*

sauce *n.* liquid added to food to enhance flavour; *inf.* impudence —*vt.* add sauce to; *inf.* be cheeky, impudent to —**sau'cily** *adv.* —**sauc'y** *a.* impudent —**sauce'pan** *n.* cooking pot with long handle

sau'cer *n.* curved plate put under cup; shallow depression

sau'erkraut [sow'ər-krowt] *n.* German dish of finely shredded and pickled cabbage

sau'na *n.* steam bath, *orig.* Finnish

saun'ter *vi.* walk in leisurely manner, stroll —*n.* leisurely walk or stroll

sau'rian *n.* one of the order of reptiles including the alligator, lizard *etc.*

saus'age [sos'-] *n.* minced meat enclosed in thin tube of animal intestine or synthetic material —**sausage roll** pastry cylinder filled with sausage

sauté [sō'tā] *a.* fried quickly with little fat

Sauternes' [sō-tern'] *n.* sweet white Fr. wine

sav'age *a.* wild; ferocious; brutal; uncivilized, primitive —*n.* member of savage tribe, barbarian —*vt.* attack ferociously —**sav'agely** *adv.* —**sav'agery** *n.*

savann'a(h) *n.* extensive open grassy plain

sav'ant *n.* man of learning

save *vt.* rescue, preserve; protect; secure; keep for future, lay by; prevent need of; spare; except —*vi.* lay by money —*prep. obs.* except —*conj. obs.* but —**sa'ving** *a.* frugal; thrifty; delivering from sin; excepting; compensating —*prep.* excepting —*n.* economy —*pl.* money, earnings put by for future use

sav'eloy *n.* type of smoked red sausage

sa'viour *n.* person who rescues another; (**S-**) Christ

sav'oir-faire' [sav'wahr-fer'] *Fr. n.* ability to do, say, the right thing in any situation

sa'vory *n.* aromatic herb used in cooking

sa'vour [-vər] *n.* characteristic

taste; flavour; odour; distinctive quality —vi. have particular smell or taste; have suggestion (of) —vt. give flavour to; have flavour of; enjoy, appreciate —sa'voury a. attractive to taste or smell; not sweet —n. savoury snack (before meal)

savoy' n. variety of cabbage

savv'y sl. vt. understand —n. wits, intelligence

saw[1] n. tool for cutting wood etc. by tearing it with toothed edge —vt. cut with saw —vi. make movements of sawing (**sawed, sawn, saw'ing**) —**saw'yer** n. one who saws timber —**saw'dust** n. fine wood fragments made in sawing —**saw'fish** n. fish armed with toothed snout —**saw'mill** n. mill where timber is sawn into planks etc.

saw[2] pt. of SEE

saw[3] n. wise saying, proverb

sax n. inf. short for SAXOPHONE

saxe n. shade of blue

sax'horn n. instrument of trumpet class

sax'ifrage n. Alpine or rock plant

Sax'on n. member of West Germanic people who settled widely in Europe in the early Middle Ages —a.

sax'ophone n. keyed wind instrument

say vt. speak; pronounce; state; express; take as example or as near enough; form and deliver opinion (**said** pt./pp., **say'ing** pr.p., **says** 3rd pers. sing. pres. ind.) —n. what one has to say; chance of saying it; share in decision —**say'ing** n. maxim, proverb

SAYE Save As You Earn

scab n. crust formed over wound; skin disease; disease of plants; offens. blackleg —**scabb'y** a.

scabb'ard n. sheath for sword or dagger

sca'bies [skā'-] n. contagious skin disease —**sca'bious** a. having scabies, scabby

sca'bious n. plant with pink, white or blue flowers

sca'brous a. having rough surface; thorny; indecent; risky

scaff'old n. temporary platform for workmen; gallows —**scaff'olding** n. (material for building) scaffold

sca'lar n. variable quantity, eg time, having magnitude but no direction —a.

scald [skawld] vt. burn with hot liquid or steam; clean, sterilize with boiling water, heat (liquid) almost to boiling point —n. injury by scalding

scale[1] n. one of the thin, overlapping plates covering fishes and reptiles; thin flake; incrustation which forms in boilers etc. —vt. remove scales from —vi. come off in scales —**sca'ly** a. resembling or covered in scales —**scale insect** plant pest which lives under scale

scale[2] n. (chiefly in pl.) weighing instrument —vt. weigh in scales; have weight of

scale[3] n. graduated table or sequence of marks at regular intervals used as reference or for fixing standards, as in making measurements, in music etc.; ratio of size between a thing and a model or map of it; (relative) degree, extent —vt. climb —vi. scale down —**scale up** or **down** increase or decrease proportionately in size

sca'lene a. (of triangle) with three unequal sides

scall'op [skol'-] n. edible shellfish; edging in small curves like edge of scallop shell —vt. shape like scallop shell; cook in scallop shell or dish like one

scall'ywag *n. inf.* scamp, rascal

scalp *n.* skin and hair of top of head —*vt.* cut off scalp of

scal'pel *n.* small surgical knife

scamp *n.* mischievous person or child —*v.* skimp

scam'per *vi.* run about; run hastily from place to place —*n.*

scam'pi *pl.n.* kind of large prawn

scan *vt.* look at carefully, scrutinize; measure or read (verse) by metrical feet; examine, search by systematically varying the direction of a radar or sonar beam; glance over quickly —*vi.* (of verse) conform to metrical rules (**-nn-**) —*n.* scanning —**scan'ner** *n.* device, *esp.* electronic, which scans —**scan'sion** *n.*

scan'dal *n.* action, event generally considered disgraceful; malicious gossip —**scan'dalize** *vt.* shock —**scan'dalous** *a.* outrageous, disgraceful

scant *a.* barely sufficient or not sufficient —**scant'ily** *adv.* —**scant'y** *a.*

scape'goat *n.* person bearing blame due to others —**scape'-grace** *n.* mischievous person

scap'ula *n.* shoulder blade (*pl.* -lae [-lē], -las) —**scap'ular** *a.* of scapula —*n.* part of habit of certain religious orders in R.C. Church

scar *n.* mark left by healed wound, burn or sore; change resulting from emotional distress —*v.* mark, heal with scar (**-rr-**) —**scarred** *a.*

scar'ab [ska'rəb] *n.* sacred beetle of ancient Egypt; gem cut in shape of this

scarce [skārs] *a.* hard to find; existing or available in insuffi-

cient quantity; uncommon —**scarce'ly** *adv.* only just; not quite; definitely or probably not —**scarce'ness, scarc'ity** *n.*

scare [skār] *vt.* frighten —*n.* fright, sudden panic —**scar'y** *a. inf.* —**scare'crow** *n.* thing set up to frighten birds from crops; badly dressed or miserable looking person —**scare'monger** *n.* one who spreads alarming rumours

scarf[1] *n.* long narrow strip, large piece of material to put round neck, head *etc.* (*pl.* **scarfs** *or* **scarves**)

scarf[2] *n.* part cut away from each of two pieces of timber to be jointed longitudinally; joint so made —*vt.* cut or join in this way —**scarf'ing** *n.*

sca'rify *vt.* scratch, cut slightly all over; lacerate; stir surface soil of; criticize mercilessly (**-fied, -fying**) —**scarifica'tion** *n.*

scar'let *n.* a brilliant red colour; cloth or clothing of this colour, *esp.* military uniform —*a.* of this colour; immoral, *esp.* unchaste —**scarlet fever** infectious fever with scarlet rash

scarp *n.* steep slope; inside slope of ditch in fortifications

scar'per *vi. sl.* depart in haste

scat *vi. inf.* (*usu. imp.*) go away

scathe [-ATH] (*usu. now as pp./a.* **scathed** & **unscathed**[1]) *n.* injury, harm, damage —*vt.* injure, damage —**sca'thing** *a.* harshly critical; cutting; damaging

scatt'er *vt.* throw in various directions; put here and there; sprinkle —*vi.* disperse —*n.* —**scatt'erbrain** *n.* silly, careless person —**scatt'y** *a. inf.* silly, useless

scav'enge *v.* search for (anything usable) *usu.* among discarded material —**scav'enger** *n.* person who scavenges; animal, bird which feeds on refuse

ScD Doctor of Science

scene [sēn] *n.* place of action of novel, play *etc.*; place of any action; subdivision of play; view; episode; display of strong emotion —**sce'nery** *n.* natural features of district; constructions of wood, canvas *etc.* used on stage to represent a place where action is happening —**sce'nic** *a.* picturesque; of or on the stage —**scenar'io** *n.* summary of plot (of play *etc.*) or plan (*pl.* **-ios**)

scent [sent] *n.* distinctive smell, *esp.* pleasant one; trail, clue; perfume —*vt.* detect or track (by smell); suspect, sense; fill with fragrance

scep'tic [sk-], US **skep'tic** *n.* one who maintains doubt or disbelief; agnostic; unbeliever —**scep'tical** *a.* —**scep'ticism** *n.*

scep'tre [sep'tər] *n.* ornamental staff as symbol of royal power; royal dignity

sched'ule [sh-] *n.* plan of procedure for a project; list; timetable —*vt.* enter in schedule, plan to occur at certain time —**on schedule** on time

sche'ma [skē'-] *n.* overall plan or diagram —**schemat'ic** *a.* presented as plan or diagram —**sche'matize** *v.*

scheme [sk-] *n.* plan, design; project; outline —*v.* devise, plan, *esp.* in underhand manner —**sche'mer** *n.*

scher'zo [sker'tso] *n. Mus.* light playful composition

schis'm [siz'm] *n.* (group resulting from) division in political party, church *etc.* —**schismat'ic** *n./a.*

schist [sh-] *n.* crystalline rock which splits into layers —**schis'tose** *a.*

schizan'thus [ski-] *n.* plant with divided leaves

schizophre'nia [skit-sō-frē'-] *n.* mental disorder involving deterioration of, confusion about personality —**schizophren'ic** *a./n.* —**schiz'oid** *a.* relating to schizophrenia

schmaltz [shm-] *n.* excessive sentimentality —**schmalt'zy** *a.*

schnap(p)s [shn-] *n.* spirit distilled from potatoes; *inf.* any strong spirit

schnit'zel [shn-] *n.* thin slice of meat, *esp.* veal, as *Wiener schnitzel*

schol'ar *n. see* SCHOOL

scho'lium [sk-] *n.* marginal annotation; note; comment (*pl.* **-lia, -liums**) —**scho'liast** *n.* commentator or annotator —**scholias'tic** *a.* pert. to a scholiast or his pursuits

school [sk-] *n.* institution for teaching children or for giving instruction in any subject; buildings of such institution; group of thinkers, writers, artists *etc.* with principles or methods in common —*vt.* educate; bring under control, train —**school'man** *n.* medieval philosopher —**schol'ar** *n.* learned person; one taught in school; one quick to learn —**schol'arly** *a.* learned, erudite —**schol'arship** *n.* learning; prize, grant to student for payment of school or college fees —**scholas'tic** *a.* of schools or scholars, or education; pedantic

school [sk-] *n.* shoal (of fish, whales *etc.*)

schoon'er [sk-] *n.* fore-and-aft rigged vessel with two or more masts; tall glass

schottische' [sho-tēsh'] *n.* kind of dance; music for this

sciat'ica [sī-] *n.* neuralgia of hip and thigh; pain in sciatic nerve —**sciat'ic** *a.* of the hip; of sciatica

sci'ence [sī'-] n. systematic study and knowledge of natural or physical phenomena; any branch of study concerned with observed material facts —**scien'tif'ic** a. of the principles of science; systematic —**scientif'ically** adv. —**sci'entist** n. one versed in natural sciences —**science fiction** stories set in the future making imaginative use of scientific knowledge —**science park** area where scientific research and commercial development are carried on in cooperation

Scientol'ogy [sī-] R religious cult

scill'a [sil'ə] n. plant with bell-shaped flowers

scim'itar [sim'-] n. oriental curved sword

scin'tillate [sin'-] v. sparkle; be animated, witty, clever —**scintilla'tion** n.

sci'on [sī'-] n. descendant, heir; slip for grafting

sciss'ion [sish'-] n. act of cutting, dividing, splitting —**sciss'ile** a.

sciss'ors [siz'-] pl.n. (esp. **pair of scissors**) cutting instrument of two blades pivoted together —n./a. (with) scissorlike action of limbs in swimming, athletics etc., eg **scissors kick**

sclero'sis n. a hardening of bodily organs, tissues etc.

scoff [sk-] vt. express derision for —n. derision; mocking words —**scoff'er** n.

scoff v. sl. eat rapidly

scold [skō-] v. find fault; reprimand, be angry with —n. someone who does this —**scold'ing** n.

scoll'op n. see SCALLOP

sconce [sk-] n. bracket candlestick on wall

scone [skon] n. small plain cake baked on griddle or in oven

scoop [-ōō-] n. small shovellike tool for ladling, hollowing out etc.; sl. profitable deal; Journalism exclusive news item —vt. ladle out; hollow out, rake in with scoop; make sudden profit; beat (rival newspaper etc.)

scoot [-ōō-] vi. sl. move off quickly —**scoot'er** n. child's vehicle propelled by pushing on ground with one foot; light motorcycle also **motor scooter**

scope n. range of activity or application; room, opportunity

scorch v. burn, be burnt, on surface; parch; shrivel; wither —n. slight burn —**scorch'er** n. inf. very hot day

score n. points gained in game, competition; group of 20; a line (esp. pl.); musical notation; mark or notch, esp. to keep tally; reason, account; grievance —vt. gain points in game; mark; cross out; arrange music (for) —vi. keep tally of points; succeed

scorn n. contempt, derision —vt. despise —**scorn'er** n. —**scorn'ful** a. derisive —**scorn'fully** adv.

Scor'pio n. (the scorpion) 8th sign of zodiac operative c. Oct. 23 – Nov. 21

scor'pion n. small lobster-shaped animal with sting at end of jointed tail

Scot n. native of Scotland —**Scot'tish** a. (also **Scotch, Scots**) —**Scotch** n. Scotch whisky —**Scots'man** n.

scotch vt. put an end to; obs. wound

scot-free' a. without harm or loss

scoun'drel n. villain, blackguard —**scoun'drelly** a.

scour vt. clean, polish by rubbing; clear or flush out

scour v. move rapidly along or over (territory) in search of something

scourge [skurj] *n.* whip, lash; severe affliction; pest; calamity —*vt.* flog; punish severely

scout *n.* one sent out to reconnoitre; (**S-**) member of **Scout Association**, organization to develop character and responsibility —*vi.* go out, act as scout; reconnoitre —**Scout'er** *n.* leader of troop of scouts

scow *n.* unpowered barge

scowl *vi.* frown gloomily or sullenly —*n.* angry or gloomy expression

scrabb'le *v.* scrape at with hands, claws in disorderly manner —*n.* (**S-**) R word game

scrag *n.* lean person or animal; lean end of a neck of mutton —**scragg'y** *a.* thin, bony

scragg'ily *a.* untidy

scram[1] *v. inf.* (oft. *imp.*) go away hastily, get out

scram[2] *n.* emergency shutdown of nuclear reactor —*v.*

scram'ble *vi.* move along or up by crawling, climbing *etc.*; struggle with others (for); (of aircraft, aircrew) take off hurriedly —*vt.* mix up; cook (eggs) beaten up with milk; render (speech) unintelligible by electronic device —*n.* scrambling; rough climb; disorderly proceeding; motorcycle race over rough ground

scrap *n.* small piece or fragment; leftover material; *inf.* fight —*v.* break up, discard as useless —*vi. inf.* fight (**-pp-**) —**scrapp'y** *a.* unequal in quality; badly finished —**scrap'book** *n.* book in which newspaper cuttings *etc.* are kept

scrape *vt.* rub with something sharp; clean, smooth thus; grate; scratch; rub with harsh noise —*n.* act, sound of scraping; *inf.* awkward situation, *esp.* as result of escapade —**scra'per** *n.* instrument for scraping; contrivance on which mud is scraped from shoes *etc.*

scratch *vt.* score, make narrow surface wound with claws, nails, or anything pointed; make marks on with pointed instruments; scrape (skin) with nails to relieve itching; remove, withdraw from list, race *etc.* —*vi.* use claws or nails, *esp.* to relieve itching —*n.* wound, mark or sound made by scratching; line or starting point —*a.* got together at short notice; impromptu —**scratch'y** *a.*

scrawl *vt.* write, draw untidily —*n.* thing scrawled; careless writing

scraw'ny *a.* thin, bony

scream *vi.* utter piercing cry, *esp.* of fear, pain *etc.*; be very obvious —*vt.* utter in a scream —*n.* shrill, piercing cry; *inf.* very funny person or thing

scree *n.* loose shifting stones; slope covered with these

screech *vi./n.* scream

screed *n.* long (tedious) letter, passage or speech; thin layer of cement

screen *n.* device to shelter from heat, light, draught, observation *etc.*; anything used for such purpose; mesh over doors, windows to keep out insects; white or silvered surface on which photographic images are projected; windscreen; wooden or stone partition in church —*vt.* shelter, hide; protect from detection; show (film); scrutinize; examine (group of people) for presence of disease, weapons *etc.*; examine for political motives; *Electricity* protect from stray electric or magnetic fields —**the screen** cinema generally

screw [-ōō] *n.* (naillike device or cylinder with) spiral thread cut to engage similar thread or to bore into material (wood etc.) to pin or fasten; anything resembling a screw in shape, esp. in spiral form; propeller; twist —vt. fasten with screw; twist around; inf. extort —**screw'y** a. inf. crazy, eccentric —**screw'driver** n. tool for turning screws —**screw up** distort; inf. bungle

scrib'ble v. write, draw carelessly; make meaningless marks with pen or pencil —n. something scribbled —**scrib'bly** a.

scribe n. writer; copyist —v. scratch a line with pointed instrument

scrimm'age n. scuffle

scrimp vt. make too small or short; treat meanly —**scrim'py** a.

scrip n. written certificate esp. of holding stocks or shares

script n. (system or style of) handwriting; written characters; written text of film, play, radio or television programme; answer paper in examination

scrip'ture n. sacred writings; the Bible —**script'ural** a.

scriv'ener n. obs. copyist, clerk

scrof'ula n. tuberculosis of lymphatic glands, esp. of neck —**scrof'ulous** a.

scroll [-ōl] n. roll of parchment or paper; list; ornament shaped thus

scro'tum n. pouch containing testicles (pl. -ta) —**scro'tal** a.

scrounge v. inf. get without cost, by begging —**scroun'ger** n.

scrub[1] vt. clean with hard brush and water; scour; inf. cancel, get rid of (-bb-) —n. scrubbing —**scrubbing brush**

scrub[2] n. stunted trees; brushwood —**scrubb'y** a. covered with scrub; stunted; inf. messy

scruff n. nape (of neck)

scrum(mage) n. Rugby re-

starting of play in which opposing packs of forwards push against each other then to gain possession of the ball; crush, crowd

scru'ple n. doubt or hesitation about what is morally right; weight of 20 grains —vi. hesitate —**scru'pulous** a. extremely conscientious; thorough, attentive to small points —**scru'pulously** adv. —**scru'pulousness** n.

scru'tiny n. close examination; critical investigation; official examination of votes etc.; searching look —**scrutineer**[1] n. examiner of votes —**scru'tinize** vt. examine closely

scu'ba n./a. (relating to) self-contained underwater breathing apparatus

scud vi. run fast; run before wind (-dd-)

scuff vi. drag, scrape with feet in walking —vt. scrape with feet; graze —n. act, sound of scuffing —pl. thong sandals —**scuffed** a. (of shoes) scraped or slightly grazed

scuf'fle vi. fight in disorderly manner; shuffle —n.

scull n. oar used in stern of boat; short oar used in pairs —v. propel, move by means of scull(s)

scull'ery n. place for washing dishes etc. —**scull'ion** n. despicable person; obs. kitchen underservant

sculp'ture n. art of forming figures in relief or solid; product of this art —v. represent by sculpture —**sculpt** v. —**sculp'tural** a. with qualities proper to sculpture —**sculp'tor** n. (**sculp'tress** fem.)

scum n. froth or other floating matter on liquid; waste part of anything; vile person(s) or thing(s) —**scumm'y** a.

scupp'er n. hole in ship's side

level with deck to carry off water
—vt. inf. ruin, destroy, kill

scurf n. flaky matter on scalp,
dandruff —**scurf'y** a.

scur'rilous a. coarse, indecently abusive —**scurril'ity** n.

scur'ry vi. run hastily (**scur'-
ried, scur'rying**) —n. bustling
haste; flurry

scur'vy n. disease caused by
lack of vitamin C —a. afflicted
with the disease; mean, contemptible

scut n. short tail of hare or other
animal

scutch'eon see ESCUTCHEON

scut'tle[1] n. fireside container
for coal

scut'tle[2] vi. rush away; run
hurriedly —n.

scut'tle[3] vt. make hole in ship
to sink it

scythe [sITH] n. manual implement with long curved blade for
cutting grass —vt. cut with
scythe

SDI Strategic Defence Initiative

SDP Social Democratic Party

SE southeast(ern)

sea n. mass of salt water covering greater part of earth; broad
tract of this; waves; swell; large
quantity; vast expanse —**sea
anemone** sea animal with suckers like petals —**sea'board** n.
coast —**sea'faring** a. occupied in
sea voyages —**sea gull** gull —**sea
horse** fish with bony plated body
and horselike head —**sea lion**
kind of large seal —**sea'man** n.
sailor —**sea'sickness** n. nausea
caused by motion of ship —**sea'-
sick** a. —**sea'side** n. place, esp.
holiday resort, on coast —**sea
urchin** marine animal, echinus
—**sea'weed** n. plant growing in
sea —**sea'worthy** a. in fit condition to put to sea

seal[1] n. piece of metal or stone
engraved with device for impres-

sion on wax etc.; impression thus
made (on letters etc.); device,
material preventing passage of
water, air, oil etc. (also **seal'er**)
—vt. affix seal to ratify, authorize; mark with stamp as evidence
of some quality; keep close or
secret; settle; make watertight,
airtight etc.

seal[2] n. amphibious furred carnivorous mammal with flippers
as limbs —vi. hunt seals —**seal'-
er** n. man or ship engaged in
sealing —**seal'skin** n. skin, fur of
seals

seam n. line of junction of two
edges, eg of two pieces of cloth,
or two planks; thin layer, stratum
—vt. mark with furrows or wrinkles —**seam'less** a. —**seam'y** a.
sordid; marked with seams
—**seam'stress** [sem'-], **semp'-
stress** n. sewing woman

se'ance [sá'ons] n. meeting of
spiritualists

sear vt. scorch, brand with hot
iron; deaden

search [-ur-] v. look over or
through to find something; probe
into, examine —n. act of searching; quest —**search'er** n.
—**search'ing** a. keen; thorough;
severe —**search'light** n. powerful electric light with concentrated beam

seas'on [sēz'-] n. one of four
divisions of year associated with
type of weather and stage of
agriculture; period during which
this happens, grows, is active
etc.; proper time —vt. flavour
with salt, herbs etc.; make reliable or ready for use; make
experienced —**seas'onable** a. appropriate for the season; opportune; fit —**seas'onal** a. depending
on, varying with seasons —**sea'-
soning** n. flavouring —**season
ticket** one for series of journeys,
events etc. within a certain time

seat n. thing for sitting on; buttocks; base; right to sit (eg in council etc.); place where something is located, centred; locality of disease, trouble etc.; country house —vt. make to sit; provide sitting accommodation for; install firmly

SEATO Southeast Asia Treaty Organization

seba'ceous [-shəs] a. of, pert. to fat; secreting fat, oil

se'cant n. Maths. (secant of an angle) reciprocal of its cosine; line that intersects a curve

sec'ateurs [or -turz'] pl.n. small pruning shears

secede' [si-sēd'] vi. withdraw formally from federation, Church etc. —**secession** n. —**seces'sionist** n.

seclude' vt. guard from, remove from sight, view, contact with others —**seclu'ded** a. remote; private —**seclu'sion** n.

sec'ond[1] a. next after first; alternate, additional; of lower quality —n. person or thing coming second; attendant; sixtieth part of minute; SI unit of time; moment; (esp. pl.) inferior goods —vt. support; support (motion in meeting) so that discussion may be in order —**sec'onder** n. —**sec'ondly** adv. —**second-hand** a. bought after use by another; not original —**second sight** faculty of seeing events before they occur

second[1,2] vt. transfer (employee, officer) temporarily

sec'ondary a. subsidiary, of less importance; developed from, or dependent on, something else; Education after primary stage —**sec'ondarily** adv.

se'cret a. kept, meant to be kept from knowledge of others; hidden; private —n. thing kept secret —**se'crecy** n. keeping or

being kept secret —**se'cretive** a. given to having secrets; uncommunicative; reticent —**se'cretiveness** n. —**se'cretly** adv.

sec'retary n. one employed by individual or organization to deal with papers and correspondence, keep records, prepare business etc.; head of a state department —**secreta'rial** a. —**secreta'riat** n. body of secretaries; building occupied by secretarial staff —**sec'retaryship** n.

secrete' vt. hide; conceal; (of gland etc.) collect and supply particular substance in body —**secre'tion** n. —**secre'tory** a.

sect n. group of people (within religious body etc.) with common interest; faction —**secta'rian** a. of a sect; narrow-minded —**sec'tary** n.

sec'tion n. part cut off; division; portion; distinct part of city, country, people etc.; cutting; drawing of anything as if cut through; smallest military unit —**sec'tional** a.

sec'tor n. part or subdivision; part of circle enclosed by two radii and the arc which they cut off

sec'ular a. worldly; lay, not religious; not monastic; lasting for, or occurring once in, an age; centuries old —**sec'ularism** n. —**sec'ularist** n. one who believes that religion should have no place in civil affairs —**seculariza'tion** n. —**sec'ularize** vt. transfer from religious to lay possession or use

secure' [-kyoor'] a. safe; free from fear, anxiety; firmly fixed; certain; sure, confident —vt. gain possession of; make safe; free (creditor) from risk of loss; make firm —**secure'ly** adv. —**secur'ity** n. state of safety; protection; that which secures; assurance; anything given as bond, caution or pledge; one that becomes surety for another

sedan[1] *n. US* saloon car —**sedan chair** *Hist.* closed chair for one person, carried on poles by bearers

sedate[1] *a.* calm, collected, serious —**sedate'ly** *adv.*

sedate[2] *vt.* make calm by sedative —**seda'tion** *n.* —**sed'ative** *a.* having soothing or calming effect —*n.* sedative drug

sed'entary *a.* done sitting down; sitting much

sedge *n.* plant like coarse grass growing in swampy ground

sedi'lia *pl.n.* stone seats on south side of altar for priests

sed'iment *n.* matter which settles to the bottom of liquid; dregs, lees —**sediment'ary** *a.*

sedi'tion [-dish'-] *n.* speech or action threatening authority of a state —**sedi'tious** *a.*

seduce[1] *vt.* persuade to commit some (wrong) deed, *esp.* sexual intercourse; tempt; attract —**seduc'tion** *n.* —**seduct'ive** *a.* alluring; winning —**sedu'cer** *n.* (**se-duc'tress** *fem.*)

sed'ulous *a.* diligent; industrious; persevering, persistent —**se-du'lity** *n.*

se'dum *n.* rock plant

see[1] *vt.* perceive with eyes or mentally; observe; watch; find out; reflect; come to know; interview; make sure; accompany —*vi.* perceive; consider; understand (**saw, seen, see'ing**) —**see'ing** *conj.* since; in view of the fact that

see[2] *n.* diocese, office, or jurisdiction of bishop

seed *n.* reproductive germs of plants; one grain of this; such grains saved or used for sowing; origin; sperm; *obs.* offspring —*vt.* sow with seed; arrange draw for

lawn tennis or other tournament, so that best players do not meet in early rounds —*vi.* produce seed —**seed'ling** *n.* young plant raised from seed —**seed'y** *a.* shabby; run to seed; *inf.* unwell, ill

seek *vt.* make search or enquiry for —*vi.* search (**sought** [sawt], **seek'ing**)

seem *vi.* appear (to be or to do); look; appear to one's judgment —**seem'ing** *a.* apparent but not real —**seem'ingly** *adv.*

seem'ly *a.* becoming and proper —**seem'liness** *n.*

seen *pp. of* SEE

seep *vi.* trickle through slowly, as water, ooze

seer *n.* prophet

seer'sucker *n.* light cotton fabric with slightly crinkled surface

see'saw *n.* game in which children sit at opposite ends of plank supported in middle and swing up and down; plank used for this —*vi.* move up and down

seethe [-TH] *vi.* boil, foam; be very agitated; be in constant movement (as large crowd *etc.*) (**seethed, see'thing**)

seg'ment *n.* piece cut off; section —*v.* [-ment'] to divide into segments —**segment'al** *a.* —**segmenta'tion** *n.*

seg'regate *vt.* set apart from rest; dissociate; separate; isolate —**segrega'tion** *n.*

se'gue [sā'gwi] *vi.* proceed from one section or piece of music to another without break (**se'gued, se'gueing**) —*n.*

seine [sān] *n.* type of large fishing net

seis'mic [sīz'-] *a.* pert. to earthquakes —**seis'mograph** *n.* instrument to record earthquakes (*also* **seismom'eter**) —**seismolog'ic-(al)** *a.* pert. to seismology —**seis-**

mol'ogist n. one versed in seismology —**seismol'ogy** n. science concerned with study of earthquakes

seize [sēz] vt. grasp; lay hold of; capture —vi. in machine, of bearing or piston, to stick tightly through overheating —**seiz'able** a. —**seiz'ure** n. act of taking, esp. by warrant, as goods; sudden onset of disease

sel'dom adv. not often, rarely

select' vt. pick out, choose —a. choice, picked; exclusive —**selec'tion** n. —**select'ive** a. —**selectiv'ity** n. —**select'or** n.

sele'nium n. nonmetallic element with photoelectric properties —**sele'nic** a.

selenog'raphy [se-li-] n. study of surface of moon

self pron., used reflexively or to express emphasis (pl. **selves**) —a. (of colour) same throughout, uniform —n. one's own person or individuality —**self'ish** a. concerned unduly over personal profit or pleasure; lacking consideration for others; greedy —**self'ishly** adv. —**self'less** a. having no regard to self; unselfish

self- (comb. form) of oneself or itself, as in

> self-addressed'
> self-assured'
> self-ca'tering
> self-cen'tred
> self-con'fident
> self-contained'
> self-control'
> self-defence'
> self-deni'al
> self-employed'
> self-ev'ident
> self-help'
> self-indul'gent
> self-in'terest

> self-pit'y
> self-rai'sing
> self-reli'ant
> self-sac'rifice
> self-sat'isfied
> self-support'ing

self-certifica'tion n. formal assertion by worker to employer that absence of up to seven days was due to sickness

self-con'scious a. unduly aware of oneself; conscious of one's acts or states

self'-determina'tion n. the right of person or nation to decide for itself

self-made' a. having achieved wealth, status etc. by one's own efforts

self-possessed' a. calm, composed —**self-possession** n.

self-respect' n. proper sense of one's own dignity and integrity

self-right'eous a. smugly sure of one's own virtue

self'same a. very same

self-seek'ing a./n. (having) preoccupation with one's own interests

self-ser'vice a./n. (of) shop or restaurant where customers serve themselves

self-suffi'cient a. sufficient in itself; relying on one's own powers

self-will' n. obstinacy; wilfulness —**self-willed** a. headstrong

sell vt. hand over for a price; stock, have for sale; make someone accept; inf. betray, cheat —vi. find purchasers (**sold, sell'ing**) —n. inf. disappointment; inf. hoax —**sell'er** n. —**sell'out** n. disposing of completely by selling; betrayal

Sell'otape R type of adhesive tape —vt.

Selt'zer (water) [-sər] n. aerated mineral water

sel'vage, sel'vedge [-vij] n. finished, unfraying edge of cloth

seman'tic a. relating to meaning of words or symbols —**seman'tics** pl.n. study of linguistic meaning

sem'aphore n. post with movable arms for signalling; system of signalling by human or mechanical arms

semasiol'ogy [si-mă-] n. semantics

sem'blance n. (false) appearance; image, likeness

se'men n. fluid carrying sperm of male animals; sperm

semes'ter n. US half-year session in many universities, colleges

sem'i n. inf. semidetached house

semi- (comb. form) half, partly, not completely, as in semicircle

sem'ibreve n. musical note half length of breve

sem'icircle n. half of circle —**semicir'cular** a.

semico'lon n. punctuation mark (;)

semidetached' a./n. (of) house joined to another on one side only

semifi'nal n. match, round etc. before final

sem'inal a. capable of developing; influential, important; rudimentary; of semen or seed

sem'inar n. meeting of group (of students) for discussion

sem'inary n. college for priests

semipre'cious [-presh'-] a. (of gemstones) having less value than precious stones

semiskilled' a. partly skilled, trained but not for specialized work

Se'mite n. member of race including Jews and Arabs —**Semit'ic** a. denoting a Semite; Jewish

sem'itone n. musical half tone

semoli'na [-lē'-] n. hard grains left after sifting of flour, used for puddings etc.

sempervi'vum n. plant with ornamental rosettes of leaves

SEN State Enrolled Nurse

sen'ate n. upper council of state, university etc. —**sen'ator** n. —**senator'ial** a.

send vt. cause to go or be conveyed; despatch; transmit (by radio) (**sent, send'ing**)

sen'eschal n. Hist. steward

se'nile a. showing weakness of old age —**senil'ity** n.

se'nior a. superior in rank or standing; older —n. superior; elder person —**senior'ity** [-o'ri-] n.

sen'na n. tropical plant; its dried leaves or pods used as laxative

señor' [sen-nyawr'] n. Sp. title of respect, like Mr. —**señor'a** n. Mrs. —**señori'ta** [-rē'-] n. Miss

sensa'tion n. operation of sense, feeling, awareness; excited feeling, state of excitement; exciting event; strong impression; commotion —**sensa'tional** a. producing great excitement; melodramatic; of perception by senses —**sensa'tionalism** n. use of sensational language etc. to arouse intense emotional excitement; doctrine that sensations are basis of all knowledge

sense n. any of bodily faculties of perception or feeling; sensitiveness of any or all of these faculties; ability to perceive, mental alertness; consciousness; meaning; coherence, intelligible meaning; sound practical judgment —vt. perceive; understand —**sense'less** a. —**sense'lessly** adv.

sen'sible a. reasonable, wise;

perceptible by senses; aware, mindful; considerable, appreciable —**sensibil'ity** n. ability to feel *esp.* emotional or moral feelings —**sen'sibly** adv.

sen'sitive a. open to, acutely affected by, external impressions; easily affected or altered; easily upset by criticism; responsive to slight changes —**sen'sitively** adv. —**sensitiv'ity, sen'sitiveness** n. —**sen'sitize** vt. make sensitive, *esp.* make (photographic film *etc.*) sensitive to light

sen'sor n. device that responds to stimulus

sen'sory a. relating to organs, operation, of senses

sen'sual a. of senses only and not of mind; given to pursuit of pleasures of sense; self-indulgent; licentious —**sen'sualism** n. —**sen'sualist** n. —**sensual'ity** n.

sen'suous a. stimulating, or apprehended by, senses *esp.* in aesthetic manner

sent *pt./pp. of* SEND

sen'tence n. combination of words, which is complete as expressing a thought; judgment passed on criminal by court or judge —vt. pass sentence on, condemn —**senten'tial** a. of sentence —**senten'tious** a. full of axioms and maxims; pithy; pompously moralizing —**senten'tiously** adv. —**senten'tiousness** n.

sen'tient a. capable of feeling; feeling; thinking —**sen'tience, sen'tiency** n.

sen'timent n. tendency to be moved by feeling rather than reason; verbal expression of feeling; mental feeling, emotion; opinion —**sentimen'tal** a. given to indulgence in sentiment and in its expression; weak; sloppy —**sentimen'talist** n. —**sentimen-**

tal'ity n. —**sentimen'talize** v.

sent'inel n. sentry

sen'try n. soldier on watch

sep'al n. leaf or division of the calyx of a flower

sep'arate [-āt] vt. part; divide; sever; put apart; occupy place between —vi. withdraw, become parted from —a. [-it] disconnected, apart, distinct, individual —**sep'arable** a. —**sep'arately** adv. —**separa'tion** n. disconnection; *Law* living apart of married people without divorce —**sep'arator** n. that which separates; apparatus for separating cream from milk

se'pia n. reddish-brown pigment made from a fluid secreted by the cuttle fish —a. of this colour

sep'sis n. presence of pus-forming bacteria in body

Sept. September

Septem'ber n. 9th month (7th in Roman calendar)

septenn'ial a. lasting, occurring every seven years

septet(te)¹ n. music for seven instruments or voices; group of seven performers

sep'tic a. of, caused by, sepsis; (of wound) infected —**septicae'mia** [-sē-] n. blood poisoning

septuagena'rian a. aged between seventy and eighty —n.

Septuages'ima [-jes'-] n. third Sunday before Lent

sep'ulchre [-kər] n. tomb; burial vault —**sepul'chral** a. of burial, or the grave; mournful; gloomy —**sep'ulture** n. burial

se'quel n. consequence; continuation, *eg* of story

se'quence n. arrangement of things in successive order; section, episode of film —**se'quent, sequen'tial** a.

seques'ter vt. separate; seclude; put aside —**sequest'rate** vt. confiscate; divert or appropriate income of property to satisfy claims against its owner **—sequestra'tion** n.

se'quin n. small ornamental metal disc on dress etc.; orig. Venetian gold coin

sequoi'a [si-kwoi'ə] n. giant Californian coniferous tree

seraglio [-rahl'-] n. harem, palace, of Turkish sultan (pl. -ios)

ser'aph [se'rəf] n. member of highest order of angels (pl. -s, ser'aphim) **—seraph'ic** a.

serenade' n. sentimental piece of music or song of type addressed to woman by lover esp. at evening **—v.** sing serenade (to someone)

serendip'ity n. faculty of making fortunate discoveries by accident

serene' a. calm, tranquil; unclouded; quiet, placid **—serene'ly** adv. **—seren'ity** n.

serf n. one of class of medieval labourers bound to, and transferred with, land **—serf'dom, serf'hood** n.

Serg. Sergeant

serge n. strong hard-wearing twilled worsted fabric

serg'eant, serj'eant [sahrj'-ənt] n. noncommissioned officer in army; police officer above constable **—sergeant major** highest noncommissioned officer in regiment **—sergeant at arms** parliamentary, court officer with ceremonial duties

se'ries n. sequence; succession; set (eg of radio, TV programmes with same characters, setting, but different stories) (pl. se'ries) **—se'rial** n. story or play produced in successive episodes or instalments **—a. —se'rialize** v. publish, present as serial **—seriat'im** adv. one after another

ser'if [se'rif] n. small line finishing off stroke of letter

se'rious a. thoughtful, solemn; earnest, sincere; of importance; giving cause for concern **—se'riously** adv.

ser'mon n. discourse of religious instruction or exhortation spoken or read from pulpit; any similar discourse **—ser'monize** vi. talk like preacher; compose sermons

ser'pent n. obs., biblical snake **—serp'entine** a. like, shaped like, serpent **—n.** green to black rock

serr'ate, serra'ted a. having notched, sawlike edge **—serra'tion** n.

serr'ied a. in close order, shoulder to shoulder

se'rum n. watery animal fluid, esp. thin part of blood as used for inoculation or vaccination

ser'val n. feline Afr. mammal

serve v. (mainly vt.) work for, under, another; attend (to customers) in shop etc.; provide; help to (food etc.); present (food etc.) in particular way; provide with regular supply of; be member of military unit; pay homage to; spend time doing; be useful, suitable enough; Tennis etc. put (ball) into play **—n.** Tennis etc. act of serving ball **—serv'ant** n. personal or domestic attendant **—serv'ice** n. the act of serving, helping, assisting; system organized to provide for needs of public; maintenance of vehicle; use; readiness, availability for use; department of State employ; employment of persons engaged in this; set of dishes etc.; form, session, of public worship **—pl.** armed forces **—vt.** overhaul **—serv'iceable** a. in working order, usable; durable **—serv'iceman** n. member of the armed forces —**service road** narrow road giving access to houses, shops etc. · —**service station** place supplying fuel, oil, maintenance for motor vehicles

serviette' n. table napkin

ser'vile a. slavish, without independence; cringing; fawning; menial —**servil'ity** n.

ser'vitude n. bondage, slavery

ser'vomechanism n. device for converting small mechanical force into larger, esp. in steering mechanisms

ses'ame [-ə-mi] n. plant with seeds used as herbs and for making oil

sess'ion [sesh'-] n. meeting of court etc.; assembly; continuous series of such meetings; any period devoted to an activity; school or university term or year

set v. (mainly tr.) put or place in specified position or condition; cause to sit; fix, point, put up; make ready; become firm or fixed; establish; prescribe, allot; put to music; (of hair, arrange while wet, so that it dries in position; of sun, go down; have direction (set, sett'ing) —a. fixed, established; deliberate; formal, arranged beforehand; unvarying —n. act or state of being set; bearing, posture; Radio, Television complete apparatus for reception or transmission; Theatre, Cinema organized settings and equipment to form ensemble of scene; number of things, persons associated as being similar, complementary or used together; Maths. group of numbers, objects etc. with at least one common property —**set'back** n. anything that hinders or impedes —**set'up** n. position; organization —**set up** establish

set(t) n. badger's burrow

settee' n. couch

sett'er n. various breeds of gun dog

sett'ing n. background; surroundings; scenery and other stage accessories; act of fixing; decorative metalwork holding precious stone etc. in position; tableware and cutlery for (single place at) table; descending below horizon of sun; music for song

set'tle vt. arrange, put in order; establish, make firm or secure or quiet; decide upon; end (dispute etc.); pay; bestow (property) by legal deed —vi. come to rest; subside; become clear; take up residence; subside, sink to bottom; come to agreement —**set'tlement** n. act of settling; place newly inhabited; money bestowed legally; subsidence (of building) —**sett'ler** n. colonist

sev'en a./n. cardinal number, next after six —**sev'enth** a. the ordinal number —**sev'enteen'** a./n. ten and seven —**sev'enty** a./n. ten times seven

sev'er v. separate, divide; cut off —**sev'erance** n. —**severance pay** compensation paid by a firm to an employee for loss of employment

sev'eral a. some, a few; separate; individual; various; different —pron. indefinite small number —**sev'erally** adv. apart from others

severe' [-er'] a. strict; rigorous; hard to do; harsh; austere; extreme —**severe'ly** adv. —**sever'ity** [-ve'ri-] n.

sew [sō] v. join with needle and thread; make by sewing (sewed pt., sewed, sewn pp., sew'ing pr.p.) —sew'ing n.

sew'age [sōō'ij] n. refuse, waste matter, excrement conveyed in sewer —**sew'er** n. underground drain to remove waste water and refuse —**sew'erage** n. arrangement of sewers; sewage

sex *n.* state of being male or female; males or females collectively; sexual intercourse —*a.* concerning sex —*vt.* ascertain sex of —**sex'ism** *n.* discrimination on basis of sex —**sex'ist** *n./a.* —**sex'ual** *a.* —**sex'ually** *adv.* —**sex'y** *a.* —**sexual intercourse** act of procreation in which male's penis is inserted into female's vagina

sexagena'rian *a./n.* (person) sixty years old

Sexages'ima [-jes'-] *n.* the second Sunday before Lent

sexenn'ial *a.* lasting, occurring every six years

sex'tant *n.* navigator's instrument for measuring elevations of heavenly body *etc.*

sextet(te)' *n.* (composition for) six singers or players; group of six

sex'ton *n.* official in charge of a church, often acting as gravedigger

sf science fiction

S. Glam South Glamorgan

shabb'y *a.* faded, worn, ragged, poorly dressed; mean, dishonourable; stingy —**shabb'ily** *adv.* —**shab'biness** *n.*

shack *n.* rough hut —**shack up (with)** live (with)

shac'kle *n.* metal ring or fastening for prisoner's wrist or ankle; anything that confines —*vt.* fasten with shackles; hamper

shad *n.* various herring-like fish

shade *n.* partial darkness; shelter, place sheltered from light, heat *etc.*; darker part of anything; depth of colour; tinge; ghost; screen; anything used to screen —*pl.* windowblind —*pl. US sl.* sunglasses —*vt.* screen from light, darken; represent shades in drawing —**sha'dy** *a.* shielded

from sun; dim; dubious; dishonest; dishonourable

shad'ow *n.* dark figure projected by anything that intercepts rays of light; patch of shade; slight trace; indistinct image; gloom; inseparable companion —*vt.* cast shadow over; follow and watch closely —**shad'owy** *a.*

shaft [-ah-] *n.* straight rod, stem, handle; arrow; ray, beam (of light); revolving rod for transmitting power; one of the bars between which horse is harnessed; entrance boring of mine

shag¹ *n.* matted wool or hair; long-napped cloth; coarse shredded tobacco —**shagg'y** *a.* covered with rough hair or wool; tousled; unkempt

shag² *n.* cormorant

shah *n.* formerly, ruler of Iran

shake *v.* (cause to) move with quick vibrations; tremble; grasp the hand (of another) in greeting; upset; wave, brandish (**shook, sha'ken**) —*n.* act of shaking; vibration; jolt; *inf.* short period of time, jiffy —**sha'kily** *adv.* —**sha'ky** *a.* unsteady, insecure

shale *n.* flaky, sedimentary rock

shall *v. aux.* makes compound tenses or moods to express obligation, command, condition or intention (**should** *pt.*)

shallot¹ *n.* kind of small onion

shall'ow [-ō] *a.* not deep; having little depth of water; superficial; not sincere —*n.* shallow place —**shall'owness** *n.*

sham *a./n.* imitation, counterfeit —*v.* pretend, feign (-**mm**-)

sham'ble *vi.* walk in shuffling, awkward way

sham'bles *pl.n.* messy, disorderly thing or place

shame *n.* emotion caused by consciousness of guilt or dishonour in one's conduct or state; cause of disgrace; ignominy; pity;

hard luck —*vt.* cause to feel shame; disgrace; force by shame (into) —**shame'ful** *a.* disgraceful —**shame'fully** *adv.* —**shame'less** *a.* with no sense of shame; indecent —**shame'faced** *a.* ashamed

shamm'y (leather) *inf.* chamois leather

shampoo' *n.* various preparations of liquid soap for washing hair, carpets *etc.*; this process —*vt.* use shampoo to wash

sham'rock *n.* clover leaf, *esp.* as Irish emblem

shan'dy *n.* mixed drink, *esp.* beer diluted with soft drink

shanghai' [-hī'] *vt.* force, trick someone to do something

shank *n.* lower leg; shinbone; stem of pipe

shantung' *n.* soft, natural Chinese silk

shant'y[1] *n.* temporary wooden building; crude dwelling

shant'y[2], **chan'ty** *n.* sailor's song with chorus

shape *n.* external form or appearance; mould, pattern; *inf.* condition, *esp.* of physical fitness —*vt.* form, mould, fashion, make —*vi.* develop (**shaped, sha'ping**) —**shape'less** *a.* —**shape'ly** *a.* well-proportioned

shard *n.* broken fragment, *esp.* of earthenware

share[1] [shār] *n.* portion; quota; lot; unit of ownership in public company —*v.* give, take a share; join with others in doing, using, something —**share'holder** *n.*

share[2] [shār] *n.* blade of plough

shark *n.* large usu. predatory sea fish; person who cheats others

shark'skin *n.* stiff rayon fabric

sharp *a.* having keen cutting edge or fine point; keen; not gradual or gentle; brisk; clever; harsh; dealing cleverly but unfairly; shrill; strongly marked, *esp.* in outline —*adv.* promptly —*n. Mus.* note half a tone above natural pitch; *sl.* cheat, swindler —**sharp'ly** *adv.* make sharp —**sharp'ly** *adv.* —**sharp'ness** *n.* —**sharp'shooter** *n.* marksman

shatt'er *v.* break in pieces; ruin (plans *etc.*); disturb (person) greatly

shave *v.* cut close, *esp.* hair of face or head; pare away; graze; reduce (**shaved, sha'ven, sha'ving**) —*n.* shaving —**sha'vings** *pl.n.* parings —**close, near shave** narrow escape

shawl *n.* piece of fabric to cover woman's shoulders or wrap baby

she *pron.* 3rd person singular feminine pronoun

sheaf *n.* bundle, *esp.* corn; loose leaves of paper (*pl.* **sheaves**)

shear *v.* clip hair, wool from; cut through; fracture (**sheared** *pt.*, **shorn, sheared** *pp.* —**shear'ing** *pr.p.*) —**shear'er** *n.* —**shears** *pl.n.* large pair of scissors; mechanical shearing, cutting instrument

shear'water *n.* various sea birds

sheath *n.* close-fitting cover, *esp.* for knife or sword; scabbard; condom —**sheathe** *vt.* put into sheath

shebang' *n. sl.* situation, matter, *esp.* **whole shebang**

shed[1] *n.* roofed shelter used as store or workshop

shed[2] *vt.* (cause to) pour forth (*eg* tears, blood); cast off (**shed, shedd'ing**)

sheen *n.* gloss —**sheen'y** *a.*

sheep *n.* ruminant animal bred for wool and meat —**sheep'ish** *a.* embarrassed, shy —**sheep-dip** *n.* (deep trough containing) solution in which sheep are immersed to kill vermin and germs in fleece —**sheep'dog** *n.* dog of various breeds *orig.* for herding sheep

—**sheep'skin** n. skin of sheep (with fleece) used for clothing, rug or without fleece for parchment

sheer [1] a. perpendicular; of material, very fine, transparent; absolute, unmitigated

sheer [2] vi. deviate from course; swerve; turn aside

sheet [1] n. large piece of cotton etc. to cover bed; broad piece of any thin material; large expanse —vt. cover with sheet

sheet [2] n. rope fastened in corner of sail —**sheet anchor** large anchor for emergency

sheik(h) [-āk, -ēk] n. Arab chief

shek'el n. Jewish weight and silver coin; money, cash

shelf n. board fixed horizontally (on wall etc.) for holding things; ledge (pl. **shelves**)

shell n. hard outer case (esp. of egg, nut etc.); husk; explosive projectile; outer part of structure left when interior is removed —vt. take shell from; take out of shell; fire at with shells —**shell'fish** n. mollusc; crustacean —**shell shock** nervous disorder caused by bursting of shells or bombs —**shell out** inf. pay up

shellac' n. lac in thin plates for use as varnish —vt. coat with shellac

shel'ter n. place, structure giving protection; protection; refuge; haven —vt. give protection to; screen —vi. take shelter

shelve vt. put on a shelf; put off; cease to employ; defer indefinitely —vi. slope gradually

shenan'igan n. sl. frolicking; playing tricks etc.

shep'herd [shep'ərd] n. man who tends sheep (**shep'herdess** fem.) —vt. guide, watch over —**shepherd's-purse** n. plant with white flowers

sher'bet n. fruit-flavoured effer-

vescent powder, as sweet or in drink

sher'iff [she'rif] n. US law enforcement officer; in England and Wales, chief executive representative of the crown in a county; in Scotland, chief judge of a district

Sher'pa n. member of a Tibetan people (pl. **-pas, -pa**)

sherr'y n. fortified wine

shew [shō] vt. old form of SHOW

shew'bread [shō'-] n. unleavened bread used in Jewish ritual

shibb'oleth n. custom, word etc. distinguishing people of particular class or group

shield n. piece of armour carried on arm; any protection used to stop blows, missiles etc.; any protective device; sports trophy —vt. cover, protect

shift v. (cause to) move, change position —n. relay of workers; time of their working; evasion; expedient; removal; woman's underskirt or dress —**shift'iness** n. —**shift'less** a. lacking in resource or character —**shift'y** a. evasive, of dubious character

shille'lagh [-lā'lə] n. (in Ireland) cudgel

shill'ing n. former Brit. coin, now 5p; monetary unit in various countries

shill'yshally vi. waver —n. wavering, indecision

shimm'er vi. shine with quivering light —n. such light; glimmer

shin n. front of lower leg —vi. climb with arms and legs —vt. kick on shin (him) —**shin'bone** n. tibia

shin'dig, shin'dy n. inf. row; noisy disturbance

shine vi. give out, reflect light; perform very well, excel —vt. cause to shine by polishing (**shone** [shon], **shi'ning**) —n.

brightness, lustre; polishing
—**shin'y** a.

shin'gle[1] [-ng'gl] n. wooden roof tile —vt. cover with shingles

shin'gle[2] [-ng'gl] n. mass of pebbles

shin'gles [-ng'glz] n. disease causing inflammation along a nerve

Shin'to n. native Japanese religion —**Shin'toism** n.

ship n. large seagoing vessel —vt. put on or send (esp. by ship) —vi. embark; take service in ship (-pp-) —**ship'ment** n. act of shipping; goods shipped —**shipp'ing** n. freight transport business; ships collectively —**ship'shape** a. orderly, trim —**ship'wreck** n. destruction of a ship through storm, collision etc. —vt. cause to undergo shipwreck —**ship'yard** n. place for building and repair of ships

shire n. county

shirk vt. evade, try to avoid (duty etc.) —**shirk'er** n.

shirr vt. gather (fabric) into parallel rows —n.

shirt n. garment for upper part of body —**shirt'y** a. sl. annoyed

shiv'er[1] vi. tremble, usu. with cold or fear; shudder; vibrate —n. act, state, of shivering

shiv'er[2] v. splinter, break in pieces —n. splinter

shoal[1] n. stretch of shallow water; sandbank or bar —v. make, become, shallow

shoal[2] n. large number of fish swimming together —vi. form shoal

shock[1] vt. horrify, scandalize —n. violent or damaging blow; emotional disturbance; state of weakness, illness, caused by physical or mental shock; paralytic stroke; collision; effect on sensory nerves of electric discharge —**shock'er** n. person or

thing which shocks or distresses —**shock absorber** device (esp. in cars) to absorb shocks

shock[2] n. group of corn sheaves placed together

shock[3] n. mass of hair —a. shaggy —**shock'headed** a.

shodd'y a. worthless, trashy, second-rate, of poor material

shoe [shoo] n. covering for foot, not enclosing ankle; metal rim or curved bar put on horse's hoof; various protective plates or undercoverings (pl. shoes) —vt. protect, furnish with shoe or shoes (shod pt./pp., shoe'ing pr.p.) —**shoe'string** a./n. very small (amount of money etc.)

shone [shon] pt./pp. of SHINE

shoo interj. go away! —vt. drive away

shook pt. of SHAKE

shoot v. hit, wound, kill with missile fired from weapon; discharge weapon; send, slide, push rapidly; photograph, film —vi. hunt; sprout (shot, shoot'ing) —n. young branch, sprout; shooting competition; hunting expedition —**shoot'er** n.

shop n. place for retail sale of goods and services; workshop, works building —vi. visit shops to buy —vt. sl. inform against (-pp-) —**shop floor** part of factory housing machines; workers in factory —**shop'lifter** n. one who steals from shop —**shop steward** trade union representative of workers in factory etc. —**shop'walker** n. overseer who directs customers etc. —**talk shop** talk of one's business etc. at unsuitable moments

shore[1] n. edge of sea or lake

shore[2] vt. prop (up)

shorn pp. of SHEAR

short a. not long; not tall; brief, hasty; not reaching quantity or standard required; wanting, lacking; abrupt, rude; friable —*adv.* suddenly, abruptly; without reaching end —*n.* drink of spirits, as opposed to beer *etc.*; short film —*pl.* short trousers —**short'age** *n.* deficiency —**short'en** *v.* —**short'ly** *adv.* soon; briefly —**short'cake, short'bread** *n.* sweet, brittle cake made of butter, flour and sugar —**short cir'cuit** *Electricity* connection, often accidental, of low resistance between two parts of circuit —**short'coming** *n.* failing; defect —**short'hand** *n.* method of rapid writing by signs or contractions —**short-handed** *a.* lacking the usual or necessary number of workers, helpers —**short list** selected list of candidates (*esp.* for job) from which final selection will be made —**short shrift** summary treatment —**short ton** US ton (2000 lb.) —**short wave** radio wave between 10 and 50 metres

shot *n.* act of shooting; missile; lead in small pellets; marksman, shooter; try, attempt; photograph; short film sequence; dose; *inf.* injection —*a.* woven so that colour is different, according to angle of light —*pt./pp.* of SHOOT

should [-ood] *pt.* of SHALL

shoul'der [-ōl'-] *n.* part of body to which arm or foreleg is attached; anything resembling shoulder; side of road —*vt.* undertake; bear (burden); accept (responsibility); put on one's shoulder —*vi.* make way by pushing —**shoulder blade** shoulder bone

shout *n.* loud cry —*v.* utter (cry *etc.*) with loud voice

shove [-uv] *vt.* push; *inf.* put —*n.* push —**shove off** *inf.* go away

shov'el [-uv'-] *n.* instrument for scooping, lifting earth *etc.* —*vt.* lift, move (as) with shovel (**-ll-**)

show [-ō] *vt.* expose to view; point out; display; exhibit; explain; prove; guide; accord (favour *etc.*) —*vi.* appear; be noticeable (**showed, shown, show'ing**) —*n.* display, exhibition; spectacle; theatrical or other entertainment; indication; competitive event; ostentation; semblance; pretence —**show'ily** *adv.* —**show'y** *a.* gaudy; ostentatious —**show'down** *n.* confrontation; final test —**show'jumping** *n.* horse-riding competition to demonstrate skill in jumping obstacles —**show'man** *n.* one employed in, or owning, show at fair *etc.*; one skilled at presenting anything in effective way —**show off** exhibit to invite admiration; behave in this way —**show-off** *n.* —**show up** reveal; expose; *inf.* embarrass; arrive

show'er *n.* short fall of rain; anything coming down like rain; kind of bath in which person stands while being sprayed with water; US party to present gifts to a person, as a prospective bride —*vt.* bestow liberally —*vi.* take bath in shower —**show'ery** *a.*

shrank *pt.* of SHRINK

shrap'nel *n.* shell filled with pellets which scatter on bursting; shell splinters

shred *n.* fragment, torn strip; small amount —*vt.* cut, tear to shreds (**shred** *or* **shred'ded, shred'ding**)

shrew [-ōō] *n.* animal like mouse; bad-tempered woman; scold —**shrew'ish** *a.* nagging

shrewd [-ōōd] *a.* astute, intelligent; crafty —**shrewd'ly** *adv.* —**shrewd'ness** *n.*

shriek *n.* shrill cry; piercing scream —*v.* screech

shrike *n.* bird of prey

shrill *a.* piercing, sharp in tone —*v.* utter in such tone —**shrill'y** *adv.*

shrimp n. small edible crustacean; inf. undersized person —vi. go catching shrimps

shrine n. place (building, tomb, alcove) of worship, usu. associated with saint

shrink vi. become smaller; retire, flinch, recoil —vt. make smaller (**shrank** pt., **shrunk'en, shrunk** pp., **shrink'ing** pr.p.) —n. sl. psychiatrist —**shrink'age** n.

shrive vt. give absolution to (**shrived, shrove** pt., **shriv'en** pp., **shri'ving** pr.p.) —**shrift** n. confession; absolution

shriv'el vi. shrink and wither (**-ll-**)

shroud n. sheet, wrapping, for corpse; anything which covers, envelops like shroud —pl. set of ropes to masthead —vt. put shroud on; screen, veil; wrap up

Shrove'tide n. the three days preceding Lent —**Shrove Tuesday** day before Ash Wednesday

shrub n. bushy plant —**shrub'bery** n. plantation, part of garden, filled with shrubs —**shrub'by** a.

shrug vi. raise shoulders, as sign of indifference, ignorance etc. —vt. move (shoulders) thus; (with off) dismiss as unimportant (**-gg-**) —n. shrugging

shrunk('en) pp. of SHRINK

shuck n. shell, husk, pod

shudd'er vi. shake, tremble violently, esp. with horror —n. shuddering, tremor

shuf'fle vi. move feet without lifting them; act evasively —vt. mix (cards); (with off) evade, pass to another —n. shuffling; rearrangement —**shuff'ler** n.

shun vt. avoid; keep away from (**-nn-**)

shunt vt. push aside; divert; move (train) from one line to another

shut v. close; bar; forbid entrance to (**shut, shutt'ing**) —**shut'ter** n. movable window screen, usu. hinged to frame; device in camera admitting light as required to film or plate —**shut down** close or stop factory, machine etc.

shut'tle n. instrument which threads weft between strands of warp in weaving; similar appliance in sewing machine; plane, bus etc. travelling to and fro over short distance —**shut'tlecock** n. small, light cone with cork stub and fan of feathers used as a ball in badminton

shy [1] a. awkward in company; timid, bashful; reluctant; scarce, lacking (esp. in card games, not having enough money for bet etc.) —vi. start back in fear; show sudden reluctance (**shied, shy'ing**) —n. start of fear by horse —**shy'ly** adv. —**shy'ness** n.

shy [2] vt./n. throw (**shied, shy'ing**)

shy'ster n. sl. dishonest, deceitful person

SI Fr. Système International (d'Unités), international system of units of measurement based on units of ten

Si Chem. silicon

Siamese [1] a. of Siam, former name of Thailand —**Siamese cat** breed of cat with blue eyes —**Siamese twins** twins born joined to each other by some part of body

sib'ilant a. hissing —n. speech sound with hissing effect

sib'ling n. person's brother or sister —a.

sib'yl n. woman endowed with spirit of prophecy —**sib'ylline** a. occult

sic Lat. thus: oft. used to call attention to a quoted mistake

sick a. inclined to vomit, vomiting; not well or healthy, physically or mentally; *inf.* macabre, sadistic, morbid; *inf.* bored, tired; *inf.* disgusted —**sick'en** v. make, become, sick; disgust; nauseate —**sick'ly** *a.* unhealthy, weakly; inducing nausea —**sick'ness** *n.* —**sick'bay** *n.* place set aside for treating sick people, *esp.* in ships

sic'kle *n.* reaping hook

side *n.* one of the surfaces of object, *esp.* upright inner or outer surface; either surface of thing having only two; part of body that is to right or left; region nearer or farther than, or right or left of, dividing line *etc.*; region; aspect or part; one of two parties or sets of opponents; sect, faction; line of descent traced through one parent; *sl.* swank, conceit —*a.* at, in, the side; subordinate, incidental —*vi.* take up cause of (*usu.* with) —**si'ding** *n.* short line of rails on which trains or wagons are shunted from main line —**side'board** *n.* piece of furniture for holding dishes *etc.* in dining room —**side'burns** *pl.n.* man's side whiskers —**side'car** *n.* small car attached to side of motorcycle —**side'light** *n. esp.* either of two small lights on front of motor vehicle —**side'line** *n.* Sport boundary of playing area; subsidiary interest or activity —**side'long** *a.* lateral, not directly forward —*adv.* obliquely —**side'slip** *n.* skid —**sides'man** *n.* Anglican Ch. man elected to help parish churchwarden —**side'track** *v.* deviate from main topic —*n.* —**side'walk** *n.* US footpath beside road —**side'ways** *adv.* to or from the side; laterally

side're al [sī-dē'ri-əl] *a.* relating to, fixed by, stars

si'dle *vi.* move in furtive or stealthy manner; move sideways; fawn

SIDS sudden infant death syndrome (*see* COT DEATH)

siege [-j] *n.* besieging of town or fortified place

sienn'a [si-en'ə] *n.* (pigment of) brownish-yellow colour

sierr'a [si-er'ə] *n.* range of mountains with jagged peaks

siest'a [si-est'ə] *n.* rest, sleep in afternoon

sieve [siv] *n.* device with network or perforated bottom for sifting —*v.* sift; strain

sift *vt.* separate (eg with sieve) coarser portion from finer; examine closely —**sift'er** *n.*

sigh [sī] *v./n.* (utter) long audible breath —**sigh for** yearn for, grieve for

sight [sīt] *n.* faculty of seeing; seeing; thing seen; view; glimpse; device for guiding eye; spectacle; *inf.* pitiful or ridiculous object; *inf.* large number, great deal —*vt.* catch sight of; adjust sights of gun *etc.* —**sight'less** *a.* —**sight-read** *v.* play, sing music without previous preparation —**sight'see** *vi.* visit (place) to look at interesting sights —**sight'seeing** *n.* —**sight'seer** *n.*

sign [sīn] *n.* mark, gesture *etc.* to convey some meaning; (board, placard, bearing) notice, warning *etc.*; symbol; omen; evidence —*vt.* put one's signature to; ratify —*vi.* make sign or gesture; affix signature

sig'nal *n.* sign to convey order or information, *esp.* on railway; that which in first place impels any action; Radio *etc.* sequence of electrical impulses transmitted or received —*a.* remarkable, striking —*vt.* make signals to —*vi.* give orders *etc.* by signals (**-ll-**) —**sig'nalize** *vt.* make notable —**sig'nally** *adv.*

sig'natory *n.* one of those who sign agreements, treaties

sig'nature n. person's name written by himself; act of writing it —**signature tune** tune associated with particular programme, person etc.

sig'net n. small seal

signif'icant a. revealing; designed to make something known; important —**signif'icance** n. import, weight; meaning —**signif'icantly** adv. —**significa'tion** n. meaning

sig'nify vt. mean; indicate; denote; imply —vi. be of importance (**sig'nified, sig'nifying**)

sig'nor [sē'nyawr] n. Italian title of respect, like Mr. —**signor'a** n. Mrs. —**signori'na** [-rē'-] n. Miss

Sikh [sēk] n. member of Indian religious sect

si'lage n. fodder crop harvested while green and stored in state of partial fermentation

si'lence n. absence of noise; refraining from speech —vt. make silent; put a stop to —**si'lencer** n. device to reduce noise of engine exhaust, firearm —**si'lent** a.

silhouette' [-lōō'-] n. outline of object seen against light; profile portrait in black

sil'ica n. naturally occurring dioxide of silicon —**sili'ceous, sili'cious** [-lish'-] a. —**silico'sis** n. lung disease caused by inhaling silica dust over a long period

sil'icon n. brittle metalloid element found in sand, clay, stone, widely used in chemistry, industry —**sil'icone** n. large class of synthetic substances, related to silicon and used in chemistry, industry, medicine

silk n. fibre made by larvae (**silkworm**) of certain moth; thread, fabric made from this —**silk'en** a. made of, like silk; soft; smooth; dressed in silk —**silk'ily** adv. —**silk'iness** n. —**silk'y** a.

sill n. ledge beneath window; bottom part of door or window frame

sill'y a. foolish; trivial; feeble-minded —**sill'iness** n.

si'lo n. pit, tower for storing fodder or grain; underground missile launching site (pl. -**los**)

silt n. mud deposited by water —v. fill, be choked with silt —**silta'tion** n. —**silt'y** a.

sil'van a. see SYLVAN

sil'ver n. white precious metal; things made of it; silver coins; cutlery —a. made of silver; resembling silver or its colour; having pale lustre, as moon; soft, melodious, as sound; bright —vt. coat with silver —**sil'very** a. —**silver birch** tree having silvery white peeling bark —**silver wedding** 25th wedding anniversary

sim'ian a. of, like apes

sim'ilar a. resembling, like —**similar'ity** n. likeness; close resemblance —**sim'ilarly** adv.

sim'ile [-i-li] n. comparison of one thing with another, using 'as' or 'like', esp. in poetry

simil'itude n. outward appearance, likeness; guise

simm'er v. keep or be just bubbling or just below boiling point; to be in state of suppressed anger or laughter

si'mony n. (sinful) buying, selling of church preferment

sim'per vi. smile, utter in silly or affected way —n.

sim'ple a. not complicated; plain; not combined or complex; ordinary, mere; guileless; stupid —**sim'pleton** n. foolish person —**simplic'ity** [-lis'-] n. simpleness, clearness, artlessness —**simplifica'tion** n. —**sim'plify** vt. make simple, plain or easy (-**plified,**

-plifying) —**simplist'ic** a. very simple, naive —**sim'ply** adv. —**simple fraction** one in which both the numerator and the denominator are integers

sim'ulate vt. make pretence of; reproduce, copy, esp. conditions of particular situation —**simula'tion** n. —**sim'ulator** n.

simulta'neous a. occurring at the same time —**simultane'ity, simulta'neousness** n. —**simulta'neously** adv.

sin n. transgression of divine or moral law, esp. committed consciously; offence against principle or standard —vi. commit sin (-nn-) —**sin'ful** a. of nature of sin; guilty of sin —**sin'fully** adv. —**sin'ner** n. —**sin-bin** n. inf. separate unit for disruptive school children

since prep. during or throughout period of time after —conj. from time when; because —adv. from that time

sincere' a. not hypocritical, actually moved by or feeling apparent emotions; true, genuine; unaffected —**sincere'ly** adv. —**sincer'ity** [-seri-] n.

sine [-I-] n. mathematical function, esp. ratio of length of hypotenuse to opposite side in right-angled triangle

si'necure n. office with pay but minimal duties

si'ne di'e Lat. with no date, indefinitely postponed

si'ne qua non' [sī'-ni-kwä-non'] Lat. essential condition or requirement

sin'ew n. tough, fibrous cord joining muscle to bone —pl. muscles, strength —**sin'ewy** a. stringy; muscular

sing vi. utter musical sounds; hum, whistle, ring —vt. utter (words) with musical modulation; celebrate in song or poetry (sang, sung, sing'ing) —**sing'er** n. —**singing telegram** greetings service in which messenger sings greetings to person celebrating —**sing'song** n. informal singing session —a. monotonously regular in tone, rhythm

singe [-nj] vt. burn surface of (singed, singe'ing) —n. act or effect of singeing

sin'gle [-ng'gl] a. one only; alone, separate; unmarried; for one; formed of only one part, fold etc.; denoting ticket for train etc. valid for outward journey only; whole-hearted, straightforward —n. single thing; gramophone record with one short item on each side; single ticket —vt. pick (out) —**sin'gly** adv. —**single file** persons, things arranged in one line —**single-handed** a. without assistance —**singles bar** bar or club that is social meeting place for single people

sing'let n. sleeveless undervest

sin'gular a. remarkable; unusual; unique; denoting one person or thing —**singular'ity** n. something unusual —**sin'gularly** adv. particularly; peculiarly

sin'ister a. threatening; evil-looking; wicked; unlucky; Heraldry on left-hand side

sink vi. become submerged (in water); drop, give way; decline in value, health etc.; penetrate (into) —vt. cause to sink; make by digging out; invest (sank pt., sunk, sunk'en pp., sink'ing pr.p.) —n. receptacle with pipe for carrying away waste water; cesspool; place of corruption, vice —**sink'er** n. weight for fishing line —**sinking fund** money set aside at intervals for payment of particular liability at fixed date

Sinn Fein [shin fān] Irish republican political movement

Sino- (*comb. form*) Chinese, of China

sin'uous *a.* curving, devious, lithe —**sin'uate** *a.* —**sinuos'ity** *n.* —**sin'uously** *adv.*

si'nus *n.* cavity, *esp.* air passages in bones of skull —**sinusi'tis** *n.* inflammation of sinus

sip *v.* drink in very small portions (**-pp-**) —*n.*

si'phon, sy'phon *n.* device, *esp.* bent tube, which uses atmospheric or gaseous pressure to draw liquid from container —*v.* draw off thus; draw off in small amounts

sir *n.* polite term of address for a man; (**S-**) title of knight or baronet

sire *n.* male parent, *esp.* of horse or domestic animal; term of address to king —*v.* beget

si'ren *n.* device making loud wailing noise, *esp.* giving warning of danger; legendary sea nymph who lured sailors to destruction; alluring woman

sir'loin *n.* prime cut of loin of beef

si'sal *n.* (fibre of) plant used in making ropes

sis'kin *n.* small olive-green bird of finch family

siss'y *a./n.* weak, cowardly (person)

sis'ter *n.* daughter of same parents; woman fellow-member *esp.* of religious body; senior nurse —*a.* closely related, similar —**sis'terhood** *n.* relation of sister; order, band of women —**sis'terly** *a.* —**sister-in-law** *n.* sister of husband or wife; brother's wife

sit *v.* (*mainly intr.*) adopt posture or rest on buttocks, thighs; perch; incubate; pose for portrait; occupy official position; hold session; remain; take examination; keep watch over baby *etc.* —**sit in**

protest by refusing to move from place —**sit-in** *n.*

sitar' *n.* stringed musical instrument, *esp.* of India

site *n.* place, location; space for, with, a building

sit'uate *v.* place, locate —**situa'tion** *n.* place, position; state of affairs; employment, post

six *a./n.* cardinal number one more than five —**sixth** *a.* ordinal number —*n.* sixth part —**six'teen'** *n./a.* six and ten —**six'ty** *n./a.* six times ten

size[1] *n.* bigness, dimensions; one of series of standard measurements of clothes *etc.*; *inf.* state of affairs —*vt.* arrange according to size —**siz(e)'able** *a.* quite large —**size up** *inf.* assess (person, situation *etc.*)

size[2] *n.* gluelike sealer, filler —*vt.* coat, treat with size

siz'zle *v./n.* (make) hissing, spluttering sound as of frying —**sizz'ler** *n. inf.* hot day

skald [-awl-] *n.* ancient Scandinavian poet

skate[1] *n.* steel blade attached to boot, for gliding over ice —*vi.* glide on skates —**skate'board** *n.* small board mounted on roller-skate wheels

skate[2] *n.* large marine ray

skedad'dle *vi. inf.* scamper off

skein [-a-] *n.* quantity of yarn, wool *etc.* in loose knot; flight of wildfowl

skel'eton *n.* bones of animal; bones separated from flesh and preserved in their natural position; very thin person; outline, draft, framework; nucleus —*a.* reduced to a minimum; drawn in outline; not in detail —**skel'etal** *a.* —**skeleton key** *n.* key filed down so as to open many different locks

skel'm [skel'əm] *n. SA sl.* rogue, rascal

skerr'y n. rocky island or reef

sketch n. rough drawing; brief account; essay; short humorous play —v. make sketch (of) —**sketch'y** a. omitting detail; incomplete; inadequate

skew vi. move obliquely —a. slanting; crooked —**skew'whiff** a. inf. aslant; crooked

skew'bald a. white and any other colour (except black) in patches (esp. of horse)

skew'er n. pin to fasten (meat) together —v. pierce or fasten with skewer

ski [skē] n. long runner fastened to foot for sliding over snow or water (pl. **skis** [-z]) —v. slide on skis (**skied, ski'ing**)

skid v. slide (sideways), esp. vehicle out of control with wheels not revolving (**-dd-**) —n. instance of this; device to facilitate sliding, eg in moving heavy objects —**skid'pan** n. area made slippery so that drivers can practise controlling skids

skiff n. small boat

skill n. practical ability, cleverness, dexterity —**skilled** a. having, requiring knowledge, united with readiness and dexterity —**skil'ful** a. expert, masterly; adroit —**skil'fully** adv.

skill'et n. small frying pan

skim vt. remove floating matter from surface of liquid; glide over lightly and rapidly; read thus —vi. move thus (**-mm-**) —**skim(med) milk** milk from which cream has been removed

skimp vt. give short measure; do thing imperfectly —**skimp'y** a. meagre; scanty

skin n. outer covering of vertebrate body, lower animal or fruit; animal skin used as material or container; film on surface of cooling liquid etc.; complexion —vt. remove skin of (**-nn-**)

—**skin'less** a. —**skinn'er** n. dealer in hides; furrier —**skinn'y** a. thin —**skin-deep** a. superficial; slight —**skin diving** underwater swimming using breathing apparatus —**skin'flint** n. miser, niggard —**skin graft** transplant of piece of healthy skin to wound to form new skin —**skin'tight** a. fitting close to skin

skint a. sl. without money

skip vi. leap lightly; jump a rope as it is swung under one —vt. pass over, omit (**-pp-**) —n. act of skipping

skip n. large open container for builders' rubbish etc.; large bucket, container for transporting men, materials in mines etc.

skipp'er n. captain of ship, plane or team —vt. captain

skirl n. sound of bagpipes

skirm'ish n. fight between small parties, small battle —vi. fight briefly or irregularly

skirt n. woman's garment hanging from waist; lower part of woman's dress, coat etc.; outlying part; sl. woman —vi. border; go round —**skirt'ing** n. vertical board round margin of floor (also skirting board); material for women's skirts

skit n. satire, esp. theatrical burlesque

skitt'ish a. frisky, frivolous

skit'tles pl.n. ninepins

skive v. evade work or responsibility

skivv'y n. female servant who does menial work

skok'iaan [skok'i-an] n. SA potent alcoholic beverage

sku'a n. large predatory gull

skuldugg'ery n. inf. trickery

skulk vi. sneak out of the way; lurk —**skulk'er** n.

skull n. bony case that encloses brain —**skull'cap** n. close-fitting cap

skunk n. small N Amer. animal which emits evil-smelling fluid; sl. mean person

sky n. apparently dome-shaped expanse extending upwards from the horizon; outer space; heavenly regions (pl. **skies**) —vt. hit (cricket ball) high —**sky'diving** n. parachute jumping with delayed opening of parachute —**sky'light** n. window in roof or ceiling —**sky'scraper** n. very tall building

slab n. thick, broad piece

slack[1] a. loose; sluggish; careless, negligent; not busy —n. loose part, as of rope —vi. be idle or lazy —**slack'ly** adv. —**slack'en** v. become looser; become slower, abate

slack[2] n. coal dust, small pieces of coal

slacks pl.n. informal trousers worn by men or women

slag n. refuse of smelted metal; sl. coarse woman

slain pp. of SLAY

slake vt. satisfy (thirst, desire etc.); combine (lime) with water to produce calcium hydroxide

slal'om [slahl'əm] n./v. race over winding course in skiing etc.

slam v. shut noisily; bang; hit; dash down; inf. criticize harshly (**-mm-**) —n. (noise of) this action —**grand slam** Cards winning of all tricks

slan'der [-ah-] n. false or malicious statement about person —v. utter such statement —**slan'derer** n. —**slan'derous** a.

slang n. colloquial language —vt. sl. scold, abuse violently

slant [-ah-] v. slope; put at angle; write, present (news etc.) with bias —n. slope; point of view; idea —a. sloping, oblique —**slant'wise** adv.

slap n. blow with open hand or flat instrument —vt. strike thus; inf. put on, down carelessly or messily (**-pp-**) —**slap'dash** a. careless and abrupt —**slap'stick** n. boisterous knockabout comedy

slash vt. gash; lash; cut, slit; criticize unmercifully —n. gash; cutting stroke

slat n. narrow strip of wood or metal as in blinds etc.

slate n. kind of stone which splits easily in flat sheets; piece of this for covering roof or, formerly, for writing on —vt. cover with slates; abuse —**sla'ter** n. woodlouse —**sla'ting** n. severe reprimand

slath'er [-ahTH'-] n. inf. large quantity —**open slather** A, NZ sl. free-for-all

slatt'ern n. slut —**slatt'ernly** a. slovenly, untidy

slaugh'ter [slaw'-] n. killing —vt. kill —**slaugh'terous** a. —**slaugh'terhouse** n. place for killing animals for food

slave n. captive, person without freedom or personal rights; one dominated by another or by a habit etc. —vi. work like slave —**sla'ver** n. person, ship engaged in slave traffic —**sla'very** n. —**sla'vish** a. servile

slav'er vi. dribble saliva from mouth; fawn —n. saliva running from mouth

slaw n. short for COLESLAW

slay vt. kill; inf. impress, esp. by being very funny (**slew, slain, slay'ing**) —**slay'er** n. killer

sleaz'y a. sordid —**sleaze** n. inf. sordidness

sledge[1], **sled** n. carriage on runners for sliding on snow; toboggan —v.

sledge[2], **sledge'hammer** n. heavy hammer with long handle

sleek a. glossy, smooth, shiny

sleep n. unconscious state regularly occurring in man and animals; slumber, repose; *inf.* dried particles *oft.* found in corners of eyes after sleeping —*vi.* take rest in sleep, slumber **(slept, sleep'ing)** —**sleep'er** *n.* one who sleeps; beam supporting rails of railway; railway sleeping car —**sleep'ily** *adv.* —**sleep'iness** *n.* —**sleep'less** *a.* —**sleep'y** *a.* —**sleeping sickness** Afr. disease spread by tsetse fly

sleet *n.* rain and snow or hail falling together

sleeve *n.* part of garment which covers arm; case surrounding shaft; gramophone record cover —*vt.* furnish with sleeves —**sleeved** *a.* —**sleeve'less** *a.* —**have up one's sleeve** have something prepared secretly for emergency

sleigh [slā] *n.* sledge

sleight [slīt] *n.* dexterity; trickery; deviousness —**sleight of hand** (manual dexterity in) conjuring, juggling; legerdemain

slen'der *a.* slim, slight; feeble

slept *pt./pp. of* SLEEP

sleuth [-ōō-] *n.* detective; tracking dog (*also* **sleuth'hound**) —*vt.* track

slew[1] *pt. of* SLAY

slew[2] *v.* swing round

slice *n.* thin flat piece cut off; share; flat culinary tool —*vt.* cut into slices; cut cleanly; hit with bat *etc.* at angle

slick *a.* smooth; smooth-tongued; flattering; superficially attractive; sly —*vt.* make glossy, smooth —*n.* slippery area; patch of oil on water

slide *v.* slip smoothly along; glide, as over ice; pass imperceptibly; deteriorate morally **(slid** *pt.,* **slid, slidd'en** *pp.,* **sli'ding** *pr.p.)* —*n.* sliding; surface, track for sliding; sliding part of mechanism; piece of glass holding object to be viewed under microscope; photographic transparency; ornamental clip to hold hair in place, hair slide —**slide rule** mathematical instrument of two parts, one of which slides upon the other, for rapid calculations —**sliding scale** schedule for automatically varying one thing (*eg* wages) according to fluctuations of another (*eg* cost of living)

slight [-īt] *a.* small, trifling; not substantial, fragile; slim, slender —*vt.* disregard; neglect —*n.* indifference; act of discourtesy —**slight'ly** *adv.*

slim *a.* thin; slight —*v.* reduce person's weight by diet and exercise **(-mm-)** —**slim'line** *a.* slim; for slimmers

slime *n.* greasy, thick, liquid mud or similar substance —**sli'my** *a.* like slime; fawning

sling *n.* strap, loop with string attached at each end for hurling stone; bandage for supporting wounded limb; rope, belt *etc.* for hoisting, carrying weights —*vt.* throw; hoist, swing by rope **(slung, sling'ing)**

slink *vi.* move stealthily, sneak **(slunk, slink'ing)** —**slink'y** *a.* sinuously graceful; (of clothes *etc.*) figure-hugging

slip[1] *v.* (cause to) move smoothly, easily, quietly; pass out of (mind *etc.*); (of motor vehicle clutch) engage partially, fail —*vi.* lose balance by sliding; fall from person's grasp; make mistake (*usu.* with up); decline in health, morals —*vt.* put on or take off easily, quickly; let go (anchor *etc.*); dislocate (bone) **(-pp-)** —*n.* act or occasion of slipping; mistake; petticoat; small piece of paper; plant cutting; launching slope on which ships are built; *Cricket* (fieldsman in) position offside and a little behind wicket covering for pillow —**slip road** narrow road giving access to motorway *etc.* —**slip'shod** a. slovenly, careless —**slip'stream** n. *Aviation* stream of air driven astern by engine —**slip'way** n. incline for launching ships

slip [2] n. clay mixed with water to creamy consistency, used for decorating ceramic ware

slipp'er n. light shoe for indoor use —**slipp'ered** a.

slipp'ery a. so smooth as to cause slipping or to be difficult to hold or catch; changeable; unreliable; crafty; wily

slit vt. make long straight cut in; cut in strips (**slit, slitt'ing**) —n.

slith'er [-TH-] vi. slide unsteadily (down slope *etc.*)

sliv'er n. thin small piece torn off something; splinter

slob n. *inf.* stupid, coarse person

slobb'er v. slaver; be weakly and excessively demonstrative —n. running saliva; maudlin speech —**slobb'ery** a.

sloe n. blue-black, sour fruit of blackthorn

slog vt. hit vigorously, *esp.* at cricket —vi. work or study with dogged determination; move, work with difficulty (**-gg-**) —n.

slo'gan n. distinctive phrase in advertising *etc.*)

sloop n. small one-masted vessel; *Hist.* small warship

sloot n. SA ditch for irrigation or drainage

slop vi. spill —vt. spill, splash (**-pp-**) —n. liquid spilt; liquid food; dirty liquid —pl. liquid refuse —**slopp'y** a. careless, untidy; sentimental; wet, muddy

slope vt. place slanting —vi. lie in, follow an inclined course; go furtively —n. slant; upward, downward inclination

slosh n. watery mud *etc.*; sl.

heavy blow; —v. splash; hit —**sloshed** a. sl. drunk

slot n. narrow hole or depression; slit for coins —vt. put in slot; sort; *inf.* place in series, organization (**-tt-**) —**slot machine** automatic machine worked by insertion of coin

sloth [-ō-] n. sluggish S Amer. animal; sluggishness —**sloth'ful** a. lazy, idle —**sloth'fully** adv.

slouch vi. walk, sit *etc.* in lazy or ungainly, drooping manner —n. —a. (of hat) with wide, flexible brim

slough [1] [-ow] n. bog

slough [2] [-uf] n. skin shed by snake —v. shed (skin); drop off

slov'en [-uv'-] n. dirty, untidy person —**slov'enly** a. untidy; careless; disorderly —adv.

slow [-ō] a. lasting a long time; moving at low speed; behind the true time; dull —v. slacken speed (of) —**slow'ly** adv. —**slow'ness** n. —**slow'coach** n. person slow in moving, acting, deciding *etc.* —**slow-motion** a. (of film) showing movement greatly slowed down

slow'worm [slō'-] n. small legless lizard, blindworm

sludge n. slush, ooze; sewage

slug [1] n. land mollusc with no shell; bullet —**slug'gard** n. lazy, idle person —**slug'gish** a. slow; lazy, inert; not functioning well —**slug'gishness** n.

slug [2] v. hit, slug —n. heavy blow; portion of spirits —**slug'ger** n. hard-hitting boxer, slogger

sluice [-ōōs] n. gate, door to control flow of water —vt. pour water over, through

slum n. squalid street or neighbourhood —vi. visit slums (**-mm-**)

slum'ber vi./n. sleep —**slum'berer** n.

slump v. fall heavily; relax ungracefully; decline suddenly in value, volume or esteem —n. sudden decline; (of prices etc.) sharp fall; depression

slung pt./pp. of SLING

slunk pt./pp. of SLINK

slur vt. pass over lightly; run together (words, musical notes); disparage (-**rr**-) —n. slight, stigma; Mus. curved line above or below notes to be slurred

slurp v. inf. eat, drink noisily

slurry n. muddy liquid mixture as cement, mud etc.

slush n. watery, muddy substance; excess sentimentality —**slush fund** US fund for financing bribery, corruption

slut n. dirty (immoral) woman —**slutt'ish** a. —**slutt'ishness** n.

sly a. cunning, wily, knowing; secret, deceitful —**sly'ly** adv. —**sly'ness** n.

smack[1] n. taste, flavour; sl. heroin —vi. taste (of); suggest

smack[2] vt. slap; open and close (lips) with loud sound —n. smacking slap; crack; such sound; loud kiss —adv. inf. squarely; directly

smack[3] n. small sailing vessel, usu. for fishing

small [-awl] a. little, unimportant; petty; short; weak; mean —n. small slender part esp. of the back —pl. inf. personal laundry, underwear —**small'ness** n. —**small'holding** n. small area of farming land —**small hours** hours just after midnight —**small-minded** a. having narrow views; petty —**small'pox** n. contagious disease —**small talk** light, polite conversation

smarm v. inf. fawn —**smarm'y** inf. a. unpleasantly suave; fawning

smart a. astute; brisk; clever, witty; impertinent; trim, well dressed; fashionable; causing stinging pain —v. feel, cause pain —n. sharp pain —**smart'en** vt. —**smart'ly** adv. —**smart'ness** n. —**smart aleck** inf. conceited person, know-all

smash vt. break violently; strike hard; ruin; destroy —vi. break; dash violently against —n. heavy blow; collision (of vehicles etc.); total financial failure; inf. popular success —**smashed** a. sl. very drunk or affected by drugs —**smash'er** n. inf. attractive person, thing

smatt'ering n. slight superficial knowledge

smear vt. rub with grease etc.; smudge, spread with dirt, grease etc. —n. mark made thus; sample of secretion for medical examination; slander —**smear'y** a. greasy

smell vt. perceive by nose; fig. suspect —vi. give out odour; use nose (**smelt** or **smelled, smell'ing**) —n. faculty of perceiving odours by nose; anything detected by sense of smell —**smell'y** a. with strong (unpleasant) smell

smelt[1] vt. extract metal from ore —**smelt'ery** n.

smelt[2] n. fish of salmon family

smew n. type of duck

smile n. curving or parting of lips in pleased or amused expression —v. wear, assume a smile; approve, favour

smirch vt. dirty, sully; disgrace, discredit —n. stain; disgrace

smirk n. smile expressing scorn, smugness —v.

smite vt. strike; attack; afflict; affect, esp. with love or fear (**smote, smitt'en, smi'ting**)

smith n. worker in iron, gold etc. —**smith'y** [-TH'-] n. blacksmith's workshop

smithereens[?] n. small bits

smock n. loose, outer garment —vt. gather by sewing in honeycomb pattern —**smock'ing** n.

smog n. mixture of smoke and fog

smoke n. cloudy mass of suspended particles that rises from fire or anything burning; spell of tobacco smoking —vi. give off smoke; inhale and expel tobacco smoke —vt. use (tobacco) by smoking; expose to smoke (esp. in curing fish etc.) —**smo'ker** n. —**smo'kily** adv. —**smo'ky** a.

smooch inf. v./n. kiss, cuddle

smooth [-TH-] a. not rough, even of surface or texture; sinuous; flowing; calm, soft, soothing; suave, plausible; free from jolts —vt. make smooth; quieten —**smooth'ly** adv.

smor'gasbord [-gəs-] n. buffet meal of assorted dishes

smote pt. of SMITE

smoth'er [-uTH-] v. suffocate; envelop; suppress —vi. be suffocated

smoul'der [-ō-] vi. burn slowly without flame; (of feelings) exist in suppressed state

smudge v. make smear, stain, dirty mark (on) —n.

smug a. self-satisfied, complacent —**smug'ly** adv.

smug'gle vt. import, export without paying customs duties; conceal, take secretly —**smug'gler** n.

smut n. piece of soot, particle of dirt; lewd or obscene talk etc.; disease of grain —vt. blacken, smudge (-tt-) —**smut'ty** a. soiled with smut, sooty; obscene, lewd

Sn Chem. tin

snack n. light, hasty meal —**snack bar** bar at which snacks are served

snaf'fle n. light bit for horse —vt. sl. appropriate, scrounge; put snaffle on

snag n. difficulty; sharp protuberance; hole, loop in fabric caused by sharp object; obstacle (eg tree branch etc. in river bed) —vt. catch, damage on snag

snail n. slow-moving mollusc with shell; slow, sluggish person —**snail-like** a.

snake n. long scaly limbless reptile, serpent —v. move like snake —**sna'ky** a. of, like snakes

snap v. break suddenly; make cracking sound; bite (at) suddenly; speak suddenly, angrily —n. act of snapping; fastener; inf. snapshot; inf. easy task; brief period, esp. of cold weather —a. sudden, unplanned, arranged quickly —**snap'per** n. perch-like fish —**snap'py** a. irritable; sl. quick; sl. well-dressed, fashionable —**snap'dragon** n. plant with flowers that can be opened like a mouth —**snap'shot** n. photograph

snare n. (noose used as) trap —vt. catch with one

snarl n. growl of angry dog; tangle, knot —vi. utter snarl; grumble —**snarl-up** n. inf. confusion, obstruction, esp. traffic jam

snatch v. make quick grab or bite (at); seize, catch —n. grab; fragment; short spell

snazz'y a. inf. stylish, flashy

sneak vi. slink; move about furtively; act in mean, underhand manner —n. mean, treacherous person; petty informer —**sneak'ing** a. secret but persistent

sneak'ers pl.n. US flexible, informal sports shoes

sneer n. scornful, contemptuous expression or remark —v.

sneeze vi. emit breath through nose with sudden involuntary spasm and noise —n.

sneeze'wood n. S Afr. tree yielding very hard wood used for fencing, gateposts etc.; this wood

snick n. small cut or notch; nick —vt. cut; clip; nick

snick'er n./v. same as SNIGGER

snide a. malicious, supercilious

sniff vi. inhale through nose with sharp hiss; (with at) express disapproval etc. by sniffing —vt. take up through nose, smell —n. —**snif'fle** vi. sniff noisily through nose, esp. when suffering from a cold in the head; snuffle —**sniffer dog** police dog trained to detect drugs or explosives by smell

snig'ger n. sly, disrespectful laugh, esp. partly stifled —v.

snip vt. cut, cut bits off (-pp-) —n. act, sound of snipping; bit cut off; inf. bargain; inf. certainty —**snipp'et** n. shred, fragment, clipping —**snips** pl.n. tool for cutting

snipe n. wading bird —v. shoot at enemy from cover; (with at) criticize, attack (person) slyly —**sni'per** n.

snitch inf. vt. steal —vi. inform —n. telltale

sniv'el vi. sniffle to show distress; whine (-ll-)

snob n. one who pretentiously judges others by social rank etc. —**snobb'ery** n. —**snobb'ish** a. of like a snob —**snobb'ishly** adv.

snoek [-ook] n. SA barracouta

snoo'ker n. game played on billiard table —vt. leave (opponent) in unfavourable position; place (someone) in difficult situation

snoop v. pry, meddle; peer into —n. one who acts thus; snooping —**snoop'er** n.

snoot'y a. sl. haughty

snooze vi. take short sleep, be half asleep —n. nap

snore vi. breathe noisily when asleep —n.

snor'kel n. tube for breathing underwater —vi. swim, fish using this

snort vi. make (contemptuous)

noise by driving breath through nostrils —n.

snot n. vulg. mucus from nose

snout n. animal's nose

snow n. frozen vapour which falls in flakes; sl. cocaine —v. tall, sprinkle as snow; let fall, throw down like snow; cover with snow —**snow'y** a. of, like snow; covered with snow; very white —**snow'ball** n. snow pressed into hard ball for throwing —v. increase rapidly; play, fight with snowballs —**snow'blindness** n. temporary blindness due to brightness of snow —**snow'drift** n. bank of deep snow —**snow'drop** n. small, white, bell-shaped spring flower —**snow fence** fence erected in winter beside exposed road —**snow goose** white N Amer. goose —**snow-in-summer** n. rock plant with white flowers —**snow line** elevation above which snow does not melt —**snow'man** n. figure shaped out of snow —**snow'shoes** pl.n. shoes like rackets for travelling on snow —**snow under** cover and block with snow; fig. overwhelm

snub vt. insult (esp. by ignoring) intentionally (-bb-) —n. —**snub'by** a. short and blunt —**snub-nosed** a.

snuff[1] n. powdered tobacco for inhaling through nose —**snuffdipping** n. practice of absorbing nicotine by retaining tobacco in mouth

snuff[2] v. extinguish (esp. candle etc.) —**snuff it** inf. die

snuf'fle vi. breathe noisily, with difficulty

snug a. warm, comfortable —**snug'gle** v. lie close to, for warmth or affection —**snug'ly** adv.

so[1] adv. to such an extent; in such a manner; very; the case being such; accordingly —conj.

therefore; in order that; with the result that —*interj.* well! —**so-called** *a.* called by but doubtfully deserving that name —**so long** **SA** *sl.* in the meantime, for the time being

so² *see* SOH

soak *v.* steep; absorb; drench; lie in liquid —*n.* soaking; *sl.* habitual drunkard

soap *n.* compound of alkali and oil used in washing —*vt.* apply soap to —**soap'y** *a.* —**soap opera** radio or television serial of domestic life

soar [sawr] *vi.* fly high; increase, rise (in price *etc.*)

sob *vi.* catch breath, *esp.* in weeping (**-bb-**) —*n.* sobbing —**sob story** tale of personal distress told to arouse sympathy

so'ber *a.* not drunk; temperate; subdued; dull, plain; solemn —*v.* make, become sober —**so'berly** *adv.* —**sobri'ety** *n.* state of being sober

so(u)'briquet [sŏ'bri-kā] *n.* nickname; assumed name

Soc. Society

socc'er *n.* game of football, with spherical ball

so'ciable *a.* friendly; convivial —**sociabil'ity** *n.* —**so'ciably** *adv.*

so'cial *a.* living in communities; relating to society; sociable —*n.* informal gathering —**so'cialite** *n.* member of fashionable society —**socializa'tion** *n.* —**so'cialize** *v.* —**so'cially** *adv.* —**social security** state provision for the unemployed, aged *etc.* —**social work** work to improve welfare of others

so'cialism *n.* political system which advocates public ownership of means of production, distribution and exchange —**so'cialist** *n./a.* —**socialist'ic** *a.*

soci'ety *n.* living associated with others; those so living; com-

panionship; company; association; club; fashionable people collectively

sociol'ogy *n.* study of societies

sock¹ *n.* cloth covering for foot

sock² *sl. vt.* hit —*n.* blow

sock'et *n.* hole or recess for something to fit into

Socrat'ic *a.* of, like Greek philosopher Socrates

sod *n.* lump of earth with grass; *sl.* person considered obnoxious; *sl.* person, as specified

so'da *n.* compound of sodium; soda water —**soda water** water charged with carbon dioxide

sodd'en *a.* soaked; drunk; heavy and doughy

so'dium *n.* metallic alkaline element —**sodium bicarbonate** white crystalline soluble compound (*also* **bicarbonate of soda**)

sod'omy *n.* anal intercourse —**sod'omite** *n.*

so'fa *n.* upholstered seat with back and arms, for two or more people

soft *a.* yielding easily to pressure, not hard; mild; easy; subdued; quiet, gentle; (too) lenient; oversentimental; feeble-minded; (of water) containing few mineral salts; (of drugs) not liable to cause addiction —**soft'en** [sof'n] *v.* make, become soft or softer; mollify; lighten; mitigate; make less loud —**soft'ly** *adv.* gently, quietly —**soft drink** one that is nonalcoholic —**soft furnishings** curtains, rugs *etc.* —**soft option** easiest alternative —**soft soap** flattery —**soft'ware** *n.* computer programs, tapes *etc.* —**soft'wood** *n.* wood of coniferous tree

SOGAT Society of Graphical and Allied Trades

sogg'y *a.* soaked with liquid; damp and heavy

soh, so, sol *n.* fifth sol-fa note

soil[1] n. earth, ground; country, territory

soil[2] v. make, become dirty; tarnish, defile —n. dirt; sewage; stain

soir'ee [swahr'ā] n. private evening party esp. with music

so'journ [soj'ərn] vi. stay for a time —n. short stay —**so'journer** n.

sol see SOH

sol'ace n./vt. comfort in distress

so'lar a. of the sun —**solariza'tion** n. —**so'larize** vt. affect by sunlight —**solar plexus** network of nerves at pit of stomach

sola'rium n. room built mainly of glass to give exposure to sun; (place with) bed for acquiring suntan by artificial means

sold pt./pp. of SELL

sol'der n. easily-melted alloy used for joining metal —vt. join with it —**soldering iron**

sol'dier [sōl'jər] n. one serving in army —vi. serve in army; (with on) persist doggedly —**sol'dierly** a. —**sol'diery** n. troops

sole[1] a. one and only, unique; solitary —**sole'ly** adv. alone; only; entirely

sole[2] n. underside of foot; underpart of boot etc. —vt. fit with sole

sole[3] n. small edible flatfish

sol'ecism n. breach of grammar or etiquette

sol'emn [-əm] a. serious; formal; impressive —**solem'nity** n. —**solemniza'tion** n. —**sol'emnize** vt. celebrate, perform; make solemn —**sol'emnly** adv.

so'lenoid n. coil of wire as part of electrical apparatus

sol-fa n. Mus. system of syllables sol, fa etc. sung in scale

solic'it [-lis'-] vt. request; accost; urge; entice —**solicita'tion** n. —**solic'itor** n. lawyer who prepares documents, advises clients, but represents them in lower courts only —**solic'itous** a. anxious; eager; earnest —**solic'itude** n.

sol'id a. not hollow; compact; composed of one substance; firm; massive; reliable, sound —n. body of three dimensions; substance not liquid or gas —**solidar'ity** [-da'ri-] n. unity of interests; united state —**solidifica'tion** n. —**solid'ify** v. make, become solid or firm; harden (-ified, -ifying) —**solid'ity** n. —**sol'idly** adv.

solil'oquy [-ə-kwi] n. (esp. in drama) thoughts spoken by person while alone —**solil'oquize** vi.

sol'ipsism n. doctrine that self is the only thing known to exist —**sol'ipsist** n.

sol'itary a. alone, single —n. hermit —**solitaire**[1] [or sol'-] n. game for one person played with pegs set in board; single precious stone set by itself —**sol'itude** n. state of being alone; loneliness

so'lo n. music for one performer; card game like whist (pl. so'los) —a. not concerted; unaccompanied, alone; piloting aeroplane alone —**so'loist** n.

sol'stice [-is] n. either shortest (winter) or longest (summer) day of year —**solsti'tial** [-stish'-] a.

solve vt. work out, explain; find answer to —**solubil'ity** n. —**sol'uble** a. capable of being dissolved in liquid; able to be solved or explained —**solu'tion** [-lōō'-] n. answer to problem; dissolving; liquid with something dissolved in it —**sol'vable** a. —**sol'vency** n. —**sol'vent** a. able to meet financial obligations —n. liquid with power of dissolving —**solvent abuse** deliberate inhalation of intoxicating fumes from certain solvents

som'bre a. dark, gloomy

sombre'ro [-â'-] n. wide-brimmed hat (pl. **-ros**)

some [sum] a. denoting an indefinite number, amount or extent; one or other; amount of; certain; approximately —pron. portion, quantity —**some'body** n. some person; important person —**some'how** adv. by some means unknown —**some'thing** n. thing not clearly defined; indefinite amount, quantity or degree —**some'time** adv. formerly; at some (past or future) time —a. former —**some'times** adv. occasionally; now and then —**some'what** adv. to some extent, rather —**some'where** adv.

som'ersault [sum'-] n. tumbling head over heels

somnam'bulist n. sleepwalker —**somnam'bulism** n. —**somnambulis'tic** a.

som'nolent a. drowsy; causing sleep —**som'nolence** n.

son n. male child —**son-in-law** n. daughter's husband

so'nar n. device like echo sounder

sonat'a [-naht'ə] n. piece of music in several movements —**sonati'na** [-tē'-] n. short sonata

son et lu'mière [son-ā-lōōm'yār] Fr. entertainment staged at night at famous place, building, giving dramatic history of it with lighting and sound effects

song n. singing; poem etc. for singing —**song'ster** n. singer; songbird —**song'stress** fem.)

son'ic a. pert. to sound waves —**sonic boom** explosive sound caused by aircraft travelling at supersonic speed

sonn'et n. fourteen-line poem with definite rhyme scheme —**sonneteer'** n. writer of this

sonor'ous a. giving out (deep) sound, resonant —**sonor'ously**

adv. —**sonor'ity** [-o'ri-] n.

sook n. inf. babyish person —**sook'y** a.

soon [-ōō-] adv. in a short time; before long; readily, quickly

soot [-oo-] n. black powdery substance formed by burning of coal etc. —**soot'y** a. of, like soot

sooth [-ōō-] n. truth —**sooth'say-er** n. one who foretells future; diviner

soothe [-ōōTH] vt. make calm, tranquil; relieve (pain etc.)

sop n. piece of bread etc. soaked in liquid; concession, bribe —vt. steep in water etc.; soak (up) (**-pp-**) —**sopp'ing** a. completely soaked —**sopp'y** a. inf. oversentimental

soph'ist n. fallacious reasoner, quibbler —**soph'ism** n. specious argument —**sophist'ical** a. —**soph'istry** n.

sophis'ticate vt. make artificial, spoil, falsify, corrupt —n. sophisticated person —**sophis'ticated** a. having refined or cultured tastes, habits; worldly wise; superficially clever; complex —**sophistica'tion** n.

soph'omore n. US student in second year at college

soporif'ic a. causing sleep (esp. by drugs)

sopra'no [-rahn'-] n. highest voice in women and boys; singer with this voice; musical part for it (pl. **-os**)

sor'bet [or -bā] n. (fruit-flavoured) water ice

sor'cerer n. magician (**sor'cer-ess** fem.) —**sor'cery** n. witchcraft, magic

sor'did a. mean, squalid; ignoble, base —**sor'didly** adv. —**sor'didness** n.

sore a. painful; causing annoyance; severe; distressed; annoyed —adv. obs. grievously, intensely —n. sore place, ulcer, boil etc.

—**sore'ly** adv. grievously; greatly —**sore'ness** n.

sor'ghum [-gəm] n. kind of grass cultivated for grain

sorr'el n. plant; reddish-brown colour; horse of this colour —a. of this colour

sorr'ow [-ō] n. pain of mind, grief, sadness —vi. grieve —**sor'rowful** a. —**sorr'owfully** adv.

sorr'y a. feeling pity or regret; distressed; miserable, wretched; mean, poor —**sorr'ily** adv. —**sor'riness** n.

sort n. kind or class —vt. classify —**sort'er** n.

sort'ie n. sally by besieged forces

SOS n. international code signal of distress; call for help

so-so a. inf. mediocre

sot n. habitual drunkard

sott'o vo'ce [-chi] It. in an undertone

sou'fflé [sōō'flā] n. dish of eggs beaten to froth, flavoured and baked

sough [sow] n. low murmuring sound as of wind in trees

sought [sawt] pt./pp. of SEEK

soul [sōl] n. spiritual and immortal part of human being; example, pattern; person; (also **soul music**) type of Black music combining urban blues with jazz, pop etc. —**soul'ful** a. full of emotion or sentiment —**soul'less** a. mechanical; lacking sensitivity or nobility; heartless, cruel

sound[1] n. what is heard; noise —vi. make sound; seem; give impression of —vt. cause to sound; utter —**sound barrier** inf. hypothetical barrier to flight at speed of sound waves —**sound track** recorded sound accompaniment of film etc.

sound[2] a. in good condition; solid; of good judgment; legal; solvent; thorough; effective; watertight; deep —**sound'ly** adv. thoroughly

sound[3] vt. find depth of, as water; ascertain views of; probe —**sound'ings** pl.n. measurements taken by sounding

sound[4] n. channel; strait

soup [sōōp] n. liquid food made by boiling meat, vegetables etc. —**soup'y** a. like soup; murky; sentimental

sour a. acid; gone bad; rancid; peevish; disagreeable —v. make, become sour —**sour'ly** adv. —**sour'ness** n. —**sour'puss** n. sullen, sour-faced person

source [-aw-] n. origin, starting point; spring

souse v. plunge, drench; pickle —n. sousing; brine for pickling

soutane [sōō-tan'] n. priest's cassock

south n. cardinal point opposite north; region, part of country etc. lying to that side —a./adv. (that is) towards south —**south'erly** [suTH'-] a. towards south —n. wind from the south —**south'ern** [suTH'-] a. in south —**south'wards** a./adv. —**South'down** n. breed of sheep

souvenir' [sōō-və-nēr'] n. keepsake, memento

sou'west'er [sow-] n. waterproof hat

sov'ereign [sov'rin] n. king, queen; former gold coin worth 20 shillings —a. supreme; efficacious —**sov'ereignty** n. supreme power and right to exercise it; dominion; independent state

so'viet n. elected council at various levels of government in USSR; citizen of USSR —a. of, pert. to USSR, its people, government —**sov'ietism** n.

sow[1] [sō] vi. scatter, plant seed —vt. scatter, deposit (seed); spread abroad (**sowed** pt., **sown**

or **sowed** *pp.,* **sow'ing** *pr.p.*)
—**sow'er** *n.*

sow[1] *n.* female adult pig

soy'a *n.* edible bean used as
meat substitute, in making
soy(a) sauce *etc.*

sozz'led [-əld] *a. sl.* drunk

spa [spah] *n.* medicinal spring;
place, resort with one

space *n.* extent; room; period;
empty place; area; expanse; region beyond earth's atmosphere
—*vt.* place at intervals —**spa'-
cious** *a.* roomy, extensive
—**space'craft, space'ship** *n.* vehicle for travel beyond earth's
atmosphere —**Space Invaders** R
game played on video screen in
amusement arcades *etc.* involving destroying aliens from outer
space —**space'man** *n.* —**space
shuttle** vehicle for repeated
space flights —**space'suit** *n.*
sealed, pressurized suit worn by
astronaut

spade[1] *n.* tool for digging
—**spade work** arduous preparatory work

spade[2] *n.* leaf-shaped black
symbol on playing card

spaghett'i [-get'-] *n.* pasta in
form of long strings

spake *obs. pt. of* SPEAK

span *n.* space from thumb to
little finger as measure; extent,
space; stretch of arch *etc.*;
abbrev. of **wingspan**, distance
from wingtip to wingtip —*vt.*
stretch over; measure with hand
(**-nn-**)

span'gle [-ng'gl] *n.* small shiny
metallic ornament —*vt.* decorate
with spangles

span'iel *n.* breed of dog with
long ears and silky hair

spank *vt.* slap with flat of hand,
esp. on buttocks —*n.* —**spank'ing**
n. series of spanks —*a.* quick,
lively; large, fine

spann'er *n.* tool for gripping
nut or bolt head

span'spek *n.* SA sweet melon

spar[1] *n.* pole, beam, *esp.* as part
of ship's rigging

spar[2] *vi.* box; dispute, *esp.* in fun
(**-rr-**) —*n.* sparring

spar[3] *n.* kinds of crystalline
mineral

spare [-âr] *vt.* leave unhurt;
show mercy; abstain from using;
do without; give away —*a.* additional; in reserve; thin; lean;
scanty —*n.* spare part (for machine) —**spa'ring** *a.* economical,
careful

spark *n.* small glowing or burning particle; flash of light produced by electrical discharge;
vivacity, humour; trace; in
internal-combustion engines,
electric spark (in **spark plug**)
which ignites explosive mixture
in cylinder —*v.* emit sparks;
kindle, excite

spar'kle *vi.* glitter; effervesce;
scintillate —*n.* small spark; glitter; flash; lustre —**spar'kling** *a.*
flashing; glittering; brilliant; lively; (of wines) effervescent

spar'row [-ō] *n.* small brownish
bird —**sparr'owhawk** *n.* hawk
that hunts small birds

sparse *a.* thinly scattered

spar'tan *a.* hardy; austere; frugal

spasm [-zm] *n.* sudden convulsive (muscular) contraction; sudden burst of activity *etc.* —**spas-
mod'ic** *a.* occurring in spasms

spas'tic *a.* affected by spasms,
suffering cerebral palsy —*n.*

spat[1] *pt. of* SPIT[1]

spat[2] *n.* short gaiter

spat[3] *n.* slight quarrel

spate *n.* rush, outpouring; flood

spathe *n.* large sheathlike leaf
enclosing flower cluster

spa'tial *a.* of, in space

spatt'er *vt.* splash, cast drops

over —*vi.* be scattered in drops
—*n.* slight splash; sprinkling

spat'ula *n.* utensil with broad, flat blade for various purposes

spav'in *n.* injury to, growth on horse's leg —**spav'ined** *a.* lame, decrepit

spawn *n.* eggs of fish or frog; *oft. offens.* offspring —*vi.* (of fish or frog) cast eggs

spay *vt.* remove ovaries from (animal)

speak *vi.* utter words; converse; deliver discourse —*vt.* utter; pronounce; express; communicate in (**spoke, spo'ken, speak'ing**) —**speak'able** *a.* —**speak'er** *n.* one who speaks; one who specializes in speech making; (*oft.* **S-**) official chairman of many legislative bodies; loudspeaker

spear *n.* long pointed weapon; slender shoot, as of asparagus —*vt.* transfix, pierce, wound with spear —**spear'head** *n.* leading force in attack, campaign —*vt.*

spear'mint *n.* type of mint

spec *inf. n.* (*esp.* **on spec**) speculation or gamble

spec'ial [spesh'əl] *a.* beyond the usual; particular, individual; distinct; limited —**spec'ialism** *n.* —**spec'ialist** *n.* one who devotes himself to special subject or branch of subject —**special'ity** *n.* special product, skill, characteristic *etc.* —**specializa'tion** *n.* —**spe'cialize** *vi.* be specialist —*vt.* make special —**spe'cially** *adv.*

spe'cie [spē'shē] *n.* coined, as distinct from paper, money

spe'cies [-shēz] *n.* sort, kind, *esp.* animals *etc.*; class; subdivision (*pl.* **spe'cies**)

specif'ic *a.* definite; exact in detail; characteristic of thing or kind —**specif'ically** *adv.* —**spec'ify** *vt.* state definitely or in detail (**-ified, -ifying**) —**speci-**

fica'tion *n.* detailed description of something to be made, done —**specific gravity** ratio of density of substance to that of water

spec'imen [-es-] *n.* part typifying whole; individual example

spe'cious *a.* deceptively plausible, but false —**spe'ciously** *adv.* —**spe'ciousness** *n.*

speck *n.* small spot, particle —*vt.* spot —**spec'kle** *n./vt.* speck

spec'tacle *n.* show; thing exhibited; ridiculous sight —*pl.* pair of lenses for correcting defective sight —**spectac'ular** *a.* impressive; showy; grand; magnificent —*n.* lavishly produced performance —**spectate'** *vi.* —**specta'tor** *n.* one who looks on

spec'tre *n.* ghost; image of something unpleasant —**spec'tral** *a.* ghostly

spec'trum *n.* band of colours into which beam of light can be decomposed *eg* by prism (*pl.* **spec'tra**) —**spec'troscope** *n.* instrument for producing, examining spectra

spec'ulate *vi.* guess, conjecture; engage in (risky) commercial transactions —**specula'tion** *n.* —**spec'ulative** *a.* given to, characterized by speculation —**spec'ulator** *n.*

spec'ulum *n.* mirror; reflector of polished metal, *esp.* in reflecting telescopes (*pl.* **-la, -lums**) —**spec'ular** *a.*

speech *n.* act, faculty of speaking; words, language; conversation; discourse; (formal) talk given before audience —**speech'ify** *vi.* make speech, *esp.* long and tedious one (**-ified, -ifying**) —**speech'less** *a.* dumb; at a loss for words

speed *n.* swiftness; rate of progress; degree of sensitivity of photographic film; *sl.* amphetamine —*vi.* move quickly; drive vehicle at high speed; *obs.* succeed —*vt.* further; expedite (**sped** *or* **speed'ed** *pt./pp.*) —**speed'ing** *n.* driving (vehicle) at high speed, *esp.* over legal limit —**speed'ily** *adv.* —**speed'o** *n. inf.* speedometer —**speed'y** *a.* quick; rapid; nimble; prompt —**speed'boat** *n.* light fast motorboat —**speedom'eter** *n.* instrument to show speed of vehicle —**speed'way** *n.* track for motorcycle racing —**speed'well** *n.* plant with small *usu.* blue flowers

spek *n. SA* bacon

speleol'ogy [spē-li-] *n.* study, exploring of caves —**speleolog'ical** *a.*

spell[1] *vt.* give letters of in order; read letter by letter; indicate, result in (**spelled** *or* **spelt** *pt./pp.,* **spell'ing** *pr.p.*) —**spell'ing** *n.* —**spell out** make explicit

spell[2] *n.* magic formula; enchantment —**spell'bound** *a.* entranced; entranced

spell[3] *n.* (short) period of time, work

spen'cer *obs. n.* overcoat; woman's undervest

spend *vt.* pay out; pass (time) on activity *etc.*; use up completely (**spent** *pt./pp.,* **spend'ing** *pr.p.*) —**spend'er** *n.* —**spend'thrift** *n.* wasteful person

sperm *n.* male reproductive cell; semen —**spermat'ic** *a.* of sperm —**sperm'icide** *n.* drug *etc.* that kills sperm

spermacet'i [-set'-] *n.* white, waxy substance obtained from oil from head of sperm whale —**sperm whale** large, toothed whale

spew *v.* vomit

sphagʹnum [sfag'-] *n.* moss that grows in bogs

sphere [sfēr] *n.* ball, globe; range; field of action; status;

position; province —**spherʹical** [sfe'ri-] *a.*

sphincʹter *n.* ring of muscle surrounding opening of hollow bodily organ

sphinx *n.* statue in Egypt with lion's body and human head; (**S-**) monster, half woman, half lion; enigmatic person (*pl.* **-es, sphinʹges** [-jēz])

spice *n.* aromatic or pungent vegetable substance; spices collectively; anything that adds flavour, relish, piquancy, interest *etc.* —*vt.* season with spices, flavour —**spiʹcily** *adv.* —**spiʹcy** *a.* flavoured with spices; *inf.* slightly indecent, risqué

spick-and-span *a.* neat, smart, new-looking

spiʹder *n.* small eight-legged creature which spins web to catch prey —**spiʹdery** *a.* —**spider plant** hardy house plant with long thin leaves

spiel [shpēl] *inf. n.* glib (sales) talk —*vi.* deliver spiel, recite —**spielʹer** *n.*

spigʹot *n.* peg or plug

spike *n.* sharp point; sharp pointed object; long flower cluster with flowers attached directly to the stalk —*vt.* pierce, fasten with spike; render ineffective; add alcohol to (drink) —**spiʹky** *a.*

spill[1] *v.* (cause to) pour from, flow over, fall out, *esp.* unintentionally; upset; be lost or wasted (**spilt** *or* **spilled** *pt./pp.*) —*n.* fall; amount spilt —**spillʹage** *n.*

spill[2] *n.* thin strip of wood, twisted paper *etc.* for lighting fires *etc.*

spin *v.* (cause to) revolve rapidly; whirl; twist into thread; prolong; *inf.* tell (a story); fish with lure (**spun, spun** *pt.,* **spun** *pp.,* **spinʹning** *pr.p.*) —*n.* spinning; (of aircraft) descent in dive with continued rotation; rapid run or ride —**spinn'ing** n. act, process of drawing out and twisting into threads, as wool, cotton, flax etc. —**spinning wheel** household machine with large wheel turned by treadle for spinning wool etc. into thread —**spin dry** spin clothes in (washing) machine to remove excess water —**spin-dryer** n.

spin'ach [-ij, -ich] n. garden vegetable

spin'dle n. rod, axis for spinning —**spin'dly** a. long and slender; attenuated

spin'drift n. spray blown along surface of sea

spine n. backbone; thin spike, esp. on fish etc.; ridge; back of book —**spi'nal** a. —**spine'less** a. lacking spine; cowardly

spin'et [or -et'] n. keyboard instrument like harpsichord

spinn'aker n. large yacht sail

spinn'ey n. small wood

spin'ster n. unmarried woman

spi'raea [-ri-ə] n. shrub, plant with small white or pink flower sprays

spi'ral n. continuous curve drawn at ever increasing distance from fixed point; anything resembling this —a. —**spi'rally** adv.

spire n. pointed part of steeple; pointed stem

spir'it n. life principle animating body; disposition; liveliness; courage; frame of mind; essential character or meaning; soul; ghost; liquid got by distillation, alcohol —pl. emotional state; strong alcoholic drink eg whisky —vt. carry away mysteriously —**spir'ited** a. lively —**spir'itless** a. listless, apathetic —**spir'itual** a. given to, interested in things of the spirit —n. negro sacred song, hymn —**spir'itualism** n. belief that spirits of the dead communi-

cate with the living —**spir'itualist** n. —**spiritual'ity** n. —**spir'itually** adv. —**spir'ituous** a. alcoholic —**spirit level** glass tube containing bubble in liquid, used to check horizontal, vertical surfaces —**spirits of salts** hydrochloric acid

spirt n. see SPURT

spit[1] vi. eject saliva —vt. eject from mouth (**spat, spit** pt./pp., **spitt'ing** pr.p.) —n. spitting, saliva —**spit'tle** n. saliva —**spittoon'** n. vessel to spit into —**spit'fire** n. person with fiery temper

spit[2] n. sharp rod to put through meat for roasting; sandy point projecting into the sea —vt. thrust through (-**tt**-)

spite n. malice —vt. thwart spitefully —**spite'ful** a. —**spite'fully** adv. —**in spite of** prep. regardless of; notwithstanding

spiv n. smartly dressed man, esp. one who makes living by shady dealings

splash v. scatter liquid about or on, over something; print, display prominently —n. sound of this; patch, esp. of colour; (effect of) extravagant display; small amount

splat n. wet, slapping sound

splatt'er v./n. spatter

splay v. spread out; slanting; turned outwards —vt. spread out; twist outwards —n. slant surface; spread —**splay'footed** a. flat and broad (of foot)

spleen n. organ in the abdomen; anger; irritable or morose temper —**splenet'ic** a.

splen'did a. magnificent, brilliant, excellent —**splen'didly** adv. —**splen'dour** n.

splice vt. join by interweaving strands; join (wood) by overlapping; sl. join in marriage —n. spliced joint

spline n. narrow groove, ridge,

strip, *esp.* joining wood *etc.*

splint *n.* rigid support for broken limb *etc.*

splint'er *n.* thin fragment —*vi.* break into fragments, shiver —**splinter group** group that separates from main party, organization, *oft.* after disagreement

split *v.* break asunder; separate; divide (**split, split'ting**) —*n.* crack, fissure; dessert of fruit and ice cream

splotch, splodge *n./v.* splash, daub —**splotch'y, splodg'y** *a.*

splurge *v.* spend money extravagantly —*n.*

splutt'er *v.* make hissing, spitting sounds; utter incoherently with spitting sounds —*n.*

spoil *vt.* damage, injure; damage manners or behaviour of (*esp.* child) by indulgence; pillage —*vi.* go bad (**spoiled** *or* **spoilt** *pt./pp.*, **spoil'ing** *pr.p.*) —*n.* booty; waste material, *esp.* in mining (*also* **spoil'age**) —**spoil'er** *n.* slowing device on aircraft wing *etc.* —**spoiling for** eager for

spoke[1] *pt.*, **spo'ken** *pp.* of SPEAK —**spokes'man** *n.* one deputed to speak for others

spoke[1] *n.* radial bar of a wheel —**spoke'shave** *n.* tool for shaping wood

spolia'tion [spō-] *n.* act of spoiling; robbery; destruction —**spo'liate** *v.* despoil, plunder, pillage

spon'dee *n.* metrical foot consisting of two long syllables

sponge [-unj] *n.* marine animal; its skeleton, or a synthetic substance like it, used to absorb liquids; type of light cake —*vt.* wipe with sponge —*v.* live menially at expense of others; cadge —**spong'er** *n. sl.* one who cadges, or lives at expense of others —**spong'y** *a.* spongelike; wet and soft

spon'sor *n.* one promoting, advertising something; one who agrees to give money to a charity on completion of specified activity by another; one taking responsibility for (*esp.* for welfare of child at baptism, *ie* godparent); guarantor —*vt.* act as sponsor —**spon'sorship** *n.*

sponta'neous *a.* voluntary; natural; not forced; produced without external force —**sponta-ne'ity** [*or* -a'-] *n.* —**sponta'neous-ly** *adv.* —**sponta'neousness** *n.*

spoof [-ōō-] *n.* mild satirical mockery; trick, hoax

spook [-ōō-] *n.* ghost —**spook'y** *a.*

spool [-ōō-] *n.* reel, bobbin

spoon [-ōō-] *n.* implement with shallow bowl at end of handle for carrying food to mouth *etc.* —*v.* lift with spoon —**spoon'ful** *n.*

spoon'erism [-ōō-] *n.* amusing transposition of initial consonants, *eg* "half-warmed fish" for "half-formed wish"

spoor *n.* trail of wild animals —*v.* follow spoor

sporad'ic *a.* intermittent; scattered, single —**sporad'ically** *adv.*

spore *n.* minute reproductive organism of some plants and protozoans

sporr'an *n.* pouch worn in front of kilt

sport *n.* game, activity for pleasure, competition, exercise; enjoyment; mockery; cheerful person, good loser —*v.* wear (*esp.* ostentatiously) —*vi.* frolic; play (sport) —**sport'ing** *a.* of sport; behaving with fairness, generosity —**spor'tive** *a.* playful —**sports car** fast (open) car —**sports jacket** man's casual jacket —**sports'man** *n.* one who engages in sport; good loser

spot *n.* small mark, stain; blemish; pimple; place; (difficult) situation; *inf.* small quantity —*vt.*

mark with spots; detect; observe (**-tt-**) —**spot'less** a. unblemished; pure —**spot'lessly** adv. —**spott'y** a. with spots; uneven —**spot check** random examination —**spot'light** n. powerful light illuminating small area; centre of attention

spouse n. husband or wife —**spou'sal** n. marriage

spout v. pour out; sl. speechify —n. projecting tube or lip for pouring liquids; copious discharge

sprain n./vt. wrench or twist (of muscle etc.)

sprang pt. of SPRING

sprat n. small sea fish

sprawl vi. lie or sit about awkwardly; spread in rambling, unplanned way —n. sprawling

spray[1] n. (device for producing) fine drops of liquid —vt. sprinkle with shower of fine drops

spray[2] n. branch, twig with buds, flowers etc.; floral ornament, brooch etc. like this

spread [-ed] v. extend; stretch out; open out; scatter; distribute; unfold; cover (**spread, spread'ing**) —n. extent; increase; ample meal; food which can be spread on bread etc. —**spread-eagle(d)** a. with arms and legs outstretched

spree n. session of overindulgence; romp

sprig n. small twig; ornamental design like this; small nail

spright'ly [-rīt'-] a. lively, brisk —**spright'liness** n.

spring vi. leap; shoot up or forth; come into being; appear; grow; become bent or split —vt. produce unexpectedly; set off (trap) (**sprang, sprung, spring'ing**) —n. leap; recoil; piece of coiled or bent metal with much resilience; flow of water from earth; first season of year

—**spring'y** a. elastic —**spring'board** n. flexible board for diving —**spring tide** high tide at new or full moon

spring'bok n. S Afr. antelope; name given to S Africans, esp. national sportsmen

sprin'kle [-ng'kl] vt. scatter small drops on, strew —**sprin'kler** n. —**sprin'kling** n. small quantity or number

sprint vt. run short distance at great speed —n. such run, race —**sprint'er** n. one who sprints

sprit n. small spar set diagonally across a fore-and-aft sail in order to extend it —**sprit'sail** n. sail extended by a sprit

sprite n. fairy, elf

sprock'et n. projection on wheel or capstan for engaging chain; wheel with these

sprout vi. put forth shoots, spring up —n. shoot —**Brussels sprout** kind of miniature cabbage

spruce[1] n. variety of fir

spruce[2] a. neat in dress

sprung pp. of SPRING

spry a. nimble, vigorous

spud n. inf. potato

spume n./vi. foam, froth

spun pt./pp. of SPIN

spunk n. courage, spirit

spur n. pricking instrument attached to horseman's heel; incitement; stimulus; projection on cock's leg; projecting mountain range; branch (road etc.) —vt. ride hard (**-rr-**)

spurge n. plant with milky sap

spur'ious [spyoor'-] a. not genuine

spurn vt. reject with scorn, thrust aside

spurt, spirt v. send, come out in jet; rush suddenly —n. jet; short sudden effort, esp. in race

sput'nik [-oo-] n. one of series of Russian satellites

sputt'er v. splutter

spu'tum n. spittle (pl. -ta)

spy n. one who watches (in rival countries, companies etc.) and reports secretly —vi. act as spy —vt. catch sight of (**spied, spy'ing**) —**spy'glass** n. small telescope

Sq. Square

squab'ble [-ob'-] vi. engage in petty, noisy quarrel, bicker —n.

squad [-od] n. small party, esp. of soldiers —**squad'ron** n. division of cavalry regiment, fleet or air force

squal'id [-ol'-] a. mean and dirty —**squal'or** n.

squall [-awl] n. harsh cry; sudden gust of wind; short storm —vi. yell

squan'der [-on'-] vt. spend wastefully, dissipate

square [-âr] n. equilateral rectangle; area of this shape; in town, open space (of this shape); product of a number multiplied by itself; instrument for drawing right angles —a. square in form; honest; straight; even; level, equal; denoting a measure of area; inf. old-fashioned, conservative —vt. make square; find square of; pay; bribe —vi. fit, suit —**square'ly** adv. —**square metre** etc. area equal to that of square with sides one metre etc. long —**square root** number that, multiplied by itself, gives number of which it is factor

squash [-osh] vt. crush flat; pulp; suppress; humiliate (person) —n. juice of crushed fruit; crowd; game played with rackets and soft balls in walled court; marrowlike plant

squat [-ot] vi. sit on heels; act as squatter (-tt-) —a. short and thick —**squatt'er** n. one who settles on land or occupies house without permission

squaw n. Amer. Indian woman

squawk n. short harsh cry, esp. of bird —vi. utter this

squeak v./n. (make) short shrill sound

squeal n. long piercing squeak —vi. make one; sl. confess information (about another)

squeam'ish a. easily made sick; easily shocked; overscrupulous

squee'gee [-jē] n. tool with rubber blade for clearing water (from glass etc.), spreading wet paper etc. —vt. press, smooth with a squeegee

squeeze vt. press; wring; force; hug; subject to extortion —n. act of squeezing; period of hardship, difficulty caused by financial weakness

squelch vi. make, walk with wet sucking sound, as in walking through mud —n.

squib n. small (faulty) firework; insignificant person

squid n. type of cuttlefish

squig'gle n. wavy, wriggling mark —vi. wriggle; draw squiggle

squint vi. have the eyes turned in different directions; glance sideways —n. this eye disorder; glance

squire n. country gentleman

squirm vi. wriggle; be embarrassed —n.

squirr'el n. small graceful bushy-tailed tree animal

squirt v. (of liquid) force, be forced through narrow opening —n. jet; inf. short or insignificant person

squish v./n. (make) soft splashing sound

Sr Chem. strontium

Sr. Senior; Sister

SRN State Registered Nurse

SS steamship

St. Saint; Strait; Street

st. stone (weight)

stab v. pierce, strike (at) with pointed weapon (**-bb-**) —n. blow, wound so inflicted; sudden sensation, eg of fear; attempt

sta'bilize vt. make steady, restore to equilibrium, esp. of money values, prices and wages —**stabiliza'tion** n. —**sta'bilizer** n. device to maintain equilibrium of ship, aircraft etc.

sta'ble[1] n. building for horses; racehorses of particular owner, establishment; such establishment —vt. put into stable

sta'ble[2] a. firmly fixed; steadfast, resolute —**stabil'ity** n. steadiness; ability to resist change of any kind —**sta'bly** adv.

stacca'to [-kaht'-] a. Mus. with notes sharply separated; abrupt

stack n. ordered pile, heap; chimney —vt. pile in stack; control aircraft waiting to land so that they fly at different altitudes

sta'dium n. open-air arena for athletics etc. (pl. **-s**, **-ia**)

staff [-ah-] n. body of officers or workers; personnel; pole; five lines on which music is written (pl. **staffs**, **staves**) —vt. employ personnel; supply with personnel

Staffs Staffordshire

stag n. male deer —a. for men only, as in **stag party**

stage n. period, division of development; raised floor or platform; (platform of) theatre; scene of action; stopping-place on road, distance between two of them; separate unit of space rocket, that can be jettisoned —vt. put (play) on stage; arrange, bring about —**sta'gy** a. theatrical —**stage whisper** loud whisper intended to be heard by audience

stagg'er vi. walk unsteadily —vt. astound; arrange in overlap-

ping or alternating positions, times; distribute over a period —n. act of staggering —pl. form of vertigo; disease of horses —**stagg'ering** a. astounding

stag'nate [or -nāt'] vi. cease to flow or develop —**stag'nant** a. sluggish; not flowing; foul, impure —**stagna'tion** n.

staid a. of sober and quiet character, sedate —**staid'ly** adv. —**staid'ness** n.

stain v. spot, mark; apply liquid colouring to (wood etc.); bring disgrace upon —n. —**stain'less** a. —**stainless steel** rustless steel alloy

stairs pl.n. set of steps, esp. as part of house —**stair'case**, **stair'way** n. structure enclosing stairs; stairs

stake n. sharpened stick or post; money wagered or contended for —vt. secure, mark out with stakes; wager, risk

stal'actite n. lime deposit like icicle on roof of cave

stal'agmite n. lime deposit like pillar on floor of cave

stale a. old, lacking freshness; hackneyed; lacking energy, interest through monotony —**stale'-mate** n. Chess draw through one player being unable to move; deadlock, impasse

stalk[1] [-awk] n. plant's stem; anything like this

stalk[2] [-awk] v. follow, approach stealthily; walk in stiff and stately manner —n. stalking —**stalking-horse** n. pretext

stall [-awl] n. compartment in stable etc.; erection for display and sale of goods; seat in chancel of church; front seat in theatre etc.; finger sheath —v. put in stall; stick fast; (motor engine) unintentionally stop; (aircraft) lose flying speed; delay; hinder; prevaricate

stall'ion n. uncastrated male horse, *esp.* for breeding

stal'wart [-awl'-] a. strong, brave; staunch —n. stalwart person

sta'men n. male organ of a flowering plant

stam'ina n. power of endurance, vitality

stamm'er v. speak, say with repetition of syllables, stutter —n. habit of so speaking —**stam'merer** n.

stamp vi. put down foot with force —vt. impress mark on; affix postage stamp; fix in memory; reveal, characterize —n. stamping with foot; imprinted mark; appliance for marking; piece of gummed paper printed with device as evidence of postage *etc.*; character

stampede' n. sudden frightened rush, *esp.* of herd of cattle, crowd —v. cause, take part in stampede

stance n. manner, position of standing; attitude; point of view

stanch [-ah-] *see* STAUNCH

stan'chion [stahn'shən] n. upright bar, support —vt. support

stand v. have, take, set in upright position; remain; be situated; remain firm or stationary; cease to move; endure; adhere to principles; offer oneself as a candidate; be symbol *etc.* of —vt. inf. provide free, treat to (**stood, stand'ing**) —n. holding firm; position; halt; something on which thing may be placed; structure from which spectators watch sport *etc.*; stop made by pop group *etc.* —**stand'ing** n. reputation, status; duration —a. erect; permanent, lasting; stagnant; performed from stationary position (as **standing jump**) —**stand in** deputize (for) (**stand-in** n.)

—**stand over** watch closely; postpone

stand'ard n. accepted example of something against which others are judged; degree, quality; flag; weight or measure to which others must conform; post; **SA** school form or grade —a. usual, regular; average; of recognized authority, competence; accepted as correct —**standardiza'tion** n. —**stan'dardize** vt. regulate by a standard

stand'pipe n. vertical pipe up which water rises, providing supply *eg* outside a building

stand'point n. point of view, opinion; mental attitude

stank pt. of STINK

stann'ous a. of, containing tin

stan'za n. group of lines of verse (pl. **-zas**)

sta'ple n. U-shaped piece of metal with pointed ends to drive into wood for use as ring; paper fastener; main product; fibre; pile of wool *etc.* —a. principal; regularly produced or made for market —vt. fasten with staple; sort, classify (wool *etc.*) according to length of fibre —**sta'pler** n. small device for fastening papers together

star n. celestial body, seen as twinkling point of light; asterisk (*); celebrated player, actor; medal, jewel *etc.* of apparent shape of star —vt. adorn with stars; mark (with asterisk); feature (as star performer) —vi. play leading role in film *etc.* (**-rr-**) —a. leading, most important, famous —**starr'y** a. covered with stars —**star'dom** n. —**star'fish** n. small star-shaped sea creature —**Star Wars** U.S. proposed system of artificial satellites armed with lasers to destroy enemy missiles in space (*also* **SDI**)

star'board n. right-hand side of

ship, looking forward —a. of, on this side

starch n. substance forming the main food element in bread, potatoes etc., and used mixed with water, for stiffening linen etc. —vt. stiffen thus —**starch'y** a. containing starch; stiff; formal; prim

stare vi. look fixedly at; gaze with wide-open eyes; be obvious or visible to —n. staring, fixed gaze —**stare out** abash by staring at

stark a. blunt, bare; desolate; absolute —adv. completely

star'ling n. glossy black speckled songbird

start vt. begin; set going —vi. begin, esp. journey; make sudden movement —n. beginning; abrupt movement; advantage of a lead in a race —**start'er** n. electric motor starting car engine; competitor in, supervisor of, start of race

star'tle vt. give a fright to

starve v. (cause to) suffer or die from hunger —**starva'tion** n.

stash vt. inf. put away, hide

state n. condition; place, situation; politically organized people; government; rank; pomp —vt. express in words —**sta'ted** a. fixed; regular; settled —**state'ly** a. dignified, lofty —**state'ment** n. expression in words; account —**state'room** n. private cabin on ship; large room in palace, mansion, used for ceremonial occasions —**states'man** n. respected political leader —**states'manship** n. his art

stat'ic a. motionless, inactive; pert. to bodies at rest, or in equilibrium —n. electrical interference in radio reception —pl. branch of physics —**stat'ically** adv.

sta'tion n. place where thing

stops or is placed; stopping place for railway trains; local office for police force, fire brigade etc.; place equipped for radio or television transmission; bus garage; post, employment; status; position in life —vt. put in position —**sta'tionary** a. not moving, fixed; not changing

sta'tioner n. dealer in writing materials etc. —**sta'tionery** n.

statist'ics pl.n. (with sing. v.) numerical facts collected systematically and arranged; the study of them —**statist'ical** a **statist'ically** adv. —**statisti'cian** [-tish'-] n. one who compiles and studies statistics

stat'ue n. solid carved or cast image of person, animal etc. —**stat'uary** n. statues collectively —**statuesque'** [-esk'] a. like statue; dignified —**statuette'** n. small statue

stat'ure n. bodily height; greatness

sta'tus n. position, rank; prestige; relation to others —**status quo** existing state of affairs

stat'ute n. written law —**stat'utory** a. enacted, defined or authorized by statute

staunch [-aw-] vt. stop flow (of blood) from —a. trustworthy, loyal

stave n. one of the pieces forming barrel; verse, stanza; Mus. staff —vt. break hole in; ward (off) (**stove, staved** pt./pp., **sta'ving** pr.p.)

stay[1] vi. remain; sojourn; pause; wait; endure —vt. stop; hinder; postpone (**stayed, stay'ing**) —n. remaining, sojourning; check; restraint; deterrent; postponement

stay[2] n. support, prop, rope supporting mast etc. —pl. formerly, laced corsets

STD subscriber trunk dialling

stead [-ed] n. place —**in stead** in

place (of) —**in good stead of** service

stead'y a. firm; regular; temperate; industrious; reliable —vt. make steady —**stead'ily** adv. —**stead'iness** n. —**stead'fast** a. firm, fixed, unyielding —**stead'fastly** adv. —**steady (on)** be careful!

steak [stāk] n. thick slice of meat, esp. beef; slice of fish

steal [-ēl] vi. rob; move silently —vt. take without right or leave (**stole, sto'len, steal'ing**)

stealth [stelth] n. secret or underhand procedure, behaviour —**stealth'ily** adv. —**stealth'y** a.

steam n. vapour of boiling water; inf. power, energy —vi. give off steam; rise in vapour; move by steam power —vt. cook or treat with steam —**steam'er** n. steam-propelled ship; vessel for cooking or treating with steam —**steam-engine** n. engine worked or propelled by steam —**steam'roller** n. large roller, orig. moved by steam, for levelling road surfaces etc.; any great power used to crush opposition —vt. crush

steed n. Poet. horse

steel n. hard and malleable metal made by mixing carbon in iron; tool, weapon of steel —vt. harden —**steel'y** a.

steel'yard n. kind of balance with unequal arms

steep[1] a. rising, sloping abruptly; precipitous; inf. difficult; (of prices) very high or exorbitant; inf. unreasonable —**steep'en** v. —**steep'ly** adv.

steep[2] v. soak, saturate —n. act or process of steeping; the liquid used

stee'ple n. church tower with spire —**stee'plechase** n. horse race with ditches and fences to jump; foot race with hurdles etc.

to jump —**stee'plejack** n. one who builds, repairs chimneys, steeples etc.

steer[1] vt. guide, direct course of vessel, motor vehicle etc. —vi. direct one's course —**steer'age** n. effect of a helm; formerly, cheapest accommodation on ship —**steering gear, wheel** etc. mechanism for steering

steer[2] n. castrated male ox

stein [stīn] n. earthenware beer mug

ste'le n. ancient carved stone pillar or slab

stell'ar a. of stars

stem[1] n. stalk, trunk; long slender part, as in tobacco pipe; part of word to which inflections are added; foremost part of ship

stem[2] vt. check, stop, dam up (**-mm-**)

stench n. evil smell

sten'cil n. thin sheet pierced with pattern which is brushed over with paint or ink, leaving pattern on surface under it; the pattern; the plate; pattern made —vt. (**-ll-**) —**sten'ciller** n.

stenog'raphy n. shorthand writing —**stenog'rapher** n. —**stenograph'ic** a.

stento'rian a. (of voice) very loud

step vi. move and set down foot; proceed (in this way) —vt. measure in paces (**-pp-**) —n. act of stepping; sound made by stepping; mark made by foot; manner of walking; series of foot movements forming part of dance; gait; pace; measure, act, stage in proceeding; board, rung etc. to put foot on; degree in scale; mast socket; promotion —pl. (**pair of steps**) portable ladder with hinged prop attached, stepladder —**step'ladder** n. four-legged ladder having broad flat steps

step'child n. child of husband or wife by former marriage —**step'brother** n. —**step'father** n. —**step'mother** n. —**step'sister** n.

steppe n. extensive treeless plain in European and Asiatic Russia

stere n. cubic metre

stereophon'ic a. (of sound) giving effect of coming from many directions —**ster'eo** a./n. (of, for) stereophonic record player etc.

stereoscop'ic a. having three-dimensional effect

ster'eotype [-ste'ri-] n. metal plate for printing cast from set-up type; something (monotonously) familiar, conventional, predictable —vt. make stereotype of

ster'ile [ste'rīl] a. unable to produce fruit, crops, young etc.; free from (harmful) germs —**steril'ity** n. —**steriliza'tion** n. process or act of making sterile —**ster'ilize** vt. render sterile —**ster'ilizer** n.

ster'ling a. genuine, true; of solid worth, dependable; in British money —n. British money

stern[1] a. severe, strict —**stern'ly** adv. —**stern'ness** n.

stern[2] n. rear part of ship

ster'num n. the breast bone

ster'ols [ster'olz] pl.n. class of complex organic alcohols, including ergosterol, cholesterol

ster'torous a. with sound of heavy breathing, hoarse snoring

stet Lat. let it stand (proof-reader's direction to cancel alteration previously made)

steth'oscope n. instrument for listening to action of heart, lungs etc. —**stethoscop'ic** a.

stet'son n. type of broad-brimmed felt hat

ste'vedore n. one who loads or unloads ships

stew n. food cooked slowly in closed vessel; state of excitement, agitation or worry —v. cook by stewing

stew'ard n. one who manages another's property; official managing race meeting, assembly etc.; attendant on ship's or aircraft's passengers (**stew'ardess** fem.)

stick n. long, thin piece of wood; anything shaped like a stick; inf. person (as **good stick** etc.) —vt. pierce, stab; place, fasten, as by pins, glue; protrude; inf. tolerate, abide —vi. adhere; come to stop, jam; remain; be fastened; protrude (**stuck** pt./pp.) —**stick'er** n. esp. adhesive label, poster —**stick'y** a. covered with, like adhesive substance; (of weather) warm, humid; inf. difficult, unpleasant

stic'kleback [-kl-b-] n. small fish with sharp spines on back

stick'ler n. person who insists on something

stiff a. not easily bent or moved; rigid; awkward; difficult; thick, not fluid; formal; stubborn; unnatural; strong or fresh, as breeze; inf. excessive —n. sl. corpse —**stiff'en** v. —**stiff'ly** adv. —**stiff'ness** n. —**stiff'-necked** a. obstinate, stubborn

sti'fle vt. smother, suppress

stig'ma n. distinguishing mark esp. of disgrace (pl. **stig'mas, stig'mata**) —**stig'matism** n. —**stig'matize** vt. mark with stigma

stile n. arrangement of steps for climbing a fence

stilet'to n. small dagger; small boring tool (pl. **-os**) —a. thin, pointed like a stiletto

still[1] a. motionless, noiseless, at rest —vt. quiet —adv. to this time; yet; even —n. photograph esp. of film scene —**still'ness** n.

—**still'born** a. born dead —**still life** painting of inanimate objects

still[2] n. apparatus for distilling —**still room** pantry, storeroom in large house

stilt n. pole with footrests for walking raised from ground; long post supporting building etc. —**stilt'ed** a. stiff in manner, pompous —**stilt'edly** adv.

stim'ulus n. something that rouses to activity; incentive (pl. **-uli** [-lī, -lē]) —**stim'ulant** n. drug etc. acting as a stimulus —**stim'ulate** vt. rouse up, spur —**stim'ulating** a. acting as stimulus —**stimula'tion** n. —**stim'ulative** a.

sting vt. thrust sting into; cause sharp pain to; sl. impose upon by asking for money, overcharge —vi. feel sharp pain (**stung**, **sting'ing**) —n. (wound, pain, caused by) sharp pointed organ, often poisonous, of certain insects and animals

stin'gy [-ji] a. mean; avaricious; niggardly —**stin'gily** adv. —**stin'giness** n.

stink vi. give out strongly offensive smell; sl. be abhorrent (**stank**, **stunk**, **stink'ing**) —n. such smell, stench; inf. fuss, bother

stink'wood n. S Afr. tree yielding hard wood used for furniture; this wood

stint vt. be frugal, miserly to (someone) or with (something) —n. allotted amount of work or time; limitation, restriction

sti'pend n. salary, esp. of clergyman —**stipend'iary** a. receiving stipend

stip'ple vt. engrave, paint in dots —n. this process

stip'ulate vi. specify in making a bargain —**stipula'tion** n. proviso; condition —**stip'ulator** n.

stir v. (begin to) move; rouse;

cause trouble —vt. set, keep in motion; excite (**-rr-**) —n. commotion, disturbance

stirr'up n. metal loop hung from strap for supporting foot of rider on horse

stitch n. movement of needle in sewing etc.; its result in the work; sharp pain in side; least fragment (of clothing) —v. sew

stoat n. small mammal with brown coat and black-tipped tail

stock n. goods, material stored, esp. for sale or later use; reserve, fund; financial shares in, or capital of, company etc.; standing, reputation; farm animals (livestock); plant, stem from which cuttings are taken; handle of gun, tool etc.; liquid broth produced by boiling meat etc.; flowering plant; lineage —pl. Hist. frame to secure feet, hands (of offender); frame to support ship during construction —a. kept in stock; standard, hackneyed —vt. keep, store; supply with livestock, fish etc. —**stock'y** a. thickset —**stock'broker** n. agent for buying, selling shares in companies —**stock car** ordinary car strengthened and modified for a form of racing in which cars often collide —**stock exchange** institution for buying and selling shares —**stock'man** n. man experienced in driving, handling cattle, sheep —**stock'jobber** n. dealer on a stock exchange —**stock'pile** v. acquire and store large quantity of (something) —**stock-still** a. motionless —**stock'taking** n. examination, counting and valuing of goods in a shop etc.

stockade' n. enclosure of stakes, barrier

stockinet' n. machine-knitted elastic fabric

stock'ing n. close-fitting cover-

ing for leg and foot —**stock'-
inged** a.

stodg'y a. heavy, dull —**stodge**
n. heavy, solid food

stoep [-oop] n. **SA** verandah

sto'ic a. capable of much self-
control, great endurance without
complaint —n. stoical person
—**sto'ical** a. —**sto'icism** n.

stoke v. feed, tend fire or furnace —**sto'ker** n.

stole [1] pt. —**sto'len** pp. of STEAL

stole [2] n. long scarf or shawl

stol'id a. hard to excite; heavy,
slow, apathetic —**stolid'ity** n.
—**stol'idly** adv.

stom'ach [-um'ək] n. sac forming chief digestive organ in any
animal; appetite; desire, inclination —vt. put up with

stomp vi. inf. stamp

stone n. (piece of) rock; gem;
hard seed of fruit; hard deposit
formed in kidneys, bladder;
weight, 14 lbs. —vt. throw stones
at; free (fruit) from stones
—**stoned** a. sl. stupefied by alcohol or drugs —**sto'nily** adv.
—**sto'ny** a. of, like stone; hard;
cold —**stone-blind** a. completely
blind —**stone'chat** n. black songbird with reddish-brown breast
—**stone deaf** a. completely deaf
—**stonewall'** vi. obstruct business; play slow game, esp. in
cricket —**stone'ware** n. heavy
common pottery —**stony-broke**
a. sl. with no money left

stood pt./pp. of STAND

stooge [stooj] n. Theatre etc.
performer always the butt of
another's jokes; sl. one taken
advantage of by another

stook [-oo-] n. group of sheaves
set upright in field to dry

stool [-oo-] n. backless chair;
excrement

stoop [-oo-] vi. lean forward or
down, bend; swoop; abase, de-

grade oneself —n. stooping carriage of the body

stop vt. check, bring to halt;
prevent; interrupt; suspend; desist from; fill up an opening —vi.
cease, come to a halt; stay (-**pp**-)
—n. stopping or becoming
stopped; punctuation mark, esp.
full stop; any device for altering
or regulating pitch; set of pipes
in organ having tones of a distinct quality —**stopp'age** n.
—**stop'per** n. plug for closing
bottle etc. —**stop'cock** n. valve to
control or stop flow of fluid in
pipe —**stop'gap** n. temporary
substitute —**stop'off, stop'over** n.
short break in journey —**stop
press** news put into a newspaper
at the last minute —**stop'watch**
n. one which can be stopped for
exact timing of race

store vt. stock, furnish, keep —n.
shop; abundance; stock; department store; place for keeping
goods; warehouse —pl. stocks of
goods, provisions —**stor'age** n.
—**store cattle** cattle bought lean
to be fattened for market

stor'ey n. horizontal division of
a building

stork n. large wading bird

storm n. violent weather with
wind, rain, hail, sand, snow etc.;
assault on fortress; violent outbreak, discharge —vt. assault;
take by storm —vi. rage
—**storm'y** a. like storm; (emotionally) violent

stor'y n. (book, piece of prose
etc.) telling about events, happenings; inf. lie; **US** same as STO-
REY

stoup [-oo-] n. small basin for
holy water

stout a. fat; sturdy, resolute —n.
kind of beer —**stout'ly** adv.
—**stout'ness** n.

stove [1] n. apparatus for cooking,
heating etc.

stove[2] _pt./pp. of_ STAVE

stow [stō] _vt._ pack away —**stow'-age** _n._ —**stow'away** _n._ one who hides in ship to obtain free passage

strad'dle _vt._ bestride —_vi._ spread legs wide —_n._

strafe [-âf, -ahf] _vt._ attack (_esp._ with bullets, rockets) from air

strag'gle _vi._ stray, get dispersed, linger —**strag'gler** _n._

straight [strāt] _a._ without bend; honest; level; in order; (of spirits) undiluted, neat; expressionless; (of drama, actor _etc._) serious; _sl._ heterosexual —_n._ straight state or part —_adv._ direct —**straight'-en** _v._ —**straight'away** _adv._ immediately —**straightfor'ward** _a._ open, frank; honest —**straightfor'wardly** _adv._

strain[1] _vt._ stretch tightly; stretch to full or to excess; filter —_vi._ make great effort —_n._ stretching force; violent effort; injury from being strained; burst of music or poetry; great demand; (condition caused by) overwork, worry _etc._; tone of speaking or writing —**strained** _a._ —**strain'er** _n._ filter, sieve

strain[2] _n._ breed or race; type (_esp._ in biology); trace, streak

strait _n._ channel of water connecting two larger areas of water —_pl._ position of difficulty or distress —_a._ narrow; strict —**strait'en** _vt._ make strait, narrow; press with poverty —**strait'-jacket** _n._ jacket to confine arms of violent person —**strait-laced** _a._ austere, strict; puritanical

strand[1] _v._ run aground; leave, be left in difficulties or helpless —_n. Poet._ shore

strand[2] _n._ one single string or wire of rope _etc._

strange [-ânj] _a._ odd; queer; unaccustomed; foreign; uncommon; wonderful; singular

stran'ger _n._ unknown person; foreigner; one unaccustomed (to) —**strange'ly** _adv._ —**strange'ness** _n._

stran'gle [-ng'gl] _vt._ kill by squeezing windpipe; suppress —**strangula'tion** _n._ strangling

strap _n._ strip, _esp._ of leather —_vt._ fasten, beat with strap (**-pp-**) —**strap'ping** _a._ tall and well-made —**strap'hanger** _n._ in bus, train, one who has to stand, steadying himself with strap provided for this

strat'agem [-jəm] _n._ plan, trick —**strat'egy** _n._ art of war; overall plan —**strate'gic(al)** _a._ —**strat'egist** _n._

strathspey' [-spā'] _n._ type of Scottish dance with gliding steps

strat'osphere _n._ upper part of the atmosphere approx. 11 km above earth's surface

strat'um [-aht-] _n._ layer, _esp._ of rock; class in society (_pl._ **-ta**) —**strat'ify** [-at'-] _v._ form, deposit in layers (**-ified, -ifying**) —**stratifica'tion** _n._

straw _n._ stalks of grain; single stalk; long, narrow tube used to suck up liquid —**straw'berry** _n._ creeping plant producing a red, juicy fruit; the fruit

stray _vi._ wander; digress; get lost —_a._ strayed; occasional, scattered —_n._ stray animal

streak _n._ long line or band; element, trace —_vt._ mark with streaks —_vi._ move fast; _inf._ run naked in public —**streak'y** _a._ having streaks; striped

stream _n._ flowing body of water or other liquid; steady flow; class, division of schoolchildren grouped together because of similar ability —_vi._ flow; run with liquid; float, wave in the air —_vt._ group (schoolchildren) in streams —**stream'er** _n._ (paper) ribbon, narrow flag

stream'lined *a.* (of car, plane *etc.*) built so as to offer least resistance to air —**stream'lining** *n.*

street *n.* road in town or village, usu. lined with houses —**street'-walker** *n.* prostitute —**street'-wise** *a.* adept at surviving in urban, oft. criminal, environment (*also* street-smart)

strength *n.* quality of being strong; power; capacity for exertion or endurance; vehemence; force; full or necessary number of people —**strength'en** *v.* make stronger, reinforce —**on the strength of** relying on; because of

stren'uous *a.* energetic; earnest —**stren'uously** *adv.*

streptococc'us *n.* genus of bacteria (*pl.* **-cocc'i** [-kok'ī])

streptomy'cin *n.* antibiotic drug

stress *n.* emphasis; strain; impelling force; effort; tension —*vt.* emphasize; accent; put mechanical stress on

stretch *vt.* extend; exert to utmost; tighten, pull out; reach out —*vi.* reach; have elasticity —*n.* stretching, being stretched; expanse; spell —**stretch'er** *n.* person, thing that stretches; appliance on which disabled person is carried; bar linking legs of chair; bar in boat for rower's feet

strew [-rōō] *vt.* scatter over surface, spread (**strewed** *pt.*, **strewn** *or* **strewed** *pp.*, **strew'ing** *pr.p.*)

stri'a *n.* small channel or threadlike line in surface of shell or other object (*pl.* **stri'ae** [-ē]) —**stri'ate** [-it], **stria'ted** *a.* streaked, furrowed, grooved —**stri'ate** [-āt] *vt.* mark with streaks; score —**stria'tion** *n.*

strick'en *a.* seriously affected by disease, grief, famine; afflicted; *pp.* of STRIKE

strict *a.* stern, not lax or indulgent; defined; without exception —**strict'ly** *adv.* —**strict'ness** *n.*

stric'ture *n.* critical remark; constriction

stride *vi.* walk with long steps (**strode**, **stridd'en**, **stri'ding**) —*n.* single step; its length; regular pace

stri'dent *a.* harsh in tone; loud; urgent

strife *n.* conflict; quarrelling

strike *v.* hit (against); ignite; (of snake) bite; arrive at, come upon; of plants (cause to) take root; attack; hook (fish); sound (time) as bell in clock *etc.* —*vt.* affect; enter mind of; discover (gold, oil *etc.*); dismantle, remove; make (coin) —*vi.* cease work as protest or to enforce demands (**struck** *pt.*, **strick'en**, **struck** *pp.*, **stri'king** *pr.p.*) —*n.* act of striking —**stri'ker** *n.* —**stri'king** *a.* noteworthy, impressive —**strike pay** allowance paid by trade union to members on strike —**strike off** remove

string *n.* (length of) thin cord or other material; strand, row; series; fibre in plants —*pl.* conditions —*vt.* provide with, thread on string; form in line, series (**strung**, **string'ing**) —**stringed** *a.* (of musical instruments) furnished with strings —**string'y** *a.* like string; fibrous

strin'gent [-j-] *a.* strict, rigid, binding —**strin'gency** *n.* severity —**strin'gently** *adv.*

strip *vt.* lay bare, take covering off; dismantle; deprive (of) —*vi.* undress (**-pp-**) —*n.* long, narrow piece —**stripp'er** *n.* —**strip-(tease')** *n.* cabaret or theatre act in which person undresses

stripe *n.* narrow mark, band;

chevron as symbol of military rank —**stri'py** a.

strip'ling n. youth

strive vi. try hard, struggle, contend (**strove, striv'en, striv'-ing**)

strobe n. apparatus which produces high-intensity flashing light

strode pt. of STRIDE

stroke n. blow; sudden action, occurrence; apoplexy; mark of pen, pencil, brush etc.; chime of clock; completed movement in series; act, manner of striking (ball etc.); style, method of swimming; rower sitting nearest stern setting the rate; act of stroking —vt. set time in rowing; pass hand lightly over

stroll n. [-ōl] vi. walk in leisurely or idle manner —n.

strong a. powerful, robust, healthy; difficult to break; noticeable; intense; emphatic; not diluted; having a certain number —**strong'ly** adv. —**strong'hold** n. fortress

stron'tium n. silvery-white chemical element —**strontium 90** radioactive isotope of strontium present in fallout of nuclear explosions

strop n. leather for sharpening razors —vt. sharpen on one (**-pp-**) —**stropp'y** a. sl. angry, awkward

stro'phe n. division of ode —**stroph'ic** a.

strove pt. of STRIVE

struck pt./pp. of STRIKE

struc'ture n. (arrangement of parts in) construction, building etc.; form; organization —v. give structure to —**struc'tural** a.

strug'gle vi. contend; fight; proceed, work, move with difficulty and effort —n.

strum v. strike notes of guitar etc. (**-mm-**)

strum'pet n. obs. promiscuous woman

strung pt./pp. of STRING

strut vi. walk affectedly or pompously (**-tt-**) —n. brace; rigid support, usu. set obliquely; strutting gait

strych'nine [-ik'nēn] n. poison got from nux vomica seeds —**strych'nic** a. —**strych'ninism** n.

stub n. remnant of anything, eg pencil, cigarette etc.; counterfoil of cheque etc. —vi. strike, as toes, against fixed object; extinguish by pressing against surface (**-bb-**) —**stubb'y** a. short, broad

stub'ble n. stumps of cut grain after reaping; short growth of beard

stubb'orn a. unyielding, obstinate —**stubb'ornly** adv. —**stubb'ornness** n.

stucc'o n. plaster —**stucc'oed** a.

stuck pt./pp. of STICK

stud [1] n. nail with large head; removable double-headed button; vertical wall support —vt. set with studs (**-dd-**)

stud [2] n. set of horses kept for breeding —**stud'book** n. book giving pedigree of noted or thoroughbred animals, esp. horses —**stud farm**

stu'dio n. workroom of artist, photographer etc.; building, room where film, television or radio shows are made, broadcast (pl. **-s**)

stud'y vi. be engaged in learning —vt. make study of; try constantly to do; consider; scrutinize (**stud'ied, stud'ying**) —n. effort to acquire knowledge; subject of this; room to study in; book, report etc. produced as result of study; sketch —**stu'dent** n. one who studies, esp. at university etc. —**stud'ied** a. carefully designed, premeditated —**stu'di-**

ous a. fond of study; thoughtful; painstaking; deliberate —**stu'diously** adv.

stuff v. pack, cram, fill (completely); eat large amount; fill with seasoned mixture; fill (animal's skin) with material to preserve lifelike form —n. material, fabric; any substance —**stuff'ing** n. material for stuffing, esp. seasoned mixture for inserting in poultry etc. before cooking —**stuff'y** a. lacking fresh air; inf. dull, conventional —**do your stuff** inf. do what is required or expected of you

stult'ify vt. make ineffectual (-**ified, -ifying**) —**stultifica'tion** n.

stum'ble vi. trip and nearly fall; falter —n. —**stumbling block** obstacle

stump n. remnant of tree, tooth etc., when main part has been cut away; one of uprights of wicket in cricket —vt. confuse, puzzle; break wicket of (batsman out of his ground in playing ball) —vi. walk heavily, noisily —**stump'y** a short and thickset

stun vt. knock senseless; amaze (-**nn-**) —**stun'ning** a.

stung pt./pp. of STING

stunk pp. of STINK

stunt[1] vt. check growth of, dwarf —**stunt'ed** a. underdeveloped; undersized

stunt[2] n. feat of dexterity or daring; anything spectacular, esp. unusual done to gain publicity

stu'pefy vt. make insensitive, lethargic; astound (-**efied, -efying**) —**stupefac'tion** n.

stupen'dous [styōō-] a. astonishing; amazing; huge

stu'pid a. slow-witted; silly; in a stupor —**stupid'ity** n. —**stu'pidly** adv.

stu'por n. dazed state; insensibility —**stu'porous** a.

stur'dy a. robust, strongly built; vigorous —**stur'dily** adv. —**stur'diness** n.

stur'geon [-jən] n. fish yielding caviare and isinglass

stutt'er v. speak with difficulty; stammer —n.

sty[1] n. place to keep pigs in; hovel, dirty place

sty[2], **stye** n. inflammation on edge of eyelid

Styg'ian [stij-] a. of river Styx in Hades; gloomy; infernal

style n. manner of writing, doing etc.; designation; sort, elegance, refinement; superior manner, quality; design —vt. shape, design; adapt; designate —**sty'lish** a. fashionable —**sty'lishly** adv. —**sty'list** n. one cultivating style in literary or other execution; designer; hairdresser —**stylis'tic** a. —**sty'lize** vt. give conventional stylistic form to —**styling mousse** foamy substance applied to hair before styling to retain shape

sty'lus n. writing instrument; (in record player) tiny point running in groove of record (pl. -**li** [-lī], -**luses**)

sty'mie vt. hinder, thwart

styp'tic a./n. (designating) a substance that stops bleeding

sty'rene n. colourless liquid used in making synthetic rubber, plastics

suave [swahv] a. smoothly polite, affable, bland —**suav'ity** n.

sub short for subeditor, submarine, subscription, substitute —n. inf. advance payment of wages, salary —inf. v. serve as substitute; grant or receive advance payment; subedit (-**bb-**)

sub- (comb. form) under, less than, in lower position, subordinate, forming subdivision etc., as in **subaqu'a** a., **subed'itor** n., **sub'heading** n., **subnor'mal** a. etc.

sub'soil n. Such words are not given here where the meaning may be easily inferred from the simple word

sub'altern [-əl-tən] n. army officer below rank of captain

sub'committee n. section of committee functioning separately from main body

subcon'scious a. acting, existing without one's awareness —n. Psychology that part of the human mind unknown, or only partly known to possessor

subcuta'neous a. under the skin

subdivide' vt. divide again —subdivi'sion [-vizh'-] n.

subdue' v. overcome —**subdued'** a. cowed, quiet; not bright or intense

sub'ject n. theme, topic; that about which something is predicated; conscious self; one under power of another —a. owing allegiance; subordinate; dependent; liable (to) —vt. [-jekt'] cause to undergo; make liable; subdue —subjec'tion n. act of bringing, or state of being, under control —subject'ive a. based on personal feelings, not impartial; of the self; existing in the mind; displaying artist's individuality —subjectiv'ity n.

subjoin' vt. add to end

sub ju'dice [-di-si] Lat. under judicial consideration

sub'jugate vt. force to submit; conquer —subjuga'tion n. —sub'jugator n.

subjunc'tive n. mood used mainly in subordinate clauses expressing wish, possibility —a. in, of, that mood

sublet' vt. (of tenant) let whole or part of what he has rented to another (sublet', sublett'ing)

sub'limate vt. Psychology direct energy (esp. sexual) into

activities considered more socially acceptable; refine —n. Chem. material obtained when substance is sublimed —sublima'tion n. Psychology unconscious diversion of sexual impulses towards new aims and activities; Chem. process in which a solid changes directly into a vapour

sublime' a. elevated; eminent; majestic; inspiring awe; exalted —v. Chem. change or cause to change from solid to vapour —sublime'ly adv. —sublim'ity, sublime'ness n.

sublim'inal a. resulting from processes of which the individual is not aware

sub-machine'-gun n. portable automatic gun with short barrel

sub'marine [or -rēn'] n. (war-) ship which can travel (and attack from) below surface of sea and remain submerged for long periods —a. below surface of sea

submerge' v. place, go under water —submer'sion n.

submit' vt. surrender; put forward for consideration —vi. surrender; defer (-tt-) —submis'sion n. —submiss'ive a. meek, obedient

subord'inate [-it] a. of lower rank or less importance —n. inferior; one under order of another —vt. [-āt] make, treat as subordinate —subord'inately adv. —subordina'tion n.

suborn' vt. bribe to do evil —suborna'tion n. —suborn'er n.

subpoe'na [-pēnə] n. writ requiring attendance at court of law —vt. summon by such order (-naed [-nəd], -naing)

subscribe' vt. pay, promise to pay (contribution); write one's name at end of document —subscri'ber n. —subscrip'tion n.

subscribing; money paid

sub'section n. division of a section

sub'sequent a. later, following or coming after in time —**sub'sequence** n. —**sub'sequently** adv.

subser'vient a. submissive, servile —**subser'vience** n. —**ser'viently** adv.

subside' vi. abate, come to an end; sink; settle; collapse —**subsi'dence** [or sub'si-] n.

subsid'iary a. supplementing; secondary; auxiliary —n.

sub'sidize vt. help financially; pay grant to —**sub'sidy** n. money granted

subsist' vi. exist, sustain life —**subsist'ence** n. the means by which one supports life; livelihood

subson'ic a. concerning speeds less than that of sound

sub'stance n. matter; particular kind of matter; chief part, essence; wealth —**substan'tial** a. considerable; of real value; solid, big, important; really existing —**substantial'ity** n. —**substan'tially** adv. —**substan'tiate** vt. bring evidence for, confirm, prove —**substantia'tion** n. —**sub'stantive** a. having independent existence; real, fixed —n. noun

sub'stitute v. put, serve in exchange (for) —n. thing, person put in place of another; deputy —**substitu'tion** n.

substrat'um [-raht'-] n. that which is laid or spread under; layer of earth lying under another; basis; subsoil (pl. **-ta, -tums**)

subsume' vt. incorporate (idea, case etc.) under comprehensive heading, classification

subtend' vt. be opposite to and delimit

sub'terfuge n. trick, lying excuse used to evade something

subterra'nean, subterra'neous a. underground; in concealment

sub'title n. secondary title of book; written translation of film dialogue, superimposed on film

subt'le [sut'l] a. not immediately obvious; ingenious, acute; crafty; intricate; delicate; making fine distinctions —**subt'lety** n. —**subt'ly** adv.

subtract' vt. take away, deduct —**subtrac'tion** n.

subtrop'ical a. of regions bordering on the tropics

sub'urb n. residential area on outskirts of city —**subur'ban** a. —**subur'bia** n. suburbs of a city

subven'tion n. subsidy

subvert' vt. overthrow; corrupt —**subver'sion** n. —**subver'sive** a.

sub'way n. underground passage; US underground railway

succeed' [sək-sēd'] vi. accomplish purpose; turn out satisfactorily; follow —vt. follow, take place of —**success'** n. favourable accomplishment, attainment, issue or outcome; successful person or thing —**success'ful** a. —**success'fully** adv. —**succes'sion** n. following; series; succeeding —**success'ive** a. following in order; consecutive —**succes'sively** adv. —**success'or** n.

succinct' [sək-singkt'] a. terse, concise —**succinct'ly** adv. —**succinct'ness** n.

succ'our vt./n. help in distress

succ'ubus n. female demon fabled to have sexual intercourse with sleeping men (pl. **-bi** [-bī])

succ'ulent a. juicy, full of juice; (of plant) having thick, fleshy leaves —n. such plant —**succ'ulence** n.

succumb' [-kum'] vi. yield, give way; die

such a. of the kind or degree

mentioned; so great, so much; so made *etc.*; of the same kind —**such'like** *inf. a.* such —*pron.* other such things

suck *vt.* draw into mouth; hold (dissolve) in mouth; draw in —*n.* sucking —**suck'er** *n.* person, thing that sucks; organ, appliance which adheres by suction; shoot coming from root or base of stem of plant; *inf.* person easily deceived or taken in

suc'kle *v.* feed from the breast —**suck'ling** *n.* unweaned infant

suc'tion *n.* drawing or sucking of air or fluid; force produced by difference in pressure

sudd'en *a.* done, occurring unexpectedly; abrupt, hurried —**sud'denly** *adv.* —**sudd'enness** *n.*

sudorif'ic *a.* causing perspiration —*n.* medicine that produces sweat

suds *pl.n.* froth of soap and water, lather

sue *vt.* prosecute; seek justice from —*vi.* make application or entreaty; beseech

suede [swād] *n.* leather with soft, velvety finish

su'et [sōō'it] *n.* hard animal fat from sheep, ox *etc.*

suffer *v.* undergo, endure, experience (pain *etc.*); *obs.* allow —**suff'erable** *a.* —**suff'erance** *n.* toleration —**suff'erer** *n.*

suffice' *v.* be adequate, satisfactory (for) —**suffi'ciency** *n.* [-fish'-] adequate amount —**suffi'cient** *a.* enough, adequate

suff'ix *n.* letter or word added to end of word —*vt.* add, annex to the end

suff'ocate *v.* kill, be killed by deprivation of oxygen; smother —**suffoca'tion** *n.*

suff'ragan *n.* bishop appointed to assist an archbishop or another bishop

suff'rage [-rij] *n.* vote or right of voting —**suff'ragist** *n.* one claiming a right of voting (**suffragette'** *fem.*)

suffuse' *vt.* well up and spread over —**suffu'sion** *n.*

sug'ar [shoog'-] *n.* sweet crystalline vegetable substance —*vt.* sweeten, make pleasant (with sugar) —**sug'ary** *a.* —**sugar beet** varieties of common beet grown for sugar —**sugar cane** plant from whose juice sugar is obtained —**sugar daddy** *sl.* wealthy (elderly) man who pays for (*esp.* sexual) favours of younger person

suggest' [-j-] *vt.* propose; call up the idea of —**suggestibil'ity** *n.* —**suggest'ible** *a.* easily influenced —**sugges'tion** *n.* hint; proposal; insinuation of impression, belief *etc.*, into mind —**sugges'tive** *a.* containing, open to suggestion, *esp.* of something indecent —**suggest'ively** *adv.*

su'icide [sōō'-] *n.* (act of) one who kills himself —**suici'dal** *a.* —**suici'dally** *adv.*

suit [sōōt] *n.* set of clothing; garment worn for particular event, purpose; one of four sets in pack of cards; action at law —*v.* make, be fit or appropriate for; be acceptable to (someone) —**suitabil'ity** *n.* —**suit'able** *a.* fitting, proper, convenient; becoming —**suit'ably** *adv.* —**suit'case** *n.* flat rectangular travelling case

suite [swēt] *n.* matched set *esp.* furniture; set of rooms; retinue

suit'or [sōōt'-] *n.* wooer; one who sues; petitioner

sulk *vi.* be silent, resentful, *esp.* to draw attention to oneself —*n.* this mood —**sulk'ily** *adv.* —**sulk'y** *a.*

sull'en *a.* unwilling to talk or be

sociable, morose; dismal; dull —**sul'lenly** adv.

sull'y vt. stain, tarnish, disgrace (**sull'ied, sull'ying**)

sul'phate n. salt formed by sulphuric acid in combination with any base

sulphon'amides n. group of drugs used as internal germicides in treatment of many bacterial diseases

sul'phur [-fər] n. pale yellow nonmetallic element —**sulphu'ric** [-fyoor'-] a. —**sul'phurous** a.

sul'tan n. ruler of Muslim country —**sultan'a** [-tahn'-] n. sultan's wife; kind of raisin

sul'try a. (of weather) hot, humid; (of person) looking sensual

sum n. amount, total; problem in arithmetic —v. add up; make summary of main parts (**-mm-**)

su'mach [sōō'mak] n. shrub with clusters of green flowers and red hairy fruits

summ'ary n. abridgment or statement of chief points of longer document, speech etc.; abstract —a. done quickly —**sum'marily** adv. speedily; abruptly —**summ'arize** vt. make summary of; present briefly and concisely —**summa'tion** n. adding up

summ'er n. second, warmest season —vi. pass the summer —**summ'ery** a. —**summ'er time** n. daylight saving time, ie time shown by clocks etc. put forward one hour during certain period of year

summ'it n. top, peak —**summit conference** meeting of heads of governments

summ'on vt. demand attendance of; call on; bid witness appear in court; gather up (energies etc.) —**summ'ons** n. call; authoritative demand

sump n. place or receptacle

(esp. as oil reservoir in engine) where fluid collects

sump'tuous a. lavish, magnificent; costly —**sump'tuously** adv. —**sump'tuousness** n. —**sump'tuary** a. pert. to or regulating expenditure

sun n. luminous body round which earth and other planets revolve; its rays —vt. expose to sun's rays (**-nn-**) —**sun'less** a. —**sunn'y** a. like the sun; warm; cheerful —**sun'bathing** n. exposure of whole or part of body to sun's rays —**sun'beam** n ray of sun —**sun'burn** n. inflammation of skin due to excessive exposure to sun —**sun'down** n. sunset —**sun'fish** n. sea fish with large rounded body —**sun'flower** n. plant with large golden flowers —**sun'spot** n. dark patch appearing temporarily on sun's surface —**sun'stroke** n. illness caused by prolonged exposure to intensely hot sun —**sun'tan** n. colouring of skin by exposure to sun

sun'dae [-dā] n. ice cream topped with fruit etc.

Sun'day n. first day of the week; Christian Sabbath —**Sunday school** school for religious instruction of children

sun'der vt. separate, sever

sun'dry a. several, various —**sun'dries** pl.n. odd items not mentioned in detail

sung pp. of SING

sunk, sunk'en pp. of SINK

sup vt. take by sips —vi. take supper (**-pp-**) —n. mouthful of liquid

su'per [sōō'-] a. inf. very good

super- (comb. form) above, greater, exceeding(ly), as in **superhu'man** a., **su'perman** n., **su'perstore** n., **su'pertanker** n. Such compounds are not given here where the meaning may be inferred from the simple word

su'perable [sōō'-] a. capable of being overcome; surmountable

superann'uate vt. pension off; discharge or dismiss as too old —**superann'uated** a. —**superannua'tion** n. pension given on retirement; contribution by employee to pension

superb' a. splendid, grand, impressive —**superb'ly** adv.

su'percharge [sōō'-] vt. charge, fill to excess —**su'percharged** a. —**su'percharger** n. (internal-combustion engine) device to ensure complete filling of cylinder with explosive mixture when running at high speed

superci'lious a. displaying arrogant pride, scorn, indifference —**superci'liously** adv. —**superci'liousness** n.

superfi'cial [-fish'-] a. of or on surface; not careful or thorough; without depth, shallow —**superfi'ciality** n.

super'fluous a. extra, unnecessary; excessive; left over —**superflu'ity** [-flōō'-] n. superabundance; unnecessary amount —**super'fluously** adv.

su'pergrass n. informer who implicates many people in terrorism or crime

superintend' v. have charge of; overlook; supervise —**superintend'ence** n. —**superinten'dent** n. esp. senior police officer

supe'rior a. greater in quality or quantity; upper, higher in position, rank or quality; showing consciousness of being so —**superior'ity** [-o'ri-] n. quality of being higher, greater, or more excellent

super'lative a. of, in highest degree or quality; surpassing; Grammar denoting form of adjective, adverb meaning 'most' —n. Grammar superlative degree of adjective or adverb

su'permarket n. large self-service store selling chiefly food and household goods

super'nal a. celestial

supernat'ural a. being beyond the powers or laws of nature; miraculous —**supernat'urally** adv.

supernu'merary a. in excess of normal number, extra —n. extra person or thing

superphos'phate n. chemical fertilizer

su'perscript n./a. (character) printed, written above the line

supersede' vt. take the place of; set aside, discard, supplant —**supersess'ion** n.

superson'ic a. denoting speed greater than that of sound

supersti'tion [-stish'-] n. religion, opinion or practice based on belief in luck or magic —**supersti'tious** a. —**supersti'tiously** adv.

su'perstructure [sōō'-] n. structure above foundations; part of ship above deck

su'pertax [sōō'-] n. tax on large incomes in addition to usual income tax

supervene' vi. happen, as an interruption or change —**superven'tion** n.

su'pervise [sōō'-] vt. oversee; direct; inspect and control; superintend —**supervi'sion** [-vizh'-] n. —**su'pervisor** n. —**supervi'sory** a.

supine' [or sōō'-] a. lying on back with face upwards; indolent —n. [sōō'-] Latin verbal noun

supp'er n. (light) evening meal —**supp'erless** a.

supplant' [-ahnt'] vt. take the place of, esp. unfairly; oust —**supplant'er** n.

su'pple a. pliable; flexible; compliant —**su'pply** adv.

supp'lement n. thing added to

fill up, supply deficiency, *esp.* extra part added to book *etc.*; additional number of periodical, usu. on special subject; separate, often illustrated section published periodically with newspaper —*vt.* add to; supply deficiency —**supplement'ary** a. additional —**supplementary benefit** money paid by the state to minimum legal levels

supp'liant a. petitioning —n. petitioner

supp'licate v. beg humbly, entreat —**supplica'tion** n. —**sup'plicatory** a.

supply' vt. furnish; make available; provide (**supplied', supply'ing**) —n. supplying, substitute, stock, store

support' vt. hold up; sustain; assist —n. supporting, being supported; means of support —**support'able** a. —**support'er** n. adherent —**support'ing** a. (of film *etc.* role) less important —**support'ive** a.

suppose' [-ōz'] vt. assume as theory; take for granted; accept as likely; (in passive) be expected, obliged; ought —**supposed'** a. —**suppos'edly** [-id-li] adv. —**supposi'tion** [-zish'-] n. assumption; belief without proof; conjecture —**supposi'tious** a. —**suppositi'tious** a. sham; spurious; counterfeit

suppos'itory [-oz'-] n. medication (in capsule) for insertion in orifice of body

suppress' vt. put down, restrain; crush, stifle; keep or withdraw from publication —**suppres'sion** [-esh'-] n.

supp'urate vi. fester, form pus —**suppura'tion** n.

supra- (*comb. form*) above, over, as in **supranat'ional** a. involving more than one nation Such words are not given here

where the meaning may easily be inferred from the simple word

supreme' a. highest in authority or rank; utmost —**suprem'acy** n. position of being supreme —**supre'mely** adv. —**supre'mo** n. person with overall authority

surcease' v. (cause to) cease, give respite —n. cessation

sur'charge n. additional charge —vt. make additional charge

sure [shoor] a. certain; trustworthy; without doubt —adv. inf. certainly —**sure'ly** adv. —**sure'ty** n. one who makes himself responsible for another's obligations

surf n. waves breaking on shore —v. swim, ride surf —**surf'er** n. one who (often) goes surfing —**surf'board** n. board used in sport of riding over surf

sur'face [-fis] n. outside face of body; exterior; plane; top, visible side; superficial appearance, outward impression —a. involving the surface only; going no deeper than surface —v. (cause to) come to surface; put a surface on

sur'feit [-fit] n. excess; disgust caused by excess —v. feed to excess

surge n. wave; sudden increase; *Electricity* sudden rush of current in circuit —vi. move in large waves; swell, billow

sur'geon [-jon] n. medical expert who performs operations —**sur'gery** n. medical treatment by operation; doctor's, dentist's consulting room —**sur'gical** a. —**sur'gically** adv.

sur'ly a. gloomily morose; ill-natured; cross and rude —**sur'lily** adv. —**sur'liness** n.

surmise' v./n. guess, conjecture

surmount' vt. get over, overcome —**surmount'able** a.

sur'name n. family name

surpass' [-ahs'] vt. go beyond; excel; outstrip —**surpass'able** a. —**surpass'ing** a. excellent; exceeding others

sur'plice [-plis] n. loose white vestment worn by clergy and choristers

sur'plus n. what remains over in excess

surprise' [-iz'] vt. cause surprise to; astonish; take, come upon unexpectedly; startle (someone) into action thus —n. what takes unawares; something unexpected; emotion aroused by being taken unawares

surre'alism n. movement in art and literature emphasizing expression of the unconscious —**surre'al** a. —**surre'alist** n./a.

surren'der vt. hand over, give up —vi. yield; cease resistance; capitulate —n. act of surrendering

surrepti'tious [-tish'-] a. done secretly or stealthily; furtive —**surrepti'tiously** adv.

surr'ogate [-git] n. deputy, esp. of bishop; substitute —**surrogate mother** woman who bears child on behalf of childless couple

surround' vt. be, come all round, encompass; encircle; hem in —n. border, edging —**surround'ings** pl.n. conditions, scenery etc. around a person, place, environment

sur'tax n. additional tax

surveill'ance [sur-vāl'-] n. close watch, supervision —**surveill'ant** a./n.

survey' vt. view, scrutinize; inspect, examine; measure, map (land) —n. [sur'-] a surveying; inspection; report incorporating results of survey —**survey'or** n.

survive' vt. outlive; come alive through —vi. continue to live or exist —**survi'val** n. continuation

of existence of persons, things etc. —**survi'vor** n. one left alive when others have died

suscep'tible [sə-sep'-] a. yielding readily (to); capable (of); impressionable —**susceptibil'ity** n.

suspect' vt. doubt innocence of; have impression of existence or presence of; be inclined to believe that; mistrust —a. [sus'-] of suspected character —n. suspected person

suspend' vt. hang up; cause to cease for a time; debar from an office or privilege; keep inoperative; sustain in fluid —**suspend'ers** pl.n. straps for supporting stockings

suspense' n. state of uncertainty, esp. while awaiting news, an event etc.; anxiety, worry —**suspen'sion** n. state of being suspended; springs on axle of body of vehicle —**suspen'sory** a.

suspi'cion [-spish'-] n. suspecting, being suspected; slight trace —**suspi'cious** a. —**suspi'ciously** adv.

sus(s) sl.n. suspect; suspicion —vt. suspect; investigate, find (out)

sustain' vt. keep, hold up; endure; keep alive; confirm —**sustain'able** a. —**sus'tenance** n. food

su'ture [sōō'-] n. act of sewing; sewing up of a wound; material used for this; a joining of the bones of the skull —**su'tural** a.

su'zerain [sōō'-] n. sovereign with rights over autonomous state; feudal lord —**su'zerainty** n.

svelte a. lightly built, slender; sophisticated

SW southwest(ern)

swab [-ob] n. mop; pad of surgical wool etc. for cleaning, taking specimen etc.; sl. low or unmannerly fellow —vt. clean with swab (-bb-) —swab'ber n.

swad'dle [-od'-] vt. swathe
—swaddling clothes Hist. long
strips of cloth for wrapping newborn baby

swag n. sl. stolen property; A inf.
bag carried by swagman
—swag'man n. A itinerant tramp

swagg'er vi. strut; boast —n.
strutting gait; boastful, overconfi-
dent manner

swain n. rustic lover

swall'ow¹ [-ol'ō] vt. cause, allow to pass down gullet; engulf;
suppress, keep back; inf. believe
gullibly —n. act of swallowing

swall'ow² [-ol'ō] n. migratory
bird with forked tail and skimming manner of flight

swam pt. of SWIM

swamp [-omp] n. bog —vt. entangle in swamp; overwhelm;
flood —swamp'y a.

swan [-on] n. large, web-footed
water bird with graceful curved
neck —vi. inf. stroll idly —swan
song fabled song of a swan
before death; last act etc. before
death —swann'ery n.

swank vi. sl. swagger; show off
—swank'y a. sl. smart; showy

swap [-op], swop inf. n./v.
exchange; barter (-pp-)

sward [-aw-] n. green turf

swarm¹ [-aw-] n. large cluster
of insects; vast crowd —vi. (of
bees) be on the move in swarm;
gather in large numbers

swarm² [-aw-] vi. climb (rope
etc.) by grasping with hands and
knees

swar'thy [-aw-] a. dark-
complexioned

swash'buckler [-osh'-] n.
swaggering daredevil person
—swash'buckling a.

swas'tika [-os'-] n. form of cross
with arms bent at right angles,
used as badge by Nazis

swat [swot] vt. hit smartly; kill,
esp. insects (-tt-)

swath [-awth] n. line of grass or
grain cut and thrown together by
scythe; whole sweep of scythe
(also swathe [-ATH])

swathe vt. cover with wraps or
bandages

sway vi. swing unsteadily; (cause
to) vacillate in opinion etc. —vt.
influence opinion etc. —n. control; power; swaying motion

swear [-ār] vt. promise on oath;
cause to take an oath —vi. declare; curse (swore, sworn,
swear'ing)

sweat [swet] n. moisture oozing
from, forming on skin, esp. in
humans —v. (cause to) exude
sweat; toil; employ at wrongfully
low wages; inf. worry (sweat or
sweat'ed pt./pp., sweat'ing
pr.p.) —sweat'y a. —sweat shirt
long-sleeved cotton jersey

sweat'er n. woollen jersey

Swede n. native of Sweden. (s-)
variety of turnip

sweep vi. effect cleaning with
broom; pass quickly or magnifi-
cently; extend in continuous
curve —vt. clean with broom;
carry impetuously (swept,
sweep'ing) —n. act of cleaning
with broom; sweeping motion;
wide curve; range; long oar; one
who cleans chimneys —sweep'-
ing a. wide-ranging; without limitations, reservations —sweep,
sweep'stake n. gamble in which
winner takes stakes contributed
by all

sweet a. tasting like sugar;
agreeable; kind, charming; fresh,
fragrant; in good condition; tuneful; gentle, dear, beloved —n.
small piece of sweet food; sweet
course served at end of meal
—sweet'en v. —sweet'ish a.
—sweet'ly adv. —sweet'bread n.
animal's pancreas used as food

—**sweet'brier** n. wild rose
—**sweet'heart** n. lover —**sweet'-meat** n. sweetened delicacy e.g. small cake, sweet —**sweet pea** plant of pea family with bright flowers —**sweet potato** trailing plant; its edible, sweetish, starchy tubers —**sweet-talk** v. inf. coax, flatter —**sweet william** garden plant with flat flower clusters

swell v. expand —vi. be greatly filled with pride, emotion (**swelled**, **swo'llen**, **swell'ing**) —n. act of swelling or being swollen; wave of sea; mechanism in organ to vary volume of sound; sl. person of high social standing —a. sl. smart, fine

swelt'er vi. be oppressed with heat

swept pt./pp. of SWEEP

swerve vi. swing round, change direction during motion; turn aside (from duty etc.) —n. swerving

swift a. rapid, quick, ready —n. bird like a swallow —**swift'ly** adv.

swig n. large swallow of drink —v. drink thus

swill v. drink greedily; pour water over or through —n. liquid pig foods; greedy drinking; rinsing

swim vi. support and move oneself in water; float; be flooded; have feeling of dizziness —vt. cross by swimming; compete in by swimming (**swam**, **swum**, **swim'ming**) —**swimm'er** n. —**swim'mingly** adv. successfully, effortlessly

swin'dle n./v. cheat —**swin'dler** n. —**swind'ling** n.

swine n. pig; contemptible person (pl. **swine**) —**swi'nish** a. —**swine'herd** n.

swing v. (cause) to move to and fro; (cause to) pivot, turn; hang; arrange, play music with (jazz) rhythm —vi. be hanged; hit out (at) (**swung** pt./pp.) —n. act, instance of swinging; seat hung to swing on; fluctuation (esp. eg in voting pattern) —**swing'er** n. inf. person regarded as modern, lively

swinge'ing a. severe; huge

swipe v. strike with wide, sweeping or glancing blow; sl. steal

swirl v. (cause to) move with eddying motion —n. such motion

swish v. (cause to) move with audible hissing sound —n. the sound —a. inf. fashionable, smart

Swiss n. native of Switzerland —a. —**Swiss roll** type of rolled-up sponge cake

switch n. mechanism to complete or interrupt electric circuit etc.; abrupt change; flexible stick or twig; tufted end of animal's tail; tress of false hair —vi. shift, change; swing —vt. affect (current etc.) with switch; change abruptly; strike with switch —**switch'back** n. road, railway with steep rises and descents —**switch'board** n. installation for establishing or varying connections in telephone and electric circuits

swiv'el n. mechanism of two parts which can revolve the one on the other —v. turn (on swivel) (**-ll-**)

swo'llen pp. of SWELL

swoon [-ōō] vi./n. faint

swoop [-ōō] vi. dive, as hawk —n. act of swooping; sudden attack

swop vt. see SWAP

sword [sawrd] n. weapon with long blade for cutting or thrusting —**sword'fish** n. fish with elongated sharp upper jaw, like sword

swore pt. **—sworn** pp. of SWEAR

swot inf. v. study hard (**-tt-**) —n. one who works hard at lessons or studies

swum pp. of SWIM

swung pt./pp. of SWING

syb'arite n. person who loves luxury **—sybarit'ic** a.

syc'amore [sik'-] n. tree allied to plane tree and maple

syc'ophant [sik'-] n. one using flattery to gain favours **—sycophan'tic** a. **—syc'ophancy** n.

syll'able n. division of word as unit for pronunciation **—syllab'ic** a. **—syllab'ify** vt.

syll'abub, sill'abub n. sweet frothy dish of cream, sugar and wine; something insubstantial

syll'abus n. outline of a course of study; programme; list of subjects studied on course (pl. **-es, -bi** [-bī])

syll'ogism [-j-] n. form of logical reasoning consisting of two premisses and conclusion **—syllogis'tic** a. **—syllogist'ically** adv.

sylph [silf] n. slender, graceful woman; sprite

syl'van a. of forests, trees

sym- see SYN-, used before labial consonants

symbio'sis n. living together of two organisms of different kinds, esp. to their mutual benefit **—symbiot'ic** a.

sym'bol n. sign; thing representing or typifying something **—symbol'ic** a. **—symbol'ically** adv. **—sym'bolism** n. use of representation by symbols; movement in art holding that work of art should express idea in symbolic form **—sym'bolist** n./a. **—sym'bolize** vt.

symm'etry n. proportion between parts; balance of arrangement between two sides; order **—symmet'rical** a. having due proportion in its parts; harmoni-

ous; regular **—symmet'rically** adv.

sym'pathy n. feeling for another in pain etc.; compassion, pity; sharing of emotion, interest, desire etc.; fellow feeling **—sympathet'ic** a. **—sympathet'ically** adv. **—sym'pathize** vi.

sym'phony n. composition for full orchestra; harmony of sounds **—symphon'ic** a. **—sympho'nious** a. harmonious

sympo'sium n. conference, meeting; discussion, writings on a given topic

symp'tom n. change in body indicating its state of health or disease; sign, token **—symptomat'ic** a.

syn- [sin-, sing-] (comb. form) with, together, alike

syn'agogue [-gog] n. (place of worship of) Jewish congregation

syn'chromesh a. (of gearbox) having device that synchronizes speeds of gears before they engage

syn'chronize vt. make agree in time —vi. happen at same time **—syn'chronism** n. **—synchroniza'tion** n. **—syn'chronous** a. simultaneous

syn'chrotron [-kro-] n. device for acceleration of stream of electrons

syn'copate vt. accentuate weak beat in bar of music **—syncopa'tion** n.

syn'cope [-kǝ-pi] n. fainting; elision of letter(s) from middle of word

syn'dicate n. body of people, delegates associated for some enterprise —v. form syndicate —vt. publish in many newspapers at the same time **—syn'dicalism** n. economic movement aiming at combination of workers in all trades to enforce demands of labour

syn'drome n. combination of several symptoms in disease; symptom, set of symptoms or characteristics

synec'doche [-nek'də-ki] n. figure of speech by which whole of thing is put for part or part for whole, eg sail for ship

syn'od n. church council; convention

syn'onym n. word with same meaning as another —**synonym'ity** n. —**synon'ymous** a.

synop'sis n. summary, outline —**synop'tic** a. of, like synopsis; having same viewpoint

syn'tax n. part of grammar treating of arrangement of words in sentence —**syntac'tic** a. —**syntac'tically** adv.

syn'thesis n. putting together, combination (pl. **-theses** [-ēz]) —**syn'thesize** v. make artificially —**syn'thesizer** n. electronic keyboard instrument capable of reproducing a wide range of musical sounds —**synthet'ic** a. artificial; of synthesis —**synthet'ically** adv.

syph'ilis n. contagious venereal disease —**syphilit'ic** a.

syr'inge [si'rinj] n. instrument for drawing in liquid by piston and forcing it out in fine stream or spray; squirt —vt. spray, cleanse with syringe

syr'up [si'rəp] n. thick solution obtained in process of refining sugar; any liquid like this, esp. in consistency —**syr'upy** a.

sys'tem n. complex whole, organization; method; classification —**systemat'ic** a. methodical —**systemat'ically** adv. —**sys'tematize** vt. reduce to system; arrange methodically —**system'ic** a. affecting entire body or organism

sys'tole [-tə-li] n. contraction of heart and arteries for expelling blood and carrying on circulation —**systol'ic** a. contracting; of systole

T

T tablespoon; temperature; Chem. tritium —**to a T** precisely, to a nicety

t. tense; ton

t tonne

TA Territorial Army

ta [tah] interj. inf. thank you

taal [tahl] n. SA language, esp. Afrikaans

tab n. tag, label, short strap —**keep tabs on** inf. keep watchful eye on

tab'ard n. (herald's) short tunic open at sides

tab'by n./a. (cat) with markings of stripes etc. on lighter background

tab'ernacle n. portable shrine of Israelites; RC Ch. receptacle containing consecrated Host; place of worship not called a church

ta'ble n. piece of furniture consisting of flat board supported by legs; food; set of facts, figures arranged in lines or columns —vt. lay on table; submit (motion etc.) for consideration by meeting —**ta'bleland** n. plateau, high flat area —**ta'blespoon** n. spoon used for serving food etc. —**table tennis** ball game played on table with small bats and light hollow ball

tab'leau [-lō] n. group of persons, silent and motionless, arranged to represent some scene; dramatic scene (pl. **-leaux** [-lō])

tab'le d'hôte' [tahb'l-dōt] Fr. meal, with limited choice of dishes, at a fixed price

tab'let n. pill of compressed powdered medicinal substance; flattish cake of soap or stone, wood etc., esp. used formerly for writing on

tab'loid n. illustrated popular small-sized newspaper with terse, sensational headlines

taboo' a. forbidden or disapproved of —n. prohibition resulting from social conventions etc.; thing prohibited —vt. place under taboo

tab'ular a. shaped, arranged like a table —**tab'ulate** vt. arrange (figures, facts etc.) in tables —**tabula'tion** n. —**tab'ulator** n.

tacho- (comb. form) speed

tach'ograph [tak'-] n. device for recording speed and distance travelled by lorries

tachom'eter [-kom'-] n. device for measuring speed, esp. of revolving shaft (in car) and hence revolutions per minute

tac'it [tas'-] a. implied but not spoken; silent —**tac'itly** adv. —**tac'iturn** a. talking little; habitually silent —**taciturn'ity** n.

tack¹ n. small nail; long loose stitch; Naut. course of ship obliquely to windward; course, direction; inf. food —vt. nail with tacks; stitch lightly; append, attach; sail to windward

tack² n. riding harness for horses

tac'kle [-kəl] n. equipment, apparatus, esp. lifting appliances with ropes; Sport physical challenge of opponent —vt. take in hand; grip, grapple with; challenge

tack'y a. sticky; not quite dry —**tack'ie** n. SA plimsoll —**tack'iness** n.

tact n. skill in dealing with people or situations; delicate perception of the feelings of others

—**tact'ful** a. —**tact'fully** adv. —**tact'less** a. —**tact'lessly** adv.

tac'tics pl.n. art of handling troops, ships in battle; adroit management of a situation; plans for this —**tact'ical** a. —**tacti'cian** n.

tac'tile a. of, relating to the sense of touch

tad'pole n. immature frog, in its first state before gills and tail are absorbed

taffe'ta n. smooth, stiff fabric of silk, rayon etc.

taff'rail n. rail at stern of ship; flat ornamental part of stern

Taff'y n. sl. Welshman

tag¹ n. label identifying or showing price of (something); ragged, hanging end; pointed end of shoelace etc.; trite quotation; any appendage —vt. append, add (on); trail (along) behind (**-gg-**)

tag² n. children's game where one being chased becomes the chaser upon being touched —vt. touch —**tag wrestling** wrestling match for teams of two, where one partner may replace the other upon being touched on hand

tail n. flexible prolongation of animal's spine; lower or inferior part of anything; appendage; rear part of aircraft; inf. person employed to follow another —pl. reverse side of coin; inf. tail coat —vt. remove tail of; inf. follow closely, trail —**tailed** a. —**tail'ings** pl.n. waste left over from some (eg industrial) process —**tail'less** a. —**tail'back** n. queue of traffic stretching back from an obstruction —**tail'board** n. removable or hinged rear board on lorry etc. —**tail coat** man's evening dress jacket —**tail end** last part —**tail'light** n. light carried at rear of vehicle —**tail'plane** n. stabilizing surface at rear of

aircraft —**tail'spin** n. spinning dive of aircraft —**tail off** diminish gradually, dwindle —**turn tail** run away

tail'or n. maker of outer clothing, esp. for men —**tailor-made** a. made by tailor; well-fitting; appropriate

taint v. affect or be affected by pollution etc. —n. defect, flaw; infection, contamination

take vt. grasp, get hold of; get; receive, assume; adopt; accept; understand; consider; carry, conduct; use; capture; consume; subtract; require —vi. be effective; please; go (**took, ta'ken, ta'king**) —n. esp. Cinema (recording of) scene, sequence photographed without interruption —**ta'king** a. charming —**ta'kings** pl.n. earnings, receipts —**take-off** n. instant at which aircraft becomes airborne; commencement of flight —**take after** resemble in face or character —**take down** write down; dismantle; humiliate —**take in** understand; make (garment etc.) smaller; deceive —**take in vain** blaspheme; be facetious —**take off** (of aircraft) leave ground; inf. go away; inf. mimic —**take to** become fond of

talc n. soft mineral of magnesium silicate; talcum powder —**talcum powder** powder, usu. scented, to absorb body moisture, deodorize etc.

tale n. story, narrative, report; fictitious story

tal'ent n. natural ability or power; ancient weight or money —**tal'ented** a. gifted

talk [tawk] vi. express, exchange ideas etc. in words —vt. express in speech, utter; discuss —n.

tal'isman [-iz-] n. object supposed to have magic power; amulet (pl. **-mans**) —**talisman'ic** a.

mour —**talk'ative** a. fond of talking —**talk'er** n. —**talking-to** n. inf. reproof

tall [tawl] a. high; of great stature; incredible, untrue, as **tall story**; inf. difficult to accomplish

tall'boy [tawl'-] n. high chest of drawers

tall'ow [-ō] n. melted and clarified animal fat —vt. smear with this

tall'y vi. correspond one with the other; keep record (**tall'ied, tall'ying**) —n. record, account, total number —**tall'ier** n.

tally-ho' interj. huntsman's cry to urge on hounds

Tal'mud n. body of Jewish law —**Talmud'ic** a.

tal'on n. claw

tam'arind n. tropical tree; its pods containing sour brownish pulp

tam'arisk n. ornamental, evergreen tree or shrub with slender branches, very small leaves and spiky flowers

tambourine' [-rēn'] n. flat half-drum with jingling discs of metal attached

tame a. not wild, domesticated; subdued; uninteresting —vt. make tame —**tame'ly** adv. in a tame manner; without resisting —**ta'mer** n.

tam-o'-shant'er, tamm'y n. brimless wool cap with bobble in centre

tamp vt. pack, force down by repeated blows

tamp'er vi. interfere (with) improperly; meddle

tam'pon n. plug of lint, cotton etc. inserted in wound, body cavity, to stop flow of blood, absorb secretions etc.

tan a./n. (of) brown colour of skin after long exposure to rays of sun etc. —v. (cause) to go brown; (of animal hide) convert to leather by chemical treatment (-nn-) — **tann'er** n. — **tann'ery** n. place where hides are tanned — **tann'ic** a. — **tann'in** n. vegetable substance used as tanning agent — **tan'bark** n. bark of certain trees, yielding tannin

tan'dem n. bicycle for two riders, one behind the other

tang n. strong pungent taste or smell; trace, hint; spike, barb — **tang'y** a.

tan'gent [-j-] n. line that touches a curve without cutting; divergent course — a. touching, meeting without cutting — **tangen'tial** a. — **tangen'tially** adv.

tangerine ['-rēn'] n. Asian citrus tree; its fruit, a variety of orange

tan'gible a. that can be touched; definite; palpable; concrete — **tangibil'ity** n.

tan'gle [-ng'gl] n. confused mass or situation — vt. twist together in muddle; contend

tan'go n. dance of S Amer. origin (pl. -gos)

tank n. storage vessel for liquids or gas; armoured motor vehicle moving on tracks; cistern; reservoir — **tank'er** n. ship, lorry etc. for carrying liquid in bulk

tank'ard n. large drinking cup of metal or glass; its contents, esp. beer

tann'in see TAN

Tann'oy R type of public-address system

tan'sy [-zi] n. yellow-flowered aromatic herb

tan'talize vt. torment by appearing to offer something desired; tease

tan'tamount a. equivalent in value or signification; equal, amounting (to)

tan'trum n. childish outburst of temper

tap [1] v. strike lightly but with

some noise (-pp-) — n. slight blow, rap

tap [2] n. valve with handle to regulate or stop flow of fluid in pipe etc.; stopper, plug permitting liquid to be drawn from cask etc.; steel tool for forming internal screw threads — vt. put tap in; draw off with or as with tap; make secret connection to telephone wire to overhear conversation on it; make connection to supply of electricity at intermediate point in supply line; form internal threads in (-pp-)

tape n. narrow long strip of fabric, paper etc.; magnetic recording of music etc. — vt. record (speech, music etc.) — **tape measure** tape of fabric, metal marked off in centimetres, inches etc. — **tape recorder** apparatus for recording sound on magnetized tape and playing it back — **tape'worm** n. long flat worm parasitic in animals and man — **have (someone) taped** inf. have (someone) sized up; have measure of

ta'per vi. become gradually thinner towards one end — n. thin candle; long wick covered with wax; a narrowing

tap'estry n. fabric decorated with designs in colours woven by needles, not in shuttles — **tap'estried** a.

tapio'ca n. beadlike starch made from cassava root, used esp. in puddings

ta'pir [-por] n. Amer. animal with elongated snout, allied to pig

tapp'et n. in internal-combustion engine, short steel rod conveying movement imparted by the lift of a cam to the valve stem

tap'root n. large single root growing straight down

tar[1] *n.* thick black liquid distilled from coal *etc.* —*vt.* coat, treat with tar (**-rr-**)

tar[2] *n. inf.* sailor

tarantell'a *n.* lively Italian dance; music for it

taran'tula *n.* any of various large (poisonous) hairy spiders

tard'y *a.* slow, late —**tard'ily** *adv.*

tare[1] *n.* weight of wrapping, container for goods; unladen weight of vehicle

tare[2] *n.* vetch; weed

tar'get *n.* mark to aim at in shooting; thing aimed at; object of criticism; butt

tar'iff [ta'rif] *n.* tax levied on imports *etc.*; list of charges; method of charging for supply of services, *eg* electricity

Tar'mac R mixture of tar, bitumen and crushed stones rolled to give hard, smooth surface to road *etc.*; (t-) airport runway

tarn *n.* small mountain lake

tar'nish *v.* (cause to) become stained, lose shine or become dimmed or sullied —*n.* discoloration, blemish

tar'o *n.* plant of Pacific islands; its edible roots

tar'ot [ta'rō] *n.* one of special pack of cards now used mainly in fortune-telling

tarpaul'in *n.* (sheet of) heavy hard-wearing waterproof fabric

tarr'agon *n.* aromatic herb

tarr'y *vi.* linger, delay; stay behind (**tarr'ied, tarr'ying**)

tar'sier *n.* nocturnal tree-dwelling mammal of Indonesia *etc.*

tart[1] *n.* small pie or flan filled with fruit, jam *etc.*; *inf. offens.* promiscuous woman

tart[2] *a.* sour; sharp; bitter

tar'tan *n.* woollen cloth woven in pattern of coloured checks,

esp. in colours, patterns associated with Scottish clans; such pattern

tar'tar[1] *n.* crust deposited on teeth; deposit formed during fermentation of wine —**tartar'ic** [-ta'rik] *a.*

tar'tar[2] *n.* vicious-tempered person, difficult to deal with

tar'trazine [-trozēn] *n.* artificial yellow dye widely used in food, soft drinks, drugs and to dye textiles

task [-ah-] *n.* piece of work (*esp.* unpleasant or difficult) set or undertaken —*vt.* assign task to; exact —**task force** naval or military unit dispatched to carry out specific undertaking —**task'master** *n.* overseer —**take to task** reprove

tass'el *n.* ornament of fringed knot of threads *etc.*; tuft

taste *n.* sense by which flavour, quality of substance is detected by the tongue; this act or sensation; (brief) experience of something; small amount; preference, liking; power of discerning, judging; discretion, delicacy —*v.* observe or distinguish the taste of a substance; take small amount into mouth; experience —*vi.* have specific flavour —**taste'ful** *a.* in good style; with, showing good taste —**taste'fully** *adv.* —**taste'less** *a.* —**ta'sty** *a.* pleasantly or highly flavoured —**taste bud** small organ of taste on tongue

tat[1] *v.* make by tatting (**-tt-**) —**tatt'er** *n.* —**tatt'ing** *n.* type of handmade lace

tat[2] *n.* ragged, shoddy article; tattiness

tatt'er *v.* make or become ragged, worn to shreds —*n.* ragged piece

tatt'le *vi./n.* gossip, chatter

tattoo'[1] *n.* beat of drum and

bugle call; military spectacle or pageant

tattoo[1][2] vt. mark skin in patterns etc. by pricking and filling punctures with indelible coloured inks (**tattooed**[1], **tattoo'ing**) —n. mark so made

tatt'y a. shabby, worn out —**tat'tiness** n.

taught pt./pp. of TEACH

taunt vt. provoke, deride with insulting words etc. —n. instance of this

Tau'rus [taw'-] n. (the bull) 2nd sign of the zodiac, operative c. Apr. 21–May 20

taut a. drawn tight; under strain —**taut'en** vt. make tight or tense

tautol'ogy n. repetition of same thing in other words in same sentence —**tautolog'ical** a.

tav'ern n. inn, public house

taw n. large marble —pl. game of marbles

taw'dry a. showy, but cheap and without taste, flashy —**taw'drily** adv. —**taw'driness** n.

tawn'y a./n. (of) light (yellowish) brown

taws(e) n. in Scotland, leather strap used esp. formerly to punish schoolchildren

tax n. compulsory payments by wage earners, companies etc. imposed by government to raise revenue; heavy demand on something —vt. impose tax on; strain; accuse, blame —**tax'able** a. —**taxa'tion** n. levying of taxes —**tax'payer** n. —**tax return** statement of personal income for tax purposes

tax'i(cab) n. motor vehicle for hire with driver (pl. **tax'is** [-iz]) —vi. (of aircraft) run along ground under its own power; go in taxi (**tax'ied** pt./pp., **tax'ying, tax'iing** pr.p.) —**taxi rank**

tax'idermy n. art of stuffing, mounting animal skins to give them lifelike appearance —**taxi'der'mal, taxider'mic** a. —**tax'idermist** n.

taxon'omy n. science, practice of classification, esp. of biological organisms

TB tuberculosis

te, ti n. seventh sol-fa note

tea n. dried leaves of plant cultivated esp. in (sub)tropical Asia; infusion of it as beverage; various herbal infusions; tea, cakes etc. as light afternoon meal; main evening meal —**tea bag** small porous bag of paper containing tea leaves —**tea'spoon** n. small spoon for stirring tea etc. —**tea tree** Aust., N.Z. tree

teach vt. instruct; educate; train; impart knowledge of —vi. act as teacher (**taught, teach'ing**) —**teach'er** n. —**teach'ing** n.

teak n. East Indian tree; very hard wood obtained from it

teal n. type of small duck; greenish-blue colour

team n. set of animals, players of game etc. associated in activity —vi. (usu. with up) (cause) to make a team —**team'ster** n. driver of team of draught animals —**team spirit** subordination of individual desire for good of team —**team'work** n. co-operative work by team acting as unit

tear[1] [ter] n. drop of fluid appearing in and falling from eye —**tear'ful** a. inclined to weep; involving tears —**tear'less** a. —**tear'drop** n. —**tear gas** irritant gas causing abnormal watering of eyes, and temporary blindness —**tear-jerker** n. inf. excessively sentimental film etc.

tear[2] [tār] vt. pull apart, rend —vi. become hurt; rush (**tore, torn, tear'ing**) —n. hole, cut or split

tease vt. tantalize, torment, irritate, bait; pull apart fibres of —*n.* one who teases —**teas'ing** *a.*

tea'sel, tea'zel *n.* plant with prickly leaves and head

teat *n.* nipple of female breast; rubber nipple of baby's feeding bottle

tech [tek] *a./n. inf.* short for technical (college)

tech. technical; technology

tech'nical *a.* of, specializing in industrial, practical or mechanical arts and applied sciences; skilled in practical and mechanical arts; belonging to particular art or science; according to letter of the law —**technical'ity** *n.* point of procedure; state of being technical —**tech'nically** *adv.* —**techni'cian** *n.* one skilled in technique of an art —**technique'** [-nēk'] *n.* method of performance in an art; skill required for mastery of subject —**technical col'lege** higher educational institution, with courses in art, technology *etc.*

Tech'nicolor [tek'-] R colour photography, *esp.* in cinema

technoc'racy [tek-] *n.* government by technical experts; group of these experts

technol'ogy [tek-] *n.* application of practical, mechanical sciences to industry, commerce; technical methods, skills, knowledge —**technolog'ical** *a.* —**technol'ogist** *n.*

tecton'ic *a.* of construction or building —**tecton'ics** *pl.n.* (used as *sing.*) art, science of building

tedd'y (bear) child's soft toy bear

te'dious *a.* causing fatigue or boredom, monotonous —**te'dium** *n.* monotony

tee *n.* Golf slightly raised ground from which first stroke of hole is made; small peg supporting ball for this stroke; target in some games, *eg* quoits —**tee off** make first stroke of hole in golf

teem *vi.* abound with; swarm; be prolific; pour, rain heavily

teens *pl.n.* years of life from 13 to 19 —**teen'age** *a.* —**teen'ager** *n.* young person between 13 and 19

tee'pee *n.* see TEPEE

tee'ter *vi.* seesaw or make similar movements; vacillate

teeth *n., pl.* of TOOTH

teethe [-TH] *vi.* (of baby) grow first teeth —**teething troubles** problems, difficulties at first stage of something

teeto'tal *a.* pledged to abstain from alcohol —**teeto'talism** *n.* —**teeto'taller** *n.*

Tef'lon R polymer used to make nonstick coatings on cooking utensils

tel. telegram; telegraph; telephone

tele- (*comb. form*) at a distance, and from far off

tel'ecast *v./n.* (broadcast) television programme

telecommunica'tions *pl.n.* (*with sing. v.*) science and technology of communications by telephony, radio, television *etc.*

tel'egram *n.* message sent by telegraph

tel'egraph *n.* electrical apparatus for transmitting messages to a distance; any signalling device for transmitting messages —*v.* communicate by telegraph —**telegraph'ic** *a.* —**telegraph'ically** *adv.* —**teleg'raphist** *n.* one who works telegraph —**teleg'raphy** *n.* science of telegraph; use of telegraph

teleol'ogy *n.* doctrine of final causes; belief that things happen because of the purpose or design that will be fulfilled by them —**teleolog'ic(al)** *a.*

telep'athy *n.* action of one

mind on another at a distance —telepath'ic a. —telepath'ically adv.

tel'ephone n. apparatus for communicating sound to hearer at a distance —v. communicate, speak by telephone —telephon'ic a. —teleph'onist n. person operating telephone switchboard —teleph'ony n.

telepho'to a. (of lens) producing magnified image of distant object

tel'eprinter n. apparatus, like typewriter, by which typed messages are sent and received by wire

Tel'eprompter n. R Television device to enable speaker to refer to his script out of sight of the cameras

tel'escope n. optical instrument for magnifying distant objects —v. slide or drive together, esp. parts designed to fit one inside the other; make smaller, shorter —telescop'ic a.

tel'esales pl.n. selling product or service by phoning potential customers

tel'etext n. electronic system which shows information, news on subscribers' television screens

Tel'etype R type of teleprinter

tel'evision n. system of producing on screen images of distant objects, events etc. by electromagnetic radiation; device for receiving this transmission and converting it to optical images; programmes etc. viewed on television set —tel'evise vt. transmit by television; make, produce as television programme

tel'ex n. international telegraph service using teleprinters —v.

tell vt. let know; order, direct; narrate, make known; discern; distinguish; count —vi. give account; be of weight, importance;

inf. reveal secrets (told, tell'ing) —tell'er n. narrator; bank cashier —tell'ing a. effective, striking —tell'tale n. sneak; automatic indicator —a. revealing

tellur'ian [-loor-] a. of the earth —tellur'ium n. nonmetallic bluish-white element —tellu'ric a. —tell'urous a.

tell'y n. inf. television (set)

temer'ity [-me'ri-] n. boldness, audacity

temp n. inf. one employed on temporary basis

temp. temperature; temporary

temp'er n. frame of mind; anger, oft. noisy; mental constitution; degree of hardness of steel etc. —vt. restrain, qualify, moderate; harden; bring to proper condition

temp'era n. emulsion used as painting medium

temp'erament n. natural disposition; emotional mood; mental constitution —temperament'al a. given to extremes of temperament, moody; of, occasioned by temperament —temperamen't'ally adv.

temp'erate a. not extreme; showing, practising moderation —temp'erance n. moderation; abstinence, esp. from alcohol —temp'erately adv.

temp'erature n. degree of heat or coldness; inf. (abnormally) high body temperature

temp'est n. violent storm —tempes'tuous a. turbulent; violent, stormy —tempest'uously adv.

temp'late, temp'let n. mould, pattern to help shape something accurately

temp'le[1] n. building for worship; shrine

temp'le[2] n. flat part on either side of forehead

tem'po *n.* rate, rhythm, *esp.* in music

tem'poral *a.* of time; of this life or world, secular —**tempo'rality** *n.*

tem'porary *a.* lasting, used only for a time —**tem'porarily** *adv.*

tem'porize *vi.* use evasive action; hedge; gain time by negotiation *etc.*; conform to circumstances —**tem'porizer** *n.*

tempt *vt.* try to persuade, entice, *esp.* to something wrong or unwise; dispose, cause to be inclined to —**tempta'tion** *n.* act of tempting; thing that tempts —**tempt'er** *n.* (**tempt'ress** *fem.*) —**tempt'ing** *a.* attractive, inviting

ten *n./a.* cardinal number next after nine —**tenth** *a./n.* ordinal number

ten'able *a.* able to be held, defended, maintained

tena'cious *a.* holding fast; retentive; stubborn —**tenac'ity** [-nas'-] *n.*

ten'ant *n.* one who holds lands, house *etc.* on rent or lease —**ten'ancy** *n.* —**ten'antry** *n.* body of tenants

tench *n.* freshwater game fish

tend [1] *vi.* be inclined; be conducive; make in direction of —**ten'dency** *n.* inclination, bent —**ten'dentious** *a.* having, showing tendency or bias, controversial

tend [2] *vt.* take care of, watch over —**tend'er** *n.* small boat carried by yacht or ship; carriage for fuel and water attached to steam locomotive; one who tends, *eg* bar tender

tend'er [1] *a.* not tough or hard; easily injured; gentle, loving, affectionate; delicate, soft —**ten'derly** *adv.* —**tend'erness** *n.* —**ten'derize** *vt.* soften (meat) by pounding or by treating (it) with substance made for this purpose —**tend'erfoot** *n.* newcomer, *esp.* to ranch *etc.*

tend'er [2] *vt.* offer —*vi.* make offer or estimate —*n.* offer; offer or estimate for contract to undertake specific work; what may legally be offered in payment

ten'don *n.* sinew attaching muscle to bone *etc.*

tend'ril *n.* slender curling stem by which climbing plant clings to anything; curl, as of hair

ten'ement *n.* building divided into separate flats

ten'et [or tē'-] *n.* doctrine, belief

tenn'er *n. inf.* ten pound note

tenn'is *n.* game in which ball is struck with racket by players on opposite sides of net, lawn tennis —**tennis elbow** strained muscle as a result of playing tennis

ten'on *n.* tongue put on end of piece of wood *etc.*, to fit into a mortise —**tenon saw**

ten'or *n.* male voice between alto and bass; music for, singer with this; general course, meaning

tense [1] *n.* modification of verb to show time of action

tense [2] *a.* stretched tight; strained; taut; emotionally strained —*v.* make, become tense —**ten'sile** *a.* of, relating to tension; capable of being stretched —**ten'sion** *n.* stretching; strain when stretched; emotional strain or excitement; hostility, suspense; *Electricity* voltage

tent *n.* portable shelter of canvas

tent'acle *n.* elongated, flexible organ of some animals (*eg* octopus) used for grasping, feeding *etc.*

tent'ative *a.* done as a trial; experimental, cautious —**ten'tatively** *adv.*

tent'erhooks *pl.n.* —**on**

tenterhooks in anxious suspense

ten'uous a. flimsy, uncertain; thin, fine, slender —**tenu'ity** n.

ten'ure n. (length of time of) possession, holding of office, position etc.

te'pee n. N Amer. Indian cone-shaped tent of animal skins

tep'id a. moderately warm, luke-warm; half-hearted

tequi'la [-ke'-] n. Mexican alcoholic spirit

ter'bium n. rare metallic element

tercente'nary a./n. (of) three-hundredth anniversary

term n. word, expression; limited period of time; period during which courts sit, schools are open etc.; limit, end —pl. conditions; mutual relationship —vt. name, designate

term'inal a. at, forming an end; pert. to, forming a terminus; (of disease) ending in death —n. terminal part or structure; extremity; point where current enters, leaves electrical device (eg battery); device permitting operation of computer at some distance from it

term'inate v. bring, come to an end —**term'inable** a. —**termina'tion** n.

terminol'ogy n. set of technical terms or vocabulary; study of terms —**terminolog'ical** a.

term'inus n. finishing point; farthest limit; railway station, bus station etc. at end of long-distance line (pl. **-ni** [-nī])

ter'mite n. insect, some species of which feed on and damage wood (also called **white ant**)

tern n. sea bird like gull

tern'ary a. consisting of three; proceeding in threes

Terr. Terrace; Territory

terr'ace n. raised level place; level cut out of hill; row, street of houses built as one block; (oft. pl.) unroofed tiers for spectators at football stadium —vt. form into, furnish with terrace

terr'a cott'a hard unglazed pottery; its colour, a brownish-red

terr'a fir'ma Lat. firm ground; dry land

terr'ain [or -ān'] n. area of ground, esp. with reference to its physical character

Terramy'cin n. R antibiotic allied to penicillin

terr'apin n. type of aquatic tortoise

terra'rium n. enclosed container in which small plants, animals are kept

terrazz'o [-ats'ō] n. floor, wall finish of chips of stone set in mortar and polished

terrest'rial a. of the earth; of, living on land

terr'ible a. serious; dreadful, frightful; excessive; causing fear —**terr'ibly** adv.

terr'ier n. small dog of various breeds, orig. for following quarry into burrow

terrif'ic a. very great; inf. good, excellent; terrible, awe-inspiring

terr'ify vt. fill with fear, dread

terr'itory n. region; geographical area under control of a political unit, esp. a sovereign state; area of knowledge —**terri-to'rial** a. of territory —**Territorial Army** locally recruited volunteer force

terr'or n. great fear; inf. troublesome person or thing —**terr'orism** n. use of violence, intimidation to achieve ends; state of terror —**terr'orist** n./a. —**terr'orize** vt. force, oppress by fear, violence

terr'y n./a. (pile fabric) with the loops uncut

terse a. expressed in few words, concise; abrupt

ter'tiary [-shər-i] a. third in degree, order etc. —n. (**T-**) geological period before Quaternary

Ter'ylene [te'rə-] R synthetic yarn; fabric made of it

tess'ellate vt. make, pave, inlay with mosaic of small tiles; (of identical shapes) fit together exactly —**tess'ellated** a. —**tessella'tion** n. —**tess'era** n. stone used in mosaic (pl. **-ae** [-ē])

test vt. try, put to the proof; carry out test(s) on —n. critical examination; means of trial —**test'ing** a. difficult —**test case** lawsuit viewed as means of establishing precedent —**test match** one of series of international sports contests, esp. cricket —**test tube** narrow cylindrical glass vessel used in scientific experiments —**test-tube baby** baby conceived in artificial womb

test'ament n. Law will; declaration; (**T-**) one of the two main divisions of the Bible —**testamen'tary** a.

test'ate a. having left a valid will —**test'acy** n. state of being testate —**testa'tor** n. maker of will (**testa'trix** fem.)

test'icle n. either of two male reproductive glands

test'ify v. declare; bear witness (to) (**-ified, -ifying**)

test'imony n. affirmation; evidence —**testimo'nial** n. certificate of character, ability etc.; gift by person expressing regard for recipient

test'is n. testicle (pl. **test'es** [-ēz])

test'y a. irritable, short-tempered —**test'ily** adv.

tet'anus n. acute infectious disease producing muscular spasms, contractions (also called lockjaw)

tête-à-tête' [tāt-ə-tāt'] Fr. private conversation

teth'er [-TH-] n. rope or chain for fastening (grazing) animal —vt. tie up with rope —**be at end of one's tether** have reached limit of one's endurance

tet'ragon n. figure with four angles and four sides —**tetrag'onal** a. —**tetrahe'dron** n. solid contained by four plane faces

Teuton'ic a. German; of ancient Teutons

text n. (actual words of) book, passage etc.; passage of Scriptures etc., esp. as subject of discourse —**text'ual** a. of, in a text —**text'book** n. book of instruction on particular subject

tex'tile n. any fabric or cloth, esp. woven —a. of (the making of) fabrics

tex'ture n. character; structure; consistency

TGWU Transport and General Workers' Union

thalid'omide n. drug formerly used as sedative, but found to cause abnormalities in developing foetus

thall'ium n. highly toxic metallic element —**thall'ic** a.

than [TH-] conj. introduces second part of comparison

thane n. Hist. nobleman holding lands in return for certain services

thank vt. express gratitude to; say thanks; hold responsible —**thanks** pl.n. words of gratitude —**thank'ful** a. grateful, appreciative —**thank'less** a. having, bringing no thanks; unprofitable —**Thanksgiving Day** public holiday in Canada, US

that [TH-] a. demonstrates or particularizes (pl. **those**) —**demonstrative** pron. particular thing meant (*pl.* those) —*adv.* as —*relative pron.* which, who —*conj.* introduces noun or adverbial clauses

thatch *n.* reeds, straw *etc.* used as roofing material —*vt.* to roof (a house) with reeds, straw *etc.* —**thatch'er** *n.*

thaw *v.* melt; (cause to) unfreeze; defrost; become warmer, or more genial —*n.* a melting (of frost *etc.*)

the [THə, THē] is the definite article

the'atre [-tər] *n.* place where plays *etc.* are performed; drama, dramatic works generally; large room with (tiered) seats, used for lectures *etc.*; surgical operating room —**theat'rical** *a.* of, for the theatre; exaggerated, affected —**theat'rically** *adv.* —**theat'ricals** *pl.n.* amateur dramatic performances

thee [TH-] *pron. obs.* objective and dative of THOU

theft *n.* stealing

their [THār] *a./pron.* of THEM; possessive of THEY —**theirs** *poss. pron.* belonging to them

the'ism *n.* belief in creation of universe by one god —**the'ist** *n.* —**theist'ic** *a.*

them *pron.* objective case of THEY; those persons or things —**themselves'** *pron.* emphatic and reflexive form of THEY

theme *n.* main idea or topic of conversation, book *etc.*; subject of composition; recurring melody in music —**themat'ic** *a.* —**theme park** leisure area designed round one subject

then [TH-] *adv.* at that time; next; that being so

thence [TH-] *adv. obs.* from that place, point of reasoning *etc.*

theoc'racy *n.* government by a deity or a priesthood —**theocrat'ic** *a.*

theod'olite *n.* surveying instrument for measuring angles

theol'ogy *n.* systematic study of religion(s) and religious belief(s) —**theolog'ical** *a.* —**theolog'ically** *adv.* —**theolo'gian** *n.*

the'orem *n.* proposition which can be demonstrated by argument —**theoremat'ic(al)** *a.*

the'ory *n.* supposition to account for something; system of rules and principles; rules and reasoning *etc.* as distinguished from practice —**theoret'ical** *a.* based on theory; speculative, as opposed to practical —**theoret'ically** *adv.* —**the'orist** *n.* —**the'orize** *vi.* form theories, speculate

theos'ophy *n.* any of various religious, philosophical systems claiming possibility of intuitive insight into divine nature

ther'apy [the'ra-] *n.* healing treatment: *usu.* in compounds as RADIOTHERAPY —**therapeu'tic** [-pyōō'-] *a.* of healing; serving to improve or maintain health —**therapeu'tics** *pl.n.* art of healing —**ther'apist** *n.*

there [TH-] *adv.* in that place; to that point —**thereby'** *adv.* by that means —**there'fore** *adv.* in consequence, that being so —**thereupon'** *conj.* at that point, immediately afterwards

therm *n.* unit of measurement of heat —**ther'mal, ther'mic** *a.* of, pert. to heat; hot, warm (*esp.* of spring *etc.*)

ther'mion *n.* ion emitted by incandescent body —**thermion'ic** *a.* pert. to thermion —**thermionic valve** electronic valve in which electrons are emitted from a heated rather than a cold cathode

thermo- (*comb. form*) related to, caused by or producing heat

thermodynam'ics *pl.n.* (*with sing. v.*) the science that deals with the interrelationship and interconversion of different forms of energy

ther·moelectric'ity n. electricity developed by the action of heat

ther'mograph n. self-registering thermometer

thermom'eter n. instrument to measure temperature —**thermomet'ric** a.

thermonu'clear a. involving nuclear fusion

thermoplas'tic n. plastic that retains its properties after being melted and solidified —a.

Ther'mos R vacuum flask

ther'mostat n. apparatus for automatically regulating temperature —**thermostat'ic** a.

thesau'rus [-aw'-] n. book containing lists of synonyms and antonyms; dictionary of selected words, topics

these [TH-] pron., pl. of THIS

the'sis n. written work submitted for degree, diploma; theory maintained in argument (pl. the'ses [-sēz])

Thes'pian a. theatrical —n. actor, actress

they [THA] pron. the third person plural pronoun

thi'amine n. soluble white crystalline vitamin of B group

thick a. having great thickness, not thin; dense, crowded; viscous; (of voice) throaty; inf. stupid, insensitive; inf. friendly —n. busiest, most intense part —**thick'en** v. make, become thick; become more involved, complicated —**thick'ly** adv. —**thick'ness** n. dimensions of anything measured through it, at right angles to length and breadth; state of being thick; layer —**thick'set** n. thick growth of small trees —**thickset'** a. sturdy and solid of body; set closely together

thief n. one who steals (pl. thieves) —**thieve** v. steal —**thiev'ish** a.

thigh [thī] n. upper part of leg

thim'ble n. cap protecting end of finger when sewing

thin a. of little thickness; slim; lean; of little density; sparse; fine; loose, not close-packed; inf. unlikely —v. make, become thin —**thin'ner** n. —**thin'ness** n.

thine [THīn] pron./a. obs. belonging to thee

thing n. material object; any possible object of thought

think vi. have one's mind at work; reflect, meditate; reason; deliberate; imagine; hold opinion —vt. conceive, consider in the mind; believe; esteem (thought [thawt], think'ing) —**think'able** a. able to be conceived, considered, possible, feasible —**think'er** n. —**think'ing** a. reflecting —**think-tank** n. group of experts studying specific problems

third a. ordinal number corresponding to three —n. third part —**third degree** see DEGREE —**third party** Law, Insurance etc. person involved by chance or only incidentally in legal proceedings etc. —**Third World** developing countries of Africa, Asia, Latin Amer.

thirst n. desire to drink; feeling caused by lack of drink; craving; yearning —v. feel lack of drink —**thirst'ily** adv. —**thirst'y** a.

thir'teen a./n. three plus ten —**thir'ty** n./a. three times ten

this [TH-] demonstrative a./pron. denotes thing, person near, or just mentioned (pl. these)

this'tle [-sl] n. prickly plant with dense flower heads

thith'er [THiTH'-] adv. obs. to or towards that place

thixotrop'ic a. (of certain liquids, as paints) having property of thickening if left undisturbed but becoming less viscous when stirred

thong *n.* narrow strip of leather, strap

thor'ax *n.* part of body between neck and belly —**thoract'ic** [-as'-] *a.*

thor'ium *n.* radioactive metallic element

thorn *n.* prickle on plant; spine; bush noted for its thorns; *fig.* anything which causes trouble or annoyance —**thorn'y** *a.*

thor'ough [thur'ə] *a.* careful, methodical; complete, entire —**thor'oughly** *adv.* —**thor'oughbred** *a.* of pure breed —*n.* purebred animal, *esp.* horse —**thor'oughfare** *n.* road or passage open at both ends; right of way

those [TH-] *pron.*, *pl.* of THAT; denoting, as a correlative of THESE, the former, as distinguished from the latter

thou [TH-] *pron. obs.* the second person singular pronoun (*pl.* **ye, you**)

though [THŌ] *conj.* in spite of the fact that, even if —*adv.* nevertheless

thought [thawt] *n.* process of thinking; what one thinks; product of thinking; meditation —*pt./pp.* of THINK —**thought'ful** *a.* considerate; showing careful thought; engaged in meditation; attentive —**thought'less** *a.* inconsiderate, careless, heedless

thou'sand [-z-] *n./a.* cardinal number, ten hundred

thrall [-awl] *n.* slavery; slave, bondsman —*vt.* enslave —**thrall'dom** *n.* bondage

thrash *vt.* beat, whip soundly; defeat soundly; thresh —*vi.* move, plunge (*esp.* arms, legs) in wild manner —**thrash out** argue about from every angle; solve by exhaustive discussion

thread [-ed] *n.* fine cord; yarn; ridge cut spirally on screw; theme, meaning —*vt.* put thread into; fit film, magnetic tape *etc.* into machine; put on thread; pick (one's way *etc.*) —**thread'bare** *a.* worn, with nap rubbed off; meagre; shabby

threat [-et] *n.* declaration of intention to harm, injure *etc.*; person or thing regarded as dangerous —**threat'en** *vt.* utter threats against; menace

three *n./a.* cardinal number, one more than two —**three-ply** *a.* having three layers (as wood) or strands (as wool) —**three'some** *n.* group of three —**three-dimensional, 3-D** *a.* having three dimensions; simulating the effect of depth

thresh *v.* beat, rub (wheat, *etc.*) to separate grain from husks and straw; thresh

thresh'old [-ōld] *n.* bar of stone or wood forming bottom of doorway; entrance; starting-point; point at which a stimulus is perceived, or produces a response

threw *pt.* of THROW

thrice *adv.* three times

thrift *n.* saving, economy; genus of plant, sea pink —**thrift'y** *a.* economical, frugal, sparing

thrill *n.* sudden sensation of excitement and pleasure —*v.* (cause to) feel a thrill; vibrate, tremble —**thrill'er** *n.* book, film *etc.* with story of mystery, suspense —**thrill'ing** *a.* exciting

thrive *vi.* grow well; flourish, prosper (**throve, thrived** *pt.*, **thriv'en, thrived** *pp.*, **thri'ving** *pr.p.*)

throat *n.* front of neck; either or both of passages through it —**throat'y** *a.* (of voice) hoarse

throb vi. beat, quiver strongly, pulsate (-bb-) —n. pulsation, beat; vibration

throes [-ōz] pl.n. condition of violent pangs, pain etc. —**in the throes of** inf. in the process of

thrombo'sis n. formation of clot of coagulated blood in blood vessel or heart

throne n. ceremonial seat, powers and duties of king or queen —vt. place on throne, declare king etc.

throng n./v. crowd

thros'tle [-sl] n. thrush

throt'tle n. device controlling amount of fuel entering engine and thereby its speed —vt. strangle; suppress; restrict (flow of liquid etc.)

through [thrōō] prep. from end to end, from side to side of; between the sides of; in consequence of; by means or fault of —adv. from end to end; to the end —a. completed; inf. finished; continuous; (of transport, traffic) not stopping —**throughout'** adv./prep. in every part (of) —**through'put** n. quantity of material processed, esp. by computer —**through ticket** ticket for whole of journey —**through train, bus** etc. train etc. which travels whole (unbroken) length of long journey —**carry through** accomplish

throve pt. of THRIVE

throw [-ō] vt. fling, cast; move, put abruptly, carelessly; give, hold (party etc.); cause to fall; shape on potter's wheel; move (switch, lever etc.); inf. baffle, disconcert (**threw, thrown, throw'ing**) —n. act or distance of throwing —**throw'back** n. one who, that which reverts to character of an ancestor; this process

thrush[1] n. songbird

thrush[2] n. fungal disease of mouth, esp. in infants; foot disease of horses

thrust v. push, drive; stab; push one's way (**thrust, thrust'ing**) —n. lunge, stab with pointed weapon etc.; cutting remark; propulsive force or power

thud n. dull heavy sound —vi. make thud (-dd-)

thug n. brutal, violent person —**thug'gery** n. —**thug'gish** a.

thu'ja, thu'ya [thōō'yə] n. various coniferous trees of N Amer. and E Asia

thumb [-m] n. first, shortest, thickest finger of hand —vt. handle, dirty with thumb; signal for lift in vehicle; flick through (pages of book etc.)

thump n. dull heavy blow; sound of one —vt. strike heavily

thun'der n. loud noise accompanying lightning —vi. rumble with thunder; make noise like thunder —vt. utter loudly —**thun'derous** a. —**thun'dery** a. sultry —**thun'derbolt, thun'derclap** n. lightning flash followed by peal of thunder; anything totally unexpected and unpleasant —**thun'derstruck** a. amazed

Thurs'day n. fifth day of the week

thus [TH-] adv. in this way; therefore

thwack vt./n. whack

thwart [-awt] vt. foil, frustrate, baffle —adv. obs. across —n. seat across a boat

thy [THI] a. obs. belonging to thee —**thyself'** pron. emphasized form of THOU

thyme [tīm] n. aromatic herb

thy'mus n. small ductless gland in upper part of chest

thy'roid gland endocrine gland controlling body growth, situated (in man) at base of neck

ti see TE

Ti Chem. titanium

tiar'a n. jewelled head ornament, coronet

tib'ia n. thicker inner bone of lower leg (pl. **-biae** [-bi-ē], **-bias**) **—tib'ial** a.

tic n. spasmodic twitch in muscles, esp. of face

tick[1] n. slight tapping sound, as of watch movement; small mark (√); inf. moment —vt. mark with tick —vi. make the sound **—tick'er tape** continuous paper ribbon **—tick off** mark off; reprimand **—tick over** (of engine) idle; continue to function smoothly

tick[2] n. small insectlike parasite living on and sucking blood of warm-blooded animals

tick[3] n. mattress case **—tick'ing** n. strong material for mattress covers

tick[4] n. inf. credit, account

tick'et n. card, paper entitling holder to admission, travel etc.; label; US list of candidates of one party for election —vt. attach label to; issue tickets to

tic'kle vt. touch, stroke, poke (person, part of body etc.) to produce laughter etc.; please, amuse —vi. be irritated, itch —n. act, instance of this **—tick'lish** a. sensitive to tickling; requiring care or tact

tidd'ler n. inf. very small fish etc. **—tidd'ly** a. tiny; inf. slightly drunk

tidd'lywinks pl.n. game of trying to flip small plastic discs into cup

tide n. rise and fall of sea happening twice each lunar day; stream; obs. season, time **—ti'dal** a. of, like tide **—tidal wave** great wave, esp. produced by earthquake **—tide over** help someone for a while, esp. by loan etc.

ti'dings pl.n. news

ti'dy a. orderly, neat; inf. of fair size —vt. put in order

tie v. equal (score of) —vt. fasten, bind, secure; restrict (**tied, ty'ing**) —n. that with which anything is bound; restriction, restraint; long, narrow piece of material worn knotted round neck; bond; connecting link; drawn game, contest; match, game in eliminating competition **—tied** a. (of public house) obliged to sell beer etc. of only one brewer; (of cottage etc.) rented to tenant only as long as he is employed by owner **—tie-dyeing** n. way of dyeing cloth in patterns by tying sections tightly so they will not absorb dye

tier [tēr] n. row, rank, layer

tiff n. petty quarrel

ti'ger n. large carnivorous feline animal

tight [tīt] a. taut, tense; closely fitting; secure, firm; not allowing passage of water etc.; cramped; inf. mean; inf. drunk **—tights** pl.n. one-piece clinging garment covering body from waist to feet **—tight'en** v. **—tight'ly** adv. **—tight'rope** n. rope stretched taut above the ground, on which acrobats perform

ti'gon n. offspring of tiger and lioness

ti'ki [tē'-] n. amulet, figurine of Maori cultures

tile n. flat piece of ceramic, plastic etc. material used for roofs, walls, floors, fireplaces etc. —vt. cover with tiles **—tiled** a. **—ti'ling** n.

till[1] prep. up to the time of —conj. to the time that

till[2] vt. cultivate **—till'age** n. **—till'er** n.

till[3] n. drawer for money in shop counter; cash register

till'er n. lever to move rudder of boat

tilt v. incline, slope, slant; tip up —vi. take part in medieval combat with lances; thrust, aim (at) —n. slope, incline; *Hist.* combat for mounted men with lances, joust

tilth n. tilled land; condition of soil

tim'ber n. wood for building *etc.*; trees suitable for the sawmill —**tim'bered** a. made of wood; covered with trees —**timber line** geographical limit beyond which trees will not grow

tim'bre [-bər, tam'brə] n. quality of musical sound, or sound of human voice

time n. existence as a succession of states; hour; duration; period; point in duration; opportunity; occasion; leisure; tempo —vt. choose time for; note time taken by —**time'ly** a. at opportune or appropriate time —**ti'mer** n. person, device for recording or indicating time —**time bomb** bomb designed to explode at prearranged time —**time-honoured** a. respectable because old —**time-lag** n. period of time between cause and effect —**time'piece** n. watch, clock —**time sharing** system of part ownership of holiday property for specified period each year; *Computers* system enabling users at different terminals to communicate with computer apparently at same time —**time'table** n. plan showing hours of work, times of arrival and departure *etc.* —**Greenwich Mean Time** world standard time, time as settled by passage of sun over the meridian at Greenwich

tim'id a. easily frightened; lacking self-confidence —**timid'ity** n. —**tim'idly** adv. —**tim'orous** a. timid; indicating fear

tim'pani, tym'pani pl.n. set of kettledrums —**tim'panist** n.

tin n. malleable metal; container made of tin or tinned iron —vt. put in tin, *esp.* for preserving (food); coat with tin (-**nn**-) —**tin'ny** a. (of sound) thin, metallic; cheap, shoddy —**tin'pot** a. *inf.* inferior, worthless

tinc'ture n. solution of medicinal substance in alcohol; colour, stain —vt. colour, tint

tin'der n. dry easily-burning material used to start fire

tine n. tooth, spike of fork, antler, harrow *etc.*

tin'ea n. fungal skin disease

ting n. sharp sound, as of bell; tinkling —vi. tinkle

tinge [-j] n. slight trace, flavour —vt. colour, flavour slightly

tin'gle [-ng'gl] vi. feel thrill or pricking sensation —n.

tin'ker n. formerly, travelling mender of pots and pans —vi. fiddle, meddle (eg with machinery) oft. inexpertly

tin'kle [-ng-k-] v. (cause to) give out series of light sounds like small bell —n. this sound or action

tin'sel n. glittering metallic substance for decoration; anything sham and showy

tint n. colour; shade of colour; tinge —vt. dye, give tint to

ti'ny a. very small, minute

tip[1] n. slender or pointed end of anything; piece of metal, leather *etc.* protecting an extremity —vt. put a tip on (-**pp**-)

tip[1] n. small present of money given for service rendered; helpful piece of information; warning, hint —vt. give tip to (-**pp**-) —**tip'ster** n. one who sells tips about races

tip[1] v. tilt, upset; touch lightly —vi. topple over (-**pp**-) —n. place where rubbish is dumped

tipp'et n. covering for the neck and shoulders

tip'ple v. drink (alcohol) habitually, *esp.* in small quantities —*n.* drink —**tip'pler** *n.*

tip'sy *a.* drunk, partly drunk

tip'toe *vi.* walk on ball of foot and toes; walk softly

tiptop' *a.* of the best quality or highest degree

TIR Transports Internationaux Routiers (*Fr., International Road Transport*)

tirade' [tī-rād'] *n.* long speech, generally vigorous and hostile, denunciation

tire *vt.* reduce energy of, *esp.* by exertion; bore; irritate —*vi.* become tired, wearied, bored —**ti'ring** *a.* —**tire'some** *a.* wearisome, irritating, tedious

ti'ro *n. see* TYRO

tiss'ue *n.* substance of animal body, plant *etc.*; fine, soft paper, *esp.* used as handkerchief *etc.*; fine woven fabric

tit[1] *n.* varieties of small birds, usu. in combination, *eg* tomtit, bluetit

tit[2] *n. vulg. sl.* female breast; *sl.* despicable, stupid person

titan'ic [tī-] *a.* huge, epic

tita'nium [tī-] *n.* rare metal of great strength and rust-resisting qualities

tit'bit *n.* tasty morsel of food; pleasing scrap (of scandal *etc.*)

tit for tat blow for blow, retaliation

tithe [-TH] *n.* tenth part *esp. Hist.* of agricultural produce paid for the upkeep of the clergy or as tax —*vt.* exact tithes from

tit'ian [tish'-] *a.* (of hair) reddish-gold, auburn

tit'illate *vt.* tickle, stimulate agreeably —**titilla'tion** *n.* —**tit'illator** *n.*

tit'ivate *v.* dress or smarten up —**titiva'tion** *n.*

ti'tle *n.* name of book; heading; name; appellation denoting rank; legal right or document proving

it; *Sport* championship —**ti'tled** *a.* of the aristocracy —**title deed** legal document as proof of ownership

titt'er *vi.* laugh in suppressed way —*n.* such laugh

tit'tle *n.* whit, detail

tit'tle-tattle *n./vi.* gossip

tit'ular *a.* pert. to title; nominal; held by virtue of a title —**tit'ularly** *adv.*

tizz, tizz'y *n. inf.* state of confusion, anxiety

T.N.T. *see* TRINITROTOLUENE

to *prep.* towards, in the direction of; as far as; used to introduce a comparison, ratio, indirect object, infinitive mood *etc.* —*adv.* to the required or normal state or position

toad *n.* animal like large frog —**toad'y** *n.* one who flatters, ingratiates himself —*vi.* do this (**toad'ied, toad'ying**) —**toad-in-the-hole** *n.* sausages baked in batter —**toad'stool** *n.* fungus like mushroom, but usu. poisonous

toast *n.* slice of bread crisped and browned on both sides by heat; tribute, proposal of health, success *etc.* made by company of people and marked by drinking together; one toasted —*vt.* crisp and brown (as bread); drink toast to; dry or warm at fire —**toast'er** *n.* electrical device for toasting bread

tobacc'o *n.* plant with leaves used for smoking; the prepared leaves (*pl.* **-cos**) —**tobacc'onist** *n.* one who sells tobacco products

tobogg'an *n.* sledge for sliding down slope of snow —*vi.* slide on one

to'by jug mug in form of stout, seated man

tocca'ta [-ah'-] *n.* rapid piece of music for keyboard instrument

toc'sin [tok's-] *n.* alarm signal, bell

today' n. this day —adv. on this day; nowadays

tod'dle vi. walk with unsteady short steps; inf. stroll —n. toddling —**todd'ler** n. child beginning to walk

todd'y n. sweetened mixture of alcoholic spirit, hot water etc.

to-do' n. inf. fuss, commotion (pl. -dos)

toe n. digit of foot; anything resembling toe in shape or position —vt. reach, touch with toe —**toe the line** conform

toff n. sl. well-dressed or upper class person

toff'ee n. chewy sweet made of boiled sugar etc.

tog n. unit used to measure insulating power of quilt, garment etc.

to'ga n. loose outer garment worn by ancient Romans

togeth'er [-TH-] adv. in company, simultaneously; inf. (well) organized

tog'gle n. small wooden, metal peg fixed crosswise on cord, wire etc. and used for fastening as button; any similar device

togs inf. pl.n. clothes

toil n. heavy work or task —vi. labour —**toil'worn** a. weary with toil; hard and lined

toil'et n. lavatory; process of washing, dressing; articles used for this

to'ken n. sign or object used as evidence; symbol; disc used as money; gift card, voucher exchangeable for goods of a certain value —a. nominal, slight

tokoloshe' [-losh'] n. **SA** malevolent imp in Bantu folklore

told pt./pp. of TELL

tol'erate vt. put up with; permit —**tol'erable** a. bearable; fair, moderate —**tol'erably** adv. —**tol'erance** n. (degree of) ability to endure stress, pain, radiation etc. —**tol'erant** a. disinclined to interfere with others' ways or opinions; forbearing; broad-minded —**tol'erantly** adv. —**tolera'tion** n.

toll' [tõl] vt. make (bell) ring slowly at regular intervals; announce death thus —vi. ring thus —n. tolling sound

toll² [tõl] n. tax, esp. for the use of bridge or road; loss, damage incurred through accident, disaster etc.

toll'ie n. **SA** steer calf

tom n. male of some animals, esp. cat

tom'ahawk n. fighting axe of N Amer. Indians —vt. strike, kill with one

tomat'o [-aht'-] n. plant with red fruit; the fruit, used in salads etc. (pl. -toes)

tomb [tõõm] n. grave; monument over one —**tomb'stone** n. gravestone

tombo'la n. lottery with tickets drawn to win prizes

tom'boy n. girl who acts, dresses in boyish way

tome [tõm] n. large book or volume

tomfool'ery n. nonsense, silly behaviour

tomm'y n. sl. private soldier in Brit. army —**Tommy gun** type of sub-machine-gun

tomorr'ow [-õ] adv./n. (on) the day after today

tom'-tom n. drum associated with N Amer. Indians or with Asia

ton [tun] n. measure of weight, 1016 kg (2240 lbs.) (also called **long ton**); **US** measure of weight, 907 kg (2000 lbs.) (also called **short ton**) —**tonn'age** n. carrying capacity; charge per ton; ships collectively

tone n. quality of musical sound; quality of voice, colour etc. general character, style; healthy condition —*vt.* give tone to; blend, harmonize (with) —**to'ner** *n.* substance that modifies colour or composition —**to'nal** *a.* —**tonal'ity** *n.* —**tone poem** orchestral work based on story, legend *etc.*

tongs [-z] *pl.n.* large pincers, *esp.* for handling coal, sugar

tongue [tung] *n.* muscular organ inside mouth, used for speech, taste *etc.*; various things shaped like this; language, speech, voice

ton'ic *n.* medicine to improve bodily tone or condition; *Mus.* keynote; first note of scale —*a.* invigorating, restorative; of tone —**tonic** (**water**) mineral water oft. containing quinine

tonight' [-nīt'] *n.* this night; the coming night —*adv.* on this night

tonne [tun, tun'i] *n.* metric ton, 1000 kg

ton'sil *n.* gland in throat —**ton'sillar** *a.* —**tonsill'itis** *n.* inflammation of tonsils

ton'sure *n.* shaving of part of head as religious or monastic practice; part shaved —*vt.* shave thus

ton'tine [-ēn] *n.* fund, subscribers to which receive annuities increasing as number of subscribers decreases

too *adv.* also, in addition; in excess, overmuch

took *pt. of* TAKE

tool [-ōō] *n.* implement or appliance for mechanical operations; servile helper; means to an end —*vt.* work on with tool, *esp.* chisel stone; indent design on leather book cover *etc.* —**tool'ing** *n.* decorative work; setting up *etc.* of tools, *esp.* for machine operation

toot [-ōō] *n.* short sound of horn, trumpet *etc.*

tooth [-ōō] *n.* bonelike projection in gums of upper and lower

jaws of vertebrates; various pointed things like this; prong, cog (*pl.* **teeth**)

too'tle [-ōō-] *inf. v.* toot —*vi.* go, proceed

top[1] *n.* highest part, summit; highest rank; first in merit; garment for upper part of body; lid, stopper of bottle *etc.*; platform on ship's mast —*vt.* cut off, pass, reach, surpass top; provide top for (-**pp**-) —**top'less** *a.* (of costume, woman) with no covering for breasts —**top'most** *a.* supreme; highest —**topdress'** *vt.* spread soil, fertilizer *etc.* on surface of land —**top'dressing** *n.* —**top hat** man's hat with tall cylindrical crown —**top-heavy** *a.* unbalanced; with top too heavy for base —**top-notch** *a.* excellent, first-class —**top-secret** *a.* needing highest level of secrecy, security —**top'soil** *n.* surface layer of soil; more fertile soil spread on lawns *etc.*

top[2] *n.* toy which spins on tapering point

to'paz *n.* precious stone of various colours

to'pee, -pi *n.* lightweight hat made of pith

to'piary *a.* (of shrubs) shaped by cutting or pruning, made ornamental by trimming or training —*n.* —**to'piarist** *n.*

top'ic *n.* subject of discourse, conversation *etc.* —**top'ical** *a.* up-to-date, having news value; of topic

topog'raphy *n.* (description of) surface features of a place —**topog'rapher** *n.* —**topograph'ic** *a.* —**topograph'ically** *adv.*

top'ple *v.* (cause to) fall over, collapse

top'sy-tur'vy *a.* upside down, in confusion

toque [tōk] *n.* small round hat

tor *n.* high, rocky hill

torch n. portable hand light containing electric battery and bulb; burning brand *etc.*; any apparatus burning with hot flame, eg for welding —**torch'bearer** n.

tore pr. —**torn** pp. of TEAR [2]

tor'eador [to'ri-] n. bull fighter

torment' v. torture in body or mind; afflict; tease —n. [tor'-] suffering, torture, agony of body or mind —**torment'or, ·er** n.

torna'do n. whirlwind; violent storm (pl. **-does**)

torpe'do n. cylindrical self-propelled underwater missile with explosive warhead, fired *esp.* from submarine (pl. **-does**) —vt. strike, sink with, as with, torpedo

tor'pid a. sluggish, apathetic —**tor'por** n. torpid state —**tor'pidity** n.

torque [-k] n. collar, similar ornament of twisted gold or other metal; *Mechanics* rotating or twisting forces

torr'ent n. a rushing stream; downpour —**torren'tial** a. resembling a torrent; overwhelming

torr'id a. parched, dried with heat; highly emotional —**torrid'ity, torr'idness** n. —**Torrid Zone** land between tropics

tor'sion n. twist, twisting

tor'so n. (statue of) body without head or limbs; trunk (pl. **-sos, -si** [-sē])

tort n. *Law* private or civil wrong

tortill'a [-tē'ə] n. thin Mexican pancake

tor'toise [-təs] n. four-footed reptile covered with shell of horny plates —**tor'toiseshell** n. mottled brown shell of hawksbill turtle used commercially —a.

tor'tuous a. winding, twisting; involved, not straightforward —**tortuos'ity** n.

tor'ture n. infliction of severe pain —vt. subject to torture —**tor'turer** n. —**torture chamber**

Tor'y n. member of Brit., Canad. conservative party; politically reactionary person

toss vt. throw up, about —vi. be thrown, fling oneself about —n. act of tossing

tot [1] n. very small child; small quantity, *esp.* of drink

tot [2] v. (with up) add up; amount to (**-tt-**)

to'tal n. whole amount; sum, aggregate —a. complete, entire, full, absolute —vi. amount to —vt. add up (**-ll-**) —**total'ity** n. —**to'talizator** n. machine to operate system of betting on racecourse in which money is paid out to winners in proportion to their stakes

totalita'rian a. of dictatorial, one-party government

tote [1] n. short for TOTALIZATOR

tote [2] vt. haul, carry

to'tem n. tribal badge or emblem —**totem'ic** a. —**totem pole** post carved, painted with totems, *esp.* by Amer. Indians

tott'er vi. walk unsteadily; begin to fall

tou'can [too'kon] n. tropical Amer. bird with large bill

touch [tuch] n. sense by which qualities of object *etc.* are perceived by touching; characteristic manner or ability; touching; slight blow, stroke, contact, amount *etc.* —vt. come into contact with; put hand on; reach; affect emotions of; deal with, handle; eat, drink; *inf.* (try to) borrow from —vi. be in contact; (with on) refer to —**touch'ing** a. emotionally moving —*prep.* concerning —**touch'y** a. easily offended, sensitive —**touch'line** n. side line of pitch in some games

—**touch'stone** *n.* criterion —**touch'wood** *n.* tinder —**touch and go** precarious (situation)

touché [tōō-shā'] *interj.* acknowledgement that blow (orig. in fencing), remark *etc.* has been successful

tough [tuf] *a.* strong, resilient, not brittle; sturdy; able to bear hardship, strain; difficult; needing effort to chew; *sl.* rough; uncivilized; violent; *inf.* unlucky, unfair —*n. inf.* rough, violent person —**tough'en** *v.* —**tough'ness** *n.*

toupée [tōō'pā] *n.* hairpiece, wig

tour [toor] *n.* travelling round; journey to one place after another; excursion —*v.* make tour (of) —**tour'ism** *n.* tourist travel; this as an industry —**tour'ist** *n.* one who travels for pleasure

tour de force *Fr.* brilliant stroke, achievement

tour'maline [toor'-] *n.* crystalline mineral used for optical instruments and as gem

tour'nament [toor'-] *n.* competition, contest usu. with several stages to decide overall winner; *Hist.* contest between knights on horseback —**tour'ney** *n. Hist.* knightly tournament

tour'niquet [toor'ni-kā] *n.* bandage, surgical instrument to constrict artery and stop bleeding

tou'sle *vt.* tangle, ruffle; treat roughly —*n.*

tout *vi.* solicit custom (usu. in undesirable fashion); obtain and sell information about racehorses —*n.* one who touts

tow[1] [tō] *vt.* drag along behind, *esp.* at end of rope —*n.* towing or being towed; vessel, vehicle in tow —**tow'age** *n.* —**tow'bar** *n.* metal bar attached to car for towing caravan *etc.* —**tow'path**

n. path beside canal, river, orig. for towing

tow[2] [tō] *n.* fibre of hemp, flax —**tow-headed** *a.* with palecoloured, or rumpled hair

towards' [tə-] *prep.* in direction of; with regard to; as contribution to (*also* **toward'**)

tow'el *n.* cloth for wiping off moisture after washing —**tow'elling** *n.* material used for making towels

tow'er *n.* tall strong structure often forming part of church or other large building; fortress —*vi.* stand very high; loom (over)

town *n.* collection of dwellings *etc.* larger than village and smaller than city —**town'ship** *n.* small town —**town clerk** chief administrative officer of town —**towns'people** *n.*

tox'ic *a.* poisonous; due to poison —**toxae'mia** [-sē'-] *n.* blood poisoning —**toxic'ity** [-is'-] *n.* strength of a poison —**toxicol'ogy** *n.* study of poisons —**tox'in** *n.* poison of bacterial origin

toxoph'ilite *n.* student, lover of archery —**toxophilit'ic** *a.*

toy *n.* something designed to be played with; (miniature) replica —*a.* very small —*vi.* act idly, trifle

trace[1] *n.* track left by anything; indication; minute quantity —*vt.* follow course, track of; find out; make plan of; draw or copy exactly, *esp.* using tracing paper —**tra'cery** *n.* interlaced ornament, *esp.* stonework of Gothic window —**tra'cing** *n.* traced copy of drawing —**trace element** chemical element occurring in very small quantity in soil *etc.* —**tracer, bullet, shell** *etc.* one which leaves visible trail so that aim can be checked —**tracing paper** transparent paper placed over drawing, map *etc.* to enable exact copy to be taken

trace[2] *n.* chain, strap by which horse pulls vehicle; *Angling* short piece of gut, nylon attaching hook or fly to line

trache'a [-kē'-] *n.* windpipe (*pl.* **trache'ae** [-kē'ē]) —**trache'al, -e'an** *a.* —**tracheot'omy** *n.* surgical incision into trachea

tracho'ma [-kō'-] *n.* contagious viral disease of eye —**trachom'atous** *a.*

track *n.* mark, line of marks, left by passage of anything; path; rough road; course; railway line; distance between two road wheels on one axle; circular jointed metal band driven by wheels as on tank, bulldozer *etc.*; course for running or racing; separate section on gramophone record —*vt.* follow trail or path of; find thus —**tracker dog** dog trained to hunt for fugitives or missing persons —**track events** athletic sports held on a track —**track record** past accomplishments of person, company *etc.* —**track'suit** *n.* warm, two-piece garment worn *esp.* by athletes

tract[1] *n.* wide expanse, area; *Anat.* system of organs *etc.* with particular function

tract[2] *n.* treatise or pamphlet, *esp.* religious one —**tract'ate** *n.* short tract

tract'able *a.* easy to manage, docile, amenable

trac'tion *n.* action of drawing, pulling —**traction engine**

trac'tor *n.* motor vehicle for hauling, pulling *etc.*

trad. traditional

trade *n.* commerce, business; buying and selling; any profitable pursuit; those engaged in trade —*v.* engage in trade; buy and sell; barter —**tra'der** *n.* —**trade-in** *n.* used article given in part

payment for new —**trade'mark, trade'name** *n.* distinctive mark (secured by legal registration) on maker's goods —**trades'man** *n.* shopkeeper; skilled worker —**trade union** society of workers for protection of their interests —**trade wind** wind blowing constantly towards equator in certain parts of globe

tradi'tion [-dish'-] *n.* unwritten body of beliefs, facts *etc.* handed down from generation to generation; custom, practice of long standing; process of handing down —**tradi'tional** *a.* —**tradi'tionally** *adv.*

traduce'[1] *vt.* slander

traff'ic *n.* vehicles passing to and fro in street, town *etc.*; (illicit) trade —*vi.* trade, *esp.* in illicit goods, e.g drugs (**trafficked, traff'icking**) —**traff'icker** *n.* trader —**traffic lights** set of coloured lights at road junctions *etc.* to control flow of traffic —**traffic warden** one employed to supervise road traffic, parking *etc.*

trag'edy [-aj'-] *n.* sad or calamitous event; dramatic, literary work dealing with serious, sad topic and with ending marked by (inevitable) disaster —**trage'dian** *n.* actor in, writer of tragedies —**trag'ic** *a.* of, in manner of tragedy; disastrous; appalling —**trag'ically** *adv.* —**tragicom'edy** *n.* play with both tragic and comic elements

trail *vt.* drag behind one —*vi.* be drawn behind; hang, grow loosely —*n.* track or trace; thing that trails; rough ill-defined track in wild country —**trail'er** *n.* vehicle towed by another vehicle; *Cinema* advertisement of forthcoming film; trailing plant

train *vt.* educate, instruct, exercise; cause to grow in particular

way; aim (gun *etc.*) —*vi.* follow
course of training. *esp.* to
achieve physical fitness for athletics —*n.* line of railway vehicles joined to locomotive; succession, *esp.* of thoughts, events *etc.*;
procession of animals, vehicles
etc. travelling together; trailing
part of dress; body of attendants
—**train'ing** *n.* —**trainee'** *n.* one
training to be skilled worker, *esp.*
in industry

traipse *vi. inf.* walk wearily

trait [trāt, trā] *n.* characteristic
feature

trait'or *n.* one who betrays or is
guilty of treason —**trait'orous** *a.*
disloyal; guilty of treachery
—**trait'orously** *adv.*

trajec'tory *n.* line of flight,
(curved) path of projectile

tram *n.* vehicle (*esp.* electrically
driven and for public transport)
running on rails laid on roadway
—**tram'car** *n.* —**tram'way** *n.*
rails for trams in street

tramm'el *n.* anything that re-
strains or holds captive; type of
compasses —*vt.* restrain; hinder
(-ll-)

tramp *vi.* travel on foot, *esp.* as
vagabond or for pleasure; walk
heavily —*n.* (homeless) person
who travels about on foot; walk;
tramping; vessel that takes cargo
wherever shippers desire

tram'ple *vt.* tread on and crush
under foot

tram'poline [-lin] *n.* tough canvas sheet stretched horizontally
with elastic cords *etc.* to frame,
for gymnastic, acrobatic use

trance [-ah-] *n.* unconscious or
dazed state; state of ecstasy or
total absorption

trann'ie *n. inf. short for* transis-
tor radio

tran'quil [-ng'kw-] *a.* calm, quiet; serene —**tranquill'ity** *n.*
—**tran'quilize** *vt.* make calm

—**tran'quillizer** *n.* drug which
induces calm, tranquil state
—**tran'quilly** *adv.*

trans- (*comb. form*) across,
through, beyond

transact' *vt.* carry through;
negotiate; conduct (affair *etc.*)
—**transac'tion** *n.* performing of
any business; that which is performed; single sale or purchase
—*pl.* proceedings; reports of a
society

transceiv'er *n.* combined radio transmitter and receiver

transcend' *vt.* rise above; exceed, surpass —**transcend'ent** *a.*
—**transcend'ence** *n.* —**transcen-
den'tal** *a.* surpassing experience;
supernatural; abstruse —**tran-
scenden'talism** *n.*

transcribe' *vt.* copy out; record for later broadcast; arrange
(music) for different instrument
—**tran'script** *n.* copy

tran'sept *n.* transverse part of
cruciform church; either of its
arms

transfer' *vt.* move, send from
one person, place *etc.* to another
(-rr-) —*n.* [trans'-] removal of
person or thing from one place
to another; design which can be
transferred from one surface to
another by pressure, heat *etc.*
—**transfer(r)'able** *a.* —**trans'-
ference** *n.* transfer

transfig'ure *vt.* alter appearance of —**transfigura'tion** *n.*

transfix' *vt.* astound, stun;
pierce

transform' *vt.* change shape,
character of —**transforma'tion**
n. —**transform'er** *n.* Electricity
apparatus for changing voltage
of alternating current

transfuse' *vt.* convey from one
vessel to another, *esp.* blood
from healthy person to one injured or ill —**transfu'sion** *n.*

transgress' *vt.* break (law);

sin —**transgres'sion** n. —**transgres'sor** n.

trans(s)hip' vt. move from one ship, train etc. to another

tran'sient [-z-] a. fleeting, not permanent —**tran'sience** n.

transis'tor n. Electronics small, semi-conducting device used to amplify electric currents; portable radio using transistors

tran'sit n. passage, crossing —**transi'tion** n. change from one state to another —**transi'tional** a. —**tran'sitive** a. (of verb) requiring direct object —**tran'sitory** a. not lasting long, transient

translate' vt. turn from one language into another; interpret —**transla'tion** n. —**transla'tor** n.

translit'erate vt. write in the letters of another alphabet —**translitera'tion** n.

translu'cent [-loo'-] a. letting light pass through, semitransparent —**translu'cence** n.

transmigrate' vi. (of soul) pass into another body —**transmigra'tion** n.

transmit' vt. send, cause to pass to another place, person etc.; communicate; send out (signals) by means of radio waves; broadcast (radio, television programme) —**transmis'sion** n. transference; gear by which power is communicated from engine to road wheels

transmog'rify vt. inf. change completely esp. into bizarre form

transmute' vt. change in form, properties, or nature —**transmuta'tion** n.

tran'som [-zəm] n. crosspiece; lintel

transpar'ent [-pa'rənt] a. letting light pass without distortion; that can be seen through distinctly; obvious —**transpar'ence** n. —**transpar'ency** n. quality of being transparent; photographic slide; picture made visible by light behind it —**transpar'ently** adv.

transpire' vi. become known; inf. happen; (of plants) give off water vapour through leaves —**transpira'tion** n.

transplant' vt. move and plant again in another place; transfer organ surgically from one body to another —n. [trans'-] surgical transplanting of organ; anything transplanted —**transplanta'tion** n.

transport' vt. convey from one place to another; Hist. banish, as criminal, to penal colony; enrapture —n. [trans'-] means of conveyance; ships, aircraft etc. used in transporting stores, troops etc.; a ship etc. so used —**transporta'tion** n. transporting; Hist. deportation to penal colony

transpose' vt. change order of; interchange; put music into different key —**transpo'sal** n. —**transposi'tion** n.

transubstantia'tion n. doctrine that substance of bread and wine changes into substance of Christ's body when consecrated in Eucharist

transverse' a. lying across; at right angles

transvest'ite n. person seeking sexual pleasure by wearing clothes normally worn by opposite sex

trap n. snare, device for catching game etc.; anything planned to deceive, betray etc.; arrangement of pipes to prevent escape of gas; movable opening, esp. through ceiling etc.; Hist. two-wheeled carriage; sl. mouth —vt. catch, ensnare (-pp-) —**trapp'er** n. one who traps animals for their fur —**trap'door** n. door in floor or roof

trapeze' n. horizontal bar suspended from two ropes for use in gymnastics, acrobatic exhibitions *etc.*

trape'zium *n.* quadrilateral figure with two sides only parallel (*pl.* **-ziums, -zia**) (US **trap'ezoid**) **trap'ezoid** *n.* quadrilateral with no parallel sides (US **trape'zium**)

trapp'ings *pl.n.* equipment, ornaments

Trapp'ist *n.* member of Cistercian order of monks who observe strict silence

trash *n.* rubbish; nonsense —**trash'y** *a.* worthless, cheap

trau'ma [-aw'-] *n.* nervous shock; injury —**traumat'ic** *a.* of, causing, caused by trauma

trav'ail *vi./n.* labour, toil

trav'el *v.* go, move from one place to another (**-ll-**) —*n.* act of travelling, *esp.* as tourist; *Machinery* distance component is permitted to move —*pl.* (account of) travelling —**trav'eller** *n.* —**trav'elogue** [-log] *n.* film *etc.* about travels

trav'erse *vt.* cross, go through or over; (of gun) move laterally —*n.* anything set across; partition; *Mountaineering* face, steep slope to be crossed from side to side —*a.* being, lying across

trav'esty *n.* farcical, grotesque imitation; mockery —*vt.* make, be a travesty of (**-esti-d, -estying**)

trawl *n.* net dragged at deep levels behind special boat, to catch fish, prawns *etc.* —*vi.* fish with one —**trawl'er** *n.* trawling vessel

tray *n.* flat board, usu. with rim, for carrying things; any similar utensil

treach'ery [trech'-] *n.* deceit, betrayal —**treach'erous** *a.* disloyal; unreliable; dangerous —**treach'erously** *adv.*

trea'cle *n.* thick syrup produced when sugar is refined —**treac'ly** *a.*

tread [tred] *vt.* set foot on; trample; oppress —*vi.* walk (**trod** *pt.,* **trodd'en** or **trod** *pp.,* **tread'ing** *pr.p.*) —*n.* treading; fashion of walking; upper surface of step; part of rubber tyre in contact with ground —**tread'mill** *n. Hist.* cylinder turned by treading on steps projecting from it; dreary routine *etc.*

tread'le [tred'l] *n.* lever worked by foot to turn wheel

trea'son [-z-] *n.* violation by subject of allegiance to sovereign or state; treachery; disloyalty —**trea'sonable** *a* constituting treason —**trea'sonably** *adv.* —**trea'sonous** *a.*

treas'ure [trezh'-] *n.* riches; stored wealth or valuables —*vt.* prize, cherish; store up —**treas'urer** *n.* official in charge of funds —**treas'ury** *n.* place for treasure; government department in charge of finance —**treasure-trove** *n.* treasure found hidden with no evidence of ownership

treat *n.* pleasure, entertainment given —*vt.* deal with, act towards; give medical treatment to; (*with of*) discourse on; entertain, *esp.* with food or drink —*vi.* negotiate —**treat'ment** *n.* method of counteracting a disease; act or mode of treating; manner of handling an artistic medium

treat'ise [-iz] *n.* book discussing a subject, formal essay

treat'y *n.* signed contract between states *etc.*

treb'le [treb'l] *a.* threefold, triple; *Mus.* high-pitched —*n.* soprano voice; part of music for it; singer with such voice —*v.* increase threefold —**treb'ly** *adv.*

tree *n.* large perennial plant with woody trunk; beam; anything (*eg* genealogical chart) resembling tree, or tree's structure —*vt.* force, drive up tree; plant with trees —**tree creeper** small songbird

tref'oil *n.* plant with three-lobed leaf, clover; carved ornament like this

trek *vi./n.* (make) long difficult journey, *esp.* on foot or **SA** *esp.* migration by ox-wagon —**trek'ker** *n.*

trell'is *n.* lattice or grating of light bars fixed crosswise —*vt.* screen, supply with one

trem'ble *vi.* quiver, shake; feel fear, anxiety —*n.* involuntary shaking; quiver; tremor

tremen'dous *a.* vast, immense; *inf.* exciting, unusual; *inf.* excellent

trem'olo *n.* quivering or vibrating effect in singing or playing

trem'or *n.* quiver; shaking; minor earthquake

trem'ulous *a.* a quivering slightly; timorous; agitated

trench *n.* long narrow ditch, *esp.* as shelter in war —*vt.* cut grooves or ditches in —**trench coat** double-breasted waterproof coat

trench'ant *a.* cutting, incisive, biting

trench'er *n.* *Hist.* wooden plate on which food was served

trend *n.* direction, tendency, inclination, drift —**trend'y** *inf. a./n.* consciously fashionable (person) —**trend'iness** *n.*

trepan' *n.* see TREPHINE

trepang' *n.* edible sea slug or bêche-de-mer

trephine' [-fēn'] *n.* instrument for cutting circular pieces, *esp.* from skull —*vt.*

trepida'tion *n.* fear, anxiety

tres'pass *vi.* intrude (on) property *etc.* of another; *obs.* transgress, sin —*n.* wrongful entering on another's land; wrongdoing

tress *n.* long lock of hair

tres'tle [-sl] *n.* board fixed on pairs of spreading legs and used as support

trews [trōoz] *pl.n.* close-fitting trousers, orig. of tartan

tri- (*comb. form*) three

tri'ad *n.* group of three; *Chem.* element, radical with valency of three

tri'al *n.* act of trying, testing; experimental examination; *Law* investigation of case before judge; thing, person that strains endurance or patience

tri'angle *n.* figure with three angles; percussion musical instrument —**triang'ular** *a.*

tribe *n.* race; subdivision of race of people —**tri'bal** *a.*

tribula'tion *n.* misery, trouble, affliction, distress; cause of this

trib'une *n.* person or institution upholding public rights —**tribu'nal** *n.* lawcourt; body appointed to inquire into and decide specific matter; seat of judge

trib'utary *n.* stream flowing into another —*a.* auxiliary; contributory; paying tribute

trib'ute *n.* sign of honour or recognition; tax paid by one state to another

trice *n.* moment —**in a trice** instantly

trichi'na [-kī'-] *n.* minute parasitic worm —**trichino'sis** *n.* disease caused by this

trick *n.* deception; prank; mannerism; illusion; feat of skill or cunning; knack; cards played in one round; spell of duty —*vt.* cheat; hoax; deceive —**trick'ery** *n.* —**trick'ster** *n.* —**trick'y** *a.* difficult, needing careful handling; crafty

trick'le *v.* (cause to) run, flow, move in thin stream or drops

tric'olour *a.* three coloured

—*n.* tricolour flag, *eg* of France

tri'cycle *n.* three-wheeled cycle

tri'dent *n.* three-pronged fork or spear

trienn'ial *a.* happening every, or lasting, three years

tri'fle *n.* insignificant thing or matter; small amount; pudding of spongecake, whipped cream *etc.* —*vi.* toy (with); act, speak idly —**tri'fler** *n.*

trig *n./a.* *short for* TRIGONOMETRY, TRIGONOMETRICAL

trigg'er *n.* catch which releases spring *esp.* to fire gun —*vt.* (*oft. with* off) start, set in action *etc.* —**trigger-happy** *a.* tending to irresponsible, ill-considered behaviour, *esp.* in use of firearms

trigonom'etry *n.* branch of mathematics dealing with relations of sides and angles of triangles —**trigonomet'rical** *a.*

trihe'dron *n.* figure formed by intersection of three planes —**trihe'dral** *a.*

trilat'eral *a.* having three sides —**trilat'erally** *adv.*

tril'by *n.* man's soft felt hat

trill *vi.* sing with quavering voice; sing lightly; warble —*n.* such singing or sound

trill'ion *n.* one million million million, 10^{18}; **US, C** one million million 10^{12}

tril'ogy [-ji] *n.* series of three related (literary) works

trim *a.* neat, smart; slender; in good order —*vt.* shorten slightly by cutting; prune; decorate; adjust; put in good order; adjust balance of (ship, aircraft) (-**mm**-) —*n.* decoration; order, state of being trim; haircut that neatens existing style; upholstery, accessories in car; edging material, as inside woodwork round doors, windows *etc.* —**trimm'ing** *n.* (*oft. pl.*) decoration, addition

tri'maran *n.* three-hulled vessel

trinitrotol'uene *n.* a high explosive derived from toluene

trin'ity *n.* the state of being threefold; (**T**-) the three persons of the Godhead —**trinita'rian** *n./a.*

trink'et *n.* small ornament, trifle —**trink'etry** *n.*

tri'o [-ē·ō] *n.* group of three; music for three parts (*pl.* -**s**)

tri'ode *n. Electronics* three-electrode valve

trip *n.* (short) journey for pleasure; stumble; switch; *inf.* hallucinatory experience caused by drug —*v.* (cause to) stumble; (cause to) make false step, mistake —*vi.* run lightly; skip; dance; *inf.* take hallucinatory drugs —*vt.* operate (switch) (-**pp**-) —**trip'per** *n.* tourist

tripar'tite *a.* having, divided into three parts

tripe *n.* stomach of cow *etc.* prepared for food; *inf.* nonsense

tri'plane *n.* aeroplane with three wings one above the other

tri'ple [trip'l] *a.* threefold —*v.* treble —**trip'let** *n.* three of a kind; one of three offspring born at one birth —**trip'lex** *a.* threefold —**trip'ly** *adv.*

trip'licate [-it] *a.* threefold —*vt.* [-āt] make threefold —*n.* state of being triplicate; one of set of three copies —**triplica'tion** *n.*

tri'pod *n.* stool, stand *etc.* with three feet

tri'pos *n.* degree examination at Cambridge University

trip'tych [-tik] *n.* carving, set of pictures (*esp.* altarpiece) on three panels hinged side by side

trite *a.* hackneyed, banal

trit'ium *n.* radioactive isotope of hydrogen

tri'umph *n.* great success; victory; exultation —vi. achieve great success or victory; prevail; exult —**triumph'al** a. —**triumph'ant** a. victorious

trium'virate [trī-] n. joint rule by three persons

triv'et n. metal bracket or stand for pot or kettle

triv'ia pl.n. petty, unimportant things, details —**triv'ial** a. of little consequence; commonplace —**trivial'ity** n.

tro'chee [trō'kē] n. in verse, foot of two syllables, first long and second short —**trocha'ic** a.

trod pt., **trodd'en, trod** pp. of TREAD

trog'lodyte n. cave dweller

Tro'jan a./n. (inhabitant) of ancient Troy; steadfast or persevering (person)

troll [-ō-] vt. fish for by dragging baited hook or lure through water

troll [-ō-] n. supernatural being in Scandinavian mythology and folklore

troll'ey n. small wheeled table for food and drink; wheeled cart for moving goods etc.; US tram —**trolley bus** bus deriving power from overhead electric wire but not running on rails

troll'op n. promiscuous or slovenly woman

trombone' n. deep-toned brass wind instrument with sliding tube —**trombo'nist** n.

troop n. group or crowd of persons or animals; unit of cavalry —pl. soldiers —vi. move in a troop, flock —**troop'er** n. cavalry soldier

trope n. figure of speech

tro'phy n. prize, award, as shield, cup; memorial of victory, hunt etc.

trop'ic n. either of two lines of latitude at 23½° N (**tropic of Cancer**) or 23½° S (**tropic of**

Capricorn) —pl. area of earth's surface between these lines —**trop'ical** a. pert. to, within tropics; (of climate) very hot

trot vi. (of horse) move at medium pace, lifting feet in diagonal pairs; (of person) run easily with short strides (**-tt-**) —n. trotting, jog —**trott'er** n. horse trained to trot in race; foot of certain animals, esp. pig

troth [-ō-] n. obs. fidelity, truth

trou'badour [trōō-] n. one of school of early poets and singers

trou'ble [trub'l] n. state or cause of mental distress, pain, inconvenience etc.; care, effort —vt. be trouble to —vi. be inconvenienced, concerned (about); be agitated; take pains, exert oneself —**trou'blesome** a.

trough [trof] n. long open vessel, esp. for animals' food or water; hollow between two waves; Meteorology area of low pressure

trounce vt. beat thoroughly, thrash

troupe [-ōō-] n. company of performers —**troup'er** n.

trou'sers pl.n. two-legged outer garment with legs reaching to the ankles

trou'sseau [trōō'sō] n. bride's outfit of clothing

trout n. freshwater sport and food fish

trow'el n. small tool like spade for spreading mortar, lifting plants etc.

troy weight system of weights used for gold, silver and gems

tru'ant [trōō-] n. one absent without leave, esp. child so absenting himself or herself from school —a. —**tru'ancy** n.

truce n. temporary cessation of fighting; respite, lull

truck n. wheeled (motor) vehicle for moving goods

truck n. barter; dealing, esp. in

have no truck with; payment of workmen in goods

truck'le vi. yield weakly (to)

truc'ulent a. aggressive, defiant

trudge vi. walk laboriously —n. laborious or wearisome walk

true [trōō] a. in accordance with facts; faithful; exact, correct; genuine —**tru'ism** n. self-evident truth —**tru'ly** adv. exactly; really; sincerely —**truth** [-ōō-] n. state of being true; something that is true —**truth'ful** a. accustomed to speak the truth; accurate, exact —**truth'fully** adv.

truf'fle n. edible fungus growing underground; sweet resembling this

trug n. long shallow basket used by gardeners

tru'ism n. see TRUE

trump[1] n. card of suit temporarily ranking above others —vt. take trick with a trump —**trump up** invent, concoct —**turn up** or **out trumps** turn out (unexpectedly) well, successfully

trump[2] n. trumpet; blast on trumpet

trum'pery a. showy but worthless —n. worthless finery, trash, rubbish

trum'pet n. metal wind instrument like horn —vi. blow trumpet; make sound like one, as elephant —vt. proclaim, make widely known

truncate[1] vt. cut short

trun'cheon n. short thick club or baton; staff of office or authority —vt. cudgel

trun'dle vt. roll, as a thing on little wheels

trunk n. main stem of tree; person's body without or excluding head and limbs; box for clothes etc.; elephant's proboscis —pl. man's swimming costume —**trunk call** long-distance telephone call —**trunk line** main line of railway, canal, telephone etc. —**trunk road** main road

truss vt. fasten up, tie up —n. support; medical device of belt etc. to hold hernia in place; package, bundle (of hay etc.); cluster of flowers at end of single stalk

trust n. confidence; firm belief; reliance; combination of producers to reduce competition and keep up prices; care, responsibility; property held for another —vt. rely on; believe in; expect, hope, consign to care —**trustee'** n. one legally holding property on another's behalf —**trustee'ship** n. —**trust'ful** a. inclined to trust; credulous —**trust'worthy** a. reliable; dependable; honest; safe —**trust'y** a. faithful; reliable

truth see TRUE

try vi. attempt, endeavour —vt. attempt; test; make demands upon; investigate (case); examine (person) in court of law; purify or refine (as metals) (tried, try'ing) —n. attempt, effort; Rugby score gained by touching ball down over opponent's goal line —**tried** a. proved; afflicted —**try'ing** a. upsetting, annoying; difficult

tryst n. appointment to meet; place appointed

tsar see CZAR

tset'se n. Afr. bloodsucking fly whose bite transmits various diseases to man and animals

T-shirt, tee-shirt n. informal (short-sleeved) sweater, usu. of cotton

T-square n. T-shaped ruler for drawing parallel lines, right angles etc.

TT teetotal; Tourist Trophy; tuberculin tested

tub n. open wooden vessel like bottom half of barrel; small round container; bath; *inf.* old, slow ship *etc.*

tu'ba *n.* valved brass wind instrument of low pitch

tube *n.* long, narrow, hollow cylinder; flexible cylinder with cap to hold liquids, pastes; underground electric railway —**tu'bular** *a.* like tube

tu'ber *n.* fleshy underground stem of some plants, *eg* potato —**tu'berous** *a.*

tu'bercle *n.* any small rounded nodule on skin *etc.*; small lesion of tissue, *esp.* produced by tuberculosis —**tuber'cular** *a.* —**tuber'culin** *n.* extraction from bacillus used to test for and treat tuberculosis —**tuberculo'sis** *n.* communicable disease, *esp.* of lungs

TUC Trades Union Congress

tuck *vt.* push, fold into small space; gather, stitch in folds; draw, roll together —*n.* stitched fold; *inf.* food —**tuck'er** *n.* strip of linen or lace formerly worn across bosom by women

Tu'dor *a.* of the English royal house ruling 1485-1603; in, resembling style of this period, *esp.* of architecture

Tues'day *n.* third day of the week

tu'fa *n.* porous rock formed as deposit from springs *etc.*

tuff'et *n.* small mound or seat

tuft *n.* bunch of feathers, threads *etc.*

tug *vt.* pull hard or violently; haul; jerk forward (**-gg-**) —*n.* violent pull; ship used to tow other vessels —**tug of war** contest in which two teams pull against one another on a rope

tui'tion [tyoo-ish'ən] *n.* teaching, instruction; private coaching —**tui'tional** *a.*

tu'lip *n.* plant with bright cup-shaped flowers

tulle [tyool] *n.* kind of fine thin silk or lace

tum'ble *v.* (cause to) fall or roll, twist *etc.* (*esp.* in play); rumple, disturb —*n.* fall; somersault —**tum'bler** *n.* stemless drinking glass; acrobat; spring catch in lock —**tumble-down** *a.* dilapidated —**tumble(r) drier** machine that dries clothes *etc.* by tumbling in warm air —**tumble to** *inf.* realize, understand

tum'brel, tum'bril *n.* open cart for taking victims of French Revolution to guillotine

tu'mefy *v.* (cause to) swell —**tumes'cence** *n.* —**tumes'cent** *a.* (becoming) swollen

tumm'y *n. inf.* childish word for stomach

tu'mour *n.* abnormal growth in or on body

tu'mult *n.* violent uproar, commotion —**tumult'uous** *a.*

tu'mulus *n.* burial mound, barrow (pl. **-li** [-lī])

tun *n.* large cask; measure of liquid

tu'na *n. see* TUNNY

tun'dra *n.* vast treeless zone between ice cap and timber line of N America and Eurasia

tune *n.* melody; quality of being in pitch; adjustment of musical instrument; concord; frame of mind —*vt.* put in tune; adjust machine to obtain most efficient running; adjust radio circuit —**tune'ful** *a.* —**tune'fully** *adv.* —**tu'ner** *n.* —**tune in** adjust (radio, television) to receive (a station, programme)

tung'sten *n.* greyish-white metal, used in lamp filaments, some steels *etc.*

tu'nic *n.* close-fitting jacket forming part of uniform; loose hip-length or knee-length garment

tunn'el *n.* underground passage,

esp. as track for railway line; burrow of a mole *etc.* —*v.* make tunnel (through) (-ll-) —**tun'nel·ler** *n.*

tunn'y *n.* large marine food and game fish

tup *n.* male sheep, ram

tur'ban *n.* in certain countries, man's headdress, made by coiling length of cloth round head or a cap; woman's hat like this

tur'bid *a.* muddy, not clear; disturbed —**turbid'ity** *n.*

tur'bine *n.* rotary engine driven by steam, gas, water or air playing on blades

turbo- (*comb. form*) of, relating to, or driven by a turbine

tur'bot *n.* large European flatfish

tur'bulent *a.* in commotion; swirling; riotous —**tur'bulence** *n. esp.* instability of atmosphere causing gusty air currents *etc.*

tureen' *n.* serving dish for soup

turf *n.* short grass with earth bound to it by matted roots; grass; *esp.* as lawn (*pl.* **turfs, turves**) —*vt.* lay with turf —**turf accountant** bookmaker —**the turf** horse racing; racecourse —**turf out** *inf.* dismiss, throw out

tur'gid *a.* swollen, inflated; bombastic —**turges'cent** *a.* —**turgid'ity** *n.*

tur'key *n.* large bird reared for food

Turk'ish *a.* of, pert. to Turkey, the Turks —**Turkish bath** steam bath —**Turkish delight** gelatin flavoured and coated with powdered sugar

tur'meric *n.* Asian plant; powdered root of this used as dye, medicine and condiment

tur'moil *n.* confusion and bustle, commotion

turn *v.* move around, rotate; change, reverse, alter position or direction (of); (*oft.* with into)

change in nature, character *etc.* —*vt.* make, shape on lathe —*n.* act of turning; inclination *etc.*; period, spell; turning; short walk; (part of) rotation; performance —**turn'er** *n.* —**turn'ing** *n.* road, path leading off main route —**turn'coat** *n.* one who forsakes his party or principles —**turn'out** *n.* number of people appearing for some purpose, occasion; way in which person is dressed, equipped —**turn'over** *n.* total sales made by business over certain period; rate at which staff leave and are replaced; small pasty —**turn'pike** *n. Hist.* (gate across) road where toll was paid —**turn'stile** *n.* revolving gate for controlling admission of people —**turn'table** *n.* revolving platform —**turn-up** *n.* turned-up fold at bottom of trouser leg —**turn down** refuse —**turn up** appear; be found; increase (flow, volume)

turn'ip *n.* plant with globular root used as food

turp'entine *n.* resin got from certain trees; oil, spirits made from this —**turps** *n. short for* turpentine

turp'itude *n.* depravity

tur'quoise *n.* bluish-green precious stone; this colour

turr'et *n.* small tower; revolving armoured tower for guns on warship, tank *etc.*

tur'tle *n.* sea tortoise

tusk *n.* long pointed side tooth of certain animals, *eg* elephant, wild boar *etc.* —**tusk'er** *n.* animal with tusks fully developed

tus'sle *n./v.* fight, wrestle, struggle

tuss'ock *n.* clump of grass; tuft —**tuss'ocky** *a.*

tu'telage *n.* act, office of tutor or guardian —**tu'telary** *a.*

tu'tor *n.* one teaching individuals or small groups —*v.* teach thus —**tutor'ial** *n.* period of instruction with tutor

tu'tu [tōō'tōō] *n.* short, stiff skirt worn by ballerinas

tuxe'do *n. US* dinner jacket

TV television —**TV game** game like tennis played on domestic TV screen using special attachment

twad'dle [twod'l] *n.* silly talk

twain *n. obs.* two —**in twain** asunder

twang *n.* vibrating metallic sound; nasal speech —*v.* (cause to) make such sounds

tweak *vt.* pinch and twist or pull —*n.*

twee *a. inf.* excessively sentimental, sweet, pretty

tweed *n.* rough-surfaced cloth used for clothing —*pl.* suit of tweed

tweet *n./vi.* chirp —**tweet'er** *n.* loudspeaker reproducing high-frequency sounds

tweez'ers *pl.n.* small forceps or tongs

twelve *n./a.* cardinal number, two more than ten —**twelfth** *a.* the ordinal number —*n.*

twen'ty *n./a.* cardinal number, twice ten —**twen'tieth** *a.* the ordinal number —*n.*

twerp, twirp *n. inf.* silly person

twice *adv.* two times

twid'dle *v.* fiddle; twist

twig[1] *n.* small branch, shoot

twig[2] *v. inf.* notice, understand (**-gg-**)

twi'light *n.* soft light after sunset

twill *n.* fabric woven so as to have surface of parallel ridges

twin *n.* one of pair, *esp.* of two children born together —*a.* being a twin —*v.* pair, be paired

twine *v.* twist, coil round —*n.* string, cord

twinge *n.* momentary sharp, shooting pain; qualm

twin'kle *vi.* shine with dancing or quivering light, sparkle —*n.* twinkling; flash; gleam of amusement in eyes —**twink'ling** *n.* very brief time

twirl *vt.* turn or twist round quickly; whirl; twiddle

twist *v.* make, become spiral, by turning with one end fast; distort, change; wind —*n.* thing twisted —**twis'ter** *n. inf.* swindler —**twist'y** *a.*

twit *n. inf.* foolish person —*vt.* taunt (**-tt-**)

twitch *v.* give momentary sharp pull or jerk (to) —*n.* such pull or jerk; spasmodic jerk, spasm

twitt'er *vi.* (of birds) utter succession of tremulous sounds —*n.* such succession of notes

two [tōō] *n./a.* cardinal number, one more than one —**two'fold** *a./adv.* —**two-faced** *a.* double-dealing, deceitful; with two faces —**two-stroke** *a.* (of internal-combustion engine) making one explosion to every two strokes of piston

tycoon[1] [tī-] *n.* powerful, influential businessman

tyke, tike *inf. n.* small, cheeky child; small (mongrel) dog

tym'pani SEE TIMPANI

type *n.* class; sort; model; pattern; characteristic build; specimen; block bearing letter used for printing; such pieces collectively —*vt.* print with typewriter; typify; classify —**type'script** *n.* typewritten document or copy —**type'write** *v.* —**type'writer** *n.* keyed writing machine —**ty'pist** *n.* one who operates typewriter —**ty'po** *n. inf.* error in typing

ty'phoid *n.* acute infectious disease, affecting *esp.* intestines

—*a.* —**ty'phus** *n.* infectious disease

typhoon' *n.* violent tropical storm or cyclone —**typhon'ic** *a.*

typ'ical *a.* true to type; characteristic —**typ'ically** *adv.*

typ'ify *vt.* serve as type or model of (**-ified, -ifying**)

typog'raphy [tī-] *n.* art of printing; style of printing —**typograph'ical** *a.* —**typog'rapher** *n.*

ty'rant [tī'-] *n.* oppressive or cruel ruler; one who forces his will on others cruelly and arbitrarily —**tyrann'ical** [ti-] *a.* despotic, ruthless —**tyrann'ically** *adv.* —**tyrann'icide** *n.* slayer of tyrant; his deed —**tyr'annize** *v.* exert ruthless or tyrannical authority (over) —**tyr'annous** *a.* —**tyr'anny** *n.* despotism

tyre *n.* (inflated) rubber ring over rim of road vehicle; metal band on rim of cart wheel

ty'ro [tī'-] *n.* novice, beginner

U

U Union; United; *Chem.* uranium

UAE United Arab Emirates

ubiq'uitous [yōō-bik'w-] *a.* everywhere at once; omnipresent —**ubiq'uity** *n.*

udd'er *n.* milk-secreting organ of cow *etc.*

UDI Unilateral Declaration of Independence

UEFA Union of European Football Associations

UFO unidentified flying object

ug'ly *a.* unpleasing, repulsive to the sight, hideous; ill-omened; threatening —**ug'lify** *vt.* —**ug'liness** *n.*

UHF ultrahigh frequency

UHT ultra heat treated

UK United Kingdom

ukule'le [yōō-kə-lā'li] *n.* small four-stringed guitar, *esp.* of Hawaii

ul'cer *n.* open sore on skin, mucous membrane that is slow to heal —**ul'cerate** *v.* make, form ulcer(s) —**ul'cerated** *a.* —**ulcera'tion** *n.* —**ul'cerous** *a.*

ull'age *n.* quantity by which a container falls short of being full

ul'na *n.* longer of two bones of forearm (*pl.* **ul'nae** [-nē])

ult. ultimate; ultimo

ulte'rior *a.* lying beneath, beyond what is revealed or evident (*eg* motives); situated beyond

ult'imate *a.* last; highest; most significant; fundamental —**ul'timately** *adv.* —**ultima'tum** [-tā-] *n.* final proposition; final terms offered (*pl* **-s, -ta**) —**ult'imo** *adv.* in last month

ultra- (*comb. form*) beyond, excessively, as in **ultramod'ern** *a.*

ultrahigh frequency (band of) radio waves of very short wavelength

ultramarine' [-ēn'] *n.* blue pigment

ultrason'ic *a.* of sound waves beyond the range of human ear

ultravi'olet *a.* of electromagnetic radiation (*eg* of sun *etc.*) beyond limit of visibility at violet end of spectrum

um'bel *n.* umbrella-like flower cluster with stalks springing from central point —**umbellif'erous** *a.*

um'ber *n.* dark brown pigment

umbil'ical *a.* of (region of) navel —**umbilical cord** cordlike structure connecting foetus with placenta of mother; cord joining astronaut to spacecraft *etc.*

um'brage *n.* offence, resentment

umbrell'a *n.* folding circular cover of nylon *etc.* on stick, carried in hand to protect against rain, heat of sun; any-thing shaped or functioning like an umbrella

um'pire n. person chosen to decide question, or to decide disputes and enforce rules in a game —v. act as umpire (in)

umpteen' inf. a. many —**ump-teenth'** a.

UN United Nations

un- (comb. form) indicating not, contrary to, opposite of, reversal of an action, removal from, re-lease or deprivation The list below contains some of the more common compounds

unan'imous a. [yoo-] in com-plete agreement; agreed by all —**unanim'ity** n.

unassu'ming a. not preten-tious, modest

unavail'ing a. useless, futile

unaware' a. not aware, unin-formed —**unawares'** adv. with-out previous warning; unexpect-edly

unbos'om [-booz'-] vt. tell or reveal (one's secrets etc.)

uncann'y a. weird, mysterious

unc'le n. brother of father or mother; husband of aunt

uncomplimen'tary a. not complimentary; insulting, de-rogatory

uncon'scionable a. unscru-pulous, unprincipled; excessive

uncon'scious a. insensible; not aware; not knowing; of thoughts, memories etc. of which one is not normally aware —n. these thoughts —**uncon'sciously** adv. —**uncon'sciousness** n.

uncouth' [-ooth] a. clumsy, boorish; without ease or polish —**uncouth'ly** adv.

unc'tion [ungk'shon] n. anoint-ing; excessive politeness; sooth-ing words or thoughts —**unc'tu-ous** a. slippery, greasy; oily in manner, gushing

undeceive' vt. reveal truth to (someone mistaken, misled)

un'der prep. below, beneath; bound by, included in; less than; subjected to; known by; in the time of —adv. in lower place or condition —a. lower

under- (comb. form) beneath, below, lower, as in underground

un'derarm a. (of measure-ment) from armpit to wrist; Sport (of bowling etc.) with hand swung below shoulder level

un'dercarriage n. landing gear of aircraft

unaccept'able	uncommitt'ed	unearned'
unaccom'panied	uncomm'only	uneat'able
unaccus'tomed	uncondi'tional	uneconom'ic
unaffect'ed	unconstitu'tional	uned'ucated
unapproach'able	unconven'tional	unemo'tional
unattached'	uncoor'dinated	unend'ing
unattrac'tive	uncrit'ical	une'qualled
unauth'orized	undeci'ded	unequiv'ocal
unbear'able	undemand'ing	uneth'ical
unbeliev'able	undeserved'	unevent'ful
unbi'as(s)ed	undesi'rable	unexpect'ed
unbreak'able	undeterred'	unexplained'
uncer'tain	undis'ciplined	unfail'ing
uncharacteris'tic	undiscov'ered	unfair'
unchar'itable	undisturbed'	unfamil'iar
uncom'fortable	undrink'able	unfa'vourable

under'charge¹ vt. charge less than proper amount —n. too low a charge

un'dercoat n. coat of paint applied before top coat

undergo¹ vt. experience, endure, sustain (-went¹, -gone¹, -go'ing)

undergrad'uate n. student member of university or college who has not taken degree

un'derground a. under the ground; secret —adv. secretly —n. secret but organized resistance to government in power; railway system under the ground

un'derhand a. secret, sly; Sport underarm

underline¹ vt. put line under; emphasize

un'derling n. subordinate

undermine¹ vt. wear away base, support of; weaken insidiously

underneath¹ adv. below —prep. under —a. lower —n.

un'derpass n. section of road passing under another road, railway line etc.

understand¹ v. know and comprehend; realize —vt. infer; take for granted (-stood¹, -stand'ing) —understand'able a. —under-

stand'ably adv. —**understand'-ing** n. intelligence; opinion; agreement —a. sympathetic

un'derstudy n. one prepared to take over theatrical part from performer if necessary —vt.

undertake¹ vt. make oneself responsible for; enter upon; promise (-took¹, -ta'ken, -ta'king) —**un'dertaker** n. one who arranges funerals —**un'dertak-ing** n. that which is undertaken; project; guarantee

un'dertone n. quiet, dropped tone of voice; underlying tone or suggestion

un'dertow n. backwash of wave; current beneath surface moving in different direction from surface current

un'derwear n. garments worn next to skin (also **un'derclothes**)

un'derworld n. criminals and their associates; Myth. abode of the dead

un'derwrite vt. agree to pay; accept liability in insurance policy (-wrote, -written, -writing) —**un'derwriter** n. agent for insurance

undo¹ [-dōō¹] vt. untie, unfasten; reverse; cause downfall of (-did¹, -done¹, -do'ing) —**undo'ing** n.

unfeel'ing	unhurt'
unfeigned'	unhygie'nic
unfin'ished	uniden'tified
unfold'	unimag'inative
unforgett'able	unimpaired'
unfor'tunate	unimpor'tant
unfound'ed	unimpressed'
ungra'cious	uninhab'ited
ungrammat'ical	uninhib'ited
unguard'ed	uninspired'
unhapp'y	uninsured'
unharmed'	unintell'igible
unhealth'y	uninten'tional
unheat'ed	unin'teresting
unhelp'ful	uninterrupt'ed
unhurr'ied	uninvi'ted

unjus'tified	
unla'belled	
unlaw'ful	
unlim'ited	
unlined'	
unluck'y	
unman'ageable	
unmarr'ied	
unmen'tionable	
unmer'ited	
unmistak(e)'able	
unmoved'	
unmu'sical	
unnamed'	
unnat'ural	
unnec'essary	

—undone' a. ruined; not performed

un'dulate [-dyoo-] v. move up and down like waves **—undulation** n. **—un'dulatory** a.

unearth' vt. dig up; discover

uneas'y a. anxious; uncomfortable

unemployed' a. having no paid employment, out of work **—unemploy'ment** n.

unerr'ing a. not missing the mark; consistently accurate

UNESCO United Nations Educational, Scientific and Cultural Organization

ungain'ly a. awkward, clumsy

un'guent [ung'gwənt] n. ointment

uni- (comb. form) one, as in unicorn, uniform etc. Such words are not given here where the meanings may easily be inferred from the simple word

UNICEF United Nations International Children's Emergency Fund

u'nicorn n. mythical horselike animal with single long horn

u'niform n. identifying clothes worn by members of same group eg soldiers, nurses etc. —a. not changing, unvarying; regular, consistent; conforming to same standard or rule **—uniform'ity** n. sameness **—u'niformly** adv.

u'nify v. make or become one (-ified, -ifying) **—unification** n.

unilat'eral [yoo-] a. one-sided; (of contract) binding one party only **—unilat'erally** adv.

u'nion n. joining into one; state of being joined; result of being joined; federation, combination of societies etc.; trade union **—u'nionism** n. **—u'nionist** n. supporter of union **—u'nionize** v. organize (workers) into trade union **—Union Jack** national flag of United Kingdom

unique' [yoo-nēk'] a. being only one of its kind; unparalleled

u'nison n. Mus. singing etc. of same note as others; agreement, harmony, concord

u'nit n. single thing or person; standard quantity; group of people or things with one purpose **—unita'rian** n. member of Christian body that denies doctrine of the Trinity **—unita'rianism** n. **—u'nitary** a.

unite' [yoo-] vt. join into one, connect; associate; cause to adhere —vi. become one; combine **—u'nity** n. state of being one;

unno'ticed	unrelent'ing	unsuit'able
unobser'vant	unrequit'ted	unsweet'ened
unobtain'able	unresolved'	unsympathet'ic
unobtru'sive	unrestrained'	unsystemat'ic
unoffi'cial	unri'valled	untrained'
unopposed'	unruf'fled	untrust'worthy
unor'thodox	unsafe'	untyp'ical
unpaid'	unsale'able	unu'sable
unpar'donable	unsatisfac'tory	unu'sual
unpleas'ant	unsched'uled	unutt'erable
unpop'ular	unselfcon'scious	unwant'ed
unprec'edented	unshak(e)'able	unwarr'anted
unprepared'	unsolic'ited	unwill'ing
unques'tionably	unspec'ified	unwind'
unrealis'tic	unspo'ken	unwise'
unrea'sonable	unsuccess'ful	unwrap'

harmony; agreement, uniformity; combination of separate parts into connected whole; *Maths* the number one —**United Nations Organization** an organization formed in 1945 to promote peace and international cooperation

u'niverse *n.* all existing things considered as constituting systematic whole; the world —**uni·ver'sal** *a.* relating to all things or all people; applying to all members of a community —**univer·sal'ity** *n.* —**univer'sally** *adv.*

univer'sity [yōō-] *n.* educational institution for study, examination and conferment of degrees in various branches of learning

univo'cal [yōō-] *a.* unambiguous

unkempt' *a.* of rough or uncared-for appearance

unless' *conj.* if not, except

UNO United Nations Organization

unrav'el *vt.* undo, untangle

unremitt'ing *a.* never slackening or stopping

unru'ly [-rōō-] *a.* badly behaved, ungovernable, disorderly

unsa'voury *a.* distasteful, disagreeable

unsight'ly *a.* ugly

unten'able *a.* (of theories *etc.*) incapable of being maintained, defended

unthink'able *a.* out of the question; inconceivable; unreasonable

until' *conj.* to the time that; (with a negative) before —*prep.* up to the time of

un'to *prep. obs.* to

untouched' *a.* not touched; not harmed —**untouch'able** *a.* not able to be touched —*n.* esp. formerly, non-caste Hindu, forbidden to be touched by one of caste

untoward' *a.* awkward, inconvenient

untram'melled *a.* not confined, not constrained

unwaged' *a.* not receiving wage or salary

unwell' *a.* not well, ill

unwield'y *a.* awkward, big, heavy to handle; clumsy

unwitt'ing *a.* not knowing; not intentional

up *prep.* from lower to higher position; along —*adv.* in or to higher position, source, activity *etc.*; indicating completion (**up' per** *comp.*, **upp'ermost** *sup.*) —**up'ward** *a./adv.* —**up'wards** *adv.* —**up against** confronted with

up- (*comb. form*) up, upper, upwards as in *uproot, upgrade etc.* Such words are not given here where the meaning may easily be found from the simple word

upbraid' *vt.* scold, reproach

up'bringing *n.* rearing and education of children

update' *vt.* bring up to date

upfront' *a. inf.* open, frank —*a./adv.* (of money) paid out at beginning of business arrangement

upgrade' *vt.* promote to higher position; improve

upheav'al *n.* sudden or violent disturbance

uphold' *vt.* maintain, support *etc.* (**upheld', uphold'ing**)

upholst'er [-ō-] *vt.* fit springs, padding and coverings on chairs *etc.* —**upholst'erer** *n.* one who fits coverings *etc.* —**upholst'ery** *n.*

up'keep *n.* act, process or cost of keeping something in good repair

up'land *n.* high land

uplift' *vt.* raise aloft —*n.* [up'-] a lifting up; mental, social or emotional improvement

upon' *prep.* on

upp'er *a.* higher, situated above

—*comp. of* UP —*n.* upper part of boot or shoe —**upp'ercut** *n.* short-arm upward blow —**upp'ermost** *a. sup. of* UP

upp'ish, upp'ity *inf. a.* self-assertive; arrogant; affectedly superior

up'right *a.* erect; honest, just —*adv.* vertically —*n.* thing standing upright, *eg* post in framework

up'rising *n.* rebellion, revolt

up'roar *n.* tumult, disturbance —**uproar'ious** *a.* rowdy —**up-roar'iously** *adv.*

upset' *vt.* overturn; distress; disrupt; make ill (**upset', upset'-ting**) —*n.* [**up'-**] unexpected defeat; confusion; trouble; overturning

up'shot *n.* outcome, end

up'stage' *a.* of back of stage —*vt. inf.* draw attention away from another to oneself

up'start *n.* one suddenly raised to wealth, power *etc.*

uptight' *inf. a.* displaying tense nervousness, irritability; repressed

ura'nium [yoo-] *n.* white radioactive metallic element, used as chief source of nuclear energy

Ura'nus *n.* Greek god, personification of sky; seventh planet from the sun

ur'ban *a.* relating to town or city —**ur'banize** *vt.* change countryside to residential or industrial area

urbane' *a.* elegant, sophisticated —**urban'ity** *n.*

urch'in *n.* mischievous, unkempt child

ur'ea [yoor'-] *n.* substance occurring in urine

ure'thra [yoor-] *n.* canal conveying urine from bladder out of body

urge *vt.* exhort earnestly; entreat; drive on —*n.* strong desire

ur'gency *n.* —**ur'gent** *a.* pressing; needing attention at once —**ur'gently** *adv.*

u'rine *n.* fluid excreted by kidneys to bladder and passed as waste from body —**u'ric** *a.* —**uri'nal** *n.* (place with) sanitary fitting(s) used by men for urination —**u'rinary** *a.* —**u'rinate** *vi.* discharge urine —**urina'tion** *n.*

urn *n.* vessel like vase, *esp.* for ashes of the dead; large container with tap for making and dispensing tea, coffee *etc.*

ur'sine *a.* of, like a bear

US, USA United States (of America)

us *pron. pl.* the objective case of the pronoun WE

use [yōōz] *vt.* employ, avail oneself of; exercise; exploit; consume —*n.* [yōōs] employment, application to a purpose; need to employ; serviceableness; profit; habit —**u'sable** [-z-] *a.* fit for use —**u'sage** [-s-] *n.* act of using; custom; customary way of using —**used** [-z-] *a.* second-hand, not new —**use'ful** [-s-] *a.* of use; helpful; serviceable —**use'fully** *adv.* —**use'fulness** *n.* —**use'less** *a.* —**use'lessly** *adv.* —**use'lessness** *n.* —**used** *to* [-s-] *a.* accustomed to —*vt.* did so formerly —**user friendly** (of computer *etc.*) easily understood and operated

ush'er *n.* doorkeeper, one showing people to seats *etc.* (**usher-ette'** *fem.*) —*vt.* introduce, announce; inaugurate

USSR Union of Soviet Socialist Republics

u'sual *a.* habitual, ordinary —**u'sually** *adv.* as a rule; generally, commonly

usurp' [yōō-z-] *vt.* seize wrongfully —**usurpa'tion** *n.* violent or unlawful seizing of power —**usurp'er** *n.*

V

u'sury [-zhə-] *n.* lending of money at excessive interest; such interest —**u'surer** *n.* money lender —**usur'ious** [-zhoor-] *a.*

uten'sil [yōō-] *n.* vessel, implement, *esp.* in domestic use

u'terus *n.* womb (*pl.* **u'teri** [-I]) —**u'terine** *a.*

util'ity [yōō-] *n.* usefulness; benefit; useful thing —*a.* made for practical purposes —**utilita'rian** *a.* useful rather than beautiful —**utilita'rianism** *n.* doctrine that morality of actions is to be tested by their utility, *esp.* that the greatest good of the greatest number should be the sole end of public action —**utiliza'tion** *n.* —**u'tilize** *vt.* make use of

ut'most *a.* to the highest degree; extreme, furthest —*n.* greatest possible amount

Uto'pia [yōō-] *n.* imaginary state with perfect political and social conditions, or constitution —**uto'pian** *a.* ideally perfect but impracticable

utt'er[1] *vt.* express, emit audibly, say; put in circulation (forged banknotes, counterfeit coin) —**utt'erance** *n.* act of speaking; expression in words; spoken words

utt'er[2] *a.* complete, total, absolute —**utt'erly** *adv.*

utt'ermost *a.* farthest out; utmost —*n.* highest degree

U-turn *n.* U-shaped turn by vehicle in order to go in opposite direction; reversal of political policy

UV ultraviolet

u'vula [-vyoo-] *n.* pendent fleshy part of soft palate —**u'vular** *a.*

uxor'ious *a.* excessively fond of one's wife

V *Chem.* vanadium

v volt

v. verb; verso; versus; very; vide

va'cant *a.* without thought, empty; unoccupied —**va'cancy** *n.* state of being unoccupied; unfilled post, accommodation *etc.* —**va'cantly** *adv.*

vacate' *vt.* quit, leave empty —**vaca'tion** *n.* time when universities and law courts are closed; **US** holidays; act of vacating

vac'cinate [vaks'-] *vt.* inoculate with vaccine as protection against a specific disease —**vac-cina'tion** *n.* —**vac'cinator** *n* —**vac'cine** [-sēn] *n.* any substance used for inoculation against disease

vac'illate [vas'-] *vi.* fluctuate in opinion; waver; move to and fro —**vacilla'tion** *n.* indecision; wavering; unsteadiness

vac'uum [-yoom] *n.* place, region containing no matter and from which all or most air, gas has been removed (*pl.* **-uums**, **-ua**) —*v.* clean with vacuum cleaner —**vacu'ity** *n.* —**vac'uous** *a.* vacant; expressionless; unintelligent —**vacuum cleaner** apparatus for removing dust by suction —**vacuum flask** double-walled flask with vacuum between walls, for keeping contents of inner flask at temperature at which they were inserted

vag'abond *n.* person with no fixed home; wandering beggar or thief —*a.* like a vagabond

va'gary [*or* və-gā'-] *n.* something unusual, erratic; whim

vagi'na [-jī'-] *n.* passage from womb to exterior —**vagi'nal** *a.*

va'grant *n.* vagabond, tramp

—a. wandering, *esp.* without purpose —**va'grancy** *n.*

vague [vāg] *a.* indefinite or uncertain; indistinct; not clearly expressed; absent-minded

vain *a.* conceited; worthless, useless; unavailing; foolish —**vain'ly** *adv.*

vain'glory *n.* boastfulness, vanity —**vainglor'ious** *a.*

val'ance *n.* short curtain round base of bed *etc.*

vale *n. Poet.* valley

valedic'tion *n.* farewell —**valedic'tory** *n.* farewell address —*a.*

va'lency, va'lence *n. Chem.* combining power of element or atom

val'entine *n.* (one receiving) card, gift, expressing affection, on Saint Valentine's Day, 14th Feb.

valer'ian *n.* flowering herb

val'et [*or* -ā] *n.* gentleman's personal servant

valetu'dinary *a.* sickly; infirm —**valetudina'rian** *n.* person obliged or disposed to live the life of an invalid

Valhall'a *n. Norse Myth.* place of immortality for heroes slain in battle

val'iant *a.* brave, courageous

val'id *a.* sound; capable of being justified; of binding force in law —**valid'ity** *n.* soundness; power to convince; legal force —**val'idate** *vt.* make valid

valise' [-ēz] *n.* travelling bag

Val'ium R drug used as tranquillizer

Valky'rie [-kē'-] *n.* one of the Norse war-goddesses who chose the slain and guided them to Valhalla

vall'ey *n.* low area between hills; river basin

val'our [-ər] *a.* bravery —**val'orous** *a.*

val'ue *n.* worth; utility; equivalent; importance —*pl.* principles, standards —*vt.* estimate value of; hold in respect; prize —**val'uable** *a.* precious; worthy; capable of being valued —*n.* (*usu. pl.*) valuable thing —**valua'tion** *n.* estimated worth —**val'ueless** *a.* worthless —**val'uer** *n.* —**value added tax** tax on difference between cost of basic materials and cost of article made from them

valve *n.* device to control passage of fluid *etc.* through pipe; *Anat.* part of body allowing one-way passage of fluids; part of radio or television which controls flow of current; any of separable parts of shell of mollusc; *Mus.* device on brass instrument for lengthening tube —**val'vular** *a.* of, like valves

vamoose', vamose' *v. sl.* depart quickly

vamp[1] *inf.* *n.* woman who deliberately allures men —*v.* exploit (man) as vamp

vamp[2] *n.* something patched up (*also* **revamp**[1]); front part of shoe upper —*vt.* patch up, rework

vamp'ire *n.* (in folklore) corpse that rises from dead to drink blood of the living —**vampire bat** one that sucks blood of animals

van[1] *n.* covered vehicle, *esp.* for goods; railway carriage for goods and use of guard

van[2] *n. short for* VANGUARD

vana'dium *n.* metallic element used in manufacture of hard steel

van'dal *n.* one who wantonly and deliberately damages or destroys —**van'dalism** *n.* —**van'dalize** *vt.*

vane *n.* weathercock; blade of propeller; fin on bomb *etc.*; sight on quadrant

van'guard *n.* leading, foremost group, position *etc.*

vanill'a *n.* tropical climbing orchid; its seed(pod); essence of this for flavouring

van'ish vi. disappear; fade away

van'ity n. excessive pride or conceit; ostentation

van'quish vt. subdue in battle; conquer, overcome —**van'quishable** a. —**van'quisher** n.

van'tage [vahn'-] n. advantage

vap'id a. flat, dull, insipid —**vapid'ity** n.

va'pour [-ər] n. gaseous form of a substance more familiar as liquid or solid; steam, mist; invisible moisture in air —**va'porize** v. convert into, pass off in, vapour —**va'porizer** n. —**va'porous** a.

va'riable see VARY

var'icose [va'ri-] a. of vein, swollen, twisted

va'riegate vt. diversify by patches of different colours —**va'riegated** a. streaked, spotted, dappled —**variega'tion** n.

vari'ety n. state of being varied or various; diversity; varied assortment; sort or kind

vario'rum a./n. (edition) with notes by various commentators

va'rious a. manifold, diverse, of several kinds

var'let n. formerly, menial servant, rascal

var'nish n. resinous solution put on a surface to make it hard and shiny —vt. apply varnish to

va'ry v. (cause to) change, diversify, differ, deviate (**va'ried, va'rying**) —**variabil'ity** n. —**va'riable** a. changeable; unsteady or fickle —n. something subject to variation —**va'riance** n. state of discord, discrepancy —**va'riant** a. different —n. difference in form; alternative form or reading —**varia'tion** n. alteration; extent to which thing varies; modification —**varia'tional** a.

—**va'ried** a. diverse; modified; variegated

vas n. vessel, tube carrying bodily fluid (pl. **va'sa**)

vas'cular a. of, with vessels for conveying sap, blood etc.

vase [vahz] n. vessel, jar as ornament or for holding flowers

vasec'tomy n. contraceptive measure of surgical removal of part of vas bearing sperm from testicle

Vas'eline [-ēn] n. **R** jellylike petroleum product

vass'al n. holder of land by feudal tenure; dependant —**vass'alage** n.

vast [-ah-] a. very large —**vast'ly** adv. —**vast'ness** n.

VAT value added tax

vat n. large tub, tank

Vat'ican n. Pope's palace; papal authority

vau'deville [vō'də-vil] n. theatrical entertainment with songs, juggling acts, dance etc.

vault[1] n. arched roof; arched apartment; cellar; burial chamber; place for storing valuables —vt. build with arched roof

vault[2] v. spring, jump over with the hands resting on something —n. such jump

vaunt v./n. boast

VC Vice Chairman; Vice Chancellor; Victoria Cross; Viet Cong

VCR video cassette recorder

VD venereal disease

VDU visual display unit

VE Victory in Europe

veal n. calf flesh as food

vec'tor n. quantity (eg force) having both magnitude and direction; disease-carrying organism, esp. insect; compass direction, course

veer vi. change direction; change one's mind

ve'gan n. strict vegetarian, who

does not eat animal products

veg'etable [vej'-] n. plant, esp. edible one; inf. person who has lost use of mental faculties; inf. dull person —a. of, from, concerned with plants —**vegetable marrow** plant with long, green-striped fruit, eaten as vegetable

vegeta'rian n. one who does not eat meat —a. —**vegeta'rianism** n.

veg'etate [vej'-] vi. (of plants) grow, develop; (of person) live dull, unproductive life —**vegeta'tion** n. plants collectively; plants growing in a place; process of plant growth —**veg'etative** a.

ve'hement [vē'im-] a. marked by intensity of feeling; vigorous; forcible —**ve'hemence** n. —**ve'hemently** adv.

ve'hicle [vē'ikl] n. means of conveying; means of expression; medium —**vehic'ular** [vi-hik'-] a.

veil [vāl] n. light material to cover face or head; mask, cover —vt. cover with, as with, veil —**veiled** a. disguised —**take the veil** become a nun

vein [vān] n. tube in body taking blood to heart; rib of leaf or insect's wing; fissure in rock filled with ore; streak; distinctive trait, strain etc.; mood —vt. mark with streaks —**ve'nous** a. of veins

veld, veldt [velt] n. elevated grassland in S Afr. —**veld'skoen** [-skoon] n. SA ankle-length boot orig. of raw hide

vell'um n. parchment of calf skin used for manuscripts or bindings; paper resembling this

veloc'ity [-os'-] n. rate of motion in given direction, esp. of inanimate things; speed

ve'lodrome n. area with banked track for cycle racing

velour(s) [-loor'] n. fabric with velvety finish

ve'lum n. Zool. membranous covering or organ; soft palate (pl. **ve'la**)

vel'vet n. silk or cotton fabric with thick, short pile —**velveteen'** n. cotton fabric resembling velvet —**vel'vety** a. of, like velvet; soft and smooth

ve'nal a. guilty of taking, prepared to take, bribes; corrupt —**venal'ity** n.

vend vt. sell —**vend'or** n. —**vending machine** one that automatically dispenses goods when money is inserted

vendett'a n. bitter, prolonged feud

veneer' n. thin layer of fine wood; superficial appearance —vt. cover with veneer

ven'erable a. worthy of reverence —**ven'erate** vt. look up to, respect, revere —**venera'tion** n.

vene'real a. (of disease) transmitted by sexual intercourse; infected with venereal disease; of, relating to genitals or sexual intercourse

ven'ery[1] n. obs. pursuit of sexual gratification

ven'ery[2] n. Hist. art, practice of hunting

vene'tian blind window blind made of thin horizontal slats arranged to turn so as to admit or exclude light

ven'geance n. revenge; retribution for wrong done —**venge'ful** a. —**venge'fully** adv.

ve'nial a. pardonable

ven'ison n. flesh of deer as food

ven'om n. poison; spite —**ven'omous** a. poisonous

ve'nous see VEIN

vent[1] n. small hole or outlet —vt. give outlet to; utter; pour forth

vent[2] n. vertical slit in garment esp. at back of jacket

vent'ilate vt. supply with fresh

air; bring into discussion —**venti-la'tion** n. —**vent'ilator** n.

ven'tral a. abdominal

ven'tricle n. cavity, hollow in body, esp. in heart or brain —**ventric'ular** a.

ventril'oquist n. one who can so speak that the sounds seem to come from some other person or place —**ventril'oquism** n.

ven'ture vt. expose to hazard; risk —vi. dare; have courage to do something or go somewhere —n. risky undertaking; speculative commercial undertaking —**ven'turesome** a. —**ven'turous** a.

ven'ue n. Law district in which case is tried; meeting place; location

Ve'nus n. Roman goddess of love; planet between earth and Mercury —**Venus's** flytrap insect-eating plant

vera'cious a. truthful; true —**verac'ity** [-as'-] n.

veran'da(h) n. open or partly enclosed porch on outside of house

verb n. part of speech used to express action or being —**verb'al** a. of, by, or relating to words spoken rather than written; of, like a verb —**verb'alize** v. put into words, speak —**verb'ally** adv. —**verba'tim** adv./a. word for word, literal

verbas'cum n. mostly perennial garden plant

verbe'na n. genus of fragrant, beautiful plants; their characteristic scent

verb'iage n. excess of words —**verbose'** a. wordy, long-winded —**verbos'ity** n.

verd'ant a. green and fresh —**verd'ure** n. greenery; freshness —**verd'urous** a.

ver'dict n. decision of a jury;

opinion reached after examination of facts

ver'digris n. green film on copper

verd'ure see VERDANT

verge n. edge; brink; grass border along a road —vi. come close to; be on the border of

ver'ger n. caretaker and attendant in church; bearer of wand of office

ver'ify [ve'ri-] vt. prove, confirm truth of; test accuracy of (-**ified**, -**ifying**) —**verifiable** a. —**verifica'tion** n.

ver'ily [ve'ri-] obs. adv. truly; in truth

verisimil'itude n. appearance of truth; likelihood

ver'itable [ve'ri-] a. actual, true, genuine —**ver'itably** adv.

ver'ity [ve'ri-] n. truth; reality; true assertion

vermicel'li [-sel'-] n. pasta in fine strands, used in soups; tiny chocolate strands used to coat cakes etc.

verm'icide n. substance to destroy worms —**verm'iform** a. shaped like a worm (eg **vermiform appendix**)

vermil'ion a./n. (of) bright red colour or pigment

ver'min pl.n. injurious animals, parasites etc. —**ver'minous** a.

ver'mouth [-məth] n. wine flavoured with aromatic herbs etc.

vernac'ular n. commonly spoken language or dialect of particular country or place —a. of vernacular; native

vern'al a. of spring

vern'ier n. sliding scale for obtaining fractional parts of subdivision of graduated scale

veron'ica n. genus of plants including speedwell

verru'ca [-roo̅-] n. wart, esp. on foot

ver'satile a. capable of or

adapted to many different uses, skills *etc.*; liable to change —**ver'satil'ity** n.

verse n. stanza or short subdivision of poem or the Bible; poetry; line of poetry —**ver'sify** v. turn into verse (**-ified, -ifying**) —**versifica'tion** n. —**versed in** skilled

ver'sion n. description from certain point of view; translation; adaptation

ver'so n. back of sheet of printed paper, left-hand page

ver'sus prep. against

vert'ebra n. single section of backbone (pl. **-brae** [-brē]) —**ver'tebral** a. of the spine —**ver'tebrate** n. animal with backbone —a.

vert'ex n. summit (pl. **vert'ices** [-sēz])

vert'ical a. at right angles to the horizon; upright; overhead

ver'tigo n. giddiness (pl. **-goes, vertig'ines** [-tij'i·nēz]) —**vertig'inous** [-ij'-] a. dizzy

ver'vain n. plant of the genus *Verbena*

verve n. enthusiasm; spirit; energy, vigour

ver'y [ve'ri] a. exact, ideal; same; complete; actual —*adv.* extremely, to great extent

ves'icle n. small blister, bubble, or cavity —**vesic'ular** a.

ves'pers pl.n. evening church service; evensong

vess'el n. any object used as a container, esp. for liquids; ship, large boat; tubular structure conveying liquids (eg blood) in body

vest n. undergarment for the trunk —vt. place; bestow; confer; clothe —**vest'ment** n. robe or official garment —**vested interest** strong personal interest in particular state of affairs

ves'tal a. pure, chaste

vest'ibule n. entrance hall, lobby

vest'ige [-ij] n. small trace, amount —**vestig'ial** a.

vest'ry n. room in church for keeping vestments, holding meetings *etc.*

vet n. short for VETERINARY SURGEON —vt. examine; check (**-tt-**)

vet. veteran; veterinary

vetch n. plant of bean family

vet'eran n. one who has served a long time, esp. in fighting services —a. long-serving

vet'erinary a. of, concerning the health of animals —**veterinary surgeon** one qualified to treat animal ailments

ve'to n. power of rejecting piece of legislation, or preventing it from coming into effect; any prohibition (pl. **-toes**) —vt. enforce veto against; forbid with authority

vex vt. annoy; distress —**vexa'tion** n. cause of irritation; state of distress —**vexa'tious** a. —**vexed** a. cross; annoyed; much discussed

vg very good

VHF very high frequency

vi'a adv. by way of

vi'able a. practicable; able to live and grow independently —**viabil'ity** n.

vi'aduct n. bridge over valley for a road or railway

vi'al n. same as PHIAL

vi'ands pl.n. food

vibes pl.n. inf. short for VIBRATIONS, VIBRAPHONE

vi'braphone n. musical instrument like xylophone, but with electronic resonators, that produces a gentle vibrato

vibrate' v. (cause to) move to and fro rapidly and continuously; give off (light or sound) by vibration —vi. oscillate; quiver —**vi'brant** a. throbbing; vibrating; appearing vigorous, lively —**vibra'tion** n. a vibrating —pl. inf.

instinctive feelings about a place, person etc. —**vibra'to** [-ah'tō] n. vibrating effect in music (pl. **-os**) —**vibra'tor** n. —**vi'bratory** a.

vibur'num n. subtropical shrub with white flowers and berrylike fruits

vic'ar n. clergyman in charge of parish —**vic'arage** n. vicar's house —**vica'rial** a. of vicar

vica'rious a. obtained, enjoyed or undergone through sympathetic experience of another's experiences; suffered, done etc. as substitute for another —**vica'riously** adv. —**vica'riousness** n.

vice[1] n. evil or immoral habit or practice; criminal immorality esp. prostitution; fault, imperfection

vice[2] n. appliance with screw jaw for holding things while working on them

vice- (comb. form) in place of, second to, as in vice-chairman, viceroy etc. These are not given here where meaning may be inferred from simple word

vice'roy [vīs'-] n. ruler acting for king in province or dependency (**vicereine'** [-rān'] n. fem.) —**vicere'gal** a. of viceroy —**vice'royalty** n.

vi'ce ver'sa [-si-] Lat. conversely, the other way round

vicin'ity n. neighbourhood

vi'cious [vish'əs] a. wicked, cruel; ferocious, dangerous; leading to vice —**vi'ciously** adv.

viciss'itude n. change of fortune —pl. ups and downs of fortune —**vicissitu'dinous** a.

vic'tim n. person or thing killed, injured etc. as result of another's deed, or accident, circumstances etc.; person cheated; sacrifice —**victimiza'tion** n. —**vic'timize** vt. punish unfairly; make victim of

vic'tor n. conqueror; winner —**victo'rious** a. winning; triumphant —**vic'tory** n. winning of battle etc.

vict'ual [vit'l] n. (usu. in pl.) food —v. supply with or obtain food (**-ll-**) —**vict'ualler** n.

vicu'na n. S Amer. animal like llama; fine, light cloth made from its wool

vi'de Lat. see —**vide infra** see below —**vide supra** see above

vide'licet [-li-set] Lat. namely

vid'eo a. relating to or used in transmission or production of television image —n. apparatus for recording television programmes —**video cassette** cassette containing video tape —**video cassette recorder** tape recorder for vision and sound signals, used for recording and playing back TV programmes and films on cassette (also **video**) —**video game** any of various games played on video screen using electronic control —**video nasty** film, usu. made for video, that is explicitly horrific and pornographic —**video tape** magnetic tape on which to record television programme —**video tape recorder** tape recorder for vision signals using open spools for TV broadcast —**vid'eotext** n. means of providing written or graphical representation of computerized information on TV screen

vie [vī] vi. (with with or for) contend, compete against or for someone, something (**vied**, **vy'ing**)

view [vyōō] n. survey by eyes or mind; range of vision; picture; scene; opinion; purpose —vt. look at; survey; consider —**view'er** n. one who views; one who watches television; optical device to assist viewing of photographic slides

—**view'finder** n. device on camera enabling user to see what will be included in photograph
—**view'point** n. way of regarding a subject; position commanding view of landscape

view'data n. service in which consumer is linked to a computer by telephone and can select information required

vig'il [vij'-] n. a keeping awake, watch; eve of feast day —**vig'ilance** n. —**vig'ilant** a. watchful, alert

vigilan'te [vij-] n. one (esp. as member of group) who unofficially takes it upon himself to enforce law

vignette' [vin-yet'] n. short literary essay, sketch; photograph or portrait with the background shaded off

vig'our [-ər] n. force, strength; energy, activity —**vig'orous** a. strong; energetic; flourishing —**vig'orously** adv.

Vi'king n. medieval Scandinavian seafarer, raider, settler

vile a. very wicked, shameful; disgusting; despicable —**vile'ly** adv. —**vile'ness** n. —**vilifica'tion** n. —**vil'ify** vt. speak ill of; slander (-**ified, -ifying**)

vill'a n. large, luxurious, country house; detached or semidetached suburban home

vill'age n. small group of houses in country area —**vill'ager** n.

vill'ain [-ən] n. wicked person; inf. mischievous person —**vill'ainous** a. wicked; vile —**vill'ainy** n.

vim n. inf. force, energy

vinaigrette' n. small bottle of smelling salts; type of salad dressing

vin'dicate vt. clear of charges; justify; establish the truth or merit of —**vindica'tion** n. —**vin-**

dicator n. —**vin'dicatory** a.

vindic'tive a. revengeful; inspired by resentment

vine n. climbing plant bearing grapes —**vine'yard** [vin'-] n. plantation of vines —**vin'tage** n. gathering of the grapes; the yield; wine of particular year; time of origin —a. best and most typical —**vint'ner** n. dealer in wine

vin'egar n. acid liquid obtained from wine and other alcoholic liquors —**vin'egary** a. like vinegar; sour; bad-tempered

vi'nyl n. plastic material with variety of domestic and industrial uses

vi'ol n. early stringed instrument preceding violin

vio'la[1] n. see VIOLIN

vio'la[2] n. single-coloured variety of pansy

vi'olate vt. break (law, agreement etc.), infringe; rape; outrage, desecrate —**vi'olable** a. —**viola'tion** n. —**vi'olator** n.

vi'olent a. marked by, due to, extreme force, passion or fierceness; of great force; intense —**vi'olence** n. —**vi'olently** adv.

vi'olet n. plant with small bluish-purple or white flowers; the flower; bluish-purple colour —a. of this colour

violin' n. small four-stringed musical instrument —**vio'la** n. large violin with lower range —**violin'ist** n. —**violoncell'o** n. see CELLO

VIP very important person

vi'per n. venomous snake

virag'o [-rahg'-] n. abusive woman (pl. -**go(e)s**)

vir'gin n. one who has not had sexual intercourse —a. without experience of sexual intercourse; unsullied, fresh; (of land) untilled —**vir'ginal** a. of, like virgin —n. type of spinet —**virgin'ity** n.

Virgin'ia creep'er climbing

plant that turns red in autumn

Vir'go n. (the virgin) 6th sign of the zodiac operative c. Aug. 22–Sept. 21

vir'ile [vi'rīl] a. (of male) capable of copulation or procreation; strong, forceful —**viril'ity** n.

virol'ogy *see* VIRUS

vir'tual a. so in effect, though not in appearance or name —**vir'tually** adv. practically, almost

vir'tue n. moral goodness; good quality; merit; inherent power —**vir'tuous** a. morally good; chaste —**vir'tuously** adv.

virtuo'so [-zō] n. one with special skill, esp. in a fine art (pl. **-sos, -si** [-sē]) —**virtuos'ity** n. great technical skill, esp. in a fine art as music

vir'ulent a. very infectious, poisonous etc.; malicious

vi'rus n. various submicroscopic organisms, some causing disease —**virol'ogy** n. study of viruses

Vis. Viscount

vi'sa [vē'zə] n. endorsement on passport permitting the bearer to travel into country of issuing government —**vi'saed** [-zəd] a.

vis'age [viz'ij] n. face

vis-à-vis [vēz-ah-vē'] Fr. in relation to, regarding; opposite to

vis'cera [vis'-] pl.n. large internal organs of body, esp. of abdomen —**vis'ceral** a.

vis'cid [vis'-] a. sticky, of a consistency like treacle —**viscid'ity** n.

vis'cose n. (substance used to produce) synthetic fabric

vis'count [vī'-] n. Brit. nobleman ranking below earl and above baron (**vis'countess** fem.)

vis'cous a. thick and sticky —**viscos'ity** n.

vis'ible [viz'-] a. that can be seen —**visibil'ity** n. degree of clarity of atmosphere, esp. for navigation —**vis'ibly** adv.

vis'ion [vizh'ən] n. sight; insight; dream; phantom; imagination —**vi'sionary** a. marked by vision; impractical —n. mystic; impractical person

vis'it [viz'-] v. go, come and see, stay temporarily with (someone) —n. stay; call at person's home etc.; official call —**visita'tion** n. formal visit or inspection; affliction or plague —**vis'itor** n.

vi'sor, vi'zor [-z-] n. front part of helmet made to move up and down before the face; eyeshade, on car; peak on cap

vis'ta n. view, esp. distant view

vis'ual [viz'-] a. of sight; visible —**visualiza'tion** n. —**vis'ualize** vt. form mental image of

vi'tal a. necessary to, affecting life; lively, animated; essential; highly important —**vi'tals** pl.n. vital organs of body —**vital'ity** n. life, vigour —**vi'talize** vt. give life to; lend vigour to —**vi'tally** adv.

vit'amin n. any of group of substances occurring in foodstuffs and essential to health

vi'tiate [vish'-] vt. spoil; deprive of efficacy; invalidate —**vitia'tion** n.

vit'reous a. of glass; glassy —**vitrifica'tion** n. —**vit'rify** v. convert into glass, or glassy substance (**-ified, -ifying**)

vit'riol n. sulphuric acid; caustic speech —**vitriol'ic** a.

vitu'perate [vi-tyōō'-] vt. abuse in words, revile —**vitupera'tion** n. —**vitu'perative** a.

viva'cious a. lively, gay, sprightly —**vivac'ity** [-as'-] n.

vi'va vo'ce [-chi] Lat. adv. by word of mouth —n. oral examination (oft. **vi'va**)

viv'id a. bright, intense; clear; lively, animated; graphic —**viv'idly** adv. —**viv'idness** n.

viv'ify vt. animate, inspire (-ified, -ifying)

vivip'arous a. bringing forth young alive

vivisec'tion n. dissection of, or operating on, living animals —**vivisec'tionist** n. —**viv'isector** n.

vix'en n. female fox; spiteful woman —**vix'enish** a.

viz. short for VIDELICET

vizier' n. high official in some Muslim countries

vi'zor see VISOR

vlei [flā] n. **SA** low, marshy ground

vocab'ulary n. list of words, usu. in alphabetical order; stock of words used in particular language etc.

vo'cal a. of, with, or giving out voice; outspoken, articulate —n. piece of popular music that is sung —**vo'calist** n. singer —**vo'calize** vt. utter with voice —**vo'cally** adv.

vocal'ic a. of vowel(s)

voca'tion n. (urge, inclination, predisposition to) particular career, profession etc. —**voca'tional** a.

voc'ative n. in some languages, case of nouns used in addressing a person

vocif'erate v. exclaim, cry out —**vocifera'tion** n. —**vocif'erous** a. shouting, noisy

vod'ka n. Russian spirit distilled from grain, potatoes etc.

vogue [vōg] n. fashion, style; popularity

voice n. sound given out by person in speaking, singing etc.; quality of the sound; expressed opinion; (right to) share in discussion; verbal forms proper to relation of subject and action —vt. give utterance to, express —**voice'less** a.

void a. empty; destitute; not le-

gally binding —n. empty space —vt. make ineffectual or invalid; empty out

voile n. light semitransparent fabric

vol. volume

vol'atile a. evaporating quickly; lively; fickle, changeable —**volatil'ity** n. —**volatiliza'tion** n. —**vol'atilize** v. (cause to) evaporate

vol-au-vent' [-ö-voh'] n. small, light pastry case with savoury filling

volca'no n. hole in earth's crust through which lava, ashes, smoke etc. are discharged; mountain so formed (pl. -no(e)s) —**volcan'ic** a. —**volcanol'ogy** n. study of volcanoes and volcanic phenomena

vole n. small rodent

voli'tion [-ish'-] n. act, power of willing; exercise of the will —**voli'tional, voli'tionary** a.

voll'ey n. simultaneous discharge of weapons or missiles; rush of oaths, questions etc.; Sports kick, stroke etc. at moving ball before it touches ground —v. discharge; utter; fly, strike etc. in volley —**voll'eyball** n. team game where large ball is hit by hand over high net

volt [-ō-] n. unit of electric potential —**volt'age** n. electric potential difference expressed in volts —**volt'meter** n.

volte-face' [-fahs'] Fr. n. complete reversal of opinion or direction

vol'uble a. talking easily, readily and at length —**volubil'ity** n. —**vol'ubly** adv.

vol'ume n. space occupied; bulk, mass; amount; power, fullness of voice or sound; control on radio etc. for adjusting this; book; part of book bound in one cover —**volumet'ric** a. pert. to measurement by volume —**volu'minous** a. bulky, copious

vol'untary a. having, done by free will; done without payment; supported by freewill contributions; spontaneous —n. organ solo in church service —**vol'untarily** adv. —**volunteer'** n. one who offers service, joins force etc. of his own free will —v. offer oneself or one's services

volup'tuous a. of, contributing to pleasures of the senses —**volup'tuary** n. one given to luxury and sensual pleasures

vol'ute [or -lōōt'] n. spiral or twisting turn, form or object

vom'it v. eject (contents of stomach) through mouth —n. matter vomited

voo'doo n. practice of black magic, esp. in W Indies, witchcraft —vt. affect by voodoo

voor'kamer [foor'kah-mə] n. SA front room of a house

voor'laaier [foor'lī-yə] n. SA muzzle-loading gun

voor'skot [foor's-] n. SA advance payment made to farmers' cooperative for a crop or wool clip

vora'cious a. greedy, ravenous —**vora'ciously** adv. —**vora'city** [-as'-] n.

vor'tex n. whirlpool; whirling motion (pl. **vor'tices** [-ti-sēz])

vo'tary n. one vowed to service or pursuit (**vo'taress** fem.) —**vo'tive** a. given, consecrated by vow

vote n. formal expression of choice; individual pronouncement; right to give it, in question or election; result of voting; that which is given or allowed by vote —v. express, declare opinion, choice, preference etc. by vote; authorize, enact etc. by vote —**vo'ter** n.

vouch vi. (usu. with for) guarantee, make oneself responsible for

—**vouch'er** n. document proving correctness of item in accounts, or to establish facts; ticket as substitute for cash —**vouchsafe'** vt. condescend to grant or do something

vow n. solemn promise, esp. religious one —vt. promise, threaten by vow

vow'el n. any speech sound pronounced without stoppage or friction of the breath; letter standing for such sound, as a, e, i, o, u

vox pop interviews with public on radio or TV programme

voy'age n. journey, esp. long one, by sea or air —vi. make voyage —**voy'ager** n.

voyeur' n. one obtaining sexual pleasure by watching sexual activities of others

vs. versus

VSO Voluntary Service Overseas

VSOP very superior old pale

VTR video tape recorder

vul'canize vt. treat (rubber) with sulphur at high temperature to increase its durability —**vul'canite** n. rubber so hardened —**vulcaniza'tion** n. —**vulcanol'ogy** see VOLCANOLOGY

vul'gar a. offending against good taste; coarse; common —**vulga'rian** n. vulgar (rich) person —**vul'garism** n. coarse, obscene word, phrase —**vulgar'ity** n. —**vulgariza'tion** n. —**vul'garize** vt. make vulgar or too common —**vul'garly** adv. —**vulgar fraction** simple fraction

Vul'gate n. fourth century Latin version of the Bible

vul'nerable a. capable of being physically or emotionally wounded or hurt; exposed, open to attack, persuasion etc. —**vulnerabil'ity** n.

vul'pine a. of foxes; foxy

vul'ture n. large bird which

feeds on carrion —**vul'turine,**
vul'turous *a.* of vulture; rapacious

vul'va *n.* external genitals of human female

v.v. vice versa

vy'ing *pr.p. of* VIE

W

W *Chem.* tungsten; watt; Wednesday; west(ern)

w. week; weight; width

WA West Africa; Western Australia

wad [wod] *n.* small pad of fibrous material; thick roll of banknotes; sum of money —*vt.* line, pad, stuff *etc.* with wad (**-dd-**) —**wad'ding** *n.* stuffing

wad'dle [wod'l] *vi.* walk like duck —*n.* this gait

wade *vi.* walk through something that hampers movement, *esp.* water; proceed with difficulty —**wa'der** *n.* person or bird that wades —*pl.* angler's high waterproof boots

wad'y, wad'i [wod'i] *n.* in the East, watercourse which is dry, except in wet season

wa'fer *n.* thin, crisp biscuit; thin slice of anything; thin disc of unleavened bread used in the Eucharist

waf'fle[1] [wof'l] *n.* kind of pancake

waf'fle[2] [wof'l] *vi. inf.* speak, write in vague wordy manner —*n. inf.* vague speech *etc.*; nonsense

waft [-ah-] *vt.* convey smoothly through air or water —*n.* breath of wind; odour, whiff

wag *v.* (cause to) move rapidly from side to side (**-gg-**) —*n.* instance of wagging; *inf.* humor-

ous, witty person —**wag'gish** *a.*
—**wag'tail** *n.* small bird with wagging tail

wage *n.* payment for work done (*oft. in pl.*) —*vt.* carry on

wa'ger *n./vt.* bet

wag'gle *vt.* wag —**wag'gly** *a.*

wag(g)'on *n.* four-wheeled vehicle for heavy loads; railway freight truck —**wag(g)'oner** *n.*

waif *n.* homeless person, *esp.* child

wail *v.* cry out, lament —*n.* mournful cry

wain *n. Poet.* wagon

wains'cot *n.* wooden lining of walls of room —*vt.* line thus (**-tt-**)

waist *n.* part of body between hips and ribs; various narrow central parts —**waist'coat** *n.* sleeveless garment worn under jacket or coat —**waist'line** *n.* line, size of waist (of person, garment)

wait *v.* stay in one place, remain inactive in expectation (of something); be prepared (for something); delay —*vi.* serve in restaurant *etc.* —*n.* act or period of waiting —*pl.* street musicians, carol singers —**wait'er** *n.* attendant on guests at hotel, restaurant *etc.* (**wait'ress** *fem.*); one who waits

waive *vt.* forgo; not to insist on —**wai'ver** *n.* (written statement of) this act

wake[1] *v.* rouse from sleep; stir up (**woke, wo'ken, wa'king**) —*n.* vigil; watch beside corpse; (*oft. pl.*) annual holiday in parts of N England —**wa'ken** *v.* wake —**wake'ful** *a.*

wake[2] *n.* track or path left by anything that has passed, as track of turbulent water behind ship

walk [wawk] *v.* (cause, assist to) move, travel on foot at ordinary pace —*vt.* cross, pass through by walking; escort, conduct by walking —n. act, instance of walking; path or other place or route for walking; manner of walking; occupation, career —**walk'er** n. —**walk'about** n. informal walk among crowd by royalty etc. —**walkie-talkie** n. portable radio set containing both transmission and receiver units —**walking stick** stick, cane carried while walking —**walk'out** n. strike; act of leaving as a protest —**walk'over** n. unopposed or easy victory

Walk'man R small portable cassette recorder with light headphones, personal stereo

wall [wawl] n. structure of brick, stone etc. serving as fence, side of building etc.; surface of one; anything resembling this —vt. enclose with wall; block up with wall —**wall'flower** n. garden flower, often growing on walls; at dance, woman who remains seated for lack of partner —**wall'paper** n. paper, usu. patterned, to cover interior walls

wall'aby [wol'-] n. Aust. marsupial similar to and smaller than kangaroo

wall'et [wol'-] n. small folding case, esp. for paper money, documents etc.

wall'eyed [wawl'-] a. squinting; having eyes with pale irises

wall'op [wol'-] inf. vt. beat soundly; strike hard —n. stroke or blow —**wall'oper** n. inf. one who wallops —**wall'oping** inf. n. thrashing —a./adv. very, greatly)

wall'ow [wol'ō] vi. roll (in liquid or mud); revel (in) —n.

wal'nut [wawl'-] n. large nut with crinkled shell splitting easily into two halves; the tree; its wood

wal'rus [wawl'-] n. large sea mammal with long tusks

waltz [wawls] n. ballroom dance; music for it —v.

wam'pum [wom'-] n. beads made of shells, formerly used by N Amer. Indians as money and for ornament

wan [won] a. pale, sickly complexioned, pallid

wand [wond] n. stick, usu. straight and slender, esp. as carried by magician etc.

wand'er [won'-] v. roam, ramble —vi. go astray, deviate —n. —**wand'erer** n. —**wand'erlust** n. irrepressible urge to wander or travel

wane vi./n. decline; (of moon) decrease in size

wan'gle [-ng'gl] inf. vt. manipulate, manage in skilful way —n. intrigue, trickery, something obtained by craft

want [wont] n. desire; lack —n. desire; need; deficiency —**want'ed** a. being sought, esp. by the police —**wan'ting** a. lacking; below standard

want'on [won'-] a. dissolute; without motive, thoughtless; unrestrained —n. wanton person

wap'iti [wop'-] n. large N Amer. deer

war [wawr] n. fighting between nations; state of hostility; conflict, contest —vi. make war (-rr-) —**war'like** a. of, for war; fond of war —**warr'ior** [wor'i-] n. fighter —**war cry** cry used by attacking troops in war; distinctive word, phrase used by political party etc. —**war'fare** n. hostilities —**war'head** n. part of missile etc. containing explosives —**war'monger** n. one fostering, encouraging war —**war'ship** n. vessel armed, armoured for naval warfare

War. Warwickshire

war'ble vi. sing with trills

—**war'bler** n. person or bird that warbles; any of various kinds of small songbirds

ward [-aw-] n. division of city, hospital etc.; minor under care of guardian; guardianship; bar in lock, groove in key that prevents incorrectly cut key opening lock —**ward'er** n. jailer (**ward'ress** fem.) —**ward'ship** n. office of guardian; state of being under guardian —**ward'room** n. senior officers' mess on warship —**ward off** avert, repel

ward'en [-aw-] n. person, officer in charge of building, institution, college etc. —**ward'enship** n.

ward'robe [-aw-] n. piece of furniture for hanging clothes in; person's supply of clothes; costumes of theatrical company

ware n. goods; articles collectively —pl. goods for sale; commodities; merchandise —**ware'-house** n. storehouse for goods prior to distribution and sale

war'lock [-aw-] n. wizard, sorcerer

warm [-aw-] a. moderately hot; serving to maintain heat; affectionate; ardent; earnest; hearty; (of colour) having yellow or red for a basis —v. make, become warm —**warm'ly** adv. —**warmth** n. mild heat; cordiality; vehemence, anger

warn [-aw-] vt. put on guard; caution, admonish; give advance information to; notify authoritatively —**warn'ing** n. hint of harm etc.; admonition; advance notice of

warp [-aw-] v. (cause to) twist (out of shape); pervert or be perverted —n. state, condition of being warped; lengthwise threads on loom

warr'ant [wo'rənt] n. authority; document giving authority —vt. guarantee; authorize, justify

—**warrantee'** n. person given warranty —**warr'antor** n. person, company giving warranty —**warr'anty** n. guarantee of quality of goods; security —**warrant officer** officer in certain armed services holding rank between commissioned and noncommissioned officer

warr'en [wo'rən] n. (burrows inhabited by) colony of rabbits

warr'ior n. see WAR

wart [-aw-] n. small hard growth on skin —**wart hog** kind of Afr. wild pig

wa'ry a. watchful, cautious, alert —**wa'rily** adv.

was pt. first and third person sing. of BE

wash [wosh] v. clean (oneself, clothes etc.) esp. with water, soap etc. —vi. be washable; inf. be able to be proved true —vt. move, be moved by water; flow, sweep over, against —n. act of washing; clothes washed at one time; sweep of water, esp. set up by moving ship; thin coat of colour —**wash'able** a. capable of being washed without damage etc. —**wash'er** n. one who, that which, washes; ring put under a nut —**wash'ing** n. clothes to be washed —**wash'y** a. dilute; watery; insipid —**wash'out** n. inf. complete failure

wasp [wosp] n. striped stinging insect resembling bee —**wasp'-ish** a. irritable, snappish —**wasp waist** very small waist

waste [wāst] vt. expend uselessly, use extravagantly; fail to take advantage of; lay desolate —vi. dwindle; pine away —n. act of wasting; what is wasted; desert —a. worthless, useless; desert; wasted —**wast'age** n. loss by use or decay; reduction in numbers, esp. of workforce —**waste'ful** a. extravagant —**waste'fully** adv.

—**wast'rel** n. wasteful person, idler

watch [woch] vt. observe closely; guard —vi. wait expectantly (for); be on watch —n. portable timepiece for wrist, pocket etc.; state of being on the lookout; guard; spell of duty —**watch'ful** a. —**watch'fully** adv. —**watch'maker** n. one skilled in making and repairing watches —**watch'man** n. man guarding building etc., esp. at night —**watch'word** n. password; rallying cry

wat'er [wawt'-] n. transparent, colourless, odourless, tasteless liquid, substance of rain, river etc.; body of water; river; lake; sea; tear; urine —vt. put water on or into; irrigate or provide with water —vi. salivate; (of eyes) fill with tears; take in or obtain water —**wat'ery** a. —**wat'erbuck** n. Afr. antelope —**water buffalo** oxlike Asian animal —**water closet** sanitary convenience flushed by water —**wat'ercolour** n. pigment mixed with water; painting in this —**wat'ercourse** n. stream —**wat'ercress** n. plant growing in clear ponds and streams —**wat'erfall** n. perpendicular descent of waters of river —**water lily** plant that floats on surface of fresh water —**wat'erlogged** a. saturated, filled with water —**wat'ermark** n. faint translucent design stamped on substance of sheet of paper —**wat'erproof** a. not letting water through —v. make waterproof —n. waterproof garment —**wat'ershed** n. line separating two river systems; divide —**water-skiing** n. sport of riding over water on ski towed by speedboat —**water sports** various sports, as swimming, windsurfing, that take place in or on water —**wat'ertight** a. so

fitted as to prevent water entering or escaping; with no loopholes or weak points

watt [wot] n. unit of electric power —**watt'age** n. electric power expressed in watts

wat'tle [wot'-] n. frame of woven branches etc. as fence; fleshy pendent lobe of neck of certain birds, eg turkey

wave v. move to and fro, as hand in greeting or farewell; signal by waving; give, take shape of waves (as hair etc.) —n. ridge and trough on water etc.; act, gesture of waving; vibration, as in radio waves, of electric and magnetic forces alternating in direction; prolonged spell of something; upsurge; wavelike shapes in the hair etc. —**wa'vy** a. —**wave'length** n. distance between same points of two successive sound waves

wa'ver vi. hesitate, be irresolute; be, become unsteady —**wa'verer** n.

wax[1] n. yellow, soft, pliable material made by bees; this or similar substance used for sealing, making candles etc.; waxy secretion of ear —vt. put wax on —**wax'y** a. like wax —**wax'bill** n. Afr. finchlike weaverbird —**wax'wing** n. small songbird —**wax'work** n. lifelike figure, esp. of famous person, reproduced in wax

wax[2] vi. grow, increase

way n. manner; method; means; track; direction; path; passage; course; route; progress; state or condition —**way'farer** n. traveller, esp. on foot —**waylay'** vt. lie in wait for and accost, attack (-**laid'**, -**lay'ing**) —**way'mark** n. symbol or signpost indicating footpath —**way'side** n. side or edge of a road —a. —**way'ward** a. capricious, perverse, wilful

—**way'wardly** adv. —**way'wardness** n.

WC water closet

we pron. first person plural pronoun

weak a. lacking strength; feeble; fragile; defenceless; easily influenced; faint —**weak'en** v. —**weak'ling** n. feeble creature —**weak'ly** a. weak; sickly —adv. —**weak'ness** n.

weal n. streak left on flesh by blow of stick or whip

weald n. obs. forested country

wealth [welth] n. riches; abundance —**wealth'iness** n. —**wealth'y** a.

wean vt. accustom to food other than mother's milk; win over, coax away from

weap'on [wep'n] n. implement to fight with; anything used to get the better of an opponent

wear [wãr] vt. have on the body; show; produce (hole etc.) by rubbing etc.; harass or weaken; inf. allow, tolerate —vi. last; become impaired by use; (of time) pass slowly (**wore, worn, wear'ing**) —n. act of wearing; things to wear; damage caused by use; ability to resist effects of constant use —**wear'er** n.

wear'y [wēr'i] a. tired, exhausted, jaded; tiring; tedious —v. make, become weary (**wear'ied, wear'ying**) —**wear'ily** adv. —**wea'riness** n. —**wear'isome** a. causing weariness

weas'el [wēz'-] n. small carnivorous mammal with long body and short legs

weath'er [weTH'-] n. day-to-day meteorological conditions, esp. temperature, cloudiness etc. of a place —a. towards the wind —vt. affect by weather; endure; resist; come safely through; sail to windward of —**weath'erboard** n. timber boards used as external cladding of house —**weath'ercock** n. revolving vane to show which way wind blows

weave vt. form into texture or fabric by interlacing, esp. on loom; fashion, construct; make one's way, esp. with side to side motion (**weaved** pt.) —vi. practise weaving (**wove, wo'ven, weav'ing**) —**weav'er** n.

web n. woven fabric; net spun by spider; membrane between toes of waterfowl, frogs etc. —**web'-bing** n. strong fabric woven in strips

we'ber [vā'-] n. SI unit of magnetic flux

wed vt. marry; unite closely (**-dd-**) —**wed'ding** n. act of marrying, nuptial ceremony —**wed'-lock** n. marriage

wedge n. piece of wood, metal etc., thick at one end, tapering to a thin edge —vt. fasten, split with wedge; stick by compression or crowding

Wedg'wood R kind of pottery with ornamental reliefs

Wednes'day [wenz'-] n. fourth day of the week

wee a. small; little

weed n. plant growing where undesired; inf. tobacco; inf. marijuana; inf. thin, sickly person, animal —vt. clear of weeds —**weed'y** a. full of weeds; inf. thin, weakly —**weed out** remove, eliminate what is unwanted

weeds pl.n. obs. (widow's) mourning clothes

week n. period of seven days, esp. one beginning on Sunday and ending on Saturday; hours, days of work in seven-day period —**week'ly** a./adv. happening, done, published etc. in a week —n. —**week'day** n. any day of week except Sunday and usu. Saturday —**weekend'** n. Saturday and Sunday, *esp.* considered as rest period

weep *v.* shed tears (for); grieve (**wept, weep'ing**) —**weep'y** *a.* —**weeping willow** willow with drooping branches

wee'vil *n.* small beetle harmful to grain *etc.*

weft *n.* cross threads in weaving, woof

weigh [wā] *vt.* find weight of; consider; raise (anchor) —*vi.* have weight; be burdensome —**weight** *n.* measure of the heaviness of an object; quality of heaviness; heavy mass; object of known mass for weighing; unit of measurement of weight; importance, influence —*vt.* add weight to —**weight'ily** *adv.* —**weight'y** *a.* heavy; onerous; important; momentous —**weigh'bridge** *n.* machine for weighing vehicles *etc.* by means of metal plate set into road —**weight'ing** *n.* additional allowance payable in particular circumstances

weir [wēr] *n.* river dam

weird [wērd] *a.* unearthly, uncanny; strange, bizarre

wel'come *a.* received gladly; freely permitted —*n.* kindly greeting —*vt.* greet with pleasure; receive gladly (**-comed, -coming**)

weld *vt.* unite metal by softening with heat; unite closely —*n.* welded joint —**weld'er** *n.* tradesman who welds; machine used in welding

wel'fare *n.* wellbeing —**welfare state** system in which the government takes responsibility for the social, economic *etc.* security of its citizens

well[1] *adv.* in good manner or degree; suitably; intimately; fully; favourably, kindly; to a considerable degree —*a.* in good health; suitable (**better** *comp.*, **best** *sup.*)

—*interj.* exclamation of surprise, interrogation *etc.* —**well'be'ing** *n.* state of being well, happy, or prosperous —**well-disposed** *a.* inclined to be friendly, kindly (towards) —**well-mannered** *a.* having good manners —**well-off** *a.* fairly rich —**well-read** *a.* having read much —**well-spoken** *a.* speaking fluently, graciously, aptly

well[2] *n.* hole sunk into the earth to reach water, gas, oil *etc.*; spring; any shaft like a well; space in a lawcourt where solicitors sit —*vi.* spring, gush

wellingto'nia *n.* the giant sequoia

well'ingtons *pl.n.* high waterproof boots

Welsh *a.* of Wales —*n.* language, people of Wales —**Welsh rabbit, rarebit** savoury dish of melted cheese on toast

welsh, welch *vi.* fail to pay debt or fulfil obligation —**welsh'er, welch'er** *n.*

welt *n.* raised, strengthened seam; weal —*vt.* provide with welt; thrash

wel'ter *vi.* roll or tumble —*n.* turmoil, disorder

wel'terweight *n. Boxing* weight between light and middle; boxer of this weight

wen *n.* cyst, *esp.* on scalp

wench *n. obs. now oft. facetious* young woman

wend *v.* go, travel

went *pt. of* GO

wept *pt./pp. of* WEEP

were imperfect indicative, plural and subjunctive sing. and pl. of BE

were'wolf [wēr'-] *n.* (in folklore) human being turned into wolf

west *n.* part of sky where sun sets; part of country *etc.* lying to this side; occident —*a.* that is toward or in this region —*adv.* to the west —**west'erly** *a.* —**west'ward** *a./adv.* —**west'wards** *adv.* towards the west —**west'ern** *a.* of, in the west *or* —*n.* film, story *etc.* about cowboys or frontiersmen in western U.S. —**go west** *inf.* disappear; die; be lost

wet *a.* having water or other liquid on a surface or being soaked in it; rainy; not yet dry (paint, ink *etc.*); *inf.* (of person) feeble, dull *etc.* (**wett'er** *comp.*, **wett'est** *sup.*) —*vt.* make wet (**wett'ed, wett'ing**) —*n.* moisture, rain —**wet blanket** *inf.* one depressing spirits of others —**wet'land** *n.* area of swamp or marsh —**wet nurse** woman suckling another's child —**wet suit** close-fitting rubber suit worn by divers *etc.*

weth'er [weTH'-] *n.* castrated ram

W. Glam. West Glamorgan

whack *vt.* strike with sharp resounding blow —*n.* such blow; *inf.* share; *inf.* attempt —**whacked** *a.* exhausted —**whack'ing** *a. inf.* big, enormous

whale *n.* large fish-shaped sea mammal —**wha'ler** *n.* man, ship employed in hunting whales —**whale'bone** *n.* horny elastic substance from projections of upper jaw of certain whales —**a whale of a** *inf.* very large, fine, example of something

wharf [-awrf] *n.* platform at harbour, on river *etc.* for loading and unloading ships —**wharf'age** *n.* accommodation or dues at wharf

what [wot] *pron.* which thing; that which; request for statement to be repeated —*a.* which; as much as; how great, surprising *etc.* —*interj.* exclamation of surprise, anger *etc.* —**whatev'er**

pron. anything which; of what kind it may be —**what'not** *n. inf.* person, thing whose name is unknown, forgotten *etc.*; small stand with shelves

wheat *n.* cereal plant with thick four-sided seed spikes of which bread is chiefly made —**wheat'en** *a.* —**wheat'ear** *n.* small songbird —**wheat germ** embryo of wheat kernel

whee'dle *v.* coax, cajole

wheel *n.* circular frame or disc (with spokes) revolving on axle; anything like a wheel in shape or function; act of turning; steering wheel —*v.* (cause to) turn as if on axis; (cause to) move on or as if on wheels; (cause to) change course, *esp.* in opposite direction —**wheel'barrow** *n.* barrow with one wheel —**wheel'base** *n.* distance between front and rear hubs of vehicle —**wheel'chair** *n.* chair mounted on large wheels, used by people who cannot walk —**wheel clamp** immobilizing device fixed to wheel of illegally parked car, driver has to pay for its removal —**wheel'house** *n.* deckhouse for steersman

wheeze *vi.* breathe with difficulty and whistling noise —*n.* this sound; *inf.* trick, idea, plan —**wheez'y** *a.*

whelk *n.* sea snail *esp.* edible variety

whelp *n.* (*oft.* jocular, disparaging) pup, cub —*v.* produce whelps

when *adv.* at what time —*conj.* at the time that; although; since —*pron.* at which (time) —**when-ev'er** *adv./conj.* at whatever time

whence *adv./conj. obs.* from what place or source; how

where *adv./conj.* at what place; at or to the place in which —**where'abouts** *adv./conj.* in what, which place —*n.* present position —**whereas'** *conj.* considering that; while, on the contrary —**whereby'** *conj.* by which —**where'fore** *adv. obs.* why —*conj.* consequently —**whereupon'** *conj.* at which point —**wherev'er** *adv.* at whatever place —**where'withal** *n.* necessary funds, resources *etc.*

wherr'y *n.* barge; light rowing boat

whet *vt.* sharpen; stimulate (-**tt**-) —**whet'stone** *n.* stone for sharpening tools

wheth'er [WETH-] *conj.* introduces the first of two alternatives, of which the second may be expressed or implied

whey [wA] *n.* watery part of milk left after separation of curd in cheese making

which *a.* used in requests for a selection from alternatives —*pron.* which person or thing; the thing "who" —**whichev'er** *pron.*

whiff *n.* brief smell or suggestion of; puff of air —*v.* smell

Whig *n.* member of British political party that preceded the Liberal Party

while *conj.* in the time that; in spite of the fact that, although; whereas —*vt.* pass (time, usu. idly) —*n.* period of time —**whilst** *conj.* while

whim *n.* sudden, passing fancy —**whim'sical** *a.* fanciful; full of whims —**whimsical'ity** *n.* —**whim'sy** *n.* whim; caprice —*a.*

whim'brel *n.* type of curlew

whim'per *vi.* cry or whine softly; complain in this way —*n.* such cry or complaint

whin *n.* gorse —**whin'chat** *n.* type of songbird

whine *n.* high-pitched plaintive cry; peevish complaint —*vi.* utter this

whinge *inf. vi.* whine, complain —*n.*

whinn'y *vi.* neigh softly (**whin'nied, whinn'ying**) —*n.*

whip *vt.* strike with whip; thrash; beat (cream, eggs) to a froth; lash; *inf.* pull, remove, insert *etc.* quickly; *inf.* steal —*vi.* dart (-**pp**-) —*n.* lash attached to handle for urging or punishing; one who enforces attendance of political party; call made on members of Parliament to attend for important divisions; elastic quality permitting bending in mast, fishing rod *etc.*; whipped dessert —**whip'lash injury** injury to neck as result of sudden jerking of unsupported head —**whipping boy** scapegoat —**whip'round** *n. inf.* collection of money

whipp'et *n.* racing dog like small greyhound

whir *v.* (cause to) fly, spin *etc.* with buzzing or whizzing sound; bustle (-**rr**-) —*n.* this sound; bustle

whirl *v.* swing rapidly round; move rapidly in a circular course; drive at high speed —*n.* whirling movement; confusion, bustle, giddiness —**whirl'igig** *n.* spinning toy; merry-go-round —**whirl'pool** *n.* circular current, eddy —**whirl'wind** *n.* wind whirling round while moving forwards —*a.*

whisk *v.* brush, sweep, beat lightly; move, remove, quickly; beat to a froth —*n.* light brush; egg-beating implement

whisk'er *n.* any of the long stiff hairs at side of mouth of cat or other animal; any of hairs on a man's face —**by a whisker** *inf.* only just

whisk'y *n.* spirit distilled from fermented cereals (*Irish*, **C**, *US* **whiskey**)

whisp'er *v.* speak in soft,

hushed tones, without vibration of vocal cords; rustle —n. such speech; trace or suspicion; rustle

whist n. card game

whis'tle [-sl] vi. produce shrill sound by forcing breath through rounded, nearly closed lips; make such a sound —vt. utter, summon etc. by whistle —n. such sound; any similar sound; instrument to make it —**whis'tler** n. —**whistle-blower** n. inf. person who informs on or puts stop to something

whit n. jot, particle (usu. in **not a whit**)

white a. of the colour of snow; pale; light in colour; having a light-coloured skin —n. colour of snow; white pigment; white part; clear fluid round yolk of egg; (**W-**) white person —**whi'ten** v. —**white'ness** n. —**whi'tish** a. —**white ant** termite —**white'bait** n. small edible fish —**white-collar** a. denoting nonmanual salaried workers —**white el'ephant** useless, unwanted, gift or possession —**white flag** white banner or cloth used as signal of surrender or truce —**white hope** one expected to bring honour or glory to his group, team etc. —**white lie** minor, unimportant lie —**white paper** government report on matter recently investigated —**white slave** woman, child forced or enticed away for purposes of prostitution —**white'wash** n. substance for whitening walls etc. —vt. apply this; cover up, gloss over, suppress

whith'er [WITH'-] adv. obs. to what place; to which

whi'ting n. edible sea fish

whit'low [-lō] n. abscess on finger, esp. round nail

Whit'sun [wit'sən] n. week fol-

lowing **Whit Sunday**, seventh Sunday after Easter

whit'tle vt. cut, carve with knife; pare away —**whittle down** reduce gradually, wear (away)

whiz(z) n. loud hissing sound; inf. person skilful at something —v. move with such sound, or make it; inf. move quickly (-zz-)

WHO World Health Organization

who [hōō] pron. relative and interrogative pronoun, always referring to persons —**whodun'it** n. inf. detective story —**whoev'er** pron. who, any one or every one that

whole [hōl] a. complete; containing all elements or parts; entire; not defective or imperfect; healthy —n. complete thing or system —**who'lly** adv. —**whole-heart'ed** a. sincere; enthusiastic —**whole'meal** a. of, pert. to flour which contains the whole of the grain —**whole'sale** n. sale of goods by large quantities to retailers —a. dealing by wholesale; extensive —**whole'saler** n. —**whole'some** a. producing good effect, physically or morally —**on the whole** taking everything into consideration; in general

whom [hōōm] pron. objective case of WHO

whoop [wōōp] n. shout or cry expressing excitement etc.

whoo'pee n. inf. gay, riotous time —**make whoopee** participate in wild noisy party; go on spree

whooping cough [hōōp'-] n. infectious disease of mucous membrane lining air passages, marked by convulsive coughing with loud whoop or indrawing of breath

whopp'er inf. n. anything unusually large; monstrous lie —**whop'ping** a.

whore [h-] n. prostitute

whorl *n.* ring of leaves or petals; turn of spiral; anything forming part of circular pattern, *eg* lines of human fingerprint

whose [hōōz] *pron.* possessive case of WHO and WHICH

why *adv.* for what cause or reason

wick *n.* strip of thread feeding flame of lamp or candle with oil, grease *etc.*

wick'ed *a.* evil, sinful; very bad; mischievous —**wick'edly** *adv.* —**wick'edness** *n.*

wick'er(work) *n.* woven cane *etc.*, basketwork

wick'et *n.* small gate; *Cricket* set of three stumps and bails; cricket pitch

wide *a.* having a great extent from side to side, broad; having considerable distance between; spacious; liberal; vast; far from the mark; opened fully —*adv.* to the full extent; far from the intended target —*n.* Cricket ball bowled out of batsman's reach —**wi'den** *v.* —**wide'ly** *adv.* —**width, wide'ness** *n.* breadth —**wide'spread** *a.* extending over a wide area

wid'ow [-ō] *n.* woman whose husband is dead and who has not married again —*vt.* make a widow of —**wid'ower** *n.* man whose wife is dead and who has not married again —**wid'owhood** *n.*

wield *vt.* hold and use; brandish; manage

Wiener schnitzel [vē'nər] thin slice of veal, crumbed and fried

wife *n.* a man's partner in marriage, married woman (*pl.* wives) —**wife'ly** *a.*

wig *n.* artificial hair for the head —**wigged** *a.*

wig'gle *v.* (cause to) move jerkily from side to side —*n.* —**wig'gly** *a.*

wight [wīt] *n. obs.* person

wig'wam *n.* N Amer. Indian's hut or tent

wild [wīld] *a.* not tamed or domesticated; not cultivated; savage; stormy; uncontrolled; random; excited; rash; frantic; *inf.* (of party *etc.*) rowdy, exciting —**wild'ly** *adv.* —**wild'ness** *n.* —**wild'cat** *n.* any of various undomesticated European and Amer. feline animals; *inf.* wild, savage person —*a.* unsound, irresponsible; sudden, unofficial, unauthorized —**wild-goose chase** futile pursuit —**wild'life** *n.* wild animals and plants collectively

wil'debeest [-di-bēst] *n.* gnu

wil'derness *n.* desert, waste place; state of desolation or confusion

wild'fire *n.* raging, uncontrollable fire; anything spreading, moving fast

wile *n.* trick —**wi'ly** *a.* crafty, sly

wil'ful *a.* obstinate, self-willed; intentional —**wil'fully** *adv.* —**wil'fulness** *n.*

will *v. aux.* forms moods and tenses indicating intention or conditional result (**would** *pt.*) —*vi.* have a wish —*vt.* wish; intend; leave as legacy —*n.* faculty of deciding what one will do; purpose; volition; determination; wish; directions written for disposal of property after death —**will'ing** *a.* ready; given cheerfully —**will'ingly** *adv.* —**will'ingness** *n.* —**will'power** *n.* ability to control oneself, one's actions, impulses

will-o'-the-wisp *n.* brief pale flame or phosphorescence sometimes seen over marshes; elusive person or hope

will'ow [-ō] *n.* tree (*eg* weeping willow) with long thin flexible branches; its wood —**will'owy** *a.* lithe, slender, supple —**willow-**

herb n. tall plant with mauve flowers

wil'ly-nill'y adv./a. (occurring) whether desired or not

wilt v. (cause to) become limp, drooping or lose strength etc.

Wilts. Wiltshire

wimp n. inf. feeble, ineffective person

wim'ple n. garment worn by nun, around face

win vi. be successful, victorious —vt. get by labour or effort; reach; allure; be successful in; gain the support, consent etc. of (**won, winn'ing**) —n. victory, esp. in games —**winn'er** n. —**winn'ing** a. charming —**winn'ings** pl.n. sum won in game, betting etc.

wince vi. flinch, draw back, as from pain etc. —n. this act

winceyette' n. cotton fabric with raised nap

winch n. machine for hoisting or hauling using cable wound round drum —vt. move (something) by using a winch

wind¹ [wind] n. air in motion; breath; flatulence; idle talk; hint or suggestion; scent borne by air —vt. render short of breath, esp. by blow etc.; get the scent of —**wind'ward** n. side against which wind is blowing —**wind'y** a. exposed to wind; flatulent; sl. nervous, scared; inf. talking too much —**wind'fall** n. unexpected good luck; fallen fruit —**wind instrument** musical instrument played by blowing or air pressure —**wind'mill** n. wind-driven apparatus with fanlike sails for raising water, crushing grain etc. —**wind'pipe** n. passage from throat to lungs —**wind'screen** n. protective sheet of glass etc. in front of driver or pilot —**wind'sock** n. cone of material flown on mast at airfield to indicate wind direction —**wind'surfing** n. sport of sailing standing up on sailboard holding special boom to control sail

wind² [wind] vi. twine; meander —vt. twist round, coil; wrap; make ready for working by tightening spring (**wound** [wownd], **wind'ing**) —n. act of winding; single turn of something wound; a turn, curve

wind'lass n. winch, esp. simple one worked by a crank

win'dow [-ō] n. hole in wall (with glass) to admit light, air etc.; anything similar in appearance or function; area for display of goods behind glass of shop front —**window-dressing** n. arrangement of goods in a shop window; deceptive display

wine n. fermented juice of grape etc. —**wine box** wine sold in cubic, usu. 3-litre, carton with tap —**wine'press** n. apparatus for extracting juice from grape

wing n. feathered limb a bird uses in flying; one of organs of flight of insect or some animals; main lifting surface of aircraft; lateral extension; side portion of building projecting from main central portion; one of sides of a stage; flank corps of army on either side; part of car body that surrounds wheels; Sport (player on) either side of pitch; faction esp. of political party —pl. insignia worn by qualified aircraft pilot; sides of stage —vi. fly; move, go very fast —vt. disable, wound slightly —**winged** a. having wings —**wing'er** n. Sport player positioned on wing

wink v. close and open (an eye) rapidly, esp. to indicate friendliness or as signal; twinkle —n. act of winking

win'kle n. shellfish, periwinkle —**winkle out** extract, prise out

winn'ow [-ō] vt. blow free of chaff; sift, examine

win'some a. charming, winning

win'ter n. the coldest season —vi. pass, spend the winter —**win'try** a. of, like winter; cold —**winter sports** sports held in open air on snow or ice

wipe vt. rub so as to clean —n. wiping —**wi'per** n. one that wipes; automatic wiping apparatus (esp. **windscreen wiper**) —**wipe out** erase; annihilate; sl. kill

wire n. metal drawn into thin, flexible strand; something made of wire, eg fence; telegram —vt. provide, fasten with wire; send by telegraph —**wi'ring** n. system of wires —**wi'ry** a. like wire; lean and tough —**wire-haired** a. (of various breeds of dog) with short stiff hair

wire'less n. old-fashioned term for radio, radio set —a.

wise[1] [wīz] a. having intelligence and knowledge; sensible —**wis'dom** n. (accumulated) knowledge, learning; erudition —**wise'ly** adv. —**wise'acre** n. one who wishes to seem wise —**wisdom tooth** third molar usually cut about 20th year

wise[2] [wīz] n. obs. manner

wise'crack n. inf. flippant, (would-be) clever remark

wish vi. have a desire —vt. desire —n. desire; thing desired —**wish'ful** a. desirous; too optimistic —**wish'bone** n. V-shaped bone above breastbone of fowl

wisp n. light, delicate streak, as of smoke; twisted handful, usu. of straw etc.; stray lock of hair —**wisp'y** a.

wiste'ria n. climbing shrub with usu. mauve flowers

wist'ful a. longing, yearning; sadly pensive —**wist'fully** adv.

wit n. ingenuity in connecting amusingly incongruous ideas; person gifted with this power; sense; intellect; understanding; ingenuity; humour —**wit'icism** n. witty remark —**wit'tily** adv. —**wit'tingly** adv. on purpose; knowingly —**wit'less** a. foolish —**wit'ty** a.

witch[1] n. person, usu. female, believed to practise, practising, or professing to practise (black) magic, sorcery; ugly, wicked woman; fascinating woman —**witch'ery** n. —**witch'craft** n. —**witch doctor** in certain societies, man appearing to cure or cause injury, disease by magic

witch[2] see WYCH

with prep. in company or possession of; against; in relation to; through; by means of —**withal'** [-awl'] adv. also, likewise —**within'** prep./adv. in, inside —**without'** prep. lacking; obs. outside

withdraw' v. draw back or out (-drew', -drawn', -draw'ing) —**withdraw'al** n. —**withdrawn'** a. reserved, unsociable

with'er v. (cause to) wilt, dry up, decline —**with'ering** a. (of glance etc.) scornful

with'ers pl.n. ridge between a horse's shoulder blades

withhold' vt. restrain; keep back; refrain from giving (-held', -hold'ing) —**withhold'er** n.

withstand' vt. oppose, resist, esp. successfully (-stood', -stand'ing)

with'y [-ᴛʜi] n. willow tree; (also **withe**) its twig

wit'ness n. one who sees something; testimony; one who gives testimony —vi. give testimony —vt. see; attest; see and sign as having seen

wiz'ard n. sorcerer, magician; conjurer —**wiz'ardry** n.

wiz'ened a. shrivelled, wrinkled

woad n. blue dye from plant

wob'ble vi. move unsteadily; sway —n. an unsteady movement —**wob'bly** a.

wodge n. inf. thick lump, chunk

woe n. grief —**woe'begone** a. looking sorrowful —**woe'ful** a. sorrowful; pitiful; wretched —**woe'fully** adv.

wog n. sl. offens. foreigner, esp. one who is not white

wold [wōld] n. open downs, moorland

wolf [woolf] n. wild predatory doglike animal of northern countries; inf. man who habitually tries to seduce women (pl. **wolves**) —vt. eat ravenously —**wolf whistle** whistle by man expressing admiration for a woman —**cry wolf** raise false alarm

wolf'ram [-oo-] n. tungsten

wol'verine [woolvə-rēn] n. carnivorous mammal inhabiting Arctic regions

wom'an [woom-] n. adult human female; women collectively (pl. **wom'en** [wim'-]) —**wom'anhood** n. —**wom'anish** a. effeminate —**wom'anize** vi. inf. (of man) indulge in many casual affairs with women —**wom'ankind** n. —**wom'anly** a. of, proper to woman —**Women's Liberation** movement for removal of attitudes, practices that preserve social, economic etc. inequalities between women and men (also **women's lib**)

womb [woōm] n. female organ of conception and gestation, uterus

wom'bat n. Aust. burrowing marsupial with heavy body, short legs and dense fur

won [wun] pt./pp. of WIN

won'der [wun-] n. emotion excited by amazing or unusual thing; marvel, miracle —vi. be curious about; feel amazement —**won'derful** a. remarkable; very fine —**won'derfully** adv. —**won'derment** n. surprise —**won'drous** a. inspiring wonder, strange —**won'drously** adv.

wonk'y a. inf. shaky, unsteady; groggy; askew; unreliable

wont [-ō-] n. custom —a. accustomed —**wont'ed** a. habitual, established

woo vt. court, seek to marry —**woo'er** n. suitor

wood n. substance of trees, timber; firewood; tract of land with growing trees —**wood'ed** a. having (many) trees —**wood'en** a. made of wood; obstinate; without expression —**wood'y** a. —**wood'bine** n. honeysuckle —**wood'cock** n. game bird —**wood'chuck** n. Amer. burrowing marmot —**wood'cut** n. engraving on wood; impression from this —**wood'land** n. woods, forest —**wood'louse** n. small grey land crustacean with seven pairs of legs —**wood'pecker** n. bird which searches tree trunks for insects —**wood pigeon** large Eurasian pigeon —**wood'wind** a./n. (of) wind instruments of orchestra, orig. made of wood —**wood'worm** n. insect larva that bores into wood

woof [-ōō-] n. the threads that cross the warp in weaving

woof'er n. loudspeaker for reproducing low-frequency sounds

wool n. soft hair of sheep, goat etc.; yarn spun from this —**wool'len** a. —**wool'ly** a. of wool; vague, muddled —n. knitted woollen garment —**wool'gathering** a./n. daydreaming —**wool'sack** n. Lord Chancellor's seat in British House of Lords

wop n. sl. offens. S European

immigrant, *esp.* Italian

Worcs. Worcestershire

word [wurd] *n.* unit of speech or writing regarded by users of a language as the smallest separate meaningful unit; term; message; brief remark; information; promise; command —*vt.* express in words, *esp.* in particular way —**word'ily** *adv.* —**word'ing** *n.* choice and arrangement of words —**word'y** *a.* using more words than necessary, verbose —**word processor** keyboard, microprocessor and VDU for electronic organization and storage of written text

wore *pt.*, **worn** *pp. of* WEAR

work [wurk] *n.* labour; employment; occupation; task; toil; something made or accomplished; production of art or science; book; needlework —*pl.* factory; total of person's deeds, writings *etc.*; *inf.* everything, full or extreme treatment; mechanism of clock *etc.* —*vt.* cause to operate; make, shape —*vi.* apply effort; labour; operate; be engaged in trade, profession *etc.*; turn out successfully; ferment —**work'able** *a.* —**work'er** *n.* —**workahol'ic** *n.* person addicted to work —**work'house** *n.* Hist. institution offering food, lodgings for unpaid menial work —**working class** social class consisting of wage earners, *esp.* manual —**working-class** *a.* —**working party** advisory committee studying specific problem, question —**work'man** *n.* manual worker —**work'manship** *n.* skill of workman; way thing is finished; style —**work'shop** *n.* place where things are made —**work to rule** adhere strictly to all working regulations to reduce rate of work as form of protest

world [wurld] *n.* the universe; the planet earth; sphere of existence; mankind, people generally; society —**world'ly** *a.* earthly; mundane; absorbed in the pursuit of material gain, advantage; carnal —**world war** war involving many countries

worm [wurm] *n.* small limbless creeping snakelike creature; anything resembling worm in shape or movement; gear wheel with teeth forming part of screw threads; *inf.* weak, despised person —*pl.* (disorder caused by) infestation of worms, *esp.* in intestines —*vi.* crawl *vt.* work (oneself) in insidiously; extract (secret) craftily; rid of worms —**worm'cast** *n.* coil of earth excreted by earthworm —**worm-eaten** *a.* full of holes gnawed by worms; old, antiquated —**worm'y** *a.*

worm'wood [wurm'-] *n.* bitter herb; bitterness

worn *pp. of* WEAR

worr'y [wu'ri] *vi.* be (unduly) concerned —*vt.* trouble, pester, harass; (of dog) seize, shake with teeth (**worr'ied, worr'ying**) *n.* (cause of) anxiety, concern —**worr'ier** *n.*

worse [wurs] *a./adv. comp. of* BAD *or* BADLY —*n.* —**worst** *a./adv. sup. of* BAD *or* BADLY —*n.* —**wors'en** *v.* make, grow worse; impair; deteriorate

wor'ship [wur'-] *vt.* show religious devotion to; adore; love and admire (**-pp-**) —*n.* act of worshipping; title used to address mayor, magistrate *etc.* —**wor'shipful** *a.* —**wor'shipper** *n.*

wors'ted [woos'tid] *n.* woollen yarn —*a.* made of woollen yarn; spun from wool

wort [wurt] *n.* obs. plant, herb; infusion of malt before fermentation

worth [wurth] *a.* having or deserving to have value specified; meriting —n. excellence; merit, value; virtue; usefulness; price; quantity to be had for a given sum —**wor'thy** [-THi] a. virtuous; meriting —n. one of eminent worth; celebrity —**wor'thily** adv. —**wor'thiness** n. —**worth'less** a. useless —**worthwhile'** a. worth the time, effort etc. involved

would [wood] v. aux. expressing wish, intention, probability; pt. of WILL —**would-be** a. wishing, pretending to be

wound[1] [woond] n. injury, hurt from cut, stab etc. —vt. inflict wound on, injure; pain

wound[2] [wownd] pt./pp. of WIND[2]

wove pt., **wo'ven** pp. of WEAVE

wow interj. of astonishment —n. inf. object of astonishment, admiration etc.; variation, distortion in pitch in record player etc.

wpm words per minute

WRAC Women's Royal Army Corps

wrack [rak] n. seaweed

WRAF Women's Royal Air Force

wraith n. apparition of a person seen shortly before or after death; spectre

wran'gle [-ng'gl] vi. quarrel (noisily); dispute; **US, C** herd cattle —n. noisy quarrel; dispute —**wran'gler** n. **US, C** cowboy

wrap v. cover, esp. by putting something round; put round (-pp-) —**wrap, wrapp'er** n. loose garment; covering —**wrapp'ing** n. material used to wrap

wrasse [ras] n. type of sea fish

wrath [roth] n. anger —**wrath'ful** a. —**wrath'fully** adv.

wreak vt. inflict (vengeance); cause

wreath [rēth] n. something twisted into ring form, esp. band of flowers etc. as memorial or tribute on grave etc. —**wreathe** [rēTH] vt. form into wreath; surround; wind round

wreck n. destruction of ship; wrecked ship; ruin; something ruined —vt. cause the wreck of —**wreck'age** n. —**wreck'er** n. person or thing that destroys, ruins; one whose job is to demolish houses, dismantle old cars etc.

Wren n. member of Women's Royal Naval Service

wren n. kind of small songbird

wrench vt. twist; distort; seize forcibly; sprain —n. violent twist; tool for twisting or screwing; spanner; sudden pain caused esp. by parting

wrest vt. take by force; twist violently

wres'tle [-sl] vi. fight (esp. as sport) by grappling and trying to throw down; strive (with); struggle —n. —**wrest'ler** n. —**wres'tling** n.

wretch n. despicable person; miserable creature —**wretch'ed** a. miserable, unhappy; worthless —**wretch'edly** adv. —**wretch'edness** n.

wrig'gle v. move with twisting action, as worm; squirm —n. this action

wright [rīt] n. obs. workman, maker, builder

wring vt. twist; extort; pain; squeeze out (**wrung, wring'ing**)

wrin'kle [-ng'kl] n. slight ridge or furrow on surface; crease in the skin; fold; pucker; inf. (useful) trick, hint —v. make, become wrinkled, pucker

wrist n. joint between hand and arm —**wrist'let** n. band worn on wrist

writ n. written command from law court or other authority

write vt. mark paper etc. with the symbols which are used to represent words or sounds; compose; send a letter —*vt.* set down in words; compose; communicate in writing (**wrote, writt'en, wri'ting**) —**wri'ter** *n.* one who writes; author —**write-off** *n. inf.* something damaged beyond repair —**write-up** *n.* written (published) account of something

writhe [rīTH] *v.* twist, squirm in or as in pain *etc.* —*vi.* be acutely embarrassed *etc.* (**writhed** *pt.*, **writhed,** *Poet.* **writh'en** *pp.*, **wri'thing** *pr.p.*)

WRNS Women's Royal Naval Service

wrong *a.* not right or good; not suitable; wicked; incorrect; mistaken; not functioning properly —*n.* that which is wrong; harm; evil —*vt.* do wrong to; think badly of without justification —**wrong'doer** *n.* one who acts immorally or illegally —**wrong'ful** *a.* —**wrong'fully** *adv.* —**wrong'ly** *adv.*

wrote *pt.* of WRITE

wrought [rawt] *pt./pp.* of WORK —*a.* (of metals) shaped by hammering or beating —**wrought iron** pure form of iron used *esp.* in decorative railings *etc.*

wrung *pt./pp.* of WRING

WRVS Women's Royal Voluntary Service

wry *a.* turned to one side, contorted, askew; sardonic, dryly humorous —**wry'neck** *n.* type of woodpecker

wt. weight

WWI World War One

WWII World War Two

wych- (*comb. form*) (of tree) with pliant branches, as **wych'elm**

wynd [-ī-] *n.* in Scotland, narrow lane, alley

X

X Christ; Christian; Cross; Roman numeral, 10; mark indicating something wrong, a choice, a kiss, signature *etc.* —*n.* unknown, mysterious person, factor

x Maths. unknown quantity

Xe *Chem.* xenon

xenog'amy *n.* pollination from another plant; cross-fertilization —**xenog'amous** *a.*

xen'on *n.* colourless, odourless gas occurring in very small quantities in air

xenopho'bia *n.* dislike, hatred, fear, of strangers or aliens

xerog'raphy *n.* photocopying process —**Xe'rox R** xerographic copying process, machine

X'mas [eks'mɔs] *n. short for* CHRISTMAS

x-rays *pl.n.* radiation of very short wavelengths, capable of penetrating solid bodies, and printing on photographic plate shadow picture of objects not permeable by rays —**x-ray** *v.* photograph by x-rays

xy'locarp *n.* hard, woody fruit —**xylocarp'ous** *a.* having fruit that becomes hard or woody

xy'lograph *n.* wood engraving; impression from wood block

xy'loid *a.* pert. to wood; woody, ligneous

xy'lophone *n.* musical instrument of wooden bars which sound when struck

Y

yacht [yot] *n.* vessel propelled by sail or power, used for racing, pleasure *etc.* —**yachts'man** *n.*

yahoo¹ *n.* crude, coarse person

Yah'weh [yah'wā] *n.* God

yak *n.* shaggy-haired, long-horned ox of Central Asia

yam *n.* large edible tuber, sweet potato

yank *v.* jerk, tug; pull quickly —*n.* quick tug

Yank, Yank'ee *a./n. sl.* American

yap *vi.* bark (as small dog); talk idly; gossip (-**pp**-) —*n.*

yard¹ *n.* unit of length, .915 metre; spar slung across ship's mast to extend sails —**yard'stick** *n.* formula or standard of measurement or comparison

yard² *n.* piece of enclosed ground, oft. attached to or adjoining building and used for some specific purpose, as garden, storage, holding livestock *etc.* —**yard'age** *n.* use of yard; charge made for this

yarn *n.* spun thread; tale —*vi.* tell a tale

yarr'ow *n.* plant with flat white flower clusters

yash'mak *n.* face veil worn by Muslim women

yaw *vi.* of aircraft *etc.*, turn about vertical axis; deviate temporarily from course

yawl *n.* two-masted sailing vessel

yawn *vi.* open mouth wide, esp. in sleepiness; gape —*n.* a yawning

yaws *pl.n.* contagious tropical skin disease

yd. yard

ye [yē] *pron. obs.* you

yea [yā] *interj. obs.* yes

year *n.* time taken by one revolution of earth round sun, about 365 days; twelve months —**year'ling** *n.* animal one year old —**year'ly** *adv.* every year, once a year —*a.* happening *etc.* once a year

yearn [yern] *vi.* feel longing, desire; be filled with pity, tenderness —**yearn'ing** *n.*

yeast *n.* substance used as fermenting agent, esp. in raising bread —**yeast'y** *a.* of, like yeast; frothy, fermenting

yell *v.* cry out in loud shrill tone; *inf.* call —*n.* loud shrill cry; *inf.* call

yell'ow [-ō] *a.* of the colour of lemons, gold *etc.*; *inf.* cowardly —*n.* this colour —**yellow fever** acute infectious disease of (sub)-tropical climates —**yell'ow-hammer** *n.* small European bunting —**yell'owwood** *n.* **SA** type of conifer; its rich yellow wood used esp. for furniture and building

yelp *vi./n.* (produce) quick, shrill cry

yen¹ *n.* Japanese monetary unit

yen² *n. inf.* longing, craving

yeo'man [yō'-] *n. Hist.* farmer cultivating his own land; assistant, subordinate

yes *interj.* affirms or consents, gives an affirmative answer —**yes man** weak person willing to agree to anything

yes'terday *n.* day before today; recent time —*adv.*

yet *adv.* now, still, besides, hitherto; nevertheless —*conj.* but, at the same time, nevertheless

yet'i *n. see* ABOMINABLE SNOWMAN

yew *n.* evergreen tree with dark leaves; its wood

Yidd'ish *a./n.* (of, in) dialect of mixed German and Hebrew used by many Jews in Europe

yield *vt.* give or return as food; produce; provide; concede; give up, surrender —*vi.* produce; submit; comply; surrender, give way —*n.* amount produced, return, profit, result

YMCA Young Men's Christian Association

yob, yobb'o n. sl. aggressive, surly youth (pl. **-s**)

yo'del, yo'dle vi. warble in falsetto tone (**-ll-**) —n. falsetto warbling as practised by Swiss mountaineers

yo'ga n. Hindu philosophical system aiming at spiritual, mental and physical wellbeing by means of certain physical and mental exercises —**yo'gi** n. one who practises yoga

yog(h)'urt [yog'at] n. thick, custard-like preparation of curdled milk

yoke n. wooden bar put across the necks of two animals to hold them together and to which plough etc. may be attached; various objects like a yoke in shape or use; fitted part of garment, esp. round neck, shoulders; bond or tie; domination —vt. put a yoke on, couple, unite

yo'kel n. disparaging term for (old-fashioned) country dweller

yolk [yōk] n. yellow central part of egg; oily secretion of skin of sheep

yon a. obs. or dial. that or those over there —**yon'der** a. yon —adv. over there, in that direction

yonks pl.n. inf. very long time

yore n. Poet. the distant past

york'er n. Cricket ball that pitches directly under bat

Yorks. Yorkshire

York'shire pudding savoury baked batter eaten with roast beef

you [yōō] pron. referring to person(s) addressed, or to unspecified person(s)

young [yung] a. not far advanced in growth, life or existence; not yet old; immature; junior; recently formed; vigorous —n. offspring —**young'ster** n. child

your [yawr] a. belonging to you —**yours** pron. —**yourself'** pron. (pl. **yourselves'**)

youth [-ōō-] n. state or time of being young; state before adult age; young man; young people (pl. **yourselves'**) —**youth'ful** a.

yowl v./n. (produce) mournful cry

yo'-yo n. toy consisting of a spool attached to a string, by which it can be spun out and reeled in while attached to the finger (pl. **-s**)

YST US, C Yukon Standard Time

YTS Youth Training Scheme

yucc'a n. tropical plant with stiff lancelike leaves

Yule n. the Christmas festival or season

Yup'pie n. young urban professional —a.

YWCA Young Women's Christian Association

Z

za'ny a. comical, funny in unusual way

zap vt. sl. attack, kill or destroy; Computers clear from screen, erase —vi. change television channels rapidly by remote control (**-pp-**)

zeal [zēl] n. fervour; keenness, enthusiasm —**zeal'ot** [zel'-] n. fanatic; enthusiast —**zeal'ous** a. ardent; enthusiastic; earnest —**zeal'ously** adv.

zeb'ra n. striped Afr. animal like a horse —**zebra crossing** pedestrian crossing marked by stripes on road

ze'bu n. humped Indian ox or cow

Zen n. Japanese school teaching contemplation, meditation

zen'ith n. point of the heavens directly above an observer; point opposite nadir; summit; peak; climax —**zen'ithal** a.

zeph'yr [zef'ər] n. soft, gentle breeze

zepp'elin n. large, cylindrical, rigid airship

ze'ro n. nothing; figure 0; point on graduated instrument from which positive and negative quantities are reckoned; the lowest point (pl. **-ro(e)s**)

zest n. enjoyment; excitement; interest, flavour; peel of orange or lemon

zig'zag n. line or course characterized by sharp turns in alternating directions —vi. move along in zigzag course (**-zagged** pt./pp., **-zagging** pr.p.)

zimm'er n. tubular frame used by the disabled or convalescents as a support for walking

zinc n. bluish-white metallic element with wide variety of uses, esp. in alloys as brass etc.

zinn'ia n. plant with daisylike, brightly coloured flowers

Zi'on n. hill on which Jerusalem stands; Judaism; Christian Church; heaven —**Zi'onism** n. movement to found, support Jewish homeland in Palestine —**Zi'onist** n./a.

zip n. device for fastening with two rows of flexible metal or nylon teeth, interlocked and opened by a sliding clip (also **zipp'er**, **zip fastener**); short whizzing sound; energy, vigour —vt. fasten with zip —v. move with zip

zir'con n. mineral used as gemstone and in industry

zith'er n. flat stringed instrument

zlot'y n. Polish coin

Zn Chem. zinc

zo'diac n. imaginary belt of the heavens along which the sun, moon, and chief planets appear to move, divided crosswise into twelve equal areas, called **signs of the zodiac**, each named after a constellation —**zodi'acal** a.

zom'bi(e) n. person appearing lifeless, apathetic etc.; corpse supposedly brought to life by supernatural spirit

zone n. region with particular characteristics or use; any of the five belts into which tropics and arctic and antarctic circles divide the earth —**zo'nal** a.

zoo n. place where wild animals are kept, studied, bred and exhibited (in full **zoological gardens**)

zoogeog'raphy [zō-ə-] n. science of geographical distribution of animals

zoog'raphy [zō-og'-] n. descriptive zoology —**zoog'rapher**, **zo-og'raphist** n. —**zoograph'ic(al)** a.

zo'olite n. fossil animal —**zoolit'ic** a.

zool'ogy [zō-ol'- or zōō-ol'-] n. scientific study of animals; characteristics of particular animals or of fauna of particular area —**zoolog'ical** a. —**zool'ogist** n.

zoom v. (cause to) make loud buzzing, humming sound; (cause to) go fast or rise, increase sharply —vi. (of camera) use lens of adjustable focal length to make subject appear to move closer or further away —**zoom lens** lens used in this way

zo'ophyte n. plantlike animal, eg sponge —**zoophyt'ic** a.

Zu'lu [zōō'-] n. member, language of native S Afr. tribe

zy'gote n. fertilized egg cell

zymot'ic [zī-] a. of, or caused by fermentation; of, caused by infection

PUNCTUATION MARKS AND OTHER SYMBOLS

, comma.
; semicolon.
: colon.
. period.
— dash.
! exclamation mark.
? interrogation or doubt.
- hyphen; as in *knick-knack.*
' apostrophe; as in *Peter's pence.*
( ) parentheses.
[ ] brackets.
{ brace. to enclose two or more lines.
´ acute accent; as in *blasé.*
` grave accent
^ circumflex } as in *tête-à-tête.*
~ tilde, used over *n* in certain Spanish words to denote the sound of *ny;* as in *señor.*
¸ cedilla, to denote that *c* is pronounced soft; as in *façade.*
" " quotation marks.
' ' quotation marks, when used within a quotation; as in *"He said, 'I will go at once' and jumped into the car."*
‾ macron, to mark length of sound; as in *cōbra.*
˘ breve, marking a short sound; as in *līnen.*
¨ diaeresis; as in *dais.*
in German, used to denote modification of the vowel sound; as in *Köln* (Cologne).
∧ caret, marking a word or letter to be inserted in the line.

.. .. — or - - - - ellipsis to indicate a break in a narrative, or an omission.
⁂ or ⁂ asterism, used to call attention to a particular passage.
... .. or - - - - leaders, to direct the eye to a certain point.
¶ paragraph.
* star, asterisk; (1) a reference mark; (2) used in philology to denote forms assumed to have existed though not recorded.
† dagger, obelisk; (1) a reference mark; (2) obsolete or dead.
‡ double dagger, a reference mark.
² superior figure, used (1) as a reference mark; (2) to indicate the number of a verse or line; as in *St. Mark* 4[16].
ᵃ superior letter.
§ section mark.
‖ parallel mark.
☞ index, hand, fist.
♯ number; space.
" ditto.
& ampersand, and.
&c et cetera.
@ at.
℀ per.
% per cent, per hundred.
© copyright.
® registered; registered trademark.
♂ male.
♀ female.

601

PUNCTUATION AND THE USE OF CAPITAL LETTERS

apostrophe The sign ('), used to indicate possession. In the singular -'s is used (eg *day's end*); in the plural the apostrophe is added to the end of the word (eg *the neighbours' dog*). Plurals that do not end in -s also take -'s (eg *sheep's eyes*). Except for a few traditional exceptions (like *Jesus', Keats'*) proper names ending in -s take -'s at the end (eg *Thomas's, the Jones's*).

brackets These serve to isolate part of a sentence which could be omitted and still leave an intelligible statement. Punctuation of the rest of the sentence should run as if the bracketed portion were not there, eg *That house over there (with the blue door) is ours.* Square brackets are used where the writer inserts his own information into a quotation, eg *I knew Pitt [the Younger] as a boy.*

capital letters These are used at the beginning of a sentence or quoted speech, and for proper names and titles of people and organizations, eg *Mr Robertson, Dr Smith, South America, British Rail.* They are not used when speaking of a general topic like *the pay of miners, the manufacture of cosmetics.* If an initial the is included in a title it has a capital, eg *We went to see The Tempest.*

colons and semicolons The function of these is to provide more of a break than a comma, and less than a full stop. The colon is used to make an abrupt break between two related statements, eg *Take it or leave it: the choice is yours.* It is also used to introduce a list, quotation, or summary and may be followed by a dash if the following matter begins on a separate line. Semicolons can be used instead of conjunctions to link two sentences or parts of them, eg *Two of the lights were working; two were out.*

commas 1. These make divisions or slight pauses in sentences, eg *She stormed out, slamming the door behind her.* 2. Commas are used to divide units in a series of nouns, adjectives, or phrases, eg *The cupboard was full of pots, pans, and crockery.* In such a series the last comma (ie before 'and' or 'or') is optional. It is not usual to place a comma between the last of a series of adjectives and the noun, eg *It was a long, hot, humid day.* 3. Commas also serve to mark off a word or phrase in a sentence which can stand grammatically complete on its own, as can dashes and brackets. Commas give the lightest degree of separation, dashes produce a jerky effect, and brackets cut off part of a sentence most firmly, eg *He hurried home, taking a short cut, but still arrived too late. It's a long time — over two years — since last we met. They both went to Athens (unaware of each other's plans) and stayed in the same hotel.* 4. When two phrases are linked by a conjunction a comma is used if there is a contrast, eg *She was dark, but her brother was fair.* 5. When addressing a person,

602

commas are used before and after the person's name or title, eg *Well, Mrs Smith, how are you today?*

exclamation marks These should only be used after genuine exclamations and not after ordinary statements

full stops (periods) Normally, these appear only at the end of a complete sentence containing a main verb, except in reported speech and where a passage takes the form of an argument, eg *You may think you can get away with it. Not a chance.* Full stops are also used after abbreviations and initial letters standing for the whole word (as in, *fig.*, *a.m.*, *R.C.*) but they are often omitted after abbreviations which include the first and last letters of a word (*Dr, Mr, ft*) and in much-used titles like *BBC, USA, TUC*. As usage is currently in a state of flux the above should be taken only as a guide to common practice.

hyphens Compound words, like *lay-by* or *manor house*, or words with a prefix, like *unpick*, may or may not contain a hyphen. It is generally used when the compound is new and dropped as it becomes familiar. When a compound adjective comes before a noun it should be hyphenated to stress that the constituent parts are not to be used independently, eg *He has a half-Italian wife.*

inverted commas (quotation marks, quotes) 1. These are used for direct quotation, not for indirect speech. It is usual to have a comma before and after a quotation if the sentence is resumed, eg *He said, "Follow me", and set off down the street.*
2. Single quotation marks can be used to indicate a title or quotation within a speech, eg *"I loved 'War and Peace'," she said, "but it took so long to read."*

question marks These are used at the end of direct questions, but not after reported ones.

PLURALS OF NOUNS

Plurals are formed by adding -s except in the following cases.

1. When a word ends in -ch, -s, -sh, -ss, or -x the plural is formed by adding -es (eg *benches*, *gases*, *dishes*, *crosses*, *taxes*).

2. When a word ends in -y preceded by a consonant the plural

form is -ies (eg *parties*, *bodies*, *policies*). When a word ends in -y preceded by a vowel the plural is formed by adding -s (eg *trays*, *joys*, *keys*).

3. When a word ends in -o the more common plural ending is -oes (eg *cargoes*, *potatoes*, *heroes*, *goes*). In many less familiar words or when the final

PLURALS OF NOUNS

-o is preceded by a vowel the plural ending is -os (eg *avocados*, *armadillos*, *studios*, *cameos*).

4. When a word ends in -f the plural is formed either by adding -s (eg *beliefs*, *cuffs*, *whiffs*) or by changing the -f to -v and adding -es (eg *wives*, *thieves*, *loaves*). Some words may take both forms (eg *scarf*, *hoof*, *wharf*).

5. When a word ends in -ex or -ix the more formal plural ending is -ices. In more general contexts -es is used (eg *appendices*, *appendixes*; *indices*, *indexes*).

6. When a word from Latin ends in -is the plural form is -es (eg *crises*, *analyses*).

With compound words (like *court-martial*) it is usually the most important part which is pluralized

(eg *courts-martial*, *lord-justices*, *mothers-in-law*).

In certain cases the plural form of a word is the same as the singular (eg *deer*, *sheep*, *grouse*) and in some words both forms end in -s (eg *measles*, *corps*, *mews*).

There are two main types of plural which take either singular or plural verbs:

a. words like *media* and *data*. These are in common use as singular nouns although, strictly, this is incorrect.

b. words ending in -ics. Generally, these are treated as plural when the word relates to an individual person or thing (eg *his mathematics are poor; the hall's acoustics are good*) and as singular when it is regarded more strictly as a science (eg *mathematics is an important subject*).

LETTER-WRITING AND FORMS OF ADDRESS

forms of address Letters to men can be addressed as follows: *Mr. Bates, Mr. T. Bates,* or *Mr. Thomas Bates.* If the courtesy title *Esq.* is used the surname must be preceded by a first name or initials, and any letters must be put after the *Esq.* eg *Thomas Bates Esq., M.A.* Young boys can be addressed as *Master.* The plural form *Messrs.* is only used with names of business firms which contain a personal name, eg. *Messrs. Jackson and Sons.*

Unmarried women and young girls can be addressed as *Miss.* Married women are often identified by their husband's first name or initial, eg *Mrs. R(obert) Henderson,* but it is increasingly common for them to appear as in *Mrs. M(ary) Henderson,* which is also the usual form for a widow. It is possible to use *Ms.* instead of *Miss* or *Mrs.*

Professional titles are used instead of *Mr.* etc., as in *Dr. H. Stevens, The Rev. Simon Clifford.* First names are always used with the titles *Sir* and *Dame,* as in *Sir Laurence Olivier, Dame Margot Fonteyn.*

Orders, decorations, degrees, qualifications, and letters denoting professions appear in that order. Degrees start with the lowest, but orders start with the highest, eg *Joseph Halliday Esq., O.B.E., D.S.O., M.A., F.S.A., M.D.* Orders and decorations are usually included in addresses, but qualifications etc. are only used where appropriate, as when writing to a person in his official capacity.

A list of some ceremonious forms of address follows at the end of this article.

postal addresses In Britain the recommended form of postal address has the Post Town in capital letters, followed by the county in small letters, followed by the postcode (where applicable), eg

Miss Joan Bannerman
6 Overton Drive
HORSHAM
Sussex
(postcode)

address of a letter The writer's address should appear in the top right-hand corner with the date underneath. The name and address of the intended recipient should come below the date, on the left-hand side of the page.

beginnings and endings These depend on the degree of formality required. The most commonly used forms are as follows:

very formal

Sir,	I am, Sir, *or*
Gentlemen,	I remain, Sir,
Madam,	Your obedient
Mesdames,	servant,

formal

Dear Sir(s),	Yours faithfully,
Dear Madam,	
Mesdames,	Yours truly,

when correspondent is known

Dear Mr.	Yours sincerely,
(Mrs. etc)–	Yours truly,

between friends

Dear–	Yours ever,
My dear–	Yours affectionately,

postscript This abbreviates to PS (not P.S.). An additional postscript is labelled PPS.

CEREMONIOUS FORMS OF ADDRESS

The Queen *Address* The Queen's Most Excellent Majesty *Begin* Madam *or* May it please Your Majesty *Refer to as* Your Majesty *End* I have the honour to remain, Your Majesty's faithful subject,

Prince *Address* His Royal Highness Prince (Christian name) *Or, if a duke* His Royal Highness the Duke of– *Begin* Sir *Refer to as* Your Royal Highness *End* I have the honour to remain, Your Royal Highness's most dutiful subject,

Princess *Address* Her Royal Highness the Princess (Christian name) *Or, if a Duchess* Her Royal Highness the Duchess of– *Begin* Madam *Refer to as* Your Royal Highness *End* I have the honour to remain, Your Royal Highness's dutiful and obedient subject,

Duke *Address* His Grace the Duke of– *Begin* My Lord Duke *Refer to as* Your Grace *End* I have the honour to be, Your Grace's most obedient servant,

Duchess *Address* Her Grace the Duchess of– *Begin* Madam *Refer to as* Your Grace *End* I have the honour to be, Your Grace's most obedient servant,

Baronet *Address* Sir (Christian name and surname), Bt. *Begin* Sir *End* I am, Sir, Your obedient servant,

Baronet's wife *Address* Lady (surname) *Begin* Madam *Refer to as* Your Ladyship *End* I am, Madam, Your obedient servant,

Knight *Address* Sir (Christian name and surname) K.C.B. *Begin, End* as Baronet.

Knight's wife as Baronet's wife.

Prime Minister according to rank.

Privy Councillor *Address* The Rt. Hon. (name or title) *Begin etc.* according to rank.

Member of Parliament *Address* according to rank, with the addition of M.P. *Begin etc.* according to rank.

Secretary of State *Address* H.M. Principal Secretary of State for (Department) *Begin* Sir *End* I am, Sir, Your obedient servant,

Ambassador, British *Address* His Excellency (rank) H.B.M.'s Ambassador and Plenipotentiary *Begin* Sir, My Lord, etc. according to rank *Refer to as* Your Excellency *End* I am. etc. (according to rank), Your. obedient servant,

Consul-General *Address* (name) Esq., H.B.M.'s Consul-General, Consul. Vice-Consul etc. *Begin* Sir *End* I am, Sir, Your obedient servant,

Lord Mayor (for London, York, Belfast, Dublin) *Address* The Rt. Hon. the Lord Mayor of– *or* The Rt. Hon. (Christian name and surname), Lord Mayor of– *Begin* My Lord *Refer to as* Your Lordship *End* I am, my Lord Mayor, Your obedient servant,

Lord Mayor (for others) The Right Worshipful the Lord Mayor of– Otherwise as above.

Lord Mayor's Wife *Address* The Rt. Hon. (or Hon. according to husband's title) The Lady Mayoress of– *Begin* My Lady Mayoress or Madam *Refer to as* Your Ladyship *End* I am, my Lady Mayoress, Your obedient servant,

Mayor *Address* (for certain cities) The Right Worshipful the Mayor of– *Begin* (Your Lordship) Sir (or Madam) *End* I am, Sir (or Madam), Your obedient servant,

GROUP NAMES AND COLLECTIVE NOUNS

barren of mules
bevy of quails
bevy of roes
brace or lease of bucks
brood or covey of grouse
brood of hens or chickens
building or clamour of rooks
bunch, company or knob of
   wigeon (in the water)
bunch, knob or spring of teal
cast of hawks
cete of badgers
charm of goldfinches
chattering of choughs
clowder of cats
colony of gulls (breeding)
covert of coots
covey of partridges
cowardice of curs
desert of lapwings
dopping of sheldrakes
down or husk of hares
drove or herd of cattle (kine)
exaltation of larks
fall of woodcocks
field or string of racehorses
flight of wigeon (in the air)
flight or dule of doves
flight of swallows
flight of dunlins
flight, rush, bunch or knob of
   pochards
flock or flight of pigeons
flock of sheep
flock of swifts
flock or gaggle of geese

flock, congregation, flight or
   volery of birds
gaggle of geese (on the
   ground)
gang of elk
haras (stud) of horses
herd of antelopes
herd of buffaloes
herd, sedge or siege of cranes
herd of curlews
herd of deer
herd of giraffes
herd or tribe of goats
herd or pod of seals
herd or bevy of swans
herd of ponies
herd of swine
hill of ruffs
host of sparrows
kindle of kittens
labour of moles
leap of leopards
litter of cubs
litter of pups or pigs
litter of whelps
murmuration of starlings
muster of peacocks
nest of rabbits
nye or nide of pheasants
pace or herd of asses
pack of grouse
pack, mute or cry of hounds
pack, rout or herd of wolves
paddling of ducks
plump, sord or sute of wildfowl
pod of whiting

GROUP NAMES AND COLLECTIVE NOUNS

pride or troop of lions
rag of colts
richesse of martens
run of poultry
school or run of whales
school or gam of porpoises
sedge or siege of bitterns
sedge or siege of herons
shoal or glean of herrings
shoal, draught, haul, run or
   catch of fish
shrewdness of apes
skein of geese (in flight)
skulk of foxes
sleuth of bears
sord or sute of mallards

sounder of boars
sounder or dryft of swine
stand or wing of plovers
stud of mares
swarm of insects
swarm or grist of bees, or flies
swarm or cloud of gnats
tok of capercailzies
team of ducks (in flight)
troop of kangaroos
troop of monkeys
walk or wisp of snipe
watch of nightingales
yoke, drove, team or herd of
   oxen

NAMES AND SYMBOLS OF METRIC UNITS

Quantity	Name of Unit	Value	Symbol
LENGTH	metre	base unit	m
	centimetre	0.01 m	cm
	millimetre	0.001 m	mm
	micrometre	0.000 001 m	μm (or um)
	kilometre	1 000 m	km
	international nautical mile (for navigation)	1 852 m	n mile
MASS (weight)	kilogram	base unit	kg
	milligram	0.000 001 kg	mg
	gram	0.001 kg	g
	tonne	1 000 kg	t
TIME	second	base unit	s
	minute	60 s	min
	hour	60 min	h
	day	24 h	d
AREA	square metre	SI unit	m^2
	square millimetre	0.000 001 m^2	mm^2
	square centimetre	0.000 1 m^2	cm^2
	hectare	10 000 m^2	ha
	square kilometre	1 000 000 m^2	km^2
VOLUME	cubic metre	SI unit	m^3
	cubic centimetre	0.000 001 m^3	cm^3
VOLUME (for fluids)	litre	0.001 m^3	l
	millilitre	0.001 l	ml
	kilolitre	1 000 l (1 m^3)	kl
VELOCITY	metre per second	SI unit	m/s
	kilometre per hour	0.27 m/s	km/h
	knot	1 n mile/h or 0.514 m/s	kn
FORCE	newton	SI unit	N
	kilonewton	1 000 N	kN
	meganewton	1 000 000 N	MN
ENERGY	joule	SI unit	J
	kilojoule	1 000 J	kJ
	megajoule	1 000 000 J	MJ

NAMES AND SYMBOLS OF METRIC UNITS

Quantity	Name of Unit	Value	Symbol
POWER	watt	SI unit	W
	kilowatt	1 000 W	kW
	megawatt	1 000 000 W	MW
DENSITY	kilogram per cubic metre	SI unit	kg/m³
	tonne per cubic metre	1 000 kg/m³	t/m³
	gram per cubic metre	0.001 kg/m³	g/m³
DENSITY (for fluids)	kilogram per litre	1 000 kg/m³	kg/l
PRESSURE	pascal	SI unit (N/m²)	Pa
	kilopascal	1 000 Pa	kPa
	megapascal	1 000 000 Pa	MPa
PRESSURE (for meteorology)	millibar	100 Pa	mb
ELECTRIC CURRENT	ampere	base unit	A
	milliampere	0.001 A	mA
POTENTIAL DIFFERENCE	volt	SI unit	V
	microvolt	0.000 001 V	µV
	millivolt	0.001 V	mV
	kilovolt	1 000 V	kV
	megavolt	1 000 000 V	MV
ELECTRICAL RESISTANCE	ohm	SI unit	Ω
	microhm	0.000 001Ω	µΩ
	megohm	1 000 000Ω	MΩ
FREQUENCY	hertz	SI unit	Hz
	kilohertz	1 000 Hz	kHz
	megahertz	1 000 000 Hz	MHz
	gigahertz	1 000 000 000 Hz	GHz
TEMPERATURE	kelvin	SI unit	K
	degree Celsius	K-273.15	°C

METRIC/IMPERIAL CONVERSION FACTORS

Imperial to Metric Units   ## *Metric to Imperial Units*

LENGTH

Imperial to Metric		Metric to Imperial	
1 in	= 25.4 mm	1 cm	= 0.394 in
1 ft	= 30.5 cm	1 m	= 3.28 ft
1 yd	= 0.914 m	1 m	= 1.09 yd
1 mile	= 1.61 km	1 km.	= 0.621 mile

MASS

1 oz	= 28.35 g	1 g	= 0.0353 oz
1 lb	= 454 g	1 kg	= 2.20 lb
1 ton	= 1.02 tonne	1 tonne	= 0.984 ton

AREA

1 in²	= 6.45 cm²	1 cm²	= 0.155 in²
1 ft²	= 929 cm²	1 m²	= 10.8 ft²
1 yd²	= 0.836 m²	1 m²	= 1.20 yd²
1 ac	= 0.405 ha	1 ha	= 2.47 ac
1 sq. mile	= 259 ha	1 km²	= 247 ac

VOLUME

1 in³.	= 16.4 cm³	1 cm³	= 0.0610 in³
1 ft³.	= 0.0283 m³	1 m³	= 35.3 ft³
1 yd³	= 0.765 m³	1 m³	= 1.31 yd³
1 bushel	= 0.0364 m³	1 m³	= 27.5 bushels

VOLUME (fluids)

1 fl oz	= 28.4 ml	1 ml	= 0.0352 fl oz
1 pint	= 568 ml	1 litre	= 1.76 pint
1 gallon	= 4.55 litre	1 m³	= 220 gallons

FORCE

1 lbf (pound-force) = 4.45 N	1N (newton) = 0.225 lbf

PRESSURE

1 psi (lb/sq in) = 6.89 kPa	1 kPa (kilo- = 0.145 psi pascal)

VELOCITY

1 mph = 1.61 km/h	1 km/h = 0.621 mph

TEMPERATURE

$$°C = \frac{5}{9}\,(°F - 32)$$ $$°F = \frac{9 \times °C}{5} + 32$$

ENERGY

1 Btu (British = 1.06 kJ thermal unit)	1 kJ (kilo- = 0.948 Btu joule)

POWER

1 hp = 0.746 kW	1 kW = 1.34 hp

FUEL CONSUMPTION

$$mpg = \frac{282}{litres/100\ km}$$ $$litres/100\ km = \frac{282}{mpg}$$

TEMPERATURE CONVERSION TABLE

CELSIUS TO FAHRENHEIT

Conversion formulae:
See METRIC/IMPERIAL CONVERSION FACTORS.

°C	°F	°C	°F	°C	°F
50	122	20	68	−10	14
49	120.2	19	66.2	−11	12.2
48	118.4	18	64.4	−12	10.4
47	116.6	17	62.6	−13	8.6
46	114.8	16	60.8	−14	6.8
45	113	15	59	−15	5
44	111.2	14	57.2	−16	3.2
43	109.4	13	55.4	−17	1.4
42	107.6	12	53.6	−18	−0.4
41	105.8	11	51.8	−19	−2.2
40	104	10	50	−20	−4
39	102.2	9	48.2	−21	−5.8
38	100.4	8	46.4	−22	−7.6
37	98.6	7	44.6	−23	−9.4
36	96.8	6	42.8	−24	−11.2
35	95	5	41	−25	−13
34	93.2	4	39.2	−26	−14.8
33	91.4	3	37.4	−27	−16.6
32	89.6	2	35.6	−28	−18.4
31	87.8	1	33.8	−29	−20.2
30	86	0	32	−30	−22
29	84.2	−1	30.2	−31	−23.8
28	82.4	−2	28.4	−32	−25.6
27	80.6	−3	26.6	−33	−27.4
26	78.8	−4	24.8	−34	−29.2
25	77	−5	23	−35	−31
24	75.2	−6	21.2	−36	−32.8
23	73.4	−7	19.4	−37	−34.6
22	71.6	−8	17.6	−38	−36.4
21	69.8	−9	15.8	−39	−38.2

SIGNS OF THE ZODIAC

♈	Aries, the Ram	21 March–19 April
♉	Taurus, the Bull	20 April–20 May
♊ ♊	Gemini, the Twins	21 May–21 June
♋	Cancer, the Crab	22 June–22 July
♌	Leo, the Lion	23 July–22 August
♍	Virgo, the Virgin	23 August–22 September
♎	Libra, the Balance	23 September–21 October
♏	Scorpio, the Scorpion	22 October–21 November
♐	Sagittarius, the Archer	22 November–21 December
♑ ♑	Capricorn, the Goat	22 December–19 January
♒	Aquarius, the Water Bearer	20 January–18 February
♓	Pisces, the Fish	19 February–20 March

ROMAN NUMERALS

I	=	1	XX	=	20
II	=	2	XXX	=	30
III	=	3	XL	=	40
IV or IIII	=	4	L	=	50
V	=	5	LX	=	60
VI	=	6	LXX	=	70
VII	=	7	LXXX	=	80
VIII	=	8	XC	=	90
IX	=	9	C	=	100
X	=	10	CC	=	200
XI	=	11	CCC	=	300
XII	=	12	CCCC or CD	=	400
XIII	=	13	D	=	500
XIV	=	14	DC	=	600
XV	=	15	DCC	=	700
XVI	=	16	DCCC	=	800
XVII	=	17	CM	=	900
XVIII	=	18	M	=	1000
XIX	=	19	MM	=	2000

CHEMICAL SYMBOLS

Each element is placed in alphabetical order of its symbol and is followed by its atomic number.

Ac actinium, 89	**H** hydrogen, 1	**Pt** platinum, 78
Ag silver, 47	**Ha** hahnium, 105	**Pu** plutonium, 94
Al aluminium, 13	**He** helium, 2	**Ra** radium, 88
Am americium, 95	**Hf** hafnium, 72	**Rb** rubidium, 37
Ar argon, 18	**Hg** mercury, 80	**Re** rhenium, 75
As arsenic, 33	**Ho** holmium, 67	**Rf** rutherfordium,
At astatine, 85	**I** iodine, 53	104
Au gold, 79	**In** indium, 49	**Rh** rhodium, 45
B boron, 5	**Ir** iridium, 77	**Rn** radon, 86
Ba barium, 56	**K** potassium, 19	**Ru** ruthenium, 44
Be beryllium, 4	**Kr** krypton, 36	**S** sulphur, 16
Bi bismuth, 83	**La** lanthanum, 57	**Sb** antimony, 51
Bk berkelium, 97	**Li** lithium, 3	**Sc** scandium, 21
Br bromine, 35	**Lr** lawrencium, 103	**Se** selenium, 34
C carbon, 6	**Lu** lutetium, 71	**Si** silicon, 14
Ca calcium, 20	**Md** mendelevium, 101	**Sm** samarium, 62
Cd cadmium, 48	**Mg** magnesium, 12	**Sn** tin, 50
Ce cerium, 58	**Mn** manganese, 25	**Sr** strontium, 38
Cf californium, 98	**Mo** molybdenum, 42	**Ta** tantalum, 73
Cl chlorine, 17	**N** nitrogen, 7	**Tb** terbium, 65
Cm curium, 96	**Na** sodium, 11	**Tc** technetium, 43
Co cobalt, 27	**Nb** niobium, 41	**Te** tellurium, 52
Cr chromium, 24	**Nd** neodymium, 60	**Th** thorium, 90
Cs caesium, 55	**Ne** neon, 10	**Ti** titanium, 22
Cu copper, 29	**Ni** nickel, 28	**Tl** thallium, 81
Dy dysprosium, 66	**No** nobelium, 102	**Tm** thulium, 69
Er erbium, 68	**Np** neptunium, 93	**U** uranium, 92
Es einsteinium, 99	**O** oxygen, 8	**V** vanadium, 23
Eu europium, 63	**Os** osmium, 76	**W** tungsten, 74
F fluorine, 9	**P** phosphorus, 15	**Xe** xenon, 54
Fe iron, 26	**Pa** protactinium, 91	**Y** yttrium, 39
Fm fermium, 100	**Pb** lead, 82	**Yb** ytterbium, 70
Fr francium, 87	**Pd** palladium, 45	**Zn** zinc, 30
Ga gallium, 31	**Pm** promethium, 61	**Zr** zirconium, 40
Gd gadolinium, 64	**Po** polonium, 84	
Ge germanium, 32	**Pr** praseodymium, 59	

MATHEMATICAL SYMBOLS

$+$	1. plus. addition sign 2. positive
$-$	1. minus. subtraction sign 2. negative
$\times$	multiplied by
$\div$	divided by; also indicated by oblique stroke (8/2) or horizontal line $\frac{8}{2}$
$=$	equals; is equal to
$\neq$	is not equal to
$\equiv$	is identical with; is congruent to
$\sim$	difference between; is equivalent to
$\simeq, \approx$	is approximately equal to
$>$	is greater than
$<$	is less than
$\not>$	is not greater than
$\not<$	is not less than
$\leqslant$	less than or equal to
$\geqslant$	greater than or equal to
$\cong$	is isomorphic to
$\because$	is to; ratio sign
$::$	as: used between ratios
∞	infinity
$\propto$	varies as. proportional to
$\therefore$	therefore
$\because$	since. because
$\angle$	angle
$\llcorner$	right angle
$\perp$	is perpendicular to

616

Symbol	Meaning
$\parallel$	is parallel to
$\bigcirc$	circle: circumference
$\frown$	arc of a circle
$\triangle$	triangle
$\square$	square
$\square$	rectangle
$\square$	parallelogram
$\sqrt{}$	radical sign (ie square root sign)
Σ	sum
$\int$	integral
$\cup$	union
$\cap$	intersection
$\in$	is a member of: is an element of: belongs to
$\subset$	is contained as subclass within
$\supset$	contains as subclass
$\{\ \}$	set braces
ϕ	the empty set
$\mid\ \mid$	absolute value of: modulus of
$\triangleleft$	is a normal subgroup of
μ	mean (population)
σ	standard deviation (population)
$\overline{x}$	mean (sample)
s	standard deviation (sample)
π	ratio of circumference of any circle to its diameter
e	base of natural logarithms
$^{\circ}$	degrees of arc or temperature
$'$	minutes of arc or time: feet
$''$	seconds of arc or time: inches

617

DISTANCES BY AIR

The flight distances shown in the following tables are quoted in kilometres via the shortest normal airline routing from airport to airport. For cities with more than one airport a mean distance is given. An asterisk indicates a maximum distance.

Distances from London

Accra	5086	Kuwait	4666
Algiers	1650	Lagos	4988
Amsterdam	370	Lisbon	1555
Auckland	24290*	Madrid	1232
Baghdad	4097	Marseilles	971
Bahrain	5084	Melbourne	25011*
Bangkok	9551	Milan	940
Barcelona	1129	Montreal	5234
Beirut	3468	Moscow	2507
Belgrade	1689	Nairobi	6825
Berlin	952	Naples	1613
Bombay	7205	New York	5564
Brisbane	23746*	Nice	1022
Brussels	340	Oslo	1175
Budapest	1476	Palma	1330
Buenos Aires	13442*	Paris	336
Cairo	3518	Prague	1037
Calcutta	11111*	Rangoon	12255*
Cape Town	12275*	Rio de Janeiro	11132*
Casablanca	2062	Rome	1436
Chicago	6364	Harare (Zimbabwe)	10707*
Cologne	525	San Francisco	10420*
Colombo	11289*	Singapore	14133*
Copenhagen	984	Stockholm	1462
Dakar	4349	Sydney	24163*
Darwin	18151*	Tehran	4408
Delhi	6730	Tel Aviv	3577
Djakarta	15208*	Tokyo	17518*
Dubrovnik	1715	Toronto	5727
Geneva	736	Tunis	1813
Hamburg	745	Venice	1135
Honolulu	11699*	Vienna	1262
Istanbul	2502	Warsaw	1465
Jamaica	7532	Washington	5889
Johannesburg	9059	Wellington	24372
Karachi	8494		

Distances from Montreal

Amsterdam	5509	New York	531
Auckland	17658*	Paris	5527
Berlin	7314*	Rio de Janeiro	9942*
Bombay	15340*	Rome	6601
Cairo	10488*	Vancouver	3684
Moscow	8832*	Zurich	6000

Distances from Sydney

Auckland	2162	Paris	21329*
Berlin	20940*	Rome	20041*
Cairo	17475*	San Francisco	14442*
Johannesburg	14685*	Singapore	6303
Moscow	20933*	Tokyo	7821
New York	19407*	Toronto	18839*

Distances from Auckland

Berlin	23535*	New York	17275*
Brisbane	2297	Paris	23923*
Buenos Aires	15809*	Rome	24588*
Cairo	20069*	San Francisco	13142*
Honolulu	7094	Singapore	10157*
Moscow	24598*	Tokyo	13584*

Distances from Johannesburg

Amsterdam	10848*	Nairobi	2914
Auckland	17161*	New York	15424*
Berlin	10930*	Paris	10600*
Cape Town	1272	Rio de Janeiro	7150
Montreal	16061*	Rome	9507*
Moscow	11162*	Tel Aviv	6506

Distances from Bombay

Auckland	14857*	Paris	9068*
Berlin	8680*	Rio de Janeiro	18444*
Cairo	4345	Rome	6182
Hong Kong	4303	San Francisco	19563*
Johannesburg	8939*	Singapore	3916
Moscow	8671*	Sydney	12262*

WORLD STANDARD TIMES

At noon, GMT, 1300 BST

For each degree of longitude, time differs by 4 minutes; west of Greenwich is earlier, east of Greenwich later, than GMT.

Place	Time	Place	Time
Adelaide	2130	Malta	1300
Algiers	1300	Melbourne	2200
Amsterdam	1300	Mexico City	0600
Athens	1400	Montevideo	0830
Auckland	2400	Montreal	0700
Beirut	1400	Moscow	1500
Belgrade	1300	Nairobi	1500
Berlin	1300	New York	0700
Bern	1300	Oslo	1300
Bombay	1730	Panama	0700
Brisbane	2200	Paris	1300
Brussels	1300	Peking	2000
Bucharest	1400	Perth, Australia	2000
Budapest	1300	Prague	1300
Buenos Aires	0800	Quebec	0700
Cairo	1400	Rangoon	1830
Calcutta	1730	Rio de Janeiro	0900
Cape Town	1400	Rome	1300
Caracas	0800	St John's, Newfoundland	0830
Chicago	0600	San Francisco	0400
Colombo	1730	Santiago	0800
Copenhagen	1300	Singapore	1930
Helsinki	1400	Sofia	1400
Hong Kong	2000	Stockholm	1300
Istanbul	1400	Sydney	2200
Jerusalem	1400	Tehran	1530
Karachi	1700	Tokyo	2100
Lagos	1300	Toronto	0700
Leningrad	1500	Vancouver	0400
Lima	0700	Vienna	1300
Lisbon	1200	Warsaw	1300
Madras	1730	Winnipeg	0600
Madrid	1300	Yokohama	2100

SELECTED MOUNTAIN HEIGHTS

	Metres		Metres
Everest, China-Nepal	8848	McKinley, USA	6190
K2 (Godwin Austen), Kashmir-Sinkiang	8611	Logan, Canada	6050
Kangchenjunga, India-Nepal	8598	Cotopaxi, Ecuador	5896
Makalu, China-Nepal	8481	Kilimanjaro, Tanzania	5895
Dhaulagiri, Nepal	8167	Bolivar, Colombia	5775
Nanga Parbat, Kashmir	8126	Citlaltépetl, Mexico	5699
Annapurna, Nepal	8091	Damavand, Iran	5670
Xixabangma, Tibet	8012	Elbrus, USSR	5642
Distaghil Sar, Kashmir	7989	Popocatépetl, Mexico	5452
Nanda Devi, India	7816	Kirinyaga (Kenya), Kenya	5200
Rakaposhi, Kashmir	7788	Ararat, Turkey	5165
Namcha Barwa, Tibet	7756	Stanley, Uganda-Zaïre	5110
Kamet, China-India	7756	Jaya (Carstensz), Indonesia	5030
Gurla Mandhata, Tibet	7728	Mont-Blanc, France-Italy	4807
Muztag (Ulugh Muztagh), Sinkiang-Tibet	7723	Klyuchev, Kamchatka, USSR	4750
Kongur (Kungur), China	7719	Monte Rosa, Italy-Switzerland	4634
Tirich Mir, Pakistan	7690	Matterhorn (Cervino), Italy-Switzerland	4477
Gongga Shan (Minya Konka), China	7556	Whitney, USA	4418
Muztagata, China	7546	Elbert, USA	4398
Pik Kommunizma, USSR	7495	Mauna Kea, Hawaii, USA	4205
Pik Pobedy, USSR-China	7439	Kinabalu, Sabah, Malaysia	4094
Aconcagua, Argentina	6960	Erebus, Antarctica	3794
Ojos del Salado, Argentina-Chile	6880	Fuji, Japan	3776
Bonete, Argentina	6872	Cook, New Zealand	3764
Huascaran, Peru	6768	Etna, Sicily, Italy	3323
Sajama, Bolivia	6542	Ben Nevis, Scotland	1343
Illampu, Bolivia	6485	Snowdon, Wales	1085
Chimborazo, Ecuador	6310	Carrantuohill, Ireland	1041
		Scafell Pike, England	978

RIVER LENGTHS

	km
Nile, Africa	6695
Amazon, S America	6516
Yangtze, Asia	6380
Mississippi-Missouri N America	6019
Ob-Irtysh, Asia	5570
Yenisey-Angara, Asia	5550
Huang Ho (Yellow River), Asia	5464
Zaïre (Congo), Africa	4667
Paraná, S America	4500
Mekong, Asia	4425
Amur, Asia	4416
Lena, Asia	4400
Mackenzie, N America	4250
Niger, Africa	4030
Missouri, N America	3969
Mississippi, N America	3779
Murray-Darling, Australia	3750
Volga, Europe	3688
Madeira, S America	3200
Yukon, N America	3185
Indus, Asia	3180
Syr Darya, Asia	3078
Salween, Asia	3060
St Lawrence, N America	3058
São Francisco, S America	2900
Rio Grande, N America	2870
Danube, Europe	2850
Brahmaputra, Asia	2840
Euphrates, Asia	2815
Pará-Tocantins, S America	2750
Zambezi, Africa	2650

	km
Amu Darya, Asia	2620
Paraguay, S America	2600
Nelson-Saskatchewan, N America	2570
Ural, Asia	2534
Kolyma, Asia	2513
Ganges, Asia	2510
Orinoco, S America	2500
Shabeelle, Africa	2490
Arkansas, N America	2348
Colorado, N America	2333
Dnieper, Europe	2285
Columbia, N America	2250
Negro, S America	2250
Irrawaddy, Asia	2150
Xi Jiang, Asia	2129
Don, Europe	1870
Orange, Africa	1860
Pechora, Europe	1809
Marañón, S America	1609
Magdalena, S America	1550
Dniester, Europe	1411
Rhine, Europe	1320
Elbe, Europe	1159
Gambia, Africa	1094
Yellowstone, N America	1080
Donets, Europe	1078
Vistula, Europe	1014
Loire, Europe	1012
Tagus, Europe	1006
Meuse (Maas), Europe	925
Oder, Europe	909
Seine, Europe	761
Severn, Wales-England	354
Thames, England	338
Liffey, Ireland	80

POPULATIONS
(estimated) of selected urban areas

New York — NE New Jersey, USA	16 121 297	Washington DC, USA	3 060 922
		Berlin, W Germany	1 869 584
Mexico City, Mexico	14 750 182	Berlin, E Germany	1 179 442
Tokyo, Japan	11 676 264	Dallas — Fort Worth, USA	2 974 805
Los Angeles — Long Beach, USA	11 497 568	Istanbul, Turkey	2 948 856
Shanghai, China	10 820 000	Montreal, Canada	2 862 300
Buenos Aires, Argentina	9 927 404	Cleveland, USA	2 834 062
Calcutta, India	9 165 650	Rome, Italy	2 830 569
Paris, France	8 510 000	Melbourne, Australia	2 803 600
Seoul, S Korea	8 364 379	Miami — Fort Lauderdale, USA	2 643 981
Bombay, India	8 227 332	Osaka, Japan	2 623 124
Moscow, USSR	8 011 000	Singapore	2 517 000
Chicago, USA	7 869 542	Shenyang (Mukden), China	2 411 000
Beijing (Peking), China	7 570 000		
São Paulo, Brazil	7 033 529	St Louis, USA	2 356 460
London, England	6 696 008	Kiev, USSR	2 355 000
Jakarta, Indonesia	6 503 449	Pittsburgh, USA	2 263 894
Delhi — New Delhi, India	5 713 581	Wuhan, China	2 146 000
		Athens, Greece	2 101 103
Philadelphia, USA	5 547 902	Budapest, Hungary	2 064 026
San Francisco — Oakland, USA	5 179 784	Havana, Cuba	1 951 373
Karachi, Pakistan	5 103 000	Bucharest, Romania	1 934 025
Rio de Janeiro, Brazil	5 093 232	Essen — Dortmund — Duisburg, W Germany	1 792 907
Cairo, Egypt	5 074 016	Barcelona, Spain	1 754 900
Hong Kong	4 986 560	Milan, Italy	1 634 638
Bangkok (Krung Thep), Thailand	4 697 071	Manila, Philippines	1 630 485
		Hamburg, W Germany	1 623 848
Detroit, USA	4 618 161	Warsaw, Poland	1 621 044
Lima, Peru	4 600 891	Lisbon, Portugal	1 611 887
Tehran, Iran	4 589 201	Vienna, Austria	1 562 000
Leningrad, USSR	4 588 000	Johannesburg, S Africa	1 441 366
Tianjin (Tientsin), China	4 280 000	Stockholm, Sweden	1 386 980
		Munich, W Germany	1 287 080
Madras, India	4 276 635	Naples, Italy	1 210 503
Boston, USA	3 448 122	Cape Town, S Africa	1 107 763
Sydney, Australia	3 280 900	Turin, Italy	1 103 520
Santiago, Chile	3 234 066	Lagos, Nigeria	1 060 848
Madrid, Spain	3 188 297	Rotterdam, Netherlands	1 024 749
Toronto, Canada	3 067 100		

COUNTRIES, RELATED NOUNS, ADJECTIVES, AND CURRENCIES

Country	Noun/Adjective	Currency Unit
Afghanistan	Afghan	afghani
Albania	Albanian	lek
Algeria	Algerian	dinar
Andorra	Andorran	franc/peseta
Angola	Angolan	kwanza
Argentina	Argentine or Argentinian	peso
Australia	Australian	dollar
Austria	Austrian	schilling
Bahamas	Bahamian	dollar
Bahrain	Bahraini	dinar
Bangladesh	Bangladeshi	taka
Barbados	Barbadian	dollar
Belgium	Belgian	franc
Benin	Beninese	franc
Bermuda	Bermudan	dollar
Bhutan	Bhutanese	ngultrum
Bolivia	Bolivian	peso boliviano
Botswana		pula
Brazil	Brazilian	cruzeiro
Brunei		dollar
Bulgaria	Bulgarian	lev
Burma	Burmese	kyat
Burundi	Burundian	franc
Cameroon	Cameroonian	franc
Canada	Canadian	dollar
Cape Verde	Cape Verdean	escudo
Central African Republic		franc
Chad	Chadian	franc
Chile	Chilean	peso
China	Chinese	yuan
China (Taiwan)	Chinese	dollar
Colombia	Colombian	peso
Congo	Congolese	franc
Costa Rica	Costa Rican	colon
Cuba	Cuban	peso
Cyprus	Cypriot	pound
Czechoslovakia	Czech, Czechoslovak or Czechoslovakian	koruna
Denmark	Dane; Danish	krone
Djibouti		franc

COUNTRIES, RELATED NOUNS & ADJECTIVES, & CURRENCIES

Country	*Noun/Adjective*	*Currency Unit*
Dominica	Dominican	dollar
Dominican Republic	Dominican	peso
Ecuador	Ecuadorean	sucre
Egypt	Egyptian	pound
El Salvador	Salvadorean	colon
Equatorial Guinea		ekpwele
Ethiopia	Ethiopian	birr
Fiji	Fijian	dollar
Finland	Finn; Finnish	markka
France	Frenchman, -woman; French	franc
Gabon	Gabonese	franc
Gambia	Gambian	dalasi
Germany, East	East German	mark
Germany, West	West German	deutschmark
Ghana	Ghanaian	cedi
Greece	Greek	drachma
Grenada	Grenadian	dollar
Guatemala	Guatemalan	quetzal
Guinea	Guinean	franc
Guinea–Bissau		peso
Guyana	Guyanese	dollar
Haiti	Haitian	gourde
Honduras	Honduran	lempira
Hungary	Hungarian	forint
Iceland	Icelander; Icelandic	krona
India	Indian	rupee
Indonesia	Indonesian	rupiah
Iran	Iranian	rial
Iraq	Iraqi	dinar
Ireland, Republic of	Irishman, -woman; Irish	pound
Israel	Israeli	pound
Italy	Italian	lira
Ivory Coast		franc
Jamaica	Jamaican	dollar
Japan	Japanese	yen
Jordan	Jordanian	dinar
Kampuchea	Kampuchean	riel
Kenya	Kenyan	shilling
Korea, North	North Korean	won
Korea, South	South Korean	won
Kuwait	Kuwaiti	dinar

COUNTRIES, RELATED NOUNS & ADJECTIVES, & CURRENCIES

Country	Noun/Adjective	Currency Unit
Laos	Laotian	kip
Lebanon	Lebanese	pound
Lesotho		rand
Liberia	Liberian	dollar
Libya	Libyan	dinar
Liechtenstein		franc
Luxembourg		franc
Madagascar	Madagascan	franc
Malawi	Malawian	kwacha
Malaysia	Malaysian	ringgit
Maldives	Maldivian	rupee
Mali	Malian	franc
Malta	Maltese	pound
Mauritania	Mauritanian	ouguiya
Mauritius	Mauritian	rupee
Mexico	Mexican	peso
Monaco	Monegasque	franc
Mongolian People's Republic	Mongolian	tugrik
Morocco	Moroccan	dirham
Mozambique	Mozambican	escudo
Nauru	Nauruan	dollar
Nepal	Nepalese	rupee
Netherlands	Dutchman, -woman, Netherlander; Dutch	guilder
New Zealand	New Zealander	dollar
Nicaragua	Nicaraguan	cordoba
Niger		franc
Nigeria	Nigerian	naira
Norway	Norwegian	krone
Oman	Omani	rial
Pakistan	Pakistani	rupee
Panama	Panamanian	balboa
Papua New Guinea	Papuan	kina
Paraguay	Paraguayan	guarani
Peru	Peruvian	sol
Philippines	Filipino or Philippine	peso
Poland	Pole; Polish	zloty
Portugal	Portuguese	escudo
Qatar	Qatari	riyal
Rumania	Rumanian	leu
Rwanda	Rwandan	franc

626

COUNTRIES, RELATED NOUNS & ADJECTIVES, & CURRENCIES

Country	Noun/Adjective	Currency Unit
San Marino	San Marinese or Sammarinese	lira
Saudi Arabia	Saudi Arabian	riyal
Senegal	Senegalese	franc
Seychelles		rupee
Sierra Leone	Sierra Leonean	leone
Singapore	Singaporean	dollar
Somalia	Somalian	shilling
South Africa	South African	rand
Spain	Spaniard; Spanish	peseta
Sri Lanka	Sri Lankan	rupee
Sudan	Sudanese	pound
Surinam	Surinamese	guilder
Swaziland	Swazi	lilangani
Sweden	Swede; Swedish	krona
Switzerland	Swiss	franc
Syria	Syrian	pound
Tanzania	Tanzanian	shilling
Thailand	Thai	baht
Togo	Togolese	franc
Tonga	Tongan	pa'anga
Trinidad and Tobago	Trinidadian, Tobagan	dollar
Tunisia	Tunisian	dinar
Turkey	Turk; Turkish	lira
Uganda	Ugandan	shilling
USSR	Russian or Soviet	ruble
United Arab Emirates		dirham
United Kingdom	Briton; British	pound
USA	American	dollar
Upper Volta		franc
Uruguay	Uruguayan	peso
Vatican City		lira
Venezuela	Venezuelan	bolivar
Vietnam	Vietnamese	dong
Western Samoa	Samoan	dollar
Yemen, People's Democratic Republic	Yemeni	dinar
Yemen, Arab Republic	Yemeni	riyal
Yugoslavia	Yugoslav or Yugoslavian	dinar
Zaire	Zairean	zaire
Zambia	Zambian	kwacha
Zimbabwe	Zimbabwean	dollar

BUILD UP YOUR GEM COLLECTION!

This dictionary is just one of over eighty titles in the bestselling series of GEM Dictionaries and Guides.

GEM Dictionaries can help you with writing and spelling – in English and many other languages.

There are also Travel Gem Dictionaries and Phrase Books to help you on holiday or business travel. And there are Colour Gem Guides too – great companions on country walks.

Every GEM is the same handy format as this dictionary – so it will fit your pocket, handbag or satchel.

This order form lists some of the most popular titles. Use it to start building up your GEM collection today!

Order Form

☐ English Dictionary	£1.95
☐ English Thesaurus	£1.95
☐ French Dictionary	£1.95
☐ French Grammar	£1.95
☐ French Verb Tables	£1.95
☐ 5000 French Words	£1.95
☐ German Dictionary	£1.95
☐ German Grammar	£1.75
☐ German Verb Tables	£1.95
☐ 5000 German Words	£1.95
☐ Spanish Dictionary	£1.95
☐ Spanish Grammar and Verb Tables	£1.95
☐ Italian Dictionary	£1.95
☐ Latin Dictionary	£1.95
☐ Portuguese Dictionary	£2.25
☐ Russian Dictionary	£2.25
☐ Greek Dictionary	£2.25

Travel Gem Dictionaries   £1.25 each
- ☐ French   ☐ German
- ☐ Italian   ☐ Spanish

Travel Gem Phrase Books   £1.25 each
- ☐ French   ☐ German
- ☐ Italian   ☐ Spanish

Gem Nature Guides
(illustrated in full colour)   £2.25 each
- ☐ Birds   ☐ Butterflies
- ☐ Mushrooms & Toadstools   ☐ Night Sky
- ☐ Trees   ☐ Wild Flowers

Gem Colour Guides
- ☐ Aircraft of World Wars I & II   £2.25
- ☐ Modern Combat Aircraft   £2.25
- ☐ Flags   £2.25

All Collins Gems are available at your local bookshop or newsagent. Or, in case of difficulty, you can order direct from the publisher. Just tick the titles required, and fill in the form below.

Name

Address

Send to: Collins Gems, Cash Sales Dept., P.O. Box 11, Falmouth, Cornwall, TR10 9EN.

Please enclose cheque or postal order to the total of the cover prices PLUS postage and packing as follows.
UK & BFPO: 50p for first book plus 25p for each additional book to a maximum of £1.75.
Overseas: 75p for first book plus 25p for each additional book.
Collins reserve the right to increase book prices from those previously advertised; and postal charges in line with current Post Office tariffs.